COSTA RICAN

NATURAL
HISTORY

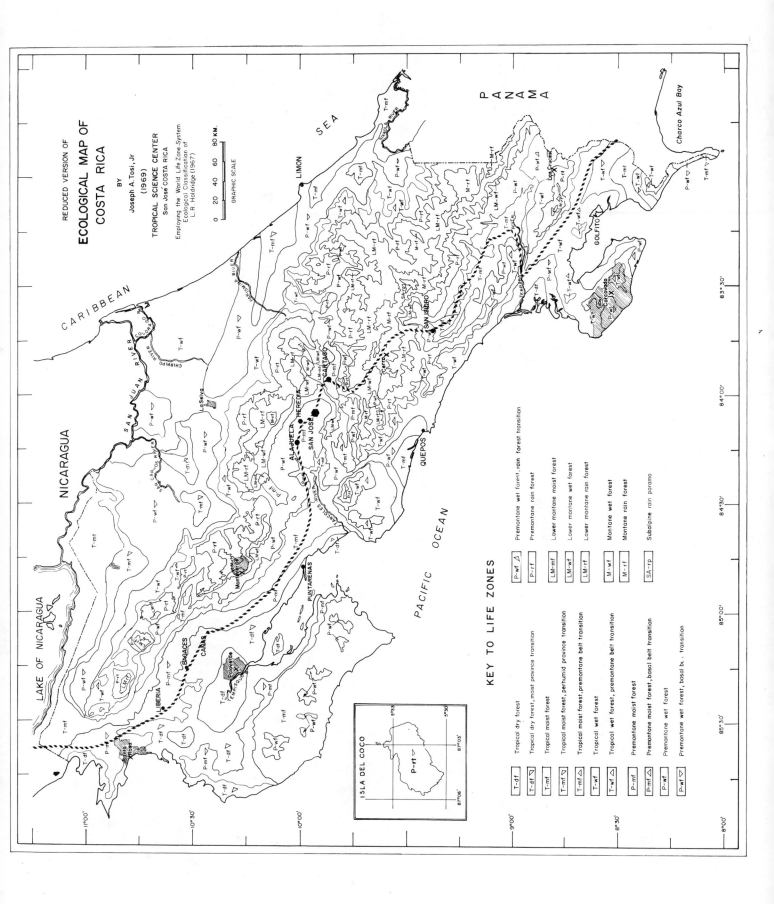

REDUCED VERSION OF

ECOLOGICAL MAP OF COSTA RICA

BY

Joseph A.Tosi, Jr
(1969)

TROPICAL SCIENCE CENTER
San José COSTA RICA

Employing the World Life Zone-System
Ecological Classification of
L.R. Holdridge (1967)

GRAPHIC SCALE

0   20   40   60   80 KM.

ISLA DEL COCO

KEY TO LIFE ZONES

T-df	Tropical dry forest
T-df ▽	Tropical dry forest, moist province transition
T-mf	Tropical moist forest
T-mf ▽	Tropical moist forest, perhumid province transition
T-mf △	Tropical moist forest, premontane belt transition
T-wf	Tropical wet forest
T-wf △	Tropical wet forest, premontane belt transition
P-mf	Premontane moist forest
P-mf △	Premontane moist forest, basal belt transition
P-wf	Premontane wet forest
P-wf ▽	Premontane wet forest, basal b. transition

P-wf △	Premontane wet forest, rain forest transition
P-rf	Premontane rain forest
LM-mf	Lower montane moist forest
LM-wf	Lower montane wet forest
LM-rf	Lower montane rain forest
M-wf	Montane wet forest
M-rf	Montane rain forest
SA-rp	Subalpine rain paramo

COSTA RICAN NATURAL HISTORY

EDITED BY

Daniel H. Janzen

WITH
174 CONTRIBUTORS

THE UNIVERSITY OF CHICAGO PRESS
CHICAGO AND LONDON

DANIEL H. JANZEN is professor of biology at the University of Pennsylvania and an associate member of the Museo Nacional de Costa Rica.

THE UNIVERSITY OF CHICAGO PRESS, CHICAGO 60637
THE UNIVERSITY OF CHICAGO PRESS, LTD., LONDON

90 89 88 87 86 85 84 83   5 4 3 2 1

Identification of cover illustrations (all photographs by Daniel H. Janzen)

1. Female *Rothschildia lebeau* (saturniid moth) in copulo. Santa Rosa National Park.
2. Last-instar caterpillar of *Rothschildia erycina* (saturniid moth). Santa Rosa National Park.
3. Dehisced fruit and seeds of *Pentaclethra macroloba* (legume tree) on forest floor. Finca La Selva.
4. Adult *Felis wiedii* (margay). Santa Rosa National Park.
5. Adult *Drymobius margaritiferus* (speckled racer) swallowing adult *Rana* (frog). Santa Rosa National Park.
6. Subadult *Welfia georgii* (welfia palm), with leaves 6 to 8 meters long, growing through late secondary succession. Finca La Selva.
7. Adult *Bradypus variegatus* (three-toed sloth). La Lola.
8. Adult *Glaucidium minutissimum* (least pygmy owl). Limón.
9. Infructescence/inflorescence of *Musa sapientum* (banana). Monteverde.
10. Last-instar caterpillar of *Automeris rubrescens* (io moth). Santa Rosa National Park.
11. Adult *Citherias menander* (satyrid butterfly). Finca La Selva.
12. Adult *Pterocarpus officinalis* (legume tree) in pterocarpus swamp. Corcovado National Park.
13. Adult *Ganoderma* (bracket fungus). Santa Rosa National Park.
14. Adult female *Odocoileus virginianus* (white-tailed deer). Santa Rosa National Park.
15. Inflorescence of *Asclepias curassavica* (milkweed) with crab spider that has just seized queen *Azteca* ant as prey. Palo Verde.

Library of Congress Cataloging in Publication Data
Main entry under title:

Costa Rican natural history.

Includes bibliographical references and index.
1. Natural history—Costa Rica. I. Janzen,
Daniel H.
QH108.C6C67   1983   508.7286   82–17625
ISBN 0–226–393321 (cloth)
ISBN 0–226–393348 (paper)

CONTENTS

PREFACE

Many biologists are now studying natural history in Costa Rica. Many more will do so. This book is an attempt to write down some of what we already know, in a form that can be quickly digested by the newcomer to Costa Rican field biology. I shudder to think that this book might become a definitive statement about Costa Rican natural history. It is neither that nor a thorough review of the literature on the subject. It is, however, an introduction to that literature, and it should give the newcomer a starting point for inquiries into the biology of Costa Rican organisms. I hope this book will be out of date in ten or twenty years; some sections were out of date as they were being written. Those who read it are the ones who will make it obsolete. In editing these various contributions from 174 authors, I have been impressed with how fragmentary is the knowledge each of us has even of our own areas of specialization and of the organisms we are supposed to be familiar with. Rather than be scornful of this sorry state of tropical biology, however, I encourage the reader to work doubly hard to rectify it.

Since the manuscript entered its odyssey of publication, six works have appeared that might have been often cited had they appeared earlier. I wish to draw the reader's attention to them:

Janzen, D. H., and Liesner, R. 1980. Annotated checklist of plants of lowland Guanacaste Province, Costa Rica, exclusive of grasses and non-vascular cryptogams. *Brenesia* 18:15–90.

Pohl, R. W. 1980. Flora costaricensis: Family number 15, Gramineae. *Fieldiana, Bot.* n.s., 4:1–608.

Savage, J. M. 1980. *A handlist with preliminary keys to the herpetofauna of Costa Rica.* Privately printed; available from the author.

Slud, P. 1980. The birds of Hacienda Palo Verde, Guanacaste, Costa Rica. *Smithsonian Contrib. Zool.,* no. 292, pp. 1–92.

Valerio, C. E. 1980. *Historia natural de Costa Rica.* San José: Editorial Universidad Estatal a Distancia.

Young, A. M. 1982. *Population biology of tropical insects.* New York: Plenum Press.

Furthermore, the pages of *Brenesia,* the biological journal of the Museo Nacional de Costa Rica, offer a steady stream of information on the natural history of Costa Rican organisms.

The protocol for this book's production was straightforward. For chapters 1–5 and the introductions to later chapters, I asked people very familiar with those aspects of Costa Rica to write down what they would say in a lecture to interested but naive graduate students. For the checklists, I asked the authors to revise old checklists or make up new ones. For each "chapterlet"—each species account—I asked a person intimately familiar with the organism concerned to write what he or she would say to a small group of graduate students new to Costa Rica when first confronted with the plant or animal in its natural habitat.

At the inception of this project, there were some who thought of it as a revision or updating of "The Book," —an out-of-print compendium of essays, checklists, keys, and data produced by the Organization for Tropical Studies (Universidad de Costa Rica, Ciudad Universitaria) for use in its courses in field biology. However, the present work should be viewed as complementary to "The Book," not as a replacement for it.

Almost everyone I asked to write consented. I chose the organisms covered to achieve a balance among life forms and major taxonomic groups, for the conspicuousness of the organisms, and according to the availability of an authority. Now I belatedly realize that I left out numerous organisms and some scientists. I hope that the many biologists who could have contributed to this book will volunteer to help with future books of this nature. The next step should be not the updating of all these accounts and the addition of more to produce a yet fatter compendium, but rather a similar effort to produce numerous new volumes, examining more species in more detail, one for each of the major taxonomic categories. If you are interested in contributing to such future projects, drop me a line and I will record your interest for the appropriate editor some years hence. Constructive commentary on this book is invited; it will be reviewed and filed for the future.

It would have been impossible to pull together this present volume without the active support and encouragement of many people and organizations. Those whose financial support has made it possible to publish this book at such a reasonable price are listed in the Acknowledgments, and I thank them here once again. They have made it possible for many students to afford this book and have thus made the research presented in it much more widely available. As a further contribution to the book, all of us who have written sections have declined to accept either fees or royalties, as have I as editor.

The Organization for Tropical Studies (OTS) has helped in many ways, tangibly by providing honoraria for section reviewers, help with photocopying, and administration of applications for financial support for the book. Special thanks are due Peter H. Raven and Donald E. Stone for their strong encouragement and their work to secure contributions to support publication.

My deepest indebtedness in the production of this book is to those students in past OTS courses who have wanted to know about this or that organism, and to all those who have cared enough to learn something rather than merely be entertained by Costa Rican natural history. I could never have undertaken this project without the certain knowledge that people out there would contribute to it.

I owe a special acknowledgment to the writers of chapters 1–5 and later chapter introductions, and to Luis Gómez, who not only volunteered many pages of writing but found more contributors. Most important of all, he served as counsel during the tortuous journey through the offices of three publishing houses that backed out on their promises, resulting in a full two years' delay in the publication date. The authors of the chapter on agricultural species planned and contributed that chapter independent of my efforts. W. Hallwachs, G. Stevens, M. Johnston, and L. Gómez served as volunteer editorial assistants. D. Gill, G. Stevens, R. Hallwachs, M. Hall-wachs, and R. Foster carried edited manuscript and proofs to me in Costa Rica to help ensure safe delivery and avoid loss of time in the mails. The secretarial staff of the Department of Biology at the University of Pennsylvania helped enormously.

Traditionally the University of Chicago Press does not allow its staff to be thanked by name in such acknowledgments as this, but I thank the Press for its great interest in this book and for extraordinary efforts on its behalf.

In a manner difficult to define, the presence of the Servicio de Parques Nacionales de Costa Rica, an organization that frequently goes far out of its way to support Costa Rican field biology studies, served as a major inspiration to me to organize and carry out this task. Likewise, the Museo Nacional de Costa Rica provided a logistical and psychological home for the project far beyond the call of duty.

Finally, I must recognize that it was Jay Savage who first brought me to Costa Rica in 1963, and that the National Science Foundation paid for it.

D. H. Janzen

A list of the contributors and their mailing addresses at the time of publication begins on page 781.

ACKNOWLEDGMENTS

Further research in tropical biology is essential if we are to understand and appreciate the biological complexity of the tropics and contribute to their preservation and wise use as well as to the preservation of the biological diversity of life on earth. Thanks are due the following individuals and institutions, whose commitment to the importance of this work is manifest in their generous support of the publication of this book:

The Animal Research and Conservation Center of the
  New York Zoological Society
The Association for Tropical Biology
George R. Cooley
Stanley R. and Lynn W. Day
Fundación de Parques Nacionales de Costa Rica
The Hershey Fund
Philip and Margaret Hess
Lewis F. Kibler
Marion Lloyd
Mr. and Mrs. J. Daniel Mitchell
Museo Nacional de Costa Rica
The Organization for Tropical Studies
E. Lisa Smith
The Smithsonian Tropical Research Institute
Catherine H. Sweeney
Typoservice Corporation
Universidad de Costa Rica
The World Wildlife Fund—United States

1 SEARCHERS ON THAT RICH COAST: COSTA RICAN FIELD BIOLOGY, 1400–1980

L. D. Gómez and J. M. Savage

The early, radical transformation of the geographical significance and the social structure of Costa Rica was produced by coffee agriculture (Hail 1978). Monocultures and their dependent economies are characteristically a predominant aspect of underdevelopment, and the exclusive exploitation of a single product like coffee generally is a poor use of physical and human resources. But the cultivation of coffee in nineteenth-century Costa Rica is an exception to this rule in that it established a social climate that has encouraged strong development of the natural sciences in this small tropical country.

Discovery and Conquest

About the mid-1400s, Spain expelled its Moors and Jews. Scientists (not to mention bankers and others) left Spain, leaving behind very little in the way of a scientific tradition to be exported to the newly discovered Neotropics. By thus confirming messianism as the role of Iberia, Spanish rulers condemned their country and its colonies to prolonged intellectual obscurantism. Nevertheless, even if we exclude as literary hyperbole Columbus's glowing comments on the exuberant scenery of his newly discovered continent (Colón 1972), as soon as the Spanish had settled in various parts of the Americas some of the literate pioneers, mostly ecclesiastics, began to write descriptions and accounts of the natural marvels of the New World. Thus we find in Father José de Acouta's *Historia natural y moral de las Indias* (1590) a man in theological quicksand, trying to explain the existence of some species such as "the dirty foxes" and how they happened to be in Peru, far from Mount Ararat, where Noah's ark had come to rest. At the northern end of the Spanish domains, Friar Bernardino de Sahagún gives detailed descriptions of the Mexicans' use of hallucinogenic fungi and peyotl.

But these authors lived in rich viceroyalties. In Central America the poor friars had little leisure for writing. The first chronicler was Gonzalo Fernández de Oviedo y Valdés, whose *Historia general y natural de las Indias, islas y tierra-firme del Mar Oceano,* written between 1535 and 1549, is a rich mélange of the earliest Americana but is nevertheless an uncoordinated array of events and descriptions, often lacking geographical precision and adorned throughout with the florid and poetic usage of sixteenth-century Spanish.

Following Oviedo's style but more focused on the Mexican–Central American region, Francisco López de Gómara's *Historia general de las Indias,* published in 1552, devotes several detailed descriptive chapters to Nicaragua and northern Costa Rica; Antonio de Remesal's *Historia general de las Indias Occidentales y particular de la gobernación de Chiapas y Guatemala* (1615–17) is valuable for its accounts of the peoples and the environment, as is Antonio de Alcedo's *Diccionario geográfico de las Indias Occidentales* (1786–89), which abounds in information of all sorts, indexed to the geographical names then in use.

Perhaps to us the most important, yet the least known, of the early chroniclers is Francisco Ximénez (1666–1729), who compiled the grammars of several aboriginal languages, discovered and published the Popol Vuh, or Mayan cosmology, and wrote the *Historia natural del reino de Guatemala.* Father Ximénez covers all aspects of Central American natural history in an orderly manner, devoting each fascicle or book to a given theme (animals, flowers, minerals, etc.) drawn from a direct, personal knowledge de rerum naturae.

Priests, army surgeons, and barbers collected, digested, and divulged the natural marvels of the New World on their own initiative. Unfortunately, the more apparent wealth of some of the viceroyalties captivated kings, who sent out royal expeditions such as those to Nueva España, Nueva Granada, or the Pacific. These were led by illustrious men of science such as Sessé, Mociño, Mutis, and La Espada and were not interested in the poor, insalubrious isthmus of the Americas.

Early Times

The numb and tattered epoch of colonial exploitation that ended for Central America in 1821 could not have been more sterile in terms of the development of local cultures and intellectual ambience. Prepotent and royal Spain

1

hardly allowed for the scant and elementary education of her subjects, while the iron hand of the church treated intellectual endeavors as works of the devil, fatal to the souls of her charges—particularly if these endeavors were contaminated by the ideas of the French Revolution and other demoniacal inspirations, such as Freemasonry. The condition of public education in Costa Rica during the colonial period is well documented by González F. (1978), and the capital importance of French liberalism in the movement for independence is presented by Láscaris (1964). Debilitated from its very inception (González F. 1978; González V. 1977; Soley 1940), the economy of the area could barely sustain the first twenty-odd years of republican life. But then, despite the fashionable efforts of the Duchess of Bedford and her cup of tea, England settled for a cup of coffee. And quite unexpectedly, too.

In 1843 William Le Lacheur, an English merchant, docked the *Monarch* in the port of Caldera on the Pacific coast of Costa Rica. The holds of the brig were almost empty for his homeward voyage, and Le Lacheur wished to obtain some cargo that would compensate him for the long and hazardous trip around Cape Horn. He rode a mule into San José, where he met Santiago Fernández, dealer in coffee. Fernández trusted Le Lacheur, and on his credit Le Lacheur departed carrying 5,505 hundredweight of Costa Rican coffee. He returned in 1845 to pay Fernández, and this time he brought more vessels and a good supply of sterling.

A new industry had been born. Ships arriving to load the coffee brought holds full of goods, including Manchester cotton fabrics, which were to open entire continents to British imperialism. And, of course, they brought people. The cash flow turned a dilapidated region into a prosperous one, changing many things as the criollos became able to barter for cultural goods as well.

Coffee was responsible for the initiation of diplomatic relations between Costa Rica and England, France, and the Hansa in 1849 and for the expansion of agricultural areas and many of the subsequent movements of the population, as well as for the opening of access roads and railways. Coffee was perhaps also responsible for the first officially recognized coup d'état in Costa Rica; J. R. Mora Fernández and R. Aguilar, partners in a coffee export firm, parted on bad terms owing to a financial disagreement. Later, Mora was given pecuniary satisfaction and eventually became president of Costa Rica, but he was deposed by a vengeful Aguilar in 1859. The importance of coffee in the development of the history and geography of Costa Rica is documented by Hall (1978) and Estrada (1965).

The Traveler-Naturalists

Why did people come to Costa Rica aboard the growing coffee fleet? A look at the history of continental Europe in the last third of the nineteenth century would provide many of the answers, but even a brief overview lies outside the scope of this chapter. Immigration of Europeans to Latin America in general, and Central America in particular, was primarily a response to the sociopolitical situation of Europe and the apparent utopian conditions of the New World. The relative stability of Central American politics, coupled with niches for the crafts and professions in the flourishing regional economy, enticed foreign entrepreneurs and scholars. Cities that had lacked elementary schools suddenly had private "academies" catering to a clientele eager to learn, be it bookkeeping or fine arts. The streets resounded with foreign names as the general stores gave way to specialized shops and cottage manufactures yielded to incipient industries. This birth of cosmopolitanism is both the cause and the effect of immigration. The Gold Rush of 1848 also fueled the demographic explosion in Central America; the way to California was either around Cape Horn, a lengthy and hazardous enterprise, or by the much faster route across southern Nicaragua (Houwaldt 1975; Folkmann 1972), along the present border between Nicaragua and Costa Rica.

But why did the traveler-naturalists come? Certainly neither Sutter's findings nor the area's economy and politics were the explanation for their presence in this part of the world. The accounts of Humboldt, La Dondamine, and other less illustrious but equally good propagandizers provide the reason. The romance of travel, exploration, and discovery, triggered by European expansionism during the seventeenth century, was rampant in the Europe of the Industrial Revolution, and such adventurous observers were far from immune to the call of the vast and unknown American continent. A glance at the titles of some then-popular books is illuminating: Bülow, *Auswanderung und Colonisation in Interesse des deutschen Aussenhandels* (1849); Bard, *Waika; or, Adventures on the Mosquito Shore* (1855); Scherzer, *Wanderungen durch die mittelamerikanischen Freistaaten* (1857); Marr, *Reise nach Zentral Amerika* (1863); Boyle, *A Ride across a Continent: Personal Narrative of Wanderings through Nicaragua and Costa Rica* (1868); Pim, *Dottings on the Roadsides of Panamá, Nicaragua . . .* (1868); Wagner, *Naturwissenschaftliche Reise in Tropical America* (1870); and many others (cf. Fernández 1972).

We cannot boast of personalities of the stature of Alexander von Humboldt, who scarcely saw the high volcanoes of Central America from his ship bound for Mexico, but, unlike that meteor of the Parisian salons, those who came usually stayed, sowing the seed of interest in natural history. To this period belong several important names: the already-mentioned Moritz Wagner, who in association with Karl Scherzer published in 1886 *Die Republik Costa Rica;* the Danish Anders Sandoe Ørsted, who visited Costa Rica from 1846 to 1848, publishing his famous opus *L'Amérique Centrale: Recherches sur sa géographie politique, sa faune et sa flora,* printed in Copenhagen under the auspices of the Costa Rican government. A somewhat unknown figure who deserves credit for his active part in advancing local natural history is William More Gabb, whose endeavors in the geology, paleontology, and zoology of the lower Talamancas (Ferrero 1978) were crowned by later publications by E. D. Cope, L. Pilsbry, and J. A. Allen, among others.

This is the period of F. Duncane Godman and Osbert Salvin, initiators of the single most comprehensive work on Central American biology, aptly entitled *Biología Centrali-Americana;* it appeared between 1879 and 1915 in many volumes, with the approval of the leading authorities on the diverse groups of fauna and flora. Karl Sapper, geologist by profession and naturalist by avocation (Termer 1956), closes the period. His collected writings on Costa Rica have been published (Sapper 1943).

The Emergence of Costa Rican Biologists
Separating this period from that covered in the previous paragraphs is highly artificial, since Costa Rican field biology stems from the causes mentioned there. In 1853, scarcely ten years after the opening of the European coffee market, President Mora Fernández welcomed two

German physicians who carried a letter of introduction from Alexander von Humboldt—Carl Hoffmann (1833–59) and Alexander von Frantzius (1821–77).

Hoffman explored the upper portions of the central volcanic ridge (Hoffman 1856, 1857), collected plants and animals that he sent to Berlin, and fought William Walker in Nicaragua in 1856. He died in 1857 and is commemorated in the names of a dozen species. His colleague von Frantizius was also very active; his botanical explorations made Costa Rica known to the scholarly world, and his faunal collections were used for one of the first annotated lists on the mammals and birds, both by himself and by the famous Cabanis of Berlin. Frantzius opened a drugstore in San José, and his apprentice, José C. Zeledón, became deeply interested in nature, later becoming known worldwide as an ornithologist. Frantzius and Zeledón's drugstore was a germination chamber from which sprang the first batch of local naturalists such as Anastasio Alfaro and J. F. Tristán (fig. 1.1).

Costa Rica was oriented toward England commercially, but culturally it was French. In the natural sciences its practitioners were truly Victorian, and soon the "drugstore gang" and their disciples were to be seen rummaging through the countryside with nets, pillboxes, and other paraphernalia.

FIGURE 1.1 Part of the "drugstore gang" at the old quarters of the Museo Nacional. *Left,* George K. Cherrie, zoologist and taxidermist; *center,* Anastasio Alfaro, first director; *right, in front,* an assistant, possibly Francisco Méndez; *far right,* José Gástulo Zeledón (photo, archives of Museo Nacional de Costa Rica).

Under the administration of Bernardo Soto, Mauro Fernández, the minister of public education, achieved one of the most significant feats in Costa Rican history. He developed the new pattern of public schooling totally sponsored by the government, compulsory for all citizens until the seventh grade, and he opened high schools for both men and women. Manuel Mária Peralta, ambassador to Europe, was commissioned to hire European teachers that were to staff the Liceo de Costa Rica and the Colegio Superior de Señoritas. This precipitated the arrival of a Swiss mining engineer, Henri François Pittier, accompanied by others whose names are very much part of Costa Rican history: Pablo Biolley, Julian Carmiol, Gustavo Michaud, and Juan Rudin. With Pittier (1857–1950) begins the golden period of Costa Rican natural history (Conejo 1972).

Determined, indefatigable, tyrannical Pittier was soon in charge of all significant scientific activity in Costa Rica. Through his enthusiasm, Pittier promoted or founded several important institutions such as the Instituto Físico Geográfico, the Sociedad Nacional de Agricultura, and the Observatorio Nacional. He planned and led a multidisciplinary approach to field biology, inspired by his years as a disciple of the typical nineteenth-century gymnasium. Botanists owe him the national herbarium and his *Primitiae Florae Costaricensis,* begun in 1891. It is the first systematic flora of the country. The cloak and dagger circumstances of the *Primitiae* are summarized by Gómez (1978a,b). Pittier and his associates in all branches of science, notwithstanding financial and technical difficulties, amassed a body of information as yet unsurpassed. Revolving around him, willingly or not, were Adolphe Tonduz, Charles Wercklé, George Cherrie, and scores of foreign researchers who at his insistence either visited the country or studied collections sent from the Instituto Geográfico or the national herbarium. Until 1904, when Pittier left the country, sciences from limnology to social anthropology flourished.

It is at this time that the Museo Nacional makes its appearance. The philosophical foundation of the Museo has been briefly reviewed by Gómez (1973), who attributed its origin to the Victorian craze for bric-a-brac and the French mania for "cabinets" of exhibits that seized the country when it plunged into the international marketing of coffee. In this context the figure of Anastasio Alfaro is of utmost importance, since it was through his efforts and persuasiveness, as well as the usual political intrigue, that President Bernardo Soto inaugurated the national museum in 1887. Alfaro, then twenty-two years old, became its first director. The liaison of Alfaro and Zeledón was in large part responsible for opening Costa Rica to North American scientific interest. Zeledón, the disciple of Frantzius, had been sent to Washington to learn under the tutelage of Robert Ridgway, and he prepared the Smithsonian grounds for Alfaro and others. From then on the flow of United States researchers has never stopped. A glance at the publication *Costa Rica en el siglo XIX* (published in 1902) informs us of the dozens of scholars who contributed their knowledge to Costa Rican field biology in the last twenty years of that century.

Three political events are noteworthy. (1) The government of Mora asked Monsignor Llorente y La Fuente to leave the country. The immediate result was the segregation of church and state in educational matters. This meant the introduction of krausism and fuller curricula into the system. (2) The government of Bernardo Soto enthroned positivism in the figure of Mauro Fernández. These two events helped to form the philosophical basis of Costa Rican republicanism. The profound consequences of these events could still be felt as late as 1921, one hundred years after independence, in the thoughts of Ricardo Jiménez (1921). (3) The same Mauro Fernández, positivist par excellence and architect of the Costa Rican educational system, was moved by political reasons to close the Universidad de Sto. Tomás in 1888. The only scholastic units to remain functioning were the school of law and the school of agriculture.

The First Half of a Bright New Century

Under the tutelage of Comte and Spencer, Costa Rica started the new century as an international merchant whose economy was based entirely on agriculture. But, paradoxically, it had just an incipient and meager school of agriculture that functioned only spasmodically owing to insufficient funding (according to an editorial in *La República* in 1890; the eventual closing of this school was due to the reallocation of its funds to the building of the national theater, a project initiated and patronized by the coffee growers' elite). The school of law was the only other faculty at the university in these early years. It produced the professionals necessary to regulate and run the recently born banking system, and commercial operations in general, and to consolidate a legalistic republican structure. Between 1898 and 1941, all the prominent personalities were lawyers, leading the Nicaraguan poet Darío to describe Costa Rica as "a land of lawyers, clerks and oxen." On such a scene the natural sciences, regardless of the prominence of the remaining partners of the "drugstore gang," were considered an amenity, and field research by local or foreign naturalists was seen as a pastime for the eccentric or the wealthy, a view that still persists.

A review of the educational system prompted President Iglesias to suggest reopening the Universidad de Sto. Tomás (presidential address of 1 May 1900), but this initiative had no success. It did, however, trigger the interests of the Costa Rican intelligentsia, and during the next two decades some of those directly influenced by Fernández sought a diversified college education in Chile or in Europe. Important participants in this emigration were Elías Leiva, J. F. Tristán, José Ma. Orozco, Emel Jiménez, Lucas R. Chacón, R. Brenes Mesén, and Carlos Monge, all directly associated with the renovation of the high-school curriculum, educational techniques, or, eventually, the renaissance of the university. In these early years, the slow disappearance of the old Europeña, or Europeanized teachers, and their direct disciples is reflected in the country's lack of intellectual tone in all but fine arts and letters.

In 1917 Phillip and Amelia Calvert published *A Year of Costa Rican Natural History,* based on a year spent studying dragonfly biology under the auspices of the Philadelphia Academy of Sciences. Their narrative, so far unexcelled, is a must for all interested in field biology as well as in the social atmosphere of Costa Rica during the first decade of this century.

Meanwhile the Costa Rican economy suffered a severe blow from the European war of 1914–18, followed by the German crisis of 1923. The magic market for coffee vanished as it had appeared, on the wings of change, propelled by the flourishing of South American competitors as well as by the banana industry (Gaspar 1979). All this motivated an orientation toward American markets and North American pragmatism. Although the 1929 Wall Street crash had serious repercussions in the Costa Rican economy, it also had beneficial effects in that the fiscal depression provoked the appearance of several non-conservative political parties (Aguilar 1978).

(Although this story of field biology may seem to be deviating into a general history of Costa Rica, our goal is to sketch the economic and political background of field biology rather than merely listing names and citing works that can be found elsewhere [González 1976; Dobles 1927; Gómez 1975a].)

The installation of other political parties meant a plurality of ideas and, more important, of attitudes to counteract the narrow concepts of the coffee oligarchy. Among these changes was the reopening of the university system. In the 1920s the lack of a university was already evident, and the inauguration of the Universidad de Costa Rica (UCR) by the socially oriented party in power took place without adequate preparation. The sudden need for professors allowed many of the high-school docents to participate in the early development of the university, which impaired the quality of the natural sciences curriculum from the very start. The role of the university in natural history studies and research during the first twenty years of its existence was nil. First, being overly concerned with arts and letters, it did not offer proper careers; second, it mismanaged the Museo Nacional (which was cared for by the university from the mid-

1940s to 1953). During this period the collections were badly curated, the libaries pillaged, and the efforts of sixty-five years of struggling dedication wasted (P. C. Standley, in litt.; J. A. Echeverría, O. Jiménez, pers. comm.). From then until the late 1960s, the Museo Nacional will be remembered by all, including some of the early participants in courses taught by the Organization for Tropical Studies (OTS), as "the pits."

Still, not all was darkness. In 1913 Clodomiro Picado Twight (Picado 1964) returned from Paris (Sorbonne, Institute of Colonial Medicine or Institute Pasteur) as a doctor of science (fig. 1.2), organized the first clinical laboratory of the San Juan de Dios Hospital, and dedicated himself to studying the natural riches of the country. His production includes a treatise *The Poisonous Snakes of Costa Rica* (1931, reprinted 1976), almost a hundred articles on diverse topics related to tropical medicine and microbiology, and, most important of all, his research on the ecology of the tank bromeliads that served as his doctoral dissertation and is considered a pioneer work in tropical ecology. Some of the important works of Picado have recently been reprinted (Gómez 1975b). Picado's activities were in full swing when the

FIGURE 1.2. Clodomiro Picado Twight, first Costa Rican academic biologist, who graduated from the Sorbonne in 1913 (photo, L. D. Gómez collection).

5

plurality in politics took place, and he did not neglect this opportunity to participate in the country's ideologies, his influence being felt more in that field than in local biology. Of his 322 published articles, 131 are on scientific matters. He was a Lamarckist (Picado and Trejos 1942), as befits a Paris-trained scientist, and most of his scientific writings were published abroad, while those issued locally were of a more popular character. His almost poetic rendering of the biographies of Pasteur and Metchnikoff (Picado 1921) like many of his newspaper articles, reveals a thinker of intense humanism, ardently longing for ampler horizons.

Unfortunately, Picado died in 1944, depriving the Universidad de Costa Rica of his enlightment in those critical years of its inception. Although for political reasons he was excluded from the planning for that institution (R. L. Rodríguez, pers. comm.), had he lived longer it is quite possible that the Universidad de Costa Rica would have had an altogether different role in the development of biological sciences in Costa Rica.

The Second World War played an important role in our story, since it disrupted markets and politics, but it also had a direct influence on the advancement of technology over the pure sciences. Costa Rica plunged, again without preparation, into the atomic age. Higher education was therefore biased toward applied sciences in the same way the economy was dominated by North American capital and markets. In 1948 the revolution of the Liberal party finally decapitated the dwindling remains of conservative ideas (Schifter 1979; Cerdas 1972), and Costa Rica moved into a technocracy that tended to neutralize a potent electorate with bureaucracy (Trudeau 1971). The establishing of a mediocre segment of the population in government positions signified the beginning of a "scientificism" at the decision-making levels that obstructed the development of true science. This massification, which could have been prevented had the politicans read Ortega y Gasset, moved inexorably toward a Jasperian *Vernunft* and *Widervernuft* of scientific advancement.

Nevertheless, the names of two courageous idealists deserve mention: Antonio Balli was an Italian biologist brought in as part of the General Studies Program during the renovation of the Universidad de Costa Rica in the 1950s. Balli was an eclectic philosopher of science whose teachings met with skepticism and outright derision, and he had no impact either on the students or on the administrative groups at the higher stages of education (Balli 1974–77).

Rafael Lucas Rodríguez, well known to OTS participants, earned his doctorate from the University of California, Berkeley, and was requested to create a department of biology for the Universidad de Costa Rica. He was responsible for the actual curriculum of that school, which was designed to produce able high-school teachers in the shortest time (R. L. Rodríguez, pers. comm.). However, paradoxically, it was biased toward zoology. Rodríguez was a devoted neo-Darwinist whose influence could have been stronger had it not met with apathy from the students. Rodríguez was intellectual father to many a research project and an inspiration to several younger scientists, and he played a decisive role in establishing OTS in Costa Rica. Although Rodríguez is celebrated for his multiple contributions to the community, particularly concerning youth, and for his unexcelled talents as a botanical illustrator, the portentous depth of his thinking was little recognized among his colleagues and students.

As with Picado and Balli, the scientific output and influence of Rodríguez is better known outside Costa Rica, a symptom that conditions are not yet ripe for the development of the propitious national attitude toward field and theoretical biology appropriate to a country whose natural heritage is of such magnificence. It may be that Charles Wercklé, writing to Nathaniel Lord Britton to congratulate the famous botanist on the founding of the New York Botanical Garden, has proved prophetic: "But only if a Nation has reached the highest degree of development, the interest in the Natural Sciences becomes general and the fact is understood by the most advanced that these sciences, real and original, are of a higher order than the Social Sciences." Thus the first half of the twentieth century closes under the resigned looks of Spencer and Comte, the faint shadow of Lamarck, and the scornful stance of Darwin.

Science and the Costa Rican

It is difficult to define the historical process of cultural integration in any society. It becomes particularly painful when such integration has been simultaneous with the consolidation of the national entity as a whole. Costa Rica stands in contrast to countries where one can easily examine and analyze the origins and development of the culture of an already constituted social system.

We have dealt at some length with the political and economic conditions under which such a cultural manifestation—the natural sciences—has evolved in Costa Rican history so as to present the ontogeny of the natural sciences or attitudes toward science in the context of science as a social phenomenon. One aspect of scientific development remains to be considered: the social characteristics that enable science to be born, to grow, or to die in a country.

None of the local sociologists (Barahona 1953; Rodríguez 1979) have touched upon the subject of science and the Costa Rican. Sancho (1935), with all his ingenuity and incisiveness, ignored the local attitude toward science, as has Láscaris in more recent times (Láscaris

1975). Nevertheless, all these authors agree, with a mixture of doubt and pessimism, that environmental, historical, and demographic elements have yielded a set of individual and collective circumstances that do not favor inquisitiveness beyond the most pragmatic reasons. Such conclusions, tinged with Lamarckism, also agree with the thoughts expressed in Clodomiro Picado's many articles in the popular press, and Picado is the landmark of this century. The characterization of an "attitude toward science" is not an exclusively local problem but concerns the entire Latin American community and offers a fascinating field of research (Cardoso, Pinto, and Sunkel 1970).

Reform and Change, 1955–80

The prevailing malaise of Costa Rican field biology was to change with the reform of the Universidad de Costa Rica in 1955. Shortly thereafter a school of biology was established. The curriculum of the school was designed in consultation with Archie F. Carr, a noted North American biologist and author. Rodríguez's role has already been mentioned. From this modest beginning has grown the well-designed and well-equipped School of Biology and the Zoological Museum, with a full-time faculty of fifteen Ph.D.s, some of whom are interested in field biology. More or less simultaneously, another native Costa Rican, Alvaro Wille, a Ph.D. from the University of Kansas, took over and developed the entomological section of the School of Agriculture. While the general trend of Costa Rican government agencies and institutions has followed that of other developing countries in emphasizing pragmatic and applied science and technology over basic science, the Universidad de Costa Rica in its latest incarnation has had a salutary effect on this attitude toward biology.

Similarly, the revitalization of the Museo Nacional in 1970 added a stimulus to both *costarricenses* and *extranjeros* to undertake modern field studies. The institution, now a semiautonomous government agency, contains the national herbarium and provides modest modern research facilities and cooperative opportunities to all field biologists. The Museo's extraordinary recovery is due in major part to the botanist Luis Diego Gómez, who has elsewhere described the origins and activities of the Museo (Gómez 1975*a*, 1978*a,b*).

There are several other agencies in Costa Rica that are contributing to the current flourishing of field studies. The Centro Agronómico Tropical de Investigación y Enseñanza (CATIE) was originally founded by the Organization for American States as the Instituto Interamericano de Ciencias Agrícolas (IICA) in Turrialba in 1942. In 1972 the Centro became an independent entity but continued its applied teaching and research program in agriculture, forestry, and wildlife management. A graduate program for the Universidad de Costa Rica is located there as well. CATIE has been host to many field biologists, both in Turrialba and at its lowland field station at La Lola on the railroad to Limón.

The Caribbean Conservation Corporation (CCC), a group of individuals dedicated to preserving and protecting the sea turtle nesting grounds at Tortuguero, was established in 1959 by Archie F. Carr, Jr. Professor Carr, the world's foremost authority on sea turtles, used this site to study many aspects of the biology and migration of turtles, especially green turtles. Many field biologists have worked at the field camp at Tortuguero, and it became part of a national park in 1970.

The Ministerio de Agricultura y Ganadería (MAG), a major department of the government, is responsible for agriculture, cattle, forestry, fisheries, and wildlife and for the National Park Service. A series of the ministry's agricultural experiment stations at various localities in Costa Rica, especially at Taboga and Los Diamantes, have been used by many field biologists. The recently created wildlife reserve Rafael Lucas Rodriguez Caballero, formerly known as Hacienda Palo Verde, is a site of many studies and will continue to be available for field research.

The Tropical Science Center (TSC) is a private consulting firm organized in 1962 by three North Americans originally associated with the IICA at Turrialba: Leslie R. Holdridge, an internationally known tropical forester; Robert J. Hunter, an agriculturalist; and Joseph A. Tosi, forester and land-use expert. Gary Hartshorn currently is associated with two of the original partners, Holdridge and Tosi, in studies of land use and forest resources. TSC operated a field station at Rincón de Osa (1966–73), and it owns and manages the Monteverde Forest Preserve (since 1971). Substantial field biology studies have been carried out at both sites. In this connection we should mention Paul Slud, whose works on the birds of La Selva (1960) and Costa Rica (1964) are classics, and whose association with Holdridge led to these synthetic works.

By 1968 the cadre of professional biologists in Costa Rica had reached a point where the group organized its own professional association, the Colegio de Biólogos, to establish standards for educational requirements and to improve the qualifications for the title (career) of *biólogo*. The college holds irregular meetings with public lectures and has led a number of significant campaigns to preserve endangered natural areas, most notably the Isla del Caño and the migratory water bird reserve at Palo Verde. Most members of the college are field biologists or are conservation oriented.

The Servicio de Parques Nacionales de Costa Rica (SPN), or National Park Service, technically a part of MAG, was established in 1970 as a response to the Costa Rican people's demand for a park system dedicated to preserving the natural areas of Costa Rica. Although several parks had been established in the past, only to be abandoned, the growing sentiment of Costa Rican conservationists, led by the remarkable and dedicated Mario A. Boza, stimulated the government of Pepe Figueres (in his second term as president after being out of office since 1958) to form the SPN in 1970. In the ensuing years, under the leadership first of Boza, then of Alvaro F. Ugalde, and most recently of José María Rodríguez, and with the support of Presidents Daniel Oduber and Rodrigo Carazo, a national system of twenty parks and reserves, unrivaled by any others in Latin America, has been developed (Boza and Bonilla 1981). Research consonant with the park's purposes is encouraged by the SPN.

Consejo Nacional de Investigaciones Científicas y Tecnológicas (CONICIT) was established in 1972 as an arm of the planning office of the Costa Rican government. It serves as a combination National Research Council and National Science Foundation, attempting to set national priorities in science and technology and providing grant support to many field-oriented research projects. Its president is Rodrigo Zeledón, a distinguished parasitologist, former dean of the School of Microbiology at UCR.

Universidad Nacional Autonoma (UNA), a second national Costa Rican university, was founded in 1973 in Heredia, with emphasis on an unusual curriculum and organization as opposed to the more familiar arrangement at the Universidad de Costa Rica. A major unit at UNA is the School of Environmental Sciences, which includes forestry and marine resources programs, among others.

One curious fact of Costa Rican history is the almost total absence of interest in marine biology. Very few studies were carried out even by foreign naturalists on Costa Rican marine organisms during the nineteenth and early twentieth centuries, except those coincidentally related to major expeditions that happened to collect in waters near the Republic. This situation doubtless derives from the concentration of the population, and of economic and cultural life, on the Meseta Central during most of Costa Rica's history. Without the convivial Costa Rican hosts enjoyed by terrestrial biologists to encourage them, marine biologists were not attracted to Costa Rican shores. For these reasons the recent establishment (1978) of a Centro de Ciencias Marinas at the university, under the vigorous leadership of Manuel M. Murillo, a noted student of crustacean ecology, and the construction of a small marine station by CONICIT at Punta Morales are encouraging.

The Organization for Tropical Studies (OTS)
In 1961 the Universidad de Costa Rica (UCR) and the University of Southern California (USC) began offering a field-oriented course in tropical biology in Costa Rica. The program was a cooperative effort by the Director of the School of Biology, Rafael L. Rodríguez, the vice-dean of Science and Letters, John deAbate, who holds a Ph.D. in zoology from Tulane University, and Jay M. Savage of USC, to stimulate the development of field studies in Costa Rica. The original program, sponsored by the National Science Foundation of the United States, brought groups of United States professors to Costa Rica for six-week periods of instruction in field biology by biologists resident in Costa Rica. Field trips to many major habitats were an integral part of the program.

At about this same time the Universities of Miami and Kansas were developing the concept of a modest field station for tropical studies in Costa Rica; Harvard University was thinking of relocating its tropical botany offerings after Castro's take-over of the Atkins Gardens in Cuba; and the Universities of Florida and Washington were looking for a tropical base. Finally, the University of Michigan had spent nearly ten years trying to establish a field station in southern Mexico, for purposes similar to those of the other institutions. Because of these interests and the success of the UCR-USC program, a series of meetings demonstrated that the common goals and individual institutional objectives could be met through a cooperative organization. As a result, the Organization for Tropical Studies (OTS) was established in 1963 as a small consortium of seven North American universities and the Universidad de Costa Rica (Smith 1978). The primary objective of the group was to develop a center for advanced graduate education and research in tropical sciences centered on basic knowledge of tropical environments. The consortium was formed because its members recognized that no single institution could provide the material and human resources necessary for the task. Principal emphasis in the beginning of OTS was on developing a cadre of knowledgeable tropical ecologists who had course and field experience in tropical environments and whose research activities would become concentrated on tropical systems.

In the intervening period OTS has grown to include twenty-seven institutions of higher education, twenty-three from the United States and four from Costa Rica. It has a central office facility in San José, Costa Rica, administrative headquarters at Duke University, and a series of field stations and other sites in key environments throughout the Republic. OTS has an annual budget of about one million dollars to operate its facilities and course programs and to provide logistic support to groups of independent researchers. In addition, the more than fourteen hundred graduate-level students who have participated in its course programs make OTS the principal developer of a new generation of tropical biologists whose knowledge is based on actual tropical field experience.

Because Costa Rica borders on both the Atlantic and the Pacific and is divided by a high mountain chain that attains an elevation of 3,918 m, it has a remarkably diverse biota including approximately 800 species of birds, 350 species of amphibians and reptiles, and 8,000 species of higher plants. About 10% of the known world butterfly fauna occurs in Costa Rica. Of the 38 major tropical plant formations, 14 are represented in the Republic, ranging from lowland deciduous and rain forests to páramo on the highest peaks. Finally, the region is of great biogeographic interest because it lies on the isthmian link that has made possible the dramatic interchange of biota between the previously separated North and South American continents.

OTS field sites aim to take advantage of these factors so that courses and researchers may visit many diverse environments within a short time. It is possible to visit almost any major terrestrial or marine habitat within a day's ride of San José and to carry out comparative ecological studies at several sites within a week. Principal sites utilized by OTS include lowland deciduous forest at Santa Rosa National Park (0–320 m); lowland deciduous forest and riverine swamp at Refugio Rafael Lucas Rodríguez Caballero (formerly Palo Verde, 3–183 m); several premontane to lower montane formations at Monteverde (1,200–1,800 m); premontane rain forest at Las Cruces (1,200 m); montane forests at Cerro de la Muerte (3,000 m); lowland evergreen forests at La Selva (29–100 m) on the Atlantic versant and Corcovado National Park on the Pacific coast (0–400 m). Principal marine sites are at Santa Rosa, Playas del Coco (Pacific), and Cahuita National Park (Atlantic), a coral reef area.

OTS's primary field station is at La Selva. It was originally owned by Leslie R. Holdridge, whose foresight in preserving a sample of undisturbed lowland forest cannot be overstated. The property was sold to OTS by Holdridge in 1968. This evergreen forest site has been selected by the National Research Council (United States) Committee on Research Priorities in Tropical Biology as one of four worldwide tropical localities for intensive long-term ecological research.

The course program of OTS, particularly its renowned "Tropical Biology: An Ecology Approach" (familiarly called the Fundamentals course), grew out of the efforts of Daniel H. Janzen and Norman J. Scott, who in the mid-sixties increased the course length to eight weeks, emphasized a full-time intensive field experience, and centered the theme on the exciting theoretical concepts of ecology that emerged in the period 1965–75. In retrospect almost every major figure in tropical biology today in the United States has been associated with the Fundamentals course.

When OTS was founded in 1963 the intent was to create a cadre of knowledgeable tropical biologists whose educational experience would be based on a common core of field-centered biology and ecology. First, it was anticipated that the training provided by direct exposure to tropical environments would generate new approaches to thinking about tropical ecology. Second, it was hoped that students and faculty would realize that field research is possible in the tropics with only slightly more effort then elsewhere. Third, it was anticipated that the development of this new generation of tropical biologists would increase basic research on tropical problems. Fourth, OTS hoped that the intellectual foment developed by course participation would increase the number and interest of Latin American scientists in tropical studies. Finally, it was anticipated that OTS graduates would become involved in planning operational aspects of renewable natural resource management.

In terms of research, OTS provided the impetus for a new wave of field studies, primarily ecological. Where almost all previous field studies in Costa Rica had been taxonomic or systematic in orientation, the new ecological theories of the 1960 and 1970s were well understood, tested, and revised, and new ideas were generated by tropical field biologists interested in this exciting area. The publication of several hundred papers based on OTS-assisted studies during the first fifteen years of its existence attests to the excitement generated by the opportunities in Costa Rica.

Less sanguine were the attempts by OTS to mount a "big science" program of coordinated ecosystem research (1968–76)—the necessary infrastructure simply failed to materialize, and, while individual components and individual principal investigators had successes, the idea of an integrated effort failed in practice. The concept of an ecosystem analysis of two tropical lowland forests, one deciduous (Palo Verde) and the other evergreen (La Selva), was sound. Its implementation failed because no single scientist emerged as the coordinator and leader for the entire project. Investigators and projects within the comparative ecological study included forest communities and primary productivity (Kenneth J. Turnbull); reproductive biology of plants (Herbert G. Baker and Gordon W. Frankie); beetle interactions (Jack E. Coster); early development of the forests (Gordon H. Orians); leaf-litter herpetofauna (Jay M. Savage and Ian R. Straughan); reproductive cycles, biomass, and food in vertebrate consumers (Henry S. Fitch); insect-plant interactions (Lawrence E. Gilbert); experiments with tropical forest litter and its biotic communities (Monte Lloyd); growth initiative in trees (James S. Bethel); mineral cycling (Dale W. Cole); biometeorology (Leo Fritschen); soils and plant nutrition (Stanley P. Gessel); plant community interactions (William H. Hatheway); insect dynamics (Daniel H. Janzen).

Subsequent studies of a more restricted and individually coordinated type, especially in population biology, have been the mode since 1976. The titles of published papers from these efforts constitute part of the bibliographies of this book; the substance of many of them is contained in the articles that follow.

The Future of Costa Rican Field Biology

The enormous and tragic devastation of tropical forest environments during the past decades (Myers 1981) promises to continue in spite of the best efforts of all who care for natural environments. Although Costa Rica now has a cadre of biologists whose orientations have been shaped by the new theoretical ecology, the ecological movement, and the stimulus of continuing contact with United States science through OTS, can they resist this trend? Through their efforts, Costa Rica now has a solid scientific base in its CONICIT, its universities, and the Museo Nacional. It has an awareness of ecological problems and the proper attitude to face this dilemma. The Costa Rican national park system gives some hope that the marvelously diverse communities of tropical organisms will be preserved for future generations to enjoy and for future scientists to study.

But can these factors overcome the pragmatism of economic man? Especially the pragmatism of the Latin culture? Can short-term economic gain be ignored for future long-term benefits to the nation? Or will Costa Rica, now ideally situated to provide an example to the rest of tropical America, succumb as well?

We do not know. Perhaps Costa Rica, among all the tropical countries, because of its history, its commitment to the preservation of natural areas, and its emerging scientific consciousness, can avoid the temptation of uncontrolled exploitation of its lands. If it succeeds where all others have failed it may be the beacon that provides guidance to others in the salvation of natural tropical environments. The pessimist may wish Costa Rica well yet believe there will be no room for field biology by the end of this century. Only fields of crops, a crowded and polluted Meseta Central, eroded hills, and silted rivers will remain. The optimist fears the worst yet remembers the changes in Costa Rican national attitudes in the past two decades, the dedicated young biological scientists and conservationists who have helped in developing the nation's environmental consciousness, and the emerging national concern for basic knowledge of the environment and its biota coupled with planning for the benefit of both man and environment. A long shot perhaps, but one that must pay off if there is to be tropical field biology in the twenty-first century.

But still—we remember the bright blue skies, the white clouds, the almost black forest on the slopes of the volcanoes, the driving rain, the green complexity of the forest canopy viewed from a mountain slope, and our own tininess within the forest's grasp. We remember the wonder and awe when a startled danta leaps up from underfoot, the morpho butterflies flit by, and the bellbird sounds from the forest top. On the trail of discovery followed by all the long line of our predecessors in the forests and on the cerros of Costa Rica, can we truly believe that man is so foolish as to completely destroy this special world? We cannot let it be so! For once gone, something special and basic about ourselves will be gone too—and afterward man himself will not survive. *Viva Costa Rica!* All success in this noble undertaking!

*

Aguilar B., O. 1978. *Costa Rica y los hechos políticos de 1948: Problematica de una década.* San José: Editorial Costa Rica.

Balli, A. 1974–77. *Ideas biológicas.* Department of Biology, University of Costa Rica. Mimeographed.

Barahona J., L. 1953, *El gran incógnito: Visión interna del campesino costarricense.* Serie Ensayos 3. San José: Editorial Universidad de Costa Rica.

Boza, M., and Bonilla, A. 1981. *The National Parks of Costa Rica.* Madrid: INCAFO.

Cardoso, F. H.; Pinto, A.; and Sunkel, O. 1970. *América Latina: Ciencia y tecnología en el desarrollo de la sociedad.* Colección Tiempo Latinoamericano. Santiago de Chile: Editorial Universitaria.

Cerdas, R. 1972. *La crísis de la democracia liberal en Costa Rica.* Series 6. San José: EDUCA.

Colón, C. 1972. *Diario de Colón.* 2d ed. Madrid: Editorial Cultura Hispánica.

Conejo G., A. 1972. Materiales para una bio-bibliografía costarricense del Dr. Henri Pittier Dormond. Tesis de grado, Universidad de Costa Rica.

Dobles S., L. 1927. *Indice bibliográfico de Costa Rica.* Vols. 1–3. San José: Lehmann.

Estrada M., L. 1965. *La Costa Rica de Don Tomás de Acosta.* San José: Editorial Costa Rica.

Fernández G., R. 1972. *Costa Rica en el siglo XIX.* 3d ed. San José: EDUCA.

Ferrero A., L. 1978. W. M. Gabb. *Talamanca: El espacio y los hombres.* Serie Nos Ven 7. San José: Ministerio de Cultura, Juventud y Deporte.

Folkman, D. I. 1970. *The Nicaragua route.* Salt Lake City: University of Utah Press.

Gaspar, J. C. 1979. *Limón 1880–1940: Un estudio de la industria bananera en Costa Rica.* San José: Editorial Costa Rica.

Gómez P., L. D. 1973. El Museo Nacional de Costa Rica. *Museum* (UNESCO) 25:182–84.

———. 1975a. *Bibliografía geológica y paleontológica de Centroamerica y el Caribe.* San José: Museo Nacional de Costa Rica.

———, ed. 1975b, Biology of Bromeliaceae. In *Historia natural de Costa Rica,* vol. 1. San José: Museo Nacional de Costa Rica.

———. 1978a. Contribuciones a la pteridología costarricense. XI. Hermann Christ, su vida, obra e influencia en la botánica nacional. *Brenesia* 12–13:25–79.

———. 1978*b*. Contribuciones a la pteridología costarricense. XII. Carlos Wercklé. *Brenesia* 14–15:361–93.

González F., L. F. 1976. *Historia de la influencia extranjera en el desenvolvimiento educacional y científico de Costa Rica*. 2d ed. Biblioteca Patria. San José: Editorial Costa Rica.

———. 1978. *Evolución de la institución pública en Costa Rica*. 2d ed. Biblioteca Patria. San José: Editorial Costa Rica.

González V., C. 1977. *Historia financiera de Costa Rica*. 2d ed. San José: Editorial Costa Rica.

Hall, C. 1978. *El café y el desarrollo histórico-geográfico de Costa Rica*. San José: Editorial Costa Rica–EUNA.

Hoffmann, Carl. 1856. Excursion nach dem Volcán de Cartago in Central America. *Bonplandia*, no. 6.

———. 1957. Eine Excursion nach dem Barba-Vulkan in Costa Rica. *Bonplandia*, no. 16.

Houwald, G. von. 1975. *Los Alemanes en Nicaragua*. Serie Histórica 2. Managua: Banco de América.

Jiménez, R. 1921. El Colegio de Cartago. *Repertorio Americano* (San José).

Láscaris C., C. 1964. *Desarrollo de las ideas Filosóficas en Costa Rica*. San José: Editorial Costa Rica.

———. 1975. *El costarricense*. San José: Editorial Universidad Centroamericana (EDUCA).

Myers, N. 1981. The hamburger connection: How Central America's forests became North America's hamburgers. *Ambio* 10:3–8.

Picado Ch., M. 1964. *Vida y obra del Doctor Clodomiro Picado*. Biblioteca Autores Costarricenses. San José: Editorial Costa Rica.

Picado T., C. 1921. Pasteur y Metchnikoff. *Repertorio Americano* (San José).

Picado T., C., and Trejos W., A. 1942. *Biología hematológica comparada*. San José: Editorial Universidad de Costa Rica.

Rodríguez, V. E. 1979. *Apuntes para una sociología costarricense*. 3d ed. San José: Editorial Universidad Estatal a Distancia.

Sancho, M. 1935. *Costa Rica, Suiza Centroamericana*. San José.

Sapper, C. 1943. *Viajes a varias partes de la República de Costa Rica 1899–1924*, ed. J. F. Trejos. San José: Universal.

Schifter, J. 1979. *La fase oculta de la guerra civil en Costa Rica*. San José: Editorial Universitaria Centroamericana (EDUCA).

Slud, P. 1960. The birds of Finca "La Selva," a tropical wet forest locality. *Bull. Am. Mus. Nat. Hist.* 121:49–148.

———. 1964. The birds of Costa Rica: Distribution and ecology. *Bull. Am. Mus. Nat. Hist.* 128:1–430.

Smith, C. M. 1978. The impact of O.T.S. on the ecology of Costa Rica. *Texas J. Sci.* 30:283–89.

Soley G., T. 1975. *Compendio de historia económica y hacendaria de Costa Rica*. 2d ed. Biblioteca Patria. San José: Editorial Costa Rica.

Termer, F. 1956. Carlos Sapper: Explorador de Centro-América (1866–1954). *An. Soc. Geog. Hist. Guatemala* 29:55–101.

Trudeau, R. H. 1971. Costa Rican voting: Its socio-economic correlates. Ph.D. diss., University of North Carolina.

2 THE CENTRAL AMERICAN DISPERSAL ROUTE: BIOTIC HISTORY AND PALEOGEOGRAPHY

P. V. Rich and T. H. Rich

The narrow strip of land that today joins the Neotropics of South America and the Nearctic of North America, two major biogeographic realms, has not always been as it is. At present Central America forms a continuous land connection between the north and the south, serving both as a corridor for terrestrial forms (Marshall et al. 1982) and as a barrier to marine forms attempting an east-west movement between the Caribbean–Gulf of Mexico and the Pacific Ocean. In times past this area has been both continuous terrestrial corridor and insular stepping-stones for land dwellers as well as both barrier and corridor for marine life. Thus it has a varied history that cannot be deduced from its present configuration.

To understand the biotic associations present today in Costa Rica, as well as in the rest of Central America, it is useful to know something of the history of the area. Thus it is appropriate that this book include sections on geologic history (see chap. 4) and on plant and animal fossils. In this chapter we deal with three major aspects of Central American history. First, we estimate what the area has looked like, both paleogeographically and paleo-environmentally, during the Phanerozoic (the past 600 million years or so). Second, we present an overview of biotic history, that is, a summary of what is known of fossil organisms, both marine and nonmarine, emphasizing the past 60 million years, the time most relevant to the development of modern faunas and floras in this area. Third, we evaluate the role this area has played in the biotic interchange between different biogeographic realms and consider how it has achieved its present unique character.

The Paleogeography of Central America during the Phanerozoic: The Past 600 Million Years

The narrow strip of land that now connects the major *terrestrial* biogeographic realms of Nearctica (North America) and Neotropica (South America) includes Costa Rica. Today this area is usually included within the Neotropical realm, but it certainly has a distinct Nearctic flavor, and it serves as a filter bridge (see Simpson 1965; Marshall et al. 1982) across which some organisms can

pass. Additionally, it now serves as a barrier to marine forms in both the Caribbean and the Pacific; but, as paleontological studies have demonstrated, its role has changed many times. Let us first try to reconstruct just how Central America looked geographically and ascertain its relationship to both North and South America through time. To this end, we will present a quick resume of several current theories, none of which has met with general acceptance.

No more than twenty years ago, a majority of biogeographers would have said that Central America has always been much as it is today. The only major changes suggested would have been occasional rises and falls in sea level and raising and lowering of the mountains that form the backbone of the area. But as for bits and pieces of Central America moving through several degrees of latitude or longitude, the prevailing opinion was "not possible!" Continents, and parts thereof, were stable—perhaps not vertically, but definitely with regard to "horizonal" position upon the earth's surface and certainly relative to one another. This "stablist" hypothesis, then, is one way of viewing the past of Costa Rica and the rest of Central America.

Plate Tectonics and Central America

More recently, a number of theories with a "mobilist" flavor have been put forward, contending that parts of Central America have moved markedly and that the present configuration cannot be assumed to extend very far into the past. All these theories assume the correctness of a major synthetic theory, *plate tectonics* (see any recent geology text for a thorough explanation of this, such as Wyllie 1976 or Tarling and Tarling 1971), and the existence of sea-floor spreading. Simply stated, this theory suggests that the earth's crust (the outer few hundred kilometers of rock) is composed of a series of plates (see fig. 2.1) that meet along three types of boundaries: ridges, trenches, and transform faults (see figs. 2.2 and 2.3). Where plates meet along ridges, new molten rock is added from below, causing the plates to grow and move in opposite directions (ridges, such as the mid-

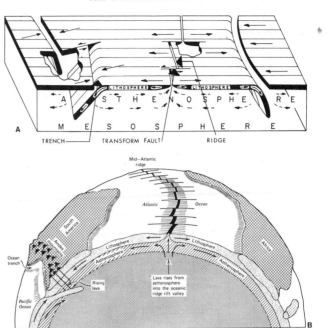

FIGURE 2.2. Cross section of a part of the upper 700 km of the earth showing major divisions between crustal plates. *a,* modified after Sykes (1972). *b,* from Wyllie (1976).

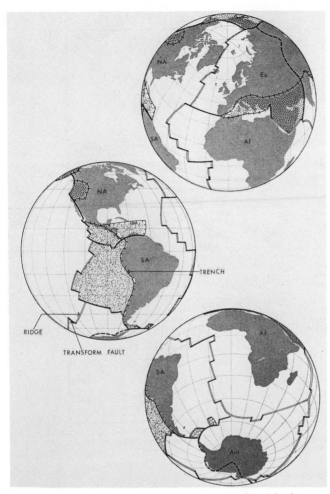

FIGURE 2.1. Major divisions (lithospheric plates) in the earth's crust that have moved relative to one another. The major boundaries are of three types: ridges, where new crustal material is added and plates grow; trenches, where crustal material slides beneath other crustal material; and transform faults, where crustal material slides past other crustal material (e.g., the San Andreas fault in California). In this diagram, ‖ represents ridges; ≠, trenches; | transform faults. From Middlemiss, Rawson, and Newall (1971).

Atlantic ridge, most often occur in ocean basins, but they can have terrestrial counterparts, as in central Iceland). Shallow earthquakes and volcanic activity often occur along such boundaries.

Trenches are boundaries where one crustal plate (lithospheric plate) dives under another, and the lower plate is consumed or remobilized. Crustal shortening occurs in these areas, and deep earthquakes are common along the plane of the descending plate. The oceanic trench off the west coast of South America is a familiar example, often associated with devastating earthquakes in Chile and other western South American countries. Not only are shallow, moderate, or deep earthquakes associated with such trenches, but so is volcanism. Behind trenches, above the area where one plate descends beneath another,

volcanoes are common, as in the Lesser Antilles, an extreme example being the tremendous explosion of Mount Pele early in this century.

Transform faults are a third boundary type, where two crustal plates move past one another laterally, generally resulting in shallow earthquakes. Most of these occur in ocean basins, but occasionally they are manifest on land such, as is supposedly the case with the San Andreas fault in California.

Detailed studies of ocean floor magnetism, volcanism, seismicity, general geology, and several other aspects of geology all suggest that plate tectonics is the best theory currently available. One major problem remaining is just what mechanism drives these plates, although many suggestions have been made (see fig. 2.4).

When the plate tectonics model is applied to the history of the area between North and South America, the Caribbean, and the Gulf of Mexico, several theories result. Most workers have dealt only with the past 100 to 200 million years of history (Dietz and Holden 1970; Fox, Schreiber, and Heezen 1971; Freeland and Dietz 1971; Malfait and Dinkelman 1972, for example), but a few have attempted reconstructions spanning 600 million years (Walper and Rowett 1972), beginning with the Paleozoic era (see figs. 2.5 and 2.6).

There certainly are Paleozoic rocks in parts of Central America, all north of central Nicaragua, some dating back to least 400 million years, into the Silurian period (Nairn and Stehli 1975). But there is a lack of understanding of just what paleogeographic relationship these

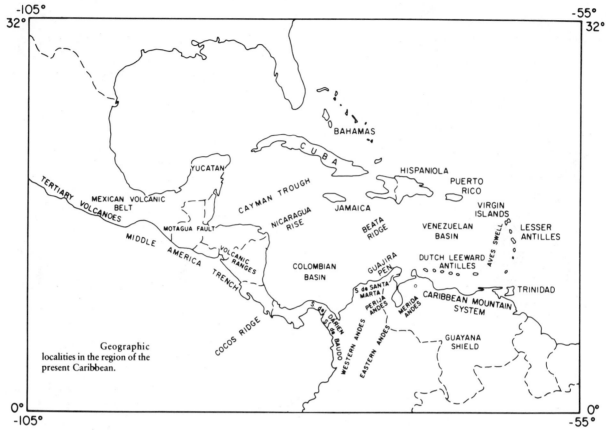

FIGURE 2.3. Important geographic features of terrestrial and marine environments in Central America and the Caribbean (after Ladd 1976).

Central American rocks had to each other and to those outside this area. For example, there is no general agreement on whether the Gulf of Mexico first formed during the Mesozoic or is a much older Paleozoic or Precambrian feature. Some workers suggest that the first and only Gulf of Mexico began in the Mesozoic and gradually enlarged as the North and South Atlantic developed over the past 200 million years. Others suggest that this was only the final history of a much older ocean that was present during the Paleozoic and may have partially or completely closed during the late Paleozoic or early Mesozoic, only to reopen again in the Mesozoic to present. According to this latter theory, there would have been a proto-Gulf as well as the modern Gulf of Mexico (see Cebull and Sherbet 1980, for a good summary of this controversy). Evidence is gradually accumulating to suggest that the proto-Gulf/Gulf hypothesis is the more tenable (Cebull and Sherbet 1980; Ross 1979).

More applicable to studies on the living biota of Central America are paleogeographic reconstructions for the late Mesozoic and Cenozoic, a time when mammals and birds as well as the flowering angiosperms radiated widely. Although there is still disagreement among mobilist geologists about the correct way to assemble and disassemble Central America, there is much more paleomagnetic data and information from general geology and fossil studies, allowing more constraints on theories proposed for the past 200 million years than on theories about earlier times.

FIGURE 2.4. Proposed mechanism for movement of lithospheric plates (after Rich 1976).

FIGURE 2.5. Geological time scale giving both names and absolute dates for the major time divisions from the beginning of the earth to the present (from McAlester 1976).

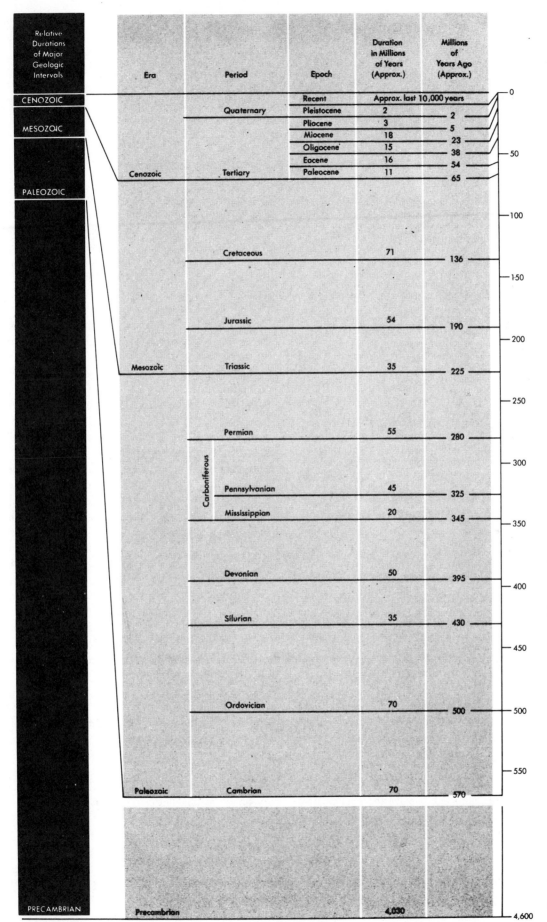

Relative Durations of Major Geologic Intervals	Era	Period	Epoch	Duration in Millions of Years (Approx.)	Millions of Years Ago (Approx.)	
CENOZOIC			Recent	Approx. last 10,000 years	0	
		Quaternary	Pleistocene	2	2	
			Pliocene	3	5	
			Miocene	18	23	
MESOZOIC			Oligocene	15	38	
	Cenozoic	Tertiary	Eocene	16	54	
			Paleocene	11	65	
PALEOZOIC		Cretaceous		71	136	
		Jurassic		54	190	
	Mesozoic	Triassic		35	225	
		Permian		55	280	
		Pennsylvanian (Carboniferous)		45	325	
		Mississippian (Carboniferous)		20	345	
		Devonian		50	395	
		Silurian		35	430	
		Ordovician		70	500	
	Paleozoic	Cambrian		70	570	
PRECAMBRIAN		Precambrian		4,030	4,600	

Millions of Years

Formation of Earth's crust about 4,600 million years ago

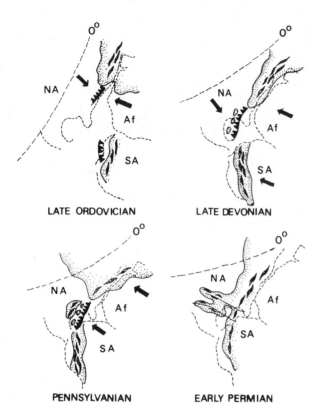

FIGURE 2.6. Inferred Paleozoic history of Central America, from 600 to 225 million years ago (after Walper and Rowett 1972).

Figure 2.7 illustrates several hypotheses on continental configurations at the beginning of the Mesozoic. Although they indicate the breadth of divergent opinions, all suggest that the separation of North and South America as well as the separation of both from Africa at this time was small, and that terrestrial forms thus probably would have had few barriers to dispersal. Pacific and Atlantic marine forms would have been affected in a variety of ways depending on the reconstruction chosen. During the Mesozoic and Cenozoic, the North and South Atlantic as well as the Gulf of Mexico and the Caribbean Sea gradually developed and increased in size (see figs. 2.8–10). Malfait and Dinkelman (1972) have suggested that during this expansion of these ocean basins the Central American area was affected by the incursion of part of the Pacific crustal plate, which determined the paleogeography of this entire area. Others workers (e.g., Gose and Scott 1979; Gose and Swartz 1977; Anderson 1978; and Schmidt 1978) do not entirely agree with this model, preferring to define a number of small crustal plates in the eastern Pacific and Caribbean area that rotate relative to one another, eventually leading to the late Cenozoic aggregation that we know today as terrestrial Central America.

Even though it is not clear which of the multiple theories are correct, it *is* clear that, from the latest Mesozoic

until sometime in the Pliocene (5–6 million years ago; Raven and Axelrod 1975), no terrestrial connection existed between North and South America via Central America (see our section on paleontology below, and Bandy and Casey 1973; Case et al. 1971, among others), although there could well have been a connection via Europe and Africa.

Plate Tectonics and Costa Rica

The geologic history of Costa Rica, unlike that of "nuclear Central America" (to the north of central Nicaragua) spans only the middle Mesozoic to Recent times. There are no known Paleozoic rocks from northern Nicaragua to Colombia (Nairn and Stehli 1975). During this time terrestrial geologic history has been tied to volcanism, as have even the marine sediments of the Mesozoic.

Most of the Mesozoic sequence, exemplified by the Nicoya complex, well exposed on the Nicoya Peninsula (see chap. 4) represents deepwater marine sediments probably associated with a trench, the volcanic rocks resulting from remobilization of oceanic crust on the descending plate behind the trench (see fig. 2.2).

Rocks from the Cenozoic (including the older Tertiary period and the younger Quaternary period) include both volcanic (as well as plutonic; see chap. 4) and terrestrial and marine sedimentary fractions. The terrestrial sediments represent volcanic debris, riverine and lake deposits flowing off the rising backbone of Central America, which continues to grow through volcanic activity. According to Malfait and Dinkelman's (1972) hypothesis, these mountains (see figs. 2.2 and 2.8–10) have resulted from upwelling of remobilized, molten material created along a descending crustal plate behind the Middle American Trench. Only in the late Pliocene did they approach their current height. Most of the terrestrial sediments deposited as these mountains rose have very small areas of outcrop (often only along streams and in roadcuts); they are otherwise covered by vegetation or may have been deeply weathered, and thus fossil localities within them are extremely rare.

Throughout most of the Cenozoic the area from Nicaragua to northern Colombia would probably have been reminiscent of the Lesser Antilles today—volcanically active, topographically and environmentally diverse, but certainly not a continuous terrestrial connection. This area was a perfect example of Simpson's (1965) sweepstakes route between North and South America, allowing only an occasional terrestrial form to pass, purely by chance, not by design.

History of the Flora of Central America: The Flowering Plants

Today the angiosperms, or flowering plants, are the dominant terrestrial plants, having retained this dominance

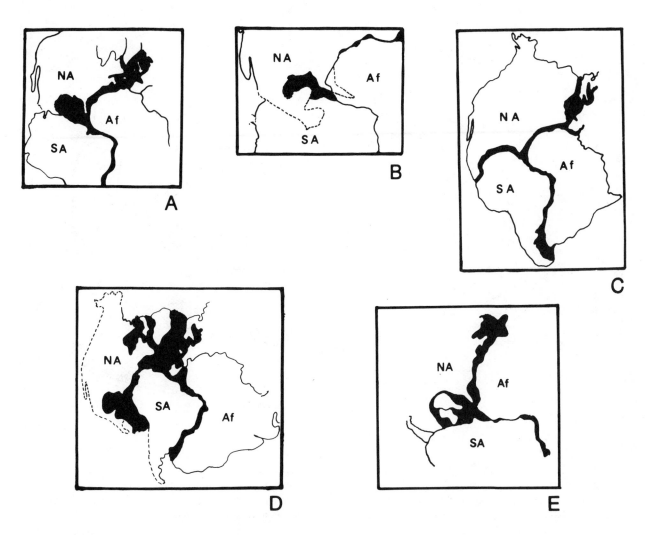

FIGURE 2.7. Five hypotheses concerning the arrangement of continents just before the last stage of major drifting, during the Triassic (early Mesozoic), about 200 million years ago. *a,* "Bullard fit" after Sherbet and Cebull 1975. *b,* "Bullard fit" after Freeland and Dietz 1971. *c,* After Walper and Rowett 1972. *d,* After Morel and Irving 1980. *e,* After Freeland and Dietz 1971.

for more than 80 million years. In Central America at present, the angiosperms—in fact the entire flora—seem most similar to those of South America. In reviewing this similarity Raven and Axelrod (1975) suggest that, ever since the beginning of angiosperms sometime during the Cretaceous, Africa and South America, and perhaps even some of the fragments of Central America yet unconsolidated, have constituted a site of evolutionary importance. Much of the world's lowland tropics were concentrated in these areas. As Africa and South America separated, from the late Cretaceous onward, and as South

America began to converge on some parts of Central America, the West Indies, and southern North America, sweepstakes dispersal occurred and South American forms moved into these areas.

Raven and Axelrod (1975) further note that the reverse dispersal, from temperate North America to South America, was not so striking. "Such genera as fir (*Abies*), alder (*Alnus*), sweetgum (*Liquidambar*), beech (*Fagus*), walnut (*Juglans*) and elm (*Ulnus*) had already reached the mountains of southern Mexico 16 million years ago" (p. 428). Some of these forms extended through Central

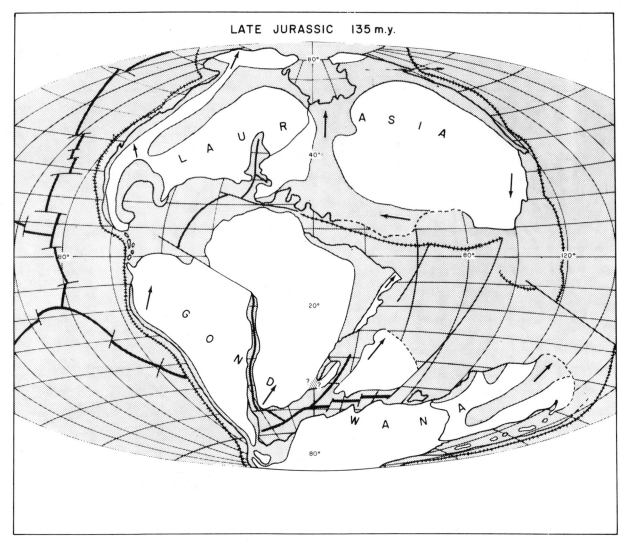

FIGURE 2.8. The world during mid-Mesozoic times, 135 million years ago. *Hatched lines* indicate oceanic trenches where crust is being consumed; *heavy lines,* spreading ridges; *light lines,* transform faults. *Arrows* indicate motion of individual crustal plates relative to one another. *White areas* are terrestrial environments (after Rich 1975).

America into South America, with walnuts reaching northern South America by at least 8 million years ago, alders by 700,000 years ago, and oaks (*Quercus*) by about 150,000 years ago. By the late Pliocene, some 2–3 million years ago, the mountains were high enough to provide a reliable corridor for montane-adapted plants.

During the Pleistocene, cool climates first appear in tropical latitudes (Raven and Axelrod 1975), and this further promoted dispersal of Montane species. Such forms as the gooseberries and currents (*Ribes*), the locoweeds (*Astragalus*), willows (*Salix*), and evening primroses (*Oenothera*) probably dispersed south from North America then sometime during the past million years.

Additionally, during the Pleistocene there were periods of greater aridity than in modern times (Raven and Axelrod 1974). Grasslands expanded, as did thorn scrub, and this environmental alteration favored the exchange both north and south of more arid-adapted animals and of grazing forms such as glypotodonts, horses, ground sloths, and camels (see below).

Rock Sequences in Central America, with Emphasis on Marine Sediments and Invertebrate Fossils: Paleozoic to Recent

Woodring (1964) summarizes well the outcrop patterns of marine rocks in Central America, which are dated primarily according to the invertebrate fossils occurring in them. Most of these fossils are foraminifers and radiolarians or mollusks (primarily bivalves and gastropods) (see fig. 2.11).

The oldest rocks in Central America occur in the deformed mountain ranges of northern Honduras, central Guatemala, and northern Nicaragua. These are definitely

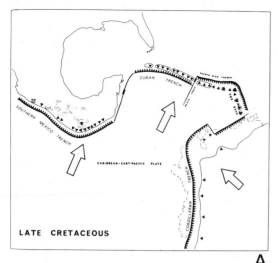

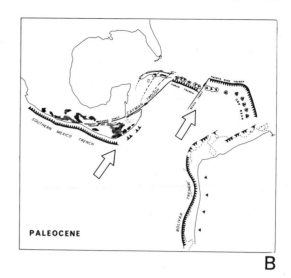

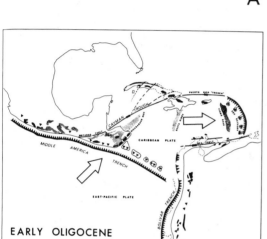

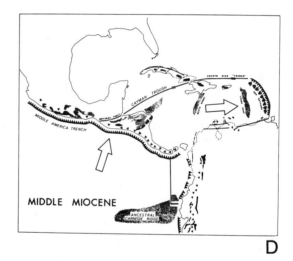

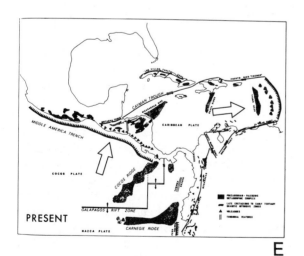

FIGURE 2.9. The history of Central America during the late Mesozoic and Cenozoic era, 80 million years ago to the present (after Malfait and Dinkelman 1972).

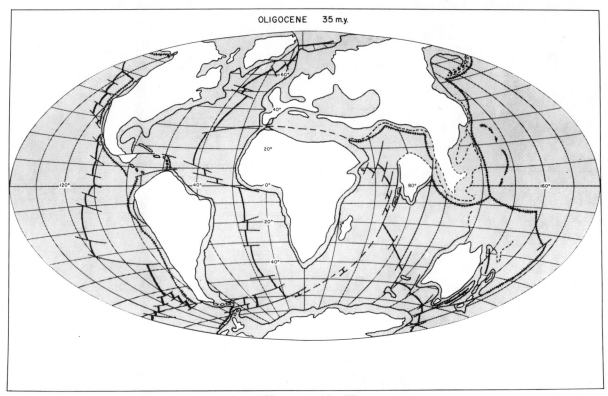

FIGURE 2.10. The world during mid-Cenozoic times (Oligocene), 35 million years ago. See figure 2.8 for legend.

older then early Permian and in fact may be Precambrian in age. Early Permian marine rocks directly overlie these older igneous and metamorphic rocks.

No Triassic rocks appear to be present in Central America, and there is a record of deformation and intrusion by granitic, and some more basic, rocks. After this deformation, nonmarine Jurassic rocks were deposited north and south of these folded ranges. These rocks contain plants of early and middle Jurassic age. Except for an undocumented report of late Jurassic sediments in Honduras, no marine Jurassic rocks are known from Central America. Early Cretaceous marine rocks are known in northern Central America, containing rhudist corals (see fig. 2.11) and the microscopic foraminifer *Orbitolina concava texana*. Although they do not crop out on land, early Cretaceous deposits dredged up off the Pacific coast of Central America have contained land-plant debris. Late Cretaceous marine deposits are known in northern Guatemala that contain the strange rudist bivalve *Barrettia* (converging with corals in external morphology) and from northwestern Panama near the Costa Rican border (dated by the contained foraminifers).

Cenozoic marine deposits are decidedly more abundant in Central America than are Mesozoic and Paleozoic deposits. Paleocene and early Eocene sediments, however, are mostly thin and limited in extent. During the mid to late Eocene carbonate deposits (limestones) were widespread, with some terrestrial sediments and volcanics. Although early Oligocene sediments of any kind are rare, marine limestones of late Oligocene or Miocene occur in Central America, along with extensive volcanics and some terrestrial sediments. Marine Pliocene deposits are generally thin; marine coralliferous rocks are known from Limón, Costa Rica. Thin marine Pleistocene deposits are widely distributed on coastal terraces. They have not been satisfactorily differentiated into early or late Pleistocene. Reef corals and mollusks are common in these deposits.

Some of the more important invertebrate localities in Central America are listed below, as are faunal lists of the better-known forms from each of these areas. Figure 2.11 illustrates a few of the characteristic invertebrate fossils from some of these locales. For more detailed coverage of this topic one should consult such references as Davies (1971–75), Olsson (1922, 1942, 1943) Jackson (1917), Coryell and Fields (1937), and Woodring (1957), both for text descriptions and for good illustrations of most species. Only a very few localities have produced Cretaceous, or pre- Cenozoic, invertebrates in Central America. The fauna includes foraminifers (*Globotruncana* and *Gümbelina*), radiolarians, and rhudist corals.

The first diverse marine invertebrate faunas from southern Central America are known from the mid to late Eocene of Panama and Costa Rica (e.g., Gatuncillo For-

20

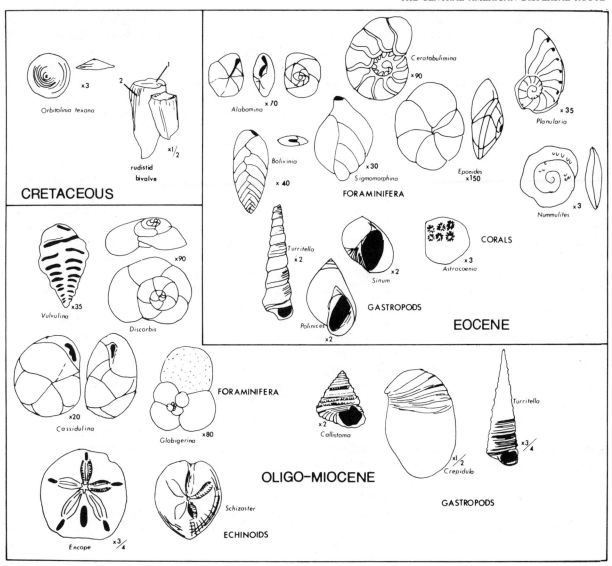

FIGURE 2.11. A selection of invertebrates most common in Central American Phanerozoic sediments. Ages are indicated for each suite.

mation) and have been dated primarily by the contained microscopic Foraminifera. Smaller Foraminifera include *Alabamin*, *Allomorphina*, *Angulogerina*, *Anomalina*, *Anomalinoides*, *Astacolus*, *Bathysiphon*, *Bolivina*, *Bulimina*, *Cassidulina*, *Cassidulinoides*, *Ceratobulimina*, *Chilostomella*, *Chilostomelloides*, *Chrysalogonium*, *Cibicides*, *Clavulinoides*, *Cornuspira*, *Cyclammina*, *Dentalina*, *Discorbis*, *Dorothia*, *Ellipsoglandulina*, *Entosolenis*, *Eponides*, *Frondicularia*, *Gaudryina*, *Glandulina*, *Globigerina*, *Globigerinoides*, *Globulimina*, *Globorotalia*, *Globulina*, *Gümbelina*, *Guttulina*, *Gyroidinoides*, *Hantkenina*, *Haplophragmoides*, *Hastigerinella*, *Höglundina*, *Karreriella*, *Lagena*, *Lagenoglandulina*, *Lagenonodosauria*, *Loxostoma*, *Marginulina*, *Marginulinopsis*, *Nodogenerina*, *Nodosaria*, *Noion*, *Orthomorphina*, *Osangularia*, *Planularia*, *Planulina*, *Plectina*, *Plecto-* *frondicularia*, *Pleurostomella*, *Pseudoglandulina*, *Pullenia*, *Pyrgo*, *Quinqueloculina*, *Robulus*, *Rotaliatina*, *Saracenaria*, *Schenckiella*, *Sigmoilina*, *Sigmomorphina*, *Siphonina*, *Siphonodosaria*, *Siphotextularia*, *Spiroloculina*, *Spiroplectammina*, *Textularia*, *Textulariella*, *Triloculina*, *Uvigerina*, *Vaginulinopsis*, *Valvulineria*, *Virgulina*. Larger foraminifers include *Yaberinella*, *Operculinoides*, *Nummulites*, *Heterostegina*, *Fabiania*, *Helicostegina*, *Lepidocyclina*, *Helicolepidina*, *Asterocycline*, and *Pseudophragmina* (Woodring 1957). Corals include *Heliopora*, *Astrocoenia*, *Astreopora*, *Diploastrea*, *Goniopora*, *Porites*, *Favia*, *Colpophyllia*, *Antillia*, and *Millepora*. Mollusks include *Velates*, *Hannatoma*, *Xenophora*, *Hipponix*, *Calyptracea*, *Polonices?*, *Neverita?*, *Sinum*, *Amaurellina?*, *Pachycrommium?*, *Turritella* cf. *carinata*, and *T.* cf. *samanensis*.

Oligocene faunas possibly are represented by the Bohio Formation in Panama, which contains a diversity of smaller Foraminifera. Although much of this formation is nonmarine, with silicified wood recorded, the marine fossils are what establish the age of these sediments. Smaller Foraminifera include *Alabamina, Ammospira, Angulogerina, Astacolus, Bathysiphon, Bolivina, Bulimina, Cassidulina, Chrysalogonium, Cibicides, Clavulinoides, Cyclammina, Dentalina, Discorbis, Eponides, Gaudryina, Glandulina, Globigerina ciperoensis, Gümbelina, Guttulina, Gyroidinoides, Karreriella, Lagena, Marginulina, Nodogenerina, Nodosaria, Nonion, Osangularia, Planularia, Plectina, Plectofrondicularia, Pleurostomella, Pseudoglandulina, Pullenia, Quinqueloculina, Robulus, Schenckiella, Sigmomorphina, Siphonina, Siphonodosaria, Spiroloculina, Uvigerina, Vaginulina, Vaginulinopsis, Virgulina,* and *Vulvulina.* Larger Foraminifera include *Heterostegina antillea, Archaias, Lepidocyclina,* and *Miogypsina.* Mollusks are primarily gastropods and include *Solariella, Neritina, Hemisinus, Crepidula, Natica, Polinices, Sinum, Globularia, Pachycrommium,* and *Turritella* cf. *altilira* (Woodring 1957).

Miocene marine faunas are markedly diverse in Foraminifera, corals, mullusks, and a few enhinoids. Some of the more important fossiliferous rock units are the Culebra, Cucaracha, Panama, and Gatún formations, mainly in Panama, especially on Barro Colorado Island and part of the Usacari Shale and the "Puerto Limón" Formation near Limón, Costa Rica. Foraminifers include *Siphogenerian transversa, Miogypsina, Lepidocyclina miraflorensis,* and several others not yet described. Corals include *Stylophora, Acropora, Porites,* and *Montastrea.* Mollusks include a particularly wide variety in the Gatún Formation: *Calliostoma, Turbo, Neritina, Teinostoma, Anticlimax, Cyclostremiscus, Solariorbis, Episcynia, Rissoina, Xenophora, Crepidula, Calyptraea, Trochita, Crucibulum, Cheilea, Natica, Stigmaulax, Tectonatica, Polinices, Neverita, Sinum, Turritella altilira* and several more species. Echinoids include *Clypeaster gatuni, Encope annectens,* and *Schizaster panamensis.* Eighteen species of ostracods have also been recorded (Coryell and Fields 1937). Other areas that have produced Miocene faunas of marked diversity include the Río Dulce (Guatemala) and Barranca (Costa Rica). Fish are also rather abundant in the Gatún Formation including selachians and teleosts (*Xenodermichthys* and *Gobius*).

The Cucaracha Formation is of particular interest because it is mainly nonmarine. Later in this chapter we will discuss fossil mammals. The formation also includes plant debris (*Taenioxylon multiradiatum*) and wood. A few marine and brackish-water fossils have been found in the lower part of the formation: *Anadara, Crassostrea* cf. *Lucina,* and *C.* cf. *Tellina.* On the basis of these few fossils the age of the Cucaracha Formation cannot be established, but it can be delimited because both the underlying Culebra Formation and the overlying Panama Formation are considered to be of Miocene age.

The Pliocene is represented by such rock units as the Chagres sandstone (Toro limestone member) of Panama, the Burica sandstone of Panama and Costa Rica, and the Moin Formation near Limón, Costa Rica. Faunas from these are primarily mollusks and a few echinoids: Mollusks include *Dentalium, Terebra, Architectonica, Cancellaria, Hanetia, Cantharus, Phos, Fusinus, Siphonalia, Turritella, Polinices, Nucula, Arca, Pecten, Chione, Luciploma thyasira,* and *Solemya.* In the Burica Formation the presence of *Dentalium (Fissidentalium) buricum* and *Nucula iphigenia* suggest a Pliocene age, while *Phos gatunensis* and *Turritella* cf. *gatunensis* suggest late Miocene affinities. Additional mollusks from the Chagres sandstone include *Turitella altilira* and *Stigmaulax fuppians.* Echinoids are represented by *Clypeaster.*

By far the most richly fossiliferous of all the Cenozoic marine rocks are those of Pleistocene age. Mollusks are by far the most diverse of any invertebrate group recorded, although a thorough search of more recent literature would probably yield additional data on Foraminifera. A typical assemblage of molluskan genera is represented by one from Monte Verde Ravine, Costa Rica, where more than 130 molluskan species are known: *Arca, Barbartia, Noetia, Pinna, Ostrea, Pecten, Plicatula, Crenella, Anomia, Placuanomia, Pandora, Thracia, Eucrassatella, Crassinella, Chama, Diplodonta, Cardium, Cyclinella, Macrocallista, Pitar, Chione, Tellina, Macoma, Semele, Tagelus, Solecurtus, Mactra, Labiosa, Corbula, Panopea, Bullaria, Terebra, Conus, Polystira, Turricula, Clathrodrillia, Crassispira, Nannodrillia, Cancellaria, Oliva, Olivella, Marginella, Lyria, Latirus, Galeodea, Hanetia, Colubraria, Cymatium, Distorsio, Engina, Cantharus, Triumphis, Nassa, Phos, Metula, Columbella, Cosmioconcha, Strombina, Murex, Phyllonotus, Thais, Seimcassis, Ficus, Cypraea, Strombus, Turritella, Architectonica, Crepidula, Crucibulum, Calyptraea, Natica, Polinices, Neritina, Circulus,* and *Dentalium.* Many species are indistinguishable from living forms. Corals are also diverse in these faunas.

When Cenozoic marine invertebrate faunas of the Central American area are examined, particulary the mollusks (Woodring 1966), it becomes clear that, although species were able to move between the Caribbean and the Pacific during the early and middle part of the Cenozoic, particularly during the Miocene, that during the latest Miocene and more recently this interchange was increasingly restricted. Interchange ceased entirely during the latest Pliocene or earliest Pleistocene, the Central American land bridge disrupting an extensive biogeographic province. This not only stifled direct interchange but also led to the impoverishment of the Caribbean province (Woodring 1966).

For further identification of invertebrate fossils from field specimens books such as those by Moore, Lalicker, and Fischer (1952), Cushman (1955), and Davies (1971) should be consulted as starting points.

The Record of Cenozoic Terrestrial Mammals in Central America

The history of terrestrial vertebrates in Central America is poorly documented by direct evidence from the fossils of animals that once lived there. Table 2.1 lists the terrestrial fossil mammal sites recorded in the literature, and figure 2.12 shows where they are situated. None of them are Mesozoic in age, and only one is older than Miocene; thus the first four-fifths of the history of mammals is completely unknown in Central America, and all but the last tenth is documented by only one locality (see figs. 2.13–16).

TABLE 2.1   Summary of the Vertebrates from Central American Cenozoic Sediments

(Information is presented in the following order: 1, name of fauna; 2, country; 3, age; 4, literature reference; 5, continental affinities of fauna; 6, faunal list.)

Eocene-Oligocene

1. Guanajuato fauna
2. Mexico
3. Uintan or Chadronian (mid-Eocene to early Oligocene)
4. Black and Stephens (1973), Fries, Hibbard, and Dunkle (1955)
5. North America and endemic
6. Class Mammalia
   Order Perissodactyla
      Superfamily Tapiroidea
   Order Rodentia
      Family Ischyromyidae
         Floresomys guanajuatoensis
      Family indet.
         Guanajuatomys hibbardi

Miocene

1. El Gramal fauna
2. Oaxaca, Mexico
3. Hemingfordian or Barstovian (early Miocene)
4. Stirton (1954), Wilson (1967)
5. North America
6. Class Mammalia
   Order Perissodactyla
      Family Equidae
         Merychippus sp.
   Order Artiodactyla
      Family Camelidae
         ?Oxydactylus
      Family ?Protoceratidae

1. Cucaracha fauna (= Gaillard Cut local fauna)
2. Panama Canal Zone
3. Hemingfordian (early Miocene)
4. Patton and Taylor (1973), Whtimore and Stewart (1965)
5. North America
6. Class Reptilia
   Order Chelonia
   Order Crocodilia
   Class Mammalia
      Order Perissodactyla
         Family Equidae
            Anchiterium
            Archaeohippus
         Family Rhinocerotidae
            Diceratherium
      Order Artiodactyla
         Family Protoceratidae
            Paratoceras n. sp.
         Family Merycoidodontidae
            Merycochoerus
            ?Brachycrus

1. Hidalgo fauna
2. Mexico
3. Clarendonian (mid-Miocene)
4. Mooser (1959, 1963)
5. North America
6. Class Mammalia
   Order Perissodactyla
      Family Equidae
         Neohipparion montezumae
         N. otomii
         N. monias

Miocene-Pliocene

1. Gracias fauna
2. Honduras
3. Hemphillian (late Miocene or early Pliocene)
4. Olson and McGrew (1941), McGrew (1944)
5. North America, endemic at the specific level only
6. Class Mammalia
   Order Carnivora
      Family Canidae
         Osteoborus cynoides
         Amphicyon sp.
   Order Perissodactyla
      Family Equidae
         Pliohippus hondurensis
         Neohipparion montezumae
      Family Rhinocerotidae
         Subfamily Teleocerinae
   Order Artiodactyla
      Family Cervidae?
      Family Camelidae
         Procamelus sp.
   Order Proboscidea
      Family Bunomastodontidae
         Rhynchotherium sp., cf. *blicki*
   Order Rodentia

23

TABLE 2.1 Continued

Pleistocene

1. Comayagna Valley fauna
2. Honduras
3. Early Pleistocene
4. Webb (1972)
5. North and South America
6. Class Mammalia
    Order Proboscidea
    Order Notoungulata
        Family Toxodontidae

1. Copan fauna
2. Honduras
3. Late Pleistocene
4. Stirton and Gealey (1949)
5. North and South America
6. Class Mammalia
    Order Edentata
        Family Megatheriidae
            Megatherium
        Family Glyptodontidae
    Order Carnivora
        Family Felidae
            Felis concolor
    Order Perissodactyla
        Family Equidae
            Equus
    Order Artiodactyla
        Family Camelidae
            Camelops?
        Family Cervidae
            Odocoileus?
    Order Proboscidea
    Order Notoungulata
        Family Toxodontidae

1. El Hatillo fauna
2. Pese, Panama
3. Late Pleistocene
4. Gazin (1957)
5. North and South America
6. Class Reptilia
    Order Chelonia
        Family Testudinidae
            Pseudemys sp.
    Class Aves
        Order Anseriformes
            Family Anatidae
                Cairina moschata
    Class Mammalia
        Order Edentata
            Family Megatheriidae
                Eremotherium rusconi
            Family Mylodontidae
                Cf. *Glossotherium tropicorum*
                Scelidotherium?

Family Glyptodontidae
    Glyptodon
Order Perissodactyla
    Family Equidae
        Equus sp.
Order Artiodactyla
    Family Tayassuidae
    Family Cervidae
        Odocoileus sp.

1. Hormiguero
2. El Salvador
3. Late Pleistocene
4. Stirton and Gealey (1949)
5. North and South America
6. Class Mammalia
    Order Edentata
        Family Megatherium
            Megatherium
    Order Carnivora
        Family Felidae
            Smilodon
    Order Artiodactyla
        Family Camelidae
        Family Bovidae
            Bison
    Order Proboscidea
        Family Gomphotheriidae
            Cuvieronius
        Family Elephantidae
            Mammuthus cf. *jeffersonii*

1. La Coca fauna
2. Ocu, Panama
3. Late Pleistocene
4. Gazin (1957)
5. North and South America
6. Class Mammalia
    Order Edentata
        Family Megatheriidae
            Eremotherium rusconi
    Order Notoungulata
        Family Toxodontidae
            Toxodon

Besides those sites listed, Stirton and Gealey (1949) mention nineteen Pleistocene sites in El Salvador but give no further information. Rodriguez (1942) records six sites in Costa Rica and one in Nicaragua that have yielded proboscidians, plus a number of others where isolated toxodont or horse remains have been found, but the information he gives about these Pleistocene occurrences is extremely scanty. Doubtless, if an effort were made to search out the information, numerous other sites of Pleistocene age could be found in Central America (cf. Janzen and Martin 1982). One nonmammalian site of interest is from the Oligocene of Costa Rica, where the tortoise *Geochelone* was recorded (Auffenberg 1971).

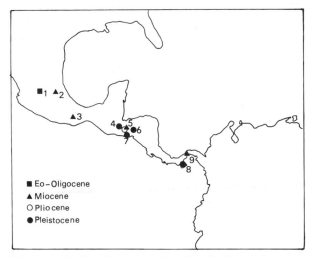

FIGURE 2.12. Fossil vertebrate localities in Central America,
1, Guanajuato; 2, Hidalgo; 3, El Gramal; 4, Copán (Cobán);
5, Gracias; 6, Comayagna valley; 7, Hormiguero; 8, El
Hatillo and La Coca; 9, Cucaracha.

Quaternary faunas in Central America reflect an inter-
mixing of elements from North and South America. This
interchange began after a land connection was established about 3 million years ago across the Bolivar
Trench, a seaway between the Atlantic and Pacific oceans
that cut through northwestern Colombia and eastern
Panama (Marshall et al. 1979).

By contrast, as far south as Panama the Central American Tertiary (pre-Pleistocene) mammal faunas show no
affinity whatever with South America. Even the early
Miocene Gaillard Cut local fauna (= Cucaracha fauna)
(fig. 2.13), collected on the bank of the Panama Canal,
consists of either five or six taxa, all congeneric with
North American forms. From just 400 km to the east in
Colombia, across the Bolivar Trench, a late Miocene
fauna has been collected that consists of genera with
exclusively South American affinities. Except for one
site, this pattern that all Central American Tertiary terrestrial mammals are congeneric with North American species is consistent. The exception is the late Eocene or
early Oligocene Guanajuato fuana of southern Mexico,
which also happens to be the oldest known terrestrial
vertebrate locality in Central America.

The Guanajuato fauna (fig. 2.14) is exceptional because the two genera recognized are not known anywhere
else. They also happen to be small mammals (rodents),
in contrast to every other Central American fossil mammal yet reported in the literature (all are medium-sized to
large forms). This suggests that the picture of a strong
North American affinity for the Central American Tertiary mammalian fauna may be an artifact of the pronounced bias toward larger genera in the other available
samples. There may be a second component to the Ter-

tiary fauna of Central America composed of smaller,
endemic mammals.

Further support for the existence of such a suite of
smaller mammals is to be found in the recognition by
Wood (1974) of three previously unknown rodent genera
in the late Eocene and early Oligocene of the Trans-Pecos
region of Texas, plus the report by Slaughter (1978) of a
middle Miocene didelphid from east Texas. It may be that
the Texas area was more closely allied with Central
America in its small mammals during the Tertiary than
were areas farther north. The evolutionary role played by
this largely unknown Central American element may
have been important in the origin of major higher groups.
As an example, *Guanajuatomys* from the Guanajuato
fauna of southern Mexico strongly supports the suggestion that the South American caviomorph rodents
(e.g., guinea pig, agouti, capybara) evolved from a stock
that entered from the north.

There is a great similarity between the Caviomorpha
and the Old World Hystricomorpha and Phiomorpha, particularly in the extreme modifications of the masseter
musculature and the associated structures of the jaw and
skull. Because of this, all these forms are grouped together in the order Hystricognathi. It has been suggested
a number of times, most recently by Lavocat (1973,
1980), that this close similarity indicates faunal interchange of the Hystricognathi across the Atlantic between
Africa and South America. In Lavocat's formulation, the
interchange would have taken place during the late Eocene, when, according to plate tectonics theory, the Atlantic would have been narrower than it is today. However, even then the gap would have been at least 3,000
km wide, imposing severe difficulties for successful interchange (Sclater, Hellinger, and Tapscott 1977), unless
intermediate islands were present to serve as stepping-
stones (McKenna 1980).

The presence of *Guanajuatomys* with a mandible structure specialized in the pattern of the Hystricognathi in the
early Tertiary at Guanajuato (Black and Stephens 1973),
and of the similarly constructed *Prolapsus* in the Trans-
Pecos area of Texas (Wood 1974), supports the idea that
a source stock did exist in Central America and southern
North America from which the Caviomorpha could have
arisen without the necessity for trans-Atlantic interchange (Wood 1980).

Even less directly, a role for Central America as a
center of origin for mammalian groups has been inferred
for an earlier time, the Paleocene. Sloan (1970) noted
that the fossil floral record of the present United States
indicates a change from a temperate to more tropical
conditions from the Paleocene to the early Eocene. Associated with this was a shifting northward in North America of the mammalian faunas through the same time period. In addition, ancestral stocks are first recorded in

FIGURE 2.13. Restorations of fossil vertebrates known from the Miocene of Central America, best represented by the Cucaracha fauna, Panama. *a,* Merycoidodont (oredont). *b, Diceratherium,* a rhinoceros. *c, Paratoceras,* a protoceratid artiodactyl. *d,* Anchitherine horse with more than a single digit and low-crowned browsing teeth, view of skull and molar tooth (top and side views). *e,* Crocodilian. *f,* Turtle. Illustrations in this figure as well as figs. 2.14–16 are based on those in Fenton and Fenton (1958) and Halstead (1978).

several instances in New Mexico and Colorado, and their presumed descendants occur in younger deposits in Wyoming and Montana. Prominent among these southern ancestral groups are the phenacodontid condylarths. They show affinities with the earliest horses (which may have arisen in southern North America) and also with the Didolodontidae of South America. All this information led Sloan to postulate the existence of a tropical mammalian fauna centered in Central America and the adjacent regions of Mexico during the Paleocene, which became widely recorded only in the fossiliferous early Eocene deposits of the United States, by which time it had spread northward as the climate ameliorated.

Because of the lack of detailed knowledge about the position or even existence of various parts of Central America during the late Mesozoic and early Tertiary, the

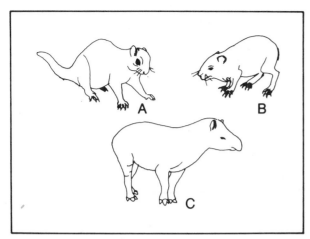

FIGURE 2.14. Restorations of fossil vertebrates known from the Eocene or Oligocene sediments of Guanajuato, Southern Mexico. *a,* rodent intermediate between squirrellike forms and gophers. *b,* hystricomorph rodent. *c,* tapir.

area's role as a route for the faunal interchanges between North and South America that did occur at that time is obscure. By the time of the late Tertiary interchanges, the scope of this role is better known.

Beginning in the late Miocene, there was a noticeable increase in the frequency of island-hopping across the Bolivar Trench. At that time in North America, one mylodontid genus and one or two megalonychid genera of ground sloths appeared, all groups clearly of South American origin. Their arrival is not marked by only a single occurrence at that time; rather, their remains are known from Florida to California. Their absence in the one Central American fauna of that age, the Gracias fauna of Honduras (fig. 2.15), merely confirms the impression that the record there is incomplete. Conceivably, they could have entered North America through the Antilles rather than island-hopping across the shorter gap of the Bolivar Trench into Central America and thus might have avoided the area altogether. However, even had they done so, it seems likely that they would have spread southward as rapidly as in the other directions they are known to have taken once they arrived in North America. The late Miocene interchange was not one-way, for a procyonid (raccoon) entered South America from the north (See Webb 1978; Marshall et al. 1979).

When faunal interchange began between North and South America because a land connection formed across the Bolivar Trench can be most accurately resolved in the terrestrial mammalian faunas of Argentina and the United States, more than 5,000 km from the scene of the event, rather than in Central America or nothern South America (Marshall 1981; Marshall et al. 1982). This paradox arises because the individual faunas are richer and more numerous in these more remote regions. With such dis-

tances between the point of the actual interchange and the place where its effects can be gauged most accurately, some have suggested that there was a delay of perhaps half a million years between each group's entry into the new continent and its first record there, as indicated by the interpretation of radiometric data in Marshall et al. (1979). But if conditions were favorable for dispersal on the new continent, this could have occurred in a geologic instant: once they arrived in Australia, rabbits crossed that continent in less than a century.

When the land connection between North and South America opened, the conditions were particulary suitable for the dispersal of savanna-adapted forms, for a nearly continuous band of savanna between North and South America right across Central America enabled forms adapted to regions at 45° latitude to spread across the equator. In the late Pliocene and early Pleistocene, at least twenty-two of the thirty-one mammalian genera involved in interchange between the two continents were savanna-adapted forms (Webb 1978).

With the severance of this band of savanna habitat during the late Pleistocene and Recent times owing to the spreading of moister tropical rain forests, the rate of interchange of mammals across the Panamanian isthmus decreased markedly. Only mammals with the broadest tolerances were than able to utilize both the environments encountered in Central America and northern South America and also the more xeric conditions farther from the equator, enabling them to pass from one continent to the other.

With separation of Central America from South America persisting at the Bolivar Trench until the late Pliocene, the fauna of Central America did not take on its Neotropical character until later. And it was not until the late Pleistocene and Recent times that the tropical rain-forest fauna of northern South America was able to move into Central America en masse as conditions there became moister (Webb 1978).

In summary, Central America played two roles with respect to the mammalian fauna. First, it served as a route of interchange between North and South America, at least during the late Cenozoic. Second, it may also have been an important center of mammalian evolution. Both these roles can be inferred only in part from the fossil record available there; they are less directly documented by the modern distribution of mammals and the occurrences of fossils thousands of kilometers from Central America.

Conclusions

From this brief and somewhat uneven coverage of Central American paleobiogeography we can draw several conclusions, all suggesting that the present-day Costa

FIGURE 2.15. Restorations of fossil vertebrates from the late Miocene–early Pliocene of Central America, best represented in the Gracias fauna of Honduras (Clarendonian or Hemphillian in age). *a, Pliohippus*, restoration and molar tooth (top view). *b, Osteoborus. c, Procamelus*, restorations and skull. *d*, Mastodont, restoration and molar tooth. *e*, Teleocerine rhinoceros.

Rican and Central American flora and fauna are a fairly recent amalgam resulting from a changeable geography and climate:

1. The configuaration of Central America has changed markedly. For much of its history the southern part of the area (south of Nicaragua, north of Colombia) has been either archipelagic or situated elsewhere. The continuous connection between North and South America that it provides today has been in existence for only the past 3 million years or so (from latest Pliocene times).

2. Probably not until the latter part of the Cenozoic did the mountainous backbone of Central America reach its present altitude, offering the variety of habitats that characterize this area today.

FIGURE 2.16. Restorations of fossil vertebrates known from the Pleistocene of Central America, mainly from El Hatillo, the Comayagna valley (Honduras), southern Nicaragua, and several Costa Rican localities. *a,* Mastodont, restoration and molar tooth. *b, Glyptodon,* restoration, skeleton, and molar tooth, relative of the living armadillo. *c,* Muscovy duck. *d, Pseudemys,* a turtle. *e,* Mylodont ground sloth, restoration and skull. *f, Neochoerus,* giant capybara. *g,* Toxodont.

3. Marine, primarily invertebrate, faunas from Central America are not well known in pre-Cenozoic rocks. Cenozoic faunas consisting primarily of foraminifers and mollusks indicate direct marine connection of the Caribbean and western Pacific well into the Pliocene.

4. Terrestrial vertebrate fossils are rare in Central America and known only from Cenozoic rocks, mainly Miocene or younger.

5. Until about 3 million years ago the Central American mammalian faunas were composed of dominantly North American forms. Only then did interchange begin and the South American vertebrates enter in any marked quantities (see fig. 2.17).

6. Very little is known of the small mammal faunas of Central America during the Cenozoic. What is known suggests that an endemic small mammal fauna might have developed in Central America and southern North America at this time and dispersed from there.

FIGURE 2.17. Representation of the interchange of terrestrial mammals that occurred during the late Cenozoic between North and South America (modified after Halstead 1978.).

7. Angiosperm floras of Central America today are most similar to those of South America, and sweepstakes dispersal from South America may have been more pronounced for plants than for animals. Unlike the situation with vertebrates, when a land connection finally formed the takeover of northern forms was not so pronounced in South America. Pleistocene cool periods in the tropics promoted dispersal of montane species such as gooseberries, currants, willows, and primroses.

8. Throughout most of the Pleistocene, especially at the height of glaciation in northern North America, savanna grassland conditions had a much broader geographic spread. This promoted the dispersal of grassland-adapted forms. Only in the later part of the Pleistocene were these grasslands fragmented by increasing precipitation.

9. Not until the later part of the Pleistocene did the humid tropical rain forest become widespread in Central America, thus decreasing the effectiveness of the terrestrial connection between North and South America and leading to the distinctive modern biotic assemblages in Central America today.

Apology and Acknowledgments

We must apologize for the rather general and hastily prepared summary of such an exceedingly complex area as Central America. We only hope that it will stimulate someone to do a more thorough job and will encourage workers in the Central American area to collect and carefully document any fossil material they happen to discover.

Thanks are due to many who helped in the preparation of this chatper: D. Janzen, S. Cebull, D. Sherbet, B. Furher, G. Earl, F. Ovenden, L. Reid, E. Lundelius, M. Fenton, B. Halstead, and L. Rich. We especially thank Eurobook Limited and M. Fenton for use of illustrations in their publications, especially fig. 2.17. M. L. Vickers patiently and rapidly typed several versions of the manuscript.

*

Anderson, T. H. 1978. Mesozoic crustal evolution of Middle America and the Caribbean: Geological considerations. *EOS* 59 (4):404.

[Anonymous]. 1964. Geological Society Phanerozoic

time scale 1964. *Geol. Soc. London Quat. J.*, 120:260–62.

Anthony, H. E. 1942. Summary of the fossil land mammals of the West Indies. *Proc. Eighth Am. Sci. Congr.* 4:359–63.

Auffenberg, W. 1971. A new fossil tortoise, with remarks on the origin of South American Testudinines. *Copeia* 1971:106–17.

Baker, R. H. 1963. Geographical distribution of terrestrial mammals in Middle America. *Am. Midland Nat.* 70(1):208–49.

Bandy, O. L., and Casey, R. E. 1973. Reflector horizons and paleobathymetric history, eastern Panama. *Geol. Soc. Am. Bull.* 84:3081–87.

Black, C. C., and Stephens, J. J. III. 1973. Rodents from the Paleocene of Guanajuato, Mexico. *Occ. Pap. Mus. Texas Tech. Univ.* 14:1–10.

Bullard, E. C., et al. 1965. The fit of the continents around the Atlantic. *Roy. Soc. London Philos. Trans.*, ser. A., 258:1–41.

Case, J. E., et al. 1971. Tectonic investigations in western Colombia and eastern Panama. *Geol. Soc. Am. Bull.* 82:2685–2712.

Cebull, S. E., and Keller, G. R. 1976. Plate tectonics models for the Ouachita foldbelt: Comment and replies. *Geology* 84:636–37.

Cebull, S. E., and Sherbet, D. H. 1980. The Ouachita Belt in the evolution of the Gulf of Mexico. In *The origin of the Gulf of Mexico and the early opening of the central North Atlantic Ocean,* ed. R. H. Pilger, Jr., pp. 17–26. Baton Rouge: Louisiana State University, School of Geosciences.

Coryell, H. N., and Fields, S. 1937. A Gatún ostracode fauna from Cativa, Panama. *Am. Mus. Novitates* 956:1–18.

Cushman, J. A. 1955. *Foraminifera: Their classification and economic use.* Cambridge: Harvard University Press.

Darlington, P. J. 1965. *Biogeography of the southern end of the world.* Cambridge: Harvard University Press.

Davies, A. M. 1971–75. *Tertiary faunas: A text-book for oilfield palaeontologists and students of geology.* 2 vols. Amsterdam: Elsevier.

Dietz, R. S., and Holden, J. C. 1970. Reconstruction of Pangaea: Breakup and dispersion of continents, Permian to present. *J. Geophys. Res.* 75:4939–56.

Donnelly, W. 1974. The geological history of the Caribbean: Old problems and new approaches. Seventh Conf. Geol. Caraibes, Abst., pp. 21–22.

Duellman, W. E. 1966. The Central American herpetofauna: An ecological perspective. *Copeia* 1966:700–719.

Durham, J. W., et al. 1955. Evidence for no Cenozoic Isthmus of Tehuantepec seaway. *Bull. Geol. Soc.Am.* 66:977–92.

Fenton, C. L., and Fenton, M. A. 1958. *The fossil book.* Garden City, N.Y.: Doubleday.

Fox, P. J.; Schreiber, E.; and Heezen, B. C. 1971. The geology of the Caribbean crust: Tertiary sediments, granitic and basic rocks from the Aves ridge. *Tectonophy* 12:89–109.

Freeland, G. L., and Dietz, R. S. 1971. Plate tectonic evolution of Caribbean–Gulf of Mexico region. *Nature* 232:20–23.

Fries, C. J.; Hibbard, C. W.; and Dunkle, D. H. 1955. Early Cenozoic vertebrates in the Red conglomerate at Guanajuato, Mexico. *Smithsonian Misc. Coll.* 123:1–25.

Gabb, W. M. 1881. Descriptions of new species of fossils from Pliocene clay beds between Limon and Moin, Costa Rica, together with notes on previously known species from there and elsewhere in the Caribbean area. *Acad. Nat. Sci. Philadelphia,* 2d ser., 8:349–80.

Gazin, C. L. 1957. Exploration for the remains of giant ground sloths in Panama. *Smithsonian Rept.* 1956: 341–54.

Gose, W. A., and Scott, G. R. 1979. The aggragation of Meso-America. *Abst. Geol. Soc. Am.* 11(7):434.

Gose, W. A., and Swartz, D. K. 1977. Paleomagnetic results from Cretaceous sediments in Honduras: Tectonic implications. *Geology* 5:505–8.

Halstead, L. B. 1978. *The evolution of the mammals.* Australia: Cassell.

Harrington, H. J. 1962. Paleogeographic development of South America. *Bull. Am. Assoc. Petrol. Geol.* 46:1773–1814.

Herschfeld, S. E., and Marshall, L. G. 1976. Revised faunal list of the La Venta fauna (Friasian-Miocene) of Colombia, South America. *J. Paleontol.* 50(3): 433–36.

Hershkovitz, P. 1972. The recent mammals of the Neotropical region: A zoogeographic and ecological review. In *Evolution, mammals and southern continents,* ed. A. Keast et al., pp. 311–431. Albany: State University of New York.

Jackson, R. T. 1917. Fossil echini of the Panama Canal Zone and Costa Rica. *U.S. Nat. Mus. Proc.* 53:489–501.

Janzen, D. H., and Martin, P. S. 1982. Neotropical anachronisms: The fruits the gomphotheres ate. *Science* 215:145–64.

Kesler, S. E. 1971. Nature of ancestral orogenic zone in nuclear Central America. *Am. Assoc. Pet. Geol. Bull.* 55:2116–29.

Ladd, J. W. 1976. Relative motion of South America with respect to North America and Caribbean tectonics. *Geol. Soc. Am. Bull.* 87:969–76.

Lavocat, R. 1973. Les rongeurs du Miocène d'Afrique orientale. 1. Miocène inférieur. *Ecole Pratique des Hautes Etudes, Inst. de Montpellier, Mém.* 1:i–iv, 1–284.

———. 1980. The implications of rodent paleontology and biogeography to the geographical sources and origin of platyrrhine Primates. In *Evolutionary biology of the New World monkeys and continental drift,* ed. R. L.

Cicochon and A. B. Chiarelli, pp. 93–102. New York: Plenum Press.

Lilligraven, J. A. 1976. A new genus of therian mammal from the late Cretaceous "El Gallo Formation," Baja California, Mexico. *J. Paleontol.* 50(2):437–43.

Lloyd, J. J. 1963. Tectonic history of the South Central–American orogen. *Am. Assoc. Petrol. Geol. Mem.* 2:88–100.

McAlester, A. L. 1976. *The history of life.* Englewood Cliffs, N.J.: Prentice-Hall.

McBirney, A. R., and Williams, H. 1965. Volcanic history of Nicaragua. *California Univ. Pubs. Geol. Sci.* 55:1–65.

McDowell, S. B. 1958. The Greater Antillean insectivores. *Am. Mus. Nat. Hist.* 115:117–214.

MacGillavry, H. J. 1970. Geological history of the Caribbean. *Koninkl. Nederl. Akademie van wetenschappen —Amsterdam, Proc.,* ser. B., 73(1):64–96.

McGrew, P. O. 1944. An *Osteoborus* from Honduras. *Geol. Ser. Field Museum Nat. Hist.* 8:75–77.

McKenna, M. 1956. Survival of primitive notoungulates and condylarths into the Miocene of Colombia. *Am. J. Sci.* 254:736–43.

———. 1972. Possible biological consequences of plate tectonics. *Bio. Sci.* 22(9):519–25.

———. 1973. Sweepstakes, filters, corridors, Noah's arks, and beached Viking funeral ships in palaeogeography. In *Implications of continental drift to earth sciences,* vol. 1, ed. D. H. Tarling and S. K. Runcorn, pp. 295–308. New York: Academic Press.

———. 1980. Early history and biogeography of South America's extinct land mammals. In *Evolutionary biology of the New World monkeys and continental drift,* ed. R. L. Ciochon and A. B. Chiarelli, pp. 43–77. New York: Plenum Press.

Maldonado-Koerdell, M. 1964. Geohistory and paleogeography of Middle America. In *Handbook of Middle American Indians,* ed. R. Wauchope and R. C. West, pp. 3–32. Austin: University of Texas Press.

Malfait, B. T., and Dinkelman, M. G. 1972. Circum-Caribbean tectonic and igneous activity and the evolution of the Caribbean plate. *Geol. Soc. Am. Bull.* 83:251–72.

Marshall, L. G. 1976. New didelphine marsupials from the La Venta fauna (Miocene) of Colombia South America. *J. Paleontol.* 50(3):402–18.

———. 1979. A model for paleobiogeography of South American cricetine rodents. *Paleobiology 5:126–32.*

———. 1981. The great American interchange—an invasion-induced crisis for South American mammals. In *Biotic crises in ecological and evolutionary time,* ed. M. H. Nitecki, pp. 133–229. New York: Academic Press.

Marshall, L. G.; Butler, R. F.; Drake, R. E.; Curtis, G. H.; and Tedford, R. H. 1979. Calibration of the Great American interchange: A radioisotope chronology for Late Tertiary interchange of terrestrial faunas between the Americas. *Science* 204:272–79.

Marshall, L. G., and Hecht, M. K. 1978. Mammalian faunal dynamics of the Great American interchange: An alternative interpretation. *Paleobiology 4:203–6.*

Marshall, L. G.; Webb, S. D.; Sepkoski, J. J., Jr.; and Raup, D. M. 1982. Mammalian evolution and the great American interchange. *Science* 251:1351–57.

Maxwell, A. E.; von Herzen, R. P.; Hsu, K. J.; Andrews, J. E.; Saito, T.; Percival, S. F., Jr.; Milow, E. D.; and Boyce, R. R. 1970. Deep sea drilling in the South Atlantic. *Science* 168:1047–59.

Mayr, E. 1964. Inferences concerning the Tertiary American bird faunas. *Proc. Nat. Acad. Sci.* 51:280–88.

Middlemiss, F. A.; Rawson, P. F.; and Newall, G. 1971. *Faunal provinces in space and time.* Liverpool: Seel House Press.

Moore, R. C.; Lalicker, C. G.; and Fischer, A. G. 1952. *Invertebrate fossils.* New York: McGraw-Hill.

Mooser, O. 1959. Un équido fósil del genero *Neohipparion* de la Mesa Central de México. *An. Inst. Biol.* 30:375–88.

———. 1963. *Neohipparion monias* n. sp., équido fósil del Pliocene de la Mesa Central de México. *An. Inst. Biol.* 34:393–96.

Morel, P., and Irving, E. 1980. Paleomagnetism of upper Paleozoic and lower Mesozoic rocks and the evolution of Pangea. In *The origin of the Gulf of Mexico and the early opening of the central North Atlantic Ocean,* ed. R. H. Pilger, Jr., pp. 75–78. Baton Rouge: Louisiana State University, School of Geosciences.

Nairn, E. M., and Stehli, F. G. 1975. *The ocean basins and margins.* Vol. 3. *The Gulf of Mexico and the Caribbean.* New York: Plenum.

Olson, E. C., and McGrew, P. O. 1941. Mammalian fauna from the Pliocene of Honduras. *Bull. Geol. Soc. Am. 52:1219–44.*

Olsson, A. A. 1922. The Miocene of northern Costa Rica. *Bull. Am. Paleontol.* 9(39):179–309.

———. 1942. Tertiary and Quaternary fossils from the Burica Peninsula of Panama and Costa Rica. *Bull. Am. Paleontol.* 27:121–36.

———. 1943. Tertiary and Quaternary fossils from the Burica Peninsula of Panama and Costa Rica. *Bull. Am. Paleontol.* 27:157–258.

Patterson, B., and Pascual, R. 1972. The fossil mammal fauna of South America. In *Evolution, mammals, and southern continents,* pp. 247–309. Albany: State University of New York.

Patton, T. H., and Taylor, B. E. 1973. The Protoceratinae (Mammalia, Tylopoda, Protoceratidae) and the systematics of the Protoceratidae. *Am. Mus. Nat. Hist. Bull.* 150(4):347–414.

Raven, P. H., and Axelrod, D. I. 1974. Angiosperm biogeography and past continental movements. *Ann. Missouri Bot. Gard.* 61:539–673.

———. 1975. History of the flora and fauna of Latin America. *Am. Sci.* 63:420–29.

Reyment, R. A., and Tait, E. A. 1972. Biostratigraphical dating of the early history of the South Atlantic Ocean. *Roy. Soc. London Philos. Trans.,* ser. B, 264:55–95.

Rich, P. V. 1975. Antarctic dispersal routes, plate tectonics, and the origin of Australia's non-passeriform avifauna. *Mem. Nat. Mus. Victoria* 36:63–126.

———. 1976. *Continental drift, sea-floor spreading, plate tectonics: Viable theory or romantic speculations?* Minneapolis: Burgess.

Rodriguez, J. V. 1942. Informe rendido a la secretaria de educación publica sobre la labor realizada in 1941. *Serie Hist. Museo Nac. Costa Rica* 1 (4):1–48.

———. 1942. Informe rendido a la secretaria de educación publica sobre la labor realizada in 1940. *Serie Hist. Museo Nac. Costa Rica* 1 (3):32–39.

Ross, C. A. 1979. Late Paleozoic collision of North and South America. *Geology* 7:41–44.

Savage, J. M. 1966. The origin and history of the Central American herpetofauna. *Copeia* 1966 (4):719–66.

———. 1974. The isthmian link and the evolution of Neotropical mammals. *Nat. Hist. Mus. Los Angeles Cty., Sci. Publ.* 260:1–51.

Schmidt, V. A. 1978. Mesozoic crustal evolution of Middle America and the Caribbean: Geophysical considerations. *EOS* 59 (4):404.

Schuchert, C. 1935. *Historical geology of the Antillean-Caribbean region.* New York: John Wiley.

Sclater, J.; Hellinger, S.; and Tapscott, C. 1977. The paleobathymetry of the Atlantic Ocean from the Jurassic to the present. *J. Geol.* 85:509–52.

Sherbet, D. H., and Cebull, S. E. 1975. The age of the crust beneath the Gulf of Mexico. *Tectonophy* 28:T25–T30.

Simpson, G. G. 1948. The beginning of the age of mammals in South America. *Am. Mus. Nat. Hist. Bull.* 85:1–350.

———. 1956. Zoogeography of West Indian land mammals. *Am. Mus. Novit.* 1759:1–28.

———. 1960. Notes on the measurement of faunal resemblance. *Am. J. Sci. Bradley* 258-A:300–311.

———. 1965. *The geography of evolution.* Philadelphia: Hilton.

———. 1966. Mammalian evolution on the southern continents. *Neues Jahrb. Geol. Palaeont. Abh.* 125:1–18.

———. 1967. The beginning of the age of mammals in South America. Part 2. *Am. Mus. Nat. Hist. Bull.* 137:1–259.

Slaughter, B. H. 1978. Occurrences of didelphine marsupials from the Eocene and Miocene of the Texas Coastal Plain. *J. Paleontol.* 53(3):744–46.

Sloan, R. E. 1970. Cretaceous and Paleocene terrestrial communities of western North America. *N. Am. Paleontol. Conv., Proc.,* part E, pp. 427–53.

Stirton, R. A. 1951. Ceboid monkeys from the Miocene of Colombia. *Univ. California Publ. Bull. Dept. Geol. Sci.* 28:315–56.

———. 1953a. Vertebrate paleontology and continental stratigraphy in Colombia. *Bull. Geol. Soc. Am.* 64:603–22.

———. 1953b. A new genus of interatheres from the Miocene of Colombia. *Univ. California Publ. Bull. Dept. Geol. Sci.* 29:265–348.

———. 1954. Late Miocene mammals from Oaxaca, Mexico. *Am. J. Sci.* 252:634–38.

Stirton, R. A., and Gealey, W. K. 1949. Reconnaissance geology and vertebrate paleontology of El Salvador, Central America. *Bull. Geol. Soc. Am.* 60:1731–54.

Sykes, L. 1972. Seismicity as a guide to global tectonics and earthquake prediction. *Tectonophys* 13 (1–4):393–414.

Tarling, D. H., and Tarling, M. 1971. *Continental drift: A study of the earth's moving surface.* Garden City, N.Y.: Doubleday.

Toula, F. 1909–11. Eine jungtertiäre Fauna von Gatun am Panama-Kanal. *K.K. Geol. Reichsanstalt Jahrb.* 58:487–530, 673–760.

Van der Hammen, T. 1974. The Pleistocene changes of vegetation and climate in tropical South America. *J. Biogeogr.* 1:3–26.

Walper, J. L., and Rowett, C. L. 1972. Plate tectonics and the origin of the Caribbean Sea and the Gulf of Mexico. *Trans. Gulf Coast Assoc. Geol. Soc.* 22:105–16.

———. 1978. A history of savanna vertebrates in the New World. Part 2. South America and the great interchange. *Ann. Rev. Ecol. Sust.* 9:393–426.

———. 1976. Mammalian faunal dynamics of the great American interchange. *Paleobiology* 2(3):220–31.

Webb, S. D. 1972. Reconnaissance of late Cenozoic vertebrate deposits in southern Honduras. *Am. Phil. Soc. Yrbk.* 1969:336.

Whitmore, F. C., and Stewart, R. H. 1965. Miocene mammals and Central American seaways. *Science* 148:180–85.

Wilhelm, O., and Ewing, M. 1972. Geology and history of the Gulf of Mexico. *Geol. Soc. Am. Bull.* 83:575–600.

Williams, H., and McBirney, A. R. 1969. Volcanic history of Honduras. *California Univ. Pubs. Geol. Sci.* 85:1–101.

Wilson, J. A. 1967. Additions to the El Gramal local fauna, Nejapa, Oaxaca, Mexico. *Bol. Soc. Geol. Mexicana* 30, no. 1:1–4, figs. 1, 2.

Wood, A. E., 1974. Early Tertiary vertebrate faunas, Vieja group, Trans-Pecos Texas: Rodentia. *Texas Mem. Mus. Bull.* 21:1–112.

———. 1980. The origin of the caviomorph rodents from a source in Middle America: Clue to the area of the origin of the platyrrhine Primates. In *Evolutionary biology of the New World monkeys and continental drift,* ed. R. L. Ciochon and A. B. Chiarelli, pp. 79–91. New York: Plenum Press.

Woodring, W. P. 1954. Caribbean land and sea through the ages. *Bull. Geol. Soc. Am.* 65:719–32.

———. 1957–64. Geology and paleontology of Canal Zone and adjoining parts of Panama. *U.S. Geol. Surv. Prof. Pap.* 306:1–145 (1957); 146–239 (1959); 246–97 (1964). Good description and analysis of Tertiary mollusks with annotated bibliography of Panamanian geology and paleontology.

———. 1966. The Panama land bridge as a sea barrier. *Proc. Am. Phil. Soc.* 110:425–33.

Woodburne, M. O. 1969. A late Pleistocene occurrence of the collared peccary, *Dicatyles tajacu* in Guatemala. *J. Mamm.* 50:121–25.

Wyllie, P. J. 1971. *The dynamic earth: Textbook in geosciences.* New York: John Wiley.

———. 1976. *The way the earth works.* New York: John Wiley.

3 CLIMATE

E. Coen

Differences in climate over the earth have been recognized since the time of the ancient Greeks. For them, climate was related to life through the duration of daylight and through temperature. Modern people have divided the earth into two hemispheres, each containing three zones: torrid (or tropical), temperate (or extratropical) and frigid (or polar). But climate as viewed today is more than a classification of climatic variation.

The climate of a region is determined by the action of the sun's rays on the atmosphere at the surface of the planet and by the interaction of air movement with heat sinks and radiators. The atmosphere is put in motion by heat from the sun, and this air mass interacts with land and oceans to yield particular weather conditions. Climate is the sum of the weather conditions for a particular region.

Meteorology is the study of the phenomena of the atmosphere, dealing with the physical processes that produce everyday events. It is related to climatology, which examines how weather is organized in time and space. There are differences in both weather conditions and climate between tropical zones and the middle latitudes. Weather differences mostly depend on the amplitude of the oscillations of certain weather parameters, the most conspicuous being the amount of insolation, or incoming solar radiation, atmospheric heat, wind, precipitation, and cloudiness. These variations generate very diverse weather in Costa Rica, and the local weather and its effects are made even more diverse through complex interactions with microtopographic relief, surface waterways, soil drainage and reflectance, elevation, and the vegetative cover.

The principal climatic control is solar radiation. Figure 3.1 shows how solar radiation is distributed through the year at various latitudes. The radiation arriving at the earth's surface is given in langleys per day and is calibrated for an air mass that (as is usual) transmits 70% of the radiation that enters it on a cloudless day.

Because the earth is closest to the sun during the Southern Hemisphere's summer (September–March) and farthest away during the summer of the Northern Hemisphere (March–September), there is more daily radiation during summer in the Southern Hemisphere than during the summer in the Northern Hemisphere. At 10° north latitude (the latitude of Costa Rica), maximum daily radiation occurs when the sun passes its zenith. This happens twice a year, once as the sun passes overhead in its trek northward in May (to reach an overhead position at the Tropic of Cancer in northern Mexico in late June), and once as it returns south in September (to reach an overhead position at the Tropic of Capricorn in southern South America in late December). The reverse occurs in the southern tropical latitudes, but the secondary maximum corresponding to the summer solstice is not so pronounced.

Oscillation in annual radiation during the year is more pronounced in the middle latitudes in both hemispheres than in tropical latitudes (fig. 3.1). Those differences in radiation unequally heat the atmosphere and the ground at different latitudes. This heating puts the air in motion, and the spinning of the earth generates a pattern similar to the well-known schematic representation of the general circulation (fig. 3.2). Winds are predominately easterly at high and low latitudes and westerly at middle latitudes.

Because tropical latitudes absorb more solar radiation than do higher latitudes, energy must continuously flow from the equator to the poles. In accordance with the law of conservation of agular momentum, the zonal circulation breaks down and forms waves and swirls with cyclonic and anticyclonic vortices. These disturbances transport the largest amount of heat and momentum away from the equator. The irregular westerlies flow around the subtropical high pressure areas, and this air flow gener-

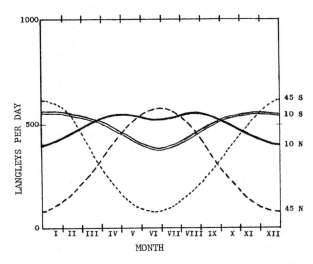

FIGURE 3.1. Solar radiation in langleys per day arriving at earth's surface when the atmosphere transmits 0.7 of a vertical beam.

35

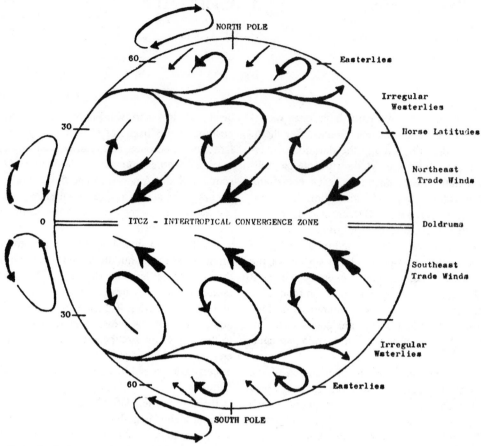

FIGURE 3.2. General wind pattern on the earth's surface.

ates the trade winds, which blow from the east toward the equator at an angle and form the intertropical convergence zone, or ITCZ (fig. 3.2). Ancient mariners called the ITCZ the doldrums. On the polar side of the westerlies, the cyclonic circulation is called the polar front (old terminology) or polar trough (new terminology). The polar trough is a wave in the westerlies that has sufficient amplitude to reach the tropics in the upper air.

These features of general air circulation are the dominant causes of weather in low and middle latitudes. Changes in weather at high latitudes are generated by air masses with thermal conditions very different from those in the tropics. Weather changes in the tropics are mostly dynamic, because differences in the temperatures of interacting air masses are less pronounced there. Also, the high temperature and humidity of the ground surface in tropical regions quickly makes the air masses more similar.

Weather at middle and high latitudes is associated with cold and warm fronts, well-organized disturbances that travel mainly from the west. When cold fronts are very intense in winter, their leading edges penetrate the tropics and may reach as far south as Costa Rica. It is clear that

warm fronts can never penetrate the tropical zone, because the warm air masses that lead the fronts are generated in the tropics. When the leading edge of a cold front penetrates the tropical zone by way of the Gulf of Mexico, the cold air mass soon warms up and takes on moisture. Nevertheless, such an air mass can be recognized by the wind patterns it still contains when it penetrates lower latitudes.

Weather in tropical regions is chiefly determined by dynamic rather than thermal phenomena. The intertropical convergence zone, waves in the easterlies, and hurricanes are the principal dynamic phenomena. Except for the effects of hurricanes, the weather in tropical regions is much less variable than that in middle and high latitudes. The air circulation pattern on any particular day departs very little from the seasonal average.

On the Meteorology of Central America and Costa Rica

In much of Central America, as in many parts of the world, a few rainy days (usually less than about 15 of 365) bring 70% or more of the total rainfall of the region (and see Portig 1965). This suggests that organized weather disturbances account for most of the rainfall in the Central American tropics, except on east-facing sides of mountain ranges, areas that receive large amounts of rain generated by winds that are driven upward by the mountains and then cooled. The principal disturbances that cause most of the weather changes as well as the average conditions in the tropics are the intertropical convergence zone, the easterly waves, and the polar trough (Dunn and Miller 1960, p. 30). Other processes also generate weather, but these three are the most important. Hurricanes generate the most severe storms, but they occur only sporadically in a particular region. Over the past ninety years, an average of only eight tropical cyclones a year have occurred in the Atlantic north of the equator, and this is far greater than the average for Central America. Over the past ten years, only five hurricanes have reached the Caribbean coast, and only one of them (hurricane Martha, 21–25 November 1969) hit the coast near the border of Costa Rica and Panama. This is the only hurricane to hit Costa Rica during the hundred years for which we have records. The Intertropical Convergence Zone (ITCZ) extends from the Caribbean to the Pacific across Central America and reaches farthest north

(12° north latitude) in August, receding to near the equator, its southernmost position, in February. The ITCZ follows the path where the sun is directly overhead, with a lag of approximately two months (Placido 1973, p. 11). It generates the regimes of rainfall in the tropical zone, which are then modified by the polar trough for certain regions in Central America.

There are two different regimes of Central American rainfall (table 3.1). The Atlantic side has the most rain during December and January, and the Pacific side has almost no rain during the northern winter (December–April). The intense November–January rains on the Atlantic coast are generated by the intensification of the cold front and the polar trough, which penetrates the air mass over the Caribbean Sea to as low as 10° N. However, in the Central American isthmus there is great variety in the microgeographic distribution of rainfall within this pattern, generated by the orientation of mountain ranges and the configuration of the coastline relative to the air-flow patterns of the season (Coen 1959, p. 14). In general, ridges are wet, lee sides of ranges are dry, and windward sides are much moister. The rainfall patterns in inland areas are a mix of the Atlantic and the Pacific

TABLE 3.1 Monthly Rainfall as a Percentage of the Mean Annual Value for Several Stations in Central America

Location	Jan.	Feb.	Mar.	Apr.	May	June	July	Aug.	Sept.	Oct.	Nov.	Dec.
Atlantic Coast												
Swan Island 18° N, 84° W	6	2	1	1	6	15	9	6	9	20	15	10
Belize 17° N, 88° W	5	3	2	2	6	12	12	8	13	18	11	8
Port Barrios 16° N, 89° W	12	5	3	1	3	16	13	8	10	10	6	13
Port Cabezas 14° N, 83° W	5	3	1	2	8	14	15	12	9	11	11	9
Blue Fields 12° N, 84° W	6	3	2	2	9	11	16	14	7	9	11	10
Port Limón 10° N, 83° W	10	6	6	8	8	8	12	8	3	6	12	13
Pacific Coast												
San Salvador 14° N, 89° W	0	0	0	5	9	16	20	17	19	11	2	0
Managua 12° N, 86° W	0	0	0	0	12	19	11	9	18	26	3	1
Puntarenas 10° N, 85° W	0	0	0	2	11	13	12	15	19	18	7	2
Vaca 88° N, 93° W	1	2	2	5	10	12	12	13	12	16	11	4
Tonosí 7° N, 80° W	1	0	0	2	12	13	11	11	11	18	16	5
Taparcal 5° N, 76° W	5	7	8	11	11	8	6	6	7	12	12	7
Restrepo 4° N, 76° W	5	4	7	13	11	9	5	6	8	14	11	7

SOURCE: Mendizabal 1973.

regimes (Coen 1951, pp. 34–37), with maximum rainfall at middle elevations on the windward sides of obstacles (Escoto 1964; Mendizabal 1973). As I mentioned previously, the rains come on the Pacific side of Costa Rica when the ITCZ arrives and the land mass is so heated that air rises, cools, and drops its water. Of course, the forces pushing moisture-laden air across Costa Rica from the northeast may also contribute to this rainfall, to the degree that this air has not already lost its water on the Caribbean side.

In all the Central American rainy seasons, there is less rain in the middle of the year than in the months just before or after: July–August or August–September (Portig 1965). This period of less rain is called *veranillo,* which means "little summer," because people call the main dry and hot season (December–May) on the Pacific side *verano* ("summer"). The sudden and annually variable *veranillo* in Central America is associated with a pronounced northerly flow in the upper troposphere (Hastenrath 1967), as well as with the most northerly extent of the ITCZ.

People in Central America also label *temporales* any nearly continuous rain that occurs during the morning (and often continues into the afternoon). There are two different kinds: *temporales del Atlantico* and *temporales del Pacifico.* In both cases the rain occurs because laterally moving air masses have encountered mountains, risen, and cooled.

The temporales del Atlantico result from an influx of cold air from the north. These winds are called *nortes* in other parts of Central America and in Mexico. The cold dry air of polar origin is rapidly modified when crossing the Gulf of Mexico as it gains latent and sensible heat from the surface (Hastenrath 1966). This air deposits its moisture when it is forced upward upon reaching the coast and high mountain ranges of Central America. When it has passed over the mountains, it brings fine, clear weather to the Pacific lowlands and valleys. On the Pacific coast such a wind is known as *papagayo* and is strongest and most frequent in January and February. It often lasts three to five days.

The temporales del Pacifico result from a change from the wind field pattern of dominant trade winds from the northeast to a pattern of a tropical depression in the Caribbean Sea, near the coast of Central America, which causes moisture-laden winds to blow from the west, off the Pacific Ocean. When this air reaches the coast, especially the western slopes of the mountains, its moisture is deposited as a heavy and persistent rain, which often lasts four to six days. The *temporales del Pacifico* occur most often in September and October and are largely responsible for the peak in annual rainfall at this time on the Pacific side of Costa Rica.

Gramzow and Henry (1971) identified, through a pentad analysis of rainfall data, the beginning, end, and duration of the rainy season in various areas of Central America. According to them, the rainy season begins earlier on the Atlantic coast and later on the Pacific coast. An exception is the northern coast of Honduras, where the rainy season begins in July. In Costa Rica the rainy season starts in late April on the Atlantic side and by the end of May on the Peninsula of Nicoya. The end of the rainy season (generally in October) comes earlier in the interior portions of southern Honduras and western Nicaragua than in other parts of Central America. In Costa Rica the rainy season ends in November on the Pacific coastal plain and in January on the Atlantic side. The period in which *veranillos* occur (July–August) is poorly defined from the Pacific coast of Panama to the Atlantic coast of Nicaragua. The highlands of Costa Rica also have a poorly defined *veranillo.*

Some Peculiarities of Costa Rican Climate
SOLAR RADIATION

The amount of solar radiation received at any point on the surface of the earth depends on factors such as latitude, time, day and year, aspect and slope of the ground, elevation, proximity of oceans and high mountain ranges, cloud thickness and height, and atmospheric composition. This means that an Angstrom equation of the form

$$Q/Q_o = a + b(s/S) \qquad (1)$$

is a model for a local site and the constants a and b must be determined from local data. In equation (1), Q is observed solar radiation, Q_o is Angot's value or the theoretical amount of radiation that would reach the surface of the earth in the absence of an atmosphere (Chang 1968, pp. 8–9), s is the observed duration of sunshine, and S is the maximum possible duration of sunshine.

In places like Costa Rica, where air pollution is not yet severe outside San José except during dry-season pasture burning, the average values may be useful. For eight stations in the country (table 3.2), the averages, with their corresponding standard deviations of the constant a and b, are

$$\overline{X}_a = 0.27 \quad s.d. = 0.04$$
$$\overline{X}_b = 0.42 \quad s.d. = 0.09.$$

If we make $s = 0$ in equation (1), then $\overline{X}_a$ is the transmission coefficient of an overcast day in Costa Rica. This is in agreement with the value of 0.25 given by Haurwitz (1948) for stratus clouds and an optical air mass of 1.1. The optical air mass at latitude 10° N at noon is 1.06 as an average for the year. The value of $a = 0.27$ is also in agreement with the value $a = 0.29 \cos \phi$, where ϕ is the latitude (Chang 1968, pp. 8–9).

TABLE 3.2   Values of the Coefficients a and b of Equation (1) for Eight Stations in Costa Rica at Different Elevations

Location	Elevation (km)	a	b	r^2	$(a+b)$
Volcán Irazú	3.40	0.30	0.54	0.97	0.84
San José	1.17	0.20	0.41	0.95	0.61
F. Baudrit	0.84	0.31	0.42	0.98	0.73
La Piñera	0.35	0.29	0.45	0.94	0.74
Nicoya	0.12	0.28	0.36	0.96	0.64
Cobal	0.06	0.25	0.32	0.85	0.57
Puntarenas	0.01	0.28	0.33	0.80	0.61
Port Limón[a]	0.01	0.21	0.55	0.82	0.76

SOURCE: 1973 records.

[a] Limón is more representative of ocean conditions than of inland conditions.

If we make $s = S$, then $(s/S) = 1$, a value we could obtain only on a cloudless day such as during the Guanacaste dry season. Here, a plus b will not necessarily be equal to one, as Fritz (1951) and other authors proposed, because Q_o is not the value proposed by Angstrom (Smithsonian 1963, p. 440); Q_o is the amount of radiation that would reach the surface of the sea in the absence of an atmosphere, and Q is the average solar radiation that reaches the site's horizontal surface on the average for all days. Thus, a plus b will be equal to the transmission coefficient, better called "atmospheric transmissivity" (Huschke 1959, pp. 589–90), at the site in question. For these reasons b must change with the elevation of the site.

In table 3.2 we can see values of a and b for eight stations at different altitudes for the year 1973. The dependence of b on the elevation H (in km) is expressed with the following equation:

$$b = 0.36 + 0.056 H, \qquad (2)$$

with a coefficient of determination (r^2) of 0.77, excluding Port Limón. Port Limón is not appropriate for the model; it has the largest value for b at sea level. In contrast, Cobal, several kilometers inland at sea level on the Atlantic side, has the lowest value for b, which suggests that clouds that develop on the Atlantic coast are pushed inland during the day by the winds. This phenomenon occurs when the *alisios* (reinforced trade winds) are strengthened by the sea breeze, producing fewer clouds during the day than during the night on the Atlantic coast. On the Pacific coast the sea breezes oppose the alisios, and cloudy skies occur more frequently during the day than during the night. This agrees with the small value for b at the Port of Puntarenas.

Thus, the "Angstrom equation" for Costa Rica, except for the very edge of the Atlantic coast, takes the following form:

$$Q/Q_o = 0.27 + (0.36 + 0.06 H)(s/S) \qquad (3)$$

Equation (3) does not take into consideration the atmospheric pollution that may occur in a valley during the day. Such turbidity of the air will probably yield low values for the sum of a and b. An example is the low value of the sum of a and b for San José. That Cobal has the lowest value suggests very high humidity rather than contaminants in the atmosphere. Above an altitude of approximately 6.2 km, equation (3) suggests a transmissivity of unity for the air on a clear day.

Coen (1977) made monthly maps of the number of hours of sunshine for Costa Rica based on some satellite photographs and the sunshine records for twenty-two stations (fig. 3.3). From the maps were read the estimated day hours of sunshine at national parks (table 3.3).

TEMPERATURES

Because Costa Rica is in the equatorial zone, the average temperature of the warmest month does not exceed the average temperature of the coolest month by more than 5° C at a given site. Figures 3.4 and 3.5 represent the variation of maximum and minimum temperatures through the year at different elevations. The data in table 3.4 were used to draw the isotherms.

It is interesting to note that, as elevation increases, the difference between the mean maximum and mean minimum monthly temperatures decreases. At sea level the average difference is approximately 10° C on both slopes. Maximum differences occur on the Pacific slope during the dry season (cloudless nights and leafless vegetation allow maximum radiation of heat from the ground, and during the day the same factors lead to maximum heating of the substrate). In all parts of the country, the coolest month may be November, December, or January; the warmest month is in March, April, or May. The small variation in the average temperature throughout the year is in striking contrast to the large diurnal variation. This variation decreases with increasing elevation (figs. 3.4, 3.5). The largest changes of temperature during the day occur in some valleys where the cold winds draining off the mountains lower the minimum daily temperatures. Examples of this phenomenon are the low values for the minimum temperatures observed in Cachí and Naranjo (table 3.5), which do not correspond to the temperatures expected for these elevations (fig. 3.4). The same thing may be happening at Volcán Buenos Aires and Cobal, at elevations of 450 m and 55 m, respectively, where minimum values are exceptionally low. Each station is at the foot of a large mountain mass.

Average temperatures for the monthly maximum are higher on the Pacific coast than on the Atlantic coast at the same elevations (fig. 3.5). For the Pacific, the mean

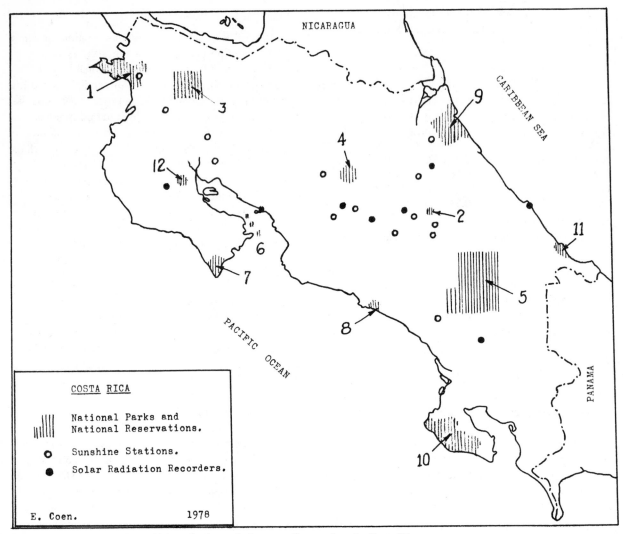

FIGURE 3.3. Location of sunshine and solar radiation recording stations in Costa Rica.

value at sea level is about 32.6° C, but on the Atlantic the mean is 29.9° C. These observations agree with the hypothesis that there are fewer clouds on the Pacific side during the dry season, allowing more solar radiation to reach the ground. On the Atlantic side the dry season is less pronounced, and there are more cloudy days during the year. These cloudy days depress the average monthly maximum temperatures.

Mean annual temperatures decrease with elevation at a rate of 6.5° C/km for the maximum and at 5.2° C/km for the minimum temperatures. Consequently, in Costa Rica the minimum and maximum average annual temperatures for the highest peak (Chirripó) are about 2.2° C and 7.2° C respectively (3,819 m elevation). With these temperatures frost is frequent, but there is no permanent ice in the soil or on ponds; nevertheless, forklore has it that snow has been seen once on Chirripó and Cerro de la Muerte.

Terrestrial radiation during the night depends to a large degree on local conditions. For a given site the minimum temperatures are more uniform through the year than are the maximums (fig. 3.4). However, lack of cloud cover during the dry season also results in cooler nights than during the rainy season.

Below elevations of 800 m on the Pacific side of Costa Rica, the mean monthly maximum temperatures are the highest of the year during February, March, and April. Between 800 m and 1,000 m the decrease in the maximum temperatures is very large (Coen 1970, pp. 66–77). This phenomenon, found on the Pacific slope at 10° N in Costa Rica, occurs on all the Pacific slopes of the mountains of Central America. It may in part be caused by the *papagayo* winds or nortes described earlier. These winds bring a cold, humid air mass over the mountains and later bring a descending dry wind that warms up the site.

TABLE 3.3   Estimated Daily Hours of Sunshine in the National Parks of Costa Rica

Number[a]	Location	$\overline{H}$[b]	Jan.	Feb.	Mar.	Apr.	May	June	July	Aug.	Sep.	Oct.	Nov.	Dec.	Average for Year
1	P.N. Santa Rosa	0.08	8.7	9.7	9.5	9.3	6.7	5.5	5.4	5.7	5.0	5.2	6.5	8.2	7.1
2	M.N. Guayabo	1.10	4.0	4.9	5.0	4.4	4.1	3.0	3.1	3.8	3.2	3.5	3.9	4.2	3.9
3	P.N. Rincón de la Vieja	1.50	7.6	8.5	8.5	8.0	5.7	4.0	4.4	4.9	4.4	4.0	5.6	6.8	6.0
4	P.N. Volcán Poas	2.00	6.0	7.0	6.6	6.4	4.6	4.4	3.9	3.9	3.4	3.8	3.9	5.4	4.9
5	P.N. Chirripó	2.50	4.3	5.0	4.5	5.4	4.0	3.0	2.4	3.1	3.0	3.0	4.0	4.0	3.8
6	R.B. Islas del Golfo	0.01	8.5	9.6	8.8	9.2	6.7	5.1	5.2	6.1	5.0	5.1	6.1	7.6	6.9
7	R.N. Cabo Blanco	0.01	8.5	8.4	9.0	9.2	6.8	4.0	5.3	6.2	4.8	5.0	5.9	7.3	6.7
8	R.N. Manuel Antonio	0.00	6.6	8.1	7.1	7.3	6.6	2.0	3.3	3.0	4.1	5.0	4.9	6.1	5.3
9	P.N. Tortuguero	0.00	4.4	4.5	5.4	5.7	4.4	3.9	2.5	5.0	4.6	4.4	4.0	4.4	4.4
10	P.N. Corcovado	0.02	6.5	8.1	6.1	6.2	5.9	3.0	4.2	4.0	4.2	4.0	4.4	5.3	5.2
11	P.N. Cahuita	0.00	4.7	6.2	6.1	5.8	5.4	4.7	4.0	4.4	4.3	5.0	4.5	4.6	5.0
12	P.N. Barra Honda	0.06	8.4	9.5	8.8	8.7	6.2	5.0	5.4	5.8	4.7	5.0	6.0	8.0	6.8
Maximum possible hours of sunshine at 10° N on the 15th day of each month			11.6	11.8	12.0	12.4	12.6	12.7	12.7	12.5	12.2	11.9	11.7	11.5	

SOURCE: Unpublished maps of sunshine for Costa Rica by E. Coen 1977.

[a] See figure 3.3

[b] Average elevation above mean sea level, in km.

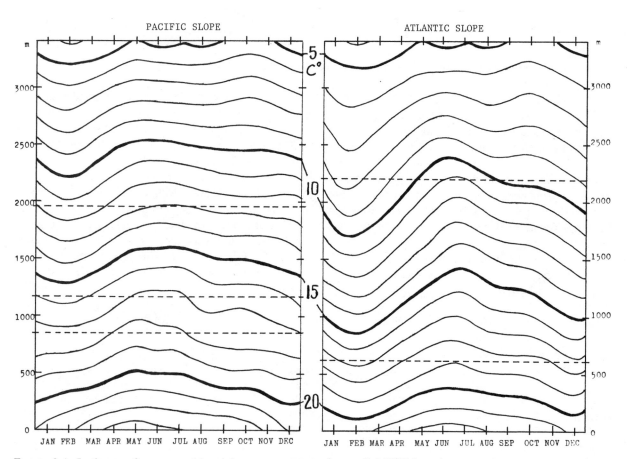

FIGURE 3.4. Isotherms of mean monthly minimum temperatures for parallel 10°N through Costa Rica (1970–73).

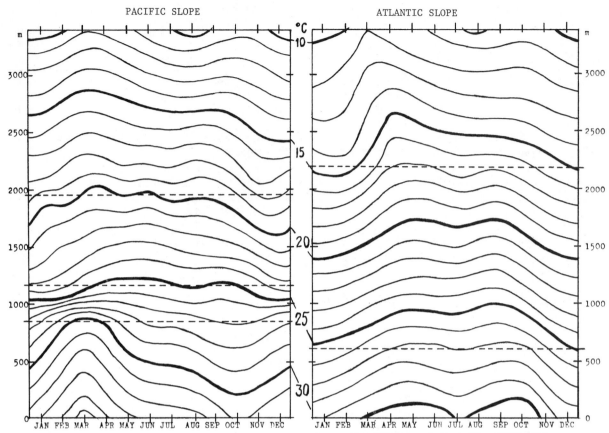

PACIFIC SLOPE ATLANTIC SLOPE

FIGURE 3.5. Isotherms of mean monthly maximum temperature for parallel 10°N through Costa Rica (1970–73).

Local Winds

The nortes or papagayo winds are more frequent and strongest in January, February, and March (see fig. 3.6). This wind is called papagayo (in Costa Rica) when it blows inland off the Pacific Ocean and nortes when it blows from inland down the slope toward the Pacific. The dry season nortes are very strong in Guanacaste, with wind speed averaging between 10 and 30 km/hr. From Las Cañas to Bagaces, at times the wind gusts reach 90 km/hr.

In Port Limón, the wind blows persistently from southwest and west as in *Bd* and *Br* in figure 3.6. A few kilometers to the north, in Cobal, the wind blows persistently throughout the year from the northeast, with an average speed of 7 km/hr as in *Ad* and *Ar* in figure 3.6.

The dry season reinforced trade winds (alisios), when crossing the Guanacaste and Central ranges, produce a fohn (chinook) effect over Guanacaste and the Central Valley (Meseta Central), with descending winds as in *Ad* in figure 3.6; however, in the valley of Perez Zeledon and Golfo Dulce, the high elevation range of the Talamancas produces a rotor (vortex with horizontal axis) on both slopes (fig. 3.6, *Bd*). Some rain falls on both regions in the dry season. The rotor on the Pacific side is stronger,

TABLE 3.4   Transect of Temperatures (C°) Near Latitude 10° N in Costa Rica

Station Name	Latitude North	Longitude West	Elevation (m)	Yearly $\overline{X}$ Maximum	Minimum	Mean
Puntarenas	09°58′	84°50′	3	32.3	22.4	27.35
F. Baudrit	10°01′	84°16′	840	28.4	17.8	23.10
San José	09°56′	84°05′	1,172	24.8	16.6	20.70
Palmira	10°13′	84°24′	1,960	19.2	12.1	15.65
Volcán Irazú	09°59′	83°42′	3,400	10.7	4.8	7.75
Cariblanco	09°57′	83°48′	2,200	16.1	9.5	12.80
Turrialba	09°53′	83°38′	602	26.6	18.0	22.30
Limón	10°00′	83°03′	5	30.1	21.6	25.80

NOTE: Figures are averages from 1970 to 1973.

TABLE 3.5   Station of Maximum Oscillation of Temperature (C°) during 1971 in Costa Rica

Station Name	Latitude North	Longitude West	Elevation (m)	Yearly $\bar{X}$ Maximum	Yearly $\bar{X}$ Mimimum	Oscillation
Naranjo	10°06'	84°24'	1,042	25.1	14.3	10.8
Cachí	09°49'	83°49'	1,018	25.7	12.8	13.7
Volcán Buenos Aires	09°13'	83°27'	450	29.7	17.8	11.9
Cobal	10°15'	83°40'	55	30.8	19.1	11.7

SOURCES: *Anuario Meteorológico* 1971.

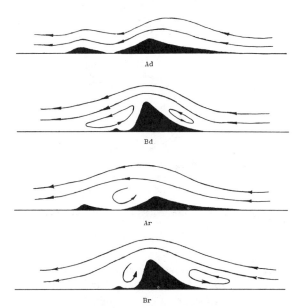

FIGURE 3.6. Trade winds crossing the mountain ranges in Guanacaste (*A*) and Talamanca (*B*). *Ad* and *Bd,* during the dry season (December, January, February, and March); *Ar* and *Br,* during the rainy season (April, May, June, July, and August).

with an average wind speed of 9 km/hr from the southwest. On the Atlantic side of Port Limón, the average speed of the wind from the southwest is 5 km/hr.

When the trade winds diminish in intensity during the rainy season, the free convection produced by differential heating of the soil and the air mass is the most significant process producing rain. The rotor on the Atlantic side of the Talamance range tends to intensify the rains at elevations above 1,000 m (fig. 3.6, *Br*). As I stated earlier, a few rainy days account for most of the total rain during the rainy season. The convectional disturbances that pro-

duce the rainy days add up to the average conditions described by the isohyets in figure 3.7.

Some Rainfall Peculiarities

The distribution of rainfall in a region is related to topography. At middle latitudes, rainfall increases with elevation. In tropical regions, the rainfall on the windward sides of mountains increases with elevation up to a certain level, then decreases. The elevation of maximum rainfall for the mountains of Central America was found by Hastenrath (1967) and Mendizabal (1973) to be at about half the average elevation of the peaks in the mountain range, or about 1,000 m elevation. This pattern probably occurs because the mountain ranges in Central America, especially those in Costa Rica, gradually slope up to this level and then break into isolated peaks and mountain passes that stop the ascending air currents by channeling the air through the passes. Such fragmentation of the air mass should diminish the rate of condensation of the water vapor carried by the wind.

Unstable air, common in the tropics, can be triggered to convective activity by encountering a slight rise in elevation as it moves inland. This is why certain localities more frequently develop thunderstorms and showers and why, when onshore air encounters the coastline, the differential heating of sea and land during the day, and the difference in surface friction between sea and land (Bergeron 1951; Coen 1959, p. 14), causes convection storms.

Examples of the first case are the high rainfall found on the slopes of the Cordillera Central and the Cordillera de Talamanca on the Atlantic side. The second case is represented by the high rainfall at Tortuguero, Valle de Parrita, and Golfito (fig. 3.7).

Minimum rainfall occurs on the floors of valleys. The valley bottom extending from Cartago through the Central Valley (Meseta Central) to the Llanuras del Guanacaste is the driest portion of the country, especially compared with the neighboring slopes.

The maximum number of days with rain, approximately 315, coincides with the area of maximum rain in the basin of the Río Macho, Río Grande de Orosí, and Río Pejivalle. The highest number of days with rain was reported at Hacienda Cedral, at an elevation of approxi-

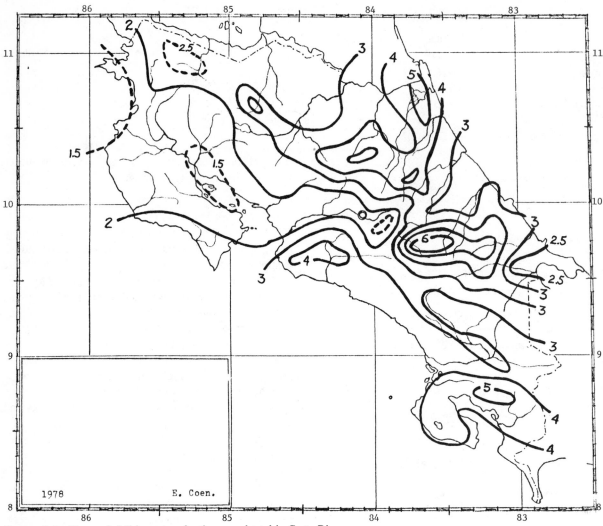

FIGURE 3.7. Mean rainfall in meters for the annual total in Costa Rica.

mately 1,100 m. Here rain fell on 351 days in 1967 and on 359 days in 1968; this may be a world record (J. F. Griffin, pers. comm.). The average number of days with rain at this station during the years 1965, 1966, 1967, and 1971 was 329. The second highest number of days with rain recorded in Costa Rica is at Buena Vista on the west slope of Volcán Poas, at 1,017 m elevation and with a northern exposure. This station reported an average of 308 rainy days from 1964 to 1968 (maximum of 344 in 1966).

When Does It Rain?

When examining national folklore, Coen (1973) found that people frequently mentioned particular rains: the rainfall around 19 and 20 March, which people call the *aguacero de los cafetaleros* (coffee grower shower), which induces coffee plants to initiate flowering; the rainfall around 11 April and the one from 27 April to 1 May (which is also the beginning of the rainy season in Guana-

caste); the lack of rain on 27 and 28 June corresponding to the *veranillo de San Juan,* and also the lack of rainfall on 2 and 3 October and 13 November. The days with rain around 8 and 12 December are called *las lagrimas de Maria* (Mary's tears). On 14 October there is believed to be a *temporal del Pacifico.*

Amador (1975, p. 56) found that oscillations in the free atmosphere have periods of four days; in the high troposphere, periods are about six days. These oscillations can be associated with the intensification of the rainfall every four to six days. Rains occur in the early afternoon in the highlands, late in the afternoon in the lowlands of the Pacific side, and during the night in the bottoms of the valleys and in the lowlands of the Atlantic side. Convection is the basic cause of rain in the tropics, and this occurs most frequently at sites where differential heating with respect to the surroundings is greatest. The sun warms the highlands faster and earlier than the lowlands, and this starts the sea breezes and valley breezes

44

moving convective clouds inland. Rain comes earlier in the day on the Pacific side than on the Atlantic side. This is in agreement with a heated-island model that includes momentum exchange (Garstang 1968); in this model, mass convergence occurs during the night and divergence occurs during the day on a windward coast; the reverse is true of the lee shore.

Relation to Biology

The effects on animal and plant biology of climate and weather in Costa Rica have scarcely been examined. Janzen (1967a) used Costa Rican weather data in constructing the hypothesis that tropical mountain ranges of a given height should be more difficult for organisms to cross than are extratropical mountain ranges of the same height. He based his hypothesis on the conjecture that, because tropical organisms are normally exposed to a narrower range of seasonal (and diel) changes in temperature than are extratropical ones, they will find it more traumatic to endure the different temperatures encountered in crossing a mountain range. In addition, he discovered that for a given difference in elevation between two Costa Rican weather stations there is less overlap in temperature regimes than for a comparable difference between two United States weather stations; the lower the absolute elevation, the more pronounced was this phenomenon, suggesting that small Costa Rican mountain ranges may be disproportionately formidable barriers to animal and plant movements.

The synchronization of flowering, fruiting, and other phenological events with the conspicuous seasonal changes in rainfall has attracted the attention of numerous field biologists in Costa Rica, as elsewhere in the tropics (e.g., Baker et al. 1982; Reich and Borchert 1982; Daubenmire 1972; Frankie 1975; Frankie, Baker, and Opler 1974a,b; Opler, Frankie, and Baker 1976, 1980; Stiles 1975, 1977, 1978). Although there is a general pattern of peaks of flowering and fruiting at the drier times of year, the pattern breaks down when we move from large woody plants to small woody plants to herbs and from deciduous forest to rain forest. Studies in progress at Monteverde (1,400–1,800 m) give us our first impression of such patterns for intermediate elevation evergreen forest in Costa Rica (W. Haber, N. Wheelwright, G. W. Frankie, P. Feinsinger, H. G. Baker). Our understanding of the causal relationships between Costa Rican weather and climate patterns and biological phenomena such as flowering and fruiting is at a very primitive stage. Janzen (1967b) argued that large woody plants may flower and fruit in the dry season largely because this is when putting resources into non-vegetative activity is least detrimental to vegetative competitive ability. Others have argued that dry season sunny days are best for pollination and least likely to damage flowers.

The microclimatic relationships between Costa Rican animals and the weather conditions they need or use has great potential for helping us understand tropical natural history. During the Guanacaste dry season, the small canyon of the ever-flowing Río Potrero (COMELCO ranch, near Bagaces) was found to have air temperatures at 10:00 A.M. of 29.6° C while the air in the deciduous forest only 90 m away was 35.3° C with a relative humidity thirty percentage points lower than the 76 relative humidity in the canyon (Janzen 1976a). It is not surprising that the insect fauna of the riparian bottomlands in Guanacaste is so different from that of the adjacent deciduous forest during the dry season (Janzen 1973, 1976b; Janzen and Schoener 1968).

But these rudimentary studies are only a minute fraction of the work that needs to be done on the interactions of Costa Rican plants and animals with climate and weather. It has long been believed that organisms in extratropical regions have major interactions with a physical environment fraught with biological harshness, while those in the tropics live in a benign physical world. However, it is clear that tropical organisms not only have to deal with severe biological challenges but also have to maintain an exact and complex relationship with the microstructure of climate and weather.

*

Amador, J. A. 1975. *Analisis espectral de las oscilaciones en la atmosfera libre sobre America Central.* Ciudad Universitaria: Escuela de Física, Universidad de Costa Rica.

Anuario Meterológico. 1964 N. San José: Servicio Meteorológico Nacional, Ministerio de Agricultura y Ganadería.

Baker, H. G.; Bawa, K. S.; Frankie, G. W.; and Opler, P. A. 1982. Reproductive biology of plants in tropical forest. In *Ecosystems of the world: Tropical forests*, ed. F. B. Golley and H. Lieth, pp. 183–215. Amsterdam: Elsevier.

Bergeron, T. 1951. A general survey in the field of cloud physics. Extrait de la Publication AIM no. 9/c. Brussels.

Chang, J. H. 1968. *Climate and agriculture.* Chicago: Aldine.

Coen, E. 1951. La meteorologia de Costa Rica. In *Atlas estadístico*, pp. 34–37. San José: Dirección General de Estadística y Censo.

———. 1959. Lluvias tormentas y vientos en Costa Rica. San José: Servicio Meteorológico, Ministerio Agricultura e Industrias.

———. 1970. Climate of Central America and Costa Rica. Atmospheric Sciences course, July–August 1970, pp. 66–77. Ciudad Universitaria: Organization for Tropical Studies.

———. 1973. El folklore Costarricense relativo al clima. *Rev. Univ. Costa Rica* 35:135–46.

———. 1977. Mapas del promedio mensual de las horas de brillo solar en Costa Rica. Unpublished manuscript, available from E. Coen.

Daubenmire, R. 1972. Phenology and other characteristics of tropical semi-deciduous forest in northwestern Costa Rica. *J. Ecol.* 60:147–70.

Dunn, G. E., and Miller, B. I. 1960. *Atlantic hurricanes.* Baton Rouge: Louisiana State University Press.

Escoto, J. A. V. 1964. Weather and climate of Mexico and Central America. In *Handbook of Middle American Indians,* vol. 1, *Natural environment and early cultures,* ed. R. C. West, pp. 187–215. Austin: University of Texas Press.

Frankie, G. W. 1975. Tropical forest phenology and pollinator plant coevolution. In *Coevolution of animals and plants,* ed. L. E. Gilbert and P. H. Raven, pp. 192–209. Austin: University of Texas Press.

Frankie, G. W.; Baker, H. G.; and Opler, P. A. 1974*a*. Comparative phenological studies of trees in tropical wet and dry forests in the lowlands of Costa Rica. *J. Ecol.* 62:881–919.

———. 1974*b*. Tropical plant phenology; Applications for studies in community ecology. In *Phenology and seasonality modeling,* ed. H. Lieth, pp. 287–96. Berlin: Springer-Verlag.

Fritz, S. 1951. Solar radiation energy and its modification by the earth and its atmosphere. In *Compendium of meteorology,* pp. 13–33. Boston: American Meteorological Society.

Garstang, M. 1968. *The role of momentum exchange in flow over a heated island.* Tallahassee: Florida State University.

Gentry, A. H. 1974. Flowering phenology and diversity in tropical Bignoniaceae. *Biotropica* 6:64–68.

Gramzow, R. H., and Henry, W. K. 1971. *The rainy seasons of Central America.* College Station: Texas A and M University.

Hastenrath, S. 1966. On general circulation and energy budgets in the area of the Central American seas. *J. Atmos. Sci.* 23:694–711.

———. 1967. Rainfall distribution and regime in Central America. *Archiv. Meteorol. Geophys. Bioklim.,* ser. B, 15:201–41.

Haurwitz, B. 1948. Transmision of solar radiation through clouds (overcast). *J. Meteorol.* 5:110; reprinted in *Smithsonian meteorological tables,* Washington, D.C.: Smithsonian Institution.

Heithaus, E. R. 1979. Community structure of Neotropical flower visiting bees and wasps: Diversity and phenology. *Ecology* 60:190–202.

Holdridge, L. R.; Grenke, W. C.; Hathaway, W. H.; Liang, T.; and Tosi, J. A., Jr. 1971. *Forest environments in tropical life zones: A pilot study.* Oxford: Pergamon Press.

Huschke, R. E. 1959. *Glossary of meteorology.* Boston: American Meterological Society.

Janzen, D. H. 1967*a*. Why mountain passes are higher in the tropics. *Am. Nat.* 101:233–49.

———. 1967*b*. Synchronization of sexual reproduction of trees with the dry season in Central America. *Evolution* 21:620–37.

———. 1973. Sweep samples of tropical foliage insects: Effects of seasons, vegetation types, elevation, time of day, and insularity. *Ecology* 54:687–708.

———. 1976*a*. The microclimate differences between a deciduous forest and adjacent riparian forest in Guanacaste Province, Costa Rica. *Brenesia* 8:29–33.

———. 1976*b*. Sweep samples of tropical deciduous forest foliage-inhabiting insects: Seasonal changes and inter-field differences in adult bugs and beetles. *Rev. Biol. Trop.* 24:149–61.

Janzen, D. H., and Schoener, T. W. 1968. Differences in insect abundance and diversity between wetter and drier sites during a tropical dry season. *Ecology* 49:96–110.

Mendizabal, M. 1973. *Distribución de la precipitación con la altura.* Ciudad Universitaria: Escuela de Física, Universidad de Costa Rica.

Opler, P. A.; Frankie, G. W.; and Baker, H. G. 1976. Rainfall as a factor in the release, timing, and synchronization of anthesis by tropical trees and shrubs. *J. Biogeog.* 3:231–36.

———. 1980. Comparative phenological studies of shrubs and treelets in wet and dry forests in the lowlands of Costa Rica. *J. Ecol.* 68:167–88.

Placido, J. M. 1973. *Sistemas sinopticos en el Atlantico Norte tropical.* Ciudad Universitaria: Escuela de Física, Universidad de Costa Rica.

Portig, W. H. 1965. Central American rainfall. *Geogr. Rev.* 55:68–90.

Reich, P. B., and Borchert, R. 1982. Phenology and ecophysiology of the tropical tree, *Tabebuia neochrysantha* (Bignoniaceae). *Ecology* 63:294–99.

Smithsonian Institution. 1963. *Meterological tables.* 6th ed. Washington, D.C.: Smithsonian Institution.

Stiles, F. G. 1975. Ecology, flowering phenology and hummingbird pollination of some Costa Rican *Heliconia* species. *Ecology* 56:285–310.

———. 1977. Coadapted competitiors: The flowering seasons of hummingbird-pollinated plants in a tropical forest. *Science* 198:1177–78.

———. 1978. Temporal organization of flowering among the hummingbird foodplants of a tropical wet forest. *Biotropica* 10:194–210.

4 GEOLOGY

R. Castillo-Muñoz

The appraisal of Costa Rican geology made here is regional in character. It describes the principal geological units that occur in Costa Rica with reference to the geological map (fig. 4.1) and a table of stratigraphic relationships of the principal formations and units that have been defined to date (fig. 4.2*a, b*), gives a detailed description of each of the principal formations and its whereabouts, and describes the tectonic structure and evolution experienced by the territory of Costa Rica as evidenced by the known geological characteristics.

Geology and Stratigraphy

The principal geological units constituting the territory of Costa Rica range in age from Jurassic to Quaternary (fig. 4.1). They can be grouped as follows by lithology and age: Mesozoic volcanic and sedimentary rocks (Jurassic-Cretaceous); Tertiary sedimentary and volcanic rocks; Cretaceous and Tertiary plutonic rocks; Quaternary sedimentary and volcanic rocks.

MESOZOIC VOLCANIC AND SEDIMENTARY ROCKS (JURASSIC-CRETACEOUS)

Volcanic Rocks (Mzvs)
Mesozoic volcanic rocks are spilitic basalts, agglomerates, basalt, and radiolarite breccia together with sedimentary rocks of dark gray graywacke, cherts, cherty shales, and aphanitic siliceous limestone. They are strongly folded together and poorly weathered. This sequence is penetrated by intrusions of gabbro, diabase, and diorite (Dengo 1962*b*).

This lithological association forms the Nicoya Complex, which outcrops extensively over the Nicoya Peninsula, in a small part of the Santa Elena Peninsula, in Punta Herradura and sites immediately to the east, in the Osa Peninsula, and in some parts of Punta Burica (figs. 4.1, 4.2).

The rocks of the Nicoya Complex vary in age from Jurassic (Middle Titonian; Galli 1977) to Upper Cretaceous (Campanian-Maestrichtian), according to Henningsen and Weyl (1967). More recently, an Upper Santonian age has been considered for these rocks (Galli and Schmidt 1977), with an isotope date of 72.5 million years (Barr and Escalante 1969).

Mesozoic Undifferentiated Sedimentary Rocks (Mzs₂)
The Mesozoic undifferentiated sedimentary rocks are pri-

marily made up of shales, siliceous sandstone and cherts with radiolarians, thin beds of conglomerate, graywackes, coarse-, medium-, and fine-grained sandstone, siltstone, calcareous shales, and limestone intercalated with volcanic rocks. These rock types occur together in a variety of interstratifications and have been assigned to the Upper Cretaceous (Campanian-Maestrichtian) (Dengo 1968, p. 28).

This undifferentiated sequence is represented by formations such as the Sabana Grande and Rivas formations that outcrop in Guanacaste and on the Nicoya Peninsula, and the Golfito and Changuinola formations that are exposed in the southeast part of the country (figs. 4.1, 4.2).

The Sabana Grande Formation, of Santonian age (Galli and Schmidt 1977), consists principally of cherts and siliceous limestone, and the overlain Rivas Formation of Santonian-Maestrichtian age (Galli and Schmidt 1977) is principally made up of layers of sandstone, shale, and some limestone beds. The two formations are separated from each other by an unconformity.

Outcrops of the Sabana Grande Formation are seen at the site bearing that name on the Nicoya Peninsula, at Guatil, along the road between Nicoya and Santa Ana to the northwest of Santa Cruz, and in the Cerros de Moracia; in the Nicoya Gulf, on Berrugate island; near Hacienda El Viejo, in the Cerros Peor es Nada and near San Lázaro (Dengo 1962*b*); outcrops are also found in the eastern part of the Cerro de Jesús south of Vigía (MacDonald 1920).

The Rivas Formation has outcrops in the northern part of the Santa Elena Peninsula, in contact with the Santa Elena Peridotite, and in various parts of the road that connects Murciélago with Playa Blanca; it is also seen in Santa Elena Bay, in the road between Santa Ana and Corralillo, in the central part of the Nicoya Peninsula, and in the valley of the Río Tempisque near Matina and Río Blanco, and in Punta Quesera (Dengo 1962*b*).

Dengo (1968) used the term Golfito Formation to designate a formation that irregularly overlies the Nicoya Complex. This formation consists, from bottom to top, of greenish gray siliceous limestone, conglomerates, shales, and siltstone, with occasional beds of stratified gray brownish sandstone with beds of siliceous limestone. This formation appears in the area of Golfito Bay, in the hills between Golfito and the railway station at El Alto, and in Punta Banco on the Burica Peninsula. There

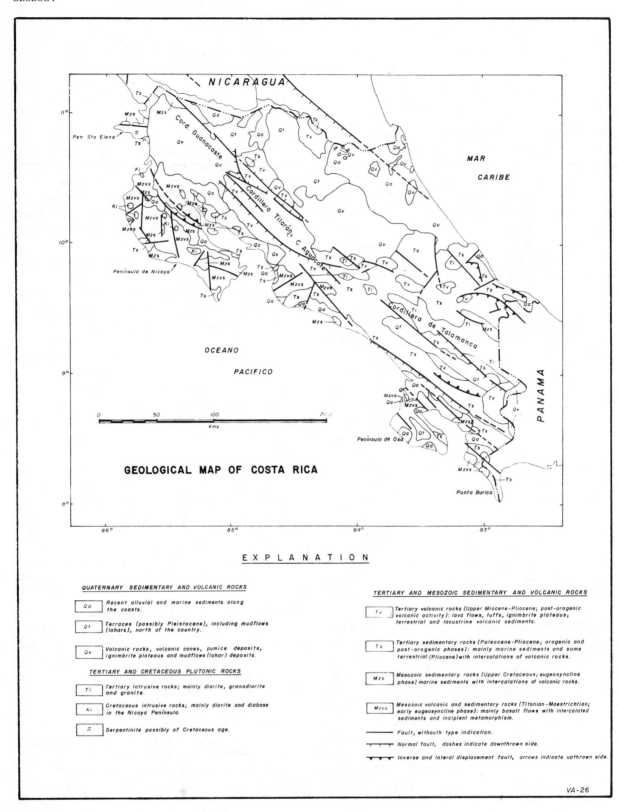

FIGURE 4.1. Geological map of Costa Rica (from Dengo et al. 1969).

is a good section between the exit of Golfito Bay and Punta Gallardo.

The Changuinola Formation, as named and described by Fisher and Pessagno (1965), is represented by limestone, usually white, grayish to clear greenish, and clear greenish yellow, with top layers of interstratified andesitic lava, and dacites and clastic sediments. These rocks are very conspicuous at the type locality in the Changuinola River and its principal tributary, the Río Peña Blanca in the northwestern part of Panama. They are also believed to occur in southeastern Costa Rica (Dengo 1968, p. 28). However, Fisher and Pessagno (1965) have found rocks similar to the Changuinola Formation in the Río Lari and think they are assignable to Tertiary sedimentary rocks, specifically Paleocene and Middle Eocene.

The Upper Cretaceous sedimentary rocks in the Nicoya Peninsula are due to volcanic detritus derived primarily from the erosion of the Nicoya Complex; however, these sediments also contain contemporary volcanic detritus and rocks, which indicates concomitant volcanic activity. In the same manner, the Changuinola Formation contains tuffaceous sandstone and intercalated andesitic lava and dacite.

TERTIARY SEDIMENTARY AND VOLCANIC ROCKS
Tertiary Sedimentary Rocks (Ts)

The Tertiary sedimentary rocks are represented principally by marine sediments and some continental sediments with intercalated volcanic rocks. These rocks, which vary in age from the Paleocene to Pliocene, appear all over the Costa Rican territory and especially in the central part of the country, such as the Pacific and Caribbean slopes (fig. 4.1).

Figure 4.2 gives the names that have been assigned to the diverse units of these rocks in different parts of the country. Each of these formations has diverse lithological characteristics that are generally associated with rudites, sandstones, and claystones, in diverse proportions and variably interstratified, and containing a major proportion of calcareous and volcanic materials.

The rocks formed in marine depositional environments, which are the predominant ones, are sandstones, siltstones, shales, and claystones, some tuffaceous in character, and limestone, all of which display diverse degrees of intercalation and outcrop in various parts of the country. The intercalated volcanic rocks, also formed in a marine habitat, were produced by various degrees of volcanic activity that influenced the sedimentary rocks as well as the continental ones. The continental Tertiary sedimentary rocks are primarily conglomerates developed on the margins of the Cordillera de Talamanca.

The volcanic rocks are those formed during the Lower Tertiary and appear in diverse parts of the country. In association with sedimentary rocks of the Eocene and some of the Oligocene, there have been found tuffs, agglomerates, andesite and basalt flows, and some diabase sills (Dengo 1962a, pp. 142–43). In this respect, the Tuis Formation on the Caribbean side contains numerous intercalations of andesite, basalt, and tuffaceous beds (Dengo 1968, p. 28).

The Barra Honda Formation is made up of stratified limestones and is found among the Paleocene sedimentary rocks on the Pacific side with extensions to the Upper Cretaceous (Maestrichtian). This unit, according to Dengo (1962b) outcrops in Guanacaste in the Cerros de Quebrada Honda, Corralillo, Quebrada Honda, Copal, Caballito, Corral de Piedra and La Cueva on the west side of the Río Tempisque, and in some small hills on the east side of the river. The lower contact of this formation is unconformable with the Rivas Formation.

Las Palmas Formation occurs in the extreme southeast portion of the Nicoya Peninsula and is Upper Paleocene in age, or possibly Lower Eocene. It is made up of thin, hard layers of siltstone and shale, well stratified, and of lenticular masses of coral reef limestone. Important examples of this formation occur 1 km from Playa Naranjo on the road to Bajo Negro; it also occurs on the Río Nacaome, to the west of Puerto Letras in the Punta Morales (Dengo 1962b). The upper contact of this formation is possibly concordant with the Brito Formation, and it is not concordant with the Barra Honda Formation (Dengo 1962b, p. 27).

It is agreed that the Eocene sedimentary rocks on the Pacific side of Costa Rica, represented primarily by the Brito Formation, are primarily clastic. However, they also contain extensive coral reef members, assigned to the Upper Eocene, which extend from Guanacaste Province, with the name Colorado Member (MacDonald 1920; Dengo 1962b), to the southeastern part of the country along with the limestone of the Fila de Cal. This formation is known in Panama as the David Formation (Dengo 1968, p. 28).

The Parritilla Limestone (Caliza de Parritilla) from the Upper Eocene is an organic limestone, dark gray to blackish and at times very fine grained, 60 m thick, with large foraminifers and calcareous algae (Malavassi 1966). It outcrops on the south and west flanks of the Cerro Caraigres, situated on the south bank of the Río Candelaria, Parritilla de Acosta (type locality), Tiquires, Escuadra, and Cangrejal. According to my observations this limestone is stratigraphically below the purple facies of the Pacacua Formation in the Cerro Caraigres, but the type of stratigraphy is unknown. Recently, Castillo (1981) has observed various limestone outcrops between Cangrejal and Escuadra that suggest that existence of more than one limestone layer intercalated with rather clastic units of unknown ages.

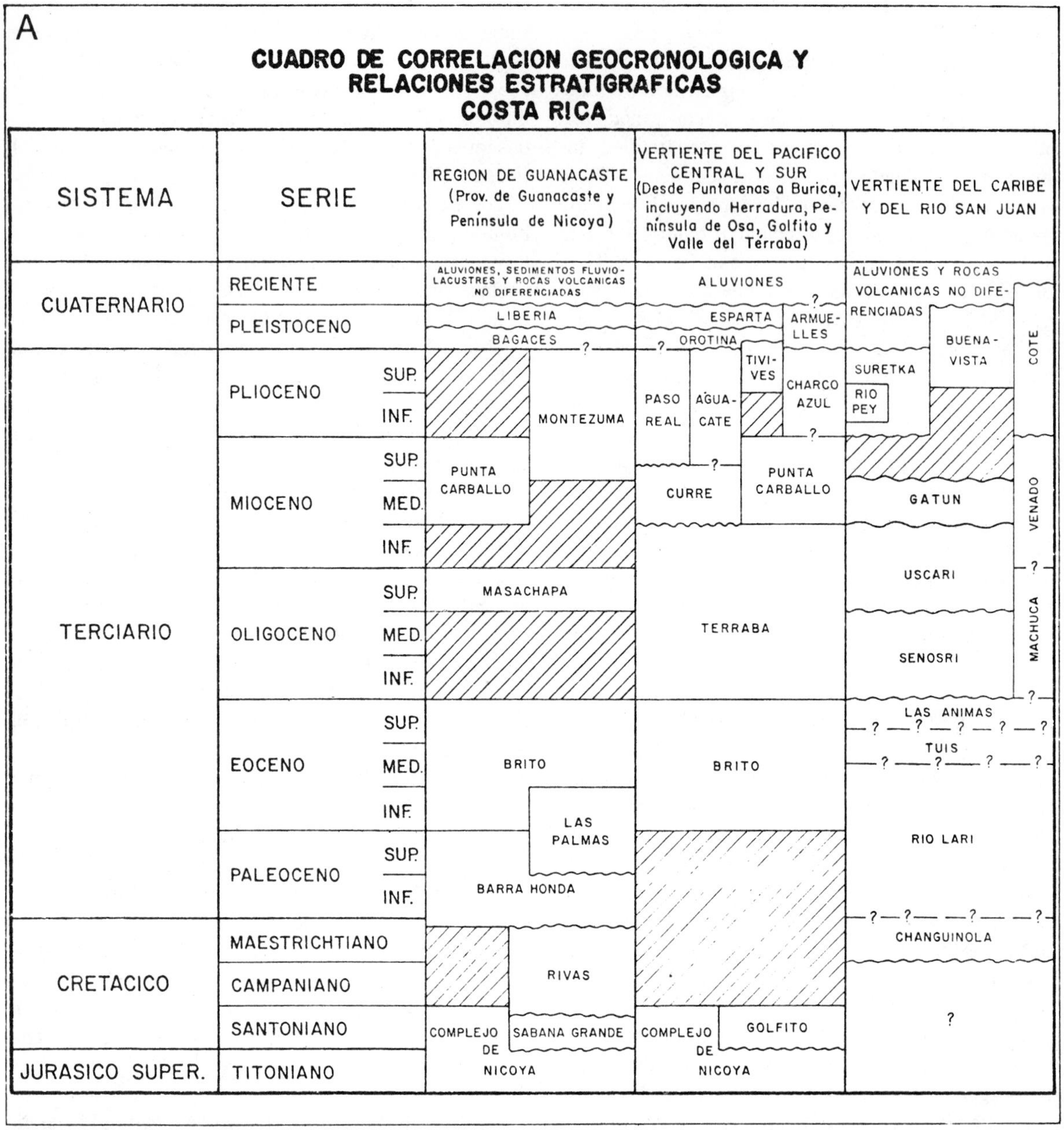

FIGURE 4.2. Geochronological and stratigraphical correlation table of Costa Rica.

Eocene sedimentary rocks on the Caribbean side of the country are represented by the Tuis Formation and the Las Animas Limestone (Caliza de las Animas).

The Tuis Formation is represented in the Turrialba area by a sequence of sandstones and tuffaceous siltstones and claystones intercalated with basalt lava flows, conglomerates, and volcanic breccias and reaching more than 3,000 m in thickness (Riviere 1973, p. 50). Although it outcrops conspicuously in Tuis of Turrialba, the type locality, the extension, and contacts with other formations are not known.

In the central part of the country sedimentary rock outcrops that have been assigned to the Eocene are grouped under the names Pacacua Formation (Castillo 1969) and Caliza de Parritilla (Malavassi 1966).

The Pacacua Formation is a sequence made up of interstratifications of breccia conglomerates and conglomeritic sandstones, sandstones, siltstones, and shales, all tuffaceous; in some places they have a characteristic purple color, and the thickness is as great as 1,148 m at the type locality on the north flank of the Cerro Pacacua. In general this formation ranges from the south and east

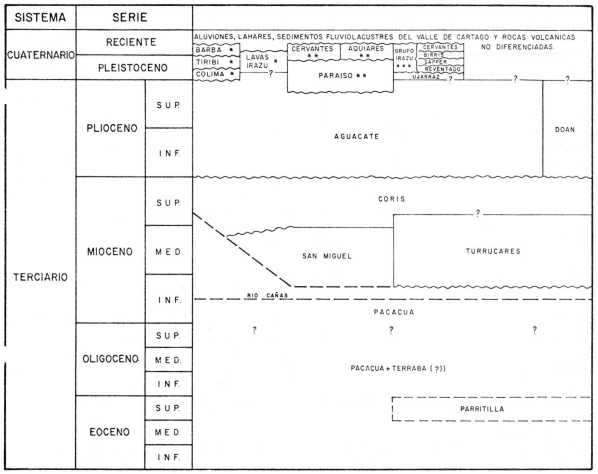

B

CORRELACION ESTRATIGRAFICA Y GEOCRONOLOGICA
PARTE CENTRAL DE COSTA RICA

(VALLE Y CORDILLERA CENTRAL, CERROS DE ESCAZU Y BUSTAMANTE)

FUENTE: DONDOLI Y TORRES, 1954; ESCALANTE, 1966; CASTILLO, 1969; KRUSHENSKY, 1972;
NACIONES UNIDAS, 1975; RIVIER, 1980.

VALLE CENTRAL OCCIDENTAL Y ORIENTAL:

* Según Naciones Unidas - Senas (1975)
** Según Dóndoli y Torres (1954)
*** Según Krushensky (1972)

Marzo 1981

of Ciudad Colón to the southwest and east of Santa Ana and to the west and east of Escazú. The lower contact of the formation is not visible in this part of the country. Recently, Riviere (1980, p. 127) assigned a Lower Miocene age to the conglomerates of the Pacacua Formation, and the whole lithologic unit, including the finer facies of sandstones and shales, was assigned to the Upper Miocene on the basis of paleontologic evidence. Castillo (1981) says that the apparently erroneous Eocenic age of the Pacacua Formation could be accentuated by the lithologic unit initially defined by Castillo in 1965 as "Río Cañas Unit" (considered in Castillo 1969 as the Térraha Formation), which is represented by a sequence of black shales, siltstones, and fine sandstone beds outcropping on the Río Cañas, southeast of Aserrí and is stratigraphically underlain by the San Miguel Limestone of Lower to Middle Miocene age; this unit was subsequently correlated in age with the Oligocene–Lower Miocene Térraba Formation only on the basis of lithologic considerations (Dengo, pers. comm.). Therefore Castillo (1981) considers it likely that a major part of the sequence of black shales, siltstone, and fine sandstone beds outcropping in various parts of the area studied by Castillo in 1965 is the lithologic equivalent of the "Río Cañas Unit," which could well be considered as the Río Cañas Formation because of its distinctive lithologic characteristics.

The Las Animas Limestone was recognized by Sjogren (Hill 1898; Hoffstetter, Dengo, and Weyl 1960, pp. 258–60); its type locality is Hacienda Las Animas in Turrialba in the Río Reventazón valley. It is a sequence made up of two layers of whitish limestone separated by layers of sandstone and conglomerate. The limestone is thin and fossil-bearing and also outcrops in the area of Azul and on the Chitaría River (Dóndoli and Torres 1954, pp. 41–42).

On the central and southern parts of the Pacific side of Costa Rica there are Oligocene to Lower Miocene rocks, represented by black shales of the Térraba Formation (Dengo 1961, p. 48), which suggests a semieuxinic environment owing to the lack of external communication of the sedimentation basin. These rocks appear extensively in the Cordillera Costeña, in the Valle de El General, and in the western foothills of the Cordillera de Talamanca. In the northwest portion of the country, in Guanacaste, the Oligocene rocks (Upper Oligocene) are represented by the Masachapa Formation, which is constituted of coarse- to fine-grained sandstones, some calcareous gray siltstones, calcareous shales, shaly limestones, and sandstones, some fossiliferous. According to Dengo (1962b), these rocks are found on the west side of the Nicoya Peninsula in two places: one in the lower part of the section from the Río Nosara to Punta Peladas, and the other from the mouth of the Río Manzanillo to Peñón de Arío. The type of contacts are unknown because they have not been examined in the places mentioned.

In the central part of the country outcrop sedimentary rocks that have been dated Oligocene–Lower Miocene, such as the Térraba Formation (Castillo 1969, pp. 11–13). They are made up of interstratified layers of sandstone, siltstone, black to dark gray calcareous shale, and some limestone. The rocks of this unit are exposed extensively in the southern part of the Valle Central in the Fila Diamante, in the Cerros de Escazú, in Tablazo, in the northern margin of the valley of the Río Tabarcia, in the north flank of Cerro Caraigres and to the west of this, and in the Fila Guaitil.

On the Caribbean side, the Oligocene sedimentary rocks are represented by the Senosri Formation and part of the Uscari and Machuca formations in the slopes of the Río San Juan.

The Senosri Formation was recognized by MacDonald (1919; also, Hoffstetter, Dengo, and Weyl 1960, pp. 287–88); the type locality is the Río Senosri, a tributary of the Río Sixaola on the Panama side. It is made up of agglomerate beds cemented by calcareous material, which locally grades into limestone. This formation has been reported by Malavassi (1967, p. 2) in a section of the Río Reventazón, in Las Animas and Peralta. It is made up of calcareous sandstone, sandstones, breccia limestones, and organic limestones with Foraminifera, algae, and shales. It has not been possible to determine precisely where this formation outcrops in Costa Rica. The nature of its contacts with other formations are not known.

The Uscari Formation, recognized by Olsson (1922), extends in age from Upper Oligocene to Lower Miocene; the type locality is in the Uscari Creek, in the Valle de Talamanca. It is primarily made up of soft shales of dark tones. However, Redfield (1923, pp. 363–64) states that the formation, beside shales, contains intercalations of limestone and calcareous sandstones. Its thickness may attain 1,500 m. The formation is typically developed on the north and east of the Cordillera de Talamanca, appearing to attain the valley of the Río Reventazón (Hoffstetter, Dengo, and Weyl 1960, p. 293) and in the area of Peralta, Chitaría, Tres Equis, and Pavones (Malavassi 1967, p. 34).

The Machuca Formation, recognized by Hayes (1899), is Oligocene in age and is made up of shales and fine sandstones. These sandstones are green, silicified, very hard, and piritized, and they lack fossils (Malavassi and Madrigal 1970, p. 6). The formation outcrops in the basin of the Río San Juan, between El Castillo Viejo and the Río Crucita del Norte. In Castillo Viejo it is overlaid by basalt (Malavassi and Madrigal 1970, p. 6), but its relationships with the other formations of the Caribbean slope are as yet unknown.

On the Pacific side, Miocene and Pliocene sedimentary rocks are represented by the Punta Carballo, Montezuma, Cirré, and Charco Azul formations. The Punta Carballo Formation, named by Dengo (1961), is Middle to Upper Miocene in age and is made up of calcareous, fine-grained sandstones, poorly stratified, greenish gray and fossiliferous in parts. They outcrop at Punta Carballo, southeast of Puntarenas. Dengo (1962b) assigned to this formation rocks of the same lithology exposed on the Isla de San Lucas in the Nicoya Gulf and in Punta Barrigona on the west side of the Nicoya Peninsula. This formation rests unconformably on the Nicoya Complex and on the Brito Formation (Dengo 1961). However, Madrigal (1970) observed it resting on rocks of the Térraba Formation.

The Montezuma Formation (Dengo 1962b), of Upper Miocene to Pliocene age, is made up of horizontal and poorly consolidated layers of conglomerate, sandstone, and siltstone. It outcrops typically near the village of Montezuma in the extreme south of the Nicoya Peninsula. The outcrops of this formation cover a good part of the southern part of the Nicoya Peninsula, and they may also be observed in villages such as Cóbano, San Isidro, and Malpais. Its lower contact is unconformable with rocks of the Nicoya Complex, and no upper contact exists because there are no younger formations over it.

The Curré Formation, named by Dengo (1962*b*), is of Middle to Upper Miocene age and made up primarily of mottled sandstones, medium grained, stratified, with minor intercalations of conglomerates and shales. These rocks reach a thickness of 830 m and outcrop in typical form in the Rí Térraba, below the Paso Real Formation (described below) between Curré and Escuadra.

The Charco Azul Formation, described by Terry (1956) in Panama, is Pliocene in age. On the Costa Rican side it is made up primarily of greenish gray shales with sandstone intercalations (Madrigal 1979, pers. comm.). It crops out in Punta Burica and in the Osa Peninsula along the Río Tigre in the extreme southern portion of the peninsula and on its eastern coastal margins. It lies unconformably over rocks of the Nicoya Complex.

Sedimentary rocks in the central part of the country belong to the San Miguel Limestone (Caliza de San Miguel) and the Turrúcares and Coris formations. The San Miguel Limestone, named by Romanes (1912*a*), is a gray bioclastic limestone, 5 to 15 m thick and poorly stratified. It is dense, generally hard with irregular jointing, and contains small fractures filled with calcite and abundant fossils. This limestone is found primarily in the east and south of Patarrá and in Loma Salitral and Loma Aserrí. This limestone has been dated as Late Lower to Middle Miocene (Carballo and Fischer 1978) and overlies the Térraba Formation. Locally it is conformably overlain by the Coris Formation and also unconformably overlain in other areas by the proper Coris Formation (Krushensky 1966, pers. comm.).

The Turrúcares Formation, named by Castillo (1969), is a sequence made up of conglomeratic sandstone and layers of conglomerates. It is approximately 200 m thick and is exposed on the east flank of the Cerros de Turrúcares. The sequence is calcareous and very fossiliferous; it has been assigned in age to the Lower Miocene, owing to the fauna identified by Woodring and Malavassi (1961, pp. 491–96). This formation rests unconformably on the Térraba Formation and probably is covered by the Coris Formation (Castillo 1969).

The Coris Formation, named by Castillo (1969), is a thick sequence of quartzitic sandstone, with thin layers of shale and some local lenses of lignite. It is clearly visible in its type locality at the Alto Coris and extends to the east to the Valle de Cartago, to the south to Cerros del Tablazo, Loma Salitral and Loma Aserrí, thence to the east to Río Azul. Local outcrops occur near Jaris in Puriscal. The formation is Middle to Upper Miocene in age (Fischer and Franco 1979) and is overlain by

volcanic rocks of the Aguacate Formation and by Quaternary volcanic and sedimentary rocks.

The sedimentary Miocene and Pliocene rocks on the Caribbean side are represented by the Uscari (described above), Gatún, Venado, and Suretka formations. The Gatún Formation, described by Olsson (1922) (Hoffstetter, Dengo, and Weyl 1960, pp. 254–56), is Middle Miocene in age. In Costa Rica it is made up primarily of sandstones and some layers of lignite and conglomerates. It also has coral facies, made up of coraline limestone and fossiliferous marl. It is encountered locally on the coast, especially at Puerto Limón (Olsson 1922). It extends along some parts of the Caribbean coast to the east of the Cordillera de Talamanca, and it seems to extend up to the Valle del Río Reventazón (Branson 1928) in the area of Turrialba, Río Bonilla, and Las Lomas. Some authors think that it unconformably overlies the Uscari Formation (Olsson 1922; Woodring 1928, p. 69), while others, such as Dengo, consider it concordant with this last formation (Hoffstetter, Dengo, and Weyl 1960, p. 254).

The Miocene Venado Formation, described by Malavassi and Madrigal (1970, pp. 5–6), is made up of a sequence of limestone, calcareous sandstones, shales, siltstones and sandstones, and layers of lignite. It outcrops between Venado, Delicias, and Jicarito de San Carlos. In the vicinity of Venado it contains caves produced by kartzic erosion. The formation is unconformably overlain by the Cote Formation and possibly by basalts assigned to the Aguacate Formation (Malavassi and Madrigal 1970, p. 5). The lower contact is unknown.

The Pliocene Suretka Formation, described by Sapper (1905) (Hoffstetter, Dengo, and Weyl 1960, pp. 288–90), derives its name from an abandoned village called Suretka, on the north bank of the Río Sixaola. It is formed by a conglomerate made up of diverse-sized fragments of andesite, basalt, and quartz diorite distributed in a siliceous sandy matrix with some lenses of claystone, sandstone, and lignitic shale interbedded with conglomerate (Redfield 192, p. 366). It outcrops in various parts of the Caribbean coast. It is exposed between the basins of the Río La Estrella and the Río Sixaola and extends for a long distance below the Duruy and Bitey rivers (tributaries of the Río La Estrella) (MacDonald 1920, p. 142). It also outcrops along the length of the Río Nanei (Nanabri) and in the higher lands to the northeast as far as Bonifacio and to the northwest as far as Bananito. It also occurs in the tunnels of the railroad to Limón (Malavassi 1967, p. 5). The formation rests unconformably over the Gatún Formation.

Tertiary Volcanic Rocks (Tv)

The Tertiary volcanic rocks constitute a continental sequence made up principally of lava flows, agglomerates, and breccias that are generally andesitic and basaltic in composition, with some tuffs and ignimbrites intruded by basalt bodies. Fluviolacustrine sedimentary rocks also appear along with these rocks.

The sequence is regarded as Miocene-Pliocene in age, and some of its principal lithological units have received diverse names such as the Aguacate, Río Pey, Paso Real (Dengo 1962b), and Doán formations (Escalante 1966). Rocks of these units outcrop in areas such as the Tilarán and Aguacate mountain ranges and to a lesser degree in the Talamanca and Costeña mountain ranges, and in the valley of the Río Térraba (fig. 4.1).

The rocks of the Aguacate Formation, named by Dengo (1962b), are andesite and basalt lava flows, agglomerates, breccias, and tuffs. They are well exposed in the Cerros del Aguacate, the type locality, in the Cordillera de Tilarán, and in parts of the Cordillera de Talamanca (fig. 4.1). Later, Madrigal (1970) grouped these rocks within the stratigraphic term Aguacate Group.

The Río Pey Formation is Pliocene in age (Dengo 1962a) and is found on the Caribbean slope, particularly in the valley of the Río Reventazón (Branson 1928) and in the Cerere and Telire rivers. The volcanic rocks of this formation are found in these rivers in the lower part of the Suretka Formation and consist primarily of agglomerates and of basaltic breccias with minor intercalations of basalt lava flows and tuffs (Dengo 1962a).

The Upper Miocene Pliocene Paso Real Formation (Dengo 1962a), found on the Pacific slope, is made up of pyroclastic rocks deposited in water, with associated agglomerates, breccias, and lava flows. It is well exposed at Río Térraba, from Quebrada Cuan to the Escuadra. It is poorly exposed between Cañas Gordas and Sabalito along the border with Panama (Dengo 1962a).

The volcanic Doán Formation, of Pliocene age (Escalante 1966, pp. 64–65), is made up of agglomerates and hard tuffs that outcrop characteristically in Cerro Doán along the southern margin of the Río Reventazón, and in other places such as Cerro Alto Araya, Copal, Cerro Cruces, Cerro Congo, Urasca, Peñas Blancas, Cerro Lajas, Alto Velo de Novia, Río Quirí (1,300–1,475 m), along the road between Tapantí and Río Tuas (1,600 m) and in the Naranjo river to Cerro Doán. Later, Krushensky (1972, pp. 12–13) assigned a sedimentary origin to this formation, but this interpretation has been rejected by Berrangé (1977, pp. 37–38), who also mapped the Tapantí quadrangle and found it to be volcanic in nature just as Escalante had proposed in 1966. This formation lies unconformably over Tertiary sedimentary and volcanic rocks (Pacacua and Aguacate formations, respectively).

In relation to these rocks, it is of particular importance that there appears to be a wide peneplain surface that developed over the Tertiary rocks in the Cordillera de Tilarán, in the Montes del Aguacate and associated foot-hills, which was a product of a period of extensive erosion and tectonic stability from the Miocene to Pliocene times in the zones referred to above.

CRETACEOUS (II AND TKI) AND TERTIARY (TI) PLUTONIC ROCKS

Plutonic Cretaceous Rocks

These rocks are the Santa Elena Periodite (II) and the bodies (TKi) of gabbro, diabase, and diorite intruding the sequence of volcanic and sedimentary rocks belonging to the Nicoya Complex mentioned earlier. The Santa Elena Periodite (II), outcropping in the northern half of the Santa Elena Peninsula, is an igneous body, partly serpentinized, with intrusions of gabro and diorite. It is considered Cretaceous in age.

The majority of the intrusive rocks (TKi) that penetrate the Nicoya Complex are small hipoabisales bodies, sills and dikes and perhaps small stocks of gabbro and diabase. Webber (1942, p. 2) discovered various olivine diabases in the Río Seco and gabbros in the southern part of Bahia Culebra. Dengo (1962a) encountered gabbros and diabases in various parts of the Nicoya Peninsula, such as at Cabo Velas, near Sardinal, near Santa Cruz, Canjel, Río Blanco, and Montezuma.

According to Dengo (1962a), intrusions similar to those in the Nicoya Peninsula occur as gabbro in Quebrada Honda de Turrúbares and in the Osa Peninsula at the headwaters of the Río Rincón, and it is possible that they may be found in other parts of the peninsula.

Tertiary Plutonic Rocks (Ti)

Stocks of granitoid intrusive rocks have been described along the length of the crest of the Cordillera de Talamanca, as a result of Gabb's (1874) explorations. These rocks were grouped by Dengo (1962b) under the name Talamanca Comagmatic Series, since the members of the association were probably initially derived from a common magma.

These rocks are principally gradodiorites, gabbros, and granites, with lesser proportions of mangerites, monzonites, diorites, and gabbrodiorites (Weyl 1957, p. 39), and intrude into the sequence of Tertiary sedimentary and volcanic rocks in the central part of the country in the cordilleras of Talamanca, Aguacate, and Talarán.

The stocks of acidic composition are found in the Cordillera de Talamanca and are named from the northwest to the southeast: the intrusives of Escazú (Castillo 1969), Monterrey (Malavassi 1966), Río Macho (Berrangé 1977), Dota, La División, Chirripó, Durika, Ujum, and Kamuk (Dengo 1962a, p. 146). The Escazú Intrusive, situated in the Escazú hills immediately to the south of San José, is made up principally of dioritic rocks, granodiorites, monzonites, and gabbros where the gabbroid rocks appear principally at the periphery of the intrusion

(Castillo 1969). The Monterrey Intrusive, to the south of San Ignacio de Acosta, on the southern margin of the Río Candelaria, between Limonal and Las Mesas, has been considered by Malavassi (1966) as a granite and is very well exposed in Monterrey de Aserrí (type locality), San Andrés, Meseta, and Ceiba Alta. The Río Macho Intrusive is basically a granodiorite grading into diorite at the margins (Berrangé 1977, p. 34). It covers an area of approximately 50 km². It is well exposed in the riverbed of the Río Macho, Río Humo, and tributaries. The Dota Intrusive (Dengo 1962a, p. 146), which varies in composition from granodiorite to quartz monzonite (Weyl 1957, p. 29), is found immediately south of Santa María de Dota. The División Intrusive (Dengo 1962a, p. 146) is made up primarily of granodiorite and granite, according to Weyl (1957, pp. 31–35), and is found on the hill of the same name; magmatite, differentiated into gabbro in the southern part and aplitic granite in the northern part, is present at the contact with the intrusive. The Chirripó Intrusive (Dengo 1962a, p. 146), which makes up the highest peak in the Talamanca Cordillera, is formed of granodiorite (Weyl 1957, p. 36). The Durika, Ujum, and Kamuk intrusives are less well known. However, Dengo (1962a, p. 146) found granodiorite on the Pacific side of these intrusions in Ujarrás, Río Ceibo, and Río Cabagra. Gabb (1874) reported granite and sienite in Kamuk.

Dengo (1962a, p. 146) also reported various intrusive bodies on the Caribbean slope of the Cordillera de Talamanca, generally of alkaline affinity, intruding into Oligocene and upper Eocene sediments and probably some of the most alkaline members of the Talamanca Comagmatic Series. Near Pico Aguila and the tributaries of the Coen, La Estrella, and Telire rivers, there are hornblendic diorite dikes that overlap the group of Victoria dikes dated as Miocene–late Pliocene. To the north of Monte Matama there is also a granite stock in the upper course of the Río Banano.

According to Dengo (1962b, p. 147), the Talamanca Comagmatic Series was emplaced during a period of strong deformation at the beginning of the Miocene. The intrusive activity produced a series of mineralizations, primarily metallic, that characterize the areas it influenced.

QUATERNARY VOLCANIC AND SEDIMENTARY ROCKS
Quaternary Volcanic Rocks (Qv)

These rocks are primarily lava flows, andesitic volcanic breccias, tuffs, and ignimbrites that grade from andesitic to rhyolitic composition, mudflow deposits, and accumulations of unconsolidated pyroclastic materials such as ash, sand, and lapilli. These rock types and the active volcanoes (Turrialba, Irazú, Poás in the central Cordillera; Tenorio, Miravalles, Rincón de la Vieja, and Orosí in the Cordillera de Guanacaste) constitute the volcanic fields of Orotina, Valle Central and Guanacaste, with a preponderance of tuffs and ignimbrites of rhyolitic, dacitic, and quartz-latitic in the last volcanic field.

The sequences of volcanic rocks in the Guanacaste volcanic field are made up of the Bagaces, Liberia, and Cote formations and the undifferentiated volcanic rocks that form the volcanic cones and other adjacent grounds in the Cordillera de Guanacaste.

The Pleistocene Bagaces Formation is made up of ignimbrites of dacitic and quartz-latitic composition in some sections (Dengo 1962a, p. 59). This formation is well exposed along the Inter-American Highway between Cañas and Bagaces, and to the northwest of Liberia in the Santa Rosa National Park.

The Pleistocene Liberia Formation rests on the Bagaces Formation and is composed of a white rhyolitic tuff that becomes ignimbritic in lower levels. This formation is well exposed in the Río Liberia and in Liberia City, for which reason it has been called the "white city," and to the north of Liberia in the Blanco and Colorado rivers.

The Quaternary Cote Formation, which is also in part Pliocene (Malavassi and Madrigal 1970, p. 4), has its type locality at Lago de Cote (north of Tilarán on the slopes of the Río San Juan). It is represented by a sequence of pyroclastic rocks made up of ash, tuffs, sands, and at times lapillis. It is also exposed in the land surrounding Laguna Arenal and to the north of the Río Arenal, covering a goodly portion of the headwaters of the tributaries of the Río Frio to near San Rafael and Jicarito (Malavassi and Madrigal 1970, geological map). This formation unconformably overlies the Tertiary sedimentary rocks of the Venado Formation.

The remaining volcanic rocks that make up the active volcanoes in the Cordillera de Guanacaste are an undifferentiated sequence of breccias, lava flows, mudflow deposit (lahars), and diverse pyroclastic materials that have not been completely differentiated and named.

The Tivives Formation and the Orotina Ignimbrites are the primary lithological units of the Orotina volcanic field. The Plio-Pleistocene Tivives Formation (Madrigal 1970, p. 29) is a mudflow containing laval fragments, mainly basalt, of various sizes (0.10 to 2.0 m) distributed in a cineritic matrix, locally enriched with pumice and clayed on the surface. It is very well exposed in the Tivives cliffs, in the Río Jesús María delta, at Peñón de Bajamar at Punta Carrizal, at Punta Loros, in the Rio Surubres, and near the confluence of the Río Machuca with the Río Jesús María. This formation rests unconformably on Tertiary sedimentary rocks (Punta Carballo Formation) and is overlain by the Orotina Ingnimbrites (Orotina Formation) (Madrigal 1970, p. 30).

The Pleistocene Orotina Ignimbrites were first recognized and described by Dengo (1961, p. 53) and were later named the Orotina Formation by Madrigal (1970). They are made up of ignimbrites of prismatic columnar structure, possibly derived from a quartz-latitic magma, similar to the magma that gave origin to the volcanic field of the Valle Central (Dengo 1961, p. 56). According to Castillo (1969) and Madrigal (1970), this formation outcrops at Hacienda Vieja and south of Orotina along the Río Grande de Tárcoles, to the south, southwest and west of Coyolar between Río Cuarros, Quebrada Huaca, and Quebrada Pozón, near the delta of the Río Jesús María on the southeast margin near the Laguna Sapo, and on the northwest side of the same river closer to the coast. This formation rests unconformably on the Tivives Formation, and over Tertiary volcanic (Aguacate Formation) and sedimentary rocks (Punta Carballo Formation). It is overlain by recent Quaternary sedimentary rocks, mainly near the coast.

The Valle Central volcanic field is made up of two sequences of rocks that outcrop in the western and eastern portions of the Valle Central (Valle Central Occidental, Valle Central Oriental), separated by the continental divide at the Alto de Ochomogo, between Tres Ríos and Cartago.

The volcanic rocks of the Valle Central Occidental are made up of andesitic and basaltic lava flows, tuff, and ignimbrites of latitic and andesitic-basaltic composition (Williams 1952, p. 155), mudflows derived from the highlands to the north and northeast, and pyroclastics recently erupted by the volcanoes of the Cordillera Central. Among this sequence of rocks some lithological units have been defined and named by a variety of authors (Colima, Tiribí, and Barba formations and the Irazú Lavas) (United Nations 1975). Other rocks of volcanic origin or nature that have not yet been named ought to be considered within the group of undifferentiated volcanic rocks of the Valle Central Occidental.

The Pleistocene Colima Formation, whose type locality is the tajo of Colima at the bridge over the Río Virilla between San Juan de Tibás and San Domingo de Heredia, is a unit made up of piroxenic-andesitic lava flows with layers of tuff and ash. It outcrops on the bottom of the canyon of the Río Virilla for more than 30 km between the delta of the Río Circuelas and the northern part of the city of San José. These lavas were called "intracanyon lavas" by Williams (1952, pp. 150–52), who considered them to be derived from Poás and Barba volcanoes. This formation lies unconformably on some Plio-Pleistocene fluviolacustrine sediments, and on Tertiary sedimentary and volcanic rocks, in several places, on the bottom of the Río Virilla canyon.

The Pleistocene Tiribí Formation has its type locality at the Río Tiribí, before it joines the Río Virilla at Electriona. It is made up primarily of tuff, poorly welded to welded ignimbrites of latitic and andesitic-basaltic composition (Williams 1952, p. 155). Some have a columnar prismatic structure, derived from cones or fractures related to the volcanic system of Poás, Barba and Irazú. This formation originated the flat and slightly undulating topography, with a slight inclination toward the south and southwest, of the Valle Central Occidental. It is distributed from the northwest of Santo Domingo to the southwest in the direction of the Río Torres and Río Tiribí in the form of a narrow belt. It is always next to the canyon of the Río Virilla until it reaches the top of the mountain mass of the Alto de Las Palomas. Also from here it is very well exposed along the canyon of the Río Virilla until it joins the Río Grande. From here it continues yet farther to the west on both sides of the Río Grande de Tárcoles, in the form of isolated patches until it blends into the Orotina Ignimbrites. This unit, described by Williams (1952, p. 53) as "glowing avalanche deposits," rests unconformably on the Colima Formation.

The Irazú Lavas together with the pyroclastic material were originated by Volcán Irazú. They are primarily andesite and outcrop to the north and east of San Isidro de Coronado to the lands adjacent to the east and south of Rancho Redondo. The stratigraphic correlation of this unit is not well established, but it could momentarily be considered contemporary with the Colima, Tiribí and Barba formations.

The Recent Barba Formation, whose type locality is the Quebrada Barba to the southeast of the village of Barba, consists of various dense, well-crystalized, massive, and fractured lava flows. They have scoriaceous and breccia facies separated by mudflows, ash, and fossil soil deposits. They extend from the southern flank of the Cordillera Central to the valley of the Río Virilla, along the length of this from Electriona to where it joins the Río Virilla, along the length of this from Electriona to where it joins the Río Ciruelas and the Río Grande to the end of the Valle Central Occidental. The rocks of this formation were called as "postavalanche lavas" by Williams (1952, pp. 162–63) and were originated from Barba and Poás volcanoes. This formation unconformably overlies the Tiribí Formation and in general is covered by ash layers of varying thickness.

Within the group of undifferentiated volcanic rocks in the Valle Central Occidental, there are mudflow deposits or "lavina," as described by Dóndoli (Dóndoli and Torres 1954), and recent ash deposits. The mudflows cover the central and northwest portions of the central valley corresponding with San José, Zapote, Curridabat, San Pedro, Guadalupe, and Moravia. They mainly consist of lava fragments of various sizes and proportions, and of volcanic gravel and sand distributed in a clayed matrix of dark brown to yellowish brown. The deposits of ash from recent eruptions reach very thick depths in some places and cover large areas of the formations described above, such as the Tiribí Formation, the Irazú Lavas, the Barba Formation, and the mudflow deposits or lahars.

The volcanic rock sequence of the Valle Central Oriental is made up of lava flows, breccias, tuffs, mudflow deposits, and recent pyroclastic material. These have been, in some cases, differentiated by stratigraphic names: for example, the Paraíso Lava Flow, the Cervantes Lava Flow, the Aquiares Lava Flow and the Irazú Group.

The lava flows mentioned above were named by Dóndoli (Dóndoli and Torres 1954). The Paraíso Lava Flow is derived from Volcán Irazú and is a fissured and fragmented andesite, massive and compact with columnar jointing and scoriaceous on the surface. It extends over the lands around Cartago and to the village of Paraíso all the way to the Río Reventazón and very near to Turrialba. It is exposed along the road between Paraíso and Orosí, approximately 1 km before arriving at the bridge over the Río Navarro, and in the road from Paraíso to Cachí.

The first flows of the Paraíso Lava Flow apparently closed off the flow of the Río Reventazón and formed a lake where were deposited the lacustrine sediments of the Ujarrás Formation (described below) which were then later covered by the more recent flows of the same Paraíso Lava Flow. The Paraíso Lava Flow lies unconformably over the Tertiary sedimentary and volcanic rocks. Dóndoli and Torres (1954) dated the Paraíso Lava Flow tentatively to the Pliocene, but Escalante (1966) placed it doubtfully in the Pleistocene.

The Cervantes Lava Flow is Recent in age; it constitutes a compact andesite internally but is scoriaceous on the surface. It is derived from the southern flank of Cerro Pasquí, a parasite cone of Volcán Irazú. It extends from the lands around the village of Cervantes and reaches the left margin of the Río Reventazón in the vicinity of the Río Parrúas. It is well exposed in the canyon of the Río Reventazón between Fajardo bridge and Santiago and in the canyon of the Río Birrís near Birrís electric plant number 2, south of Birrís (Krushensky 1972). Between Yas and Santiago the formation shows numerous circular depressions and collapsed lava canals. According to Krushensky (1972), the collapsed tubes generally do not exceed 1 km in length and a few dozen meters in width. Exceptional collapsed tubes 2 km long and 200 m wide can be observed from the Finca Leda on to the Camino del Cerro, south of Boquerón. Another collapsed tube 3.4 km long extends from the Fuentes road to the west of Arrabara along the western limit of the Cervantes Formation, to the Camino del Pedregal near Yas. This tube is about 200 m wide. The Cervantes Lava Flow lies unconformably over Tertiary volcanic rocks and over the

Unarrás Formation, which is described below, and the Paraíso Lava Flow.

The Aquiares Lava Flow is Recent in age and is an andesite, similar to the Cervantes Lava Flow. It extends from the northern part of Aquiares to the southeast in the direction of Santa Rosa and the city of Turrialba, to the other side of the Río Reventazón at the place called Angostura. The unit is dissected by the Río Turrialba and its tributary, the Río Aquiares. The Aquiares Lava Flow rests on a conglomerate made up of fragments of andesite and basalt, intruded by basalt dikes, which can be assigned to Tertiary volcanic rocks (Aguacate Formation).

Later, Krushensky (1972) introduced the term Irazú Group to classify the group of lava flows and andesitic and basaltic breccias, tuffs and mudflows derived from the Irazú and Turrialba volcanos. The Irazú Group covers the flanks of Volcán Irazú and includes four formations, from oldest to most recent: Reventado, Sapper, Birrís, and Cervantes, the last described earlier.

The Reventado Formation (Krushensky 1972, pp. 18–23) is made up of andesitic-basaltic lava, ash, and mudflow deposits. It is mainly visible in the canyon of the Río Reventado and includes three members: a lower member that corresponds to the Paraíso Lava Flow described earlier; an intermediate ash member that covers the lands around Paraíso to the east and to Caballo Blanca and Concavas and most resembles a lateritic soil produced by the laterization of the Paraíso Lava Flow (Berrangé 1977, pp. 45–46); and an upper member made up of lavas and breccias of andesitic basaltic composition and mudflow deposits intercalated, distributed as a continuous surface layer to the northwest, north, and northeast of Cartago, where are found villages such as San Rafael, Rancho Redondo, Tierra Blanca, San Juan de Chicuá, Potrero Cerrado, Cot, Pacayas, Capellades, Santa Teresa, and others (Krushensky 1972). The Reventado Formation is late Pleistocene in age and rests unconformably over the Ujarrás Formation.

The Sapper Formation (Krushensky 1972, pp. 23–26) consists of andesitic-basaltic lava flows, ash, and mudflows. The formation is very well exposed at the Cerro Sapper, 1.7 km southwest of the active crater of the Irazú volcano; in the headwaters of the Río Reventado it lies unconformably over the Reventado Formation. The type locality of the Sapper Formation is in the upper part of the canyon of the Río Reventado, about 250 m below the confluence of the Quebrada Pavas and Río Reventado to the crest of the Volcán Irazú–Cerro Pica Piedra. Also there are excellent exposures in the Río Retes, in the headwaters of the Sucio and Blanco rivers to the north of Cerro Retes, on the north face of Cerro Cabeza de Vaca, and in the headwaters of the Durazno and Cajón rivers.

The Birrís Formation is made up mainly of andesitic-basalitic lavas and outcrops in characteristic form in the canyon of the Río Birrís, from the Lechería Birrís to an unnamed quebrada that borders the Cerro Noche Nueva to the east. Good exposures are also visible in Gonzalez, Roscaván, Central and Laguna Tapada quebradas (Krushensky 1972, p. 26). This Holocene formation rests unconformably over the Sapper Formation.

Other volcanic rocks have been defined and described by Krushensky (1972, p. 13), such as the Toba de Avalancha de Piroclastos de San Jerónimo, in the Río Reventazón valley, and the Toba de Avalancha de Piroclásticos del Río Aguacaliente, which can also be seen in the Congo and in the valley of the Río Reventazón. However, Krushensky considers these units of uncertain stratigraphic position.

Quaternary Sedimentary Rocks (Qa and Qt)
These Pleistocene rocks are made up primarily of alluvial materials (Qa), coluvial-alluvial materials (Qt), and fluvial-lacustrine deposits. The coluvial-alluvial materials appear in the form of very clear elevated terraces such as in the north of the country on the slope of the Río San Juan and in the south in the El General valley. In the northern part of the country these materials include mudflows.

In the northern part of the country on the side of the drainage basin of the Nicaragua Lake and the Río San Juan, the coluvial-alluvial materials and mudflows of the Plio-Pleistocene have been grouped and named by Malavassi and Madrigal (1970, p. 34) under the stratigraphic name Buenavista Formation. They include materials of great heterogeneity in size and nature, pieces of andesitic and basaltic lava boulders distributed in a sandy and clayed matrix and intermediate fractions.

Among the Quaternary sedimentary rocks on the Pacific slope in northern Guanacaste, there is the Pleistocene Cañas Dulces Diatomite (Segura 1945; Madrigal 1960) that appears in the area of Las Brisas–Cañas Dulces and in the Camastro hill (Loma Camastro) (Salazar 1977). The diatomite is white to grayish white to yellow and violet. It was formed in a lacustrine environment developed over volcanic Quaternary rocks, such as tuffs, breccias, and lavas. It contains some impurities such as clay, quartz, volcanic ash, and metallic oxides and occurs intercalated with thin layers of lacustrine continental origin and covered by volcanic rocks of more recent Quaternary origin, as occurs at Loma Camastro. Deposits similar to diatomite have been reported near Tilarán (Salazar 1977, pers. comm.).

On the Pacific slope, specifically on the Osa Peninsula, there are rocks of the Pleistocene Armuelles Formation. Mentioned by Hoffstetter, Dengo, and Weyl (1960), the type locality is Puerto Armuelles in Panama. According to Madrigal (1978, p. 162), it is made up of conglomerates of a clayed matrix that is stratified with greenish gray, coarse-grained sandstones. These rocks are not as well stratified as those of the Charco Azul Formation, and they rest unconformably over it.

In the central part of the country, the sedimentary rocks of the Quaternary are principally alluvial, mudflows, and fluviolacustrine deposits. These intercalate with or rest principally on Quaternary volcanic rocks. Less frequently they rest on Tertiary sedimentary and volcanic rocks. Within this group are the Esparta and Ujarrás formations, the fluvial lacustrine sediments of the Cartago Valley or El Guarco, the lahares (mudflows) of the Valle Central, and the alluvial and uplifted terraces of the Río Reventazón.

The Pleistocene Esparta Formation (Madrigal 1970, p. 34) was called Terraza de Esparta by Dóndoli (1958) and is made up of a mudflow consisting primarily of phaneritic basalt fragments up to 0.40 m in size, subrounded and subangular, distributed in a reddish yellow sandy clay matrix and deeply laterized on the surface. This unit, which is a characteristic flat plain, is very evident at the type locality to the south of the park in Esparza (Esparta) on the road to Chumical (Artieda), exactly where it descends to the Río Esparta. Also it is very evident at diverse sites such as along the Inter-American Highway between Esparza and the entrance to Punta Morales. This formation discordantly overlays the Punta Carballo Formation, and to the east of the Río Jesús María also rests unconformably on the Tivives and Orotina formations.

In the area of Palmares and Turrúcares there are lacustrine Pleistocene sediments with diatomite layers. These sediments are covered by volcanic rocks of recent Quaternary age, which reveals the past existence of a lake or lakes on the west side of the western Valle Central. In the old Lago de Palmares (Dóndoli 1951) there are mastodont fossils that reveal that this site contained a remnant of the early Quaternary fauna.

The Ujarrás Formation was described by Escalante (1966, p. 62) and assigned to the Pleistocene. It is made up of a very poorly consolidated conglomerate that is clear yellowish gray to clear brown and of local breccia, irregularily intercalated with poorly sorted friable sandstone and with claystone. Near the Río Chirí and Río Birrisito, close to Loaiza, and in the small banks near Joyas, the exposures are mainly very poorly consolidated conglomerates, and conglomeratic sandstone or nonconsolidated gravel. The rocky fragments are andesites (commonly peripheral and young). The lithic fragments are andesitic, commonly porphyritic and fresh, and resemble rocks of the Aguacate and Doán formations, but differ from those of the overlying Sapper, Birrís, and Cervantes formations. The stratigraphic position of the Ujarrás Formation has not been clearly established, but according to some evidence it appears that the Ujarrás Formation is overlain by the Reventado Formation (Paraíso Member) (Escalante 1966, p. 62; Krushensky 1972, p. 17). The Ujarrás Formation overlies unconformably the Aguacate Formation and appears to overlie unconformably the Aguacaliente tuff.

The fluviolacustrine sediments of the Cartago valley or Valle del Guarco developed as a result of an old lake that was formed by the stopping up of the valley of the Río Aguacaliente (Dóndoli and Torres 1954). This was done by some of the lava emission coming from Volcán Irazú that later produced the Paraíso Lava Flow. At the end of the Quaternary, the Río Aguacaliente cut through the obstacle, permitting the draining of the lake and the exposure of the plain that is the valley of Cartago.

During the Pleistocene and Recent in the Valle Central, there were some mudflows or flows of those coluvial-alluvial materials called "lavina" by Dóndoli (Dóndoli and Torres 1954), which were previously described along with other volcanic rocks of the Valle Central.

Finally, during Recent times a series of alluvial terraces was developed in the eastern Valle Central, principally along the valle of the Río Reventazón on the lands near Orosí and Cachí, between Santiago and Turcurrique, and in the valley of Turrialba.

In the El General valley there is a Pleistocene unit made up of coluvial-alluvial materials or fanglomerates derived primarily from the Cordillera de Talamanca. This unit has developed a set of flat terraces that are dissected by epirogenic uplifts with a slight inclination principally to the southwest. However, some recent movements have modified in some places the original slope of these terraces (Madrigal 1977). These materials are old mudflows with fragments of primarily igneous nature, of various sizes and produced during the last glacial retreat that affected the Cordillera de Talamanca. On this formation develop yellowish to reddish brown laterites that ought to be aluminum ore. This formation rests unconformably on sedimentary, volcanic, and intrusive rocks of Tertiary age.

In various parts of the country there are alluvial and marine (Qa) Recent sediments that cover the oldest rocks mentioned above. However, they attain the most extensive coverage on the Caribbean plains and near the Río San Juan, the Tempisque Valley, the area of Puntarenas-Esparza, Parrita-Quepos, Limón-Sixaola section, and the southeast portion of the country next to the Cordillera Costeña to the Panamanian border and the Osa Peninsula.

TECTONIC STRUCTURE

The major tectonic features of the Central American Orogen in Costa Rica (Dengo 1962a) follow an arced orientation from northwest to southeast. However, they are interrupted by an approximately east-west tectonic trend as represented by the Valle Central and the Peninsula de Santa Elena. The tectonic structure of the orogen can be understood and included under the following tectonic and stratigraphic features: the Outer Arc, the Inner Arc, the Térraba Trough, and the Limón Basin.

Outer Arc

This area is on the Pacific side of the orogen and corresponds to the Jurasic-Cretaceous rocks of volcanic, sedimentary, and intrusive origin of the Nicoya Complex and the Santa Elena Periodotite.

Inner Arc

The inner arc is the principal structure of the orogen and extends to the northeast of the external arc on its concave side. The border between the two arcs is defined by a series of faults running from northwest to the southeast, probably of lateral displacement (Dengo 1962a, p. 136). Within the inner arc are recognized various structural subdivisions: the Cordillera de Talamanca and its foothills, made up primarily of sedimentary rocks (Ts), volcanic rocks (Tv), and plutonic rocks (Ti) of Tertiary age; the Valle Central, made up principally of Tertiary volcanic rocks (Tv$_1$) and Quaternary volcanic rocks (Qv), as well as some Tertiary sedimentary rocks (Ts); the volcanic cordilleras to the northwest, made up of Tertiary (Tv) and Quaternary (Qv) volcanic rocks.

The Térraba Trough

The Térraba Trough, southwest of the Cordillera Talamanca, extends from San Isidro de El General and the coastal lands to the west down to the province of Chiriquí in Panama. It is made up primarily of Tertiary sedimentary rocks (Ts), diabase dikes, and volcanic rocks of Upper Tertiary age (Tv) in the central part of the trough. The boundary between the trough and the Cordillera de Talamanca is marked by subparallel faults that are oriented northwest to southwest, with the downthrown block on the side of the trough. The border between the trough and the outer arc is the Faralla Fault, which is oriented northwest-southeast.

Limón Basin

The Limón Basin is a structural feature that extends to the east and northeast of the inner arc, on its concave side. It displays a geosyncline of rapid development, with intense volcanic activity, where there were deposited thick accumulations of primarily Tertiary sediments (Ts) with an addition of rudaceous continental sediments (Suretka Formation) that occurred at the time of the final main uplift of the Cordillera Talamanca. The faulting and contemporary folding also affected rocks of late Upper Tertiary (Pliocene) in the same basin.

Tectonic History

According to Dengo (1962*a*), the tectonic history of Costa Rica can be visualized considering the following igneous tectonic sequence: a prototectonic phase, an orogenic phase, and a postorogenic phase.

Prototectonic Phase

The prototectonic phase began in the Jurassic with the formation of an insular volcanic arc with the concave side toward the Caribbean. It was the product of the elevation of the ocean floor crust in this area. This initial tectonic event produced a combination of subaerial and marine volcanic activity, erosion of the resulting rocks, and sedimentation of the detritus as well as carbonates and siliceous materials originated directly from the ocean. These processed produced the ophiolitic association called the Nicoya Complex. This association was partially metamorphized by tectonic forces during the Upper Cretaceous (Dengo 1968, p. 27). The intrusive episode that took place in this phase and that characterizes the rocks of the Nicoya Complex also produced the Santa Elena Periodotite. According to Dengo (1962*b*), this last unit represents an outcrop of the upper mantle, in other words, rocks that normally are found below the Mohorovicic discontinuity that came to the surface along the length of a fault zone aligned with the Clipperton fracture of the Pacific Ocean. This emplacement of the peridotite took place during the early stages of the deformation, before the deposition of the undifferentiated Upper Cretaceous sedimentary rocks (Dengo 1962*a*).

Orogenic Phase

According to Dengo (1968, p. 28), the separation between the prototectonic and orogenic phases is largely artificial. However, the first term has been used for convenience to describe the initial events in the history of the area and the second to define the tectonic episodes that it is possible to identify with strong certainty. Both phases are in reality part of a continuous process, and the limits, established with difficulty, are arbitrary.

Dengo (1968, p. 28) considers that the orogenic phase really began with the tectonic disturbances during the last part of the Cretaceous, reaching its climax during the Eocene contemporaneous with the Laramidic orogenesis. This phase began during the Upper Cretaceous with an uplift of the axis of the orogen and with a displacement to the east of the principal area of sedimentation. This formed a deposition basin on the concave part of the insular volcanic arc influenced by intermittent volcanic activity and is where the sedimentary rocks of Upper Cretaceous and Tertiary age (Paleocene to Miocene) originated.

The tectonic movements and the displacement of the volcanic axis to the northeast produced a fragmentation of the area into two deposition basins separated by the emerging Cordillera Talamanca and the volcanoes of the inner arc: the Limón Basin to the east and the Térraba Trough to the west. During this time the Caribbean Sea and the Pacific Ocean remained connected across various canals that linked the minor sedimentation basins that may have impeded continuous terrestrial travel throughout the isthmus.

The climax of the orogenic phase (Miocene) was accompanied by an intrusive activity (Ti) represented primarily by granodiorite, gabbro, and granite along with axis of the orogen. In the late stages of the orogenic phase, at the end of the Miocene and the Pliocene epochs, there was strong volcanic activity (Tv) characterized by andesitic and basaltic lavas, agglomerates, breccias, and tuffs, intruded by basalt dikes.

Postorogenic Phase

The postorogenic phase extends from the Upper Pliocene to the Recent (Dengo 1962*a*, p. 133) and refers to the events that occurred after the orogenic phase of mountain building and deals with diverse events such as normal taphrogenic faulting and extensive volcanism. This volcanism (Qv) involved emission of lava flows, ash-flow tuff and ignimbrite avalanches, and air-fall pyroclastic eruptions. This phase is characterized more by deformations owing to tensions in the crust than to compression. During this phase the Guanacaste and Central cordilleras were formed and produced the volcanoes we now know.

The terrestrial connection between North and South America took place in the Miocene or more probably during the Pliocene (Dengo 1968, p. 30). According to Woodring (1966), the small areas of Pliocene deposits indicate that the area of Central America corresponding to Costa Rica would have emerged almost in totality during this period.

*

Barr, K. W., and Escalante, G. 1969. Contribucíon al esclarecimiento del problema del Complejo de Nicoya, Costa Rica. *Publ. Geol. ICAITI* 2:43–47.

Berrangé, J. P. 1977. *Reconnaissance geology of the Tapantí Quadrangle, Talamanca Cordillera, Costa Rica.* Institute of Geological Sciences, Overseas Division.

Branson, E. B. 1928. Some observations on the geography and geology of middle-eastern Costa Rica. *Univ. Missouri Stud.* 3:30–72.

Carballo, M. A., and Fischer, R. 1978. La Formación San Miguel (Mioceno, Costa Rica). *Inf. Semest. Inst. Geograph. Nac.*, January–June.

Castillo, R. 1969. *Geología de los mapas básicos Abra y parte de Río Grande, Costa Rica.* Informes Técnicos y Notas Geológicas no. 33. San José: Ministerio de Economía, Industria y Comercio.

———. 1981. Sinopsis sobre la geología de Costa Rica. *Rev. Univ. Costa Rica,* in press.

Dengo, G. 1961. Notas sobre la geología de la parte central del litoral del Pacífico de Costa Rica: Inst. Geogr. de Costa Rica. *Inf. Semest., Inst. Geograph. Nac.,* July–December, pp. 43–63.

———. *1962a.* Tectonic-igneous sequence in Costa Rica. *Buddington Vol., Geol. Soc. America,* pp. 133–61.

———. 1962*b. Estudio geológico de la región de Guanacaste, Costa Rica.* San José: Instituto Geographico.

———. 1968. *Estructura geológica, historia tectónica y morfología de América Central.* San José: Centro Regional de Ayuda Técnica (AID)

Dengo, G., et al. 1969. Mapa Metalogenético de América Central. *Publ. Geol. ICAITI.*

Dóndoli, C. 1951. *Zona de Palmares, estudio geoagromómico.* Technical bulletin no. 5, 16. San José: Ministerio de Agricultura e Industrias.

———. 1958. Breve reseña geológica. In *Estudio semidetallado de los suelos de la región comprendida entra los ríos Barranca y Lagarto.* San José: Ministerio de Agricultura e Industrias.

Dóndoli, C., and Torres, J. A. 1954. Estudio geoagronómico de la región oriental de la Meseta Central. Technical bulletin no. 32. San José: Ministerio de Agricultura e Industrias.

Escalante, G. 1966. Geología de la cuenca superior del Río Reventazón, Costa Rica. *Publ. Geol. ICAITI* 1 (Guatemala):59–70.

Fischer, R., and Franco, J. C. 1979. La Formación Coris (Mioceno; Valle Central, Costa Rica). *Inf. Semest. Inst. Geograph. Nac.,* January–June.

Fisher, S. P., and Pessagno, E. A. 1965. Upper Cretaceous strata of northwestern Panama. *Am. Assoc. Petrol. Geol.* 49:433–44.

Gabb, W. M. 1874. On the geology of Costa Rica: *Am. J. Sci.* 7:438–39; 8:388–90; 9:198–204.

Galli, C. 1977. Edad de emplazamiento y período de acumulación de la ofiolita de Costa Rica. *Cienc. Tec.,* vol. 1, no. 1.

Galli, C., and Schmidt-Effing, R. 1977. Estratigrafía de la cubierta sedimentaria supra ofiolítica cretácica de Costa Rica. *Cienc. Tec.* vol. 1, no. 1.

Hayes, C. W. 1899. Physiography and geology of region adjacent to the Nicaragua canal route. *Geol. Soc. Am. Bull.* 10:285–348.

Henningsen, D., and Weyl, R. 1967. Ozeanishe Kruste im Nicoya-Komplex von Costa Rica (Mittelamerika). *Geol. Rdsch.* 57:33–47.

Hill, R. T. 1898. The geological history of the isthmus of Panama and portions of Costa Rica. *Mus. Comp. Zool. Harvard Coll. Bull,* 28:151–285.

Hoffstetter, R.; Dengo, G.; and Weyl, R. 1960. *Léxico estratigráfico de América Central.* San José.

Krushensky, R. 1972. Geology of the Istarú Quadrangle, Costa Rica. *U.S. Geol. Surv. Bull.,* no. 1358.

MacDonald, D. F. 1920. *Informe final geológico y geográfico de Costa Rica.* San José: Revista Costa Rica.

Madrigal, R. 1960. *Algunas localidades de diatomita de Costa Rica.* Informes Técnicos y Notas Geológicas, no. 5. San José: Ministerio de Agricultura e Industrias.

———. 1970. *Geología del mapa básico Barranca, Costa Rica.* Informes Técnicos y Notas Geológicas, no. 37. San José: Ministerio de Industria y Comercio.

———. 1977. Evidencias geomórficas de movimientos tectónicos recientes en el Valle de El General. *Cienc. Tec.* 1, no. 1; 97–108.

———. 1978. Terrazas marinas y tectonismo en la Península de Osa, Costa Rica. Instituto Panamericano de Geográfia e Historia, *Rev. Geograf.* 86–87: 161–66.

Malavassi, E. 1966. *Geología de la hoja Caraigres.* San José: Ministerio de Industria y Comercio. Restricted report.

———. 1967 Reseña geológica de la zona de Turrialba. Informes Técnicos y Notas Geológicas no. 27. San José: Ministerio de Industria y Comercio.

Malavassi, E., and Madrigal, R. 1970. Reconocimiento geológico de de la zona norte de Costa Rica. Informes Técnicos y Notas Geológicas no. 38. San José: Ministerio de Industria y Comercio.

Olsson, A. A. 1922. The Miocene of northern Costa Rica. *Bull. Am. Paleontol* 9, no. 39:9–20.

Redfield, A. H. 1923. The petroleum possibilities of Costa Rica. *Econ. Geol.* 18, no. 3:81–101.

Riviere, F. 1973. Contribución estratigráfica sobre la geología de la Cuenca de Limón, zona de Turrialba, Costa Rica. *Publ. Geol. ICAITI* 4:144–59.

———. 1980. Geología del area norte de los Cerros de Escazú, Cordillera de Talamanca, Costa Rica. *Inf. Semest., Inst. Geograph. Nac.* January–June.

Romanes, J. 1912*a.* Geology of a part of Costa Rica. *Geol. Soc. London Quart. J.* 68:105–23.

———. 1912*b.* Geological notes on the Peninsula of Nicoya, Costa Rica. *Geol. Mag.* 9:258–65.

Salazar, A. 1977. Geología de los depósitos de diatomita de la Brisas-Cañas Dulces y la Loma Camastro, Liberia, Guanacaste y su evaluación preliminar. [Corporación Costarricense de Desarrolo] *Bol. Geol. Recurs. Mineral.* 1:296–319.

Segura, A. 1945. Rápidos apuntes sobre los mármoles de Guanacaste y otros aspectos geológicos. *Rev. Inst. Defensa Café.* 15:337–47.

Terry, R. A. 1956. *A geological reconnaissance of Panamá.* Occasional Paper no. 23. San Francisco: California Academy of Sciences.

United Nations–Senas. 1975. *Investigaciones de aguas subterráneas en zonas seleccionadas.* DP/UN/COS 65-502/1.

Webber, B. M. 1942. Manganese deposits in Costa Rica, Central America. *Am. Inst. Min. Met. Tech. Pub.* 1445:339–45.

Weyl, R. 1957. *Contribución a la geología de la Cordillera de Talamanca de Costa Rica.* San José: Instituto Geográfico de Costa Rica.

Williams, H. 1952. Volcanic history of the Meseta Central Occidental, Costa Rica. *Univ. California Publ. Geol. Sci.* 29, no. 4:145–80.

Woodring, W. 1928. Miocene molluscs from Bowden, Part 2. Publication 385. Washington, D.C.: Carnegie Institution.

———. 1966. The Panamá land bridge as a sea barrier. *Am. Philos. Soc. Proc.* 110, no. 6:425–33.

Woodring, W., and Malavassi, E. 1961. Miocene foraminifera, mollusks and a barnacle from the Valle Central, Costa Rica. *J. Paleontol* 35, no. 3:489–97.

5 SOILS

A. Vásquez Morera

The distribution of the various Costa Rican soil types described here can be seen in the general soil map of Costa Rica (fig. 5.1). This study was compiled from the information base in the Dirección de Riego y Drenaje del Ministerio de Agricultura y Ganadería (Section of Irrigation and Drainage of the Ministry of Agriculture and Livestock) Dóndoli and Torres (1954), Vargas and Torres (1958), Sander et al. (1966), Nuhn et al. (1977) Centro Científico Tropical (1968), Pérez, Alvarado, and Ramirez (1978) and Morge (1978).

In spite of the different levels of study that have provided information, the map's level of cartographic generalization is not uniform for the entire country. In isolated cases, and in areas of very difficult access, the summaries are very approximate, such as occurs in some extreme northwest zones and in the central region of the southeastern part of the country.

The soils are separated into four large categories, based on relief. These are then subdivided according to drainage, texture, and depth among other local characteristics. The soils are classified to the level of suborders and in accordance with the soil taxonomy of the United States Department of Agriculture.

Classification and Description

The classification and description of the principal categories of Costa Rican soils, with their map symbols, is as follows:

1. Soils on flat relief
   a) Soils of alluvial origin
      A-1 Well-drained, deep, dark, fertile, friable, medium-texture soils, rich in organic matter, with slopes of 0–2% (Udolls, Ustolls, Tropepts).
      A-2 Moderately drained, brown, clayey, moderately fertile soils, with slopes less than 2%, susceptible to occasional flooding (Tropepts, Aquepts).
      A-3 Poorly drained, light-colored, clayey, hydromorphic soils, with weak morphogenetic development, and susceptible to flooding, with slopes less than 1% (Aquepts).
      A-4 Very poorly drained, dark-colored, heavy-textured, hydromorphic soils, without morphogenetic development and with slopes less than 1% (Aquents).
      A-5 Marshy soils, occurring frequently near oceans and often under mangroves (Aquents).
      A-6 Very light-textured soils formed mainly as elongated belts along littoral beaches (Psamments).
   b) Soils of fluviolacustrine origin:
      A-7 Flat, dark, very heavy-textured soils, very poorly permeable to water, lumpy when dry and sticky when wet (shrinking and swelling clays); fertile but difficult to farm. The external drainage is moderate to poor and the slopes are less than 2% (Usterts, Uderts).
   c) Soils of organic origin
      A-8 Soils formed from organic materials in an advanced state of decomposition, poorly drained, flooded (Saprist, Hemist).
2. Soils on undulating relief
   B-1 Soils of coluvial-alluvial origin, on slightly undulating terrain, with slopes of 2–8%, well drained, deep, medium to moderately heavy in texture, moderately fertile, brownish (Tropepts).
   B-2 Soils developed from volcanic ash deposits on gently undulating terrain, with slopes of 3–15%; well drained, deep, dark colors, rich in organic matter, of medium texture, friable, moderately fertile (Andepts).
   B-3 Soils developed from volcanic tuffs, on almost flat to gently undulating terrain, with slopes of 3–15%, moderate to shallow in depth, brownish, medium to moderately light in texture, well to excessively drained, with low fertility (Tropepts).
   B-4 Soils developed from old coluvial-alluvial materials, on gently undulating relief, formed in areas of longitudinally dissected piedmonts, with slopes of 3–15%, highly weathered, well drained, deep, red, clayey-textured, with low fertility (Humults, Tropepts).
   B-5 Soils developed over ancient eroded terraces and forming a softly undulating terrain of low hills, with slopes of 3–15%. They are deep, somewhat excessively drained, reddish, heavy-textured, and have low fertility (Humults, Udults).

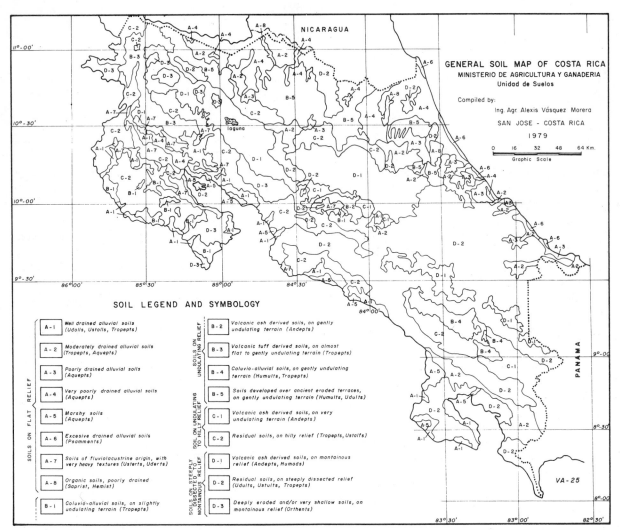

FIGURE 5.1. General soil map of Costa Rica.

3. Soils on undulating to hilly relief

    C-1 Soils developed on volcanic ash deposits, very undulating terrain, slopes of 15–30%, deep, well drained, rich in organic material, dark colored, medium-textured, friable, moderately fertile (Andepts).

    C-2 Residual soils on hilly relief, with slopes of 15–40%, moderately deep to deep, very eroded, brownish red, medium- to heavy-textured, with low fertility and excessive external drainage (Tropepts, Ustalfs).

4. Soils on steeply dissected to mountainous relief

    D-1 Soils developed from volcanic ash deposits, mountainous relief with slopes of 30–80%, dark, deep, rich in organic matter, medium-textured, moderately fertile, excessively drained (Andepts).

    D-2 Residual soils, on terrain steeply dissected to mountainous, with slopes of 40–80% or greater, deep to very shallow, with excessive external drainage, reddish, heavy-textured, with very low fertility and strongly eroded (Udults, Ustults, Tropepts).

    D-3 Very eroded or shallow or both, where the parent rock is commonly visible, with slopes greater than 50%, on mountainous terrain (Orthents).

*

Centro Científico Tropical. 1968. *Investigación preliminar de la zona norte de las provincias de Alajuela y Heredia.* San José: Centro Científico Tropical.

Dóndoli B., C., and Torres, J. A. 1954. *Estudio geogronómico de la región oriental de la Mesta Central.* San José: Ministerio de Agricultura e Industria.

Morge V., L. A. 1978. Cartografía y clasificación de suelos del Vallede Parrita: Estudio a nivel de reconocimiento. Thesis, Escuela de Fitotécnia, Facultad de Agronomía, Universidad de Costa Rica.

Nuhn, H.; Pérez, S.; and others. 1977. *Estudio geográfico regional zona Atlántica Norte de Costa Rica*. San José: Instituto de Tierras y Colonización.

Pérez, S.; Alvarado, A.; and Ramírez, E. 1978. *Asociación de subgrupos de suelos de Costa Rica (mapa preliminar)*. San José: OPSA/MAG Instituto Geografico Nacional.

Sander, G.; Nuhn, H.; et al. 1966. *Estudio geográfico regional de la zona norte de Costa Rica*. San José: Instituto de Tierras y Colonización.

United States Department of Agriculture, Soil Conservation Service. 1975. *Soil taxonomy*. Agriculture Handbook no. 436. Washington, D.C.: U.S. Government Printing Office.

Vargas Vaglio, O., and Torres, J. A. 1958. *Estudio preliminar de suelos de la región occidental de la Meseta Central*. Boletín Técnico no. 22. San José: Ministerio de Agricultura e Industria.

Vásquez M, A., and Lara C., L. D. 1977. *Mapa de reconocimiento de suelos: Cuenca Baja del Río Tampisque*. San José: Sección de Suelos, Dirección de Riego y Drenaje, Ministerio de Agricultura y Ganadería.

6 AGRICULTURE

INTRODUCTION

D. H. Boucher, M. Hansen, S. Risch, and J. H. Vandermeer

We will begin with a short history of the development of the major crops and cropping systems of Costa Rica, followed by a geography of agriculture, including the amount of land in production and the distribution of major crops. Next we will discuss the major types of ecosystems—small farm, plantation, and pastures and savannas—then present some principles of ecology as they apply to agro-ecosystems and assess their potential use as research tools for the ecologist.

History

The agricultural history of Costa Rica extends well back into pre-Columbian times. A variety of recent evidence indicates that the area was a meeting place of cultures, supporting a substantial human population. Much of the Atlantic coastline was cultivated when the Spaniards came (Sauer 1966), and archaeological evidence in the form of large roads and of jade, gold, pottery, and other artifacts at such sites as Guayabo de Turrialba (now a national park) shows that Costa Rica was an important trading area (Stone 1972). The boundary between Meso-

American and South American cultures ran more or less north–south through western Costa Rica. To the northwest, in what is now the province of Guanacaste, lived the Chorotega, a people whose basic food plant was maize, which they ground and made into tortillas, combined with chocolate in the drink *chicha,* or used in a variety of other ways. All other peoples in Costa Rica—the Huetares and Talamancas of the Atlantic coast and central highlands, the Diquis of the Térraba Valley, and others—depended on yuca (*Manihot*) and other tubers and on the pejibaye palm. This agricultural division also corresponds to linguistic boundaries and to the limits of a variety of ethnographic traits. The line was more or less preserved during the Spanish Conquest, with Guanacaste being part of the territory of Nicaragua until 1824.

The Conquest, beginning in Costa Rica in the 1560s, reduced the Indian population by as much as 95% (Parsons 1975). War, disease, and slavery were the immediate causes, and intermarriage of the few survivors with the conquistadores virtually eliminated what remained of the Indian cultures. The forest grew back over most of the cultivated areas, and Costa Rica was to remain very sparsely populated until after independence. Initial settlement was mostly on the Meseta Central, and small family farms growing subsistence crops such as wheat

View southwest from the Esquinas Forest Reserve, across the Golfo Dulce, with the Osa Peninsula in the background. *Foreground:* Terminal cattle pasture, the consequence. *Middle:* Squatter's ranch, the proximate cause. *Distant background:* Smoke plume from cut and burning pristine forest, the mechanism. Is this what we should be doing with the last remnants of 70 million years of evolution? (photo, D. H. Janzen).

and corn were the rule (Hall 1976). Cacao beans were used for a small amount of local trade, but in the early 1700s a colonial governor complained that there was so little exchange that he was forced to grow his own food or else starve. Guanacaste was sparsely settled (only five hundred persons about 1800) but probably was extensively deforested, since large cattle ranches were established there and valuable woods (brazil, mahogany, Spanish cedar) were logged out.

The one major export of Costa Rica in colonial times was cacao, which was grown in the Matina region of the Atlantic lowlands in the eighteenth century, but the plantations were constantly threatened by English pirates and had already declined in productivity by the nineteenth century. When Costa Rica received word in 1821 that it was independent (by mail from Guatemala) it was a small, isolated nation, unimportant in world trade.

All this changed with the introduction of coffee. Merely a curiosity when it was first brought to Costa Rica in the late 1700s, the plant became a significant export crop by the 1830s, and within a few decades Costa Rica was the world's leading coffee exporter. The entire crop went to Europe via the port of Puntarenas. A small ruling class, tracing its ancestry to the conquistadores but deriving its power from the growing and especially the processing and export of coffee, came to dominate Costa Rican political and economic life (Stone 1976).

Dependence on Great Britain was the fundamental fact of the Costa Rican economy through the nineteenth century and into the twentieth. But the future tie to the United States was foreshadowed by the contracts signed with the Keith family in the late 1800s for building a railroad to the Atlantic—ironically, given its importance to the future banana industry, to promote the export of coffee. Minor Keith, who finally completed the job by bringing in Jamaican and Chinese workers to Limón Province, obtained substantial amounts of land from the government as part of the bargain. He used this land to establish plantations of bananas, which were exported through Limón to Boston, and this fruit soon came to rival coffee in its importance to Costa Rica. This was the beginning of the United Fruit Company (now United Brands). With growing United States investment in Central America, and with military interventions becoming common to protect this investment, Costa Rica became a classic example of a neocolonial "banana republic."

The depression of the 1930s severely affected both coffee prices and the situation of Costa Rican workers. Organizing a banana workers' union by the growing Communist Party, as well as increasing problems with fungal disease in its plantations, convinced the United Fruit Company that the time had come to leave the Atlantic lowlands. A deal with the government allowed it to move its operations to the Pacific side, recruit a new labor force, and start new plantations. As a result, Limón Province sank into a depression that was only partially alleviated by the renewal of banana cultivation in the 1950s (this time by Standard Fruit Company) and by the conversion of banana plantations to cacao.

The years since World War II have seen some diversification of the export economy (Araya Pochet 1976). Particularly rapid growth occurred in sugar in the 1960s after the United States reassigned Cuba's sugar import quota to other countries when it imposed the economic blockade on the island. However, the most striking change is undoubtedly the enormous expansion of pasture for the export beef market. Beef cattle production more than doubled from the early 1960s to 1972, and area in planted pasture increased 62% over ten years. All the increase in production and more went to exports, so that domestically available beef actually declined slightly (Parsons 1976). Pasture expansion has resulted in the final cutting of the forest in the traditional cattle-raising areas as well as in rapid expansion into new areas such as the Valle del General and more recently the Atlantic lowlands. Between 1961–65 and 1976 the area in permanent pasture has increased by 589,000 ha, mostly at the expense of forest (FAO 1978), and it has been predicted that by 1990 most of the remaining rain forest will have been destroyed (Parsons 1976). Most Costa Rican beef is grass-fed and thus is lean and graded low in the United States import market. This means that the cattle, the cause of the final destruction of the Costa Rican rain forest, are mostly being converted into fast-food hamburgers, TV dinners, and pet food.

Geography

Costa Rica has a total land area of approximately 5 million ha, but only 3.1 million ha were included in any sort of farm at the time of the 1973 census. At that date 158,000 ha, about 3% of the country's land area, were planted to annual crops, with 125,000 ha (2.5%) lying fallow. About 207,000 ha (4% of the country) were in permanent crops (perennials). By far the largest part of the agricultural land was pasture, totaling 1,558,000 ha, or about 31% of the nation. According to the FAO study of Costa Rica's land-use potential (Plath and van der Sluis 1968; table 6.1), 20% of the nation is suitable for annual crops—more than three times the acreage so employed. On the other hand, only an additional 33% is suitable for permanent cropland and pasture combined, a figure that has already been exceeded.

Virtually all the cultivated land is found in the Meseta Central, where the provinces of Alajuela, Heredia, San José, and Cartago come together; Guanacaste Province; the General Valley in southwest Costa Rica; on the San Carlos Plains in northern Alajuela Province; and near the ports of Puntarenas and Puerto Quepos. This land can be

TABLE 6.1   Potential Land Use

Use Type		Area (1,000 km²)	Percentage of Total
I	Intensive	11.5	22.9
IA	Annual crops	7.7	15.2
IP	Perennial crops and pasture	3.8	7.5
II	Extensive	15.2	29.9
IIA	Annual crops	2.5	4.9
IIP	Perennial crops and pasture	12.7	25.0
III	Forest	18.8	37.0
IV	Very extensive	5.3	10.4
	Total	50.8	100.0

SOURCE: Plath and van der Sluis 1968.

TABLE 6.2   Area, Total Production, and Mean Yields for Major Crops, 1977

Crop	Area (1,000 ha)	Production (1,000 tons)	Yields (kg/ha)
Coffee	82	79	971
Rice	63	130	2,063
Corn	43	61	1,419
Banana (including plantain)	42[a]	1,294	30,809
Sugarcane	37	2,160	58,378
Beans	35	15	429
Coconuts	25	—	—
Cacao	20	8	400
Sorghum	20	37	1,841

SOURCE: FAO 1978.

[a] 1973 data.

broken up into four main regions—Meseta Central, Atlantic lowlands, Guanacaste, and the Pacific southwest.

As can be seen from table 6.2, coffee is the most important crop in terms of area. Table 6.3 lists the distribution of principal crop production by provinces. Although coffee production appears fairly evenly spread out in four provinces, it is actually very much concentrated in the Meseta Central, with the major coffee region covering about 400 km² around the cities of San José, Heredia, and Alajuela between the altitudes of 900 and 1,100 m (Blutstein et al. 1970). The second major coffee-producing area is in the Turrialba Valley, in the province of Cartago, at an elevation of 500–800 m. In Puntarenas the two main areas are San Vito de Java on the Panamanian border and Ureña, on the Pacific side of the Talamanca Mountains. There are also some large plantations around San Carlos in Heredia Province.

Sugarcane, while fairly unimportant in terms of area planted, is an important export crop, and its production has been expanding at an increasing rate over the last ten years. In 1967–68, 1.627 million tons were produced

(Blutstein et al. 1970); by 1974 production had risen to 1.76 million tons (FAO 1975a); by 1977 the figure had jumped to 2.16 million tons, a 29% increase over the 1974 figure. As with coffee, production is concentrated in the Meseta Central, with 75% of land for sugarcane being around the cities of San José, Cartago, and Alajuela (Blutstein et al. 1970).

Like sugarcane, bananas are an important export crop, and the total production figures and the area devoted to them have steadily increased over the past fifteen years. From 1963 to 1973, area in banana production increased from 25,600 ha to 40,000 ha, a 56% increase, while total production leaped from 476,000 tons to 1,300,000 tons, a 173% increase (FAO 1975b). Much of the increase has occurred in the coastal lowland regions so that today production occurs primarily on the Atlantic and Pacific coasts, though bananas grow all over the country except in the driest regions of Guanacaste. Virtually all production occurs on large plantations like the ones outside Golfita and Puerto Quepos, both on the southwest coast,

TABLE 6.3   Distribution by Province: Area in Major Crops (1,000 ha), Number of Livestock (1,000 head), Number of Farms (1,000s) and Area in Farm Property (1,000 ha)

	Total	San José	Alajuela	Cartago	Heredia	Geste	Punta	Limón
Crop								
Coffee	83	26	25	14	9	2	6	—
Rice	66	3	5	—	—	26	31	—
Corn	52	11	7	2	—	12	15	5
Bananas	42	1	3	1	3	—	13	22
Sugarcane	40	3	18	9	—	5	4	—
Beans	28	7	5	—	—	7	8	—
Cacao	20	—	2	—	—	—	—	17
Livestock								
Cattle	1,593	157	372	75	45	629	343	72
Pigs	215	31	41	12	6	56	55	14
Number of farms	82	19	20	8	4	12	14	5
Area in farms	3,122	322	648	148	135	909	681	245

SOURCE: Dirección General de Estadistica y Censos 1973.

Río Frio in the Sarapiqui region, and Limón and Cahuita, both on the southeast coast.

Cacao is yet another important export. In fact, Costa Rica is the largest cacao producer and exporter in all of Central America. A vast majority (89%) of production takes place in Limón Province; the rest is scattered through the provinces of Puntarenas and Alajuela (table 6.3).

Corn, beans, and rice are the three most important staple foods for the average Costa Rican. Of the three, corn has the most area devoted to its production—43,000 ha were planted in 1977 (table 6.2). Production occurs anywhere from sea level to 8,400 feet, with 60% being grown on the Pacific side. Puntarenas is the leading area (29%), followed by Guanacaste. The Meseta Central accounts of 25% of production, with most (19%) corn being grown in San José Province along hillsides. The rest is grown in the Atlantic lowlands in Limón Province.

Beans (both red and black varieties) are grown throughout the country in small plots; 99% of production occurs on farms smaller than 3 ha (Blutstein et al. 1970). Bean produciton is confined primarily to the Meseta Central and the Pacific coast, in the provinces of Puntarenas and Guanacaste.

In terms of area, rice is the third most important crop, with 63,000 ha grown in 1977. Very little of this is paddy rice, since 90% of it is grown without irrigation. Guanacaste has been the traditional rice area, accounting for over 53% of production in 1963. New areas were developed on the Pacific coast in Puntarenas Province as a result of unpredictable rains in the northwest. By 1968 the new area had increased so that 50% of production occurred in Puntarenas Province and 35% came from the new area. Rice is also grown in the Sarapiqui region of Heredia Province, in the vicinity of the La Selva field station.

The Food and Agriculture Organization (FAO) study of the land-use potential of Costa Rica (Plath and van der Sluis 1968), though somewhat out of date, provides some indication of the productive potential of Costa Rican agriculture. The FAO classification uses four main categories: Intensive Use, Extensive Use, Forest, and Very Extensive Use. Intensive Use land (type I) can produce high yields with modern technologies of crop production, while Extensive Use land (type II) can produce moderate yields per hectare. Type III lands are best used for commercial timber production, and type IV lands can produce only low yields even with modern technologies and are best reserved for watershed protection or perhaps low-intensive animal and timber production.

The FAO classificaiton of Costa Rica (table 6.1) shows about 23% of the country as type I; this includes almost all the Meseta Central and alluvial plains and valleys in various other areas. Type II land, found mostly on the

Atlantic slope of the volcanoes and on the Nicoya Peninsula, contributes an additional 30%. The remaining (types III and IV) areas are predominantly montane; interestingly enough, a substantial part of northern Guanacaste, which has been used for cattle ranching for hundreds of years, is considered type IV.

Small Farms

By far the majority of agriculturists in Costa Rica are "small farmers" who own or lease less than 5–10 ha of land. Agriculture as practiced by these farmers contrasts sharply with plantation agriculture and cattle production in several important ways. First and most obviously, the landholdings are considerably smaller. Second, the food items produced in a given area are much more diverse. Third, small farmers frequently produce a significant percentage of the food they consume. In these ways small farm agriculture resembles to some degree the farming practices of traditional agriculturists centuries ago. Yet the small farmer in Costa Rica, like large landowners, is by and large integrated into the market economy of the country. Agricultural inputs such as fertilizer, pesticides, herbicides, and farming implements are purchased (and frequently bank financed), and at least part of the produce is sold on the market. There are very few subsistence farmers in Costa Rica who are completely self-sufficient.

A "typical" small farm in the Atlantic lowlands includes a variety of crops. Throughout the year, one could probably find small patches of cassava, taro, and pineapple and several chickens, representing the "understory" of the diverse assemblage. Banana, plantain, papaya, pejibaye, and perhaps a few citrus trees would make up the overstory. In drier areas corn and peppers are also frequently grown year-round. Beans and squash and sometimes tomatoes are found only during the dry season and in the drier areas of this zone. Occasionally one also sees a breadfruit tree or manzana de agua. A typical small farm on the Meseta Central contrasts sharply with one in the lowlands. Understory elements include a variety of "north temperate" vegetables—cabbage, tomatoes, peppers of all kinds, carrots, broccoli, corn, beans, and squash—plus a few chickens. Bananas, plantain, papaya, and citrus are also a common part of a small farm at this elevation. In addition, the farmer will sometimes have a small patch (several hectares) of coffee.

To provide a background for understanding the ecology and cultural evolution of the kind of agriculture practiced by small farmers, we will summarize some of the ideas of Harris (1972) and Boserup (1965) on the development of agriculture in tropical areas. Before the invention of agriculture (about 7000 B.C.), people lived as hunter-gatherers in "natural ecosystems" characterized by a relatively balanced cyclic flow of nutrients. Nutrients were added to the soil mainly from leaf and branch fall. Most of these nutrients were immediately picked up near the soil surface by plant roots, and those that leached farther down were intercepted by deep tree roots. Small amounts were lost to the system altogether through erosion and leaching, but the loss was on the whole balanced by the inflow from N_2 fixation by microbes and movement of animals into the system. With the advent of agriculture this pattern changed radically. Humans directly removed from the system a large amount of nutrients in the form of food harvest, and by simplifying the agricultural environment (which often meant removing trees) they increased losses of nutrients owing to erosion and leaching. These changes resulted in a large net outflow of nutrients, and we may in some sense look at the evolution of agriculture as the development of techniques to remedy this nutrient imbalance.

The well-known methods of slash-and-burn agriculture are perhaps the oldest way of dealing with this problem. Large trees and shrubs are killed by cutting or girdling and the vegetation is then burned, thus releasing a large amount of nutrients into the soil. Crops can be grown on the land for several years, until nutrient levels fall. The farmer then moves to a new area and repeats the process, allowing natural vegetation to colonize the previously cultivated land. Nutrient levels are gradually reestablished in these areas as tree roots bring up leached nutrients from deep in the soil, large numbers of animals are attracted into the area, and microbes fix free nitrogen. Under ideal conditions, farmers do not return to the area for many years, until relatively large trees have grown up and the supply of nutrients in the soil and the above-ground vegetation has been replenished. But as the numbers of farmers per unit of land increase, the tendency is for fallow time to decrease. We thus see a slow progression over historical time from forest fallow to shrub fallow to grass fallow to permanent cultivation.

Accompanying this gradual decrease in fallow time was the rise of problems associated with fertilizing and weeding. With a short period of fallow there is not sufficient time for natural replenishment of soil nutrients, and other mechanisms must be found for reestablishing soil fertility. Weeds also become more of a problem. Weeding is virtually unnecessary under forest fallow and rarely needed in bush fallow with a short period of cultivation, since burning will essentially kill all the old vegetation. By contrast, weeding is indispensable under intensive types of bush fallow and grass fallow. In these systems burning is not an efficient technique for removing the natural grass vegetation that accumulates during the fallow, since the grass roots are left intact; plowing therefore becomes necessary. Partly in response to problems with grasses under the short fallow cycle of intensive agriculture, some peoples in the New World

tropics have developed a fallow cycle of about eight years in which the land is cultivated eight years in a row and then allowed to lie fallow for eight years. During the eight-year period of intensive cultivation, grass does not have time to establish itself between seasons. And since the fallow period is relatively long, this allows ecological succession to proceed to the shrub-small tree stage, vegetation that is easily killed by burning.

Harris (1972) argues that, in addition to the gradual decrease in length of fallow, the evolution of agriculture in the tropics has been characterized by a change in the *kinds* of plants grown. There are essentially two distinct kinds of agriculture that first arose more or less independently of one another. Seed culture (grains such as corn, wheat, and rice) apparently evolved in the dry subtropics (e.g., Mexico in the New World). Tropical areas with distinct dry seasons (e.g., Central America including Costa Rica) gave rise to vegeculture (cultivation of starch-rich cultigens with enlarged tubers or stems such as manioc, sweet potato, taro, and yams). Harris points out that the ecology of seed culture differs in several important ways from vegeculture and that these differences have affected the dynamics of agricultural evolution: (1) Traditional vegeculture is characterized by more species-rich and structured polycultures than is seed culture. Typically, ground-covering vine crops, small shrubs, and taller crops (like manioc) all are grown in the same plot, which usually results in less soil erosion and weed invasion. (2) Vegeculture is also less energy-draining, since it mostly removes carbohydrates rather than protein-rich seeds. In addition, swidden areas in vegeculture as opposed to seed cultivation are usually burned less intensively and thus have more organic material in the soil. (3) Finally, vegeculture but not seed culture must coexist with protein hunting or gathering or both, and this restricts this kind of agriculture to areas that provide predictable animal protein sources. Harris argues that since vegeculture requires an additional and usually "spatially fixed" protein source, it is not a very mobile type of agriculture. However seed cultivation can more easily spread, since it contains a nearly complete complement of nutrients, and historically it appears that there has been a tendency for seed culture to spread and take over areas once dominated by vegeculture. There are now few places in the tropics where vegeculture is exclusively practiced.

Although vegeculture may once have been the dominant form of agriculture in Costa Rica, most small farmers now engage in complex mixtures of seed culture and vegeculture and frequently interplant the two kinds of plants. In addition, little real slash-and-burn agriculture is still practiced, the fallow cycle having been reduced until one and often two crops are usually grown in the same field each year. While one still sees forests being cut and burned and crops later planted in the area, this usually happens when a farmer has purchased new land and is turning it into permanently cultivated fields or pastures.

That most small farmers frequently interplant a variety of crops (in contrast to large-scale farmers, who more commonly grow monocultures) has a number of important ecological implications. As we have already mentioned, this practice usually results in less soil erosion and fewer weed problems because ground cover is more complete. Other benefits of polycultures include: (1) more complete use of the total amount of light reaching one area, especially in complex, vertically structured polycultures in which shade-tolerant crops are grown beneath less shade-tolerant crops; (2) transfer of fixed nitrogen from legumes to nonlegumes interplanted in the same field; (3) better use of the entire spectrum of available soil nutrients; and (4) decreased problems with insect pests (e.g., recent work in Costa Rica has shown that there were significantly fewer pest beetles on corn, beans, and squash grown in polycultures than on those grown in monocultures [Risch 1979]). (For reviews of the literature on polycultures see Igbozurike 1971; Trenbath 1974; Perrin 1977; Kass 1978; and Cromartie 1981.)

There has recently been a tendency among small farmers in various parts of the country to develop production cooperatives. Land is still privately owned, but some of the farm work and usually all the marketing is organized by the local cooperative organization.

Plantations

Despite the commonness of small family farms and their associated polycultures, in terms of dollar value of product the plantation agro-ecosystem is far more important in Costa Rica. Two of the country's three top exports, coffee and bananas, are grown in plantations. Driving on almost any road one will find oneself going through plantations or second growth derived from plantations.

The plantation habitat is a unique ecosystem in and of itself, especially in a tropical region. In the midst of the much-touted tropical diversity sits a group of monocultures. And these internally homogeneous (relatively) monocultures are scattered about much like islands in an ocean of primary and secondary vegetation. Frequently they require a great deal of pesticide to keep them producing, presumably in accord with the well-known speculations about monoculture susceptibility in the tropics. They are usually involved with important features of human ecology—labor camps next to banana plantations or migrant workers in coffee fields.

The productive plantation is also a potentially important ecosystem for the ecologist. Since most plantations are monocultures, they usually have a relatively uniform physical environment in their understories. They frequently provide the sort of environmental controls that never could be found in a natural forest. For this reason a large number of research projects have already been done in the cacao and pejibaye plantations on the La Selva field station.

But perhaps what comes after the plantation is more important, at least to the ecologist. While a temperate zone bias looks at "second growth" as something resembling an old field and sees secondary succession as remarkably close to the way Clements and Shelford described it, most inhabited tropical zones are substantially different. Second growth frequently occurs as an understory of a rather closed-canopy planation. Thus it may seem strange to refer to an old cacao plantation, with its extremely dark understory, as second growth and to vegetation changes therein as secondary succession. But from an ecological point of view the ecosystems generated by abandoned plantations are indeed second growth, and the vegetation changes that go on within them, though frequently not well understood, must be called succession.

Furthermore, the effects of various plantation types on subsequent second growth are as variable as the plantations themselves. At one extreme is the banana plantation. Besides being notoriously hard on the soil, the plantation itself leaves little evidence of its former presence once it is abandoned. At the other extreme is the cacao plantation. Typically a thick mat of vines grows over the canopies of the cacao trees, making the understory extremely dark, more so than in a well-kept cacao grove. Between these two extremes are tall-statured plantations with a relatively diffuse canopy such as pejibaye palm and coconuts, short-statured "woodland" types of plantations like coffee, and the oil palm plantations with their very dark but patchy understories.

The dominant animal associated with plantations is *Homo sapiens*. Unique socioeconomics relations characterize most plantation agriculture. For example, banana plantations are generally the property of large corporations—in Costa Rica, United Brands on the Pacific coast and Standard Fruit on the Atlantic. Such companies are among the most vertically integrated in the world, controlling all aspects of the banana industry from production to packaging to rail transport to shipping.

Workers in the banana industry typically live permanently on or near the plantation in labor camps that resemble some of the better-kept migrant labor camps in the United States. In Costa Rica the banana workers have a long history of unionization (unlike some other Central American countries) and currently are members of one of the strongest unions in Costa Rica. The entire process of production and packaging is frequently observed by OTS classes at the Río Frio plantation (about an hour's drive from La Selva).

In contrast to banana plantations, coffee plantations present a substantially different socioeconomic picture. Hundreds of small and medium-sized holdings can be observed along any highway in the Meseta Central or the southern highlands (e.g., near San Vito). The owners of these holdings typically hire migrant labor to pick the coffee fruits, which are sold directly to the processing plant (*beneficio*). At the beneficio the coffee fruits are shucked, dried, packaged, and sold to shippers, thus only indirectly linking the farmer to the world coffee trade. Absent is the striking vertical integration so characteristic of the banana industry.

Also different from the banana industry is the situation of coffee workers. Mostly migrant or temporary seasonal labor, the coffee pickers lack adequate union representation and thus receive little compensation for their labor. Like seasonal farm labor in the developed world, coffee pickers seem barely able to survive from season to season.

Savannas and Pastures

The most extensive modifications of Costa Rican ecosystems by humans have been for the benefit of cattle. While small areas of "natural" savanna may have existed in Guanacaste at the time of the Conquest, in extremely rocky or seasonally inundated areas and perhaps on the highest mountaintops, the vast majority of the country was covered by forest. This has been progressively replaced by grasslands of various types, first in Guanacaste and the Meseta Central, and more recently in wet forest areas.

Savannas result from cutting and burning forests, leaving only scattered trees in the resulting grassland. A characteristic set of trees is found in savannas throughout the Neotropics, including *Byrsonima crassifolia, Curatella americana, Crescentia alata,* and the palm *Acrocomia vinifera.* These species have in common their resistance to fire and to herbivory. Well-defended shrubs such as *Acacia farnesiana, Mimosa pigra,* and the ant-acacias become common in overgrazed areas. A variety of other shrubby species, often with clumped distributions, are also found, as well as umbrella-shaped shade trees such as *Enterolobium cyclocarpum* and *Pithecellobium saman.*

The original post-Conquest savannas of Costa Rica were dominated by native grasses, but in the first few decades of this century they were replaced with other, mostly West African species. These include jaragua, *Hyparrhenia rufa;* guinea, *Panicum maximum;* and pará, *Panicum purpurascens.* Jaragua is extremely fire-resistant but also has a high silica content, whereas pará is of high quality nutritionally but generally grows well only in wet areas. More recently other grasses have been introduced, and some work has been done on possible introduction of forage legumes.

Savannas are generally dominated by one grass and a few woody species. Under annual burning or normal grazing pressure or both they will generally maintain themselves indefinitely. A lessening of fire frequency (or burning earlier in the dry season, which is less destructive to the shrubs) will allow better growth of the woody species in the intervals between fires. A critical point seems to be when the shrubs can grow large enough between fires that their postfire sprouting is from the branches rather than from the base (Boucher, unpublished). In this case their cumulative height growth and increasing canopy coverage will eventually shade out the grasses. Under frequent burning, on the other hand, each year's fire will kill the above-ground parts of the shrubs, so that sprouting (from the base) serves only to increase the number of stems. Under these conditions the fire-resistant grasses can maintain and even extend their coverage as savanna fires damage trees on the forest edge each year. The balance of species in grasslands varies from region to region. In middle- and high-elevation pastures managed for dairy cattle, a more diverse set of grasses and legumes is found, and problems with woody vegetation seem to be less. In the wet lowlands, maintaining the pasture against invading species, both woody and herbaceous, can be a major problem.

Movement of cattle from one area to another according to season dates back to colonial times, when the cows wandered freely through the forest from lower elevations in the wet season to the slopes of the Cordillera de Guanacaste in the dry season. Fences were rare, and management consisted mostly of rounding up the herd for branding and sales each year. This system has disappeared totally only since World War II and has been somewhat replaced by the expansion of pasture into wet forest areas. Often this process has involved temporary agriculture, with small farmers being allowed to cut down the forest and plant crops for a few years before they are forced to move on as yields drop and large landowners establish pasture grasses on the now-cleared land. These wet forest areas are used both for seasonal pastures, especially when there is a drought in Guanacaste, and for fattening calves. Thus the old pattern of rotating pasture use has been expanded from a regional to a national scale. A particular subject of controversy in recent years has been the effect of year-round use of wet lowland pastures on soil structure, nutrient status, and mycorrhizal populations, and the implications of this for long-term yields.

Agro-ecosystems as Research Sites

Without doubt the agro-ecosystem is fast becoming the predominant system in the world. For this reason alone it deserves much more intensive study than it currently receives. But far more important is that by its very nature it provides the community ecologist with an important experimental tool. Agro-ecosystems are manipulable and controllable and can be used for serious scientific study, enabling the ecologist to perform controlled experiments. Owing to the recent rapid expansion of this habitat, numerous experimental situations are either already available or easily set up. Agro-ecosystems thus provide the opportunity for detailed studies of ecological interactions, studies that are often much more difficult to carry out in the more "pristine" environments commonly chosen as objects of study.

Additionally, although our understanding is far from complete, in comparison with other ecosystems a considerable amount is known about how agro-ecosystems function. Besides the standard application of western scientific technique to agriculture, there exists a rich collection of associated folk knowledge in many areas of the tropics.

Finally, one should note that it is in the study of agro-ecosystems that the science of human ecology is brought into clear focus. If one is to understand a functioning agro-ecosystem, one must include questions of factors and relations of production. *Homo sapiens* enters into the deliberations at a very early point. And in a world characterized by a variety of imbalances among people and between people and the rest of the natural world, ecologists must assume a certain responsibility. *Homo sapiens* is influenced by and influences ecological processes in vitally important ways. It would be naive and short-sighted to initiate ecological investigations that ignore such an important component of the ecosystem.

*

Araya Pochet, C. 1976. *Historia económica de Costa Rica, 1950–1970*. 2d ed. San José: Editorial Fernandez Arce.

Blutstein, H. I.; Anderson, L. C.; Betters, E. C.; Dombrowski, J. H.; and Townsend, C. 1970. *Area handbook for Costa Rica*. Washington, D.C.: American University.

Boserup, E. 1965. *The conditions of agricultural growth*. Chicago: Aldine.

Cromartie, W. J. 1981. The environmental control of insects using crop diversity. In *Pest management*, ed. D. Pimentel, 1:233–51. C.R.C. Handbook Series in Agriculture. Boca Raton, Fla.: C.R.C. Press.

Dirección General de Estadistica y Censos. 1973. *Censo Agropecuario, 1973*. San José: Dirección General de Estadistica y Censos.

Food and Agriculture Organization (FAO). 1974. *Monthly Bulletin of Agricultural Economic Statistics* 23, 1 (January):23

———. 1975a. *Monthly Bulletin of Agricultural Economic Statistics* 23, 1 (January):23.

———. 1975b. *Monthly Bulletin of Agricultural Economic Statistics* 24, 7/8 (July/August):17.

———. 1978. *Production Yearbook, 1977*. Vol. 31. Rome: FAO.

Hall, C. 1976. El Café y el desarrollo histórico-geográfico de Costa Rica. San José: Editorial Costa Rica.

Harris, D. R. 1972. The origins of agriculture in the tropics. *Am. Sci.* 60:181–93.

Igbozurike, M. V. 1971. Ecological balance in tropical agriculture. *Geogr. Rev.* 61:519–27.

Kass, D. C. L. 1978. Polyculture cropping systems: Review and analysis. *Cornell Int. Agricu. Bull.* 32:1–18.

Parsons, J. J. 1975. The changing nature of New World tropical forests since European colonization. In *The use of ecological guidelines for development in the American humid tropics*, pp. 28–38. IUCN Publications, new series no. 31. Morges, Switzerland. IUCN.

———. 1976. Forest to pasture: Development or destruction? Simposio internacional sobre la ecológia de la conservación y el desarrollo en el Istmo Centroamericano. *Rev. Biol. Trop.*, vol. 24, suppl. 1.

Perrin, R. M. 1977. Pest management in multiple cropping systems. *Agroecosystems* 3:93–118.

Plath, C. V., and van der Sluis, A. 1968. *Uso potencial de la tierra del Istmo Centroamericano*. Rome: FAO.

Risch, S. J. 1979. Effect of plant diversity on the population dynamics of several beetle pests in monocultures and polycultures of corn, beans, and squash in Costa Rica. Ph.D. thesis, University of Michigan, Ann Arbor.

Sauer, C. 1966. *The early Spanish Main*. Berkeley: University of California Press.

Stone, D. 1972. *Pre-Columbian man finds Central America: The archeological bridge*. Cambridge, Mass.: Peabody Museum Press.

Stone, S. 1976. *La dinastia de los conquistadores*. 2d ed. San José: Editorial Universitaria Centroamericana.

Trenbath, B. R. 1974. Biomass productivity of mixtures. *Adv. Agron.* 26:177–210.

SPECIES ACCOUNTS
African Oil Palm (Palma de Aceite)

J. Vandermeer

The oil palm, *Elaeis guineensis* (fig. 6.1a), is becoming one of the most abundant trees in Costa Rica. Its rapid spread is due to a particularly effective dispersal agent, *Homo sapiens,* organized in a particularly effective way for such activity. The Standard Fruit Company and especially the United Fruit Company are rapidly expanding

FIGURE 6.1. *Elaeis guineensis. a,* Interior mature plantation near Quepos, Costa Rica. *b,* Maturing plantation near Que- pos, Costa Rica. *c,* Freshly harvested racemes. La Virgin, Sarapiquí District, Costa Rica (photos, D. H. Janzen).

their oil palm plantations (fig. 6.1*b*), converting much old banana land.

Originally domesticated in Africa, *Elaeis* was transported to the New World with the slave trade. Palm oil was one of the products that were developed as a replacement for the slave trade during the Industrial Revolution. It was an important component in cementing the colonial link between Europe and Africa, being the primary oil in industrial use at that time. Large plantations have been developed in Latin America since 1960.

Within Costa Rica *Elaeis* occurs in the wet areas of the Atlantic side and the southwestern lowlands. It is always associated with human habitation; I have never seen it outside a plantation. Small plantations exist between San Miguel and Puerto Viejo on the way to the La Selva field station, and near Palmar Sur the United Fruit Company has extensive plantations that can be seen as one comes out of the mountains on the way to the Pan American Highway from San Vito.

In its natural state the species is apparently riverine, often associated with *Raphia*. It can withstand flooding provided the water does not stagnate, and it does well in the presence of a fluctuating water table. It cannot regenerate in primary forest. In wild or semiwild conditions yields are much lower than in plantations (Purseglove 1972).

Oil palms grow adequately on a wide range of tropical soils. Wet but not waterlogged areas are best. Frequently oil palms are grown in soils that supply only marginally adequate nutrients (e.g., in Ghana and western Nigeria the better soils are usually reserved for cocoa production). They tolerate a wide range of soil pH (4–6).

The root system is highly variable and depends upon local conditions. Primary roots go deep unless the water table is high. Other primary roots extend laterally and grow up to 20 m from the trunk. Secondary roots ascend to the surface of the soil from these lateral branches. Subsequent extensive branching creates a dense surface mat. Most of the root mass is found in the top 15 cm of soil.

The trunk is formed after about three years of establishment growth, at least in open conditions. Increase in height then occurs at a rate of 25–50 cm per year. Leaf bases usually adhere to the trunk, making a very rough stem usually saturated with epiphytes.

Seedling leaves are bifid and are produced monthly for about the first six months. Subsequently, more pinnae are formed until in the mature palm the usual long leaf with large numbers of pinnae is evident. The pattern seems to be similar to that in *Welfia georgii*. In a mature individual, the leaves unfurl at a rate of approximately two per month.

Inflorescences emerge from the bases of the petiole and consist of a central spike with 100–200 spikelets arranged spirally around it. An inflorescence primordium is produced in the axil of each leaf at the time the leaf primordium is produced. When the inflorescence reaches 6–12 cm it frequently aborts, depending on environmental conditions and the health of the tree. The inflorescence is enclosed in a sheath until about one month after it emerges from the petiole base (6 weeks before anthesis).

The inflorescences are either male or female (occasionally hermaphroditic), both types occurring on the same tree. Male inflorescences have a series of small spikelets, each resembling a "fuzzy" aroid spadix, 10–20 cm long. Each spikelet contains 700–1,200 small male flowers. The anthers protrude beyond the petals, and the flowers are densely packed, giving the spikelet its fuzzy appearance. The female inflorescence is about 30 cm long with thick fleshy spikelets. Each female flower appears with two male flowers, both of which abort. Usually a given tree will contain one sex or another at a given time. The sex of an inflorescence is determined two years before anthesis. The cues that determine the sex ratio are a mystery.

Most pollen is shed during a 2–3-day period, principally in the afternoons. The female flowers are receptive for 36–48 h, and all flowers on a given inflorescence open within 24 h. Apparently all pollination is accomplished by wind. Bees are frequently seen visiting the male flowers, but they rarely visit female flowers.

The fruit (fig. 6.1c) develops to maturity in 5–6 months. The fruit is spherical to ovoid, 2–5 cm long, and 3–30 g in weight. The unripe fruit is deep violet to black, turning orange on its lower half when ripe. Each fruit contains a single seed surrounded by a pulp high in oil (35–60%). A variety of frugivorous birds eat the fruits with relish, and climbing rats frequently are important pests. Fruits that fall to the ground are rapidly eaten (usually including the seed itself) by mammals.

Extraction techniques have become varied and complicated. Because of chemical changes continually occurring in the harvested fruit, the method of extraction determines to a great extent the quality of the extracted oil. For example, if the fruits are allowed to become free of the infructescence naturally, free fatty acids are produced that make the oil less valuable. All modern extraction techniques consist of ten steps, though the details vary considerably within any one step. The steps are (1) sterilization of branches, (2) stripping of branches, (3) digestion and mashing of fruit, (4) extraction of mesocarp oil, (5) clarification of the palm oil, (6) separation of fiber from the nuts, (7) nut drying, (8) nut grading and cracking, (9) kernel separation and discarding of the shell, (10) kernel drying and bagging.

Before World War II oil palms were virtually free of disease. With the increase in acreage, the number of important diseases has risen dramatically. Insect pests are frequently the same as those that attack coconuts.

*

Purseglove, J. W. 1972. *Tropical crops: Monocotyledons.* Vol. 1. New York: John Wiley.

Banana (Plátano, Banano)

J. Vandermeer

In June of 1870, Captain Lorrenzo Dow Baker picked up a couple of bunches of green bananas while docked at Port Morant, Jamaica. Eleven days later he sold those bunches in New York for ten to fifteen times what he paid for them. Such a modest beginning is dwarfed by the subsequent accomplishments of the establishment that eventually evolved from Captain Baker's initial exchange—the United Fruit Company, today known as United Brands. Through this company and its competitor, Standard Fruit (a subsidiary of Castle and Cook), the banana has become in many ways the most important plant in Central America, especially in Costa Rica. Whether it be the country's extensive railways built by Minor Keith, one of United Fruit's founders, or the hundreds of acres of second growth in the Atlantic lowlands that were left when Panama disease ravaged the United Fruit Company's plantation, almost anywhere one goes in Costa Rica, one sees the indirect effects of bananas.

The banana apparently originated through a complex series of hybridization events, resulting in the diverse group of cultivars that exists today. Two wild species are involved: *Musa acuminata* Colla is widely distributed from India to the Philippines, while *M. balbisiana* is native in eastern India and Burma but is notably absent from the area in which *M. acuminata* is common.

According to Simmonds (1962), the beginnings of domestication arose at the western edge of the range of *M. acuminata,* with the emergence of a parthenocarpic variety. The characteristics of edibility were selected for in this variety, and eventually male-fertile clones were transported throughout the range, giving rise to new cultivars. Humans continually selected for edibility and vegetative propagation.

During the course of this selection, triploid strains were found. It has been shown experimentally that certain almost sterile diploids tend to exhibit female restitution, forming triploid progeny, possibly similar to the origin of the original triploid strains. The triploids have larger fruits and are more vigorous and hardy than their diploid parents. Numerous triploid strains have developed alongside the various diploid strains.

The two basic genomes of *M. acuminata,* then, are the diploid (symbolized as AA) with $2n = 22$, and the triploid (symbolized as AAA) with 2n = 33. Each genome is represented by numerous varieties around the world, having been transported originally throughout southern tropical Asia. Such transportation caused *M. acuminata* (both diploids and tetraploids) to come into contact with wild populations of *M. balbisiana*. The normal diploid genome of *M. balbisiana* (symbolized here as BB) is not edible, and no evidence has come forward for the existence of *M. balbisiana* triploids. Natural hybridization produced genomes AB, AAB, and ABB. Thus there are five basic genomes of all known cultivars of bananas today: AA, AAA, AB, AAB, and ABB.

While both parent species (*M. acuminata* and *M. balbisiana*) are tropical in origin, the second species is more typical of monsoon climates and thus is hardier and more resistant to droughts than *M. acuminata*.

Bananas were not present in the new world in pre-Columbian times. The first clones were introduced into Hispaniola in 1516. Many further introductions occurred, and by the time of the Industrial Revolution the banana was commonly grown all over tropical America, setting the stage for its development as one of the most important export commodities in the world.

Some of the more important cultivars in Central America are as follows. "Gros Michael," an AAA genome, had been the main producer in Latin America until it was decimated by Panama disease. Most Gros Michaels have now been replaced with one of the "Cavendish" cultivars, especially the "robusta" and "Valery" clones in Central America and the "Dwarf Cavendish" clone in South America. The Cavendish cultivars are all AAA genomes and are resistant to Panama disease. The plantain type "silk" is widely distributed but not common. It is of the genome AB. The cultivar "Bluggoe" is genome ABB and is an extremely vigorous and hardy clone. It is common in the Old World tropics but is rarely seen in the New World.

The banana root system is superficial, the abundant adventitious roots forming a dense mat near the soil surface. An underground stem is the origin for the many adventitious roots. Stems or rhizomes are commonly formed but do not grow horizontally for any appreciable distance. Thus results the typical clumping habit.

The leaves are borne in a left-handed spiral. The number of functional leaves in an adult remains relatively constant at about 10–15. New leaves are produced every 7–10 days. The total number of leaves each stem produces before flowering is thirty-five to fifty.

The inflorescence consists of a stout central shaft with flowers arranged in nodal clusters. Each cluster is subtended by a large bract. The clusters are borne spirally, no single cluster encircling the central shaft. The first five to fifteen basal clusters produce female flowers (fig. 6.2), and the distal clusters produce only male flowers. In

FIGURE 6.2. *Musa sapientum* female flower (parthenocarpic) before it enlarges to form the familiar banana. Palmar Sur, Costa Rica (photo, D. H. Janzen).

cultivated bananas male flowers only rarely contain pollen. Nectar is abundantly secreted in both sexes, making the inflorescence attractive to a variety of animals (bats, birds, ants, bees, wasps, and other insects). The two parent species seem to be adapted for bat pollination.

Time from the emergence of flowers to harvesting of fruit is about 90 days. Pollination is superfluous in cultivated bananas, and vegetative parthenocarpy produces a fruit that lacks seeds. The small black spots on the insides of the fruit are the old ova, long since aborted. In some clones (e.g., gross Michel) slight fertility remains, and if a male fertile diploid is available about one seed per infructescence is produced.

The domestic banana is, in a sense, an ecologically demanding species. It requires abundant moisture, high temperatures, and soil with abundant nutrients. If bananas are grown without rotation on the same land for any length of time, it is common to find substantial mineral deficiencies (calcium, iron, magnesium, nitrogen, phosphorous, potassium, and zinc) in that soil. In general bananas require much water, although genetic contributions to the genome from *M. balbisiana* confer a certain degree of drought resistance.

Two major diseases affect bananas, Panama disease and Sigatoka disease. The Panama disease is caused by *Fusarium oxysporum*. It is soil-borne and initially attacks the banana roots, growing into the corm, up the stems, and eventually into the leaves. Attacked corms are stained purple, and attacked leaves turn yellow and then collapse. There is no effective control of the disease, and it has been combated only by planting resistant strains.

Sigatoka disease (leaf spot) is also fungal, caused by *Mycosphaerella musicola*. Faint yellowish spots first appear on the young leaves, followed by large yellow lesions with decayed centers, parallel to the lateral veins. The disease causes premature ripening of the fruit and lowers productivity, but it rarely kills the plant.

Ascospores of *M. musicola* are produced during the viral and late wet season and are dispersed by wind. They gain entrance to the leaf through the stomata and require at least a thin film of water to germinate. Conidiophores are produced throughout the wet season and are dispersed by water. For those cultivars that are resistant to Panama disease, Sigatoka disease is the most serious they face. It is controlled mainly by aerial spraying of mineral oil.

More than two hundred insect species have been recorded as attacking bananas. The most important is the banana weevil, *Cosmopolites sordidus* (the banana borer or banana beetle). A native of Southeast Asia, this species has been spread throughout the world by human agency. Eggs are laid at the base of the stem, and hatched larvae bore holes into the stem and pupate in the tunnels so created.

In Costa Rica bananas grow in two patterns, as plantations or as isolates. The plantations are operated by either United Brands (on the west coast) or Standard Fruit (on the east coast). Though extensive in occurrence, the banana plantation as an ecological habitat has been little studied. The almost ubiquitous occurrence of individual banana plants in backyard gardens has also received little attention from an ecological point of view.

As an element of the broad picture of human ecology one could hardly find a more important plant. From its use as a subsistence backyard crop to its role in international politics (McCann 1976), the banana has left its imprint on human ecology throughout Latin America. If one studies human ecology in Latin America, it is likely that the banana will be included no matter what level the study addresses.

*

McCann, T. P. 1976. *An American company: The tragedy of United Fruit*. New York: Crown.

Purseglove, J. W. 1972. *Tropical crops: Monocotyledons*. Vol. 1. New York: John Wiley.

Simmonds, N. W. 1962. *The evolution of the bananas*. London: Longman.

Beef Cattle (Ganado)

J. J. Parsons

Cattle raising has always been the most prestigious of occupations in Latin America, and Costa Rica is no exception. But it is only with the inauguration of large-scale exports of frozen boneless meat in the past twenty years that the country's cattle industry has taken on its present proportions. Today beef exports are surpassed only by coffee and bananas as producers of foreign exchange. The nation's herd in 1979 approached two million head, approximately equal to the country's human population. It has more than doubled in twenty years. The original criollo breed has been substantially upgraded by Zebu (fig. 6.3), Charolais, shorthorn, Hereford, and other bloods. Costa Rica has recently become an exporter of

quality breeding stock to other countries of tropical America.

Guanacaste Province, with its long dry season, traditionally has been the heartland of the Costa Rica cattle industry, and it still contains more than one-third of the country's cattle. Increasingly its large haciendas have developed improved pastures of imported African pasture grasses, while adopting fencing, rotational grazing, supplemental feeding, and sanitary programs that have substantially improved productivity. A planned 125,000 ha irrigation project on the Río Tempisque floodplain is representative of the move toward more intensive use of the land in this, the most progressive cattle-raising area in Central America.

The initiation of beef exports to United States markets in 1957 provided a major new economic incentive to the industry. Cattle people, almost always from the moneyed elite, began to cast their eyes toward the new colonization zones where subsistence crops and coffee had been the principal focus of land use. As new roads were pushed into the Valle del General and Coto Brus, to Turrúbares, Puriscal, and Parrita, to San Carlos and the Sarapiquí and Arenal colonization fronts, these areas became increasingly devoted to pasture. Only the much rainier Atlantic slope was largely spared from the stockmen's encroachment. In one decade, between 1963 and 1973, the area in pasture in Costa Rica increased 62%, much of it extremely rugged country of steep slopes that would much better have been left in forest, if only for watershed protection. Today some 70% of the country's farmland is in pasture, with forests continuing to be destroyed at the rate of some 52,000 ha a year (Departamento de Aprovechamiento Forestal). Unless institutional brakes are soon placed on the *potreroismo* that is sweeping the country, it is projected that within twenty years the virgin forests of Costa Rica will have almost completely disappeared.

This rush into cattle raising has been encouraged by low-interest loans from the national banking system and has been further supported by the Agency for International Development, the World Bank, and similar international development institutions. More than half the cattle slaughtered each year in Costa Rica go to foreign markets. The country has become the leading Latin American beef exporter, accounting for some 5% of all United States meat imports in 1977 (a much larger share comes from Australia and New Zealand). In addition to the 30,000 tons allowed into the North American market under the congressionally established quota system, other markets are beginning to develop. In 1977 Venezuela for the first time became a major outlet for Costa Rican beef, accounting for one-fourth of total sales. Shipments to Israel were also substantial. Originally all the beef moved by refrigerated trailers from slaughter-

FIGURE 6.3. *Bos taurus* adult female with calf (variety cebu) in brushy pasture in mid dry season, Guanacaste Province, Costa Rica (photo, D. H. Janzen).

houses in San José and Barranca up the Pan American Highway to ports on the Caribbean coast of Guatemala. From here it moved, with meat from other Central American republics, to Tampa or to Puerto Rico. More recently waterborne shipments out of Limón have become substantial as its port facilities and highway links with the interior have improved.

Although the surge in raising cattle for export has been strongly supported by the government, its human and ecologic consequences have come under increasing scrutiny. Paradoxically, despite the increased size of the nation's herd, the per capita consumption of beef in Costa Rica declined from 27 lb to 19 lb in the period between 1962 and 1972. These consumption figures may exclude, however, the low-priced viscera (entrails) such as liver, kidney, tripe, tongue, and brains, which are an important source of animal protein for many consumers who cannot afford red meat. Costa Rica's foreign exchange balance may have improved, and the cattle people may be prospering (though they complain of low prices for steers sold for export), but the man in the street seems not to be benefiting from this shift to cattle raising. At the same time, his country is being stripped of much of its original vegetative mantle. It was the good fortune of the aboriginal inhabitants, as Alexander Skutch has observed, that they did not know domestic livestock, so that they had no incentive to convert the forested lands to pasture. Today cattle raising dominates much of the rural scene, above all in the tierras calientes of the drier Pacific lowlands. Not only is it profitable, but it is a prestigious activity within the Latin American system of values. It is also a way of life that is relatively easy to enter. The coffee ruling class that so long controlled the country has been increasingly replaced with the "cattle-ranching bourgeoise."

The ecological impact of the expansion of cattle ranching has been incalculable, leading to serious problems of soil erosion, nutrient depletion, and ground compaction. Social ills also follow, such as the intensified flow of people from the country to the city and declining production of traditional food crops. Small farmers tend to be driven off the land wherever cattle raising becomes dominant, because there is little need for manpower to maintain cattle. They usually grow subsistence crops in the first few years after clearing an area, then sell off the depleted land to expanding cattle operations, moving on to colonize other virgin forest areas. With the loss of soil structure and anchoring roots, erosion in higher rainfall areas may wash more than 100 lb of topsoil per hectare per year to the sea. The destructive floods that have become increasingly frequent in lowland Costa Rica (e.g., October 1978 in the Zona Sur; November 1977 in Guápiles) can generally be traced to the "cattle mania" that has been sweeping the land.

There is increasing awareness of the irreversible ecological deterioration that the traditional extensive cattle raising may leave in its wake. More intensive production techniques could undoubtedly greatly increase returns and eliminate the need for continuing forest destruction. The San José press has been full of accounts of what has been going on, and both politicians and the general public are being increasingly alerted to what it threatens for the countryside. But meanwhile, as ecologists Joseph Tosi and Ricardo Quesada have noted, "the innocent looking beef cow is at the center of a destructive ecological cycle that is slowly strangling Costa Rica" (*Tico Times*, 3 November 1978). The potential consequences of this "grassland revolution" that the expanding cattle industry has induced in Costa Rica and elsewhere in the American tropics must be of major concern for everyone dedicated to the aims and purposes of the Organization for Tropical Studies.

*

Myers, N. *The sinking ark.* 1979. Oxford and New York: Pergamon Press. (Chaps. 9 and 10 are on Costa Rica.)

Nations, J. D. 1980. Tropical moist forest destruction in Middle America: Current patterns and alternatives. A report to the Tinker Foundation and the Inter-American Foundation. Mimeographed.

Parsons, J. J. The spread of African pasture grasses into the New World tropics. 1972. *J. Range Manag.* 20:13–17.

———. 1976. Forest into pasture: Development or destruction? (With commentary by Joseph A. Tosi, Jr.) *Rev. Biol. Trop.* 24, Suppl. 1:121–38.

"Sacred cow" causing ecological disaster in Costa Rica, local experts say. 1978. *Tico Times,* 3 November.

Shane, D. R. 1980. *Hoofprints on the forests: The beef cattle industry in tropical Latin America.* Washington D.C.: Department of State.

West, R. C. 1976. Recent developments in cattle raising and the beef export trade in the Middle American region. *Actes du XLII Congrés International des Americanistes* (Paris) 1:391–402.

Black Beans (Frijoles Negros)

D. H. Boucher

Phaseolus vulgaris (common, kidney, navy, snap, or pole bean) is an herbaceous annual of the subfamily Papil-ionoideae (or Faboideae) of the Leguminosae. It grows under a wide variety of conditions but does best in cool regions with 1,000 mm or more of rain annually. The plant has tendrils and climbs readily; both vine (pole, guìa, voluble, trepador) and bush (arbustivo) varieties are grown. The flowers have their keel petal, which encloses the anthers, twisted through 360° or more and are self-pollinating. Flowering generally begins 35 to 40 days after germination, and maturity (for dry beans) is reached at 80 to 90 days. The seeds (fig. 6.4) are rich in protein and have an amino acid composition complementary to that of most cereal grains, which are low in lysine. Both red and black beans are commonly eaten in Costa Rica, the red being more expensive. Black beans generally grow better than red beans in lowland areas (Rachie and Roberts 1974). Hundreds of varieties are known, differing in such traits as seed color, growth habit, time to maturity, and disease and pest resistance.

P. vulgaris is mutualistic with nitrogen-fixing bacteria of the "species" (actually cross-inoculation group) *Rhizobium phaseoli,* "fast-growing" bacteria that do best at moderate to high pHs. The *Rhizobium,* which are aerobic, can live saprophytically in the soil, but they multiply rapidly when the proper legume species are planted and enter the plant through the root hairs. One or a very few bacteria are generally considered sufficient to nodulate a bean plant under normal conditions (Vincent 1970). The bacteria live within the roots in more or less round nodules, which are a distinct pink inside owing to the leg-hemoglobin pigment the bacteria use for oxygen transport. They fix atmospheric nitrogen that is taken up by the plant and in turn receive carbohydrates that their energy needs. A bean plant generally has from one hundred to one thousand nodules, with a total nodule weight

FIGURE 6.4. Mature fruits of *Phaseolus vulgaris,* split from drying and with loose black beans ready to fall out at harvest. Potrerillos, Guanacaste, Costa Rica (photo, D. H. Janzen).

of about 5 g. An estimate of total nitrogen fixed by a bean monoculture over the growing season is 45 kg/ha, compared with three or four times that amount for clover in the same area (Russell 1973). Furthermore, most of the nitrogen fixed in the bean plant's nodules will be removed in its seeds at harvest, so that, unlike the case with perennial legumes, the agricultural importance of the *Rhizobium* nodulation mutualism in beans is the production of high-protein seeds, not soil enrichment. Nodulation is generally reduced at high levels of soil nitrate, with the plant presumably controlling nodule formation in accordance with the relative efficiency of different ways of obtaining nitrogen. Thus responses to nitrogen fertilization are generally less impressive for beans than for cereal grains.

In Costa Rica (and in most of Latin America) beans are a peasant crop, grown mostly on small farms (under 5 ha) and often in polyculture with corn (CIAT 1975, 1976; Moreno 1977). They can be (and are) grown throughout the country, but commercial production is limited mostly to middle elevations with a dry season, such as the Meseta Central and the Coto Brus and Arenal valleys. Subsistence production generally involves criollo vine-type varieties associated with corn, while larger farms producing beans commercially tend to grow monocultures of bush varieties, which can be planted at high densities (250,000 to 400,000 plants/ha) and harvested by machine. Countries where mechanized production predominates (e.g., Chile, the United States) generally have yields of 1,100 to 1,500 kg/ha or more, whereas the mean for Latin America in 1971 was 620 kg/ha (CIAT 1975). Yield for Costa Rica at this date was 403 kg/ha (FAO 1978); the figures for 1955 and 1963 were 320 and 390 kg/ha, respectively. In the latter year 43,811 ha were planted to beans in Costa Rica, compared with 81,200 ha for coffee and 53,053 ha for corn (Committee for the World Atlas of Agriculture 1969). Experimental stations generally attain yields of about 3,000 kg/ha, and over 5,000 kg/ha has been reached with vine beans growing on wire frames, planted at densities of more than 1,000,000 per ha (CIAT 1975). Bean yields in Latin America have increased much less rapidly than those of cereal grains in the past twenty years.

The most important biological factor limiting yields and the range of commercial production seems to be disease. Among the major diseases in Costa Rica are common bean mosaic virus (CBMV), yellow mosaic virus, common wilt (*Xanthomonas*), blight (*Uromyces*), anthracnose (*Colletotrichum*), and powdery mildew (*Erysiphe*). Although several of these diseases are transmitted on seeds, there is little use of certified disease-free seed (CIAT 1975). In collections of seeds from seventy-seven Costa Rican farms for testing, Sanchez and Pinchinat (1974) found only 68% germination. One of the sup-

posed advantages of polyculture is reduced disease losses, but the problem is not a simple one. For example, Moreno (1977) found increased incidence of angular leaf spot (*Isariopsis griseola*) in polycultures with corn, but reduced incidences in polycultures with sweet potato or manioc, compared with monocultures. The major insect pests in Costa Rica are *Empoasca*, *Diabrotica*, and cutworms (CIAT 1975). Losses of stored beans to weevils can also be a serious problem.

Beans have been found with corn in archaeological deposits dating back six thousand years or more, and the ranges of beans and teocinte in Mexico are quite similar, so that it is probable that bean-cereal diets have been a staple in the New World for millennia. In Costa Rica beans and rice are at present the basic foods of working people, both rural and urban. Beans are cooked by soaking them in water overnight and then boiling them for several hours. They may also be mashed and/or refried and eaten with rice (*gallopinto*, *moros y cristianos*). The price of beans is fixed by the Costa Rican government, and a substantial portion of the crop is purchased by the Consejo Nacional de Producción and sold through its *expendios*. In some years recently it has been necessary to import substantial amounts, generally from Mexico, Honduras, or other Central American nations, while in other years there has been a "surplus." Increases in the government-fixed price, as well as hoarding and selling above this price, are frequently an important issue in Costa Rican politics. Beans are considered one of the "basic grains" (*granos basicos*) and as such have been a focus of development programs, and increases in yield of 4% per year have been projected for Latin America as a whole (CIAT 1975). Certainly there is an enormous gap between present yields and those attained on experiment stations and in other countries. However, lack of access to capital by the peasants who are the continent's major bean producers is a fundamental limit to the potential for increased production.

*

Centro Internacional de Agricultura Tropical (CIAT). 1975. *Programa de sistemas de producción de frijol.* Series FS-5 Cali, Colombia: CIAT.
———. 1976. Estabilidad de producción en el sistema de frijol/maiz asociado. *Noti-CIAT,* ser. AS-1, pp. 1–2.
Committee for the World Atlas of Agriculture. 1969. *World atlas of Agriculture.* Vol 3. *Americas.* Novara, Italy: Istituto Geográfico de Agostini.
Food and Agriculture Organization (FAO). 1978. *Production yearbook, 1977.* Vol. 31. Rome: FAO.
Moreno, Raul A. 1977. Efecto de diferentes sistemas de cultivo sobre la severidad de la mancha angular del frijol (*Phaseolus vulgaris* L.), causada por *Isariopsis griseola* Sacc. *Agron. Costarricense* 1:39–42.

Russell, E. W. 1973. *Soil conditions and plant growth.* 10th ed. London and New York: Longman.

Sanchez, F. R., and Pinchinat, A. M. 1974. Bean seed quality in Costa Rica. *Turrialba* 24:72–75.

Vincent, J. M. 1970. *A manual for the practical study of root-module bacteria.* Oxford: Blackwell Scientific.

Chocolate (Cacao)

M. Hansen

The cacao tree, *Theobroma cacao,* though now an important export crop throughout the tropics, is believed to have originated in the Amazon basin on the eastern equatorial slopes of the Andes. It has been cultivated by Indian cultures from Mexico to the southern border of Costa Rica for upward of two thousand years (León 1968). Many tribes believed the plant came from the gods, hence the name *Theobroma,* meaning "food of the gods." It has formed the base of both hot and cold beverages and of a pasta, as well as being used as currency by many Indian societies, including the Aztecs and the Mayas. It is thought to have been brought to Costa Rica from Mexico by the Nahua Indians in A.D. 1350. After the Spanish conquest of the country in the mid- to late 1500s, cacao became the most important cash crop in the country. Throughout the 1700s the seeds were still used as currency. Coffee was introduced in the late 1700s and slowly replaced cacao as the important export crop, so that by the late 1800s cacao production had virtually ceased. However, in 1944 cacao was replanted in the Atlantic lowlands, and production increased until by 1968 Costa Rica was the major producer and exporter of cocoa in Central America, accounting for 1% of world production (Blutstein et al. 1970). The major producers, however, are Ghana, Brazil, and Nigeria.

Ecologically, *T. cacao* is a small understory tree of wet tropical lowland evergreen forests with little seasonality. It is truly tropical, with the bulk of production occurring between 10° N and 10° S latitude. It is extremely shade-tolerant and moisture-loving, usually occurring in clumps along riverbanks. It requires humidity year-round and must be cultivated in areas with over 150 cm of rain annually, spread out fairly evenly throughout the year so that no month has rainfall of less than 10 cm. Optimum average temperature range is 20–24° C, with the minimum no lower than 15° and with little seasonal or diurnal fluctuation. The bulk of cultivation occurs at altitudes below 300 m, although it is cultivated at up to 1,000 m in Colombia and Venezuela. In Costa Rica the vast majority of *T. cacao* is grown in the Atlantic lowlands, with 89% of production occurring in Limón Province, primarily outside the coastal cities of Limón and Cahuita (Blutstein et al. 1970).

T. cacao ranges in size from 6 to 8 m, although some cultivars in West Africa and Ecuador reach 12–14 m. The growth form is fairly distinctive, since the tree has strongly dimorphic branches. When it is grown from a seed, there is a single stem axis that contains leaves and grows until it reaches approximately 1.5 m in height. At this point vertical growth stops, and the apical meristem breaks up into three to five pieces that develop into lateral branches, creating a flat, fan-shaped effect called a jorquette. The lateral branches themselves often have a highly branched growth form and may be nearly horizontal. Further growth in height takes place when an axillary bud, situated just beneath the jorquette, develops into a vertical lateral shoot, called a chupon, the apical meristem of which breaks down into three to five pieces, forming another jorquette. There may be from four to six layers of branches.

The lateral and vertical branches differ primarily in the way the leaves are arranged on the stems. The leaves on the vertical branches emerge in a pattern of three/eight (every group of eight consecutive leaves represent three rotations around the branch) while those on the horizontal branches emerge in a pattern of one/two. One also observes this difference in branching pattern in vegetatively propagated trees. If one uses lateral branches for propagation the tree will have a fan-shaped growth form. Vertical branches, or chupons, result in trees with the same growth form as a tree grown from a seed.

The type of propagation, whether by seed or vegetatively, also affects the growth form of the root system. If the tree is grown from a seed there will be a main taproot up to 2 m long, providing soil conditions are good and the water table is not too high. Axillary or secondary roots occur primarily within 20 cm of the surface and are often highly branched and up to 5–6 m long, forming a dense mat of superficial roots. When trees are grown by vegetative means they lack the taproot; the root system is primarily superficial and highly branched.

T. cacao is deciduous, with new leaf growth occurring in flushes on the lateral branches from two to four times throughout the year; the leaves are usually shed after two flushes. Mature leaves are simple, glabrous, bright green, and basically oblong, averaging from 10 to 20 cm long and 5 to 12 cm wide, with shade leaves, which occur in the interior of the tree, being longer than sun leaves, which occur in the canopy. The petioles vary in length from 1 to 5 cm, being longer for leaves on the chupons than for those on the lateral branches. Young leaves are usually reddish, owing to large quantities of anthocyanin pigments, and hang down vertically when they first come out (fig. 6.5a). Both attributes are thought to be adaptations to minimize the damage done to the young leaves by intense sunlight.

The adult leaves as well as the young ones have the ability to raise and lower themselves from a nearly hori-

FIGURE 6.5. *Theobroma cacao. a,* New red leaves (pendant) held stiffly downward on a new shoot, with older green leaves horizontal. *b,* Mature fruit (pod) with hole chewed in it by a squirrel seeking fruit pulp or seeds. Finca La Selva, Sarapiquí District, Costa Rica (photos, D. H. Janzen).

zontal to a nearly vertical position depending on the amount of sun. As the intensity of sunlight increases the leaves usually start to droop, depending on the amount of sunlight hitting them. There is a pulvinus, a swollen area of specialized spongy cells that can change its degree of turgor, at each end of the petiole, distal and terminal, and these are responsible for the leaf's movement. In general pulvini are much rarer in temperate-zone plants than in tropical plants, being common in such families as the Leguminoseae.

The inflorescences appear to grow directly out of the main trunk and lateral branches, a condition known as cauliflory. Inflorescences always occur on the older parts of the tree, never on the new growth. They are reduced cymes and may contain forty to sixty small, odorless, white hermaphroditic flowers 6–8 mm long with a pedicel 1–1.5 cm long. The petals each contain two purple guidelines and are cup-shaped at the base. The anthers are in these pouches and the stigmata are surrounded by the staminal tubes, or staminodes, thus making pollination difficult. Ceratopogonids feed on these staminodes and the guidelines and are believed to be the pollinators, although other small crawling insects may be pollinators as well. Pollination occurs in the early morning, the flowers falling off in 24 h if pollination does not occur. A large number of flowers are produced, but pollination success is very low, from 2% to 3% at the beginning of flowering but increasing throughout the season. Few of the pollinated flowers will set seed.

Fruits (fig. 6.5*b*) are 10–30 cm long and develop within 4 to 5 months of fertilization and, once full size, take another month to ripen. Though they are produced throughout the year, the main harvest occurs near the end of the wet season, which lasts from November to February in Costa Rica. They are extremely variable in shape, surface texture, and color, depending on the cultivar type. They range from spherical to oblong, with pointed to blunt tips and a smooth to warty surface. In some cultivars there are five longitudinal ridges and in others ten. Immature fruits are white, green, or red turning green, yellow, red, or purple as they ripen, again depending on the variety. In Costa Rica the predominant variety, which is called a criollo, is oblong with pointed ends and turns from green to yellow or red as it ripens. From twenty to sixty oval seeds grow in five rows in the center of the pod. In ripe fruits the seeds are surrounded by a sugary mucilaginous substance that must be fermented off (fig. 6.6) before the seeds can be roasted and processed into cocoa. The seeds are dispersed by small mammals and monkeys, which break through the pod wall and eat the sugary pulp, leaving the seeds behind.

There are many pests and diseases of cacao; they attack all parts of the plant. Hill (1975) lists twenty-two major and minor insect pests, and this does not include the many insects known to attack *T. cacao* that do not cause large losses in production. In addition there are about eleven viruses, bacteria, and fungi that can cause major problems (Frohlich et al. 1970). In Costa Rica the

FIGURE 6.6. *Theobroma cacao* seeds drying and fermenting on large drying rack (*foreground*) that can be rolled under roof at right in case of rain. La Lola, Limón Province, Costa Rica (photo, D. H. Janzen).

main pests are black pod disease, black root rot, witch's broom disease, and cacao thrips. Black pod disease is caused by a phycomycete fungus, *Phytophthora palmivora*. The disease first appears as a small dark brown spot anywhere on the pod, which gradually spreads until the whole pod is brown. Both the internal tissues and the seeds also show a brownish discoloration. As the disease progresses the pods turn black, shrivel up, and fall off the tree. If the fungus passes through the petiole of the fruit it causes soft brown spongy spots, or cankers, on the bark. Black root rot, caused by the fungus *Rosellinia pepo*, is a severe problem in Central America. It appears as a gray coating of mycelium on the roots. Witch's broom disease, caused by the fungus *Marasmius perniciosus*, attacks the flowers, fruits, and twigs, causing a characteristic thickening of the twigs that gives them a broomlike appearance. It also causes a thickening of the floral pedicels and a consequent deformation of the fruits. The three fungal diseases do not kill the tree, although the whole harvest may be lost. Cacao thrips, *Selenothrips rubrocinctus*, on the other hand, can kill the tree. They are small insects, slightly over 1 mm long, and feed on the undersides of the leaves, causing them to wither slightly and turn a rusty color on the undersides. The leaves also will bear many black spots of excreta. Since the insects are parthenogenetic and produce about ten generations per year, and since the motile stages (larvae and adults) rarely disperse, infestations worsen with time. The populations build up, and eventually the leaves start falling off the tree from the distal end of the branches toward the proximal end, entire branches being denuded in the process. Eventually the tree weakens and dies. The thrips also cause the fruits to turn a yellowish brown, making it difficult to determine how ripe the fruit is, which in turn causes problems with the harvest.

*

Blutstein, H. I.; Anderson, L. C.; Betters, E. C.; Dombrowski, J. H.; and Townsend, C. 1970. *Area handbook for Costa Rica*. Washington, D.C.: American Unviersity.

Hardy, F. 1960. *Cacao manual*. Turrialba: IICA

Hill, D. 1975. *Agricultural insect pests of the tropics and their control*. New York: Cambridge University Press.

Frolich, G.; Rodewald, W.; et al. 1970. *Pests and diseases of tropical crops and their control*. Oxford: Pergamon Press.

León, J. 1968. *Fundamentos botanicos de los cultivos tropicales*. San José: Instituto Interamericano de Ciencias Agricolas de la OEA.

Purseglove, J. W. 1968. *Tropical crops: Dicotyledons*. Vol. 1. New York: John Wiley.

Citrus Fruits (Lima, Limón, Toronja, Mandarina, Naranja)

C. R. Carroll

The domestication of citrus fruits probably began on the southern slopes of the Himalayas in northeast India and Burma. The ancestors of the modern oranges and mandarins spread north into China, while the forerunners of the modern limes, lemons, and citrons spread south into the region of Malaysia (Ziegler and Wolfe 1975). From these two centers of distribution, the various citrus fruits spread throughout the tropical and subtropical world. The Spanish name for the orange, *naranja*, comes from the Sanskrit *nagarunga* through the Persian *naranj*. Oranges, lemons, and limes were brought to Latin America with the earliest Spanish and Portuguese voyages. Limes are especially productive in Latin America, with Mexico being the world's largest producer.

In Costa Rica little citrus is grown for export. It is unusual to see citrus plantations of more than a few dozen trees, although sizable plantations of several hundred lime and orange trees occur on the central plateau. Much more commonly, citrus trees—usually limes and occasionally oranges—are simply integrated into kitchen gar-

FIGURE 6.7. Mature tree of *Citrus sinensis* (sweet orange) in a Guanacaste farmyard; ripe oranges are scattered over the dense crown (photo, D. H. Janzen).

dens. A single tree will normally provide enough fruit for a family. Citrus fruits contain, of course, large amounts of vitamins C and A. The latter vitamin is inadequate in many Third World diets, and a consequence of this dietary deficiency is blindness or at least impaired vision. Vitamin C is well known as a preventative for scurvy, and it is also thought to be useful in improving resistance to disease. Mature citrus fruits can be left on the tree for many weeks without losing nutritional value. This feature is particularly important for peasant families, for whom food storage (in the unusual case where any surplus exists) is difficult.

Citrus trees begin bearing fruit within a year or two after planting and tolerate a wide range of soils. In poorly drained soils, however, they are susceptible to various kinds of bacterial and fungal root rot. To increase resistance to these pathogens, sweet oranges and grapefruits are often grafted onto resistant rootstock of limes. Citrus trees are attacked by a large variety of pests. Kranz, Schmutterer, and Koch (1977) list more than fifty important tropical pests of citrus. Several of the more damaging pests in Costa Rica are the Mexican fruit fly (*Anastrepha ludens,* Tephritidae), citrus blackfly (*Aleurocanthus woglumi,* Aleyrodidae), citrus nematode (*Tylenchulus semipenetrans,* Tylenchulidae), citrus mealybug (*Planococcus citri,* Pseudococcidae), and leaf-cutting ants (*Acromyrmex* and *Atta* spp., Formicidae).

Citrus fruit fly larvae cause rotten spots in the fruit and premature fruit drop. The citrus black fly and the citrus mealybug, through their copious production of sugary secretions, cause extensive black sooty mold that interferes with leaf physiology and produces a general decline in productivity. These last two insects may be the principal factors that limit production in the Costa Rican wet lowlands. They are both heavily parasitized by at least five species of wasps, and in other Latin American republics (Panama and Mexico) they are controlled by these parasites. A curious variant of *P. citri* in some Old World tropical countries attacks the roots of coffee and citrus. In coffee, an associated root fungus often kills the bush. In Costa Rica, as in other countries, ants frequently visit the whitefly and mealybug nymphs to collect their sugary secretions. Where ants are particularly abundant, their numbers may prevent the build-up of these secretions on the leaf surface and thereby reduce the damage done by the pests. However, many species of ants tend these nymphs with aggressive workers that chase off predators and parasites of the nymphs as well as removing parasitized nymphs. Thus these ants tend to increase populations of the blackfly and the mealybug. This interaction needs to be explored, especially in light of the obvious success that ants have had in controlling other pests on other tropical tree crops.

The remaining two pests are very localized in their effects. Nematodes are highly influenced by soil conditions and, in high abundance, produce symptoms similar to water stress and low mineral nutrition. Leaf-cutting ants are, of course, patchy, since their incidence on citrus is determined by the distribution of colonies. These ants are particularly attracted to the rinds, especially the white inner rind. The ants will occasionally remove the rind from the pulp and leave the peeled fruit hanging on the tree. Limes are usually not attacked. Much more serious is their defoliation of young trees.

In large commercial citrus regions, such as California and Florida, attempts to control pests have been largely through chemical pesticides. Since the pesticides largely eliminate biological control agents and select for pesticide resistance, attempts to control citrus pests with pesticides have become increasingly difficult and costly. This is particularly ironic since, as far back as the ninth century, the Chinese successfully used tailor ants (*Oecophylla* sp.) to control insect pests. Recently, more integrated methods of pest control have been introduced into commercial citrus regions. Since pesticide corporations have a history of irresponsible promotion of their products, especially in Third World countries, citrus growers in Costa Rica may be particularly vulnerable to inheriting the legacy of the California and Florida pest problems. Biological control of pests should be an integral part of the program of the Costa Rican Ministry of Agriculture. In particular, the small-scale production of citrus, as it occurs in a matrix of diverse vegetation, is appropriate for biological control.

*

Kranz, J.; Schmutterer, H.; and Koch, W. 1977. *Diseases, pests and weeds in tropical crops*. Verlag Paul Parey.

Ziegler, L., and Wolfe, H. 1975. *Citrus growing in Florida*. Gainesville: University Presses of Florida.

Coconut (Coco)

J. Vandermeer

Anywhere one travels in the tropics, one is bound to encounter the coconut palm (*Cocos nucifera*). Although most common (indeed almost ubiquitous) near tropical beaches, the coconut can and does live in almost any tropical climate. Although the original range of the species is still a matter of debate, it occurred in both Old and New World tropics before 1492. However, at the time of Columbus's landing it was known only from western Panama in the Americas, and it has reached its pantropical distribution within historical times. In Costa Rica, coconuts are found in all lowland habitats, but large plantations are situated only near the oceans. Its existence is almost always the result of human planting, although wild individuals may be established along coastlines.

Although the species is usually found near the sea, it in no sense requires salt for satisfactory establishment. Rather, it seems that the species is a poor "competitor," living mainly where conditions are not suitable for other species. Nevertheless, it has been suggested that certain structures are particularly adapted to "beach living" (Purseglove 1972, p. 452). The roots require aerated soil with a continuous supply of fresh water. The abundant supply of groundwater with high nutrient content, usually found near beaches, provides excellent habitat. The species requires a large amount of sunlight and cannot tolerate shade from other species. As long as they are well drained and aerated, coconuts can be grown on almost any kind of soil.

Coconuts have a single trunk that is evident after a few years of establishment growth. It is grayish brown, 20–40 cm in diameter, and usually leans toward the light or away from the direction of prevailing winds. Internodes are short, and adventitious roots are produced at the lowest nodes. The height of the trunk increases rapidly until the individual reaches maturity, after which growth continues slowly until the onset of senility. Any damage to the truck is "recorded" as a permanent and obvious scar (since there is no cambium), and a reduction in nutrients is reflected permanently by a narrowing of the trunk diameter—thus much of the history of an individual can be ascertained from the trunk.

The leaves are large (4.5–6 m long) and heavy, with clasping petioles that channel water to the crown. Leaf primordia are differentiated approximately 30 months before emergence, and the full unfurling takes 4–6 months. An individual leaf remains on the tree for 2.5–3 years, depending on conditions. An average adult contains a total of twenty-eight to thirty-six leaves, a one-year-old seedling eight to ten leaves.

The leaves are positioned spirally. As one views the crown from below the spiral is either clockwise (in which case inflorescenses are on the right of petiolar bases) or counterclockwise (in which case the inflorescences are on the left of petiolar bases). Whether the spiral is clockwise or counterclockwise is *not* a genetically determined character. The angle between successive leaves is about 140°.

Flowering begins at 6–10 years of age and proceeds at the rate of about one inflorescence a month. The inflorescence is monoecious, with predominantly male flowers. Each inflorescence consists of 40 lateral branches, each of which contains two hundred to three hundred male flowers along its proximal surface and one or a few female flowers at the distal end.

Male flowers open before female flowers. The male flowering period is 16–22 days. The male flower sheds its pollen in the bud, to be dispersed when the bud opens. Pollen shedding and bud opening take one day. The female flowers are receptive for 24 h but usually do not open until the male flowering period on the same inflorescence is over. Thus cross-pollination is the usual rule.

Approximately 50–60% of the female flowers fall before they begin to mature into fruit. Another fraction of fruits fall as immature nuts, leaving three to six fruits per inflorescence at maturity. Six months after fertilization the fruit reaches its full size. Of the three ovule primordia, only one remains functional, the other two degenerating. The embryo sac of the functional ovule expands, and its central cavity fills with fluid, the "coconut milk." The endosperm is fully formed after 10 months, and the fruit is fully ripe after 12 months.

Natural dispersal of the fruit has long been a matter of debate. It has been repeatedly demonstrated that coconuts can traverse short distances (up to 5,000 km) without losing their germinating ability. But excessively long distances are more difficult to imagine. For example, coconuts on the deck of Thor Heyerdahl's *Kon Tiki* remained capable of germination for 101 days, but those below deck with the waves constantly washing over them were ruined by the seawater. Natives of Polynesia and Malaysia routinely take coconuts along for food and drink on voyages. They frequently plant excess ones on any shore they visit.

Modern dispersal is, of course, accomplished almost totally by man. Propagation for plantations is always by seed. The seed nuts are planted in nurseries completely open to sunlight. They are replanted in the plantations when they are 6–12 months old. Young plantations are routinely interplanted with cassava, sweet potatoes, maize, and other crops. Although it is uncommon in Costa Rica, in other tropical regions coconuts are interplanted with other crops, both tree crops (cocoa, rubber, mango, cashew, breadfruit, citrus) and others (corn, banana, sugarcane). Occasionally pastures are established in the interior of plantations.

The major product of *Cocos* is copra, the dried endosperm of the seed. The usual production method is first to remove the husk (exocarp) immediately after harvest. The husked nuts (consisting of mesocarp, endocarp, and seed) can be stored. The nut is then split in half, the milk is drained, and the two halves are placed so that the endosperm is exposed to the sun. It takes about 60–80 h of sunshine to dry the endosperm. Sometimes the copra is dried over open fires or in kilns.

The copra contains 60–68% oil, and with current extracting techniques a 64% extraction rate is possible. The oil is classified as an edible-industrial oil. Below 24° C it is a white to yellowish solid fat, and at higher temperatures it melts to a colorless or brownish yellow oil.

Extracting oil from copra is one of the oldest seed-crushing industries in the world. In the Western world its first important use was for soap manufacture (patent granted in 1841). It is currently used to make margarine, as a confectionery fat, as a substitute for cocoa butter, and to make candles. It is also used in the manufacture of detergents, resins, cosmetics, and hair oil.

Lepesme (1947) list 750 species of insects recorded on *Cocos*. A variety of diseases have been known worldwide for some time, yet most are still incompletely understood.

In most countries, including Costa Rica, the bulk of the crop is owned by medium to small landowners. There is only a small international trade in fresh coconuts, but the international market in copra has grown to major proportions since 1850. At present the area in coconuts worldwide is estimated to be about 4.5 million acres, with more than 500 million trees in production. As noted by Purseglove (1972), "Coconuts produced the largest tonnage in oil equivalent of all fats and oils entering world trade until 1962, when they were surpassed by soya beans."

*

Child, R. 1964. *Coconuts*. London: Longmans.
Lepesme, P. 1947. *Les insectes des palmiers*. Paris: Lechevalier.
Lever, R. J. A. W. 1969. *Pests of coconuts*. Rome: FAO.
Purseglove, J. W. 1972. *Tropical crops: Monocotyledons*. Vol. 2. New York: John Wiley.

Coffee (Café)

D. H. Boucher

Coffee is a crop that, as Hall puts it, "has contributed both to the development and to the underdevelopment of Costa Rica" (Hall 1976). It was the country's first major export crop, and its only export of any consequence in the nineteenth century. Although some diversification of the economy has taken place since then, coffee still accounts for 20% of Costa Rican agricultural production, measured in dollars (Araya Pochet 1976), and fluctuations in the world market price for coffee have major repercussions on the Costa Rican economy.

The heart of the coffee-producing region is the central part of the Meseta Central, an area stretching roughly from Alajuela to Tres Ríos. In this area coffee is the dominant crop. Eastward to the Turrialba valley and west to San Ramón it shares importance with other crops, notably sugarcane, and in recent years new producing areas have been planted, such as the Coto Brus and General valleys and even parts of the San Carlos region on the Atlantic slope and the Nicoya Peninsula in Guanacaste. Nevertheless, the Meseta Central still accounts for 75% of the land area in coffee and 85% of total production (Araya Pochet 1976).

Coffee farms tend to be smaller than those growing other export crops, and in economic structure they are intermediate between the enormous plantations of banana, oil palm, or cacao owned by single companies and the tiny peasant farms that produce most of Latin America's food grains. However there is a clear tendency toward dominance of coffee production by a relatively small number of large farms. In 1955 the 324 largest producers produced more coffee than all the remaining 21,656 combined, and the largest 13.5% of farms controlled 67% of the land in coffee. In reality the concentration of economic control is substantially even greater than these figures show, for two reasons. First, the separate owners of the coffee farms as registered in census data are in fact mostly members of a few extended families (Stone 1976). Furthermore, these families control most of the major *beneficios* (processing plants) and the infrastructure of transport, finance, and export. In fact, the major locus of economic power associated with coffee is not production at all, but rather the postproduction phases. This also continues to be the source of the political power held by the coffee-based ruling class (now diversifying into cattle, manufacturing, and other pursuits), as it has been for nearly 150 years (Hall 1976; Cerdas 1972; Stone 1976).

Coffee grows widely in both the subtropics (Brazil is the world's leading producer) and the tropics, but the best beans in tropical regions come from middle elevations between 800 and 1,500 m in altitude that have a distinct dry season. The importance of the dry season to coffee production illustrates the interaction of biological and economic factors in agriculture. Drought serves to make flowering relatively synchronous at the start of the rainy season (May–June in Costa Rica). This means that fruit maturation will occur over only a few months in the following dry season. Despite the Colombian Coffee Institute's television commercials that show Juan Valdez climbing the mountain every day to pick the few beans that have ripened overnight, it is a distinct disadvantage to coffee growers to have the harvest spread out over a long time. A short harvest period means one can employ large numbers of temporary workers, at a time when competition for jobs will keep wages down, without having to pay many workers during the rest of the year. Not coincidentally, the school vacation in Costa Rica is at the beginning of the dry season, and many of those who find temporary work picking coffee are women and children. Thus the dry season, in addition to reducing the costs of coffee harvesting and processing, also ensures that work will be temporary and undependable for many Costa Ricans.

In fact, coffee can be grown in a variety of climates; I have even seen families with a few plants, producing coffee for home consumption only, in the Corcovado basin of the Osa Peninsula. Nevertheless there is no doubt that Costa Rica's Meseta Central is one of the best places in the world for commercial production, and the beans it produces compare favorably with the top grades ("strictly hard bean") of Colombian coffee, acknowledged as the best. In addition to the proper seasonality as discussed above, this area has about the right amount of rainfall (between 1,500 and 2,500 mm per year is optimal for coffee) and fertile soils derived from the surrounding volcanoes, with substantial organic matter and good drainage (Hall 1976).

Coffea arabica is an allopolypolid, with $2n = 44$, whereas all other species of the genus have $2n = 22$ (León 1968). The species originated in the highlands of Ethiopia and apparently was domesticated only in the past millennium. The introduction of coffee to Europe and America was relatively recent, in the seventeenth century, but the drink quickly became very popular (the craze for it was satirized in Johann Sebastian Bach's *Coffee Cantata*). The first plantations in the New World probably originated from a small number of plants of what is now called the variety typica. Thus the coffee plant has undergone little evolutionary change since its introduction to the Americas.

Coffee is a shrub that can reach a height of 5 m if unpruned. It has a single main trunk and nearly horizontal lateral branches, from which grow short shoots that bear many white flowers (fig. 6.8). These open early in the morning and last one to two days. Most flowers are self-pollinated, with the percentage of cross-pollination (owing mostly to wind) being less than 6% (León 1968). The fruit, an ellipsoid drupe, contains two seeds and is 10 to 20 mm long. Originally green, it becomes orange and then red at maturity. The pulp must be removed and the beans dried at a beneficio before they can be exported or roasted. This processing was formerly done by hand, using the heat of the sun for drying, but depulping, drying, and polishing are now mechanized in the larger operations. However, the industry as a whole remains comparatively labor-intensive, since seeding, planting, cultivation, picking, and sorting are still done by hand (Griffith 1974).

The shiny, dark green leaves, borne opposite each other on the lateral branches, have prominent stipules like those of many other members of the Rubiaceae. The roots reach a depth of 50 to 60 cm and a radius of about 2.5 m. A coffee plant will begin to bear fruit at 3 years and will be productive for 6 to 10 years. While it is possible to lengthen productivity somewhat by pruning, older plantations are often replaced simply to introduce new varieties. The lag time involved in growth to fruiting size, combined with fluctuations in world demand, has led to frequent crises of overproduction that have made prices highly variable in recent years. Although the International Coffee Organization, with headquarter in London, brings together the major producers, it is not strong enough to prevent the market from oscillating substantially in response to, for example, rumors of a frost in Brazil.

Coffee prices often fall considerably more than those of other commodities when there is a worldwide recession. An explanation of the vulnerability of Costa Rica to recessions, which I first heard propounded by Rodrigo Carazo, now Costa Rica's president, might be called the "dessert model." It is based on the fact that Costa Rica's main export crops—coffee, bananas, sugar, and chocolate—are all products that are eaten at the end of a meal rather than as staple parts of the diet. When people in industrialized nations must cut back their spending on food owing to reduced real incomes, it is logical for them to eat fewer chocolate eclairs rather than fewer potatoes. Thus countries exporting dessert crops will be particularly vulnerable to recession-induced price collapses. Whether consumers in fact behave in this way, and whether this explains the world price of coffee, remains to be explored, however, as do the implications of the model for diversification into new crops like macadamia nuts.

Fungal diseases are a major problem in coffee growing. The leaf spot ojo de gallo (*Mycena citricolor* [Ber. & Cur.] Sacc.) is a constant threat, generally kept within reasonable limits by heavy applications of pesticides such as lead arsenate. The roya de cafe (*Hemileia*

FIGURE 6.8. *Coffea arabica* in full flower near Alajuela, Costa Rica (photo, D. H. Janzen).

vastatrix), another fungal disease, has caused serious damage in the Old World, and it appeared in Nicaragua in the mid-1970s. It is regarded as a serious threat to coffee production in other Central American nations, and quarantines and spraying have been used to try to prevent it from spreading. Biological controls have been used against various insect pests in Africa, including stinkbugs, mealybugs, and leaf miners, but with limited success (Hill 1975).

The coffee plantation is often a two-story pseudoforest, with an overstory of "shade trees" over a fairly continuous layer of coffee plants. The shade trees undoubtedly affect pests and diseases, as well as coffee plants directly, through their effects on the microclimate. This is a fairly complicated problem; shade trees are considered in some areas to be absolutely necessary and in others to be positively harmful. As important as their shade may be that they are usually legumes, with nitrogen-fixing bacteria mutualistic in their roots. *Erythrina,* for example, is a very commonly used shade-tree genus (both native red-flowered species and the introduced purple-flowered species) that has very large nodules and could be providing substantial amounts of fixed nitrogen.

*

Araya Pochet, Carlos. 1976. *Historia económica de Costa Rica, 1950–70*. 2d ed. San José: Editorial Fernandez Arc.

Cerdas, Rodolfo. 1972. *La crisis de la democracia liberal en Costa Rica.* San José: Editorial Universitaria Centroamericano.

Griffith, William J. 1974. Coffee industry (Central America). In *Encyclopedia of Latin America,* ed. Helen Delpar, pp. 145–46. New York: McGraw-Hill.

Hall, Carolyn. 1976. *El Café y el desarrollo histórico-geográfico de Costa Rica.* San José: Editorial Costa Rica.

Hill, Dennis. 1975. *Agricultural insect pests of the tropics and their control.* Cambridge: Cambridge University Press.

León, Jorge. 1968. *Fundamentos botánicos de los cultivos tropicales.* Turrialba: IICA.

Stone, Samuel. 1976. *La dinastía de los conquistadores.* 2d ed. San José: Editorial Universitaria Centroamericana.

Corn (Maíz)

S. Risch

Corn (*Zea mays*) is a stout annual grass, 1 to 4 m tall (fig. 6.9). The stem of modern corn is solid, with clearly

FIGURE 6.9. *Zea mays* field in second year of use after slash-and-burn clearing, after 3 months of growth; weeds have been cut to ground level in foreground, exposing the surviving corn plants. Lowland Veracruz, Mexico (photo, D. H. Janzen).

defined nodes and internodes (averaging fourteen). Leaves are borne alternately on each side of the stem at the nodes and number eight to twenty-one. Corn has well-developed adventitious roots that develop from the lowest nodes of the stem about 2.5 cm below the soil surface. Some roots grow horizontally for 0.5 m to 1 m and then turn downward; others grow almost vertically to a depth of up to 2.5 m and branch profusely. At the time of rapid stem elongation, the two or three nodes above-ground produce whorls of prop and brace roots that enter the ground and behave like ordinary roots (Purseglove 1972).

Corn is monoecious, with male and female flowers borne in separate inflorescences on the same plant. The male inflorescence, called a tassel, is a terminal panicle up to 40 cm long, of which the central axis is a continuation of the stem, bearing a variable number of lateral branches. Paired spikelets, each with two glumes, occur in several rows on the main axis and on lateral branches. Each glume contains two staminate flowers. In corn vari-

eties commonly grown in Costa Rica, the staminate flowers on a given tassle typically start to open about 65 days after planting and have completed dehiscing about 8 days later.

The female inflorescence, called the ear, is a modified spike produced from a short lateral branch in the axil of one of the largest foliage leaves, about halfway down the stem. Sometimes two or even three buds may develop into ears, usually from above downward. The branch has short internodes at the base, with eight to thirteen modified leaves at the lowest nodes forming the overlapping husks that enclose and protect the inflorescence. The central axis or cob is a thickened modified stem that bears paired spikelets in longitudinal rows. The paired spikelets are identical with two glumes that enclose two florets, the upper one of which is sterile. The fertile floret is pistillate, with a single basal ovary and a long thread-like style or silk that grows up to 45 cm long and emerges from the top of the husk. The silk may be green, yellow, red, brown, or purple and is receptive throughout most of its length.

The pollen of corn is shed before the silk is receptive, but, since there is some overlap, up to 5% self-pollination can occur. The tassel spreads fully before anthesis begins. An anther usually begins shedding pollen about sunrise and finishes within a few hours. A tassel continues to shed pollen for about 5–8 days, with maximum shedding about the third day. A single anther produces about 2,500 grains of pollen and a tassel about 2–5 million, so that there are 20,000 to 30,000 pollen grains for each silk. Pollen remains viable for 24 h. Under favorable conditions, all silks emerge during a period of 3–5 days; they are receptive on emergence and can remain so for 14 days. The pollen grains are caught on the moist, sticky stigmatic hairs and germinate immediately. The silk dries up upon germination. In calm weather, most of the pollination is effected from neighboring plants, but with a high wind pollen can be carried up to 500 m.

The fruit is known as the kernel and is mature about 50 days after fertilization. The kernels are borne in an even number of rows, four to thirty, along the length of the cob, having been derived from the single fertile flower of each pair of spikelets. The mature ear is usually 8–42 cm long, with three hundred to one thousand grains. The grain is usually dried before being stored (to less than 20% moisture for cobs and less than 13% moisture for shelled grain). The composition of grain on a dry weight basis is 77% starch, 2% sugar, 9% protein, 5% fat, and 2% ash.

There are an extremely large number of corn cultivars, including the familiar popcorn, sweet corn (in which conversion of some of the sugar to starch is prevented), and a variety of field corn types (dent, flint, pod, wax, etc., classified according to grain structure).

Corn has never been found growing wild, but what appear to be the true wild ancestors of modern corn have been found in cave deposits in southern Mexico dating about 6000 B.C.

Corn is the most important cereal grain in Costa Rica after rice and is used as a staple human food, as a raw material for many industrial products, and to some extent as feed grain for livestock and poultry (about two-thirds as much corn as rice is grown in Costa Rica). In Costa Rica corn is prepared and consumed in a multitude of ways. The whole grain is sometimes boiled or roasted and at times is fermented. Most frequently the grain is ground and pounded, and the resulting meal is eaten as a gruel or porridge, is made into a dough and baked as thin cakes (tortillas), or is steamed as tamales. Immature "green" ears (with husks still on) are roasted and eaten.

Corn produces a number of important industrial products, including dextrins, syrups and sugars, starches (for food, sizing, and urethane plastics), oil (for food, soaps, or glycerine), various fermentation products (alcohols and acids), synthetic fibers of high tensil strength, and a substitute for shellac. However, only a few of these are produced in Costa Rica.

The many cultivars of corn have different maturity periods and are adapted to slightly different ecological conditions, so that corn can be cultivated in a wide variety of environmental conditions. It is grown in nearly all parts of Costa Rica from sea level to about 2,000 m. Rainfall during the growing season should not fall below 200 mm, and 450–600 mm is preferred, but corn does well even with up to 1 m and more of rain. Corn grows adequately in a wide variety of soils but does best on well-drained, well-aerated, deep, warm loams and silt loams containing adequate organic matter and well supplied with available nutrients. High yields of corn make a heavy drain on soil nutrients, and corn has a high nitrogen requirement. It is usually grown during both the wet and the dry seasons; planting is done in May and November. During the past few years, Costa Rica has produced an average annual yield of 900,000 metric tons on about 60,000 ha of land (about 25% of the permanently cropped land in Costa Rica) (FAO 1978).

Most of the corn is grown on small to medium-sized farms (fig. 6.10). The larger of these farms are in relatively flat areas with the best soils and are usually mechanized to some degree. On a typical small farm or subsistence plot corn is planted using a digging stick, which is plunged into the ground to make a hole 3–6 cm deep (fig. 6.10). Two or three seeds are normally planted in each hole. Row width in corn monocultures is typically about 1 m with 0.25 to 0.5 m spacing between hills in a row. When the corn silk has turned completely black and

ears have filled out completely, the plants are usually bent in half and the corn is allowed to dry in the field for about 4–6 weeks.

Especially on small farms, corn is commonly interplanted with other crops, frequently with beans (during the dry season) or squash or both, in which case spacing between corn plants is considerably increased. Squash and beans are sometimes planted at the same time as corn, the squash providing a good ground cover and considerably decreasing weed growth. Climbing or bush beans (*Phaseolus* or *Vigna*) are planted in this case, and there is some evidence that they increase the nitrogen in the soil. Sometimes climbing beans are not planted until the corn is bent over to dry.

Experiments conducted at the Central American Institute for Research and Training in Tropical Agriculture (CATIE) in Turrialba, Costa Rica, have shown that interplanting beans with corn produces greater total biomass than planting them separately (Soria et al. 1975). The detailed mechanisms through which this intercropping advantage is achieved have yet to be fully explored, but Risch (1980) has shown that there are significantly fewer leaf-eating beetle pests (Chrysomelidae) per bean and squash plant when they are interplanted with corn than when they are monocropped. The differences apparently result not from differences in rates of parasitism or predation on the beetles, nor from differences in beetle birthrates, but principally from differences in overall patterns of adult movements (Risch 1981). It was shown experimentally that beetles avoided feeding on shaded host plants and that the cornstalks themselves in some way interfered with flight movements of the insects.

Interplanting crops with corn also apparently increased both the abundance and the diversity of parasitoids in field plots at CATIE. Risch (1979) demonstrated higher abundance and diversity of parasitoids in corn–sweet potato dicultures than in either monoculture, and Hansen (1979) showed greater abundance of parasitoids in tricultures of corn, beans, and squash than in the respective dicultures and monocultures without corn. I have observed large numbers of small parasitoids (Chalcids and Braconids) on male corn inflorescences.

While a number of diseases attack corn in Costa Rica (leaf blights, corn smut, leaf spot, etc.), they are not generally considered as serious a problem as insect pests, probably owing to utilization of resistant corn varieties.

Probably the most serious insect pests during the rainy season are the larvae of scarabaeid beetles (*Phyllophaga* sp.). These beetles are univoltine; the adults emerge with the onset of the rainy season in May–June and lay their eggs in the soil near corn. The larvae feed on corn roots during the rainy reason until about September and then are dormant until the onset of the next rainy season, when they emerge as adults. Whole fields of corn are com-

FIGURE 6.10. *Zea mays. a,* Two slash-and-burn fields newly cut out of virgin forest for corn planting. *b,* Dibble-stick-planted corn (down slope, left half of photograph) and beans (right half of photograph) in newly cleared and burned virgin forest. Central Costa Rica (photo, D. H. Janzen).

monly damaged unless soil insecticides are used. The large scoliid wasps are common external parasites of these larvae. They are frequently seen flying low over the ground in cornfields, stopping when they apparently sense the presence of underground larvae, and burrowing 15 cm or more to locate and oviposit on their host.

Diabrotica balteata and *Diabrotica viridula* also feed on corn roots as larvae and are common pests throughout the year. *D. viridula* is more common on the Atlantic side of the country, but *D. balteata* is widespread throughout Costa Rica. Both species eat very young corn leaves as adults, and high numbers can severely damage crops. Ants (*Solenopsis* sp. and *Pheidole* sp.) were important predators of *Diabrotica* eggs at Turrialba and may be important predators of rootworm eggs throughout Costa Rica (Risch 1981). A tachinid fly parasitizes the adult beetles but seems to be rare.

Other important pests of corn in Costa Rica are *Heliothis zea* larvae, which feed on the terminal grain in the developing ear, and *Diatraea lineolata* larvae, which are stem borers. *Heliothis* eggs are laid on the silk, and the larvae burrow into the developing ear, cannibalizing conspecifics until only one is left grazing on the ear. The proportion of ears affected by *H. zea* was high at Turrialba, but only in corn maturing in February and March; however, the proportion of grains destroyed was low (10–15%) *D. lineolata* was found in 40–60% of the stems. Both *Diatraea* and *Heliothis* larvae have tachinid parasites.

Young corn plants (until about 10 days after emergence) can be severely damaged by noctuid cutworm larvae (*Agrotis* and *Spodoptera*), and whole fields of young corn are frequently destroyed by blackbirds. Blackbirds can also eat the fruit just as the corn is starting to ripen.

*

Coen, Elliot. 1968. *Zonas potenciales del cultivo del maiz y epocas de siembra en Costa Rica*. Publicaciónes de la Universidad de Costa Rica. Serie Agronómia no. 9. San José: Universidad de Costa Rica.

Food and Agriculture Organization (FAO). 1978. *Production yearbook, 1977*. Vol. 31. Rome: FAO.

Hansen, M. K. 1979. Abundance of insect predators and parasitoids in monocultures and polycultures of corn, beans, and squash in Costa Rica. In preparation.

Purseglove, J. W. 1972. *Tropical crops: Monocotyledons*. New York: Vol. 2. Longman.

Risch, S. J. 1979. A comparison, by sweep sampling, of the insect fauna from corn and sweet potato monocultures and polycultures. *Oecologia* 42:195–211.

———. 1980. The population dynamics of several herbivorous beetles in a tropical agroecosystem: The effect of intercropping corn, beans and squash in Costa Rica. *J. Appl. Ecol.* 17:5a3–612.

———. 1981. Insect herbivore abundance in tropical monocultures and polycultures: An experimental test of two hypotheses. *Ecology* 62:1325–40.

Cotton (Algodón)

Evaristo Morales M.

Cotton belongs to the order Malvales, to the family Malvaceae, and to the genus *Gossypium*. The name *Gossypium*, taken from the Arabic language, was given to cotton by Pliny.

Linnaeus divides the genus *Gossypium* into three species: *G. herbaceum* (the American upland and Peruvian cotton); *G. barbadense* (the Sea Island cotton), and *G. arboreum* (the tree cotton of Asia). But the most commonly used classification is that of the United States Bureau of Plant Industry, which divides the genus into *G. hirsutum* (the American upland), *G. barbadense* (or Sea Island cotton), and *G. peruvianum* (or Peruvian cotton).

The cotton plant has an erect stem with a variable number of lateral limbs or branches (fig. 6.11). The plant varies from 1 m to 2.5–3 m tall, depending upon soil fertility, water content, and variety. The leaves are of medium size, petiolate, palmate, and arranged spirally on the branches. The size of the leaves varies depending on variety, the position of the leaf on the stem, the vigor of the plant, and the age of the leaf. A full-grown leaf will vary in size from 7 cm in length and 4 cm in width to 16 cm in length and 11 cm in width. Leaves are developed that are three-, five-, or seven-lobed, and three-, five-, or seven-veined. Near the base of the midvein, on the underside of the leaf, may be found a small dark green gland. These glands may or may not be present on the other veins. Some varieties lack these glands. The color of the leaf will vary from brownish red to light green, depending upon the vigor of the plant and the variety.

The flowers of cotton are large and attached by short peduncles to the branches at the nodes accesory to the petioles. The first flowers appear about 7 to 10 weeks after planting. The flower buds may be distinguished 3 or 4 weeks before the opening of the flowers. The number of stigmata varies from three to five. They always grow together and thus determine the number of loculi in the boll. The number of flowers per plant depends on the size and vigor of the plant and on the variety.

The flowers open just before or at sunrise, close at night, and never open again. The flowers always turn dark with age; even the white ones become reddish purple by the second or third day after opening. The cotton boll (the fruit) resembles a small hen's egg. The boll varies from about 2 to 5 cm in length and from 2 to 5 cm in width. The cotton fiber, or lint, is a white, tubelike, unicellular structure of great strength arising from the epidermis of the seed coat. When the valves of the bolls

FIGURE 6.11. *a*, Field of mature *Gossypium* plants. *b*, Dehisced fruit of *Gossypium* (*below*) and maturing cotton fruit (*above*). Liberia, Guanacaste, Costa Rica (photos, D. H. Janzen).

first open, the cotton appears as a moist, pearly white, or in some cases brown, compact mass, but upon exposure to the air a great deal of water is lost from the fiber. The length of the fiber varies with the variety and species, but 2–5 cm is a general average in many varieties of cotton.

Attached to the seed is a covering of very short fibers called linters or fuzz, which makes up about 10% of the total weight of the fiber and varies from white to grayish green. The seeds are attached to the boll at the inner angle of each compartment. The seed is divided into three parts: the outer coating or hull, called the testa; the nucellus; and the embryo.

The major part of the cotton of Costa Rica grows in Guanacaste Province, with smaller amounts in Puntarenas and Alajuela. Cotton is planted from 0 m to 150 m above sea level (in extreme cases it can be planted at 900 m above sea level).

Culture of cotton is determined by several factors, such as ecology, soil texture, soil drainage, soil humidity, topography, access roads, hand labor, equipment for combat of pests, diseases, weeds, and soil preparation.

The cotton plant prefers deep soils (1.2–3 m deep), friable and well drained. Land where superficial water accumulates must be avoided, or the cotton plant will be damaged. Soils must have enough organic matter, but too high a content may make the plant grow too tall. Soil must hold enough water that the plant can resist periods of dryness. The water-holding capacity can be increased by good soil preparation (subsoiling, etc.). Cotton plants do better in loam soils (loam-arcillo-arenoso), with a pH of 5.3 to 8. The land should be flat or almost flat to permit the use of machinery for soil preparation, planting, fertilizing, combating pests, diseases, and weeds, and harvest and transport.

Good climatic conditions for cotton include a temperature ranging from 24° to 28° C (maximum limits 20–30° C). The optimum temperature for seed germination is about 30°C, and for the seedling it is 25–30°C. The adult plant thrives at 25°C. A temperature exposure of two hours or more at temperature higher than 30° C can produce toxins that interfere with normal metabolism. Rainfall has to be well distributed throughout the growth period. The water requirement is high during the growing and blooming periods, but too much water at these times can prevent normal pollination of flowers and cause young fruits to fall. The weather should be dry while the bolls open so they will dry well and ripen normally. Even sporadic rains during the opening period can cause severe damage to the bolls, preventing normal opening. When the bolls are open they can accumulate dust, and rain will damage the fiber, which will lose brightness and color. The rainfall necessary for cotton varies from 900 to 1,300 mm during its growth period. Cotton plants need at least 50–60% full sunlight. In the cotton areas of Costa Rica it usually rains regularly during the afternoon, after a sunny morning with a hot and humid atmosphere.

Planting is done from 20 June to 20 August, with small variations according to the moisture in the soil and to the rains. Harvesting starts during November or December.

In certain areas of Guanacaste, such as Cañas and Bagaces, cotton plantations can suffer from strong winds at the end of the year (after November), which cause a heavy fall of open bolls and fiber. Wind increases leaf evaporation and makes the stomata close. The stomata open again when humidity returns to normal. The closing of the stomata stops the plant metabolism, so the plant produces less fruit and the crop is reduced. Harvest must start as soon as bolls are ripe, after the bolls are completely open and there is a high percentage of open bolls on the plant.

Several species of weeds damage cotton after its emergence, especially when the number of plants per area is low because seed germination was poor or when the plants are not vigorous. In these cases the blank spaces in the cotton fields are invaded by weeds.

Insects are the principal enemies of the cotton plant; they can cause damage anytime after germination. Soon after the plants emerge they are attacked by cutworms, wire worms, white worms, and aphids. Once the plants have grown, foliage pests become a problem, such as aphids, cotton leafhoppers, cotton leafworms, yellow-striped armyworms, salt-marsh caterpillars, cotton stainers, white flies, spider mites, and thrips. Just after the blooming, when square formation starts, insects of the flowers, squares and bolls arrive, such as cotton bollworms, yellow-striped armyworms, cotton boll weevils, cotton stainers, and many others.

Diseases of cotton are of minor importance in Costa Rica. One of the most important, caused by *Rhyzoctonia* sp., attacks the stem of the young plants. Sometimes cotton boll rot can be a problem. This disease is produced by several fungi, such as *Aspergillus* sp., *Colletotrichum* sp., *Fusarium* sp., and *Phythophthora* sp. Sometimes cotton fields are attacked by a virus disease transmitted by the white fly.

Honeybees (Abejas de Miel)
M. Winston

The honeybee, *Apis mellifera* (Apidae), is one of the more common bees of Costa Rica, although it is not native to the New World and is not often found nesting in nonmanaged situations. The local honeybees are descended from imported European races (mostly yellow Italian bees and the darker German bee) and do not do well on the wet tropical Atlantic side of Costa Rica. There are approximately twenty thousand beehives throughout the country, concentrated in Guanacaste, Puntarenas, and the central plateau around San José.

Two types of beekeeping are practiced in Costa Rica, modern movable-frame beekeeping (85% of all beekeeping; Drescher 1976; Kent 1973) and less-technical fixed-comb beekeeping (15%; Kent 1979). Movable-frame beekeeping is similar to that found in the United States, although not as well developed. Bees are kept in standard boxes (supers), each containing ten frames of comb attached to wooden bars that can be removed for inspection or honey extraction. A bee colony (which consists of one queen, twenty to eighty thousand workers, and some males, or drones, during parts of the year) will generally rear its broods in the bottom super and store honey in the top ones. When the honey supers are full, beekeepers remove the supers, uncap the honey, and spin the honey-laden frames in a centrifugal extractor. The honey is then either bottled for local sale or exported to Europe in fifty-five-gallon drums.

Fixed-comb beekeeping is more primitive in that bees are kept under seminatural conditions, without removable frames of comb. Such colonies are kept in hollow logs, boxes, or clay pots, and the bees build combs suspended from the tops of these hives. Management consists solely of cutting out honeycomb once or twice a year and either eating it as comb honey or squeezing out the honey and discarding the comb (a wasteful practice, since considerable energy goes into producing wax for comb). None of this honey is exported (Kent 1979).

Guanacaste is the best beekeeping region in Costa Rica, with colonies using largely dry-season tree flowers to produce high honey yields. There have been a number of problems with beekeeping in Guanacaste, however; in 1963 and 1968 volcanic eruptions destroyed between six thousand and eight thousand colonies (Drescher 1976). Also, recent heavy application of pesticides for cotton pests has killed nearby bee colonies, and this problem is increasing. Beekeeping is also popular in Puntarenas and the Central Plateau; in the latter region coffee flowers provide much of the honeyflow.

The average Costa Rican beekeeper maintains between ten and one hundred colonies, producing approximately 60 lb of honey annually per colony. There are very few large-scale commercial beekeepers, and only one with more than one thousand colonies. Since honey currently sells for about 35 ¢/lb wholesale, the average beekeeper with one hundred colonies could earn about $2,000 a year before expenses. This is considerably less than the potential income from beekeeping, since well-managed colonies should produce averages of 75–100 (Central Plateau) or 130–50 (Guanacaste) lb of honey annually. The reason for this disparity between potential and actual production is lack of proper management; most beekeepers do not stop swarming (colony reproduction, which diminishes honey production), requeen colonies (old queens do not produce as many workers as younger queens), or feed bees to build up the colony population before the honeyflows.

Beekeeping in Costa Rica will change considerably in four to five years with the arrival of Africanized honeybees, which are spreading northward from South America (Winston 1979). These bees are aggressive, swarm readily, and often abscond (abandon the hive completely), and they can cause serious problems for bee-keepers. Unless some sort of assistance is made available, it is likely that many Costa Rican beekeepers will abandon their colonies. Although it is possible to keep Africanized bees with some changes in management techniques (Taylor and Levin 1978), anyone considering starting beekeeping in Costa Rica should be aware of the problems Africanized bees will cause.

*

Drescher, W. 1976. The use of movable frame hives in development programs (Africa and Latin America). In *Apiculture in tropical climates*, ed. Eva Crane, pp. 23–30. London: International Bee Research Association.

Kent, R. B. 1973. Beekeeping with honey bees in a tropical environment—the case of Costa Rica. Master's thesis, Department of Geography, University of California at Davis.

———. 1979. Technical and financial aspects of fixed comb and movable frame beekeeping in Costa Rica. *Am. Bee J.* 119:36–38, 43, 127–28, 135.

Taylor, O. R., and Levin, M. D. 1978. Observations on Africanized honey bees reported to South and Central American government agencies. *Bull. Ent. Soc. Am.* 24:412–14.

Winston, M. L. 1979. The potential impact of the Africanized honey bee on apiculture in Mexico and Central America. *Am. Bee J.* 119:584–86, 642–45.

Mango (Mango)

M. Hansen

The mango tree, *Mangifera indica*, a member of the Anacardiaceae, is a moderately large evergreen tree with a life span of up to 100 years that is grown for its fruits throughout the tropics from sea level to elevations of 1,500 m. Although it will grow in a wide variety of habitats, it does best in areas below 2,000 ft that have a distinct dry season and a soil pH of 5.5–7.5. Although it is grown throughout Costa Rica, it is most common on the Pacific coast in the provinces of Guanacaste and Puntarenas. It is at present believed to have originated in India or Burma, since it grows wild throughout India but especially in the hilly areas of the northeast (Singh 1960). It is postulated to have arrived in the New World by two routes: from the Philippines to Mexico, via the Spaniards and from West Africa to Brazil via the Portuguese (León 1968, pp. 256–59).

There are two growth forms, depending on whether it is grown from a seed or a graft. When grown from a seed, the tree is 10–40 m tall with an erect trunk, many branches, and a tightly packed, dome-shaped canopy. Grafted individuals are shorter and more sparsely branched and have a more open canopy. The bark is grayish brown and deeply ridged and contains many resinous glands. It has a long taproot (6–8 m) that allows the plant to get water during the dry season, as well as an extensive superficial root system up to 20 m in diameter that is used to gather water and nutrients during the rainy season.

The shiny green, leathery leaves are spirally arranged and are produced in flushes toward the ends of the branches and branchlets. The size of the leaves is extremely variable; they tend to be narrowly elliptical or lanceolate with a prominant midrib, ranging in size from 8–40 cm by 2–10 cm. Leaves appear to be relatively expensive to make and so to be well protected, since they have life spans of over a year and are filled with secondary compounds. Young leaves are often pink or red, turning green as they age, a phenomenon well known in tropical plants and thought to be a protective adaptation to intense sunlight, since ultraviolet is most harmful to a growing leaf.

The inflorescences (fig. 6.12) are arranged in a widely branched terminal panicle from 10 to 60 cm long and contain anywhere from one thousand to five thousand small yellowish or pinkish flowers arranged in cymes on the ends of the branchlets. The flowers are sweet-smelling and come in two forms, staminate or hermaphroditic. Both types of flowers are 5–8 mm in diameter and have an extremely short peduncle. There are

FIGURE 6.12. a, Inflorescence of *Mangifera indica*. b, Infrutescence of *M. indica* with young fruits a few weeks old. Liberia, Guanacaste, Costa Rica (photos, D. H. Janzen).

usually five sepals and five petals (3–6 mm long and 1–2 mm wide) that are cream-colored, with three to five yellow ridges on the inside, and turn pinkish as they age. The center of the flowers contains a fleshy, five-lobed disk between the corolla and the androecium. Hermaphroditic flowers contain a single pistil and usually five stamens. The single pistil, curved and situated on the center of the disk, contains a lateral style and a simple stigma. Of the five stamens around the outer edge of the disk, usually only one or two are fertile; these are longer than the sterile ones and contain pink anthers that turn purple at anthesis. Hot, sunny conditions are necessary for anthesis; rain reduces pollination and fruit set, which explains why the tree does so poorly in the Caribbean lowlands. In Costa Rica flowering is concentrated in July and August, during the *veranillo* or short dry season. The flower opens in late evening and early morning, with peak anthesis between 8:00 a.m. and noon. Pollination is entomophilous, and dipterans appear to be the primary pollinators (Purseglove, 1968, pp. 24–32).

Fruits take 2–5 months to develop, depending on the temperature and the cultivar. Flowering and setting fruit is very costly, energetically speaking, and can be done only ever 2–4 years. Not only is a high carbon-to-nitrogen (C/N) ratio necessary to initiate flowering, but few flowers, even if fertilized, make mature fruits; most are aborted before this, and only 0.25 to 0.1% ever reach maturity. In addition, new leaf growth, which is synchronous, must occur in the "off years" between flowering, since it too requires a high C/N ratio.

The fruit is a fleshy drupe, consisting of an exocarp, mesocarp, endocarp, and seed, and comes in a variety on sizes, shapes, and colors. It is from 5 to 30 cm long and rounded to oblong, often with a pronounced lateral compression and an unequal profile, the dorsal part convex and the ventral part with a concavity toward the apical end. The base color of the exocarp is usually yellowish, with patches of varying sizes of green and red depending on environmental conditions as well as cultivar type. The thick exocarp also contains many small clear patches whose abundance is a varietal factor; they are really large cells filled with resin canals that contain high concentrations of terpenoids (Singh 1960). These glands give the mango its turpentinelike flavor. The mesocarp, or edible part of the fruit, is orange to yellow and varies in thickness, texture, and flavor, ranging from sweet and juicy to fibrous and turpentine-flavored, depending on variety. The fibers in the mesocarp are attached to the woody endocarp; the quantity and size of these fibers varies with varietal type. Usually there is a single seed within the endocarp.

There are two main means of propagation: seeds and grafts. Grafting is the preferred means of cultivation, since it produced fruits identical with the maternal type, whereas trees produced from seeds do not usually yield fruits identical to the parental type; lower-quality fruits thus are often produced. The economic life of a plant is extremely variable, depending on the clone. Ordinarily, fifteen to twenty fruits will be produced in the 4th or 5th year if the mango is grafted, or in the 7th or 8th year if it is grown from a seedling. The yield increases steadily until at age 10 a tree produces four hundred to six hundred fruits during an "on" year. Yields increase until the 20th year, then level off until age 40, after which production steadily declines (Singh 1960).

Although a number of pests and diseases attack *M. indica*, only a few are serious. The worst are two species of fungi, *Gloeosporium mangifera* and *Erysiphe cichoracearum* (Fröhlich and Rodewald 1970). *G. mangifera*, a deuteromyocete, is particularly bad where the humidity is very high; thus it is a serious problem in areas of the wet tropical lowlands. It first appears as dark brown spots on the leaves and black spots on the twigs and flowers. As the disease progresses the flowers turn black and wither, as do the young twigs and fruits. The black spots spread to the fruits, causing the young ones to abort; older fruits remain on the trees. Powdery mildew, *E. cichoracearum*, an ascomycete, is also a serious problem in many areas, causing losses of 5–20%. It attacks young flowers and fruits, appearing as powdery white spots. The hairy tips of unopened flowers are first infected, then the fungus slowly travels down the floral axis to the peduncle and feeds on the outer cells of flowers and very young fruits. Fruit flies of the genus *Ceratitis* in the Mediterranean and *Anastrepha* in South America, Mexico, and the West Indies reproduce in the fruits, making them inedible. Destroying the fallen infested fruits often reduces the problem. Mango-hoppers of the genus *Idiocerus* are serious pests of the flowers, and weevils of the genus *Cryptorhynchus* are serious pests of the seeds.

*

Frölich, G.; Rodewald, W.; et al. 1970. *Pests and diseases of tropical crops and their control*. Oxford: Pergamon Press.

León, J. 1968. *Fundamentales botanicos de los cultivos tropicales*. San José: Instituto Interamericano de Ciencias Agricolas de la OEA.

Purseglove, J. W. 1968. *Tropical crops: Dicotyledons*. Vol. 1. New York: John Wiley.

Singh, L. B. 1960. *The mango*. London: Leonard Hill.

Papaya (Papaya)

S. Risch

Papaya is a short-lived, quick-growing, soft-wooded tree 2–10 m in height; it is usually unbranched. *Carica papaya* has never been found in the wild, but Purseglove (1968) says it probably originated in southern Mexico and Costa Rica. The stem is straight and cylindrical, with prominent leaf scars (fig. 6.13). The leaves are deeply and palmately lobed and cluster near the apex of the trunk in a spiral arrangement. The tree occurs at mid to low elevations throughout Costa Rica on well-drained, fertile soils. On the dry Pacific side it sometimes requires irrigation for adequate production. The tree grows well only in complete sun; when it is found as an escape in natural second growth, the tree does not produce if there is any shade.

Papaya is usually dioecious, but hermaphroditic forms do occur. The small white or yellowish, very fragrant flowers are produced in abundance near the trunk apex. Male flowers are borne in great numbers on long, drooping flower stalks, and female flowers are produced on short, branched stalks in the leaf axils. Interestingly, both male and hermaphroditic trees (but never females) can undergo sex reversal; the type of flower produced on one tree apparently depends on age, season, and probably other variables as well. In hermaphroditic trees, female sterility is favored by warm weather, and such trees may become female-fertile in cool months. Whether the tree

FIGURE 6.13. Female *Carica papaya* with nearly mature cauliflorous fruits. Liberia, Guanacaste, Costa Rica (photo, D. H. Janzen).

is male, female, or hermaphroditic cannot be determined until flowering commences.

The method of natural pollination is not known with certainty. It is variously stated that papaya is wind-pollinated, that small insects like thrips may assist, and that the sweet-scented nocturnal flowers are pollinated by moths. Isolated female trees have set fruit when they were 800 yards from the nearest male tree (Purseglove 1968).

The plant produces large, fleshy berries 7–30 cm long and weighing up to 9 kg (the fruits from pistillate flowers are ovoid-oblong to nearly spherical; those from hermaphroditic flowers are pear-shaped or cylindrical). The skin is thin, smooth, and green, turning yellowish or orange when ripe. The edible flesh is yellow to reddish orange, of the consistancy of butter, with a mild, pleasant flavor.

The ripe fresh fruits are eaten throughout Costa Rica. They are also used in making soft drinks, jams, and ice cream, and the crystallized fruits are canned in syrup. The edible portion of the fresh fruit contains approximately 88% water, 10% sugars, 0.5% protein, 0.1% fat, 0.6% ash and 0.7% fiber. It is high in vitamins A and C. Young leaves of the tree can be eaten like spinach.

Papain, which is prepared from the dried latex of immature fruits, is a proteolytic enzyme used in meat tenderizers, chewing gum, and cosmetics, as a drug for digestive ailments, in the tanning industry for bathing hides, for degumming natural silk, and to give shrink resistance to natural wool. The production of papain is not an established industry in Costa Rica.

The many seeds are parietal and are attached in five rows to the interior wall of the ovary. They are sperical, about 5 mm in diameter, and enclosed in a gelatinous mass formed from the outer integument. About twenty dried seeds weigh 1 g.

The major diseases of papaya are several mosaic viruses and mildews, both of which have a variety of insect vectors, including aphids, thrips, and probably other insects as well. The most serious insect pest in Costa Rica is the fly *Toxotrypana curvicauda* (Gerstaecker) (Tephritidae). The female fly is approximately 2.5 cm in length, with an ovipositor about 1.3 cm long. Eggs are deposited inside the young fruit, and larvae develop there, emerging when completely developed and falling to the ground to pupate. If the female leaves her ovipositor in the fruit for any length of time, the plant latex coagulates upon contact with air; it appears to bind her ovipositor, and sometimes she cannot dislodge herself (Ponciano 1966). Egg to adult fly development requires 45–60 days. Adult females are active only one hour before and after dawn and sunset, whereas males are generally active throughout the day. Females fly only short distances, and it appears likely that important dispersers of the fly are the many animals and birds that carry off rotting fruits with developing fly larvae. Mites and pseudococcids (frequently tended by ants) are other important arthropod pests of papaya, and birds occasionally attack healthy fruits.

In rural Costa Rica, papaya is frequently grown for local consumption as one of the many crops on subsistence and small farms. It is common to see several trees growing alongside a farmer's house. Papaya is grown for market on medium to large fruit farms, frequently in combination with avocados and mangoes. FAO estimates that Costa Rica has produced an average of 3,000 metric tons of papaya per year over the past ten years (FAO 1978).

Papayas are normally propagated by seed. These may be planted in wooden flats, then transplanted to small individual containers after 3 weeks, and after another 3 to 4 weeks they are ready to plant in the orchard. Ultimately, one male plant is allowed for every 25–100 female plants. Yields per tree vary between 30 and 150 fruits per year, giving up to 15 tons of marketable fruit per acre. Intercropping is sometimes practiced and seems to be especially advantageous during early growth of the young trees. Mulching is common and apparently useful.

For papain production, tapping commences when the unripe fruits are 10 cm or more in diameter. It is done by making three or four vertical cuts about 0.25 cm deep. The latex may be caught on a cheesecloth-covered tray mounted on a wire frame clamped onto the trunk. The latex coagulates and is scraped off. Developing fruits are retapped between the previous cuts about once a week. Ripe fruits have little latex, but tapped fruits still are edible when they ripen. A tree produces 50% of its total production of papain in its first year of cropping, 30% in its second year, and 20% in its third year, after which the crop is replanted. Yields of dry papain are 27–54 kg per acre.

*

Food and Agriculture Organization (FAO). 1978. *Production yearbook, 1977.* Vol. 31. Rome: FAO.

León, J. 1968. *Fundamentales botanicos de los cultivos tropicales.* San José: Instituto Interamericano de Ciencias Agricolas de la OEA.

Ponciano, P. A. M. A. 1966. Mosco o avispa de la papaya. *Rev. Agric.* 38(2):78–80.

Purseglove, J. W. 1968. *Tropical crops: Dicotyledons.* Vol. 1. London: Longman.

Pejibaye Palm (Pejibaye)

J. Vandermeer

During Costa Rica's wet season it is common to see small, reddish palm fruits for sale at the market and in the streets of San José. This delicious and popular fruit, from the pejibaye palm, is one of the few foods that are almost completely Costa Rican. Although the species (*Bactris gasipaes*) ranges from Nicaragua to Bolivia (Seibert 1950), only in Costa Rica—and to a lesser extent in Panama—has it become a popular food item (Popenoe and Jimenez 1921; Kitzke and Johnson 1975). Although several aboriginal tribes in South America (Venezuela, Colombia, Ecuador), use it as a staple food source (Popenoe and Jimenez 1921), as did some Costa Rican Indians, westernized segments of the society do not readily accept it as food, and in some areas people regard it as nothing more than pig food (Johannessen 1966*a*).

The species ranges from sea level to 1,000 m, although individuals tend to be stunted above 700 m (Johannessen 1966*a*). The trees thrive best in high-rainfall lowland areas. From South America through Panama single trees can be found growing wild in forests, but in Costa Rica I have observed them only in association with humans. Some of the best sites are on the lower terraces of the major rivers, such as the Reventazón, San Carlos, and El General. Growth and yield are apparently greatly influenced by soil type, and young loamy soils developed from river alluvium seem to be best (Johannessen 1966*a,b*).

On the drive from San José to Puerto Viejo de Sarapiquí, after descending the eastern slope of the mountains, one notices that this species (fig. 6.14*a*) is one of the commonest trees along the roadside. Most individuals are associated with homesites; almost every family between San Miguel and Puerto Viejo has at least one pejibaye palm in the backyard. This method of growth—isolated individuals associated with small farm plots—is undoubtedly the most common existence for the species in Costa Rica, but large plantations are also common (Johannessen 1966*a*) and account for much of the commercial production. Thus, from an ecological point of view, the species exists in two modes—as isolated individuals widely scattered across the countryside and in large monocultures. Both modes exist at the La Selva field station.

The trunk of the species grows 10–15 m tall and almost always occurs in multiples. That is, suckers usually

FIGURE 6.14. Pejibaye palm. *a*, Adult tree with two racemes about 1 m below lowest leaves. *b*, Trunk of young tree showing spines that apparently deter some climbing rodents. Finca La Selva, Sarapiquí District, Costa Rica (photos, D. H. Janzen).

develop at the base of the trunk, eventually creating an individual with up to six stems originating from the same base. The existence of suckers has prompted horticulturists to develop techniques for vegetative propagation, with questionable results. Usually the trunks are armed with densely packed spines (fig. 6.14b), growing in annular bands 5–15 cm wide between the attachment points of the leaf petioles. At least one variety of spineless or nearly spineless pejibaye has been found and is currently being propagated (G. S. Hartshorn, pers. comm.).

The leaf is a large spine-laden, pinnately compound leaf, with the pinnae coming off the midrib at various angles, as is common in the genus. The pinnae occur in groups of two to seven, groups being separated by a gap of 1 to 1.5 cm. A new leaf is produced every 2 to 4 weeks, depending on conditions. Young leaves are morphologically distinct from older leaves, having the typical bifid appearance so common in the seedling stage of many palm species (Tomlinson 1961).

The root system appears to consist of a central root mass extending several meters downward, plus a superficial lateral extension of roots. The lateral extension can occupy an area significantly larger than the ground level projection of the canopy of the tree (Vandermeer 1977).

The flower-bearing raceme develops on the trunk directly above the center of the insertion of the petiole. Staminate flowers are most abundant except at the terminus of each rachillus. Only pistillate flowers occur on the last few inches of each rachillus, whereas on the rest of the inflorescense male and female flowers are interspersed more or less at random. Male flowers drop off the raceme within 24 h. They are usually so synchronous in their dropping that they produce a "rain" of flowers under the tree (J. Beech, pers. comm.). Although the flowers are visited by a large number of insects, no published accounts of the details of the pollinating mechanism are available at this time.

The fruit contains a single seed surrounded by fibrous edible material. It may be 2 to 6 cm in diameter and length. It may be rounded, nippled, cylindrical, or pyramidal. Fruit color tends to be constant for a given tree but fruit may vary from yellow to green to orange to red on different trees. Occasionally a fruit contains two fused seeds or is totally seedless.

A variety of animals eat the fruits. I have observed parrots and oropendolas pecking at the fruits on the tree. Although toucans and aracaris are commonly seen in pejibaye trees, I have never observed them actually eating the fruits. Apparently arboreal mammals are discouraged by the spiny armament on the trunks and leaves, but fruits that fall to the ground are a prime food source for ground-dwelling mammals. Captive pocket mice (*Heteromys desmarestianus*), armored rats (*Hoplomys gymnurus*), and agoutis (*Dasyprocta punctata*) ate pejibaye fruits with relish, and livestock are known to thrive on them. At the La Selva field station, one of the best places to observe wild agoutis is in the pejibaye plantations.

The two parts of the tree with potential or actual commercial value are the fruit and the heart. Locally, fermented drinks are made from the sap when the trunk is cut down, the flowers are occasionally cut very young and cooked with eggs, and the outer layers of the trunk provide hard yet flexible wood. Lances, bows, and arrows were commonly made from the wood by Indians in the country.

The fruit is highly variable in its nutritional content (Johannessen 1967). In a sample of eighteen trees Johannessen obtained the following figures for fresh fruit: water, 56%; fat, 6%; crude fiber, 1%; protein, 2%; ash, 0.7% (figures based on weight of fresh fruit). More significant than these mean values was the variability. There was a fivefold range in fat content, an eightfold range in carotene, and a twenty-three-fold range in vitamin C. The protein content is relatively high (range = 0.31 to 2.85%) for a food that is considered basically a source of starch.

In addition to the fruit, the palm heart (*palmito*) is a prized delicacy and recently has found a niche in commercial production. The heart (the tissue immediately surrounding and including the meristem) is tender and delicious. It is boiled or eaten raw.

Yields of pejibaye plantations rival those of commercial cornfields (Hunter 1969), and a recent report by the National Academy of Sciences includes the species among relatively unknown tropical crops with potential economic value (NAS 1975). From a strictly ecological point of view the species is now important both because of the wide occurrence of isolated trees and because of the unique habitat it produces when grown as a plantation. If, as is expected, its abundance and distribution increase in future years, we need to know a great deal more about its autecology and the ecology of the habitat it creates.

*

Hunter, J. R. 1969. The lack of acceptance of the pejibaye palm and a relative comparison of its productivity to that of maize. *Econ. Bot.* 23:237–44.

Johannessen, C. L. 1966a. Pejibayes in commercial production. *Turrialba* 16(2):181–87.

———. 1966b. Pejibaye palm: Yields, prices, and labor costs. *Econ. Bot.* 20(3):302–15.

———. 1967. Pejibaye palm: Physical and chemical analysis of the fruit. *Econ. Bot.* 21:371–78.

Kitzke, E. D., and Johnson, D. 1975. Commercial palm products other than oils. *Principes* 19:3–24.

National Academy of Sciences. 1975. *Underexploited tropical crops with promising economic value.* Washington, D.C.: NAS.

Popenoe, W., and Jimenez, O. 1921. The pejibaye, a neglected food-plant of tropical America. *J. Hered.* 12(4):151–66.

Seibert, R. J. 1950. The importance of palms to Latin America: Pejibaye a notable example. *Ceiba* 1(2):65–74.

Tomlinson, P. B. 1961. Essays on the morphology of palms. III. Seedling leaves and juvenile foliage. *Principes* 5:8–12.

Vandermeer, J. H. 1977. Observations on the root system of the pejibaye palm (*Bactris gasipaes* in H.B.K.) in Costa Rica. *Turrialba* 27:239–42.

Pigs (Chanchos, Cerdos)

R. Rice

The pig (fig. 6.15) is a even-toed ungulate belonging to the order Artiodactyla. The family is Suidae, which refers to Old World pigs, since known fossil remains of pigs are restricted to the Old World (Mount 1968). Pigs are known to have been domesticated in the Near East by 7000 B.C. (some 1,500 years after sheep). The oldest known evidence indicating domestication of the pig has been found in what is now Turkey.

Hafez (1962) relates that the domestic pig (*Sus domesticus*) found in the Western Hemisphere today is descended from the European wild pig (*Sus scrofa*) and the Far Eastern pig (*Sus vittatus*). There seems to be some evidence that the Indians of Costa Rica "had in their power" the indigenous wild pig upon the arrival of the Spaniards (Maroto 1970), although it is unclear whether the pig was actually domesticated.

FIGURE 6.15. Small adult *Sus scrofa* exhibiting escape behavior. Potrerillos, Guanacaste, Costa Rica (photo, D. H. Janzen).

In Costa Rica today the pig business is for the most part a sideline; very few commercial farms exist. The main market adjoins a packing plant near Alajuela. Pigs belonging to small farm owners can be found roaming free along roadsides, in pastures or forests, and even along beaches, where, according to the local people, pigs search out and eat crabs.

Pigs generally receive little care in rural Costa Rica. Seldom are they fed grain of any kind, since it is either a human staple (corn) or too expensive to give to an animal that can survive by foraging. The usual supplementary hog feed consists of plantains and bananas, which produce fairly good results. Pigs also do relatively well on tuber crops, which grow well and fast in the wet lowland areas. The protein supplied by these feeds is unbalanced, however, so that growth is slow and productivity reduced. A satisfactory single protein source is difficult to find, so individual hog growers must adapt their feed rations to whatever is available. Soybeans—an excellent protein source—do not grow well in Costa Rica. Milo grain is available, but chicken growers compete for that. Bone meal and fish meal are sometimes available but the quality is not consistent. Hence the greatest problem facing a pig grower is finding an adequate supply of satisfactory protein. This problem is evidenced by the fact that it takes more than a year for a pig to grow to 150 lbs (R. Baker, pers. comm.).

Costa Rican weather is favorable to pig raising, since it is never too extreme for the animal. Even so, annual slaughter is about eighty thousand pigs, which yields only 4,000 metric tons of pork. The average number of pigs per hectare in Costa Rica is twelve, compared with eighty-seven cows per hectare and nine horses per hectare (Maroto 1970). Large numbers of pigs are imported, mostly from Nicaragua. There is no hog cholera in Costa Rica. Other diseases and parasites do exist, but apparently they present no more of a threat than in the United States.

*

Hafez, E. S. E., ed. 1962. *The behavior of domestic animals.* Baltimore: Williams and Wilkins.

Maroto, A. S. 1970. *Historia agricola de Costa Rica.* Ciudad Universitaria: "Rodrigo Facio."

Mount, L. E. 1968. *The climatic physiology of the pig.* Baltimore: Williams and Wilkins.

Pineapple (Piña)

D. H. Boucher

Pineapples are members of the monocot family Bromeliaceae, which consists primarily of small epiphytic species, often called "air plants" (Padilla 1973). The genus *Ananas* is centered in South America, and a number of wild species with small fruits are known. The domesticated pineapple, *A. comosus,* is not found in the wild, although it probably originated in the Amazon or Paraná basin. It was already cultivated widely throughout the Americas when Columbus arrived, and he brought it to the Old World on his second voyage. It is now cultivated throughout the tropics, with Hawaii and Malaysia being among the major producing regions.

Costa Rica is not important to the world market, but it does export small amounts of fruit, both fresh and canned, and juice. Estimated 1977 production was 9,000 metric tons, up from 5,000 tons in 1969–71 (FAO 1978). Most commercial plantations are in the Meseta Central west of Alajuela and in the Río Grande de Tárcoles valley, and in adjacent parts of Puntarenas Province.

The pineapple is a rosette plant (fig. 6.16) with long leaves, short internodes, and rather shallow roots. A single large inflorescence grows from the center of the rosette. Between one hundred and two hundred flowers are produced, generally a few each day over a month or more. Although they produce abundant nectar and are visited by pollinating insects, they rarely set viable seeds. Propagation is thus totally by vegetative means. The fruit is multiple, formed by the fusion of all the flowers including their subtending bracts. Mature pineapples are generally yellow, but there are also red-fruited varieties.

Most varieties have originated by somatic mutation, and breeding is difficult owing to the general lack of hybrids. In the most commonly grown variety, the cayenne, both spiny-leaved and spineless types were formerly known, but only the spineless ones ("smooth cayenne") were selected, and now the spiny type is not found in cultivation (León 1968).

The specific name *comosus* means "long-haired" and refers to the trichomes on the undersides of the leaves. These are whitish and can easily be brushed off. Their function has not been established. The upper side of the leaves has a thick cuticle that reduces water loss, and substantial amounts of water can be stored within the leaves. The white fibers in the interior of the leaves can be made into rope or even cloth, though they are seldom exploited commercially as are agave fibers.

The roots are relatively shallow, and toppling of the entire plant can be a problem. Although the fruit may continue to grow, the upper side will suffer from "sunburn." Sowing the plants very densely so that they support each other is helpful. Adventitious roots that grow out near the base can enter the soil and function as normal roots, while those originating higher up on the stem often wind around it.

Propagation can be done in a number of ways. Shoots (called "suckers" and "slips") that grow from the stem can be allowed to root and produce new plants adjacent to the old (the "ratoon crop"). The shoots can also be cut off and planted. In this case it takes 1.5 to 2 years before the first fruit can be harvested.

FIGURE 6.16. *Ananas comosus* plantation in Puerto Rico (photo, D. H. Janzen).

Pineapples grow in a relatively wide range of climates and soils and are raised for home consumption in many parts of Costa Rica. The plant does not tolerate freezing or long periods of drought, but it can grow well in partial shade. Fertilization increases yields but is often unnecessary in fertile volcanic soils. The plant may also be able to absorb nutrients from the rainwater that collects in the axils of the leaves and in the center of the rosette.

The major pests are nematodes, which can cause severe damage. Mealy bugs, scale insects, and mites may also reduce yields. Various fungal diseases cause rotting of the leaves, base, and fruit (Hayes 1960).

The fruit is high in water content and in sugars (8 to 15%). Maturity is indicated by the outside color. Experienced buyers can also detect watery or overripe pineapples by thumping them and listening to the sound.

*

Food and Agriculture Organization (FAO). 1978. *Production yearbook, 1977*. Rome: FAO.

Hayes, W. B. 1960. *Fruit growing in India*. 3d ed. Allahabad: Kitabistan.

León, J. 1968. *Fundamentos botanicos de los cultivos tropicales*. San José: Instituto Interamericano de Ciencias Agricolas de la OEA.

Padilla, V. 1973. *Bromeliads*. New York: Crown.

Potatoes (Papas)

M. T. Jackson

The potato (*Solanum tuberosum*) is a member of the family Solanaceae, as are tomato, pepper, eggplant, and tobacco. Unlike other solanaceous crops, potatoes reproduce both sexually and asexually, although at present commercial potato production is dependent upon the vegetative propagation of the crop through tubers. The life of the individual potato plant begins with the initiation of a tuber on a stolon of the mother plant. The tuber is an underground stem, much enlarged and modified as a food storage organ, with minute scalelike leaves and buds or "eyes." Stolons are underground stems that can become aerial should they reach the surface of the soil. Tubers arise as swellings between the terminal bud and the penultimate expanding internode of the stolon. Potato leaves are imparipinnately compound. The typical inflorescence is a terminal cyme, borne on a peduncle of varying length depending upon the variety.

In Costa Rica two varieties are commonly grown, atzimba and rosita, although the former represents about 85% of all potatoes produced. Atzimba has large light green leaves and is of medium height; its growth is erect. The flowers are white (fig. 6.17a). The tubers are oblong, with smooth white skins and a yellowish flesh; the eyes are of medium depth. The foliage of rosita is a darker green, and its growth habit is also erect. Flowers are lilac. Tubers are oblong, with smooth pink skins; the eyes are deeper than those of atzimba. Unlike many North American and European varieties, flowering is abundant in both these varieties.

In Costa Rica, as in other Central American countries, potatoes are cultivated on less than 1% of the total cropland. However, in Cartago Province, potato cultivation is one of the most important agricultural activities and provides work and income for a considerable sector of the rural population.

In 1976 it was estimated that 3,000 ha of potatoes were planted, with a total production of approximately 50,000 metric tons, of which 98% was produced in Cartago Province. Most potatoes are grown on the slopes of the Irazú volcano (fig. 6.17b), between 1,400 and 3,000 m, where the climate is cool and humid with only a brief (2–4 months) dry season. Other potato areas are found in Heredia Province, in Zarcero, and on the slopes of the Turrialba volcano. The concentration of potato cultivation in a relatively small area of the Central Valley is due to climatic and soil factors as well as to tradition and the proximity of markets in the metropolitan area of San José.

Growing seasons depend not only upon climate, but also upon altitude. The east-facing slopes of the Irazú volcano, around Pacayas, and the Turrialba volcano, are influenced by the Atlantic and are generally wetter. South- and west-facing slopes of the Irazú volcano (Llano Grande, Tierra Blanca, Cot, Potrero Cerrado) and other areas of the Central Valley are influenced by the Pacific climatic regime and have a dry season from January to April.

Between 1,400 m and 2,000 m (Cartago to Potrero Cerrado), planting is done in May and the crop matures in approximately 3.5 months. From Potrero Cerrado to San Juan de Chicuá (2,000 m to 2,800 m) the main season is from April to October, with the crop harvested after 4 months. Above 2,800 m, the duration of the growing cycle is approximately 5 to 6 months, owing to lower temperatures and lower light intensity caused by almost continuous cloud cover. However, the presence of clouds, and consequently humidity, allows the crop to be planted here as early as February or March.

Much of potato cultivation is on steep slopes, and consequently mechanization is used only for land preparation before planting where this is possible. Oxen are commonly utilized for planting, as well as hand labor. Distances between rows are generally 70–80 cm, but distances between plants vary depending upon whether the crop is for seed production or ware production (i.e., for consumption). A distance of 30 cm is generally used to produce ware potatoes. Approximately 2 metric tons of seed potatoes (size 40–60 g) are needed to plant one

FIGURE 6.17. *Solanum tuberosum. a,* Flowers and leaves. *b,* Field in full flower. Above Cartago, Costa Rica (photos, D. H. Janzen).

hectare. Seed potatoes are produced at the highest elevations on the Irazú volcano because insect vectors of virus diseases, as well as wilt-causing bacteria, are less prevalent there.

Potatoes are grown on ridges to give sufficient room for the new tubers and to leave a layer of soil above them. Such a layer helps to prevent green tubers and infection by various pathogens. Planting depths vary according to area, variety, and growing season. Fertilizers and soil insecticides and fungicides are applied in the bottom of the furrow at planting. Tubers are then placed in the furrow and covered with soil to form a small ridge. A layer of loose soil is added to the ridge when plants are 20–40 cm high. Weed growth is also controlled by ridging, carried out by hand or with a ridging implement pulled by oxen.

The potato is subject to many diseases and pests in Costa Rica, and without the efficient use of fungicides and insecticides it is impossible to cultivate potatoes successfully. The major fungal disease, late blight, is caused by *Phytophthora infestans* (Mont.) De Bary. Atzimba was originally bred in Mexico for resistance to late blight. In Costa Rica two factors—the widespread cultivation of this one variety and local climatic conditions—have contributed to the selection of physiological races of the pathogen that overcome the genetic resistance of the variety. Conditions on many parts of the Irazú volcano are ideal for sporulation of the fungus, and weekly fungicide spraying is necessary. Early blight, caused by *Alternaria solani* (Ell. and G. Martin) Sor., is of less importance and is controlled by the same fungicides as late blight. Stem canker, caused by *Rhizoctonia solani* Kühn, is present in many soils because it is easily disseminated on tubers. It causes considerable damage to emerging sprouts when the soil is cold and wet.

Two important bacterial diseases of potato—bacterial wilt, caused by *Pseudomonas solanacearum* E. F. Smith, and blackleg, caused by *Erwinia carotovora* var. *atroseptica* (Van Hall) Dye—are found in Costa Rica. The former is found below 2,220 m and can persist in the soil for many years. Only rotations, including pasture grasses, and the use of healthy seed reduce the severity of attack. Blackleg is a serious problem at altitudes over 2,500 m. It is carried on the surface of the seed tuber and causes a general yellowing and wilting of the plant through a rotting of the stems, which eventually may pass to the tubers.

There are many virus diseases of the potato, of which PLRV (potato leafroll virus), PVX, PVY, and PVS are the most important. Viruses are especially important in seed production, since they cause a degeneration of potato varieties—that is, a reduction in vigor, cropping capacity, and disease resistance over a period of time if tubers from a diseased crop are used as seed for the next. PLRV is prevalent in Costa Rica, and it is estimated that 95% of all potatoes are infected with the virus. It is transmitted by aphids, principally the green peach aphid, *Myzus persicae* Sulzer, and consequently seed tubers are produced in isolated areas, generally at the highest altitudes, where insect vectors are uncommon. PLRV can cause yield reductions of up to 90%. In combination, PVY and PVX can also cause severe yield reductions.

A number of insect pests are common in all potato-producing areas. The most important are the two species of tuber moth, *Phthorimaea operulella* Zeller and *Scrobibalpopsis solanivora* Povolni. These insects attack both the foliage and the developing tubers. *Phthorimaea* larvae often burrow through the stems to the tubers, but it is more common for the female to lay her eggs on exposed tubers, as with *Scrobibalpopsis*. The damage done by both moths is considerable, rendering tubers unmarketable.

Rice and beans are the staple foods in Costa Rica, and consequently potato is utilized as a vegetable. Because of high production costs, it remains expensive and is not a regular food in the diet of the rural poor, despite its high nutritive value. Most potatoes are sold fresh at harvest, as there are no ware potato storage facilities in the country. Only a small portion of the crop is processed, mainly to produce potato chips and frozen french fries.

Current research in Costa Rica is concerned with developing late blight- and virus-resistant varieties, producing healthy seed potatoes, and adapting potatoes to hot, humid conditions. With the development of adapted varieties with genetic resistance to various pests and diseases, the potato has the potential to become a more important component in the diet of a larger proportion of the Costa Rican population.

Rice (Arroz)

J. Stout

Rice (fig. 6.18), the second most important crop grown in Costa Rica in terms of area planted, is a member of the family Gramineae. At germination a seminal root forms, after which secondary root development occurs at stem nodes. These tillers begin forming after the plant has developed four or five leaves. The number of tillers increases as leaves develop on the main stem; the maximum number produced coincides with plant anthesis. Tillers become independent from the parent stem once they develop three leaves and four or five roots of their own. With sufficient sun and water and proper temperature, the capacity to tiller depends on nitrogen and phosphorus concentrations in the soil. Active tillering, important to crop yields, requires more than 3.5% nitrogen and more than 0.25% phosphorus in the soil.

At anthesis one flower is borne on each spikelet, developing laterally from the main panicle. An optimum temperature for pollination and fertilization is 31–32° C. Fertilization success is high if there is sufficient moisture; if a drought or low temperatures occur during this time, crop yields can be severely reduced.

The rice grain is rather invariant in size, unlike grains of wheat and barley, in that the inner and outer glumes containing the developing grain do not expand beyond the size of glume, which assumes maximum size approximately five days before anthesis. Thus rice yields are much more closely related to numbers of tillers, panicles, and spikelets than to individual grain size.

Details on the origin of rice, the basic food plant of Southeast Asia, remain more obscure than for other grain crops in spite of its agricultural importance. It definitely existed as early as 5000 or 3500 B.C. in Thailand, but its origins could date back much farther. From China, rice was introduced to Japan and to Europe during the second century B.C. Rice was brought to the New World soon after the Spanish Conquest.

Oryza sativa, the primary species used in world rice production, is grown principally in the provinces of Guanacaste and Puntarenas on the Pacific side of Costa Rica. In the 1950s Guanacaste Province produced more than 50% of the country's rice. However, there were often severe drought years in that province. During those times, imports of rice were necessary, causing price increases. In the 1960s rice production extended southward along the Pacific Coast at sites where conditions allowed the production of dry rice. (Only about 10% of rice produced in Costa Rica comes from paddy or wetland methods of production). By 1968 Puntarenas Province, south of Guanacaste Province, produced 50% of Costa Rica's rice. Although in Costa Rica rice is second only to coffee production in terms of area under cultivation (63,000 ha versus 82,000 ha), rice is produced for domestic use rather than being an export crop. In fact, rice is often imported to Costa Rica to supplement domestic production.

Most Costa Ricans use rice and beans, either separately or combined in a dish called *gallo pinto,* at every meal. Breakfast usually is gallo pinto; lunch and supper consist of beans and rice served separately, along with fried plantains and possibly a piece of meat or a vegeta-

FIGURE 6.18. *Oryza sativa* plantation near Bagaces, Guanacaste Province, Costa Rica
(photo, D. H. Janzen).

ble. When the price of rice goes up, substitutes can be used, such as yuca, bananas, or plantains, but in normal economic circumstances these are not acceptable replacements.

Rice is grown on large farms in Guanacaste Province, but it is not unusual to see small-acreage farmers growing rice for personal consumption and, in good yield years, for commercial sale. Cultivating and harvesting rice in small fields is a labor-intensive operation. Harvesting often takes place in the intense humidity of the wet season; swinging machetes, bending backs, sweat mixed with chaff in 99% humidity has caused more than one North American OTS staff member to gain respect for the rice she/he ate every day, after experiencing for a few hours the life of a small acreage rice farmer on the Osa Peninsula.

Many pest species attack *O. sativa*. Pentatomid bugs (*Solubea poecila*) sucking on leaves and stems can retard the growth of panicles and damage grains. Noctuid moth larvae can attack leaves and cause serious damage, especially after heavy rains followed by extensive drought. One of the worst diseases of rice is caused by a virus.

Hoja blanca, as the disease is called, can inflict losses up to 75% of the potential yield. As was true for the banana problem in Central America, the best method of preventing the rice viral diseases is to plant varieties that are resistant to the virus.

Large farms, especially in Guanacaste Province (fig. 6.12), make extensive use of fertilizers and insecticides, both of which can increase production of rice for a time, but these expensive methods also reduce the net gain on the sale of the crop. The Costa Rican government is making efforts to develop disease-resistant varieties.

Sugarcane (Caña)

E. D. McCoy

Sugarcane (*Saccharum officinarum* L.) (fig. 6.19) is a perennial grass (Gramineae: Andropogoneae) of Old World origin, most probably originating in New Guinea. The genus *Saccharum* includes six species; four of which are cultigens, unable to survive long in a wild state (*S. officinarum*, *S. barberi* Jeswiet, *S. sinense* Roxb., and *S. edule* Hassk.). *S. spontaneum* L. is widely distributed

FIGURE 6.19. *Saccharum officinarum. a,* Sugarcane fields near Alajuela. *b,* Mature plants with inflorescences near Alajuela; person is reaching to a height of about 2 m. *c,* Tradi- tional manner of taking harvested cane to a small mill, near Heredia, Costa Rica. *d,* A large sugarcane mill in lowland Veracruz, Mexico (photos, D. H. Janzen).

Fig. 6.19 c–d continued next page.

through Africa, Asia, and the Pacific; *S. robustum* Brandes and Jeswiet is confined to New Guinea and neighboring islands. Almost all the commercial cultivars of sugarcane now grown are interspecific hybrids.

Most cultivars are tall (2.5–6 m), and all have a solid, jointed culm. The size, shape, and color of the joints vary with the cultivar and with environmental factors. Sugarcane is grown in a wide variety of climates and soils, mostly between 35°N and 35°S. However, highest yields are obtained in heavy but well-drained, highly fertile soils (fertilizers are often applied) in areas with high temperatures, abundant sunlight, and heavy rainfall (the plants require at least 1,525 mm of rain per year unless grown with irrigation).

The principal sugarcane growing regions are Australia and southern Asia, the West Indies, South America, and the lower part of North America (Mexico and the United States). Central America has never been a major sugarcane-growing region, and the present total area in cultivation there is less than half that in Mexico.

Costa Rica and other Central American countries have substantially increased the production of sugarcane, particularly within the past ten years, and the crop has become relatively important in Costa Rica's economy. Cane sugar production in the country increased steadily but slowly until the early 1950s, when a decline in production began. This decline was halted in the late 1950s, and since then production has accelerated. For instance, output in 1962–63 was about 96,000 metric tons; in 1970–71 it was about 168,000 metric tons.

The relatively low production of sugarcane in Costa Rica in the past has been attributed to several factors (McPherson 1960): the high altitude of much of the cane-growing region, which delays maturity for 15 to 18 months; the irregular topography of the region, which does not allow efficient cultivation; transportation distances; and lack of capital. The decline in production in the early 1950s resulted from the shifting of cultivation from cane to coffee on the small fincas of the Meseta Central. Subsequent increased production in the Pacific provinces, the principal area of sugarcane farming, and a rapid proliferation of production in the Atlantic provinces, particularly San José, Heredia, and Alajuela, accounts for the recent increasing trend in cane sugar output in Costa Rica.

A large suite of diseases and pests of sugarcane are recorded. The major diseases and many of the nematode pests are widespread, but most insect pests are localized (Strong et al. 1977; Williams et al. 1969). Detailed information on cane-associated diseases is available in Hughes et al. (1964) and on cane-associated nematodes in Williams et al. (1969). Box (1953) records only six species of insects as feeding on sugarcane in Costa Rica: *Brassolis isthmia* (Lepidoptera: Brassolidae); *Diatraea guatamalella* and *D. tabernella* (Lepidoptera: Pyralidae); *Saccharicoccus sacchari* (Homoptera: Pseudococcidae); *Phera obtusifrons* (Homoptera: Cicadellidae); and (?) *Ectecephala tripunctata* (Diptera: Chloropidae). *D. lineolata* and *Schistocerca paranensis* (Orthoptera: Acrididae) probably also feed on sugarcane in Costa Rica (Williams et al. 1969). It may well be that the actual number of insect pest species there is larger; about thirty species are known from all of Central America. Central America is relatively depauperate in recorded numbers of pest spe-

cies for many crops, indicating that the region's agricultural pests may be poorly collected. Little work has been done on the biological control of Costa Rican sugarcane pests, but *Trichogramma fasciatum* (Hymenoptera: Trichogrammatidae) and *Paratheresia claripalpus* (Diptera: Tachinidae) are known to parasitize *Diatraea* spp. there.

Rodents are serious pests of sugarcane in many parts of the world. Costa Rica is no exception, and a rich mammalian pest fauna has been recorded for the country. In addition to the ubiquitous *Rattus rattus* and *R. norvegicus* (Rodentia: Muridae), native species of *Zygodontomys* (Rodentia: Cricetidae), and *Heterogeomys* and *Macrogeomys* (Rodentia: Geomyidae) have been observed destroying cane.

*

Barnes, A. C. 1974. *The sugar cane*. New York: Halsted Press.

Box, H. E. 1953. *List of sugar cane insects*. London: Commonwealth Institute of Entomology.

Fernandez, O. J. E. 1906. Estudio de los taladradores de la cana de azúcar del genero *Diatraea* (Pyralidae: Lepidoptera) y su importancia económica en Costa Rica. Thesis, Univsidad de Costa Rica.

Hughes, G. C., et al., eds. 1964. *Sugar cane diseases of the world*. Amsterdam: Elsevier.

Humbert, R. P. 1968. *The growing of sugar cane*. Amsterdam: Elsevier.

McPherson, W. K. 1960. *Informe sobre el cultivo de la cana de azúcar y el desarrollo de la industria azucarera en Costa Rica*. San José: Ministro de Agricultura y Industrias.

Strong, D. R., et al. 1977. Time and the number of herbivore species: The pests of sugar cane. *Ecology* 58:167–75.

Williams, J. R., et al., eds. 1969. *Pests of sugar cane*. Amsterdam: Elsevier.

Vegetables (Legumbres)

M. Holle

Vegetables, defined as perishable plant products that particularly contribute minerals and vitamins to the diet, are found throughout Costa Rica in four characteristic situations:

1. *The homestead garden.* Such gardens are apparently disorganized arrays of plants next to homes, including fruit trees, ornamentals, vegetables, and medicinal and miscellaneous plants. Careful description and analysis of such plantings are lacking for Costa Rica, but they exist for Guatemala (Anderson 1950), Java (Soemarwoto et al. 1975), and the Philippines (Sommers 1978). Casual observation here shows that the important vegetables are chayote (*Sechium edule*), hot peppers (mainly *Capsicum sinense* and *C. frutescens* in the lower altitudes and

C. pubescens above 1,500 m), cherry tomatoes (*Lycopersicon esculentum* var. *cerasiforme*), squash (*Cucurbita* spp.), herbs like "ruda" (*Ruta graveolens*) and roots like cassava (*Manihot esculenta*), sweet potato (*Ipomoea batata*), and some weed forms like *Solanum nigrum,* whose shoots and flowers are occasionally consumed as *picadillo* (a mixture of chopped vegetables with or without scrambled eggs or meat). Most of these plants are managed as perennial crops and can produce throughout the year.

2. *The market-oriented vegetable production system* (*truck farm*). The producer cultivates more than five species at any one time and intends the produce for the local market, mainly larger cities of the Central Valley area (San José, Cartago, Alajuela, Heredia). These operations are scattered, but they are found most often in the areas of:

Cartago: Cervantes (potatoes, tomatoes); Paraíso (leaf crops); Tejar (cabbage, green corn, squashes, snap beans, etc.); Volcán Irazú (potatoes, root crops, cabbage); Guayabo (cabbage, tomatoes, snap beans).

San José: Santa Ana de Escazú (onions); San Antonio de Belén (sweet potatoes, miscellaneous).

Heredia: Santo Domingo (garlic).

Alajuela: Zarcero (a variety of species); La Garita de Alajuela (tomatoes).

Limón: Guápiles/Siquirres (tropical root crops, hot peppers).

In most of these areas production is concentrated in the rainy season (April through December) unless water is available for irrigation. Landholdings are rarely above 15 ha. Tables 6.4 and 6.5 summarize varieties used, agronomic practices, and some of the main disease and insect problems.

3. *The mixed farm.* Normally agronomic crops are alternated with intermittent vegetable crops. This usually constitutes a gamble and provides an opportunity to learn the management of a different and more intensive operation. These units can be found anywhere in the country. Plots rarely are more than 0.5 ha. Crops and characteristics are the same as described above for truck farms.

4. *The industry contract plot.* The farmer arranges with a processor to grow vegetables such as tomatoes, broccoli, hot peppers, cucumbers, and peas for commercial canning, pickling, or freezing. Such operations can sometimes be seen in the Meseta Central and in Guanacaste. There is interest in this type of production, but at this time it is not regular or concentrated, although it will probably continue to develop, possibly in the Guanacaste area (drier than the rest of the country) in connection with irrigation projects.

*

Anderson, E. 1950. An Indian garden at Santa Lucia, Guatemala. *Ceiba* (Honduras) 1:97–103.

Folquer, F. 1976. *Clasificacion botanica y varietal de las hortalizas.* Miscellanea no. 62. Tucuman, Argentina: Facultad de Agronomia y Zootecnia, Universidad Nacional de Tucuman.

Smith, P. G., and Welch, J. E. 1964. Nomenclature of vegetables and condiment herbs grown in the United States. *Proc. Am. Soc. Hort. Sci.* 84:535–48.

Soemarwoto, O., et al. 1975. The Javanese homegarden as an integrated agroecosystem. Paper presented at the International Congress of Scientists on the Human Environment, 16–26 November 1975, Kioto, Japan.

Sommers, P. 1978. Description and analysis of the home garden in four areas of the Philippines. M.S. thesis, University of the Philippines at Los Baños, Institute of Human Ecology (tentative title).

Terrell, E. E. 1977. *A checklist of names for 3,000 vascular plants of economic importance.* Agriculture Handbook no. 505. Washington, D.C.: Agricultural Research Service, USDA.

TABLE 6.4 Common (Spanish and English) and Scientific Names of Plants Grown as Vegetables in Costa Rica

Spanish Name	Scientific Name	English Name	Family
Vegetable Crops			
Acelga	*Beta vulgaris* L.	Swiss chard	Chenopodiaceae
Ají, pimiento, chile	*Capsicum* spp.[a]	Pepper, chili pepper, red pepper	Solanaceae
Ajo	*Allium sativum* L.	Garlic	Liliaceae
Apio	*Apium graveolens* L. (dulce group)	Celery	Umbelliferae
Arveja	*Pisum sativum* L.	Pea, garden pea	Leguminosae
Arracacha	*Arracacia xanthoriza*	—	Umbelliferae
Ayote, zapallo	*Cucurbita* spp.[b]	Squash	Cucurbitaceae
Berenjena	*Solanum melongena*	Eggplant	Solanaceae
Broccoli	*Brassica oleracea* L. (italica group)	Broccoli	Cruciferae
Camote, batata	*Ipomoea batatas* L. (Poir)	Sweet potato	Convolvulaceae

TABLE 6.4—cont.

Spanish Name	Scientific Name	English Name	Family
Caupi, rabiza, frijol de costa	*Vigna sinensis* (Stickm.) Savi Hassk.	Cowpea, southern pea	Leguminosae
Cebolla	*Allium cepa* L. (common onion group)	Onion	Liliaceae
Chayote	*Sechium edule* (Jacq.) Sw.	Chayote	Cucurbitaceae
Coliflor	*Brassica oleracea* (botrytis group)	Cauliflower	Cruciferae
Condeamor	*Momordica charantia* L.	Balsam pear, bitter melon	Cucurbitaceae
Jicama	*Pachyrrhizus erosus* L. (Urban)	Jicama, yam bean	Leguminosae
Lechuga	*Lactuca sativa* L.	Lettuce	Compositae
Maíz (dulce, choclo, elote)	*Zea mays* L.	Sweet corn	Graminae
Melón	*Cucumis melo* L. (reticulatus group)	Melon, muskmelon, cantaloupe	Cucurbitaceae
Okra, quimbombo	*Hibiscus esculentus*	Okra, gumbo	Malvaceae
Papa	*Solanum tuberosum* L.	Potato, Irish potato, white potato	Solanaceae
Pepinillo, pepino	*Cucumis sativus* L.	Cucumber	Cucurbitaceae
Pepino (mata serrano)	*Solanum muricatum* Ait.	Pepino, melon shrub	Solanaceae
Porro, puerro	*Allium ampelloprassum* L. (leek group)	Leek	Liliaceae
Rábano	*Raphanus sativus*	Radish	Cruciferae
Remolacha, betarraga	*Beta vulgaris* L.	Garden beet, table beet	Chenopodiaceae
Repollo (col)	*Brassica oleracea* L. (capitata group)	Cabbage	Cruciferae
Repollo, (col china, pe-sai)	*Brassica campestris* L. (pekinensis group)	Chinese cabbage, pe-tsai	Cruciferae
Sandía, patilla	*Citrullus lanatus* (Thunb.) (Mansf./C. vulgaris)	Watermelon	Cucurbitaceae
Tomate	*Lycopersicon esculentum* Mill.	Tomato	Solanaceae
Vainita, ejote	*Phaseolus vulgaris* L.	Snap bean, green bean, string bean	Leguminosae
Zanahoria	*Daucus carota* L.	Carrot	Umbelliferae

Herbs
(partial list)

Spanish Name	Scientific Name	English Name	Family
Albahaca	*Ocimun bailicum* L.	Basil	Labiatae
Berro de agua	*Nasturtium officinale* R. Brown	Watercress	Cruciferae
Culantro, cilantro	*Coriandrum sativum* L.	Coriander	Umbelliferae
Perejil	*Petroselinum crispum* (Mill.)	Parsley	Umbeliferae
Ruda	*Ruta graveolens* L.	Common rue	Rutaceae

NOTE: Useful supplements to this checklist are Terrell 1977; Folquer 1976; and Smith and Welch 1964.

[a] The species of this genus found cultivated in Costa Rica are *Capsicum annuum* L.; *C. frutensens* L.; *C. baccatum* L. var. *pendulum* (wild) Eshbaugh; *C. pubescens*, Ruiz and Pavón. The first two are most common.

[b] The species of this genus found cultivated in Costa Rica are *Cucurbita moschata* (Duch.) Duch. ex Poir; *C. pepo* L.; *C. ficifolia*—Bouché (chiverre); *C. maxima* Duch.; *C. mixta* Pang. The first two species are the most common.

TABLE 6.5   Descriptive Data for Costa Rican Vegetable Crops

Vegetable (Spanish Name)	Cultivar Commonly Seen	Areas Where Commonly Seen	Type of Farm System	Uses in Local Dishes	Problems with Other Biological Organisms[8]
Acelga	Lucullus	Cartago	2, 1, 2, 3, 4	Cooked, salad, cooked hot sauce	IF, DE, IF, V, N
Ajo	Local (criollo)	Volcán Irazú	2	Condiment	DF
Apio	Tall Utah 52–7 OR, Washington self-blanching	Paraíso	2	Soup, salad (limited)	DF, N
Arracacna	Local	—	1	Cooked	Information limited
Arveja	Reserve early perfection, sprite	Cartago		Soup, cooked, canning	DS, IF
Ayote	Local, sello de oro	Cartago/Tejar, generalized	1, 2, 3	Soup, dessert, cooked	DF, IF, V, N
Berenjena	Black beauty	Cartago (rarely seen)	2	Cooked (limited)	IL
Broccoli	Gem	Meseta Central (rarely seen)	2, 4	Frozen (limited)	IF
Camote	C-15	San Antonio de Belén	2	Cooked	IS, N
Caupi (rabiza)	Centa 105	Rarely seen	1, 2	Same as snap bean	*Atta* spp., DF
Cebolla	Yellow granex, tropicana	Volcán Irazú, Cartago	2	Cooked	DF, DS
Chayote	Local	Ujarrás, generalized	1, 4	Cooked, pickled	DS, IS, DF, N, V
Coliflor	Snowball, X, Y	Volcán Poás	2	Cooked (limited)	IF
Col de bruselas	Jade cross	Meseta Central (rare)	2, 4	Frozen (rarely used)	IF
Cubaces	Local	Above 1,200 m	1, 2	Green seeds cooked	Information limited
Lechuga	White bouton, Great Lakes	Meseta Central	2, 3	Salad	DF, V, IF
Maíz (elote)	Local white and yellow corn varieties	Generalized	2, 3	Cooked, tamales	If
Melón	?	Dry Pacific	3, 4	Fruit	IS, IF, N, DS, V, DF
Okra	Clemson spineless	Rare	2	Rare	IF
Papa	Atzimba	Volcán Irazú	3	Cooked	DF, DS, IF, V
Pepino	Poinsett	Meseta Central	2, 3	Salad, pickled (limited)	Same as melon
Pepino	Local	Rare	1	Fruit	IL
Paerro	American flag	Rare	2	Cooked (limited)	DF, IL
Rábano	Cherry belle	Meseta Central (Cervantes)	2	Salad, fresh	IS, N
Remolacha	Detroit dark red	Meseta Central (Cervantes)	2	Cooked (limited), salad	IS, N

Sowing Practice	Days to Transplant	Days to Harvest	Distance between Rows (m)	Distance within Row (m)	Fertilization (kg/ha) N	P	Number of Applications
Transplant	30	90–120	0.7	0.3	Home garden		—
Direct	120	—	—	—	—	—	—
Direct	45–60	100–150	1.0–1.2	0.4–0.5	200	300	3
Direct (roots)	—	240 130–65	0.15	0.08	90	250	2
Direct	—	60–80	0.2	0.2[1]	150	225	2
Direct	—	90–120	2–3	2–3	100	200	1
Transplant	—	90–180	1.0–1.2	0.6–0.8	n.d.[3]	n.d.	n.d.
Transplant	30	60–90	0.75	0.3	125	300	2
Transplant	—	120–80	0.5	0.2	40	50[7]	1
Direct	—	100–140	0.5	0.1	90	90	2
Transplant	60	90–120	0.10–0.15	0.10–0.15	200 300[2]	300 600	3
Direct	—	Months	Home garden	Home garden[4]	—	—	—
Transplant	30	80–110	0.4	0.6	168	400	2
Transplant	30	90–140	0.5	1.0	200	300	3
Direct	—	Home garden	Home garden	Home garden	—	—	—
Transplant	30	75–90	0.25–0.3	0.25–0.3	100	100	2
Direct	—	100–140	1.0	0.5	90	90	2
Direct	—	120–80	2–3	0.5–1.0	n.d.	n.d.	n.d.
Direct	—	120–80	1.5–2	0.5–1.0	n.d.	n.d.	n.d.
Direct	—	90–120	0.7–1.0	0.2	260	640	1
Direct	—	60–90	1.2	0.2	150	500	2
Transplant	—	Home garden	—	—	—	—	—
Transplant	—	90–150	0.15	0.15	n.d.	n.d.	n.d.
Direct	—	30	0.3	0.1	n.d.	n.d.	n.d.
Direct	—	60–80	0.25	0.03	100	50[6]	2

113

TABLE 6.5—cont.

Vegetable (Spanish Name)	Cultivar Commonly Seen	Areas Where Commonly Seen	Type of Farm System	Uses in Local Dishes	Problems with Other Biological Organisms[8]
Repollo	Golden acre, Copenhagen market	Meseta Central, Zarcero	2, 3	Cooked, salad	IF, DF
Sandía	Charleston gray	Guanacaste	2, 3	Fruit	V, IF, DF, N
Tomato	Tropic floradel, manapal, tripigro, tropared	Meseta Central, Tilaran, Bijagua	2, 3	Cooked, salads, processed	DF, DD, IF, V, N
Vainita	Tendergreen, harvester, Guaria, extender, contender	Meseta Central, Tejar, Guayabo, Volcán Irazú	2, 3	Cooked	DF, DS, IF, V
Zanahoria	Chantanay	Volcán Irazú	2	Cooked soup	IS, DF
Hierbas de sabor	Local	Generalized	1		IL

SOURCE: Most of this information was adapted from O. Pérez Arguedas and C. González Villalobos, *Recomendaciónes para la siembra de hortalizas* (San José: MAG-UCR, 1978.) Additional comments from: W. Canessa and J. Hernández (Estación Experimental Fabio Baudrit, Universidad de Costa Rica, Alajuela, Costa Rica, 1980).
1. Beds 0.9–1.0 m wide.
2. If grown for storage, add 100 kg K_2O/ha.
3. N.d. = no data.

Yuca (Yuca, Cassava)

M. Hansen

In the tropics throughout the world, root tubers frequently are an important source of carbohydrates. In the New World and Africa the most important root crop is *Manihot esculenta* (= *M. utilissima*), of the family Euphorbiaceae, commonly known as yuca, cassava, or manioc (fig. 6.20). It has been under cultivation for so long that it can no longer be found in the wild. The genus is strictly American, although *M. esculenta* is cultivated throughout the tropics, with two centers of specialization: northeastern Brazil and western and southern Mexico. *M. esculenta* is believed to have originated in the former, since a greater variety of cultivars or clones and more uses of the plant exist there, and since the species most closely related to it are also found there (León 1968). Grown in all tropical climates, it is extremely drought resistant and does well in areas where there is a long dry season or rains are sporadic and where the soil is of moderate to poor quality. Although primarily a lowland tropical crop, it can be grown at elevations up to 2,000 m in the Andes. Because it can be grown on very poor soils that are unsuitable for other crops, it is often the last crop planted before a fallow cycle begins or is often the only crop grown. It is cultivated throughout Costa Rica and appears to be most abundant on the west coast.

M. esculenta is a short-lived shrub 1–5 m in height, with large palmate leaves. It is extremely variable in all its characters. The growth form is highly variable depending on clonal variety and method of propagation. Plants grown from seed tend to have a single stout trunk with perhaps a small amount of branching at the apex, whereas those grown vegetatively tend to have a trunk that branches once or twice, with these branches then dividing further into an umbrella-shaped growth form. The latter form is more common, since most propagation by humans is vegetative. Whether the trunk bifurcates close to the ground or higher up, the angle of the branches to the main stem and the angle of leaves to the branches are varietal characters, determining whether the plant has an erect or a spreading growth form.

The leaves are extremely variable in size, shape, color, number of lobes, shape of lobes, and so forth, depending on clonal variety. In general they are near the apex of the branches and are spirally arranged. In form they are large, glabrous, and palmate with from three to eleven lobes, five to seven being average. Shape of the lobes can vary from strictly linear-lanceolate to obovate-lanceolate; in some varieties there is even a distinct bulge than may occur anywhere along the length of the lobe from base to apex (Rogers 1963). The size of a lobe ranges from 4 to 20 cm. Both position on the trunk and environmental conditions affect the number of lobes per leaf. As one

Sowing Practice	Days to Transplant	Days to Harvest	Distance between Rows (m)	Distance within Row (m)	Fertilization (kg/ha)		Number of Applications
					N	P	
Transplant	30	90–120	0.25	0.25	n.d.	n.d.	n.d.
Direct	—	120–50	2–4	1–2	300[5]	600	3
Direct	22	90–150	1.2	0.5	70–150	200	—
Direct	—	60–90	0.1–0.2	—	100	100	2
Direct	—	75–90	0.3	0.3	100	100	2
Direct	—	Home garden	—	—	—	—	—

4. Specialized production practices in Ujarrás/Cartago.
5. Additional foliar applications of Poliboro (500 g per 200 l water) and molybdenum (10 g per 200 l water).
6. If less than 50 ppm of P in soil analysis.
7. Add 100 kg K_2O/ha.
8. IF = foliar insects; IS = soil insects; V = virus; DF = foliar diseases; DS = soil diseases; N = nematodes.

advances up the trunk, the number of lobes per leaf increases; it is not uncommon to find cultivars in which the basal leaves are entire. In addition, the number of lobes is generally smaller during the rainy season than during the dry season. This phenomenon is noticeable within a clone, since the average life of a leaf is only 1–2 months.

The leaves are bicolored, with the top ranging from a bright green to green with a tinge of red to green and yellow variegation, while the underside is more glaucous, ranging from gray to bluish. Color of the midrib and the veins is also variable, ranging from green to yellow to red. In some clones there may be intraleaf variation in the vein color, with a different color on each side of the midrib (León 1968). The petiolar color varies from purple to red to green and from uniform to splotched depending on the variety. The petiole is usually longer than the lamina, being from 20 to 40 cm long. At the base are a pair of lateral stipules that are long or short, have smooth or dentate edges, and usually have three to five lanceolate lobes each. The leaf scars are very noticeable and variable in color, ranging from gray to greenish yellow to dark green, red to dark brown, or streaked with purple.

The inflorescences commonly are in the axils of the leaves, though they may also be near the ends of the branches. They are panicles, or a loose, several-times-branched inflorescence with stalks that are 5–15 cm long and bear approximately fifty to sixty small unisexual flowers, the majority being male, with the female ones situated at the base of the panicle. Hermaphroditic flowers occur in some clones, as do panicles with only staminate flowers. All floral types lack petals; the sepals look like petals. There are five glabrous sepals that vary from greenish to yellow; in some clones they may be tinged with red or purple, either in the center or around the edges. Sepals also contain latex glands, as do most of the other parts of the plant.

Staminate flowers are smaller than pistillate flowers and have a short, straight pedicel 0.5–1.0 cm long and a calyx 6–8 mm long. In the center of the flower is a fleshy orange disk with nectaries; around this are two whorls of stamens, alternately short and long. Pistillate flowers have a long curved pedicel 1–2.5 cm long and a calyx 1 cm or more in length. In the center of the flower is a large yellowish or reddish ten-lobed disk, on which sits an elliptical six-sided ovary 3–4 mm long that contains three carpels, each with a single ovule. The pistil contains a short style that is divided into three finely lobed stigmata. The primary pollinators, thought to be dipterans, visit the flowers, which open for 2–3 h around midday for 8–10 consecutive days. Female flowers open 6–8 days before the male flowers. Very few flowers set seed, a process that takes 5 months. The fruit is a green

FIGURE 6.20. *Manihot utilissima. a,* View under canopy of mature crop. *b,* Tubers (on ground) and sectioned tubers (white ends on table) in market. Guanacaste Province, Costa Rica (photos, D. H. Janzen).

oval capsule 1.5 cm in length and contains three seeds. Upon maturation, the hard capsule explodes and ejects the mottled grayish seeds, which are flat and elliptical, 1 cm long, and have large caruncles attached to them.

When grown from a seed, *M. esculenta* usually has a single main root; tubers develop as swellings on some of the secondary or adventitious roots. When the plant is grown vegetatively, pieces of the stem 20–30 cm long are planted with a few inches sticking out of the top of the soil; adventitious roots, some of which develop into tubers, form from the leaf scars. Extensive variability exists in tuber size, number, shape, color, flavor, and amount of secondary compounds. The average number of tubers per plant is five to ten, each being 5–100 cm long and either cylindrical, branched, or tapering. The tuber consists of two parts: the cortex, or rind, which is variable in color, ranging from white to dark brown or pink to red, and containing the phloem; and the xylem, which is the edible portion of the tuber and composes approximately 80% of total tuber weight. The xylem contains few latex glands. The carbohydrate content, however, is very high; it can supply more calories per area planted than corn, rice, or other tubers. Protein content, on the other hand, is low, averaging 2% of fresh weight. The leaves may contain up to 18% protein and are eaten in parts of Africa in addition to the tubers. Leaves also make excellent cattle fodder owing to their high protein content. The tubers themselves are rich in vitamin B, iron, and phosphorous but are low in calcium (León 1968).

For a long time people thought there were two forms of yuca—one with soft, white, sweet xylem, the other with a tougher, more yellow, bitter xylem—but now it is realized that there is a gradient from the bitter form to the sweet form. The bitterness is due in part to the presence of hydrogen cyanide (HCN) and varies with environmental conditions. In the sweet forms HCN is usually restricted to the rind or cortex, but in the bitter form it is also usually found in the xylem, which must be processed to remove it. The bitter form is found predominantly in areas with very poor soil conditions and can be grown where other crops will not grow. It is long-lived, requiring a year or more to produce tubers. Tuber production may last 3 to 4 years without deterioration in the tuber quality. The sweet form, in contrast, is short-lived, faster growing, and occurs primarily in areas with better soil conditions. Tubers may be harvested after as little as 6 months, but after 9–11 months the tuber quality starts to deteriorate. The flavor of a variety or clone can also

116

change according to environmental conditions—in areas with poorer soils sweet forms may be more bitter but still have the HCN confined to the cortex, while bitter forms may become sweeter when grown in richer soil, independent of the distribution of HCN.

Yuca may be prepared for eating in a number of ways. Sweet yuca can be peeled and eaten raw, whereas bitter yuca must be cooked and repeatedly washed to remove the HCN. Sweet or bitter forms may be cut into strips or sections and boiled, cooked, or fried. Flour can be made from sun-dried slices. Starch is extracted by grinding washed, peeled tubers and then squeezing them in repeated changes of water. It is then cooked or fried before eating. Yuca is also used as a broth for making a type of vegetable stew. In Indonesia it is heated on iron plates, which causes it to agglutinate into small balls, forming tapioca. The major nations importing tapioca are the United States and countries of Europe, where it is used as a dessert and in the manufacture of various confectionery products. The major producer and exporter of tapioca before World War II was Indonesia.

Two viruses are the major serious pests of *M. esculenta*. In many areas the mosaic virus can be a serious problem, causing up to 95% mortality on susceptible cultivars. Vectors for the virus are whiteflies of the genus *Bemisia*. It can also be spread by the use of infected cuttings for propagation. The virus attacks only young leaves, with symptoms occurring in 2–3 weeks if the infection is bad enough and if there are enough vectors. Withered spots first appear on the young leaves and then increase in size, gradually spreading down the petiole into the stem and the root. Infected leaves are usually deformed and small. Brown streak virus is also a serious pest, especially in the coastal regions of Africa. It attacks older leaves, turning them yellow, but no deformation of the leaf blade occurs. Brown streaks appear in the cortical stem tissue and congeal into patches, followed by shrinkage and death of internodal tissue and discolored areas in the roots. The virus also makes the plants sensitive to cold. Mammals such as rats and wild pigs kill much sweet yuca. Few insects are real pests of the plant. *M. esculenta* is cultivated throughout Africa, partially because of its resistance to locusts. There are a number of programs for breeding *M. esculenta* with other species in the same genus in an attempt to produce strains with resistance to the mosaic and black streak viruses as well as to increase the protein content of the leaves.

*

León, J. 1968. *Fundamentos botanicos de los cultivos tropicales*. San José: Instituto Interamericano de Ciencias Agricolas de la OEA.
Purseglove, J. W. 1968. *Tropical crops: Dicotyledons*. Vol. 1. New York: John Wiley.
Rogers, D. J. 1963. Studies of *Manihot esculenta* Grantz and related species. *Bull. Torrey Bot. Club* 90:43–54.

7 PLANTS

INTRODUCTION

G. S. Hartshorn

This chapter is meant to introduce the reader to the vegetation of Costa Rica. Major emphasis is given to the description and ecological understanding, or lack thereof, of the vegetation of the seven field sites on which OTS courses have focused.

General descriptions of tropical forest vegetation can be found in the pantropical coverage by Richards (1952) and Baur (1968) or in the regional treatments by Whitmore (1975) and Longman and Jeník (1974). Though no regional treatment of Neotropical vegetation exists, here I shall attempt to provide a cursory hemispheric perspective.

A significant proportion of our ecological understanding of the vegetation of Costa Rica is a direct consequence of studies done over the past fifteen years by OTS students, professors, and researchers. Studies oriented toward natural history and evolutionary ecology have dominated OTS sponsored or affiliated research. Except for the Holdridge et al. (1971) pilot study of tropical life zones, practically nothing is known of forest ecosystem functions or the ecophysiological processes of tropical plants in their natural habitats (Mooney et al.

1980). By both design and necessity, this chapter takes an evolutionary ecological approach.

The seven sites frequented by OTS courses and emphasized in this chapter are: *Santa Rosa* National Park, *Palo Verde* National Wildlife Refuge (recently renamed Refugio Rafael Lucas Rodriguez Caballero), *La Selva* Biological Reserve, *Corcovado* National Park, *Monteverde* Cloud Forest Reserve, *Las Cruces* Field Station and Tropical Botanical Garden, and the *Cerro* de la Muerte ("Hill of Death"). The shortened vernacular title shown here in italics—for example, La Selva—will be used throughout the chapters on vegetation and plants to represent the correct and longer title, unless specifically stated otherwise.

Botanical Exploration

The middle and late nineteenth century brought many interesting, often eccentric, but very competent European naturalists to Costa Rica (Pittier 1957). The first naturalist to publish an account of the vegetation of Costa Rica was the Danish botanist Andres Oersted (1871), who in 1846–48 made the first substantial collections of Costa Rica's flora. Other notable foreign botanists who collected in Costa Rica include the Polish gardener Warscewicz, the German physician Carl Hoffmann, the

Monospecific stand of *Pterocarpus officinalis* trees in the swamp between the mangroves and the mixed forest at Llorona, Corcovado National Park, Osa Peninsula, Costa Rica (photo, D. H. Janzen).

German gardeners Hermann Wendland and Jules Carmiol, and the German professor Helmut Polakowsky. The German naturalists Moritz Wagner and Carl Scherzer (1856) explored Costa Rica during 1853–54, offering a fascinating account of their arduous journey from Puerto Viejo de Sarapiquí to the Meseta Central.

A new era began in 1887 with the arrival of the Swiss educator, botanist, and naturalist Henri Pittier, the founding of the Museo Nacional, and the official involvement of Costa Rican botanists. Anastasio Alfaro's 1888 listing of higher plants and ferns known from Costa Rica totaled 1,218 species. Standley (1937–38) suggests that three-fourths of the species Alfaro listed were discovered by Oersted. Pittier's laudatory writings indicate a strong and productive collaboration with Anastasio Alfaro that not only greatly increased the knowledge of the Costa Rican flora but was a profound stimulus to Costa Rican botanists and naturalists such as Juan Cooper, Adolfo Tondúz, Pablo Biolley, Carlos Wercklé, and Alberto Brenes. Pittier (1957) culminated sixteen years in Costa Rica with a remarkable essay on the useful plants of Costa Rica (published in 1908). The extraordinary impact of Pittier and Alfaro on Costa Rican botany can be gleaned from Standley's comments that the Costa Rican National Herbarium in 1903 was unequaled south of the Río Grande del Norte (Mexico) and increased the known flora of Costa Rica to about 5,000 species.

After Pittier's departure in 1903, Alberto Brenes made the first systematic collections for Central America in the mountains around San Ramón. Brenes's fine work is evident in the substantial number of endemic species based on his collections and in the fact that some of the new species collected by him in the 1900s have not been collected again. Other Costa Rican botanical contributors of the early 1900s were Otón Jiménez, Ruben Torres Rojas, Juvenal Valerio Rodriguez, and Manuel Valerio.

The 1920s brought the prolific botanist Paul Standley to Costa Rica during the Chicago winters of 1923–24 and 1925–26. Standley's prodigious collecting of 15,000 plants led to the 1937–38 publication of his *Flora of Costa Rica,* an annotated listing of 5,815 species of higher plants native to Costa Rica. Present estimates of the Costa Rican higher plant flora are about 8,000 species (W. Burger, pers. comm.). Such an extraordinarily rich flora in so small a country (51,100 km^2) is truly remarkable and no doubt is still an important attraction to botanists. The Chicago Field Museum of Natural History has recently undertaken to publish a new Flora Costaricensis under the direction of William Burger. Two issues covering fifteen families have been published to date (Burger 1971, 1977).

The first attempts to describe the phytogeography of Costa Rica differentiated a few floristic regions, primarily on the basis of altitude. Pittier (1957) recognized three

altitudinal belts: (1) a basal zone from sea level to 1,000 m with mean annual temperatures between 28° and 21°C; (2) an intermediate or mountainous zone from 1,000 to 2,600 m with mean annual temperatures between 21 and 14°C; and (3) a superior or Andean zone above 2,600 m and mean annual temperatures between 15° and 5°C.

In an enlightened essay on the phytogeographic regions of Costa Rica, Wercklé (1909) describes four regions. (1) Atlantic or Caribbean region from sea level to 800 m; (2) Pacific region from sea level to 800 m; (3) temperate region from 800 to 1,500 m; and (4) cold region above 1,500 m. Wercklé gives 2,000 m as the lower limit of frost. He also says there are no paramos in Costa Rica—a statement no doubt generated by his experience in Colombia and his unfamiliarity with the highest parts of the Talamancas.

Standley (1937–38) follows Wercklé's phytogeographic divisions but states that the cold region must be subdivided into lower and upper belts. Standley is the first to point out the difficulty of assigning a single altitudinal limit to a particular type of vegetation.

Holdridge Life Zones

L. R. Holdridge's dissatisfaction with existing vegetation classification systems applied to the mountainous regions of Haiti led to the development of a new classification system based on simple climatic data (Holdridge 1947). In Latin America, Holdridge's classification system has been extensively used to prepare ecological maps of twelve countries and as a basis for detailed studies of land-use capability, natural resources management, and environmental impact assessment. Preliminary ecological mapping and trial applications of the Holdridge system have also been successfully conducted in Nigeria, Thailand, and East Timor. Because of the objectivity, applicability, and generality of the Holdridge classification system, it is used here as a framework for describing the vegetation of Costa Rica.

Holdridge's classification system gives first importance to temperature and rainfall and the seasonal variation and distribution of these two climatic parameters as the primary determinants of the world vegetation. The bioclimatically defined units are called Life Zones. Although a Holdridge Life Zone may be somewhat analogous to the plant geographer's "formation" or the ecologist's "biome," Holdridge avoids the botanical bias of the former term. Each Holdridge Life Zone has a distinctive vegetation physiognomy and structure that occurs wherever similar bioclimatic conditions exist. Since Holdridge's Life Zone system is independent of floristic relationships, the same Life Zone may occur on opposite sides of the world—for example, the tropical moist forest Life Zone in Latin America, Africa, and Southeast Asia.

119

Holdridge (1967) states that associations of naturally evolved communities of plants and animals are recognizable in the tropics, and he defines an association as a unique ecosystem within a Life Zone that has distinctive environmental conditions and associated plants and animals. Associations form a lower level in the Holdridge classification system. The difference in scale between the Life Zone level and the association level is so great that Tosi has added an intermediate level termed an "association grouping" that is analogous to the "catena" sequence in soil science. The "association grouping" level is particularly useful for medium-scale ecological mapping (Tosi 1976; Hartshorn 1977).

The Life Zone, association grouping, and association levels in Holdridge's hierarchical system are all concerned with natural, undisturbed, or primary vegetation. Man's pervasive and usually disruptive influence on natural vegetation enters into the Holdridge classification system as a fourth-order component. Altered types of vegetation such as pasture or crops and secondary successional stages are described in relation to the naturally occurring associations they replace.

Holdridge's Life Zone system is probably known best for the deceptively simple diagram (fig. 7.1) depicting some thirty hexagonal Life Zones. Actually, the diagram is considerably more complex than it appears, for it is a three-dimensional model of the approximately 116 Life Zones on earth. The diagram consists of three parameters scaled logarithmically and arranged isogonally. Mean annual biotemperature in degrees Celsius is defined as the mean of unit-period temperatures, with zero substituted for all unit-period values below 0° C and above 30° C. Mean annual precipitation in millimeters is used as the second independent parameter. The third parameter in the Life Zone diagram, potential evapotranspiration ratio, is dependent on the two independent parameters; it is the ratio of mean annual potential evapotranspiration (PET) to mean annual precipitation. Since PET is dependent on temperature, Holdridge et al. (1971) derived the constant 58.93 to be multiplied by mean annual biotemperature to give PET in millimeters of precipitation. The PET ratio is a biologically meaningful index of moisture availability; for example, a PET ratio of 1.0 occurs when the mean annual precipitation is equal to the PET, and it also separates humid (PET ratio < 1.0) and subhumid (PET ratio > 1.0) humidity provinces.

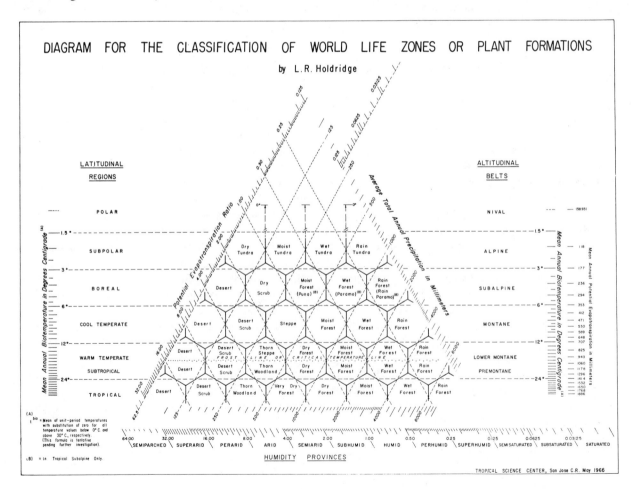

FIGURE 7.1. Diagram of Holdridge Life Zones (Tropical Science Center).

The intersection of any two logarithmic isograms in the diagram forms a boundary point for a Life Zone. A Life Zone is circumscribed by a hexagon formed by a line bisecting the acute angle between any two isograms. The six small triangles formed within each hexagon (between the dashed and solid lines in fig. 7.1) are called transitional areas by Holdridge. In a clockwise sequence from the twelve o'clock position, the transitional areas are termed cool, cool-wet, warm-wet, warm, warm-dry, and cool-dry.

In the Life Zone diagram (fig. 7.1), latitudinal regions are listed on the left and altitudinal belts on the right. Although there appears to be equivalency between latitudinal regions and altitudinal belts, for example, cool temperate and montane, it is important to note the absence of an altitudinal belt equivalent to the tropical latitudinal region. By definition a basal latitudinal region does not have an equivalent altitudinal belt; for example, a cool temperate latitudinal region can have only subalpine, alpine, and nival altitudinal belts, but not a cool temperate montane Life Zone.

The subtropical and warm temperate latitudinal regions, as well as the tropical premontane and lower montane altitudinal belts, are divided by a vague frost line or critical temperature line. Although shown on the diagram at approximately 17° C, the critical temperature line can occur between 12° and 18° C because it is determined by the frequency of killing frosts. In Costa Rica the critical temperature line coincides very well with the upper limit of coffee plantations, the tropical premontane altitudinal belt. Above the "coffee line," land is used for pasture or for frost-tolerant crops such as potatoes and cabbage. Costa Rica's "coffee line" illustrates the advantage of not associating life zone boundaries with specific elevations or degrees of latitude. In the Meseta Central the coffee line is about 1,500 m, but in the protected Dota Valley, coffee extends up to 1,800 m.

At the equator, the theoretical upper limits of altitudinal belts would be 1,000 m for the tropical basal belt, 2,000 m for tropical premontane, 3,000 m for tropical lower montane, 4,000 m for tropical montane, 4,500 m for tropical subalpine, and 4,750 m for tropical alpine. However, these upper altitudinal limits decrease as one moves poleward, until at about 12–13° north latitude tropical premontane becomes the subtropical basal belt (fig. 7.2).

To name a Life Zone, entries for two of the three parameters are required to locate a point within a hexagon. Determination of altitudinal belt and latitudinal region is made by increasing the biotemperature to its sea-level value using the appropriate adiabatic lapse rate.

Holdridge Life Zones in Costa Rica

Because students in OTS courses visit several different ecological areas in Costa Rica, it is appropriate to offer generalized descriptions and distributions for each of the twelve Life Zones that occur in Costa Rica. Table 7.1 gives the areal extent of each Life Zone. Holdridge et al. (1971) is the primary source of the following descriptions.

TROPICAL DRY FOREST

Centered on the lower Río Tempisque, this Life Zone is barely dry. The Tropical Dry Forest Life Zone is ringed by a variable band of cool-wet transitional forest, occurring as a narrow fringe around the Golfo de Nicoya and along the Pacific coast from the head of the Nicoya Peninsual to the Nicaraguan border. Six effectively dry months per year is only about one month longer than for the climatic association in this Life Zone. Edaphic associations occur south of Liberia on soils derived from rhyolitic ash and on the black montmorillonite clay soils in the Tempisque basin. Hydric associations of mangroves occur in the Golfo de Nicoya and in protected bays along the Pacific coast.

The Tropical Dry Forest is a low, semideciduous forest with only two strata of trees. Canopy trees are usually 20–30 m tall, with short, stout trunks and large, spreading, flat-topped crowns, usually not in lateral contact with each other. Many canopy trees have thin, often compound leaves that are dry-season deciduous. Bipinnately leaved mimosoid and caesalpinioid leguminous trees are the most conspicuous canopy component. Understory trees are 10–20 m tall, with slender crooked or leaning trunks and small open crowns with more evergreen species than in the canopy. Rubiaceae is a prominent understory family. The shrub layer is 2–5 m tall, dense in openings, often multiple-stemmed, and armed with thorns or spines. The ground layer is sparse except in openings. Woody vines are common, but herbaceous vines are uncommon. Epiphytes are occasional, with bromeliads the most conspicuous.

TROPICAL MOIST FOREST

Tropical Moist Forest is not only the most extensive Life Zone in Costa Rica but also the most discontinuous. Substantial tracts of Tropical Moist Forest occur on the Nicoya Peninsula, the lower valleys of the Río Grande de Tárcoles, south of Lake Nicaragua, the El General valley and delta of the Río Grande de Térraba, near the mouth of the Golfo Dulce, the coastal lowlands south of Puerto Limón, and the Estrella and Sixaola valleys. Tropical Moist Forest, cool transition occurs on the Pacific flank of the Tilarán and Guanacaste cordilleras between Atenas and Santiago, and in the Turrialba valley. Tropical Moist Forest, cool-wet transition, occurs northwest of Limón, in San Carlos, and around Upala and Lago Caño Negro. The Tropical Moist Forests on the Pacific flank of the cordilleras are mostly an atmospheric association due to a longer than typical dry season caused by rain-shadow

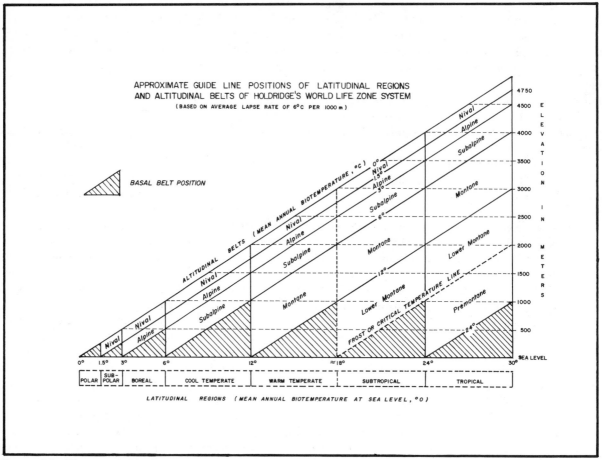

FIGURE 7.2. Diagram of altitudinal distribution of Life Zones with respect to latitude (Tropical Science Center).

effects. The remaining areas of Tropical Moist Forest are close to the climatic association.

Tropical Moist Forest is a tall, multistratal, semi-deciduous or evergreen forest. Canopy trees are 40–50 m tall, mostly with wide crowns and tall, slender boles unbranched for 25–35 m, mostly less than 100 cm dbh, often with high, thin buttresses and smooth, light-colored bark. Subcanopy trees are to 30 m tall, mostly with narrow crowns. Palms, especially *Scheelea rostrata,* are usually abundant, except in cool transitional areas. Understory trees are mostly 8–20 m tall, with round to conical crowns; leaves often have long drip tips. The shrub layer consists of dwarf palms and giant broad-leaved herbs. The ground layer is generally bare except for occasional ferns. Herbaceous vines and woody lianas are abundant, as are epiphytes.

TROPICAL WET FOREST

The second most extensive Life Zone in Costa Rica is the Tropical Wet Forest, with two large blocks at opposite ends of the country: the Sarapiquí and Tortuguero plains in the northeast, and the lowlands surrounding the Golfo

Dulce. Tropical Wet Forest also extends up the Pacific coastal lowlands to the mouth of the Golfo de Nicoya. A substantial band of tropical Wet Forest, cool transition, occurs in the Atlantic foothills all the way from the Panama border to Volcán Orosí. Other Tropical Wet Forest, cool transitional, areas occur inland of the Tropical Wet Forests in the southern Pacific lowlands. In a general sense, most of the Tropical Wet Forest Life Zone in Costa Rica is near the climatic association with a brief effective dry season (Pacific side) or no effective dry season (Atlantic side).

Tropical Wet Forest is a tall, multistratal, evergreen forest. A few canopy species are briefly deciduous, but this does not change the overall evergreen aspect of the forest. Canopy trees are 45–55 m tall, with round to umbrella-shaped crowns, and have clear boles to 30 m and attaining 100–200 cm dbh. Smooth, thin, light-colored bark and high buttresses are common. Subcanopy trees are 30–40 m tall, with round crowns and slender trunks, generally lacking buttresses. Understory trees are 10–25 m tall, with narrow conical crowns and slender boles, often twisted or crooked, usually with

TABLE 7.1. Extent of Life Zones in Costa Rica

Life Zone	Unit km² (%)	Total km² (%)
Tropical Dry Forest		5,263 (10.3)
Tropical Moist Forest		12,366 (24.2)
Nontransitional	10,373 (20.3)	
Cool-dry transition	153 (0.3)	
Cool-wet transition	307 (0.6)	
Cool transition	1,533 (3.0)	
Tropical Wet Forest		11,549 (22.6)
Nontransitional	8,892 (17.4)	
Cool transition	2,657 (5.2)	
Tropical Premontane Moist Forest		2,402 (4.7)
Nontransitional	716 (1.4)	
Warm transition	1,686 (3.3)	
Tropical Premontane Wet Forest		6,950 (13.6)
Nontransitional	2,606 (5.1)	
Warm transition	4,344 (8.5)	
Tropical Premontane Rain Forest		5,008 (9.8)
Tropical Lower Montane Moist Forest		102 (0.2)
Tropical Lower Montane Wet Forest		767 (1.5)
Tropical Lower Montane Rain Forest		3,781 (7.4)
Tropical Montane Wet Forest		51 (0.1)
Tropical Montane Rain Forest		2,759 (5.4)
Tropical Subalpine Rain Páramo		102 (0.2)

SOURCE: Holdridge et al. 1971.

smooth, dark bark, occasionally cauliflorous. Stilt-rooted palms are often abundant. Shrub layer is 1.5–2.5 m tall with abundant dwarf palms; unbranched treelets and giant broad-leaved herbs are occasional. The ground layer is sparse, with a few ferns and *Selaginella*. Woody lianas are not common, and epiphytic shrubs and strangling trees are rare. Tropical Wet Forest is the most species-rich Life Zone in Costa Rica.

TROPICAL PREMONTANE MOIST FOREST

Nontransitional Tropical Premontane Moist Forest is restricted in Costa Rica to two intermountain basins—the densely populated Meseta Central from San José to Turrúcares, and the San Ramón valley. An extensive band of Tropical Premontane Moist Forest, warm transition occurs in the northwestern lowlands between the Tropical Dry Forest, cool-wet transition, and the Tropical Moist Forest. The juxtaposition of a Premontane Life Zone between two basal belt Tropical Life Zones is a consequence of the geometry of Holdridge's diagram. The diagram shows that the biotemperature does not decrease below 24° C as the rainfall increases from about 1,500 mm to more than 2,200 mm. The nontransitional Tropical Premontane Moist Forests are the most altered Life Zone in Costa Rica, with no significant areas of primary forest remaining. The nontransitional Tropical Premontane Moist Forest Life Zone is considered near the climatic association.

Tropical Premontane Moist Forest is a two-layered, semideciduous, seasonal forest of medium height. Canopy trees are mostly dry-season deciduous, about 25 m tall, with characteristically broad, flat, or umbrella-shaped crowns and relatively short, stout trunks, often with thick, fissured, or flaky bark. Compound leaves are very common. Understory trees are 10–20 m tall, evergreen, with round to conical crowns and short, twisted, or crooked boles with smooth or moderately rough bark. The shrub layer is dense, 2–3 m tall, of single- or multiple-stemmed woody plants, some armed with spines. The ground layer is sparse. Epiphytes are rare. Tough, supple, thin-stemmed woody vines are abundant.

TROPICAL PREMONTANE WET FOREST

Nontransitional Tropical Premontane Wet Forest occurs in three areas of Costa Rica: the lower slopes of the El General valley in a position peripheral to Tropical Moist Forest; in the Turrialba area; and in a broad arc on the lower slopes of the Meseta Central, extending in a narrow band along the Pacific flank of the Tilarán and Guanacaste cordilleras. Premontane Wet Forest, warm transition, occupies a large part of the San Carlos lowlands; the Santa Clara plains from Parismina to Puerto Viejo de Sarapiquí, near Guápiles, through Siquirres and Puerto Limón south to the Panamanian border; a narrow band from San Isidro to the Río Cabagra in the El General valley; a substantial band in the Puerto Cortes-Palmar-

Sierpe area; the Corcovado basin and eastern and southern portions of the Osa Peninsula; three areas south of Ciudad Neily adjoining Panama; and an arc from the Río Turrubaritos of Quepos. Tropical Premontane Wet Forest, warm-wet transition, occurs in the San Vito–Coto Brus area. Most of the Tropical Premontane Wet Forest Life Zone can be considered near to the climatic association, although some areas of an atmospheric association occur.

Tropical Premontane Wet Forest is medium to tall, semievergreen forest with two or three strata, with a few canopy species dry-season deciduous. Canopy trees are mostly 30–40 m tall, with mostly round to spreading crowns and relatively short clear boles. Buttresses are common but small. Bark is mostly brown or gray, moderately thick and flaky or fissured. Leaves are often clustered at the twig ends. Understory trees are 10–20 m tall with deep crowns and smooth, often dark bark. Stilt roots and long, strap-shaped leaves are common. Tree ferns are occasional. The shrub layer is 2–3 m tall and often dense. The ground layer is generally bare except for ferns. Epiphytes are present but not conspicuous. Climbing herbaceous vines are abundant. Most trees are covered by a thick layer of moss.

TROPICAL PREMONTANE RAIN FOREST

This Life Zone occurs along the Atlantic slope of the Talamanca, Central, and Tilarán cordilleras; completely rings each volcano in the Guanacaste Cordillera; and occurs in relatively narrow bands on the Pacific slope of the Talamanca Cordillera and the Fila Costeña (coastal range separating the El General valley and the Pacific coast) as far northwest as Cerro Turrúbares. The Tropical Premontane Rain Forest Life Zone is near the climatic association.

Tropical Premontane Rain Forest is an evergreen forest, intermediate in height, with two or three strata. Canopy trees are mostly 30–40 m tall, with round or umbrella-shaped crowns and straight branches. Buttresses are common but small. Bark is brown, black, or gray, moderately thick, mostly flaking or fissured. The subcanopy is very dense, with trees 15–25 m tall, having slender trunks often unbranched for most of their length; narrow, round to conical crowns; and thin light- or dark-colored bark. Palms are common in well-drained situations. Understory is also very dense and may be difficult to distinguish from the subcanopy stratum. Understory trees are 8–15 m tall, often with leaning, crooked, or twisted trunks and relatively long crowns with horizontal branches; many trees have stilt roots. Tree ferns are common in the understory. The shrub layer is 2–3 m tall and very dense. Dwarf palms are uncommon in the shrub layer. The ground layer consists of a nearly complete cover of ferns, *Selaginella* and broad-leaved herbs, often with bluish leaves. Epiphytes, woody vines, and herbaceous climbers are very abundant. Moss and epiphytes cover practially all surfaces.

TROPICAL LOWER MONTANE MOIST FOREST

This Life Zone occurs in three small areas of Costa Rica—north and southwest of Cartago and around the town of Zarcero. These small areas are considered near the climatic association for the Life Zone.

Tropical Lower Montane Moist Forest is an open evergreen forest of intermediate height with two tree strata. Canopy trees are mostly *Quercus,* 30–35 m tall, with heavy, gnarled branches and thick, twisted boles and thick, scaling, or rough bark. The understory is fairly open, with evergreen trees to 20 m in height, having slender trunks and round to conical crowns. The shrub layer is 2–5 m tall, fairly dense, with soft-wooded plants and often with large leaves. The ground layer is mostly open, with scattered broad-leaved herbs and grasses. Although a few epiphytic trees occur, epiphytic herbs and mosses are inconspicuous.

TROPICAL LOWER MONTANE WET FOREST

The Tropical Lower Montane Wet Forest Life Zone is primarily restricted to central Costa Rica, with the most substantial area along the southwest flank of the Central Cordillera; also south of San José and Cartago and in the Dota valley. Small outliers occur on the Pacific flank of the Tilarán Cordillera, in the upper valley of the Río Chirripó del Pacífica, and on the Pacific flank of the Talamanca Cordillera near the Panama border. These forests are considered to be the climatic association for this Life Zone.

Tropical Lower Montane Wet Forest is an evergreen forest of intermediate height with two tree strata. Canopy trees are mostly 20–25 m tall, but some *Quercus* are taller, with short, stout trunks dividing into numerous long, heavy, twisting, ascending branches, producing wide, umbrella-shaped, billowing crowns. Buttresses are uncommon. Bark is thick, mostly flaking or fissured. The understory is fairly open, with trees 5–10 m tall, having spreading crowns. The shrub layer is relatively dense, 2–3 m tall, and palms are uncommon. The ground layer is well-covered with ferns, *Begonia,* aroid vines, and a thick layer of moist, rotting leaves. Small orchids, bromeliads, and ferns are common epiphytes. A thin layer of moss grows on tree trunks. Herbaceous vines, especially Araceae, are common at and near ground level. Large, coiled lianas are occasional to common.

TROPICAL LOWER MONTANE RAIN FOREST

This Life Zone occurs extensively on the windward flanks of the Central Cordillera, both flanks of the Talamanca Cordillera, the top of the Tilarán Cordillera, and around the volcanic summits in the Guanacaste Cordillera. The forests are mostly in the climatic association for this Life Zone.

Tropical Lower Montane Rain Forest is an evergreen forest of low to intermediate height, with two tree strata. Canopy trees are mostly 25–30 m tall, but *Quercus* may reach 50 m, having short, stout, often twisted trunks with rough, dark bark. Branches are thick, sinuous, and relatively short. Crowns are relatively small and compact. Buttresses are uncommon. Understory stratum is often dense, with trees 10–20 m tall. Trunks are slender, straight or sinuous, with small, brushlike crowns of twisted branches. Bark is smooth, thin, and mostly dark. Suckers are common at the base of the trunk. The Shrub layer is very dense, 1.5–3 m tall, often with flat sprays of small leaves. The ground layer is very well covered with ferns, sedges, delicate trailing herbs, and patches of moss. Epiphytes (orchids, bromeliads, gesneriads, and aroids) are common in the moss covering trunks and branches. Ericaceae and Melastomataceae are abundant shrubby epiphytes. Large-leaved vines are occasional, but large lianas are uncommon.

TROPICAL MONTANE WET FOREST

This Life Zone is restricted in Costa Rica to the summit and upper southwest slopes of Volcán Irazú. Most of the vegetation near the Irazú crater was destroyed or severely damaged by the volcanic eruptions of 1963–65; hence no data is available for this Life Zone.

Tropical Montane Wet Forest should be an evergreen forest of intermediate height and two tree strata. The canopy should be dominated by *Quercus* spp. Bamboos should be abundant in the shrub layer.

TROPICAL MONTANE RAIN FOREST

The Tropical Montane Rain Forest Life Zone occurs extensively in the high Talamancas, with small outliers round the summits of Turrialba, Irazú, Barba, and Poás volcanoes. The Life Zone in Costa Rica is considered to be the climatic association, except near the active volcanic craters.

Tropical Montane Rain Forest is an evergreen forest of low to intermediate height with two tree strata. Canopy trees are 25–30 m tall, having short, stout, unbuttressed trunks with rough bark. Crowns are small, compact, and rounded, with many thick, short, twisting branches. Leaves are often clustered at the twig tip. The understory is fairly open, with trees mostly 5–15 m tall, having slender, crooked trunks and compact, much-branched, brushlike crowns. Tree ferns are common in the understory. The shrub layer is dense, with dwarf bamboos up to 5 m tall. The ground layer is open under the bamboo. Trunks and branches of trees are thickly covered with moss and small herbaceous epiphytes; orchids and ferns are common in the moss. Large epiphytes are restricted

to a few species of bromeliads. Woody vines with thick, fleshy leaves are common as canopy epiphytes.

TROPICAL SUBALPINE RAIN PÁRAMO

This Life Zone is the northernmost occurrence of Andean Páramo, originally restricted to the highest peaks (Chirripó) of the Talamancas, but extending downward in the Cerro de la Muerte region owing to human disturbance. Páramo refers to cold, inhospitable, and humid landscape above the tree line. In the northern Andes and in Costa Rica páramo is dominated by shrubs where drainage is adequate, but bogs occur where drainage is poor. Andean páramos are best known for the tree espeletias (Compositae), which dominates the landscape. Costa Rican páramos and their floristic and physiognomic relationships with Andean páramos are described in detail by Weber (1959).

Site Descriptions
SANTA ROSA

Santa Rosa National Park (fig. 7.3) is in northern Guanacaste Province, between the Golfo de Papagayo and the Inter-American Highway, with geographical coordinates 10°45' to 11°00' N and 85°30' to 85°45' W. The 10,700 ha national park was created by executive decrees no. 1562-A on 20 March 1971 and no. 7013-A on 4 May 1977. Boza and Bonilla (1978) give a detailed description of the unique setting Santa Rosa has had in Costa Rican history, as well as several superb color photographs of the more important habitats in the park. Elevations range from 317 m to sea level.

An approximately east-west physiographic transect starts with an extensive upper plateau formed by Plio-Pleistocene lava flows and aeolian ash deposits from the Cordillera de Guanacaste. West of the upper plateau are a series of lower terraces derived from basalt parent material with substantial inputs of ash. The lower terraces are interspersed among low but rugged basalt hills that extend to the coast, forming the rocky headlands protecting small beaches.

According to the ecological map of Costa Rica (Tosi 1969), the upper plateau of Santa Rosa is mapped as tropical premontane moist forest, warm transition, whereas a substantial band of tropical dry forest, cool-moist transition, occurs along the Pacific coast. These two life zones are very similar climatically, receiving between 1,500 and 2,000 mm of average annual rainfall, but the upper plateau has a slightly cooler mean annual biotemperature.

The vegetation of the upper plateau is dominated by the African pasture grass jaragua (*Hyparrhenia rufa*) with occasional islands of trees. It is quite clear that no natural savannas exist in nonswamp areas of Guanacaste because of the necessity for burning the pastures annually to pre-

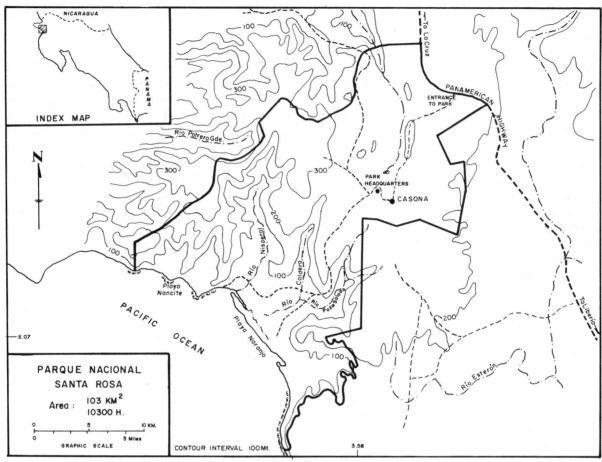

FIGURE 7.3. Map of Santa Rosa National Park (Tropical Science Center).

vent woody encroachment and colonization (Daubenmire 1972). The jaragua grasslands on the upper plateau were no doubt derived from the evergreen oak (*Quercus oleoides*) forest characteristic of the pumice/ash soils of the seasonally dry lowlands of Central America (Montoya Maquín 1966). The species-poor oak forest that originally covered parts of the upper plateau can be considered an edaphic-atmospheric association because of the poor soils and a longer than average dry season. Table 7.2 provides compositional information on a remnant stand near the entrance to Comelco Ranch, Bagaces, that I believe is representative of the oak forest that once covered the upper plateau of Santa Rosa. Within the grasslands on the plateau occur patches of *Crescentia alata* (Bignoniaceae) trees forming an edaphic-hydric association on dimensionally unstable montmorillonite clay soils. Scattered, fire-resistant trees of *Byrsonima crassifolia* (Malpighiaceae) and *Curatella americana* (Dilleniaceae) dot the jaragua grasslands.

As the upper plateau drops off to the west and north, a complex series of habitats and vegetation types occur on varied physiography ranging from small colluvial terraces and intermittent stream valleys to rocky outcrops and sheltered coves. The actual vegetation of this region is further complicated by a long history of uncertain and varied activities including the more obvious forest clearing for pasture and the less obvious selective logging and the browsing of hungry bovines during the severe dry season (fig. 7.4). The degree of disturbance spans a broad spectrum, making it difficult to comment on the naturalness of the vegetation. D. H. Janzen (pers. comm.) believes the most undisturbed vegetation occurs in the lower valleys and north-facing slopes of the Río Poza Salada watershed.

The heterogeneous forests on the lower slopes are the most biologically diverse habitats in Santa Rosa. Even though the forest is well developed on the basalt-derived soils, it must still be considered an atmospheric association owing to the longer-than-normal dry season. Some of the trees attain 30 m in height, but the canopy is generally about 20 m tall. Common tree species include *Bombacopsis quinatum, Calycophyllum candidissimum, Casearia arguta, Chomelia spinosa, Croton reflexifolius, Enterolobium cyclocarpum, Eugenia salamensis, Gua-*

TABLE 7.2. Stand Characteristics of a 4 Ha Plot 0.5 Km North of the Entrance to Comelco Ranch, 10 Km Northwest of Bagaces, Guanacaste Province

Species	Density Stems (%)	Frequency Subplots (%)	Basal Area m^2 (%)	Importance Value (%)
Quercus oleoides	279 (34)	81 (18)	29.2 (58)	36.77
Byrsonima crassifolia	99 (12)	51 (11)	3.2 (6.3)	9.99
Apeiba tibourbou	92 (11)	48 (11)	3.0 (5.9)	9.33
Spondias mombin	61 (7.5)	35 (7.9)	3.3 (6.6)	7.32
Cordia alliodora	43 (5.3)	33 (7.4)	0.9 (1.8)	4.82
Guazuma ulmifolia	24 (3.0)	18 (4.1)	1.1 (2.1)	3.04
Luehea candida	19 (2.3)	15 (3.4)	1.1 (2.1)	2.61
Annona reticulata	24 (3.0)	17 (3.8)	0.4 (0.9)	2.54
Luehea speciosa	16 (2.0)	12 (2.7)	1.0 (2.0)	2.21
Cochlospermum vitifolium	12 (1.5)	12 (2.7)	0.9 (1.7)	1.96
Subtotal: top 10 species	669 (82)	322 (73)	44.1 (87)	80.59
Subtotal: other 34 species	145 (18)	118 (27)	6.6 (13)	19.41
Total: 44 species	814 (100)	440 (100)	50.7 (100)	100.00

zuma ulmifolia, Jacquinia pungens, Luehea candida, Piper amalago, Pithecellobium saman, Tabebuia ochracea, T. rosea, Thouinidium decandrum, Trichilia colimana, and Zanthoxylum setulosum. The canopy trees are generally deciduous except in the moist coves, where the evergreen trees Andira inermis, Ardisia revoluta, Ficus, Hymenaea courbaril, Mastichodendron capiri, and Manilkara zapota are locally abundant. Unfortunately, no studies have been made of the forest vegetation of Santa Rosa; thus it is impossible to comment upon forest dominance and diversity patterns.

Near the coast the valleys broaden, with appreciable areas of fertile alluvial flatlands crossed by meandering wet-season creeks. Remnant and probably degraded patches of the natural forest exist along the roads to Playa Naranjo. This edaphic association supports an impressive forest with a general canopy of about 30 m, although some trees may exceed 35 m, a fairly high density of large trees, and many evergreen species. Some of the more prominent tree species are Brosimum alicastrum, B. guianense, Hura crepitans, Licania arbora, Manilkara zapota, and Terminalia oblonga. Many of the larger M. zapota trees bear the scars of chicle tapping. The chicleros no doubt entered the small fertile valleys from the coast.

Coastal access by boat also brought in several farmers who practiced slash-and-burn agriculture over much of the valley bottomlands; however, it is unlikely that a true shifting cultivation occurred. Many of the small fields (1–5 ha) cleared in the 1960s are now in the early stages of secondary succession with an abundance of pioneer and shade-intolerant tree species such as Castilla elastica, Cecropia peltata, Cochlospermum vitifolium, Guazuma ulmifolia, and Muntingia calabura. The secondary forest

just southwest of the main fork in the road to opposite ends of Playa Naranjo was in active cultivation for agriculture in 1970 (R. Peck, pers. comm.).

As drainage becomes poorer nearer the foredunes, the mixed bottomland forest grades to a swamp forest, dominated by Caesalpinia coriaria and Prosopis juliflora. With the influence of brackish and salt water, there occur small fringe areas of mangroves containing the characteristic tree species Rhizophora mangle, Avicennia germinans, Laguncularia racemosa, and Conocarpus erecta (Pool, Snedaker, and Lugo 1977). The absence of permanent freshwater streams is probably an important restriction on the extent of mangroves and swamp forest in Santa Rosa.

The coastal strand vegetation is quite representative of tropical beaches, with Ipomoea pes-caprae, Canavalia maritima, Hibiscus tiliaceous, and Hippomane mancinella.

The rocky headlands have perhaps the most xeric vegetation in Costa Rica owing to the paucity of soil and exposure to dry winds. The stunted, shrubby vegetation consists of distinctive dwarf trees of Bursera permollis, Euphorbia schlechtendalii, and Haematoxylon brasiletto, plus cacti and agaves.

PALO VERDE

The Refugio Rafael Lucas Rodriguez Caballero (Palo Verde National Wildlife Refuge) lies in the lower Tempisque depression near the head of the Golfo de Nicoya in south-central Guanacaste Province. Geographical coordinates are 10°19′ to 10°24′N and 85°18′ to 85°25′W, covering an area of 4,757 ha. Palo Verde was the southern end of an enormous ranch established by David Russell Stewart in 1923 that extended from the Río Tem-

FIGURE 7.4. *a,* Deciduous forest, 70–100 years of age, on 1 May 1980 (8 days before the first rain at the end of the dry season) in the uplands of Santa Rosa National Park. There are at least twenty-five species of woody plants in this photograph; the large tree just to the left of center is *Ateleia herbert-smithii* (photo, D. H. Janzen). *b,* Deciduous forest, 70–100 years of age, on 1 June 1980 (22 days after the first rain of the year) in the uplands of Santa Rosa National Park. There are at least thirty species of woody plants in this photograph; the large crown slightly to the left of upper center is *Tabebuia ochracea* (photo, D. H. Janzen).

pisque to the slopes of Volcán Miravalles. The property is commonly known as Finca Wilson, because Stewart temporarily used the pseudonym George Wilson in the 1920s. In 1968 the Organization for Tropical Studies chose the Palo Verde area as the dry forest site for a comparative ecosystem study. An OTS–Comelco contractual agreement leased Palo Verde and several other sites on the Comelco ranch to OTS for research and teaching operations; OTS completed the construction of a field station adjacent to the airstrip during the 1971 dry season. The Costa Rican government expropriated much of the Comelco ranch, including Palo Verde in 1975 for an ITCO agricultural colonization project. The Palo Verde National Wildlife Refuge (fig. 7.5) was created by executive decree on 29 April 1977. Since that time numerous reports and promises of major extensions to the northwest and southeast have emanated from government

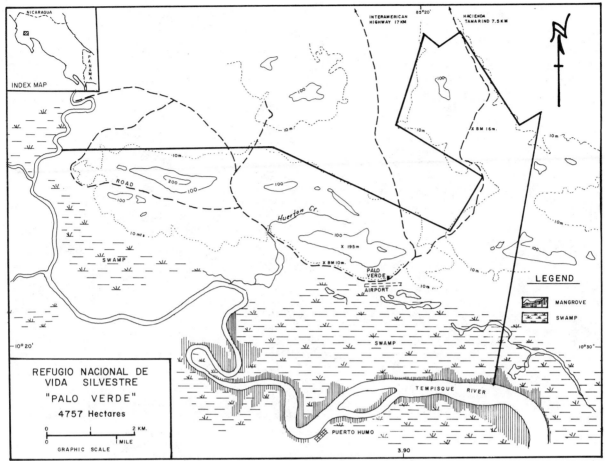

FIGURE 7.5. Map of Palo Verde National Wildlife Refuge (Tropical Science Center).

officials, but to date no extensions have been added to Palo Verde.

The uniqueness of Palo Verde lies in the juxtaposition of a large seasonal swamp between the Río Tempisque and abrupt limestone hills (fig. 7.6a). The isolated chain of hills more of less paralleling the dominant west–east course of the Tempisque consist of hard, porous Eocene limestone. Maximum elevations are about 200 m. The ridges and upper slopes generally lack soil, so it is an extremely xeric habitat during the dry season. The colluvial deposits on the lower slopes and at the base of the hills are derived from the limestone with admixtures of clay and silt sediments. Away from the bases of the limestone hills are vast expanses of dimensionally unstable black soils consisting almost entirely of montmorillonite clay. The 2×2 lattice structure of the clay micelles permits considerable incorporation of water molecules during the wet season and a substantial dry-season loss of water, producing large cracks in the soil.

The entire Palo Verde area is mapped as tropical dry forest (Tosi 1969), with expected mean annual rainfall between 1,000 and 1,500 mm and mean annual bio-

temperature above 24° C. The lower Tempisque basin is in the driest area of Costa Rica. The entire area is an atmospheric association because of the six-month dry season (December–May) and the strong, dry trade winds that parch the Guanacaste lowlands from December to March. Although the rainy season usually starts abruptly in April or May (local farmers say 6 weeks after Easter), a less-rainy spell of 2 or 3 weeks, called the *veranillo,* often occurs in July. The heavy rains and associated flooding caused by Pacific storms occur in September and October.

On the exposed limestone outcrops occur agaves and stunted trees similar to the vegetation on the dry ridges of the rocky coastal headlands of Santa Rosa. *Euphorbia schlectendalii* and *Rehdera trinervis* are two of the conspicuous small trees in this habitat. Many of the limestone ridges and upper slopes are composed of very sharp, deeply creviced "dogtooth" limestone, often with surface scalloping strikingly suggestive of the lapping of waves. The deep crevices in the porous limestone permit deep rooting, with the consequence of a taller (10–15 m), more closed forest than on the shallow basalt outcrops in

129

FIGURE 7.6. *a*, Palo Verde marsh viewed from limestone cliff early in the dry season; note airstrip in foreground and gallery forest along Río Tempisque at top of photo. *b*, Palo Verde marsh and limestone hills in the middle of the rainy season; note absence of trees (photos, G. S. Hartshorn).

130

Santa Rosa. Probably the most distinctive plant growing on the dogtooth limestone is the endangered "lignum vitae" tree *Guaiacum sanctum*, associated with *Lemaireocereus aragonii, Bursera simaruba, Bombacopsis quinatum,* and *Astronium graveolens.*

As soil depth increases on the lower slopes and at the base of the limestone hills, a much better developed, more species-rich forest occurs. Protected coves (fig. 7.6*b*) occur on the south side of the limestone hills, with several evergreen species of trees, such as *Brosimum alicastrum, Garcia nutans, Manilkara zapota, Sapindus saponaria,* and *Trophis racemosa.* These moist evergreen coves are important dry-season refugia for arboreal and flying herbivores.

Along the south side of the limestone hills is a 100–200 m wide band of deep soils between the base of the hills and the seasonal marshes and floodlands. These well-drained colluvial soils in the vicinity of the hacienda are now mostly in pasture, but about 8 km west of the field station is a beautiful forest that could well be the least-disturbed lowland dry forest in Guanacaste. Common tree species include *Bombacopsis quinatum, Caesalpinia eriostachys, Calycophyllum candidissimum, Capparis odoratissima, Casearia arguta, Chomelia spinosa, Croton reflexifolius, Enterolobium cyclocarpum, Erythroxylon havanense, Eugenia salamensis, Guazuma ulmifolia, Jacquinia pungens, Luehea candida, Piper amalago, Tabebuia ochracea, T. rosea, Thouinidium decandrum, Trichilia colimana,* and *Zanthoxylum setulosum.* The most important tree species on a 4 ha permanent inventory plot in this forest (along the old road to the former apiary) are given in table 7.3. Along the numerous intermittent streams draining the limestone hills, the following tree species are locally abundant:

Ardisia revoluta, Brosimum alicastrum, Licania arborea, Manilkara zapota, and *Sloanea terniflora.* Notably absent from the Palo Verde forest is *Hymenaea courbaril;* it is not known whether *H. courbaril* will not grow on limestone-derived soils or whether it was unable to reach Palo Verde over the extensive montmorillonite clay flatlands.

Between the limestone hills and the Río Tempisque are large seasonally flooded, herbaceous marshes dominated by a Juncaceae, *Typha latifolia,* and *Thalia geniculata.* The woody shrub *Ipomoea* sp. and the Palo Verde tree, *Parkinsonia aculeata,* are scattered through the marsh. High water levels occur in September or October, with moist areas remaining until March.

Narrow bands of mangroves with the characteristic species *Rhizophora mangle, Avicennia germinans, Laguncularia racemosa,* and *Conocarpus erecta* occur along the Río Tempisque owing to tidal action and brackish water. The natural levee supports a much taller and more heterogeneous riparian forest with some unusual tree species that have yet to be identified.

As is true for all of Guanacaste, fire and cattle browsing have had pervasive influences on the vegetation, yet those effects appear to have been minimal in Palo Verde. Fires regularly (annually?) sweep south toward Palo Verde, but they seem to seldom cross the limestone hills. The exceptional forest along the apiary road had a light ground fire in 1978, the first since the plot was established in 1970. The browsing effect of cattle is more difficult to determine. Comelco cattle would move into the forest to browse after the pastures dried up. We were unable to find seedlings or small saplings of *Brosimum alicastrum* in the inventory plot (G. S. Hartshorn, unpub. data), suggesting that cattle browsing may have ad-

TABLE 7.3　Stand Characteristics of a 4 Ha Plot along the Apiary Road, Palo Verde Wildlife Refuge, Guanacaste Province

Species	Density Stems (%)	Frequency Subplots (%)	Basal m^2 (%)	Importance Value (%)
Calycophyllum candidissimum	55 (6.3)	41 (5.9)	16.6 (20.8)	11.02
Licania arborea	55 (6.3)	39 (5.6)	5.9 (7.4)	6.43
Brosimum alicastrum	32 (3.7)	20 (2.9)	7.5 (9.4)	5.33
Spondias mombin	45 (5.1)	31 (4.5)	4.2 (5.3)	4.99
Guazuma ulmifolia	53 (6.1)	35 (5.1)	2.7 (3.4)	4.86
Thouinidium decandrum	42 (4.8)	29 (4.2)	1.4 (1.8)	3.61
Caesalpinia eriostachys	26 (3.0)	19 (2.8)	4.0 (5.0)	3.56
Luehea candida	36 (4.1)	30 (4.3)	1.4 (1.7)	3.39
Tabebuia ochracea	36 (4.1)	29 (4.2)	0.9 (1.2)	3.15
Bombacopsis quinatum	15 (1.7)	14 (2.0)	4.4 (5.5)	3.07
Subtotal: top 10 species	395 (45)	287 (42)	49.0 (62)	49.41
Subtotal: other 58 species	480 (55)	404 (58)	30.4 (38)	50.59
Total: 68 species	875 (100)	691 (100)	79.4 (100)	100.00

versely affected the regeneration of palatable species. Comelco cattle also moved into the seasonal marsh during the dry season. F. G. Stiles (pers. comm.) believes cattle have played an important role in maintaining areas of open water in the marsh.

CORCOVADO

Corcovado National Park (fig. 7.7) is in southern Puntarenas Province, on the Pacific side of the Osa Peninsula, with geographical coordinates 8°26′ to 8°39′N and 83°25′ to 83°45′W. The 43,735 ha national park was created by executive decree number 5357 on 24 October 1975. The original area of 36,000 ha was enlarged by executive decree on 5 February 1980, adding 7,735 ha of rugged highlands in the center of the peninsula. Elevations range from sea level to 745 m on the Cerros Rincón and Mueller in the Fila Matajambre. A detailed study of land use and conservation on the Osa Peninsula has recently been completed (Lewis 1982). The Osa is part of the area treated by P. H. Allen (1956) in his excellent book *The Rain Forests of Golfo Dulce,* though there is no record of his working on the peninsula.

The park includes the entire drainage of the Corcovado "plain," a sediment-filled oceanic embayment between Punta Llorona and Punta Salsipuedes that extends 5–10 km inland. The Corcovado plain covers about 10,000 ha ringed with steep and broken uplands on three sides and the Pacific Ocean on the southwest. Intense geological weathering has produced a physiography of narrow ridges, long and steep slopes, and a dense drainage network that dominates practically all of the uplands except for an undulating plateau in the northwest part of the park.

Tosi (1973) and Vaughn (1979) recognize and briefly describe thirteen major ecosystems within Corcovado National Park: intertidal (both rocky and sandy), mangroves, lagoon with floating herbaceous vegetation, herbaceous swamp, palm swamp, swamp forest, low forest on poorly drained alluvium, forest on well-drained terraces and alluvial plains, forest on undulating plateau, forest on low broken hills, forest on low steep hills, mountainous forest, and cloud forest. Detailed studies of the vegetation of Corcovado will probably yield twenty-five to thirty discernible associations. Although no

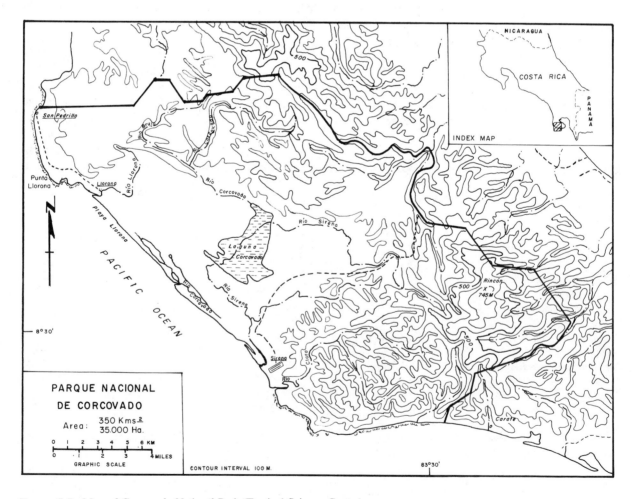

FIGURE 7.7. Map of Corcovado National Park (Tropical Science Center).

weather stations exist within the park, the Corcovado plain is mapped as tropical premontane wet forest, warm transition, whereas the uplands are mapped as tropical wet forest (Tosi 1969). Recent impressions of T. J. Lewis on the vegetation of the highest peaks in the center of the peninsula strongly suggest the occurrence of tropical premontane rain forest. The Corcovado plain should receive an average annual rainfall between 3,000 and 3,800 mm; the tropical wet forest uplands receive more than 4,000 mm. The actual vegetation suggests that annual rainfall in the high interior of the peninsula could be between 5,000 and 6,000 mm. Essentially all of the uplands can be considered to be the climatic association, while the Corcovado plain consists of several edaphic and hydric associations.

The lowlands of southern Costa Rica are the only wet forests still extant on the Pacific side of Central America. The abundant rainfall coupled with a short three-month dry season seems to be ideal for tree growth, for these forests are by far the most exuberant in Central America. In fact, the Corcovado forests are just as impressive in height as the best forests I have seen in the Amazon basin or the dipterocarp forests of Malaysia and Indonesia. The Pacific lowland wet forests in southern Costa Rica have strong floristic affinities with the Colombian Chocó. South American tree genera such as *Anthodiscus, Batocarpus, Cariniana, Caryocar, Chaunochiton, Couratari, Crematosperma, Huberodendron, Iryanthera, Parkia, Peltogyne, Uribea,* and *Vantanea* all reach their northern limits in southern Costa Rica. Many of these genera occurred in the El General valley (L. R. Holdridge, pers. comm.), but wholesale deforestation in southern Costa Rica probably means they will remain only in Corcovado National Park.

The Corcovado forests exemplify the popular conception of the tropical rain forest, with a multitude of species, very tall trees, spectacular buttresses, large woody lianas, and abundant herbaceous vines. Holdridge et al. (1971) report that the most outstanding feature of their upland study site about 5.5 km west of Rincón near the northwest corner of the Golfo Dulce is the extreme height of the forest; they encountered twenty-two species over 50 m tall, five species that exceeded 60 m, and one, *Minquartia guianensis,* that reached 73 m. The most important tree species on Holdridge's study site 8A are given in table 7.4. The complete absence of dominance is characteristic of the upland forests in Corcovado; however, the particular species most important in Holdridge's small sample are not necessarily the most important species in the park. Common tree species on the uplands of Corcovado include *Ardisia cutteri, Aspidosperma megalocarpon, Brosimum utile, Heisteria longipes, Iriartea gigantea, Poulsenia armata, Socaratea durissima,* and *Sorocea cufodontisii.*

Holdridge et al. (1971) report the results (table 7.5) of a small inventory on a very narrow ridge in the Cerros de Salsipuedes that appears to be representative of the narrow ridges in Corcovado. *Brosimum utile* and *Scheelea rostrata* are distinctive tree species characteristic of the narrow ridges. *Caryocar costaricense* does just as well on the knife ridges as it does on the plateau and in the plain. The well-drained ridges often support giant trees that are well-anchored on both sides of the ridge.

The forest on the undulating plateau north of Llorona is particularly impressive, even awe-inspiring, because of a very high density of large trees. In 1978 I established a 1 ha permanent inventory plot in the best stand along the Llorona–San Pedrillo trail. The most important spe-

TABLE 7.4. Stand Characteristics of Three Strips Totaling 0.75 Ha near Ricón, Osa Peninsula, Puntarenas Province

Species	Density Stems/ha (%)	Frequency (%)	Basal Area m^2/ha (%)	Importance Value (%)
Symphonia globulifera	27 (5.4)	13 (4.7)	2.7 (6.7)	5.6
Virola sp.	35 (7.0)	14 (5.0)	0.9 (2.2)	4.7
Unidentified	—	—	—	4.5
"Nispero"	21 (4.2)	12 (4.3)	1.9 (4.7)	4.4
Brosimum spp.	25 (5.0)	12 (4.3)	1.5 (3.7)	4.3
Vochysia hondurensis	5 (1.0)	7 (2.5)	3.3 (8.2)	3.9
Protium spp.	21 (4.2)	13 (4.7)	0.9 (2.2)	3.7
Iriartea gigantea	27 (5.4)	13 (4.7)	0.4 (1.0)	3.6
Peltogyne purpurea	17 (3.4)	11 (4.0)	1.3 (3.2)	3.5
Manilkara sp.	4 (0.8)	3 (1.1)	3.9 (9.7)	3.4
Subtotal: top 10 species	182 (36)	98 (35)	16.8 (41.6)	41.6
Subtotal: other 92 species	321 (64)	179 (65)	23.6 (58.4)	58.4
Total: 102 species	503 (100)	277 (100)	40.4 (100)	100.00

SOURCE: Data recalculated from Sawyer and Lindsay 1971; same as Holdridge et al. 1971, site 8A.

TABLE 7.5.   Stand Characteristics of a 0.2 Ha Plot on a Narrow Ridge near Rincón, Osa Peninsula, Puntarenas Province

Species	Density Stems (%)	Frequency (%)	Basal Area m^2 (%)	Importance Value (%)
Peltogyne purpurea	2 (1.4)	1.75	1.6 (15)	6.09
Protium copal	12 (8.7)	6.14	0.25 (2.4)	5.74
Sorocea pubivena	11 (8.0)	6.14	0.17 (1.7)	5.25
Talisia nervosa	8 (5.8)	5.26	0.37 (3.5)	4.85
Brosimum utile	2 (1.4)	1.75	1.2 (11.2)	4.79
Subtotal: top 5 species	35 (25.3)	—	3.6 (33.7)	26.72
Subtotal: other 56 species	103 (74.7)	—	7.0 (66.3)	73.28
Total: 61 species	138 (100)	—	10.6 (100)	100.00

SOURCE: Data recalculated from Holdridge et al. 1971, site 8F.

cies are given in table 7.6. The tallest tree on the plot was *Vantanea barbourii* at 65 m.

Casual observations of the trees of Corcovado suggest appreciable floristic differences between the plateau in the northwest and the very dissected uplands south of Sirena. *Anaxagorea costaricensis, Calophyllum longifolium, Cariniana pyriformis, Chrysochlamys* sp., *Qualea paraense, Symphonia globulifera, Tetragastris panamensis,* and *Vantanea barbourii* are common trees on the plateau that are rare or absent south of Sirena. The rare trees *Anthodiscus* sp., *Chaunochiton kappleri, Huberodendron patinoi,* and *Parkia pendula* are known only from the northern region of the park.

Peripheral to the small, open-water lagoon east of the center of the Corcovado plain is an extensive floating mat of herbaceous vegetation, dominated by a *Pennisetum* sp. As the depth of water decreases, a more heterogeneous vegetation is rooted in the muck soil. The slightly higher

natural levees of the streams feeding the lagoon support a pure linear stand of *Inga vera*.

Surrounding the herbaceous swamp is an extensive area dominated by the Yolillo palm, *Raphia taedigera,* estimated by Vaughan (1979) to vary between 200 and 1,500 m in radius. The Yolillo palm forms monospecific stands in areas receiving appreciable floodwaters for a few months each year (R. Myers, pers. comm.); the *Raphia* swamp does dry out briefly during the dry season to the stage that it is relatively easy to walk on the mucky swamp soil. Peripheral to the pure *Raphia* swamp where flooding is less in duration or magnitude or both, dicot tree species such as *Andira inermis, Carapa guianensis, Crataeva tapia,* and *Luehea seemannii* begin to dilute the dominance of *Raphia*.

With the lessening occurrence of *Raphia,* the vegetation takes on the appearance of typical swamp forest with large, well-buttressed canopy trees, stilt-rooted sub-

TABLE 7.6   Stand Characteristics of a 1 Ha Plot in Virgin Forest on a Plateau near Punta Llorona, Corcovado National Park, Puntarenas Province

Species	Density Stems (%)	Frequency Subplots (%)	Basal Area m^2 (%)	Importance Value (%)
Vantanea barbourii	10 (2.82)	8 (2.67)	9.23 (20.2)	8.55
Qualea paraense	21 (5.93)	12 (4.00)	5.89 (12.9)	7.60
Brosimum utile	23 (6.50)	16 (5.33)	3.53 (7.71)	6.51
Welfia georgii	23 (6.50)	16 (5.33)	0.55 (1.20)	4.34
Symphonia globulifera	20 (5.65)	12 (4.00)	1.34 (2.92)	4.19
Aspidosperma megalocarpon	6 (1.70)	5 (1.67)	3.32 (7.30)	3.56
Minquartia guianensis	6 (1.70)	6 (2.00)	1.88 (4.10)	2.60
Carapa guianensis	9 (2.54)	7 (2.33)	1.34 (2.90)	2.59
Caryocar costaricense	2 (0.56)	2 (0.67)	2.87 (6.27)	2.50
Trichilia sp.	12 (3.39)	10 (3.33)	0.16 (0.35)	2.36
Subtotal: top 10 species	132 (37)	94 (31)	30.11 (66)	44.80
Subtotal: other 98 species	222 (63)	206 (69)	15.67 (34)	55.20
Total: 108 species	354 (100)	300 (100)	45.78 (100)	100.00

TABLE 7.7. Stand Characteristics of a 0.2 Ha Plot on Recent Alluvium near the Quebrada Vanegas, Osa Peninsula, Puntarenas Province

Species	Density Stems (%)	Frequency %	Basal Area m^2 (%)	Importance Value (%)
Cryosophila guagara	21 (24.7)	14.7	0.2 (2.4)	13.93
Hieronyma oblonga	1 (1.2)	1.47	1.5 (18.6)	7.09
Mortoniodendron anisophyllum	4 (4.7)	4.41	0.6 (7.8)	5.63
Grias fendleri	4 (4.7)	4.41	0.3 (3.7)	4.28
Batocarpus costaricense	3 (3.5)	4.41	0.4 (4.8)	4.26
Subtotal: top 5 species	33 (39)	—	3.0 (36)	35.19
Subtotal: other 31 species	52 (61)	—	5.3 (64)	64.81
Total: 36 species	85 (100)	—	8.3 (100)	100.00

SOURCE: Data recalculated from Holdridge et al. 1971, site 8E.

canopy trees, and a fairly open understory of abundant palms. Common tree species include *Carapa guianensis, Cryosophila guagara, Erythrina lanceolata, Grias fendleri, Mouriri* sp., *Prestoea decurrens, Pterocarpus officinalis* (see Janzen 1978c), and *Virola koschnyi*. The latter two species form monospecific stands in certain poorly drained areas associated with the Río Llorona. The Holdridge et al. (1971) study site 8E near the Quebrada Vanegas (table 7.7) appears to have similar vegetation on imperfectly to poorly drained alluvial soil.

On the briefly flooded but adequately drained natural levees bordering the major rivers crossing the Corcovado plain occurs a distinctive forest type characterized by giant *Anacardium excelsum* trees. Other large trees of *Basiloxylon excelsum, Caryocar costaricense, Ceiba pentandra, Hernandia didymantha,* and *Terminalia oblonga* also occur in this forest type. Possibly the largest tree in Central America, *Ceiba pentandra*, measuring 80 m tall and 3 m in diameter above 10 m tall buttresses, occurs on the Corcovado plain (Boza and Bonilla 1978). The Holdridge et al. (1971) study site 8D2 (table 7.8) on a

levee of the Río Rincón appears quite representative of the same habitat in Corcovado.

Mangroves occur in association with the tidal estuaries of the Llorona, Corcovado, and Sirena rivers and have the typical tree species *Rhizophora mangle, Avicennia germinans, Pelliciera rhizophorae, Laguncularia racemosa,* and *Conocarpus erecta*. Although the mangrove forest is particularly well developed near the mouth of the Río Llorona, it is evident that *Rhizophora* trees were felled for their bark (used in leather tanning). *Mora oleifera* commonly occurs in the swamp forest behind the mangroves, but *Prioria copaifera* is notably absent from this forest type in Corcovado.

The coastal strand vegetation is highly disturbed owing to human interventions, but it contains the characteristic naturalized tree species *Cocos nucifera* and *Terminalia catappa* in addition to native *Chrysobalanus icaco, Enallagma latifolia,* and *Hibiscus tiliaceous*.

Even though the Corcovado National Park was established in 1975 and more than a hundred families of colonists were moved out in 1976, it was not until May 1978

TABLE 7.8 Stand Characteristics of a 0.1 Ha Plot on a Natural Levee along the Río Rincón, Osa Peninsula, Puntarenas Province

Species	Density Stems (%)	Frequency %	Basal Area m^2 (%)	Importance Value (%)
Anacardium excelsum	4 (4.5)	6.1	5.0 (41)	17.16
Cryosophila guagara	22 (25)	15.2	0.2 (1.8)	13.97
Guarea sp.	8 (9.1)	6.1	0.4 (3.1)	6.07
Trichilia pittieri	4 (4.5)	6.1	0.7 (6.1)	5.58
Hernandia didymantha	2 (2.3)	3.0	1.3 (10.3)	5.21
Subtotal: top 5 species	40 (45)	—	7.6 (63)	47.99
Subtotal: other 19 species	48 (55)	—	4.6 (37)	52.01
Total: 24 species	88 (100)	—	12.2 (100)	100.00

SOURCE: Data recalculated from Holdridge et al. 1971, site 8D2.

that the cattle were removed from the park. Most of the pastures and croplands were concentrated in the Sirena–Río Pavo area, although young secondary forest as well as degraded forest occurs patchily throughout the flatlands. Vaughan (1979) estimates 2,000 ha of clearings in the park; however, park personnel use a figure of 3,000 ha, and Herwitz (1979) reports 500 ha. Many of the trails departing from Sirena and Llorona go through undercut forest (*bosque socolado*) where the colonists had cut the undergrowth in preparation for sowing pasture grass and felling the forest. Herwitz (1979) uses a figure of 400 ha of undercut forest, but I think it totals less than 100 ha, though its prevalence along trails give the impression that it is quite extensive. Unfortunately, no studies of the secondary successions occurring in Corcovado have been initiated.

LA SELVA

The La Selva Biological Reserve (fig. 7.8) is in northern Heredia Province at the confluence of the Sarapiquí and Puerto Viejo rivers, with geographical coordinates 10°26′ N and 83°59′ W. The 730.5 ha La Selva area includes the topographic changeover from the low, steep foothills of the Cordillera Central to the extensive Sarapiquí coastal plain extending north to the Río San Juan and east to Tortuguero. Elevations range from 35 m on the recent (or A) terrace of the Río Puerto Viejo to roughly 150 m. Basalt bedrock is the parent material of the residual soils covering the southern two-thirds of La Selva. Closer to the Río Puerto Viejo the basalt is overlain by an old alluvial terrace (i.e., no longer flooded and presumably of Pleistocene origin) and by the recent alluvium that is occasionally flooded. The basalt bedrock impedes creek drainage of several swampy areas in La Selva (fig. 7.8); the swamps may be forested as in plot II or naturally treeless, as along the River Road East just before the Quebrada El Salto.

La Selva is owned and administered by the Organization for Tropical Studies, which purchased the core property from L. R. Holdridge in 1968. OTS added two additions—Annex A along the east side in 1970 and Annex B on the southern end in 1973. Holdridge purchased the property in 1953 with the original intention of making it a commercial production forest and fruit farm. By 1956 he had decided the virgin forest had more value as a scientific reserve but continued to develop cacao (*Theobroma cacao*), pejibaye (*Bactris gasipaes*), and laurel (*Cordia alliodora*) plantations on the alluvial terraces. According to Petriceks (1956), most of the recent alluvium bore 18–20-year-old secondary forest that originated after the abandonment of banana plantations owing to a *Fusarium* blight that wiped out the banana industry in the 1920s and 1930s.

The ecological map of Costa Rica (Tosi 1969) shows La Selva with two Life Zones; Tropical Wet Forest on the west side and Tropical Premontane Wet Forest, warm transition, to the east. Mean annual rainfall at La Selva (taken near Rafael's house) is 3,991 ± 748 mm (n = 22 years). The vegetation of La Selva can be considered to be an atmospheric association owing to the absence of an effective dry season and the prevalence of condensation drip practically every night, possibly related to cold air drainage associated with the Río Puerto Viejo. The fertile recent alluvium is an edaphic association, whereas the swamps are hydric associations.

Approximately 89% of the La Selva property is virgin forest (fig. 7.9) with three major forest types on residual, swamp, and old alluvial soils. *Pentaclethra macroloba* dominates all three types of virgin forest with importance values between 18 and 23% (tables 7.9, 7.10, 7.11, 7.12); its dominance is attributed to a combination of tolerance of infertile soil, lack of an effective dry season, permitting a swamp species to extend to slopes and ridges, and the lack of significant seed predation (Hartshorn 1972). The most striking aspect of the La Selva forest is the richness and abundance of subcanopy, understory, and dwarf palms, particularly *Welfia georgii*, *Socratea durissima*, *Iriartea gigantea*, *Geonoma congesta*, *Synecanthus warscewiczii*, *Asterogyne martiana*, and *Calyptrogyne sarapiquensis*. Characteristic trees on the well-drained basalt and old alluvial soils include *Anaxagorea costaricensis*, *Capparis pittieri*, *Cassipourea elliptica*, *Dendropanax arboreus*, *Dipteryx panamensis*, *Dussia macroprophyllata*, *Faramea suerrensis*, *Goethalsia meiantha*, *Guarea rhopalocarpa*, *Hernandia didymantha*, *Inga thibaudiana*, *Laetia procera*, *Perebea angustifolia*, *Protium pittieri*, *Quararibea bracteolosa*, *Rinorea pubipes*, *Swartzia simplex*, and *Warscewiczia coccinea*. The very well drained or excessively drained soils on narrow ridges have *Euterpe macrospadix*, *Ryania speciosa*, *Trophis involucrata*, *Vochysia ferruginea*, and *Macrocnemum glabrescens* as characteristic tree species. This ridgetop complement of tree species is completely different from the tree species occupying a similar habitat in Corcovado.

The 58 ha of swamp forest are characterized by the subdominance of *Carapa guianensis* and the abundance of *Adelia triloba*, *Astrocaryum alatum*, *Bactris longiseta*, *Dialyanthera otoba*, *Piper cenocladum*, and *Pterocarpus officinalis*. In the deforested swamp on Annex A (between lines 1,800 and 2,000, east of the East Trail) the terrestrial aroid *Spathiphyllum* sp. is especially abundant. The swamp palm, *Raphia taedigera*, was formerly very abundant in the sloughs and old river channels of the Río

FIGURE 7.8. Map of La Selva biological reserve (Tropical Science Center).

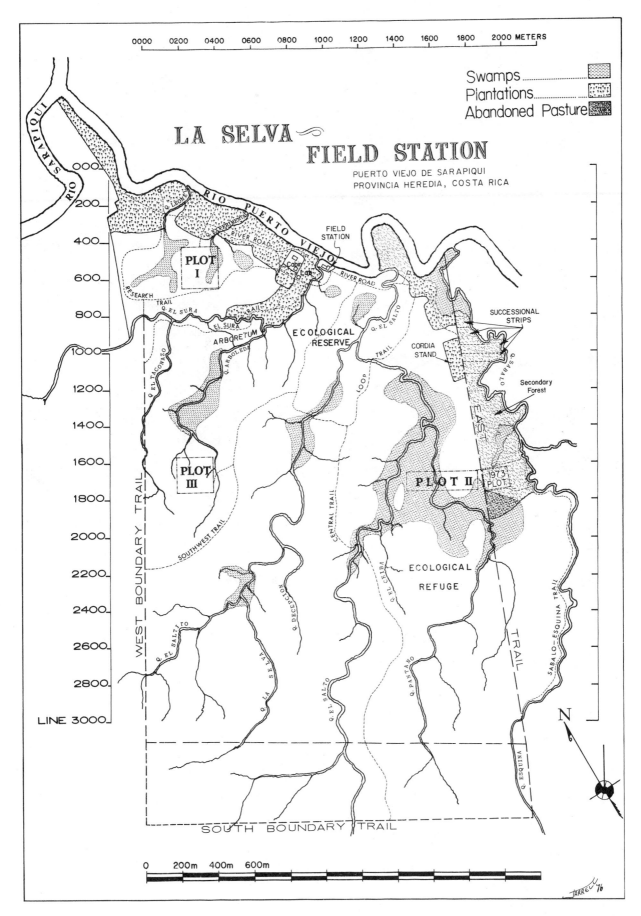

LA SELVA FIELD STATION

PUERTO VIEJO DE SARAPIQUI
PROVINCIA HEREDIA, COSTA RICA

Swamps ....
Plantations ....
Abandoned Pasture

0000 0200 0400 0600 0800 1000 1200 1400 1600 1800 2000 METERS

FIELD STATION

PLOT I

RIO PUERTO VIEJO

RIVER ROAD

ECOLOGICAL RESERVE

SUCCESSIONAL STRIPS

CORDIA STAND

Secondary Forest

PLOT III

PLOT II

1973 PLOT

ECOLOGICAL REFUGE

WEST BOUNDARY TRAIL

SOUTHWEST TRAIL

CENTRAL TRAIL

SABALO-ESQUINA TRAIL

TRAIL

LINE 3000

SOUTH BOUNDARY TRAIL

0   200m   400m   600m

N

Tarrell 76

FIGURE 7.9. Oblique aerial photo of La Selva forest with Rio Puerto Viejo in foreground. Tower (40 m) is at center right, just to the right of huge, light-colored *Dipteryx panamensis* crown (photo, G. S. Hartshorn).

TABLE 7.9. Stand Characteristics of a 4 Ha Plot (I) in Virgin Forest on an Old Alluvial Terrace in La Selva, Heredia Province

Species	Density Stems (%)	Frequency Subpolts (%)	Basal Area m^2 (%)	Importance Value (%)
Pentaclethra macroloba	194 (14.7)	78 (9.73)	44.96 (44.5)	22.99
Welfia georgii	214 (16.2)	75 (9.35)	4.85 (4.80)	10.11
Socratea durissima	159 (12.1)	68 (8.48)	2.35 (2.32)	7.64
Protium pittieri	55 (4.17)	40 (4.99)	2.51 (2.48)	3.86
Warscewiczia coccinea	56 (4.25)	30 (3.74)	1.28 (1.27)	3.07
Goethalsia meiantha	32 (2.43)	19 (2.37)	2.91 (2.88)	2.55
Dendropanax arboreus	31 (2.35)	23 (2.87)	2.06 (2.04)	2.44
Casearia arborea	36 (2.73)	26 (3.24)	0.98 (0.97)	2.32
Laetia procera	19 (1.44)	15 (1.87)	3.46 (3.42)	2.26
Virola sebifera	29 (2.20)	21 (2.62)	0.98 (0.97)	1.92
Subtotal: top 10 species	825 (63)	395 (49)	66.34 (66)	59.16
Subtotal: other 78 species	494 (37)	407 (51)	34.74 (34)	40.84
Total: 88 species	1319 (100)	802 (100)	101.08 (100)	100.00

TABLE 7.10.   Stand Characteristics of a 2 Ha Plot (IIa) in Virgin Swamp Forest at La Selva, Heredia Province

Species	Density Stems (%)	Frequency Subplots (%)	Basal Area m^2 (%)	Importance Value (%)
Pentaclethra macroloba	122 (17.3)	42 (9.05)	19.82 (29.2)	18.51
Carapa guianensis	62 (8.78)	27 (5.82)	13.16 (19.4)	11.33
Pterocarpus officinalis	25 (3.54)	18 (3.88)	11.27 (16.6)	8.01
Astrocaryum alatum	61 (8.64)	29 (6.25)	0.85 (1.25)	5.38
Iriartea gigantea	35 (4.96)	23 (4.96)	0.90 (1.33)	3.75
Welfia georgii	20 (2.83)	20 (4.31)	0.44 (0.65)	2.60
Dialyanthera otoba	22 (3.12)	14 (3.02)	0.69 (1.02)	2.39
Apeiba membranacea	13 (1.84)	11 (2.37)	1.92 (2.83)	2.35
Pterocarpus hayesii	5 (0.71)	4 (0.86)	3.26 (4.80)	2.12
Colubrina spinosa	20 (2.83)	14 (3.02)	0.28 (0.41)	2.09
Subtotal: top 10 species	385 (55)	202 (44)	52.59 (77)	58.53
Subtotal: other 105 species	321 (45)	262 (56)	15.32 (23)	41.47
Total: 115 species	706 (100)	464 (100)	67.91 (100)	100.00

Sarapiquí around the town of Puerto Viejo (Anderson and Mori 1967); however, it is notably absent from comparable habitats in La Selva, such as the slough near line 800 and the River Road East. *Raphia taedigera* seems to have poor seed dispersal (R. Myers, pers. comm.), and it is likely that natural seed dispersers have not crossed the Sarapiquí and Puerto Viejo rivers into La Selva.

Disturbed habitats on the north and east edges of La Salva include assorted plantations of cacao, laurel, and pejibaye (8 ha), cacao plantations (40 ha) abandoned in 1968, young secondary forest (12 ha) on Annex A pastures abandoned between 1966 and 1968, five 0.5 ha successional strips between lines 900 and 1,200 in Annex A that are cut on a five-year rotation in order to maintain patches of early successional vegetation, an experimental succession plot (1.4 ha) established in 1973 between lines 1,600 and 1,800 in Annex A, about 15 ha of treeless swamp, and a 3.5 ha arboretum bearing the name of Dr. L. R. Holdridge, former owner of La Selva and premier dendrologist in tropical America.

The Holdridge Arboretum was a small area of cacao with an exceptionally rich overstory of native shade trees. After the cacao was removed in 1968 to aid the phenological study of Frankie and Baker, approximately 100 species were identified among the more than 650 trees remaining. Since 1970 I have planted seedlings of many La Selva tree species in the Holdridge Arboretum, bringing the totals to more than 1,000 individuals of about 240 species—more than two-thirds of the native tree species at La Selva. All trees are numbered with

TABLE 7.11.   Stand Characteristics of a 2 Ha Plot (IIb) in Virgin Forest at La Selva, Heredia Province

Species	Density Stems (%)	Frequency Subplots (%)	Basal Area m^2 (%)	Importance Value (%)
Pentaclethra macroloba	122 (14.4)	44 (7.15)	20.32 (31.8)	17.80
Iriartea gigantea	94 (11.1)	37 (6.02)	2.54 (3.98)	7.04
Goethalsia meiantha	38 (4.50)	24 (3.90)	5.20 (8.14)	5.51
Welfia georgii	51 (6.04)	33 (5.37)	1.21 (1.89)	4.43
Macrolobium costaricense	32 (3.79)	24 (3.90)	1.09 (1.71)	3.13
Apeiba membranacea	12 (1.42)	12 (1.95)	3.63 (5.68)	3.02
Pourouma aspera	18 (2.13)	16 (2.60)	1.95 (3.05)	2.59
Protium panamense	18 (2.13)	16 (2.60)	1.20 (1.88)	2.20
Carapa guianensis	9 (1.07)	8 (1.30)	2.44 (3.82)	2.06
Pterocarpus hayesii	14 (1.66)	12 (1.95)	1.22 (1.91)	1.84
Subtotal: top 10 species	408 (48)	226 (37)	40.80 (64)	49.62
Subtotal: other 108 species	437 (52)	389 (63)	23.07 (36)	50.38
Total: 118 species	845 (100)	615 (100)	63.87 (100)	100.00

TABLE 7.12.   Stand Characteristics of a 4 Ha Plot (III) in Virgin Forest on Residual Soils at La Selva, Heredia Province

Species	Density Stems (%)	Frequency Subplots (%)	Basal Area m^2 (%)	Importance Value (%)
Pentaclethra macroloba	285 (14.6)	95 (7.47)	44.03 (40.0)	20.71
Socratea durissima	197 (10.1)	85 (6.68)	2.66 (2.41)	6.40
Welfia georgii	136 (6.99)	76 (5.97)	3.10 (2.82)	5.26
Iriartea gigantea	134 (6.88)	66 (5.19)	3.24 (2.94)	5.00
Protium pittieri	94 (4.83)	61 (4.80)	2.73 (2.49)	4.04
Protium panamense	73 (3.75)	50 (3.93)	2.43 (2.21)	3.30
Euterpe macrospadix	97 (4.98)	48 (3.77)	1.11 (1.01)	3.25
Warscewiczia coccinea	88 (4.52)	47 (3.69)	1.48 (1.35)	3.19
Pourouma aspera	47 (2.41)	35 (2.75)	3.11 (2.83)	2.66
Naucleopsis naga	40 (2.05)	36 (2.83)	0.93 (0.85)	1.91
Subtotal: top 10 species	1,191 (61)	599 (47)	64.82 (59)	55.72
Subtotal: other 102 species	756 (39)	673 (53)	45.22 (41)	44.28
Total: 112 species	1,947 (100)	1,272 (100)	110.04 (100)	100.00

permanent metal tags, listed with scientific name and size (diameter or height), and located to the nearest meter in a 25 × 25 m reference grid. An up-to-date listing of trees in the Holdridge Arboretum is maintained in the field station. The herbaceous ground cover is cut three times a year, maintaining a parklike landscape. The openness in the Holdridge Arboretum makes it easier to view the tree crowns, contributing to its attractiveness for bird watchers and making it next in popularity to the field station porch and balconies.

Although no virgin forest remains on the recent alluvial terraces in La Selva, it is possible to list the more common species present in the abandoned cacao plantations and to infer that they are normal components in the undisturbed forest type on recent alluvium. Characteristic tree species are expected to include *Alchornea costaricensis, Bravaisia integerrima, Bursera simaruba, Castilla elastica, Chamaedorea exorrhiza, Cordia alliodora, Croton schiedeanus, Erythrina cochleata, Hernandia stenura, Hura crepitans, Inga densiflora, I. oerstediana, Lonchocarpus oliganthus, Spondias radlkoferi, Terminalia oblonga, Trophis racemosa,* and *Zanthoxylum panamense.*

The banks of the Río Puerto Viejo are lined with large trees of *Pithecellobium longifolium* and *Ficus glabrata,* often leaning over the river and contributing to the attractiveness of boat rides. The two riparian tree species are restricted to the banks of the river, but *Sickingia maxonii* and *Ficus tonduzii* are frequently associated with the creeks.

The early successional strips go through a succession starting with abundant *Erechtites hieracifolia,* followed by dominance of *Phytolacca rivinoides* toward the end of the first year and extending well into the second. Small, precocious trees such as *Acalypha* spp., *Colubrina spinosa, Hamelia patens, Miconia affinis, Neea laetevirens, Piper* spp., and *Solanum rugosum* become prominent in the second year, as do the pioneer trees *Cecropia obtusifolia, Heliocarpus appendiculatus,* and *Ochroma lagopus.* Years one and three are the "machete" stage, an appropriate name because it is impossible to move through without cutting a trail. As the pioneer and gap species close and raise the canopy, the understory becomes more open.

In August of 1975 I established a 0.6 ha (60 × 100 m) permanent plot in the young secondary forest of Annex A, between lines 1,200 and 1,400. The few large trees left when the original forest was cut were not included in the stand analysis (table 7.13). If the minimum diameter limit is reduced to 5 cm, the top four species are the same, but *Miconia affinis* takes over as the fifth most important tree. Four of the second set of five tree species are the same as with the larger 10 cm minimum diameter limit.

The experimental succession plot was established during September–November 1973 by cutting down the young secondary forest on an area 120 by 120 m. Six replicates of the following six treatments were imposed: (1) one large tree from the original forest not cut and all organic debris left on the subplot; (2) all trees cut and all organic debris left on the subplot; (3) all trees cut and organic debris burned; (4) all trees cut and all aboveground debris removed; (5) same as treatment 4, plus soil surface heterogenized by garden forking; and (6) same as treatment 5, plus soil sterilization with methyl bromide. The secondary forest is well developed on all except the sterilized subplots, which are still covered by the spiny fern *Hypolepis* sp. and other perennial herbs.

TABLE 7.13.   Stand Characteristics of a 0.6 Ha Plot (IV) in Twelve-Year-Old Secondary Forest, La Selva, Heredia Province

Species	Density Stems (%)	Frequency Subplots (%)	Basal Area m^2 (%)	Importance Value (%)
Goethalsia meiantha	44 (18.6)	7 (6.7)	2.3 (35)	20.26
Rollinia microsepala	44 (18.6)	8 (7.7)	1.0 (15)	13.89
Casearia arborea	27 (11.4)	12 (11.5)	0.35 (5.5)	9.48
Pentaclethra macroloba	17 (7.2)	10 (9.6)	0.37 (5.8)	7.53
Stryphnodendron excelsum	18 (7.6)	9 (8.7)	0.39 (6.1)	7.46
Hieronyma oblonga	18 (7.6)	8 (7.7)	0.30 (4.7)	6.67
Laetia procera	13 (5.5)	5 (4.8)	0.19 (2.9)	4.41
Inga sapindoides	9 (3.8)	5 (4.8)	0.26 (4.0)	4.20
Apeiba membranacea	8 (3.4)	6 (5.8)	0.11 (1.7)	3.62
Simarouba amara	4 (1.7)	2 (1.9)	0.10 (1.6)	1.74
Subtotal: top 10 species	202 (86)	72 (69)	5.37 (84)	79.26
Subtotal: other 25 species	34 (14)	32 (31)	1.05 (16)	20.74
Total: 35 species	236 (100)	104 (100)	6.42 (100)	100.00

MONTEVERDE

The Monteverde Cloud Forest Reserve straddles the low continental divide in the Cordillera de Tilarán where the provinces of Puntarenas, Guanacaste, and Alajuela meet. In the Monteverde region the Cordillera de Tilarán is a loaf-shaped range with undulating topography up to 3 km wide and flanked on both Pacific and Atlantic sides by very steep slopes and deep valleys. Elevations within the Monteverde Reserve range from isolated peaks above 1,800 m to 1,200 m in the Peñas Blancas valley. The reserve takes its name from the nearby Monteverde Quaker community founded in 1951 as a dairy-farming colony.

The Monteverde Reserve was initiated in March 1972 by George and Harriet Powell to preserve in perpetuity some of the remarkable cloud forest habitats and biota in the Tilarán mountains. The Powells' dedicated and persistent quest for funds to establish the Monteverde Reserve was actively supported by United States conservation organizations and individuals. The 2,500 ha Monteverde Reserve (fig. 7.10) is owned and administered by the Tropical Science Center (TSC), a San José based scientific and conservation association.

The exposed position atop the Cordillera de Tilarán and the steep valleys draining both sides, coupled with five months of strong, moisture-laden Atlantic trade winds, has produced a remarkable array of altitudinally compressed life zones. The protected Pacific valleys and slopes are in a dry season rain shadow nearly as severe as in the Guanacaste lowlands. Only near the continental divide do the moisture-laden winds spill over to bathe the uppermost Pacific slopes in a nourishing mist that seems incongruous with the bright, sunny weather. Those same moisture-laden winds forced up the Atlantic valleys and slopes have produced a beautifully sculptured and streamlined elfin forest on the exposed upper Atlantic slopes.

The ecological map of Costa Rica (Tosi 1969) shows the following Life Zones in the Monteverde area: (1) Tropical Premontane Moist Forest in the upper San Luís valley and along the cliff edge; (2) Tropical Premontane Wet Forest encompasses most of the extended community and farms; (3) Tropical Lower Montane Wet Forest on the upper Pacific slopes such as in the vicinity of the TSC field station and much of the Sendero (trail) Bosque Nuboso; (4) Tropical Lower Montane Rain Forest along the divide and mountains generally above 1,500 m, including the Elfin Forest; and (5) Tropical Premontane Rain Forest in the upper Peñas Blancas valley. The first three Life Zones in the Monteverde area, as well as the elfin forest, should be considered atmospheric associations owing to the strong influence of the dry-season trade winds. The relatively level, swampy area along the Sendero Pantanoso is a hydric association. Most of the continental divide and upper Pacific slopes have had substantial inputs of andesitic volcanic ash, suggesting that they are largely edaphic associations. Perhaps only the Tropical Premontane Rain and the more easterly Lower Montane Rain Life Zones are close to the respective climatic associations.

Practically the entire Monteverde Reserve can be considered cloud forest because of the prevalence of moisture-bearing clouds throughout the year. During the April–November rainy season the trade winds lessen in velocity but still contribute substantial moisture to the Monteverde area. Convectional thunderstorms bring almost daily rain during May to October with a slight *veranillo* in July. The physiographic complexity of the

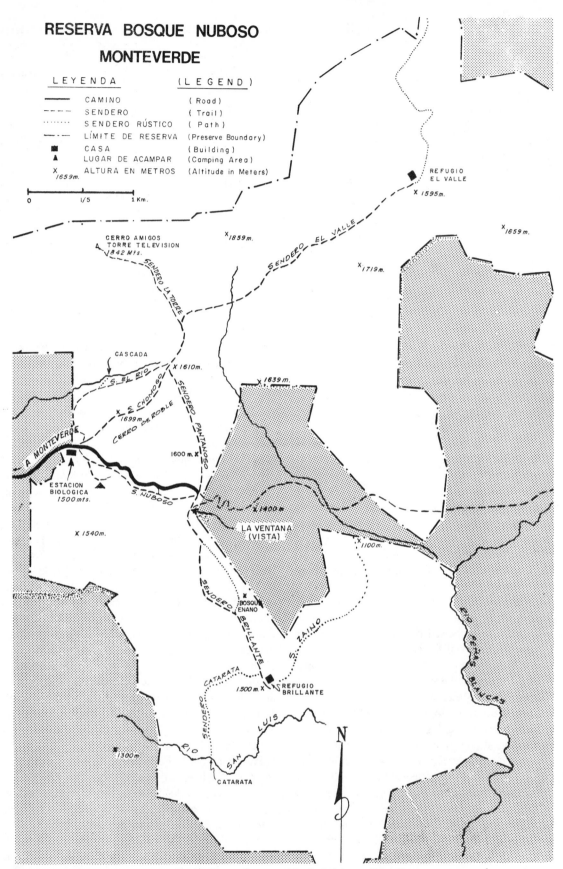

FIGURE 7.10. Map of Monteverde Cloud Forest Reserve (Tropical Science Center).

Tilarán Cordillera accentuates the dominant role of wind and clouds in determining the types of forest in the Monteverde area. The incredible abundance and diversity of both vascular and bryophytic epiphytes—some growing on top of each other amid dense carpets of soft mosses 10 cm thick—imparts a characteristic aeriel-draped cloud forest where it is sometimes impossible to locate the leaves of the host tree. Of the major cloud forests in tropical America produced by the northeast trade winds (Rancho Grande in Venezuela, the Blue Mountains of Jamaica, and the Luquillo Mountains in Puerto Rico), cloud forest is most luxuriantly developed in Monteverde.

Within the Monteverde Reserve, Lawton and Dryer (1980) describe the vegetation of six forest types: cove, leeward cloud, oak ridge, windward cloud, elfin, and swamp forests. The following summaries are based on the Lawton and Dryer descriptions. Cove forest within the Monteverde Reserve is restricted to the protected western base of Cerro Roble and the upper, west-facing slope of Quebrada Alondra. The forest is well developed, 30–40 m tall, and evergreen despite the dry-season loss of moisture. Characteristic tree species include the huge strangler *Ficus tuerckheimii, Meliosma vernicosa, Quararibea platyphylla, Sapium oligoneuron,* and *S. pachystachys,* as well as several members of Lauraceae, Myrtaceae, and Sapotaceae. Of the six forest types, the cove forest has the least-developed epiphytic load; bryophytes cover less than 30% of trunk surfaces, while canopy epiphytes are mostly drought-resistant, shrubby forms.

Leeward cloud forest is more exposed to the trade wind spillover than is the cove forest and occurs in a broad, irregular arc from Cerro Sin Nombre to the Brillante Gap. This forest (fig. 7.11*a*) has a more open canopy, is shorter (25–30 m), and has heavier epiphyte loads than cove forest. Byrophytes cover 50–70% of the tree trunks, reflecting a much less stressful dry season. The authors claim the leeward cloud forest is transitional from tropical Lower Montane Wet to Lower Montane Rain Life Zone. Typical tree species include *Calocarpum viride, Citharexylum macradenium, Daphnopsis americana,* the strangler *Ficus crassiuscula, Guarea tuisana, Meliosma vernicosa, Persea americana, Quararibea platyphylla, Sapium pachystachys, Sloanea medusula,* and several members of the Lauraceae and Myrtaceae.

FIGURE 7.11. Profile of upper Peñas Blancas valley in Monteverde; the very steep, uppermost slopes are covered with elfin forest (photo, G. S. Hartshorn).

143

Oak ridge forest occurs on the exposed ridges of Cerros Sin Nombre, Amigo, and Roble. The dominant oaks, *Quercus corrugata* and *Q. seemannii*, may attain 1 m dbh and 25 m in height on the less windswept ridges. Epiphyte cover is practically complete on all surfaces, including the ground: 75–100% for bryophytes and 30–80% for angiosperms. Other tree species include *Billia hippocastanum*, *Brunellia costaricensis*, the strangler *Ficus crassiuscula*, *Guatteria consanguinea*, *Hieronyma poasana*, *Oreopanax xalapensis*, *Persea americana*, *P. schiedeana*, the stilt-rooted *Tovomita nicaraguensis*, *Weinmannia pinnata*, *W. wercklei*, *Zanthoxylum melanostichum*, and members of the Lauraceae and Myrtaceae.

Windward cloud forest is the most extensive type within the lower montane rain life zone in the Monteverde Reserve. It is an extremely saturated habitat with a very discontinuous canopy, seldom more than 20 m tall, and a dense understory. Many of the tree species are the same as those in the leeward cloud forest; typical tree species include *Alchornea latifolia*, *Ardisia palmana*, *Citharexylum macradenium*, *Daphnopsis americana*, *Dendropanax gonotopodus*, the strangler *Ficus crassiuscula*, *Guarea tuisana*, *Guatteria consanguinea*, *Hieronyma poasana*, *Inga longispica*, *Meliosma* sp., *Persea schiedeana*, *Sapium pachystachys*, *Weinmannia wercklei*, *Zanthoxylum melanostichum*, and several members of the Lauraceae. Windward cloud forest has the most luxuriant load of epiphytes, including beautiful *Begonia estrellensis* and *Hydrangea peruviana*, plus carnivorous *Utricularia* spp.

Elfin forest occurs along the crest of the Brillante Gap as well as on other very exposed ridges. It is a short, gnarled, dense, sodden forest whose canopy appears sculptured and streamlined by the relentless wind. The smooth profile of the elfin forest viewed (fig. 7.11*b*) from the overlook on the old road cut to Peñas Blancas belies the tangled mass of roots, branches, and fallen dwarfs that is nearly impenetrable. The plants that make up the elfin forest are the same ones as in the windward cloud forest, except for those species such as *Cecropia polyphlebia* and *Heliocarpus popayensis* that are unable to tolerate the wind stress. Stilt-rooted *Clusia alata* trees may protrude above the low canopy as true emergents, especially on the ridge crest above elfin forested slope. The Araliaceae, *Didymopanax pittieri*, *Oreopanax nubigenum*, and *O. sanderianus* are common trees in the elfin forest.

Swamp forest occupies the poorly drained plateau between Cerro Roble and Cerro Sin Nombre. The authors note that the western drainage is a blackwater tributary to the Río Guacimál. The forest is a mosaic of scattered patches of trees to 25 m tall among lower thickets of small trees. Characteristic tree species include *Alchornea*

latifolia, *Clusia alata*, *Conostegia* spp., *Dendropanax arboreus*, *D. gonatopodus*, *Guatteria consanguinea*, *Hieronmya poasana*, *Magnolia* sp., *Persea schiedeana*, *Podocarpus oleifolius*, *Quercus corrugata*, *Q. seemannii*, *Sapium pachystachys*, *Tetrorchidium* sp., *Tovomita nicaraguensis*, and *Weinmannia wercklei*. Lawton and Dryer (1980) do not include descriptions of the Tropical Premontane Rain Life Zone in the upper Peñas Blancas valley or the Tropical Premontane Wet Life Zone around the Monteverde community. The Peñas Blancas valley is so poorly known botanically and ecologically that it is presumptuous to try to characterize the forests there. Suffice it to say that the forest is taller and that huge strangler figs are much less frequent than in other Monteverde forest types. Only remnant patches of forest remain around the Monteverde community, but they clearly indicate that it was a magnificent forest, extremely rich in species of Lauraceae and Sapotaceae, as well as huge strangling *Ficus*. The tree species in the vicinity of the Monteverde community are reasonably well documented in the checklist of trees found later in this chapter.

LAS CRUCES

The tropical premontane rain forest that covered the upper Coto Brus valley has been virtually exterminated in the past fifteen years. One of the few remaining remnants occupies 100 ha of Las Cruces. It is a tall forest (30–35 m) with abundant *Quercus* spp. and Lauraceae. The epiphyte load is appreciably less than at Monteverde, presumably because of the slight dry season and absence of wind-driven mist at Las Cruces. L. J. Poveda is preparing a report on the Las Cruces forest.

CERRO

Pensión La Georgina is close to the present transition from oak forest to páramo. The Holdridge et al. (1971) Villa Mills study site just south of the pensión illustrates (table 7.14) the complete canopy dominance of *Quercus costaricensis*. Most of the oak forests along the Inter-American Highway have been severely degraded by logging and charcoal-making. The scandent bamboo, *Swallenochloa* sp., aggressively dominates the shrub layer of the degraded and open oak stands and appears to be inhibiting the regeneration of oaks.

Páramo vegetation on the Cerro is often dominated by *Hypericum* shrubs 1–1.5 m tall with occasional emergent (to 5–8 m) trees. The drier, rocky hillsides are covered by clump grasses with occasional forbs. Bogs have an interesting assemblage of plants such as *Cirsium* sp., *Puya dasylirioides*, and the Andean fern, *Jamesonia*. Circumstantial evidence suggests that man's frequent use of fire on the Cerro is effectively lowering the tree line. Regeneration after fire is extremely slow (Janzen 1973).

TABLE 7.14   Stand Characteristics of a 0.4 Ha Plot at Km 97 of the Inter-American Highway on the Cerro, Cartago Province

Species	Density Stems (%)	Frequency (%)	Basal Area m^2 (%)	Importance Value (%)
Quercus costaricensis	101 (41.2)	20.43	10.93 (61)	40.89
Miconia bipulifera	39 (15.9)	15.05	1.78 (9.9)	13.63
Vaccinium consanguineum	25 (10.2)	11.82	0.71 (3.9)	8.66
Weinmannia pinnata	16 (6.5)	8.60	1.75 (9.8)	8.30
Didymopanax pittieri	10 (4.1)	6.45	0.85 (4.8)	5.10
Subtotal: top 5 species	191 (78)	62.35	16.02 (89)	76.58
Subtotal: other 15 species	54 (22)	37.65	1.90 (11)	23.42
Total: 20 species	245 (100)	100.00	17.92 (100)	100.00

SOURCE: Data from Holdridge et al. 1971, site 6.

Physiognomic Features and Patterns

Distinctive tropical forest features such as buttresses, crown shapes, drip tips, epiphytes, and lianas have long attracted naturalists, phytogeographers, and plant ecologists (Schimper 1903; Richards 1952), leading to considerable speculation on the functional significance or evolutionary advantage of particular structures. Unfortunately, our understanding of some tropical forest features has not progressed much beyond the speculative stage. Notwithstanding the dearth of testable hypotheses, such features as buttresses, drip tips, and epiphyte distribution often attract OTS students. In this section the more prominent physiognomic features are briefly reviewed to highlight hypotheses, point out ecological patterns, and serve as entrées to the pertinent literature.

BUTTRESSES AND STILT ROOTS

Of all the distinctive or interesting physiognomic features of tropical forests, none has elicited more conjecture and speculation than the question, "Why do some tropical trees have buttresses?" Buttressing (fig. 7.12) is largely restricted to the tropical basal belt in Costa Rica and is best developed in tropical Moist and Wet Life Zones. Buttress height is well correlated with trunk diameter (Holdridge et al. 1971), but not all canopy trees are buttressed. Buttressing is more prevalent in poorly drained areas, but some exceptionally well buttressed trees, for example, *Dussia macroprophyllata* and *Huberodendron patinoi,* occur on well-drained sites. The height, thickness, form, and degree of bifurcation of buttresses are generally very useful in species identification. Buttress growth is strongly epinastic (Richards 1952), that is, the anatomical center of the buttress is at or near ground level and growth is strongly skewed to the upper edge of the buttress.

The various explanations of buttress formation are grouped into four theories, discussed in Richards (1952): (1) adaptive responses to wind or gravity stresses;

(2) negative geotropism; (3) conduction shortcut; and (4) mechanical stimulation of strains caused by winds. Smith (1972) updates and reviews the buttressing theories. An analysis of buttresses using engineering models indicates buttresses are excellent support structures (Henwood 1973). Smith (1979) found a strong negative correlation between buttressing and bark thickness, suggesting why thick-barked temperate trees are not buttressed.

It is a common generalization (Corner 1940; Richards 1952; Spruce 1908; Whitmore 1975) that taprooted trees do not form buttresses, and vice versa. A common misconception holds that buttresses are attached to the central trunk: "In felling tropical timber trees the cut is necessarily made above the buttresses, so the amount of waste is considerable" (Richards 1952, p. 74). A recent paper by Black and Harper (1979) indicates that the misconception is still alive and well. Most well-buttressed trees completely lack a central bole.

Stilt roots differ from buttresses in that the former are adventitious roots. Some stilt roots elongate in a vertical plane such that they may appear as raised buttresses. The best known example of stilt roots occurs on the red mangrove, *Rhizophora mangle,* sometimes originating more than 5 m above "ground" level and making passage extremely difficult. Stilt roots occur in other dicot trees such as *Bravaisia integerrima, Protium* spp., *Symphonia globulifera, Tovomita pittieri, Virola surinamensis,* and nonepiphytic species of *Clusia. Virola surinamensis* and *Protium* spp. usually have vertically elongated stilt buttresses. Numerous palms also have stilt roots, for example, *Chamaedorea* spp., *Cryosophila albida, Euterpe macrospadix, Iriartea gigantea,* and *Socratea durissima.* In the latter, the original stem below the stilt roots actually dies, so that all support and translocation is through the adventitious stilt roots.

As with buttresses, there is considerable speculation on why stilt roots have evolved. In palms at least the

145

FIGURE 7.12. Tree line lowered by fire at Cerro de la Muerte (photo, G. S. Hartshorn).

answer seems obvious, for monocots cannot make secondary xylem; for example, *Welfia georgii* take many years to make a large trunk below ground before the trunk emerges like a telephone pole. The stilt-rooted palms are much more shade-intolerant and must grow fast on an inverted cone to take advantage of canopy openings. The evolution of adventitious stilt roots in monocots (corn is a good example) allows fast growth without building a final stem diameter at or below ground level. Holdridge et al. (1971) report that in the Tropical Premontane Rain Forest Life Zone about 10% of the tree species have stilt roots, but Tropical Dry, Premontane Moist, and Lower Montane and Montane Forest Life Zones do not have stilt-rooted trees.

BARK

"The bark of rain-forest trees is usually remarkably thin and is generally smooth and light-coloured" (Richards 1952, p. 58). That gross generalization is still widely repeated (see Walter 1973 for a recent restatement) even though it is incorrect. Isolated trees do have light, sun-bleached bark that appears deceptively smooth, but the same species in the forest generally do not have light bark. Bark color, texture, and thickness, along with odor

and sap, are sufficiently varied yet species-specific that they are useful diagnostic characters for species identification. If the quoted generalization were true, how is it that local tree finders so competently use those same characters for species identification?

In Costa Rica bark colors are predominantly dark, ranging from black to various hues of red, brown, and gray. Very few species have light-colored bark, although white, red, or blue crustose lichens may camouflage the bark. Bark thickness is generally between 5 and 10 mm, with some species having thinner bark, but very few have bark thicker than 10 mm. Smith's (1979) observation that thick-barked trees do not have buttresses appears to be valid for Costa Rican species.

Bark texture is probably more varied than are color and thickness; some examples are: coarsely fissured (e.g., *Lecythis costaricensis*), finely fissured (e.g., *Calophyllum brasiliense*), shaggy (e.g., *Lysiloma divaricata*), coarsely lenticulate (e.g., *Hernandia didymantha*), finely lenticulate (e.g., most Moraceae and Mimosaceae), minutely exfoliating (e.g., *Bursera simaruba, Inga coruscans, Pithcellobium pedicellare*), exfoliating in scalloped or concentric patterns (e.g., *Carapa guianensis, Albizzia caribaea*), and exfoliating in huge

146

thin sheets (e.g., *Terminalia oblonga*). Trees with exfoliating bark consistently have fewer epiphytes and climbing vines on the trunk and branches than do trees without exfoliating bark. Some bark surfaces bear spines, (e.g., *Bombacopsis quinatum, Hura crepitans, Pithecellobium dulce,* and *Zanthoxylum* spp.), while other species have conspicuous spines as juveniles but exceedingly few or none as mature trees (e.g., *Ceiba pentandra, Jacaratia costaricensis, Lacmellea panamensis,* and *Zanthoxylum mayanum*). A few genera (e.g., *Cryosophila* spp. and *Xylosma* spp.) have multiple-branched spines.

LEAVES

It is well documented that the overwhelming majority of tropical tree leaves are mesophylls—that is, between 20 and 182 cm^2 in upper surface area (Beard 1945; Richards 1952; Greig-Smith 1952). Many compound leaves have leaflets of mesophyll size. Compound leaves are generally more common in tropical lowlands than in tropical montane forests (Cain et al. 1956; Grubb et al. 1963), but Tasaico (1959) found that simple and compound leaves occur in the same proportion in tropical montane areas as in the lowlands. Compound leaves occur commonly not only in areas with a dry season, but on species that depend on rapid increase in height (Givnish 1978).

With increasing altitude, average leaf length decreases at a rate of about 0.5 cm per 100 m (Tasaico 1959). Entire leaf margins, drip tips, and thin leaves are most frequent in wet lowland forests. The adaptive significance of drip tips has long been associated with more rapid runoff and drying of the leaf surface (Richards 1952). An experiment with *Machaerium arboreum* (Fabaceae) leaflets confirms the role of drip tips in speeding water runoff and drying of the leaf surface (Dean and Smith 1978).

The occurrence of tropical forest understory or ground cover leaves with red spots or red undersurface has interested ecologists. Lee, Lowry, and Stone (1979) have recently shown that the abaxial anthocyanin layer enhances photosynthesis by functioning as a reflective surface that bounces light back through the mesophyll.

CROWN SHAPE

According to Richards (1952), canopy or emergent tree crowns are wider than they are deep and often are umbrella-shaped; subcanopy tree crowns are deeper than wide, or are equal; and understory tree crowns are conical, much deeper than wide. In their analyses of useful physiognomic and structural features, Holdridge et al. (1971) report a rough positive correlation of branching angle with trunk shape (trunk shape defined as clear bole length divided by trunk diameter), a slight negative correlation of crown diameter with trunk shape, and a stronger negative correlation of crown volume with trunk

shape. They found that the largest crown volumes occur in Tropical Moist and in poorly drained alluvial associations in Tropical Wet Life Zones. The smallest crown volumes occur in Tropical Lower Montane Rain and Premontane Rain Life Zones. Tropical Wet (well-drained associations) and Premontane Wet are intermediate in crown volume.

The generalization that a tree changes crown shape to conform with the characteristic shape in each stratum as it grows to the canopy (Richards 1952) appears to completely ignore gap-phase regeneration (Hartshorn 1980). The recognition of the ecological differences between monolayer and multilayer crowns (Horn 1971) also contradicts Richards's generalization. Monolayer crowns are characteristic of shade-tolerant "climax" species and shade-intolerant pioneer species, whereas multilayer crowns are common in shade-intolerant gap species. The ecological rationale is that in the low-light conditions of the forest understory it pays to maximize the coverage of the photosynthetic surface area, that is, in a monolayer, while in the better light regime in gaps it pays to stack one or more additional layers of leaves below the uppermost layer. The latter rationale would intuitively hold for pioneer species, except that they are often in such a strong competitive milieu that only the uppermost layer of leaves is important for photosynthesis.

STRATIFICATION

The presence or absence of strata (layers, stories, and tiers are used synonymously with strata) of trees, shrubs, and herbs has engendered considerable controversy. Richards (1952) states that three tree strata occur in most humid tropical forests, whereas two tree strata is the rule for temperate forests. Shrubs and herbs are considered to form one stratum each; hence they are ignored in virtually all discussions of forest stratification. Richards (1952, p. 23) defines a stratum as "a layer of trees whose crowns vary in height between certain limits" and says that "in a several-layered forest each stratum will have a distinctive floristic composition." However, he admits that the presence of juveniles can considerably obscure the well-defined strata. Other authors such as Mildbraed (1922, cited in Richards 1952) state that strata have no objective basis. Strata are most easily recognized in species-poor secondary forest, but they become increasingly cryptic (if they exist) in heterogeneous, mature forest.

Because it is so difficult for a ground observer to see tree strata in the forest (an interesting twist to not seeing the trees for the forest) Davis and Richards (1933, 1934) constructed profile diagrams depicting all the trees on a 7.6 × 61 m strip of forest as an aid to recognizing tree strata. Major problems with profile diagrams are the impossibility of replicating even two sample strips within the same heterogeneous forest and that dynamic phases are either ignored or avoided.

Holdridge et al. (1971) avoided the problems of actual profile diagrams by using only mature individuals to prepare an idealized profile diagram. Sketches of mature individuals of the most "important" species are placed together in a profile to represent species richness, basal area, density, and frequency on actual 10 × 100 m sample strips. The idealized profile diagram is used to define the height limits of tree strata. However, Sawyer and Lindsey (1971), using the same tree height and crown depth data, often give different height limits for strata and, in a few instances, disagree on the number of tree strata.

The polemic on the presence of tree strata has avoided the more fundamental question of their importance—if they do indeed exist. What are the ecophysiological and competitive consequences of numerous tree crowns in the same stratum? Is reproductive biology hindered in a dense stratum of tree crowns? Is herbivory affected by the density of tree crowns in a stratum?

Despite the difficulty with observing tree strata, the multistratal concept has produced a terminology for the upper height limit attained by mature individuals within a forest. The differentiation of a forest into abstract canopy (and/or emergent), subcanopy, and understory strata, without necessarily defining height limits, is an ecologically meaningful positioning of the hundreds of tree species in a tropical forest. Canopy, subcanopy, and understory tree species may have different modes of regeneration, reproductive syndromes, root systems, and so on, that are discussed in other sections of this chapter. It is in this spirit that subjective assignments to the canopy, subcanopy, or understory are made in the next section.

EPIPHYTES

The abundance and richness of the epiphytic flora is much more pronounced in the Neotropics than in the Paleotropics (Brieger 1969). Epiphytic Bromeliaceae are strictly Neotropical, and only the epiphytic cactus *Rhipsalis* occurs in Africa and Sri Lanka. A preliminary comparison (table 7.15) with tropical West Africa and Java clearly demonstrates the richness of dicot epiphytes in Costa Rica.

Dicot families with prominent epiphytic members in the Neotropics include the Araliaceae, Begoniaceae, Cactaceae, Ericaceae, Gesneriaceae, Melastomataceae, Piperaceae, and Solanaceae. Monocot epiphytes are most rich in the Araceae, Bromeliaceae, and Orchidaceae, with about 1,200 Costa Rican species in the latter family. Costa Rica also has an incredibly rich array of epiphytic ferns and mosses.

Epiphytes are most conspicuous in biomass and species richness in Premontane and Lower Montane Rain Life Zones, probably reflecting a correlation with available moisture. Cloud cover and wind-driven mist are more important to epiphytism than is rainfall (Grubb et al. 1963; Grubb and Whitmore 1966; Sudgen and Robins 1979). Epiphytic loads appear heavier in La Selva than in Corcovado, even though total rainfall is approximately the same. The nearly year-round presence of condensation drip at La Selva and the three-month dry season at Corcovado may account for the difference in epiphyte abundance. Epiphyte abundance and richness are drastically less in the Dry and Moist Life Zones, although a very few species of Bromeliaceae, Cactaceae, and Orchidaceae may be fairly abundant. Large tank bromeliads holding up to 1,000 ml of water are most conspicuous in the Montane Rain Life Zone. Epiphytic shrubs such as Ericaceae and Araliaceae are largely restricted to Lower Montane and Montane Wet and Rain Life Zones.

The interesting observations of Perry (1978) suggest that arboreal mammals, primarily monkeys, may play an important role in preventing epiphyte dominance on upper branch surfaces used as canopy highways.

OTS courses have generated numerous attempts to determine the degree of host specificity between epiphytes and trees, but I am not aware of any publications reporting detailed studies of epiphyte distribution and abundance in the Neotropics. Hazen (1966) found a species of *Guzmania* to have a random distribution of four branches of an isolated tree on CATIE grounds near Turrialba. On a larger scale, there does appear to be a remarkable fidelity of most epiphytic species with Life Zones (J. Utley, pers. comm.).

Epiphylls are tiny epiphytes occurring on leaf surfaces and by-and-large are restricted to lower plants such as mosses, liverworts, lichens, and algae. Epiphylls are

TABLE 7.15.   Preliminary Comparison of Dicot Epiphyte Floras of Costa Rica, Java, and Tropical West Africa

	Costa Rica	Java	Tropical West Africa
Total area (km^2)	51,100	130,987	ca. 1,000,000
Total dicot families	155	153	154
Epiphytic families	19	12	9
Epiphytic genera	51	22	16
Epiphytic species	247	107	58

SOURCE: Burger 1980.

most prominent in the perhumid and superhumid life zones without an effective dry season, but they are not nearly as common in the cooler montane altitudinal belt. Understory trees and shrubs have the heaviest loads of epiphylls, not only because of the shaded conditions, but also because they are slow-growing hosts whose leaves appear to be held longer than those of canopy members. Epiphylls appear especially abundant on shade-tolerant members of the Rubiaceae and Palmae.

The classic literature on epiphylls (as cited in Richards 1952) generally viewed them as detrimental to the host leaves. In the extremely low light conditions of the forest understory, an epiphyllous covering must seriously hinder photosynthesis in the host leaf. Richards (1952) summarized by stating that most epiphylls are at least partially parasitic on the host leaf. Drip tips are purportedly adaptive in that they enhance surface runoff of rainwater, which in turn reduces the availability of moist substrate for epiphyllous colonization. Edmisten (1970) found that blue green algae among the epiphylls fix atmospheric nitrogen, suggesting a beneficial input to the host leaf. Barbara Bentley and Amos Bien are at present investigating the role of nitrogen-fixing epiphylls in the La Selva understory.

Canopy lichens also contribute significant quantities of fixed nitrogen to tropical ecosystems. Foreman (1975) found that canopy lichens in a Colombian forest fixed about as much atmospheric nitrogen (roughly 5 kg/ha/yr) as enters the ecosystem through rainfall inputs. Canopy lichens occur mostly on twigs and branches in the 3–12 cm diameter range and generally do not occur in the understory.

CLIMBERS

Herbaceous and woody climbers—the latter also called vines, lianas, and bush ropes—are conspicuous and integral components of tropical forests. The distinction between herbaceous and woody is diffuse, more often related to size than to taxonomic affinity, yet some delicate vines are remarkably strong. Climbers occur in more families than do epiphytes, with Apocynaceae, Araceae, Bignoniaceae, Combretaceae, Convolvulaceae, Dilleniaceae, Hippocrateaceae, Leguminosae, Malpighiaceae, Passifloraceae, Sapindaceae, Smilacaceae, Ulmaceae, and Vitaceae being well represented among the climbers. Bignoniaceae usually has the greatest number of climbing species (about twenty in any tropical forest; Gentry 1976).

The gymnosperm *Gnetum* is a canopy liana in La Selva and Corcovado. *Rourea glabra* (Connaraceae), *Combretum farinosum* (Combretaceae), and *Davilla kunthii* (Dilleniaceae) are common lianas in the Tropical Dry Forests. Climbing palms—the rattáns of the tropical Far East—are very depauperate in the Neotropics, with only

Desmoncus costaricensis present at La Selva and Corcovado. In contrast to the erect, emergent stature of some of the Old World rattáns, Neotropical canopy lianas, including *Desmoncus,* are scandent, draping themselves over tree crowns.

Lianas tend to be more frequent in the dry forest of the tropical lowlands, yet the thickest "stems" (30–40 cm in diameter) are found in Tropical Wet Forests. Because of their very slow diameter increment, the presence of thick lianas is considered an excellent indicator of undisturbed forest (Budowski 1965).

In contrast to shade-intolerant lianas, the herbaceous climbers are often shade-tolerant and restricted to the forest understory. Some understory climbers locate suitable hosts by growing toward dark areas (Strong and Ray 1975). Most climbers have the remarkable ability to greatly vary internode length. In dense shade, internode length is long and leaf size reduced; in sunny patches, internodes are drastically shortened and leaf size is increased (see Givnish and Vermeij 1976). Herbaceous climbers in *Monstera* (Araceae) have appressed, disklike juvenile leaves that effectively cover the terminal meristem. In apparently more favorable light regimes 5–10 m above the ground, *Monstera* produces more typical aroid leaves perpendicular to the climbing stem.

STRANGLERS

Some species of *Ficus* (Moraceae) and *Clusia* (Guttiferae) start out as epiphytes but send down woody, clasping roots that anastomose around the host trunk. The host tree often dies, and after it rots away, a hollow shell of anastomosed roots supports an independent tree. Although these are generically termed "strangler figs," the actual cause of death of the host tree has not been elucidated. Constriction of the trunk seems unlikely; root competition is possible; but I think crown competition may be a more likely cause. Stranglers seem able to easily overtop the host crown with a dense monolayer of evergreen leaves.

Stranglers are most frequent in Tropical Moist and Premontane Wet Life Zones, where they may be among the tallest trees in the forest. The greater abundance of stranglers in Corcovado than in La Selva suggests that an effective dry season may be ideal for seedling establishment as epiphytes.

PARASITES AND SAPROPHYTES

Parasitic shrubs in several genera of the Loranthaceae are well represented in the wetter Life Zones of Costa Rica from the Tropical basal belt to Lower Montane. *Gaiadodendron poasense* is a parasitic tree with beautiful yellow flowers that grows in Lower Montane and Montane Rain Life Zones. All the other Costa Rican Loranthaceae are crown parasites, often forming dense shrubby clusters. Loranthaceae are much more prevalent in isolated trees left standing in pastures and such, than in undisturbed forest. I am unaware of any evidence for host specificity.

Among Costa Rican members of the Olacaceae, root parasitism has been documented for *Schoepfia schreberi* (Werth, Baird, and Musselman 1979) and *Ximenia americana* (DeFillips 1969), but no evidence of host specificity has been found for these two genera.

Achlorophyllous saprophytic plants are rare in Costa Rica. I have seen *Leiphaimos* (Gentianaceae) only in virgin forest above Punta Llorona in Corcovado. An obligate association with mycorrhiza may restrict the occurrence of *Leiphaimos* to small areas (D. Janos, pers. comm.).

Community Ecology

PRIMARY PRODUCTIVITY AND NUTRIENT CYCLING

No studies of primary productivity of natural forests have been done in Costa Rica, nor are data on plant biomass (standing crop) available. Scarcity of data, of course, has not hindered generalizations for tropical forests (e.g., Rodin and Bazilevich 1967; Kira and Ogawa 1971; Rodin, Bazilevich, and Rozov 1975; Golley 1975). Annual gross primary productivity for humid tropical forests appears to range between 75 and 150 tons/ha/yr, yielding net primary productivity of 25–50 tons/ha/yr. Dry forests appear to have productivity values roughly half those for moist and wetter forests. Total plant biomass appears to range between 600 and 1,200 tons/ha. Estimates available are crude at best and tell us practically nothing about the variability of primary productivity and total plant biomass in different Life Zones, or about the ecology of the site.

Productivity studies in El Verde, Puerto Rico (Odum and Pigeon 1970), Darien, Panama (Golley et al. 1975), Amazonian Brazil near Manaus (Klinge et al. 1975), and the Río Negro region of Amazonian Venezuela (Herrera et al. 1978) should not be considered representative of Costa Rican forests. All four study areas are on soils much poorer in nutrients than most Costa Rican soils.

The hypothesis of direct nutrient cycling (Went and Stark 1968) and the realization that luxuriant tropical forests may occur on quite infertile soils have stimulated considerable investigation of nutrient cycling in tropical forests. Most of the productivity studies mentioned above also include information on nutrient (or mineral) cycling. Jordan and Kline (1972) review the state of knowledge about nutrient cycling in tropical forests. My earlier expression of caution about generalizing from productivity studies to Cost Rican forests is even more appropriate to nutrient cycling. The infertile Ultisols near Manaus and the mosaic of practically sterile white sands (Spodosols) and lateritic (Oxisols) soils in the Río Negro region of Venezuela and Brazil are very different from the relatively fertile soils of Costa Rica (Harris, Neumann, and Stouse 1971).

In an analysis of nutrient status on volcanic (andesitic) soils in San Carlos, Costa Rica, Krebs (1975) found that permanent agriculture did not cause serious deterioration of soil nutrients. On a fairly fertile soil near Turrialba, Costa Rica, Harcombe (1973) found that early secondary succession accumulated nutrients in approximately equal proportions from decomposition of organic debris and from external inputs such as rain, dust, and soil mineralization.

As part of the OTS comparative ecosystem project, investigators from the University of Washington's College of Forest Resources collected considerable quantities of data on nutrient cycling, primarily at La Selva and secondarily at Palo Verde. The few publications that have come out of that project are based on rather short data runs lasting a few days to a few weeks. Substantial quantities of nutrients are leached out of the canopy by intense rainfall and moved by throughfall and stemflow into the soil and to a lesser degree on through the watershed by groundwater (McColl 1970). Carbonic acid is postulated as the primary cation leaching agent in noncalcareous tropical soils by Johnson, Cole, and Gessel 1975). These authors report that litter decomposition accounts for only 25–50% of the CO_2 produced in the soil; the remainder is attributed to root respiration and microbial activity. CO_2 entrapment and buildup occurs because of poor diffusivity in the soil. Passage of a wetting front creates appreciable quantities of carbonic acid that leaches cations through the soil profile. The authors report that CO_2 evolution is an order of magnitude greater in La Selva soil than in a Douglas fir forest soil in western Washington state. Carbonic acid leaching of tropical forest soils may be an overlooked flux in the current polemic over whether tropical forests are a source or sink for the global carbon cycle.

PHENOLOGY

Phenological studies of the periodicity of leaf production and senescence, flowering, and fruiting of tropical trees in Costa Rica were stimulated by Janzen's (1967) paper on the synchronization of sexual reproduction with the strong dry season in Guanacaste. Despite the inimical physical conditions caused by severe annual drought, numerous tree species flower during the dry season. Janzen (1967) interpreted dry-season flowering as in part an optimum time for pollinator activity, but, more important, he pointed out the advantage of being reproductive at a time when adjacent tree crowns are not engaging in vegetative competition because they are quiescent and leafless.

Knowledge of tropical tree and forest phenology has been greatly advanced by the considerable efforts of Gordon Frankie, Herbert Baker, and Paul Opler (1974a,b), who in 1968 initiated detailed phenological monitoring of a majority of tree species in a tropical dry forest area (the front part of Comelco ranch, near Bagaces) and in a tropical wet forest (La Selva). Only 8% (N = 331) of the tree species in La Selva are deciduous, and virtually all of them are canopy species; hence the canopy remains evergreen with scattered deciduous crowns during the driest time of year. The dry forest canopy is almost entirely deciduous during the long dry season, while the understory is partially deciduous. Periodicity of leaf fall coincides well with the onset of the primary dry season at each site, even though February–March is seldom effectively dry at La Selva. In the wet forest leaf flushing peaks in January, a generally wet month, but in the dry forest it occurs just before and after the rainy season.

In the wet forest, Frankie, Baker, and Opler (1974a) differentiate seasonally flowering ($\bar{x} = 6.5$ weeks) from extended-flowering species ($\bar{x} = 23$ weeks) and report that the length of flowering is very similar for overstory and understory tree species. Seasonally flowering species have a slight peak during February–March and gradually taper off through the rest of the year. Extended-flowering species have a major peak during May–August. A definite fruiting peak occurs in September–October.

Dry forest flowering has two peaks—a broad, mid-dry-season period and a sharp peak immediately after the rainy season starts. Sporadic light rain showers in the few weeks before the heavy rains start are the proximal cue to synchronization of flowering of many tree species at the end of the dry season (Opler, Frankie, and Baker 1976). The peak of fruit maturation is spread through the dry season.

The most complete phenological study of all flowering plants was done on Barro Colorado Island, Panama (Foster 1973; Croat 1975). Barro Colorado has a double peak of flowering activity—one in the dry season and one in the wet season—that corresponds well with its intermediate situation (tropical moist forest) between dry and wet sites studied by Frankie's team. Croat (1975) reports that more species flower and fruit in the rainy season than in the dry season, although the greater dry-season synchrony produces a higher peak. Foster's (1973) detailed study demonstrates that an unusually wet "dry season" in 1970 prevented many species from flowering and fruiting, with drastic consequences for frugivore populations.

Detailed phenological studies of indigenous species are very few (e.g., Mori and Kallunki 1976) and gener-

ally report unusual behavior. The dry forest understory tree *Jacquinia pungens* (Theophrastaceae) is deciduous during the rainy season but produces leaves, flowers, and fruit during the dry season; *Jacquinia* has a very long taproot, which enables it to be in full leaf below the deciduous canopy (Janzen 1970a). Being dormant during the rainy season, even in full shade, costs the tree about a third of its starch reserves (Janzen and Wilson 1974).

Some trees regularly flower and fruit once in two years (e.g., *Andira inermis* and *Hymenolobium pulcherrimum*, both Fabaceae); others do so irregularly once in three to six years (e.g., *Licania* sp., Chrysobalanaceae, *Ouratea lucens*, Ochnaceae). However, almost no Neotropical tree species synchronously produce mast fruiting at long intervals like the tropical Far Eastern Dipterocarpaceae (see Janzen 1974).

Perennial plants that flower once before dying, such as bamboos and some palms, have long attracted the attention of biologists (Janzen 1976a). Among the few dicot trees that are monocarpic, that is, die after reproducing once, *Tachigalia versicolor* (Caesalpiniaceae) cohorts appear to be four years offset from each other (Foster 1977). Some individuals in a population flower, then die as the large fruit crop matures. In some trees only a branch or part of the crown is reproductive and then dies, while the nonreproductive branches remain healthy.

Phenological patterns may be important components of community organization, such as with nectivorous guilds of birds (Feinsinger 1976; Stiles 1978), or the high species richness of sympatric species (Gentry 1974, 1976).

REPRODUCTIVE BIOLOGY

Research on the reproductive biology of tropical plants has focused on three aspects: breeding systems, pollination, and seed dispersal and predation. The generally held interpretation that individuals of a species are hyperdispersed in species-rich tropical forests (e.g., Richards 1952) gave rise to the assumption that most tropical tree species must be self-compatible (e.g., Baker 1959; Fedorov 1966). The pioneering studies of Kamal Bawa on tropical tree breeding systems indicates that self-incompatibility mechanisms are more prevalent in tropical dry forest than in temperate forests and that dioecy is surprisingly frequent for biotically pollinated species (Bawa 1974; Bawa and Opler 1975). Recent studies demonstrate that bees are effective long-distance pollinators (Janzen 1971a; Frankie, Opler, and Bawa 1976). Evidence is also accumulating that tropical tree species are not spatially hyperdispersed but are generally regularly or randomly distributed, or even occasionally clumped (Hubbell 1979), but nevertheless are much farther apart than it they grew in proportion to the density of their seed shadows (Janzen 1971*d*).

The predominance of biotic pollination in lowland tropical forests has led to spectacularly coevolved pollination systems involving very complex floral attractions and deceptions. Some of these systems, such as for orchids and bees, have received much attention; others are not nearly as well known, such as for figs and wasps (Janzen 1979). It is impossible to adequately review the fascinating field of pollination here, but some recent papers on tropical pollination systems should provide the necessary entrée to the abundant literature (Cruden et al. 1976; Essig 1971; Gentry 1978; Gilbert and Raven 1975; Janzen 1968; Linhart 1973; Opler, Baker, and Frankie 1975; Toledo 1977; Uhl and Moore 1977).

The relationship of seed predation and spacing of tropical trees has received considerable attention, particularly owing to Janzen's prolific research on insect seed predation in tropical dry forests. Host-specific predators devastate seed crops unless seeds escape in space or time or both via dispersal or toxicity or satiating the predators (Janzen 1969, 1971*b,c,e*, 1972, 1975*a,b*; Janzen and Wilson 1977; Silander 1978). The high degree of seed and seedling predation precludes establishment of regeneration near the parent tree, hence herbivores may have an important effect on species-packing in tropical forests (Janzen 1970*b*, 1971*d*). Much less is known about vertebrate predation on seeds (e.g., Higgins 1979).

Vertebrates are extremely important vectors for seed dispersal in tropical forests. Wind dispersal of tree seeds accounts for 31% of dry forest trees (Frankie, Baker, and Opler 1974*a*) and only 8% for La Selva trees (Hartshorn 1978). Including wind-dispersed canopy lianas and epiphytes would be expected to raise the percentage a few points, but the floras are still too poorly known to permit a more complete analysis of dispersal modes. For La Selva trees ($N = 320$ species) Hartshorn (1978) estimates that 50% have diaspores of the type dispersed by birds and 13% have those of the type dispersed by bats. The remainder are dispersed by arboreal and terrestrial mammals or by wind. Only the riparian *Ficus glabrata* (Moraceae) appears to be fish-dispersed. This contrasts, not unexpectedly, with the important role Amazonian fish play in dispersal of varzea forest seeds (Gottsberger 1978).

A few detailed studies of seed dispersal by birds have been done in Costa Rica on *Casearia corymbosa* in the Flacourtiaceae (Howe and Primack 1975; Howe 1977; Howe and Vande Kerckhove 1979) and on *Stemmadenia donnell-smithii* in the Apocynaceae (McDiarmid, Ricklefs, and Foster 1977; Cant 1979). Bats are effective dispersal agents of aggregate fruits like *Ficus* and *Piper*, as well as of large single-seeded fruits such as *Dipteryx* and *Andira* (e.g., Morrison 1978; Vasquez-Yanes et al.

1975). The propensity of bats to carry diaspores to night feeding roosts often produces discernible seed shadows (Janzen et al. 1976; Janzen 1978*a,b*). I have also encountered substantial concentrations of *Brosimum alicastrum* (Moraceae) and *Calophyllum brasiliense* (Guttiferae) seeds under trees of different species obviously used as feeding roosts by bats.

Terrestrial mammals can be important seed dispersal agents, as in the scatter-hoarding of seeds by agoutis (Smythe 1970) or the diaspores that easily attach to passersby (Bullock and Primack 1977).

Species characteristic of swamps and coastal habitats often have diaspores that float (e.g., *Carapa guianensis*, Meliaceae; *Prioria copaifera*, Caesalpiniaceae). Mangrove species have dispersal properties that are well adapted to their habitat preferences (Rabinowitz 1978).

TREE ARCHITECTURE

Hallé and Oldeman's (1970) characterization of tropical trees by architectural models has recently appeared in an expanded English version (Hallé, Oldeman, and Tomlinson 1978) that is a veritable gold mine of information on tropical trees. For the thousands of tropical tree species, only twenty-three architectural models have been found. Each architectural model is based on a set of morphological characters that includes the life-span of meristems and the degree and type of differentiation of vegetative meristems; the latter involves sexual versus vegetative differentiation, plagiotropy (horizontal axes) versus orthotropy (vertical axes), rhythmic (episodic) versus continuous growth, and chronology of branch development.

Some examples of well-represented architectural models are Corner's model (*Carica papaya*, *Cocos nucifera*, *Welfia georgii*); Tomlinson's model (*banana*); Koriba's model (*Hura crepitans*); Nozeran's model (*Theobroma cacao*); Aubreville's model (*Terminalia catappa*); Massart's model (*Araucaria heterophylla*, *Ceiba pentandra*); and Cook's model (*Castilla elastica*).

Architectural models are most easily determined in young, free-growing trees. Mature trees in the forest are more difficult to categorize because of vegetative plasticity and responses to competition and damage; however, reiteration of the basic architectural model is evident in vegetative sprouting.

An intriguing potential use of tree architecture models is in the investigation of forest dynamics and management. Do pioneer, gap, and climax tree species represent different models? Are shade-tolerant and shade-intolerant tree species mutually exclusive models? Are there optimum mixtures of architectural models for photosynthetic efficiency? Are forest strata occupied by trees with different architectural models? The use of architectural analysis should stimulate some exciting new areas of research on tropical trees and forests.

Because of our considerable ignorance about the root systems of tropical trees (but see Longman and Jeník 1974; Jeník 1978), architecture models only vaguely address root systems. In Neotropical forests, buttresses and taproots appear to be mutually exclusive. Non-buttressed canopy trees—for example, *Bertholletia excelsa, Lecythis costaricensis* (both Lecythidaceae), *Sterculia recordiana* (Sterculiaceae), *Chaunochiton kappleri* (Olacaceae), and *Sacoglottis trichogyna* (Humiriaceae) —have a well-developed system of feeder roots near the soil surface. In contrast, nonbuttressed subcanopy trees with a large conical taproot, for example, *Naucleopsis naga* (Moraceae) and *Grias fendleri* (Lecythidaceae), do not have extensive surface feeder roots. Slow-growing, shade-tolerant subcanopy trees may be obtaining nutrients from the subsoil rather than competing for nutrients from litter decomposition. Even less is known about the root systems of understory trees, but I have seen no evidence of taproots on shade-tolerant species. Fast-growing, shade-intolerant understory trees and treelets appear to have superficial root systems.

Janzen (1976b) suggests that hollow trunks may be adaptive by providing a roosting site for bats, whose guano could then be tapped by the "host" tree's roots. There is some evidence that a hollow tree's roots exploit the nutrient resources beneath the hollow trunk (Dickenson and Tanner 1978).

DOMINANCE AND DIVERSITY
Single-species dominance is most pronounced in tropical montane rain forest on the Cerro (table 7.14), where *Quercus costaricensis* (Fagaceae) has an important value of 41%, precisely triple the value of the second most important species, *Miconia bipulifera* (Melastomataceae). The only lowland tropical oak, *Quercus oleoides,* dominates the dry forest on pumice and rhyolitic ash soils with an importance value of 37% (table 7.2), more than three and a half times the value of *Byrsonima crassifolia* (Malpighiaceae), the second most important species.

Pentaclethra macroloba (Mimosaceae) dominates the virgin forests of La Selva (tables 7.9–12) (Hartshorn 1972), with importance values between 18% and 23%, more than double the values of the second most important species, except in the swamp (table 7.10), where *Carapa guianensis* (Meliaceae) has an importance value of 11%. In the Palo Verde forest, *Calycophyllum candidissimum* (Rubiaceae) is nearly twice as important (11%) as the second-ranked species (table 7.3).

Of the four sites with adequate plot data, Corcovado's forests show the weakest dominance. Dominant species are evident where restrictive site factors substantially reduce species diversity (tables 7.7 and 7.8; also Janzen 1978c). It is clear (tables 7.4 and 7.5) that dominance does not occur in the forests of the Corcovado uplands.

Species diversity is greatest in the upland forests of Corcovado—undoubtedly the richest forest in Central America. Dominance of the La Selva forests by *Pentaclethra macroloba* greatly reduces the alpha diversity of trees in the La Selva forest. Even though the heterogeneous forests of Palo Verde and Santa Rosa lack a strongly dominant species, the alpha diversity of these forests is less than at La Selva because of lower species richness in the dry forests. It is hoped that more plot data will become available for Monteverde, Corcovado, and Santa Rosa that will then permit much more detailed analyses of patterns in Costa Rican tree species diversity.

Analyzing the wealth of data on tree species diversity and soil nutrients from the Holdridge et al. (1971) study sites in Costa Rica, Huston (1980) found a strong negative correlation between tree species diversity and soil fertility. This pattern of lower species diversity on more fertile soils appears equally valid within sites (e.g., Corcovado) and between sites and typifies Amazonian forests as well. Even the species-rich forests of Corcovado (100–120 species/ha) pale in comparison with Amazonian forests, where the number of species 10 cm and larger in diameter ranges between 150 and 200 per hectare.

FOREST SUCCESSION AND DYNAMICS
Several papers summarizing important aspects of Neotropical secondary succession appeared in a supplemental issue of *Biotropica* (Ewel 1980), hence it would be presumptuous to attempt to review here this vast field. Much less attention has been given to successional and dynamic processes in late secondary and mature forests. In the same *Biotropica* supplement, I review our present understanding of Neotropical forest dynamics. (Hartshorn 1980).

Based on my travels to many forests in tropical America, I believe La Selva is at the fast end of the range of Neotropical forest dynamics; that is, tree falls are more frequent in La Selva than in any other mature forest I have visited in tropical America. That of course excludes obvious successional forests such as the *Euterpe* palm breaks on the windward ridges of Puerto Rico maintained by hurricanes. In Corcovado, tree falls do not appear to be as prevalent as in La Selva. Drier forests (e.g., Palo Verde, Santa Rosa) and midelevation forests (e.g., Monteverde) do not appear to be as dynamic as La Selva; however, long-term monitoring will be necessary to determine if gaps are any less important to species regeneration elsewhere than at La Selva.

Forest dynamic processes in western Amazonia (western Brazil, northern Bolivia, eastern Peru and Ecuador, and southern Colombia) appear to be similar to those found to be important in Costa Rican forests (see Hartshorn 1978, 1980). However, in central and northeastern Amazonia on much poorer soils, gap-phase dynamics are strikingly different. Near San Carlos de Río Negro, Venezuela, on white sand soils (Spodosols) I noticed most trees die while still standing rather than being uprooted or having the entire crown snap off. The gradual crown attrition of dead branches followed by the fall of a branchless bole does not open up a substantial canopy gap, nor does it cause high mortality of nearby trees. A small, one-crown canopy gap is filled by competing pole-sized trees that survived the death of the canopy tree. This type of canopy replacement suggests that most tree species must be shade-tolerant, which is quite different from the abundance of shade-intolerant species in the La Selva forest. A greater proportion of shade-tolerant canopy species would indicate more deterministic forest dynamics than occurs in the highly stochastic forests of Central America and western Amazonia.

*

Allen, P. H. 1956. *The rain forests of Golfo Dulce.* Gainesville: University of Florida Press.

Anderson, R., and Mori, S. 1967. A preliminary investigation of *Raphia* palm swamps, Puerto Viejo, Costa Rica. *Turrialba* 17:221–24.

Baker, H. G. 1959. Reproductive methods as factors in speciation in flowering plants. *Cold Spring Harbor Symp. Quant. Biol.* 24:177–91.

Bauar, G. N. 1968. *The ecological basis of rainforest management.* Sydney: Forest Commission of New South Wales, Australia.

Bawa, K. S. 1974. Breeding systems of tree species of a lowland tropical community. *Evolution* 28:85–92.

Bawa, K. S., and Opler, P. A. 1975. Dioecism in tropical forest trees. *Evolution* 29:167–79.

Beard, J. S. 1945. *The natural vegetation of Trinidad.* Oxford Forest Memoir no. 20. Oxford: Oxford University Press.

Black, H. L., and Harper, K. T. 1979. The adaptive value of buttresses to tropical trees: Additional hypotheses. *Biotropica* 11:240.

Boza, M. A., and Bonilla, A. 1978. Los parques nacionales de Costa Rica. Madrid: INCAFO.

Brieger, F. G. 1969. Patterns of evolutionary and geographical distribution in Neotropical orchids. *Biol. J. Linn. Soc.* 1:197–217.

Budowski, G. 1965. Distribution of tropical American rain forest species in the light of successional processes. *Turrialba* 15:40–42.

Bullock, S. H., and Primack, R. B. 1977. Comparative experimental study of seed dispersal on animals. *Ecology* 58:681–86.

Burger, W., ed. 1971. Flora costaricensis. *Fieldiana, Bot.* 35:1–227.

———, ed. 1977. Flora costaricensis. *Fieldiana, Bot.* 40:291.

Cain, S. A.; Oliveira Castro, G. M. de; Murça Pires, J.; and Tomas de Silva, N. 1956. Application of some phytosociological techniques to Brazilian rain forest. *Am. J. Bot.* 43:911–41.

Cant, J. G. H. 1979. Dispersal of *Stemmadenia donnell-smithii* by birds and monkeys. *Biotropica* 11:122.

Corner, E. J. H. 1940. *Wayside trees of Malaya.* 2 vols. Singapore: Government Printing Office.

Croat, T. B. 1975. Phenological behavior of habit and habitat classes on Barro Colorado Island (Panama Canal Zone). *Biotropica* 7:270–77.

Cruden, R. W.; Kinsman, S.; Stockhouse, R. E., II; and Linhart, Y. B. 1976. Pollination, fecundity, and the distribution of moth-flowered plants. *Biotropica* 8:204–10.

Daubenmire, R. 1972. Ecology of *Hyparrhenia rufa* (Nees) in derived savanna in north-western Costa Rica. *J. Appl. Ecol.* 9:11–23.

Davis, T. A. W., and Richards, P. W. 1933. The vegetation of Moraballi Creek, British Guiana: An ecological study of a limited area of tropical rain forest. Part I. *J. Ecol.* 21:350–84.

———. 1934. The vegetation of Moraballi Creek, British Guiana: An ecological study of a limited area of tropical rain forest. Part 2. *J. Ecol.* 22:106–155.

Dean, J. M., and Smith, A. P. 1978. Behavioral and morphological adaptations of a tropical plant to high rainfall. *Biotropica* 10:152–54.

DeFillips, R. 1969. Parasitism in *Ximenia*. *Rhodora* 71:439–43.

Dickinson, T. A., and Tanner, E. V. J. 1978. Exploitation of hollow trunks by tropical trees. *Biotropica* 10:231–33.

Edmisten, J. 1970. Preliminary studies of the nitrogen budget of a tropical rain forest. In *A tropical rain forest,* ed. H. T. Odum and R. F. Pigeon, chap. H-211-215. Washington, D.C.: USAEC.

Essig, F. B. 1971. Observations on pollination in *Bactris*. *Principes* 15:20–24.

Ewel, J. 1980. Special issue on tropical succession. *Biotropica* 12 (suppl.):1.

Fedorov, A. A. 1966. The structure of the tropical rain forest and speciation in the humid tropics. *J. Ecol.* 54:1–11.

Feinsinger, P. 1976. Organization of a tropical guild of nectarivorous birds. *Ecol. Monogr.* 46:257–91.

Foreman, R. T. T. 1975. Canopy lichens with blue-green algae: A nitrogen source in a Colombian rain forest. *Ecology* 56:1176–84.

Foster, R. B. 1973. Seasonality of fruit production and seed fall in a tropical forest ecosystem in Panama. Ph.D. diss., Duke University.

———. 1977. *Tachigalia versicolor* is a suicidal Neotropical tree. *Nature* 268:624–26.

Frankie, G. W.; Baker, H. G.; and Opler, P. A. 1974a. Comparative phenological studies of trees in tropical wet and dry forests in the lowlands of Costa Rica. *J. Ecol.* 62:881–919.

————. 1974*b*. Tropical plant phenology: Applications for studies in community ecology. In *Phenology and seasonality modeling,* ed. H. Lieth, pp. 287–96. New York: Springer-Verlag.

Frankie, G. W.; Opler P. A.; and Bawa, K. S. 1976. Foraging behaviour of solitary bees: Implications for outcrossing of a Neotropical forest tree species. *J. Ecol.* 64:1049–57.

Gentry, A. H. 1974. Flowering phenology and diversity in tropical Bignoniaceae. *Biotropica* 6:64–68.

————. 1976. Bignoniaceae of southern Central America: Distribution and ecological specificity. *Biotropica* 8:117–31.

————. 1978. Anti-pollinators for mass-flowering plants? *Biotropica* 10(1):68–69.

Gilbert, L. E., and Raven, P. H., eds. 1975. *Coevolution of animals and plants.* Austin: University of Texas Press.

Givnish, T. J. 1978. On the adaptive significance of compound leaves, with particular reference to tropical trees. In *Tropical trees as living systems,* ed. P. B. Tomlinson and M. H. Zimmermann, pp. 351–80. London: Cambridge University Press.

Givnish, T. J., and Vermeij, G. J. 1976. Sizes and shapes of liane leaves. *Am. Nat.* 110:743–78.

Golley, F. B. 1975. Productivity and mineral cycling in tropical forests. In *Productivity of world ecosystems,* pp. 106–15. Washington, D.C.: NAS.

Golley, F. B.; McGinnis, J. T.; Clements, R. G.; Child, G. I.; Duever, M. J.; plus Duke, J.; Ewel, J.; and Gist, C. 1975. *Mineral cycling in a tropical moist forest ecosystem.* Athens: University of Georgia Press.

Gottsberger, G. 1978. Seed dispersal by fish in the inundated regions of Humaita, Amazonia. *Biotropica* 10:170–83.

Greig-Smith, P. 1952. Ecological observations on degraded and secondary forest in Trinidad, British West Indies. I. General features of the vegetation. *J. Ecol.* 40:283–315.

Grubb, P. J.; Lloyd, J. R.; Pennington, T. D.; and Whitmore, T. C. 1963. A comparison of montane and lowland rain forest in Ecuador. 1. The forest structure, physiognomy and floristics. *J. Ecol.* 51:567–601.

Grubb, P. J., and Whitmore, T. C. 1966. A comparison of montane and lowland rain forest in Ecuador. 2. The climate and its effects on the distribution and physiognomy of the forests. *J. Ecol.* 54:303–33.

Hallé, F., and Oldeman, R. A. A. 1970. *Essai sur l'architecture et la dynamique de croissance des arbres tropicaux.* Paris: Masson.

Hallé, F.; Oldeman, R. A. A.; and Tomlison, P. B. 1978. *Tropical trees and forests: An architectural analysis.* New York: Springer-Verlag.

Harcombe, P. A. 1973. Nutrient cycling in secondary plant succession in a humid tropical forest region (Turrialba, Costa Rica). Ph.D. diss., Yale University.

Harris, S. A.; Neumann, A. M.; and Stouse, P. A., Jr. 1971. The major soil zones of Costa Rica. *Soil Sci.* 122:439–47.

Hartshorn, G. S. 1972. The ecological life history and population dynamics of *Pentaclethra macroloba,* a tropical wet forest dominant and *Stryphnodendron excelsum,* an occasional associate. Ph.D. diss., University of Washington.

————. 1977. *Critérios para la clasificación de bosques y la determinación del uso potenciál de tierras en Paraguay.* Informe técnico 8. Asunción: FAO/FO:DP/PAR/72/001.

————. 1978. Tree falls and tropical forest dynamics. In *Tropical trees as living systems,* ed. P. B. Tomlinson and M. H. Zimmermann, pp. 617–38. London: Cambridge University Press.

————. 1980. Neotropical forest dynamics. *Biotropica* 12 (suppl.):23–30.

Hazen, W. E. 1966. Analysis of spatial pattern in epiphytes. *Ecology* 47:634–35.

Heithaus, E. R. 1979. Community structure of Neotropical flower visiting bees and wasps: Diversity and phenology. *Ecology* 60:190–202.

Henwood, K. 1973. A structural model of forces in buttressed tropical rain forest trees. *Biotropica* 5:83–93.

Herrera, R.; Jordan, C. F.; Klinge, H.; and Medina, E. 1978. Amazon ecosystems: Their structure and functioning with particular emphasis on nutrients. *Interciencia* 3:223–31.

Herwitz, S. 1979. The regeneration of selected tropical wet forest tree species in Corcovado National Park, Costa Rica. M.A. thesis, University of California, Berkeley.

Higgins, M. L. 1979. Intensity of seed predation on *Brosimum utile* by mealy parrots (*Amazona farinosa*) *Biotropica* 11:80.

Holdridge, L. R. 1947. Determination of world plant formations from simple climatic data. *Science* 105:367–68.

————. 1967. *Life zone ecology.* Rev. ed. San José: Tropical Science Center.

Holdridge. L. R.; Grenke, W. C.; Hatheway, W. H.; Liang, T.; and Tosi, J. A., Jr. 1971. *Forest environments in tropical life zones: A pilot study.* Pergamon Press.

Horn, H. S. 1971. *The adaptive geometry of trees.* Princeton: Princeton University Press.

Howe, H. F. 1977. Bird activity and seed dispersal of a tropical wet forest tree. *Ecology* 58:539–50.

Howe, H. F., and Primack, R. B. 1975. Differential seed dispersal by birds of the tree *Casearia nitida* (Flacourtiaceae). *Biotropica* 7:278–83.

Howe, H. F., and Vande Kerckhove, G. S. 1979. Fecundity and seed dispersal of a tropical tree. *Ecology* 60:180–89.

Hubbell, S. P. 1979. Tree dispersion, abundance, and diversity in a tropical dry forest. *Science* 203:1299–1309.

Huston, M. 1980. Soil nutrients and community structure in Costa Rican forests. *J. Biogeogr.* 7:147–57.

Janzen, D. H. 1967. Synchronization of sexual reproduction of trees within the dry season in Central America. *Evolution* 21:620–37.

————. 1968. Reproductive behavior in the Passifloraceae and some of its pollinators in Central America. *Behaviour* 32:33–48.

———. 1969. Seed-eaters versus seed size, number, toxicity and dispersal. *Evolution* 23:1–27.

———. 1970*a*. *Jacquinia pungens,* a heliophile from the understory of tropical deciduous forest. *Biotropica* 2:112–19.

———. 1970*b*. Herbivores and the number of tree species in tropical forests. *Am. Nat.* 104:501–28.

———. 1971*a*. Euglossine bees as long-distance pollinators of tropical plants. *Science* 171:203–5.

———. 1971*b*. Escape of *Cassia grandis* L. beans from predators in time and space. *Ecology* 52:964–79.

———. 1971*c*. The fate of *Scheelea rostrata* fruits beneath the parent tree: Predispersal attack by bruchids. *Principes* 15:89–101.

———. 1971*d*. Seed predation by animals. *Ann. Rev. Ecol. Syst.* 2:465–92.

———. 1971*e*. Escape of juvenile *Dioclea megacarpa* (Leguminosae) vines from predators in a deciduous tropical forest. *Am. Nat.* 105:97–112.

———. 1972. Escape in space by *Sterculia apetala* seeds from the bug *Dysdercus fasciatus* in a Costa Rican deciduous forest. *Ecology* 53:350–61.

———. 1973. Rate of regeneration after a tropical high elevation fire. *Biotropica* 5:117–22.

———. 1974. Tropical blackwater rivers, animals, and mast fruiting by the Dipterocarpaceae. *Biotropica* 6:69–103.

———. 1975*a*. Intra- and interhabitat variations in *Guazuma ulmifolia* (Sterculiaceae) seed predation by *Amblycerus cistelinus* (Bruchidae) in Costa Rica. *Ecology* 56:1009–13.

———. 1975*b*. Behavior of *Hymenaea courbaril* when its predispersal seed predator is absent. *Science* 189:145–47.

———. 1976*a*. Why bamboos wait so long to flower. *Ann. Rev. Ecol. Syst.* 7:347–91.

———. 1976*b*. Why tropical trees have rotten cores. *Biotropica* 8:110.

———. 1978*a*. The size of a local peak in a seed shadow. *Biotropica* 10:78.

———. 1978*b*. A bat-generated fig seed shadow in rainforest. *Biotropica* 10:121.

———. 1978*c*. Description of a *Pterocarpus officinalis* (Leguminosae) monoculture in Corcovado National Park, Costa Rica. *Brenesia* 14–15:305–9.

———. 1979. How to be a fig. *Ann. Rev. Ecol. Syst.* 10:13–51.

Janzen, D. H.; Miller, G. A.; Hackforth-Jones, J.; Pond, C. M.; Hooper, K.; and Janos, D. P. 1976. Two Costa Rican bat-generated seed shadows in *Andira inermis* (Leguminosae). *Ecology* 57:1068–75.

Janzen, D. H., and Wilson, D. E. 1974. The cost of being dormant in the tropics. *Biotropica* 6:260–62.

———. 1977. Natural history of seed predation by *Rosella sickingiae* Whitehead (Curculionidae) on *Sickingia maxonii* (Rubiaceae) in Costa Rican rainforest. *Coleopt. Bull.* 31:19–23.

Jeník, J. 1978. Roots and root systems in tropical trees: Morphologic and ecologic aspects. In *Tropical trees as living systems,* ed. P. B. Tomlinson and M. H. Zimmermann, pp. 323–49. London: Cambridge University Press.

Johnson, D.; Cole, D. W.; and Gessel, S. P. 1975. Processes of nutrient transfer in a tropical rain forest. *Biotropica* 7:208–15.

Jordan, C. F., and Kline, J. R. 1972. Mineral cycling: Some basic concepts and their application in a tropical rain forest. *Ann. Rev. Ecol. Syst.* 3:33–50.

Kira, T., and Ogawa, H. 1971. Assessment of primary production in tropical and equatorial forests. *Proc. UNESCO Brussels Symp.*, pp. 309–21.

Klinge, H.; Rodrigues, W. A.; Brunig, E.; and Fitthau, E. J. 1975. Biomass and structure in a central Amazonian rain forest. In *Tropical ecological systems: Trends in terrestrial and aquatic research,* ed. F. B. Golley and E. Medina, pp. 115–22. New York: Springer-Verlag.

Krebs, J. E. 1975. A comparison of soils under agriculture and forests in San Carlos, Costa Rica. *In Tropical ecological systems: Trends in terrestrial and aquatic research,* ed. F. B. Golley and E. Medina, pp. 381–90. New York: Springer-Verlag.

Lawton, R., and Dryer, V. 1980. The vegetation of the Monteverde Cloud Forest Reserve. *Brenesia* 18:101–16.

Lee, D. W.; Lowry, J. B.; and Stone, B. C. 1979. Abaxial anthocyanin layer in leaves of tropical rain forest plants: Enhancer of light capture in deep shade. *Biotropica* 11:70–77.

Lewis, B. E. 1982. Land-use and conservation on the Osa Peninsula, Costa Rica. Ph.D. diss., University of California, Berkeley.

Linhart, Y. B. 1973. Ecological and behavioral determinants of pollen dispersal in hummingbird-pollinated *Heliconia. Am. Nat.* 107:511–23.

Longman, K. A., and Jeník, J. 1974. *Tropical forest and its environment.* London: Longman.

McColl, J. G. 1970. Properties of some natural waters in a tropical wet forest of Costa Rica. *Bioscience* 20:1096–1100.

McDiarmid, R. W.; Ricklefs R. E.; and Foster, M. S. 1977. Dispersal of *Stemmadenia donnell-smithii* (Apocynaceae) by birds. *Biotropica* 9:9–25.

Montoya Maquín, J. M. 1966. Notas fitogeográficas sobre el *Quercus oleoides* Cham. y Schlecht. *Turrialba* 16:57–66.

Mooney, H. A.; Björkman, O.; Hall, A. E.; Medina, E.; and Tomlinson, P. B. 1980. The study of the physiological ecology of tropical plants—current status and needs. *Bioscience* 30:22–26.

Mori, S. A., and Kallunki, J. A. 1976. Phenology and floral biology of *Gustavia superba* (Lecythidaceae) in central Panama. *Biotropica* 8:184–92.

Morrison, D. W. 1978. Foraging ecology and energetics of the frugivorous bat *Artibeus jamaicensis. Ecology* 59:716–23.

Odum, H. T., and Pigeon, R. F., eds. 1970. *A tropical rain forest: A study of irradiation and ecology at El Verde, Puerto Rico*. Washington, D.C.: U.S. Atomic Energy Commission.

Oersted, A. S. 1871. *L'Amérique centrale, recherches sur sa flore et sa géographie physique: Résultats d'un voyage dans les Etats de Costa Rica et de Nicaragua, exécuté pendant les années 1846–1848*. Copenhagen.

Opler, P. A.; Baker, H. G.; and Frankie. G. W. 1975. Reproductive biology of some Costa Rican *Cordia* species (Boraginaceae). *Biotropica* 7:234–47.

Opler, P. A.; Frankie, G. W.; and Baker, H. G. 1976. Rainfall as a factor in the synchronization, release, and timing of anthesis by tropical trees and shrubs. *J. Biogeogr.* 3:231–36.

Perry, D. R. 1978. Factors influencing arboreal epiphytic phytosociology in Central America. *Biotropica* 10:235–37.

Petriceks, J. 1956. Plan de ordenación del bosque de la Finca "La Selva." M. Agr. thesis, Instituto Interamericano de Ciencias Agrícolas, Turrialba.

Pittier, H. 1957. *Ensayo sobre plantas usuales de Costa Rica*. 2d ed. San José: University of Costa Rica. Originally published 1908.

Pool, D. J.; Snedaker, S. C.; and Lugo, A. E. 1977. Structure of mangrove forests in Florida, Puerto Rico, Mexico and Costa Rica. *Biotropica* 9:195–212.

Rabinowitz, D. 1978. Dispersal properties of mangrove propagules. *Biotropica* 10:47–57.

Richards, P. W. 1952. *The tropical rainforest: An ecological study*. Cambridge: Cambridge University Press.

Rodin, L. E., and Bazilevich, N. I. 1967. *Production and mineral cycling in terrestrial vegetation*. Edinburgh: Oliver and Boyd.

Rodin, L. E.; Bazilevich, N. I.; and Rozov, N. N. 1975. Productivity of the world's main ecosystems. In Productivity of world ecosystems, pp. 13–26, Washington, D.C.: NAS.

Sawyer, J. O., and Lindsey, A. A. 1971. Vegetation of the life zones of Costa Rica. *Indiana Acad. Sci. Monogr.* no. 2.

Schimper, A. R. W. 1903. *Plant geography upon a physiological basis*. Oxford: Clarendon Press.

Silander, J. A., Jr. 1978. Density-dependent control of reproductive success in *Cassia biflora*. *Biotropica* 10:292–96.

Smith, A. P. 1972. Buttressing of tropical trees: A descriptive model and new hypotheses. *Am. Nat.* 106:32–46.

———. 1979. Buttressing of tropical trees in relation to bark thickness in Dominica, B.W.I. *Biotropica* 11:159–60.

Smythe, N. 1970. Relationships between fruiting seasons and seed dispersal methods in a Neotropical forest. *Am. Nat.* 104:25–35.

Spruce, R. 1908. *Notes of a botanist on the Amazon and Andes*. 2 vols. London.

Standley, P. C. 1937–38. *Flora of Costa Rica*. Chicago: Field Museum of Natural History.

Stiles, F. G. 1978. Temporal organization of flowering among the hummingbird foodplants of a tropical wet forest. *Biotropica* 10:194–210.

Strong, D. R., Jr.; and Ray, T. S., Jr. 1975. Host tree location behavior of a tropical vine *Monstera gigantea* by skototropism. *Science* 190:804–6.

Sugden, A. M., and Robins, R. J. 1979. Aspects of the ecology of vascular epiphytes in Colombian cloud forests. I. The distribution of the epiphytic flora. *Biotropica* 11:173–88.

Tasaico, H. 1959. La fisionomía de las hojas de árboles en algunas formaciónes tropicales. M. Agr. thesis, IICA, Turrialba.

Toledo, V. M. 1977. Pollination of some rain forest plants by non-hovering birds in Veracruz, Mexico. *Biotropica* 9:262–67.

Tosi, J. A., Jr. 1969. *Mapa ecológico, República de Costa Rica: Según la clasificación de zonas de vida del mundo de L. R. Holdridge*. San José: Centro Científico Tropical.

———. 1973. *The Corcovado basin on the Peninsula de Osa*. San José: Tropical Science Center.

———. 1976. *La zonificación ecológica preliminar de la región de Darién en la República de Colombia*. San José: Centro Científico Tropical.

Uhl, N. W., and Moore, H. E., Jr. 1977. Correlations of inflorescence, flower structure, and floral anatomy with pollination in some palms. *Biotropica* 9:170–90.

Vasquez-Yanes, C.; Orozco, A.; Francois, G.; and Trejo, L. 1975. Observations on seed dispersal by bats in a tropical humid region in Veracruz, Mexico. *Biotropica* 7:73–76.

Vaughan, C. 1979. Plan maestro para el manejo y desarrollo del Parque Nacional Corcovado, Península de Osa, Costa Rica. M.S. thesis, CATIE, Turrialba.

Wagner, M., and Scherzer, C. 1856. La República de Costa Rica en Centro America (1974 transl.) Vol. 1. San José: Ministera de Cultura, Juventud y Deportes.

Walter, H. 1973. *Vegetation of the earth in relation to climate and the ecophysiological conditions*. New York: Springer-Verlag.

Weber, H. 1959. Los páramos de Costa Rica y su concatenación fitogeográfica con los Andes Suramericanos. San José: Instituto Geografico.

Went, F. W., and Stark, N. 1968. Mycorrhiza. *Bioscience* 18:1035–39.

Wercklé, C. 1909. La subregion fitogeográfica costarricense. San José: Sociedad Nacional de Agronomia.

Werth, C. R.; Baird, W. V.; and Musselman, L. J. 1979. Root parasitism in *Schoepfia* Schreb. (Olacaceae). *Biotropica* 11:140–43.

Whitmore, T. C., and Burnham, C. P. 1975. *Tropical rain forests of the Far East*. London: Oxford University Press.

CHECKLIST OF TREES

G. S. Hartshorn and L. J. Poveda

We attempt to provide a reasonably up-to-date checklist of trees known at the seven major sites described in the preceding section. Rather than limiting our effort to a simple presence list, we have incorporated information on canopy stature and abundance of mature individuals, plus major habitats where the species occur. These three categories and their classes are:

1. Typical physiognomic position attained by mature individuals

    C = canopy (or emergent)

    S = subcanopy

    U = understory

    T = treelet (< 10 cm dbh or 5 m tall)

2. Abundance of mature individuals

    c = common (> 10/ha)

    f = frequent (1–10/ha)

    o = occasional (0.1–1/ha)

    r = rare (0.1–0.01/ha or between 1/10 ha and 1/100 ha)

    v = very rare (< 0.01/ha or < 1/100 ha)

3. Habitats

    R = riparian (streamside)

    A = alluvial (floodable, but good drainage)

    W = swamp (floodable, but poor drainage)

    P = plateau or flatlands (slopes ≤ 5%, moderate drainage)

    L = slope (slopes > 5%, good drainage)

    I = ridge (well drained to excessive drainage)

    O = open country, cultivated areas, pastures, etc.

    G = secondary forest

The information above is presented in the checklist as a three-part code: category 1 by an upper-case letter, category 2 by a lower-case letter, and category 3 by one or more upper-case letters. As an example, *Pentaclethra macroloba* (Mimosaceae) at La Selva has the code CcWLI, which means mature individuals (1) are canopy trees, (2) are common, and (3) occur in swamps and on slopes and ridges. In some instances we are uncertain about the abundance or habitat preferences of a species; hence we have simply left blank those parts of the code.

Let us stress that the checklist is not complete for any single site. A site such as La Selva is much better known floristically than is Corcovado or Monteverde. Such differences are readily apparent when one looks at the checklist entries for plant families with numerous species of small trees and treelets, such as the Rubiaceae, Piperaceae, or Melastomataceae.

Aereal extent and habitat diversity also affect the species richness at a site: La Selva is small, but the trees are reasonably well known; Corcovado is huge and should have at least five hundred species of trees; Monteverde includes three life zones and should also have at least five hundred species of trees; Las Cruces is very small and not very well known. It should be evident that it is not valid to use the presence data in our checklist to make any detailed comparisons of the tree flora between sites.

We thank Luís Diego Gómez for making available to us his informative list of tree ferns for the seven sites. We also thank Valerie Dryer and Bill Haber for valuable help with Monteverde trees. Finally, we welcome corrections and additions to this checklist.

Taxa	Santa Rosa	Palo Verde	Corcovado	La Selva	Monteverde	Las Cruces	Cerro de La Muerte
Acanthaceae							
Aphelandra deppeana Schlecht. & Cham.	TfPL			TfA	TvO		
Bravaisia integerrima (Spreng.) Standl.			CoA	CfA			
Justicia aurea Schlecht.				TrAG	ToLG		
Razisea spicata Oerst.				ToPL	TcPLG		
Actinidiaceae							
Saurauia veraguasensis Seem.					UfLIO		
Anacardiaceae							
Anacardium excelsum (Bert. & Balb.) Skeels		CfRA	CfRA				
Astronium graveolens Jacq.	CfL	CfPLI	CrLI				
Mauria heterophylla HBK.					SoOGI		
Spondias mombin L.	CfPLO	CfPLO	CfA	CrA			
Spondias purpurea L.	UoPLO	UoPLOAP	UrO				

Taxa	Santa Rosa	Palo Verde	Corcovado	La Selva	Monteverde	Las Cruces	Cerro de La Muerte
Spondias radlkoferi							
Donn. Smith		CfRA		CoA			
Spondias sp.			Crl				
Tapirira brenesii Standl.			SrR		CoPL		
Annonaceae							
Anaxagorea crassipetala Hemsl.			UfPL	UfPLI			
Anaxagorea phaeocarpa Mart.				UfLI			
Annona holosericea Safford		UrA	SrPLI				
Annona purpurea							
Moc. & Sessé	SoPL	SfPL					
Annona reticulata L.	SoPL	SoPL					
Annona sp.				UoLI			
Crematospermum sp.			SrL				
Cymbopetalum costaricense							
(Donn. Smith) Fries			UrA	UrA			
Cymbopetalum sp.				TrAPL			
Desmopsis bibracteata							
(Rob.) Safford	TrA				UoP		
Desmopsis maxonii Safford				UrAWP			
Desmopsis microcarpa Fries						UoL	
Guatteria aeruginosa Standl.				SoPL			
Guatteria amplifolia							
Triana & Planch.			UrPL				
Guatteria consanguinea							
Klotzsch.					SoWPL		
Guatteria costaricensis Fries					UoO		
Guatteria inuncta Fries			UfPL				
Guatteria tonduzii Diels						UoOL	
Guatteria verrucosa Fries					ToLP		
Rollinia microsepala Standl.			CoAL	CoAP; fG			
Sapranthus campechianus							
(HBK.) Standl.				UoAW			
Sapranthus palanga Fries	SoPL	SoPL					
Unonopsis pittieri Safford				SrAPL			
Xylopia sericophylla							
Standl. & L. Wms.			CrLI	CrPL			
Apocynaceae							
Aspidosperma megalocarpon							
Muell. Arg.			CfPL	CvP			
Aspidosperma myristicifolium							
(Markgr.) Woodson			CvLI				
Lacmellea panamensis							
(Woods.) Markgr.			CrPL	CoPL			
Plumeria rubra L. var.							
acutifolia (Ait.) Woods.	SoPLI	SoLI					
Rauvolfia purpurascens Standl.				SoPL			
Stemmadenia alfari							
(Donn. Sm.) Woodson					ToL		
Stemmadenia donnell-smithii							
(Rose) Woodson			UoA	SoAP			
Stemmadenia glabra Benth.					UvPLOG		
Stemmadenia macrantha							
Standl.				TvP			

159

Taxa	Santa Rosa	Palo Verde	Corcovado	La Selva	Monteverde	Las Cruces	Cerro de La Muerte
Stemmadenia obovata (Hook. & Arn.) Schum.	UoPL	UfPLRO					
Tabernaemontana arborea Rose				CrP			
Tabernaemontana chrysocarpa Blake	ToPR						
Tabernaemontana sp. (Dryer 1349)					S		
Thevetia ovata (Cav.) A. DC.	ToPL	TrPL					
Aquifoliaceae							
Ilex lamprophylla Standl.					SoPL		
Ilex skutchii Edwin				CrPL			
Ilex vulcanicola Standl.					SrP		
Araliaceae							
Dendropanax albertii-smithii Nevl.					SrLI		
Dendropanax arboreus (L.) Dcne. & Planch.			SoPL	SfPL	SoPLI	SoPL	
Dendropanax gonatopodus (D. Sm.) A. C. Smith					SoPL	SoPL	
Dendropanax praestans Standl.					SrI		
Dendropanax stenodontus (Standl.) A. C. Smith				UrR			
Didymopanax pittieri March.					CfLI		CfLI
Oreopanax nubigenum Standl.					SoLI		
Oreopanax oerstedianum March.					UoPL		UoPL
Oreopanax xalapensis (HBK.) Dcne. & Pkanch.					CoLI	SrPL	
Sciadodendron excelsum Griseb.	CoL	SrLI					
Betulaceae							
Alnus acuminata HBK.					SrRG		CcLIG
Bignoniaceae							
Crescentia alata HBK.	CfWO						
Enallagma latifolia (Mill.) Small	UoA		UfA				
Enallagma sp. (Dryer #1160)					UvPL		
Godmania aesculifolia (HBK.) Standl.	SoLI	SoPI					
Jacaranda copaia (Aubl.) D. Don			CrPL	CvL			
Parmentiera valerii Standl.			UoA				
Tabebuia guayacan (Seem.) Hemsl.			CrL	CrL			
Tabebuia impetiginosa (Mart.) Standl.	CoP	CfPL					
Tabebuia ochracea (Cham.) Standl.	CfPL	CfPL					
Tabebuia rosea (Vertol.) DC.	CfPL	CfAPL	CrW	CrW		CrPL	

160

Taxa	Santa Rosa	Palo Verde	Corovado	La Selva	Monteverde	Las Cruces	Cerro de La Muerte
Bixaceae							
Bixa orellana L.	UoOG	UoO					
Bombacaceae							
Bombacopsis quinatum (Jacq.) Dugand	CfPL	CfPL					
Ceiba aesculifolia (HBK.) Britt. & Baker	CvA						
Ceiba pentandra (L.) Gaertn.	CrAL	CoAP	CoA	CrAL		CoL	
Huberodendron patinoi			CvPLI				
Ochroma lagopus Swartz	CoAP		CfA; cG	CoWA		CoL	
Pachira aquatica Aubl.			CoAW	CrWA			
Pseudobombax septenatum (Jacq.) Dugand	CfPL	CfPL	CvW; fI				
Quararibea asterolepis Pittier			CfWA				
Quararibea bracteolosa (Ducke) Cuatr.				SfPL			
Quararibea sp.				UvR			
Quararibea parvifolia Standl.				TvR			
Quararibea platyphylla Pitt. & D. Sm.					SoLPG		
Boraginaceae							
Bourreria costaricensis (Standl.) A. Gentry					CoP		
Bourreria quirosii Standl.	SrPL	CvL					
Cordia alliodora (R. & P.) Oken	SfPL	SoPL		CcA			
Cordia bicolor DC.			SoPL	CoPL			
Cordia collococca L.		SrPL; cOG					
Cordia cymosa (D. Sm.) Standl.					SoPLG	SoPL	
Cordia dwyeri Nowicke			SoPL	SoPL			
Cordia gerascanthus L.	SfPL	SfPL	CrA				
Cordia lucidula I. M. Johnston				SrPL			
Cordia nitida Vahl.				ToPL			
Cordia panamensis Riley	UfPL	UoPL					
Ehretia austin-smithii Standl.					SoPO		
Tournefortia glabra L.			ToLO		ToPLG		
Tournefortia ramonensis Standl.					TrO		
Brunelliaceae							
Brunellia costaricensis Standl.					SoIL		ScPL
Brunellia standleyana Cuatr.						SfPLR	
Burseraceae							
Bursera graveolens (HBK.) Triana	TrI	SrI					
Bursera simaruba (L.) Sarg.	CfLI	CfPLI	CrA; fI	CrA			
Bursera permollis Standl. & Steyerm.	UfI	UfI					
Bursera tomentosa (Jacq.) Triana & Planch.	SoPL						

Taxa	Santa Rosa	Palo Verde	Corcovado	La Selva	Monteverde	Las Cruces	Cerro de La Muerte
Protium costaricense (Rose) Engler				UrPL			
Protium glabrum (Rose) Engler				SrPL			
Protium panamense (Rose) I. M. Johnston			SoAPL	SfPL			
Protium pittieri (Rose) Engler			SoPL	SfPL			
Protium sp.				UrAR			
Protium sp.				CoLI			
Tetragastris panamensis (Engl.) O. Kuntze			SfPL				
Tetragastris tomentosa D. M. Porter				CrLI			
Trattinnickia aspera (Standl.) Swart.			CrAL				
Cactaceae							
Lemaireocereus aragonii (Weber) Britt. & Rose	UoLI	UoI					
Caesalpiniaceae							
Ateleia herbert-smithii Pittier	ScP						
Bauhinia ungulata L.	UfPLO						
Caesalpinia coriaria (Jacq.) Willd.	SfR; rP						
Caesalpinia eriostachys Benth.		CfPL					
Caesalpinia exostemma DC.	TfR						
Cassia emarginata L.	ToPL	TrPL					
Cassia fruticosa Mill.			UoA	UoAP			
Cassia grandis Lf.	CoL	CrAP	CvL				
Cassia papillosa (B. & R.) Standl.	UrRPL	UoRPL					
Cassia reticulata Willd.			UfRAO			UrO	
Copaifea aromatica Dwyer			CoL				
Cynometra hemitomophylla (D. Sm.) Britt. & Rose			CoL				
Dialium guianense (Aubl.) Steud.			CoPL				
Haematoxylon brasiletto Karst.	SoAI	SrI					
Hymenaea courbaril L.	CfPL		CrPL				
Macrolobium costaricense W. Burger				SoL			
Mora oleifera (Triana) Ducke			CcRA				
Parkinsonia aculeata L.		CcA					
Peltogyne purpurea Pittier			CrL				
Schizolobium parahybum (Vell.) Blake			CoG				
Sclerolobium sp.				CrL			
Swartzia cubensis (Britt. & Wils.) Standl.	UrI			CrPL			
Swartzia simplex (Swartz) Spreng.			UrPL	UfPL			
Tachigalia versicolor Standl. & L. Wms.			CoPLI				

Taxa	Santa Rosa	Palo Verde	Corcovado	La Selva	Monteverde	Las Cruces	Cerro de La Muerte
Capparidaceae							
Capparis baducca L.		TrG					
Capparis indica							
(L.) Fawc. & Rendle	UoAP	UoA	UfA				
Capparis odoratissima Jacq.	UoAW	UfAW					
Capparis pittieri Standl.				UfPL			
Capparis pseudocacao Schum.					SrP		
Crataeva tapia L.	UoA	UoA	SoW	SfR			
Forchhammeria pallida Liebm.	CoA						
Morisonia americana L.	TrRA						
Caprifoliaceae							
Sambucus mexicana Presl.					UoR		
Viburnum costaricanum							
(Oersted.) Hemsl.					UfIG		
Caricaceae							
Jacaratia dolichaula							
(D. Sm.) I. M. Johnston			UoL	UoPL			
Jacaratia costaricensis							
I. M. Johnston			SrAL	CvAPL			
Caryocaraceae							
Anthodiscus sp.			CrPL				
Caryocar costaricense							
Donn. Smith			CfAPLI				
Celastraceae							
Alzatea verticellata R. & P.					CrL		
Crossopetalum tonduzii							
(Loes) Lundell					SrL		
Cuervea kappleriana							
(Miq.) A. C. Smith		UrP					
Euonymous costaricensis							
Standl.					TrP		
Maytenus woodsonii Lundell							TrLI
Maytenus sp. (Hartshorn 1470)					SoLO		
Maytenus sp. (Dryer #1125)					CoPLG		
Perrottetia longistylis Rose					SrPL	CoL	
Zinowiewia integerrima Turcz.					CoPL		
Chloranthaceae							
Hedyosmum costaricense							
C. E. Wood						UoLI	
Hedyosmum montanum							
W. Burger						UoLI	
Hedyosmum scaberrimum							
Standl.				UoPL			
Chrysobalanaceae							
Chrysobalanus icaco L.			ToA				
Couepia polyandra							
(Kunth.) Rose				CvPL			
Hirtella lemsii							
L. Wms. & Prance			UoPL	UoPL			
Hirtella racemosa Lam.	UrPL						

163

Taxa	Santa Rosa	Palo Verde	Corcovado	La Selva	Monteverde	Las Cruces	Cerro de La Muerte
Licania arborea Seem.	CfAL	CcAP	CrL				
Licania hypoleuca Benth.				SrL			
Licania platypus (Hemsl.) Fritsch			CoA				
Clethraceae							
Clethra lanata Mart. & Gal.			CoL	CrL	SoPL	CoLI	
Cochlospermaceae							
Cochlospermum vitifolium (Willd.) Spreng	SoPL; fO	SoP; fO					
Combretaceae							
Conocarpus erecta L.	SoA	SoRA	SoA				
Laguncularia racemosa (L.) Gaertn.	SfA	SfRA	SfA				
Terminalia amazonia (J. F. Gmel.) Exell			CoL	CoL			
Terminalia bucidioides Standl. & L. Wms.			CrAL	CvAL			
Terminalia oblonga (R. & P.) Steud.	CoRA	CrR	CoA	CfA			
Compositae							
Clibadium leiocarpum Steetz					TrLOG		
Critonia daleoides DC.					UrPL		
Eupatorium angulare Rob.					ToPLIOG		
Eupatorium hebabotryum (DC.) Hemsl.					UrLP		
Eupatorium hylonomum Robinson					UoLP		
Eupatorium morifolium Mill.	ToP			TrR			
Eupatorium pittieri Klatt					TfLPG		
Lasianthaea fruticosa (L.) K. Becker	ToPG			ToO	ToOG		
Senecio arborescens					UrL		
Senecio cooperi Greenm.					TfOG	TfOG	
Verbesina oerstediana Benth.					TrOGI		
Cornaceae							
Cornus disciflora DC.					CrPL		
Cunoniaceae							
Weinmannia pinnata L.					CoPLGO		CoPL
Weinmannia wercklei Standl.					CoPLGO		
Cyatheaceae (sensu lato)							
Cnemidaria choricarpa			T	T	T	T	
Cnemidaria cochleana			T				
Cnemidaria grandifolia					T		
Cnemidaria horrida				T			
Cnemidaria mutica			T	T	T	T	
Culcita coniifolia						T	T
Cyathea divergens			T	T			
Cyathea fulva					T	T	

Taxa	Santa Rosa	Palo Verde	Corcovado	La Selva	Monteverde	Las Cruces	Cerro de La Muerte
Cyathea holdridgeana							T
Cyathea multiflora			T	T	T	T	
Cyathea suprastrigosa							T
Dicksonia gigantea					T	T	T
Dicksonia lobulata							T
Metaxya rostrata			T				
Nephelea cuspidata				T			
Nephelea erinacea				T	T	T	
Nephelea mexicana	UrR		UoL	UoPL		UfL	
Nephelea polystichoides				T	T		
Sphaeropteris brunei					T		T
Sphaeropteris elongata				T			
Sphaeropteris horrida					T		
Trichipteris costaricensis	T						
Trichipteris microdonta				T	T		
Trichipteris schiedeana				T		T	
Trichipteris stipularis	T			T	T	T	T
Trichipteris trichiata				T			
Trichipteris ursina				T			
Trichipteris wendlandii				T		T	
Trichipteris williamsii						Tr	

Dichapetalaceae
Dichapetalum axillare Woodson

Taxa	Santa Rosa	Palo Verde	Corcovado	La Selva	Monteverde	Las Cruces	Cerro de La Muerte
Dichapetalum axillare Woodson				ToWAP	UrL		
Dichapetalum brenesii Standl.				UfPL			
Dichapetalum nervatum Cuatr.				TrL			

Dilleniaceae

Taxa	Santa Rosa	Palo Verde	Corcovado	La Selva	Monteverde	Las Cruces	Cerro de La Muerte
Curatella americana L.	CfPO						

Ebenaceae

Taxa	Santa Rosa	Palo Verde	Corcovado	La Selva	Monteverde	Las Cruces	Cerro de La Muerte
Diospyros nicaraguensis Standl.	SrP	SrP					
Diospyros sp. (Dryer #1178)					UrGO		

Elaeocarpaceae

Taxa	Santa Rosa	Palo Verde	Corcovado	La Selva	Monteverde	Las Cruces	Cerro de La Muerte
Muntingia calabura L.	SrPL; fO	SrP; fO	SoR				
Sloanea faginea Standl.				SoAP			
Sloanea fragrans Rusby				CrL			
Sloanea laurifolia (Benth.) Benth			CvL	CvP			
Sloanea medusula Schum. & Pitt.					CrPL		
Sloanea picapica Standl.			CrPL				
Sloanea terniflora (Moc. & Sessé) Standl.	CoPL	CfP					
Sloanea zuliaensis Pittier			SvL				

Ericaceae

Taxa	Santa Rosa	Palo Verde	Corcovado	La Selva	Monteverde	Las Cruces	Cerro de La Muerte
Vaccinium consanguineum Klotzch							CfL; CcI

Erythroxylaceae

Taxa	Santa Rosa	Palo Verde	Corcovado	La Selva	Monteverde	Las Cruces	Cerro de La Muerte
Erythroxylon amplum Benth.				UrAP	UoPL		

165

Taxa	Santa Rosa	Palo Verde	Corcovado	La Selva	Monteverde	Las Cruces	Cerro de La Muerte
Erythroxylon fimbriatum Peyr.				UrPL			
Erythroxylon havanense Jacq.	ToP	TcL					
Erythroxylon lucidum HBK.		TrAPl					
Erythroxylon rotundifolium Lunan	SrL						
Euphorbiaceae							
Acalypha diversifolia Jacq.			TfG	TfG			
Acalypha macrostachya Jacq.			UoAG	UfAG			
Acalypha schiedeana Schlecht.	T						
Adelia triloba (Muell. Arg.) Hemsl.				UfAW			
Alchornea costaricensis Pax & Hoffm.			SoRL	SoA			
Alchornea latifolia Swartz					CoPL	SoL	
Croton gossypiifolius Vahl.					SfO	SoL	
Croton killipianus Croisat				SvL			
Croton reflexifolius HBK.	UfLR	UfPL					
Croton schiedeanus Schlecht			SoAL	SfA			
Drypetes standleyi Webster				SrRL			
Euphorbia schlechtendalii Boiss.	TrPI	UfI					
Garcia nutans Rohr	UoA	UcAL					
Gymnanthes lucida Swartz	UoPL						
Hieronyma guatemalensis Donn. Smith					CrIL		
Hieronyma oblonga var. *benthamii* (Tul.) Muell. Arg.			CoPL	CoPL			
Hieronyma poasana Standl.					CoLI		
Hippomane mancinella L.	CoA	CoRA	CrA				
Hura crepitans L.	CrAL	CrL	CrA	CrA			
Jatropha aconitifolia Mill.	ToA						
Jatropha curcas L.	ToP						
Mabea occidentalis Benth.			ToL	ToL			
Manihot carthagenesis (Jacq.) Muell. Arg.	ToP						
Margaritaria nobilis (L. f.) Muell. Arg.	SoA	SoA					
Phyllanthus valerii Standl.					TrWG		
Richeria cf. *racemosa* (P. & E.) Pax & Hoffm.				SrPL			
Sapium jamaicense Swartz			CoAL	CoAP			
Sapium macrocarpum Muell.	CoPL	CfPL					
Sapium oligoneuron Schum. & Pitt.				CrW	CoLPO		
Sapium pachystachys Schum. & Pitt.					CoPL		
Sapium thelocarpum Schum. & Pitt.					CoP		
Stillingia zelayensis (HBK.) Muell. Arg.		TrL					
Tetrorchidium euryphyllum Standl.				SrPL			

Taxa	Santa Rosa	Palo Verde	Corcovado	La Selva	Monteverde	Las Cruces	Cerro de La Muerte
Tetrorchidium sp. (Dryer #1071)					SoILW		
Veconcibea pleiostemona (D. Sm.) Pax. & Hoffm.			CoL	CoPL		CrPL	
Fabaceae							
Acosmium panamense (Benth.) Yakoul.	CoP	CrPL					
Andira inermis (Swartz) HBK.	SoPL	SoAP	SoWA	UrAPL			
Dalbergia retusa Hemsl.	CoPL	CoLI					
Dalbergia tucurrensis Donn. Smith				CvL			
Diphysa robinioides Benth.	CoPL						
Dipteryx panamensis (Pitt.) Record				CfP			
Dussia cuscatlanica (Standl.) Standl. & Steyerm.				CrPL			
Dussia macroprophyllata (D. Sm.) Harms			CfP; oL	CoPL	CoPLI		
Erythrina cochleata Standl.			SoA	CoA			
Erythrina fusca Lour.		CfW					
Erythrina lanceolata Standley			UrW		UoPLRO	TrL	
Gliricidia sepium (Jacq.) Steud.	SoPLO	SoPO					
Lonchocarpus acuminatus (Schlecht.) Sousa	Ur						
Lonchocarpus costaricensis (D. Sm.) Pittier	CoP	CfP					
Lonchocarpus minimiflorus Donn. Smith	SfPO	SoP					
Lonchocarpus oliganthus Hermann				SoRA			
Lonchocarpus orotinus Pittier	UoPL						
Lonchocarpus pentaphyllus (Poir.) DC				UoP			
Lonchocarpus eriocarinalis Micheli	SrRA						
Lonchocarpus rugosus Benth.	TrPI						
Lonchocarpus velutinus Benth.				CvA			
Machaerium biovulatum Micheli	SoPL	SoP					
Muellera sp.				SvL			
Myrospermum frutescens Jacq.	UoP	UrP					
Ormosia velutina Rudd				CrL			
Ormosia sp.			CoPL				
Ormosia sp.					CoPL		
Piscidia carthagenensis Jacq.	SoL	UoP					
Platymiscium pinnatum (Jacq.) Dugand			CoAL				
Platymiscium pleiostachyum Donn. Smith	CrPL	CrPL					

Taxa	Santa Rosa	Palo Verde	Corcovado	La Selva	Monteverde	Las Cruces	Cerro de La Muerte
Pterocarpus hayesii Hemsl.			CoPL	CoPL			
Ptericarpus officinalis L.			CcW	CfW			
Pterocarpus rohrii Vahl.	CrPL	CrP					
Sweetia (see Acosmium)							
Uribea tamarindoides Dugand & Romero			CvL				
Willardia schiedeana (Schlecht.) Hermann	CrPL						
Fagaceae							
Quercus brenesii Trel.					CoLI		
Quercus copeyensis C. H. Mull.							CcLIO
Quercus corrugata Hooker					CoPL		
Quercus costaricensis Liebmann					CfPLI	CcLIO	CcLIO
Quercus guglielmi-treleasei C. H. Muller						CoL	
Quercus insignis Mart. & Gal.					CrLI		
Quercus oleoides Schlecht. & Cham.	CcP						
Quercus oocarpa Liebm.					CoPL	CoL	
Quercus pilarius Trel.					CrLI		
Quercus seemannii Liebmann					CoPL		
Flacourtiaceae							
Abatia parviflora Ruíz & Pavón							UcPLO
Banara guianensis Aubl.	UoPL						
Carpotroche platyptera Pittier			ToPL	ToPL			
Casearia aculeata Jacq.	ToPL	ToPL					
Casearia arborea (Rich.) Urban				SfPL			
Casearia arguta HBK.	TfPL	TfPL					
Casearia corymbosa HBK.	ToPL	UrR		SoA			
Casearia sylvestris Swartz	ToPL	ToPL			SrPL		
Casearia tremula (Griseb.) Wright	SrPL						
Hasseltia floribunda HBK.			UoPL	UrALP	SoPL	SoL	
Laetia procera (Poeppig) Eich.			CoPL	CfPL			
Laetia thamnia (L.) Amoen.		SfP					
Lozania (see Lacistemaceae)							
Lunania mexicana Brandg.						UoL	
Macrohasseltia macroterantha (Standl. & L. Wms.) L. Wms.					CrPL		
Pleuranthodendron mexicana (Gray) L. O. Wms.			SoAP				
Prockia crucis L.	ToLI						
Ryania speciosa var. *panamensis* Monach.				SfLI			
Samyda sp. (Dryer #1155)					SrPL		
Tetrathylacium costaricense Standl.			UoAL				

Taxa	Santa Rosa	Palo Verde	Corcovado	La Selva	Monteverde	Las Cruces	Cerro de La Muerte
Xylosma flexuosa (HBK.) Hemsl.	UoPL	SoP					
Xylosma hemsleyana Standl.				UrL			
Xylosma intermedium (Tr. & Pl.) Griseb.					SoPL		
Zuelania guidonia (Sw.) Britt. & Millsp.	SrPL						
Garryaceae							
Garrya laurifolia Hartweg							SoPL
Guttiferae							
Calophyllum brasiliense var. *rekoi* Standl.			CoLI	CrAL		CfLI	
Calophyllum longifolium Willd.			CoAP				
Chrysochlamys sp.			UfPL				
Hypericum sp.							TcPL
Marila pluricostata Standl. & L. Wms.				TvR			
Rheedia edulis Triana & Planch.	UrR		SoAPL		SrP	UoL	
Rheedia intermedia Pittier				SoAP			
Symphonia globulifera Lf.			CfWAPL	ToPL	ToPLR	UoRL	
Tovomita glauca (Oerst.) L. Wms.						UoL	
Tovomita macrophylla L. Wms.			UoPL				
Tovomita nicaraguensis (Oerst.) L. Wms.			ToPL		UoLIPW	UoL	
Tovomita pittieri Engler				UoI			
Tovomitopsis multiflora Standl.				ToPL			
Tovomitopsis sp. (Dryer #640)					TrPR		
Vismia baccifera (L.) Tr. & Pl.	TrP		UoO	UrO			
Vismia latifolia Choisy				SrPL			
Vismia sp.					SrWO		
Hernandiaceae							
Hernandia didymanthera Donn. Smith				CfAPL			
Hernandia stenura Standl.				CoAP			
Hippocastanaceae							
Billia colombiana Planch. & Lind.			CoPL		CoPL		
Billia hippocastanum Peyritsch					CoPLW	CoPL	
Hippocrateaceae							
Hemiangium excelsum (HBK.) A. C. Smith	UoPL	UfPL					
Humiriaceae							
Sacoglottis trichogyna Cuatr.			C	CrAWL			
Vantanea barbourii Standl.			CfP; oL				

169

Taxa	Santa Rosa	Palo Verde	Corcovado	La Selva	Monteverde	Las Cruces	Cerro de La Muerte
Icacinaceae							
Calatola costaricensis Standl.			CrL		SrP		
Juglandaceae							
Alfaroa costaricensis Standl.					CrLI		
Alfaroa williamsii Molina					Cr		CoLI
Lacistemaceae							
Lacistema aggregatum (Berg.) Rusby				UoPL			
Lozania montana Standl.					TrIL		
Lozania mutisiana R. & S.			UoAL	TrA			
Lauraceae							
Aiouea costaricensis (Mez) Kostermans					SrPL		
Beilschmiedia costaricense					CoL		
Beilschmiedia mexicana (Mez) Kostermans					CoPL		
Licaria sp.			CoL				
Nectandra davidsoniana C. K. Allen					SoP		
Nectandra gentlei Lundell				SrP	SoLP		
Nectandra reticulata (R. & P.) Mez				CoA			
Nectandra salicina C. K. Allen					CoLP		
Nectandra smithii C. K. Allen					SoP		
Ocotea atirrhensis Mez & Donn. Smith				TfPL			
Ocotea austinii C. K. Allen					CfPL		
Ocotea bernoulliana Mez				UoAP	UoPL		
Ocotea cernua (Nees) Mez				SoA	CoPL		
Ocotea cooperi C. K. Allen				SoPL			
Ocotea endresiana Mez					S		
Ocotea ira Mez & Pittier			CoL	CrP	SoPL		
Ocotea mollifolia Mez & Pittier				CfPL			
Ocotea nicaraguensis Mez				SvRAL			
Ocotea pedalifolia Mez				TfPL			
Ocotea stenoneura Mez & Pittier					SrLP		
Ocotea tonduzii Standl.					C		
Ocotea veraguensis (Meissn.) Mez	UrRA	UrR					
Ocotea wachenheimii R. Benoist				CrL			
Persea americana Mill.			CrLI	CvL	CoPL		
Persea caerulea (R. & P.) Mez					SoPL		
Persea schiedeana Nees					CfPLWI		
Phoebe mexicana Meissn.			SoPL			CoL	
Phoebe neurophylla Mez & Pittier					CrPL		
Phoebe valeriana Standl.				SrL	SoPL		
Lecythidaceae							
Cariniana pyriformis Miers			CfPL				

Taxa	Santa Rosa	Palo Verde	Corcovado	La Selva	Monteverde	Las Cruces	Cerro de La Muerte
Couratari panamensis Standl.			CoPL				
Eschweilera calyculata Pittier			CrPL	SrPL			
Grias fendleri Seem.			SoWAP	SvWP			
Gustavia brachycarpa Pittier			UrP				
Lecythis ampla Miers				CrPL			
Lecythis minor Jacq.			CoPL				

Leguminosae (see Mimosaceae, Caesalpiniaceae, and Fabaceae)

Loganiaceae

Taxa	Santa Rosa	Palo Verde	Corcovado	La Selva	Monteverde	Las Cruces	Cerro de La Muerte
Buddleia alpina Oerst.							CoPL; cO

Loranthaceae

Taxa	Santa Rosa	Palo Verde	Corcovado	La Selva	Monteverde	Las Cruces	Cerro de La Muerte
Gaiadendron poasense Donn. Smith							SoL

Magnoliaceae

Taxa	Santa Rosa	Palo Verde	Corcovado	La Selva	Monteverde	Las Cruces	Cerro de La Muerte
Magnolia poasana (Pitt.) Dandy					CvW		CoPL
Talauma sambuensis Pittier			SoPL	UvL	CvP		

Malpighiaceae

Taxa	Santa Rosa	Palo Verde	Corcovado	La Selva	Monteverde	Las Cruces	Cerro de La Muerte
Bunchosia biocellata Schlecht.	UoPL						
Bunchosia macrophylla Rose				UrPL			
Bunchosia pilosa HBK					ToPL		
Bunchosia swartziana Griseb.				ToA			
Bunchosia ternata					TfPL		
Bunchosia sp. (Hartshorn 1904)					SrPL		
Byrsonima aerugo Sagot				CvL			
Byrsonima crassifolia (L.) DC.	CoPO	CoI	CrIO				
Malpighia glabra L.	UrA	TrP			UoPL		
Malpighia lundellii Morton		TvL					
Spachea sp.				CvL			
Tetrapteris schiedeana					ToPLG		

Malvaceae

Taxa	Santa Rosa	Palo Verde	Corcovado	La Selva	Monteverde	Las Cruces	Cerro de La Muerte
Hampea appendiculata (D. Sm.) Standl.			CrPL; cG	CrPL; cG	CfG	CfPL	
Hibiscus tiliaceus L.	UcA		UcA				
Malvaviscus arboreus Cav.	ToG	ToG	ToG	ToG	UoPLRG		
Wercklea insignis Pittier & Standl.					SrLI		

Melastomataceae

Taxa	Santa Rosa	Palo Verde	Corcovado	La Selva	Monteverde	Las Cruces	Cerro de La Muerte
Centronia phlomoides Triana					ToPIW		
Conostegia formosa Macf.				SrAP	SoLI		
Conostegia hirtella Cogn.					ToLI		
Conostegia macrantha Berg					T		
Conostegia oerstediana Berg					UfPL		
Conostegia pittieri Cogn.					UoPLI		
Conostegia vulcanicola Donn. Smith					ToLI		
Conostegia xalapensis (Bonpl.) D. Don					SoLIO		
Graffenrieda micrantha					UrI		

171

Taxa	Santa Rosa	Palo Verde	Corcovado	La Selva	Monteverde	Las Cruces	Cerro de La Muerte
Henriettella tuberculosa Donn. Smith				UoPL			
Miconia affinis DC.				UfG			
Miconia appendiculata Tr.				ToG			
Miconia argentea (Sw.) DC.	SoPL	SoPL	UvA				
Miconia bipulifera Cogn.							U
Miconia brenesii Standl.					TrL		
Miconia calvescens DC.				SoPL			
Miconia centrodesma Naud.				ToG			
Miconia costaricensis Cogn.					TrLI		
Miconia elata (Sw.) DC.				SrG			
Miconia flavida Cogn.					TrL		
Miconia glaberrima (Schlecht.) Naud.					ToLIO		
Miconia gracilis Triana				ToG			
Miconia serrulata (DC.) Naud.				TrG			
Miconia tonduzii Cogn.					TrL		
Mouriri parvifolia Benth.	T						
Mouriri sp.			UfPW				
Topobea brenesii Standl.	UoOP						
Meliaceae							
Carapa guianensis Aubl.			CoAPL; fW	CrAl; cW			
Cedrela mexicana Roem.	CoAPL	CoPL	CrAW	CrAW			
Cedrela tonduzii C. DC.					CrPLR	CoPL	
Guarea brevianthera C. DC.				UvA			
Guarea bullata Radlk.				SfPL			
Guarea chichon C. DC.				CrA			
Guarea excelsa HBK.	UoPL	UoR					
Guarea glabra Vahl.·					UrWL		
Guarea microcarpa C. DC.				UrL	SrPL		
Guarea rhopalocarpa Radlk.				UfPL	SoPL		
Guarea tonduzii C. DC.					SoPL		
Guarea trichiloides L.				CfPL			
Guarea tuisana C. DC.					CrPL		
Ruagea caoba (C. DC.) Harms					CoPLI		
Swietenia macrophylla King	CrPL	CrP					
Trichilia colimana C. DC.	SfPL	SfPL					
Trichilia cuneata Radlk.	SfPL	SoPL					
Trichilia havanensis Jacq.					SoPLI		
Trichilia hirta L.	SoPL	SfPL					
Trichilia moritzii C. DC.			SoL	SoPL			
Trichilia trifolia L.	ToPL	TrP					
Menispermaceae							
Hyperbaena tonduzii Diels		UfPL					
Hyperbaena sp.			UoLI				
Mimosaceae							
Acacia collinsii Safford	UcOPLIG	UcOPLIG					
Acacia cornigera (L.) Willd.	UcOPL	UcOPL					
Acacia farnesiana (L.) Willd.	TcO	ToO					
Albizzia adinocephala (D. Sm.) Britt. & Rose	SrP			CvL			

172

Taxa	Santa Rosa	Palo Verde	Corcovado	La Selva	Monteverde	Las Cruces	Cerro de La Mierte
Albizzia caribaea (Urban) Britt. & Rose	CoA	CoP					
Albizzia guachapele (HBK.) Little		CrP					
Calliandra costaricensis (Britt. & Rose) Standl.	SoP		U				
Enterolobium cyclocarpum (Jacq.) Griseb.	CoPLO	CoPO					
Inga coruscans Willd.			CoPL	CoP			
Inga densiflora Benth.				SfAP	SrPL		
Inga goldmanii Pittier					SrLI		
Inga longispica Standl.				CoL	CoPLWI		
Inga marginata Willd.			SoWA	UoWA			
Inga mortoniana J. León					UrPL		
Inga oerstediana Benth.				CfA	SrPO		
Inga paterno Harms					SrP		
Inga punctata Willd.					SoPL		
Inga ruiziana G. Don				SoRA			
Inga sapindoides Willd.			SoAPL	SfPL			
Inga thibaudiana DC.				CfPL			
Inga tonduzii Donn. Smith					CrPLO		
Inga venusta Standl.				UrL			
Inga vera var. *spuria* (Willd.) J. León	UfR	UfR	UoA; cW				
Lysiloma desmostachys Benth.	UoPL	UoP					
Lysiloma seemannii Britt. & Rose	CoPL	CfPL					
Parkia pendula Benth.			CrPL				
Pentaclethra macroloba (Willd.) Kuntze.				CcWPL			
Pithecellobium arboreum (L.) Urban			CrL				
Pithecellobium brenesii Standl.					UrLR		
Pithecellobium catenatum Donn. Smith				UrPL			
Pithecellobium costaricense (Britt. & Rose) Standl.					UoLPI		
Pithecellobium dulce (Roxb.) Benth.	SfP	SfPL					
Pithecellobium gigantifolium (Schery) J. León				UoPL			
Pithecellobium longifolium (Humb. & Bonpl.) Standl.		SoR		CcR			
Pithecellobium macradenium Pittier			C	CvPL			
Pithecellobium mangense (Jacq.) MacBr.	SvP						
Pithecellobium pedicellare (DC.) Benth			CrLI	CoLI			
Pithecellobium saman (Jacq.) Benth	CfOAP	CoOP					
Pithecellobium valerioi (Britt. & Rose) Standl.				SoW			
Prosopis juliflora (Sw.) DC.	UoA						
Stryphnodendron excelsum Harms				CoPL			

173

Taxa	Santa Rosa	Palo Verde	Corcovado	La Selva	Monteverde	Las Cruces	Cerro de La Muerte
Monimiaceae							
Mollinedia costaricensis Donn. Smith				TrP			
Siparuna nicaraguensis Hemsl.				ToPL	ToIL		
Siparuna pauciflora (Beurl.) A. DC.				ToPL			
Siparuna tonduziana Perkins				TrAP	ToPLG		
Siparuna sp. (Dryer #600)				TrPG			
Moraceae							
Batocarpus costaricensis Standl. & L. Wms.			SoLI				
Brosimum alicastrum Swartz	CfAL	CfAL	CoAL	CrA			
Brosimum costaricanum Liebm.			CoAL				
Brosimum guianense (Aubl.) Huber	CoA						
Brosimum lactescens (Moore) Berg				CoPL			
Brosimum utile (HBK.) Pittier			CfLI				
Castilla elastica Sessé	CoA			CfA; rP			
Castilla tuna Hemsl.			SoAPL				
Cecropia insignis Liebm.			SrPL	CrPLI		CfLG	
Cecropia obtusifolia Bertol.			SrAPL; CG	CrPL; fG	SoPLGO	CfLG	
Cecropia peltata L.	CfG	CfG					
Cecropia polyphlebia Donn. Smith					CfGO		
Chlorophora tinctoria (L.) Gaud.	CfPL	CfPL	SvA				
Clarisia biflora R. & P.				CvAPL			
Ficus brevibracteata Burger				SrA			
Ficus crassiuscula Warb.					CoPLI	CoL	
Ficus dugandii Standl.				CrO			
Ficus glabrata HBK.	CoR	CrR		CcR			
Ficus goldmanii Standl.	CfO	CfO					
Ficus hartwegii (Miq.) Miq.					CrL	CrL	
Ficus insipida Willd.				SvR			
Ficus macbridei Standl.			CrLI		CrL		
Ficus maxima P. Miller			SrL		SrL		
Ficus ovalis (Liebm.) Miq.	CoP	CoPL					
Ficus schippii Standl.			UvW	UvR			
Ficus tonduzii Standl.			SrAP	SrA			
Ficus tuerckheimii Standl.					CoPL		
Ficus turrialbana Burger				CrPL			
Ficus velutina H. & B.					CrPL		
Ficus yoponensis Desv.					SrPL		
Maquira costaricana (Standl.) C. C. Berg				UoPL			
Naucleopsis naga Pittier			SoPL	SoPL			
Perebea angustifolia (Poep. & Endl.) C. C. Berg			UoPL	UfPL			
Poulsenia armata (Miq.) Standl.			CfAPL				
Pourouma aspera Trecul			SoPL	CoPL			
Pourouma minor Benoist				SoPL			
Pseudolmedia oxyphyllaria Donn. Smith					SoL	SoL	

Taxa	Santa Rosa	Palo Verde	Corcovado	La Selva	Monteverde	Las Cruces	Cerro de La Muerte
Sorocea cufodontisii W. Burger			UfLI				
Sorocea pubivena Hemsl.				UoP			
Sorocea trophoides W. Burger					UoL		
Trophis involucrata W. Burger				TcLI			
Trophis racemosa (L.) Urban	SrP	SrP		SoA			
Myricaceae							
Myrica phanerodonta Standl.					UrI		
Myrica pubescens Humb. & Bonpl.					ToI		
Myristicaceae							
Composneura sprucei (A. DC.) Warb.			UoPL	UoPL			
Dialyanthera otoba (Humb. & Bonpl.) Warb.			CoPL	CrPW		CoPL	
Iryanthera sp.			SrAL				
Virola guatamalensis (Hemsl.) Warb.			CoPL				
Virola koschnyi Warb.			CoPL	CoAWPL			
Virola sebifera Aubl.				SoPL			
Myrsinaceae							
Ardisia auriculata Donn. Smith				ToL			
Ardisia compressa HBK.					UoPLIWG		
Ardisia cutteri Standl.			UfLI				
Ardisia dodgei Standl.			S				
Ardisia glanduloso-marginata Oerst.					ToPL		
Ardisia granatensis Mez				UvPL			
Ardisia nigropunctata Oerst.				ToAP			
Ardisia palmana Donn. Smith					UoPLW		
Ardisia pittieri Mez					ToL		
Ardisia revoluta HBK.	UfRA	UfR					
Parathesis adenanthera					UrLIG		
Parathesis chrysophylla Lundell				SoPL			
Parathesis glabra Donn. Smith				ToPL			
Rapanea ferruginea (R. & P.) Mez					SfPLOG		
Rapanea juergensenii Mez					UrIG		
Weigeltia spectabilis (Standl.) Lundell				TrAP			
Myrtaceae							
Calyptranthes pallens Griseb.	ToR						
Eugenia salamensis Donn. Smith	SfPL	SfPL					
Eugenia sp.				SrL			
Myrcia carnea DC.				UoAPL			
Myrcia splendens (Sw.) DC.				UrRA		UrPL	

175

Taxa	Santa Rosa	Palo Verde	Corcovado	La Selva	Monteverde	Las Cruces	Cerro de La Muerte
Myrcianthes fragrans (Sw.) McVaugh					SrPOG		
Nyctaginaceae							
Neea amplifolia Donn. Smith			UrLI	UoPL	ToPL		
Neea laetevirens Standl.				TfG			
Pisonia aculeata L.					UfP		
Pisonia macranthocarpa Donn. Smith	UoPL	UfPL					
Torrubia costaricana					TfPL		
Ochnaceae							
Cespedesia macrophylla Seem.			SrL	CrPL			
Ouratea crassinervia Engl.				ToL			
Ouratea lucens (HBK.) Engler	ToPL		SoW	SvPL			
Ouratea valerii Standley			WA				
Olacaceae							
Chaunochiton kappleri (Sagot) Ducke			CrLI				
Heisteria acuminata Humb. & Bonpl.					TfPL		
Heisteria concinna Standl.				SrAP			
Heisteria longipes Standl.			UcLI				
Minquartia guianensis Aubl.			CrL	CrL			
Schoepfia schreberi Gmel.	UoPL	UoPL					
Ximenia americana L.	SrL	SrL	SoA				
Oleaceae							
Linociera panamensis Standl.					CoLP		
Opiliaceae							
Agonandra macrocarpa L. O. Wms.	CvPL						
Palmae							
Acrocomia vinifera Oerst.	CoPO	CoPLO					
Asterogyne martiana Wendl.			TcPL	TcPL			
Astrocaryum alatum Loomis			UoW	UcAW			
Astrocaryum standleyanum L. H. Bailey			UoPL	SrPL			
Bactris guinensis (L.) H. E. Moore	ToA	TcO					
Bactris longiseta Wendl.				TfAW			
Bactris major Jacq.			UfW				
Bactris porschiana Burret				UoPL			
Calyptrogyne sarapiquensis Wendl.				TcAW			
Chamaedorea exorrhiza Wendl.				UfAW			
Cryosophila albiba Bartlett				UoWPL			
Cryosophila guagara Allen			UfA				
Elaeis melanococca Oerst.			UcA				
Euterpe macrospadix Oerst.				ScI			
Geonoma ferruginea Wendl.				TvL			
Geonoma interrupta Ruíz & Pavón				UvA			

Taxa	Santa Rosa	Palo Verde	Corcovado	La Selva	Monteverde	Las Cruces	Cerro de La Muerte
Geonoma longevaginata Wendl.				UoPL			
Geonoma seleri Burret					ToPLW	ToL	
Iriartea gigantea Wendl.			SfPL	ScL			
Oenocarpus panamensis L. H. Bailey			SoPL				
Pholidostachys pulchra Wendl.				UfL			
Raphia taedigera Martius			UcAW				
Scheelea rostrata (Oerst.) Burret	SvA		SfI				
Socratea durissima (Oerst.) Wendl.			SfPL	ScPL			
Synecanthus warscewiczianus Wend.			UoPL	UfL			
Welfia georgii Wendl.			SoPL	ScPL			
Papaveraceae							
Bocconia frutescens L.					UfGO		
Piperaceae							
Piper amalago L.	TcPL	TcPL					
Piper arboreum Aublet			TrL	UrL			
Piper augustum Rudge				ToPL			
Piper auritum HBK.			TcO	TcO	TfO		
Piper biolleyi C. DC.				TrL			
Piper biseriatum C. DC.				ToPL	TrLP		
Piper carrilloanum C. DC.				ToPL			
Piper cenocladum C. DC.				TcAW			
Piper colonense C. DC.				UoPL			
Piper euryphyllum C. DC.				TfPL	TrIL		
Piper imperiale (Miq.) C. DC.				UoPL			
Piper obliquum Ruíz & Pavón				UoPL			
Piper reticularum L.			ToPL	ToPL			
Piper sancti-felicis Trel.			TcO	TcO			
Piper sinugaudens C. DC.				ToPL			
Podocarpaceae							
Podocarpus oleifolius Don.					ColW		
Polygonaceae							
Coccoloba caracasana Meissn.	UrP	UfRW					
Coccoloba floribunda (Benth.) Lindau	UoALO	SoAW					
Coccoloba padiformis Meissn.	SoA	UrP					
Coccoloba tuerckheimii Donn. Smith					SvPA		
Ruprechtia costata Meissn.		SrR					
Triplaris melaenodendron (Bertol.) Standl. & Steyerm.	SoPL	SoPL					
Proteaceae							
Panopsis costaricensis Standl.					CoPL		
Panopsis sp.			SrP				
Roupala glaberrima Pittier					CoPL		
Roupala montana Hubl.	CoOP						

Taxa	Santa Rosa	Palo Verde	Corcovado	La Selva	Monteverde	Las Cruces	Cerro de La Muerte
Quiinaceae							
Lacunaria panamensis Standl.				UoL			
Quiina sp.			UrA	UrL			
Rhamnaceae							
Colubrina spinosa Donn. Smith				UfAWPL; cG			
Karwinskia calderoni Standl.	CoPL	CoPLI					
Zizyphus guatemalensis Hemsl.	SrRA	CrPL					
Rhizophoraceae							
Cassipourea ellipitica Poir.				UfPL			
Cassipourea guianensis Aubl.					UoPL		
Rhizophora mangle L.	CcA	CcRA	CcA				
Rosaceae							
Prunus annularis Koehne					SrL	CrL	
Prunus cornifolia Koehne					SrLPI		
Rubiaceae							
Alibertia edulis (L. Rich.) A. Rich.	ToPL		ToA				
Bertiera guianensis Aubl.				TrPL			
Calycophyllum candidissimum (Vahl) DC.	CfPL	CcPL					
Cephaelis elata Swartz				UoL	ToPLI		
Cephaelis tomentosa (Aubl.) Vahl				ToO			
Chimarrhis latifolia Standl.			CrL				
Chimarrhis parviflora Standl.	S			SrAW			
Chione costaricensis Standl.			U	UfPL	UoPL		
Chomelia spinosa Jacq.	UcPL	UcPL					
Coussarea austin-smithii Standl.				UoLW			
Coussarea impetiolaris Donn. Smith				UrPW			
Coussarea talamancana Standl.				ToPL			
Coussarea taurina Standl. & Wms.				UoPL			
Duroia panamensis Dwyer				UrL			
Elaeagia auriculata Hemsl.					SoL	SoPL	
Exostema mexicana Gray	SoPL						
Faramea occidentalis (L.) Rich.				UfPL	UoP		
Faramea quercetorum Standl.					UoPL		
Faramea suerrensis Donn. Smith				UcPL			
Faramea talamancarum Standl.				ToL			
Ferdinandusa panamensis Standl. & L. Wms.				UcL			

Taxa	Santa Rosa	Palo Verde	Corcovado	La Selva	Monteverde	Las Cruces	Cerro de La Muerte
Genipa americana L.	SoP	SoPL	SrA	CvA			
Gonzalagunia rosea Standl.					UoPLG		
Guettarda macrosperma Donn. Smith	SoPL	SfPL					
Guettarda poasana Standl.					SoLIG		
Hamelia patens Jacq.	ToA	UrL	TcAO	UcAO	ToOG	ToO	
Hamelia xerocarpa Kuntze				TrAP			
Hillia valerii Standl.					SfLI		
Ixora nicaraguensis Standl.				ToPL			
Ladenbergia valerii Standl.					SrWI		
Palicourea sp. *angustifolia* HBK.					ToPL		
Pentagonia donnell-smithii Standl.				UoAPL			
Pentagonia gymnopoda Standl.			ToAP				
Posoqueria grandiflora Standl.				UoPL			
Posoqueria latifolia (Rudge) Roem. & Schult.			UoR	UoR	SrP		
Psychotria carthaginensis Jacq.	T						
Psychotria chiapensis Standl.				UfA			
Psychotria grandistipula Standl.				UoPL	ToPL		
Psychotria luxurians Rusby				UoPL			
Randia armata (Swartz) DC.				ToPL			
Randia grandifolia Standl.				UvA			
Randia karstenii Polak	ToL	ToPL					
Randia lasiantha Standl.	UoPL	UfPL					
Rondeletia amoena (Planch.) Hemsl.					TrILG		
Rondeletia buddleioides Benth.					UrPLIR		
Rondeletia calycosa Donn. Smith					ToPLI		
Rondeletia torresii Standl.					UoIL		
Rudgea cornifolia (Humb. & Bonpl.) Standl.				UrPL			
Simira maxonii Standl.			SoA	SfAP			
Tocoyena pittieri (Standl.) Standl.			UrA				
Warscewiczia coccinea (Vahl) Klotzsch.			SoPL	ScPL			
Rutaceae							
Casimiroa edulis Llave & Lex.					SrPL		
Esenbeckia litoralis Donn. Smith	U						
Zanthoxylum belizense Lundell			CAL				
Zanthoxylum elephantiasis Macfad.				SfA	SvP		
Zanthoxylum mayanum Standl.				CrA			
Zanthoxylum melanostichum Schlecht. & Cham.					UoPL		
Zanthoxylum panamense P. Wilson				SfAPL			

Taxa	Santa Rosa	Palo Verde	Corcovado	La Selva	Monteverde	Las Cruces	Cerro de La Muerte
Zanthoxylum setulosum P. Wilson	SoPL	SfPL			UoP		
Sabiaceae							
Meliosma donnell-smithii Urb.				UoPL			
Meliosma glabrata (Liebm.) Urb.					UoPL		
Meliosma ira (Liebm.) L. Wms.					TfP		
Meliosma vernicosa (Liebm.) Griseb.				CrL	CfPL		
Sapindaceae							
Allophyllus occidentalis (Sw.) Radlk.	UoAL	UoAP					
Allophyllus psilospermus Radlk.				UrA			
Cupania costaricensis Radlk.				UrA			
Cupania glabra Swartz					SoPL		
Cupania guatemalensis Radlk.	UrPL	UrPL					
Dipterodendron costaricense Radlk.	SrPL		CrWA				
Exothea paniculata (Juss.) Radlk.					CoP		
Matayba oppositifolia (A. Rich.) Britt.					CfP		
Matayba sp.				UoPL			
Sapindus saponaria L.	CoAL	CfAPL					
Talisia nervosa Radlk.			UoPL				
Thouinidium decandrum (Humb. & Bonpl.) Radlk.	CfPL	CcPL					
Sapotaceae							
Calocarpum mammosum (L.) Pierre			SoO		CoP		
Calocarpum viride Pittier					CfPL		
Chrysophyllum brenesii Cron.	CrP						
Chrysophyllum panamense Pittier			CrL				
Dipholis parvifolia Standl.					CoPL		
Manilkara zapota (L.) van Royan	CcA	CfPL	CoL				
Mastichodendron capiri (A. DC.) Cron.	CoAPL	CoPL					
Mastichodendron sp.					CoP		
Pouteria campechiana (HBK.) Baehni				SoPL			
Pouteria lucentifolia (Standl.) Baehni				UfPL			
Pouteria lucuma (R. & P.) Ktze. & Baehni					SrL		
Pouteria neglecta Cronquist			CoL	CoPL			
Pouteria standleyana (Pitt.) Baehni				CfPL			

Taxa	Santa Rosa	Palo Verde	Corcovado	La Selva	Monteverde	Las Cruces	Cerro de La Muerte
Pouteria unilocularis (D. Sm.) Baehni					CoPL		
Saxifragaceae							
Escallonia poasana Donn. Smith							CcLI
Simaroubaceae							
Alvaradoa amorphoides Liebm.		SoPL					
Picramnia allenii D. M. Porter	TrA						
Picramnia carpinterae Polak					TfPL	TfL	
Picramnia latifolia Tulasne			UrRA		UrL		
Simaba cedron Planch.			UoAP				
Simarouba amara Aubl.			CrL	CrAPL			
Simarouba glauca DC.	CoPL	CoPL					
Solanaceae							
Acnistus arborescens (L.) Schlecht.					UfOG	UfO	
Cestrum megalophyllum Lingelsh.				ToPL	ToPLOG		
Cestrum racemosum Standl.			UoA	UoAP	UoPLOG		
Cestrum rugulosum					TrPLR		
Cyphomandra hartwegii Donn. Smith				UrAPL			
Solanum accrescens Standl. & Morton					ToPLOG		
Solanum antillarum O. E. Schulz	ToRG						
Solanum arboreum H. & B.					ToPLOG		
Solanum brenesii Morton & Standl.			ToGO		ToPLOG		
Solanum hazenii Britt.	TrPOG						
Solanum nudum HBK.					TfPOG		
Solanum rugosum Dunal.			UfG	UfG			
Witheringia cuneata (Standl.) Hunz.					ToPLG		
Witheringia riparia HBK.					ToPLG		
Staphyleaceae							
Turpinia occidentalis (Sw.) Don.					SrPL		
Sterculiaceae							
Basiloxylon excelsum Standl. & L. Wms.			CrAL				
Guazuma ulmifolia Lam.	ScPLO	ScPLO					
Herrania purpurea (Pitt.) R. E. Schultes			TrPL	TfL			
Sterculia apetala (Jacq.) Karst.	CoAL	CoPL					
Sterculia mexicana R. Br.			CrPL				
Sterculia recordiana Pittier			CrAL	CrAP			
Theobroma bicolor Humb. & Bonpl.				SvL			

181

Taxa	Santa Rosa	Palo Verde	Corcovado	La Selva	Monteverde	La Cruces	Cerro de La Muerte
Theobroma mammosum Cuatr. & J. León				UoPW			
Theobroma simiarum Donn. Smith			SrLI	SrAP			
Styracaceae							
Styrax argentea Presl.	SoL				CoP		
Styrax glabrescens Benth.					UrL		
Symplocaceae							
Symplocos sp.				UrL			
Theaceae							
Freziera candicans Tulasne					UrOP		
Freziera friedrichsthaliana (Szysz.) Kobuski					SrOGIL		
Laplacea semiserrata (Murt. & Succ.) Cambess.						CfPL	
Pelliciera rhizophorae Triana & Planch.			ScA				
Symplocarpon brenesii					SrLPI		
Ternstroemia tepezapote Schlecht. & Cham.					SrLO		
Theophrastaceae							
Jacquinia pungens Gray	UfPL	UcPL					
Thymelaeaceae							
Daphnopsis americana					CoPL		
Tiliaceae							
Apeiba membranacea Spruce			CoAL	CoPL			
Apeiba tibourbou Aubl.	SoPL	SoP	SoAP				
Goethalsia meiantha (D. Sm.) Burret				CfPL			
Heliocarpus appendiculatus Turcz.			CfG	CfG		CfOG	
Heliocarpus popayanensis HBK.					CfPG		
Luehea candida (DC.) Mart.	UfL	UcPL					
Luehea seemannii Triana & Planch.			CoWA	CoWA			
Luehea speciosa Willd.	UfL	UrPL					
Mortoniodendron anisophyllum (Standl.) Standl. & Steyerm.			CoA				
Mortoniodendron costaricense Standl. & Wms.				UvA	UoPL		
Ulmaceae							
Ampelocera hottlei (Standl.) Standl.				CrPL			
Celtis schippii Standl.				CrRA			
Trema micrantha (L.) Blume	SrL	CoA	CoAP	CoAP	SoPLOG		

Taxa	Santa Rosa	Palo Verde	Corocovado	La Selva	Monteverde	Las Cruces	Cerro de La Muerte
Ulmus mexicana (Liebm.) Planch.						CoPL	
Umbelliferae							
Myrrhidendron donnell-smithii Coult. & Rose							SoLI
Urticaceae							
Myriocarpa longipes Liebm.				UcAG			
Urera alceifolia Gaud.					UrG		
Urera baccifera (L.) Gaud.	T			TfGO		ToL	
Urera caracasana (Jacq.) Griseb.				ToG			
Urera elata (Sw.) Griseb.				TrA	ToPL		
Verbenaceae							
Aegiphila facata Donn. Smith				UoG			
Aegiphila martinicensis Jacq.	T			TrPL			
Aegiphila paniculata Moldenke	T						
Avicennia germinans (L.) L.	CcA		CcA				
Citharexylum costaricense Moldenke					SrPL		
Citharexylum donnell-smithii Greenm.					SoP		
Citharexylum macradenium Greenm.					SrPL; fG		
Citharexylum macrophyllum Poir.					CoPL		
Citharexylum viride Moldenke			UrO				
Cornutia grandifolia (Schlecht. & Cham.) Schau.	TrLI						
Lippia torresii Standl.						CoOG	
Rehdera trinervis (Blake) Moldenke	CoPL	CoPL					
Vitex cooperi Standl.			CoPL	CoPL			
Violaceae							
Amphirrhox longifolia Spreng.				TrL			
Gleoaspermum diversipetalum Standl. & L. Wms.				ToPL			
Rinorea pubipes Blake				UcPL			
Vochysiaceae							
Qualea paraense Ducke			CfPLI	CvLI			
Vochysia ferruginea Mart.			CoPLI	CoPLI			
Vochysia hondurensis Sprague			CoAPL	CrAP			
Winteraceae							
Drimys winteri Forst.					UrOI		UcI
Zygophyllaceae							
Guaiacum sanctum L.		UfLI					

SPECIES ACCOUNTS
Acrocomia vinifera (Coyol)

D. H. Janzen

There are two large single-trunked palms in the Guanacaste lowlands, *Acrocomia vinifera* and *Scheelea rostrata* (palma real). *S. rostrata* attains a height of up to 20 m (more commonly 10–15 m), has oval fruits and seeds, has the leaflets arranged in one plane, and occurs only in riparian vegetation along permanent streams (where it is now almost extinct in Guanacaste; cf. Janzen 1971; Wilson and Janzen 1972). *S. rostrata* also occurs in central Panama (where it is called *S. zonensis*), and in Costa Rica it occurs in more upland and hilly habitats where the rainfall is higher.

A. vinifera (fig. 7.13*a*) is most common in the Guanacaste lowlands (below about 500 m) but extends southward in pasture habitats. It ranges from Mexico (where it is called *A. mexicana*) at least to Panama. I suspect it was introduced into Costa Rica by the pre-Columbian Indians, since it is never found in any habitat except sites disturbed by humans: pastures, old fields, roadsides, house sites. It rapidly invades pastures that are not burned annually—the young plants bear copious amounts of long spines (fig. 7.13*b*) on the leaves and are only weakly browsed by cattle. The seeds are carried into pastures by cattle (cf. Janzen and Martin 1982). These animals eat the fruits (fig. 7.13*c*) whole when very hungry and pass the nuts in their dung, intact and viable. *A. vinifera* is easily distinguished from all other Costa Rican

palms by a sparsely spiny trunk and numerous (3–10 cm long) spines on the underside of the rachis (a few on the top side), densely spiny petioles, perfectly spherical glabrous fruits 3 cm in diameter, and heavily compound leaves 2–3 m long with leaflets leaving the rachis in four different directions (so they look like a bottle brush). A fruit contains a single spheroidal nut 20–28 mm in diameter ($\bar{X} = 7.64$ g fresh nut weight, s.d. = 0.48, $N = 20$). It is made up of a very hard, bony endocarp 3–5 mm thick and filled with translucent white, moderately hard moist seed contents ($\bar{X} = 2.41$ g fresh seed weight, s.d. = 0.20, $N = 20$). The seed contents taste like bland, sugar-free coconut meat. Pre-Colombian Indians ate them, and *Liomys* mice can maintain body weight on a diet of them alone.

Newly opened inflorescences may be found on coyol palms from March through June, with the major flowering period being about April–May (Santa Rosa National Park). The inflorescence pops open and is immediately visited heavily by *Trigona* bees collecting pollen from the male flowers. These bees are probably the pollinators, and coyol may set a heavy fruit crop when the nearest other tree is many hundreds of meters away. A representative healthy-appearing inflorescence from a large coyol at Santa Rosa had about 52,500 male flowers on 95 branchlets (average of 550 flowers per branch, s.d. = 36.0). It bore 449 female flowers (4.47 per branch, s.d. = 1.05). All branchlets were very similar (cluster of female flowers at the base, male flowers beyond these) except that the terminal branchlet (end of the inflorescence central axis) bore 743 male flowers and 29

FIGURE 7.13. *Acrocomia vinifera. a,* Adult plant growing in jaragua grassland; top of tallest leaf is 6 m tall. *b,* Spines on underside of leaf midrib, sapling. *c,* Bunch of mature fruit; ruler is 15 cm long. May 1980, Santa Rosa National Park, Guanacaste Province, Costa Rica (photos, D. H. Janzen).

female flowers). The inflorescence produces pollen for at least two days and perhaps longer. It is heavily infested by a tiny yellow weevil, but it is not known what this animal does for a living.

Mature coyol inflorescences bear 20 to 250 fruits that mature and fall in March–June of the year after flowering (one to ten inflorescences per plant). In cattle-free habitats they lie under the parent tree and rot. In some cases unknown small rodents (probably *Liomys salvini* or *Sigmodon hispidus*) chew off the slightly moist, sweet-starchy pulp from the nut but do not enter the nut. Collared peccaries will both chew off the pulp and crack the nuts between their molars. They do not appear to ever swallow the nuts whole. However, if cattle have access to coyol trees, the fruits rarely stay under the tree for long. The nuts pass through cattle, but it is not known whether some are digested. I believe none are digested, since other hard large seeds make the trip unharmed. *Scheelea rostrata* nuts are attacked by two species of large bruchid beetles (the egg is laid on the nut and the larva bores through the nut wall into the seed); on rare occasions one of these bruchids also attacks *A. vinifera* nuts, but often it does not appear able to exit as a larva and newly emerged adult. However, at Santa Rosa National Park there is a regular infestation of 1–2% of the coyol nuts by one of these bruchids (*caryobruchus buscki*) when the tree is growing in second-growth forest. Curiously, it never attains the high levels of infestation found in *Scheelea rostrata* nuts, but it has the ability to escape from the nut. I suspect that the fruit pulp and the nut contents were major food items for some large Pleistocene mammals (Janzen and Martin 1982). The nut is so hard that it takes heavy blows with a hammer to open it. The cow, avidly eating the fruits and passing as many as fifteen nuts in one fecal pat, is probably a moderately good ecological analogue of one of these animals.

The habitat occupied by *A. vinifera* is often burned over by fires set by people. Light grass fires have little or no effect on the plant; more intense fires often scorch or even consume the leaves, but the shoot apex, buried deep among the leaf bases, is not damaged. Within a month a new green leaf appears at the top of the crown. A severe fire may burn into the trunk, which lacks a cambium and is therefore unable to repair itself. Repeated intense fires, even at intervals of several years, will kill the palm by gradually eroding its water-conducting capacity and sometimes by burning right through the trunk.

The resources used in fruit and flower production are stored in the trunk. In some species of palm the tree can be felled, a troughlike groove cut down its length, and the carbohydrate-rich liquid that flows into the trough fermented to produce a palm wine. Tradition has it, however, that *A. vinifera* palm wine was made by climbing the tree, cutting out the shoot apex, and collecting the

fluid that accumulates in the pit. This fluid, which was bearing nutrients for developing flowers or fruits, was then fermented to various degrees before drinking. In addition to this use, I suspect that the Indians were heavy predators on *A. vinifera* palm nuts for both the nutrient-rich mesocarp and the oil-rich seed. The seed is easily extracted by cracking the nut between two stones.

*

Janzen, D. H. 1971. The fate of *Scheelea rostrata* fruits beneath the parent tree: Predispersal attack by bruchids. *Principes* 15:89–101.

Janzen, D. H., and Martin, P. S. 1982. Neotropical anachronisms: The fruits the gomphotheres left behind. *Science* 215:19–27.

Wilson, D., and Janzen, D. H. 1972. Predation on *Scheelea* palm seeds by bruchid beetles: Seed density and distance from the parent palm. *Ecology* 53:954–59.

Acrostichum aureum (Negra Forra, Helecho Mangle, Marsh Fern)

L. D. Gómez

Acrostichum aureum, described by Linnaeus in his *Species Plantarum* of 1753, is found on all tropical and some subtropical seashores. It is a terrestrial fern with a short, stout, and woody erect rhizome clothed with scales. The fronds are very large (up to 2 m), simply pinnate with large entire pinnae, thick and leathery in texture, glabrescent and with a fine uniformly reticulate venation.

The sporangia are borne on the entire dorsal surface of the fertile pinnae (fig. 7.14), producing a compact layer of spore cases, not as in other ferns such as *Polypodium*, where one can see discrete sori. This condition is referred to as the "acrostichoid" state. The sporangia are mixed

FIGURE 7.14. *Acrostichum aureum*, fertile fronds bearing droplets of salty water excreted early in the morning. Llorona, Corcovado National Park, Osa Peninsula, Costa Rica (photo, D. H. Janzen).

with capitate-lobed paraphyses, interpreted as abortive sporangia. The spores are large, minutely tuberculate, and tetrahedral.

The genus consists of a few species, of which two are found in Costa Rica: *A. aureum,* with all the pinnae in one frond fertile and never imbricating, and *A. danaefolium,* with only the distal pinnae fertile and all pinnae somewhat overlapping at least at their bases. The species *aureum* is found all along the Pacific coast, while *danaefolium* is more abundant on the Caribbean seashore. There are no records of mixed populations or hybrid swarms.

Pteridologists have not reached an agreement on the delimitation of the major groups of ferns, but Copeland (1947) places this genus in his Pteridaceae, Holttum (1949) places it in his subfamily Pteridoideae of Dennstaedtiaceae, and Ching (1940) places it in a family of its own, the Acrostichaceae, to cite the three most important modern attempts at fern classification.

Regardless of their panoceanic distribution, the species of *Acrostichum* have similar biologies. A brackish marsh in the northern parts of Australia or nearby islands will have *A. speciosum* in the same place where *aureum* or *danaefolium* would grow in the American tropics. The marsh fern, *A. aureum,* synthesizes the biology of these bizarre plants: they are typically part of the "strand" vegetation, where organisms are constantly subject to salt deposited from the atmosphere, as is the case of San Ramón in the Philippine Islands (Copeland 1907) or are decidely salt-marsh ferns conspicuous in what Schimper (1903) names the *"Nipa* formation" and subject to the direct influence of the tides at least for part of the year, such as the landward edge of the mangroves, estuaries, and sandy beaches.

Acrostichum is structurally very well adapted to its habitat, which is part watery and part arid (high temperatures, desiccating winds, full exposure to sun and hot soils). The number of stomata per square millimeter can be as high as 220, equivalent to 35% of the frond surface. There are thick layers of epidermal tissue, underlain above by two layers of irregular hyaline endodermis and underneath by one incomplete layered endodermis. This is characteristic of ferns adapted to xerophytic habitats, but in this case it seems to be directed more toward insolation than toward water balance, judging from the high density of stomata.

Even if the epidermal layers are devoid of chloroplasts, this does not interfere with photosynthetic rates, nor does the xerophytic structure of the epidermal layers, if we are to judge from the appearance of the often densely clumped plants.

The petioles of *Acrostichum* often have a narrow, light-colored longitudinal strip of tissue near the base. This is called a pneumatophore and serves the same purpose of the synonymous structures in the mangrove trees: regulation of gaseous exchange. Only occasionally, and in very silted soils, one or two roots of each clump of marsh fern grow upward above the ground level.

The regulation of salts in the cellular fluids of the fern has never been studied or explained. The marsh ferns do not have salt-secreting glands like *Rhizophora* and other mangrove higher plants. Apparently the salts accumulate in the tissues, rendering them very incombustible, a property discovered by Central American indians, who sometimes use the fronds to thatch those areas of their huts where the fire or hearth will be set. The new settlers adopted this custom and named the fern *negra forra,* referring to the blackened sooty appearance of the fronds after months of use.

As in most ferns, there is no apparent damage by insects in the populations of marsh ferns, owing to the presence of various secondary compounds and possibly to the high concentration of salts, plus the thick epidermis. Nevertheless, in areas where the swamp lily (*Crinum erubescens*) or the Caribbean lilly (*Hymenocallis caribaea*) or both grow with the ferns, a black and red large locust, the juveniles of which forage on those monocots, may chew a few tender shoots of *Acrostichum.*

On continental shores, fiddler crabs (*Uca* spp.) and swamp or beach crabs (*Ocypode* spp.) are often seen pruning shoots that grow too close to their burrows. Why those crabs do this and not *Cardisoma crassum* or *Uca panamensis* in the brackish swamps of Cocos Island, under similar population densities and microtopography conditions, remains unexplained.

On Cocos Island the fronds (petioles, rachises, and pinnae) are severely parasitized by a fungus of the Hypocreales, *Nectria* sp. I have found no records of fungal parasitism in other continental or insular habitats.

Since it is a pantropical genus, it seems logical to think that the wide distribution of the species of *Acrostichum* is due to airborne spores as well as to vegetative propagation when fragments of the rhizomes are carried long distances by ocean currents after storms, landslides, or river floodings. Pioneer marsh fern plants will establish themselves near the higher tide marks and from there disperse with the first sporulation, colonizing open spaces, where they may grow so thick as to prevent the growth of other vegetation. It has never been recorded from transient landforms such as sand dunes, even if these are in close proximity to large populations of the fern, and this opens a possibility of using the highly resistant marsh fern to stabilize sandy soils.

Any fern flora of the tropics will list species of the genus as typical seashore plants, and Gams (1938) proclaims it an obligate halophyte. Still, there are isolated populations of *A. aureum* growing exuberantly far from the ocean and at considerably higher elevations. For instance, in the environs of Desamparados in the Central Valley of Costa Rica, and in Salitral de Santa Ana at the western edge of the valley, records have been obtained at altitudes ranging from 800 to 1,200 m and at least 100 km from the nearest shore. The only plausible explanation is related to edaphic conditions: to richness of mineral salts, mainly sodium and potassium chlorides and nitrates, and to microclimates.

Several experiments can be done with *Acrostichum* that would lead to a better understanding of its biology. For instance, Why do the millions of spores produced per plant per population not produce thousands of gametophytes around the parent plants? What proportion of these spores are sterile, favoring stoloniferous establishment of clonal populations? What salinity gradients affect the viability of rhizomes and of spores? How do non-perisporial spores of *Acrostichum* resist long-term transportation over oceans and endure the great physiological stress of high temperatures and desiccating climates?

The biology of the gametophytic phase, as in most other ferns, may give valuable clues to population biology of marsh fern species.

*

Ching, R. C. 1940. On the natural classification of the family Polypodiaceae. *Sunyatsenia* 5(4):201–5.

Copeland, E. B. 1907. The comparative ecology of San Ramón Polypodiaceae. *Philippine J. Sci.* 2(1):1–76.

———. 1947. *Genera filicum.* Waltham, Mass.: Chronica Botanica.

Gams, H. 1938. Okologie der extratropischen Pteridophyten. In *Manual of pteridology,* ed. Fr. Verdoorn, pp. 382–419. The Hague: M. Nijhoff.

Holttum, R. E. 1949. The classification of ferns. *Biol. Rev.* 24:267–96.

Schimper, A. F. W. 1903. *Plant-geography upon a physiological basis.* English ed. Oxford: Clarendon Press.

Adiantum concinnum (Alientos, Culantrillos, Common Maidenhair Fern)

W. H. Wagner

The most abundant maidenhair fern in Central America, *Adiantum concinnum* is widely scattered in occurrence and turns up even on walls in cities.

This fern is small and delicate, with bi- or tripinnate fronds (fig. 7.15) of pale green ranging up to 40 cm long and 10 cm wide. The fronds can become fertile and produce sporangia when very young and small. The stem is compact and usually bears five to fifteen fronds, the old ones turning brownish after death. The new fronds are reddish to apricot-colored during development. The petiole is short. All axes are black, shiny, and wirelike. The

FIGURE 7.15. *Adiantum concinnum* growing on rock wall. Santa Rosa National Park, Guanacaste Province, Costa Rica (photo, W. H. Wagner).

parts of the blade overlap, and the inner segments overlap the midrib. The individual segments are ovate to fan-shaped and more or less deeply scalloped, with projections 1–2 mm wide.

Reproduction is by abundant sori, these being kidney-shaped with the narrow sinus on the outer edge along the blade margin. The spore cases are covered by a specialized flap of the blade margin, the false indusium. The spores are obtained at the right stage by drying the fronds in paper; they are tetrehedral, fairly smooth, and 30–40 μ in diameter.

Young prothallial stages are abundant in shady crevices of soil banks and rocky surfaces. It is easy to find the tiny sexual plants—very delicate, dull green, and about 1–3 mm across—on which the young ferns are attached. The outline of the sexual plants is like a broad heart.

Adiantum concinnum prefers rocky soil and crevices in rocks. In the natural habitats it is most commonly found on rocky outcrops and stream banks, but it is often abundant in man-made sites such as roadbanks and rock walls.

Some thirty species of maidenhair ferns have been reported from Costa Rica. Most species occur in the lowland forests, a number of them in habitats more or less similar to that of *A. concinnum.* Some of the giant species of maidenhair ferns reach 1 m in height and have segments up to 6 × 10 cm. A number of the species have become popular conservatory plants in temperate-zone botanical gardens.

Alfaroa costaricensis (Gaulín)

D. E. Stone

The genus *Alfaroa* ranges from Mexico to Colombia in mid-elevation, premontane rain-forest habitats. Four species of this member of the walnut family have been described from Costa Rica, along with two species of the winged-fruited *Oreomunnea* (*Engelhardia*). Curiously, no

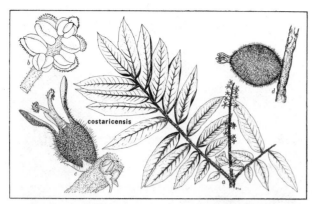

FIGURE 7.16. *Alfaroa costaricensis. a,* Branch shoot with opposite, pinnately compound leaves; leaflets serrate, truncate, and revolute at base; pistillate inflorescence terminal, with numerous reduced flowers. *b,* Single male flower removed from staminate catkin, six stamens partially enveloped in subtending floral segments. *c,* Single female flower subtended by three-lobed sessile bract; petals absent; four sepals fused at base to form husk and free at tips to shelter bifurcate stigma and style. *d,* Fruit about 25 mm long, ellipsoidal, pubescent; persistent calyx at apex and three-lobed bract at base.

walnuts (*Juglans*) are native here; the black walnut group skips from Guatemala to Colombia and Venezuela and then south to Bolivia and Argentina. *J. boliviana* (C. DC.) Dode was introduced to Turrialba in 1948 and has since been planted successfully in San José and San Vito de Java.

A. costaricensis is a large tree (to 23 m tall and 90 cm dbh) with a well-developed crown and weakly developed buttresses. It is only one of twenty-one species of Costa Rican trees recognized by Holdridge and Poveda (1975) that have opposite, pinnately compound leaves (fig. 7.16*a*). The leaflets are coarsely serrate and pubescent on the lower surface. Vivid reddish flushes of new growth appear in January at the beginning of the dry season. February marks the period of peak flowering. The highly reduced male flowers (fig. 7.16*b*; up to fifty) are congested on an axis to form numerous catkins that are borne either terminally on the shoots or laterally subtending the female spike. The tiny female flowers lack petals but bear four sepal lobes at the apex (fig. 7.16*c*). The female spike often persists after flowering has ceased (fig. 7.16*a*). The fruits that reach maturity are eight-chambered, ovoid, up to 22 cm in diameter and 3 cm long, and bear a dense coat of fine hairs (fig. 7.16*d*). The husk and shell are thin, and the nutmeat is bitter. The cotyledons of the germinating seed remain buried in the soil, leaving only the young epicotyl exposed to predation; new adventitious shoots are produced if the epicotyl is destroyed. This feature of hypogeous cotyledons is derived in the Juglandaceae. The more primitive Old World members such as *En-*

gelhardia, Platycarya, and *Pterocarya* all have seedlings with epigeous cotyledons.

Pollination is by wind in *Alfaroa* and all other members of the family, though a gardenialike odor has been detected in fresh male catkins of one of the Costa Rican species (*A. guanacastensis*). The small (ca. 25 mμ) triporate grains with sculpturing of minute spinules are typical of windborne pollen. It may be, however, that individuals of *Alfaroa* are self-compatible. The closely related taxon *Oreomunnea pterocarpa* is represented by a flowering specimen in the Botanic Garden of the Universidad de Costa Rica in San José, and this isolated tree sets viable fruit.

The wood of *A. costaricensis* is fine grained, with white sapwood and pink heartwood. The lumber is of cabinet quality, and few extensive stands remain. Isolated trees are occasionally encountered between 600 and 2,220 m elevation. The most extensive stand I have seen was in the Muñeco region south of Cartago, but logging in the past several years has considerably reduced the population. Numerous trees still stand in the pasture on the north slopes of Varablanca, and magnificent specimens have been seen in the exquisite cloud forest at Monteverde.

*

Holdridge, L. R., and Poveda A., L. J. 1975. *Arboles de Costa Rica.* Vol. 1. San José: Centro Científico Tropical.

Manning, W. E. 1957. A Bolivian walnut from Peru growing in Costa Rica. *Brittonia* 9:131.

———. 1959. *Alfaroa* and *Engelhardtia* in the New World. *Bull. Torrey Bot. Club* 86:190–98.

Stone, D. E. 1972. New World Juglandaceae. III. A new perspective of the tropical members with winged fruits. *Ann. Missouri Bot. Gard.* 59: 297–321.

———. 1973. Patterns in the evolution of amentiferous fruits. *Brittonia* 25:371–84.

———. 1977. Juglandaceae. In Flora costaricensis, ed. W. C. Burger. *Fieldiana, Bot.* 40:28–53.

Stone, D. E., and Broome, C. R. 1975. Juglandaceae A. Rich. ex Kunth. *World Pollen and Spore Flora* 4:1–35.

Whitehead, D. R. 1969. Wind pollination in the angiosperms: Evolutionary and environmental considerations. *Evolution* 23:28–35.

Alnus acuminata (Jaul, Alder)

W. C. Burger

The Betulaceae, a largely north temperate family that includes birches, alders, and hazelnuts, is represented by only a single species in Costa Rica. These trees (fig. 7.17), growing to about 20 m tall, are found between 1,500 and 3,100 m elevation and often dominate second-growth areas and old landslide scars through oak forests.

FIGURE 7.17. *Alnus acuminata* left standing in a pasture as the forest was cut 15 km north of Heredia, Costa Rica (photo, D. H. Janzen).

The open, well-spaced branches and small leaves (gray green) are characteristic of some second-growth trees and suggest a fairly rapid growth rate. However, we know very little about the biology of these plants. If they are similar to their northern congeners, then one would expect the Costa Rican species to be wind-pollinated and to have root nodules associated with nitrogen-fixing bacteria (young plants have nodules, D. H. Janzen, pers. comm.). The latter feature allows the northern species to pioneer on recently disturbed, nitrogen-poor substrates such as gravel bars and may explain why the Central American species is often found on old roadcuts and landslides, where the upper humus-rich soil layers have been removed. Wind pollination appears to be rare in the tropics and is associated with species that occur in nearly pure stands or are codominants in forests with relatively few tree species, as in the high-altitude oak forests of Costa Rica. In the mountains above Heredia, the *Alnus* population is occasionally subject to extensive total defoliation by leaf-eating insect larvae (D. H. Janzen, pers. comm.)

A. acuminata is not known to occur north of Volcán Barva (Barba) in Costa Rica, though the species ranges northward to Mexico. The lack of populations in the Sierra de Tilarán and along the northern part of the Meseta Central may reflect the fact that, for wind pollination to be effective, this species must grow in populations with a considerable number of individual trees in close proximity. Then again, the species may be lacking in northwestern Costa Rica because the areas above 1,500 m are smaller, so that, as on small islands, the chance for extinction is greater and the chance for immigration smaller. *A. acuminata* is an important timber tree in the highlands around San José.

Anacardium excelsum (Espavél, Espavé, Acajou)

G. S. Hartshorn and A. H. Gentry

The Anacardiaceae is a chiefly tropical family of seventy-three genera and approximately six hundred species. The type genus, *Anacardium,* is native to tropical America, with eight or nine species, only two of which occur in Central America. *A. excelsum* extends from Ecuador and the Guianas through northern South America to Honduras. In Central America it occurs as a riparian tree in the tropical dry life zone, on slopes and alluvium in tropical, premontane, and subtropical moist life zones, and only on alluvium in the tropical wet life zone.

A. excelsum is one of the truly giant trees of tropical America, reaching 50 m in height and 3 m dbh on fertile alluvium in tropical wet forests such as the Corcovado plain. The cylindrical bole is not buttressed, though the base may be slightly fluted or have a minor butt swell. The outer bark is dark gray to black and vertically fissured, though not as prominently as *Caryocar costaricense* or *Calophyllum* spp. The inner bark is thick, pink, and slightly resinous, with the turpentinelike odor typical of the family. The wood is used for rough construction timber, but it does not finish smoothly because of its fibrous character. Cots made of espavél wood caused skin rashes when used by students in some early OTS courses.

Leaves are simple, alternate, and obovate, to 30 cm long, clustered at the branch tips. Large, open, terminal panicles of small, cream-colored flowers are borne from February to mid-April in Guanacaste (Frankie, Baker, and Opler 1974). Such small, inconspicuous flowers are typical of a great many tropical trees whose pollination biology is little known, and its significance to community organization is even less well understood.

The fruit is a curved, single-seeded nut similar to the seed of the cashew apple (*A. occidentale*), borne distally on a small, fleshy receptacle or hypocarp that is an

189

FIGURE 7.18. *a*, Terminal inflorescence of *Anacardium excelsum* (approximately 40 cm in length). *b*, Mature fruit; the large curved object is a resin-rich covering over the wild cashew (seed) while the structure strongly curled in the horizontal plane is the receptacle of the fruit (homologous to the "cashew apple" of *Anacardium occidentale*, the commercial cashew) and is the part eaten by the bats that disperse the seeds. *c*, Mature foliage of *A. excelsum;* the longest leaves are about 25 cm in length. Southern Guanacaste, Costa Rica (photos, D. H. Janzen).

acrescent pedicel (fig. 7.18). The raw seeds of both species are highly toxic, but roasting removes the toxicity. There are reports of blindness and severe allergic reactions among cashew processors who come into contact with the vapors of roasting cashew nuts. The large, fleshy receptacle of marañon (*A. occidentale*) is delicious eaten raw and is the source of a canned fruit drink of the same name. The fleshy receptacle of *Anacardium* is carried by bats to feeding roosts, where the untouched seeds are dropped after the frugivorous bat eats the receptacle.

*

Brealey, O. 1972. *Manuál de dendrología para las especies arbóreas de la Península de Osa, Costa Rica.* San José: Organization for Tropical Studies.

Frankie, G. W.; Baker, H. G.; and Opler, P. A. 1974. Comparative phenological studies of trees in tropical wet and dry forests in the lowlands of Costa Rica. *J. Ecol.* 62:881–919.

Record, S. J., and Hess, R. W. 1943. *Timbers of the New World.* New Haven: Yale University Press.

Anguria and *Gurania* (Rain-Forest Cucumber)

L. E. Gilbert

Among the few bird and butterfly pollinated cucurbits are two primarily wet-forest vine genera, *Anguria* (now changed to *Psiguria*) and *Gurania*.

These genera are in need of taxonomic revision, so the specific names used here may change in the future. Within a Costa Rican site, however, there is no problem in separating the four coexisting species, two of each genus. *Gurania* species typically have large, pubescent leaves that are often three-lobed or nearly so. Single tendrils at each node do not branch as they do in other cucurbits. There are no stipules or nectaries. *Gurania* male flowers (fig. 7.19*b*) are borne on long, erect peduncles and are produced continually for several months at the rate of 0.3 to 1.0 flowers per day. Female flowers are produced two per node on branches that had been male at some period. The switch is so complete that botanists have regarded these plants as dioecious rather than delayed monoecious, as most now appear to be.

Gurania flowers have bright orange calyces and yellow petals that at first appear to be anthers. Pollen is shed in 100 μ tetrads. The most commonly seen species in Costa Rica are *Gurania leyvana,* a hummingbird-pollinated species that can become a robust liana in rain-forest canopy, and *Gurania costaricense,* a smaller plant that occupies forest edges and earlier succession. *G. leyvana* possesses calyx lobes that inhibit butterfly visitors, whereas *G. costaricense* has smaller flowers with more accessible nectar and pollen. It is heavily visited by pollen-feeding *Heliconius* butterflies and an occasional hummingbird. Fruits ripen green and are dispersed by bats.

Anguria species (= *Psiguria* of other literature) are identical to *Gurania* in type of tendril, lack of stipules and nectaries, type of male and female inflorescences, pollen morphology, and seed dispersal by bats. *Anguria* may be distinguished by glabrous, shiny, dark green, leathery leaves. Also, flowers have *green,* rather than orange, calyces and orange or red petals (fig. 7.19*a*) that are well developed compared with the small yellow petals of *Gurania*.

Anguria pachyphylla is a canopy vine with three-lobed leaves—usually entirely divided. Male flowers may be available at one inflorescence for five months and may

FIGURE 7.19. *a, Anguria* male inflorescence with one open flower and buds of various ages. Sirena, Corcovado National Park, Osa Peninsula, Costa Rica. *b, Gurania* male inflorescence; interior Corcovado National Park, Osa Peninsual, Costa Rica (photos, D. H. Janzen).

remain on one plant for much longer. A large individual of this species may be seen on the forest margin immediately southeast of the station building at La Selva. It has been in female condition several times since 1974. One female branch was seen to alternate flowering and fruiting until it attained a length of about 15 m and reached ground level. *A. pachyphylla* is a major pollen and nectar source for *Heliconius* butterflies.

Anguria warscewiczii occupies the edges of small streams and rivers. It is smaller than *A. pachyphylla,* forming female branches at 5–10 m rather than 20–30 m high. Leaves are also three-lobed but have a characteristic angular form. Petals are orange rather than red. *A. warscewiczii* is the only species of either genus to invade the deciduous forests of Guanacaste, being found along some streams in places like Taboga near Cañas.

All *Anguria* provide accessible resources for *Heliconus* butterflies and are heavily visited by them. Though hummingbirds are not mechanically excluded, they appear to not to compete well with the insects. For some *Gurania* with no devices to exclude *Heliconius,* it appears that both hummingbirds and butterflies can be important pollinators. At the extreme, one Peruvian *Gurania* not only

excludes butterflies with calyx lobes of the sort seen in Costa Rica *G. leyvana,* but actually fails to open, so that only birds can force their way into the flower. *Heliconius* butterflies are totally prevented from removing pollen.

Parasites and predators of *Anguria* and *Gurania* appear to be largely the same over their range. A showy iridescent green coreid bug with an orange bar across its elytra is an important parasite of these vines. These *Paryphes* species injure flowers, fruits, shoots, and young leaves. Tephritid fruit flies, *Blephoneura* species, attack male and female flowers. A species of Pyralididae (Lepidoptera) related to the pickleworm (*Diaphania*) is a major defoliater of *Anguria* and possibly of *Gurania.* Several flea beetles also attack them. Squirrels and parrots appear to be the major predators on immature fruit, and pollination experiments must be protected with heavy wire cages around female inflorescences.

The time from seed to sexual maturity may be as short as six months in some successional *Anguria* species under greenhouse conditions. For larger canopy species in the field, many years must intervene between germination and fruit production.

Some interesting problems that are worth doing with these plants include: (1) comparative demography of *Anguria/Gurania* of different successional habitats; (2) relationship of herbivory to flower production and sexual condition; (3) comparative phenology of sympatric species; (4) sorting out the relative importance of apparent pollinators.

*

Heywood, V. H. 1978. *Flowering plants of the world.* New York: Mayflower Books. This contains a color illustration of female flowers of *Gurania.*

Asclepias curassavica (Bailarina, Mata Caballo, Mal Casada, Milkweed)

M. F. Willson and M. N. Melampy

Asclepias curassavica (fig. 7.20) is widely distributed in the Neotropics and subtropics, from near sea level to about 2,000 m, and has been introduced into the Old World. Woodson (1954) calls it an annual, but pruned plants and those in greenhouses may live several years, and we suspect it is probably perennial. It is a weedy species, often found on roadsides and in pastures, blooming at any time of the year. The flowers are reddish orange (corolla) and yellow (gynostegium) and commonly are visited by butterflies (and moths), bees and wasps, flies, and beetles.

Milkweed flowers have five "hoods" that contain nectar and separate five stigmatic chambers arranged around the gynostegium. Above each stigmatic chamber is a dark "spot," which is the corpusculum that connects

191

FIGURE 7.20. *Asclepias curassavica*, adult plant growing along irrigation ditch. Finca La Pacifica, near Cañas, Guanacaste Province, Costa Rica (photo, D. H. Janzen).

each pair of pollinia to each other, the pollinia themselves lying in cavities on each side of the stigmatic chamber. When insects visit the flower for nectar, they often slide their legs or proboscides down the side of the gynostegium between the hoods; when the appendage is withdrawn, it frequently extracts a pair of pollinia with it. These dry and twist in a way that supposedly enhances proper insertion into a stigmatic chamber if the pollinia vector walks on another flower; successful fertilization reportedly occurs only if the proper (the more sharply convex) side of the pollinium is inserted first.

There are usually seven to ten flowers (range about two to fifteen) in an *A. curassavica* inflorescence, with no evidence of geographic variation among our sites in Costa Rica. Nectar concentrations in four samples at San Vito in July 1973 ranged from 8% to 24% sugar (P. Hoch, pers. comm.). Although more than one young pod (follicle) may be initiated on an inflorescence, seldom did more than one mature (in July 1973); however, in January and February of 1975 near Monte Verde, multiple pods

were much more common, averaging 1.9 pods per inflorescence at Río Negro, 1.3 at Pensión, and 1.7 at San Luís (where the maximum was four). Each flower contains two ovaries with numerous ovules, but development of both ovaries into mature pods is rare.

Pod initiation increased slightly with inflorescence size at some sites, but not at others. No trends were apparent at San Vito or La Virgen in July 1973. Three sites near Monte Verde were studied in January–February 1975: San Luís at about 900 m, Pensión at 1,400 m, and Río Negro at 1,600 m. At San Luís and Pensión, we obtained a correlation coefficient of 0.22 for pods initiated as a function of the number of flowers per inflorescence. Obviously this accounts for little of the variance in numbers of young pods; and at Río Negro the correlation was not significant. Inflorescence size was even less closely related to pod maturation: at San Luís, the correlation coefficient was .12; at the other two sites there was no significant correlation (Willson and Price 1977).

Sample counts of total seeds per pod (all in July 1973) were: Cartago, $\bar{x} = 96$ (*S.E.*, 2.62, $N = 15$); San Vito de Java, $\bar{x} = 102$ (*S.E.*, 1.96, $N = 77$); La Pacifica, near Cañas, $\bar{x} = 97$ (*S.E.*, 2.05, $N = 20$); La Virgen, near Puerto Viejo, $\bar{x} = 62$ (*S.E.*, 4.70, $N = 16$); in January and February 1975, the following counts were obtained near Monte Verde: San Luis, $\bar{x} = 81$ (*S.E.*, 1.7, $N = 152$); Pensión, $\bar{x} = 66$ (*S.E.*, 3.0, $N = 40$); Río Negro, $\bar{x} = 57$ (*S.E.*, 4.3, $N = 18$).

Studies of three North American milkweeds (*Asclepias syriaca, A. verticillata, A. incarnata*) have demonstrated that pod production (an estimate of the plant's reproductive success as a female) is limited (in Illinois) not by pollinator activity but by energy and nutrients (e.g., Willson and Price 1977, 1980; Willson and Bertin 1979). These three species and *A. curassavica* all exhibit a low percentage of pod initiation, even though (at least in the North American species) most flowers are pollinated. The three North American species all abort many (usually about 70%) of the young pods that do form. This is less true for *A. curassavica*, which matured about 40% of its young pods (except at the Río Negro site, where fewer than 10% survived). We do not know if *A. curassavica* pod production is limited by pollinators or by "food" resources. However, the following observations are germane (and experimental resolution would be easy). First, the failure of an inflorescence to initiate a pod was generally higher for *A. curassavica* than for the three species in Illinois. Usually fewer than 40% of inflorescences (except for the very smallest ones) failed in Illinois; in *A. curassavica*, however, commonly 50–90% of inflorescences failed to initiate pods (only inflorescences of eleven or more flowers had a higher average pod-initiation rate). Second, pollinia removal in *A. syriaca* typically averaged two to four pairs of pollinia per flower

(Willson and Price 1977; Willson and Bertin 1979). For *A. curassavica* in 1975, pollinia removal per flower was noticeably lower than that and decreased with increasing altitude: San Luís, $\bar{x} = 1.72$ (*S.E.*, 0.08, $N = 352$); Pensión, $\bar{x} = 1.09$ (*S.E.*, 0.06, $N = 314$); Río Negro, $\bar{x} = 0.90$ (*S.E.*, 0.09, $N = 155$). Of course, not all the pollinia removed are inserted properly into a receptive stigmatic chamber, but the trends are probably indicative. Thus these data suggest that pollinator limitation of pod production may be more likely in *A. curassavica* than in the Illinois species.

The gradient in pod development and pollinia removal from Río Negro to San Luís at Monte Verde probably reflects the striking changes in climate between these sites. The Río Negro site and, to a lesser extent, the Pensión site are frequently subjected to mist and low temperatures (near 60°F) during overcast and windy days in the dry season. Río Negro is near the top of the continental divide, and the Pensión site is below and adjacent to the Monte Verde settlement. The San Luís site is much drier and warmer, since it is situated in a valley on the Pacific side of the continental divide below Monte Verde. Because of the dry, hot winds at San Luís, herbivores like aphids, which cannot tolerate desiccation, were absent on *A. curassavica*. But in the more mesic environment of the Pensión and Río Negro sites, aphids were common. Other herbivores, such as monarch butterfly larvae, also seemed to be more abundant and to do greater damage at Pensión and Río Negro. Pollinators, especially butterflies, also seemed to be less active at Pensión and Río Negro than at San Luís, which could be attributable to the lower temperatures at the higher elevations.

Another factor affecting reproductive success in *A. curassavica* is the interaction of nectar robbers with legitimate pollinators. Wyatt (1974), at Palo Verde, found that *A. curassavica* inflorescences that were protected with tangle-foot from nectar-robbing ants had a slightly lower rate of pollinia removal than unprotected inflorescences. However, protected inflorescences, which contained relatively large quantities of nectar, had slightly more pollinia inserted than unprotected inflorescences. Nectar robbing seems to force legitimate pollinators to visit more flowers, but high nectar volumes probably result in longer pollinator visits that increase the probability of pollinia insertion. Therefore, nectar robbers can reduce pod production in *A. curassavica*.

*

Willson, M. F., and Bertin, R. I. 1979. Flower visitors, nectar production, and inflorescence size of *Asclepias syriaca* L. *Can. J. Bot.* 57:1380–88.

Willson, M. F., and Price, P. W. 1977. The evolution of inflorescence size in *Asclepias* (Asclepiadaceae). *Evolution* 31:495–511.

———. 1980. Resource limitation of fruit and seed production in some *Asclepias* species. *Can. J. Bot.* 58: 2229–33.

Woodson, R. E. 1954. The North American species of *Asclepias* L. *Ann. Missouri Bot. Gard.* 41:1–211.

Wyatt, R. 1974. The impact of nectar-robbing ants on the pollination system of *Asclepias curassavica*. OTS Coursebook 74-1.

Bixa orellana (Achiote, Annatto)

B. L. Bentley

Bixa orellana is a monospecific genus in the family Bixaceae. It is an attractive large shrub (up to 10 m tall) with glossy green ovate leaves. The large (5–8 cm) pink or whitish flowers (fig. 7.21) are produced on terminal panicles at the end of the wet season (October–November in Guanacaste) or for more extended periods in wetter areas.

The flowers open before dawn and are visited by large euglossine and ptiloglossine bees. Later in the morning smaller bees, such as *Trigona*, also visit the flowers. Since the flowers do not have nectaries, the "reward" for the pollinators is pollen—which is produced copiously. The flowers wilt by midday, and the corolla falls by late afternoon.

Because it has been grown as an ornamental and as a source of red dye (achiote or annatto), *Bixa* is common throughout Costa Rica below 1,500 m. In Guanacaste it

FIGURE 7.21. *Bixa orellana* flower and buds (spheres). Finca La Pacifica, near Cañas, Guanacaste Province, Costa Rica (photo, D. H. Janzen).

is most common near river courses, while in the Atlantic lowlands it is a common roadside shrub, especially near rural houses (e.g., along the road approaching Puerto Viejo). If not native to Guanacaste, it is thoroughly naturalized.

The spiny fruits are quite variable in size (1.5–5 cm in diameter) and shape (from a "pinchushion" to "*corazon de Jesús*"). Because the fruits are often bright red as well, the plant can be easily identified even when not in flower. The seeds are attacked by coreid bugs when immature and by a bruchid beetle (*Stator championi*) after the capsule opens.

The plant has extrafloral nectaries on the stem at the node and on the peduncle of the flower and fruit. The nectaries on the stem are active only when the foliage is very young, but those on the peduncle are active from bud maturity through to drying of the fruit capsule. Ants attracted to these nectaries (most notably *Ectatomma tuberculatum, E. ruidum,* and various species of *Camponotus* and *Crematogaster*) reduce the effects of insect herbivores on the buds and developing fruits.

The oily red dye on the seed has been used throughout tropical Latin America since pre-Columbian times for body decoration and as a food color. Today it is used to color *arroz con pollo* and is being explored as a possible "natural" dye for such foods as margine (it is yellow when dilute) and other products requiring an oil-soluble dye.

*

Bentley, B. L. 1977. The protective function of ants visiting the extrafloral nectaries of *Bixa orellana* (Bixaceae). *J. Ecol.* 65:27–38.

Blakea (San Miguel)

C. Lumer

Blakea (Melastomataceae), a genus of hemiepiphytes, is essentially a Neotropical montane genus with scattered lowland species throughout Central and South America. Five species grow in and around the Monteverde Cloud Forest Reserve (*B. anomala, B. gracilis, B. chlorantha, B. grandiflora,* and *B. tuberculata*). The plants are sun-loving and grow at various levels in the canopy, including the uppermost canopy. However, they are often found growing on fallen logs or tree stumps in light gaps caused by tree falls or human clearing. It is in these areas that they are available for study. We are often unaware of these plants in the canopy unless our attention is drawn to fallen petals, fruit, or leaves on the ground.

With one exception (*B. chlorantha*), those species found in the Monteverde area have relatively large, showy flowers (fig. 7.22) ranging from white to pink. Like most members of the Melastomataceae, these

FIGURE 7.22. *Blakea gracilis* flower with amphitheater effect of stamens, which is typical of most (but not all) *Blakea* species. Monteverde, Puntarenas Province, Costa Rica (photo, C. Lumer).

flowers lack nectar and have anthers that release their pollen through terminal pores.

Many species of bees visit these flowers. These include *Xylocopa* sp., *Epicharis* sp., *Melipona fasciata,* two species of *Bombus,* two species of *Trigona,* and three species of *Eulaema*. The bees alighting on the anthers vibrate their indirect flight muscles, causing pollen to be released from the anther pores. The bees then clean themselves and collect the pollen.

Three of the five species (*B. anomala, B. gracilis, B. chlorantha*) have a rather long flowering period of six to eight months. While the blooming period is basically synchronous for a species, the start and finish may vary by as much as two months from plant to plant within a species.

The other two species (*B. grandiflora* and *B. tuberculata*) both have one very short blooming period during the wet season.

Except for *B. chlorantha,* the floral biology of the plants is similar, that is, they are self-compatible, have open, showy flowers, lack nectar, and are pollinated by bees. *Blakea chlorantha,* however, has nectar, has small green, bell-shaped flowers, and is pollinated by rodents that visit the flowers at night for nectar. In these flowers the pollen shoots out from the pores when slight pressure is applied on the outside of the petals or when the base of the anthers is probed. This occurs when the rodent grasps the flower in its front paws, putting pressure on the petals, and probes for nectar with its tongue.

Blakea gracilis is not found in the reserve at all, but it is common in the lower, drier woods of the San Luís valley. In the Monteverde area it is often seen in pastures growing on tree stumps, where the cows eat the buds, flowers, fruit, and leaves. The local people call it "San Miguel" and also find the plants tasty. The flavor is the slightly acidic taste of oxalic acid.

All five species of *Blakea* in Monteverde have attractive red fruits that contain approximately a thousand seeds per fruit. Close inspection of a "plant" often shows that many plants make up what, to the casual observer, seems to be one. This is probably due to the method of seed dispersal. That is, one fruit with many seeds is eaten by a bird or other animal, which then defecates or regurgitates, dropping a number of seeds in one spot.

This method of dispersal and consequent habit raises an interesting question about pollination and gene flow. Many of the small bees, such as *Melipona fasciata*, that seem to spend a lot of time on "one plant" might actually be moving pollen between closely growing plants, while the larger bees, which visit fewer flowers per "plant" are probably involved in gene flow between widely dispersed plants.

*

Almeda, F. 1974. A new epiphytic *Blakea* (Melastomataceae) from Panama. *Brittonia* 26:393–97.

Gleason, H. A. 1945. On *Blakea* and *Topobea*. *Bull. Torrey Bot. Club* 72:383–93.

Janzen, D. H. 1971. Euglossine bees as long distance pollinators of tropical plants. *Science* 171:203–5.

Lumer, C. 1980. Rodent pollination of *Blakea* (Melastomataceae) in a Costa Rican cloud forest. *Brittonia* 23:512–17.

Wille, A. 1963. Behavioral adaptations of bees for pollen collecting from *Cassia* flowers. *Rev. Biol. Trop.* 11:205–10.

Bromelia pinguin and *B. karatas*
(Chiras, Piñuelas)

W. Hallwachs

Like ant-acacias (*Acacia*) with their stinging ants and mala mujer (*Cnidoscolus urens*) with its urticating hairs, the terrestrial bromeliads *Bromelia pinguin* and *B. karatas* are easy to remember after a first encounter. They are among the spiniest of the spiny plants characteristic of Guanacaste deciduous habitats (others are *Randia* "echinocarpa," *Bombacopsis quinatum* and *Xanthoxylum setulosum*, *Bactris minor* and *Acrocomia vinifera*, *Chomelia spinosa*, *Mimosa pigra*, *Pithecellobium mangense*, *Jacquinia pungens*, various cacti, *Agave*, etc.).

The straplike leaves (100–140 cm long in large plants) (fig. 7.23) have pointed tips and bear hooked thorns on their margins. These may not only deter potential grazers but also repel large mammals that might be merely passing by but could bend, break, or trample the leaves if there were no reason to avoid the plant. The large, tough-looking plants are in fact probably very vulnerable to physical damage of this sort. Bromeliads are monocots; their thin, flattened leaves are made up of long parallel fibers. A monocot leaf with the dimensions and high

weight of *B. pinguin* and *B. karatas* leaves is probably easily damaged by twisting or bending. Furthermore, there is only one meristem (at the center of the plant between the leaf bases). Unlike a dicotyledon branch of similar biomass, a fully grown bromeliad leaf cannot be repaired by sprouting new leaves or branchlets. Protection is increased by the tendency of the spiny terrestrial species to reproduce vegetatively on short runners, forming dense patches of plants. Insects and small to medium vertebrates (Smythe 1970, p. 32) take refuge in these patches, and other plants may be sheltered from large herbivores by the bromeliads' spines.

The plants are easy to identify from a distance. They are the largest species of bromeliad in Santa Rosa National Park and the only terrestrial ones. (They are also found throughout the deciduous forested Pacific lowlands of the rest of Costa Rica, a region that is relatively species poor in bromeliads.) The crown of a large plant is almost 1 m tall and has a diameter of 2–2.5 m with more than fifty living leaves, the largest of which is 130–40 cm long and about 8 cm wide at the base. They are sometimes planted in hedges, and it is believed that they were planted as barriers around Indian villages, since potsherds and other Indian relics are often found near large patches of the plants. Both species usually grow in monospecific patches in open or lightly shaded habitats. Under the light shade of an open-crown tree like *Crescentia alata* the plants can reproduce. When shaded by dense, low herbs, however, the plants are small, with narrow and slightly blue-tinted leaves, and probably do not flower. Several plants growing on a west-facing cliff-top exposed to full sun and the dry-season wind had lost much turgidity by the end of the dry season but were still alive (May 1980, Santa Rosa National Park). Other plants growing a few meters back from the same cliff edge, but lightly shaded and somewhat shielded from the wind, were as turgid as those growing in open areas in the forest.

As in pineapples and all other bromeliads, new leaves appear at the center of the crown. In *B. pinguin* and *B. karatas*, new leaves are produced one at a time and in a spiral pattern with a little more than 120° between leaves. A new leaf is therefore not directly above and shading the leaves below it until one moves down several tiers in the helix. In a sample of twenty-four plants, there were nearly equal numbers of right-handed and left-handed growth spirals. An offshoot produced vegetatively may have the same handedness as its parent or the opposite. In 1980 established *B. pinguin* plants produced about eight new leaves during the Santa Rosa rainy season (May to December). Plants that have produced a flower bud are not capable of putting out new leaves, but the vegetative offshoots from such plants grow very quickly; one produced twenty leaves over a 7-month period.

FIGURE 7.23. *Bromelia pinguin. a,* Maturing large plant; the trap at its base is 20 cm long. *b,* Inflorescence with numerous old and newly opening flowers (uppermost flowers) (May). Santa Rosa National Park, Guanacaste Province, Costa Rica (photos, D. H. Janzen).

Mature leaves are almost vertical at the base but grow outward as well as upward until they form a gentle curve bending back to the ground. Leaves are usually curved into a U in cross section, especially at the base. Water and debris are channeled naturally down this trough to the cups formed between the base of the leaf and the center of the plant. While these bromeliads may gather some moisture and nutrients from what collects in these leaf axils, they are not elaborately designed for it as are the epiphytic tank bromeliads, and they do not have specialized trichomes capable of absorbing water from the broad leaf surfaces as many epiphytic bromeliads do (Benzing 1977; Benzing and Burt 1970; Benzing and Renfrow 1971). However, channeling of rainwater by the leaves should maximize the amount of water that arrives at the roots.

Crassulacean acid metabolism occurs in *B. pinguin,* just as in all other species of the subfamily Bromelioideae studied (Medina 1974).

Aging undamaged leaves die slowly from the tip inward; old leaves usually have brown tips. *B. pinguin* is the host plant of *Dynastor darius* (Satyridae) (Aiello and Silberglied 1978). The caterpillars eat from the spiny leaf margins inward; the larval feeding period is probably throughout the last two-thirds of the rainy season. Though the plants are evergreen, there was no sign of larval feeding in the dry season of 1980. Of twenty-four plants, two, which were adjacent and were both dying after fruiting and flowering, had leaf-miner tunnels.

B. pinguin and *B. karatas* reproduce sexually and also grow new plants vegetatively. A medium to large plant sends out an offshoot from near its base; the offshoot is connected to the parent plant by a stalk like a garden hose. Recent offshoots are recognizable even after they are firmly rooted, by the presence of this stalk and by the shortness of the oldest leaves at the base of rooted offshoots. I have found one large plant with a fruit stalk that had two dead and one living offshoots, and two live plants that are clearly offshoots of a single plant now rotted almost to oblivion; but in general one live offshoot at a time is usual. The offshoots may take root as little as 28 cm away, but the average distance, center of offshoot to center of parent, is 85 cm.

As in many other bromeliads, the youngest upper leaves of *B. pinguin* flag a flowering plant by turning pinkish red when the inflorescence is developing. The

196

inflorescence of *B. pinguin* (fig. 7.23*b*) is an upright stalk with about a hundred pink flowers deeply buried in whitish gray bracts; one to four flowers open each day for several weeks. They are visited by pierid butterflies (*Eurema diara* and *Phoebus* spp.) and by hummingbirds. When ripe, the fruits are 2–3 cm in diameter, yellow spheroids designed to be eaten by a large vertebrate. Each contains an acidic-sweet, white juicy pulp and five to fifteen black, smooth seeds 3–4 mm in diameter to which the pulp clings. There are five to twenty fruits to a spike. Plants die slowly after fruiting but usually leave a living offshoot. The inflorescence of *B. karatas* is sessile, and this is by far the best way to recognize this rarer species. *B. karatas* leaves seem narrower and more heavily ridged and lack a type of leaf damage—a spreading oval spot of brown dead leaf tissue, possibly caused by a fungus— that is characteristic of *B. pinguin,* and the thorns on the leaf margins are farther apart (4.5–5 cm versus ca. 3 cm on full-grown leaves).

Patches of *B. pinguin* and *B. karatas* may be formed from a great deal of vegetative spreading or from a combination of vegetative growth and short-distance seed dispersal. Although there may be a number of genetically identical plants in the same patch, the fact that plants must grow large before flowering and that fruiting may not be highly seasonal gives plants a chance of outcrossing between patches; two individuals in the same patch are not likely to be in flower at the same time.

Bromelia pinguin is both widespread and common; it occurs in dry habitats from Mexico to Venezuela and on Caribbean islands as well (Foster 1952). An analogous spiny large terrestrial bromeliad with sweet fruits, *Aechmea magdalenae,* grows in Central American rain forests. Humans eat young inflorescences of *B. pinguin* as a vegetable (Spencer 1981). Terrestrial bromeliads are grown for fiber as well as hedges, and a vermifuge is prepared from members of the genus *Bromelia,* as from the pineapple. All bromeliad fruits known are edible (Spencer 1981), and some are delicious, though not easy for a large mammal to harvest, as described in 1857 by a Middlebury College professor, I. F. Holton:

I came to another plant [*Bromelia karatas*] with stiff, thorny leaves, much like those of the century plant. The inner leaves were red, and within is a dense head of flowers six inches in diameter, which give place to scores of fruits as large as a finger. It bears the name of pinuela, and is one of the best fruits of the land, being among the sweetest in the world, with a good supply of a very aggreable acid. The drawbacks are that each fruit must be peeled—and the operation covers the fingers with sirup—and that there is rather an abundance of seeds. . . . It makes a formidable hedge, and it often costs more to cut your way with a long machete to the center of a vigorous plant than all the fruits are worth. I have seen where boys have cut a sort of dog-hole to creep in, six or eight feet under the leaves, and it seemed to me an operation worthy of Baron Trenck [Nally 1955].

*

Aiello, A., and Silberglied, R. E. 1978. Life history of *Dynastor darius* (Lepidoptera: Nymphalidae: Brassolinae) in Panama. *Psyche* 85:331–56.

Benzing, D. H. 1977. Bromeliad trichomes: Structure and function. *J. Bromeliad Soc.* 27:122–8, 170–9.

Benzing, D. H., and Burt, K. M. 1970. Foliar permeability among twenty species of the Bromeliaceae. *Bull. Torrey Bot. Club* 97:269–79.

Benzing, D. H., and Renfrow, A. 1971. The significance of photosynthetic efficiency to habitat preference and phylogeny among tillandsioid bromeliads. *Bot. Gaz.* 132:19–30.

Burt-Utley, K., and Utley, J. F. 1975. Supplementary notes: Phytogeography, physiological ecology and the Costa Rican genera of Bromeliaceae. *Hist. Nat. Costa Rica* (Museo Nacional de Costa Rica) 1:9–30.

Foster, M. B. 1952. Nomenclature clarification no. 3. *Bromeliad Soc. Bull.* 2:34.

Medina, E. 1974. Dark CO_2 fixation, habitat preference and evolution within the Bromeliaceae. *Evolution* 28: 677–86.

Nally, J. 1955. Notes from Julian Nally. *Bromeliad Soc. Bull.* 5:96–96.

Symthe, N. D. 1970. Ecology and behavior of the agouti (*Dasyprocta punctata*) and related species on Barro Colorado Island, Panama. Ph.D. diss., University of Maryland.

Spencer, M. 1981. Bromeliads: Edible and therapeutic. *J. Bromeliad Soc.* 31:147–51.

Bromeliads (Piña silvestre, Piñuelas, Chiras, Wild Pineapple)

J. F. Utley and K. Burt-Utley

The family Bromeliaceae contains about two thousand species that range from tropical to warm-temperate regions of the New World. They vary from terrestrial species (fig. 7.23) with mesophytic to strongly xerophytic adaptations through taxa that are highly modified for an epiphytic existence (fig. 7.24, 7.25). This variety of lifestyles is accompanied by a concomitant diversity of morphological and physiological adaptations. The xerophytic and epiphytic species are the most highly modified taxa in the family, and, since many of the challenges an epiphyte faces involve acquiring and conserving water, it is frequently hypothesized that the former condition was an evolutionary precursor to the latter. Xerophytic adaptations that are frequently encountered include water-storage tissue in the leaves, giving them a succulent nature, well-developed spines (protection from grazing

FIGURE 7.24. Bromeliads. *a,* Adult plants festooning inner crown branches of a large tree; each leafy rosette is one plant, and each is about 50 cm wide. Puerto Viejo, Sarapiquí District, Costa Rica. *b,* Adult plants perched on a small horizontal branch in cloud forest. Volcán Poás, Costa Rica (photos, D. H. Janzen).

predators in a water-scarce environment?), and crassulacean acid metabolism (CAM). CAM is a modified form of carbon fixation that permits the stomata to remain closed during the day when elevated temperatures would result in greater water losses during gas exchange (Medina 1974).

The adaptations encountered in epiphytic species include those mentioned above and a number of other modifications that result in a series of adaptive types. These adaptive syndromes range from the atmospheric, highly reduced, densely pubescent species such as *Tillandsia caput-medusae* E. Morr., *T. circinnata* Schlecht., and *T. pruinosa* Sw. to the large tank- or cistern-forming taxa (e.g., *Vriesea gladioliflora* [Wendl.] Ant. and *V. kupperiana* Suessen.). The atmospheric syndrome depends on a reduced surface-to-volume ratio coupled with a dense indumentum of absorptive trichomes, and it is usually associated with CAM. The second adaptive syndrome, the tank or cistern, utilizes a series of tightly overlapping leaf bases (fig. 7.25*b*) on a shortened stem to form a rosette, the central portion of which consists of a series of water-impounding reservoirs. Collectively these reservoirs hold significant quantities of water and detritus that can serve as the plant's moisture supply between periods of precipitation, as well as being a potential source of nutrients. This syndrome may be, but frequently is *not,* associated with CAM. In all cases absorption of water and nutrients is faciliatated by absorptive foliar trichomes. The general structure of bromeliad trichomes has been described by Tomlinson (1969) and Benzing (1976) and illustrated with great clarity by Ehler (1977). These highly modified hairs have a specialized pattern of cutinization that directs absorbed water and solutes into the leaf interior, and they are thus partially analogous to the roots of terrestrial plants. Moreover, this cuticular pattern coupled with hygroscopic changes in orientation of the trichomes enables these structures to function as "one-way valves" in water and solute uptake (Benzing 1976). In addition to absorptive trichomes, some tank forms develop a system of tank or axillary roots that emerge from the stem and ramify within the tank areas formed by the overlapping leaf sheaths (pers. obs.). It seems likely that these unusual roots serve to absorb both moisture and dissolved nutrients from the impounded solution.

The two adaptive syndromes, atmospheric and tank, represent the extremes of an intergrading spectrum of adaptation to epiphytism in the Bromeliaceae. Although

FIGURE 7.25. Bromeliads. *a,* Seedling growing on side of vertical trunk in rain forest. *b,* Vertical section through leaf whorl of adult-sized plant; note leaves accumulated in central axils. Finca La Selva, Sarapiquí District, Costa Rica (photos, D. H. Janzen).

the syndromes are quite different in approach, they are by no means mutually exclusive in their distribution. Both atmospheric and tank species can occur in the same area and perhaps in the same tree; this is demonstrated by the occurrence of *Vriesea gladioliflora* and *Tillandsia pruinosa* at Finca la Selva near Puerto Viejo, Costa Rica. Although these two species are sympatric, it is difficult to imagine that they are ecologically equivalent. Their mutual presence may be promoted by microenvironmental gradients within the canopy.

The foregoing modifications have dealt largely with water balance; however, those minerals obtained from soil by terrestrial plants are not directly available to an epiphyte. Because of this, the epiphytic environment is extremely poor in mineral nutrients, and the Bromeliaceae demonstrate a number of adaptations that help them accumulate these substances. In addition to the detritus present in the tanks of some species, bromeliads are capable of exploiting other sources of mineral nutrients. Precipitation that has passed through the forest can-

opy (leachate) contains carbohydrates and organic and amino acids as well as all required minerals (Tukey and Mecklenburg 1964) and is a source of nutrients for both atmospheric and tank forms. While leachate may be the primary mineral source for atmospheric species, fine, wind-blown particulate matter is also a possbile source of minerals. But the most interesting adaptation for acquiring a nutrient supply involves cohabitation with a faunal associate or potentially a variety of them. The association of ants with many species of bromeliads (especially atmospheric *Tillandsia* spp.) has been noted by plant collectors as well as entomologists (cf. Wheeler 1942), and recent studies strongly indicate that the by-products of these faunal associates are readily available to the plant host (Benzing 1970). The association of one or a few animal taxa with a bromeliad is not uncommon; Picado (1913) enumerated 250 animal species found in the tanks of bromeliads, and McWilliams (1974) briefly considered the potential for coevolution of bromeliads and their associated fauna. Moreover, the work of Laessle (1961) on

199

the associated fauna (and flora) of bromeliads suggests that the tank environment may approximate a miniature ecosystem. With or without an associated fauna, however, epiphytic bromeliads (and epiphytes in general) exist in a nutrient desert. In fact, recent research has indicated that some atmospheric species of *Tillandsia* approach the "outer limits" of nutrient availability and have evolved mechanisms to effectively partition reproductive efforts in the face of these and other constraints (Benzing and Davidson 1979).

Because of a paucity of water and mineral salts, the epiphytic environment is potentially one of the harshest and least hospitable situations in which plants exist. The Bromeliaceae have met the challenge of scarce or patchy supplies of water and mineral nutrients through a variety of morphological and physiological adaptations. These and many other facets of bromeliad biology as well as general corollaries to an epiphytic existence are discussed in Benzing (1976), Burt-Utley and Utley (1977), Smith and Downs (1974), and Pittendrigh (1948).

Costa Rica has the richest bromeliad flora of any comparable political area in Central America; the entire range of adaptive syndromes, from mesophytic pitcairnias to extreme atmospheric species of *Tillandsia,* can be found within the country (Burt-Utley and Utley 1977). The most painfully obvious members of the family are the bromelias, which are good examples of xerophytic species previously discussed. Both *Bromelia pinguin* L. and *B. plumieri* (Morren) L. B. Smith are native to the seasonally dry areas of the country and, because of their viciously spinose leaves, are widely planted in hedgerows. The tank syndrome is well represented in Costa Rica; all species of *Guzmania,* most species of *Vriesea,* and many species of *Tillandsia* form tanks. The most abundant tank species are *Vriesea gladioliflora and V. ororiensis* (Mez) L. B. Smith and Pittendrigh. The former species is found from sea level to the lower montane slopes, and the latter occurs throughout the wet middle and upper montane slopes, and the latter occurs throughout the wet middle and upper montane regions. The atmospheric syndrome is best represented by *Tillandsia caput-medusae,* which is weedy throughout the dryer portions of the Meseta Central and much of the Pacífico Seco. *Tillandsia circinnata,* one of the most-studied atmospherics, is found in the seasonally dry regions of Guanacaste Province, especially between the Pan American Highway and Tenorio and Miravalles volcanoes.

*

Benzing, D. H. 1970. Foliar permeability and the absorption of minerals and organic nitrogen by certain tank bromeliads. *Bot. Gaz.* 131:23–31.

———. 1976. Bromeliad trichomes: Structure, function and ecological significance. *Selbyana* 1:330–48.

Benzing, D. H., and Davidson, E. A. 1979. Oligotrophic *Tillandia circinnata* Schlecht (Bromeliaceae): An assessment of its patterns of mineral allocation and reproduction. *Am. J. Bot.* 66:386–97.

Burt-Utley, K., and Utley, J. F. 1977. Phytogeography, physiological ecology and the Costa Rican genera of Bromeliaceae. *Hist. Nat. Costa Rica* 1:9–29.

Ehler, N. 1977. *Bromelienstudien.* Vol. 2. *Neue Entersuchungen zur entwickling Struktur und Funktion der Bromelien-Trichome.* Tropische und subtropische Pflanzenwelt 20. Mainz: Akademie der Wissenschaften und der Literatur.

Laessle, A. M. 1961. A micro-limnological study of Jamaican bromeliads. *Ecology* 42:499–517.

McWilliams, E. L. 1974. Evolutionary ecology. In *Pitcairnioideae (Bromeliaceae),* ed. L. B. Smith and R. J. Downs, pp. 40–55. Flora Neotropica, Monograph no. 14. New York: Hafner Press.

Medina, E. 1974. Dark CO_2 fixation, habitat preference and evolution within the Bromeliaceae. *Evolution* 28: 677–86.

Picado, C. 1913. Les Broméliacées épiphytes considérées comme milieu biologique. *Bull. Sci. France Belgique,* ser. 7, 47:216–360.

Pittendrigh, C. S. 1948. The bromeliad-Anopheles-Malaria complex in Trinidad. I. The bromeliad flora. *Evolution* 2:58–89.

Smith, L. B., and Downs, R. J. 1974. *Pitcairnioideae (Bromeliaceae).* Flora Neotropica, Monograph no. 14. New York: Hafner Press.

Tomlinson, P. B. 1969. Commelinales-Zingiberales. In *Anatomy of the monocotyledons,* ed. C. R. Metcalfe. Oxford: Clarendon Press.

Tukey, H. B., Jr., and Mecklenburg, R. A. 1964. Leaching of metabolites from foliage and subsequent reabsorption and redistribution of the leachate in plants. *Am. J. Bot.* 51:737–42.

Wheeler, W. M. 1942. Studies of Neotropical ant-plants and their ants. *Bull. Mus. Comp. Zool. Harvard* 90: 1–262.

Brosimum utile (Baco, Mastate, Milk Tree)

G. S. Hartshorn

The Moraceae genus *Brosimum* consists of thirteen species ranging from Mexico and the Greater Antilles to southern Brazil. All species of the genus produce copious white latex that is more or less drinkable and have useful wood and edible fruit.

Bromosium utile is the famous cow tree (*palo de vaca*) discovered in Venezuela at the beginning of the nineteenth century by Alexander von Humboldt (see Record and Hess 1943, p. 381, for an English translation of Humboldt's description of the use of *B. utile* latex). The species ranges from the Amazon basin through Colombia to southwestern Costa Rica, where it is restricted to the tropical wet life zone in the Pacific lowlands.

In Corcovado National Park, *B. utile* is the most abundant canopy tree on well-drained slopes and ridges, attaining 50 m in height and 1.5 m dbh. The cylindrical bole is moderately fluted at the base (fig. 7.26), with reddish gray bark and large, prominent lenticels that are more noticeable on the roots. The orange red roots are similar to the characteristic red roots of *Clarisia* spp. (Moraceae).

Leaves are simple and alternate, with united stipules to 2 cm in length. The elliptical leaf blade is very large for the genus, 30 cm long and 10 cm broad; the apex is acute and the base is broadly rounded, with numerous prominent, parallel secondary veins.

Inflorescences are bisexual, subglobose to 1 cm in diameter; the male flowers cover most of the inflorescence; the female flower is solitary in the distal center of the inflorescence. Flowering is reported between November and January (Brealey 1972). The fruit is borne within the globose succulent infructescence, to 3 cm in diameter and green to brown at maturity. The pulp surrounding the single large seed is edible and has a sweet flavor (Brealey 1972).

Seed germination appears to be excellent, judging from the carpet of seedlings often found under mature trees on the more open ridges.

The thick (1–2 cm) bark of *B. utile* was used by Indians for blankets (F. Godínez, pers. comm.). A section of bark was removed from the tree and placed in a stream for several days of leaching. It was then dried and beaten to soften the bark, resulting in a warm, flexible blanket.

*

Brealey, O. 1972. *Manual de dendrología para las especies arbóreas de la Península de Osa, Costa Rica.* San José: Organization for Tropical Studies.

Burger, W. C. 1977. Moraceae. In *Flora costaricensis. Fieldiana, Bot.* 40:118–19.

Record, S. J., and Hess, R. W. 1943. *Timbers of the New World.* New Haven: Yale University Press.

Bursera simaruba (Indio Desnudo, Jiñocuave, Gumbo Limbo)

G. Stevens

Bursera simaruba is a dioecious tree occurring mainly in dry forests but also found occasionally in wetter forests throughout Costa Rica. It is common at Santa Rosa National Park and can also be found at Corcovado National Park, Monteverde, and Tortuguero. It ranges from California and Florida to Argentina and is well known to tropical biologists as "that tree with the orange bark." The tree is leafless (fig. 7.27a) in Santa Rosa National Park from late November to May, and during this period the tree continues to photosynthesize, utilizing the chloroplasts under the surface of the bark. Leaves flush in early May before the rains begin.

Flowering occurs in late April to May in Santa Rosa National Park. The flowers are 1–2 mm in diameter, yellow green to white, and grow in clusters at the ends of the branches. The male and female flowers look alike; the female has nonfunctional stamens, but the male produces much more nectar and at an earlier time each day than does the female. Nectar production starts before dawn, and the flowers last only one day. Male plants produce many more flowers (up to five thousand at one time) than do females (rarely more than one thousand at a time) and also flower for longer periods, starting before and finishing after all the females in the area. The flowers attract large numbers of *Trigona* and *Hypotrigona* (stingless bees) as well as flies, ants, and some small cerambycid beetles.

Once the flowers have been pollinated the fruits expand to full size in less than a week (about 9 mm in diameter) and remain on the tree a full eight months

FIGURE 7.26. *Brosimum utile* buttresses in undisturbed forest near Llorona, Corcovado National Park, Osa Peninsula, Costa Rica (photo, G. S. Hartshorn).

FIGURE 7.27. *Bursera simaruba. a,* Large leafless adult bearing a large fruit crop (June). *b,* Immature fruits with filled and nearly mature seeds (January); sectioned fruit wall shows resin pockets. Santa Rosa National Park, Guanacaste Province, Costa Rica (photos, D. H. Janzen).

before they ripen and are dispersed. The embryo of these fully expanded fruits is minute and remains that way until just before the fruit ripens (fig. 7.27*b*). I assume this reduces seed predation by making the nutrient-rich embryo unavailable to seed-eating animals.

On some trees the number of fruits produced can reach sixty thousand, but the average is closer to six hundred (1977, $\bar{x} = 635.4$, $s^2 = 969.7$, $N = 171$), the fruits mature in the middle of the dry season in Santa Rosa National Park, beginning in January and continuing to March, and become a major food item for *Cebus capucinus* (white-faced monkey) at that time (K. Overall, pers. comm.). Other seed dispersers include *Ateles geoffroyi* (spider monkey), *Sciurus variegatoides* (squirrel), and several species of birds. The tough seed of the fruits can also be found in the feces of *Tayassu tajacu* (collared peccary); the peccaries eat fruits from branches that monkeys have broken off while feeding. Both monkeys and peccaries eat the fruits whole, whereas all other seed dispersers strip off the outer covering and drop the hard seed. No known insect seed predators feed on *B. simaruba* (D. H. Janzen, pers. comm.).

Cebus capucinus is also known to eat the young branch tips of the tree in May when the leaves are just flushing (K. Overall, pers. comm.), and there is extensive damage to the tree at this time. Some trees are completely defoliated by the monkeys, but a second defoliation has never been observed. *B. simaruba* contains volatile terpenes, as is evidenced by the turpentine smell and taste of the leaves and branches.

The smooth bark of this tree is also used as a nest site for *Synoeca* wasps. In some areas (Comelco Ranch near Cañas) up to 20% of the *B. simaruba* trees have this species of wasp associated with them. Whether the tree benefits from this association is unknown; these wasps are known to nest primarily on smooth surfaces (A. Forsyth, pers. comm.).

Byrsonima crassifolia (Nance, Nancite, Shoemaker's Tree)

W. R. Anderson

This plant of the family Malpighiaceae is a shrub or a small tree about 7 m tall, though it reportedly grows up to 10 m (fig. 7.28*c*). Interpreted broadly to include closely related segregates, it ranges from Mexico south to Paraguay. It grows in lowland savannas and open, semideciduous woods; indeed, in Central America *Byrsonima crassifolia* (L.) H. B. K. and *Curatella americana* (Dilleniaceae) dominate many savannas. Like most savanna plants, *B. crassifolia* is resistant to fire, and it often shows the twisted, even gnarled architecture of savanna trees. The mature fruit (fig. 7.28*b*) is a small orange drupe with an edible exocarp and a single stone containing one to three seeds. Birds disperse the fruits, and it seems likely that small ground animals do too, though no one has reported such observations. The flesh is slightly oily and astringent but not unpleasant, and the fruits are sold in markets in Central America (*nance*) and the Amazon (*murucí*). In the same regions a drink is made by removing the stones and mashing the flesh in water with sugar; this is delicious, either straight or fermented. Horses eat these fruits readily (D. H. Janzen, pers. comm.). In Belém one can relish the ultimate in exotica, murucí ice cream. The cortex of the stem has astringent chemicals that make it useful in tanning hides (*byrsa* is Greek for "leather"); this may explain its use in the preparation of various folk remedies such as febrifuges.

The yellow and orange flowers of *Byrsonima crassifolia* (fig. 7.28*a*) are typical of those of the Malpighiaceae, in which the flowers are very conservative relative to other structures (Anderson 1979). The only rewards for pollinators are pollen and an oil that collects in blisters on

FIGURE 7.28. *a,* Flower of *Byrsonima crassifolia. b,* Fruit of *B. crassifolia. c,* Large adult *B. crassifolia* at entrance to Santa Rosa National Park, Guanacaste, Costa Rica. *d,* Mature foliage (photos, D. H. Janzen).

the large glands borne on the abaxial side of the sepals. *Trigona* bees take pollen from the flowers (K. S. Bawa, B. Gates, pers. comm.), but it is not certain whether they are effective pollinators. The oil is collected by the females of certain anthophorid bees, most commonly *Centris* spp. (Vogel 1974; K. S. Bawa, S. L. Buchmann, B. Gates, pers. comm.). The bee alights on the flower, orienting with her head toward the flag petal and grasping its claw with her mandibles. Reaching between the clawed petals with her front two pair of legs, she scrapes the glands, depositing the oil in special structures on her hind legs. The oil is mixed with pollen to make food for her larvae; the adult bee herself feeds on sugary nectars obtained from other species of flowering plants (Vogel 1974). Some species of *Byrsonima* have eglandular flowers, either throughout the species or only in certain individuals or populations. It would be interesting to study the pollination biology of such species, especially in populations with both glandular and eglandular plants, as in *B. chrysophylla* on the campus of INPA in Manaus. There are several hypotheses that could explain such polymorphism, some of them tied to the behavior of the oil bees. In this connection it is important to note that Bawa (1974) found *B. crassifolia* to be self-compatible. Also see Anderson (1980).

Many genera of Malpighiaceae have extrafloral nectaries on the petiole or blade of the leaf. These large glands secrete a sugary nectar and are visited by ants. Costa Rican genera with such glands are *Banisteriopsis, Heteropterys,* and *Stigmaphyllon;* all are vines with samaroid fruits. *Byrsonima* and a few of its closest relatives have lost (or never had?) such nectaries, and the only glands on the plant are the calyx glands.

Byrsonima is a very large genus (130 species or more), probably the largest in the Malpighiaceae. It has achieved a level of diversity and distribution far greater than its more primitive relatives in the subfamily Byrsonimoideae. This seems likely to be related primarily to its evolution of bird-dispersed fruits, whereas most members of the subfamily have little or no adaptation for efficient dispersal. Two other genera of Malpighiaceae, *Malpighia* and *Bunchosia,* have evolved bird-dispersed fruits. They are not closely related to *Byrsonima* or to each other, and fleshy fruits very probably evolved three times in parallel in this family (Anderson 1978). Although some species of *Byrsonima* inhabit wet forests, the great majority grow in savannas, where they vary from fairly large trees down to twiggy subshrubs with subterranean stems, forming a matlike covering on termite mounds in central Brazil.

203

*

Anderson, W. R. 1978. Byrsonimoideae: A new subfamily of the Malpighiaceae. *Leandra* 7:5–18.

———. 1979. Floral conservatism in Neotropical Malpighiaceae. *Biotropica* 11:219–23.

———. 1980. Cryptic self-fertilization in the Malpighiaceae. *Science* 207:892–93.

Bawa, K. S. 1974. Breeding systems of tree species of a lowland tropical community. *Evolution* 28:85–92.

Vogel, S. 1974. Ölblumen und ölsammelnde Bienen. *Trop. subtrop. Pflanzenwelt* 7:1–547.

Calathea insignis (Hoja Negra, Hoja de Sal, Bijagua, Rattlesnake Plant)

H. Kennedy

Calathea insignis is a commonly encountered large understory herb belonging to the family Marantaceae (prayer plant or arrowroot family). This species occurs from Mexico to Ecuador and is prevalent in lowland Costa Rica from sea level, on the Osa Peninsula, to about 1,500 m at Monteverde and near San Vito, in semideciduous to premontane wet forests. Individuals from the Atlantic lowlands and Monteverde are larger, ranging up to 4 m, than those on the Pacific side from the Osa Peninsula and San Vito, where they usually are less than 2.5 m tall. The Atlantic population has been described as a distinct species, *C. quadraspica*. The Atlantic and Pacific populations, however, are interfertile, and intermediates are still present.

Flowering occurs mainly during the rainy season, May through November, but in the wetter areas a small percentage of the population can be found in flower at other periods of the year. The bright yellow, laterally flattened, rectangular inflorescences consist of a series of conduplicately folded bracts (fig. 7.29a). Each bract subtends eight to ten pair of flowers (fig. 7.29b) and developing flower buds. Flower maturation (anthesis) begins at the base of the inflorescence with the flower pair (buds) nearest the axis and proceeds up the inflorescence in an orderly fashion. Each day the next higher bract, or bracts, "flowers." (Occasionally a flower in the uppermost bract will mature first.) After six to nine days the second pair of flower buds in the lowermost bract matures. Thus there are "waves" of flowering. When the third pair of flowers in the basal bracts opens, the bracts halfway up the inflorescence are in their second flowering, while the uppermost bracts may have just begun to mature. Thus the number of flowers produced per day varies sinusoidally. The number of flowers can vary between one and nine per inflorescence, with an average of five ($\sigma = 2.3$) per day. The young inflorescences have a slightly sweet odor that disappears with age. The odor differs between the San Vito and La Selva populations and is very pronounced in the closely related species *C. similis*. This odor may serve to attract pollinators to the inflorescences at the beginning of the flowering season. *Calathea insignis* exhibits dimorphism in flower color, with yellow and pinkish purple morphs in parts of its range. Both color morphs occur in the Osa Peninsula population and in Panama populations, though most populations are monomorphic for yellow flowers. Populations monomorphic for the pinkish purple form are as yet unknown, as is the significance of this dimorphism.

The flower structure is highly modified and is well adapted to bee pollination. There is a single fertile stamen and three modified sterile staminodes that make up the showy portion of the flower. The petals reflex at anthesis and are fused basally, forming a corolla tube. The ovary is inferior, with three locules, and bears three nectaries apically. The nectar collects in the base of the corolla tube. The pollination mechanism is one of explosive secondary pollen presentation. Within the bud, the pollen is shed, between 1700 and 2100, into a depression in the style just behind the terminal, scoop-shaped stigmatic depression. At anthesis the style is under tension and is held in place by the cucullate (hooded) staminode, which is also under tension but is "pulling" in the opposite direction. During pollination the bee inserts its head and proboscis into the flower, displacing the appendage on the cucullate staminode—the "trigger"—and thus releasing the style. The bee first inserts its proboscis into the corolla tube, and when it forces its head farther into the flower to probe the nectar it trips the mechanism. The released style snaps upward, bringing the stigma into contact with the pollen previously deposited on the pollinator's body and simultaneously depositing its own pollen in the same place. In *Calathea insignis* the style enters the groove beneath the bee's head that houses the base of the proboscis, the proboscidial fossa (Kennedy 1973, 1978). The pollen is placed in this groove and is covered and protected by the base of the proboscis when the bee is flying between plants. The pollen has a very thin wall and will desiccate and become inviable within 1 to 2 h.

The flowers are visited solely for their nectar. The nectar production is similar to that described by Feinsinger (1978) as "bonanza-blank." Some flowers have a full complement of nectar, others have none or nearly none. In *Calathea insignis* the nectar volume per flower varies between 0 and 4 μl, with most flowers falling into the 3–4 μl or the 0–1. μl class, a clearly nonrandom distribution. The production or lack of production of nectar in the flower did not seem to follow any clear pattern, though there appeared to be a trend for reduced nectar volume in those flowers with a high probability of setting capsules, within that bract (see following dis-

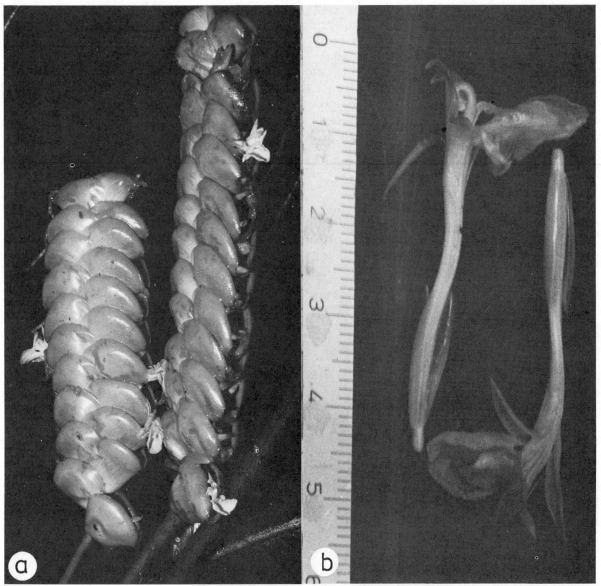

FIGURE 7.29. *Calathea insignis. a,* Inflorescences bearing several flowers that have been visited by pollinators. *b,* Florets that have been visited and had their floral mechanisms sprung. Costa Rica (photos, H. Kennedy).

cussion of seed set). The correlation was not statistically significant. The percentage of sucrose in the nectar generally ranged from 34% to 38% (Kennedy, unpublished data).

At low to mid elevations (ca. 800–1,000 m) *Calathea insignis* is pollinated mainly by euglossine bees. Sixteen species of *Euglossa,* three species of *Eulaema,* and a *Euplusia* species have been observed to pollinate it (Kennedy and Dressler, unpublished data). At higher elevations (San Vito and Monteverde) a ground bee, *Thygater* sp. (and occasionally *Bombus pullatus*) replaces the euglossines as the main pollinator. The bees frequently work the inflorescences in a systematic manner, starting with the lower flowers on one side of the inflorescence and proceeding upward, then flying to the other side and proceeding again from base to top. This type of behavior leads to a fair amount of geitonomgamy, the genetic equivalent of selfing. *Calathea insignis* is self-compatible. Because of the morphology of the flower, it is mechanically impossible, under natural conditions, for a flower to be pollinated with its own pollen. However, not all the flowers visited are always tripped or pollinated. *Calathea insignis* is generally pollinated between 0600 and 1000. In the populations at Monteverde, San Vito, and Osa Peninsula, on the average only one-third of the flowers produced are pollinated. Of the tripped flowers, fewer than 50% have pollen in their stigmata. The percentage of flowers pollinated or visited within a population varies considerably depending on weather conditions, position of the plant in the population, time of year, and so forth. Visits by both pollinators and robbers were fewer on rainy days, as might be expected. Plants growing at the disturbed forest edge received more visits on the average than those a few meters into the forest. Tripped but not pollinated flowers are often the result of robbing visits (Kennedy 1978). Hummingbirds are one of the most common nectar robbers at the Osa Peninsula, and they nearly always trip the flower when robbing it. *Calathea insignis* flowers are commonly robbed by longer-tongued bees such as *Eulaema cingulata* and *Exaerete smaragdina* at San Vito and on the Osa Peninsula, where the smaller-flowered forms of *C. insignis* occur. The Atlantic lowland populations of *C. insignis,* which have larger and longer-tubed flowers, are pollinated by *Eulaema*. Occasionally ants or other small insects inadvertently trip the mechanism and are caught in the curled style. The percentage of flowers destroyed by phytophagous insects is usually about 2% (up to 6% in some populations). From about 1030 to 1200 the unpollinated flowers abscise and fall from the inflorescence.

The pattern of seed set is not, however, what would be expected from random pollinations. The position of the capsules set in an inflorescence is highly ordered (significantly nonrandom; Travis, pers. comm.). The common pattern of capsule placement within a bract is (*a*) a single capsule matured per flower pair, even if both are pollinated; (*b*) no capsules set by the next two flower pairs following the maturing capsule; and (*c*) a capsule set by one of the next two flower pairs (third and fourth pairs following the capsule). Thus the pattern is capsule, 0, 0, capsule or C, 0, 0, 0, C. This pattern is of course not absolute, but it clearly predominates (Kennedy, unpublished data). The physiological control mechanism is as yet unknown, but the developing fruit could produce a hormone that causes the later-fertilized ovaries to abscise. This spacing of fruit might be selected for because of the physiological inability of the plant to mature a large number of seeds at one time or because there is greater seed or seedling survival when the seeds are dispersed a few at a time over a long period. Generally it takes about fifty days from pollination to seed set. The yellow capsule dehisces, exposing three bright blue seeds with white arils, which presumably are bird-dispersed. An unidentified "small brown bird" at San Vito has been observed to take the seed.

In exposed areas with plenty of light, a plant can go from a single-leafed seedling to a mature, flowering plant within two years (Kennedy, unpublished data). This species is one of the more widespread, "weedy" members of the genus and appears to be generally adapted for pollination by a variety of small bees. This relative lack of specificity with regard to pollinators has probably contributed to its ability to spread geographically.

*

Feinsinger, P. 1978. Ecological interactions between plants and hummingbirds in a successional tropical community. *Ecol. Monogr.* 48:269–87.

Kennedy, H. 1973. Notes on Central American Marantaceae I. *Ann. Missouri Bot. Gard.* 60:413–26.

———. 1978. Systematics and pollination of the "closed-flowered" species of *Calathea* (Marantaceae). *Univ. California Publ. Bot.* 71:1–90.

Standley, P. C. 1937. Marantaceae. In Flora of Costa Rica. *Fieldiana, Bot.* 18:191–96.

Carapa guianensis (Cedro Macho, Caobilla)

L. A. McHargue and G. S. Hartshorn

This important timber tree of the mahogany family (Meliaceae) occurs in the lowland wet Neotropics from Belize to Amazonian Brazil and in the Antilles (Whitmore and Hartshorn 1969). It is predominantly a species of swampy or periodically inundated land. At La Selva *C. guianensis* Aubl. is a canopy tree that attains 2 m in diameter and 45 m in height. It is occasionally found along streams and is very common in the swamp forest of plot II, second only to *Pentaclethra macroloba* in abundance and basal area. *Carapa guianensis* can be found growing on slopes and ridges at La Selva, probably because of the area's high rainfall throughout the year (Hartshorn 1972). In Corcovado National Park *C. guianensis* occurs in swampy areas with *Mora oleifera* and *Pterocarpus officinalis* and in the swamp forest behind the abandoned new airstrip at Sirena. The tree is made conspicuous by its fruit valves, which look like thick, woody cantalope segment rinds, and by its large seeds.

The *C. guianensis* population at La Selva produces good seed crops about every other year; in 1971, 1974, and 1976 almost all mature trees produced abundant seeds, but in 1973 and 1975 very few trees fruited. The trees produce fruit in May–August, eight months after the previous year's flowering (Frankie, Baker, and Opler 1974). The fruit (fig. 7.30) is 10–14 cm in diameter, a brown, corky capsule that falls from the tree when ripe and breaks into four segments. Each segment holds one to three, usually two, large (4–5 cm across) seeds that are flattened on three sides and rounded on a fourth, with a smooth brown coat that Fanshawe (1947) reported formed 29% of the seed. Seeds can weigh as much as 62 g (fresh weight) but are commonly 25–35 g. A bitter oil expressed from seeds has been used for making soap and insecticidal washes, treating skin diseases, insect-proofing wood, and, by Indians in Guyana, as an insect repellant and for lighting (Fanshawe 1947).

Trees 60 to 100 cm dbh produce about two thousand to four thousand seeds; fruits drop to the ground below the tree's crown, where 80–90% of the seeds are rapidly

FIGURE 7.30. *Carapa guianensis* seeds in cross section (white interiors), intact seeds (two just above pen, which is 13 cm long), and fruit split open (two seeds inside upper section of fruit). August 1980, Sirena beach drift, Corcovado National Park, Osa Peninsula, Costa Rica (photo, D. H. Janzen).

dustlike frass coming out of 1–3 mm diameter holes in the seed coat through which larvae emerge. Larvae usually complete their life cycle in forty days but may go into diapause for up to five months (Becker 1973). Recently fallen seeds can contain up to forty-six larvae, with an average of five larvae per infested seed (McHargue and Hartshorn 1981). Seeds can contain a few plump larvae and nothing else, being completely hollowed out by the insects' activity. Seeds can sustain some reduction in their reserves by moth larvae or rodents and still germinate, although the resultant seedling is proportionately smaller. Germinating seeds can produce at least three successive shoots in response to apical meristem loss. In common with other large-seeded swamp species such as *Prioria copaifera, Pachira aquatica,* and *Mora oleifera,* a germinating *C. guianensis* puts up a tall shoot before the first leaves are produced. The large seeds of all these species may be advantageous by producing tall shoots that place the seedling's leaves above flood levels.

*

Becker, V. O. 1973. Estudios sobre el barrenadór *Hypsipylla grandella* Zeller, Lep., Pyralidae. XVI. Observaciónes sobre la biología de *H. ferrealis* Hampson, una espécie afín. *Turrialba* 23:154–61.

Fanshawe, D. B. 1947. Studies of the trees of British Guiana. 1. Crabwood (*Carapa guianensis*). *Trop. Woods* 90:30–40.

Frankie, G. W.; Baker, H. G.; and Opler, P. A. 1974. Comparative phenological studies of trees in tropical wet and dry forests in the lowlands of Costa Rica. *J. Ecol.* 62:881–919.

Hartshorn, G. S. 1972. The ecological life history and population dynamics of *Pentaclethra macroloba,* a tropical wet forest dominant and *Stryphnodendron excelsum,* an occasional associate. Ph.D. diss., University of Washington.

McHargue, L. A., and Hartshorn, G. S. 1981. Seed and seedling ecology of *Carapa guianensis. Turrialba,* in press.

Whitmore, J. L., and Hartshorn, G. S. 1969. *Literature review of common tropical trees.* Seattle: College of Forest Resources, University of Washington.

removed or eaten by vertebrate herbivores (McHargue and Hartshorn 1981). Spiny rats (*Hoplomys gymnurus*) feed on germinating seeds. Scatter-hoarding by agoutis is probably responsible for most seed removal, but collared and white-lipped peccaries, pacas, and smaller rodents probably also contribute to the mortality and dispersal of seeds. The seeds will float until they rot (Fanshawe 1947), and they are found among drift seeds on the Atlantic coast at Tortuguero and along the beach in Corcovado, especially near the mouths of watercourses.

Carapa guianensis seeds have no dormancy and germinate very quickly on top of the soil underneath the parent tree if it is moist enough, often resulting in dense stands of juveniles under the adults. Seeds will not germinate if they are submerged in waterlogged soil or if they dry out. If protected from drying—by being buried by an agouti, for example—seeds will germinate in exposed sites. Seedlings grow rapidly with high insolation. The planted trees on the south side of the laboratory building in the pejibaye grove at La Selva are 10–15 cm in diameter, about 7–10 m tall, and 6 years old, the same age as a group of shaded seedlings in the plot II swamp, most of which are below 1 m in height. The seedlings are probably shade-tolerant for many years.

The larvae of the moth *Hypsipyla ferrealis* Hampson (Pyralidae) are commonly found in the seeds of *C. guianensis*. Infested seeds are easily recognized by the saw-

Caryocar costaricense (Ajillo, Ajo, Ají)

G. S. Hartshorn

The Neotropical family Caryocaraceae consists of only two genera, *Anthodiscus* and *Caryocar,* both present in Corcovado National Park; species richness centers in the Amazon basin, with fifteen species of *Caryocar* ranging from Costa Rica to Paraguay and eight species of *Anthodiscus* in Costa Rica, Colombia, Venezuela, the Guianas, and the upper Amazon basin. Most of the species are canopy trees. The genus *Caryocar,* especially *C. nu-*

FIGURE 7.31. *Caryocar costaricense* tree base in undisturbed rain forest on level terrain. Llorona, Corcovado National Park, Osa Peninsula, Costa Rica (photo, G. S. Hartshorn).

ciferum, is best known for its tasty, oily nuts, called butternuts in English. Prance (1976) reports that the fruit of at least three species of *Caryocar* is used as a fish poison by Amazonian Indian tribes.

Caryocar costaricense occurs in the tropical wet life zones of the Pacific lowlands of Costa Rica and in the low eastern San Blas mountains of Panama. It is a conspicuous tree in Corcovado National Park, with vertically fissured dark gray bark and a very columnar bole arising abruptly from prominent, thick buttresses less than 1 m tall (fig. 7.31). In Corcovado it may reach 50 m in height and 2 m dbh, occurring in a wide variety of habitats—freshwater swamp, alluvium, plateau, and ridges. The inner bark has a characteristic vinegar smell. The wood is readily accepted in Costa Rica and is reported to be resistant to water (Brealey 1972).

The leaves are opposite, long-petiolate, and trifoliate, with two prominent glands where the three leaflets join. The leaflets are borne on short petiolules, and the leaflet margins are serrate. Inflorescences are terminal racemes of thirty to thirty-five light yellow, hermaphroditic flowers with numerous showy stamens. The common name *ajo* comes from the strong garlic odor of the flowers. *C. costaricense* flowers in January–March in Corcovado. Prance (1976) reports that the genus is bat-pollinated.

Fruits are four locular drupes, with only one or two locules developing a single seed. The mesocarp is yellow, thick, and oily, and the endocarp is woody. Fruits mature in April–June in Corcovado.

Although *C. costaricense* is an important tree in Corcovado, I have seen very little regeneration in mature forest. Virtually nothing is known about its ecology.

*

Brealey, O. 1972. *Manual de dendrología para las especies arbóreas de la Península de Osa, Costa Rica.* San José: Organization for Tropical Studies.

Holdridge, L. R., and Poveda, L. J. 1975. *Arboles de Costa Rica.* San José: Centro Científico Tropical.

Prance, G. T. 1976. Caryocaraceae. In Flora of Panama. *Ann. Missouri Bot. Gdn.* 63(3, part 6):541–46.

Casearia corymbosa (Cerito, Raspa Lengua)

D. H. Janzen

Flacourtiaceous shrubs and treelets (*Casearia, Prockia, Xylosma,* etc.) are prominent members of Costa Rican lowland forest understory vegetation. Of these, *Casearia corymbosa* is probably the most widespread in Costa Rica, the most locally abundant, and the best studied (Howe 1977; Howe and Vander Kerckhove 1979).

In rain-forest sites, such as the vicinity of Puerto Viejo de Sarapiquí (e.g., Finca La Selva), *C. cormybosa* (*C. nitida* of older Costa Rican literature) is a canopy-member tree attaining as much as 30 m in height in primary forest and late secondary succession. The trees flower in May–June and bear ripe fruit in December through early February, then are largely leafless in February–March. The 10–15 mm diameter fruits are borne in large clusters, and each day a few from each cluster split open to expose one or more cream-colored seeds completely enclosed in a soft, oily (internally) orange red aril. The arillate seed remains within the opened fruit valves for several days if not picked. Birds eat the arillate seeds whole, the gizzard strips off the aril, and the large seeds are regurgitated intact. A large tree may bear as many as twenty thousand fruits in a crop. There is minor predispersal seed predation by a weevil (*Anthonomus sallei*), but it appears that the seeds are toxic to mice and birds. In a study by Howe (1977), the masked tityra (*Tityra semifasciata*) was the best dispersal agent because it regurgitated viable seeds at a distance from the parent tree, was a regular and common visitor to the fruit crop throughout the fruiting season and ate many fruits. Twenty-one other consumers of *C. cory-*

mbosa fruit were apparently "deficient dispersers." Parrots ate the arils but dropped the seeds below the parent; fourteen species of birds visited only occasionally. Toucanoids and flycatchers regurgitated intact seeds but were only occasional visitors and tended to drop seeds below the parent. While it is tempting to view this tree and its fruit as being of great importance to these birds, especially the masked tityra, during its fruiting season, one must consider the difficult question of what happens to the birds in years when the tree does not fruit. Although this tree was used as a primary food source for a long period, the birds may have used some other food source in the general area had *C. corymbosa* failed to fruit (as it surely must have done in some years).

In the deciduous forests of Santa Rosa National Park, *C. corymbosa* is the most common of the flacourtiaceous shrubs, especially in late secondary succession and along breaks in the forest caused by cliffs and ravines. Many of the younger plants do not bear fruit in a fruiting year, making the plant appear scarcer than it really is. It is easily distinguished from the other Guanacaste *Casearia* by its nearly sessile leaves and its somewhat angled ovoid spheroidal fruits that are orange on the outside and dehisce to display a red orange aril bearing one to two seeds. In contrast to *C. corymbosa* of the rain forest, *C. corymbosa* in deciduous forest is a shrubby treelet that rarely grows more than 5 m tall and is more commonly 2–3 m tall when reproductive. It stands leafless during the dry season and flowers (fig. 7.32*a*) at the beginning of the rainy season (May). It bears gradually enlarging green fruit from May through August, when the fruits (fig. 7.32*b*) begin to turn yellow orange. The fruits mature in September–October, and the seeds are dispersed at this time. The seeds are relatively soft and begin to germinate within a few days; they have about three months of growth on moist soil before the dry season sets in. I doubt they could survive the dry season as dormant seeds. There are some plants in fruit every year, but good fruiting years such as 1976, studied by Howe and Vander Kerckhove (1979), and 1979 alternate with years of almost no fruits (e.g., 1977, 1980).

Howe and Vander Kerckhove (1979) found that, out of 1,956 visits by birds, the yellow-green vireo (*Vireo flavoviridis*) was the most reliable disperser and took some 65% of the seeds that were removed. The streaked flycatcher (*Myiodynastes maculatus*), golden-fronted woodpecker (*Melanerpes aurifrons*), and pale-fronted flycatcher (*Myiarchus nuttingi*) also stripped off the oily arils in the gut and regurgitated viable seeds in the forest. Another ten species of birds also removed seeds from the trees. At seventeen closely monitored plants, birds removed 91% of the accessible seeds (crop sizes 1–2,700 fruits). When measured in terms of seeds removed, dispersal success was highest among plants of intermediate

FIGURE 7.32. *Casearia corymbosa. a,* Inflorescences with many flower buds and some open flowers; wasp visitor just to right of center. May 1980. *b,* Mature leaves and full-sized (but unopened, green) fruits. July 1980, Santa Rosa National Park, Guanacaste Province, Costa Rica (photos, D. H. Janzen).

fecundity; birds missed the smallest crops, and the largest crops apparently satiated them (Howe and Vander Kerckhove 1979).

There is mild predispersal seed predation by a weevil in southern Guanacaste (*Conotrachelus* sp.), but *C. corymbosa* should be viewed as a plant in which nearly all the seeds produced are available for dispersal. In contrast, the foliage of *C. corymbosa* has a rich fauna of insect herbivores (it is not, however, eaten by horses, peccaries, or tapirs). In 1978 at Santa Rosa National Park, virtually every plant in the park lost 20% to 100% of its first leaf crop to a single species of pyraustine pyralid leaf-rolling caterpillar; not only did they eat substantial parts of the leaf crop, but the caterpillars rolled up many uneaten leaves in a manner that probably greatly reduced their photosynthetic activity. Later in the same year, many upland park plants were heavily defoliated by the large sphingid caterpillar *Manduca lefeburei*. In the 1979 growing season, neither the pyralids nor the sphingids were abundant, but there was a spectacular outbreak of the saturniid *Hylesia lineata*. Among the numerous hosts of the caterpillars of this moth, it appears that *C. corymbosa* is one of the most favored; *C. corymbosa* was the recipient of at least half of the egg masses laid by *H. lineata* at the beginning of the 1979 dry season and again during the population peak in July 1979 (Janzen 1980). An egg mass of *H. lineata* contains one hundred to three hundred eggs, and the resulting caterpillars from one mass can easily remove from half to all of the leaves from a 2 m semi-insolated *C. corymbosa* within a month. The obvious prediction is that 1980 will not be a heavy fruiting year for *C. corymbosa*. Although I was not there at the final time of fruit ripening, it appeared that much of the 1979 fruit crop was aborted from the *C. corymbosa* plants that had been defoliated.

*

Howe, H. F. 1977. Bird activity and seed dispersal of a tropical wet forest tree. *Ecology* 58:539–50.

Howe, H. F., and Vander Kerckhove, G. A. 1979. Fecundity and seed dispersal of a tropical tree. *Ecology* 60:180–89.

Janzen, D. H. 1981. Patterns of herbivory in a tropical deciduous forest. *Biotropica*: 13:271–82.

Cassia biflora (Abejón)

D. H. Janzen

This common small, caesalpinaceous perennial shrub is at present widespread in the dry lowlands of the Pacific coast of Costa Rica and ranges from Mexico into northern South America. It is easily distinguished from the other fourteen species of *Cassia* native to Guanacaste in that it bears its flowers (fig. 7.33*a*) in pairs on a thin, 2 cm long stalk, has yellow orange petiolar nectaries 2–3 mm long on the distal part of the rachis, and has thin (3–4 mm wide), 6–8 cm long dehiscent brown fruits with a raised X over each seed on the immature and dry fruit (fig. 7.33*b*). There are six or seven pairs of 2–3 cm long oval leaflets on the 5–6 cm long once-compound leaves. The vulgar name is also applied to *Cassia obtusifolia* and *C. leptocarpa*, two annual species of *Cassia*.

Cassia biflora was probably once a rare shrub on natural breaks in the deciduous forest (cliff edges, creek banks, marsh edges), but it has become extremely common in old fields and pastures, where it may constitute nearly monospecific stands a hectare or more in extent. The plant is not generally eaten by cattle or horses, and is difficult to remove since it sprouts readily from burned or cut rootstock.

The bright yellow flowers first appear by July, plants are in full flower by November, and an individual plant may continue to flower well into April if there is any noticeable soil moisture. The fruits develop continuously from the time of first flowering and require about two months to reach maturity (most plants have full-length green fruits by the end of December). Almost every flower sets a fruit in pollinator- and sun-rich habitats. The flowers are visited early in the morning by large bees

(*Melipona, Eulaema, Xylocopa, Ptiloglossa*), which get at the pollen by holding onto the tubular anthers with their feet and buzzing their wings (Wille 1963; Michener, Winston, and Jander 1978; Buchman and Hurley 1978). The pollen shoots out of the terminal pore of the anther and hits the bee on the chest, then is brushed off and transferred to pollen baskets on the bee's hind legs (scopae or corbiculae). Several species of these bees have been shown to visit *C. biflora* more readily if the flowers are high (canopy level) off the ground than if they are at ground level (Frankie and Coville 1979). In 1963 and 1965, large bees were much more common visitors to the large roadside and pasture stands of *C. biflora* than at present. In present-day habitats, other food sources for the bees have been so decimated that it appears they have largely disappeared, despite the presence of certain food plants like *C. biflora*. For example, *C. biflora* is only a pollen source, and the bees must also have nectar, which is generally not available in large pastures with only scattered trees.

An insolated *C. biflora* shrub may produce a crop of many hundreds of pods, but a more usual crop size is twenty to one hundred pods. Each pod contains six to twenty-nine hard, dry flat rectangular seeds (with a raised X on the surface). These are dumped on the ground by dehiscion of the dry, thin pod. However, while the pod is still green but starting to mature, as many as five different species of small bruchid beetles (Janzen 1980) may glue eggs to the pod surface, and the larvae bore through the pod wall and into the seed. A single larva develops in a single seed. It eats out the contents and sometimes part of the soft seed coat. The larva pupates in the seed or seed cavity in the fruit, and the newly emerging adult is dumped out by dehiscion or may cut a hole through the pod wall. Silander (1978) has shown that the predation intensity of these beetles is most intense on plants that are far from other *C. biflora* in a pasture habitat. The widely separated plants also appear to have reduced pollination; it appears that a *C. biflora* plant that is a member of a group or small clump has the highest fitness, though this conclusion does not consider the fate of the numerous seedlings generated by such a clump compared with the fewer produced by a plant far from conspecifics.

*

Buchmann, S. L., and Hurley, J. P. 1978. A biophysical model for buzz pollination in angiosperms. *J. Theoret. Biol.* 72:639–57.

Frankie, G. W., and Covill, R. 1979. An experimental study on the foraging behavior of selected solitary bee species in the Costa Rican dry forest. *J. Kansas Ent. Soc.* 52:591–602.

Janzen, D. H. 1980. Specificity of seed-attacking beetles in a Costa Rican deciduous forest. *J. Ecol.* 68:929–52.

FIGURE 7.33. *Cassia biflora. a,* Flower with polymorphic anthers and long curved style. *b,* Intact green fruits, longitudinally sectioned green fruits, mature fruit (*far right*) and loose seeds (scale in mm). Santa Rosa National Park, Guanacaste Province, Costa Rica (photos, D. H. Janzen).

Michener, C. D.; Winston, M. L.; and Jander, R. 1978. Pollen manipulation and related activities and structures in bees of the family Apidae. *Univ. Kansas Sci. Bull.* 51:575–601.

Silander, J. A. 1978. Density-dependent control of reproductive success in *Cassia biflora. Biotropica* 10: 292–96.

Wille, A. 1963. Behavioral adaptations of bees for pollen collecting from *Cassia* flowers. *Rev. Biol. Trop.* 11: 205–10.

Cayaponia racemosa (Wild Bitter Gourdlet)

D. H. Janzen

This annual cucurbitaceous vine and its spherical-fruited congener *Cayaponia attenuata* (fig. 7.34) are occasional members of vine tangles in tree falls, forest edges, and riparian vegetation. They are common also in anthropogenic vegetation on roadsides, old fields, and abandoned pastures. The bright yellow orange to red glabrous fruits (ovoids on *C. racemosa,* spheriods on *C. attenuata*) are 1–2 cm in diameter, have a thin but tough rind, and contain one to four seeds embedded in a juicy beige pulp. A single plant often bears hundreds to thousands of ripe fruits during the last half of the dry season when *Cayaponia* and most other deciduous forest plants are leafless. These large sprays of fruit are occasionally visited by birds that eat entire fruits or break fruits open and swallow the contents. An unknown fraction of the seeds then pass undamaged through the bird and are defecated quite clean of the extremely bitter-tasting pulp that is loosely attached to them while still in the fruits. These seeds germinate when the rains begin, provided they have not been found by the small forest rodents that are professional seed predators (e.g., *Liomys salvini*) and readily

211

FIGURE 7.34. *Cayaponia attenuata* full-sized and nearly ripe fruits, near Bagaces, Guanacaste Province, Costa Rica (photo, D. H. Janzen).

eat *Cayaponia* seeds. The seedling rapidly grows into a large climbing vine that sprawls to a height of 1–3 m on the vegetation and spreads its moderate-sized, heavily lobed leaves in full sun. It may hang off the edge of a tree crown as a pendant sheet of foliage.

Cayaponia, in contrast to other Costa Rican wild cucurbits, is not free of predispersal seed predation. When the green immature fruits are full-sized, a moderate-sized cryptic brown mottled weevil (*Phymatophosus scapularis,* Clark 1977) lays an egg in a white irregular covering on the fruit's rind. The larva develops inside the fruit, eating both fruit pulp and seeds. After pupating and emerging in the fruit, the adult weevil cuts a hole 4–5 mm in diameter through the side of the fruit and leaves about the time the undamaged fruits are beginning to ripen.

As is commonplace among cucurbit fruits in Costa Rica, *Cayaponia* fruits hang on the dead vine for many months if not taken by dispersal agents, and their bright orange signal may still be seen as much as two months after the rains turn the habitat green at the end of the dry season. One is left with the impression that *Cayaponia*

fruits are not high on the list of delectable food items in the deciduous forest. *Cayaponia racemona* is most abundant in the Santa Rosa National Park region of Guanacaste, while *C. attenuata* is more abundant to the south, especially in large marshes.

*

Clark, W. E. 1977. Revision of the weevil genus *Phymatophosus* Faust (Coleoptera: Curculionidae). *Syst. Entomol.* 3:103–30.

Ceiba pentandra (Ceyba, Ceiba, Kapok Tree)

H. G. Baker

This very large canopy member or emergent tree is occasionally encountered in the forests of both coasts of Costa Rica, occurring in wet forests and in locally moist areas of dry forest. The first item to catch one's attention is the extremely well-developed "plank" root buttresses at the base of the stout gray trunk. There is some evidence (Baker 1973) that these are larger on the side of the tree toward the prevailing wind, but this needs further study. Closer up, one notices that the trunk bears occasional conical spines, and that these thickly cover the horizontally borne branches. The biological significance of these dense aggregations of spines on branches and younger trunks (fig. 7.35*b*) is another matter that needs elucidation.

Ceiba pentandra is unusual in occurring naturally in tropical America (from southern Mexico to the southern boundary of the Amazon basin) and in West Africa, as well as being grown as a plantation tree in Southeast Asia (Baker 1965).

Since it demands light, the kapok tree is also found on forest margins and riversides. It is a pioneer in secondary successions, growing from seed blown into the cleared area. Its rapid growth in height (4 m per year has been recorded for young trees in Africa; Chipp 1927) more than keeps pace with the regeneration of the forest, so that this pioneer tree persists in the canopy or as an emergent in the climax forest. It may reach a height of 60 m.

Kapok trees have digitately compound leaves on flexuous petioles; there are five to eight leaflets in each leaf. The leaves are frequently attacked by phytophagous insects, and in extreme cases trees may be defoliated. They are normally deciduous during the dry season (a synchrony that is more obvious in the dry forest than in the wet). The timing of leaf drop and the flushing of new leaves vary with the onset of the dry season. Flower buds form (on trees that are more than 4–10 years old) in well-lighted habitats while the trees are still leafy, but their maturation apparently triggers leaf fall. The flowering and subsequent fruiting take place in the leafless phase, usually in January or February (with fruits maturing about 4–6 weeks later; Frankie, Baker, and Opler 1974). However, a tree does not flower every year, and as many as 5–10 years may pass between flowering episodes. If flowers are not produced, the flushing of new leaves may take place within 2 weeks of leaf fall if the climate is moist. Consequently, leaf fall may be looked upon as providing for not only free access to the flowers by pollinators (and also for unimpeded dispersal of the seeds), but also renewal of the leaf canopy after diseased or parasitized leaves are shed.

The flowers are white or pink on the outsides of the five petals (which are densely brown on the inside). They are about 3 cm long and open in the evening to disclose five anthers (well supplied with pollen) and a single style. There is abundant nectar production, and the flowers have a sour smell. The pollination of *Ceiba pentandra* flowers by bats of the suborder Megachiroptera in West Africa has been studied carefully by Baker and Harris (1959). These bats consume pollen and nectar while crawling among the flowers. Pollination by Microchiroptera in Brazil has been studied by Carvalho (1960), and the pollination of *Ceiba acuminata* by other Microchiroptera has been described pictorially by Baker, Cruden, and Baker (1971). The nectar of *C. pentandra* contains sugar at a concentration of 15–18% (sucrose

equivalent, weight by total weight), with the following proportions: sucrose .130; glucose .401; fructose .438. The concentration of amino acids in the nectar is low (all chemical analyses by I. Baker and H. G. Baker, unpublished data).

Only a few flowers in a cluster on a branch will be open on the same night, and flowers on the same tree may open over a period of two to three weeks. Each flower closes in the morning, but before this happens, scavenging birds, bees, and other insects may visit the flowers and take what rewards remain. The style often falls with the withered flower during the day, so it is important that pollen tubes have penetrated the ovary by that time. Toxopeus (1950), working with plantation trees in the East Indies, showed that fertilization takes place within 12 h at temperatures at or above 20° C, but that at 16° C the flowers fall before fertilization occurs. These plantation trees, as well as trees experimentally pollinated in West Africa, are self-compatible.

Evidence that a complex assortment of visitors frequent flowers of *C. pentandra* in the Vera Cruz rain forests in Mexico is provided by Toledo (1977). Hummingbirds and passerines were observed, along with bees, wasps, and beetles, an opossum, mustelids, and squirrels (as well as bats). For the most part these visit the remnant flower resources in the morning, and there is reason to believe that by this time the flowers have already been pollinated. Garrido (1955) observed on cultivated trees in the Philippines that the stigmata are receptive to pollen even before the flowers open.

Each flower is capable of giving rise to a fruit, although there is usually much "voluntary shedding" of fruits in various stages of development. Nevertheless, a mature tree may produce from five hundred to four thousand fruits (fig. 7.35a) at the same time, each containing two hundred or more seeds. Botanically, the fruit is an oval capsule, up to 18 cm in length and 3–5 cm in diameter, with a prominent nipplelike constriction at the style end. The fruits open on the tree (most often in March or April in Costa Rica) by five longitudinally running valves, and the grayish white kapok fibers, with seeds loosely embedded in them, blow away in the wind.

The kapok "fibers" that surround the brownish black seeds are not attached to them (in contrast to fibers and seeds of cotton, *Gossypium*) but are derived from the inside wall of the fruit and, in the mature state, are dry and air-filled. As a consequence, they serve admirably to disperse the seeds (until these fall out of the fiber mass) on the winds that sweep *over* the forest canopy or through forest clearings. The leafless condition of the tree at the time of seed dispersal assists this process.

The kapok fibers are 1.5–3 cm in length and have a silken sheen, owing to a waxy covering, but they are too short, too smooth, and too little twisted to be spun for

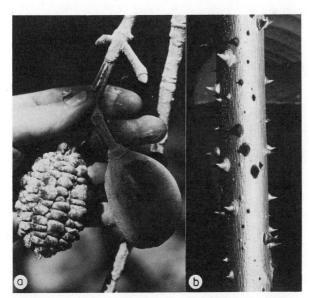

FIGURE 7.35. *Ceiba pentandra. a,* Mature fruits; on left is fruit with outer hull dehisced but the fluff and seeds remaining tightly packed together; on right is fruit before shedding the fruit hull. Bebidero, Guanacaste Province, Costa Rica. *b,* Stem of 3 m tall sapling growing in a tree-fall clearing. Finca La Selva, Sarapiquí District, Costa Rica (photos, D. H. Janzen).

making textile thread. But being only one-eighth as heavy as cotton, kapok is used as a stuffing for cushions, mattresses, life preservers, upholstery, and saddles. The ease with which the seeds can be removed (there is no need for the "ginning" necessary with cotton) is valuable in this regard. The kapok insulates well against sound and heat and is water-repellent, so it is valuable for stuffing pillows to be used in areas of high heat and humidity (as well as in life preservers). Even after prolonged immersion, its fluffiness is easily restored by drying. Unopened fruits (which may fall from a tree when nearly ripe) can float indefinitely in fresh water or seawater without the water's penetrating the mass of fibers. This may indicate that the dispersal of the kapok tree from the American tropics to West Africa could have been by floating fruit.

The seeds (average diameter 5 mm) are rich in oil (about 20% of dry weight), which is edible as well as being used for soap making and for lighting. Kapok-seed cake, from which the oil has been pressed, is a moderately rich protein source (about 26%) for livestock.

Kapok tree wood is soft and absorbent, very light and easy to work with crude tools, but it is not durable and is often attacked by a fungus living on the tree (producing "blue wood"). It is brittle when dry. Consequently it has not been exploited as a timber tree and may be left standing when other members of the forest are cut for lumber. This places it in an excellent position to contribute to secondary succession. However, because of the softness of the wood and the straightness of the trunk, it is used in making coffins, carvings, and dugout canoes. The term *ceiba* is said to be an old word for "canoe" in the Caribbean region.

The pantropical distribution of *Ceiba pentandra* has probably been achieved from an American origin (all other species in the genus are limited to the American tropics), probably by floating of fruits across the Atlantic Ocean (possibly when it was narrower than it is now). Transport to Southeast Asia seems to have been by human agency in about the tenth century A.D. (Baker 1965). There it is known only in cultivation, in a form that is spineless, fruits every year, and has a fruit that stays closed at maturity. This syndrome of characters, useful in collection of kapok for human use, would be suicidal for the species in nature. The cultivated form was probably selected by West African natives from hybrids between a forest race and a savanna race and brought into cultivation there before being carried by Arab traders across Africa and across the Indian Ocean (Baker 1965).

The chromosome number of *Ceiba pentandra* is not constant: $2n = 80$ and $2n = 88$ have been counted in material from the American tropics (Baker and Baker 1968). Numbers ranging from $2n = 72$ to $2n = 88$ have been counted elsewhere. Consequently, some chromosome duplication may be expected.

In Africa the fallen seeds (and to a lesser extent the immature fruits) of *Ceiba pentandra* are attractive to heteropterans of the genus *Dysdercus* (so-called red bugs or cotton stainers, of the family Pyrrhocoridae). Most of the damage is done by the insects' feeding on the seeds, although they also stain the kapok with excrement and encourage fungal growth. Insects of this kind should be looked for in Costa Rica. It may be that the "strategy" of massive flowering and seeding at irregular intervals of years provides some escape from seed predators of this kind.

The germination of the seeds of *Ceiba pentandra* is epigeal (phanerocotylar) and takes place within a few days if a light stimulus is received along with adequate moisture. Otherwise the seeds may lie dormant but viable in the soil for a "considerable period" (Budowski 1965).

*

Baker, H. G. 1965. The evolution of the cultivated kapok tree: A probable West African product. In *Ecology and economic development in Africa,* ed. D. Brokensha, pp. 185–216. Research Series no. 9. Berkeley: Institute of International Studies, University of California.

———. 1973. Buttressing in trees of *Ceiba pentandra* in Ghana. Appendix to K. Henwood, An engineering perspective on the value of buttressing in tropical rain forest trees. *Biotropica* 5:89–93.

Baker, H. G., and Baker, I. 1968. Chromosome numbers in the Bombacaceae. *Bot. Gaz.* 129:294–96.

Baker, H. G.; Cruden, R. W.; and Baker, I. 1971. Minor parasitism in pollination biology and its function: The case of *Ceiba acuminata. BioScience* 21:1127–29.

Baker, H. G., and Harris, B. J. 1959. Bat pollination of the kapok tree, *Ceiba pentandra* (L.) Gaertn. (sensu lato), in Ghana. *J. West Science Assoc.* 5:1–9.

Budowski, G. 1965. Distribution of tropical American rainforest species in the light of successional processes. *Turrialba* 15:40–42.

Carvalho, C. T. de. 1960. Das visitas de morcegos às flôres (Mammalia: Chiroptera). *Anais Acad. Brasil. Cienc.* 32:359–77.

Chipp, T. F. 1927. *The Gold Coast forest: A study in synecology.* Oxford Forestry Memoirs no. 7, Oxford: Clarendon Press.

Frankie, G. W.; Baker, H. G.; and Opler, P. A. 1974. Comparative phenological studies of trees in tropical wet and dry forests in the lowlands of Costa Rica. *J. Ecol.* 62:881–919.

Garrido, T. G. 1955. Progress report on kapok breeding. *Philippine J. Agric.* 20:233–67.

Pijl, L. van der. 1936. Fledermäuse und Blumen. *Flora* 131:1–40.

Toledo, V. M. 1977. Pollination of some rainforest plants by non-hovering birds in Veracruz, Mexico. *Biotropica* 9:262–67.

Toxopeus, H. J. 1950. Kapok. In *Die Landbouw in de Indische Archipel*, ed. C. J. J. van Hall and C. van de Koppel. vol. 3., The Hague: N. V. Uitgeverij, W. Van Hoeve.

Cochlospermum vitifolium (Poro-poro, Cochlospermum, Silk Tree, Cotton Tree)

K. S. Bawa and G. W. Frankie

Cochlospermum vitifolium, "poro-poro," is a small deciduous tree (to 10 m) common to thickets and forests of the Pacific slope, ascending to 1,000 m. The tree is generally found in early successional habitats, and it ranges from Mexico to northern South America (Bawa and Frankie, pers. obs.; Standley 1938).

In the lowland dry forest in Costa Rica, most individuals of *C. vitifolium* lose their leaves (fig. 7.36a) in December and January before the onset of flowering in January and February (Frankie, Baker, and Opler 1974). However, in semideciduous Panamanian forests and under greenhouse conditions, *C. vitifolium* may retain most of its leaves during the flowering period (Frankie, pers. obs.).

In Costa Rica, an average-sized tree bears flowers for about 6 weeks, producing relatively few new ones each day. The large (10 cm) yellow hermaphroditic flowers (fig. 7.36b), borne at the terminals of branches, begin opening just before 0500 central standard time. They are not fully opened until 0600–0630. Pollen, which is the only reward offered to visitors and pollinators, is produced after 0700 when the anthers begin to dehisce apically. Pollen is shed progressively throughout the first half of the day. Each flower lasts a day, and the plants are genetically self-incompatible (Bawa 1974).

Medium to large female bees of the family Anthophoridae are the primary pollinators of *C. vitifolium* in Guanacaste Province. Examples of anthophorids that commonly forage from the flowers include *Centris adani*, *C. aethyctera*, *C. flavifrons*, *C. fuscata*, *C. heithausii*, *C. inermis*, *C. segregata*, *C. trigonoides subtarsata*, *Xylocopa fimbriata*, *X. gualanensis*, *X. muscaria*, and *X. viridus*. Most of these bees visit the flowers by "buzzing" them for pollen (see Wille 1963 for a description of this behavior) between 0630 and 1100; however, some

FIGURE 7.36. *Cochlospermum vitifolium*. *a*, Leafy crown of sapling (July). *b*, Open flower (*right*) and flower bud (*left*) (March). *c*, Mature fruits; some open with fiber and seeds still present (April). *a* and *c*, Santa Rosa National Park, Guanacaste Province, Costa Rica (photos, D. H. Janzen). *b*, near Bagaces, Guanacaste Province (photo, G. W. Frankie).

stragglers may continue foraging until midafternoon. A few stingless bees forage from *C. vitifolium* flowers, but many of their visits occur on two-day-old flowers. Since the stigma is thought to be receptive only in one-day-old flowers, it is believed that stingless bees play an insignificant role in the pollination of *C. vitifolium*. Further, the relatively great separation between the stigma and the anthers and the small size of these bees makes them unlikely pollinators even on one-day-old flowers.

The fruits, which are capsules with numerous seeds (one hundred to three hundred per fruit), mature 6–8 weeks after pollination (Frankie, Baker, and Opler 1974). When mature, the capsules dehisce (fig. 7.36c), exposing seeds with white pappi, which aid in their dispersal by wind. An unidentified small bruchid beetle enters the dehiscing fruit and oviposits on the newly exposed seeds; the adults emerge about a month later (D. H. Janzen, pers. comm.). There is no marked post-dispersal predation of seeds by insects (Janzen 1978), but they are eaten by *Liomys salvini* (D. H. Janzen, pers. comm.). Seeds usually germinate without any pretreatment. Two 8-month-old seedlings grown in a Boston greenhouse once produced two to three flowers, supporting Standley's (1938) early observations that the juvenile period of this plant is very short.

The trees bear new leaves in May after flowering and fruiting are terminated. This event occurs just before the start of the rains (Frankie, Baker, and Opler 1974).

Cochlospermum vitifolium has at least one potential enemy in Guanacaste. In some habitats a woody, broom-like black gall, which may be caused by a bacterial or possibly a fungal infection, is known to occur on trunks and branches of affected trees. Some trees may become so severely affected that substantial branch die-back results. In Santa Rosa National Park, many *C. vitifolium* branches are killed by mistletoe (*Phoradendron* sp.) (D. H. Janzen, pers. comm.).

*

Bawa, K. S. 1974. Breeding systems of tree species of a lowland tropical community. *Evolution* 31:52–63.

Frankie, G. W.; Baker, H. G.; and Opler, P. A. 1974. Comparative phenological studies of trees in tropical wet and dry forests in the lowlands of Costa Rica. *J. Ecol.* 62:881–919.

Janzen, D. H. 1978. Seeding patterns in tropical trees. In *Tropical trees as living systems,* ed. P. B. Tomlinson and M. H. Zimmerman, pp. 83–128. Cambridge: Cambridge University Press.

Standley, P. C. 1938. Flora of Costa Rica. *Fieldiana, Bot.* 18:1–1616.

Wille, A. 1963. Behavioral adaptations of bees for pollen collecting from *Cassia* flowers. *Rev. Biol. Trop.* 11: 205–10.

Cocos nucifera (Coco, Cocotero, Coconut)

J. Sauer

The world tropics have several palm species adapted to brackish tidal swamps and dune swales, but the coconut (fig. 7.37) is the only palm that evolved as a pioneer of ocean beaches. Its sole natural habitat is a narrow zone, commonly only a meter or so wide, at the outer edge of a beach-ridge thicket. Emerging above the spray-shorn shrub canopy, the coconut palms usually lean toward the sea owing to positive tropism to both sun and wind. Thus they overhang the sparse outpost vegetation of beach vines and herbs, and they drop their ripe nuts within reach of the waves. The coconut is a classic example of a disseminule adapted for dispersal by ocean currents. The fruit or ovary is differentiated into three layers, the tough, smooth outer skin or exocarp, the buoyant fibrous husk, or mesocarp, and the impervious stony shell or endocarp (fig. 7.38). Within these the single seed may float in the sea for moths before germinating. In small-scale experiments, coconuts have remained afloat and

FIGURE 7.37. *Cocos nucifera* adults growing wild on Ile la Digue, Seychelles, within the Indian Ocean region where the species may have originated (photo, J. Sauer).

216

range sea dispersal (Sauer 1971; Whitehead 1976; Harries 1978).

A stranded coconut may remain a self-potted plant for several months after germination, the roots remaining within the husk after the photosynthetic shoot emerges. The husk provides some mineral nutrients, mainly potash, but the seedling gets most of its minerals, as well as water, growth substances, and food, from the milky sap and oily endosperm within the seed. Thus, before finally rooting in the sand, a coconut can be repeatedly shifted up the beach to the limit of wave reach, to the same zone its parents occupied (Sauer 1971; Purseglove 1972).

Colonization of a new volcanic island by drift coconuts was observed on Krakatau and Anak Krakatau (Docters van Leeuwen 1936).

Once rooted, a coconut palm becomes incredibly well anchored in the loose sand. It puts out several thousand primary adventitious roots, about 1 cm in diameter, with great tensile strength, extending up to 20 m from the trunk. The palms are rarely uprooted or blown over, even by hurricanes. The root system tolerates occasional saltwater flooding during storms but needs a regular supply of fresh water. In the rainy climates where coconuts are native, a lens of fresh water is generally present under the beach above the denser salt water; this lens floats up and down with the tide, aerating the zone where the palm roots grow. Coconut beaches generally have negligible clay and organic colloids to function in ion exchange; chemical analyses of the sand usually show little or no nutrient content. The roots must get their nutrients from the circulating soil water as from a hydroponic solution. Water intake is great, especially in sunny, windy weather, when coconuts photosynthesize and grow best. Stomates are all on the lower side of the leaf; pinnae of the leaf have basal motor cells that cause a leaf under stress to fold downward and greatly reduce transpiration. However, coconuts are not adapted to cope with prolonged drought; their reproductive cycle is particularly vulnerable: it takes more than a year from inflorescence initiation to anthesis and another year from pollination to fruit maturity; the process can be aborted at any stage by water stress (Copeland 1906; Purseglove 1972; Murray 1977).

A healthy tree has about three dozen expanded leaves, adding a new one and dropping an old one about once a month. Thus the age of a palm in years can be approximated by dividing the total number of leaves and leaf scars by twelve. A seedling coconut begins flowering when it is about 6 to 12 years old. Each leaf has an axillary inflorescence with numerous unisexual flowers. In each inflorescence the male flowers have usually withered before the female flowers are receptive, but there can be a little self-pollination. The flowers are nec-

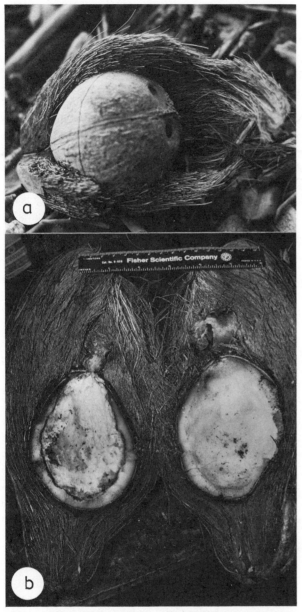

FIGURE 7.38. *Cocos nucifera. a,* Nut with its husk battered off by surf action on a rocky beach; germination pores are visible on right. *b,* Germinating seed (fruit, nut, and seed split in half) with cavity occupied by spongy tissue that takes up the liquid endosperm. Corcovado National Park, Osa Peninsula, Costa Rica (photos, D. H. Janzen).

viable after several months at sea, no maximum limits being established before termination of the experiments. Data on germination of plantation coconuts show a mean of 4 or 5 months and a maximum of more than 7 months between nut fall and shoot emergence. Since coconuts have a nonseasonal life cycle and fruit year round, seed dormancy has no apparent adaptive value except in long-

tariferous and fragrant and are visited by *Apis indica* and many other insects; wind pollination is thought to occur also. Only a few fruits in each inflorescence are held to maturity; a normal palm will drop one or two ripe nuts a week (Purseglove 1972).

After much controversy, it is now generally agreed that the species is native to the western Pacific and eastern Indian Ocean. There are Tertiary and Quaternary fossils from that region and much indirect supporting evidence, including concentration there of the greatest genetic diversity in *Cocos nucifera* and the greatest number of its parasites; more than 150 insect species that are specific to the coconut are reported there. (Incidentally, *Rattus rattus* is now and perhaps always was a major predator of coconut flowers and nuts.) Wild coconut palms were present on a whole constellation of uninhabited Indian Ocean islands when they were discovered in the sixteenth and seventeenth centuries. Centuries before, groves of wild coconut palms presumably offered the only food and drink on waterless Pacific atolls and made possible their colonization by the Polynesians (Chiovenda 1921–23; Sauer 1971).

In its native region, the species acquired innumerable traditional folk uses. For example, coir fiber from the husk is made into saltwater-resistant marine cordage, the endocarp is carved and polished into drinking cups and ceremonial objects, the leaves are woven into sails and mats, the trunks are used for timber, and sap from an injured inflorescence is tapped for an alcoholic toddy. For such uses and for its edible and drinkable seeds, the species was taken into cultivation at many different times and places. Often the local wild groves were simply extended by clearing adjacent competing vegetation and planting unselected nuts. It was formerly widely believed that the large nut size was due to artificial selection, but this assumption is now discounted. Selection under cultivation evidently has had little effect on overall nut size, though it may have increased the proportion of endosperm and reduced the thickness of the husk; this may have produced varieties quicker to germinate and less able to float long distances (Safford 1905; Burkill 1935; Harries 1978).

There were no coconut groves anywhere is the Atlantic Ocean basin until the Portuguese rounded Africa and brought nuts back from the Indian Ocean. The subsequent spread of the species through the Caribbean in the European colonial period is well documented (Bruman 1944; Patiño 1963; Whitehead 1976).

Widespread commercial planting of coconuts for oil and copra, the dried endosperm, began in the nineteenth century; until overtaken by soybean oil in 1962, *Cocos nucifera* was the leading source of vegetable oil and fat in international commerce. It is estimated there are now more than 500 million coconut palms planted on nearly 5 million ha, an area second only to coffee among tree crops. However, the species is still only an incipient domesticate: the bulk of the plantation trees are not genetically distinct from their wild seashore progenitors. Mutant cultivars such as the Malayan dwarfs are being planted, but deliberate breeding has scarcely begun. The species is expected to be intractable material for systematic breeding because of its outcrossing behavior, long generation time, and poorly known genetics (Purseglove 1972; Whitehead 1976).

In Costa Rica, the common coconut varieties of the Caribbean and Pacific coasts arrived from opposite directions and are quite distinct. The Caribbean variety is the Jamaica tall, which is shared with West Africa and the western Indian Ocean; Costa Rica is at the end of the chain of historic westward introductions initiated by the Portuguese. On the Pacific coast, the Pacific tall, also called the Panama tall variety, is most closely related to coconuts of the central and western Pacific. Such coconuts may, of course, have been introduced repeatedly to the New World during the Spanish colonial period. However, coconut groves were already present on the Pacific coast when Balboa crossed the isthmus; they were encountered by the earliest Spanish explorers at various beaches, including Punta Burica on the Panama–Costa Rica border and on Isla del Coco. The nuts were immediately recognized as being like those Vasco da Gama's men had brought back, under the name *coco,* from the Indian Ocean. The Spanish took it for granted that the Central American palms had grown from nuts cast up by the sea. Neither they nor later French and English buccaneers who described these groves reported any local Indian names or any Indian use of these palms (Bruman 1944; Patiño 1963; Whitehead 1976; Harries 1978; Richardson, Harries, and Balsevicius 1978).

Four centuries after these groves were discovered, Paul Allen described those just west of Punta Burica: "Coconut palms are the dominant element along sandy beaches in the entire Golfo Dulce region, forming small picturesque groves or . . . stretching out in a thin line for miles in front of the darker, broad-leaved vegetation. The trees have every appearance of being wild and are universally believed to be so by the local inhabitants, since they regenerate spontaneously without the aid of man, far from any present habitation" (Allen 1956).

The lack of any evidence of aboriginal human connection has not kept these groves from being invoked as evidence of prehistoric transpacific voyages. A leading early proponent of such voyages recognized them as wild and suggested they were the original source from which ancient American Indians had introduced the coconut along with other crops to Asia (Cook 1901). Heyerdahl (1966) embellished the story by postulating aboriginal coconut plantations on Isla del Coco; this was based on an assumption that palm groves sighted from a distance in the interior of the island were coconuts; actually they belong to *Euterpe macrospadix* (synonym: *Rooseveltia frankliniana*). Recently, proponents of prehistoric transpacific crop introductions have usually argued for human carriage of the coconut in the other direction, from the Pacific Islands to Central America (Dennis and Gunn 1971; Carter 1977). However, a coconut on its own would probably have as much chance of completing the voyage as a raft or canoe would, and the number setting forth would have been several orders of magnitude greater. The Equatorial Counter Current, the most likely vector from the Pacific islands to Central America, is neither fast nor steady, but it has lots of time. It is true that the eastern Pacific disjunction in the range of the coconut is very wide, but such disjunctions are commonplace in tropical beach pioneers. The beaches of Isla del Coco and the adjacent mainland share other equally disjunct species with the Pacific islands: *Hibiscus tiliaceus, Canavalia maritima, Caesalpinia bonducella, Ipomoea pescaprae*. The localized distribution of coconuts in Central America at the time of Balboa is not good evidence of recent arrival. In Costa Rica, for example, most of the coast has too long a dry season for coconut palms; also, it has too few storms and too constant offshore winds to provide a habitat for much of any pioneer beach vegetation (Sauer 1975).

*

Allen, P. H. 1956. *The rain forests of Golfo Dulce*. Gainesville: University of Florida Press.

Bruman, H. J. 1944. Some observations on the early history of the coconut in the New World. *Acta Americana* 2:220–43.

Burkill, I. H. 1935. *A dictionary of the economic products of the Malay Peninsula*. London: Crown Agents for the Colonies.

Carter, G. F. 1977. Kilmer's law: Plant evidence of early voyages. *Oceans* 12(4):8–12.

Chiovenda, E. 1921–23. La culla del coco. *Webbia* 5:199–294, 359–449.

Cook, O. F. 1901. The origin and distribution of the cocoa palm. *Contrib. U.S. Nat. Herb.* 7:257–93.

Copeland, E. B. 1906. On the water relations of the coconut palm. *Philippine Sci.* 1:6–57.

Dennis, J. F., and Gunn, C. R. 1971. Case against transPacific dispersal of the coconut by ocean currents. *Econ. Bot.* 25:407–13.

Docters van Leeuwen, W. M. 1936. Krakatau, 1883 to 1933. *Ann. Jard. Bot. Buitenzorg* 16:1–506.

Harries, H. C. 1978. The evolution, dissemination and classification of *Cocos nucifera* L. *Bot. Rev.* 44:265–319.

Heyerdahl, T. 1966. Notes on pre-European coconut groves on Coco Island. *Reports, Norwegian Archaeological Expedition to Easter Island and the East Pacific* 2:461–67.

Murray, D. B. 1977. Coconut palm. In *Ecophysiology of tropical crops*, ed. P. Alvim and T. T. Kozlowski, pp. 387–407. New York: Academic Press.

Patiño, V. M. 1963. *Plantas cultivadas y animales domésticos en America Equinoccial*. Vol. 1. *Frutales*. Cali: Imprenta Departmental.

Purseglove, J. W. 1972 *Tropical crops: Monocotyledons*. Vol. 2. New York: John Wiley.

Richardson, D. L.; Harries, H. C.; and Balsevicius, E. 1978. Variedades de cocoteros en Costa Rica. *Turrialba* 28:87–90.

Safford, W. E. 1905. The useful plants of the island of Guam. *Contrib. U.S. Nat. Herb.* 9:1–417.

Sauer, J. D. 1971. A reevaluation of the coconut as an indicator of human dispersal. In *Man across the sea*, ed. C. L. Riley et al. Austin: University of Texas Press.

———. 1975. Remnant seashore vegetation of northwest Costa Rica. *Madroño* 23:174–81.

Whitehead, R. A. 1976. Coconut. In *Evolution of crop plants*, ed. N. W. Simmonds, pp. 221–25. London: Longman.

Cordia alliodora (Laurel)

P. A. Opler and D. H. Janzen

Cordia alliodora (Ruiz and Pavo) Cham. (Boraginaceae) ranges from South America to Sinaloa and San Luís Potosí in Mexico. Throughout much of Central America it occurs on both Atlantic and Pacific slopes, ranging from sea level to about 1,500 m elevation.

It is an erect tree that reaches 30 m in height and 90 cm dbh in rain forest, but it is smaller and more bushy in deciduous forests. It has a finely fissured gray trunk, often bearing lichens, and a rounded crown of ovate lanceolate leaves up to 17 cm long. Swollen nodes (fig. 7.39) occur at each branching juncture and are conspicuous on smaller-diameter twigs and branchlets. The leaves have a sandpapery feeling and are distinctly whitish below. The white, fragrant flowers occur in axillary or terminal panicles (Pennington and Sarukhan 1968). Flowering occurs during January and February in Guanacaste and during the same months on the Atlantic slope. The aerially dispersed tiny, single-seeded fruits are shed parachute fashion in April; the persistent scarious corolla (now brownish) becomes the parachute.

In many ways *C. alliodora* is a generalist tree, as is shown by its wide geographic range and its occurrence in several life zones, yet in other ways it is highly specialized. It is a hermaphroditic species with a variable compatibility system. Some individuals are almost completely self-fertile, while others are almost completely self-infertile. Compatibility with different neighboring individuals also varies widely (Opler, Baker, and Frankie 1975).

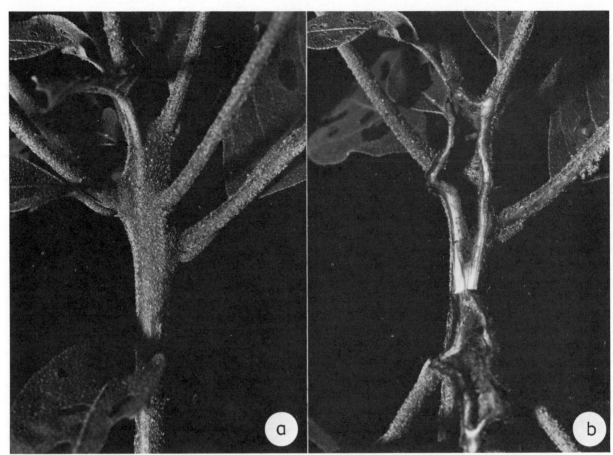

FIGURE 7.39. *Cordia alliodora. a,* Swollen node and internode at branch end on sapling. *b,* Swollen node sliced open to show inner natural cavity that later may become occupied by arboreal ants. Santa Rosa National Park, Guanacaste Province, Costa Rica (photos, D. H. Janzen).

Cordia alliodora appears to be adapted for pollination by small moths (fragrant, white flowers and early morning anthesis), yet its stigmata remain receptive after dawn, and some pollination by bees, butterflies, and small beetles may occur.

While the hundreds of thousands of flowers in a single tree's crown may produce a crop of hundreds of thousands of seeds, as many as 50% of the seeds may perish through predispersal seed predation by the larvae of tiny bruchid beetles (*Amblycerus* spp). The beetles glue one or two eggs directly to the corolla around the maturing fruit, and a single bruchid larva develops within. Several species of seed chalcids (parasitic Hymenoptera) also prey on the seeds before dispersal. This seed predation occurs in *C. alliodora* crops in both the deciduous and the rainforest habitats it occupies in Costa Rica, but it has never been monitored with care in either habitat. Once the seeds are on the ground, they are probably preyed on by small rodents.

Seedlings appear in the first year of pioneer succession after burning or felling, and it is probable that this tree is a light-gap species (Tschinkel 1965). Young trees are fast growing and may be easily recognized by the swollen nodes at each branching point. When the first swollen nodes appear, many are quickly cut into by founding queens of *Azteca longiceps* and a variety of other genera of ants. If the *Azteca* colony becomes established, there will be a queen in one swollen node and her brood in many others. Mealybugs (Pseudococcidae) and scale insects (Coccidae) are reared in the hollow cavity (nectar and protein source for the ants), and ant trash is dumped in the bottom. We suspect that the tree benefits by taking up some of the materials released by the decomposition of this trash heap, as is the case with some southeast Asian ant plants (Janzen 1974). In addition, the ants are generally agressive toward vines that climb on the plant. Wheeler (1942) was of the general opinion that the ants were of no positive significance to *C. alliodora*, but the subject certainly deserves experimental study. The matter is made more complicated by the observation that *C. alliodora* without an *Azteca* colony seems to fare better in general than do *Cecropia* and ant-acacias without their ant colonies. Further, it is clear that many ant species that occupy the hollow nodes of *C. alliodora* have no potential as "protective agents."

For a fast-growing tree, *C. alliodora* has particularly fine wood, not only for construction, but for furniture. Its wood is a beautiful combination of orangish and yellow tones. Because of this, many have felt that *C. alliodora* is the native tree best suited for reforestation in the American tropics. In fact, some small plantations exist, such as at the OTS La Selva field station. It has annual growth rings that are recognizable with careful technique (Tschinkel 1966). The young trees were often left when forest was cleared on the Atlantic slopes, and their straight white trunks stand as gaunt reminders of what once was.

*

Janzen, D. H. 1974. Epiphytic myrmecophytes in Sarawak: Mutualism through the feeding of plants by ants. *Biotropica* 6:237–59.

Opler, P. A.; Baker, H. G.; and Frankie, G. W. 1975. Reproductive biology of some Costa Rican *Cordia* species (Boraginaceae). *Biotropica* 7:234–47.

Pennington, T. D., and Sarukhan, J. 1968. *Los arboles tropicales de México*. Mexico, D.F.: Institutio Nacional Investigaciónes Forestales.

Tschinkel, H. M. 1965. Algúnos factores que influyen en la regeneración natural de *Cordia alliodora* (Ruiz and Pav.) Cham. *Turrialba* 15:317–24.

———. 1966. Annual growth rings in *Cordia alliodora*. *Turrialba* 16:73–80.

Wheeler, W. M. 1942. Studies of Neotropical ant-plants and their ants. *Bull. Mus. Comp. Zool., Harvard* 90: 1–262.

Costus laevis (Caña Agria, Wild Ginger)

D. W. Schemske

This tall (2–4 m) monocot is common in light gaps and along roadsides and streams in wet, lowland forest. Large clones are often formed through vegetative propagation of subterranean rhizomes. The striking spiral arrangement of the long acuminate leaves is typical of the genus. Young, rolled leaves are attacked by hispine beetles (see Strong 1977), and mature leaves are attacked by larvae of *Agoraea* sp. (Lepidoptera: Arctiidae). *Agoraea* has occasionally defoliated entire plants in central Panama.

The pine-cone-like inflorescence (fig. 7.40) is produced at the apex of the stem. The "cone" analogy is functionally correct—the *Costus* inflorescence consists largely of broadly overlapping bracts that cover immature flowers and fruits. In all Neotropical species of *Costus*, each bract subtends a single flower. The *C. laevis* flower

is broadly striped with yellow and red, tubular, 50–70 mm long, with a single stamen and fan-shaped stigma suspended from the "roof." As I have found in all other Central American species of *Costus*, generally one flower (rarely two) is produced per inflorescence per day for an extended period. In central Panama, most individuals flowered in the early to middle rainy season (May–August) for periods up to 3.5 months. Flowers open at dawn and generally fall by early afternoon. Peak nectar production is in midmorning, with a daily average of 30–60 μl of nectar per flower at a concentration of 40% sugar. Female euglossine bees are the primary pollinators, with *Euglossa imperialis* responsible for over 95% of all visits in central Panama. Hummingbird visits are rare and usually illegitimate.

Observations and experiments carried out on Barro Colorado Island, Panama, suggest that *Costus laevis* and *C. allenii* have converged in floral characters to use the same pollinator. These species occupy the same habitats, flower synchronously, are identical in flower color, morphology, and nectar-secretion patterns, share the same

FIGURE 7.40. *Costus laevis* inflorescence from Barro Colorado Island, Panama. Note ants at extrafloral nectaries (photo, D. W. Schemske).

pollinator (*Euglossa imperialis* females) and have strong barriers to hybridization (Schemske 1981). Low flower density and extreme floral predation have probably selected for floral similarity and pollinator-sharing in these two species.

A large black-and-yellow weevil, *Cholus cinctus,* is an important floral predator, drilling through bracts into flower buds. It occasionally destroys inflorescences, but more often it decreases total flower production per inflorescence and increases the day-to-day variance in flower output.

Costus laevis is self-compatible but not self-pollinating (autogamous). In central Panama, seed set from outcrossed flowrs was significantly greater than that from selfed flowers—fifty-three versus thirty-six seeds per fruit.

The hard, black seeds are 2–3 mm long, surrounded by a waxy white aril, and are bird-dispersed. Fruit are "displayed" from September to October when the bracts open. The bright red inner surface of the bracts contrasts sharply with the white fruit and probably increases the conspicuousness of the fruit display. The blue-black grosbeak (*Cyanocompsa cyanoides*), an understory finch, commonly eats both immature and mature fruit before the bracts open, crushing seeds—a parrot analogue.

Each bract has a single vertically oriented, extrafloral nectary. In general, only those bracts near a mature flower have active nectaries, and all nectaries cease production when the inflorescence terminates flower production. The extrafloral nectar is extremely rich in amino acids—ninety times the concentration of floral nectar. The rate of production varies tremendously between individuals, but it can exceed 150 μl per day.

A variety of ants harvest the extrafloral nectar (fig. 7.40) and presumably protect the plant from predispersal seed predators. In central Panama, approximately twenty-six ant species were observed at *C. laevis* nectaries, with *Ectatomma ruidum* and *E. tuberculatum* most abundant. Ants provide little defense against the weevil, *Cholus cinctus;* only *Azteca*-occupied inflorescences were free from attack. An experimental study of *Costus woodsonii,* a species restricted to Atlantic beaches, indicated that plants with ants excluded had significantly higher seed predation than ant-tended controls (Schemske 1981). The sole predator on *C. woodsonii* was *Euxesta* sp. (Diptera: Otitidae), a fly specific to this plant. Females oviposit beneath the bracts on immature fruit, and larvae attack seeds and arils. Preliminary collections from central Panama indicate that *Costus laevis* may also be attacked by a specific *Euxesta.*

In addition to *Costus laevis, C. pulverulentus* (= *ruber* of Stiles 1978) and *C. malortieanus* are both common at La Selva. *Costus malortienaus* is much shorter than either of the other two, rarely exceeding 1 m, and has short, broad leaves. *Costus pulverulentus* is generally 1–2 m tall, with narrower leaves. At La Selva, *C. malortieanus* is abundant in cacao and disturbed forest bordering the palm plantation. The flowers of *C. laevis* and *C. malortieanus* are very similar, both yellow and red striped, while *C. pulverulentus* flowers are uniform red, slender-tubed, with the stamen and stigma extending beyond the edge of the floral "tube." The inflorescences of all species are greenish, and that of *C. pulverulentus* is sharply pointed compared with the globose inflorescences of *C. laevis* and *C. malortieanus.* Stiles (1978) considers *C. pulverulentus* and *C. malortieanus* to be hummingbird-pollinated, though the latter species is also visited commonly by euglossine bees. At La Selva, Stiles (1978) found that *C. pulverulentus* flowered from May to July and *C. malortieanus* from August to November. All three species have extrafloral nectaries, bear black seeds with white arils, and are subject to floral predation by the weevil, *Cholus cinctus.* For further details concerning the taxonomy and distribution of Neotropical species of *Costus,* see Maas (1972).

*

Maas, P. J.M. 1972. Costoideae (Zingiberaceae). *Flora Neotrop.,* monograph no. 8.

Schemske, D. W. 1980. The evolutionary significance of extrafloral nectar production by *Costus woodsonii* (Zingiberaceae): An experimental analysis of ant protection. *J. Ecol.* 68:959–68.

———. 1981. Floral convergence and pollinator sharing in two bee-pollinated, tropical herbs. *Ecology* 62: 946–54.

Stiles, F. G. 1978. Temporal organization of flowering among the hummingbird food plants of a tropical wet forest. *Biotropica* 10:194–210.

Strong, D. R. 1977. Rolled-leaf hispine beetles (Chrysomelidae) and their Zingiberaceae host plants in middle America. *Biotropica* 9:156–69.

Crescentia alata (Jícaro, Guacal, Gourd Tree)

D. H. Janzen

This shrubby tree (fig. 7.41*b*) ranges from central Mexico well into South America, though its natural distribution is very hard to define or determine because the plant is widely planted and because the seeds are dispersed by horses and therefore likely to be moved into previously unoccupied areas. These statements also apply to its somewhat more shade-tolerant and moisture-loving congener *Crescentia cujete* (which can be distinguished from *C. alata* by having fruits 15–25 cm in diameter and simple leaves).

Being a bignoniaceous tree, *C. alata* is pollinated by animals, and in this case by small bats (*Glossophaga* and

FIGURE 7.41. *Crescentia alata. a,* Seedlings about 3 weeks old growing from a pile of dung from a horse that had been eating fruits of *C. alata* (June). *b,* Adult tree shortly after beginning to leaf out at the end of the dry season; full-sized fruits are numerous on the lower large branches (May). Santa Rosa National Park, Guanacaste Province, Costa Rica (photos, D. H. Janzen).

1982*a*), a small percentage of which are within reach of the bug from the outside of the fruit. A pyralid moth larva mines into the fruit base at its point of connection with the peduncle.

Once the fruits have dropped to the ground in contemporary natural habitats, they lie there indehiscent and rot. A few are moved about by heavy surface runoff during torrential rains, and a few are moved by rodents that chew open the fruits to prey on the seeds (they chip and grind them up (Janzen 1982*a*); Only rarely does one of these fruits release a viable seed and seedling, and saplings are extremely rare. These populations of trees are very restricted in distribution and generally are found only in select grasslands and along marsh edges.

However, when horses range free in the habitat occupied by *C. alata,* the story is quite different. After the fruit has lain on the ground for a few weeks to several months, it ripens properly. The internal beige, nonsweet material turns a slimy black, with a strong odor and dense, sweet flavor. The small mature, viable seeds (thin disks 5–6 mm in diameter) are imbedded throughout. Horses break the hard shell in their mouths (Janzen

FIGURE 7.42. *Crescentia alata,* nearly mature fruits in nearly leafless crown in end of the dry season (April). Santa Rosa National Park, Guanacaste Province, Costa Rica (photo, D. H. Janzen).

Artibeus). The pollen is in the dorsal side of the flower and placed on the head and shoulders of the bat. The large yellow green and brown purple cauliflorous flowers are borne by a single tree for several months and often for two periods in a year. There is usually a major flowering in the population during the first and last two months of the rainy season (Santa Rosa National Park). Many hundreds of flowers are borne on a tree that will produce a mature fruit crop of zero to one hundred fruits. The immature fruits, hard green spheres up to 15 cm in diameter (fig. 7.42), hang on the tree about five to seven months before turning yellow and eventually falling off as they begin to ripen.

While the green fruits hang, they are fed on by large brown-and-yellow bugs of the family Coreidae. These bugs have puncturing stylets (mouthparts) 1–2 cm in length and apparently reach in to kill seeds by sucking out part of their contents. The fruit contains from several hundred to as many as one thousand seeds (Janzen

1982*b*) and swallow the ball of seed-rich pulp with eagerness and little chewing. A tethered range horse may eat ten to twenty of these fruit balls in a meal, twice a day. Within two or three days its dung is rich in the seeds, which germinate into hundreds of healthy seedlings (fig. 7.41*a*) with the first rains. In grasslands rich in horses, *C. alata* recruitment is conspicuous, and adults can become very abundant. It is an easy inference that *C. alata* was a horse-dispersed tree up until the Pleistocene megafaunal extinction and that after the loss of horses it became local and rare (Janzen and Martin 1982). It is interesting in this context that cattle show no interest in *C. alata* fruits or in the pulp if the fruit is broken open for them.

Crescentia alata has a giant shrub life form, and the entire leaf presentation morphology reflects a plant that harvests light coming from all directions. Each branch is clothed in a dense coat of leaves borne on relatively thick branches. The leaves are borne well into severe dry seasons, and new ones appear with the first hint of rain. When the leaves first appear they are fed on lightly by the adults of a scattered population of a small chrysomelid beetle that soon stops its parasitization as the leaves harden. The beetle appears to then persist as underground larvae and as scattered individuals feeding on occasional new leaves. However, if a tree is artificially defoliated, and therefore produces a flush of new leaves during the middle of the rainy season, at this time it may suffer very heavy defoliation by the adult beetles that concentrate on it (Rockwood 1974). This kind of defoliation and artificial defoliation both have a conspicuous depressant effect on fruit production (Rockwood 1973). Another defoliator is the larva of an undescribed *Eulepte* (Pyralidae) that webs several leaves together and lives inside while eating the leaf tissue. It is found almost entirely on low saplings and may destroy most of a leaf crop.

Something about the *Crescentia* branches results in a high density of epiphytes on their surface, perhaps the highest of any species of deciduous forest tree. It is commonplace to find four species of orchids and a bromeliad on a single *Crescentia* tree in Santa Rosa National Park; their distribution among trees appears to conform to expectations of organisms occupying islands of various sizes and ages.

*

Janzen, D. H. 1982*a*. Fruit traits, and seed consumption by rodents, of *Crescentia alata* (Bignoniaceae) in Santa Rosa National Park, Costa Rica. *Am. J. Bot.* 69:1258–68.

———. 1982*b*. How and why horses open *Crescentia alata* fruits. *Biotropica* 14:149–52.

Janzen, D. H., and Martin, P. S. 1982. Neotropical anachronisms: The fruits the gomphotheres ate. *Science* 215:19–27.

Rockwood, L. L. 1973. The effect of defoliation on seed production of six Costa Rican tree species. *Ecology* 54:1363–69.

———. 1974. Seasonal changes in the susceptibility of *Crescentia alata* leaves to the flea beetle, *Oedionychus* sp. *Ecology* 55:142–48.

Cryosophila guagara (Guagara, Guagra, Fan Palm)

G. B. Williamson

This fan-leaved palm (fig. 7.43) produces ten to fifteen fronds from a single slender trunk up to 10–15 m tall (Allen 1956). It is easily recognized by its fronds, which are dark glossy green above and silvery white below. The large fronds, about 1 m in diameter, with long petioles, make excellent roofing thatch. Inflorescences are elongate and pendulous, covered with many papery yellow bracts. Fruits are waxy and round and hang in bare clusters, since the bracts fall before fruit matures.

FIGURE 7.43. *Cryosophila guagara* growing in a tree fall around a fallen tree trunk (*on left and at rear of photo*). Costa Rica (photo, B. W. Williamson).

The *Cryosophila* palms often have straight or curved thorns along the trunk that are really adventitious roots, spiked with hardened rootcaps (Corner 1966). In the lower portion of the trunk some of these grow to the ground and function as roots, while those on the upper portion serve as a spiny deterrent to climbing mammals bent on reaching the tree's apical meristem and reproductive tissues. *Cryosophila guagara* is unarmed except for the rare development of root spines near the base of the trunk. (*Cryosophila albida,* a similar species from the wet lowlands of eastern Costa Rica, always shows extensive development of root spines, often several meters up the trunk.)

Young saplings and seedlings of *C. guagara* are trunkless, appearing much like ground palms, and are often confused with *Carludovica palmata* (Cyclanthaceae), which also has fanlike leaves that are green both above and below.

Cryosophila guagara is abundant in the wet lowland understory, averaging four or five trunkless saplings per 10 × 10 m quadrat, and trees are rather evenly distributed over the forest floor. Larger-trunked individuals are about half as abundant, but they usually occur in large clumps.

All monocot trees are limited by an absence of lateral growth on the trunk, so they must produce a trunk of a certain diameter and add height increments through terminal bud growth. For *Cryosophila* species that grow in the shade of the wet lowlands, trunk growth appears to be restricted to times when the overstory canopy is opened by a tree fall, thereby releasing the young saplings. The saplings apparently grow rapidly and achieve maturity at about 10 m. Fruiting may then occur for many years even after the canopy has once again closed above them.

The growth strategy of *Cryosophila guagara* is suggested by the height distribution of individuals under closed canopy, which is sharply bimodal: more than three-fourths of the individuals trunkless, and of those that have trunks about three fourths over 8 m tall (Richards and Williamson 1975). But in light gaps there are many intermediate-sized individuals with small trunks.

In the Osa lowlands it is common to encounter many intermediate-sized *C. guagara* in tree-fall areas; these are often more abundant at the base end of the tree fall and rarer at the crown end, where the falling tree crown kills many understory plants. These clumps of *C. guagara* mature in gaps and can be spotted many years later as large groves 10–15 m high in the dense shade from canopy trees above (fig. 7.43). The groves often cover up to 500 m² of understory.

*

Allen, P. H. 1956. *The rain forests of Golfo Dulce.* Gainesville: University of Florida Press.

Corner, E. J. H. 1966. *The natural history of palms.* London: Weidenfeld and Nicolson.

Richards, P., and Williamson, B. 1975. Treefalls and patterns of understory species in a wet lowland tropical forest. *Ecology* 56:1226–29.

Cyatheaceae and Dicksoniaceae (Rabos de Mico, Tree Ferns)

L. D. Gómez

The tree ferns are a large group of spectacular ferns with shapes that have struck the imagination and writings of most travelers—particularly the naturalists who have visited the tropics and subtropics. They are a common sight in Costa Rica, where they are generally known as *rabo de mico,* literally translated "monkey-tail" ferns, an allusion to the uncurling young fronds. In some places they form one of the major components of the vegetation. Tree ferns prefer the high-rainfall forests and extend from coastal areas to the subandine conditions encountered in the high Talamancas. Only rarely found in the wetter fringes of the tropical dry and tropical moist forests, most species are found in clearings of the wet and rain forests, since they are light-gap pioneers.

Tree ferns have an upright habit of growth, and the most obvious feature of this is the trunk or caudex. Some specimens that have grown undisturbed for long periods reach as much as 20 m. Still, some ferns that by other characters belong in the group of the tree ferns lack the trunk, or it is reduced to a short, compact rootstalk (*Trichipteris ursina, Lophosoria quadripinnata, Metaxya rostrata*). The trunk is hard on the outside, often made up of masses of aerial roots, much sought after by orchid growers, and has a pithy center where bizarre strands of mechanical tissues can be seen if the caudex is cut transversely. This trunk may have sharp spines, long and shiny, or blunt prickles and tubercular processes, the scars of fallen fronds or the persistent remains of them. It may have trichomes or scales densely clothing at least the upper third of the stem. At the top of the caudex there is a spread of numerous long, finely divided fronds, and in their midst is the corona or crown of fiddleheadlike young fronds.

The fronds may mature one after the other (*Trichipteris stipularis*) or in flushes of as many as twenty at a time (*Nephelea erinacea*), unwinding upward from a skirtlike mass of dead old leaves. The segmentation of the frond is quite variable, from simply pinnate (*Metaxya*) to four times pinnate (*Lophosoria*). Like the trunks, the frond petioles can be glabrous or have an indumentum of trichomes or scales, smooth or tuberculate or else spiny or prickly. The petiolar scales can be persistent or deciduous. In the fronds, the venation may be free toward the

225

margins or have anastomoses near the costa or midrib of a segment. The sori, which are always discrete, can be near the costa (*Metaxya*), more or less medial between the costa and the margins (*Trichipteris*), nearly marginal, as in most species of *Cnemidaria* (submarginal in some literature), or completely marginal as in *Dicksonia* and *Culcita*. These sori are protected by a membrane called the indusium, the shape and size of which have served since the early days of pteridology to set the major genera of tree ferns apart. The indusium may be lacking or may be reduced to a scalelike process under the mass of sporangia.

All the characters so far mentioned or described here are of taxonomic value, and anyone trying to identify a specimen should bear this in mind. Only the commonest species can be determined in the absence of this information.

There are approximately seven hundred species of tree ferns in the world, and they all belong in the families Cyatheaceae and Dicksoniaceae (Tryon 1970), sometimes merged into Cyatheaceae in the sense of Holttum and Sen (1961), an affinity suggested by Bower as early as 1935 and now gaining ground among botanists. Copeland (1947) includes the dicksonioid tree ferns in his Pteridaceae on the basis of their marginal sori and the morphology of their indusia, grouping the tree ferns with submarginal to medial sori in the family Cyatheaceae, a very artificial concept. Gómez (1976) divides Cyatheaceae into subfamilies Dicksonieae (includes *Dicksonia*, *Culcita*, *Cibotium*, and the rare *Thyrsopteris* of the Juan Fernandez Islands) and Cyatheaeae, which comprises all the other genera except *Metaxya*, which is placed in Metaxyeae. Regardless of which taxonomical system is correct, the genera of tree ferns found in Costa Rica can be identified by the following key:

1. Trunk and petioles with scales 2
1'. Trunk and petioles without scales but with trichomes 7
2. Scales conform in size and color . . . *Sphaeropteris*
2'. Scales with center (body) and margins of different colors 3
3. Petiolar scales often with an apical seta 4
3'. Petiolar scales never with apical seta, apex filamentous at the most 5
4. Spines of petiole black and shiny . . . . *Nephelea*
4'. Spines absent, replaced by blunt tubercular processes or if present with a scale attached to tip of the spine . . . . *Alsophila*
5. Veins forming a net near the costa . . . . *Cnemidaria*
5'. Veins free 6
6. Indusium present. Rarely as a minute scalelike process . . . . *Cyathea*
6'. Indusium absent . . . . *Trichipteris*
7. Fronds simply pinnate . . . . *Metaxya*

7'. Fronds 2–4-pinnate 8
8. Sori medial, without indusium . . . . *Lophosoria*
8'. Sori medial, with bivalvate indusium 9
9. Trunk well developed, with the persistent bases of old leaves and tufts of golden brown long trichomes . . . . *Dicksonia*
9'. Trunkless ferns or at most reduced to short ascending, feeble rootstalk, with scars of fallen fronds, glabrous . . . . *Culcita*

There are no records of *Cibotium* from Costa Rica, but the genus is represented in northern Nicaragua by *C. regale*, a common tree fern in Guatemala. Some of these genera have been monographed or revised: *Nephelea* (Gastony 1973), *Cnemidaria* (Stolze 1974), *Trichipteris* (Barrington 1978), *Sphaeropteris*, partly (Windisch 1977), *Cyathea* (Tryon 1976), *Alsophila*, partly (Riba 1969). Some genera are either monotypic (*Lophosoria quadripinnata*, *Metaxya rostrata*) or have only one species is the area, *Alsophila salvinii*.

Except for the brief paragraphs that deal with the geographical distribution of the species in monographs and revisions or the even briefer mention of data in the citation of specimens, an unfortunate failure of the Harvard school of pteridologists, there is no account on the ecology of tree ferns as such.

In Costa Rica the observations of Nisman (1965) and myself indicate that most species of tree ferns live in wet to very wet environments, from premontane to just below frost-line elevations. The diversity of species increases with increasing rainfall and temperature, while density of specific stands increases with a decrease of mean temperatures and an increase in elevation. The only exceptions are *Metaxya rostrata* in the Pacific lowland rain forests and its vicarious form, *Trichipteris ursina*, in the Atlantic lowland forests. A similar distribution has been noticed by Eyre (1968) in Kenya, by Benl (1977) in the Cameroon highlands, and by Parris (1976) in New Zealand. The altitudinal distribution of Costa Rican tree ferns is tabulated in terms of Holdridge's life zone ecology system in table 7.1.

Above the frost line, indicated in the Costa Rican highlands by the tree *Escallonia poasana* and more or less corresponding to Holdridge's "critical temperature line," only *Dicksonia* spp. and *Culcita coniifolia* are found, and here only in protected situations, very much like some rare stands of *Trichipteris stipularis*, *T. costaricensis*, and *Nephelea mexicana* are occasionally encountered in microclimates of the tropical dry forest, where, as in the paramos, water is not readily available. In general tree ferns are terrestrial plants, but there are isolated cases of epiphytism (*Sphaeropteris brunei* on *Quercus copeyensis*) in places where the humus content of the ground and that of debris-laden branches and trunks are equivalent. Epixylism also occurs (*T. ursina* frequently grows on fallen logs in the floodplains of rivers. Tree ferns also grow in aquatic habitats of various kinds: *T. stipularis* in fresh water and *Nephelea erinacea* in brackish water in Tortuguero. Most species of riparian habitats tolerate periodic flooding.

All tree ferns reproduce by spores, and a single fertile frond has an astronomical output of airborne propagules of this kind, all viable and readily germinated in cultures. This accounts for the wide geographical distribution of some species (*Lophosoria* is nearly cosmopolitan, *Cyathea multiflora* is Neotropical) in continental land masses and in far distant oceanic islands, but it does not explain the highly localized and reduced distribution of most endemics (for instance, *Cyathea holdridgeana* is not known from anywhere but roughly a square mile along the Inter-American Highway near the Cerro de la Muerte), those of small islands being excluded for obvious reasons. Even a species common in one crevice of one mountain may not be present in the next depression of the same mountain, even if winds favor such distribution. Several factors may contribute to this. Tree ferns are light-gap pioneers in the forest and abandoned fields, and availability of water, first atmospheric (high relative humidity) and then edaphic, marks the success or failure of the gametophyte and subsequent plantlets. Also, a mechanism of allelopathy is involved. My studies on fern succession in landslides indicate the following processes: A fresh landslide in Tapantí, Province of Cartago, 1,300 m elevation, receives, among other nonarborescent fern species, the spores of *T. stipularis,* which germinate easily intermixed with those of *Lophosoria quadripinnata*. A mixed population of these two species is soon established; all the plantlets that were initially side-by-side *horizontally* reach maturity, but not those that were placed below the stand. Spores of either one of the species will not grow immediately below mature plants of the same species, but spores sown above the clumps did germinate. The leaching of allelopathic toxins down the natural drainage of the landslide prevented the growth of more plants. That is why we so often see landslides and the narrow canyons of the quebradas with dense populations of tree ferns, but with the shape of an inverted funnel, wider side down. I observed this phenomenon in Polynesian species, too. In flat areas there will be more or less dense clumps (light the limiting factor) of one species, but never or seldom we will find clumps of mixed species, especially if they are of different genera. This may also account for the paucity of records of intrageneric and interspecific hybridization in the tree ferns. Although the fact that tree ferns grow better on inclined grounds has been well applied by gardeners, there has been no systematic study to explain it (Gómez, unpublished data).

Tree ferns remind us of landscapes of the past, and indeed they have a long geological history. Together with the cycads, they probably served as food for many a prehistoric beast; and, like the cycads, tree ferns have evolved a complex biochemistry. Unfortunately, little has been done on this subject; the few records are listed in Swain and Cooper-Driver (1973). Like most other ferns, the arborescent pteridophytes do not suffer much predatory activity of insects. A microlepidopteran mines the pinnules of *Sphaeropteris brunei* and of *Cnemidaria choricarpa,* the life cycle taking thirty-five days from oviposition. Caterpillars from *Sphaeropteris* will accept fronds of *Cnemidaria* and vice versa, but when offered *Lophosoria* (which, like *Sphaeropteris,* has chemically similar cuticular secretions less one phytosterol; Gómez, unpublished data) will reject it. Gómez (1970) describes an unidentified moth laying green eggs in rows mimicking the soral disposition in the rare *Cyathea holdridgeana.*

Cattle will usually refuse tree fern fronds as fodder, and no local vertebrate is known to forage on the foliage or trunk, but hummingbirds will readily take the silky trichomes of *Dicksonia* and the more pliable scales of other genera to build their nests (Riba and Herrera 1973).

Humans use tree ferns for ornamental gardening, including exploitation of the fibrous roots for planting orchids on slabs or preparing mulch for potting. In Polynesia and South America they are used for the beams of huts; in Guatemala the fast-congealing exudate from trunk wounds or cuts is used as glue; and throughout their range the Cyatheaceae are a sporadic source of food, the croziers being eaten after boiling, which rids the tender shoots of their high sapogenin content.

A perusal of the fern floras of the world reveals a high number of endemics in the tree ferns, a condition particularly evident in insular floras (Gómez 1975; Gómez, in prep.). The problems of endemism and geographical speciation have been treated by Tryon (1972) for the American tropics.

Common tree fern species in selected sites in Costa Rica:

San Rosa National Park
Trichipteris stipularis
T. costaricensis
Nephelea mexicana

Cocos Island
Cyathea alphonsiana
C. notabilis
Trichipteris nesiotica

San Vito de Java
Cyathea fulva
C. multiflora
Cnemidaria mutica
Cn. choricarpa
Culcita coniifolia

Dicksonia gigantea
Nephelea erinacea
N. mexicana
Trichipteris stipularis
T. schiedeana
T. wendlandii
T. williamsii (rare)

Cerro de la Muerte
Cyathea holdridgeana
C. suprastrigosa
Culcita coniifolia
Dicksonia gigantea
Dicksonia lobulata
Sphaeropteris brunei
Trichipteris stipularis

PLANTS

Corcovado National Park
  Cyathea divergens
  C. multiflora
  Cnemidaria mutica
  Cn. choricarpa
  Cn. cocleana
  Metaxya rostrata
  Nephelea mexicana
Monteverde
  Cyathea fulva
  C. multiflora
  Cnemidaria mutica
  Cn. choricarpa
  Cn. gradifolia
  Dicksonia gigantea
  Nephelea erinacea
  Sphaeropteris brunei
  Sph. horrida
  Trichipteris microdonta
  T. stipularis

La Selva Puerto Viejo
  de Sarapiquí
  Cyathea multiflora
  C. divergens
  Cnemidaria mutica
  Cn. choricarpa
  Cn. horrida
  Nephelea cuspidata
  N. polystichoides
  N. erinacea var.
    tryoniana
  N. mexicana
  Sphaeropteris elongata
  Trichipteris ursina
  T. stipularis
  T. schiedeana
  T. microdonta
  T. wendlandii
  T. trichiata

*

Barrington, D. 1978. A revision of the genus Trichipteris. Contrib. Gray Herb. 208:3–94.

Benl, C. 1977. Ferns of the Cameroons. 2. Pteridophytes of the evergreen forests. Br. Fern Gaz. 11:231–45.

Bower, F. O. 1935. The ferns. Vol. 2. Cambridge: Cambridge University Press.

Copeland, E. B. 1947. Genera filieum. Waltham, Mass.: Chronica Botanica.

Eyre, S. R. 1968. Vegetation and soils: A world picture. 2d ed. London: Arnold.

Gastony, G. J. 1973. A revision of the fern genus Nephelea. Contrib. Gray Herb. 203:81–148.

Gómez P., L. D. 1970. Two new tree ferns from Costa Rica. A. Fern J. 61:166–70.

———. 1975. Contribuciónes a la pteridología costarricense. 7. Pteridofitos de la Isla de Cocos. Brenesia 6:33–48.

———. 1976. Contribuciónes a la pteridología centroamericana. 1. Enumeratio filicum nicaraguensium. Brenesia 8:41–57.

Holdridge, L. R. 1964. Life zone ecology. Preliminary ed. San José: Tropical Science Center.

Holttum, R. E., and Sen, U. 1961. Morphology and classification of the tree ferns. Phytomorphology 11: 406–20.

Nisman, C. 1965. Estudio taxonómico y ecológico de los helechos arborescentes (Cyatheaceae & Dicksoniaceae) de Costa Rica. Thesis, Universidad de Costa Rica.

Parris, B. S. 1976. Ecology and biogeography of New Zealand pteridophytes. Br. Fern Gaz. 11:231–45.

Riba, R. 1969. The Alsophila swartziana complex (Cyatheaceae). Rhodora 71:7–17.

Riba, R., and Herrera, T. 1973. Ferns, lichens and hummingbirds' nests. A. Fern J., 63:128.

Stolze, R. G. 1974. A taxonomic revision of the genus Cnemidaria (Cyatheaceae). Fieldiana, Bot. 37:1–98.

Swain, T., and Cooper-Driver, G. 1973. Biochemical systematics in the Filicopsida. In The phylogeny and classification of the Ferns, ed. A. C. Jermy et al. pp. 111–34. London.

Tryon, R. M. 1970. The classification of the Cyatheaceae. Contrib. Gray Herb. 200: 3–53.

———. 1972. Endemic areas and geographical speciation in tropical America. Biotropica 4:121–31.

———. 1976. A revision of the genus Cyathea. Contrib. Gray Herb. 206:19–101.

Windisch, P. G. 1977. Synopsis of the genus Sphaeropteris (Cyatheaceae) with a revision of the Neotropical exindusiate species. Bot. Jahrb. 98:176–98.

Cydista diversifolia (Bejuco de Cuatro Filos, Jalapa)

A. H. Gentry

One of the commonest dry-forest vine species, Cydista diversifolia is an exceedingly conspicuous mass flowerer. It has a "multiple bang" flowering strategy, blooming at sporadic intervals through the year, with all flowers opening during the same few days and most individuals of the species in an area blooming at the same time. Despite its showy magenta flowers, it is rarely visited by any potential pollinators, which has proved a great frustration to various OTS students who attempted to study its pollination biology. The species lacks the nectar-producing disk typical of the family and is apparently a mimic that depends for pollination on occasional visits by naive bees investigating a potential new nectar source. Such a strategy is enhanced by short synchronized flowering bursts and is also advantageous in avoiding nectar thieves. An interesting question has yet to be addressed: Why are the "multiple bang," "mimic" species of Bignoniaceae almost invariably the commonest species in a community rather than the rarest ones, as might be expected of mimics?

Although successful pollination—and consequently fruit set—is rare, the species and its sympatric congener Cydista aequinoctialis (L.) Miers, which has the same flowering strategy, are extremely common. One reason may be that vegetative reproduction is important in many lianas. It is not uncommon to find several individual lianas of C. diversifolia whose bases, though not connected, form a straight line through the forest and must have sprouted from a vine that fell out of the canopy and lay flat on the ground. Intermediate stages may also be seen. The seeds, when produced, are winged and wind-dispersed, as in many canopy vines.

Cydista diversifolia, which ranges from Mexico to Venezuela, can be identified by its sharply tetragonal

228

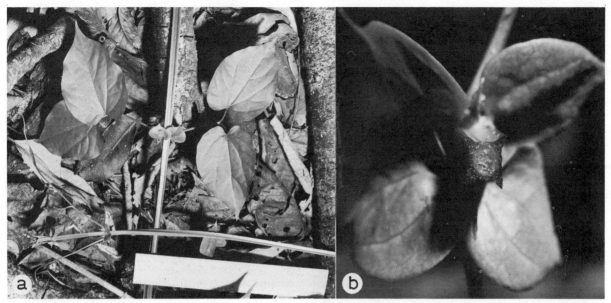

FIGURE 7.44. *a,* Stem of *Cydista diversifolia* growing across the forest floor in search of a tree fall; the shoot tip moving from right to left is from the same plant. *b,* Cross section of stem in *a.* Santa Rosa National Park, Guanacaste, Costa Rica (photos, D. H. Janzen).

stems and the green, leafy, stipulelike growths at the base of its opposite two-foliolate compound leaves (fig. 7.44). These are termed "pseudostipules" (since Bignoniaceae are not supposed to have stipules) and are modified bud scales.

This species is representative of Bignoniaceae, the most important family of lianas in Costa Rica, especially in dry forest. The vines of this family climb by means of leaf tendrils that replace the terminal leaflet of a compound leaf. Another noteworthy family character is the anomalous pattern seen in stem cross sections, which results from failure of portions of the cambium to produce secondary xylem. In *C. diversifolia* there are sixteen (or thirty-two in large stems) phloem arms or rays radiating out from the center. Some other genera have four phloem arms. Presumably this interruption of the xylem cylinder gives more flexibility, an obvious advantage to a climber.

*

Gentry, A. H. 1973. Bignoniaceae in flora of Panama. *Ann. Missouri Bot. Gard.* 60:781–977.
———. 1974. Coevolutionary patterns in Central American Bignoniaceae. *Ann. Missouri Bot. Gard.* 61:728–59.

Dalbergia retusa (Cocobolo, Rosewood)

G. S. Hartshorn

The leguminous genus *Dalbergia* (Papilionoideae or Fabaceae) is of pantropical distribution, with about two hundred species. The genus is the source of rosewood, renowned as a quality cabinet wood in both the Old World and the New. *Dalbergia retusa* occurs in the tropical and subtropical moist and dry forests in the Pacific lowlands of Central America, Panama, and Mexico.

Because of the considerable value of cocobolo wood throughout its range, it is impossible to state the upper size limits of the tree. It appears to be a shade-tolerant, subcanopy tree, perhaps growing to 20 m in height and 50 cm dbh, based on the few trees that remain.

D. retusa leaves are imparipinnate and alternate, with seven to fifteen alternate, ovate, reticulate leaflets; the margins revolute. The small white flowers are borne in panicles during the months of March and April (Frankie, Baker, and Opler 1974). The fruits expand to full size (fig. 7.45) shortly after, but they do not mature until the following dry season (D. H. Janzen, pers. comm.). Fruit is a narrowly oblong legume, up to 13 cm long, with one to three seeds.

Cocobolo heartwood (fig. 7.46) is a beautifully rich dark brown with numerous black traces weaving through the wood. Several types of cocobolo wood (e.g., cocobolo negro, rojo, oscuro, etc.) are distinguished by the woodworking industry based on color and abundance of black lines; however, they all appear to be the same *D. retusa*.

*

Frankie, G. W.; Baker, H. G.; and Opler P. A. 1974. Comparative phenological studies of trees in tropical wet and dry forests in the lowlands of Costa Rica. *J. Ecol.* 62:881–919.

FIGURE 7.45. *Dalbergia retusa* fruit-bearing branch with full-sized but green (immature) fruits, most of which are single-seeded. July 1980, Santa Rosa National Park, Guanacaste Province, Costa Rica (photo, D. H. Janzen).

FIGURE 7.46. *Dalbergia retusa* cross section through trunk of large adult; the dark heartwood is dead tissue, the part usually used in woodworking, and it has been laid down as an intrusion into the lighter sapwood where fungal damage has penetrated the sapwood (*upper center left*). Guanacaste Province, Costa Rica (photo, D. H. Janzen).

Holdridge, L. R., and Poveda, L. J. 1975. *Arboles de Costa Rica*. San José: Centro Científico Tropical.

Record, S. J., and Hess, R. W. 1943. *Timbers of the New World*. New Haven: Yale University Press.

Dalechampia scandens (Ortiguilla, Bejuco de Pan)

W. S. Armbruster

Dalechampia (Euphorbiaceae) is a primarily Neotropical genus containing about one hundred species. There are about twelve species in Mexico and Central America, and probably nine species in Costa Rica. *Dalechampia scandens* L. is a perennial, twining vine that is fairly common in many secondary, or naturally open, tropical habitats. This species is the most widespread member of the genus; it occurs from lowland tropical Mexico and the Antilles south to southern Brazil and Paraguay. Similar material from Africa, Madagascar, and the East Indies has also been placed in this species, though this placement may be suspect. *Dalechampia scandens* is a highly variable species; local differentiation of populations has resulted in a mosaic of variation in vegetative, reproductive, and ecological characters. At least seven varieties have been described from the Neotropics (Pax and Hoffmann 1919), but most of these taxa are of dubious integrity.

Dalechampia scandens is the most drought-resistant member of the genus in Central America. It is facultatively deciduous; in areas with very pronounced dry seasons, the plants die back to the woody stems during the adverse season. In regions with less severe dry season, *D. scandens* may continue to put out new leaves throughout the year.

Dalechampia scandens is the only *Dalechampia* species to occur in the xeric communities of Central America. However, in wetter sites *D. scandens* may occur with, or be "replaced" by, other species of *Dalechampia*. For example, in Santa Rosa National Park *D. scandens* alone occurs in the open savanna woodland, but at the margins of more humid forest it may occur sympatrically with a related species, *D. tiliifolia* Lam. In the moist regions of eastern Costa Rica, *D. scandens* seems to be absent; instead we find *D. tiliifolia*, *D. heteromorpha* Pax and Hoffmann, and, less frequently, *D. dioscoreifolia* Poepp. and Endl. and *D. friedrichsthalii* Mull. Arg. A sixth species, *D. spathulata* (Scheid.) Baill., has been collected in rain forest in western Costa Rica. Three additional species that are at present undescribed occur in the rain forests of the Caribbean slope of Costa Rica; one of these has also been collected from the Osa Peninsula.

The stems and foliage of *D. scandens* are covered with crystalliferous stinging trichomes (cf. Webster and Webster 1972). *Dalechampia scandens* is one of the most irritating (to human touch) of the Central American species of *Dalechampia*. It apparently has a greater density of stinging trichomes than do most other Central American species. Although these trichomes presumably serve a protective function, their precise role in deterring herbivore attack has not yet been established. *D. scandens* may be somewhat less prone to attack by generalist insect herbivores such as Orthoptera, which at times do considerable damage to certain species of *Dalechampia* with lower densities of trichomes. Flea beetles (Alticinae, Chrysomelidae) are common herbivores on *Dalechampia* species. Although large flea beetle populations may cause extensive foliar damage in some species of *Dalechampia, D. scandens* does not seem quite as susceptible, again perhaps because of its greater density of trichomes.

There are at least two genera of common oligophagous Lepidoptera that feed on *D. scandens* and other viny species of *Dalechampia: Hamadryas* and *Dynamine* (both Nymphalidae). The adult *Hamadryas* lays eggs singly or in stacks (depending on the species), usually on the underside of the expanded leaves of *Dalechampia.* The larvae hatch and remain either solitary or gregarious (corresponding to the single or mass oviposition by the adult); they feed on the mature or young leaves of *Dalechampia* (Muyshondt and Muyshondt 1975*a,b,c*). As many as four or five species of *Hamadryas* may occur sympatrically, utilizing the same food resource. At Santa Rosa National Park at least five species of *Hamadryas* are common (*H. amphinome* L., *H. arethusa* Cr., *H. februa* Hbn., *H. glauconome* Bates, and *H. guatemalena* Bates), and several, if not all, of these species feed on *D. scandens.* (*Dalechampia tiliifolia* also occurs here, and it too is utilized by several of the *Hamadryas* species.) Extensive defoliation of the plants often takes place, especially when it is a gregarious species that is abundant.

In contrast to *Hamadryas,* larval *Dynamine* feed primarily on the inflorescences or the very young leaves. These larvae are much smaller, usually less than 1 cm long. The eggs are placed singly on young inflorescences or leaf buds; the larvae remain solitary. Those larvae that hatch from eggs placed on inflorescences commence feeding on staminate flowers and the associated "gland" structures. They later feed on the developing seeds. The damage inflicted on a given plant that are infested by *Dynamine* larvae is highly variable, but it is not uncommon for it to exceed 50%.

At least two other genera of Lepidoptera have been reported to feed on *Dalechampia scandens.* Muyshondt and Muyshondt (1975*a*) report that *Catonephele nyctimus* Westwood and *Mestra anymone* Menetries use *D. scandens* as larval food.

The inflorescence structure of *Dalechampia* is unique in the Angiospermae. What appears at first to be a single flower with two large petals is actually an inflorescence of nine to ten staminate flowers and three pistillate flowers, subtended by two bracts (cf. Webster and Webster 1972). These bracts open and close in a diurnal cycle;

in *D. scandens* the bracts of most inflorescences are open from late morning to about sunset and closed the rest of the time. The bracts of *D. scandens* vary from white to greenish, depending on the population. The bracts of inflorescences in early bud and in fruit are green. The bracts serve a dual function: advertisement for pollinators when open, and protection of the flowers from herbivores when closed.

The inflorescences (fig. 7.47) of *D. scandens* open daily for about a week. During the first two or three days when an inflorescence opens, the pistillate flowers are receptive for pollination, but no staminate flowers have yet opened. On about the third or fourth day after an inflorescence has opened for the first time, the first staminate flower opens and sheds pollen. On subsequent days usually two new staminate flowers open each day; old staminate flowers fall off a few days after they have opened. Thus the inflorescence is effectively protogynous, receptive for pollination for two or three days before release of pollen by that inflorescence. During this time only cross-pollination is possible. During the following five or more days the inflorescence is in an effectively bisexual condition, and self-pollination may occur. Although this is the common phenology among most Central American species of *Dalechampia,* there is some departure from this pattern toward elimination of the protogynous period in some populations of *D. scandens* in South America.

Above the staminate flowers is a glandlike structure that, in *D. scandens* and other viny species, secretes a viscid resin throughout the receptive period of the inflorescence. This resin functions as the pollinator at-

FIGURE 7.47. *Dalechampia scandens. a, Trigona* sp. collecting resin from inflorescence in the female condition; this bee only rarely effects pollination. Note the resin-bearing gland, the staminate flowers in bud, and the receptive pistillate flowers. *b, Trigona* sp. collecting resin from the inflorescence in the bisexual condition. Note the open staminate flower. Oaxaca, Mexico, 1976 (photos, W. S. Armbruster).

tractant; *D. scandens* and other viny species are visited by female bees that collect resin to use in building their nests. In Oaxaca, Mexico, *D. scandens* was visited and pollinated by *Hypanthidium mexicanum* (Cresson) (Megachilidae), *Euplusia mexicana* (Mocsary) (Apidae), *Euglossa viridissima* Friese (Apidae), and *Trigona* sp. (Apidae) (in order of importance; Webster and Armbruster 1977; Armbruster, Ms.). At study sites in Amazonian Brazil and northern Venezuela, *D. scandens* was visited and pollinated only by *Hypanthidium* spp. (Armbruster and Webster 1981). On the pacific slope of Ecuador, *D. scandens* was pollinated by the large euglossine bee *Eulaema cingulata* (Fabricius) and, to a lesser extent, by *Euglossa* spp. (Armbruster and Webster 1982). Nothing is yet known about visitation and pollination of *D. scandens* in Costa Rica.

Resin secretion as a mode of pollinator attraction is apparently uncommon among the angiosperms. Thus far only *Dalechampia* and the unrelated genus *Clusia* (Guttiferae) have been shown to produce resins that function in this manner (Armbruster and Webster 1979; Skutch 1971). As such, resin production constitutes a distinct class of pollinator attractant, to be listed along with nectar secretion, pollen production, oil secretion, odor production, and deception as a system of pollinator attraction exhibited by angiosperm taxa.

The resin secreted by *Dalechampia scandens* is probably a mixture of terpenoid compounds. Unlike the terpenoid resins produced by Burseraceae, Leguminoseae, and other families, which harden soon after exposure to the air, the resin secreted by *Dalechampia* remains viscous and "workable" for more than a week after its secretion. The chemistry of the hardening process is not yet understood, nor have the chemical differences between cambial tree resins and the floral resin of *Dalechampia* been elucidated (cf. Langenheim 1969). However, the ecological and evolutionary significance of the nonhardening resin secreted by *Dalechampia* is seemingly evident. For the resin to remain attractive throughout the period of inflorescence receptivity, which may exceed a week, it must remain soft and collectable. A workable, waterproof resin, such as that secreted by *Dalechampia*, may be a very important resource for bees that use resins in nest construction. It is not surprising that euglossine bees will travel several kilometers to collect *Dalechampia* resin.

Dalechampia scandens is self-compatible; self-pollination and seed set are achieved in the absence of insect vectors for a considerable percentage of inflorescences. After the last few staminate flowers on an inflorescence have opened and shed their pollen, the entire staminate cymule, including the gland, abscises, leaving only the three pistillate flowers within the bracts. The bracts cease their diurnal movements and close over the developing pistillate flowers. The bracts remain closed throughout the development of the fruit. As the fruit develop, the calyxes of the pistillate flowers expand, producing numerous sharp, irritating spines and, in some forms, gland-tipped lobes. Both closed bracts and the spiny calyxes apparently protect the developing seeds. If full pollination has occurred, each inflorescence will produce nine seeds: three seeds in each of three capsules.

It takes about 3 to 4 weeks after pollination for the capsules to grow to full size (about 1 cm in diameter). After one or more weeks of further development, the capsules have dried brown, the bracts have withered back out of the way, and the calyx lobes have spread back away from the capsules. The capsules then dehisce explosively, shooting the smooth, round seeds up to several meters away. Usually all the developed capsules dehisce within a few days of each other. Thus, in *D. scandens*, as in most other viny *Dalechampia*, the development and dispersal of all the seeds produced by a given inflorescence is approximately simultaneous (Armbruster 1982). As few as one or as many as nine seeds may be produced by one inflorescence, apparently depending on the density and distribution of pollen grains on the stigmata.

Very little is known about the germination requirements of *D. scandens*. Seeds usually germinate immediately upon wetting, without any apparent dormancy. Seedling growth is rapid; the first leaves are produced from closely spaced nodes. After about five to ten leaves have been produced, the internode lengths elongate markedly and the viny habit is assumed.

It is not known whether *D. scandens* in Costa Rica reproduces in its first year of growth, although many other populations will flower during the first year if light conditions are favorable. The flowering season of *D. scandens* is somewhat variable, depending on the population and the local rainfall patterns. In seasonal scrub communities *D. scandens* blooms from the middle or late rainy season into the early dry season. However, in wetter habitats it may bloom throughout the dry season. In Santa Rosa National Park *D. scandens* blooms in the early dry season, from about November to about February.

*

Armbruster, W. S. 1982. Seed production and dispersal in *Dalechampia* (Euphorbiaceae): Divergent patterns and ecological consequences. *Am. J. Bot.* 69:1429–40.

Armbruster, W. S., and Webster, G. L. 1979. Pollination of two species of *Dalechampia* (Euphorbiaceae) in Mexico by euglossine bees. *Biotropica* 11:278–83.

———. 1981. Systemas de polinazação de duas espécias sympátricas de *Dalechampia* (Euphorbiaceae) no Amazonas, Brazil. *Acta Amazon.* 11:13–17.

———. 1982. Divergent pollination systems in sympatric species of South American *Dalechampia* (Euphorbiaceae). *Am. Midl. Nat.* 108:325–37.

Langenheim, J. H. 1969. Amber: A botanical inquiry. *Science* 163:1157–69.

Muyshondt, A., and Muyshondt, A., Jr. 1975*a*. Notes on the life cycle and natural history of butterflies of El Salvador. IB. *Hamadryas februa* (Nymphalidae-Hamadryadinae). *New York Ent. Soc.* 83:157–69.

———. 1975*b*. Notes on life cycle and natural history of butterflies of El Salvador. IIB. *Hamadryas guatemalena* Bates (Nymphalidae-Hamadryadinae). *New York Ent. Soc.* 83:170–80.

———. 1975*c*. Notes of life cycle and natural history of butterflies of El Salvador. IIIB. *Hamadryas amphinome* L. (Nymphalideae-Hamadryadinae) *New York Ent. Soc.* 83:181–91.

Pax, F., and Hoffmann, K. 1919. Euphorbiaceae-Dalechampieae. *Das Pflanzenreich* 4, 147, 12 (Heft 68):1–59.

Skutch, A. F. 1971. *A naturalist in Costa Rica*. Gainesville: University of Florida Press (pp. 261–62).

Webster, G. L., and Armbruster, W. S. 1977. Pollination ecology of some species of *Dalechampia* (Euphorbiaceae). *Bot. Soc. Misc. Ser. Publ.* 154:71.

Webster, G. L., and Webster, B. D. 1972. The morphology and relationships of *Dalechampia scandens* (Euphorbiaceae). *Am. J. Bot.* 59:573–86.

Didymopanax pittieri (Papayillo, Didymopanax)

R. Lawton

Didymopanax pittieri is a shade-intolerant tree (fig. 7.48) of lower montane and montane rain forests in Costa Rica and western Panama. On Volcán Poás it is a common constituent of the regenerating forest around the crater; along the Pan American Highway between El Empalme and the páramos of Cerro de la Muerte it is a common colonist following roadside disturbance. In the absence of human or volcanic disturbance *D. pittieri* is most commonly found in low "dwarf" or "elfin" forests on windswept ridges.

In the Monteverde Cloud Forest Reserve *D. pittieri* flowers and fruits throughout the year. Flowering, however, is concentrated in the rainy season and fruiting in the early dry season. The small (3–4 mm across), perfect flowers are borne in umbels on large terminal panicles, which support three thousand to twenty thousand blossoms. The flowers are visited on sunny days by large numbers of bees (including trigonids), flies, beetles, and butterflies. Fruits mature in 3–4 months, turning purple. They are globose, 3–4 mm in diameter, and contain two to seven seeds, 40–60% of which are inviable. The seeds are dispersed by birds; mountain robins (*Turdus plebejus*), black-and-yellow silky flycatchers (*Phainoptila melanoxantha*), common and sooty-capped bush tanagers (*Chlorospingus opthalmicus* and *C. pileatus*), emerald tou-

canets (*Aulacorhynchus prasinus*), and black guans (*Chamaepetes unicolor*) have been observed eating *D. pittieri* fruits at Monteverde.

Didymopanax pittieri leads a split existence; both terrestrial and hemiepiphytic individuals occur. In the cloud forest of Monteverde (Lawton and Dryer 1980), where canopy trees are 20–30 m tall, *D. pittieri* is found only as an epiphyte. Seedlings and saplings are generally undetectable from the ground. Trees larger than 10 or 15 cm in trunk diameter occur at a density of two to three trees per hectare. Such hemiepiphytic trees are 5–10 m tall and are generally perched 15–20 m above the ground in major crotches of large canopy trees.

In the forests exposed to the trade winds, *D. pittieri* is a common terrestrial tree, occurring in isolated populations on the order of 1 km long and 100 m wide along windswept ridge crests where the forest is 5–12 m tall. The terrestrial population occurs at a density of forty-five to fifty trees larger than 15 cm dbh per hectare but is not distributed uniformly over the ridges. The trees are most common along the ridge crests, where they account for

FIGURE 7.48. *Didymopanax pittieri* juvenile in usual forest habitat; scale at base of tree is 5 ft tall. Monteverde area, Puntarenas Province, Costa Rica (photo, R. Lawton).

30–50% of the canopy. On both the windward and the leeward flanks of the ridges, the trees become progressively less common as the forest becomes taller. When the forest reaches 15–20 m in height, *D. pittieri* is found only as an occasional hemiepiphyte. This transition takes 5–10 m on the lee flanks of ridges and 50–100 m on the windward side. In the windward margins of populations the proportion of saplings is higher than on ridge crests. The restriction of terrestrial individuals to the exposed portions of ridges appears to be due to the inability of *D. pittieri* saplings, with a wood density of 0.5–0.7 gm/cm^3, to compete with mechanically weaker (wood densities of 0.25–0.45 gm/cm^3) and faster-growing trees in protected locales. In tree fall gaps in the taller forests, *D. pittieri* saplings are rapidly overtopped by weedy trees like *Guettarda poasana* (Rubiaceae) and *Cecropia polyphlebia* (Moraceae), and by giant composites like *Eupatorium sexangulare* and *Verbesina oerstediana*. On exposed ridge crests these weaker trees are badly battered by the wind.

On elfin forested ridges *D. pittieri* seedlings get a head start on other shade-intolerant light-gap colonists by utilizing the trunk and branches of collapsed trees as nurse logs. Some epiphytic saplings even survive the collapse of their substrate. Shifting of nurse logs as they rot is one of the chief sources of sapling mortality. Individual light gaps are generally colonized by several saplings, and as a result the sapling population is conspicuously clumped at the scale of tree-fall clearings. High winds tend to erode the lee edges of ridge crest light gaps, providing space for successive *D. pittieri* invasions.

Saplings keep pace with the regenerating thicket. The frist branching occurs when the saplings are 2–4 m tall. A terminal inflorescence bud is produced, and a whorl of branches arises from axillary buds below it. The first several inflorescence buds are apparently always aborted; subsequent whorls of branches are accompanied by terminal inflorescences.

Growth is slow by lowland standards. Demographic modeling based on size-specific rates of mortality and growth indicates that vigorous canopy trees 30–40 cm dbh and 7–10 m tall are probably 25–40 years old. Growth rates are quite variable within size classes. In general, however, height increments are greatest (to 1 m/year) for trees 5–10 cm dbh and 3–5 m tall. Diameter increments are greatest (to 1.2 cm/year) in trees 15–30 cm dbh.

Growth is adjusted in accordance with wind stress (Lawton 1982). Wind speeds through the forest canopy are highest on ridge crests, and trees of a given height have thicker trunks if they grow nearer ridge crests. They also have thicker branches and twigs. These responses are produced in part by slower elongation of twigs exposed to stronger winds, and they suggest that the elfin

stature of wind-exposed montane rain forests is an adaptive response to high wind stresses.

Adult canopy trees are occasionally killed by lightning but are more commonly uprooted or snapped off. Strong winds, which commonly gust over 100 kph in the period from November through February, may also erode trees slowly, limb by limb. Many trees are extensively scarred on their trunks and major limbs as the result of abrasion by adjacent stems. These wounds may become infected; fruiting bodies of *Fomes* sp., a wood-rotting fungus, are occasionally found on the trunks of live, but sickly, individuals.

In the last stage of gap succession on wind-exposed ridges the shade-tolerant, strong-wooded, facultative strangler, *Clusia alata* overtops the shade-intolerant gap colonists like *D. pittieri*. The gaps formed by the collapse of large *Clusia* offer prime sites for the establishment of *D. pittieri* seedlings. Demographic modeling indicates that natural populations of *D. pittieri* at Monteverde have stable size-class distributions (Lawton 1980). This suggests that the short-statured elfin forests are a stable vegetation type, in equilibrium with the disturbances that allow regeneration of *D. pittieri*.

*

Lawton, R. 1980. Wind and the ontogeny of elfin stature in a Costa Rican lower montane rain forest. Ph.D. diss., University of Chicago.
————. 1982. Wind stress and elfin stature in a montane rain forest tree: An adaptive explanation. *Am. J. Bot.* 69:1224–30.
Lawton, R., and Dryer, V. 1980. The vegetation of the Monteverde Cloud Forest Reserve. *Brenesia* 18: 101–16.

Dieffenbachia (Loterías, Dumb Cane)

T. B. Croat

This conspicuous genus is generally present as an understory herb in most moist or wet life zones in Costa Rica. It is most common in wetter areas and may form dense stands. There are a few highly variable species in the genus in Costa Rica, but the state of the taxonomy is poor.

Dieffenbachia (fig. 7.49*a*) is in the subfamily Philodendroideae and is most closely related to the much larger genus *Philodendron*, both having a similar inflorescence with a convolute spathe that completely covers the inflorescence except at flowering time. *Dieffenbachia* is distinguished from *Philodendron* by being consistently terrestrial, by having a stem that does not root at all the nodes, and by having pistillate flowers sparsely scattered on the spadix and bearing usually club-shaped staminodia (fig. 7.49*b*). Inflorescences are borne in the leaf axils on

FIGURE 7.49. *Dieffenbachia. a, D. longispatha,* full habit, 2 m tall. *b, D. pittieri* inflorescence at the beginning of the second day of flowering when the staminate flowers are open (photos, T. B. Croat).

short peduncles, and the numerous, unisexual flowers are borne on a more or less club-shaped spadix that is subtended and enveloped by a boat-shaped, convolute, usually green spathe. The pistillate portion of the spadix is fused to the lower part of the spathe, and the pistillate flowers are usually relatively few in number and naked, consisting of cushion-shaped, usually yellow or orange, two- or three-carpellate pistils with broad sessile stigmata. They are subtended and surrounded by three to five club-shaped, usually white staminodia. The upper staminate part of the spadix is club-shaped and densely flowered with the flowers contiguous, four- or five-sided, and truncate at the apex. Each flower bears four fused stamens. Between the upper staminate flowers and the lower pistillate flowers is a small area of sterile staminate flowers that are similar to the fertile staminate flowers but are somewhat more irregular and produce no pollen. The convolute spathe opens wide at flowering time (Croat 1978) when the stigmata of the pistillate flowers are receptive. On the first day the plants attract large, awkward, ruteline or dynastine beetles, which may be found

in the inflorescence in relatively large numbers. As many as twenty-six beetles, all of the same species, have been found in a single inflorescence. The insects are presumably attracted to the inflorescence by a pleasant aroma given off at anthesis, though it is believed that they are aggregating for sexual purposes, since there appears to be little reward for them in the inflorescence. In related genera they have been observed chewing off the sterile staminate flowers. Jim Beach (personal communication) reports the same behavior in a species observed at Finca La Selva, Costa Rica.

The emission of this aroma is probably synchronized with thermogenetic behavior of the spadix familiar in the genus *Philodendron* and other aroid genera (Engler 1920). In the cases studied thermogenetic behavior was rhythmical, with the spadix heating up on the first day when the pistillate flowers were receptive and again on the second day when the staminate flowers released their pollen (Sheridan 1960). The thermogenetic behavior is the result of an increased rate of respiration owing to rapid oxidation of starch (Hacket 1957;   Smith and

235

Meeuse 1966; Meeuse and Buggeln 1969; Meeuse 1975).

It is a fair assumption that the same type of pollination behavior is taking place in *Dieffenbachia* as in *Philodendron,* because the same species of insects are found in both.

By the morning of the second day when the anthers of the staminate flowers are opening, the spathe of *Dieffenbachia* has already begun to close, and the lower part of the spathe (called the tube) is essentially closed. This is presumably to prevent insects now visiting the staminate part from crawling into the tube. However, before the spathe completely closes the beetles in the tube squeeze out through the small space left between the spathe and spadix, and in doing so they are covered with pollen before flying away (presumably to become entrapped in another plant in the pistillate phase).

After the spathe of the fertilized inflorescence closes, it remains tightly closed until the fruits are mature. The staminate part of the inflorescence rots in situ, and part of the debris associated with this often accumulates in the spathe tube. Both the staminate part of the spadix and the accumulation of debris in the spathe tube harbor numerous small insects (perhaps at least in part larval stages of insects that oviposit directly into the staminate inflorescence when it is still open).

When the fruits mature (still enclosed within the closed spathe), the spathe, now sometimes orange or reddish, reopens and generally breaks up to expose the commonly fleshy red seeds. Although most plant parts are inedible owing to high concentrations of oxalic acid in the sap, the fruits are edible and tasty. They are colorful and seemingly well suited for bird dispersal, but they probably attract larger animals as well.

Seeds germinate readily and have even been known to germinate on the spadix where dispersal agents are lacking. Plants often form dense stands and are quick to reproduce vegetatively by sucker shoots. Animals commonly break up and trample the brittle stems, which separate easily. Vegetative reproduction is thus further enhanced, since even the smallest parts soon produce new plants by regrowth from node branches.

*

Croat, T. B. 1978. *Flora of Barro Colorado Island.* Stanford: Stanford University Press.

Engler, A. 1920. Araceae: Pars generalis et index familiar generalis. *Das Pflanzenreich* 4, 23A (Heft 74): 1–71.

Hacket, D. P. 1959. Respiratory mechanism in the aroid spadix. *J. Exp. Bot.* 8:157.

Meeuse, B. J. D. 1975. Thermogenetic respiration in aroids. *Ann. Rev. Plant Physiol.* 26:117–26.

Meeuse, B. J. D., and Buggeln, R. G. 1969. Beetle

pollination in *Dracunculus* and *Sauromatum* (Araceae). *Coleopt. Bull.* 14:70–74.

Sheridan, W. F. 1960. The occurrence of a temperature fluctuation in the spadix of *Philodendron selloum.* Master's thesis, University of Florida.

Smith, B. N., and Meeuse, B. J. D. 1966. Production of volatile amines and skatole at anthesis in arum lily species. *Plant Physiol.* 39:1024–30.

Drymys winteri (Quiebra Muelas, Muelo, Chile Muelo, Drymys)

G. S. Hartshorn

Winteraceae is a small family of seven genera and ninety species closely related to Magnoliaceae. The bulk of the family is Southeast Asian, with only two genera, *Drimys* and *Illicium,* in the New World. *Drimys* occurs in Central and South America, Australia, New Zealand, and Malaysia. The family is a botanical curiosity, since two genera, *Drimys* and *Zygogynum,* are the only Dicotyledonae lacking vessels.

Drimys winteri (sensu lato) ranges from Oaxaca and Veracruz, Mexico, through the Andes to the Straits of Magellan. It is a subcanopy tree in lower montane rain and montane rain life zones in Costa Rica. One finds it most commonly as a small living fence post propagated vegetatively.

Leaves are simple, alternate, clustered at the twig ends, narrowly elliptical, and white beneath. Flowers are hermaphroditic, in axillary umbels. Standley (1920) reports that the flowers are a source of perfume.

D. winteri furnished the Winter's bark sold commercially for treating scurvy. The aromatic and pungent bark is chewed in rural regions to alleviate toothache and is used to make an infusion for stomach ailments (Standley 1937).

*

Record, S. J., and Hess, R. W. 1943. *Timbers of the New World.* New Haven: Yale University Press (pp. 553–54).

Standley, P. C. 1920. Trees and shrubs of Mexico. Contrib. U.S. *Nat. Herb.* 23:276.

———. 1937. Flora of Costa Rica. *Fieldiana, Bot.* 18:1–1616.

Eichhornia crassipes (Jacinto de Agua, Choreja, Lirio de Agua, Water Hyacinth)

S. C. H. Barrett

The water hyacinth (*Eichhornia crassipes* [Mart.] Solms) is a free-floating aquatic perennial (fig. 7.50) in the

most serious aquatic weeds (Holm et al. 1977), and considerable annual expenditure is invested in attempts to eradicate its extensive floating mats from reservoirs, canals, and rivers.

The genus *Eichhornia* is of New World origin and is composed of seven species of freshwater aquatics, of which *E. crassipes* is the only widespread weed. Three species of *Eichhornia* occur in Costa Rica, the natives *E. azurea* (fig. 7.50d) and *E. heterosperma*, and *E. crassipes*, which is almost certainly introduced in Central America (see later). The native species are rare in Costa Rica, occurring in marshes and ponds. *E. crassipes*, in contrast, is fairly widespread and is common in river systems, canals, and marshes, particularly in Guanacaste and Limón provinces. Some of the most impressive populations occur in marshes associated with the River Tempisque and in canals between Limnón and Tortuguero. In neighboring Nicaragua, *E. crassipes* infests most of the large inland lakes and is particularly serious in Lake Nicaragua.

Although all thirty-four species of Pontederiaceae are freshwater aquatics, only *E. crassipes* is truly free-floating. It possesses a rosette growth form with long plumose roots, short naked stems, and suborbicular to broadly elliptic leaves. The leaves often have large inflated petioles (bladders or floats) owing to the development of spongy aerenchymatous tissue in the leaf bases. These inflated petioles give the plants their buoyancy and free-floating habit. Factors that inhibit swelling of petioles include low light intensity, high temperature, rooting in soil, and low concentrations of gibberellic acid (Pieterse 1978). At the periphery of water bodies, terrestrial populations of *E. crassipes* frequently occur. Here rooted plants, particularly if at high density, develop tall, narrow petioles and upright leaves that can reach 2 m in height. In contrast, floating plants, especially at the edge of mats, are dwarfed and prostrate in form, with large bladders. There is a series of intermediate types between these different growth forms, reflecting well-developed phenotypic plasticity in the species.

Clonal growth in *E. crassipes* is by the formation of daughter rosettes on stolons. The stolons arise from lateral buds formed in the axils of leaves on the main shoot axis. The stolons are brittle and easily severed, so that daughter plants soon become physiologically independent. This process is particularly prevalent in riverine habitats, where mats are continually fragmented by swift currents. In the Amazon basin, where flooding and instability of aquatic habitats is particularly evident, a major mode of dispersal is by vegetative propagules. As a result, *E. crassipes* clones are widely distributed, and individual genotypes are exposed to a broad range of ecological conditions. Establishment in new sites is en-

FIGURE 7.50. *Eichhornia crassipes. a,* Mass flowering. *b,* Inflorescences of the three floral forms (from left to right—long-, mid-, and short-styled morphs). *c,* Clonal growth and the free-floating habit. *d,* Inflorescence of *Eichhornia azurea,* long-styled form (photos, S. C. H. Barrett).

monocotyledonous family Pontederiaceae. During the past century it has spread from its native range in lowland tropical South America to become one of the most widespread and troublesome aquatic weeds (Sculthorpe 1967). Recently it has extended its range into warm temperate zones such as Australia, California, New Zealand, and Portugal. The dramatic spread of *E. crassipes* has largely been caused by man's intentional transport of plants for ornamental purposes, followed by rapid clonal propagation once the species has "escaped" to a suitable aquatic habitat. Today *E. crassipes* is among the world's

hanced by high phenotypic plasticity and rapid powers of clonal growth.

Water hyacinths can proliferate in water of a wide range of pH values, but a growth optimum of pH 7 has been demonstrated (Chadwick and Obeid 1966). Under favorable conditions, ten plants can produce an acre of plants in eight months (Penfound and Earle 1948). One hectare of medium-sized plants may contain 2 million plants with a total wet weight of 270–400 metric tons. *Eichhornia crassipes* is one of the most productive photosynthetic organisms and may produce as much as 7.4 to 22.0 g/m^2 of organic matter per day (Pieterse 1978). The striking productivity and clonal growth rates are the major factors responsible for the species' aggressive, weedy behavior. For example, in the Sudan a 1,000 km section of the Nile River was infested within two years. Similar reports of the explosive increase of *E. crassipes* populations are frequent, particularly in nutrient-rich water bodies in the adventive range of the species.

Under favorable conditions, flowering in *E. crassipes* occurs 2–3 months after seed germination. The inflorescence is composed of two to thirty-five flowers with large yellow nectar guides on the banner petals. An inflorescence takes one or two days to complete flowering, and clones often flower synchronously, producing spectacular floral displays. Factors responsible for cueing these flowering episodes are unknown but may be associated with changes in the nutrient status of water. Flowering plants can be observed throughout the year in Costa Rica. In the native range, the major insect visitors to flowers are long-tongued bees, predominantly *Ancyloscelis gigas* and Megachilidae (Barrett 1977). However, in Costa Rica, despite its showy flowers, visitors to *E. crassipes* are infrequent, although *Apis mellifera* and *Trigona* spp. do visit flowers and effect pollination (Barrett 1979, 1980*b*).

Eichhornia crassipes possesses a rare outbreeding mechanism known as tristyly (Barrett 1977). Tristylous species occur in only eight genera of flowering plants in three plant families, Lythraceae, Oxalidaceae, and Pontederiaceae (Ganders 1981). Populations of tristylous species usually contain three floral morphs, often in equal proportions, which differ in style length, anther height, pollen size, and incompatibility type. In *E. crassipes,* which is tetraploid (2n = 4x = 32), this genetic polymorphism is controlled by two loci (S, M) with S epistatic to M. A short, mid, long sequence of dominance occurs at the two loci (Barrett, unpublished data). The development of vigorous clonal growth and the free-floating habit in *E. crassipes* prevent the normal functioning of tristyly, since these traits favor the establishment of populations in which a single morph predominates (Barrett 1977). High levels of self-compatibility in the three floral morphs further disrupt

outcrossing by allowing self-fertilization to occur (Barrett 1977, 1979).

In Costa Rica and the rest of Central America, only mid- and long-styled forms occur (Barrett 1977). Mids are more frequently encountered than longs. The absence of the short form, which is restricted to lowland South America, as well as the absence of specialized pollinators of *E. crassipes,* can be used as evidence that Central America is part of the alien, rather than the native, range of *E. crassipes*.

Evolutionary modifications of tristyly have been documented in populations of *Eichhornia crassipes* (Barrett 1979) and *E. azurea* (Barrett 1978) in Costa Rica. In a population of *E. crassipes* at Palo Verde Marsh, the spatial separation of anthers and stigmata in the mid form appears to be breaking down to give autogamous semi-homostylous forms. Selection for autogamy, owing to inefficient and limited pollinator service, may account for the development of semihomostylous forms of *E. crassipes* (Barrett 1979).

At the completion of flowering, inflorescences of *E. crassipes* bend downward (geniculation) and in floating populations are usually thrust under water within 24–48 h. The adaptive significance of the downward curvature of the floral axis, which occurs in several other members of the Pontederiaceae, is unknown, but it may be related to escape from pest attack. In the Lower Amazon, predation on aerial inflorescences of *E. crassipes* by *Cornops aquaticum* (Orthoptera) and *Tetraonyx chrysomelinus* (Coleoptera) is far more severe than in those that are submerged. Under controlled conditions, seed production in aerial versus submersed infructescences is not significantly different, indicating that submersion is not necessary for normal seed maturation (Barrett 1980*a*). The small seeds (0.5 × 1.0 mm) mature within 18–25 days and usually sink once they are released from the capsule. Despite low pollinator levels in many Costa Rican populations, some seed is usually produced. In a survey of four populations at Aranjuez, Arenal, Palo Verde, and Turrialba, average fruit set and average seed set per fruit were 1.4, 62.7, 76.7, 73.4 and 9.6, 30.8, 61.0, 43.2 respectively (Barrett 1980*b*).

Despite its high reproductive potential, most colonies of *E. crassipes* are formed by clonal growth of floating vegetative propagules. Sexual reproduction is prevented in many populations, particularly in the adventive range, by the absence of suitable ecological conditions for seed germination and seedling establishment. Most seeds accumulate in the organic debris of mats or sink. Low temperatures in deep water and shading by dense foliage inhibit germination. Specific requirements for germination are complex, but generally under field conditions, water temperatures of 28–36° C and bright sunlight are necessary. Sexual reproduction does occur in seasonal

238

habitats, such as those found in parts of Palo Verde Marsh in Guanacaste Province, where fluctuations in water level provide periods of warm, shallow water. In these types of habitats, clones are periodically destroyed by desiccation owing to water level changes, and seeds play an important role in reestablishing populations. Sexual reproduction is favored in regions such as the Amazon basin, the Pantanal of Brazil, and the Llanos of Venezuela, where large annual water level fluctuations are a characteristic feature of aquatic habitats.

*

Barrett, S. C. H. 1977. Tristyly in *Eichhornia crassipes* (Mart.) Solms (water hyacinth). *Biotropica* 9:230–38.

———. 1978. Floral biology of *Eichhornia azurea* (Sw.) Knuth. (Pontederiaceae). *Aquat. Bot.* 5:217–28.

———. 1979. The evolutionary breakdown of tristyly in *Eichhornia crassipes* (Mart.) Solms (water hyacinth). *Evolution* 33:499–510.

——— 1980*a*. Sexual reproduction in *Eichhornia crassipes* (water hyacinth). I. Fertility of clones from diverse regions. *J. Appl. Ecol.* 17:101–12.

———. 1980*b*. Sexual reproduction in *Eichhornia crassipes* (water hyacinth). II. Seed production in natural populations. *J. Appl. Ecol.* 17:113–24.

Chadwick, M. J., and Obeid, M. A. 1966. A comparative study on the growth of *Eichhornia crassipes* Solms and *Pistia stratiodes* L. in water cutlure. *J. Ecol.* 54:563–75.

Holm. L. G.; Plucknett, D. L.; Pancho, J. V.; and Herberger, J. P. 1977. *The world's worst weeds: Distribution and biology.* Honolulu: University Press Hawaii.

Ganders, F. R. 1981. The biology of heterostyly. *New Zealand J. Bot.* (In press.)

Penfound, W. T., and Earle, T. T. 1948. The biology of the water hyacinth. *Ecol. Monogr.* 18:447–72.

Pietarse, A. H. 1978. The water hyacinth (*Eichhornia crassipes*): A review. *Abstr. Trop. Agric.* (Royal Tropical Institute, Amsterdam, the Netherlands) 4:9–42.

Sculthorpe, C. D. 1967. *The biology of aquatic vascular plants.* London: E. Arnold.

Elaphoglossum (Helecho Lengua, Paddle Fern, Hart's Tongue)

W. H. Wagner

Paddle ferns (fig. 7.51) make up one of the most prevalent and diverse epiphytic plant groups in tropical America. There are many species, all variations on the same stereotype. *Elaphoglossum* is the largest genus of Costa Rican epiphytic ferns.

The fronds of *Elaphoglossum* vary from 3 cm to more than 50 cm long, with blades 1–15 cm broad. The stem is usually compact, with a varying number of tufted fronds, but it may also be a creeping rhizome in some

FIGURE 7.51. *Elaphoglossum lingua,* with dimorphic fertile frond in upper left with shorter sterile fronds at base. El Empalme (Cartago to Cerro de la Muerte), Costa Rica (photo, W. H. Wagner).

species, the fronds then being separated from each other along the axis. The leaves may be glabrous, or they may be provided with more or less elaborate scales, either all over the surfaces or along the margins. The fronds are always simple, their blades oval to linear and supported by long or short petioles. The veins are practically always free, not netted. If the veins are netted, there are no included veinlets in the areoles.

The fronds are usually strongly dimorphic, the sterile leaves having larger and broader blades and shorter petioles than the fertile ones (sporophylls). Commonly the plants have only sterile leaves (trophophylls), the fertile ones being produced only during certain years.

Reproduction is accomplished by the production of millions of spores from the undersides of the sporophylls. The fertile blades are densely covered underneath with black or brown spore cases that form a layer about 0.5 mm thick. When the spores are still embryonic and being formed, the covering of sporangia is whitish or greenish. After the spores have been discharged the color of the sporangial covering changes to pale brown or tan. The spores are bilateral and usually covered with a rugged

239

wall covering that can be seen under a compound microscope. Germination takes place in the crotches of trees, usually in mossy places. The sexual plants may sometimes be discovered by detecting very young stages of immature paddle ferns.

Most species of *Elaphoglossum* occur on woodland tree trunks, boughs, and crotches. Some may be found upon relict tree trunks in upland pastures where the forest has been destroyed. A few of the common species are common on steep banks, growing with various club mosses (*Lycopodium*) and staghorn ferns (*Gleichenia*).

Between sixty and seventy species have been recorded in Costa Rica. The genus is interesting for its basic uniformity and stereotyped structure; it can usually be recognized instantly because of the combination of paddlelike leaves of two types, trophophylls and sporophylls, and the free veins (which can best be seen by holding the fronds up to the light). Field ecologists should be warned that some simple-leaved polypodioid ferns resemble elaphoglossums. True polypodioid ferns, however, possess finely reticulate veins, and the meshes of the network contain included veinlets that are connected only at one end. With few exceptions, they have separate round or oval sori, and they tend to have scattered rather than clustered fronds, although there are a number of exceptions.

Encyclia cordigera (Semana Santa, Easter Orchid)

D. H. Janzen

This medium-sized epiphytic orchid (fig. 7.52*a*) is one of the four common orchids found on deciduous forest trees in Guanacaste Province (others are *Brassavola nodosa, Laelia rubescens, Oncidium cebolleta*). It ranges from southern Mexico to Venezuela, and over this range it is found in the same deciduous forest habitat. The spheroidal pseudobulbs are tightly appressed to the substrate and bear two leaves each. As one end of the plant grows, the other dies and falls off. Even the largest plants carry tissue only up to about four years old. *Encyclia cordigera* may be found growing on many species of trees, but it seems to attain highest density on *Crescentia alata* and *Guazuma ulmifolia* (especially in Santa Rosa National Park).

The flowers (fig. 7.52*b*) have three olive brown sepals and two olive brown petals; the three-lobed lip is white

FIGURE 7.52. *Encyclia cordigera. a*, Adult plant (epiphyte) with vertical old flower stalk bearing a single fruit. *b*, Unpollinated flowers. March, Santa Rosa National Park, Guanacaste Province, Costa Rica (photos, D. H. Janzen).

240

and lavender, marked and shaped so as to strongly resemble a flower of *Gliricidium sepium* (Leguminosae), a common tree that grows in the same habitat and flowers at the same time. The flowers of *E. cordigera* are visited by medium-sized female *Xylocopa* bees, and sticky material from the rostellum glues the caudicles of the pollinarium to the top of the bee's head (frons) or the anterior portion of the prothorax. All visitations observed to date have been in the late afternoon; these bees visit *G. sepium* very heavily during the early morning hours.

The bee usually visits one orchid flower per inflorescence and then moves on to another orchid in another tree. The reward is unknown but is presumed to be nectar. If the pollinarium is removed, the flower remains true to color, but it turns yellow within 24 h once a pollen sac (pollinium) has been placed on the stigma. Unpollinated flowers remain receptive for at least a week. The flowers are hermaphroditic (perfect), and there are usually two to eight per inflorescence, although I have seen up to sixteen on one inflorescence.

If hand-pollinated, selfed flowers set 85% fruit; if outcrossed by hand, they set 92–97% fruit, depending on the number of parents (Janzen et al. 1980). The fruits require 12–13 months to mature, and they dry to dehisce and disperse seeds in the month following flowering (the last month of the dry season). Flowering is in March, after the lavender-flowered *Laelia rubescens* in the same habitat has flowered. It is very rare in nature to encounter more than three fruits per infructescence. There are about 500,000 seeds per fruit (D. Gladstone, pers. comm.).

In Santa Rosa National Park an unidentified rodent feeds heavily on the pseudobulbs that bore leaves the previous year. This damage occurs toward the end of the rainy season (December–February). No herbivory has been observed of the leaves, flowers, or ripening fruits except for a very rare bite by some mandibulate insect.

The flower bases all have well-developed nectaries, and these are tended by ants (*Crematogaster, Pseudomyrmex, Camponotus*).

*

Janzen, D. H.; DeVries, P.; Gladstone, D. E.; Higgins M. L.; and Lewinsohn, T. M. 1980. Self- and cross-pollination of *Encyclia cordigera* (Orchidaceae) in Santa Rosa National Park, Costa Rica. *Biotropica* 12:72–74.

Enterolobium cyclocarpum
(Guanacaste, Ear Fruit)

D. H. Janzen

This enormous canopy member, an indigenous mimosaceous legume tree (fig. 7.53*a*), is rare but very conspicuous in the lowland deciduous and semideciduous

FIGURE 7.53. *Enterolobium cyclocarpum. a*, Large adult tree in full leaf. *b*, Open inflorescence and inflorescence buds (May 1980). *c*, Mature fruit sectioned longitudinally to show seeds in the cavities (March 1980). Santa Rosa National Park, Guanacaste Province, Costa Rica (photos, D. H. Janzen).

forests of the Costa Rican Pacific coastal plain. The inconspicuous white spherical inflorescences (fig. 7.53*b*) are produced in March and April, at the time when the new leaves are appearing on branches that have been bare for 1–3 months of the dry season; new leaf production therefore begins 4–8 weeks before the beginning of the rainy season. At about the time of new leaf production, the full-sized fruits (fig. 7.53*c*) from last year's flowering also begin to mature and turn brown. After flower production, the minute green fruits remain less than 2 cm in length until January, at which time they expand rapidly to a green fruit 10–14 cm diameter, containing as many as twenty-two seeds (an undamaged fruit most commonly contains ten to sixteen seeds). These green fruits are rich in (protective?) saponins, but the full-sized green seeds are heavily preyed on by *Amazona* parrots in intact forest (e.g., the lowlands of Santa Rosa National Park); the birds cut out the green seed contents, leaving the fruit and seed coat behind. The mature dark brown glabrous, indehiscent dry fruits fall in March–April, and in pastureland habitats (e.g., Guanacaste lowlands) they are eagerly eaten by cattle and horses (Janzen 1981a,b, 1982c). In contemporary habitats lacking these introduced animals, the fallen ripe fruits remain largely unharvested; presumably at one time they were harvested by the extensive fauna of Neotropical large mammals that occupied Central American forests more than ten thousand years ago (Janzen and Martin 1982). Peccaries prey on *E. cyclocarpum* seeds by breaking the seeds with their molars (Janzen and Higgins 1979). An unknown percentage of the hard seeds can survive the trip through the gut of a large animal. Tapirs eat occasional fruits, but they digest most of the *Enterolobium* seeds they swallow (Janzen 1981c). Horses pass many seeds intact and ungerminated (Janzen 1981b), but those that begin to germinate in the horse are often killed by the digestive process.

The mature brown ovoid seeds weigh 300–1,100 mg (specific gravity about 1.3); 63% of their dry weight is seed coat. The living contents of seeds of *E. cyclocarpum* contain about 2% dry weight of albizzine (Rehr et al. 1973) and 1% pipecolic acid, an uncommon toxic amino acid (E. A. Bell, pers. comm.). In Costa Rica they are not attacked by bruchids or other insects (except rarely by a phycitine pyralid moth larva that eats the mature fruit) (see Janzen 1969; Hatheway and Baker 1970). However, the smaller seeds of the rain-forest species *Enterolobium schomburgkii* Benth. in Panama are attacked in the fruit by a bruchid (*Mimosestes* sp.). The seeds of *E. cyclocarpum* in the soil are attacked by the bruchid *Stator generalis* in Panama (C. D. Johnson, pers. comm.). A large number of flowers are destroyed by the gall-forming cecidiomyid fly *Asphondylia enterolobii* (Gagne 1978); the galls are 12–18 mm in diameter and display the same delayed development as the developing fruits.

The hard, dormant seeds do not germinate unless the seed coat has been scarified by wear, gut passage, or mechanical filing. However, if the seed coat has been penetrated, there is 100% germination in a moist habitat. Some seeds germinate immediately after the beginning of the rains; these seeds have had their seed coats broken by abrasion in the soil, microorganism activity, or passage through an animal.

In Santa Rosa National Park, the seeds are heavily preyed upon by a small terrestrial rodent, *Liomys salvini* (Heteromyidae). These animals harvest the seeds from newly fallen pods, old rotten pods, horse dung, and litter. They may be eaten hard on the spot or stored in an underground burrow to be eaten later. The cached seeds are later notched and then eaten after they have softened in the early stages of germination (Hallwachs and Janzen 1983). Seed predation by *L. salvini* is sufficiently intense (Janzen 1982a,b) that it is very unlikely that the plant can reproduce itself in the forest habitats occupied by this rodent. However, seeds left in open pastures are sometimes missed because the density of *L. salvini* is lower there. However, this also does not ensure population recruitment, because seedlings in open pasture are very susceptible to fire and desiccation.

Enterolobium cyclocarpum trees grow quickly. A pasture tree 1 m dbh in Santa Rosa National Park may be as little as 60 years old. In intact forest they tend to be most abundant in areas of frequent local disturbance (such as swamp, river, and creek edges) but are found occasionally in almost all types of habitats. In progressing from the deciduous forests of Guanacaste to evergreen forests such as those on the Osa Peninsula, guanacaste trees become progressively rarer and more restricted to disturbed sites. For example, the only very large adult *E. cyclocarpum* trees in Corcovado National Park are four trunks (one root system) growing on the banks of the estuary at the lower end of the Río Sirena drainage; they may have come from a seed introduced by settlers. Large adult trees may be found up to about 700–1,100 m elevation if the climate is dry (e.g., on the Meseta Central). They have been widely planted in Costa Rica and the rest of the world. The tree appears, however, to be native from Mexico to Brazil.

The dark red brown heartwood is quite fungus-resistant, but the sapwood is quickly destroyed by fungi and insects when a log is left on the ground. Wounds in the trunk of a living tree are sealed by a water-soluble gum. Entire leaf crops are commonly eaten off by the larvae of a single species of moth (*Coenipita bibitrix*, Noctuidae) in July in Guanacaste.

There are still numerous large adults scattered about the pastures in Guanacaste. However, there is almost no reproduction from seed from these trees. Apparently the seedlings are killed by trampling, fire, desiccation (no forest to shade them in the dry season), and competition with grasses (perhaps grazing as well). Except in the parks and in gardens, the tree will probably be extinct in Costa Rica within one hundred years as the large adults senesce and die or are cut for posts, fuel, and lumber.

Gagne, R. J. 1978. A new species of *Asphondylia* (Diptera: Cecidomyiidae) from Costa Rica with taxonomic notes on related species. *Proc. Entomol. Soc. Washington* 80:514–16.

Hallwachs, W., and Janzen, D. H. 1983. Adequacy of *Enterolobium cyclocarpum* seeds as diet for *Liomys salvini. Brenesia,* in press.

Hatheway, W. H., and Baker, H. G. 1970. Reproductive strategies in *Pithecollobium* and *Enterolobium:* Further information. *Evolution* 24:253–54.

Janzen, D. H. 1969. Seed-eaters versus seed size, number, toxicity and dispersal. *Evolution* 23:1–27.

———. 1981*a*. Seed swallowing by Costa Rican range horses. *Ecology* 62:587–92.

———. 1981*b. Enterolobium cyclocarpum* seed passage rate and survival in horses, Costa Rican Pleistocene seed dispersal agents. *Ecology* 62: 593–601.

———. 1981*c*. Digestive seed predation by a Costa Rican Biard's tapir. *Biotropica* 13 (suppl.):59–63.

———. 1982*a*. Attraction of *Liomys* mice to horse dung and the extinction of this response. *Anim. Behav.* 30: 483–89.

———. 1982*b*. Removal of seeds by tropical rodents from horse dung in different amounts and habitats. *Ecology*, in press.

———. 1982*c*. Differential seed survival and passage rates in cows and horses, surrogate Pleistocene dispersal agents. *Oikos* 38:150–56.

Janzen, D. H., and Higgins, M. L. 1979. How hard are *Enterolobium cyclocarpum* seeds? *Brenesia* 16:61–67.

Janzen, D. H., and Martin, P. S. 1982. Neotropical anachronisms: The fruits the gomphotheres ate. *Science* 215:19–27.

Rehr, S. S.; Bell, E. A.; Janzen, D. H.; and Feeny, P. P. 1973. Insecticidal amino acids in legume seeds. *Biochem. Syst.* 1:63–67.

Epidendrum radicans (Bandera Española, Gallito)

C. A. Todzia

Epidendrum radicans Pavon ex Lindl. is one of the most common and noticeable orchids in Costa Rica (fig. 7.54). Its sprawling weedy growth is seen in disturbed areas, and it is especially abundant on the roadsides from San Pedro to Cartago and along the Pan American Highway from Tejar to Cerro de la Muerte. In Costa Rica the species is ubiquitous, occurring on both the Atlantic and the Pacific sides from 3,000 m in the Talamanca range to 300 m in wet lowland regions, most commonly between 1,000 and 2,000 m. It ranges from Mexico through Central America to Panama and blooms more or less throughout the year, with peaks in January–February and August–September.

FIGURE 7.54. *Epidendrum radicans* inflorescence with four flowers. San Vito de Java, Costa Rica (photo, D. H. Janzen).

The plant grows terrestrially in dense masses on open soils, rocks, and brushy banks. Although rarely epiphytic, it sometimes does occur so in light gaps of montane forests. Its stems are subscandent, prostrate or climbing, twining in masses from about 1 dm to 1 m in length, simple or branched, usually slender and leaf-bearing on the newer growth, provided with long white roots that originate opposite the bases of some of the leaves. These roots can function both for storing water and food and for support (Withner 1974).

The inflorescence is a simple, densely flowered raceme supported by a long peduncle (Ames and Correll 1952). Flowers vary in color from yellow to red, mostly on the orange red end of the spectrum. The variable lip is three-lobed (terminal lobe is itself bilobulate) and fringed, the disk provided with two short, rounded flaplike calli at its base, and with a thin or thick erect keel extending along the center from the base to about the center of the middle lobe. Red spots dot the center of this orange lip. The capsule is obliquely ellipsoid, 2.5–4 cm long, and contains tens of thousands of minute wind-dispersed seeds. This dry capsule dehisces along longitudinal sutures, the valves remaining united above and below.

Epidendrum radicans is easily confused with *E. ibaguense* HBK; the two differ in that *E. ibaguense* has a straight column, erect habit, and no lateral roots. Also, the distribution of *E. ibaguense* is more southerly, ranging from Colombia to Brazil (R. L. Dressler, pers. comm.).

This *Epidendrum* is believed to be butterfly-pollinated, and in Costa Rica pollinia are not infrequently found on the probosces of roadside butterflies (P. J. DeVries, pers. comm.). It exhibits the classic psychophilous syndrome, which includes diurnal anthesis, horizontal landing place, vivid colors, nectar present but less than in sphingid-visited flowers, long, narrow nectar tube, simple nectar guides, sexual organs not protuding and well enclosed, and flower erect (van der Pijl and Dodson 1966). The four pollinia adhere to the proboscis of the pollinator by means of a viscid disk. Figure 59 in van der Pijl and Dodson (1966) shows a hummingbird visiting *E. radicans* for nectar; this implied pollination is highly improbable owing to the narrowness of the nectary opening (G. Stiles, pers. comm.).

After a flower has been pollinated, the lip, normally a much lighter orange than the sepals and petals, turns darker, thus resembling the other perianth parts and becoming less attractive to pollinators. Of particular interest is the operation of the inflorescence as a unit. Lower flowers of the very compact raceme open first and thus are visited first. After pollination they turn a uniform color, forming a darker outside ring around the center, freshly opened flowers with their bright orange lips. The inflorescence thereby becomes more of a target for the butterfly (R. L. Rodriguez, pers. comm.). This phenomenon is similar to that displayed by *Lantana camara,* as discussed by Barrows (1976), who states: "the color change may indicate to pollinators that orange and reddish-orange flowers do not contain nectar, which would cause pollinators to concentrate their activities on the yellow flowers which are ready for pollination."

Flower color variation exists between plants growing in higher and lower elevations. The dark orange and red color components are more distinctly marked at high elevations; at lower elevations the entire flower is more orangish. There are also some genetic groups that are buff red (R. L. Rodriguez, pers. comm.). A possible explanation for this could be that the difference in flower color helps attract replacement pollinators.

Epidendrum radicans at certain localities frequently grows together with *Lantana camara* L., *Asclepias curassavica* L., or both, and also, though not so commonly, *Senecio hoffmanii* Klatt. and *Hiladgoa ternata* Llave and Lex. All these species use the same orange and red combination as a pollinator attractant. Some of the butterflies that visit these species indiscriminately when they grow together are *Anartia fatima, Danaus* spp., and *Papilio polyxenes. Epidendrum radicans* is a supposed Batesian mimic, since it apparently contains the least nectar (P. Bierzychudek, pers. comm.).

In a recent study of the very similar *E. ibaguense* in Panama, Boyden (1980) concluded that "these observations, although limited, suggest that *E. ibaguense* may be a bona fide mimic of *L. camara* and *A. curassavica* and that monarch butterflies are deceived by the mimicry." On the other hand, Bierzychudek (1981) came to the opposite conclusion after finding that the flowers of *E. radicans* were not visited any more frequently when in the presence of *L. camara* and *A. curassavica* than when by themselves. However, it needs to be added that, since *E. radicans* does not produce nectar, any visitation at all is an example of mimicry (D. Janzen, pers. comm.).

Hymenopteran parasites (*Eurytoma*) have been collected from the seed pods in April from some populations throughout the country. These wasps, numbering about twenty is each infested pod, usually had eaten the entire contents of the pod by the time they reached adulthood. Apparently they are dispersed when the pods mature and split open (P. Bierzychudek, pers. comm.).

Hawkes (1952) reported that *E. radicans* crossed with itself produces thousands of viable seeds. The progency from a single capsule exhibit a wide spectrum of shades and new colors. This raises the unanswered question of the relative importance of genetic versus environmental control of flower color.

*

Ames, O., and Correll, D. C. 1952. Orchids of Guatemala. *Fieldiana, Bot.* 26:333–35.

Barrows, E. M. 1976. Nectar robbing and pollination of *Lantana camara* (Verbanaceae). *Biotropica* 8:132–34.

Bierzychudek, P. 1981. *Asclepias, Lantana* and *Epidendrum:* A floral mimicry complex? *Biotropica* 13 (suppl.):54–58.

Boyden, T. C. 1980. Floral mimicry by *Epidendrum ibaguense* (Orchidaceae) in Panama. *Evolution* 34: 135–36.

Hawkes, A. D. 1952. An orchid new to Panama. *Orchid J.* 1:149–50.

Van der Pijl. L., and Dodson, C. H. 1966. *Orchid flowers: Their pollination and evolution.* Coral Gables: University of Miami Press (pp. 87–90).

Withner, C. L., ed. 1974. *The orchids: Scientific studies.* New York: John Wiley (pp. 334–35).

Gliricidia sepium (Mata Ratón, Madero Negro, Gallinitas)

D. H. Janzen

This small deciduous forest tree is perhaps one of the most enigmatic in Costa Rica. As a wild tree, it ranges from middle to late succession throughout very dry deciduous forest on dry lowland hills in Guanacaste. As a domesticated tree it ranges all over the tropics. In Costa Rica it is very widely distributed, below about 1,800 m elevation, as a living fencerow tree. A branch cut off the tree and stuck in the ground grows, flowers, and fruits. However, these plants never produce a wild or feral population. By this means of propagation, apparently, the species has been moved all over the world. I have seen it as a fencerow tree in Nigeria, Uganda, India, and peninsular Malaysia. I do not know, however, if it sets viable seed away from Costa Rica.

The tree is leafless (fig. 7.55a) from early January to May (or whenever the first rains come) in Guanacaste Province. The first flowers (fig. 7.55b) appear in early January, and by late February it is in full flower. The fruits (fig. 7.55a) mature rapidly thereafter, opening by twisting well before the end of the dry season. The flowers are white, yellow, and lavender, in 10–20 cm long inflorescences of twenty to forty. One branch may bear as many as forty inflorescences (twenty is a common number) and these mature progressively, from the base to the most distal. The flower spikes are produced proximal (basal) to where there was a tuft of leaves in the rainy season. The flowers are visited heavily by *Xylocopa* bees (early in the morning), wasps, some small bees, and a miscellany of other insects for nectar during the day. I suspect that the large *Xylocopa* are the real pollinators. *Aratinga canicularis* parrots eat the ovaries out of the flowers. The mature fruits look like beans 10–20 cm long by 1–2 cm wide. The large green seeds (Janzen 1982) are occasionally preyed on by the larvae of an unidentified pyralid moth.

In some years the new leaves (fig. 7.55c) of *G. sepium* are heavily fed on by a single unidentified species of chrysomelid beetle about a month after they are produced. If the entire leaf crop is manually removed from a tree early in the season, it is replaced within 2–3 weeks. If the leaf crop is removed twice in a season, there is a severe reduction in the size of the fruit crop produced in the following dry season (Rockwood 1973). Livestock do not eat the foliage of *G. sepium*. Glander (1977) has noticed that within the foraging range of a troop of howler monkeys at Finca La Pacifica there are many *G. sepium* trees but the monkeys eat the foliage of only four of them. At Santa Rosa National Park, the females

FIGURE 7.55. *Gliricidia sepium*. *a*, Nearly full-sized (10 cm long) green fruits and inflorescences on a leafless tree in the dry season (March). *b*, Hesperiid butterfly (skipper) visiting flowers. *c*, Leafy branch from adult. Santa Rosa National Park, Guanacaste Province, Costa Rica (photos, D. H. Janzen).

of *Hylesia lineata* (Saturniidae), during a population explosion, laid more than seventeen egg masses (one hundred to four hundred eggs each) on one of the twenty-four *G. sepium* trees in a fencerow while laying none on the others. The chosen tree was heavily defoliated. There are skipper (Hesperiidae) and arctiid moth larvae that regularly feed on *G. sepium*. There is an unknown compound in the foliage that is known locally as a good rodenticide (the foliage is dried and ground up and put in food) that is harmless to other animals even if eaten.

The wood is extremely hard and is termite- and fungus-resistant. It is highly valued for short telephone poles, corner fence posts, and house supports.

*

Glander, K. E. 1977. Poison in a monkey's Garden of Eden. *Nat. Hist. N.Y.* 86:34–41.

Janzen, D. H. 1982. Ecological distribution of chlorophyllous developing embryos among perennial plants in a tropical deciduous forest. *Biotropica* 14:232–36.

Rockwood, L. L. 1973. The effect of defoliation on seed production of six Costa Rican tree species. *Ecology* 54:1363–69.

Guarea rhopalocarpa (Caoba, Caobillo, Cóbano)

K. S. Bawa and S. H. Bullock

This is an understory tree, up to 20 m high and 25 cm dbh, growing in tropical lowland wet evergreen and premontane wet forests of Costa Rica and western Panama. Densities at La Selva were estimated at 7.5 reproductive trees per hectare on level areas of old alluvial soil, and 3.5/ha on a steep site with residual soils. No trees were found there in swamps. The species is dioecious.

An unusual feature of the species is its multiple flowering and fruiting each year. Flowers may be produced in January, March, May, August, September, and October, but the timing of flowering episodes is not consistent from year to year. Flowering within a population during the same flowering cycle may be asynchronous, but typical episodes are probably less than 4 weeks in duration for a population. Also, during a given flowering period some mature-sized plants may not flower. The most intense flowering, both in number of flowers per tree and in number of trees in flower, occurs in September or October.

Inflorescences are borne on the trunk and older branches. The average length of racemes is twice as great among male trees (16 cm) as among females (8 cm), but the flowers are more sparse on males than on females so the males bear less than twice as many flowers per raceme (70) as females (56). The male and female flowers are very similar. Both have a small four-lobed calyx, four to six free petals, a staminal tube, and a pistil. The petals are pink and the staminal tube is white.

The staminal tube bears eight to ten anthers on the inside. The pistil has a disk-shaped stigma and a short style holding the stigma at the end of the staminal tube; the ovary has four to five locules, with two ovules in each locule. The staminal tube in female flowers is generally shorter than that in male flowers. The anthers on the staminal tube in female flowers are without pollen and do not dehisce. The stigma is sticky in female flowers but dry in male flowers. The ovary in functionally male flowers contains ovules that turn black when exposed to air in freshly cut sections; no such change in color occurs in ovules contained in female flowers.

Why do female flowers have a staminal tube and male flowers a well-developed pistil? In the Meliaceae the petals are free, and apparently the functions of a tubular corolla, such as holding nectar, have been taken up by the staminal tube. For the retention of pistil in the male flowers, there are two possible reasons. First, the ovary is covered with glandular hairs that probably secrete nectar. Second, the stigma (and style) may aid in the pollination, either by providing a landing ground for the pollinators or by limiting access to the nectar to legitimate pollinators.

The flowers open at night (1800–1900), and moths are probably the main pollinators. Hummingbirds also visit the flowers in the morning. Flowers typically last two nights. Male and female flowers produce the same quality and quantity of nectar.

The fruits are fully developed in 6–8 weeks, but they remain on trees for another 4 weeks or more before they dehisce and disperse the seeds. The fruit is a six to eight valved, thick-walled capsule with one to two seeds per locule. It dehisces on the tree, exposing the seeds with small arillodes. The seeds are dispersed by birds.

The major seed predators are weevil larvae, which heavily infest the developing seeds. A single larva may eat several seeds, and there may be several larvae per fruit. Pupation occurs in the ground.

The alternate, even-pinnate leaves of the genus *Guarea* have the very unusual feature of intermittent growth from the rachis tip. *Guarea* leaves elongate from the end of the rachis for each new flush of leaflets, and the leaf may persist up to 5 years; however, the leaflets have a normal life span of less than one year. The compound leaves of different lengths are a good diagnostic vegetative character for the genus.

The account of the species is based on observations of 119 marked trees at the OTS La Selva Field Station, where there are at least six more species of *Guarea*.

Guazuma ulmifolia (Guácimo, Guácima, Caulote, Tapaculo)

D. H. Janzen

This common deciduous, sterculiaceous forest tree (fig. 7.56) occupies the dry lowlands from central Mexico to Panama. In Costa Rica it ranges from central Puntarenas Province to the Nicaraguan border, throughout the deciduous forests below about 1,000 m elevation. It is extremely common in pastures and fencerows because it stump-sprouts very readily, forest shade is not required for seedling establishment and growth, and its foliage and fruits are valuable cattle and horse fodder and therefore it is not rogued out of pastures. When in a fully insolated site, it has a very spreading life form and rarely grows more than 8 m tall. In forest it may attain a height of 15 m, but the trunk remains twisted and deeply grooved.

FIGURE 7.56. *Guazuma ulmifolia*. *a*, Nearly horizontal leafy branch in crown of adult tree; young fruits on stalks at branch base; leaf herbivory was done by *Phelypera distigma* weevil larvae when branch was young (photo in December). *b*, Flowers, one or two of which may become fruits (photo in May). *c*, Mature fruit with *Amblycerus* bruchid exit hole (*bottom*), fruit core and intact seeds (*center*), and hard fruit wall fragments and seed parts left by *Amblycerus* larva (*top*). d, Sibling larvae of the weevil *Phelypera distigma* eating the leaf edge. *e*, Cluster of cocoons made by *Phelypera* sibling larvae; adults emerging. *f*, Newly emerged sibling adults of *Phelypera* feeding on *Guazuma* leaf (*d–f*, photos in June). Santa Rosa National Park, Guanacaste Province, Costa Rica (photos, D. H. Janzen).

In Guanacaste, guacimo leaf drop is generally during January, though if the tree is growing in a well-watered site it may retain its leaves nearly until the new leaf crop in May. On dry sites, a flush of bright green new leaves (alternate, unequal-based, pointed dentate ovals 10–20 cm long) generally appears in late April or early May, with a few individuals leafing out in March. Trees in pastures continue to produce new leaves until mid-June or even July, but in closed-canopy forest nearly all leaf production and branch elongation has ceased by about 3 weeks after the rains begin. Saplings and young trees have very incomplete deaf drop during the dry season even in the driest sites.

The heaviest flowering occurs when the tree is largely leafless during March–April, but scattered flowers and flowering individuals occur well into June and as early as

January. Hundreds of thousands of small cream to yellow flowers are produced by a single tree. They might be wind pollinated, since there is little sign of insect activity on them despite their large numbers. The small green spherical fruits appear immediately after flowering but remain only 4–8 mm in diameter through late November. At this time they rapidly enlarge, so that by February–March there are many mature fruits on the tree and many have fallen. There is, however, great intertree variation in this timing. Some trees will have a few mature fruits as early as January, while a few are still bearing tiny dormant green fruits at this time. In March a tree may have dropped all its fruits while another only a few feet away is just maturing its fruit.

The ripe fruit is a tough ovoid (2–3 cm diameter) with a woody texture but a thin layer of sweet molasses-flavored black pulp over the outer surface. The fruit has five columns of 2–3 mm diameter smooth, hard spheroidal gray seeds inside ($\bar{x} = 59.8$ seeds per undamaged fruit, $s.d. = 13.9$, $N = 37$). The outer portion of the fruit is saturated with small, very hard V, Y, and W shaped structures that pass through a horse undigested. Inside the seed-filled locules there is a rock-hard core about 8 mm long and 3–4 mm wide. I suspect that both these hard parts protect the seeds from being milled by the molars of a horse or other large Pleistocene dispersal agent (Janzen 1982). The fruits are eaten whole and chewed up by collared peccaries and tapirs in the wild. In captivity, a tapir will eat fifty to two hundred ripe *G. ulmifolia* fruits in a meal, and a collared peccary will eat twenty to thirty. It is not known if the seeds survive the molars and the trip through the gut of these two animals. Captive white-tailed deer reject them, but this may be because they have alternate food; Guanacaste cowboys state the wild deer eat them. Agoutis and squirrels, in captivity and in the wild, gnaw the outer sweet pulp off the fruits and discard the portion containing the seeds. However, I suspect that the real dispersal agent for *G. ulmifolia* fruits was the horse or a horselike animal. Range horses in Santa Rosa National Park will eat eight hundred to two thousand fruits in a single meal and repeat this twice a day. Many of the seeds pass through the animal intact and germinate shortly thereafter if placed on moist soil. Cattle also avidly consume the fallen fruits. If the fruits are finely ground, they can be added to chick diets and are nontoxic (Bressani and Navarette 1959).

The foliage of *G. ulmifolia* is consumed very readily by cattle, horses, collared peccaries, and tapirs. A corralled tapir would consume twenty to fifty branch ends 10–15 cm long in a meal, each with three to six leaves on it. At the time of new leaf production at the end of the dry season, *G. ulmifolia* branches begin to elongate, producing single large leaves along the way. At about the tenth new leaf (late May or early June in Santa Rosa

National Park), females of the weevil *Phelypera distigma* lay clutches of eggs on the branches (the description of *P. distigma* eggs in Janzen 1979 is an error). These immediately hatch into groups of twenty to forty larvae that eat the newest leaves just as moth larvae would. Within about 2 weeks, the larvae pupate in small masses to two to fifteen spun silk cocoons on the undersides of leaves. They emerge as adults a few days later, feed awhile on *Guazuma* leaves, and within a week or two have moved into the habitat in general to wait 11 months to produce the next generation. They can be found inside rolled leaves, under bark, and in crevices at this time. It is striking that they do not oviposit on the new leaves that are produced farther out on the branches in June and over the next 3 months. The large yellow-and-red larvae of the moth *Lirimiris truncata* (Notodontidae) also eat the foliage of *G. ulmifolia* in June–July, as do the urticating larvae of *Hylesia lineata* (Saturniidae) and a variety of microlepidopterans. One large chrysomeline chrysomelid appears to feed (in Santa Rosa) only on the leaves of *G. ulmifolia* while it is a larva. The green fruits, bark, and leaves contain substantial amounts of a clear mucilage that has the property, when immersed in fresh sugarcane juice, of binding impurities and is used for this purpose in rural sugar manufacture.

*

Bressani, R., and Navarrete, D. A. 1959. Composición química y digestibilidad del fruto del caulote o guacimo (*Guazuma ulmifolia* Lam.) y su uso en raciónes para polluelos. *Turrialba* 9:12–16.

Janzen, D. H. 1979. Natural history of *Phelypera distigma* (Boheman), Curculionidae, a Costa Rican defoliator of *Guazuma ulmifolia* Lam. (Sterculiaceae). *Brenesia* 16:213–19.

———. 1982. Natural history of guacimo fruits (Sterculiaceae: *Guazuma ulmifolia*) with respect to consumption by large mammals. *Am. J. Bot.* 69:1240–50.

Gynerium sagittatum (Caña Brava, Cane)

R. W. Pohl

Gynerium sagittatum is a giant, evergreen, rhizomatous grass that forms large clonal colonies. The species ranges from southern Mexico to Peru and Paraguay and through the West Indies. The only similar grasses in Costa Rica with which *Gynerium* could possibly be confused are sugarcane, which bears leaves rather uniformly along the culm and has sweet stems, and *Arundo donax*. *Gynerium* bears all its leaves in a fan-shaped cluster near the apex of the culm, and its solid stems are not sweet. *Arundo donax* (giant reed), cultivated for ornament, has broad-based leaf blades and hollow stems. Unlike most grasses,

FIGURE 7.57. *Gynerium sagittatum,* reproductive parts (courtesy Field Museum, Chicago).

Gynerium is dioecious, the colonies being unisexual. It is presumed to be wind pollinated. Blooming is apparently yearlong, but many stems do not flower. In both sexes, the panicles (fig. 7.57) are very large, up to 2 m long, borne on elongated terminal peduncles, and have a plumelike appearance with slender, drooping branches. Panicles of pistillate plants have a fuzzy appearance because of the hairy lemmas, which fall from the panicle at maturity. The panicles of staminate plants, while grossly similar, have nonhairy lemmas, and the spikelets do not disarticulate.

This species forms conspicuous large colonies along the margins of major rivers and occasionally elsewhere, from sea level up to about 1,100 m elevation. It may be seen commonly along the road from Siquirres to Limón and along disturbed rain-forest creeks on the Osa Peninsula. A colony (clone) spreads by sending out horizontal leafless runners for as much as 20 m. These runners then turn upward at the ends to produce vertical leafy shoots. The stiff, solid stems are harvested in large quantities and are used in rustic construction and as banana props. Dry panicles are sold in the United States for ornaments.

*

Conert, H. J. 1961. *Die Systematik und Anatomie der Arundinae.* Weinheim: Cramer Verlag.

Pittier, H. 1957. *Ensayo sobre plantas usuales de Costa Rica.* 2d ed. San José: Editorial Universitaria.

Pohl, R. W. 1980. Flora costaricensis: Family number 15, Gramineae. *Fieldiana, Bot.,* n.s., 4:1–608.

Heliconia latispatha (Platanillo, Wild Plantain)

F. G. Stiles

Plants of the genus *Heliconia* (family Musaceae or Heliconiaceae) are among the most striking and characteristic features of the Neotropical landscape, with their large bananalike leaves and bizarre, colorful inflorescences. Some thirty species of *Heliconia* occur in Costa Rica, mostly in wet lowlands and foothills; one species (*H. lankesteri*) reaches 2,000 m elevation. As a group, the heliconias can be characterized as plants of forest streams, light gaps, and shady second growth. *H. latispatha* (fig. 7.58) is the most heliophilous member of the genus in Costa Rica, often growing in full sun, where it is frequently exposed to high temperatures and desiccation. Its natural habitat is the young second growth and scrub along the banks and sandbars of rivers, where periodic flooding prevents the establishment of large trees. It has also been quick to invade young, man-made second growth, often becoming a dominant plant of roadsides, overgrown pastures, field borders, and such. Because of its tolerance for heat and drought, *H. latispatha* is the only heliconia to occupy the tropical dry forests of Gua-

FIGURE 7.58. *Heliconia latispatha* inflorescence with flowers projecting upward from bracts. Sirena, Corcovado National Park, Osa Peninsula, Costa Rica (photo, D. H. Janzen).

nacaste, where it occurs mostly in river bottoms and other edaphically moist sites. It also occurs locally up to 1,300 m along roads and streams on the Caribbean slope, and to about 1,100 m on the Pacific slope. Although a plant of open areas, once established *H. latispatha* may persist for years in regenerating forests.

H. latispatha is a medium-sized heliconia, with shoots averaging 3–4 m in height; plants average taller (to 6 m) at high elevations on the Caribbean slope and shorter (often 2 m or less) in Guanacaste. A plant of *H. latispatha* actually consists of one to many leafy shoots (each of which bears an inflorescence) connected by an underground rhizome; the whole is often called a clone or "clump." *H. latispatha* rapidly forms large clumps, since the rhizome typically grows 10–30 cm before putting up a new shoot, so that the clone quickly spreads and attains vegetative dominance over an area of several square meters. Each shoot consists of a pseudotrunk formed by the imbricated petiole bases and several leaves 0.5 to 1.5 m in length and 20–35 cm in width. The leaves are stiff, containing large amounts of cellulose and probably tannins, and thus are of low nutrient value of herbivores. When the shoot is about a year old it produces an inflorescence, which is carried on a stiff peduncle at or above the level of the leaves. The inflorescence consists of twelve to seventeen showy branch bracts arranged spirally about a rachis 35–60 cm in length. The branch bracts decrease in length from about 30 cm in the basal bract (which often bears a small leaf blade as well) to 5–10 cm at the tip; the whole inflorescence is thus shaped like an inverted cone. The stiff, slender, boat-shaped branch bracts provide the main visual signal to pollinators, with their colorful outer surfaces: orange, red, and/or yellow, with a yellowish to greenish rachis. Each branch bract bears about twenty yellow to greenish flowers that ripen sequentially (usually one every 2 days) and last one day each. The flowers are tubular, the perianth averaging 40–45 mm in length with a swollen nectar chamber at the base; the distance between the mouth of the tube and the nectar averages about 30 mm. Each flower secretes about 75 μl of sucrose-rich nectar with a sugar concentration equivalent to 0.90 M sucrose (at sea level; plants from higher elevations secrete more dilute nectar). Before ripening, each flower is enclosed by a small, membranaceous floral bract that continues to cover the ripening fruit after the perianth falls or rots away. The fruit requires about 2–3 months to ripen, at which time it suddenly turns from green to blue black. By this time the floral bract has rotted or been pushed aside, exposing the fruit to dispersers. The total lifetime of an inflorescence is thus about 4 months, after which the shoot dies. The clone pushes up new shoots just before or during the flowering season; when the old shoots die, the new ones are large enough to maintain vegetative domi-

nance, and the clone can persist until overwhelmed by vines and shaded out by taller vegetation.

Heliconia plants are eaten by few herbivores, and rarely does one encounter a severely damaged plant. Most ubiquitous are hispine chrysomelid beetles, called "rolled-leaf hispines" because larvae and adults eat only the surface layers of tender young leaves before they unroll and harden. The number of species feeding on *H. latispatha* varies from four in wet lowlands to three or fewer in drier areas; there is no evidence that competition within or between beetle species occurs. The water-penny-like larvae take a long time to develop (200 days for *Chelobasis perplexa*), presumably owing to the low nutrient content of the leaves. Also slow developers are the larvae of certain satyrid (e.g., *Pierella*) and brassolid (*Opsiphanes, Caligo*) butterflies, which occasionally cause leaf damage far more extensive than the superficial feeding scars of the beetles. These butterflies may become pests in banana plantations, as is also the case with the fungus *Fusarium oxysporum*, a common pathogen of wild *Heliconia* that produces the disease called "*Fusarium* wilt" or (in bananas) "Panama disease."

All Costa Rican *Heliconia* are hummingbird pollinated, but different species are adapted in various ways for pollination by hermits or nonhermits. Nonhermit-pollinated species typically grow in small, scattered clones and have small numbers of nectar-rich flowers available during the blooming season, the flowers having long and/or curved corollas. Nonhermit-pollinated species have shorter, straighter flowers that are produced in greater numbers; they tend to grow in larger clones with more inflorescences, thus often attracting territorial birds, since one or a few adjacent clones can supply all of a bird's daily energy needs. *H. latispatha* is a classic nonhermit *Heliconia* whose major pollinator in most areas is *Amazilia tzacatl*. A variety of other nonhermits also visit *H. latispatha* in most localities (e.g., *Amazilia amabilis, A. decora, A. rutila; Thalurania furcata, Florisuga mellivora*); *Heliodoxa jacula* is important in the highlands, and the little hermit, *Phaethornis longuemareus*, is important in Guanacaste. Other hermits visit *H. latispatha* occasionally if no territorial nonhermits are present.

H. latispatha blooms mainly in the early rainy season, from June to August (although occasional inflorescences occur in any month, especially on the Pacific slope). Most species of *Heliconia* bloom at this season, raising the possibility of competition for pollinators and hybridization. The nonhermit-pollinated species most often sympatric with *H. latispatha*, and blooming at the same time, is *H. imbricata*. Although the latter tends to grow in shadier habitats and differs in pollen placement (dorsal surface of the head and bill in *H. imbricata*, ventral surface in *H. latispatha*), hybridization between the two

250

sometimes occurs, especially in areas of human disturbance.

Branch bracts of *H. latispatha* sometimes contain water and support small communities of aquatic insects (beetle, fly, and mosquito larvae) and protozoa that feed on the rotting detritus (old perianth tubes, branch bracts, etc.). The volume of water is far less, and the animal community more depauperate, than in species with deep cup- or boat-shaped bracts like *H. imbricata* and *H. wagneriana*, which seem far more specialized as "tanks" whose probable function is to protect the flower against nectar-robbing birds and bees (although fly larvae themselves will eventually eat into the flowers and take the nectar), and the developing fruit against herbivores.

The fruit of *Heliconia* is a berry containing three large, very hard-coated seeds surrounded by a rather thin, dry pulp that seems to be relished by some birds out of all proportion to its volume. At La Selva some twenty-eight species of birds have been noted taking the fruit of *H. latispatha*, including finches, tanagers, flycatchers, a cotinga, and so forth. The birds swallow the fruit whole and later regurgitate the seeds, or less often (finches) may mash up the fruit and drop the seeds in situ. The seeds require 6–7 months to germinate, since the embryo is very immature when the fruit is dispersed. This amounts to a period of seed dormancy that increases the probability of germination at a favorable time. For *H. latispatha*, flowering in July–August will produce ripe fruits in September–October and germination between about April and June, as the rains are beginning, allowing the seedling to become established before the really heavy rains in July.

Heliconia leaves have long had a variety of uses among indigenous peoples: as building and thatching material, as coverings or wrappings for food, and so on. Some species are reputed to have medicinal value as well. In the modern world, the most important use seems to be as ornamentals; many species have been grown and hybridized in cultivation (providing no end of nomenclatural confusion). *H. latispatha*, in particular, is often regarded as a pestiferous weed; but eventually we may learn to take advantage of those very qualities that make it the bane of the campesino—its hardiness and rapid growth, as well as its relative freedom from herbivores.

*

Daniels, G. S. and Stiles, F. G. 1979. The *Heliconia* taxa of Costa Rica: Keys and descriptions. *Brenesia* 15, suppl. 1.

Linhart, Y. B. 1973. Ecological and behavioral determinants of pollen dispersal in hummingbird-pollinated *Heliconia*. *Am. Nat.* 107:511–23.

Seifert, R. P., and Seifert, F. H. 1976. Natural history of insects living in the inflorescences of two species of *Heliconia*. *J. N.Y. Ent. Soc.* 84:233–42.

Stiles, F. G. 1975. Ecology, flowering phenology, and hummingbird pollination of some Costa Rican *Heliconia* species. *Ecology* 56:285–301.

———. 1978. Notes on the natural history of *Heliconia* (Musaceae) in Costa Rica. *Brenesia* 15, suppl. 1.

Strong, D. R. 1977. Insect species richness: The hispine beetles of *Heliconia latispatha*. *Ecology* 58:573–82.

Strong, D. R., and Wang, M. D. 1977. Evolution of insect life histories and host plant chemistry: Hispine beetles on *Heliconia*. *Evolution* 31:854–62.

Waite, B. H. 1963. Wilt of *Heliconia* spp. caused by *Fusarium oxysporum* f. *cubense* race 3. *Trop. Agric.* 40:299–305.

Hura crepitans (Jabillo, Sandbox Tree)

G. S. Hartshorn

Hura crepitans (Euphorbiaceae) is widely distributed from Costa Rica to the Amazon basin and in the West Indies. The only other species of the genus, *H. polyandra*, occurs in subtropical Central America from Nicaragua to Mexico. In Costa Rica *H. crepitans* occurs on alluvial soils and on slopes in tropical dry and tropical moist life zones. In the tropical wet life zone, it is restricted to recent alluvium, where it may attain 3 m in diameter and 45 m in height.

The cylindric bole has a slight butt swell at its base. The bark is densely covered with small conical spines. The inner bark contains a watery latex that is caustic and is also used to stupefy fish (Standley 1937).

Leaves are simple, alternate, very long-petiolate, and ovate, with a crenate margin. Inflorescences are monoecious with staminate flowers in terminal, long-pedunculate, fleshy, conical spikes; the pistillate flower in terminal, long-pedunculate, fleshy, conical spikes; the pistillate flower has a prominent maroon stylar column tipped by a fleshy, lobed disk (fig. 7.59*a*).

FIGURE 7.59. *Hura crepitans. a,* Flower stigma and leaf bases. Puerto Viejo, Sarapiquí District, Costa Rica (photo, G. S. Hartshorn), *b,* Full-sized green fruit with streaks of dried latex on the green surface. Santa Rosa National Park, Guanacaste Province, Costa Rica (photo, D. H. Janzen).

The fruit is an explosively dehiscing woody capsule (fig. 7.59*b*). The English common name, sandbox tree, is derived from the colonial practice of hollowing out immature capsules to make containers for blotting sand. In the Atlantic lowlands of Costa Rica, large *H. crepitans* trees are used for making dugout canoes.

H. crepitans is a shade-intolerant tree that requires openings in the forest canopy for successful regeneration. Juveniles have an unusual growth of trichotomous branching. One of the three branches becomes dominant and more vertical but continues to branch trichotomously. Despite the substantial branching away from the vertical, all trees have very straight boles.

*

Frankie, G. W.; Baker, H. G.; and Opler, P. A. 1974. Comparative phenological studies of trees in tropical wet and dry forests in the lowlands of Costa Rica. *J. Ecol.* 62:881–919.

Record, S. J., and Hess, R. W. 1943. *Timbers of the New World*. New Haven: Yale University Press (p. 160).

Standley, P. C. 1937. Flora of Costa Rica. *Fieldiana, Bot.* 18:1–1616.

Whitmore, J. L., and Hartshorn, G. S. 1969. *Literature review of common tropical trees*. Contribution 8. Seattle: University of Washington, College of Forest Resources (pp. 57–59).

Hylocereus costaricensis (Pitahaya Silvestre, Wild Pitahaya)

W. A. Haber

The cacti are represented in Costa Rica by about thirty-five species; however, most of these are slender-stemmed epiphytes of the rain-forest canopy very unlike the chunky terrestrial forms of the North American deserts (Standley 1938). Most species have large white flowers pollinated by sphinx moths or bats (fig. 7.60). A few are pollinated by hummingbirds, and another few species are probably highly specialized and unique.

Hylocereus costaricensis is an epiphytic, spiny shrub of the dry Pacific lowlands (northwestern Costa Rica) similar in appearance to *H. undatus,* the cultivated "pitahaya." The plant consists of spiny stems, triangular in cross section, each angle narrowed into a flange. The stems branch frequently at distinct nodes. The outer soft, fleshy tissue covers a tough, woody inner core that actually supports the plant. This cactus grows on limbs and in crotches of trees, attaching itself to the bark by numerous small roots originating at arioles along the stems. The cactus stems often dangle in midair 1–2 m from the supporting tree. Large, healthy individuals are common on *Pithecellobium saman* and *Bombacopsis quinatum* trees at the Taboga MAG station southwest of Cañas.

FIGURE 7.60. *Acanthocereus pentagonus* (similar to *Hylocereus costaricensis*). *a,* Adult *Manduca rustica* hovers over nocturnal open flower with tongue extended into flower. *b,* Same as *a* but moving to other flower. *c,* Moth drops into flower, presumably to get at nectar deep in flower. Near Cañas, Guanacaste Province, Costa Rica (photos, W. A. Haber).

The outstanding feature of these plants is their flowering biology. The flowers are among the largest in the world, some 30 cm long and weighing about 100 g each. Flowering occurs throughout the wet season (May–October) but is concentrated in July and August in the Cañas area. Individual plants can produce flowers periodically for 2 to 3 months. The flowers have a long narrow tube (12–14 cm) that spreads into a funnel-shaped corolla (15–17 cm long) made up of dozens of thin white petals splaying outward in all directions from the throat. The general aspect of the corolla is of a many-pointed star some 25 cm in diameter.

Each flower is active for only about 5 h on a single night. Buds open after it is completely dark (1930–2000) and close at dawn (0500). The process of opening requires only a few minutes. Plants may have as many as ten flowers at once, but usually only one to three buds mature at the same time. Plants in an area usually open their flowers synchronously (on the same night), even though these flowering episodes may be weeks apart. Flower opening is probably synchronized by heavy showers several days before opening.

On opening, a tremendously potent fragrance is released from the flowers that reminds one of jasmine and other nocturnal moth flowers. The odor of one flower can easily be detected by humans from 100 m downwind.

Large sphinx moths begin visiting the flowers as soon as they are open. The normal behavior of these moths during nectar feeding is to hover over the flower while extending the long tongue into the base of the corolla to extract the nectar. At *Hylocereus* flowers the moths hover for only a few seconds while pointing the tongue into the corolla, then literally dive into the flower and crawl as far as they can into the throat. The moths spend from 5 to 20 sec inside the flower drinking nectar before backing out and taking off. This procedure ensures that the body and wings of every moth are coated with thousands of pollen grains, since the inside of the corolla is ringed with a dense mat of several hundred dehisced anthers. The huge ten to eleven lobed stigma (1.5 cm long) projects from the corolla to just beyond the anthers and points toward the center of the corolla so that each moth rubs the undersurface of its body and wings across the stigma as it enters the flower and again as it leaves.

Each flower may be visited as many as ten times, most visits occurring between 2000 and 2230. Nectar secretion and frequency of moth visits decline markedly after 2300 and virtually cease in most flowers by 0300. Total nectar production per flower is small compared with that of other large sphingid flowers, ranging from 100 to 150 μl. Sugar concentration ranges from 29% to 34%. Odor also diminishes after 2300 and is undetectable by 0300.

The most common species of hawk moths that visit *Hylocereus* flowers (see fig. 7.60) are *Manduca sexta, M. rustica,* and *M. ochus,* which have mean tongue lengths of 108, 142, and 145 mm, respectively. Several other species of long-tongued sphingids occur in the area of *Hylocereus* (one with a tongue up to 25 cm long), but the behavior of these species at the flowers has not been observed.

About 90% or more of the *Hylocereus* flowers set fruit. The mature fruits are 6–10 cm long, purple red on the outside and bright scarlet inside. The fruit lacks spines but has about a dozen soft flangelike extensions. The soft inner tissue has up to three thousand small, black seeds embedded in it. The fruit is edible for humans and is eaten by birds and mammals. The fruit of this and related species of Cactaceae is used for making an excellent-tasting fruit drink by mashing the inner tissue and seeds with water. The seeds are consumed along with the rest.

The flower buds are often eaten by insects (grasshoppers) and various mammals including range cattle. Nectar-producing glands on the buds attract vicious stinging ants such as *Solenopsis* that guard the buds and in doing so may deter some of the bud predators.

*

Standley, P. C. 1938. Flora of Costa Rica. *Fieldiana, Bot.* 18:1–1616.

Hymenaea courbaril (Guapinol, Stinking Toe)

D. H. Janzen

This large caesalpinaceous legume tree (fig. 7.61*a*) of the Pacific coastal lowlands is most famous for producing the resin that, when fossilized, is the source of most Neotropical amber (Langenheim 1969, 1973). *Hymenaea courbaril* ranges from the lowlands of western Mexico to central South America and is the only member of the genus in Central America and on the Caribbean Islands (Lee and Langenheim 1975). There is one species of *Hymenaea* in Africa, which used to be known as *Trachylobium* (see Langenheim 1973, Martin and Langenheim 1974). In Costa Rica, *H. courbaril* ranges up to about 1,000 m elevation in the foothills of the Cordillera de Guanacaste, and to about 500 m elevation on the hills above Palmar Norte. It appears that when the forest was continuous (pre-Columbian) *H. courbaril* had a continuous distribution on the Pacific coast of Costa Rica, all the way from the Nicaraguan border to the forests of the Osa Peninsula (extensive stands still occur at Manuel Antonio National Park and in the hills just above Palmar Norte). It still maintains a breeding population in Corcovado National Park. In the deciduous forest habitats, it is most abundant along intermittent and ever-flowing watercourses, with occasional trees on hillsides. It is not found, however, on limestone hills (e.g., immediate vicinity of Palo Verde Wildlife Refuge) and in the sea level coastal flats of evergreen or semideciduous forest such as the lowlands of Santa Rosa National Park or the old floodplains of the Río Tempisque at the head of the Golfo de Nicoya. In the rain forests of the Osa Peninsula, it is generally restricted to ridges several hundred meters above sea level and several kilometers inland, though there is one large adult only 100 m from the ocean at La Sirena in Corcovado National Park.

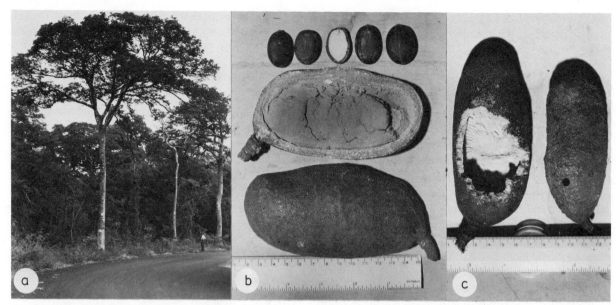

FIGURE 7.61. *Hymenaea courbaril. a,* Large adult tree in full leaf. *b,* Intact mature pod (*bottom*); mature pod split open to show dry pulp around seeds (*center*); seeds cleaned of their fruit pulp (*top,* center seed split open). *c,* Mature pod chewed open by agouti (*left*) and mature pod with *Rhinochenus transversalis* weevil exit hole (*right*). Santa Rosa National Park, Guanacaste Province, Costa Rica (photos, D. H. Janzen).

Adult *H. courbaril* in deciduous forest are evergreen and among the largest trees, with their crowns generally at the level of the canopy or even emergent (up to 40 m tall). "Evergreen" is no more literally applicable to *H. courbaril* than to *Manilkara zapota, Andira inermis, Mastichodendron capiri, Ficus* spp., and other deciduous forest trees called "evergreen." Like these other trees, *H. courbaril* has a highly synchronized (within a crown, less so between crowns) leaf drop, followed by releafing in the next 1–2 weeks. *H. courbaril* usually drops its leaves in late December to mid-January. If the dry season is not coming on too severely or too fast, the new leaves expand fully and the tree has a normal photosynthetic surface. If conditions are too dry, however, the leaves only partly expand, leading to a diffuse and unfilled crown for the rest of the year. It is most perplexing that these adult trees demonstrate that their leaves are functional and gather resources for a profit even during the driest weather, yet exchange them for new ones each year.

Flowering occurs from late December through June, as a plant collector would measure it. However, each population tends to have a peak flowering time of about 2 months, with two long tails on this distribution. It is not clear whether the members of these tails ever set fruit. In the highlands, such as from Villa Colón to Alajuela to Grecia, the guapinoles have their peak flowering from about December through early February. In the Guanacaste lowlands in general it occurs about late January through March. In Santa Rosa National Park, flowering is in February through April, but the peak may be displaced as much as a month in either direction, depending on the year.

An individual tree bears flowers for about 1.5 months, producing two to five flowers each night from each cluster of 50–150 buds. The white flowers are about 2–4 cm across when open and have white stamen filaments 2 cm long. The anthers are large and put pollen on the chest and head fur of the nectarivorous bats (e.g., *Glossophaga*) that visit the flowers (cf. Heithaus, Fleming, and Opler 1975). All evidence points toward guapinoles being self-incompatible, though crossing tests are very difficult unless one is working with trees in fully insolated sites (e.g., in pastures). Fully insolated trees have a much higher likelihood that the experimental season will be a fruiting season. Virtually all large adult *H. courbaril* trees flower each year, but most do not bear fruit each year. Annual flowering is presumably part of acting like a male, and the tree that aborts all its flowers after flowering is presumably selected for by being one of the male parents for the few fruit-bearers in its vicinity or for a fruiting subpopulation in some neighboring area (cf. Janzen 1975).

If a tree is going to bear a fruit crop, a cluster of 50–150 flowers normally produces one to ten small, flat green fruits, all but one to five of which are aborted within a month. The remaining fruits expand to nearly full size within 4–6 weeks of flowering and remain green in a fully insolated position throughout the following rainy season. The seeds are gradually increasing in size within. They are translucent (young) or white (older) at this time, but the outer fruit wall is certainly photo-synthesizing. In November–December the fruits begin to turn reddish brown, and the fruit wall hardens (the resin solidifies as well). The pulp around the seeds (fig. 7.61*b*) changes from starch rich to sweet and floury moist. The ripe pods fall to the ground without breaking open; if not opened by an animal (fig. 7.61*c*), they lie there and rot in the coming rainy season. Usually the germinating seeds cannot push such a pod apart, and if they do, their roots are not in a good place for seedling development.

The fruit-bearing pattern is complex (though probably representative of a number of other deciduous forest tree species; Janzen 1978). In Santa Rosa National Park, from which I have the best records, it appears that the trees that will fruit in a given minor drainage system do so at 2–5-year intervals, and this subpopulation is not neces-sarily in synchrony with the others in its area. More to the south, in Guanacaste, among the trees that have been left in narrow strips of riparian forest through the pastures, the same pattern persists, but there are more trees that fruit in "nonfruiting" years. In the same general area, there are large old trees standing fully insolated in open pastures with no competing trees. Some of these may fruit for as many as four consecutive years before skip-ping a couple of years. I assume that fruiting is triggered by the tree's accumulating enough reserves to make a large fruit crop, and that these large trees can do this almost every year. However, there may also be some kind of physical cueing system operating, in view of the syn-chronization of subpopulations in the forests at Santa Rosa National Park.

There are six major sources of death for *H. courbaril* seeds before germination in Guanacaste, and a multitide of minor ones. There are three species of *Anthonomus* weevils (Curculionidae) whose larvae develop in the buds. These buds are shed by the plant before they open, and the adult weevils emerge from them on the ground. In the sixth or seventh month of life of the full-sized green fruit (October–November), two large weevils at-tack. *Rhinochenus transversalis* lays one egg in a hole cut in the pod, and the larva bores through the pod wall to mine through the pulp and the seeds. It cuts a notch out of each seed (killing almost all seeds), cuts an exit hole for the adult almost through the pod wall, and pupates inside the fruit. The single new adult emerges through the hole in the indehiscent ripe pod (fig. 7.61*c*), often before the fruit drops from the tree. Pods attacked by *R. trans-versalis* are easy to census in November, since they turn brown whereas unattacked pods remain green or reddish green for another month. *Rhinochenus stigma* females lay batches of about six eggs in the pod wall and the larvae bore into one or two seeds, where they spend their larval life (several clutches may be laid in one pod). This beetle tends to kill only part of the seeds in the fruit. The larvae

pupate in the seeds and, after emerging from the seed, walk about inside the fruit waiting for a vertebrate to chew or break it open (Janzen 1974). When this happens they run very rapidly away from the pod (if caught by an agouti, *Dasyprocta punctata,* that is opening the pod, they are eaten). Agoutis eat the dry yellow pulp around the seeds, eat some seeds, and bury some seeds 2–4 cm deep in the soil and litter. The pulp is of sufficiently high quality that a laboratory rat can live on it alone for as long as a month (Janzen, unpub. data). Some of the hard seeds are dug up later and eaten by the agoutis. Peccaries also break the pods by crushing them with their molars. The fate of these seeds is unknown, but the seed is probably killed or spit out by the peccary. It would not be sur-prising to find that this fruit was once opened by one of the large extinct mammals (Janzen and Martin 1982). The story is much the same for the rain-forest *H. cour-baril* in Corcovado National Park, but the *Anthonomus* weevil has not been found there, and there are three, instead of two, species of *Rhinochenus* in the fruits.

When the rains come, some of the remaining seeds germinate. Many of them are eaten at this time by rodents that clip off the cotyledons shortly after they protrude above the ground. If the seedling survives until it has about four leaves, it may live for at least 3 years without growing more than about 30 cm tall in shade, but it grows much faster if in a light gap. In nearly full sun at the edge of a pasture, a guapinol seedling can probably become a 5 m tall shrubby treelet in 25–35 years and start flowering (but not fruiting) at this time.

The new leaves are harvested by *Atta* leaf-cutter ants while they are still pale, but once hard they are not harvested by these insects. As mentioned elsewhere, it appears that *H. courbaril* is the host of the sap-sucking lantern fly, *Fulgora laternaria.* Mature leaves are fed on by larvae of *Hylesia lineata* (Saturniidae) (Santa Rosa National Park) and other saturniids. It is commonplace for a *H. courbaril* leaf crop to be essentially undamaged by herbivores at the time it drops. Stubblebine and Lan-genheim (1977) and Langenheim, Foster, and McGinley (1980) have shown that *H. courbaril* leaf resins are toxic to a generalist moth caterpillar (*Spodoptera*). The foliage was also rejected by captive peccaries and a tapir (Janzen 1982). Variation in leaf resin kind and composition, and in the resins of other parts of the plant, has been exten-sively studied (Langenheim et al. 1978; Martin, Lan-genheim, and Zavarin 1974; Langenheim 1980).

*

Heithaus, E. R.; Fleming, T. H.; and Opler, P. A. 1975. Foraging patterns and resource utilization in seven spe-cies of bats in a seasonal tropical forest. *Ecology* 56:841–54.
Janzen, D. H. 1974. The deflowering of Central Amer-ica. *Nat. Hist.* 83:48–53.

———. 1975. Behavior of *Hymenaea courbaril* when its predispersal seed predator is absent. *Science* 189: 145–47.

———. 1978. Seeding patterns of tropical trees. In *Tropical trees as living systems,* ed. P. B. Tomlinson and M. H. Zimmerman, pp. 83–128. New York: Cambridge University Press.

Janzen, D. H. 1982. Wild plant acceptability to a captive Costa Rican Baird's tapir. *Brenesia.* In press.

Janzen, D. H., and Martin, P. S. 1982. Neotropical anachronisms: The fruits the gomphotheres ate. *Science* 215:19–27.

Langenheim, J. H. 1969. Amber: A botanical inquiry. *Science* 163:1157–69.

———. 1973. Leguminous resin-producing trees in Africa and South America. In *Tropical forest ecosystems in Africa and South America: A comparative review,* ed. B. J. Meggers, E. S. Ayensu, and W. D. Duckworth. Washington, D.C.: Smithsonian Institution Press.

———. 1980. Terpenoids in the Leguminosae. In *Proceedings of the International Legume Conference, Royal Botanic Gardens, Kew, England,* in press.

Langenheim, J. H.; Stubblebine, W. H.; Lincoln, D. E.; and Foster, C. E. 1978. Implications of variation in resin composition among organs, tissues and populations in the tropical legume *Hymenaea. Biochem. System. Ecol.* 6:299–313.

Langenheim, J. H.; Foster, C. E.; and McGinley, R. 1980. Effects of different quantitative compositions of *Hymenaea* leaf resins on a generalist herbivore *Spodoptera exigua. Biochem. System. Ecol.* 8:385–96.

Lee, Y. T., and Langenheim J. H., 1975. A systematic revision of the genus *Hymenaea* (Leguminosae; Caesalpiniodeae; Detarieae). *Univ. California Publ. Bot.* 69:1–109.

Martin, S. S., and Langenheim, J. H. 1974. Enantio-8(17), 13(16), 14-labdatrien-18-oic acid from trunk resin of Kenyan *Hymenaea verrucosa. Phytochemistry* 13:523–55.

Martin, S. S.; Langenheim, J. H.; and Zavarin, E. 1974. Quantitative variation in leaf pocket resin composition in *Hymenaea courbaril. Biochem. System. Ecol.* 3: 760–87.

Stubblebine, W. H., and Langenheim, J. H. 1977. Effects of *Hymenaea courbaril* leaf resin on the generalist herbivore *Spodoptera exigua* (beet armyworm). *J. Chem. Ecol.* 3:633–47.

Hyparrhenia rufa (Jaraguá)

R. W. Pohl

Jaragua is the commonest cultivated pasture grass in all of the dry or mesic portions of Costa Rica at elevations up to 900 m. It is of African origin, as are many other cultivated forage grasses in the American tropics. During the long-day parts of the year, jaragua produces only large, dense tufts of basal foliage, ungrazed clumps becoming up to 1 m tall. About October, the plants begin to produce flowering culms (fig. 7.62). This initiation is very widespread in many differing climatic regimes and is apparently day-length dependent and not associated with drought. By flowering time, the culms have reached a height of up to 2 m. The foliage has a pronounced reddish or brownish hue. Although sparse flowering can be observed during the long-day period (rainy season), the massive synchronous culm production and blooming occurs only during short days.

Jaragua is the dominant cultivated pasture grass in many areas of Costa Rica, especially in Guanacaste, where is not only covers the pastures but is abundant on roadsides. At times these roadside stands along the carretera are cut for seed production. While there are more productive pasture grasses, there are few in Costa Rica that will stand abuse and overgrazing as well. Other introduced pasture grasses that have attracted more recent attention and are being planted in competition with jaragua are pangola (*Digitaria decumbens* Stent) and estrella africana (*Cynodon nlemfuensis* Vanderyst). Neither is likely to replace jaragua.

*

Daubenmire, R. 1972. Ecology of *Hyparrhenia rufa* (Mees.) in derived savannah in northwestern Costa Rica. *J. Appl. Ecol.* 9:11–13.

Pohl, R. W. 1980. Flora costaricensis: Family number 15, Gramineae. *Fieldiana, Bot.,* n.s., 4:1–608.

Hypericum (Culandro Cimarrón, Saint-John's-Wort)

G. B. Williamson

The genus *Hypericum* is predominantly temperate, but representatives occur throughout the Neotropics at higher elevations. The taxonomy of these mountaintop colonizers, whose habitats are islands in the vast sea of tropical lowlands, is still primitive, so brief diagnostic descriptions follow for three species from the "páramo" vegetation at Cerro Asunción in Costa Rica:

1. *Hypericum irazuense,* the dominant, branched shrub up to 4 m (fig. 7.63*b*); leaves 2 mm wide; styles longer than stamens (fig. 7.64).
2. *Hypericum strictum,* the common, branched shrub up to 0.5 m (fig. 7.63*a*); leaves 1 mm wide; styles shorter than stamens (fig. 7.64).
3. *Hypericum caracasanum,* the rare, often unbranched shrub up to 0.5 m; leaves 4–6 mm wide; styles stout and about the same length as stamens (fig. 7.64).

Vegetational transects from the top of Cerro Asunción (3,396 m) down the slope in different directions to about 3,340 m elevation show the relative densities of *H. irazuense, H. strictum,* and *H. caracasanum* to be about 13:3:2, respectively. *H. strictum* dominates the windward eastern slope, which is dryer and probably subject to

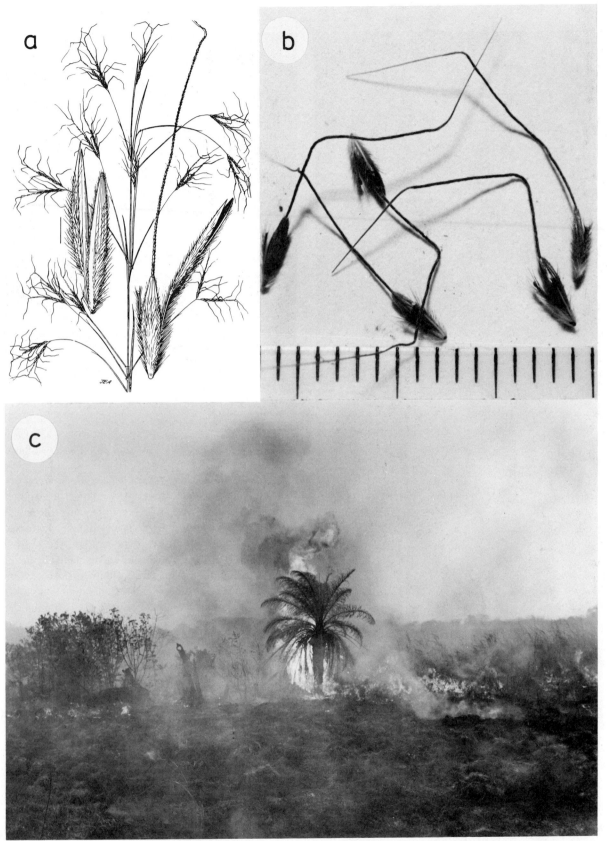

FIGURE 7.62. *a, Hyparrhenia rufa*, reproductive parts
(courtesy Field Museum). *b,* Newly fallen mature fruits
(with other floral parts still attached) of *H. rufa*. Santa Rosa
National Park, Guanacaste, Costa Rica. *c,* Dense stand of
jaragua that has just burned (still burning on right), burning
most of the crown of a coyol (*Acrocomia vinifera*) along
with it (same site as *b*) (photos, D. H. Janzen).

257

FIGURE 7.63. *Hypericum. a, H. strictum. b, H. irazuense.* Cerro de la Muerte (3,250 m elevation), Costa Rica (photos, D. H. Janzen).

FIGURE 7.64. *Hypericum* flowers with petals removed to reveal floral structure: *H. strictum* (*upper left*); *H. caracasanum* (*upper right*); and *H. irazuense,* freshly opened flower (*lower left*), and older flower (*lower right*) (photo, B. W. Williamson).

was found only in cleared pockets along an abandoned jeep trail on the moist western slope.

It appears that *H. caracasanum* and *H. strictum* are both early colonizers of disturbed ground, the former having larger, elliptical leaves and growing on moist, protected sites and the latter having needlelike, appressed leaves and growing on drier, wind-exposed faces. Both species are likely to be overtopped and excluded by larger shrubs, including *H. irazuense.* However, succession through seed colonization and regeneration by sucker shoots is exceptionally slow. For example, 1.5 m tall *H. irazuense* (Janzen's [1973] *H. caracasanum*) had recovered to only 0.5 m 3 years after a fire, and patches of bare ground were still uncolonized (Janzen 1973). Thus, seral replacement of *H. caracasanum* on moist sites and of *H. strictum* on dry sites by *H. irazuense* and its associates may require decades without further disturbance or fire.

Pollination of all three *Hypericum* species comes from visitation by *Bombus ephippiatus,* which services more than twenty-five plant species on Cerro Asunción (E. R. Heithaus, pers. comm.). Of the *Hypericum* species, *H. irazuense* is highly preferred by the bees. Pollen-foraging bees at *H. irazuense* make their next visit to the same species 88% of the time, whereas bees on *H. strictum* make their next visit to *H. strictum* only 60% of the time. Furthermore, bees leaving *H. strictum* move on to *Vaccinium consanguinium,* a nectar source, 21% of the time, while bees leaving *H. irazuense* moved to *V. consan-*

more frequent fires. *H. irazuense* dominates the moist western slope and all lower elevations free of fire. Older burn lines suggest that fires occur on the upper reaches of eastern slopes and often are extinguished when reaching western slopes and lower elevations. *H. caracasanum*

guinium only 2% of the time. Comparable data for *H. caracasanum* are not available.

Bee preference was confirmed further in an experimental floral arrangement (a case of beer bottles) with twelve flowers each of *H. strictum* and *H. irazuense*. The ratio of visits for *strictum:irazuense* was 4:16 on day one, 7:24 on day two, and 6:39 on day three. That the ratios are significantly different from 1:1, but not from each other, indicates that the bees have a preference that is not changing daily.

An interesting outcome of bee preference is that *H. strictum* is visited more frequently when it is growing alongside *H. irazuense* than when it is growing alone: mean visits per flower (for flower lifetime) was determined to be 3.5 in mixed stands and only 0.5 when grown alone.

The consequence for *H. strictum* is that cross-pollination is more likely when it is being succeeded than when it is dominant in early seral plots. In fact, if bee visits per flower follow a random (Poisson) distribution among the flowers of a species, then cross-pollination, based on mean visitation rates above, could occur in 95% of the *H. strictum* flowers when the plants are being succeeded, but in only 36% of the flowers when the plants are dominant. This result implies that the species may produce more genetically variable seeds as it is locally eliminated through succession. If such a mechanism were operating through natural selection, then *H. strictum* might benefit from production of less-preferred pollen.

Little is known about selfing in these *Hypericum* species, but bagged *H. strictum* flowers began seed development before the experiment had to be terminated prematurely. The short styles of *H. strictum* (fig. 7.64) would promote selfing, since even light rain would effect pollen transfer. In contrast, the longer styles of *H. irazuense* reach beyond the anthers and are curved away from them when the flowers open; only after many of the anthers have fallen from the filaments are the styles straight so as to contact bee visitors (fig. 7.64).

The *Hypericum* species on Neotropical mountains are often available to cattle, although there is no indication of grazing damage at Cerro Asunción. Other *Hypericum* species around the world are notoriously troublesome because they contain hypercin (Scheel 1973), which produces sores and sometimes causes death (Harris, Peschken, and Milrog 1969).

*

Harris, P.; Peschken, D.; and Milrog, J. 1969. The status of biological control of the weed *Hypericum perforatum* in British Columbia. *Canad. Entomol.* 101:1–15.

Janzen, D. H. 1973. Rate of regeneration after a tropical high elevation fire. *Biotropica* 5:117–22.

Scheel, L. D. 1973. Photosensitizing agents. In *Toxicants occurring naturally in foods,* pp. 558–72. Washington, D.C.: National Academy of Sciences.

Inga (Guaba, Guajiniquil, Caite, Paterno)

S. Koptur

There are about four hundred species of *Inga* (Fabaceae: Mimosoideae) in the Neotropics; twenty-five to thirty occur in Costa Rica (León 1966). *Inga* species are canopy and subcanopy trees recognizable by their alternate, even-pinnate, once-compound leaves, sometimes bearing a winged rachis (fig. 7.65a), and usually having glands between opposite leaflets. All the Costa Rican species have nectaries, but not all individuals of each species have them (e.g., *I. oerstediana* Benth. ex Seem. on the road up Volcán Turrialba, near Santa Cruz). The closely related genus *Pithecellobium* has glands also, but its leaves are bipinnate.

Inga flowers are arranged in inflorescences that are "puffballs": the main part of each flower is the stamens, and it is the white filaments of the numerous stamens (25–130 per flower) that provide the visual attraction. Some species of *Inga* have inflorescences borne singly (e.g., *I. brenesii* Standl., *I. mortoniana* J. León, *I. quaternata* Poeppig.); others have them grouped in compound inflorescences (*I. densiflora* Benth., *I. punctata, I. longispica* Standl.). *Inga* flowers secrete nectar that serves as a reward for visitors. *Inga* flowers often have a

FIGURE 7.65. *Inga vera. a,* Fully expanded leaf 20 cm long. *b,* Full-sized but immature fruit 10 cm long. Santa Rosa National Park, Guanacaste Province, Costa Rica, July 1980 (photos, D. H. Janzen).

distinctive odor: most are sweet-smelling (suggesting moths as pollinators), others are yeasty (suggesting bats), and the rest have only a very faint odor or none (perhaps odor is not important to the hummingbirds and butterflies that visit them). *Inga* pollen is arranged in polyads, clusters of pollen grains that are dispersed as a unit (containing sixteen, twenty-four, or thirty-two grains; León 1966; Koptur, unpub. data), as is the pollen of other advanced mimosoid legumes (Elias 1972). There are eight polyads in each anther. *Inga* stigmata are discoid. The style is slightly thicker than the stamens but is sometimes difficult to distinguish in the small-flowered species. Some species of *Inga* have individuals with styles of very different lengths (*I. brenesii, I. oerstediana*).

Inga fruits (fig. 7.65*b*) are leguminous pods of many shapes and sizes. They can be flat green pods, square brown fuzzy pods, or long twisted pods (fuzzy or glabrous) (León 1966; Holdridge and Poveda 1975). The seeds are usually covered with white, sweet pulp that aids in their dispersal by birds and mammals. Humans also enjoy eating the fruits, which are commonly known as "guaba."

Many species of *Inga* are economically important as shade trees in coffee and cacao plantations. In recent years *Inga* has been partially replaced by *Erythrina* spp. as shade, but one still sees many trees of *I. oerstediana, I. punctata,* and *I. ruiziana* in cafetales. Such trees that support that "ant mosaic" may promote protection of crop plants by natural enemies (Leston 1974). The trees are also planted for their fruit. It is difficult to grow *Inga* from stem cuttings (therefore they are rarely seen as living fence-post trees). Reproduction from seed is usually very good, and transplanting small saplings meets with fair success.

In areas of Costa Rica where nectar-drinking ants are abundant (low to mid elevations, especially dry areas), *Inga* trees benefit from ant associations (Koptur, unpub. data; see review by Bentley 1977). The extrafloral nectaries function on the new leaves; nectar secretion usually ceases when the leaves become mature. Ants visit the nectaries and patrol the leaves of *Inga* trees, protecting the leaves from a variety of insect herbivores. *Solanopteris brunei,* a myrmecophytic fern, is a common epiphyte in *Inga* trees (Gómez 1974). Different species of *Inga* use ant protection to different degrees; it also seems that there may be a trade-off between ant protection and other defenses (mechanical, chemical, etc) at different elevations (ants are not present in significant numbers at high elevations). My studies at Monteverde, Puntarenas, show that there is a higher rate of parasitization by caterpillars eating *Inga* at 1,550 m (in the cloud forest, where ants are very rare) than at 1,300 m (where ants are more abundant). The ant-related trait of extrafloral nectar secretion is not lost at higher elevations; parasitic wasps

and flies are seen at nectaries and honey baits at the higher elevations. The continued functioning of the nectaries in an antless habitat promotes another form of biotic defense. Parasites that are attracted to plants bearing extrafloral nectar may be more likely to find larvae on these plants and may oviposit more on or in these herbivores (Koptur, unpub. data: see review by Price et al. 1981).

It should be noted that the ants are not necessarily resident in or on the *Inga* trees; often they nest in the ground nearby, in a log, or in other trees. However, *I. brenesii* frequently has a resident ant population (*Myrmelachista* sp.) that lives in galls on the branches and twigs. *Inga sapindoides* Willd. sometimes has ants residing in formicaria (small domiciles of their own construction) at the base of the leaves. And, of course, nests may be built in *Inga* tree branches or trunks. Many kinds of ants are associated with and protect *Inga,* including *Crematogaster limata palans, Camponotus substitutus, Pheidole biconstricta,* and *Solenopsis* sp.

Inga leaves are subject to damage by many types of herbivores. Folivores include grasshoppers, katydids, lepidopteran larvae, beetles, monkeys, and sloths (Koptur, unpub. data; Milton 1978; Montgomery and Sunquist 1978). Leaves are also bound together by spiders, small orthopterans, skipper larvae, and microlepidoptera. Leaf-binding lepidopterans usually scrape the leaf tissue (upper epidermis and mesophyll), leaving bare brown sections. It is interesting to note that in areas where ants on *Inga* trees are abundant, leaf binders are the most common (at times, the only) type of caterpillar found on *Inga* leaves. Leaf-cutting ants and bees sometimes use *Inga* leaves. Leaf miners often find a home in the mesophyll of an *Inga* leaf. Galls of many shapes and sizes also occur, caused by wasps or small flies. These may be in the lamina of the leaflets or inside the rachis and petiole.

My studies on tagged leaves have shown that a substantial amount of damage takes place while the young leaves are developing (especially "chomping"). Leaf binders are usually found on old growth (though there are certain ones that specialize on stem tips). Leaf miners appear later in a leaf's life, as do most galls. Many lepidopteran larvae have been found to prefer young leaves in earlier instars and to eat both old and young in later instars. Major lepidopteran herbivore families are Pieridae, Hesperiidae, Megalopigidae, Saturniidae, Notodontidae, and Geometridae (sixteen families were reared in my study).

Although one might expect exclusively nocturnal anthesis for sweet-smelling white flowers with nectar as their reward, *Inga* flowers are extremely diverse in their behavior. *Inga vera* has large flowers and nocturnal anthesis, and it is visited by hawkmoths and bats during the night (Salas 1967, 1974). *I. brenesii* has large flowers that open throughout the day and night and appears to employ several "shifts" of pollinators: hummingbirds (Feinsinger 1978), large bees, and butterflies during the day; hawkmoths at dawn and dusk; and hawkmoths, other moths, and bats at night (Koptur, unpub. data). *I. punctata* is a small-flowered, sweet-smelling species with both early-morning and early-evening anthesis: it is visited by small hawkmoths at both times, butterflies during the day, and many small moths at night. *I. densiflora* is very similar to *I. punctata* is size and arrangement of flowers but has principally morning anthesis: its major visitors are butterflies and hummingbirds. *Inga mortoniana* has flowers that open very slowly from the afternoon of one day until the midmorning of the following day: they are visited primarily by butterflies (and, to a much lesser extent than other species, by hummingbirds).

In many of these species the flowers may continue to secrete nectar and be visited for many hours after the pollen has disappeared and hours after the stigma is past being receptive, giving the false impression that pollination is taking place. Most *Inga* trees are visited by many more organisms than pollinate them. The visitors that are actually pollinating are those whose periods of activity match the floral events (anthers dehiscing, stigmata receptive), whose bodies and behavior enable pollen to be placed on the stigmata, and (for all species studied so far) who move pollen from one individual to another (since these *Inga* trees are largely self-incompatible: *I. brenesii, I. punctata, I. densiflora, I. mortoniana,* and *I. oerstediana*). In some species (*I. brenesii* and *I. punctata*) I have found that closely adjacent individuals have very little success in setting fruit with crossing by hand pollination—perhaps they are too similar genetically. The incompatibility system is gametophytic.

Fruit development in all *Inga* species so far observed takes place in a characteristic way: first the fruit itself develops (it grows large, then becomes hard, fuzzy, or whatever); then the seeds develop; and finally the white, sweet pulp develops. Some pods dehisce on the tree, where the pulpy seeds can be removed and dispersed by birds and mammals. Mature fruit may be opened by squirrels or monkeys and the pulp eaten. Fruit predators include porcupines (which eat the fruit while it is still immature; B. Guindon, pers. comm.). Seed predators include wasps, beetles, and organisms that ingest and digest the soft seeds (which germinate well without any sort of endozoochorical treatment).

*

Bentley, B. L. 1977. Extrafloral nectaries and protection by pugnacious bodyguards. *Ann. Rev. Ecol. Syst.* 8:407–27.

Elias, T. S. 1972. Morphology and anatomy of foliar nectaries of *Pithecellobium macradenium* (Leguminosae). *Bot. Gaz.* 133:28–42.

Feinsinger, P. 1978. Ecological interactions between plants and hummingbirds in a successional tropical community. *Ecol. Monog.* 48:269–87.

Gómez, L. D. 1974. Biology of the potato-fern, *Solanopteris brunei*. *Brenesia* 4:37–61.

Holdridge. L. R., and Poveda, Luis J. 1975. *Arboles de Costa Rica.* Vol. 1. San José: Centro Cientifico Tropical.

León, J. 1966. Central American and West Indian species of *Inga* (Leguminosae). *Ann. Missouri Bot. Gard.* 53:365–59.

Leston, D. 1973. The ant mosaic—tropical tree crops and the limiting of pests and diseases. *Pest Art. News Summ. (PANS)* 19:311–41.

Milton, K. 1978. Behavioral adaptations to leaf-eating by the mantled howler monkey (*Alouatta palliata*). In *The ecology of arboreal folivores,* ed. G. G. Montgomery. Washington, D.C.: Smithsonian Institution Press.

Montgomery, G. G., and Sunquist, M. E. 1978. Habitat selection and use by two-toed and three-toed sloths. In *The ecology of arboreal folivores,* ed. G. G. Montgomery. Washington, D.C.: Smithsonian Institution Press.

Price, P. W.; Bouton, C. E.; Gross, P.; McPheron, B. A.; Thompson, J. N.: and Weis, A. E. 1980. Interactions among three tropic levels: Influence of plants on interactions between insect herbivores and natural enemies. *Ann. Rev. Ecol. Syst.* 11:41–65.

Salas, S. 1967. *Inga* sp. as a bat pollinated tree in Cañas, Costa Rica. OTS project report, mimeographed.

———. 1974. Analisis del sistema de polinizacion de *Inga vera* ssp. *spuria*. Thesis, Universidad de Costa Rica.

Ipomoea pes-caprae (Pudre Oreja, Beach Morning Glory)

D. E. Wilson

This convolvulaceous vine is one of two striking components of coastal strand vegetation in Costa Rica and throughout the tropics. The other is *Canavalia maritima,* which grows tightly entangled with *Ipomoea pes-caprae* to form the *pes-caprae* association of sandy beaches. The two species are very similar in growth form. Both have creeping prostrate stems that may extend 10 m or more in length along the sand. Stems growing toward the ocean often make a 180° turn when they approach within about 10 m of the high-tide line. The plants often extend underground, presumably buried by shifting sands. The sinuous and subterranean life form makes it extremely difficult to tell where one plant ends and the next begins.

In addition to habit, the two species look remarkably similar and grow in large intertwined mats at the inland edge of the beach. Their superficial leaf morphology is similar, with the succulent leaves raised off the sand on erect petioles. However, *Canavalia* leaves are alternate and pinnately trifoliate, whereas *Ipomoea* leaves are simple with an apical sinus or cleft giving them a supposed resemblance to a goat's hoof (hence the name *pes-caprae*).

The flowers of both are the same shade of pinkish purple and are superficially similar. This suggests shared pollinators, in spite of quite different morphologies. The flowers of *Ipomoea pes-caprae* have fine green sepals that are tightly overlapping, forming a narrow cup at the base of the corolla. This cup may hinder nectar robbers and also retard nectar evaporation. The five pink petals are completely united to form the corolla, and five darker pink stripes radiate out from the base to the edges of the petals. These may function as nectar guides, for the plants are apparently pollinated during the day. The odorless flowers last only one day and are not open at night.

The five separate stamens are united basally with the petals, and the corolla tube narrows around the ovary. At the base of the filaments are hairy swellings that enclose the ovary; these may serve to protect the nectar from nonpollinators.

One of the strangest aspects of the flower design of *Ipomoea* is the consistent heterogeneity of stamen filament length. Of the five anthers, one is above the stigma, one is at the level of the stigma, and three are below the stigma. We can only speculate on the function of this design, but it may facilitate pollination by a variety of insect species. In addition, any differential maturation of these stamens (with the tallest maturing last) could provide an emergency selfing mechanism if cross-pollination has not been effected. Robertson and Gooding (1963) suggest a similar system for *I. tiliacea* in the Caribbean region.

The anthers open toward the petals and away from the stigma, which is offset to one side. This may also facilitate outcrossing. Pollen grains of *Ipomoea* are large, sperical, and spinulose. The nectar is secreted by a yellow annular nectary surrounding the base of the ovary. The ovary itself is about 2 mm long, and the narrow style is about 15 mm long. The large capitate stigma is about 2 mm in length and in diameter.

The stamens and pistil are deeply recessed in the narrow, tubular portion of the corolla; an insect probably must completely enter the flower for pollination to occur.

On both coasts of Costa Rica, *Ipomoea pes-caprae* and *Canavalia maritima* produce large numbers of flowers during the rainy season (July–November) and set large seed crops that mature in the dry season (December–April). The two plants differ markedly in their reproductive strategies. *Canavalia* has apparently evolved a variety of chemical defenses against insect attack on seeds. *Canavalia maritima* seeds contain a toxic non-protein amino acid, canavanine. Probably this compound contributes to the general toxicity of the plant to insects.

Ipomoea appears to suffer a great deal of insect damage to flowers, leaves, and seeds, whereas *Canavalia* does not. *Ipomoea* flowers are often missing stamens and pistils by midday, probably owing to feeding by grasshoppers. Adult bruchid beetles (*Megacerus leucospilus*) can also be found in the flowers, but they probably are not feeding on them.

The differential rate of seed predation in *Canavalia* and *Ipomoea* is striking. *Canavalia* is not attacked at all, and the number of apparently viable seeds found on the ground during most of the year is substantial. On the other hand, seeds of *Ipomoea pes-caprae* are heavily damaged by the larvae of the bruchid *M. leucospilus*. Predation rates range from 15% to 85% in samples from both coasts of Costa Rica.

These findings, coupled with other observations, suggests that there might be fundamental differences in the reproductive strategies of these species. The hypothesis is that *Canavalia maritima* relies on successful seed germination, whereas *Ipomoea pes-caprae* relies more heavily on vegetative growth from the runners of a parent plant. *Ipomoea* has a much higher frequency of root nodes than does *Canavalia*, both per meter and per leaf node, suggesting more root production.

Although at first glance the two species seem to be intermingled at random, *Ipomoea* is in fact more dominant closer to the water, and *Canavalia* dominates on the inland side of the clumps.

*

Gates, F. C. 1915. Notes from the tropical strand: *Ipomoea pes-caprae* and *Canavalia lineata. Torreya* 15:27–28.

Robertson, E. T., and Gooding, E. G. B. 1963. *Botany for the Caribbean*. London and Glascow: Collins Clear-type Press.

Wilson, D. E. 1977. Ecological observations of the tropical strand plants *Ipomoea pes-caprae* (L) R. Br. (Convolvulaceae) *Canavalia maritima* (Aubl.) Thou. (Fabaceae). *Brenesia* 10/11:31–42.

Ipomoea trifida (Churristate, Pudre Oreja, Morning Glory)

D. H. Janzen

This common roadside, riverbank, and pasture-edge herbaceous, convolvulaceous twining vine adds lavender color to the lowland countryside from Mexico to Panama from September through January (or March in wet sites). In Costa Rica, below about 1,500 m elevation, it is very common in deciduous forest areas and occurs in weedy areas derived from rain forest. In Corcovado National Park it occurs as a member of primary succession on riverbanks and old riparian gravel bars, and in Santa Rosa National Park it occurs on banks of steep rocky ravines through nearly undisturbed forest. The vine sprawls across low vegetation up to 2–3 m high and, when in flower, may have as many as one hundred flowers per square meter of foliage-filled surface. The flowers (fig. 7.66) last only one day and are usually wilted shut by early afternoon. The lavender corolla lip deepens to dark lavender at the base of the 1.5 cm diameter corolla tube. An occasional plant has pure white flowers. The flower is about 3.5–4.5 cm wide at the front and 4.5–5 cm long. The anthers open well inside the throat of the corolla (rather than being exerted as in the hummingbird-visited morning glories). The upright peduncle is 3–8 cm long and holds the flowers well above the vegetation.

Shortly after the flowers open (before dawn, about 0430–0500, in the dark) they are visited by a few small sphinx moths (Sphingidae) and nocturnal and matinal skipper butterflies (Hesperiidae). These insects move rapidly over large areas of flowers and between flower patches and are probably effective cross-pollinators. However, I suspect that major pollinators are the male and female *Ptiloglossa* spp. bees (Colletidae) that appear about the time the flowers can barely be seen in the faintest early morning light. They have a distinct, loud buzzing flight, and they visit half a dozen flowers within a few square meters, move on a few meters and repeat the process, then move to a quite different patch. The fe-

males are often carrying heavy pollen loads from other plant species when they visit *I. trifida* for nectar (e.g., *Cassia, Solanum, Bixa*). They are very hairy bees, and both males and females become heavily coated with *I. trifida* pollen. Both sexes appear to seek only nectar from the flowers, and to do this they crawl down the broad corolla tube to its base. These bees have a brushy short, forked tongue that appears to be designed for sopping up large amounts of nectar quickly. They visit these and other nectar sources (e.g., *Passiflora foetida, Manihot aesculifolia,* and various Sapindaceae in Santa Rosa National Park) as the first bees of the morning, and therefore are probably getting the greatest amount of nectar per flower of any bee species. *Ptiloglossa* have generally stopped foraging on *I. trifida* by sunrise and usually remain in the nest for the rest of the day. About sunrise, *I. trifida* is then visited for nectar and pollen by a variety of *Trigona,* Halictidae, Anthophoridae, and other small bees, but I suspect that many, if not all, of these are not pollinators. Any patch of *I. trifida* will be reliably visited by *Ptiloglossa* in the early dawn light anywhere in Central America. In Corcovado National Park the bees start working the flowers in the dark (along with *Megalopta,* a nocturnal halictid) and may be gone before it is light enough to see the flowers easily.

The number of flowers produced and the seed set seems strongly related to the overall wetness of the year's rainy season. In a dry year plants are small and have few flowers. In a wet year the same plant may cover tens of square meters with thousands of flowers for several months at a time.

The seeds of *I. trifida* are small for morning-glory seeds. They are dark brown black, glabrous, and smooth. Four seeds are enclosed in each small, dry beige papery capsule, which shatters in the dry season as the herbaceous aboveground parts of the plant die back. They are attacked sparingly by the larvae of *Megacerus ricaensis.* The beetle glues single eggs on the green capsule, and the larvae burrow into the hardening and full-sized seeds. The new adult emerges about the same time that the seeds are being dispersed. There appears to be one or at the most two generations per year, and this beetle has not been reared from any other species of plant in Santa Rosa (there are, however, a number of other species of *Megacerus* feeding on the seeds of a number of other species of Convolvulaceae in the park; Janzen 1980).

The flowers of *I. trifida* are eaten extensively by a large black meloid beetle in Santa Rosa National Park. Among the leaf-eaters are the sphingid larva *Agrius cingulatus* (pink-spotted hawkmoth), several arctiid larvae, and several chrysomelid beetles. The foliage is readily eaten by captive collared peccaries, white-tailed deer, and a tapir—in nature the first two species have been seen to do the same (Santa Rosa, 1978, 1979).

FIGURE 7.66. *Ipomoea trifida* flowers and foliage. January 1980, Santa Rosa National Park, Guanacaste Province, Costa Rica (photo, D. H. Janzen).

The leaves of an *I. trifida* plant are shaped like one- to three-pointed spearheads, are small and glabrous, and are on long petioles. The branches come off a main stem that is connected to a large tuber, the size and shape of a large sweet-potato tuber (a fat spindle, with the long axis at a right angle to the soil surface, weighing 0.2–1 kg). The tubers are 30–50 cm below the soil surface and quite woody. If baked in an oven, they give off a strong aroma of baking sweet potato but do not soften noticeably. The relationship of this plant to domestic sweet potatoes is unclear.

*

Janzen, D. H. 1980. Host-specificity of seed-attacking beetles in a Costa Rican deciduous forest. *J. Ecol.* 68:929–52.

Schlising, R. A. 1970. Sequence and timing of bee foraging in flowers of *Ipomoea* and *Aniseia* (Convolvulaceae). *Ecology* 51:1061–67.

Jacaratia dolichaula (Papaya Silvestre, Papaya de Venado, Wild Papaya)

K. S. Bawa

Jacaratia dolichaula is a small understory tree to 8 m in height and 25 cm dbh occurring in tropical moist, tropical wet, premontane wet, and premontane rain forests of Central America. It typically occurs in gaps created by tree falls but may persist in mature forests for several years after the canopy is closed. It also occurs occasionally in young secondary vegetation. The species is dioecious, and male and female plants differ profoundly in floral morphology, floral rewards, average number of flowers per plant, and flowering periodicity.

Flowering starts in November and lasts until June, but the individual plants generally do not flower for more than 8 weeks. The male plants generally flower earlier than the female plants. For example, at the La Selva Field Station, on 30 December 1977, only 22% of the female plants were in flower compared with 55% of the male plants. The male plants also bear many more flowers than the female plants. The ratio varies from 1:700 in the early part of the blooming period to 1:5 at the peak of flowering. The bias in flower ratio is also in part due to an excess of male over female plants. The male plants generally lose all their leaves before they flower, but female plants are never leafless.

The male flowers (fig. 7.67) are sessile and are borne in clusters. They have a white corolla tube, up to 100 mm long, terminated by five reflexed corolla lobes. Stamens are in two whorls of five each, outer ones longer than the inner. The pistil is rudimentary, consisting of a poorly developed ovary and a stylelike projection.

The female flowers (fig. 7.67) are borne singly on stalks up to 40 mm long. The female flowers lack the corolla tube: the petals, which are up to 40 mm long, are

FIGURE 7.67. *Jacaratia dolichaula* flowers, female flower on left, male flower on right. Finca La Selva, Sarapiquí District, Costa Rica (photo, K. W. Bawa).

completely free and are pale green. The ovary, however, bears five large white, petaloid stigmatic lobes that, when viewed from above, appear similar to the corolla lobes of the male flowers.

The male flowers open between 1700 and 1800, last for two nights, then abcise. Nectar is secreted soon after anthesis, and the corolla tube usually contains up to 10 μl of nectar. The female flowers are probably receptive for 4–5 days as judged from the condition of the stigmata. They lack nectar but produce some stigmatic sap that in a related species, *Carica papaya,* is known to contain amino acids (Baker 1976). It is uncertain if the sap serves as a floral reward, or aids in pollen germination and pollen tube growth, or both. Female flowers have the same odor as male flowers.

The primary pollinators are sphingid moths. Butterflies have been observed to visit flowers, but it is doubtful if they play a role in pollination.

The female flowers apparently offer little or no reward to the pollinators but mimic male flowers in order to get pollinated. The moths must be attracted to the female flowers by their odor and white petaloid stigmatic lobes. They probably extend their probosces inside the stigmatic canal, which lines the ovary longitudinally, to draw nectar, but before they realize their "mistake" pollen is deposited inside the canal. Baker (1976) has termed this type of pollination system in *Carica papaya* "mistake pollination." The basic floral biology of different species of *Carica* and *Jacaratia* in the Caricaceae is the same, and it appears that "mistake pollination" or the mimicry of male flowers by female flowers is widespread within the family.

The mimicry has apparently evolved owing to disparity in the number of male and female flowers; disparity itself may be due to differences in allocation of resources toward reproduction by male or female plants, to intrasexual competition among males, resulting in greater and greater production of flowers, or to both (Bawa 1980). The early flowering by male plants can also be explained in terms of intrasexual competition (Bawa 1980).

The fruits have the same morphology as papaya except that they are smaller and are pale orange on the outside and white inside. Approximately 12 weeks are required for fruits to mature after pollination. There is some evidence for parthenocarpy, which is well known in papaya, but it remains to be confirmed. The fruit contains numerous soft seeds (up to two hundred) that germinate readily without any pretreatment. Seeds from some fruits (parthenocarpic?) show 0% viability. The seeds are highly polymorhic in color and surface; seeds from the same tree, however, are monomorphic for these characters.

The seed-dispersal agents are not known, but parrots have been seen feeding on fruits. Seed coats devoid of seeds are frequently found scattered under the trees. There is a possibility that seed-dispersal agents are also seed predators. Damage to the seeds by insects has not been observed.

Variation in sex expression of trees, though common in *Carica papaya* (Story 1977), has not been noted on any of the more than eighty plants in which sex expression has been followed for three blooming periods.

In summary, the differences between male and female plants are pronounced. Along with other members of the family, the species constitutes interesting material for investigating the problems of sexual dimorphism and sexual selection in plants.

*

Baker, H. G. 1976. "Mistake" pollination as a reproductive system with special reference to the Caricaceae. In *Tropical trees: Variation, breeding and conservation,* ed. J. Burley and B. T. Styles, pp. 161–69. London: Academic Press.

Bawa, K. S. 1980. Mimicry of male by female flowers and intrasexual competition for pollinators in *Jacaratia dolichaula* (D. Smith) Woodson (Caricaceae). *Evolution* 34:467–74.

Bullock, S. H., and Bawa, K. S. 1981. Sexual dimorphism and the annual flowering pattern in *Jacaratia dolichaula* (D. Smith) Woodson (Caricaceae) in a Costa Rican rain forest. *Ecology* 62:1494–1504.

Story, W. B. 1977. Papaya. In *Evolution of crop plants,* ed. N. W. Simmonds, pp. 21–24. London: Longman.

Jacquinia pungens (Burriquita, Siempre Viva, Siempre Verde, False Evergreen Needle Bush)

D. H. Janzen

What is probably only one species, but has many names applied to it from Mexico through Panama, is a theophrastaceous understory shrub-treelet (fig. 7.68) that is most often discovered by backing into it in the dry sea-

son. Each leathery, lanceolate leaf has a needle-sharp tip. *J. pungens* is also conspicuous for bearing leaves in the dry season in the deciduous lowland forests it occupies; however, it stands leafless through the rainy season (fig. 7.68*b*), making its Spanish common name a misnomer.

Jacquinia pungens has a distinctly shrublike life form, with multiple branches and many twigs one above the other. The small leaves are borne in tufts, throughout a deep crown. This lifeform, so atypical for a forest understory plant, is not at all surprising considering that *J. pungens* grows in a seasonally available desert (Janzen 1970). By leafing out in the dry season, the plant is harvesting a huge energy source that passes by the leafless overstory largely unused. This heliophile drops its leaves as the rains begin (as the overstory leafs out) and sits dormant during the rainy season. This dormancy is not a free ride. The starch reserves of the plant fall steadily during the rainy season, and sitting through a hot rainy season costs the dormant plant as much as 50% of the carbohydrate reserves in its stems (Janzen and Wilson 1974). At this time it is not even harvesting upper soil and litter reserves, since it does not have lateral roots in the litter or upper soil layers. Rather, it has a long, thick taproot that penetrates many meters to where moisture still exists to feed its leaves in the dry season.

The orange-to-red, somewhat tubular flowers (fig. 7.69*a*) of *J. pungens* are produced when the plant is fully leafed out and are believed to be hummingbird pollinated, though no observations are recorded to support this hypothesis. When the flower first opens, the anthers are clustered tightly over the stigma and block access to it. Several days later the anthers split apart and are moved to the sides of the mouth of the corolla tube, exposing the stigma for pollen deposition. Spherical fruits 2–3 cm diameter appear soon after flowering, and they begin to ripen to yellow at the end of the dry season. Some fruits do not ripen until several months into the rainy season. The ripe indehiscent fruits have a thick, hard rind (fig. 7.69*b*), a sweet, juicy endocarp or aril, and two to ten smooth, flattened oval seeds (about 100 mg weight). Presumably the fruits are eaten by birds or mammals that pass the seeds intact. The immature fruits taste horrible and probably contain the same fish poisons (saponins?) found in the green foliage.

J. pungens is a common plant in relatively undisturbed heavily deciduous forest, but it certainly does not form an unbroken understory layer. The puzzle is why it is no more common if the forest is effectively absent when it is photosynthesizing and harvesting with its roots. Furthermore, why is such a way of harvesting resources so scarce? Only terrestrial cacti, various epiphytes (cacti, orchids, bromeliads) and some strongly green-barked trees (e.g., *Bursera* spp., *Parkinsonia aculeata, Prosopis juliflora*) are apparently major dry-season photosynthesizers in deciduous forest. The large and nearly ever-

FIGURE 7.68. *Jacquinia pungens. a,* Fully leafed crown as it appears during the dry season. *b,* Leafless crown as it appears during the rainy season. Finca La Pacifica, near Cañas, Guanacaste Province (photos, D. H. Janzen).

green trees, such as *Hymenaea courbaril, Ficus* spp., *Andira inermis, Manilkara zapota, Mastichodendron capiri,* and *Brosimun alicastrum,* are usually associated with moister sites within the deciduous forest.

*

Janzen, D. H. 1970. *Jacquinia pungens,* a heliophile from the understory of tropical deciduous forest. *Biotropica* 2:112–19.

Janzen, D. H., and Wilson, D. E. 1974. The cost of being dormant in the tropics. *Biotropica* 6:260–62.

Lantana camara (Cinco Negritos, Lantana)

D. W. Schemske

This weedy shrub, probably of West Indian origin (Moldenke 1973), is now distributed worldwide in disturbed habitats. It is frequent in pastures and roadsides throughout Costa Rica and is especially common at Santa Rosa National Park, La Pacifica, and the Osa. Plants are generally 1–2 m tall and occasionally are armed with short thorns. Flowering and fruiting continue throughout the year, generally "peaking" in the first two months of the rainy season. Inflorescences are axillary and broadly rounded, almost composite (capitate) (fig. 7.70). Hand pollination of laboratory plants has indicated that the species is an obligate outcrosser (Barrows 1976). Butterflies are the primary pollinators, with infrequent visits by hummingbirds.

Flowers are yellow when they first open and gradually change color to orange, then red, over a 24 hr period. They remain on the inflorescence about three days, creating a "bulls-eye" display with yellow flowers at the center surrounded by successive whorls of orange, then red, flowers. Only young, yellow flowers secrete nectar; thus pollinators rarely probe orange or red flowers. Müller (1877) suggested that the multicolor floral display may be more attractive to pollinators, but the experiment of comparing visitation rates to experimentally produced one-color (yellow) inflorescences with visits to natural, multicolored inflorescences has not been performed. There is some speculation that *Lantana camara,* the milkweed *Asclepias curassavica,* and an orchid, *Epidendrum ibaguense* or *E. radicans,* form a mimicry complex of orange-flowered species (Boyden 1980). The inter-

FIGURE 7.69. *Jacquinia pungens. a,* Flowers. *b,* A broken fruit with mature seeds and pulp visible around the seeds. Finca La Pacifica, near Cañas, Guanacaste Province, Costa Rica (photos, D. H. Janzen).

pretation is that floral convergence increases "effective" plant density with respect to potential pollinators and increases visitation rates. However, the largely non-overlapping distributions of these species usually observed in the field do not suggest that selection for color mimicry would significantly improve pollination probabilities.

The centripetal pattern of floral maturation and retention of flowers past their nectar-producing period increases the size of the landing platform and the visitation rate of large butterflies. On the Osa, large butterflies visited *Lantana camara* preferentially over blue-flowered *Lantana trifolia,* a syntopic species with narrower inflorescences, fewer nectar-producing flowers per inflorescence, and shorter flowers (Schemske 1976). The average body length of butterflies from *Lantana camara* was 18.3 mm compared with 12.2 mm for *L. trifolia.* Approximately twenty-four species of butterflies were observed visiting *Lantana camura* on the Osa, with three nymphalids (*Anartia jatrophae, A. fatima,* and *Agraulis vanillae*), three pierids (*Eurema daira, Phoebis sennae,* and *Ascia monuste*), and several species of hesperiids in the genus *Urbanus* accounting for a total of 85% of all visits (Schemske 1976).

In addition to increasing the size of the landing platform, retention of nectarless flowers on the periphery of the inflorescence protects inner flowers from *Trigona fulviventris,* a meliponine bee that steals nectar by biting through the corolla. On the Osa, 34% of flowers examined ($N = 1,500$) were robbed, but only 23% of the yellow flowers on inflorescences bordered by older, nectarless flowers were robbed, compared with 71% of those

FIGURE 7.70. *Lantana camara* inflorescence with unopened buds in center, yellow newly opened flowers peripheral to that, and the oldest red orange flowers on the outside. Santa Rosa National Park, Guanacaste Province, Costa Rica (photo, D. H. Janzen).

from new, yellow-only inflorescences (Barrows 1976). There was no indication that pollinators avoided flowers that were robbed.

The bird-dispersed fruit is a spherical (3–6 mm diameter), two-seeded, fleshy drupe that matures rapidly, changing color from dark green to purple. Manakins (Pipridae) and tanagers (Thraupidae) are most frequently seen taking *Lantana* fruits, with occasional visits by the more frugivorous flycatchers (Tyrannidae). Leck (1972) lists the manakin *Manacus vitellinus,* the flycatchers *Tyrannus melanocholicus* and *Myiodynastes maculatus,* the honey-creepers (Coerebidae) *Chlorophanes spiza* and *Dacnis cayana,* and the tanagers *Tangara inornata* and *Euphonia fulvicrissa* as the major exploiters of *Lantana camara* fruits in a clearing on Barro Colorado Island, Panama Canal Zone. A similar but richer assemblage can be expected in Costa Rica, with ecological replacements for the Panamanian species of *Manacus* and *Euphonia*, plus many more tanagers (especially *Ramphocelus passerinii*) and several flycatchers (probably *Myiozetetes similis*).

The leaves are rich in alkaloids and remarkably free from herbivore damage. This virtual immunity to herbivory is largely responsible for the plant's pest status throughout the Old World tropics. Numerous accounts of *Lantana* poisoning in cattle and sheep have been recorded.

*

Barrows, E. M. 1976. Nectar robbing and pollination of *Lantana camara* (Verbenaceae). *Biotropica* 8: 132–35.

Boyden, T. C. 1980. Floral mimicry by *Epidendrum ibaguense* (Orchidaceae) in Panama. *Evolution* 34: 135–36.

Leck, C. F. 1972. Seasonal changes in feeding pressures of fruit- and nectar-eating birds in Panama. *Condor* 74:54–60.

Moldenke, H. H. 1973. Verbenaceae. In Flora of Panama, ed. R. E. Woodson and A. W. Echery. *Ann. Missouri Bot. Gard.* 60:41–148.

Müller, F. 1877. Letters to the editor. *Nature* 17:78–79.

Schemske, D. W. 1976. Pollinator specificity in *Lantana camara* and *L. trifolia* (Verbenaceae). *Biotropica* 8: 260–64.

Lecythis costaricensis (Jicaro, Olla de Mono, Monkey Pot)

G. S. Hartshorn,

The genus *Lecythis* is one of ten Lecythidaceae genera endemic to the Neotropics. Although a small family with about two hundred species, it is well known for large trees, distinctive operculate fruit, and edible nuts. Best known, of course, is the Brazil nut (*Bertholletia excelsa*), one of the most widespread and easily recognized trees of the Amazon basin. Some species of *Lecythis* (e.g., *L. zabucajo*) are highly favored for sapucaia, paradise, or cream nuts. The seeds of *L. minor,* however, are known to contain toxic quantities of silenium (Kerdal-Vargas 1966); loss of fingernails and hair are the most prominent symptoms caused by eating them.

Lecythis costaricensis Pittier occurs in the tropical wet life zone in the Atlantic lowlands of Panama, Costa Rica, and Nicaragua, the northernmost range of the forty-five species in the genus. Mori (1970) reports that "almost pure stands" of *L. costaricensis* occur occasionally, giving an example above San Clemente (Limón Province), but generally it occurs at very low densities. At La Selva it is a rare canopy tree to 175 cm in bole diameter and 45 m tall (fig. 7.71).

FIGURE 7.71. *Lecythis costaricensis* trunk and base (center photo, deeply ridged bark) in undisturbed rain forest (palm trunk on right is *Welfia georgii*). Finca La Selva, Sarapiquí District, Costa Rica, May 1974 (photo G. W. Hartshorn).

The outer bark of *L. costaricensis* is dark brown, with distinctive vertical fissures (fig. 7.71) that make the large trees easy to recognize. The distinctively fissured outer bark does not develop in young trees smaller than about 40 cm dbh. The light tan to yellow inner bark consists of numerous thin, fibrous layers characteristic of the family. Long strips of inner bark of *Lecythis* and *Eschweilera* are commonly used for strong cord straps in the Amazon basin. Lecythidaceae inner bark is also used for oakum, cigarette papers, tinder, and tanning (Record and Hess 1943).

L. costaricensis leaves are simple, alternate, without stipules, on 5 mm petioles; the 7–8 cm blade is glabrous, thin, and oblong-lanceolate, with a distinctive crenulate and serrate margin. It is one of the few tropical wet forest deciduous trees to lose all its leaves during the rainy season. Leaves are rather abruptly shed just before a 2 week flowering period in May–August.

Lecythidaceae flowers have a distinctive staminal hood concealing a disk of stamens surrounding the pistil. *L. costaricensis* flowers are light blue and white and are borne in terminal panicles. The difficulty of opening the staminal hood suggests large euglossine bees as probable pollinators.

L. costaricensis fruit is an ovoid pyxidium, 12–20 cm across and 20–30 cm deep, with a woody wall 2–3 cm thick, brown and smooth on the outside (fig. 7.72). The pyxidium is capped by a domelike operculum, 2–3 cm high and 8–10 cm across, with a central, four-winged column. The fruit hangs "upside down" so that when the seeds are mature in March–April the operculate "lid" drops off, exposing twenty to fifty funiculate seeds.

L. costaricensis seeds are 4–5 cm long and 1.5–2 cm thick and have a thick brown, grooved seed coat. A thick, white, oily funiculus firmly attaches the seed to the proximal (upper) inside end of the pyxidium (fig. 7.72). Fru-

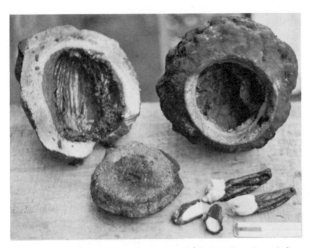

FIGURE 7.72. *Lecythis costaricensis* fruit (sectioned on left, intact on right), fruit cap, and seeds (two intact with white aril, two sectioned). Finca La Selva, Sarapiquí District, Costa Rica (photo, D. H. Janzen).

givorous bats, especially *Artibeus jamaicense,* land on the rim of the pyxidium to pull out a seed and its attached funiculus, then carry both to a night feeding roost to eat the funiculus and drop the seed. Sapucaia nut dispersal by *Phyllostomus hastatus* has been studied in Trinidad (Greenhall 1965).

L. costaricensis seeds are relished by terrestrial rodents, as is evidenced by agouti teeth marks on the occasional fallen pyxidium with its operculum still intact. Rodents feeding on fallen or dropped seeds near *L. costaricensis* trees are said to also attract bushmaster snakes (P. Slud, pers. comm.).

The "monkey pot" name refers to monkeys grasping a seed in the pyxidium and being unable to extract the closed hand, or to the empty pyxidium supposedly being used with bait to catch monkeys.

The more common genus, *Eschweilera,* has smaller, more flattened pyxidia that also drop the operculum at maturity. The genera *Cariniana* and *Couratari* have much narrower, tubular pyxidia containing numerous small winged seeds. The genus *Couroupita* bears cannonball pyxidia on strictly reproductive branches surrounding the lower bole.

Many large Lecythidaceae are valuable as timber. Abarco wood (*Cariniana pyriformis*) has been exported from the Colombian Chocó to Western Europe for the furniture trade for more than a decade. *L. costaricensis* wood is light yellow; it is used in heavy construction and for railway ties. The genera *Bertholletia, Cariniana, Couratari, Eschweilera,* and *Lecythis* contain many good-quality timber trees.

*

Greenhall, A. M. 1965. Sapucaia nut dispersal by greater spear-nosed bats in Trinidad. *Carib. J. Sci.* 5:167–71.

Kerdal-Vargas, F. 1966. The depilatory and cytotoxic action of coco de mono (*Lecythis ollaris*) and its relationship to chronic seleniosis. *Econ. Bot.* 20: 187–95.

Mori, S. 1970. The ecology and uses of the species of *Lecythis* in Central America. *Turrialba* 20:344–50.

Record, S. J., and Hess, R. W. 1943. *Timbers of the New World.* New Haven: Yale University Press (pp. 226–27).

Whitmore, J. L., and Hartshorn, G. S. 1969. *Literature review of common tropical trees.* Contribution no. 8. Seattle: University of Washington College of Forest Resources (pp. 60–61).

Luehea candida (Guácimo Molenillo, Molenillo)

W. A. Haber and G. W. Frankie

Luehea candida, "Guácimo molenillo," ranges from Mexico to Colombia; it ascends to 1,100 m (Standley 1937–38). In Costa Rica it is a common tree in the tropical dry forest of Guanacaste and northern Puntarenas provinces. It occurs on dry uplands (semideciduous forest) as well as along larger rivers where the forest is mostly evergreen. Adults are of moderate size (10–20 m), reaching the lower canopy of the forest. Most individuals have several trunks or a conspicuous low-branching growth form. Diagnostic characters include the large pubescent, toothed leaves with palmate venation; large white flowers (7–8 cm in diamater) with five petals and several hundred stamens and staminodes (fig. 7.73*a*); and the 5–8 cm long, woody, five-ridged fruits coated with golden brown pubescence.

Flowering occurs from late May to early July, following the first heavy rains of the wet season (Frankie, Baker, and Opler 1974). Occasional individuals may be found in flower during February and March if they grow

FIGURE 7.73. *Luehea. a, L. candida,* newly opened flower at night. *b, L. seemannii,* newly opened flower at night. Costa Rica (photos, W. A. Haber and G. W. Frankie).

along irrigation ditches or in fields watered during the dry season.

The flowers open 1 to 2 h after dark and immediately release a strong, sweet fragrance. Large amounts of nectar and the scent attract many species of hawkmoths (Sphingidae), which are the primary pollinators (Haber and Frankie 1980). Nectar secretion ceases shortly after dawn, but residual pollen and nectar attract large numbers of diurnal visitors including hummingbirds, bees, and butterflies. These visitors, however, pollinate very few flowers (Haber and Frankie 1982).

Fruits develop slowly during the remaining part of the wet season and into much of the dry season. They mature in February and March, about 7 months after pollination (Frankie, Baker, and Opler 1974). The woody pod dehisces on the tree along the five longitudinal ridges, allowing the winged seeds to drop out, a few at a time, when the fruits are jostled by the strong trade winds of the dry season. This event coincides with the period of general leaflessness of many dry forest trees. Seeds germinate shortly after the first rains (May) of the wet season begin (Frankie, Baker, and Opler 1974).

L. candida, like most trees of Guanacaste Province, is leafless for part of the year. Trees lose their leaves from January to April (Frankie, Baker, and Opler 1974). New leaves flush in May during the onset of the first rains so that most individuals have a complete set of new leaves when flowering begins.

Herbivores include tapirs and howler monkeys, as well as a variety of moth larvae. One caterpillar species is particularly destructive to flowers. Larvae burrow down the style into the ovary and eat the ovules. Another species of moth oviposits on immature fruits in July. The caterpillars eat into the fruit while it is still soft and may consume the developing seeds. The seeds are readily eaten by rodents and monkeys (D. Janzen, pers. comm.).

Two other species of *Luehea* occur sympatrically with *L. candida* in Guancaste Province. *L. speciosa* Willd., "Guácimo macho," is very similar in appearance to *L. candida,* but the leaves are smaller, stiffer, and more retuse, and most individuals have a single, straight trunk. The fruits are small (3–4 cm long), with indistinct ridges. Flowers of *L. speciosa* are almost identical to those of *L. candida,* but *L. speciosa* blooms early in the dry season (November to January) (Frankie, Baker, and Opler 1974). The range within Costa Rica is more extensive than that of *L. candida. L. speciosa* reaches higher elevations (to about 1,400 m) and is found commonly in the Central Valley near Alajuela.

L. seemannii Triana and Planch, "Guácimo," grows along rivers and in wet bottomlands of Guanacaste Province, where it is one of the tallest trees in the semievergreen forest (35–40 m). The leaves are similar to those of the other two species; however, they are conspicuously olive green and shiny above the rusty brown below. Fruits are slightly smaller than those of *L. speciosa* and have prominent ridges like those of *L. candida.* The white flowers (January to March) are only 1.5–2 cm in diameter, with inconspicuous petals, and look like small, round shaving brushes because of their numerous stamens (fig. 7.73*b*). *L. seemannii* is a more characteristic element of tropical wet and moist forest life zones of the Atlantic lowlands (Puerto Viejo and Upala areas) and southern Pacific lowlands (Puntarenas to the Osa Peninsula) (Holdridge et al. 1971; Allen 1956; authors' observations). It is becoming uncommon in the dry forest because its habitat is suitable for sugarcane (Finca Taboga, Comelco Property). A few roadside examples are prominent among the Pan American Highway between Barranca and Cañas and in forest patches northwest of Barranca.

*

Allen, P. H. 1956. *The rain forests of Golfo Dulce.* Stanford: Stanford University Press.

Frankie, G. W.; Baker, H. G.; and Opler, P. A. 1974. Comparative phenological studies of trees in tropical wet and dry forests in the lowlands of Costa Rica. *J. Ecol.* 62:881–919.

Haber, W. A., and Frankie, G. W. 1982. Pollination ecology of luehea (Tiliaceae) in Costa Rican dry forest: Significance of adapted and non-adapted pollinators. *Ecology,* in press.

Holdridge, L. R.; Grenke, W. C.; Hatheway, W. H.; Liang, T.; and Tosi, J. A., Jr. 1971. *Forest environments in tropical life zones: A pilot study.* Oxford: Pergamon Press.

Standley, P. C. 1937–38. *Flora of Costa Rica.* Chicago: Field Museum of Natural History.

Lycopodium (Licopodio, Club Mosses)

J. M. Beitel

The club mosses (*Lycopodium* in the broad sense) make up one of the largest genera of pteridophytes in number of species (about sixty) in Costa Rica. The genus is very diverse in morphology, life history, life form, and habitats, and for this reason it is often broken into segregate genera. As a group, the club mosses are perennial herbs with spirally arranged leaves possessing a single vein (microphylls) and kidney-shaped sporangia borne singly in leaf axils on the upper side of the leaf. The sexual generation is notably diverse in both morphology and nutrition. The gametophytes, which germinate from the spores produced by the more familiar sporophyte generation, range from minute photosynthetic, superficial pincushions to mycorrhizal, subterranean (or epiphytic) branching rods. The latter type may be long-lived, growing for 7–10 years before producing a sporophyte.

The habitats in which club mosses are commonly found in Costa Rica are the rain forest, from lowland to cloud forest, high elevation páramolike shrub formation, and roadside banks. The rainforest species are primarily pendant epiphytes with the bases of the plants attached by a mass of roots to boughs and crotches of supporting trees. Branching is strictly dichotomous (a characteristic of most of the members of the segregate genus *Huperzia*), and plants often hang down 50–100 cm, with new branches arising throughout the year at the base of the old branches. The fertile regions may be totally undifferentiated from the sterile region as in *L. dichotomum* and *L. verticillatum* (fig. 7.74a) or modified into loose tassels as in *L. callitrichaefolium*.

The gametophytes of the epiphytic species found so far have been mycorrhizal, freely branching rods growing in the humus accumulated on limbs and in the crotches of rain-forest trees. The branching nature of the gametophyte and the small, specialized gametophytic dispersal

FIGURE 7.74. *Lycopodium. a, L. verticillatum*, an epiphytic club moss with undifferentiated fertile regions; note isodichotomous branching and new branches arising from base of plant. *b, L. reflexum*, a terrestrial club moss with isodichotomous branching and sporangia in axils of undifferentiated leaves. *c, L. thyoides*, a creeping rhizome with upright branches extremely flattened and greatly reduced leaves in four ranks. *d, L. cernuum*, a common roadside plant; note differentiated strobili at tips of drooping branches. *e, L. contiguum*, with creeping rhizome and upright branches; note sessile differentiated strobili. Costa Rica (photos, J. M. Beitel).

bodies (gemmae) probably represent the bulk of the vegetative reproduction in the epiphytic species, since the sporophyte lacks a creeping rhizome. The pendant branches do possess the potential for rooting if broken off, owing to the production of adventious roots, though this type of reproduction is rarely seen.

Approximately two-thirds of the *Lycopodium* species reported from Costa Rica are rain-forest epiphytes. They are reminiscent of orchids in that there are many species, most of which are rare. Populations are made up of scattered individuals, and large colonies or clones are rarely formed. Terrestrial species, on the other hand, are fewer in number, forming large clones through vegetative reproduction. The commonest species are those that reproduce best in disturbed situations such as roadside banks in rain-forest and cloud-forest areas.

A pantropical weed on roadside banks is the nodding club moss, *Lycopodium cernuum* (fig. 7.74d). Resembling small Christmas trees with strobili hanging from the tips of the lateral branches, the plants reproduce vegetatively, forming large clones, by aboveground stolons. The only perenniating organ is the stolon tip; the rest of the plant turns yellow and dies after spore release. The spores germinate on exposed mineral soil to form tiny green pincushionlike gametophytes (a characteristic of the segregate genus *Lycopodiella*).

The familiar staghorn club moss, *L. clavatum*, scrambles over the roadside banks, reproducing chiefly by a vigorous creeping rhizome. Sterile evergreen branches, upright and branched like deer antlers, are covered with numerous leaves, each with a long hairlike tip. The fertile leaves are aggregated into strongly differentiated strobili borne on long, naked stems, three to five on a stem. The gametophyte of *L. clavatum* is subterranean and mycorrhizal, about the size, shape, and color of a walnut meat.

The other species commonly found on moist, disturbed roadcuts is *L. reflexum* (fig. 7.74b), closely related to the epiphytic species in lacking a strongly defined rhizome and in producing new branches from the base of the old branches. Its clumps of upright evergreen branches, always forking into two equal parts, resemble clusters of bottle brushes owing to their numerous leaves and their lack of a strobilus. The only insect interaction reported so far in the genus *Lycopodium*, a genus well endowed with complex alkaloids, involves *L. reflexum* and a weevil (Coleoptera: Curculionidae: Cryptorhynchinae) in Costa Rica. The larvae of this new species of weevil burrow into the stem, causing reddish, weakened areas in the upright branches. The weevil emerges from the plant as an adult and feeds on the young leaves and growing tip of the plant.

The club mosses in the high elevation, bamboo-dominated, páramolike areas such as are found on Cerro de la Muerte form an important and conspicuous element of the herb layer. *L. clavatum* and a related species, *L. contiguum* (fig. 7.74*e*), with sessile strobili, as well as the running pine *L. thyoides,* are common. *L. thyoides* (fig. 7.74*c*) has extremely flattened upright branches, the small leaves fused in four ranks (one ventral, one dorsal, and two lateral) and strobili on long, naked stems. Although the gametophytes of *L. thyoides* have not been found, closely related species in the north temperate zone (all in the segregate genus *Diphasiastrum*) have subterranean gametophytes shaped like tiny carrots.

The diverse and taxonomically confused species related to *L. reflexum* in these high elevation areas, such as *L. hippurideum, L. erythraeum, L. crassum,* and *L. saururus,* form clumps up to 40 cm in height and 40 cm in diameter, with shoots in some up to 2 cm in diameter. Although most of the species branch evenly into two equal upright portions like *L. reflexum* and most terrestrial members of *Huperzia,* in one species of uncertain identity one of the branches of each dichotomy serves as a creeping rhizome and the other forms upright branches.

*

Beitel, J. M. 1979. Incidence of epiphytism in the lycopsids. *Am. Fern J.* 69:83–84.

Beitel, J. M., and Bruce, J. G. 1978. Snout beetle herbivory in the clubmoss *Lycopodium reflexum. Bot. Soc. Am., Misc. Ser.* 156:16 (abstr.).

Bruce, J. G., and Beitel, J. M. 1979. A community of *Lycopodium* gametophytes in Michigan. *Am. Fern J.* 69:33–41.

Ollgaard, B. 1979. Studies in Lycopodiaceae. 2. The branching patterns and infrageneric groups of *Lycopodium* sensu lato. *Am. Fern J.* 69:49–61.

Wee, Y. C. 1979. The development of plantlets from strobilus branches in *Lycopodium phlegmaria. Am. Fern J.* 69:80–82.

Macfadyena unguis-cati (Uña de Gato, Cat-claw Bignone)

A. H. Gentry

A common dry forest liana, *M. unguis-cati* is also widespread, though sporadic, in moist and wet forest. It occurs from Mexico to Argentina, a typical distributional phenomenon for wind-dispersed species.

Macfadyena unguis-cati is a "big bang" flowerer, blooming near the end of the dry season; many plants bloom at the same time, and the flowering period lasts a few days. The brilliant orangish yellow tubular-campanulate flowers are bee pollinated. The linear fruits are incredibly long, up to 100 cm or more, and have bialate wind-dispersed seeds.

"Uña del gato" is unusual in having two distinct juvenile forms. The young seedlings are erect, with a few largish opposite, simple leaves. This seedling stage (fig. 7.75) then gives rise to a wiry vine with tiny bifoliolate leaves, each leaf with a trifid tendril having hooked "cat's-claw" tips. This juvenile stage is strongly photophobic and crawls across the ground directly toward the

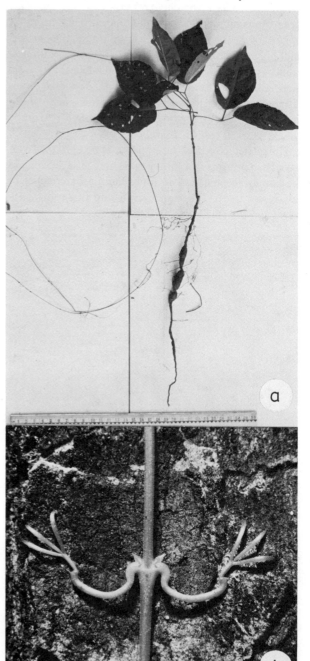

FIGURE 7.75. *Macfadyena unguis-cati. a,* Old seedling that has just put out the terminal leader that will become the climbing vine; tubers on roots become flaccid at this time (ruler is 30 cm long). *b,* Hold fast—climbing structures on small branch of mature *M. unguis-cati.* Guanacaste, Costa Rica (photos, D. H. Janzen).

nearest light-blocking object, usually a tree trunk, and then straight up that object, climbing with its cat's-claw tendrils. This juvenile form is so distinctive that it was described as a new genus, *Microbignonia*. The adult form has much larger bifoliolate leaves, usually without tendrils, and is usually more or less free hanging. The juvenile form is much more frequently encountered than the adult stage and may persist for a number of years.

Interestingly, the "big-bang" flowering strategy of *M. unguis-cati* breaks down in wet forest regions, where synchronization between different individuals, and even of flowering season, is lost. The species rarely produces seeds or seedlings in wet forest habitats even though it is perfectly capable of growing under these conditions. It has been suggested that this is an example of a species whose reproductive success and thus distribution are largely determined by the presence of a dry season cue strong enough to trigger precisely synchronized flowering.

M. unguis-cati has both diploid (2n = 40) and tetraploid (2n = 80) forms, the only case of polyploidy in its family. This is the exception that proves the rule: high chromosome numbers, rarity of polyploidy, and intrafamilial stability of chromosome number are typical not only of Bignoniaceae but of most woody tropical plants, as would be predicted for k-selected fitness specialists such as are supposed to predominate in the tropics.

The second Costa Rican species of *Macfadyena*, *M. uncata*, has a similar juvenile form and morphology, but "steady-state" flowering and thicker, water-dispersed seeds. It is restricted to swamps and streamsides in moist and wet forest habitats and also ranges from Mexico to Argentina. Until recently these two species were considered different genera because of the difference between water and wind-dispersed seeds, a good example of the fallibility of herbarium taxonomy.

Macfadyena unguis-cati is often cultivated as an ornamental in tropical or subtropical regions and in the past few years has started to become a weed along the Gulf Coast of the United States.

*

Gentry, A. H. 1974. Coevolutionary patterns in Central American Bignoniaceae. *Ann. Missouri Bot. Gard.* 61:728–59.

Mangroves (Mangles, Mangroves)

D. S. Simberloff

Mangroves (figs. 7.76, 7.77) are a group of unrelated woody plants that grow on protected tropical coasts (fig. 7.76c); they generally occur in physical habitats that in temperate regions would be occupied by salt marshes. Why mangroves do not occur in temperate zones is unknown. There are many more mangroves in tropical Asia and Australia than in the Americas (as many as sixty species in a single swamp), but in Costa Rica one commonly can see five species. "Mangrove" is not a precise taxonomic classification; generally any tree that grows directly from a subtidal or intertidal substrate may be termed a mangrove.

FIGURE 7.76 Mangroves. *a,* A five-species mangrove forest growing in the delta of the Río Térraba seaward of Palmar Sur, Costa Rica. *b,* Interior of a young Panamanian mangrove forest; note that the entire shrub layer is made up of *Acrostichum aureum. c,* Stump of dead adult *Rhizophora mangle.* Llorona, Corcovado National Park, Osa Peninsula, Costa Rica (photos, D. H. Janzen).

FIGURE 7.77. Mangroves. *a,* Pure stand of *Rhizophora mangle,* British Virgin Islands, Caribbean Sea. *b, Pelliciera rhizophorae* seedling germinating on estaurine mud bank, near Hacienda Palo Verde, Guanacaste Province, Costa Rica. *c,* Buttresses of *Pelliciera rhizophorae* at low tide (adult trees) in Boca Barranca, near Puntarenas, Costa Rica (photos, D. H. Janzen).

On the Pacific coast of Costa Rica (e.g., at Golfito) one can see the red mangrove (*Rhizophora harrisonii* = *R. brevistyla*), the tea mangrove (*Pelliciera rhizophorae*), the black mangroves (*Avicennia germinans* and *A. bicolor*), the white mangrove (*Laguncularia racemosa*), and, rarely, the buttonwood mangrove (*Conocarpus erecta*). Certain regions have only a subset of these species. For example, at Chomes both *Pelliciera* and *Conocarpus* were not seen, and at Playas del Coco only a few

small *Rhizophora* were found. On the Atlantic coast there are only four mangroves, red (*Rhizophora mangle*), black (*Avicennia germinans*), white (*Laguncularia racemosa*), and buttonwood (*Conocarpus erecta*). On both coasts one occasionally sees the fern *Acrostichum aureum* in higher areas within a mangrove swamp, and epiphytic orchids and bromeliads grow in the mangrove trees themselves.

Living in such close association with the sea has caused the evolution of unusual traits among mangroves. Some are clearly adaptive for a coastal existence; others have obscure value but, by virtue of their frequent occurrence among unrelated mangrove species and rarity elsewhere in the plant kingdom, one can deduce that they are advantageous for a marine habitat. The most obvious problems are physiological and were recognized early: "What is the reason that the sea nourishes not trees? Is it not for the same reason that it nourishes not earthly animals? For Plato, Anaxagorus, and Democritus think plants are earthly animals. Nor, though seawater be aliment to marine plants, as it is to fishes, will it therefore nourish earthly plants, since it can neither penetrate the roots, because of its grossness, nor ascend, by reason of its weight, for this among other things, shows seawater to be heavy and terrane, because it more eastly bears up ships and swimmers" (Plutarch, *Moralia,* A.D. 70). Mangroves do not *require* salt; in the laboratory, in fact, several of them grow better in fresh water than in seawater (leading to the interesting question, beyond the scope of this introduction, of why mangroves are restricted to seacoasts and not found in fresh water or on high land). There are three main ways they deal with salt: (1) toleration of higher concentrations in sap than for most plants, (2) removal by storage in older leaves before they fall, and (3) active secretion from leaves and roots. Different mangroves employ different mixes and variations of these three mechanisms. *Avicennia,* for example, concentrates salt and secretes it from leaf glands, while *Rhizophora* actively excludes it from being taken up by the roots and gets rid of what *is* taken up by leaf storage and abscission. Consequently old *Rhizophora* leaves are succulent.

Among anatomical traits the most striking feature of mangroves is the frequent occurrence of unusual root morphology. Red mangrove has aerial roots ("prop" roots) that arch from the trunk and branch into two or more roots (figs. 7.76*c,* 7.77*a*), which may themselves undergo this process; as many as seven levels of such branching may be observed. There are also "drop" roots that descend from upward of 10 m, also undergoing one or more branching episodes en route to the ground. Although such profuse and branched roots must provide support for the trees, their main function is to assist aeration. *Avicennia* does not have drop or prop roots, but its underground roots, radiating out several meters from the plant, produce slender branches called "pneumatophores" that stick up out of the ground in great number, as if they were nails on wheel spokes, and that aid in gas exchange by the roots. *Pelliciera* has buttresses that aid in aeration (fig. 7.77c). *Laguncularia* has pneumatophores similar to those of *Avicennia,* but they rarely emerge from the soil.

Finally, most mangroves have viviparous seedlings (the seed develops into a small plant while still attached to the parental tree) and water dispersal of the seedlings (propagules). Red mangrove seedlings are long and pointed and can float for at least 12 months, then implant in suitable substrate and grow. Tea mangrove seedlings, among the largest dicot seeds known, resemble heavy, sharply pointed, large onions (fig. 7.77b). White mangrove seedlings are small, lens-shaped, and buoyant by virtue of their pericarps, while black mangrove seedlings are shaped like lima beans and are about the same size. All these propagules float and will implant if they lodge in the substratum firmly enough so that waves and tides do not displace them while roots develop. White and black mangrove seedlings form roots even while they are floating.

One might expect mangroves to be zoned along a gradient with those with larger propagules seaward and those with smaller propagules landward, in the order in which they hit the substratum. This is generally true, particularly where there is a steady, pronounced elevational gradient. Where the gradient is very gradual or irregular (as at Golfito) or where currents are peculiar or heterogeneous or both, zonation is poorly expressed or absent except that the seaward fringe will usually be *Rhizophora.* Where small islands are formed offshore they are almost always *Rhizophora,* although islands very near shore or in lagoons may be *Avicennia.*

Mangrove roots constitute an important and unusual marine habitat. Sponges, oysters, tunicates, corals, barnacles, algae, and other sessile organisms commonly colonize the roots of red mangrove and, to a lesser extent, tea mangrove, although, in areas with very fine silt, settling on roots is less pronounced. Once such an "epiphytic" community exists, it is itself colonized by more mobile species—fishes, polychaetes, amphipods, isopods, crabs, lobsters, shrimps, octopi—that either feed on the attached organisms or shelter in them. Leaf fall and subsequent microbial and fungal decomposition, plus the fact that immatures of many fishes and invertebrates live there, make mangrove swamps and islands extremely important contributors to marine productivity. Their destruction in Costa Rica (e.g., at Chomes) and elsewhere always changes greatly the nature of the surrounding marine ecosystem.

Among the root dwellers, perhaps the most interesting is the wood-boring isopod *Sphaeroma terebrans,* found primarily on the margins of swamps and responsible for the many holes in *Rhizophora* prop and drop roots, making them look like Swiss cheese. These isopods kill many of the roots before they can implant in the substrate, and they have been accused both of destroying existing mangrove swamps and of preventing mangroves from further colonization. However, the branching root pattern that typifies *Rhizophora* depends critically on boring of roots, since branching is initiated *only* by damage, of which root boring by isopods is by far the most common cause *below* the water. In fact, for every root killed by boring, more than one root on average is produced by virtue of the induced branching. Furthermore, even without boring the probability that a particular root will implant in the substrate is low, because the encrusting organisms or the abrasion induced by hard substrates frequently kill it.

Although mangrove swamps typically contain far fewer species of birds than do other tropical forests, they are nonetheless interesting because of the high densities of seabirds that roost there, occasionally producing so much guano that the fertilized mangroves grow faster in spite of daily tidal flushing. Cormorants, frigate birds, pelicans, and numerous herons and egrets are all commonly found in mangrove swamps. Kingfishers, pigeons, and a variety of passerines frequently feed there, though nesting is not as common as in adjacent habitats. Other vertebrates found in the trees, particularly in the rear of swamps, are raccoons, snakes, lizards, and bats.

Insects and other arthropods, however, dominate the arboreal habitat:

We found several bogs, and swamps of salt water, upon which, and by the sides of the lagoon, grows the true mangrove, such as is found in the West Indies, and the first of the kind that we had met with. In the branches of these mangroves there were many nests of a remarkable kind of ant, that was as green as grass: when the branches were disturbed they came out in great numbers, and punished the offender by a much sharper bite than ever we had felt from the same kind of animal before. [*Lieutenant Cook's Voyage,* 1770]

The weaver ants that Cook saw in Australia are mercifully absent from New World mangroves, but their place is ably taken by various species of *Pseudomyrmex* on *Rhizophora* and *Azteca* on *Pelliciera.* Ants of many other species are found on both of these mangroves; black and white mangroves harbor fewer colonies. Other prominent mangrove ants include species of *Crematogaster, Camponotus, Paracryptocerus* (with shield-shaped heads), *Tapinoma, Xenomyrmex,* and *Monomorium.* Almost all colonies are found in hollow twigs, with larger species therefore restricted to larger hollow twigs.

More woodborers and herbivores are found on *Rhizophora* than on the other mangroves, in spite of *Rhizophora*'s high tannin content. Leaves are eaten primarily by macrolepidopteran caterpillars, fruits are bored by the host-specific scolytid beetle *Poecilips rhizophorae,* shoots are bored by moth caterpillars, roots are bored by both *Poecilips* and caterpillars (inducing branching, just as the isopods do below the water), twigs are bored by anobiid, buprestid, and cerambycid beetle larvae, and myriad other insects (thrips, crickets, termites, bugs) abound. There are also abundant spiders, millipedes, centipedes, mites, scorpions, and pseudoscorpions. Small *Rhizophora* islands have subsets of the species pool found in the swamps; the smaller or more isolated the island, the fewer the species. It is important to emphasize that there is no supratidal ground in a mangrove swamp, so that all resident species must lead some form of arboreal existence.

Special mention must be made of the mangrove tree crab, *Aratus pisonii*, that climbs to the very top of mangrove trees of all species, jumps from branch to branch when threatened, and eats mangrove leaves, primarily of red and black mangrove. It is frequently present in great abundance and may, in such dense situations, be the major herbivore of red mangrove. *Aratus* need not even come down to the water to breathe, and though it swims well and its larvae are marine, it is truly an arboreal animal. At some locations (e.g., Golfito), *Aratus* is restricted to the very tops of trees by the predatory activities of another arboreal crab, *Goniopsis pulchra*, that eats both *Aratus* and mangrove leaves. Both crab species occasionally take large insects such as crickets.

*

Chapman, V. J. 1976. *Mangrove vegetation*. Weinheim: Cramer Verlag.

Collins, J. P.; Berkelhamer, R. C.; and Mesler, M. 1977. Notes on the natural history of the mangrove *Pelliciera rhizophorae*. *Brenesia* 10/11:17–29.

Gill, A. M., and Tomlinson, P. B. 1969. Studies on the growth of red mangrove (*Rhizophora mangle* L.). I. Habit and general morphology. *Biotropica* 1:1–9.

Organization for Tropical Studies. 1979. *Tropical biology*. Course book 77-3 (pp. 223–26, 231–32, 235–46).

Rabinowitz, D. 1978. Dispersal properties of mangrove propagules. *Biotropica* 10:47–57.

Simberloff, D. S.; Brown, B. J.; and Lowrie, S. 1978. Isopod and insect root-borers may benefit Florida mangroves. *Science* 201:630–32.

Simberloff, D. S., and Wilson, E. O. 1969. Experimental zoogeography of islands. II. The colonization of empty islands. *Ecology* 50:278–95.

Manilkara zapota (Níspero, Chicle Tree)

G. S. Hartshorn

Manilkara of the Sapotaceae is an important source of timber and latex in both the Old and the New World tropics. *M. zapota* (*Achras zapota* L. is a synonym) is famous as the source of chicle, the natural base of chew-

ing gum before the advent of synthetics. The species is native from Mexico to Costa Rica. The bulk of the chicle came from the Yucatán Peninsula of Mexico and the Petén of Guatemala. Its abundance in the region is thought to be due in part to the preference of the Mayan Indians for its wood and fruit.

In Costa Rica it is a canopy tree (fig. 7.78*a*) of the tropical dry and tropical moist life zones, attaining 30 m in height and 80 cm dbh. The bark is black with narrow vertical cracks; its inner bark is pink, with copious white latex. The leaves are simple, alternate, clustered at the end of sympodially branched twigs, long-elliptic, and evergreen.

Solitary flowers (fig. 7.78*b*) are borne in the leaf axils in June (Frankie, Baker, and Opler 1974). Fruit is brown, to 4 cm long, edible, and matures in November; the one to six seeds are brown and shiny, and have a lateral scar.

M. zapota trees were tapped for chicle once every 2–3 years by making a series of ascending zigzag cuts in the

FIGURE 7.78. *Manilkara zapota. a,* Large adult that grew up in intact forest, leafless for several weeks during the rainy season near the time of flowering, July 1980. *b,* Freshly fallen flowers from the night before, June 1979. Santa Rosa National Park, Guanacaste Province, Costa Rica (photos, D. H. Janzen).

FIGURE 7.79 Lower trunk of living *Manilkara zapota* that was tapped for chicle (latex) 1960–70 (photo 1982). Santa Rosa National Park, Guanacaste, Costa Rica (photo, D. H. Janzen).

bark (fig. 7.79). Tapping scars are noticeable on some of the níspero trees along the road to Playa Naranjo in Santa Rosa National Park.

*

Frankie, G. W.; Baker, H. G.; and Opler, P. A. 1974. Comparative phenological studies of trees in tropical wet and dry forests in the lowlands of Costa Rica. *J. Ecol.* 62:881–919.

Record, S. J., and Hess, R. W. 1943. *Timbers of the New World*. New Haven: Yale University Press (pp. 495–96.)

Mimosa pigra (Zarza, Dormilona)

D. H. Janzen

This spreading, spiny mimosaceous legume shrub (to 2 m tall) (fig. 7.80*a*) once was a plant of the banks of large rivers and marsh edges, habitats similar to the contemporary roadsides and marshy spots in open pastures that it now occupies as well. It is probably much more common now than it was when the lowlands of Costa Rica were undisturbed by European man. Even in the driest parts of Guanacaste, *Mimosa pigra* is evergreen most of the year. The sites where it survives, however, are usually moister than the habitat in general. The seeds apparently are spread by road construction equipment, making the distribution probably much greater now than it was 300 years ago. At present it is largely a roadside plant, below 700 m elevation, all over Costa Rica. Since it occurs only in roadsides and nearby pastures in the San Miguel–Puerto Viejo region (Atlantic lowland foothills), it is tempting to think of it as a recent introduction to this part of Costa Rica. But there is a distinctive species of bruchid in its seeds there, and the seeds are smaller than in Guanacaste Province, implying that it is a longtime resident.

The pink, spherical, bee-pollinated inflorescences, 2 cm in diameter, last one day each and are produced continuously from June through October–November in Guanacaste. It is the only *Mimosa* that flowers in the early rainy season in Guanacaste. Each long main branch produces about one new inflorescence per day. There is a progression of new flower buds to full-sized pods down the branch. The pods are 8–15 cm long, about 1.5 cm wide, flat, and very densely covered with multicellular stiff hairs 2–4 mm long (fig. 7.80*b*). They contain eight

FIGURE 7.80. *Mimosa pigra*. *a*, Adult roadside shrub; the spreading life form is usual in fully insolated plants. *b*, Nearly mature fruits (about 10 cm long) and flowers on the same branches (June). Santa Rosa National Park, Guanacaste Province, Costa Rica (photos, D. H. Janzen).

to twenty-four seeds. When mature, the fruit fragments into indehiscent single-seeded segments, leaving behind the rim that outlines the pod margin. Pods are mature by September but continue to ripen through January in the lowlands. In evergreen forest areas, *M. pigra* remains seasonal in flower and fruit production, but some flowers and fruits can be found throughout the year.

In Guanacaste many of the seeds germinate when they are first wetted, but if 100% germination is desired, a small notch must be filed in the seed coat before moistening. In the wetter areas, the seeds seem to germinate with less delay, and large pod fragments may be found on the ground with many seedlings growing from the segments (in wet areas the pods do not fracture so neatly).

The foliage of *M. pigra* is made up of fine leaflets with many sharp, recurved spines on the undersides of the petioles, petiolets, and stems. *M. pigra* foliage has been rejected by odor by captive collared peccaries, white-tailed deer, and a tapir. Cattle and horses not browse it even when the pasture is extremely dry and food very scarce, but the leaflets are fed on by several species of chrysomelid beetles. It is becoming a serious weed, as an introduced plant, in tropical Australia.

In the moist northwestern corner of Guanacaste, north of La Cruz, the seeds of *M. pigra* are heavily preyed on by the larvae of *Acanthoscelides zebrata*. The adult bruchid lays its eggs among the hairs on the pods, and the larvae bore through the pod wall and into the seeds when full sized but not yet hard. There is one bruchid larva per seed, and it eats all of the seed content. South of La Cruz, throughout Guanacaste and Puntarenas provinces, *M. pigra* seeds are preyed on by the larvae of *Acanthoscelides pigrae* (Janzen 1980). In the area of San Miguel to Puerto Viejo, Heredia Province, the seeds are eaten by the smaller *Acanthoscelides pigricola* (Kingsolver 1980). In Costa Rica these bruchid beetles prey on no other species of seed. Immature seeds are occasionally killed by sucking Hemiptera (Pentatomidae) that puncture the green fruits.

Each *Mimosa pigra* bush seems to have a subset of the local population of adult *Acanthoscelides pigrae* or whichever species of bruchid beetle is associated with it. At dawn, just after the inflorescences have opened, the adult beetles can be found climbing about over the inflorescences, presumably eating pollen and nectar. If captured, they are replaced by another group of beetles the next morning. If this is repeated for several mornings, the number abruptly declines on the third or fourth morning; the small number that appear each subsequent morning probably represent the daily immigration input to the bush (Janzen 1975).

*

Janzen, D. H. 1975. Interactions of seeds and their insect predators/parasitoids in a tropical deciduous forest. In *Evolutionary strategies of parasitic insects and mites*, ed. P. W. Price, pp. 154–86. New York: Plenum Press.
———. 1980. Specificity of seed-attacking beetles in a Costa Rican deciduous forest. *J. Ecol.* 68:929–52.
Kingsolver, J. M. 1980. The *quadridentatus* group of *Acanthoscelides*: Descriptions of three new species, notes, synonomies, and a new name (Coleoptera: Bruchidae). *Brenesia* 17:281–94.

Monstera tenuis (Chirravaca, Mano de Tigre, Monstera)

T. Ray

The genus *Monstera* (fig. 7.81) includes about twenty-two species and is about the same size as the genus *Syngonium*. Like *Syngonium*, *Monstera* is restricted to the Neotropics and has its center of diversity in Central America. However, there is a much greater diversity of growth habits within the genus *Monstera* than within *Syngonium*.

I will begin by using the species *Monstera tenuis* (formerly *M. gigantea*) to illustrate some points. *M. tenuis* produces large infructescences, about 30 cm long, containing about one thousand fruits each. In the cacao groves at La Selva, where *M. tenuis* has attained a very high population density, the fruit is poorly dispersed. The seeds tend to fall in great density directly below the parent plant. The seeds, about 1 cm long, have no dormancy and germinate to produce a long, slender sprout, about 1 mm in diameter, with tiny bractlike leaves at the nodes, which are spaced at 6 cm intervals. These sprouts are green but have very little photosynthetic surface and so are almost entirely dependent on seed reserves. This contrasts with the *Syngonium* habit of establishing a rosette of leaves first.

The *M. tenuis* seedling is capable of reaching a length of 1 or 2 m on seed reserves. The seedlings do not produce leaves until they reach a tree; thus the seedling will die if it does not encounter a tree while on seed reserves. This not only means that a seedling must fall within 1 or 2 m of a tree if it is to survive, but also that it must grow directly toward the tree lest it waste its reserves in aimless wanderings. It is not surprising that these seeds are strongly skototropic (Strong and Ray 1975). This is strikingly displayed when the seeds fall in dense clusters around the base of a tree. The green seedlings stand out against the brown leaf litter and all point toward the tree, looking like short spokes of a wheel with the tree at the hub.

Upon reaching a tree, the seedling begins to produce small round leaves (2 cm in diameter) that are pressed flat against the tree trunk and cover the stem. Along with leaf production comes a shortening of the internodes and the

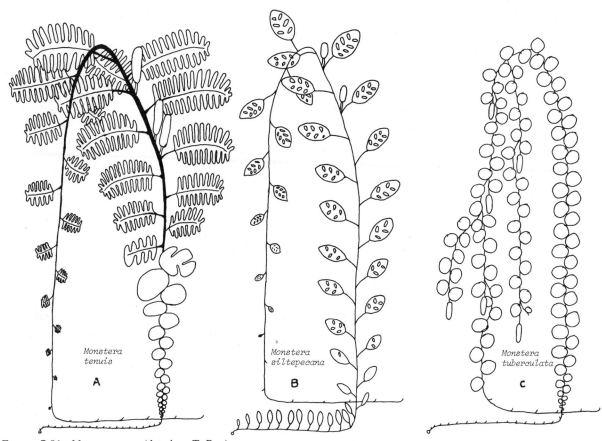

FIGURE 7.81. *Monstera* spp. (drawing, T. Ray).

beginning of stem thickening. Successive leaves will be of increasing size as the stem climbs the tree. As in *Syngonium*, the climbing stem retains the ability to switch to the leafless form and return to the ground if it reaches the top of a tree. When the successive leaves attain a diameter of about 25–30 cm, a dramatic change in leaf form occurs. The leaves develop deep clefts and become pinnatifid, having the appearance of fern fronds (fig. 7.81a). Unlike the round leaves, these are held away from the trunk of the tree on their petioles. The size of successive leaves continues to increase after the change in form, until the leaves reach a length of as much as 125 cm. At this size the petiole will be 60 cm long and the stem will be 8 cm in diameter.

As in *Syngonium*, flowering is terminal, but the branch is continued by an axillary shoot, and the stem flowers and fruits repeatedly as it climbs. Also, should the stem reach the top of the tree, even the most mature stem is capable of returning to the ground, with a change in stem form involving internode elongation and reduction of stem diameter and leaf size. In such cases the mature leaf form is retained in successively smaller leaves, even when the leaf size has been reduced well below that size

at which the change to mature leaf form occurred. By the time the hanging stem reaches the ground, the leaves will have been reduced to bracts, and the internodes will be long and slender. This resembles the leafless seedling, but on a larger scale; the internodes are longer (20 cm) and thicker (9 mm). These stems are analagous to type A_h of *Syngonium*.

The dramatic change in leaf form, from round appressed leaves to pinnatifid leaves, has atracted considerable attention. The common folklore that has arisen states that the leaves change form in response to higher light levels that the stem encounters when it climbs a tree. A simple observation should cast doubt on this hypothesis. A tree standing in an open field receives rather uniformly high insolation on the lower portion of the trunk. Yet, when *M. tenuis* grows on such a trunk, it does not switch to the mature leaf form at the base of the tree. We still see the same progression of gradually increasing leaf sizes, and the switch in form still occurs when the leaves are about 25–30 cm in diameter (Oberbauer et al. 1980). At the higher light levels, however, the increase in leaf size will occur more rapidly, so that the change in leaf form will occur lower on the trunk.

These observations can be more clearly understood if we make a distinction between changes of form induced by a change in environmental conditions and changes of form resulting from the unfolding of a developmental process. Under the strict definitions that I will use in this paper, the term heterophylly will refer only to those changes of form that are induced by some change in environmental conditions, and heteroblasty will refer to those changes that will occur even in a perfectly uniform environment. The latter are generally developmental changes that occur as the plant matures. The changes of form that occur in a climbing stem are heteroblastic changes. The stem need not encounter higher light levels as it climbs. Light may affect the rate at which the changes occur, but it does not affect their nature.

Thus we may consider *M. tenuis* to be composed of three heteroblastic series: the leafless seedling, the climbing stem, and the descending stem and ground runner. Switching between these three forms is stimulated by gaining or losing contact with a tree trunk. Thus the change in form from the leafless seedling to the leafy climber may be considered heterophyllic change, since it is induced by a change in the environment—contact with a tree. This change in form will not occur in a uniform environment.

A heteroblastic series is essentially an ontogenetic pathway. In some cases the end form is reached quite rapidly, after which the form no longer changes. When the *M. tenuis* seed germinates, for example, there is a short series of segments with increasing internode length, after which there is no further change. In other cases there will be a cycling of forms. Form A of *Syngonium* for example, alternates between forms T_1 and T_2. To sum up, changes in form need not be interpreted as a response to changes in environmental conditions. They may be ontogenetic changes that will occur even in a uniform environment, though the rate of change may be affected by environmental factors.

The most significant differences between the growth habit of *M. tenuis* and that of *Syngonium* is that the *M. tenuis* seedling does not make leaves until it reaches a tree. However, there are species of *Monstera* that make leaves before reaching a tree. But, unlike *Syngonium,* the leaves are more or less evenly spaced along the stem (fig. 7.81b) rather than clumped into rosettes alternating with "leafless" stems.

There are additional species of *Monstera* that exhibit yet another variation in growth habit. In some species the pendant stems do not go through the reduction in leaf size and internode diameter characteristic of *Syngonium,* but continue to produce leaves, and even fruit, while descending to the ground. In *M. tuberculata* (fig. 7.81c) flowering occurs only in pendant stems. The various growth habits found in *Monstera* have been described by

Michael Madison (1977) in his revision of the genus. The work includes an excellent key to the species, as well as photographs of each species.

*

Madison, M. 1977. A revision of *Monstera* (Araceae). *Contrib. Gray Herb. Harvard Univ.,* no. 207.

Oberbauer, S.; Boring, L.; Herman, K.; Lodge, D.; Ray, T.; and Trombulak, S. 1980. Leaf morphology of *Monstera tenuis.* In *Tropical biology: An ecological approach,* no. 79.1, pp. 24–28. Ciudad Universitaria: Organization for Tropical Studies.

Strong, D. R., and Ray, T. S. 1975. Host tree location behavior of a tropical vine (*Monstera gigantea*) by skototropism. *Science* 190:804–6.

Mora megistosperma (Alcornoque, Mora)

D. H. Janzen

This large, cesalpinaceous legume tree (= *Mora oleifera*) grows immediately behind the mangroves on the Golfo Dulce and in postmangrove habitats on the sides of the Osa Peninsula facing the Pacific Ocean. It has been studied only in Corcovado National Park, but other species of *Mora* have been studied in northern South America (Rankin 1978). It may also be found as a riverbank tree (fig. 7.82a) in estuarine areas free of mangroves (e.g., Boca Sirena, southern Corcovado National Park). The largest adults have a dbh of 2–4 m, but these plants almost always have the tops snapped off 5–10 m above the ground and are hollow (they stump sprout heavily from the stump top). More normal-appearing trees occur in nearly pure stands, and large reproductives may attain a height of 30–45 m and be 1–2 m in diameter just above the buttresses. The bole is straight and cylindrical but covered with knobs from which small adventitious shoots are persistently produced even in heavy shade.

The leaves normally have four large opposite leaflets. In late November they all turn yellow and drop, leaving the trees synchronously leafless for 1–2 weeks. The new leaves are very bright green when first produced.

The 8–12 cm long "catkin" of tiny, white flowers is produced in May. A large flower crop would be five hundred inflorescences (one hundred to three hundred flowers per inflorescence). Only a small fraction of these are open on the tree on any given day. They are presumably pollinated by moths at night or by miscellaneous small insects during the day. As many as fifteen tiny fruits may be set per inflorescence, but most are quickly shed. By August each tree has a small crop of enormous brown fruits. A large tree with a fully insolated crown (isolated on a riverbank) may bear up to five hundred, but in intact

FIGURE 7.82. *Mora megistosperma. a,* Pure stand of very young adults (flowering but rarely setting fruit) at the edge of the Río Sirena estuary at high tide (shrubby understory is a pure stand of *Tabebuia palustris*). *b,* Nearly mature single-seeded fruit and old but living leaflets; undeveloped and soon-to-be-shed small fruits are also present on the infrutescence (August 1980). Sirena, Corcovado National Park, Osa Peninsula, Costa Rica (photos, D. H. Janzen).

forest the mean crop size for large trees is twenty to thirty fruits. At least 99% of the fruits contain only one seed.

The fruits (fig. 7.82*b*) dehisce and drop the black brown, smooth seeds in late August and September (Corcovado). Mature seeds weigh 300–1,000 g ($N = 126$, $\bar{x} = 526$ g, s.d. $= 168$ g) and are about 45% water. They have an air space inside and are floated by the highest tides for dispersal. In late August and September seeds are common in ocean beach drift near the mouths of rivers that have *Mora* forest behind their estuarine mangroves. The seeds germinate during the month following dispersal and produce seedlings 1–2 m tall in the first 2–4 months. The seedlings then remain about this height for a least 3 years. The cotyledons or their remains are present at the base of the seedlings for at least 3 years.

There is no sign of predispersal seed or fruit predation. On the ground in *Mora* forest, the only biotic damage to juveniles is caused when tapirs enter the swamp and browse off the seedling tops 15–50 cm above the ground. The same happens if the seeds are planted in mixed, upland forest. In upland forest the cotyledons may also be partly eaten by unidentified rodents (probably agoutis or pacas).

When the leaves are very new they contain the same amount of tannin (very high, 23% dry weight) as they do when middle-aged and senescent (newly fallen). Notwithstanding, the new pale green leaves on large trees are eaten by the larvae of two species of moths and the larvae of a pierid butterfly (*Phoebis* sp.). During the rest of the year the leaves are very nearly free of insect damage but suffer necrotic fungus (?) damage. *Mora* heartwood, bark, and leaves are the richest part of the adult plant for tannins (18–30% dry weight). However, the embryo of the seedling contains as much as 40% dry weight condensed tannin (P. Waterman, pers. comm.).

The roots of seedlings do not have nodules, but the roots of adults form a dense mat that appears mycorrhizal.

*

Rankin, J. M. 1978. The influence of seed predation and plant competition on tree species abundances in two adjacent tropical rainforest communities in Trinidad, West Indies. Ph.D. thesis, University of Michigan.

Ochroma lagopus (Balsa)

J. L. Whitmore

Ochroma lagopus is a very common, extremely fast growing pioneer species (fig. 7.83*a*), the source of the lightest of commercial woods. The natural range extends from Bolivia to southern Mexico, the West Indies, and (according to one source) the southern tip of Florida. A common invader of disturbed areas, it is also occasionally found as a component of mature forests, and it can occur in pure stands.

The early nomenclature of this taxon is complicated by the inability to establish priority between *O. lagopus* Sw. and *O. pyrimidale* (Cav.) Urban. Whitmore and Hartshorn (1969) follow Pierce's (1942) suggestion of maintaining *O. lagopus* Sw. and reducing *O. pyrimidale* (Caf.) Urban to synonymy under it, since the priority is uncertain, since Urban's combination was based on a mistaken date, and since *O. lagopus* is widely used in commercial literature. However, Robyns (1964) expresses a different opinion, as do Little and Wadsworth (1964).

The literature claims a dozen or so species of *Ochroma,* although the tendency is now to consider the genus monotypic. There may well be several populations that differ at the varietal level throughout the extensive range of the genus.

Costa Rican populations of balsa flower in December–January (Frankie, Baker, and Opler 1974) and are pollinated by bats. Balsa trees are often precocious, initiating flowering when only 3–4 years old. The solitary flowers (fig. 7.83*b*) are hermaphrodite, 4–11 cm long, erect, whitish, and fleshy, with five petals. The fruit is an elongate capsule, five-valved, black and glabrous before opening, 16–25 cm long. Its interior is lanate. Upon ripening and dehiscing (January–March in Costa Rica) the fruit (fig. 7.83*c*) resembles a rabbit's foot, thus the name "lagopus." Seeds are numerous, about five mm in diameter, and attached to long hairs that carry them great distances. The light brown kapok is used for filling mattresses and pillows (Robyns 1964).

Balsa seed can be wind-carried for great distances, is reputed to remain viable in the soil for years, and may then germinate after a burn or a clearning occurs. The result can be a tree 2–5 m tall after the first year, up to 10 m after the second, and perhaps 30 m after 6–10 years. In Ecuador's Guayas River basin, where more than 95% of the world's commercial balsa wood is cut, trees 5–7 years old are harvested.

Older trees develop a property called "water heart," considered commercially to be a defect. An increment borer sample of an older balsa will demonstrate a waterlogged, dark red brown heartwood that is the "water heart." This apparently coincides with the development of a taproot and indicates to a logger that the tree's wood is denser than desired for commercial purposes (Whitmore 1968). In extreme cases, water will actually gush out of the hole when the borer sample is removed.

Balsa is native to humid lowland tropical and subtropical areas, rarely above 1,000 m, and in dry areas it grows only in riparian situations. It usually is found in mixed stands in association with other pioneer species such as *Cecropia* spp. and *Trema micrantha.* As is true of many other tropical tree species, balsa exhibits no distinct growth increment rings in its cross section. Age determination therefore is a major problem in any study of balsa.

The word "balsa" is the Spanish equivalent of "raft," which for centuries was the main use for the balsa tree. During the early part of the twentieth century other uses were found: hydroplane pontoons, mine floats, streamlining for struts and braces of airplanes, and insulation products, for example. During World War II the demand rose sharply, and both United Fruit and International Balsa Corporation established large balsa plantations near Guácimo, Costa Rica, which were abandoned after the war. Recently the demand has risen again. It seems that supertankers develop static charges owing to wave action. This causes explosions that can be prevented by using balsa liners as insulation.

Ochroma lagopus is a tree up to 30 m tall and at times well over 1 m dbh (at Playa Dominicál in Costa Rica, for example), sometimes buttressed slightly, with smooth gray bark and with large leaves forming a distinctive monolayer (sensu Horn). The leaves are simple and alternate, with broadly ovate stipules. The blade is cordate and palminerved, occasionally with two slight lobes near the apex and with tufted hairs.

*

Frankie, G. W.; Baker, H. G.; and Opler, P. A. 1974. Comparative phenological studies of trees in tropical wet and dry forests in the lowlands of Costa Rica. *J. Ecol.* 62:881–919.

Little, E. L., Jr., and Wadsworth, F. H. 1964. *Common trees of Puerto Rico and the Virgin Islands.* Agricultural Handbook no. 249. Washington, D.C.: USDA–Forest Service.

Pierce, J. H. 1942. The nomenclature of balsa wood (*Ochroma*). *Trop. Woods* 69:1–2.

Robyns, A. 1964. Bombacaceae. In Flora of Panama, ed. R. E. Woodson, Jr., and R. W. Schery. *Ann. Missouri Bot. Gard.* 51:64–67.

Whitmore, J. L. 1968. Density variation in the wood of Costa Rican balsa. School of Natural Resources master's thesis. University of Michigan. (See also *Wood Sci.* 5 (1973):223–29.)

Whitmore, J. L., and Hartshorn, G. S. 1969. *Literature review of common tropical trees.* Contribution no. 8. Seattle: University of Washington, College of Forest Resources.

Orchidaceae (Orquídeas, Orchids)

K. S. Walter

The Orchidaceae are the largest family of flowering plants; they represent one line of evolution within the monocotyledons, being related to, although not derived from, the Burmanniaceae, Corsiaceae, Geosiridaceae, Iridaceae, and, perhaps more closely, the Liliaceae. There are some twenty thousand to thirty thousand species. Although native to every major land mass except Antarctica, orchids reach by far their greatest diversity and development as tropical epiphytes. Malaysia and northern South America represent two major centers of diversity for this family.

Vegetative and especially reproductive diversity within this vast assemblage is unparalled by any other plant family. Plants range in size from less than 1 cm when in full flower (*Platystele jungermannioides* from southern Central America including Costa Rica) to upright herbs

FIGURE 7.83. *Ochroma lagopus. a,* Seedling several months old on gravel bar. Corcovado National Park, Osa Peninsula, Costa Rica. *b,* Flower with dehisced anthers. Finca La Pacifica, near Cañas, Guanacaste Province, Costa Rica. *c,* Intact central portion of a ripe fruit after valves have been shed; the seeds are imbedded in the hairs. Corcovado National Park (photos, D. H. Janzen).

7.7 m tall (*Grammatophyllum speciosum* from Malaysia). Some orchid vines may reach 30 m in length. Flower size and shape vary to such an extent that the general biologist sometimes fails to recognize many of them as orchid flowers. The pollinator spectrum includes (in order of decreasing importance) bees, flies, moths, butterflies, wasps, birds, and beetles; wind, water, and bat pollination are unreported for this family.

No single character separates all orchids from all other plant families. However, *most* orchids can be characterized as follows: relatively long-lived perennial, herbaceous, mycorrhizal plants bearing zygomorphic, usually resupinate, flowers composed of three sepals, three petals (one of which is variously modified to form the lip or labellum), and, most important, a fusion production of male and female tissues (called the column) that is composed of one (seldom two) fertile anther(s) and three fused styles and stigmata; upon pollination and fertilization, the inferior ovary producing a one-locular (seldom three-locular) capsule that dehisces at maturity to release numerous minute wind-dispersed seeds lacking endosperm. Although many groups are only poorly known cytologically, the family seems to show a high degree of polyploidy.

COSTA RICA'S ORCHIDS

Costa Rica has an especially rich orchid flora, the richest in Central America (Dressler 1981). The Orchidaceae form the largest angiosperm family in the country, with over 1,100 species in some 125 to 130 genera reported; it is certain that many more species await discovery. Some of these will be new to science (e.g., see Luer 1979); others will represent range extensions from neighboring countries.

Orchids can be found in Costa Rica from sea level (*Brassavola nodosa* and *Bletia purpurea* grow within the zone of salt spray) to over 3,500 m in Chirripo (*Malaxis soulei, Telipogon monticola*). However, they reach their greatest diversity at mid elevations (ca. 800–2,000 m) as humid forest epiphytes. On the Cerro de la Muerte (ca. 2,500 m) and in other localities, *Epidendrum exasperatum* plants may grow more than 3.5 m tall. Flower size ranges from less than 1 mm across (*Platystele jungermannioides*) to more than 25 cm (*Sobralia macrantha,* whose flowers last only one day). Another native, *Phragmipedium caudatum,* has pendant petals that can reach more than 50 cm long.

An estimated 12% of Costa Rica's orchids are terrestrial; the remaining 88% are epiphytic (those species growing on rocks are here grouped with the epiphytes). Often the same species may be found terrestrially or epiphytically depending upon the growth conditions; however, "normal" epiphytes are encountered growing on the ground more often than "normal" terrestrials are found up in the trees. No orchids grow as free-floating aquatics, although many species of *Spiranthes* and *Habe-*

283

naria occur as emergents from seasonal pools. The four species of *Vanilla* (fig. 7.91*f*) in Costa Rica are succulent vines.

MYCORRHIZAL ASSOCIATIONS AND NUTRITION

In nature, all orchids studied to date have proved to be mycorrhizal, at least during seed germination and seedling establishment. This mycorrhizal association usually lasts throughout the life of the plant, so to label mature orchids "autotrophs" may be somewhat misleading; however, some orchids have been shown to lose their fungal symbionts as they mature. It appears that the fungal partner does little for the adult orchid plant, although more data are needed here. Plants raised from asymbiotically sown seed on nutrient agar media presumably lack mycorrhizae entirely; such horticulturally grown plants appear to grow and function the same as do their wild-grown counterparts.

Virtually no work has yet been reported on the mycorrhizal associates of Costa Rican orchids, but in other parts of the world little specificity has been shown between fungus and plant, in spite of what is often stated (Hadley 1970). The fungal symbionts (endomycorrhizal basidiomycetes) are apparently controlled by the plant's production of phytoalexins. An excellent review of orchid mycorrhizae is given in Burgeff (1959).

One of the Spanish common names for epiphytic orchids is parásitos, and it has been suggested (see Cook 1926; Ruinen 1953; Benzing and Seemann 1978) that certain leafless orchid epiphytes may be partly parasitic on their host. This phenomenon of "epiphytosis" in which the host tree gradually declines under epiphytic loads is most visible with *Campylocentrum* (fig. 7.89*e*) and other leafless, supposedly autotrophic, genera (photosynthesis is carried on by the roots and highly reduced stems). If this is true, it can only be via the fungal symbiont, since no organic connections between orchid and host have been demonstrated. At least some orchid symbionts can, in certain cases, be pathogenic (Sanford 1974), so it is not unlikely that these fungi might adversely affect the host tree. However, to call these orchids parasites is unjustified, at least in light of present data. Examples of terrestrial orchids "parasitizing" nearby trees through their fungal partners are given by Sanford (1974, p. 32).

ORCHID HABITATS AND PLANT ADAPTATIONS

Certain orchid species tend to occur together under particular environmental regimes, but the correlation is often not particularly strong: expected species may be absent, or unexpected species may be present in certain circumstances. Thus, orchids tend not to be good indicator species.

General abiotic factors in determining the orchid species composition of a habitat (or series of microhabitats) include temperature (several of Costa Rica's orchids, both terrestrial and epiphytic, can withstand subfreezing temperatures), precipitation, insolation (some orchids only grow on dark forest floors; others need the intense insolation of the unshaded sun in order to flower), pH of the substrate, and nutrient availability. Biotic factors include mycorrhizal relationships; competition with other plants for light, water, nutrients, and pollinators; and chemical competition via allelopathic exudates. These factors apply to both terrestrial and epiphytic species, although to varying degrees.

Terrestrial orchids are "unusual" today in the tropics, although the family is almost certainly primitively terrestrial. The roots of terrestrial orchids often have root hairs (lacking in most epiphytes) and may be invested with a thin velamen (layer[s] of absorptive and protective dead cells). Often these roots swell up into tuberoids (underground storage organs), while the aboveground parts tend to be thin-textured and ephemeral. Stems are relatively flexible and are generally not swollen into pseudobulbs (thickened water and food storage organs). The leaves are often replaced each year. Inflorescences are often scapose (on a leafless stalk), the flowers generally numerous but small. Flowers are most often white or green (exceptions such as the scarlet *Stenorrhynchos navarrensis* and *S. speciosa* exist). Pollination of terrestrial orchids is not well documented but seems to be relatively unspectacular. Important terrestrial genera in Costa Rica include *Cranichis, Erythrodes, Goodyera, Govenia, Habenaria* (fig. 7.85*d,e*), *Liparis, Malaxis* (fig. 7.85*c,f*), *Ponthieva, Spiranthes* (fig. 7.85*b*), and *Stenorrhynchos* (fig. 7.85*a*). Although terrestrial orchids range from near sea level to 3,000 m elevation in Costa Rica, few species occur below 1,000 m; the greatest numbers are found between 1,200 m and 2,000 m. Some of these plants are found in disturbed areas, but most are native to moist, undisturbed forests.

Epiphytic orchids are much more numerous both in number of species and in number of individuals; they occupy a wider diversity of habitats, and they show a far greater diversity than is true of terrestrial orchids in Costa Rica. Roots are covered with velamen, and plants growing in more exposed habitats tending to have thicker velamen layers. Stems are often swollen into one- to many-noded pseudobulbs. Leaves tend to have a thicker cuticle than do those of terrestrial species, and, especially in those species lacking pseudobulbs (e.g., *Masdevallia, Pleurothallis, Stelis*), are fleshy and capable of water storage; stomates are often sunken. A few epiphytic genera (e.g., *Catasetum, Cycnoches, Gongora, Mormodes*) native to seasonally dry areas such as Guanacaste Province have thin-textured, deciduous leaves. Crassulacean acid and C_4 metabolism have been reported for some epiphytic orchids (Neales and Hew 1975; Sanders 1979). Inflorescence types and flowers are extremely variable, and bizarre and often highly specific pollination mechanisms may be present.

Nutrient input, often a limiting factor for epiphytes, may be augmented by certain morphological modifications. Several orchids (e.g., some species of *Catasetum*, *Oncidium*, and *Schomburgkia*) have two types of roots: (*a*) those that are tightly appressed to the substrate and attach the plant to its host; and (*b*) those that stick out into the air away from the host. These thinner, upward-pointing roots form a sort of basket and apparently serve to collect leaf litter and other humus-producing (and mineral-releasing) materials. Other autotrophic epiphytes are associated with ants. Examples include some species of *Coryanthes*, *Laelia*, and *Schomburgkia*. Many of these plants have hollow pseudobulbs that are utilized by the ants (*Camponotus*, *Crematogaster*, *Azteca*, and other genera) as nests. These well-protected plants presumably also benefit from the accumulated detritus and frass from these ant colonies.

Moisture absorption and retention are critical factors in the distribution patterns of epiphytic orchids. Holttum (1960) states that the greatest numbers of epiphytic species are found in areas with at least 250 mm of rain annually with no month receiving less than an average of 5–7.5 mm. Actual precipitation is not as important as atmospheric humidity such as mists and clouds, since the velamen layer can take up water from moisture in the air as well as from dew and condensation (Barthlott 1976).

The evenness of this moisture is of special importance. The greatest diversity of orchid species is found in forests that receive a year-round supply of moisture. Seasonally deciduous forests such as those found in Guanacaste Province support a much poorer orchid flora; the same is true for those rain forests that are contantly dripping wet, like those around Guápiles.

On a given tree, one often finds a gradient from thinner-leaved, nonspeudobulbous species growing down in protected crotches of moss-covered trunks to thicker-leaved, pseudobulbous orchids growing in exposed positions in the canopy; these more xerophytic species tend also to be slower growing.

Little is known about host tree specificity. However, some species (such as *Citrus* spp.) are known to be "good" hosts, while others are not. Dunsterville (1961) records forty-seven orchid species growing on a single tree (species not given) in Venezuela. Several factors influence these distributional patterns of epiphytes. Bark exudates and leachates have been shown by Frei (1973*a*, *b*) to have a strong effect on orchid seed germination; the

pH of these compounds can also affect seed germination and seedling establishment. Bark surface texture is another consideration; smooth-barked species, especially those whose bark is periodically sloughed off, are relatively poor orchid hosts. It is often stated that "bromeliad trees" are not good "orchid trees" and vice versa. Whether this is due to chemical factors of bark composition and allelopathic compounds secreted by other epiphytes, to microhabitat succession on the host tree, or to environmental factors such as exposure and moisture availability is not clear. Epiphytic orchids must compete with bromeliads, ferns, bryophytes (especially mosses), lichens, and, to a lesser extent, with aroids and gesneriads for water, nutrients, and sunlight.

FLORAL STRUCTURE

The three sepals of the orchid flower are generally similar in size and shape (fig. 7.84). The two lateral petals are similar to one another and may be either larger or smaller than the sepals. The third, median, petal is modified into a distinct (usually larger) structure called a lip or labellum that functions as a landing platform, an orientation device, or both. In bud, the lip is uppermost (i.e., closest to the inflorescence stalk), but it is generally brought into the lowermost position by the time the flower opens; this process, known as resupination, involves twisting of the inferior ovary, bending of the inflorescence stalk, or both.

The central portion of the orchid flower is composed of a complex fusion product of male and female tissues called the column or gynandrium. All but two of Costa Rica's native orchids have a single fertile anther (the other species have two fertile anthers and one sterile anther), borne at the apex of the column on the side away from the lip (although the anther is often bent at a right angle to the column, bringing it closer to the lip). Proximal to the terminal anther is a sunken sticky area, the stigma; this stigmatic surface faces the lip. The anther contains two to eight pollen masses, or pollinia; these pollinia may be soft and easily separated as in *Habenaria* (fig. 7.84*c*) or very hard and waxy as in *Oncidium*. Pollinia usually have a projecting tip, or caudicle, composed of an elastic matrix in which may be embedded nonviable pollen grains. The caudicles may attach the pollinia to the visitor directly, or they may themselves be attached to a nonsticky strap of columnar tissue called the stipe. A specialized projecting portion of the stigma, called the rostellum, serves to glue the caudicles or stipe to the visitor. In highly specialized orchids (as in *Catasetum*, *Maxillaria*, and *Oncidium*), a sticky pad (the viscidium, derived from the rostellum) is detached as a unit with the pollinia. The entire unit of pollinia and associated structures (stipe and/or viscidium) is called a pollinarium.

PLANTS

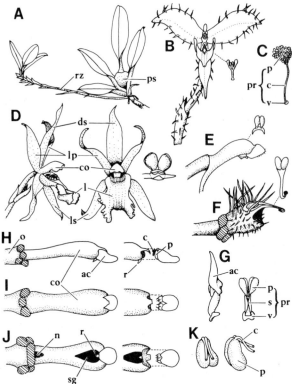

FIGURE 7.84. *a, Maxillaria wrightii* showing rhizome (*rz*)
and pseudobulb (*ps*). *b, Ponthieva diptera,* a nonresupinate
flower. *c,* Pollinarium (*p*), elongate caudicle (*c*), and small
circular viscidium (*v*). *d, Chondrorhyncha aromatica,* showing flower parts, and the pollinarium removed on a needle;
co = column; *ds* = dorsal sepal; *l* = lip; *lp* = lateral petals;
ls = lateral sepals. *e,* Side view of the column of *Maxillaria
reichenheimii,* showing the elongate column foot and sickle-
shaped viscidium. *f,* Side view of the column of *Telipogon*
sp. showing the projecting rostellum, sunken stigmatic area,
and pollinarium. *g,* Pollinarium (*pr*) of *Catasetum maculatum,* showing the anther cap (*ac*), pollinium (*p*), stipe
(*s*), and viscidium (*v*). *h–j,* Column of *Cattleya skinneri*
showing anther cap (*ac*), caudicles (*c*), column (*co*), opening to internal nectary (*n*), inferior ovary (*o*), pollinia (*p*),
rostellum (*r*), and sunken stigmatic area (*sg*). *h,* = side
view; *i,* = view from above; *j,* = view from below (i.e.,
from the lip side). *k,* Pollinia (*p*) of *Cattleya skinneri*
with caudicles (*c*). (Magnifications various) (photos,
K. S. Walter).

REPRODUCTION AND DISPERSAL

The specificity of orchid pollination is often given as a
prime example of coevolution, for in extreme cases (e.g.,
Catasetum, Coryanthes, Ophrys, Stanhopea) it is bizarre
and sometimes hard to believe (see Darwin 1862 and van
der Pijl and Dodson 1966 for examples). However, we
really know very little about the pollination systems of
most of the family, and while a one species of pollinator/
one species of orchid correlation holds for many orchids,

it certainly is less specific in other orchid groups (notably
temperate and tropical terrestrials).

Sympatric species are generally not reproductively isolated through physiological means as is usually the case
in other plants; rather, the isolation is brought about
through ethologic and morphologic adaptations. Different pollinators may be attracted to different species on the
basis of specific combinations of odor compounds (Dodson 1970; Dodson et al. 1969; Dodson and Hills 1966;
Hills et al. 1972; Walter, n.d.). Such specific relationships between plant and pollinator usually involve, in the
Neotropics, *Euglossa, Eulaema,* and *Eufriesia* (Apidae:
Euglossini). In other cases, morphologic configurations
of the flowers are such that a single insect cannot effect
hybridization even if it does visit both species. Sympatric
species may "utilize" the same insect visitor without
hybridization because each orchid species attaches its
pollinarium to a specific portion of the insect's body; up
to thirteen such locations have been shown for a single
bee species (Dressler 1968).

Species may also avoid hybridization through phenological separation as in the March-flowering *Cattleya skinneri* (Costa Rica's national flower) and the closely related
October-flowering *C. patinii.* Synchronization of
flowering over large areas is shown by some species of
Sobralia (fig. 7.91*d*); on certain days, nearly all plants of
a particular species will be in flower. Such gregarious
flowering may be offset by several days between sympatric species, but since these flowers generally last only
one day, the chances of hybridization are slim.

There is no single peak period for orchid flowering in
Costa Rica. Depending upon the locality, the beginning
of the dry season (especially in the very wet rain forests)
or the beginning of the wet season may be particularly
favorable times.

Outcrossing is favored by the pollination mechanisms
employed by most orchids. In certain cases it is assured
by means of unisexuality (e.g., *Catasetum, Cycnoches*)
or functional dichogamy (in *Orchis, Stanhopea, Vanda,*
and many other genera, the pollinarium must undergo a
reorientation of the stipe or caudicles or both before the
pollinia are correctly positioned to be inserted in the
stigmatic area, during which time the would-be pollinator
would likely have left the original inflorescence and have
flown to another).

The extreme specializations shown by most orchids
to promote outcrossing notwithstanding, some species
(approximately 3% of the family) are regularly self-
pollinating. These autogamous individuals lose their genetic variability but are freed from their dependence upon
the often rare and erratic visits of animals. Autogamy can
involve either chasmogamous (open) (as in *Masdevallia
walteri,* fig. 7.78*c*) or cleistogamous (closed) flowers (as
in *Cattleya aurantiaca,* which produces both open-

286

flowered, outcrossing plants and closed-flowered, autogamous plants).

Orchid pollen is nearly always clumped into pollinia and is thus unavailable to flower visitors as a food source. In its place, nectar, lipids, ethereal oils (fragrance compounds), and wax bodies are offered as a reward. A great many orchids, however, offer no rewards and thus attract visitors through deceit. Mimicry of nectar-producing flowers is reported in several orchid genera. Sexual mimicry is also well known in European (*Ophrys*) and Australian (*Cryptostylis*) genera. A similar phenomenon is hypothesized for the Neotropical genera *Telipogon* (fig. 7.91e) and *Trigonidium,* but field observations are lacking as yet.

Some orchid flowers last a single day (e.g., *Fregea amabilis,* many *Sobralia* species), while others may last several weeks if they are not pollinated. Upon pollination, a rather rapid series of physiological changes takes place, including a cessation of odor production, a withering of the sepals and petals, and (often) a swelling of the column to cover the stigmatic surface. Pollen tubes may take several days to several months to reach the ovary, during which time the ovules are formed (they are not present before pollination). Fertilization is followed by capsule maturation and dehiscence. The seeds are minute but very numerous (3.7 million seeds have been recorded from a single fruit of the Central American *Cycnoches chlorochilon*). These seeds generally lack endosperm and have an undeveloped embryo surrounded by a loose-fitting seed coat.

Dispersal is by air, although water may be effective in some cases. Published reports are contradictory, but cool, desiccated orchid seeds seem able to remain viable for long periods of time, so that dispersal over several hundreds or thousands of miles is at least theoretically possible.

HYBRIDIZATION

Hybridization in nature is rare, but many examples exist, even between genera. As noted above, most reproductive isolation is via prepollination mechanisms and does not involve postpollination incompatibilities, so that when habitats are disturbed and previously separated species are thrown together, hybrids and hybrid swarms may result. Introgression undoubtedly has occurred in many of the taxonomically "messy" groups such as the *Stanhopea wardii/S. oculata* complex (fig. 7.90d) and the *Epidendrum paniculatum* complex (fig. 7.86g).

Artificial hybridization has been attempted more intensively in the orchids than in any other plant group. Since 1856, when the first artificial orchid hybrid bloomed, more than fifty-three thousand artificial crosses have been registered. Some of these crosses involve five distinct genera in their parentage.

BIOLOGICAL PRINCIPLES AND THE IMPORTANCE OF ORCHIDS IN COSTA RICA

Most general biologists, especially temperate scientists in Costa Rica for only a short time, completely avoid the family, thinking it is too numerous, too difficult, or too "weird"; and yet orchids offer a virtually endless supply of biological problems to attack.

We know extremely little about mycorrhizal associations in Neotropical orchids; likewise, we know virtually nothing about host specificity and competitive interactions. Possible dormancy before seed germination and the whole area of seedling establishment are both *terra incognita.* Seed dispersal distances and rates are at present only guessed at. Even though many papers and books have been written on orchid pollination, we really know very little about this most important part of the life cycle. Nor do we understand why so many orchids occur in widely dispersed, isolated colonies, while a few (such as *Epidendrum radicans*) grow as weeds over large areas. And what is a workable definition of species (and of genus) in the orchids?

Perhaps most important, we do not understand how and why there are so many orchids in the world. Why should this family have "exploded" evolutionarily into some twenty thousand to thirty thousand species when its critical dependence upon specific interactions with fungi, other plants, and animals seems to argue against success? Many factors are undoubtedly at work (fig. 7.92), but we are far from understanding the subtle interactions between them. There is much to be done and little time in which to do it.

APPENDIX: NOTEWORTHY ORCHID GENERA OF COSTA RICA AND THEIR SUPERFICIAL FIELD CHARACTERS

Note: This is not intended as a field key or field guide to the orchids of Costa Rica; such a work is being prepared for publication elsewhere. What follows is a listing of the orchid genera most commonly encountered in Costa Rica, along with some superficial distinguishing characters. Not all members of these genera will "fit" these descriptions (this is especially true in large genera such as *Epidendrum* and *Pleurothallis*), and in other cases closely related genera not described herein will seem to "fit" some of these descriptions.

Spiranthes (fig. 7.85b): terrestrial; roots clustered, swollen; stems erect, leafy, leaves commonly petiolate and spotted or striped; inflorescences terminal, spiraled; flowers generally small, often white or greenish, often with a prominent "chin" (formed by a nectary that is united to the ovary); pollinia four, soft; stipe absent, viscidium present; about twenty-three taxa in Costa Rica; all elevations. (A taxonomic nightmare—some authors

FIGURE 7.85. *a, Stenorrhynchos navarrensis. b, Spiranthes* sp. *c, Malaxis tipuloides. d, Habenaria monorrhiza. e, Habenaria lankesteni* (?). *f, Malaxis parthonii. g, Maxillaria wrightii. h, Maxillaria variabilis* (photos, K. S. Walter).

lump this group into one polymorphic genus, *Spiranthes;* others split it into more than twenty different genera.)

Habenaria (fig. 7.85*d,e*): terrestrial; oblong root-stem tuberoids present; stems unbranched, upright; leaves cauline (along the stem) or at the base, relatively thin-textured; inflorescences terminal, racemose; flowers small to medium; dorsal (uppermost) sepal often forming a hood over the column; lip basally extended into a distinct nectar spur; column short, the single anther split into two distinct projecting arms, each locule producing one soft pollinium that is attached to a distinct viscidium; about eighteen taxa in Costa Rica, low to mid elevations.

Malaxis (fig. 7.85*c,f*): terrestrial, stems basally swollen into corms; leaves fleshy but flexible, often paired halfway up stem; inflorescence terminal, either flat-topped or elongate, few- to many-flowered; flowers small, resupinate or not, often green; pollinia four; stipe absent; viscidium present; about sixteen taxa in Costa Rica; mid to high elevations.

Maxillaria (fig. 7.85*g,h*): epiphytic; generally ovoid pseudobulbs often spread apart from one another by elongate rhizomes, usually subtended by one to several foliaceous bracts; inflorescences lateral from the base of the pseudobulbs; generally erect; flowers one to several; col-

umn usually extended into a distinct column foot to which the lip is basally fused; pollinia four, often in two unequal pairs; stipe and viscidium (often sickle-shaped) present; about seventy-five taxa in Costa Rica; all elevations.

Epidendrum (fig. 7.86*a–g*): epiphytic; no pseudobulbs (very rarely present); leaves one to many, distichous (arranged in two vertical rows on opposite sides of the stem) and usually fleshy; inflorescence terminal, single-flowered to a much-branched panicle; flowers small to large; lip fused the entire length of the column; lip often three-lobed; pollinia two, caudicles present; no stipe or viscidium; about one hundred taxa in Costa Rica; found at all elevations; generally pollinated by butterflies or moths; one species, *E. radicans* (discussed elsewhere in this book), is a common roadside weed at mid elevations. (Plants superficially similar to *Epidendrum* but with pseudobulbs and little fusion between lip and column are referred to *Encyclia* [fig. 7.86*h*].)

Pleurothallis (fig. 7.87*a–e*): epiphytic; rhizomes (horizontal stems) short, the leaves thus clustered; plants generally small; no pseudobulbs; leaves minute to medium sized, fleshy, usually narrowed to a petiole; plants often forming dense mats; inflorescences arising from the

FIGURE 7.86. *a, Epidendrum misserimum. b, E. falcatum. c, E. difforme. d, E. radicans. e, E. pseudepidendrum. f, E. exasperatum. g, E. paniculatum. h, Encyclia cordigera* (photos, K. S. Walter).

FIGURE 7.87. *a, Pleurothallis amparoana* (the "furry toilet seat orchid"). *b, P. dolichopus. c, P. rowleei. d, P. tribuloides. e, P. biflora* (photos, K. S. Walter).

FIGURE 7.88. *a, Barbosella geminata. b, Brachionidium valerioi. c, Lepanthes* sp. *d, Stelis* sp. *e, Lepanthes* sp. *f, Stelis* sp. *g, Restrepia xanthophthalma. h, Lepanthes* sp. (photos, K. S. Walter).

top of the petiole or (seemingly) from the middle of the leaf blade; flowers small (occasionally larger); petals generally smaller than the sepals; lip hinged; flowers exceptionally variable in size, shape, and color; pollinia two, with short caudicles; no stipe or viscidium; about 140 taxa in Costa Rica; all elevations, although most common at mid to high elevations. Several genera have been segregated from *Pleurothallis: Barbosella* (fig. 7.88*a*) has elongate rhizomes and produces single-flowered inflorescences; the flowers of *Brachionidium* (fig. 7.88*b*) have elongate "tails" on the sepals and petals and produce eight pollinia; *Restrepia* (fig. 7.88*g*) has fused lateral sepals; the petals are linear with a fattened tip, and the lip is small and jointed at its base.

Lepanthes (fig. 7.88*c,e,h*): epiphytic; rhizomes short, the leaves thus clustered; no pseudobulbs, stems covered with small, persistent funnel-shaped bracts; leaves single, lanceolate to cordate; inflorescences usually many-flowered, zigzag, often borne underneath the leaf; flowers small to medium sized; sepals large, petals smaller and crescent-shaped; lip small but complex, surrounding the short column; pollinia two, with short caudicles; no stipe or viscidium; about forty-five taxa in Costa Rica; mid to high elevations. (A difficult, poorly known genus; few binomials can be assigned to our species with certainty.)

Stelis (fig. 7.88*d,f*): epiphytic; rhizomes short, the

leaves thus clustered; no pseudobulbs; leaves of variable size and shape, somewhat fleshy; inflorescences arising at the base of the blade, racemose; flowers minute to small, often triangular in outline; sepals larger than the petals and lip; dorsal sepal usually basally fused with the laterals; pollinia two, with short caudicles; stipe and viscidium lacking; about fifty taxa in Costa Rica; mid to high elevations.

Masdevallia (fig. 7.89*a–d*): epiphytic; rhizomes extremely short, the leaves thus clustered; plants small to medium sized; no pseudobulbs; leaves single, fleshy, petiolate, usually with a large basal sheath; inflorescences arising at the base of the petiole, often single-flowered, less commonly successive-flowering; sepals basally fused and usually narrowed apically to form distinct "tails"; petals and lip smaller than the sepals; lip hinged; pollinia two, with short caudicles; no stipe or viscidium; about thirty-five taxa in Costa Rica; mid to high elevations (similar plants with thinner leaves and horizontal to pendant, often hairy flowers are referred to *Dracula*.)

Catasetum (fig. 7.90*a,b*): epiphytic (often on palms or exposed rotting tree trunks); pseudobulbs elongate, of

289

FIGURE 7.89. *a, Masdevallia rafaeliana. b, M. calura.*
c, M. walteri (note swollen ovaries in freshly opened
flowers). *d, M. ecaudata. e, Campylocentrum fasciola* (photos, K. S. Walter).

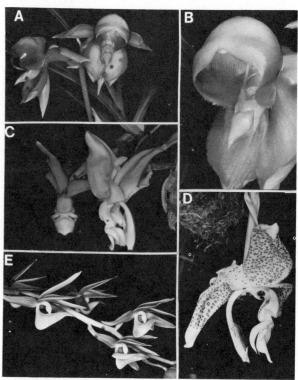

FIGURE 7.90. *a, Catasetum viridiflavum,* male. *b, Catasetum viridiflavum,* male, showing trigger for shooting pollinarium. *c, Stanhopea intermedia. d, S. oculata* (?). *e, Mormodes colossus* (photos, K. S. Walter).

several internodes, becoming ridged with age, topped by
"spines" from the fallen leaves; leaves several, thin-textured, pleated, deciduous; inflorescences lateral,
erect, bearing several showy flowers in a raceme (unbranched inflorescence); plants generally producing all
male or all female flowers at any given flowering, the
unisexual flowers usually quite distinct (female flowers
less commonly encountered than male flowers); female
flowers nonresupinate and generally similar between species; male flowers resupinate or not, distinct in different
species, provided with two sensitive antennae (projections from the column) that when depressed cause the
pollinaria to shoot out of the flower; pollinia two, stipe
and viscidium well developed; about five taxa in Costa
Rica; low to mid elevations.

Stanhopea (fig. 7.90*c,d*): epiphytic; pseudobulbs
broadly ovoid, often ridged, unifoliate; leaves large,
pleated, deciduous; inflorescences lateral from the base
of the pseudobulb, pendant; flowers large, waxy, short-lived, extremely fragrant; the winged column forming a
"chute" with the complex three-part fleshy lip; pollinia
two, oblong; stipe, and viscidium easily discernible;
about eight (?) taxa in Costa Rica; most common at low
elevations; specific pollination systems in which euglossine bees are attracted on the basis of floral odors.

Mormodes (fig. 7.90*e*): epiphytic; pseudobulbs elongate, of several internodes, relatively massive; leaves
several, thin-textured, pleated, deciduous; inflorescence
lateral, erect, bearing several fleshy flowers in a raceme;
flowers bisexual, the lip and column usually touching
apically but twisted in opposite directions, the flowers
thus asymmetric; pollinia two; stipe and viscidium well
developed; about eight taxa in Costa Rica; low to mid
elevations.

Elleanthus (fig. 7.91*a*): epiphytic or terrestrial; plants
small to large; stems elongate, erect, woody, leafy; leaves
distichous (arranged in two vertical rows on opposite
sides of the stem) and pleated; inflorescences terminal,
many flowered; flowers spiraled in colorful bracteate
heads or racemes; perianth thin-textured, short-lived, often red; lip often with two basal calluses; pollinia eight,
soft; stipe absent; viscidium usually present; about sixteen taxa in Costa Rica; mid to high elevations, common
along roadside banks, generally bird pollinated.

Sobralia (fig. 7.91*a*): epiphytic or terrestrial; plants
often large; stems reedlike, erect, no pseudobulbs; leaves
few, large, leathery, plicate; inflorescence terminal,
single-flowered or successive-flowering; flowers medium
to large, sometimes extremely showy (often resembling
a *Cattleya*), short-lived (102 days); pollinia eight, soft;

FIGURE 7.91. *a, Elleanthus* sp. *b, Dichaea muricata.*
c, Lockhartia amoena. d, Sobralia macrantha. e, Telipogon
sp. *f, Vanilla planifolia g, Oncidium ornithorrhynchum.*
h, O. cristigalli (photos, K. S. Walter).

soft; stipe absent; viscidium present; about twenty taxa in
Costa Rica; low to mid elevations.

Dichaea (fig. 7.91*b*): epiphytic; stems branched, elongate, often pendant, not swollen into pseudobulbs; leaves
many, distichous, persistent or deciduous; inflorescences
lateral, arising opposite a leaf, single-flowered; flowers
small but complex; sepals and petals more or less equal
in size; lip three-part; a column foot occasionally present;
pollinia four; stipe and viscidium present; about thirty (?)
taxa in Costa Rica; low to mid elevations. (*Lockhartia*
[fig. 7.91*c*] has much the same general appearance as
Dichaea; however, its leaves are imbricate and equitant;
flowers in *Lockhartia* are usually borne in panicles with
conspicuous bracts and are often yellow; pollinia two.)

Telipogon (fig. 7.91*e*): epiphytic; no pseudobulbs,
stems leafy, often clambering, somewhat fleshy; inflorescences lateral, several-flowered; sepals small, usually
hidden behind the large striped petals; lip very similar in
size and coloration to the other two petals; column short,
often jet black (along with the base of the petals) and
hairy, ending in a projecting hooked rostellum; pollinia
two; stipe and viscidium well developed; probably pseu-
docopulatory; mid to high elevations; about fifteen taxa
in Costa Rica.

PRESUMED INTERACTIVE FACTORS RELATING TO
HYPERSPECIATION IN THE ORCHIDACEAE

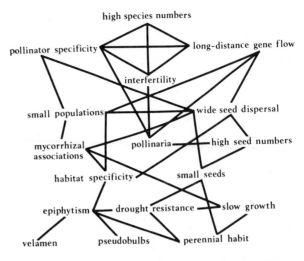

FIGURE 7.92. These factors are presumed to interact with
one another and, to varying extents, to affect the extremely
high species numbers encountered in the Orchidaceae.

Oncidium (fig. 7.91*g,h*): epiphytic; plants small to
large, pseudobulbs laterally compressed (occasionally
lacking), usually unifoliate; one to several sheathing
leaves below each pseudobulb; inflorescences lateral
from the base of the pseudobulb and racemose or pa-
niculate; flowers small to large, often yellow; generally
odorless; sepals and petals large and flat; lip larger or
smaller than the other petals, also usually flattened, and
provided basally with a callus (a swollen, fleshy out-
growth); column short, winged, oriented more or less at
a right angle to the lip; pollinia two, ovoid, with well-
developed stipe and viscidium; about forty-five taxa in
Costa Rica; all elevations. (An unnatural collection of
species belonging to several different genera.)

*

Barthlott, W. 1976. Struktur und Funktion des Velamen
Radicum der Orchideen. In *Proceedings of the Eighth
World Orchid Conference,* pp. 438–43. Frankfurt: Ger-
man Orchid Society.

Benzing, D. H., and Seemann, J. 1978. Nutritional pi-
racy and host decline: A new perspective on the
epiphyte-host relationship. *Selbyana* 2:133–48.

Burgeff, H. 1959. Mycorrhiza of orchids. In *The orchids:
A scientific survey,* ed. C. L. Withner, pp. 361–96.
New York: Ronald Press.

Cook, M. T. 1926. Epiphytic orchids as a serious pest on
citrus trees. *J. Dept. Agric. Puerto Rico* 10:5–9.

Darwin, C. R. 1862. *The various contrivances by which
orchids are fertilized by insects.* London: John Murray.

Dodson, C. H. 1970. The role of chemical attractants in
orchid pollination. In *Biochemcial coevolution,* ed. K.

L. Chambers, pp. 83–107. Corvallis: Oregon State University Press.

Dodson, C. H., et al. 1969. Biologically active compounds in orchid frangrances. *Science* 164:1243–49.

Dodson, C. H., and Hills, G. 1966. Gas chromatography of orchid frangrances. *Am. Orchid Soc. Bull.* 35: 720–25.

Dressler, R. L. 1968. Pollination by euglossine bees. *Evolution* 22:202–10.

———. 1981. *The orchids—natural history and classification.* Cambridge: Harvard University Press.

Dunsterville, G. C. K. 1961. How many orchids on a tree? *Am. Orchid Soc. Bull.* 30:362–63.

Frei, J. K. 1973a. Orchid ecology in a cloud forest in the mountains of Oaxaca, Mexico. *Am. Orchid Soc. Bull.* 42:307–14.

———. 1973b. Effect of bark substrate on germination and early growth of *Encyclia tampensis* seeds. *Am. Orchid Soc. Bull.* 42:701–8.

Hadley, G. 1970. Non-specificity of symbiotic infection in orchid mycorrhiza. *New Phytol.* 69:1015–23.

Hills, G., et al. 1972. Floral fragrance and isolating mechanisms in the genus *Catasetum* (Orchidaceae). *Biotropica* 4:61–76.

Holttum, R. F. 1960. The ecology of tropical epiphytic orchids. In *Proceedings of the Third World Orchid Conference,* pp. 196–204. London: Royal Horticultural Society.

Luer, C. L. 1979. Miscellaneous new species in the Pleurothallidinae. *Selbyana* 5:145–94.

Neales, T. F., and Hew, C. S. 1975. Two types of carbon fixation in tropical orchids. *Planta* 123:303–6.

Pijl, L. van der, and Dodson, C. H. 1966. *Orchid flowers: Their pollination and evolution.* Coral Gables: University of Miami Press.

Ruinen, J. 1953. Epiphytosis: A second view of epiphytism. *Ann. Bogorienses* 1:101–57.

Sanders, D. J. 1979. Crassulacean acid metabolism and its possible occurrence in the plant family Orchidaceae. *Am. Orchid Soc. Bull.* 48:796–98.

Sanford, W. W. 1974. The ecology of orchids. In *The orchids: Scientific studies,* ed. C. L. Withner, pp. 1–100. New York: John Wiley.

Walter, K. S. n.d. The chemistry and biology of floral fragrances. In preparation.

Parasitic Plants (Parásitas Verdaderas)

L. D. Gómez

Hid in the leafy darkness of a tree, there is a golden bough, the leaves and stem also of gold, and sacred to the queen of the infernal realm. [Vergil, *Aeneid*, 6:205]

In such dramatic and poetic terms Vergil describes *Viscum album*, a common European mistletoe believed to have magical properties and the center of many a tradition, from classical times to the Christmas kisses of today. Parasitic plants have attracted the attention of the layman as well as of the naturalist because of their elusive biology; the mountain of literature dealing with them confirms this interest. Parasitic plants, excluding fungi and other lower organisms, include what are probably the most bizarre structures of the plant kingdom: the giant flowers of *Rafflesia* in the steamy forest of tropical Asia or the minute ones of *Pilostyles* in the Neotropics attest to the diversity and complexity found among these unusual forms of flowering plants.

Classic references to the flowering parasitic plants include those by Sperlich (1925) and Pax (1935). There is a clear though partial treatment of the subject by Christmann (1960) and a general account of their biology by Kuijt (1969), who emphasizes the santalalean groups.

Two kinds of parasitism are recognized: hemiparasitism, where the parasitic plants are also capable of some photosynthesis and are thus autotrophic to some extent, and the holoparasites, devoid of assimilative pigments and on the whole heterotrophic. The santalalean parasites (Santalaceae and related groups) are hemiparasites; the rest of the flowering plants that exhibit parasitism are holoparasites. Both categories, hemi- and holoparasites, are found only in the Santalaceae, Loranthaceae, Lauraceae, Scrophulariaceae, and Orobanchaceae.

Delimitation of parasitism versus saprophytism may in some cases be difficult: the Monotropaceae, or Indian pipes, were considered parasites for many years until it was found that they were in fact saprophytes. Of course the somewhat metaphysical question arises whether a holosaprophyte is parasitic on its associated mycorrhizal fungus.

Parasitism in the flowering plants is distributed as shown in table form on page 293.

The arrangement, following Engler and Prantl, shows there are 9 orders, 16 families, about 142 genera, and approximately 2,500 species of parasitic flowering plants as well as one gymnospermous species. There are no parasitic pteridophytes or monocotyledons.

Podocarpaceae. *Podocarpus ustus,* endemic to New Caledonia, is found as a parasite of *Dacrydium taxoides,* another conifer. Gray (1959) and DeLaubenfelds (1959) report on this rare plant.

Krameriaceae. Placed among the Rosaceae by some and among the Leguminosae by others because of its papilionaceous flower, the genus *Krameria* is now assigned to its own family. Its parasitism was first reported by Cannon (1910), and the best account of the genus is by Kuntz (1913). These plants are of distinctive xerophytic preferences, found from the southern United States to Costa Rica, throughout the Caribbean into arid South America. Pollination is by bees in Costa Rica, and dispersal of the spiny fruits is by mammals and occasionally by birds. Upon germination, the seedling re-

Taxon	Hemiparasites		Holoparasites	
Gymnosperms				
Podocarpaceae	1 g.,	1 sp.		
Angiosperms				
Rosales				
Krameriaceae	1 g.,	15 spp.		
Santalales				
Olacaceae-Opiliaceae	5 g.,	22 spp.		
Myzodendraceae	1 g.,	10 spp.		
Santalaceae	30 g.,	400 spp.	2 g.,	10 spp.
Loranthaceae	35 g.,	1,000 spp.		3 spp.
Balanophorales				
Balanophoraceae			18 g.,	100 spp.
Myrtales				
Cynomoriaceae			1 g.,	1 sp.
Aristolochiaceae				
Rafflesiaceae			8 g.,	60 spp.
Mitrastemonaceae			1 g.,	2 spp.
Hydnoraceae			8 g.,	? spp.
Laurales				
Lauraceae	1 g.,	30 spp.		
Ericales				
Lennoaceae			3 g.,	4 spp.
Tubiflorales				
Convolvulaceae (Cuscutaceae)			1 g.,	80– 100 spp.
Scrophulariaceae	10 g.,	ca. 500 spp.	6 g.,	50– 60 spp.
Orobanchaceae	8 g.,	ca. 150 spp.	2– 3 g.,	? spp.

mains autotrophic for some time until it can parasitize another plant by root grafting.

Olacaceae-Opiliaceae, Myzodendraceae. The family Myzodendraceae is restricted to the antarctic beech forests of South America. Hooker (1846) offers a detailed account of the family. Pollinated by small insects, the fruit is "pushed" upward by the subtending placental column, and upon maturation it develops three setae covered by long trichomes (thus the name "feathery mistletoes") that aid dispersal by wind and passing animals. *Myzodendron* attaches itself to parts of *Nothofagus* in such way that parasite and host separate easily, leaving a scar similar to the woodroses of Loranthaceae. In Chile, *Myzodendron* mistletoes are called "angel's beards" and are thought by many to be magical.

Other than morphological or anatomical accounts such as those by Fagerlind (1947, 1948) and Agarwal (1963), little is known about the biology of the Olacaceae-Opiliaceae, united into the single family Olacaceae by some botanists and in my opinion deserving exactly the opposite. The group is represented by Costa Rica by *Heisteria* (six species), *Minquartia guianensis, Schoepfia* (two species), and *Ximenia americana*. Pollination is effected by beetles, bees, and birds, and the drupes are dispersed by small mammals and by omnivorous birds as

well as by gravity. How the Olacaceae sensu lato become parasites is not known. I suspect that root grafting, as in Krameriaceae, is an important mechanism. In the genera represented in our area the only documented case of parasitism is by Barber (1907) for *Ximenia*.

Santalaceae. The family of the sandalwoods has received more attention, and an excellent review of the biology of the representative *Exocarpus bidwillii* is given by Fineran (1962–63). The Santalaceae are plants of the Old World, with the exception of several Patagonian genera.

Loranthaceae. The true mistletoes belong in this family, divided by some authors into Loranthaceae and Viscaceae. If such separation is accepted, the Costa Rican mistletoes fall into Loranthaceae (groups I, *Gaiadendron, Peristethium, Struthanthus;* II, *Phthirusa, Orycthanthus;* IV, *Psittacanthus;* III, *Oxycanthus* [not yet recorded]); and Viscaceae (the remaining genera: *Antidaphne, Dendrophthora, Phoradendron,* fig. 7.93).

The Loranthaceae sensu lato are more or less woody and of variable habit. Some are herbaceous, others are erect shrubs or treelets or scrambling and vinelike. The leaves are entire, coriaceous, and evergreen in the rain forest, whereas those of the tropical dry and moist forests tend to be deciduous (but see fig. 7.93). The species with

FIGURE 7.93. *Phoradendron* mistletoes (Loranthaceae), leafy during the dry season in the crown of a leafless *Guazuma ulmifolia* host tree. May 1980, Santa Rosa National Park, Guanacaste Province, Costa Rica (photo, D. H. Janzen).

persistent leaves usually resemble their hosts' foliage and are often deceptive until they bloom, sometimes with brilliant colors.

In rain forests of normal, even density and shadiness, the mistletoes grow as high canopy plants, except in the light gaps and in riparian habitats. Richards (1936, 1952) has observed the altitudinal distribution of mistletoes in the heath and dipterocarp forests of Borneo. Obviously light is important to a hemiparasite, and light levels (Evans, Whitmore, and Wong 1960; Whitmore 1968) must play an important role as limiting factors as part of the microclimatic layering of the tropical forest (Oye 1921). Mistletoe distribution is also related to the behavior of birds dispersing seed. It must be noted here that mistletoes are epiphytes from the time the seed is deposited on the host until functional haustoria emerge. However brief this lapse may be, depending on the amount of reserves of the seed, mistletoes are undoubtedly subject to the series of factors governing the establishment of the epiphytic synusia (Allen et al. 1968; Dudgeon 1923; Gore 1968; Greendale and Nye 1964; Hosokawa 1968; Klinge 1963; Madison 1977; Visser 1964).

Pollination is occasionally effected by insects seeking nectar in the tubular flowers (I have seen *Papilio burchelli* feeding on *Psittacanthus* and *Trigona* bees foraging on *Phoradendron*), and bats probably visit the large white flowers of *Elythranthe albida*. Nevertheless, the loranthacean flower shows the typical adapatations of the bird-pollination syndrome: hummingbirds in the Neotropics and flowerpeckers (Dicaeidae) and sunbirds (Nectariniidae) in the Old World (Docters van Leeuwen 1954; Evans 1895). Sunbirds and flowerpeckers also disperse the seed; tanagers and thrushes take their place in the New World.

The family Loranthaceae sensu lato has a very wide range of hosts and thus occurs on trees of diverse genera and families. Some mistletoes even parasitize members of their own families, and this hyperparasitism may be of the second degree (parasite on parasite on parasite). The following is a list of Costa Rican mistletoes and their host families as recorded on herbarium specimens:

Antidaphne viscoidea P. & E., Moraceae, Anonnaceae, Fagaceae, Myrtaceae

Dendrophthora ambigua Kuijt, Saxifrangaceae

D. squamigera (Benth.) Ktze., Ericaceae, Myrsinaceae, Myrtaceae, Rosaceae

D. costaricensis Urban spp. *poasensis* Kuijt, Myrtaceae, Ericaceae, Melastomataceae, Solanaceae, Saxifragaceae

Gaiadendron punctatum (R. & P.) G. Don, Araliaceae, Cornaceae, Fagaceae, Myrtaceae, terrestrial, ferns

Orycthanthus alveolatus (HBK) Kuijt, hosts not recorded

O. amplexicaulis (HBK) Eichler, Malvaceae

O. botryostachys Eichler, Sterculiaceae

O. cordifolius (Presl) Urban, Sapindaceae

O. occidentalis (L.) Eichler, Anonnaceae, Sterculiaceae, Myrtaceae, Rutaceae, *Phoradendron*

O. spicathus (Jacq.) Eichler, Betulaceae, Fagaceae, Melastomataceae, Leguminosae

Phoradendron acinacifolium Eichler, Fagaceae

Ph. cooperi Trel., Compositae

Ph. crassifolium (Pohl) Eichler, Moraceae, Rutaceae

Ph. dipterum Eichler, Euphorbiaceae

Ph. flavans (Sw.) Griseb., Melastomataceae

Ph. obliquum (Presl) Eichler, hosts not recorded.

Ph. piperoides (HBK) Trel., Moraceae, Malvaceae, Sterculiaceae, Leguminosae, Dilleniaceae

Ph. quadrangulare (HBK) K. & U., Sterculiaceae, Tiliaceae, Nyctaginaceae, Leguminosae

Ph. quinquenervium Krause, Melastomataceae

Ph. robustissimum Eichler, Sterculiaceae, Leguminosae, Salicaceae

Ph. tonduzii Trel., Melastomataceae, Euphorbiaceae

Ph. undulatum Eichler, Fagaceae, Myrtaceae, Melastomataceae, Euphorbiaceae

Phthirusa pyrifolia (HBK) Eichler, Rubiaceae, Punicaceae, Rutaceae, Myrtaceae, Euphorbiaceae, Sterculiaceae, *Struthanthus*

294

Psittacanthus allenii Woods. & Scher., Pinaceae, Fagaceae

P. calyculatus (DC) G. Don, Burseraceae, Anacardiaceae

P. laterifolius Woods. & Scher., hosts not recorded

P. quadrifolius Kuijt, hosts not recorded

P. scheeryi Woodson, hosts not recorded

P. schiedeanus (Schlecht. & Cham.) Blume, Myrtaceae, Fagaceae, Winteraceae, Hippocastanaceae, Betulaceae

Peristethium leptostachyum (HBK) G. Don, Melastomataceae, Rhizophoraceae

Struthanthus costaricensis Handley, Lauraceae, Betulaceae, Sterculiaceae, Rutaceae, Rubiaceae

St. marginatus (Desr.) Blume, Fagaceae, Rutaceae, Solanaceae, Clethraceae

St. oerstedii (Oliver) Stand., Rosaceae, Euphorbiaceae, Salicaceae, Myrtaceae

St. orbicularis (HBK) Blume, Sterculiaceae, Anacardiaceae, Leguminosae, Rutaceae, Moraceae, Combretaceae, Malvaceae

St. polystachyum (R. & P.) Blume, Rubiaceae, Myrtaceae, Leguminosae

St. quercicola (Cham. & Schlecht.) Blume, Chloranthaceae, Fagaceae, Melastomataceae, Salicaceae, Solanaceae

St. woodsonii Cuf., hosts not recorded

When we arrange the recorded host families in a given sequence such as Hutchinson's, out of a total of 342 families of dicots 42 would be hosts, dispersed from the most primitive to the most advanced. Nevertheless, several systems tried indicate some consistent clustering, the significance of which needs further investigation, particularly in the phytochemical relationships between hosts and parasites (cf. Harris 1934).

GAIADENDRON PUNCTATUM: A CASE HISTORY

This mistletoe inhabits the upper cloud forests, being abundant between 2,500 and 3,000 m in the *Quercus* forests of Talamanca but also frequent elsewhere in mixed forests. It is the only treelike mistletoe in the country, and when in flower, with its large inflorescences of thirty to fifty golden brown flowers arranged in opposite triads, it is very striking. The racemes are usually terminal, and this tendency leads to a pseudo-dichotomous branching. The flowers have six to seven perianth segments about 16 mm long, recurved until their tips nearly touch the base of the flower. The stamens, implanted on the perianth members around the middle, are exerted and slightly oblique to the slender and straight style. This arrangement makes the glistening drops of nectar at the base of the style conspicuous. The structure does not warrant pollination by insects, since most of them could take the nectar without ever touching stamens or stigmata. Bumblebees are sometimes seen near the

flowers. In Talamanca the hummingbird *Eugenes fulgens* is the commonest visitor, but other unidentified birds also frequent the plants. Birds are particularly relevant in the high mountains, where insect activity is reduced by rains and low temperatures. The fruit is globose, about 1 cm in diameter and yellowish orange. The fleshy part is sweet, and birds (*Turdus grayi, Ptylogonis caudatus, Thraupis* sp.) swallow it whole. Seeds lack viscid qualities, and rains can wash them away from branches after they are voided by birds. This may account for the high incidence of terrestrial plants of *Gaiadendron*. Germination and initial growth are rapid, approximately 2 mm/week of radicle growth. Then the upper part of the roots swells and forms a tuber 3–5 cm long and about 1 cm thick. Its function is unknown, and it has no parallel among Loranthaceae, except maybe in the Australian *Nuytsia floribunda*. It is on the roots arising from this tuber that the first haustoria are formed, not always on living objects, and often on other *Gaiadendron* plants, an example of self-hyperparasitism. Hosts include Fagaceae, Saxifragaceae, and ferns. (Excerpted from Kuijt 1963.)

Predators. Apart from a score of fungal maladies, mistletoes are not sought after by predators. The pierid *Catasticta* uses Loranthaceae as host food plants in the American subtropics, as does *Delias,* its Old World analogue. A lycaenid (*Thecla*) feeds on *Phoradendron,* as does the larva of a saturniid moth (*Citheronia*).

Balanophoraceae. Widely distributed, members of this tropical and subtropical group of angiosperms have been the target of many morphological and anatomical studies because of their peculiar fungoid structures but have escaped the attention of ecologists. Represented in Costa Rica by the genera *Helosis* (*H. cayennensis*), *Corynaea* (2 species, fig. 7.94) and *Langsdorffia* (*L. hypogaea*), their taxonomy and distribution is given by Gómez (1983*a*). The species of *Helosis* and *Corynaea* in the area are pollinated by flies (Tachinidae); the pollinators of *Langsdorffia* are as yet unknown. Dispersal of seed is mostly by rain wash after the infructescences are debilitated by boring beetles (Staphylinidae, Scolytidae), but winds occasionally blow the minute seeds away, and ants may act sporadically as vectors. Herbivory is discouraged by the high concentration of secondary compounds such as abundant latex and bitter principles, plus the fact that the reserve substances of the plant are almost entirely of balanophorine, a glyceride. For a comprehensive review of the biology of these plants see Gómez (1979).

Cynomoriaceae. This monotypic Old World family was once considered part of the Balanophoraceae, which it resembles in several ways. Also of fungoid appearance, it was known among Europeans as *Fungus melitenses* (Maltese fungus). Little is known about this plant (Jouel 1902, 1910; Weddell 1858–61).

FIGURE 7.94. *Corynaea crassa* (Balanophoraceae) simultaneously parasitic on a palm and a bamboo (photo, L. D. Gómez).

Rafflesiaceae. Because of the remarkable size and structure of the flowers of *Rafflesia,* this is by far the best-known family of parasitic plants. In Costa Rica it is represented by the rare *Bdallophyton americanum,* parasitic on Burseraceae in the coastal cliffs of the tropical dry forest. Pollination is by flies, and the dispersal mechanisms are unknown (Gómez 1983*b*). *Pilostyles* and *Apodanthes,* parasitic on trunks and branches of Flacourtiaceae, Leguminosae, and others, are known from Panama and Honduras but have not yet been recorded in Costa Rica, but *Apodanthes* parasitizes *Casearia* in our rain forests.

Mitrastemonaceae. This monogeneric family is not always recognized but is sometimes merged with Rafflesiaceae (Kuijt 1969). *Mitrastemon matudai* was described from Chiapas and is known to occur in Guatemala. A parasite on roots of *Quercus,* it may be eventually found also in Costa Rica. Nothing is known of its biology (cf. Matuda 1947).

Hydnoraceae. Restricted to the Ethiopian region (*Hydnora*) and to Patagonian South America (*Prosopanche*), the family Hydnoraceae is quite unknown biologically. The flowers of *Hydnora* are subterranean and much sought after as food; those of *Prosopanche* are not utilized (Burkart 1963; Cocucci 1965). Pollination is effected by beetles.

Lauraceae. Only one genus of this large family is a hemiparasite. *Cassitha,* of circumpacific distribution, is also known from Puerto Rico. Being of economic importance as a pest, it is well known biologically. It is probably pollinated by both wind and small insects, and the seeds are dispersed by ocean currents. As Standley (1937) points out, it has not yet been recorded from Costa Rica. Plants resemble dodders (*Cuscuta*) and are a perfect example of convergent evolution.

Lennoaceae. Together with Krameriaceae and Myzodendraceae, the Lennoaceae is one of the three strictly American groups of parasitic angiosperms. Originally described from Mexico, and known to occur in the southwest of the United States, *Lennoa caerulea* is also known from Colombia (Blake 1926). None of the three genera in the family are known from Costa Rica.

Convolvulaceae. True dodders, often placed in their own family Cuscutaceae, are among the best known of the higher parasites. Their rapid development, strangling and damaging hosts, has given them superstitious names, such as *Teufelszwirn* and *Duivelsnaaigaren,* German and Dutch for "devilish twine or yarn." In Costa Rica they are given the more prosaic name *fideos* (spaghetti). Dodders can cover entire trees in a drapery of spaghettilike strands, measuring up to 500 m or more in length (Dean 1942) if all the branches of dodder were placed end to end. As a parasite it is voracious, including as hosts anything from *Chara* to orchids. Yuncker (1920) reports wasps as pollinators, and I have seen *Trigona* bees as well as ants visiting the flowers of some dodders in Costa Rica. Kuijt (1969) summarizes the knowledge on this parasite.

Scrophulariaceae. The differences between the figworts (Scrophulariaceae) and the broomrapes (Orobanchaceae) are tenuous. Kuijt (1969) lists twenty-six genera of scrophs as of documented parasitism, a number of them of economic importance. *Pedicularis* is well known to most temperate-zone residents. A large family in Costa Rica, only *Castilleja* (Heckard 1962) may be parasitic. Some are known as witch-weeds.

Orobanchaceae. The only Costa Rican representative of this family is *Conopholis panamensis,* a root parasite of *Quercus* in the high mountains of Talamanca, pollinated by bumblebees (*Bombus* sp.). The seeds are dispersed by rainwash as in the Balanophoraceae, and upon germination they require a mycorrhizal association (*Tricholoma, Clitocybe,* etc.) plus chemotropy to infect the host. The subterranean tuberous stems of *Conopholis* can grow very large and are long-lived, producing flushes of new inflorescences as soon as the previous ones reach maturity. The process is very slow and gives the impression of being annual rather than perennial. Acorns germinating under parasitized trees first develop the mycorrhizae that enable seedlings to be infected. This "recycling" affair between parent host and parent parasite accounts for the tendency of *Conopholis* to be reported on one kind or group of *Quercus* trees (e.g., black versus white oaks) only (Gómez 1979). *Orobanche* is known from montane pastures, where it parasitizes clover.

Angiospermic parasites and parasitism per se pose a series of intriguing problems beyond the sphere of mere taxonomy or systematics, such as the reduction of the vegetative parts versus a development of the reproductive structures and mechanisms; the morphology and histology of the parasitic relationship; physiology of the host/parasite duet and, along the same line, the phytochemistry of the alliance in relation to host selection; not to mention cytology or phenology.

The importance of the higher parasitic plants as one of the well-defined synusia of the tropical and subtropical environment has not as yet been properly investigated and offers a fascinating field of study that, in view of the somewhat esoteric assembly of bearded angels, witch-weeds, diabolical entanglements, and strangling spaghetti, should best be attempted with bell, book, and candle at hand.

*

Agarwal, S. 1963. Morphological and embryological studies in the family Olacaceae. I. *Olax.* II. *Strombosia. Phytomorphology* 13:185–96, 348–56.

Allen, S. E.; Carlisle, A.; White, E. J.; and Evans, C. C. 1968. The plant nutrient content of rainwater. *J. Ecol.* 56:497–504.

Barber, C. A. 1907. Parasitic trees in southern India. *Proc. Cambridge Phil. Soc.* 14:246–56.

Blake, S. F. 1926. *Lennoa caerulea* in Colombia. *Proc. Biol. Assoc. Wash.* 39:146.

Burkart, A. 1963. Nota sobre *Prosopanche bonacinae* Speg. (Hydnoraceae). Su area y parasitismo sobre algodón. *Darwiniana* 12:633–38.

Cannon, W. A. 1910. The root habits and parasitism of *Krameria canescens* Gray. *Carnegie Inst. Wash. Publ.* 129:5–24.

Christmann, C. 1960. *Le parasitisme chez les plantes.* Paris: Leclerc.

Cocucci, A. E. 1965. Estudios en el género *Prosopanche* (Hydnoraceae). I. Revision taxonómica. *Kurtziana* 2:53–73.

Dean, H. L. 1942. Total length of stem developed from a single seedling of *Cuscuta. Proc. Iowa Acad. Sci.* 49:127–28.

DeLaubenfelds, D. J. 1959. Parasitic conifer found in New Caledonia. *Science* 130:97.

Docters van Leeuwen, W. M. 1954. On the biology of some Javanese Loranthaceae and the roles birds play in their life-history. *Beaufortia Misc. Publ.* 4:105–207.

Dudgeon, W. 1923. Successions of epiphytes in the *Quercus incana* forest at Landour, Western Himalayas. *J. Indian Bot. Soc.* 3:270.

Evans, G. C., Whitmore, T. C.; and Wong, T. 1960. The distribution of light reaching the ground vegetation in a tropical forest. *J. Ecol.* 48:193–204.

Evans, M. S. 1895. The fertilisation of *Loranthus kraussianus* and *L. dregei. Nature* (London) 51:235–36.

Faegri, K., and Pijl, L. van der. 1966. *The principles of pollination ecology.* Oxford: Pergamon.

Fagerlind, F. 1947. Gynöceummorphologische und embryologische Studien in der Familie Olacaceae. *Bot. Notiser* 1947:207–30.

———. 1948. Beiträge zur Kenntnis der Gynaeceummorphologie und Phylogenie der Santalales-Familien. *Svensk. Bot. Tidskr.* 42:195–229.

Fineran, B. 1962–63. Studies on the root parasitism of *Exocarpus bidwillii* Hk.f. I–IV. *Phytomorphology* 12:339–54; 13:30–41, 42–54, 249–67.

Gómez, L. D. 1979. On the pollination and seed dispersal of the Balanophoraceae. In preparation.

———. 1983*a.* Balanophoraceae. In Flora costaricensis, ed. W. C. Burger. *Fieldiana, Bot.,* in press.

———. 1983*b.* Rafflesiaceae. In Flora costaricensis, ed. W. C. Burger. *Fieldiana, Bot.,* in press.

Gore, A. J. P. 1968. The supply of six elements by rain to an upland peat area. *J. Ecol.* 56:483–95.

Gray, N. E. 1959. A report on the morphology and anatomy of an unusual parasitic gymnosperm from New Caledonia, *Podocarpus ustus. Ninth Int. Bot. Congr.,* Montreal, p. 141.

Greendale, D. J., and Nye, P. H. 1964. Organic matter and nutrient cycles under moist tropical forest. *Proc. Tenth Int. Bot. Congr. Edinburgh,* p. 248.

Harris, J. A. 1934. *The physio-chemical properties of plant saps in relation to phytogeography.* Minneapolis: Blakeston.

Heckard, L. R. 1962. Root parasitism in *Castilleja. Bot. Gaz.* 124:21–29.

Hooker, J. D. 1847. *Flora antarctica.* Part 2, pp. 289–302. London: Reeve.

Hosokawa, T. 1968. Ecological studies of tropical epiphytes in forest ecosystems. In *Proceedings of the Symposium on Recent Advances in Tropical Ecology* II, ed. R. Misra and B. Gopal, pp. 482–501. Varanasi:

Jouel, O. 1902. Zur Entwicklungsgeschichte des Samens von *Cynomorium. Beih. Bot. Centralbl.* 13:194–202.

———. 1910. *Cynomorium* und *Hippuris. Svensk. Bot. Tidskr.* 4:151–59.

Klinge, H. 1963. Uber Epiphytenhumus aus El Salvador. *Pedobiologia* 2:102–7.

Kuijt, J. 1963. On the ecology and parasitism of the Costa Rican tree mistletoe, *Gaiadendron punctatum* (R. and P.) G. Don. *Can. J. Bot.* 41:927–38.

———. 1969. *The biology of parasitic flowering plants.* Berkeley: University of California.

Kuntz, M. 1913. Bie systematische Stellung der Gattung *Krameria* unter besonderer Berücksichtigung der Anatomie. *Beih. Bot. Zentralbl.* 30:412–27.

Madison, M. 1977. Vascular epiphytes: Their systematic occurrence and salient features. *Selbyana* 2:1–13.

Matuda, E. 1947. On the genus *Mitrastemon. Bull. Torrey Bot. Club* 74:133–41.

Oye, P. van 1921. Influence des facteurs climatiques sur la répartition des épiphytes á la surface des troncs d'arbres á Java. *Rev. Gen. Bot.* 33:161–76.

Pax, F. 1935. Reihen Santalales, Arsitolochiales, Balanophorales. In *Die Naturlichen Pflanzenfamilien,* ed. A. Engler and K. Prantl. Leipzig: W. Englemann.

Pijl, L. van der. 1972. *Principles of dispersal in higher plants.* New York: Springer-Verlag.

Richards, P. W. 1936. Ecological observations on the rain forests of Mount Dulit, Sarawak, I–II. *J. Ecol.* 24:1–37, 340–60.

———. 1952. *The tropical rain forest.* Cambridge: Cambridge University Press.

Sperlich, A. 1925. Die Absortionsorgane der parasitischen Samenpflanzen. *Handb. Pflanzenanat.* 11(2).

Standley, P. C. 1937. *Flora of Costa Rica.* Chicago: Field Museum of Natural History.

Visser, S. A. 1964. Origin of nitrates in tropical rain water. *Nature* 201:35.

Weddell, H. A. 1858–61. Mémoire sur le *Cynomorium coccineum,* parasite de d'ordre des Balanophorées. *Arch. Mus. Hist. Nat.* 10:269–308.

Whitmore, T. C. 1968. A study of light conditions in forests in Ecuador with some suggestions for further studies in tropical forests. In *Light as an ecological factor,* ed. R. Bainbridge et al., pp. 235–47. Oxford: Blackwell.

Yuncker, T. G. 1904. Revision of the North American and West Indian species of *Cuscuta. Ill. Biol. Mon.* 6:1–141.

Passiflora foetida (Bombillo, Calzoncillo, Ñorbo, Granadilla del Monte, Passion Flower)

J. T. Smiley

Growing in sunny lowland habitats, the vine *Passiflora foetida* may be recognized by its unbranched tendrils, slightly three-lobed leaves, and leafy stipules with gland-tipped filaments along their margins. Typical Costa Rican specimens are coated all over with fine glandular hairs and are foul smelling and sticky. The plants are common in pastures and other disturbed habitats. This "weedy" species is distributed throughout the tropics of the world and is highly variable geographically. More than forty named varieties are found in the Neotropics, the presumed ancestral home of the species (Killip 1938). *Passiflora foetida* (2n = 20) has an atypical chromosome number for the genus *Passiflora,* which typically has 2n = 12 or 2n = 18 (Beal 1973; Storey 1950).

P. foetida flowers when it is relatively small (stems less than 6 mm in diameter) and continues flowering as the plant grows, so long as conditions are favorable. The purple and white flowers (fig. 7.95) are 2–3 cm across and are partially enclosed in a lacelike shell of glandular, sticky bracts. The flowers open at dawn and are visited by *Ptiloglossa* bees (Colletidae), which appear to be specifically adapted for *P. foetida* pollination, at least in

FIGURE 7.95. *Passiflora foetida* flower after dawn, with the anther filaments bent well downward to place the anthers between the stigmata. Hacienda Palo Verde, Guanacaste Province, Costa Rica (photo, D. H. Janzen).

Guanacaste Province (Janzen 1968). These and other large bees such as *Xylocopa* reach the nectar by probing with their probosces and prying open the doughnut-shaped nectar chamber. The bees run around the rim of the flower to obtain all the nectar, and as they do so pollen is deposited on their thoraxes, wings, and abdomens by the anthers that hang down. At first the stigmatic surfaces are raised well above the anthers, preventing pollination. After a variable period of time the styles bend down so as to bring the stigmatic surfaces to the level of the anthers, at which time they receive pollen from the pollinators or directly from the anthers. By this time the pollinators have visited several flowers, and outcrossing occurs (Janzen 1968).

This mechanism of pollination in *P. foetida* was also described in Knuth (1908). However, Raju (1954) claims that pollination may occur just before bud opening, when the stigmatic surfaces are pressed against the opening anthers. These possible differences in pollination mechanism are probably real and may be due to differences among the varieties of *P. foetida* that have been investigated. In any case, the degree of self-compatibility is not known for the different varieties, although some are probably self-compatible.

After pollination, the fruits of *P. foetida* mature in about one month, still enclosed in the sticky bracts. The ripe fruit is about 3 cm in diameter and is red or yellow. It is palatable, though acidic like many other *Passiflora,* and it is difficult to separate the pulpy arils from the seeds.

P. foetida is unusual among *Passiflora* species in several ways. Its weedy, pantropical distribution has already been mentioned. The lack of extrafloral nectar glands is also unusual, though in *P. foetida* this is fully consistent with the antiherbivore strategy of secreting foul-smelling, sticky chemicals that trap small insects (Janzen 1968). *P. foetida* also appears to be unusually well-defended chemically, since it is inedible to most of the typical *Passiflora*-feeding herbivores (Smiley 1978a,b). There is some evidence that the chemical defense is related to the sticky secretions and the foul odor, since nonsticky, nonodorous varieties of *P. foetida* are palatable to many of the *Passiflora*-feeding invertebrate herbivores mentioned above (pers. obs.). Even starving horses reject the plant (D. H. Janzen, pers. comm.).

The butterflies *Agraulis vanillae* and *Euptoita hegesia* are able to circumvent the chemical defenses of *P. foetida,* with *A. vanillae* being the dominant herbivore in most localities. *E. hegesia* typically feeds on plants related to the Passifloraceae, such as Turneraceae, Violaceae, Linaceae, and others (Ehrlich and Raven 1964). The white stripe along the side of the *E. hegesia* larva will distinguish it from the reddish brown or slate-colored *A. vanillae* larvae, as will the length of the head spines, which are about the same length as the body spines in *A. vanillae* but are much longer in *E. hegesia.*

*

Beal, P. R. 1973. Cytology of the native Australian and several exotic *Passiflora* species. 3. Morphology of satellite chromosomes. *Queensland J. Agric. Anim. Sci.* 30:19–24.

Ehrlich, P. R., and Raven, P. H. 1964. Butterflies and plants: A study in coevolution. *Evolution* 18:586–608.

Janzen, D. H. 1968. Reproductive behavior in the Passifloraceae and some of its pollinators in Central America. *Behavior* 32:33–48.

Killip, E. P. 1938. The American species of Passifloraceae. *Field Mus. Nat. Hist. Bot. Ser.* 19:1–613.

Knuth, P. 1908. *Handbook of flower pollination.* Vol. 2. English translation. Oxford.

Raju, M. V. S. 1954. Pollination mechanism in *Passiflora foetida* L. *Proc. Nat. Inst. Sci. India* 20:431–36.

Smiley, J. T. 1978a. Host plant ecology of *Heliconius* butterflies in northeastern Costa Rica. Ph.D. diss., University of Texas.

———. 1978b. Plant chemistry and the evolution of host specificity: New evidence from *Heliconius* and *Passiflora. Science* 201:745–47.

Storey, W. B. 1950. Chromosome numbers of some species of *Passiflora* occurring in Hawaii. *Pacific Sci.* 4:37–42.

Passiflora vitifolia (Granadilla del Monte, Passion Flower)

J. T. Smiley

The large, brilliant red flowers of *Passiflora vitifolia* (fig. 7.96) are commonly seen in low to middle elevation moist forests in Costa Rica. This species ranges from Nicaragua to northern South America (Killip 1938). The flowering plant is a medium-sized vine (trunk diameter 2–3 cm) with serrate, three-lobed leaves that resemble those of the cultivated grape. Most foliage is found growing in the forest canopy, while the flowers usually are borne on the lower branches or nonvegetative shoots in the understory. The flowers are primarily hummingbird pollinated. As with other *Passiflora,* the nectar is secreted within a doughnut-shaped chamber. In this species the chamber is surrounded by erect filaments that bar access to most insects but allow entry to the long beak and tongue of the hummingbird (Janzen 1968; Sazima and Sazima 1978). Flowering is most frequent during February–May (Stiles 1978), but occasional flowers may be observed at any time of year. Flowers are self-incompatible (East 1940), yet they also show delayed stigmatic deflection, a mechanism to increase outcrossing (see *P. foetida*).

FIGURE 7.96. *Passiflora vitifolia* flower at midday, with two anthers eaten off by an insect and holes eaten in the petals by another insect; the leaf on the right belongs to the same vine. Sirena, Corcovado National Park, Osa Peninsula, Costa Rica (photo, D. H. Janzen).

The fruits of *P. vitifolia* are 5–10 cm in diameter, egg-shaped, and have very thick, tough skin. Mature fruits are mottled with yellow and purple; however, even such "mature" fruits may have undeveloped (or perhaps sterile?) seeds. The mature seeds are dark brown to black, flattened, and about 1 cm long, and there are one hundred to five hundred seeds per fruit. It is not uncommon to find fruits that have been chewed open, apparently by mammals. This, plus the understory habitat and fruit toughness, indicates that seed dispersal may be accomplished primarily by arboreal or terrestrial mammals.

After germination, *P. vitifolia* seeds grow into a compact plant with internodal distances of 1 cm or less. Under low light conditions in the forest understory this type of growth persists for many months or perhaps years (understory leaves of tropical plants may last several years, growing at a rate of three to four leaves per year; Bentley 1979). With more light the internodal distance lengthens after about ten nodes, tendrils develop in the leaf axils, and the plant develops a vine growth form. The leaves under these conditions are unlobed, but as vegetative growth accelerates the leaves develop with first one and then two lateral lobes. Vigorously growing plants add three to four leaves per week to their growing tips. Growth is retarded when the growing tip droops downward, and growth of axillary buds begins at the highest points along the stem (pers. obs.).

Like other *Passiflora, P. vitifolia* plants have extrafloral nectaries. On the petioles of the leaves are large, ear-shaped nectaries that are very attractive to ants and other insects. Smaller nectaries are also found in the sinuses between the lobes of the leaves and on the floral bracts. The extrafloral nectar produced by *Passiflora* species is very rich in amino acids (Durkee 1978), which may help explain their attractiveness to ants and other insects. The nectaries protect the plant by attracting predaceous insects that eat herbivorous insects (Benson, Brown, and Gilbert 1976; Bentley 1977), and they also appear to attract parasitic hymenoptera that parasitize the juvenile stages of the herbivores (Gilbert 1977; Smiley 1978; Gilbert and Smiley 1979).

The two principal types of herbivores feeding on *P. vitifolia* are heliconiine butterfly larvae and adults and larvae of flea beetles (Alticini, Chrysomelidae). The adult flea beetles of several species feed upon the new shoots, and the numerous, tiny feeding holes made by these insects are quite distinct from the typical jagged-edged feeding damage of a heliconiine larva. However, the very small larvae of two of the heliconiines may also chew holes in the leaves.

Of the heliconiines, *Heliconius cydno* and *H. hecale* often lay their eggs on the tendrils and leaf tips of *P. vitifolia* new growth, and the larvae eat the young leaves and tendrils. The egg placement cited above is probably a defense against ant predation (Benson, Brown, and Gilbert 1976; Smiley 1978a). *Eueides aliphera* and *Philaethria dido* lay their eggs on the mature leaves of the plant, and the larvae feed on these older leaves. Table 7.16 gives more complete information on the herbivores of *P. vitifolia*. One unusual characteristic of herbivory on *P. vitifolia* is that in much of Costa Rica there is no herbivore that feeds on it alone, although such herbivores are known from South America. This is in contrast to most other common, widespread species of *Passiflora*, which usually possess host-specific herbivores in Costa Rica (Smiley 1978a,b).

*

Benson, W. W.; Brown, K. S.; and Gilbert, L. E. 1976. Coevolution of plants and herbivores: Passion flower butterflies. *Evolution* 29:659–80.

Bentley, B. L. 1977. Extrafloral nectaries and protection by pugnacious bodyguards. *Ann. Rev. Ecol. Syst.* 8:407–27.

———. 1979. Longevity of individual leaves in a tropical rainforest understory. *Ann. Bot.* 43:119–21.

Durkee, L. T. 1978. The structure and function of extrafloral nectaries of *Passiflora*. Ph.D. diss., University of Iowa.

East, E. M. 1940. The distribution of self-sterility in the flowering plants. *Proc. Am. Phil. Soc.* 82:449–518.

Gilbert, L. E. 1977. The role of coevolution in the organization of ecosystems. In *Le comportement des*

TABLE 7.16   Common Herbivores of *Passiflora vitifolia* in Costa Rica

Species	Appearance	Where Found
Flea beetles		
Altica sp., adult	Dark blue green, small (5 mm long)	Shoot tips
Monomacra sp., adult	Yellow, slender, medium sized (7–8 mm long)	Shoot tips
Strabala sp., adult	Yellow, robust, medium sized (8–9 mm long)	Shoot tips
Heliconiine butterflies		
Dione moneta	Larva: dark brown	Under new leaves
	Adult: orange, silver spots on outer wing surface	
Philaethria dido	Larva: white with orange spots; spines	Mature/old leaves
	Adult: wings light green and black, large	Forest inhabiting
Euiedes aliphera	Larva: brown with yellow spots; spines	Mature/old leaves
	Adult: wings orange, small	Forest edge/clearings
Heliconius cydno	Larva: opaque whitish with black spots and spines	New growth
(Caribbean slope;		
northern Costa Rica)	Adult: wings black with white patch on forewing	Forest/forest edge
Heliconius pachinus	Larva: same as *H. cydno*	New growth
(Pacific slope south of Puntarenas)	Adult: black with broad yellow bars	Forest/forest edge
Heliconius hecale	Larva: whitish without spots dorsally; spines	Forest edge/clearings
	Adult: wings dark orange and black with white spots on hind wing	

*Taxonomy poorly known—tentative identifications only, Smithsonian Institution staff.

insects et les signaux issus du milieu tropique, ed. V. Labeyrie. Tours: Colloque International CNRS.

Gilbert, L. E., and Smiley, J. T. 1979. Determinants of local diversity in phytophagous insects: Host specialists in tropical environments. In *Diversity of insect faunas*, ed. L. A. Mound and N. Waloff, pp. 89–104. London: Blackwell.

Janzen, D. H. 1968. Reproductive behavior in the Passifloraceae and some of its pollinators in Central America. *Behavior* 32:33–48.

Killip, E. P. 1938. The American species of Passifloraceae. *Field Mus. Nat. Hist. Bot. Ser.* 19:1–613.

Sazima, M., and Sazima, I. 1978. Bat pollination of the passion flower *Passiflora mucronata* in southeastern Brazil. *Biotropica* 10:100–109.

Smiley, J. T. 1978a. Host plant ecology of *Heliconius* butterflies in northeastern Costa Rica. Ph.D. diss., University of Texas.

———. 1978b. Plant chemistry and the evolution of host specificity: New evidence from *Heliconius* and *Passiflora*. *Science* 201:745–47.

Stiles, F. G. 1978. Temporal organization of flowering among the hummingbird foodplants of a tropical wet forest. *Biotropica* 10:194–210.

Pentaclethra macroloba (Gavilán)

G. S. Hartshorn

The leguminous genus *Pentaclethra* has only two species: *P. macrophylla* Benth. in tropical West Africa and *P. macroloba* in the Neotropics. The two species are very similar morphologically (D. Janzen, pers. comm.). *P. macroloba* has three disjunct populations in tropical America: (*a*) the largest area extends from northeastern Venezuela (and Trinidad) across the Atlantic lowlands of the Guianas into the eastern Amazon basin; (*b*) a second population occurs in the Chocó Department of western Colombia and the wetter part of the adjacent Darién province of Panama; and (*c*) in the Atlantic lowlands of southeastern Nicaragua, Costa Rica, and western Panama. In eastern Costa Rica, *P. macroloba* occurs naturally from sea level to about 500 m elevation.

P. macroloba exhibits some ecological and possibly genetic differences among the disjunct American populations. The Venezuelan-Guianan-Brazilian population consists of medium-sized (subcanopy) trees in medium densities on recent alluvial terraces. The Chocó population consists of subcanopy trees (maximum dbh of 65 cm) in low densities, but not restricted to recent alluvium. The Central American population consists of canopy trees (to 130 cm dbh and 40 m tall) that form an important or dominant component of the tropical wet and premontane wet forests.

P. macroloba appears to be restricted to relatively infertile soils without an effective dry season (e.g., La Selva, Chocó), or to swamps (e.g., Tortuguero) and infertile alluvium (e.g., the Guianas) with adequate moisture. The absence of *P. macroloba* from the fertile floodplains of eastern Costa Rica may be due to its poor competitive ability on the rich deposits of andesitic volcanic ash. Farmers in the Atlantic lowlands of Costa Rica use *P. macroloba* as an indicator species of low soil fertility.

The La Selva forests on old alluvial soil, on residual soils derived from basalt, and in freshwater swamp are all dominated by *P. macroloba* with importance values—

301

IV = (% density + % frequency + % basal area)/3 — of 19–23%, more than twice the values of the second most important species. The dense, monolayer (sensu Horn) crowns of mature *P. macroloba* tend to form the base of the La Selva forest canopy at roughly 30 m above ground level.

The tree usually has a spreading, irregularly fluted base with modest buttresses. Many trees, particularly in swamps, have a fairly open base, which may indicate that seedling establishment occurred on a "nurse" log that has long since disappeared. The fairly short bole is irregularly cylindric with white, lenticulate bark and red inner bark. Heartwood is dark red and very resistant to decomposition: logs on the forest floor last for 10–20 years.

Leaves are alternate, bipinnate, without glands (atypical of Mimosaceae), and have very small leaflets (about 2 × 10 mm). The leaves of the only other small-leaflet leguminous trees at La Selva, *Pithecellobium pedicellare* and *Stryphnodendron excelsum*, are much less densely covered with leaflets than are the leaves of *P. macroloba*.

Flowers of *P. macroloba* (fig. 7.97a) have prominent white staminodes and purple calyces and are borne densely on 15 cm spikes in terminal and subterminal inflorescences. Flowers open between 0200 and 0400, but the pollinator is unknown. From the approximately two hundred flowers on a spike develop zero to five fruits (one or two most frequently). The two-valved, flattened, woody legume, 2–3 cm long and 4 cm wide (fig. 7.97b), contains several large seeds ($\bar{x} = 3.8$, range 1–7). Mature legumes dehisce elastically, throwing seeds up to 10 m from the crown periphery.

The large, rhomboid brown seeds contain an alkaloid and a free amino acid (D. Janzen, pers. comm.) that are toxic in a strict diet to the abundant native heteromyid rodent *Heteromys desmarestianus*. The toxicity of *P. macroloba* seeds contributes to the conspicuous abundance of seeds and seedlings on the forest floor. On occasion I have found clear-winged moth (Sesiidae) larvae feeding on *P. macroloba* cotyledons; however, germination is not hindered by the moth larvae, and the opening of the cotyledons exposes the larvae to ground-foraging animals.

I (Hartshorn 1972, 1975) have used a projection matrix approach to analyze the population dynamics of *P. macro-*

FIGURE 7.97. *Pentaclethra macroloba*. *a*, Open flowers (white), buds (narrow inflorescence to left), and old flowers (*right*) in branch-end array of inflorescences. *b*, Naturally opened pod value (*left*) and two living seeds on the forest floor. Finca La Selva, Sarapiquí District, Costa Rica (photos, D. H. Janzen).

loba on La Selva plot I (4 ha). I found that both the population numbers and size distributions of *P. macroloba* are essentially stable. The calculation of $\lambda_1 = 1.002$ for *P. macroloba* is the first valid estimate for any natural plant population. Sensitivity analyses indicate that increased seed mortality would not have important effects on population numbers. A surprising result of the demographic study is that approximately half of *P. macroloba* juvenile mortality is caused by falling debris—branches, palm fronds, and trees.

The success of *P. macroloba* in dominating much of the La Selva forest is due to (*a*) excellent seedling establishment in the absence of serious seed predation, (*b*) tolerance of relatively infertile soils that are probably restrictive to potentially competing species, (*c*) well-distributed and abundant rainfall that enables a swamp species such as *P. macroloba* to extend to the ridgetops, and (*d*) shade tolerance that enables *P. macroloba* saplings to survive and even grow in the dense primary forest (Hartshorn 1972). The inability of *P. macroloba* to completely dominate the La Selva forest canopy, that is, to form a pure stand, is due to its very slow growth and the fast turnover rate of the La Selva forest. The frequency of tree falls allows other, faster-growing canopy tree species to colonize gaps and mature before *P. macroloba* makes it to the canopy (Hartshorn 1978).

*

Hartshorn, G. S. 1972. The ecological life history and population dynamics of *Pentaclethra macroloba,* a tropical wet forest dominant, and *Stryphnodendron excelsum,* an occasional associate. Ph.D. diss., University of Washington.

———. 1975. A matrix model of tree population dynamics. In *Tropical ecological systems: Trends in terrestrial and aquatic research,* ed. F. B. Golley and E. Medina, pp. 41–51. New York: Springer-Verlag.

———. 1978. Tree falls and tropical forest dynamics. In *Tropical trees as living systems,* ed. P. B. Tomlinson and M. H. Zimmerman, pp. 617–38. New York: Cambridge University Press.

Whitmore, J. L., and Hartshorn, G. S. 1969. *Literature review of common tropical trees.* Contribution no. 8. Seattle: College of Forest Resources, University of Washington (pp. 76–77).

Piper (Candela, Candelillos, Piper)

T. H. Fleming

Plants of the genus *Piper* (Piperaceae) are common and widespread members of the understory of tropical forests. The genus is pantropical, but most species (about five hundred) occur in the New World tropics (Burger 1972). The Costa Rican flora contains about ninety-three species whose growth forms range from small herbs to small trees; most species are shrubs 2–3 m tall (Burger 1971). Ranging from sea level to over 2,000 m, the genus is best represented in Costa Rica in moist or wet lowland forests. More than forty species are known from Finca La Selva, for example, whereas there are probably fewer than ten species (and only four common ones) at Santa Rosa National Park.

Although often found in disturbed habitats, different *Piper* species appear to be successional specialists. Three of the four common species at Santa Rosa, for example, appear to have different "preferred" habits: *P. marginatum* is most common in open, disturbed habitats; *P. amalago* is most common in the shady understory of relatively mature forest; and *P. jacquemontianum* is restricted to humid ravines (pers. obs.). The fourth species, *P. pseudofuligineum,* is a habitat generalist, occurring at low density in a variety of different habitats. Major habitat differences also characterize the common species at La Selva.

The inflorescences of *Piper* species are distinctive solitary, leaf-opposed spikes (hence the Spanish name "candela") that contain numerous small, usually crowded, perfect flowers. The few Neotropical species whose floral biology has been studied are self-incompatible (Gomez-Pompa and Vasquez-Yanes 1974). The minute flowers are visited by *Trigona* and other small bees, small beetles, and drosophilid flies (Semple 1974; pers. obs.). In Guanacaste, sympatric species of *Piper* (e.g., *P. amalago, P. pseudofuligineum,* and *P. tuberculatum*) tend to have different flowering seasons and differ in their flower visitors (E. R. Heithaus, pers. comm.).

The erect, spikelike infructescence bears numerous single-seeded drupaceous fruits (fig. 7.98). This spike can be easily removed from the plant only when the fruits are ripe. Although there are reports of *Piper* fruits being eaten by birds (e.g., Leck 1972; Snow and Snow 1971), it is probable that phyllostomatid bats are the major dispersal agents of animal-dispersed *Piper* species throughout the Neotropics. Among these bats, members of the genus *Carollia* (e.g., *C. perspicillata*) are "piperphiles," often basing the bulk of their diet on *Piper* fruits. *Carollia* and other bats remove ripe *Piper* fruits by grabbing them with their mouths in flight. The fruits are usually eaten away from the parent plant in night roosts. Germination success of seeds is high whether or not they pass through bats.

In both wet and dry forest, most *Piper* species have seasonal periods of flowering and fruiting. At Santa Rosa National Park, three sympatric species have temporally displaced fruiting periods: *P. amalago* in July, *P. pseudofuligineum* in August, and *P. marginatum* in September (Fleming, Heithaus, and Sawyer 1977 and unpublished data). *P. amalago* has a second fruiting cycle later in the wet season. On any given night, only about 5% of a

FIGURE 7.98. *Piper tuberculatum* infrutescence shortly before being eaten by a bat. Santa Rosa National Park, Guanacaste Province, Costa Rica (photo, D. H. Janzen).

Fleming, T. H. 1981. Fecundity, fruiting pattern, and seed dispersal in *Piper amalago* (Piperaceae), a bat-dispersed tropical shrub. *Oecologia* 51:42–46.

Fleming, T. H.; Heithaus, E. R.; and Sawyer, W. B. 1977. An experimental analysis of the food location behavior of frugivorous bats. *Ecology* 58:619–27.

Gomez-Pompa, A., and Vasquez-Yanes, C. 1974. Studies on the secondary succession of tropical lowlands: The life cycle of secondary species. *Proc. First Intern. Congr. Ecology,* pp. 336–42.

Leck, C. F. 1972. Seasonal changes in the feeding pressures of fruit- and nectar-eating birds in Panama. *Condor* 79:54–60.

Semple, K. S. 1974. Pollination in Piperaceae. *Ann. Missouri Bot. Gard.* 61:868–71.

Snow, B. K., and Snow, D. W. 1971. The feeding ecology of tanagers and honeycreepers in Trinidad. *Auk* 88:291–322.

Piper auritum (Anisillo, Hinojo, Sabalero, Hoja de la Estrella, Anise Piper)

W. C. Burger

Among Costa Rica's ninety-four species of pipers, *Piper auritum* (Piperaceae) is easily recognized by its large (20–50 cm) leaves unequally lobed at the base (fig. 7.99), its preference for open to partly shaded secondary growth, and the very characteristic sarsaparilla or anise-like odor of crushed leaves. In Costa Rica the species ranges from near sea level to about 1,500 (rarely 2,000) m elevation in evergreen and partly deciduous formations or in wet sites in the deciduous formations of Guanacaste. The species ranges from Mexico to Colombia and appears to be quite uniform throughout this range with no evidence of subspecific or varietal differentiation.

These plants grow to about 6 m in height with a single main stem that often has small prop roots near the base. The large leaves are borne in two alternate ranks and are often held horizontally on horizontal upper branches, thus forming a broad light-intercepting crown with relatively few large leaves. *Piper auritum* appears to be a fast-growing, relatively short-lived, treelet of early successional habitats (cf. Gomez Pompa 1971). When found in a forest, it is never found in dark, deeply shaded sites but rather grows in areas that have an opening in the canopy or are fairly well illuminated. The flowers are very small and tightly packed in long, slender arching or drooping spikes borne opposite the leaves. We know very little about the pollination of specific pipers but, in general, small pollen-collecting bees and small beetles appear to be most important (Burger 1972; Semple 1974). The fruits are very small (less than 1 mm) and tightly packed on the spike. The fruits of this species and many

plant's fruits ripen and disappear. Each plant thus bears ripe fruit for about 3 weeks, and for species like *P. amalago* ripe fruit is available for about 4 weeks. At Santa Rosa bats such as *C. perspicillata* and *Glossophaga soricina* switch immediately from fruits of one *Piper* species to another as one species' fruiting period ends and another's begins. For bats at Santa Rosa and elsewhere in the Neotropics, *Piper* fruits tend to be a low-density resource, but one whose spatiotemporal predictability is high. Because *Piper*-eating bats are excellent at finding all the available ripe fruits on a given night (by using olfactory cues?), seeds produced by isolated plants are just as likely to be dispersed as are those on plants growing in the middle of *Piper* clumps (Fleming, Heithaus, and Sawyer 1977). The nutritional rewards that *Piper* fruits provide bats are not yet known.

*

Burger, W. 1971. Piperaceae. *Fieldiana, Bot.* 35:5–227.
———. 1972. Evolutionary trends in the Central American species of *Piper* (Piperaceae). *Brittonia* 24:356–62.

FIGURE 7.99. *Piper auritum* leaf, immature inflorescences (drooping) and mature inflorescences, near Golfito, Costa Rica (photo, D. H. Janzen).

*

Burger, W. 1972. Evolutionary trends in the Central American species of *Piper. Brittonia* 24:356–62.

Gomez Pompa, A. 1971. Posible papel de la vegetación secundaria en la evolución de la flora tropical. *Biotropica* 3:125–35.

Janzen, D. 1978. The size of a local peak in a seed shadow. *Biotropica* 10:78.

Semple, K. 1974. Pollination in Piperaceae. *Ann. Missouri Bot. Gard.* 61:868–71.

Pithecellobium saman (Cenízero, Genízero, Raintree)

D. H. Janzen

Prominent as a very spreading tree in Guanacaste pastures, *Pithecellobium saman* is a huge mimosaceous tree (fig. 7.100*a,b*) closely related to *Enterolobium cyclocarpum*. It is native to the dry lowlands of Costa Rica and Central America (Mexico to northern South America) but has been widely introduced as a shade and garden tree throughout the tropics. It is sometimes called *Samanea saman* and appears on the cover of *Biotropica*. It is deciduous in deciduous forest but evergreen where planted in rain forest. The large leaves bear large, slightly tomentose leaflets that thoroughly close up at night. The leaves have well-developed petiolar nectaries. The heartwood is beautifully but subtly grained and is prized as furniture wood and paneling, especially by foresters in Malaysia.

The tree bears a crop of tens of thousands of white and pink flowers (inflorescences) in the same weeks when it refoliates and shortly after maturing the fruits, in the last 2 months of the dry season (March–April). A few florets in many inflorescences produce minute fruits that remain small (3–5 cm long) for at least 8 months (through the rainy season following flowering) and then rapidly enlarge and mature their seeds (Janzen 1978, 1982; fig. 7.100*c*). By March (middry season of the following year) the mature fruits are falling from the leafless branches. Adjacent trees may, however, be out of phase with each other by at least a month. Also, different branches within the same tree may be out of phase by a month.

The brown indehiscent, glabrous strap-shaped fruits are variously twisted and lie on the ground in the blazing sun and dry winds of the dry season. The fruits are 10–20 cm long and theoretically bear about nineteen to twenty seeds (fig. 7.100*d*). However, the full-sized pods normally contain five to ten full-sized seeds; seed abortions and predispersal seed predation by bugs and moth larvae are largely responsible for these losses. In natural habitats, the bulk of these fallen fruits lie below the parent tree and eventually rot when the rainy season begins. A few are carried off by rodents, and the fruit pulp and

other pipers are known to be eaten by bats, which play the major role in seed dispersal (Janzen 1978).

Piper auritum is sometimes encountered in fairly large even-age stands, dominating smaller secondary growth. But the species may also be very scattered, with only isolated individuals in a given area. This patch distribution (despite its status as a very common second-growth species) is a common pattern in a small tropical country that boasts almost half as many species of flowering plants as the entire United States.

Despite the fact that these are common plants in the moister parts of Central America, we know very little about the life history of this species. We have a good idea of its geographical range and ecological preferences, its morphological characteristics, and its possible relationships, but there are many simple questions for which we have no data; for example: How fast do these plants grow, and how long do they live? How many disseminules does an average individual produce, and how often are these the result of cross-pollination? What are the primary factors determining successful growth and reproduction?

seeds are partly or completely eaten (ground up). A few are eaten by tapirs, and some seeds survive the trip through the animal to be dispersed. Peccaries eat a few fruits but grind up the seeds in the process.

Again, as with *Crescentia alata,* in habitats containing domestic animals the story is quite different. Range cattle are avid consumers of *P. saman* fruits, and they pass most of the seeds intact. Horses eat them sparingly but reject them strongly when other fruits are available. Whatever the preferences, where livestock have access to *P. saman,* the fruits never accumulate below the tree. The obvious inference is that this tree was also dispersed by Pleistocene large mammals (Janzen and Martin 1982).

About the time the fruits are full-sized and the seeds are filling, a bruchid (*Merobruchus columbinus*) oviposits on the fruits and the larvae kill 50–70% of the seeds in most crops (Janzen 1977). If the fruits are opened so that the seeds are exposed, the seeds are oviposited on by a second, much smaller bruchid (*Stator limbatus*).

P. saman leaves are generally free of conspicuous herbivory, but the common name "raintree" derives from its general high susceptibility to Homoptera that suck out large amounts of sap and defecate it in a steady drizzle after extracting some of the nitrogen-rich compounds. Sucker shoots from cut stumps often have clusters of bright red, orange, and blueblack nymphs of a coreid bug feeding on their shoot tips. Leafcutter ants occasionally harvest some *P. saman* leaves, and howler monkeys eat flowers and young leaves (Rockwood and Glander 1979). The flowers are generally believed to be moth pollinated at night (W. A. Haber, pers. comm.). The very young fruits are galled by an unknown insect.

Large *P. saman* trees growing in the open (pastures, swampy sites) have large, long, and spreading branches covered with rough bark. These appear to make excellent substrate for epiphytes; orchids (*Brassavola nodosa* and *Laelia rubescens*) and large cacti (*Hylocereus costaricensis, Deamia testudo*) are commonly encountered on the branches. When large branches break off, large cavities develop in the trunk that are favorite night roosts for large *Ctenosaura similis* lizards that bask on the trunk and usually descend to the ground to forage nearby for herbaceous plants.

*

FIGURE 7.100 *Pithecellobium saman. a,* Adult tree in full foliage (June). *b,* Same adult tree, leafless in mid dry season (March); tree bears a full fruit crop and has new leaf buds just beginning to open. *c,* Nearly full-sized green (immature) fruits (long ones) and nearly dormant fruits (small thin ones) in January from the previous flowering in April (ruler is 15 cm long). *d,* Bruchid beetle exit hole in mature pod (*upper*); lateral longitudinal and dorsoventral longitudinal sections through mature pods showing intact seeds, seed with bruchid beetle exit hole, and aborted seed (*middle*); cross section through mature pod (*lower*) (upper scale of rule is mm). Santa Rosa National Park, Guanacaste Province, Costa Rica (photos, D. H. Janzen).

Janzen, D. H. 1977. Intensity of predation on *Pithecelobium saman* (Leguminosae) seeds by *Merobruchus columbinus* and *Stator limbatus* (Bruchidae) in Costa Rican deciduous forest. *Trop. Ecol.* 18:162–76.
———. 1978. The ecology and evolutionary biology of seed chemistry as relates to seed predation. In *Biochemical aspects of plant and animal coevolution,* ed. J. B. Harborne, pp. 163–206. London: Academic Press.

———. 1982. Cenízero tree (Leguminosae: *Pithecellobium saman*) delayed fruit development in Costa Rican deciduous forests. *Am. J. Bot.* 69:1269–76.

Janzen, D. H., and Martin, P. S. 1982. Neotropical anachronisms: The fruits the gomphotheres ate. *Science* 215:19–27.

Rockwood, L. L., and Glander, K. E. 1979. Howling monkeys and leaf-cutting ants: Comparative foraging in a tropical deciduous forest. *Biotropica* 11:1–10.

Posoqueria latifolia (Boca de Vieja, Guayaba de Mico, Fruta de Mono)

J. Beach

Posoqueria is a genus of ten to fifteen species of Neotropical trees belonging to the tribe Gardenieae of the large pantropicical family Rubiaceae (Hallé 1967; Willis 1973). *P. latifolia* is a small tree, usually to about 7 m tall, that is commonly found along streams and riverbanks in the Atlantic and Pacific lowlands of the country. It is occasionally planted for ornamental purposes, for example, along the steps leading up the south bank of the Río Puerto Viejo at the OTS La Selva field station.

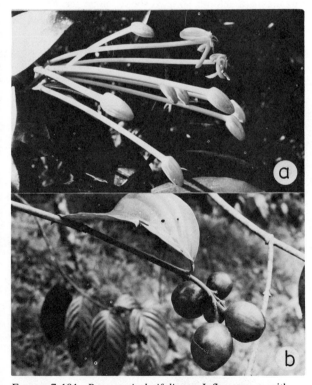

FIGURE 7.101. *Posoqueria latifolia. a,* Inflorescence with flower buds and open flowers. *b,* Infructescence with fully enlarged but green fruits. Finca La Selva, Sarapiquí District, Costa Rica (photo, J. Beach). *c (right), Posoqueria latifolia* floral morphology (adapted from Müller 1866).

In the Atlantic lowlands, the species flowers two or three times each year, in contrast to *P. grandiflora,* an understory forest species also found at La Selva that flowers at supra-annual intervals (Opler, Frankie, and Baker 1980; pers. obs.). The flowers are monomorphic and exhibit fairly typical characteristics of the moth-pollination syndrome. The white corolla tubes (fig. 7.101*a*) are about 4 mm in diameter, commonly 13 to 18 mm long, and have five lobes that reflex at anthesis (fig. 7.101*c*). The inflorescences terminate the branch and consist of a cluster of twenty to forty flowers.

The flowers begin to open in the late afternoon, about an hour before dusk, and shortly thereafter fill the night with an intoxicatingly sweet odor. Most flowers remain open for two or three nights before the corolla dehisces from the rim of the inferior ovary. The flowers produce a total of 0 to 25 μl of nectar with a 15–21% sugar concentration as measured by a hand refractometer. The reproductive biology of the species is currently under study, but available data indicate that the species is self-incompatible and to some extent protandrous.

Perhaps the most outstanding feature of the floral biology of *Posoqueria* is its specialized pollen dehiscence mechanism. This caught the attention of Fritz Müller more than one hundred years ago in Brazil (Müller 1866; also see Hallé 1967). The stamens are exposed after the five enclosing corolla lobes "pop" back as the flower opens. The anthers are coherent by their lateral margins to form a narrow cone that is slightly reflexed downward (fig. 7.101*c*). They remain in this position until they are even lightly disturbed, at which point the anther cluster explosively splits apart and the lowermost stamen rams a cohesive pollen mass into whatever is in the vicinity of the mouth of the corolla (fig. 7.101*c*). The force behind the fifth stamen's propulsion is very strong and sufficient to powder the anterior of a visiting hawkmoth with pollen. I have seen hawkmoths visit the flowers on several trees, but I have never been close enough to see their reaction to the explosive discharge. Ubiquitous *Trigona* bees frequently visit open flowers for pollen leftovers.

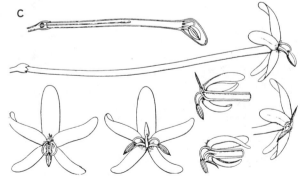

The fruit/flower ratio is low, as is the case with other self-incompatible trees (Bawa and Opler 1975). In this species the fruits are globose and range in size from 3 to 6 cm in diameter (fig. 7.101*b*). The diameter of the fruit largely reflects the number of seeds inside, four to twenty-one. At maturity the exocarp turns from green to yellow and has the strength and texture of a thin orange (*Citrus*) peel. The seeds are about 1.5 cm by 2 cm, weigh 0.5 to 1.4 g, and are very hard but covered with a thin, soft seed coat. A captive, but well-fed, parrot happily tore open the fruits and gnawed and ingested the seed coats before dropping the seeds. Fruits and seeds are probably naturally dispersed by large frugivorous birds, but I have yet to observe this. The seeds are mostly endosperm and show nearly 100% germination within 3 weeks. Plants can reach reproductive size within 5 years.

*

Bawa, K. S., and Opler, P. A. 1975. Dioecism in tropical forest trees. *Evolution* 29:167–79.

Hallé, F. 1967. Etude biologique et morphologique de la tribu des Gardéniées (Rubiaceae). *Mem. ORSTOM* (Abidjam, Ivory Coast) 22:1–146.

Müller, F. 1866. Über die Befruchtung der *Martha* (*Posoqueria*?) *fragrans. Bot. Zeit.* 24:129–32.

Opler, P. A.; Frankie, G. W.; and Baker, H. G. 1980. Comparative phenological studies of shrubs in tropical wet and dry forests in the lowlands of Costa Rica. *J. Ecol.* 68:167–88.

Willis, J. C. 1973. *A dictionary of the flowering plants and ferns.* Rev. by H. K. Airy Shaw. Cambridge: Cambridge University Press.

Pteridium aquilinum (Helechón, Helecho Alambre, Alambrón, Bracken Fern)

L. D. Gómez

The brake, common brake, or bracken (fig. 7.102) is probably the most widely distributed of the ferns and, likely, of all the vascular plants, since it is found throughout the world, arctic ice and deserts excluded.

It is even present in literature, from classical Greece to today, Shakespeare included ("We have the receipt of fern-seed, we walk invisible," *Henry IV*), and bracken pervades much of the medieval medical and herbalist writings for its imaginary magical properties as well as its medicinal value, since it reputedly killed "the broade and long wormes of the body." The antihelminthic action of a variety of ferns, including that of bracken, is known, but they are seldom so used today, since the *Filicicum acidum* of the old pharmacopoeias has been replaced by

FIGURE 7.102. *Pteridium aquilinum* fern fronds growing in an old field. Costa Rica (photo, L. D. Gómez).

safer remedies. There is also the alleged aphrodisiac power of the common brake (Cameron 1900).

Of the thousands of fern species, bracken is the only one that is troublesome to man, particularly in agricultural areas and where livestock range. Perhaps owing to this immediate effect on people's subsistence activities, *Pteridium* is the best known of all the pteridophytes (Long and Fenton 1938).

The history of bracken goes far beyond the written record of man's endeavors. It is known from pre-Quaternary times, and the fossil record extends to the late Miocene (Long and Fenton 1938). Its geographical distribution in past times was highly influenced by the glacial and interglacial periods that are undoubtedly responsible for its present distribution on earth.

Pteridium is a genus of terrestrial ferns with long-creeping subterranean rhizomes clothed with hairs. The fronds are pinnately compound, leathery, and more or less hairy, with veins free except for a marginal strand. The sorus is marginal and continuous, borne on the connecting vein and protected by a double indusium, of which the outer flap (a false indusium) is formed by the reflexed margin of the frond and the inner one (the true indusium) has a different ontogeny and may or may not be present or obsolescent. There are no paraphyses in the sorus, the sporangia are slender-stalked, and the spores are smooth, tetrahedral or slightly globose. Phylogenetically it belongs in the Pteridaceae sensu Copeland (1947) with several other closely allied genera (*Paesia, Pteris, Histiopteris, Hypolepis,* etc.). Taxonomically and as generally construed, it comprises one highly variable species, *Pteridium aquilinum* (L.) Kuhn, and a few others. The taxonomy has been revised by Tryon (1941) and by Page (1976).

In Costa Rica there are *P. aquilinum* varieties *aquilinum, arachnoideum,* and *caudatum.* In Honduras and northern Nicaragua, the pine savannas have the variety *latiusculum,* also found in some Caribbean islands and possibly extending its range to Costa Rica.

It is apparent from the study of the geographical ranges of the varietal taxa that while some are rather discrete over large geographical areas, they overlap in other places, with evident morphological intergradation that has led to some confusion over what names and ranks need to be applied to the plants in question. If the various names indeed represent different species, they hybridize freely. If *P. aquilinum* is a polymorphic species, the genome has extraordinary plasticity in phenotype expression, triggered by ecological factors or by ploidal levels or combinations thereof. The genome, n = 52 is known from diploids, tetraploids, and octoploids (Löve and Kjellqvist 1972; Chapman, Klekowski, and Selander 1979; Manton 1950; Jarrett, Manton, and Roy 1968).

Like most other ferns, *Pteridium* has two mechanisms of dispersal: a long-distance dispersal by airborne spores and a more local vegetative reproduction by fragmentation of the rhizome. This organ has a peculiar behavior, showing a continual new shoot forking and die-back of older parts (Watt 1940) that often carries the full burden of population dispersal, being more efficient than the spores. The production of spores in bracken varies from locality to locality, depending partly on habitat and season, where that applies. Dring (1965) found that spore fertility decreased with increasing shade, while the rhizomatous propagation increased in shaded habitats. In Costa Rica, where bracken is typically a sun fern, the production of spores is extremely low in number and fertility. I think that the rate of spore/rhizome propagation is regulated genetically in each population as a response to certain as yet unknown environmental conditions. Phenology in temperate zones indicates peaks of sporulation during summer. In Costa Rica, the homogeneous climatic factors and photoperiod yield a year-round spore production where a high percentage of the spores are produced for long-distance colonizing, while the producing population invades nearby grounds exclusively by stoloniferous growth.

As the name suggests (*Brache* is Old German for "wasted land"), *Pteridium* easily invades ground where agriculture has been abandoned or clearing done. This fern, popularly known in Costa Rica as "helechón" (big fern), "helecho alambre" ("wiry fern") or simply as "alambrón" ("thick wire") is a frequent pioneer of the abandoned maize and bean slash-and-burn fields. It is particularly an after-fire plant (Das 1947; Vogl 1964). In ranching areas it invades pastures, where thick colonies are established in marginal situation first by spores and then in all directions by the hypogeous growth of the rhizomes, shooting fronds everywhere. If these pastures are not being grazed, these fronds grow above the grass and are then avoided by cattle; but if grazing is permanent, the foraging animals ingest the juvenile, often uncurled, fronds, and given time a herd may be poisoned. Wherever the system of rotating or alternating grazing enclosures is practiced, this fern growth/grass growth phase explains the illness of one herd and not another. The poisoning in known as the thiaminase-mediated syndrome (Evans 1976).

The accumulative toxicity of bracken in cattle is complicated because the fern elaborates several compounds harmful to livestock. The enzyme thiaminase I breaks the thiamine (vitamin B complex) molecules (Evans, Jones, and Evans 1950), inhibiting the normal functioning of the nervous system. Animals ingesting bracken may develop a severe avitaminosis B_1 (horses, pigs). The CBPF, or cattle bracken poisoning factor (Evans et al. 1958), characterized by high body temperatures, petechial hemorrhages of mucous membranes, severe leukopenia, and trombocytopenia, leading to death, is another effect of this fern in ranches. Also, there is an apparent correlation between low-level long-term ingestion of bracken and occurrence of certain tumors caused by carcinogenic chemicals (Evans and Mason 1965), a fact that may be also responsible for the high incidence of gastric cancer in human populations where bracken is eaten. The Japanese (Hirono et al. 1972) consider it a delicacy and call the young fronds *warabe*.

Some sheep herds have developed a degenerative disease of the neuroepithelium of the retina, leading to blindness. This is called the "bright blindness disease" and is attributed to bracken ingestion, possibly linked with hemopoietic depressions involved in the CBPF syndrome.

Concentration of the lethal chemicals of bracken varies from plant to plant, in different parts of a plant, and in different populations. This variation may be seasonal (Smith and Fenton 1944) in the temperate zones. In Costa Rica the paucity of records of cattle poisoning suggests a nonperiodic fluctuation of lethal compounds, possibly related to the flush of new growth linked with the beginning of the rainy season, not so much because of the season as because of the increased probability of ingestion by the cattle.

The fluctuations may also explain the variations of the arthropod community structure that exerts herbivory pressure at various times of the year and on different parts of the bracken plant (Lawton 1976; Wiczorek 1973).

As many as forty taxa of arthropods are known to prey, directly or indirectly, on *Pteridium,* with predominance of Lepidoptera (micro), Hymenoptera, Homoptera, and Diptera. Some of these animals may be facultative feeders, also eating other ferns and higher plants. Research should be aimed at locating the obligate predators with the idea of developing successful biological controls of bracken.

Pteridium fronds have nectaries at the base of the pinnae (Schremmer 1969); the ecological meaning of these structures is in need of detailed research. In Costa Rica I have seen ants (*Pheidole, Camponotus*) visiting these secretory organs. Secretions follow a diurnal pattern, much influenced by insolation, and though there are no anatomical studies done I suspect that the bracken "nectaries" are modified pneumatophores combining functions in the gas and liquids exchange balance. The chemical composition of the brake has been extensively studied, mainly in relation to the poisons and carcinogenic compounds, but other chemicals are listed by Swain and Cooper-Driver (1973) and by Cooper-Driver (1976).

The confirmed presence of ecdysones in *Pteridium* (Williams 1972) and the implications for insect feeding offer a fascinating field of research.

Herbivory by animals other than cattle, insects, and rabbits (Sheail 1971) is not documented except for man. The New Zealand Maoris ate a bread made of the powdered rhizomes (Hooker 1861), and in a similar way this "flour" was mixed with barley and baked in the Canary Islands (Lindley 1838) and in Normandy (Lightfoot 1777; Hendrick 1919). Schery (1954) reports some American Indians eating the rhizomes, and during World War I recipes for cooking bracken were published in British newspapers (Braid 1934). I have already mentioned the food value attributed to bracken by Orientals, who sell it by the ton in their markets, importing enormous quantities when local production is low.

In terms of other plants, *Pteridium* has allelopathic effects on the surrounding vegetation, and by this mechanism it can dominate a wide variety of plants. In temperate areas allelopathic toxins are released seasonally, whereas in tropical and subtropical settings, such as Costa Rica, there is year-round production and release of phytotoxins (Gliessman 1972). Population biology of bracken in terms of allelopathy may be affected by leaching/rainfall, rainfall/soil lixiviation, and topography/drainage ratios as well as the composition of the surrounding vegetation (Watt 1965). In my opinion most ferns, bracken included, regulate the numbers of prothallia of their same species and particularly of their same parental stock by self-directed allelopathic mechanisms affecting the sexual cycle. A hint of this is found in the isolation of antheridiogenic substances from *Pteridium* and the variable results obtained when this is applied to *Pteridium* or other fern gametophytes.

*

Braid, K. W. 1934. Bracken as a colonist. *Scot. J. Agric.* 17:59–70.

Cameron, J. 1900. *Gaelic names of plants.* Edinburgh.

Chapman, R. H.; Klekowski, E. J.; and Selander, R. K. 1979. Homoeologous heterozygosity and recombination in the fern *Pteridium aquilinum. Science* 204: 1207–9.

Cooper-Driver, G. 1976. Chemotaxonomy and phytochemical ecology of bracken. *Bot. J. Linn. Soc.* 73:35–46.

Copeland, E. B. 1947. *Genera filicum.* Waltham, Mass.: Chronica Botanica.

Das, P. 1947. Panvin burning in some upper Simla hill states. *Indian Forest.* 73:121–22.

Dring, M. J. 1965. The influence of shaded conditions on the fertility of bracken. *Brit. Fern Gaz.* 9:222–27.

Evans, I. A. 1976. Bracken thiaminase-mediated neurotoxic syndromes. *Bot. J. Linn. Soc.* 73:113–31.

Evans, I. A.; Jones, N. R.; and Evans, R. A. 1950. The mechanism of antianeurin activity of bracken (*Pteris aquilina*). *Biochem. J.* 46:38.

Evans, I. A., and Mason, J. 1965. Carcinogenic activity of bracken. *Nature* 208:913–14.

Evans, W. C.; Evans, I. A.; Thomas, A. J.; Watkin, J. E.; and Chamberlain, A. T. 1958. Studies on bracken poisoning in cattle, IV. *Brit. Vet. J.* 114:180–267.

Gliessman, S. R. 1972. The role of phytotoxins in the interference with associated plants by bracken (*Pteridium aquilinum* [L.] Kuhn). Ph.D. thesis, University of California, Santa Barbara.

Hendrick, J. 1919. Bracken rhizomes and their food value. *Trans. Highl. Soc. Scot.* 5:227–36.

Hirono, I.; Shibuya, C.; Shimizu, M.; and Fushimi, K. 1972. Carcinogenic activity of processed bracken used as human food. *J. Nat. Canc. Inst.* 48:1245–50.

Hooker, W. J. 1861. *The British ferns.* London.

Jarrett, F. M.; Manton, I.; and Roy, S. K. 1968. Cytological and taxonomical notes on a small collection of living ferns from Galapagos. *Kew Bull.* 22:475–80.

Lawton, J. H. 1976. The structure of the arthropod community on bracken. *Bot. J. Linn. Soc.* 73:186–216.

Lightfoot, J. 1777. *Flora scotica.* Vol. 2. London.

Lindley, J. 1838. *Flora medica.* London.

Long, H. C., and Fenton, E. W. 1938. The story of the bracken fern. *J. Roy. Agric. Soc.* 99:15–36.

Löve A., and Kjellqvist, E. 1972. Cytotaxonomy of Spanish plants. 1. Introduction: Pteridophytes and gymnosperms. *Lagascalia* 2:23–25.

Manton, I. 1950. *Problems in cytology and evolution of the Pteridophytes.* Cambridge: Cambridge University Press.

Page, C. N. 1976. Taxonomy and phytogeography of bracken: A review. *Bot. J. Linn. Soc.* 73:1–34.

Schery, R. W. 1954. *Plants for man.* London: Allen and Unwin.

Schremmer, F. 1969. Extranuptiale Nectarien: Beobachtungen an *Salix elegans* Scop. und *Pteridium aquilinum* (L.) Kuhn. *Oest. Bot. Zeit.* 117:205–22.

Sheail, J. 1971. *Rabbits and their history.* London: Newton Abbot.

Smith, A. M., and Fenton, E. W. 1944. The composition of bracken fronds and rhizomes at different times during the growing season. *J. Soc. Chem. Ind. London* 63:218–19.

Swain, T., and Cooper-Driver, G. 1973. Biochemical systematics in the Filicopsida. In *The phylogeny and classification of the ferns,* ed. A. C. Jermy, J. A. Crabbe, and B. A. Thomas, pp. 111–34. London: Academic Press for the Linnean Society of London.

Tryon, R. M. 1941. A revision of the genus *Pteridium.* *Rhodora* 43:1–31.

Vogl, R. 1964. The effects of fire on the vegetational composition of bracken-grasslands. *Wisconsin Acad. Sci. Arts Letters* 53:67–82.

Watt, A. S. 1940. Contribution to the ecology of bracken (*Pteridium aquilinum*). 1. The rhizome. *New Phytol.* 39:401–22.

———. 1965. Bracken versus heather, a study in plant sociology. *J. Ecol.* 43:490–506.

Wiczorek, H. 1973. Zur Kenntniss der Adlerfarninsekten: Ein Beitrag zur Probleme der biologischen Bekämpfung von *Pteridium aquilinum* (L.) Kuhn in Mitteleuropa. *Z. Angew. Entomol.* 4:337–58.

Williams, C. M. 1972. Hormonal interactions between plants and insects. In *Chemical ecology,* ed. E. Sondheimer and J. B. Simeone, pp. 103–32. London: Academic Press.

Pteridophytes (Helechos, Ferns)

W. H. Wagner and L. D. Gómez

As a group these plants are ecologically much less versatile than the flowering plants. There are no parasites or saprophytes except for the mycorrhizal gametophytes of certain ferns and club mosses, and no carnivores. Ecological interactions with animals are much less diverse, since the complex insect and vertebrate interactions involving pollen and fruit dispersal are absent.

The pteridophyte life cycle is simple, involving merely production of spores and short-lived, free-living sexual plants. Costa Rica is rich in variety of pteridophytes in part because of its great array of climates and habitats, but especially because of the extensive development of rain forests of various types. The rain forests everywhere in the tropical world yield the prime requirements for the massive development of pteridophytes, which are mainly plants of shaded, moist habitats with plenty of free water in the form of dew and rain. Compared with all of North America north of Mexico, there are more than twice as many pteridophyte species in a country smaller than the state of West Virginia. What the actual number may be is unknown, but Costa Rica probably has more than eight hundred species all together. Many new finds have been made in the past decade, and discoveries will probably continue far into the future. Types wholly unknown in temperate North America are prominent—horsetails 5–6 m tall, ferns with stems 10 m tall or leaves 15 m long (climbing to the canopy of the forest), and club mosses dangling from the boughs of trees. Represented are all the major pteridophyte orders: Ophioglossales, Marattiales, and Polypodiales, the ferns; Lycopodiales, Selaginellales, the Isoetales, the club mosses and their relatives; Equisetales, the horsetails; and Psilotales, the whisk ferns. By far the largest group is Polypodiales, the higher or common ferns, which occur in Costa Rica in a multitude of families and genera. The smallest are the Equisetales with four or five species and hybrids, and the Psilotales with two species.

In the sexual life cycle, fertilization depends upon free water through which the sperm can swim. The sperm and eggs are produced on the overlooked minute sexual plants or gametophytes, which arise directly from the wind-borne spores, germinating in appropriate microhabitats characteristic of each species. Sperm produced on one gametophyte may swin to another gametophyte and cross-fertilize an egg. Also, sperm from the male organs of one gametophyte may swin to eggs in the female organs of the same gametophyte and self-fertilize. In any event, a new fern plant arises and the gametophyte dies, being an ephemeral plant that functions only to produce the next generation of sporophytes. The only exceptions are found in some environmental conditions where the gametophytes may become perennial clones, like those of mosses and liverworts, reproducing by tiny propagules or gemmae that form new gametophytes. The same gametophytes may also produce sporophytes that propagate vegetatively too. Thus the same fern species may exist in gametophytic clones and sporophytic clones. This is unusual, however, and in most species it is the familiar fern sporophyte that is perennial. So far as we know, a given fern sporophyte that has the capacity for vegetative propagation can live for decades or centuries in favorable habitat.

In Costa Rica the gametophytes are to be seen in greatest numbers on shady, mineral sites where competition is minimal or absent. The best places to see the sexual life cycle taking place are roadbanks, landslides, and stream banks in moderate to heavily rainy areas. The gametophytes appear as tiny, flat green kidney- or heart-shaped plants, 1–2 mm across and mostly one cell thick except in the center. Many of them will have young sporophytes with one to many small leaves growing from them. There are numerous variations of gametophytes that go hand-in-hand with different ecological requirements. The nonphotosynthetic types have strong mycorrhizal relationships and are subterranean; they are very rarely observed by ecologists. The algalike filamentous types occur exculsively in deeply shaded, damp sites, usually growing in close association with mosses and liverworts. The heterosporous types, in which the gametophytes are rudimentary—male ones produced in microspores and female ones produced in much-enlarged, food-filled megaspores—occur in various habitats, but especially in the rain forest and in aquatic situations like ponds and vernal pools. The heterosporous life cycle ensures cross-fertilization between gametophytes, sperm swimming from the male spores to the female spores; thus there is never any intragametophytic fertilization.

The growth forms and patterns of development of Costa Rican pteridophytes tend to be correlated with specific microhabitats. The sporophytes are generally small to medium-sized herbaceous plants, but the tissues of many of them, especially their stems and rachises, are commonly hard or wiry owing to abundant development of mechanical tissue. Soft, succulent pteridophytes are uncommon. The tallest Costa Rican ferns are some of the Cyatheaceae, which may reach 10 m or more in height, because of the extensive upright stem development, producing the habit of a palm. Other types, to be discussed below, form enormous sprawling or climbing leaves. The smallest ferns and club mosses are so small that they are sometimes confused with mosses or liverworts. Their stems are reduced to narrow threads.

The basic stem of all pteridophytes is the rhizome, a type of stem that creeps over the ground or underground. The rhizomes of eiphytic ferns grow tightly rooted on the bark of tree trunks and branches. The internodes may be long and drawn out, thus producing fronds remote from each other. Or they may be so short and compact that the fronds arise in clusters of few to many. The rhizomes of most Costa Rican ferns are poorly known because they often require laborious excavation, and many of them are massive, hardly suited for routine collection or mounting on an herbarium sheet. Some species start life on the ground and then form vines, climbing into the crowns of trees. Other species start out as epiphytes and form wholly epiphytic vines. Dozens of species of the latter type of development may be encountered on the crotches of roadside trees and pollards in wet regions at middle altitudes, including species of polypodies (*Polypodium, Pleopeltis, Phlebodium*), spleenworts (*Asplenium*), and shoestring ferns (*Vittaria*). In the same regions, the club mosses (*Lycopodium*) tend to form tassles up to 1 m long of stringy stems covered with short, pale green, needle-like leaves, pendant from boughs of trees. Thus not all epiphytic pteridophytes have long vinelike rhizomes; some have short, clustered rhizomes instead. Short rhizomes are especially common in the epiphytic paddle ferns (*Elaphoglossum*) and sword ferns (*Nephrolepis*).

Erect, trunklike stems with palmlike clusters of fronds are common in Costa Rican forest and bog species of ferns. The best known and most common are the tree ferns (*Cyathea, Dicksonia,* discussed elsewhere in this book), but similar, though smaller, forms are found in other groups, such as lady ferns (*Athyrium*) and spleenworts (*Asplenium*). Upright trunks of treelike ferns vary from 10 cm to 10 m or more. The bogs in the Cerro de la Muerte are noted for their spectacular cycadlike ferns, *Blechnum buchtienii,* with massive trunks 1–2 m tall and thick, leathery one-pinnate fronds.

Most pteridophytes, terrestrial or epiphytic, form clones. Epiphytic clones tend to be smaller than terrestrial ones, because of the narrow dimensions of the epiphytic habitat. Terrestrial clones may reach many meters in diameter, especially in uniform sites like fields and swamps. The main agent of vegetative propagation is the rhizome. In Costa Rica the most illustrative clones are those of club mosses (e.g., *Lycopodium cernuum*), horsetails (*Equisetum giganteum, E. bogotense*), bracken ferns (*Pteridium arachnoideum*), and forking staghorn ferns (*Gleichenia* spp.), all common in wet regions in open fields and meadows. In the rain forest most clones are much smaller, usually interrupted by trees, rocks, steep banks, and the like.

Epiphytic clones commonly form narrow roots that can spread over the bark and proliferate tiny buds at their tips. This is especially common in certain groups like the spleenworts (*Asplenium*) and especially the dwarf polypodies (*Grammitis*). The extensive terrestrial clones of adder's-tongue (*Ophioglossum*) ferns are also produced by root proliferation, in this case, however, by thick, fleshy roots that extend underground to form buds.

Another mode of clone formation involves the fronds. This usually happens in ferns that have short upright rhizomes. Buds form at definite places along the leaf, depending upon the species. Costa Rican maidenhair ferns (e.g., *Adiantum philipense*), spleenworts (*Asplenium radicans*, with many forms), and certain filmy ferns (*Feea diversifolia*) produce long, whiplike tips 5–20 cm long on certain leaves, at the tips of which plantlets form. The long, taillike leaf tip (up to 0.5 m long) in the common terrestrial fern of wet forests, *Bolbitis portoricensis*, may touch down several times and produce a new plant at each contact with the soil. Many ferns simply form seemingly useless buds at the middle or base of the leaf blade. It is not immediately obvious how these buds propagate the plant, but apparently when the bud-bearing leaf begins to die and lies down, the buds can reach the substratum and take root, giving rise in this way to large colonies.

Pteridophytes are said to have two basic leaf types — *microphylls*, with single central veins (e.g., club mosses, horsetails), and *megaphylls*, usually much larger, with complex *systems* of veins, either free or netted. The basic fern leaf is a megaphyll, usually designated as a frond or pteridophyll, which has a more or less massive central axis or rachis, plus lateral stalks, leaflets, or pinnae. The modifications of pteridophylls in Costa Rica are legion, many of them closely correlated with specialized habitats or growth habits. Many of the species have no true pinnae, but only lobes, and others — a very large number of species — are without either leaflets or lobes, being entirely simple. Perhaps one-fifth of Costa Rican ferns have simple fronds. Most lobed or simple fronds belong to epiphitic ferns. In contrast, most finely dissected fern leaves, four to five times compound, belong to terrestrial species.

Some of the most extreme modifications of fronds are found in the filmy ferns (Hymenophyllaceae), most of which are delicate plants growing as epiphytes low on trunks of rain-forest trees in deep shade. Even primitive filmy ferns, which are terrestrial and look like miniature tree ferns, have the characteristic blade anatomy — translucent and, except along veins, one cell layer in thickness. The most extreme modifications of filmy fern leaves are those so finely divided as to have capillary segments (*Trichomanes capillaceum*) and those with flat, platelike simple leaves with no midrib or obviously pin-

nate vein pattern (*Trichomanes membranaceum*), the veins all dichotomizing. In many respects the filmy ferns are among the most highly evolved of the polypodiales, some of them having even lost their roots phylogenetically, the entire plant being made up of strongly modified simple leaves and hairlike rhizomes. Ecologically they occur closely associated with bryophytes, some of which they resemble. The spores of filmy ferns are formed in little pocketlike involucres at the edges of the leaves. They are green owing to chlorophyll visible through the very thin, transparent walls. There is little or no stored food, and the spores are short-lived; if they do not germinate soon after discharge and before drying out, they will die. The gametophytes of filmy ferns are variously specialized: some look like fine ribbonlike liverworts, others like filamentous algae. They reproduce themselves by tiny few-celled propagules or gemmae. The filmy ferns include many species of wet dark forests everywhere in Costa Rica, especially at middle altitudes.

The most conspicuous fern fronds are those of the sprawling ferns, seen in open fields, eroding rocky slopes, second-growth areas, and roadbanks. These sprawling fronds lie upon or lean upon other vegetation. Such examples as bracken (*Pteridium*) and its relatives (e.g., *Dennstaedtia*, *Paesia*) form enormous populations at middle altitudes. The most abundant sprawling leaves are those of the staghorn ferns (*Gleichenia*), which flourish on steep hillsides. The staghorn leaves are indeterminate in growth. The wiry rachises produce pairs of pinnae, and each of these soon produces additional pairs, thus making a falsely dichotomous branching system. Dormant buds can be observed in the forkings. Some sprawling ferns (e.g., *Odontosoria*, *Dennstaedtia*) are prickly, with fine spinelike outgrowths whose functions are not clear. Perhaps they aid in climbing over other vegetation. All the sprawling ferns seem to be succession plants, appearing in abandoned fields, steep roadbanks, and landslides. Woody plants germinate in the soil below the frond canopy, and the forest returns. After some time the growth of the sprawlers becomes attenuated, and the ferns gradually disappear with the expanding forest except where there are blowdowns.

Climbing ferns have extremely long, indeterminate leaves reaching up to 20 m tall. These actually climb by twining and by hooking their leaflets to the adjacent vegetation. The two most important genera are *Lygodium* (Schizaeaceae) and *Blechnum* (syn. *Salphichlaena volubile*, Blechnaceae). All lygodiums are climbers, except in the juvenile stage. Blechnums are not climbers, with this one exception.

The major pteridophyte habitats are terrestrial, epiphytic, and aquatic. Most pteridophytes are terrestrial and grow in a great variety of habitats, including rocky slopes and rock cliffs. Epiphytic pteridophytes are most prominent in the wet forest, where they grow mainly with orchids and bromeliads. Probably the commonest single fern species in Costa Rica is the simple-leaved polypody *Pleopeltis astrolepis* (discussed in detail elsewhere in this book).

The aquatic pteridophytes of Costa Rica are of several ecological types. Some live at edges at lakes and ponds and in very wet marshes, like the giant leather ferns (*Acrostichum*) of the lowland inlets and swamps. Other aquatic pteridophytes live rooted below the surface of the water, such as quillworts (*Isoetes*) in high mountain ponds or the so-called aquarium ferns (*Ceratopteris*) of lowland marshes and ditches. Pteridophytes that float on the surface of the water are the ovate-leaved water spangles (*Salvinia*) and the tiny mosquito ferns (*Axolla*). Water spangles may choke artificial reservoirs and ponds because of unrestrained growth under certain conditions. *Azolla* is important as an indirect supplier of nitrogen nutrition in rice paddies because of the blue-green algae contained between the lobes of the minute leaves. Economically, because of its agricultural use in the improvement of rice culture, *Azolla* may develop into the most valuable pteridophyte. Its use is spreading to vari-

ous areas of the tropics from China, where its value was first recognized. Some pteridophytes occur only in wet-season ponds and lie invisible and dormant during extended dry periods, such as the water clovers (*Marsialia*, fig. 7.103).

The metropolis of pteridophytes in general is the rain forest. Epiphytes constitute roughly one-third to one-fourth of the species. The lowland rain forest is, however, poor in species diversity. Lowland epiphytes are few, and terrestrial species are limited to several genera, especially maidenhair ferns (*Adiantum*) and halberd ferns (*Tectaria*). At higher elevations more and more epiphytes occur, and the overall total of pteridophytes increases greatly. The surfaces of rocks, soil, and tree trunks become covered with algae, lichens, liverworts, and mosses, and pteridophytes become a highly conspicuous element of the vegetation.

Magnificent rich, middle-elevation rain forests are present on the slopes and ravines of the volcanos near San José, and many excellent localities can be reached in a short time by car if the roads are in good condition. Hundreds of pteridophytes species may be readily observed. Where the forest has been cut, remaining stumps

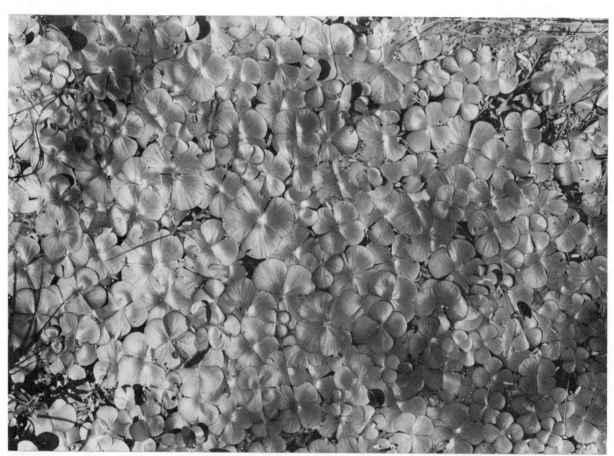

FIGURE 7.103. *Marsilea deflexa*, a heterosporous water fern on the surface of a puddle in an old road. November 1980, Santa Rosa National Park, Guanacaste Province, Costa Rica (photo, D. H. Janzen).

of massive trees become clothed with mosses and many rare and unusual epiphytes of wide ecological diversity. One of the most peculiar is the hand fern (*Ophioglossum palmatum*), which differs from all the other Costa Rican members of its genus by being epiphytic rather than terrestrial, in occurring in rain forest rather than open pastures and fields, and in having large, pendant, handlike fronds rather than small, upright, ovate or cordate leaves. Hand-fern habitat is deeply shaded cavities of old, rotting forest tree trunks (Gómez 1976a; Mesler 1974).

Even small trees that are planted along roads in areas that once were rain forests will become loaded with various epiphytes. The more conspicuous genera are club mosses (*Lycopodium*), polypodies (*Polypodium, Pleopeltis*), dwarf polypodies (*Grammitis, Cochlidium*), and filmy ferns (*Trichomanes, Hymenophyllum*). Tree ferns (*Cyathea, Dicksonia*) are especially common in wet, middle-elevation ravines, especially where there has been disturbance or erosion in the recent past.

Dry and exposed areas tend to be poor in pteridophyte diversity, but those that occur in these areas are often highly characteristic. In Guanacaste pools that dry up in drought periods become alive with water clovers when the rainy season begins. Dry forests are characterized by mainly terrestrial pteridophytes—maidenhair ferns (*Adiantum*), halberd ferns (*Tectaria*), maiden ferns (*Thelypteris*), and brakes (*Pteris*). The best development of climbing ferns of the genus *Lygodium* in Costa Rica is in lowland semidry forest along forest edges and stream banks.

Dry rocky sites, such as the cliffs along the Virilla River in San José Province and in various places in Guanacaste Province, have xerophytic pteridophytes, many of them capable of curling up and becoming desiccated and dormant during the dry season. The prominent xerophytic pteridophytes are certain spike mosses (e.g., *Selaginella pallescens*), dwarf maidenhair (*Adiantum concinnum*; see detailed discussion of this species), cliff brakes (*Pellaea*), lip ferns and cloak ferns (*Cheilanthes, Mildella, Aleuritopteris, Notholaena*), and strawberry ferns (*Hemionitis*). Many of the same species turn up on steep, rocky river and stream banks and roadbanks. Such places also have well-developed populations of blechnums (especially *B. occidentale*), silver-back ferns (especially *Pityrograma calomelanos*), and anemias (*Anemia phyllitidis* and *A. tomentosa*).

Dry rocky streambeds that occasionally flood provide the typical habitat for the goldenrod fern (*Trismeria trifoliata*), which reaches between 1 and 2 m tall. It forms huge clones by its extensive root system. The three-dimensional arrangement of the leaflets on strict, upright squarish rachises is found in no other Costa Rican fern. Goldenrod fern hybridizes readily with silver-back ferns (*Pityrogramma*) to produce abundant intermediates, as

along the Parismina River near Siquirres. The hybrid ferns are capable of forming large patches by inheriting the propagation method of the goldenrod fern (Gómez 1979).

At very high altitudes, as for example at the Cerro de la Muerte, open páramolike vegetation dominated by the bamboo, *Swallenochloa,* has a wholly distinctive pteridophyte community.

Terrestrial club mosses (*Lycopodium*) are especially well developed, including typical club mosses (group of *L. clavatum*), running cedars (generic segregate *Diphasiastrum*), and fir club mosses (generic segregate *Huperzia*). The most interesting lycopods are the hyperzias of the group of *L. saururus,* which lack a normal rhizome and have no distinction of the spore-bearing parts from the non-spore-bearing parts. The sporophylls differ from the trophophylls only in the presence of axillary spore cases.

Among the genera well developed at the Cerro de la Muerte is the striking *Jamesonia*, a fern distantly related to maidenhair ferns and cliff brakes, but characterized by stiffly erect, extremely linear, sticklike, fuzzy fronds, about 20–40 cm tall. The fronds, which look like narrow grass leaves when viewed from a short distance away, can be recognized by the bulging tips. The fiddlehead frond tips never completely unroll, so that they remain curled over and dormant. There are several species of *Jamesonia* at the Cerro de la Muerte. Not only do they readily hybridize with each other, but they also hybridize with the very different-looking ferns of the genus *Eriosorus*, in which the fronds are more ordinarily fernlike, broad and several times divided (Gómez 1979). The hybrids are vigorous and combine the parental characters.

Phenology of growth and reproduction in Costa Rican pteridophytes, as in tropical regions in general, is probably considerably less precise than in flowering plants. For example, there is no specialized flowering time to coordinate with insect pollination. Nevertheless, there are definite seasonal rhythms. These seasonal rhythms probably are rarely as pronounced as the abrupt seasonal growth stages of pteridophytes in north temperate regions in April, May, and June. Many ferns and spike mosses curl up and become dormant during the dry season. These are commonly called "resurrection ferns" or "resurrection plants," because they "come alive" when wetted, even after the plants have died. Some of the selaginellas roll up into a tight ball. Many of the epiphytic polypodies become so tightly curled that they are unrecognizable to species unless resurrected. When soaked in water for a few hours they will resume their normal frond forms.

In general the rainy periods in all habitats are the periods of maximum activity, including stem growth, leaf development, spore production, and gametophyte function. As to details of phenology in specific groups, little is known, largely because the necessary data are unavailable. We do know that different groups do differ considerably. For example, at the Cerro de la Muerte near the end of the rainy season in November we find some ferns (e.g., *Eriosorus, Jamesonia, Histiopteris*) that are actively producing new growth and forming spores. Others (*Polypodium, Elaphoglossum*) have evidently stopped new growth, and all their fronds appear to be at least 1 or 2 months old. Most species of adder's-tongue ferns (*Ophioglossum*), plants of open fields and pastures, appear during the height of the rainy season during June through September, being dormant the rest of the year. However, in unusually wet years they may be stimulated to expand their growth period or to develop out of season.

Many Costa Rican pteridophytes produce specialized spore-producing parts such as cones or highly modified sporophylls. These specialized reproductive structures are short-lived, and when they have discharged their spores they turn brown and papery and die. The vegetative shoots or unmodified trophophylls continue to function photosynthetically for many months. Some pteridophyte species have such long-lived trophophylls that the blade surfaces ultimately become covered with heavy growths of algae, lichens, and bryophytes.

Fungus-pteridophyte relationships have not been investigated in Costa Rica, although there is much descriptive evidence from studies elsewhere that mycorrhizal relationships are important.

Fungus hyphae are found in and around the roots and stems of many pteridophytes, some of which have few root hairs or none.

Although there are no wholly "saprophytic" sporophytes, the gametophytes of a number of pteridophyte genera are without chlorophyll and grow 1–4 cm below the soil surface. In these plants the relationship is probably one of parasitism, the gametophyte being entirely dependent on the mycorrhizal fungus for nutrition. Underground, nonchlorophyllous mycorrhizal gametophytes are found in Costa Rica in the adder's-tongue family, Ophioglossaceae (*Botrychium, Ophioglossum*); curly grass family, Schizaeaceae (*Actinostachys, Lophidium*); whisk fern family, Psilotaceae (*Psilotum*); and club moss family, Lycopodiaceae (*Lycopodium*, segregates *Lycopodium, Diphasiastrum,* and *Huperzia*). These presumably parasitic gametophytes are usually 1–4 mm in maximum diameter, pillow-shaped or thickly rod-shaped, ivory to brownish, and more or less covered with fine hairs. The sex organs are inconspicuous and sunken. They can be found in disturbed, open ground in the vicinity of the parents by detecting tiny juvenile sporophytes projecting from the ground and digging in the soil around and below them. The mycorrhizal gametophytes of the epiphytic species are exceedingly difficult to find.

Animal-plant relationships involving pteridophytes are much less complex than those in flowering plants because of the absence of flowers with pollen and nectar foods and of fruits and seeds with pericarp and embryo foods. The traditional dogma, in fact, is that ferns and fernlike plants are free from grazers, but this is not entirely true and is actually misleading. Grazers have been observed on many ferns, and insect-damaged leaves are commonly observed in a number of genera (Balick, Furth, and Cooper-Driver 1978). A misinterpretation of the experience of any herbarium collectors that dried ferns are not attacked by the regular museum pests may be responsible for the traditional opinion. (It is generally not necessary to fumigate pressed pteridophyte specimens in the herbarium because of their freedom from attack.)

Nectaries or nectarylike structures have not yet been studied in detail except in a few Costa Rican species (*Diplazium, Polypodium, Pteridium*), although they are well known in brackens and certain polypodies in other parts of the world. These extrasoral nectaries occur along the rachises at the bases of pinnae, and the fluids secreted are rich in various sugars and amino acids.

Relationships with ants are rare, but one of Costa Rica's most famous ferns produces modified rhizomes that accommodate ants. This fern, *Solanopteris brunei*, is a simple-leaved polypody that grows along the boughs of tall trees. Superficially it resembles many similar polypodies of the same habitat. However, in addition to the regular rhizomes, it has numerous, crowded hairy balls, 2.5–3.2 cm in diameter, that are actually highly modified stem branches. The balls contain several chambers wherein the ants are found. The unmodified rhizomes of *Solanopteris* send numerous roots into the ant chambers through large holes in the balls. These roots creep along the sides of the chambers and absorb nitrogenous substances generated by the ants (Gómez 1974, 1977; Wagner 1972). (NOTE: The foregoing material was written during the tenure of a joint NSF–CONICIT grant under the Latin American Cooperative Science Program)

Relationships with other animals include the pteridophytes as host plants for butterfly larvae (e.g., *Selaginella Euptychia*), moths (Gómez 1980), and beetles (Beitel, in prep.; Gómez 1978), and a group of grasshoppers has specialized in fern-grazing (H. Rowell, pers. comm.). It is in relation to herbivory that a word on secondary metabolites of the pteridophytes is in order.

CHEMICAL COMPOUNDS IN PTERIDOPHYTES

Pteridophytes are much less versatile biochemically than the angiosperms. One reason for their apparent simplicity is that fern allies and ferns do not need elaborate chemicals to aid in fruit dispersal or to attract pollinators. Ferns do not synthesize alkaloids, which are restricted to a few species of *Lycopodium,* and the number of mono-

and sesquiterpenes is relatively low among the pteridophytes, though these plants produce a singular series of triterpenoids and phytoecdysones.

Like many other plants, the pteridophytes synthesize different kinds of phenolic compounds, acylphloroglucinols, a few nonprotein amino acids and cyanogenic glycosides, and a large number of peculiar flavonoids. Berti and Bottari (1968) list the known chemical compounds found in the pteridophytes, and Swain and Cooper-Driver (1973) discuss their significance in biochemical systematics.

OTHER ADAPTATIONS

Because of the perennial, herbaceous nature of most fern species and the predominance of the tropical habitats, pteridophytes have not developed many adaptations to the environment. Resistance to fire is known in *Pteridium* (Gliessman 1978), discussed elsewhere is this book. Other pteridophytes of the open fields, whether páramo or lowland savanna, have tuberous roots that are fire resistant.

The humus-collecting epiphytes, such as the common bird's nest (*Asplenium nidus*) and the staghorn ferns (*Platycerium* spp.), have Neotropical representatives in various species of *Elaphoglossum, Niphidium, Asplenium,* and even the tree ferns (e.g., *Dicksonia*).

NUMBER OF SPECIES AND ENVIRONMENT

The pteridophytes are one of the largest groups of vascular plants in Costa Rica. With an estimated eight hundred taxa, the ferns are next in number to the orchids, grasses, and composites. Such a large number of species ellicits two hypotheses: (*a*) pteridophytes have been and are a predominantly tropical and subtropical group of plants, thence the diversity of species in these habitats; (*b*) pteridophytes, regardless of their geographical origin, have become such good competitors and so free of herbivore pressure as to be an important element of the herbaceous vegetation of the tropics. These hypotheses are not mutually exclusive. Gómez (1975, 1979, 1980) suggests that the conditions of the tropical and subtropical environments have remained homogeneous over a very long period, allowing speciation and life-form diversification of the pteridophytes. The relative paucity of records of rain-forest hybrids contrasts with the number of hybrids found in areas of seasonal climates and, within the tropics, in extreme microclimatic conditions.

The development of large numbers of epiphytes (in Costa Rica approximately 70% of the taxa are obligate or facultative epiphytes) is interpreted by Gómez as an indication of the long period of evolutionary time the adoption of such life form requires. Comparing several tropical fern floras, he proposes an "index of dimorphy" (percentage of species with dimorphic fronds in any given flora), or ID, as an indicator of floristic saturation of an area. For instance, the ID for Southeast Asia is 32.4; this area is considered by all biogeographers to be the center of origin and distribution for most of the paleotropical fern floras. In Costa Rica the ID is 28.1 and, as in any floristically "mature" vegetation, there is a high positive correlation between the ID and number of epiphytes. Thus Costa Rica, with its several hundred species, represents an almost saturated pteridophyte flora whose biogeographical affinities have been discussed by Wercklé (1909), Christ (1910), and Lellinger and de la Sota (1969).

PTERIDOPHYTES AND LIFE ZONE ECOLOGY

There are no checklists of the ferns typically present in any of the life zones of the Holdridge system. Nevertheless, the fern flora of the Guanacaste lowlands (Janzen and Liesner 1980) corresponds to taxa of the tropical dry to tropical moist life zones. Elsewhere in this chapter, the species common to the páramo and subpáramo have been partially listed. By far the greatest diversity of species is found between the 500 and 2,000 m elevations, in contrast to the lowlands, which have large populations of fewer species. As with other groups of plants, there is no correlation between life zones and particular groups of ferns, the páramo being the only exception; but see Page (1979).

*

Balick, M. J.; Furth, D. G.; and Cooper-Driver, G. 1978. Biochemical and evolutionary aspects of arthropod predation on ferns. *Oecologia* (Berlin) 35:55–89.

Berti, G., and Bottari, F. 1968. Constituents of ferns. In *Progress in phytochemistry,* 1:590–623. London: Academic Press.

Christ, H. 1910. *Die Geographie der Farne.* Jena (pp. 96–99).

Gliessman, S. R. 1978. The establishment of bracken following fire in tropical habitats. *Am. Fern J.* 68: 41–44.

Gómez, L. D. 1974. The biology of the potato-fern *Solanopteris brunei. Brenesia* 4:37–61.

———. 1975. Contribuciónes a la pteridología costarricense. VIII. La hibridación en el trópico. *Brenesia* 6:49–57.

———. 1976a. Variation in Costa Rican *Ophioglossum palmatum* and nomenclature of the species. *Am. Fern J.* 66:89–92.

———. 1977. The *Azteca* ants of *Solanopteris brunei. Am. Fern J.* 67:31.

———. 1978. Some insect interactions with *Azolla mexicana. Am. Fern J.* 68:60.

———. 1979. Contribuciónes a la pteridología centroamericana. III. Novitates. *Brenesia* 16:95–100.

———. 1980. Contribuciónes a la pteridología costarricense. XV. Distribución geográfica y ecología. In preparation.

Janzen, D. H., and Liesner, R. 1980. Annotated check-list of plants of lowland Guanacaste Province, Costa Rica, exclusive of grasses and non-vascular crypto-gams. *Brenesia* 18:15–90.

Lellinger, D. B., and de la Sota, E. 1969. The phy-togeography of the pteridophytes of the Departamento del Chocó, Colombia. *National Soc. Res. Rep., Projects* 1969:381–87.

Mesler, M. R. 1974. The natural history of *Ophioglossum palmatum* in South Florida. *Am. Fern J.* 64:33–39.

Page, C. N. 1979. The diversity of ferns: An ecological perspective. In *The experimental biology of ferns*, ed. A. F. Dyer, pp. 9–56. London: Academic Press.

Swain, T., and Cooper-Driver, G. 1973. Biochemical systematics. In The phylogeny and classification of the ferns, ed. C. A. Jermy et al. *Bot. J. Linn. Soc. London* 67, suppl. 1: 111–34.

Wagner, W. H. 1972. *Solanopteris brunei,* a little-known fern epiphyte with dimorphic stems. *Am. Fern J.* 62:33–43.

Wercklé, C. 1909. *La subregión fitogeográfica costar-ricense*. San José: Sociedad Nacional de Agricultura.

Quercus costaricensis (Encino, Roble, Oak)

W. C. Burger

This species (fig. 7.104) is black oak (subgenus *Erythro-balanus*) distinguished by hard dark-colored bark and by acorns that often take two growing seasons to mature. The leaves are very stiff, and the venation often becomes impressed above. The leaves are usually less than 10 cm long and are rounded at the tip. While forests dominated by a single species are rare in Costa Rica, *Quercus cos-taricensis* can be a dominant at elevations between 2,700 and 3,300 m. We know little about its flowering behavior, but I did see the results of a massive acorn crop just below Chirripó Grande, where the ground was densely littered with the large (2–3 cm in diameter) acorns of this spe-cies. The rarity of acorns in collections and the large numbers seen on this one occasion make me wonder if this species fruits irregularly but synchronously as a herbivore-satiation strategy. The wood of this and other Costa Rican oak species has a density that produces an excellent slow-burning charcoal. This characteristic has been a major factor in the rapid destruction of oak forests in the acessible areas of Costa Rica. Of the dozen species of *Quercus* in Costa Rica, only *Q. oleoides* is found in the seasonally very dry and deciduous formations of the Pacific lowlands of Guanacaste; all the other species are found in evergreen montane formations above 600 m elevation.

Quercus is one of the most successful of plant genera, whether success is measured in numbers of species (*Quercus* has hundreds), number of individuals, or sheer

FIGURE 7.104. *Quercus* crown left fully insolated following lumbering of surrounding high-elevation *Quercus* forest; note bromeliads growing on trunk and branches; 2,000 m eleva-tion, near El Empalme, road from Cartago to Cerro de la Muerte, Costa Rica (photo, D. H. Janzen).

biomass. Few other tree genera are in the same league (probably *Acacia, Ficus, Pinus,* and a few others). But this success is limited: the oaks are essentially a north temperate group, with only a species or two reaching Colombia, none in Africa south of the Sahara, and none in the Australia–New Guinea region. Their counterpart in the southern half of the world is *Nothofagus,* also a genus of the Fagaceae family.

For those who have worked with them the oaks are notorious—the species are adept at hybridizing, hybrid populations are not uncommon in many areas, and identification is often more art than science. This hybrid-ization is only within subgenera and not between sub-genera (little consolation, since the subgenera contain hundreds of species). One might think that botanists have been a bit backward or cowardly and that they should have lumped all those species that misbehave into the same single species defined by reproductive isolation. But this would create a greater problem; clearly recog-nizable morphological entities playing consistent (often sympatric) ecological roles would become parts of huge population systems, the "edges" of which might be impossible to define precisely (cf. Burger 1975). It seems that the Costa Rican species do not hybridize very much, or perhaps we simply do not know them well enough. In any event the charcoal burners will render the problem irrelevant.

*

Burger, W. C. 1975. The species concept in *Quercus*. *Taxon* 24:45–50.

Quercus oleoides (Roble Encino, Oak)

D. H. Boucher

Quercus oleoides Cham. and Schlect. (fig. 7.105) is the only lowland oak in the American tropics. It ranges from about 23° N in Tamaulipas on the Gulf coast of Mexico, to 10.5° N in Guanacaste province, Costa Rica, in climates varying from semiarid (700 mm rainfall, 7 dry months per year) to rain forest (over 3,000 mm, no dry months) (Montoya 1966). Populations in southern Texas and eastern Cuba have sometimes been considered subspecies of *Q. oleoides* but are now assigned to other species. The distribution of encino is divided into many disjunct patches, of which the southernmost three are in Costa Rica. The largest, centered on Liberia, is about 25

FIGURE 7.105. *Quercus oleoides,* Mature leaves and full-sized immature fruits (acorns). July, Santa Rosa National Park, Guanacaste Province, Costa Rica (photo, D. H. Janzen).

km in diameter and corresponds roughly to the Liberia Formation, an area of white volcanic tuffs derived from the ash of Volcán Rincón de la Vieja. The second patch, about 5 km in diameter, is in and around the northern part of Santa Rosa National Park, while the smallest patch, only about 2 km across, is along the Pan American Highway about 5 km south of La Cruz. The soils on which encino occurs are generally poor throughout its range, though they are of many different types. In Mexico it is found growing adjacent to rain forest, and the boundaries sometimes (but not always) correspond to a change from well-drained to *either* poorly drained or excessively drained soils. In Costa Rica it generally occurs on plateaus but not in valleys, and often it is on thin soils with limited root space to bedrock (von Borries 1967).

Encino is unusual among tropical trees in that it occurs in high densities and is the dominant in all forests in which it occurs. *Q. oleoides* forests ("encinares") range from about 30% encino to nearly pure stands, but, unlike other tropical single-dominant forests (e.g., mangroves), they generally contain many other tree species also. The encino forests in Santa Rosa National Park include at least eighty species of trees, nearly all of which except *Q. oleoides* also occur in the adjacent tropical deciduous forest. Thus the pattern of occurrence of encino forest cannot by explained simply by its tolerance of poor soils.

Encino is also unusual among upland dry forest trees in being evergreen, as are its closest relatives, the live oaks of the southeastern United States (Muller 1961). The leaves are sclerophyllous, shiny green above and brown-pubescent below, and about 5 cm long. The bark is thick, rough, and quite fire-resistant, enabling encino to survive when encinares are converted to savannas. Male flowers are long yellow aments borne on the year-old twigs, while the female flowers are tiny, lack nectar and petals, and are borne on the new twigs. Pollination is probably by wind, though *Trigona* bees have been observed visiting the male flowers. The acorns are thin-walled, somewhat bitter, and about 2.5 cm long with a shallow cap. The radicle elongates rapidly after germination and reaches a depth of 4 to 8 cm, after which it thickens into a small carrot-shaped tuber as the seed reserves are transferred into it from the acorn. Only after this transfer does the shoot begin to grow upward, and if the acorn in pulled away from the tuber, shoot growth can still occur. The seedlings resprout well from the roots after burning and can survive several years of fire in a row.

Leaf renewal is concentrated in the early part of the wet season, and the canopy of an encino forest becomes distinctly sparser in the late dry season. However, the forest floor remains fairly shady year-round. Flowering time varies both from place to place and from year to year in a complicated and as yet not well-described manner. The Santa Rosa population generally flowers in June, with the acorns falling to the ground about the end of the dry season and not germinating till the following rainy season. On the other hand, the Comelco area G population, near Bagaces, generally flowers in December and January, with acorns dropping in April and germinating soon thereafter. However, there are often exceptions to these patterns, and in fact herbarium specimens from Costa Rica show flowering in seven different months. Wet-season flowering tends to occur earlier as one goes from northwest to southeast within the Liberia patch— that is, toward where the wet season begins earlier. The variability in flowering time is reduced as one moves north, and in northern Mexico the phenological pattern resembles the temperate zone pattern of spring flowering and fall fruit drop (Boucher 1982a). The variations in flowering time imply substantial differences in the length of time acorns lie on the ground exposed to predators before germinating. A mature tree can produce from a few hundred to more than ten thousand acorns. It is not known if there are mast cycles as in temperate oaks.

The peculiar distribution and abundance pattern of encino probably reflects its relationships with various other organisms. *Quercus* species, including *Q. oleoides,* are ectomycorrhizal, unlike most tropical trees, which are endomycorrhizal. Thus encino cannot form mycorrhizae with endogonaceous fungi as do most of the species with which it occurs, but rather requires its own fungal species. An unidentified microlepidopteran seed predator occasionally destroys substantial numbers of accorns. This insect sometimes oviposits in the cracks formed when the radicle breaks the tip of the shell upon germination, but it has also been found inside ungerminated acorns. Early seedling growth may often involve a "race" between eating of the seed contents by the larva of this species and transfer of seed reserves into the tuber. The Costa Rican populations of encino apparently lack both the curculionid beetle seed predators found on North American oaks and the web-forming caterpillars that can severely defoliate *Quercus oleoides* in southern Mexico.

Many mammals eat the acorns, including variegated squirrels, agoutis, deer, peccaries, and even white-faced monkeys. The monkeys descend from the trees, fill both hands with acorns, and reascend to eat them, occasionally dropping one or two in the process. The mammals probably act exclusively as seed predators in most circumstances. In areas such as Santa Rosa National Park, where substantial mammal populations remain, isolated encinos in deciduous forest cannot produce enough acorns to satiate these seed predators, and the only offspring of these trees come from acorns that are dispersed far from the parent trees and thus not found by mammals. This is probably very rare, and these trees can

be considered effectively sterile. Trees in encino forest, on the other hand, are aided in satiation by their conspecific neighbors, and thus some seeds (perhaps 2–10%) survive to germinate below their canopies. Where mammal populations have been reduced (e.g., Comelco area G), survival of acorns to germination is much higher—30–70% or more (Boucher 1982b).

Most *Quercus oleoides* forests have now been converted to savannas (OTS 1968). This imposes a new set of selective forces on encino, including fire, competition from grass, direct insolation of seedlings, cattle browsing, and reduced seed predation from native mammals. Judging from the number of seedlings found in these savannas, encino seems to be maintaining at least its relative dominance with respect to other tree species, but it is not known whether the adult trees are replacing themselves. Since they generally occur on soils unsuitable for crops but adequate for pasture grasses such as *Hyparrhenia rufa,* almost all *Quercus oleoides* areas in Costa Rica are now used for producing low-grade beef cattle for export. Your next hamburger at McDonald's may well have come from a cow that replaced a hectare of *Quercus oleoides* forest.

*

Boucher, Douglas H. 1982a. The reproductive phenology of *Quercus oleoides* Cham. and Schlect, a Neotropical lowland oak. In preparation.

———. 1982b. Seed predation by mammals and forest dominance by *Quercus oleoides,* a tropical lowland oak. Oecologia 49:409–414.

Montoya Maquin, J. M. 1966. Notas fitogeográficas sobre el *Quercus oleoides* Cham. y Schlecht. *Turrialba* 16:57–66.

Muller, Cornelius H. 1961. The live oaks of the series Virentes. *Am. Midl. Nat.* 65:17–39.

Organization for Tropical Studies (OTS). 1968. Analysis of a *Quercus oleoides* stand. In *Tropical biology: An ecological approach,* section 2. July–August 1968 course book.

von Borries Guillen, Oscar H. 1967. Estudio de las características ecológicas de la asociación de encino (*Quercus oleoides* Schlecht y Cham.) en Guanacaste, Costa Rica. M.S. thesis, IICA, Turrialba.

Sapranthus palanga (Palanco, Guineo, Plátano, Turrú)

D. H. Janzen

This small to moderate-sized annonaceous tree (fig. 7.106a) is widely scattered through the deciduous forests of Guanacaste and even persists in a few fencerows. *Sapranthus* ranges from Mexico to Panama. Like other large annonaceous plants in Guanacaste (*Annona reticulata, A. purpurea, A. holosericea*), *S. palanga* has large fruits containing large seeds that I suspect were once

FIGURE 7.106. *Sapranthus palanga. a,* Adult large tree bearing cauliflorous flowers on much of trunk and cluster of full-sized but green (immature) fruits near base (May 1980). *b,* Cauliflorous flowers; light green flowers are maturing, and dark purple flower (*extreme left*) is mature. Santa Rosa National Park, Guanacaste Province, Costa Rica (photos, D. H. Janzen).

dispersed by Pleistocene mammals (Janzen and Martin 1982). It is the only tree in Guanacaste with large purple black cauliflorous flowers (fig. 7.106*b*).

S. palanga begins to flower in the early dry season (late December), and an individual may bear flowers as long as 5 months. They are large (up to 15 cm long) and hang on a 2–3 cm peduncle below the large branches and off the trunk. Dark purple black when mature (bright green when immature), the flowers have an extremely strong musky odor (like a rotting carcass). They are presumed to be pollinated by flies or beetles (W. A. Haber, pers. comm.), but no one has seen pollinators in them. The plants begin bearing flowers when they are only 3–4 m tall and 5–10 dbh, but these plants, which are generally much more common than the large trees, have never been observed to bear fruit.

The trees that bear fruit are 15–35 cm dbh and up to 20 m tall. They are usually found in 75–100-year-old secondary succession. The flowers that will produce fruit are those 1–4 m from the ground on the main trunk. There are five to fifteen fruits produced from a single many-carpeled flower, and each fruit is about the size of a large stubby banana (5–15 cm long cylinder). They are gray green and extremely hard from middry season (March) until the midrainy season (August–September), when they mature. The large flattened seeds ($2 \times 1 \times 0.5$ cm) are borne ten to twenty to a fruit in a sweet, juicy fruit matrix. In contemporary forests, the fruits eventually fall off the tree and rot on the ground, though some may be eaten by peccaries and rodents (seed fate is unknown in this case).

The densely tomentose large leaves are fed on by the larvae of several species of Sphingidae and at least two swallowtail butterflies (*Eurytides*). The leaves are generally rejected by leafcutter ants (G. Stevens and S. Hubbell, pers. comm.) and were rejected by a captive tapir (Janzen 1982). The flowers are mined by the larvae of a small pyralid moth.

Janzen, D. H. 1982. Wild plant acceptability to a captive Costa Rican Baird's tapir. *Brenesia,* in press.

Janzen, D. H., and Martin, P. S. 1982. Neotropical anachronisms: The fruits the gomphotheres ate. *Science* 215:19–27.

Sesbania emerus (Guanacastillo, Pata de Garza)

D. H. Janzen

Guanacastillo is the tallest annual herb (fig. 7.107) in Guanacaste and perhaps in all of Costa Rica. It ranges from western Mexico down through Céntral America, patchily, and is very abundant in the Guanacaste lowlands. The minute seeds (5 to 10 mg dry fresh weight) germinate with the first rains (end of May). Dense lawns of seedlings appear in places where no adult plants have been seen for at least 2 years. Presumably the hard seeds are dormant in the soil surface; since they commonly appear on sites where the grass has been burned off during the previous dry season, they are probably scarified by heat. Dense stands of seedlings also appear on ground left bare by the drying of a large marsh; it seems likely that the drying of the seed coat after a number of years of continuous soaking scarifies the seeds.

The lawn of seedlings gains height at about the same rate as other herbaceous vegetation and grasses, reaching a height of 20–40 cm by mid-June. By the end of July, differential height increment rates among the plants are becoming evident, with some individuals as tall as 1.5 m and others still only 20 cm tall (these short ones either germinated late or are in the lower center of a monospecific stand of *S. emerus* seedlings). By August the guanacastillo teenage plants are well over the top of other herbaceous vegetation and continue to add height until they are 3.5–6 m tall and begin flowering in late October.

At the time of flower opening, the mature plant may bear as many as three hundred once-compound leaves 15–25 cm long. Leaves on the main axis bear about sixty opposite leaflets, while those on lateral branches have about half as many. The leaflets are elongate ovals 2–3 cm long by 1 cm wide. The glabrous stem is 2–3 cm in diameter and filled with a very light pith. The vertical crown projection covers 0.5 to 2 m in area, depending on how crowded the plants are. There may be as many as ten large plants per square meter, though in most stands two to five per square meter is more usual. A stand produces sufficiently dense shade that other plants hardly develop below; walking through is like walking through a shady forest of bamboo canes 50–100 cm apart. Commonly guanacastillo stands appear on sites where a solid stand

of jaragua was burned in the previous dry season; in this case the shaded jaragua rhizomes survive but produce a very flimsy leaf crop. Outside the *S. emerus* stand, the jaragua will be 2 m tall and extremely dense if not grazed.

Each plant bears twenty to forty short horizontal branches when ready to flower. A small inflorescence is produced at the axil of nearly every leaf, and each inflorescence bears three to eight flowers (four or five is very common). Most flowers on an inflorescence are open simultaneously. On healthy plants it is commonplace for one or two of the flowers on each inflorescence to produce a normal fruit. There can be as many as six hundred fruits on a large plant growing well isolated from other guanacastillo plants, but those in dense stands have thirty to three hundred fruits per crown. The first flowers

FIGURE 7.107. *Sesbania emerus. a,* View through a monospecific stand (to right of old road) that is nearly leafless and bearing fruits. *b,* Mature plant (3 m tall) with heavy fruit crop. *c,* Immature but full-sized fruits, one sectioned longitudinally (*on left*); mature fruits, one split open to expose seeds (*on right*). Santa Rosa National Park, Guanacaste Province, Costa Rica (photos, D. H. Janzen).

appear in mid-October (Santa Rosa National Park), and flowering is essentially completed by the end of the second week in November (though a few individuals may bloom as late as early December). Large numbers of mature fruits are available by the end of November, and virtually all fruits are mature by mid-December. They dehisce when dry and brown, and most seeds are on the ground by mid-January. Each fruit contains thirty to fifty cylindrical smooth, mottled green brown seeds lying loosely in individual compartments; a count of the compartments in a dehisced fruit gives an accurate count of the number of seeds that were borne by that fruit. Fruits with small numbers of seeds are rare, and only rarely are there aborted seeds or gaps in the row of good seeds.

The flowers are yellow (red tip to the petal enclosing the sexual parts) and finely spotted with brown on the backs of the petals. They are heavily visited by at least three species of carpenter bees (*Xylocopa*) from dawn until nearly sunset. It looks as if the bees are collecting only nectar. They usually visit all the flowers in one to three inflorescences on a plant before moving on to another plant. Judging from the uniformity of fruit numbers of each inflorescence (one to four, with the vast preponderance being one or two) and the fact that almost every inflorescence produces a fruit, I suspect that the number of pods set, even in dense stands, is at best only weakly pollinator limited. The plants are often close enough that the branches of different individuals interdigitate. Compatibility has not been tested.

As the pods dehisce, a bruchid beetle (*Acanthoscelides griseolus*) deposits eggs in the locules. The larvae hatch and bore into the seed, completing their development after the seed has fallen to the ground. The adults emerge about 3 weeks after oviposition, and this species may have two generations per year, since there are susceptible pods for at least 6 weeks. The larvae feed only on guanacastillo seeds. If a beetle can oviposit next to the seeds on the ground, then there may be even more generations per year. A second bruchid (*Stator pruininus*) glues its eggs directly to the seed in the newly dehiscing pod or on the ground. This bruchid may have many successive generations on the seeds until they are covered or germinate in the next rains. It likewise develops inside the seed and emerges as an adult about 3 weeks later. *S. pruininus* larvae prey on at least six other species of Guanacaste legume seeds.

Once on the ground, the seeds may be preyed on by spiny pocket mice (*Liomys salvini*), although these mice do not abundantly leave the forest to forage in the patches of *Sesbania* in the open grassland. However, *S. emerus* seeds are rich in the uncommon amino acid canavanine, and this may prevent or depress seed predation by rodents and doves.

If a guanacastillo plant is growing without crown competition from other plants, mild herbivory of the shoot tip often produces a more shrubby plant with more branches and more fruits. Cattle, horses, and stem-boring moth larvae, among others, may eat shoot tips, causing such branching. Foliage herbivory is usually light. However, patchy severe defoliation may occur late in the growth cycle (Windsor 1978).

The natural habitat of guanacastillo appears to be the margins of large swamps such as the one at Palo Verde Wildlife Refuge. There are commonly nearly monospecific stands many hectares in extent that appear on the bare or nearly bare ground left by drying of the swamp during the dry season with less thorough refilling in the following rainy season. From this habitat the plant appears to have spread into pastures throughout Guanacaste and northern Puntarenas Province, wherever the soils are sometimes waterlogged, the grasses are occasionally but not annually burned, and woody vegetation is not dense.

The root system of guanacastillo is shallow, penetrating to about 10–15 cm and spreading over about 0.5–1 m². The rootlets are heavily nodulated with rust-red, healthy appearing nodules (November–December, C. Walters, pers. comm.).

*

Windsor, D. M. 1978. The feeding activities of tropical insect herbivores on some deciduous forest legumes. In *The ecology of arboreal folivores*, ed. G. G. Montgomery, pp. 101–13. Washington, D.C.: Smithsonian Institution Press.

Sickingia maxonii (Guaytil Colorado)

D. H. Janzen

This common rubiaceous tree spreads its large-leafed crown just below the general forest canopy in evergreen lowland Atlantic forests of Costa Rica and is especially easy to find in the vicinity of Puerto Viejo de Sarapiquí and Finca La Selva. The crown of a *S. maxonii* is often interdigitated between the lower portions of two allospecific higher crowns and therefore is in moderate shade. The plant is most abundant along small forest streams, and I suspect it is here that the tree has the best chance of finding a slight break in the general canopy.

The single yellow flowers are produced continually for 1–2 months in July to September. Normally the only branches to bear flowers are those that happen to be directly insolated at least part of the day by a shaft of light from above. The result is that most of the branches in the crown never bear flowers or fruit. The flowers are visited by large long-tongued bees (at least Euglossini). Normally zero to ten fruits (fig. 7.108a) are set per branch that bears flowers. These reach nearly full size (5–7 cm in diameter) within a month and remain as hard gray green spheres for 8 months or more. When they ripen, the

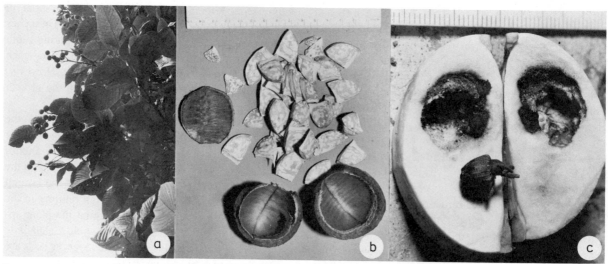

FIGURE 7.108. *Sickingia maxonii. a,* Looking through margin of crown of fruit-bearing, heavily insolated tree. *b,* Mature fruit broken open; dry fruit walls (*lower right*); central partition (*upper left*); seeds in dry pulp (*center*). *c,* Mature fruit broken open showing hole left by weevil larva mining through seeds and adult weevil that was in the cavity. Puerto Viejo, Sarapiquí District, Costa Rica (photos, D. H. Janzen).

fruit wall shrivels and browns and eventually rots apart on the tree (this process is speeded by alternate wetting and drying from rain and sun), or else the fruit falls largely intact but mature. If the fruit falls apart on the tree, the heavy seeds (fig. 7.108*b*), each with a wing remnant (or partly evolved wing), spins off to the ground. Most fruits contain twenty to thirty-five seeds ($\bar{x} = 27.08$, s.d. $= 7.64$, $N = 103$) (Janzen 1977). The seeds are readily eaten by rain-forest terrestial rodents (T. Fleming, pers. comm.) but were emphatically rejected by *Liomys salvini* at Santa Rosa National Park (Janzen, unpublished data).

If the forest is removed next to an adult *S. maxonii,* it promptly produces a huge flower and fruit crop on the side that is insolated. One tree near Puerto Viejo bore 1,625 fruits on its insolated side and 225 on its shady side (Janzen 1977). This suggests that the tree is programmed to respond branch by branch to sunlight, a sunlight that normally appears only in small, discrete patches on the crown. Certainly shade-tolerant is probably a better description than shade-loving.

When the fruits are full sized but still rather immature, a brown stocky weevil 1 cm long (Curculionidae: *Rosella sickingiae*) appears and feeds through the fruit rind into the fruit pulp. Its mandibulate proboscis does not reach the seeds. *R. sickingiae* then lays one to a few eggs in the fruit in one of its feeding holes. The larva(e) mine through the fruit, eating the seed contents as they encounter them (fig. 7.108*c*). Where the fruit and seeds have been cut by the larvae, and therefore exposed to the air, they turn from cream ivory to bright pink red, a color change that gives the tree its name.

Fruits containing one to three larvae normally lose 25–90% of their seeds. The larva pupates in the fruit and emerges a few weeks later as an adult through a hole it cuts through the rind. By this stage the fruit is too old to reattack, but it appears that the weevil can attack other younger fruits on the same tree. *R. sickingiae* probably spends the time between *S. maxonii* fruit crops wandering around the habitat (and perhaps feeding on the tree's young foliage). This weevil is present in about 95% of the fruits on trees in intact forests and kills about 30% of the seeds in them. However, the percentage of fruit attack was 16.6 to 66.6 on the large crops of the four trees exposed to the sun by forest clearing near Puerto Viejo (Janzen 1977).

I have seen no evidence of predation on the immature fruits of *S. maxonii,* but they appear to be the sort of fruit a parrot might rip apart. The fruit hull is particularly rich in the red compound mentioned above, and this chemical may serve as a deterrent to vertebrate predispersal seed predators.

*

Janzen, D. H. 1977. Natural history of seed predation by *Rosella sickingiae* Whitehead (Curculionidae) on *Sickingia maxonii* (Rubiaceae) in Costa Rican rainforest. *Coleopt. Bull.* 31:19–23.

Solanum ochraceo-ferrugineum (Berenjena de Pasto, Berenjena de Monte)

W. A. Haber

Solanum ochraceo-ferrugineum (Dun.) Fern. ranges from Mexico in the north, throughout Central America, and into northern South America (D'Arcy 1973; Gentry and Standley 1974; Standley and Morton 1938). In Costa

Rica this weedy shrub or treelet is one of the most prominent of the roadside and second-growth examples of the genus *Solanum* (fig. 7.109) from the lowlands to about 1,400 m in elevation (Haber 1978; Standley and Morton 1938). The species can be recognized by its oval, faintly emarginate, fuzzy leaves, stems and leaves with sparse, recurved spines, and leaves and twigs covered with dense pubescence of stellate hairs (often brownish yellow). Flowers are produced on lateral inflorescences arising between the leaf nodes. The flowers of an inflorescence open one or two at a time, maturing first at the base and progressing to the tip. Flowers are 2–3.5 cm in diameter with five white petals fused to their midpoint by a membranous flap. The five yellow anthers (5–7 mm long) cluster around the exerted style in the center of the flower. Fruits are subspherical, glabrous, 1–2 cm in diameter, green when immature and yellow when mature (D'Arcy 1973; Gentry and Standley 1974).

S. ochraceo-ferrugineum grows commonly in pastures, along roadsides, and in clearings. However, the natural habitat of this species includes the forest clearings caused by tree falls, landslides, and especially the washed-out areas along rivers, colonized by successional vegetation (Haber 1978). It is intolerant of deep shade but can survive and reproduce on depleted soils.

Flowering individuals are found throughout the year, even in Guanacaste Province, where the dry season is severe (little or no rain from December to April). Many individuals cease flowering for 1 or 2 months during the year, usually when large numbers of fruits are maturing. On well-drained sites away from rivers in Guanacaste some individuals of *S. ochraceo-ferrugineum* are leafless during part of the dry season.

The flowers are pollinated by medium to large bees including *Melipona* (Meliponini), *Centris* and other anthophorids, *Ptiloglossa* (Colletidae), *Euglossa* (Euglossini), and the larger species of Halictidae (Janzen 1971). Like most species of *Solanum*, the flowers of *S. ochraceo-ferrugineum* produce no nectar. Thus they attract only female bees that collect pollen. The anthers dehisce from small terminal pores so that pollen deep within the anther remains hidden from generalized visitors. Bees remove pollen by vibrating the anthers (using their thoracic muscles) while clinging to the flower. The audible buzzing of the bee causes the pollen to issue from the anther pores, where it catches among the hairs on the bee's body. The bee then combs the pollen from its body and packs it into the pollen baskets on its hind legs. The "buzz flower" adaptation also occurs among species of Melastomataceae and *Cassia* (Caesalpinaceae).

Most flowers on an individual plant are hermaphroditic, containing functional staminate and pistillate parts. A small proportion of flowers on *S. ochraceo-ferrugineum*, however, are functionally stami-

FIGURE 7.109. *a,* Inflorescence of *Solanum* sp. (petals white, anthers yellow). *b,* Foliage of *Solanum* sp. Santa Rosa National Park, Guanacaste, Costa Rica (photos, D. H. Janzen).

325

nate (male). Such flowers are recognized by a shorter style (hidden among the anthers) and a slight reduction in size of the ovary and ovules. The combination of hermaphroditic and staminate flowers on one plant, termed andromonoecy (Proctor and Yeo 1972), occurs in several other species of *Solanum* in Costa Rica.

Each flower of *S. ochraceo-ferrugineum* is active for only one day. The flowers open at about 0500 and close shortly after sundown. Flowering continues for many months on one individual, each plant producing a small number of fresh flowers every day. This type of flowering pattern conforms to the traplining strategy (Janzen 1971). Presumably, bees can increase their efficiency in collecting pollen by learning the locations of individual plants and returning to them day after day as a predictable pollen source.

Fruits mature slowly over several months so that one plant usually bears fruits of all stages simultaneously. The mature, yellow fruits are probably adapted for dispersal by birds, but they are also commonly eaten by bats (Haber 1978; Heithaus, Fleming, and Opler 1975). Most ripening fruits are removed (presumably by bats) before they reach the yellow, fully mature stage. The round, flat seeds (2.5 mm in diameter) are much like those of the tomato (*Lycopersicon esculentum*) and range from fifty to four hundred per fruit.

Herbivores of *S. ochraceo-ferrugineum* include the larvae of various moths and butterflies (especially Sphingidae, Geometridae, Ithomiinae), adult leaf beetles of many species (Chrysomelidae), and weevils (Curculionidae). Mammals (including cattle) seldom eat the leaves because they contain toxic and bitter-tasting alkaloids (Haber 1978). As a consequence, the plants become a pest weed in pastures. The insects that feed on this species tend to specialize on various species of *Solanum*, and many of them, e.g. Ithomiinae, Chrysomelidae, Hemiptera, are unpalatable members of Müllerian mimicry complexes (Haber 1978). Flowers and fruits are attacked by the larvae of minute weevils and microlepidopterans. Sibling aggregations of nymphal Hemiptera often concentrate on immature fruits, sucking the juices. These bugs are usually brightly colored in red, orange, and black as a warning that they can spray toxic chemicals if disturbed.

S. ochraceo-ferrungineum extends from the lowlands of both the Atlantic and the Pacific drainages to about 1,400 m. From 1,400 m to about 1,800 m this species is replaced by *S. hispidum* Pers. Young plants of the two species are easily confused, but *S. hispidum* is distinguished by its very large, deeply emarginate leaves and stout, abundant spines on stems and leaves. In the Guanacaste lowlands, *S. hirtum* Vahl is similar in appearance to *S. ochraceo-ferrugineum*, but it can be differentiated by its more herblike growth form, dense, straight spines, and red fruit. *S. torvum* sw., common in the Atlantic lowlands, may be very difficult to separate from *S. ochraceo-ferrugineum* except by the presence of glandular hairs on the pedicels and calyces of *S. torvum* flowers (D'Arcy 1973). The two species may occasionally hybridize together and with *S. hispidum* (D'Arcy 1973).

*

D'Arcy, W. G. 1973. Flora of Panama. Solanaceae. *Ann. Missouri Bot. Gard.* 60:573–780.

Gentry, J. L., Jr., and Standley, P. C. 1974. Flora of Guatemala. Solanaceae. *Fieldiana: Bot.* 24 (part 10, nos. 1–2): 1–151.

Haber, W. A. 1978. Evolutionary ecology of tropical mimetic butterflies (Lepidoptera: Ithomiinae). Ph.D. diss., University of Minnesota.

Heithaus, E. R.; Fleming, T. H.; and Opler, P. A. 1975. Foraging patterns and resource utilization in seven species of bats in a seasonal tropical forest. *Ecology* 56:841–54.

Janzen, D. H. 1971. Euglossine bees as long-distance pollinators of tropical plants. *Science* 171:203–5.

Proctor, M., and Yeo, P. 1972. *The pollination of flowers*. New York: Taplinger.

Standley, P. C., and Morton, C. V. 1938. Solanaceae. In Flora of Costa Rica, ed. P. C. Standley, pp. 1035–99. *Fieldiana, Bot.* 18:1–1616.

Solanum siparunoides (Tomatillo Araño, Spider Wild Tomato)

W. A. Haber

The approximately 120 species of the family Solanaceae that are native to Costa Rica form a prominent component of almost every plant community. The genus *Solanum* includes about 65 Costa Rican species of herbs, vines, shrubs, trees, and lianas. *Solanum siparunoides* Ewan is one of the more conspicuous of the liana species (a liana is a perennial, woody climber) throughout the moist, wet, and rain forest life zones of Costa Rica from the lowlands to about 1,700 m (Haber 1978; Standley and Morton 1938). This species naturally occupies tree-fall and forest-edge habitats, ascending to subcanopy and canopy height as a straggling climber. It also occurs as a pasture and roadside weed, where it assumes the growth form of a sprawling shrub. The stems, petioles, and leaves are festooned with strong, sharp, recurved spines that aid the plant in climbing and possibly serve as a defense against mammalian herbivores. It is easily recognized as the plant that is sticking to your clothes and skin as you walk through second-growth vegetation at La Selva and Monteverde.

In addition, the leaves and stems are densely coated with large, stellate hairs up to 4 mm long. Leaves are usually paired at nodes, with one leaf obviously larger than the other, 10–20 cm long, simple, alternate, with a few marginal points. The flowers are borne on lateral racemes arising between the leaf nodes. Flowers are large for the genus, 1.5–3 cm long, lavender white, the five free petals covered with purple, stellate hairs on the outside surface. The spherical fruits are red orange when mature, bitter tasting, and 1.5–2.5 cm in diameter.

S. siparunoides ranges from southern Central America to northern South America (D'Arcy 1973). In Costa Rica it is abundant in lowland wet forest (La Selva field station) and through intermediate vegetation zones to about 1,700–1,800 m (Monteverde) as well as in the less seasonal Pacific slope forests—for example, San Vito field station (Haber 1978; Standley and Morton 1938).

This species specializes in colonizing tree falls. Seedlings are common in recent tree falls within mature, undisturbed forest (La Selva, Monteverde). As successional vegetation overgrows the tree fall, *S. siparunoides* clambers over it, eventually reaching the canopy as the clearing fills in. Older tree falls frequently contain small to medium-sized individuals that begin reproducing while they ascend rapid-growing successional trees. Large individuals, though scarce within mature forest, occasionally occur as lianas that reach the canopy with stem diameters of 4 cm. Reproductive individuals are found more commonly in clearings, flowering while only 2–3 m long.

The flowers are typical *Solanum* "buzz flowers" (Buchmann, Jones, and Colin 1977). A few flowers open each day for several to many months on a single plant, conforming to the traplining strategy (Janzen 1971). The principal pollinators are large bees (Anthophoridae, Euglossini, and, at mid elevations, bumblebees (*Bombus*). The flowers produce no nectar and no odor; pollen is the only reward. Thus only female bees visit the flowers. The anthers dehisce from minute terminal pores. This adaptation requires the bees to buzz the anthers by vibrating the thoracic muscles while clinging to the flower. The vibration forces pollen to flow from the minute openings and to spread over the bee's hairy body. Flowers begin opening early in the morning and continue to open throughout the day. Each flower is active for at least 2 days.

Fruits are bright red orange berries with numerous flat, yellow seeds (fifty to two hundred per fruit). Fruit set is high so that peduncles usually bear tight clusters of developing fruits. The fruits are dispersed by large birds such as toucans. The fruits are not conspicuously juicy (compared with naranjillas, *Solanum quitoense*, for example); and since the mature fruits may remain on the plant for many weeks until eaten, they gradually shrivel and turn brown. Local residents generally state unequivocally that the fruits are poisonous.

Despite the formidable array of spines and stellate hairs, *S. siparunoides* is the larval host of numerous species of insects, including ithomiine butterflies, geometrid and other moths, and chrysomelid beetles (Haber 1978). At least six species of ithomiine butterflies use it as a specific host plant in Costa Rica (Haber 1978). Larvae eat the stellate hairs along with leaf tissue. As a group, members of the genus *Solanum* produce a variety of biologically active alkaloids as an antiherbivore defense (Haber 1978; Schreiber 1968; Habermehl 1973). However, specialized herbivores such as the Ithomiinae can tolerate high levels of these alkaloids and may store them as a defense against predators of the adult butterflies (Haber 1978; Brower and Brower 1964). Many of the species of insects that feed on *S. siparunoides* are warningly colored and unpalatable to birds, serving as models in common tropical mimicry complexes (Haber 1978). More generalized herbivores such as cows and tapirs refuse to eat the leaves of most species of *Solanum* (W. Haber and D. Janzen, pers. obs.).

Two other species of lianas in the genus *Solanum* may be confused with *S. siparunoides* in Costa Rica. Both species are armed with recurved spines. *Solanum lancaeifolium* Jacq. is very similar in general appearance, but it normally has a much less dense pubescence, the leaves are smaller, the flowers are pure white and smaller, and the fruits are smaller than those of *S. siparunoides*. The two species, however, are largely sympatric. *Solanum wendlandii* Hook. f. is a glabrous, soft-stemmed liana with deeply emarginate leaves that look compound along with some simple leaves on the same plant, and with large blue flowers with fused petals (3–5 cm in diameter). This dioecious species is known as a native only from the slopes of Volcán Irazú, but because of its showy flowers (each lasts 5–6 days) it has been widely dispersed as an ornamental and is now pantropical (D'Arcy 1973; Gentry and Standley 1974; Standley and Morton 1938).

*

Brower, L. P., and Brower, J. V. Z. 1964. Birds, butterflies, and plant poisons: A study in ecological chemistry. *Zoologica* 49:137–59.

Buchmann, S. L.; Jones, C. E.; and Colin, L. J. 1977. Vibratile pollination of *Solanum douglasii* and *S. xanti* (Solanaceae) in southern California. *Wasmann J. Biol.* 35:1–25.

D'Arcy, W. G. 1973. Flora of Panama. Solanaceae. *Ann. Missouri Bot. Gard.* 60:573–780.

Gentry, J. L., Jr., and Standley, P. C. 1974. In Flora of Guatemala. Solanaceae. *Fieldiana: Bot.* 24 (part 10, nos. 1–2):1–151.

Haber, W. A. 1978. Evolutionary ecology of tropical mimetic butterflies (Lepidoptera: Ithomiinae). Ph.D. diss., University of Minnesota.

Habermehl, G. G. 1973. Steroid alkaloids. In *Organic chemistry*, ser. 1, vol. 9. *Alkaloids*, ed. K. F. Wiesner, pp. 235–72. Baltimore: University Park Press.

Janzen, D. H. 1971. Euglossine bees as long-distance pollinators of tropical plants. *Science* 171:203–5.

Schreiber, K. 1968. Steroid alkaloids: The *Solanum* group. In *The alkaloids*, ed. R. H. F. Manske, pp. 1–192. New York: Academic Press.

Standley, P. C., and Morton, C. V. 1938. Solanaceae. In Flora of Costa Rica, ed. P. C. Standley, pp. 1035–99. *Fieldiana, Bot.* 18:1–1616.

Stemmadenia donnell-smithii (Huevos de Caballo, Cojones de Chancho)

M. S. Foster and R. W. McDiarmid

This widespread tree of the family Apocynaceae grows at low elevations from southern and eastern Mexico through Central America to Panama. Together with *S. obovata*, it is found commonly on the Pacific side of Costa Rica in a wide range of habitats including semievergreen and riparian forests, open forest and second-growth woodland, forest edge, and pasture. In the dry forests of Guanacaste, *S. donnell-smithii* (Rose) Woodson is restricted to riparian bottomlands, whereas *S. obovata* is more widely distributed in the deciduous forests. *Stemmadenia obovata* has smaller fruits and larger flowers and leaves than does *S. donnell-smithii*, but in other ways they are very similar. The trees of *S. donnell-smithii* are components of middle-level strata, reaching heights of about 20 m, though size and growth form vary with habitat. Among trees with equivalent dbh's, those in open habitats (second-growth woodland, pasture, edges, etc.) tend to be shorter and to have much broader crowns than those in forested areas. Leaves are lanceolate and opposite; inflorescences are terminal. The inflorescences, comprising one to five yellow flowers with tubular corollas 3–4 cm deep, generally produce a pair of large

FIGURE 7.110. *Stemmadenia donnell-smithii*. *a*, Full-sized mature and nearly mature fruits on leafy branch; note that leaves are about the same length as the fruits (in contrast to the very similar *S. obovata*, which has leaves much larger than the fruits). *b*, Naturally opening fruit with arillate seeds inside. Finca Taboga, near Cañas, Guanacaste Province, Costa Rica (photos, M. S. Foster and R. W. McDiarmid).

ovoid fruits (fig. 7.110). All plant parts, when damaged, produce copious amounts of a sticky white latex.

Flowering phenology varies considerably both within and between sites. At Palmar Norte in southern Costa Rica, trees flower in March and April, at the end of the dry season and beginning of the wet season (Allen 1956). On the other hand, in Guanacaste Province in northwestern Costa Rica, flowering has been observed in March and April in the dry season and in June, July, and August in the wet season. Blooms probably are present at almost any time of the year (McDiarmid, Ricklefs, and Foster 1977). Fruit development is slow, requiring several months. In Palmar Norte the peak period of ripe fruit is in August–September. Ripe fruits have been observed in Guanacaste in March through September, though production peaks in the late dry season.

The fruits are large (7–10 cm long × 5–8 cm in diameter; 52–215 g, wet weight; $\bar{x} = 143$ g, $N = 20$), rounded, and covered with a thick (1–1.6 cm) greenish brown, woody husk (McDiarmid, Ricklefs, and Foster 1977) (fig. 7.110a). The latter forms the bulk of the fruit (77–88% wet weight). The thickness of the husk, together with its extrusion of latex when damaged, probably is effective in preventing damage to immature seeds by insects and may discourage some vertebrate predation. Parrots and white-faced capuchins, *Cebus capucinus*, are known to eat the fruits. When the fruits are ripe, they dehisce along the distal margin to reveal a tightly packed mass of fleshy, bright red orange arils, each almost completely enclosing a dark brown seed (fig. 7.110b). The aril is stringy, extremely oily, and highly nutritious (mean nutrient composition/g dry weight tissue = 7.9% ash, 63.9% lipid, 10.95% protein, 8.5% TCA-soluble carbohydrate, 8.3% structural carbohydrate). On a calorie/g ash-free dry weight basis, the greatest amount of energy is put into the aril for dispersal, followed by the seed for germination, and then the husk for protection. In terms of total expenditure, however, the plant channels the most calories into protection (husk), followed by germination (seed), and then dispersal (aril). Percentage of nutrient composition and caloric content of husks and seeds are relatively uniform, whereas the lipid, protein, and caloric content of the aril varies among fruits, habitats, and years. This variation may be important in allowing the plant to maintain protection and seed quality while maximizing seed production under varying environmental conditions (McDiarmid, Ricklefs, and Foster 1977).

Crop size varies with annual differences in the weather and also between habitats, the average number of fruits per tree increasing from forest to open forest to pasture. Mean crop size also is correlated directly with dbh. The average number of fruits opening per tree per day ranges from 0 to 10.3, both relative and absolute rates of opening increasing with increasing crop size and from forest to forest-edge to pasture. Thus, on a large tree with a sizable fruit crop, freshly opened fruits will be available during most of the fruiting season of the species.

Although the slit formed when the fruit dehisces may reach 10 cm in width, the seeds and aril nearly always are removed completely when the slit measures only 1–2 cm. Thus, use is restricted to those bird species with long, relatively narrow bills (e.g., some flycatchers, motmots) and those whose heads are small enough to be inserted at least partway into the fruit (e.g., honeycreepers, manakins). Feeding is restricted further to those birds large enough to perch on the fruit and feed (e.g., woodpeckers) and birds that hover-feed (e.g., some flycatchers, manakins). Twenty-two bird species were recorded using these fruits in Guanacaste.

Birds are the primary agents of seed dispersal for *S. donnell-smithii*. (There is little to no dispersal of seeds from fruits on the ground. Ants may harvest the aril, but usually the seeds remain. In the dry season, the unused aril shrivels and dries rapidly, whereas in the wet season the pulp rots and is inhabited by fly larvae.) Birds also seem to enhance seed germination by removing the aril, scarifying the seed coat, or both (McDiarmid, Ricklefs, and Foster 1977). In return, the aril of the fruit provides the birds with an estimated 16–25% of their daily energy expenditure as well as meeting a substantial portion of their requirement for nitrogen.

The peak of fruit ripening falls in the late dry season. Therefore fruit is most abundant when birds, especially insectivores facultatively using fruit, may experience a period of insect scarcity. This plus its occupancy of edge habitats, morphological characteristics, and relatively high nutrient quality support the idea that *Stemmadenia* has evolved to capture for seed dispersal the largest number of opportunistically frugivorous insectivores. Opportunistic use by these facultative frugivores has preadapted the tree to grow in second-growth habitats where insectivorous birds are common and probably accounts for the relative success of this species in disturbed habitats today.

A comparison of the flowering and fruiting phenologies and dispersal systems of the two species of *Stemmadenia* would be very interesting and could provide insight into the population dynamics of a plant and its pollination and dispersal systems in the contrasting deciduous and riparian forests of Guanacaste.

*

Allen, P. H. 1956. *The rain forests of Golfo Dulce*. Gainesville: University of Florida Press.

McDiarmid, R. W.; Ricklefs, R. E.; and Foster, M. S. 1977. Dispersal of *Stemmadenia donnell-smithii* (Apocynaceae) by birds. *Biotropica* 9:9–25.

Swallenochloa subtessellata (Chusquea, Batamba, Matamba)

D. H. Janzen

This miniature bamboo, along with *Chusquea tonduzii,* is a conspicuous part of the disturbed vegetation along the Pan American Highway at high elevations as the highway goes from Cartago over the Cerro de la Muerte to San Isidro del General, Costa Rica.

A *Swallenochloa subtessellata* plant is manifest as a clump (fig. 7.111a) covering 1–2 m², containing several hundred stiff 1–2 cm diameter, nearly vertical stems 1.5–3 m in height. The life form is that of a huge upside-down shaving brush. The center of the clump is packed with very slowly decomposing old leaf (fig. 7.111b) fragments. On the uppermost parts of the Cerro de la Muerte, there are several km² of nearly pure stands of these clumps (clones), especially around the radio-television

FIGURE 7.111. *Swallenochloa subtessellata. a,* 10-year-old plant (clone) that is 2 m tall and has hundreds of stems. *b,* Leafy shoot. *c,* Inflorescence. Cerro Asunción, Cerro de la Muerte, Costa Rica (photos, D. H. Janzen).

relay tower (3,000 m or more elevation). Mixed in with these clumps are three species of *Hypericum* and a variety of shrubs in the Ericaceae and Compositae. This vegetation, and the more species-rich vegetation a few meters lower in elevation, is often referred to as "páramo," but it is clearly just old regeneration following clearing of the original low forest.

A clump of *S. subtessellata* grows vegetatively and relatively sedentarily for an undetermined, but genetically fixed, period of probably about 15 years (if I may infer from other small, high-elevation bamboos; Janzen 1976) and then flowers (fig. 7.111c), seeds, and dies. Occasional individuals may be seen doing this in most years, but the bulk of the population will do it en masse at regular intervals. Those that are out of phase with the general population virtually never set seed (probably owing to a pollen shortage from other plants— it is wind pollinated), and if they were to do so most of the seeds or seedlings would probably be eaten by seed or seedling predators. Since each seeding clone of *S. subtessellata* is very small, it has no chance of satiating consumers, and its offspring could escape only by being inconspicuous.

If the habitat is burned every 15–100 years (e.g., Janzen 1973), as it probably has to be for survival of the *S. subtessellata* population, the clones sprout new shoots 5–15 cm tall within 1–2 months (and thereby have one of the fastest regrowth rates in the vegetation). These shoots attain a height of 50–100 cm after 2–3 years, and the clump very slowly adds bulk and height after that. Even fully insolated, a clone requires at least 8 years to return to its preburn adult size. If the top of a clump is mowed off at 40 cm above the ground, 3 years later it will have attained about 70% of its original height, and the cut stems will still be standing. That is to say, *S. subtessellata* grows in a climate (Janzen 1967) where growth and decomposition rates are very slow (about like northwestern Scotland).

S. subtessellata is only very lightly browsed by cattle and horses, but both, along with rabbits (*Silvilagus*), will eat the young shoots that appear shortly after a fire. The new leaves of mature plants are fed on by the adults of a small black hispine chrysomelid beetle that appears abundantly is sweep samples in vegetation rich in *S. subtessellata.* If a site is not burned (or otherwise cleared) at long intervals, *S. subtessellata* is eventually shaded out by woody, slow-growing dicots (Ericaceae, Rosaceae, Hypericaceae, Compositae, Lauraceae). I suspect that originally it was a plant of the highest rocky cliff and peak edges, where erosion and exposure led to a small amount of habitat where it could persist in its nonspreading life form.

Moving downward in elevation from the top of the Cerro de la Muerte, one encounters, at about 2,900 to

2,800 m, a much more scandent species of slightly larger bamboo, *Chusquea tonduzii*. *C. tonduzii* clones have the same general sexual reproductive biology as postulated and described for *S. subtessellata* above, but a more space-occupying vegetative biology. A clone produces aerial stems 3–8 m long that grow vertically at first and then fall out away from their source to sprawl over other nearby woody plants (protovine). One plant may occupy as much as 100 m² of canopy in this manner. However, *C. tonduzii* also sends out horizontal rhizomes through the litter that may carry parts of the clones as much as 30 m from the site of the original seedling. Therefore when one clone flowers and dies, a large gray yellow irregular patch of *Chusquea* dies on a hillside; this patch may be as much as 80 m across but generally is interwoven with other (living) *C. tonduzii* clones and other large woody plants. A general flowering of this species has not been observed on the Cerro de la Muerte, but in March 1980 there were several hundred dying (in full flower) clones between Pensión La Georgina and Cerro Asunción. The clones were in a fairly tight patch of perhaps 10 ha and might well represent a single cohort.

C. tonduzii resprouts very well after cutting and burning, and the lanes under the power lines cut early in 1970 are choked with pure stands of this plant that rapidly invaded (vegetatively) after the taller trees were cleared away. The plant would be regarded as a severe economic pest (weed) if there were an agricultural population there to be bothered by it. It persists as scattered clones in the understory of oak forest (even under canopies as much as 30 m tall) but clearly grows best in tree falls, edges of landslides, and other naturally open areas.

As *C. tonduzii* approaches its upper elevational distribution limit it becomes a more dwarfed and short-branched clone. As *Swallenochloa subtessellata* approaches its lower elevational limit, the branches become longer, and the clones begin to sprawl out over other plants. The area of interface is about 2,800–3,000 m, varying with slope and exposure. It would not surprise me to discover that they are in fact the same species and that the vegetative differences we observe are eco-phenotypic expression of the changes in climate over the same gradient.

Chusquea is the largest genus of Neotropical bamboo (more than ninety species, from Mexico to Chile and on Caribbean islands), and most species occur at high elevations (Calderón and Soderstrom 1980). *Swallenochloa* is apparently derived from *Chusquea* and is so similar that there is doubt whether it should be made a separate (higher and colder elevation yet) genus (Pohl 1976; Soderstrom and Calderón 1978a). There are eight genera of bamboos in Costa Rica (Pohl 1976; Soderstrom and Calderón 1978b), and we know next to nothing about their supra-annual flowering periodicity (intermast pe-

riod), seed predation and seed survival, vegetative capacity for recovery following damage, competitive ability, or relationships with herbivores.

*

Calderón, C. E., and Soderstrom, T. R. 1980. The genera of Bambusoideae (Poaceae) of the American continent: Keys and comments. *Smithsonian Contrib. Bot.* 44:1–27.

Janzen, D. H. 1967. Why mountain passes are higher in the tropics. *Am. Nat.* 101:233–49.

———. 1973. Rate of regeneration after a tropical high elevation fire. *Biotropica* 5:117–22.

———. 1976. Why bamboos wait so long to flower. *Ann. Rev. Ecol. Syst.* 7:347–91.

Pohl, R. W. 1976. The genera of native bamboos of Costa Rica. *Rev. Biol. Trop.* 24:243–49.

Soderstrom, T. R., and Calderón, C. E. 1978a. Chusquea and *Swallenochloa* (Poaceae: Bambusoideae): Generic relationships and new species. *Brittonia* 30:297–312.

———. 1978b. The species of *Chusquea* (Poaceae: Bambusoideae) with verticillate buds. *Brittonia* 30: 154–64.

Swietenia macrophylla and *S. humilis* (Caoba, Mahogany)

J. L. Whitmore

Swietenia (fig. 7.112) is of the Meliaceae, a family long famous for its cabinet-quality woods and its stubborn taxonomic problems (Pennington and Styles 1975). In Costa Rica two of the three species of *Swietenia* are native. The Honduras or bigleaf (*S. macrophylla*) ranges from Gulf Coast Mexico (22° N) to Amazonian Bolivia (17° S). The Pacific coast mahogany (*S. humilis*) is less well known commercially and occurs along the Pacific coast of Mexico and Central America in a narrow band from 24° N to 9° N, with a small disjunct population near Lake Izabal in eastern Guatemala. The native ranges of both species join in northwestern Costa Rica (Guanacaste and adjacent parts of Puntarenas), where hybridization apparently occurs (Lamb 1966; Whitmore and Hinojosa 1977). Mahogany is absent from most or all of the rest of Costa Rica. Individuals of less than commercial size are relatively frequent on the better soils in northwestern Costa Rica and are usually left standing when forests are cleared for pasture or agriculture.

The usual habitat of *Swietenia* is the lowland tropical or subtropical forest, either dry, moist, or wet (a range of approximately 1,000–2,500 mm annual precipitation), although it can also be found in more extreme areas, wetter or drier. Mahogany can become a very large tree to 45 m tall and 2 m in diameter (e.g., Bosque Nacional Alexander von Humboldt, eastern Peru). An undisturbed

FIGURE 7.112. *Swietenia humilis* × *macrophylla. a,* Full-sized mature fruit (*left*) and another ripe fruit with one valve broken out to expose tightly packed winged seeds (knife is 9 cm long). Santa Rosa National Park, Guanacaste, Costa Rica (photo, D. H. Janzen). *b,* Leaves highly variable in size and shape from a tree growing in pasture near Puntarenas, Costa Rica. Scale is in cm (photo, J. L. Whitmore).

forest will have few mature mahoganies per square kilometer (true for eastern Peru). In the subtropical moist forest at the base of the Bolivian Andes, they average 1–1.5/ha. In the Petén of Guatemala, Mayan slash-and-burn agriculture produced conditions favorable to mahogany regeneration, and a density of one mature mahogany per hectare is common. Bawa (1974), Bawa and Opler (1975), Styles (1972), and Styles and Khosla (1976) discuss the reproductive biology of tropical trees where mature individuals of a given species are widely separated from potential breeding partners.

Fruits are ripe in northwestern Costa Rica in January–March, generally contain about forty wind-dispersed seeds, are woody capsules with five values (rarely four or six), and are rather variable in size (usually 10–15 cm long and 6–10 mm in diameter). When mature they stand out above the crown and provide an easy identification feature. Seed number per kg (dewinged) averages slightly over 2,300 in the Costa Rican mahogany. It is usually easy to collect viable and undamaged seed. Touching one to the tongue may indicate why they escape predation but is not recommended, since the astringent taste lingers for hours. However, at Santa Rosa National Park, some rodents do eat the seeds. Both fruits and leaves of Costa Rican mahogany tend to be smaller than usual for *S. macrophylla,* and in dry site plantations this local mahogany survives better than in other *S. macrophylla* provenances.

Leaves are paripinnate and average five or six leaflets per leaf. The tree is leafless briefly in wetter areas, for longer periods where the dry season is pronounced. Leaflets are entire and glabrous.

Flowers are minute, rarely visible from a distance of 10 m, and appear with new leaf formation just at the end of the dry season. Floral morphology has only recently (Lee 1967) been described correctly. The flower appears to be perfect, but in fact the development of either the anthers or the stigma is stunted in each flower. Both male and female flowers can be found in a single inflorescence. The number of staminate flowers greatly exceeds the number of pistillate flowers on a given tree.

There have been many attempts to plant mahogany on a large scale, most of which have failed. One reason for failure is the mahogany shootborer, *Hypsipyla grandella* (Zeller) Lep. Pyralidae. Large populations of this insect build up where seedlings of mahogany (and certain other species in the subfamily Swietenioideae) are planted in the open and at close spacing. The borer attacks the tender terminal shoot and kills it, causing excessive branching and poor form from a commercial point of view. The many studies on, and attempts to control, this borer are described in Grijpma (1973) and Whitmore (1976).

*

Bawa, K. S. 1974. Breeding systems of tree species of a lowland tropical community. *Evolution* 28:85–92.

Bawa, K. S., and Opler, P. A. 1975. Dioecism in tropical forest trees. *Evolution* 29:167–79.

Grijpma, P., ed. 1973. Studies on the shootborer *Hypsipyla grandella* (Zeller) Lep. Pyralidae. Vol. 1. *IICA Misc. Publ.* no. 101.

Lamb, F. B. 1966. *Mahogany of tropical America: Its ecology and management.* Ann Arbor: University of Michigan Press.

Lee, H.-Y. 1967. Studies in *Swietenia* (Meliaceae): Observations on the sexuality of the flowers. *J. Arn. Arbor.* 48:101–4.

Pennington, T. D., and Styles, B. T. 1975. A generic monograph of the Meliaceae. *Blumea* 22:419–540.

Styles, B. T. 1972. The flower biology of the Meliaceae and its bearing on tree breeding. *Silvae Genet.* 21:175–82.

Styles, B. T., and Khosla, P. K. 1976. Cytology and reproductive biology of Meliaceae. In *Tropical trees: Variation, breeding and conservation,* ed. J. Burley, and B. T. Styles, pp. 61–67. London: Academic Press.

Whitmore, J. L., ed. 1976. Studies on the shootborer *Hypsipyla grandella* (Zeller) Lep. Pyralidae. Vols. 2 and 3. *IICA Misc. Publ.* no. 101.

Whitmore, J. L., and Hinojosa, G. 1977. *Mahogany (Swietenia) hybrids.* Forest Service Research Paper ITF-23. Washington, D.C.: U.S. Department of Agriculture.

Syngonium triphyllum (Mano de Tigre)

T. Ray

The life history patterns described here refer to *Syngonium triphyllum* in particular but may be considered to apply in general to all climbing aroids, which in the New World are principally in the four genera *Anthurium, Monstera, Syngonium,* and *Philodendron.* Earlier I discussed these growth patterns with respect to the genus *Monstera.*

S. triphyllum moves both horizontally and vertically in order to reproduce sexually. The seeds germinate on the forest floor, but the plant matures high on the trunks of trees. From its site of germination the plant grows across the ground to a tree, then grows up the tree before flowering. Most of the plants that are climbed by *S. triphyllum* are too small to support the vine to maturity, but it has the flexibility to return to the ground to seek another tree. These growth patterns may be considered a

foraging strategy for light and support structures (trees).

A plant of *S. triphyllum* can be considered to be composed of a series of "segments" placed end to end. Each segment consists of an internode with a leaf, an axillary bud, and a pair of rootlets at the distal end. Branching occurs only rarely. The vine grows at the distal end while dying off through senescence and herbivory at the proximal end (new roots are produced at the nodes as the stem elongates). Thus, although no part of the plant (other than the apex) actually moves, the plant as a whole becomes displaced over time.

Figure 7.113 shows the important components of the life history. When a seed germinates on the ground, it first produces a series of about ten small leaves. Each new leaf is larger (about 3–15 cm long), and they are packed close together on a stem about 2.5 mm in diameter (type T_l, terrestrial leafy, fig. 7.113). Subsequent segments are then produced in a quite different form, consisting of long, slender internodes, each about 8 cm long and 2 mm in diameter, with leaves only 5 mm long (type T_s, terrestrial stemmy, fig. 7.113). These stems are skototropic (grow toward darkness) as a means of encountering tree trunks rapidly (Strong and Ray 1975). If the stem does not encounter a tree after producing about thirty of these slender segments, it will revert to its original leafy form. It will remain in the leafy form for

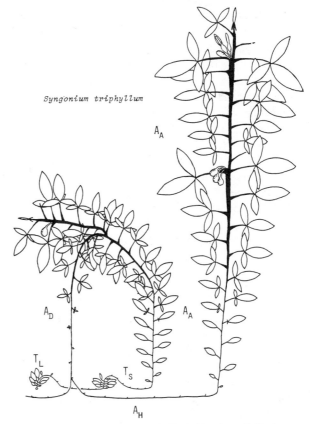

FIGURE 7.113. *Syngonium triphyllum* (drawing, T. Ray).

roughly another ten to fifteen segments, after which it will switch back to the leafless form. The stem will continue to alternate indefinitely between these two forms until the leafless form encounters a tree.

Upon encountering a tree, the stem begins to climb. Successive segments have gradually thicker stems and larger leaves. The internodes remain roughly 7 cm in length, until at about 20 cm the lamina develops lateral lobes. The central lobe may reach a length of 28 cm, and the lateral lobes grow to about 20 cm (type A_a, arboreal ascending, fig. 7.113). Occasionally a second rank of lateral lobes may occur, resulting in a palmately five-lobed leaf, but these outermost lobes rarely reach 10 cm in length.

When the stem reaches a diameter of roughly 14 mm, the plant is capable of flowering. Inflorescences are produced terminally, and the axis of the stem is continued by an axillary branch. The successive segments again increase in diameter until, after about ten segments, the stem again reaches a size capable of fruiting and the cycle is repeated. At each flowering, one to four spadices are produced. Each infructescence contains 50–150 fruits. Pollen is transferred by *Cyclocephala* sp. (Scarabaeidae), and fruits are dispersed by the collared aracari, *Pteroglossus torquatus*.

When a climbing stem reaches the top of a tree, usually a small tree, the stem ultimately becomes detached from the tree and hangs down in the air (this often happens before the stem flowers). Successive internodes then rapidly decrease in diameter to about 3 mm and increase in length to about 18 cm. At the same time, the successive leaves decrease in size but retain their mature form until they virtually disappear into the petiole (type A_d, arboreal descending, fig. 7.113). The stem retains this form after reaching the ground, where it elongates rapidly until it reaches a tree (type A_h, arboreal horizontal, fig. 7.113). These stems do not appear to be skototropic but rather grow horizontally in a straight line. Upon reaching a tree, the stem goes through the process of stem thickening (establishment growth) described earlier for type A_a. If a branch of type A_h becomes disconnected from the arboreal part of the stem, as when the stem breaks, the terrestrial portion of the stem assumes a form indistinguishable from type T.

Branching occurs regularly in only two situations. First, when a stem reaches the top of a tree and begins to dangle, an axillary branch is generally released from the arboreal part of the stem, near the top of the tree. This new branch will be of type A_a and will remain so until it also reaches the top and is forced to hang down. Second, the terrestrial type A_h has a tendency to branch, often after the stem has been cut, as commonly happens in nature. The new branch is of type A_h.

As the plant moves through the forest, the successive segments change size and shape in a consistent pattern as described above. All changes in form are completely reversible. Under the right conditions, stem of any form can change, through the appropriate intermediate stages, to a stem of any other form. Before examining the ecological significance of these changes in form, it is useful to consider in detail the precise geometry of the changes. Exactly what aspects of the form are changing, and what are the constraints on those changes?

None of the three component parts—internode, petiole, and leaf—is strongly correlated in its size (measured as dry weight), but an important and unifying correlation can be found. The dry weight of the entire segment is tightly correlated with the diameter of the internode. With this relationship between diameter and total weight, there are strong geometric constraints on the way the form of the segment may vary. The plant may produce a long (heavy) internode with a small leaf, or a large (heavy) leaf with a short internode, but it may not produce a long internode with a large leaf. There is a direct trade-off between leaf size and internode length. The ratio of the leaf weight to the internode weight often changes significantly from one segment to the next. It is by adjusting the weight of the segments, and the distribution of the weight among the parts of the segments, that *S. triphyllum* is able to tune its growth form to meet the varying conditions it encounters as it moves between microhabitats in the forest.

This trade-off between producing a large leaf and a long internode creates a morphological conflict between satisfying the plant's need for mobility and its need for photosynthesis. This conflict is particularly apparent in the case of type T, a small terrestrial plant that must provide all of its own photosynthate while moving to a tree. It is apparently for this reason that there arises a "division of labor" among adjacent groups of segments. Segments of forms T_l and A_a are specialized for photosynthesis, while segments of forms T_s and A_h are specialized for mobility.

The growth of type T is probably limited by photosynthate, since it has a small leaf surface area and lives on the shady forest floor. I have shown that the two forms, T_l and T_s are optimizing their use of photosynthate, in the sense that within the range of morphologies available to *S. triphyllum,* type T_l is the form in which leaf surface area per unit dry weight (cm^2/g) is maximized, and type T_s is the form in which segment length per unit of dry weight (cm/g) is maximized.

Type A_d can be considered transitional between forms A_a and A_h. Types A_a and A_h do not exhibit morphologies that optimize the use of photosynthate. However, I have shown that type A_a maximizes the time rate of production of leaf surface (cm^2/day) and type A_h maximizes the time rate of elongation of the stem (cm/day). Thus while the small forms, T_s and T_l, maximize elongation and leaf production with respect to utilization of dry matter, the large forms, A_a and A_h, maximize those parameters with respect to time.

An important function of type A_a is seed production. A comparison of several species indicates that those species that have thicker stems at maturity fruit more often and produce more seeds at each fruiting. Thus stem thickening is an important prerequisite for sexual reproduction. The ecological significance of type A_a can not be fully understood until the processes of stem thickening and seed production are studied in more detail. The genus *Syngonium* is very uniform in its growth habit. All species show the stages indicated in figure 7.113. The species vary primarily in maximum size attained (measured as stem diameter or leaf size), and this is correlated with the frequency of fruiting and number of fruits produced. The species with the largest size at maturity produce seven to eleven fruits at a node, and they produce fruits at every second or third node once maturity is reached. *S. triphyllum* is a medium-sized species that usually produces one fruit at a node (though it may produce as many as four), and it fruits only occasionally, fruits generally being separated by at least ten nodes. The smallest species apparently never, or at least rarely, fruit. In these species new individuals are established by spreading and fragmentation of existing individuals.

At La Selva, one such "asexual" species is *S. stenophyllum*. There is no evidence of seed production in the La Selva population of *S. stenophyllum*—that is, one cannot find infructescences or seeds. Furthermore, it occurs only in the primary forest and is completely lacking in the cacao groves where the seed-producing species of *Syngonium* attain abnormally high densities. Transplants do well in the cacao groves, suggesting that the species is absent because it lacks the seed dispersal necessary for colonization. On rare occasions one can find 4 mm long aborted vestigial inflorescences in this species. In 1977 I planted several individuals of *S. stenophyllum* in a palm grove where light levels are much higher than in the primary forest. Three years later one of these individuals was collected in flower, but it is not known if it would have produced viable fruit. It appears that under exceptional conditions the small species produce fully developed flowers and may produce fruit.

The genus *Syngonium* was revised in 1955 (Birdsey 1955), but many more species have turned up since then. There appear to be about ten species in Costa Rica. The genus has recently been revised again by Tom Croat (1982).

*

Birdsey, M. R. 1955. The morphology and taxonomy of the genus *Syngonium* (Araceae). Ph.D. diss., University of California at Berkeley.

Croat, T. B. 1982. A revision of *Syngonium* (Araceae). *Ann. Missouri Bot. Garden,* in press.

Strong, D. R., and Ray, T. S. 1975. Host tree location

behavior of a tropical vine (*Monstera gigantea*) by skototropism. *Science* 190:804–6.

Tabebuia ochracea ssp. *neochrysantha*
(Guayacán, Corteza, Cortes, Corteza Amarilla)

A. H. Gentry

This is one of three closely related species of yellow-flowered *Tabebuia* that occur in Costa Rica. The three species replace each other in different life zones—*T. ochracea* is in dry forest, *T. guayacan* in moist forest, and *T. chrysantha* (in Costa Rica) in wet forest. All three are "big bang" mass flowerers in which all individuals of the species bloom on the same day and the flowers (fig. 7.114) last only about 4 days. They bloom in the dry season while deciduous (usually 4 days after one of the infrequent dry season showers) and are an unbelievable mass of color for their few days of flowering. Sometimes there are two or three flowering bursts in a single dry season. *T. ochracea* and its allies are pollinated by a variety of bees, especially euglossines and anthophorids, and are robbed by hummingbirds and xylocopids. The seeds have membranaceous wings and are wind dispersed.

Tabebuia ochracea ranges from El Salvador to Brazil; the subspecies *neochrysantha* ranges from El Salvador to northwestern Venezuela. It has leaves (fig. 7.115) densely stellate pubescent beneath (appearing tannish) and has golden woolly calyxes and fruits with long hairs. *T. chrysantha* (Mexico to Peru and Venezuela) has stellate hairs scattered over the leaves and short reddish stellate hairs on calyxes and fruits. *T. guayacan* (Mexico to Venezuela) has stellate hairs only in the leaf axils, thick stellate calyx trichomes, and a rough, spiny fruit that has very few or no stellate hairs.

T. ochracea is one of the commonest species in upland Guanacaste dry forests (frequency of 100% for 100 m^2 quadrats and densities of thirty-four individuals over 1 in dbh/1,000 m^2 at La Pacifica) and its seedlings can literally cover the ground in the dry season (e.g., at La Pacifica in 1972 there were an average of forty-eight seedlings/m^2 shortly after seed release).

The woods of these species are among the hardest and heaviest in the Neotropics. Specific gravities up to 1.5 mean that the wood "sinks like a rock." The wood is also exceptionally durable—for example, nearly all the dead trees still standing in Gatún Lake from the forests inundated by the construction of the Panama Canal are *Tabebuia guayacan*. The dark brown heartwood of these species contrasts strikingly with the white sapwood and is much prized for furniture and household untensils. In coastal Ecuador, where this esteem has led to serious depletion of the *Tabebuia* populations, fake "guayacan"

FIGURE 7.115. Mature leaves of *Tabebuia ochracea* ssp. *neochrysantha* moderately damaged by leaf-eating beetle and moth larvae. Santa Rosa National Park, Guanacaste, Costa Rica (photo, D. H. Janzen).

FIGURE 7.114. *Tabebuia ochracea* ssp. *neochrysantha*, newly opened flowers in a leafless crown approximately 7 days after a late dry season rain. May 1980, Santa Rosa National Park, Guanacaste Province, Costa Rica (photo, D. H. Janzen).

articles are made for sale to unwary tourists by painting dark brown bands or patches on articles made of other kinds of wood.

Terminalia oblonga (Surá, Quiura, Guayabo de Monte)

G. S. Hartshorn

Terminalia, of the Combretaceae, is a pantropical genus of important timber trees. The best-known member is *T.*

catappa, the Indian almond, commonly planted in low-land towns and naturalized on ocean foredunes of the Neotropics.

T. oblonga is a canopy tree to 45 m tall and 1.3 m dbh, ranging from Guatemala to the Amazon basin. It is planted as a shade and timber tree in coffee plantations of El Salvador and Guatemala. In Costa Rica it is restricted to well-drained recent alluvium in tropical wet and premontane wet life zones; in tropical moist areas it extends onto slopes, and in tropical dry areas it is restricted to riparian sites.

It is one of the most attractive trees in the tropical forest, with its very smooth, light brown bark and well-developed but very thin buttresses (fig. 7.116). Actually, the bark exfoliates in long thin sheets, cascading down around the base of the tree.

Leaves are simple, alternate, strongly clustered at the end of sympodially branched twigs, obovate, and briefly deciduous. The small, yellow green flowers are borne on axillary spikes 7–10 cm long in December and January. Fruits have two wings about 2 × 2 cm (fig. 7.117); mature fruits are wind dispersed in February and March. I have been unsuccessful in my attempts to germinate *T. oblonga* seeds at La Selva; seed viability appears to be very low.

T. oblonga heartwood is heavy, resistant, and a rich brown in color. It is popular for flooring and paneling. Chemical analyses of the wood by the College of Forest Resources, University of Washington, show a very high accumulation of calcium (13% by dry weight).

FIGURE 7.116. *a,* Buttresses of large adult *Terminalia chiriquensis;* the buttresses of *T. oblonga* are similar but usually fewer in number. Santa Rosa National Park, Guanacaste, Costa Rica. *b,* Exfoliation pattern of bark in *a* (ruler 15 cm long) (photos, D. H. Janzen).

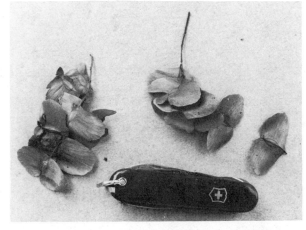

FIGURE 7.117. *Terminalia oblonga* mature fruits. Finca La Selva, Sarapiquí District, Costa Rica (photo, G. S. Hartshorn).

*

Brealey, O. 1972. *Manual de dendrología para las especies arbóreas de la Península de Osa, Costa Rica.* San José: Organization for Tropical Studies.

Whitmore, J. L., and Hartshorn, G. S. 1969. *Literature review of common tropical trees.* Contribution no. 8. Seattle: College of Forest Resources, University of Washington.

Trema micrantha (Jucó)

G. S. Hartshorn

The Ulmaceae is a predominately temperate family of about fifteen genera and two hundred species. The pantropical genus *Trema* has only a single species in Central America. *T. micrantha* ranges from Mexico and the West Indies to southern Brazil and northern Argentina. In Costa Rica it occurs in tropical moist, tropical wet, premontane wet, premontane rain, and lower montane wet life zones. At La Selva it can attain 30 m in height and 70 cm dbh.

Large specimens have slight buttresses and lightly fissured bark; the fissured bark is occasionally spiraled slightly from the base of the tree. Open-grown trees have an ample monolayer crown (*sensu* Horn). *T. micrantha* is a pioneer species that may form monospecific stands in premontane wet or rain life zones. Height growth is rapid, but not as fast as in *Cecropia*.

FIGURE 7.118. Sterile growing branch of *Trema micrantha*. Santa Rosa National Park, Guanacaste, Costa Rica (photo, D. H. Janzen).

FIGURE 7.119. *Trema micrantha,* fruit-bearing branch and full-sized green and mature fruit. Finca Taboga, near Cañas, Guanacaste, Costa Rica (photo, D. H. Janzen).

Leaves are simple, alternate, broadly lanceolate, distichous, palmately nerved, and have stipules (figs. 7.118–19); the margin is serrate and the base is usually not equilateral. Twigs and leaves have stiff gray hairs.

Inflorescences are bisexual or unisexual (Burger 1977), with small, axillary cymes. *T. micrantha* is often reported to flower continuously, but Frankie, Baker, and Opler (1974) report flowering at La Selva between May and July. Fruit (fig. 7.119) is a small, globose, 2 mm drupe, orange or red at maturity and very attractive to frugivorous birds. Seeds are thought to have a dormancy mechanism.

The strong, fibrous inner bark was formerly used for cord.

*

Burger, W. 1977. Ulmaceae. In Flora costaricensis. *Fieldiana, Bot.* 40:90–92.

Frankie, G. W.; Baker, H. G.; and Opler, P. A. 1974. Comparative phenological studies of trees in tropical wet and dry forests in the lowlands of Costa Rica. *J. Ecol.* 62:881–919.

Whitmore, J. L. and Hartshorn, G. S. 1969. *Literature review of common tropical trees.* Contribution no. 8. Seattle: College of Forest Resources, University of Washington.

Trophis involucrata (Morilla)

K. S. Bawa

Trophis involucrata is a small understory tree to 6 m in height and 8 cm dbh known only from the type locality, La Selva, where it is common on well-drained slopes in the mature-phase forest as opposed to gaps. Plants grow at an extremely slow rate; no marked changes in size (height or diameter of the stem) have been found in plants kept under observation for several years.

The species is dioecious and is unusual in being wind pollinated, since anemophily is assumed to be absent in tropical lowland wet forests (Janzen 1975; Whitehead 1969). The flowers are produced in January–February; a small proportion of plants (probably fewer than 15%) flower again in July–August.

The male flowers, borne in pendulous catkins up to 30 mm in length, are up to 5 mm long and 4 mm across (fig. 7.120*b*). Each flower has four greenish white sepals that alternate with four stamens. In a bud that is ready to open, the anther filaments are held under tension. At anthesis the filaments spring outward and release pollen in a small cloud.

FIGURE 7.120. *Trophis involucrata. a,* Female flowers along underside of branch. *b,* Male flowers in inflorescences. Finca La Selva, Sarapiqui District, Costa Rica (photos, K. S. Bawa).

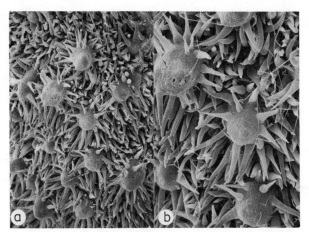

FIGURE 7.121. *Trophis involucrata*. *a*, Scanning electron microscope photograph of ovary showing glands on surface. *b*, SEM photo enlarged to show stomata at tips of glands (photos, K. S. Bawa).

The female flowers are borne in axillary clusters of two or three and are 2–3 mm long and 2 mm across. They are green, devoid of any perianth, and inconspicuous; the flower consists only of an ovary with two feathery stigmata (fig. 7.120*a*) The surface of the stigma is considerably enlarged by the presence of numerous papillae. No nectar is secreted by the flowers, but the outer surface of the ovary bears glandular structures terminated by stomata (fig. 7.121). These structures of unknown function progressively enlarge after fertilization.

Apart from the explosive dispersal of pollen, other observations also suggest wind pollination. Flowers enclosed in nylon mesh bags, to exclude insects and other animals, set fruits (Bawa and Crisp 1980). Also, female trees without male trees nearby do not set fruits. Further, no insects or other animals were found to visit female flowers that were observed for many hours.

The fruits, one-seeded black drupes, mature 8–10 weeks after pollination (March–April) and remain on the trees for a very short period, being either rapidly dropped or dispersed. It is thus not surprising that the fruits of this species have not so far been described in the taxonomic treatments (Burger 1978). The seeds, as judged from fruit morphology, are probably dispersed by birds. Predation of seeds or young fruits (or flowers) has not been observed; however, young fruits are aborted in large numbers before maturation.

The species is patchily distributed and occurs at fairly high densities at the La Selva field station. The average distance between male and female plants (trunks) is 6.6 ± 3.3 m ($N = 64$). The male and female plants appear to be randomly distributed with respect to each other, though occasionally female plants have been found to be clumped.

It should be noted here that wind pollination is not confined to *Trophis involucrata* in the lowland evergreen forests. At La Selva there is some evidence for anemophily in species of *Chamaedorea* (Palmae) and *Myriocarpa* (Urticaceae), and I suspect a few more species in the Moraceae are wind pollinated. Wind pollination is assumed to be widespread in the Moraceae of the lowland tropical forests of Africa (D. Leston, pers. comm.). Several species in the Rhizophoraceae and Pandanaceae in lowland humid forests are also, apparently, anemophilous (Tomlinson, pers. comm.).

The name of this species has recently been disputed. However, W. M. Burger, who originally described the species from La Selva, feels that the present name should be retained until the taxonomic problem is resolved. The voucher specimen of this species (Beach #1423) has been deposited in the herbarium of the Field Museum of Natural History.

*

Bawa, K. S., and Crisp, J. E. 1980. Wind-pollination in the understorey of a rain forest. *J. Ecol.* 68:871–76.

Burger, W. 1978. Moraceae. *Fieldiana, Bot.* 40:94–215.

Janzen, D. H. 1975. *The ecology of plants in the tropics.* London: Edward Arnold.

Whitehead, D. R. 1969. Wind pollination in the angiosperms: Evolutionary and environmental considerations. *Evolution* 23:28–35.

Vantanea barbourii (Caracolillo)

G. S. Hartshorn

Humiriaceae is a small Neotropical family, with the exception of one species of *Sacoglottis* that occurs along the West African coast. The genus *Vantanea* contains fourteen species from southern Brazil to Costa Rica. *V. barbourii* is known only from the tropical wet life zone of southwestern Costa Rica. It is one of the tallest trees in Corcovado National Park, to 65 m in height and 2 m dbh. The moderate buttresses coalesce into the irregularly fluted lower bole. The outer bark is dark brown, exfoliating in rectangular plates exposing large but sparse lenticels (fig. 7.122).

Leaves are simple, alternate, entire, coriaceous, and elliptical. Inflorescences are axillary panicles of hermaphroditic flowers. Calyx lobes are ciliate; petals are white and stamens numerous. Brealey (1972) reports that *V. barbourii* flowers twice a year—in June and from November to January. I observed several trees in full flower in March 1978.

The fruit is an ovoid, smooth drupe, to 3 cm long; the endocarp is woody and resistant to decomposition. The persistence of old seed on the ground makes it an easy tree to identify. I have found practically no regeneration of *V. barbourii* in Corcovado National Park.

FIGURE 7.122. *Vantanea barbourii*, buttresses of adult tree in undisturbed forest. Llorona, Corcovado National Park, Osa Peninsula, Costa Rica, March 1978 (photo, G. S. Hartshorn).

*

Brealey, O. 1972. *Manual de dendrología para las especies arbóreas de la Penínsual de Osa, Costa Rica.* San José: OTS (pp. 158–60).

Gentry, A. 1975. Humiriaceae. In Flora of Panama. *Ann. Missouri Bot. Gard.* 62:35–44.

Vesicular-Arbuscular Mycorrhizal Fungi (Hongos Micorrhízicas Arbusco-vesicular)

D. P. Janos

The lushness of lowland tropical rain-forest vegetation is striking, especially considering the infertility of lowland tropical soils. Phosphorus is often unavailable in these acid soils because it forms complexes with iron and aluminum. Moreover, the sole source of phosphorus, unweathered parent material, is scarce. The vegetation's ability to extract sufficient phosphorus and other minerals is related to a profusion of feeder roots just below the litter and in the uppermost few centimeters of soil. Stark and Jordan (1978) have documented the importance of a thick mat of superficial roots for mineral retention by vegetation on old, highly leached Venezuelan soils. However, solid root mats characterize relatively few sites, and an additional mechanism accounts for the success of tropical forests in mineral uptake from soil.

Under the low power of a compound microscope, fungal hyphae can be seen associated with the superficial, ultimate rootlets of almost any rain-forest tree, forming mycorrhizae—literally, "fungus roots." These are mutualistic fungi that, in return for energy-supplying carbon compounds from a host, increase the host's water uptake and augment the supply of minerals, especially phosphorus. Although almost all plants, including ferns, lycopods, and mosses are capable of forming mycorrhizae, dependence on the most common type of mycorrhizal association, vesicular-arbuscular (VA) mycorrhizae, for mineral uptake by lowland tropical rain-forest trees is extreme (Janos 1977, 1980a) (fig. 7.123a). The seedlings of many tree species may not survive without mycorrhizal associations.

Vesicular-arbuscular mycorrhizal fungi can be distinguished from all other root-inhabiting fungi by their typical dimorphic hyphae: ephemeral, narrow, thin-walled clear hyphae that may be septate arise from unilateral angular projections on large-diameter (10–15 μm), thick-walled, aseptate hyphae that are often yellow or brown (fig. 7.123b). Presence of typical hyphae on a root surface, however, does not necessarily indicate mycorrhiza formation; infection structures—vesicles and arbuscles—must be present within root cortices (fig. 7.123e–f). It is often difficult to see these structures without decolorizing and staining (see Phillips and Hayman 1970), because tropical tree roots are often coarse or heavily pigmented.

Although VA mycorrhizae have been called "endomycorrhizae," the term is somewhat misleading. Other kinds of mycorrhizae (orchid and ericaceous) formed by fungi in different taxonomic classes than VA mycorrhizal fungi have also been called endomycorrhizae, although they are physiologically distinct from VA mycorrhizae. In addition, although the diagnostic features of VA mycorrhizae are internal, the term "endo-" belies the importance of hyphae extending from the root into the substrate. VA mycorrhizae owe their efficiency in mineral uptake to an extensive, well-distributed absorbing network of subtrate hyphae. Rhodes and Gerdemann (1975) demonstrated transfer of radioactive phosphorus across 10 cm of hyphae to a root. Hyphae are better able to take up immobile ions or those in low concentrations than are root hairs. Root hairs may extend only 1–2 cm into the soil and can compete severely with each other because their phosphorus-depletion zones overlap more than

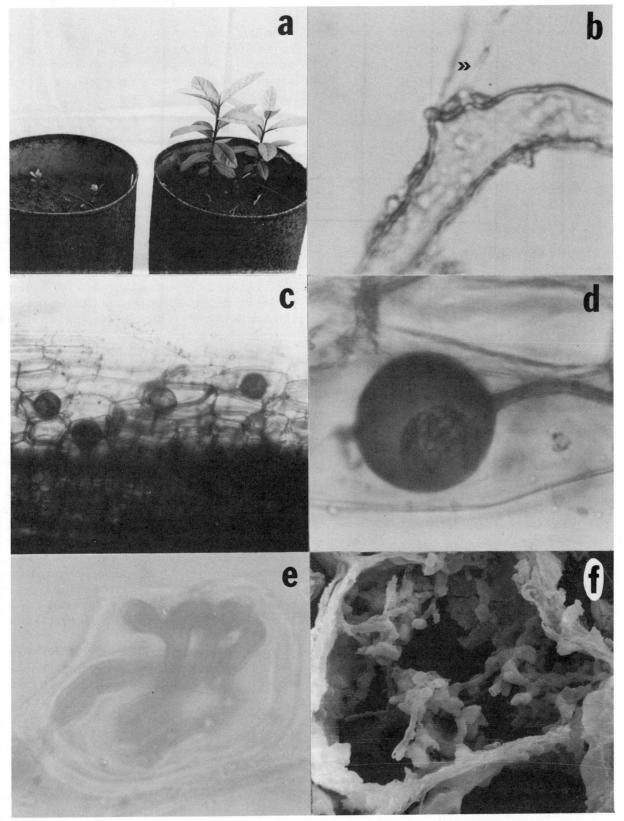

FIGURE 7.123. Features of vesicular-arbuscular (VA) my-corrhizae. *a*, Comparison of inoculated (*right*) and unin-oculated guava (*Psidium guajava*) seedlings 4 months after treatment. *b*, Typical VA mycorrhizal fungus dimorphid hypha with a small-diameter, thin-walled hypha (*arrow*) aris-ing from a unilateral angular projection on a large-diameter thick-walled hypha, × 1,000. *c*, Vesicular infection after staining in the outer cortex of a *Pentaclethra macroloba* root, × 100. *d*, Spherical vesicle, × 500. *e*, Hyphal coil within a root cortical cell of *Bactris gasipaes*, × 500. *f*, Scanning electron micrograph of arbuscles within a *Zea mays* root cortical cell, × 3,500.

those of hyphae. Root hairs are scarce or completely lacking on the roots of many tropical trees.

Root hairs are more advantageous than VA mycorrhizae where fertility is temporarily elevated, as in slash-and-burn agricultural clearings, recent volcanic deposits, and possibly in portions of tree-fall gaps (Janos 1980*b*). At high fertility levels some plants may reject mycorrhizal infection and employ root hairs or profusely branched root systems for mineral uptake, avoiding the carbon cost of the fungi. Many crop plants, pioneer grasses and other herbs, woody plants such as *Carica papaya, Trema* spp., *Cecropia* spp., other Moraceae, weedy composites, and melastomes may act in this manner.

Many species in the Commelinaceae, Cyperaceae, and Juncaceae among the monocots, and the Aizoaceae, Amaranthaceae, Brassicaceae, Caryophyllaceae, Chenopodiaceae, Fumariaceae, Nyctaginaceae, Phytolaccaceae, Polygonaceae, Portulacaceae, and Urticaceae among dicots never form mycorrhizae. They may have lower mineral requirements or other adaptations for mineral uptake that are effective in infertile soils. By not utilizing mycorrhizae, as colonizing species they attain a competitive advantage over mycorrhiza-requiring plants, which may experience growth lag while awaiting infection. Many pioneer species are nonmycorrhizal.

Nonmycorrhizal plants can affect the availability of VA mycorrhizal fungi to mycorrhiza-requiring species by direct chemical antagonism against the fungi or, more commonly, by not supplying carbon compounds to the fungi (Janos 1975*a*). Several lines of evidence suggest that VA mycorrhizal fungi are obligate root associates and cannot grow saprobically. The fungi cannot be grown in axenic culture without a host. Moreover, hyphae are never seen to leave roots after penetration as might be expected if they were able to exploit external carbon sources. Penetration of root cortical cells need not indicate cellulolytic activity, because it can be accomplished by purely physical means, as the formation of appressoria (physical penetration structures) by the fungi attests. In addition to nonmycorrhizal species, plant species that do not sustain infection at high levels of fertility may diminish fungus populations.

Succession could be directed in part by mycorrhizal interactions (Janos 1980*b*). The proportion of plants in a community that do not support mycorrhizal fungi can affect fungus population size and, hence, subsequent inoculum availability. Mycorrhizal inoculum availability and soil fertility may then interact to influence the outcome of competition among hosts that depend on mycorrhizae to different degrees. The inherent efficiency of mycorrhizae in extracting minerals from old, infertile soils probably results in strongly mycorrhiza-dependent tree species having greatest success in mature forest.

Because most plants form VA mycorrhizae, VA mycorrhizal fungi may be sparse only in disturbed sites, in permanently flooded areas, or at high elevations. Disturbance can lead to reduced mycorrhizal fungus populations either by favoring nonmycorrhizal plants, as in the case of sedge dominance of overgrazed pastures (Janos 1975*a*), or by involving a high fertility pulse that causes plants to not sustain mycorrhizae. Recent volcanic deposits, such as at Volcán Arenal, probably lack VA mycorrhizal fungi for some time, to judge by the composition of species colonizing the ash. Subsoil exposure by landslides, bulldozing, or deep plowing may also reduce mycorrhizal inoculum because VA mycorrhizal fungi are obligately aerobic, which restricts them to the uppermost soil horizons. For this reason the fungi are probably absent from permanently flooded sites as well, although infection of some aquatics, salt marsh plants, and swamp species has been reported. The occurrence of mycorrhizal infection in tropical swamp forest trees and mangroves has not been investigated.

The fungi that form VA mycorrhizae belong to a single family, the Endogonaceae, which is in the same order as the common black bread mold (*Rhizopus nigricans*). Species of four genera form VA mycorrhizae: *Acaulospora* Gerdemann and Trappe, *Gigaspora* Gerdemann and Trappe, *Glomus* Tul. and Tul., and *Sclerocystis* Berk and Broome. I have found members of all four genera at La Selva, including two new *Acaulospora* species. It is likely that these genera occur throughout Costa Rica, although no general survey for them has been done. A fifth monotypic genus may be found on the Atlantic coast beaches (see Boedijn 1930); *Glaziella aurantiaca* (Berk. and Curtis) Cooke produces large (1.5–5 cm in diameter) hollow sporocarps that are bright orange. It has not been demonstrated to form VA mycorrhizae, but it may associate with *Cocos nucifera*, which can be expected to require mycorrhizae (see Janos 1977). *G. aurantiaca* may be water dispersed and, if so, could be important to plants colonizing beaches.

Spores and sporocarps of the known VA mycorrhizal genera are not as spectacular as those of *Glaziella* but are the only structures by which species can be identified. Sporocarps, clusters of spores enclosed by hyphae, may be formed by species of *Glomus* and *Sclerocystis* (fig. 7.124*a*–*c*). *Sclerocystis* sporocarps usually occur in aggregations. Neither sporocarps nor their aggregations ordinarily exceed 2 cm in diameter. They may be white initially, turning tan or dark brown at maturity, and are rare and inconspicuous at the soil surface. I have found *Sclerocystis* only twice in the field at La Selva, both times slightly above the soil surface encrusting a support, in one instance the edge of the boardwalk in the ecological reserve. *Sclerocystis* sporocarps can contain thirty to one hundred spores, but *Glomus* sporocarps may contain thousands.

At La Selva production of single naked spores in the soil by species of *Glomus*, *Acaulospora*, and *Gigaspora* is more common that sporocarp formation by the sporocarpic genera (fig. 7.124*d–f*). Spores may be extracted from the soil by collecting appropriate size fractions of soil particles by wet sieving and searching them for spores with a dissecting microscope. Spores of VA mycorrhizal fungi are among the largest of those of any soil fungi; they range from slightly under 0.10 mm to over 0.5 mm in diameter. I found an average of 2.6 spores of the most common species in 400 ml forest soil samples from La Selva, but I found 11.5 spores in similar samples from an adjacent second-growth area.

Sporulation of VA mycorrhizal fungi is correlated with discontinuous root growth. Sporulation is greatest in seasonal environments and in cultivated soils and is least in wet forest. Although I found most spores at La Selva in an area where vegetation had been cut, possibly causing much root death, the number of spores was nonetheless two orders of magnitude less than could be expected in some temperate agricultural soils. Factors limiting sporulation and persistence of spores in the tropics are not well understood. Spores may not survive long; many are found encrusted with other fungi and bacteria or in fragments. Spores are probably lipid-rich and represent a large resource to soil organisms.

Sporocarps represent a greater resource than single spores and may be rodent dispersed (Maser, Trappe, and Nussbaum 1978). During some seasons in the north temperate zone, sporocarps constitute a major portion of rodent diets. Hyphae are digested, but spores are passed intact in feces. *Sclerocystis* species in the tropics may be most likely to have animal vectors because the hard aggregated sporocarps are covered by many hyphae. I have observed gryllacridids and blattids feeding on *Glomus* sporocarps in Panama, but the sporocarps presented little hyphal reward, and these organisms may be spore predators. Sparse sporocarp production in the tropics suggests opportunist consumption by generalists rather than by specific predators or vectors.

Spores can be moved indirectly by any agents moving soil. Although spores are too large and heavy for wind dispersal, wind and especially water erosion might effect long-distance movement of spores. Worms and ants can move spores a limited distance, and wasps and birds move spores contained in soil farther (McIlveen and Cole 1976). These are probably insignificant vectors, however, because of the low numbers of spores in tropical soils and the small amount of soil moved. No instances of spores being moved along with seeds of a mycorrhiza-dependent host have been reported. This might be advantageous to a host, but spores are produced so far from most fruits that its chance evolution is unlikely. VA mycorrhizal fungi do not penetrate host vascular tissue in the manner of pathogenic fungi, and they have no way of passing from feeder roots to stems or branches. Rhizoflorous plants, however, might be examined for this phenomenon.

Poor dispersal of VA mycorrhizal fungi seems inconsistent with their inability to live saprobically, but they do not need to find specific hosts. The same VA mycorrhizal fungus will infect and stimulate the growth of both corn and tulip tree. At La Selva I have recovered only four species of VA mycorrhizal fungi from inoculated plants of twenty-eight species (nineteen families) that showed a positive growth response to mycorrhizae. Even if only one fungus species infected any single host species, these findings still argue for broad fungus host ranges (Janos 1975*b*, 1977, 1980*a*).

VA mycorrhizal fungi do not exhibit host specificity, but some fungus species are better able than others to spread through certain soil types. For example, species of *Acaulospora* grow best in acid soil. Such differences in tolerance of soil conditions among VA mycorrhizal fungi may lead to differences in infectiveness, the amount of infection developed by a set amount of inoculum, and in effectiveness, the ability to stimulate host growth. Differences in effectiveness have been confused with host specificity. VA mycorrhizal fungus species are able to infect almost any host, even though they may not improve host growth under some conditions. All that is required for a host to not act against a fungus species is that it repay its carbon cost to the host, which need not be manifested as a growth increase. Furthermore, hosts cannot anticipate infection by an optimal fungus associate, so they should not reject suboptimal mutualists. Thus, species composition of VA mycorrhizal fungus populations may influence plant community composition by increasing the competitive abilities of those hosts with which fungus species are most effective. It is less likely that hosts will affect the species composition of the fungus community unless they do so indirectly by modification of soil conditions such as acidity.

Fresh fragments of field-collected infected feeder roots and spores serve as VA mycorrhizal inoculum. The fungi will grow away from drying root fragments to infect live roots. It is uncertain, however, if the death of infected roots is necessary in the field to stimulate the fungi to infect new roots. Although the fungi should tap additional carbon sources as they become available, lack of points of egress from intact roots suggests that root death and fragmentation increase infectiveness. In contrast to root fragments that may remain infective for only a short time, spores are like tiny time capsules. Some spores will germinate within several days, but the range in germination time is great. Delayed germination maintains inoculum potential. Nevertheless, very large numbers of spores are probably required to equal the short-term inoculum potential of well-infected root fragments. Factors stimulating spore germination are poorly understood.

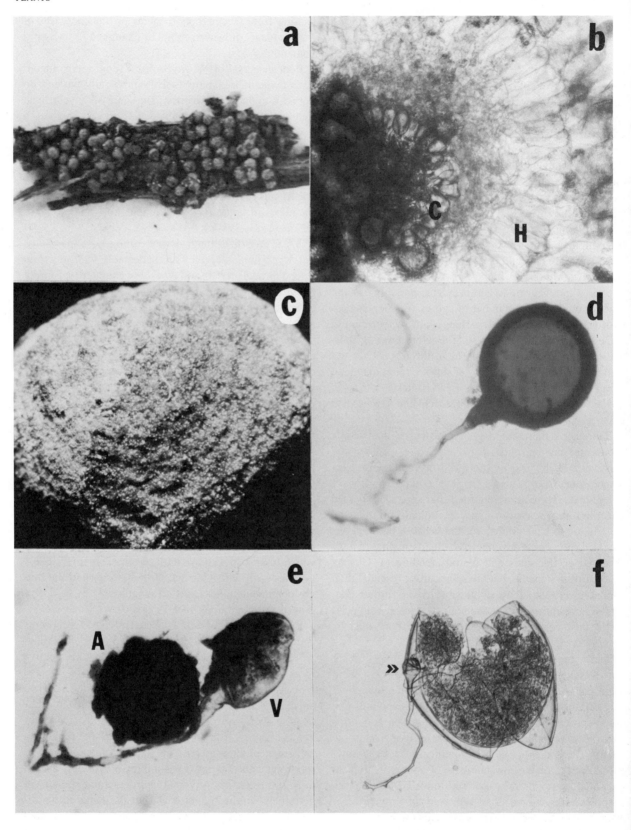

Neither hyphae emerging from germinating spores nor those from root fragments are attracted to roots.

Little is known about how infection varies around a single tree. Plants in pots develop asymmetrically infected root systems if inoculum is placed on one side. VA mycorrhizal infection does not spread rapidly along roots, but depends instead on repeated reinfection from the soil from additional fungus propagules. Thus the spread of mycelium in the substrate, upon which the effectiveness of mycorrhizae in mineral uptake depends, is maintained. How much infection (usually measured as the percentage of infected root length) is necessary to stimulate host growth is unknown, but Gerdemann (1968) has cautioned that even a low percentage of infection can amount to a large number of mycorrhizae when extrapolated to a tree's entire root system. The number of connections between roots and hyphae in the substrate may more closely reflect capacity to aid in mineral uptake than percentage of infection. Infection can be diminished by shading hosts. Light-gap species may require full sunlight in part so increase the number of mycorrhizae they support.

Several species of VA mycorrhizal fungi can simultaneously infect the same host and even the same root tip. Relative to the number of host species in lowland tropical forests, there are few VA mycorrhizal fungus species. At present only about sixty species have been described worldwide, many of which are cosmopolitan. Because the fungi have broad host ranges, it is likely that most hosts within a habitat exploit the same fungus associates and therefore have similar abilities to obtain minerals. Except for hyphal breakage, it is conceivable that several different host species might have mycorrhizal bridges connecting their roots, effectively making them competing shoots attached to a common root system. From consideration of VA mycorrhizal relationships it seems unlikely that tropical forest species richness can be accounted for by niche differentiation with respect to mineral uptake, even though tropical rain forest may owe its existence to vesicular-arbuscular mycorrhizae.

*

Boedijn, K. B. 1930. Die Gattung *Glaziella* Berkeley. *Bull. Jard. Bot. Buitenzorg.*, ser. 3., 11:57–66.

Gerdemann, J. W. 1968. Vesicular-arbuscular mycorrhiza and plant growth. *Ann. Rev. Phytopath.* 6:397–418.

Janos, D. P. 1975a. Vesicular-arbuscular mycorrhizal fungi and plant growth in a Costa Rican lowland rainforest. Ph.D. diss., University of Michigan.

———. 1975b. Effects of vesicular-arbuscular mycorrhizae on lowland tropical rainforest trees. In *Endomycorrhizas*, ed. F. E. Sanders, B. Mosse, and P. B. Tinker, pp. 437–46. London: Academic Press.

———. 1977. Vesicular-arbuscular mycorrhizae affect the growth of *Bactris gasipaes*. *Pincipes* 21:12–18.

———. 1980a. Vesicular-arbuscular mycorrhizae affect lowland tropical rain forest plant growth. *Ecology* 61:151–162.

———. 1980b. Mycorrhizae influence tropical succession. *Biotropica* 12(suppl.):56–64.

McIlveen, W. D., and Cole, H., Jr. 1976. Spore dispersal of Endogonaceae by worms, ants, wasps and birds. *Can. J. Bot.* 54:1486–89.

Maser, C.; Trappe, J. M.; and Nussbaum, R. A. 1978. Fungal–small mammal interrelationships with emphasis on Oregon coniferous forests. *Ecology* 59: 799–809.

Phillips, L. H., and Hayman, D. S. 1970. Improved procedures for clearing roots and staining parasitic and vesicular-arbuscular mycorrhizal fungi for rapid assessment of infection. *Trans. Brit. Myc. Soc.* 55: 158–61.

Rhodes, L. H., and Gerdemann, J. W. 1975. Phosphate uptake zones of mycorrhizal and non-mycorrhizal onions. *New Phytol.* 75:555–61.

Stark, N. M., and Jordan, C. F. 1978. Nutrient retention by the root mat of an Amazonian rain forest. *Ecology* 59:434–37.

FIGURE 7.124. Sporocarps and spores of vesicular-arbuscular mycorrhizal fungi. *a,* Sporocarps of *Sclerocystis coremioides* Berk. and Broome on a wood fragment, × 5. *b,* Cross section of a *Sclerocystis dussii* (Pat.) von Höhn. Sporocarp delimited by an outer layer of radially arranged inflated hyphal ends (*H*) that enclose chlamydospores (*C*) in a single-layered hemisphere around a central plexus of hyphae, × 100. *c,* Cross section of a *Glomus pulvinatus* (Hennings) Trappe and Gerdemann sporocarp. Note that single spores are discernible, × 7. *d,* Chlamydospore of *Glomus mosseae* (Nicol. and Gerd.) Gerdemann and Trappe wet sieved from soil, × 300. *e,* Azygospore (*A*) of an *Acaulospora* sp. from soil laterally attached to its subtending hypha, which terminates in a partially collapsed vesicle (*V*), × 250. *f,* Broken *Gigaspora* sp. azygospore showing a double wall and the bulbous suspensor (*arrow*) characteristic of the genus, × 150.

Virola sebifera (Fruta Dorada, Wild Nutmeg)

G. S. Hartshorn

Myristicaceae is a small pantropical family best known as the source of nutmeg that comes from *Myristica fragrans*, native of the East Indian Moluccas. *Virola* (fig. 7.125) is the largest of the five Neotropical genera, with most of the species in the Amazon basin. *V. sebifera* ranges from Bolivia and southern Brazil to Nicaragua. In Costa Rica *V. sebifera* occurs in tropical moist, tropical wet, premontane wet, and premontane rain life zones. It is a canopy tree to 40 m in height and 80 cm dbh, with a very straight, cylindric bole and slight buttresses.

FIGURE 7.125. *Virola sebifera* flowering branch (*upper*, October 1973) and *Virola* fruit (*lower*); fruit has been split open the way it dehisces to show the arillate seed (*right*) and the naked seed (*upper*). Finca La Selva, Sarapiquí District, Costa Rica (upper photo, G. S. Hartshorn; lower photo, D. H. Janzen).

All Neotropical Myristicaceae have distinctively whorled, horizontal branches about a strongly monopodial stem. Most, including *V. sebifera,* have a watery red sap in the inner bark. *V. sebifera* has simple, alternate, entire leaves, without stipules, with evenly spaced, parallel secondary veins averaging less than 1 per cm along the

midrib. Twigs and leaves have abundant rust golden pubescence.

Individuals are dioecious with very small flower (fig. 7.125). Frankie, Baker, and Opler (1974) report flowering in La Selva from December to March. Fruit is a bivalved, dehiscent capsule about 8–10 mm long (fig. 7.125). The single seed is covered by a bright red, lacinate aril that is very attractive to medium and large frugivorous birds. Birds pluck out the seed from the partially opened valves, ingest the aril-covered seed to remove the aril in the crop, then regurgitate the seed. Occasionally the seed passes through the gut. Mature fruits occur from June to October in La Selva.

V. sebifera seedlings are shade-tolerant but respond vigorously to canopy opening.

*

Duke, J. A. 1962. Myristicaceae. In Flora of Panama. *Ann. Missouri Bot. Gard.* 49:221–22.

Frankie, G. W.; Baker, H. G.; and Opler, P. A. 1974. Comparative phenological studies of trees in tropical wet and dry forests in the lowlands of Costa Rica. *J. Ecol.* 62:881–919.

Whitmore, J. L., and Hartshorn, G. S. 1969. *Literature review of common tropical trees.* Contribution no. 8. Seattle: College of Forest Resources, University of Washington.

Welfia georgii (Palmito, Palma Conga, Welfia Palm)

J. Vandermeer

Welfia georgii ranges from the Chocó in western Colombia to the San Juan River in Southern Nicaragua (Wessels Boer 1968). Usually it is a relatively rare component of pristine tropical forests, as are many tree species. On the Osa Peninsula it occurs as just such a species. But occasionally it occurs in extreme relative abundance. The watershed of the Sarapiquí River is one such area, with the La Selva field station representing an area of high density of this species. Only *Pentaclethra macroloba* is more abundant, and on some parts of the field station *Welfia* is even more abundant than *Pentaclethra*. It requires a habitat with relatively high rainfall and is thus totally absent from Guanacaste Province. In Costa Rica, then, *W. georgii* is rare in the southern Pacific lowlands, rare in the flat peripheral areas of the eastern lowlands, absent in the higher elevations and dry forests, and extremely abundant in the high-rainfall areas near the bases of the east-facing mountains in the Atlantic lowlands.

Its habitat is wet pristine forests, although it persists as adults in cleared fields. Along with *Socratea durissima* and *Iriartea gigantia, Welfia* trees are frequently left standing when forest is cleared. It seems to be especially abundant in those forests in which small light gaps are frequently formed, that is, where the turnover rate of light gaps is high.

Welfia seems to grow best under medium- to well-lighted conditions. Considering the dynamic structure of the forest, it might be called a "minor light gap" species, since it grows well in patches of diffuse light under the cover of larger trees. In larger light gaps it grows quite well but typically becomes overtopped by a variety of fast-growing second-growth species. When a seedling (fig. 7.126*a*) becomes established in a relatively dark climax situation, it apparently grows very slowly, if at all, until a light gap is created after a tree falls. The locally increased light regime then permits the seedling to grow rapidly. It continues such growth until it is either out-competed by a second-growth species or until that light gap becomes closed above the seedling. If the light gap closes before a second-growth species takes over, the seedling (now somewhat larger) again grows very slowly until another tree falls. But if the seedling becomes overtopped by some fast-growing second-growth species—

likely to happen in a large or "major" light gap—that seedling dies (Vandermeer, Stout, and Miller 1975).

Just as the species seems to be affected by the general forest structure, it also contributes a great deal to the generation of that structure. For example, an adult forms a very dense canopy, creating relatively dark conditions around its base. Also, the large and heavy fronds cause a great deal of physical damage when they fall, frequently killing seedlings and small saplings of their own species as well as other species (Hartshorn 1975; Vandermeer 1977).

The growth habit of this species is similar to that of other palms that undergo a so-called establishment phase. At germination, one leaf containing two leaflets appears. The next few leaves each have two leaflets, the width of the leaflet becoming larger with each successive leaf. The rate at which the leaflet becomes larger with new leaf emergence depends on local light conditions (Vandermeer, Stout, and Miller 1975). After a certain number of leaves have been produced and a certain leaflet width is attained, subsequent leaves show an increase in leaflet number. Each succeeding leaf, under appropriate light

FIGURE 7.126. *Welfia georgii. a,* Seedling–very young sapling, forest floor. Finca La Selva, Sarapiquí District, Costa Rica. *b,* Section of infructescence (*top*) and opened fruit showing husk and nut. Corcovado National Park, Osa Peninsula, Costa Rica (photos, D. H. Janzen).

conditions, has more leaflets than the previous leaf up to a certain life stage, at which point the tree begins to grow upward. A similar pattern is described for palms in general by Tomlinson (1960) and for *Iguanura geonomaeformis* Mart., by Kiew (1972) and has been elaborated elsewhere (Vandermeer, Stout, and Miller 1975). The tree then grows upward to a height of 8 to 20 m, at which point it begins fruiting. For purposes of discussion I have divided the stages of growth into (1) seedlings, those individuals whose leaves contain no more than two leaflets, (2) saplings, those individuals whose leaves contain more than two leaflets and lack a recognizable trunk, (3) juveniles, those individuals that have a recognizable trunk but have not reached fruiting size, and (4) adults, those individuals large enough to bear fruit. Preliminary data indicate an annual survival rate of about 62% for seedlings, about 94% for saplings, and over 99% for juveniles and adults.

The inflorescence is composed of a four- to six-branched raceme. Each rachis contains a large number of facets, each facet containing four flowers, three males and a female. When an individual comes into flower, the following sequence of events is usual. First, on a section of each rachis male flowers open. The male flower is a one-day flower, white, with long, obvious anthers. On each rachis a clump of new male flowers opens each day for about 10–15 successive days. Subsequently, the inflorescence is in a dormant state for 1 or 2 days—neither male nor female flowers are produced during this time. Then all the female flowers bloom simultaneously. Female flowers remain on the inflorescence for 2 to 4 days. The female flower resembles the male both in color and in the drawn-out nature of the petals, which makes them look very much like anthers. It has been suggested that the female flowers are actually mimics of the male flowers (M. Baudoin, pers. comm.). After a group of bees has set up a foraging territory that includes a male flowering *Welfia,* when the tree switches to female flowering, the insect is presumably tricked into visiting what appear to be male flowers.

A large number of insect species (mainly bees) have been observed visiting *Welfia* flowers, but the most common are *Trigona* bees and small curculionid beetles. It seems that the bulk of the pollination is accomplished by the bees, but the long-distance dispersal of pollen may be accomplished by the beetles. I have one record of a beetle transferring *Welfia* pollen more than 300 m.

Fruits are borne on large infructescences (fig. 7.126*b*) attached below the crown. Each nut is covered by a pulpy, sweet mesocarp that, in turn, is covered by a relatively soft ectocarp, easily removed by various birds and mammals. When the fruits ripen they fall to the ground; sometimes they are jarred loose by animals, but they always fall directly beneath the parent tree. The nut is never attacked by insect seed predators, although the mesocarp is frequently attacked by a small beetle larva before the ripe fruit falls from the tree.

At least nine different species of mammals and birds are thought to be involved in the process of seed dispersal. I have seen kinkajous (*Potos flavus*) and squirrels (*Sciurus* sp.) shucking fruits, eating the mesocarp, and dropping the nuts to the ground. Observations were also made of monkeys (*Cebus capucinus*) breaking off an entire rachis, chewing the ectocarp off individual fruits, eating the mesocarp, and dropping the undamaged nuts and the broken rachis to the ground. Agoutis (*Dasyprocta punctata*) were observed picking up fruits from the ground, shucking them, eating the mesocarp, and either eating the nut or dropping it to the ground. Three small rodent species (*Heteromys desmarestianus, Hoplomys gymnurus,* and *Proechimys semispinosus*) and agoutis have been trapped using *W. georgii* fruits as bait. Whether captive agoutis, *H. desmarestianus,* and *H. gymnurus* eat the mesocarp and the nut itself is highly dependent on numbers of fruits offered and availability of other food resources. The nuts are frequently found in bird feces under fruiting *Welfia* trees. Captive parrots (*Amazona* sp.) remove the ectocarp, scrape off the mesocarp, and drop the nut to the ground. Although no direct observations have been made on toucans (*Ramphastos sulfuratus*), I suspect that the feces containing nuts come from them.

Major fruit fall occurs in July, August, and September (Vandermeer, Stout, and Risch 1979). Most seeds fall as ripe fruits, although a significant fraction fall as nuts, having been shucked by arboreal animals. The daily rates at which seeds or fruits placed on the ground are removed can vary from year to year (average 70–80% in one year to 7–8% in the next year). But the daily pickup rate is significantly correlated with the number of seeds falling in a given area, supporting the notion that the tree is satiating both dispersers and predators.

A preliminary analysis of a large body of demographic data for this species at the La Selva field station shows that the species is not at a stable age distribution. Furthermore, the population seems to be expanding at a slow but positive rate.

*

Hartshorn, G. S. 1975. A matrix model of tree population dynamics, In *Tropical ecological systems: Trends in terrestrial and aquatic research,* ed. F. B. Golley and E. Medina. New York: Springer-Verlag.

Kiew, R. 1972. The natural history of *Iguanura geonomaeformis* Martius: A Malayan undergrowth palmlet. *Principes* 16:3–10.

Tomlinson, P. B. 1960. Essays on the morphology of palms. II. The early growth of the palm. *Principes* 4:140–43.

Vandermeer, J. H. 1977. Notes on density dependence in *Welfia georgii,* a lowland rainforest palm from Costa Rica. *Brenesia* 10/11:1–15.

Vandermeer, J. H.; Stout, J.; and Miller, G. 1975. Growth rates of *Welfia georgii, Socratea durissima,* and *Iriartis gigantea* under various conditions in a natural rainforest in Costa Rica. *Principes* 18:148–54.

Vandermeer, J. H.; Stout, J.; and Risch, S. 1979. Seed dispersal of a common Costa Rican rainforest palm (*Welfia georgii*). *Trop. Ecol.* 20:17–26.

Wessels Boer, J. G. 1968. The geonomid palms. Verhand. *Koninklijke Nederl. Akad. Wetensch. Afd. Natuurk. Tweede Reeks,* 58, no. 1:1–202.

Zamia skinneri and *Z. fairchildiana*
(Zamia, Palmera Siempre Verde, Cycad)

P. J. DeVries

The cycad genus *Zamia* (Cycadaceae) occurs from the southern United States through tropical South America. Cycads are some of the oldest living plants, being well represented in the fossil record, and are often referred to as "living fossils." The Costa Rican species of *Zamia* occur as understory plants in the wet forest from sea level to about 1,000 m elevation. They superficially resemble small palms, have long taproots, are evergreen, and are dioecious. *Z. skinneri* occurs on the Atlantic drainage, has stiff, dark green corrugated leaves, and has an average stem height of less than a meter in mature plants. *Z. fairchildiana* occurs on the Pacific drainage from about Punta Quepos south to Panama. It does not enter those parts of the deciduous forest that have a strongly marked dry season. *Z. fairchildiana* has thinner, noncorrugated leaves and may attain 2 m in height in Corcovado National Park.

In both species the erect, conelike inflorescences (fig. 7.127) are emergent from the base of the fronds, roughly from February until May. Male plants produce from one to six cones in sequence, dehiscing pollen over a continuous period of 4 to 6 weeks. The literature considers all cycads to be wind pollinated. I have seen *Trigona* bees gathering pollen from male inflorescences on the Osa Peninsula. These observations, the relatively wind-free rain-forest habitat of the Costa Rican *Zamia* species, and the fact that Chamberlain (1965) reports that the pollination droplet has a high sugar content makes me suspect these species are at least in part reliant on insects as pollen vectors. There is no published field study on the pollination of *Zamia* from anywhere in the world. Ovules will develop into full-sized fruits without being pollinated, but the seeds are hollow. As the female cone swells, the bright red seed coats are exposed through the peltate portions of the cone and may remain intact for more than a year in the field.

In the field the seeds are apparently dispersed when the cone parts rot away. The seeds fall off the plant and eventually form clusters of seedlings around the female plants. Some seeds are carried farther from the plants by rolling down a hill or are carried away by water for those plants growing along rivers. In the Talamancas, on the Osa Peninsula, and in other mountainous areas of Costa Rica, plants commonly grow on ridgetops and are absent in the valleys and intervening areas. I have not seen a seed of either species damaged by bird beak marks, animal claws, or teeth, or any other sign that indicates a potential vertebrate dispersal agent. This is curious in that the seeds look as though they would be highly attractive to animals. The only mention of a possible disperser of a cycad is Chamberlain (1965), who cites baboons as major seed predators of the Old World cycad *Encepha-*

FIGURE 7.127. *Zamia* female immature infructescence. San Pedrillo, Corcovado National Park, Osa Peninsula, Costa Rica (photo, D. H. Janzen).

lartos caffer. There is nothing published concerning anything eating or dispersing *Zamia* seeds.

All *Zamia,* and cycads in general, are chemically well protected by azoxyglycosides (Dossaji 1974). These toxins cause paralysis and death in cattle (Mason and Whiting 1966) and are highly toxic to humans. The leaves, stems, cone parts, and seed coat are eaten by the butterfly larvae of *Eumaeus minyas* (Lycaenidae). These larvae are thought to gain chemical protection via the plant toxins (DeVries 1976), as has been shown for the moth *Seirarctia echo* by Teas (1967). Successive defoliations by *E. minyas* larvae can be fatal to the plant. The leaves are also mined by an unidentified dipteran (G. Vogt, pers. comm.). Besides these two examples, I have seen no other signs of herbivory on the *Zamia* species in Costa Rica.

Economically, the roots are used as a starchy food after successive boilings, and the Cabecar and Bribri Indians in the Talamancas use an extract as a treatment for snakebite.

*

Chamberlain, C. J. 1965. *The living cycads.* New York: Hafner.

DeVries, P. J. 1976. Notes on the behavior of *Eumaeus minyas* (Lepidoptera: Lycaenidae) in Costa Rica. *Brenesia* 8:103.

Dossaji, S. F. 1974. The distribution of azoxyglycosides, amino acids, and biflavinoids in the order Cycadales: Their taxonomic, phylogenetic, and toxocological significance. Ph.D. diss., University of Texas.

Mason, M. M., and Whiting, M. G. 1966. Demyelination in the bovine spinal cord caused by *Zamia* neurotoxicity. *Fedn. Proc.* 25:533.

Teas, H. 1967. Cycasin synthesis in *Seirarctia echo* (Lepidopitera) larvae fed methylazoxymethanol. *Biochem. Biophys. Res. Comm.* 26:687–90.

8 REPTILES AND AMPHIBIANS

Adult *Boa constrictor* killing an adult coati (pisote; *Nasua narica*) in the forest understory, Finca Taboga, Guanacaste Province, Costa Rica (photo, D. H. Janzen).

INTRODUCTION

N. J. Scott and S. Limerick

Costa Rica has been a center of interest to field-oriented biologists for many years. Few places in the world combine such a great diversity of habitats with so rich a tropical fauna and flora. Seacoasts and coral reefs, rain forests and páramo are all represented within a few hours' drive on good roads. The herpetofauna is no exception to the general pattern. Several generations of Costa Rican and foreign scientists have taken advantage of opportunities to study the speciose fauna, and as a result there is a great deal of information available on the reptiles and amphibians.

Much of the voluminous herpetological literature will be reviewed in one way or another in the following accounts of individual species, but it is appropriate here to single out three publications that summarize the ecological and evolutionary backdrop of the Costa Rican herpetofauna. Savage (1966) portrayed the historical faunal elements and geological forces that combined to create the modern herpetofauna, and Duellman (1966a) mapped the ecological divisions of Central America and described the associated herpetofaunal patterns. Scott (1976) compared Costa Rican faunas with those studied in other tropical regions.

This paper is designed to serve as an introduction to some aspects of the ecology and evolution of the Costa Rican herpetofauna. The choice of subjects was guided by several criteria: our own interests, broad taxonomic scope, availability of information, group "importance," and ease of study. In each section the information is placed into an ecological-evolutionary framework that is designed to generate hypotheses for future studies. The section on amphibian breeding examines the varied reproductive modes and discusses the selective pressures and opportunities faced by amphibians in a diverse array of habitats. This area of study has a rich literature, but many aspects of amphibian breeding biology remain unknown. The part discussing anuran defenses serves to introduce a rapidly expanding field that has received little attention until recently. We predict that in the future the ecological aspects of how amphibians avoid predation will receive a great deal of attention. Diurnal lizards are often very easy to work with, and many scientists have taken advantage of the opportunity. This is another area that should yield much information. The final section on turtles and crocodilians was included because their biological traits tend to be similar and they are the most important reptiles from the viewpoints of economics and conservation.

Several general terms need to be defined. In this introduction, lowland refers to elevations below about 800 m, intermediate to elevations from 600 to 1,700 m, and highland to elevations above 1,700 m. "Dry" refers to areas receiving less than about 2,000 mm of annual rainfall (most of lowland Guanacaste Province, northern Puntarenas Province, and the floor of the Meseta Central), and "wet" includes the rest of the country.

Breeding Biology of Amphibians

North American frogs have a generalized life history that is familiar to most people. Male frogs call near a pond, females approach, a pair goes into amplexus, and eggs are fertilized as they are laid. After a few days the tadpoles hatch from the eggs, feed on detritus and algae, and grow. They transform into frogs after a variable period. The metamorphosed froglets grow into adults, usually on land. This scenario, with minor variations, describes the reproductive biology of the great majority of United States frogs. However, in the southwestern United States

and in Florida there is a small group of frogs that are the only United States mainland representatives of the tropical American family Leptodactylidae, a group that shows a quite different breeding behavior. The cliff and barking frogs (*Syrrhophyus, Halactophryne*) and the introduced greenhouse frog (*Eleutherodactylus*) lay large-yolked eggs on land in moist situations. The tadpole stage develops within the egg, and the egg hatches a froglet. This mode of reproduction is called *direct development*. In the remaining United States genus in this family, *Leptodactylus,* the male whips up a foam nest from mucous secretions of the female and semen. The nest protects the eggs and young tadpoles until they become large enough to move out into the pond.

The generalized pattern described above could fit many United States salamanders too. Quite a few, however, lay terrestrial eggs that hatch either into larvae that complete their development in water or into fully terrestrial young that have the same body form as do the adults. Other differences between salamander and generalized frog reproduction are the courtship patterns (salamanders, unlike most anurans, do not call) and fertilization (all except one species of United States salamander have internal fertilization). Several species and populations of salamanders are aquatic during their entire life.

TABLE 8.1   Reproductive Modes of Costa Rican Amphibians

Site of Development	Gymnophiona Caeciliidae	Caudata Plethodontidae	Anura Rhinophrynidae	Anura Microhylidae
I. Eggs and larvae in water				
A. Unconstrained body of water				
1. Temporary pond			1	2
2. Stream				
3. Permanent pond				
B. Arboreal water				
1. Tree cavities				
2. Bromeliads				
C. Constructed basins				
II. Eggs out of water, larvae develop in water				
A. Eggs on vegetation over water				
1. Temporary pond				
2. Stream				
B. Eggs in foam nest				
C. Eggs on land, larvae carried to water				
III. Neither eggs nor larva in water				
A. Direct development		24		
B. Viviparity	3			
IV. Unknown				
Total	3	24		

SOURCES: Data for caecilians from Wake (1977); salamanders from Wake and Lynch (1976); *Rhinophrynus* from Stuart (1961); microhylids from personal observations and Nelson (1972); leptodactylids from Heyer (1969), Starrett (1973), and Breder (1946); bufonids from personal observations, Starrett (1967), Novak and Robinson (1975), and Zug and Zug (1979); hylids from personal

In contrast, Costa Rican amphibians show an incredible diversity of reproductive behavior that is only hinted at in United States amphibians. One of the two leptodactylid breeding adaptations described above occurs in more than forty species, and other forms of reproduction are common. Here we will examine these patterns, suggest adaptive trends, and speculate on the selective forces that produce such a great diversity of breeding types.

The clearest trend in the breeding biology of Costa Rican amphibians is a progression of specializations leading away from dependence on a body of permanent water and toward increased terrestriality. A summary of reproductive modes will define this trend. The changes from completely aquatic to terrestrial breeding are accompanied by several specific adaptive traits, including an increase in parental care, a change from oviparity to viviparity, and changes from an aquatic larval state to direct development on land.

REPRODUCTIVE MODES

Crump (1974; modified by Duellman 1978) tabulated the reproductive modes found in an Ecuadorian anuran community. Her classification, with minor modifications, can be used for the Costa Rican amphibian fauna (table 8.1). In some cases we have added breeding types not found in Crump's Ecuadorian frogs, such as viviparity and bromeliad breeding; in other instances we have subdivided some of her modes into ecologically meaningful subdivisions, such as permanent versus temporary water and pond versus stream habitats. We have likewise deleted modes found in Ecuadorian frogs but not found in Costa Rican frogs, such as egg transportation by adults. We could not even guess the breeding mode for four species (*Bufo fastidiosus, Hyla colymba, Crepidophryne epioticus,* and *Glossostoma aterrimum*), but where available evidence allowed us to make a reasonable guess we did so. Some species breed in two or more types of aquatic habitat; in those cases they were assigned to the most common developmental site.

Mode IA: Reproduction in Unconstrained Bodies of Water

The most generalized mode of reproduction is similar to that described earlier for most North American anurans. Eggs and larvae are found in ponds or streams. Chorusing males gather at the breeding site and are joined by the females. There is no known extended courtship or parental care in this group.

In Costa Rica most of the mode IA species deposit eggs in temporary ponds, which eliminates some fish and aquatic insect predation, but the eggs and larvae may

		Anura				
Leptodactylidae	Bufonidae	Hylidae	Dendrobatidae	Centrolenidae	Ranidae	Totals
	8	13			1	25
	3	2			1	6
	1				2	3
		2				2
		3				3
		1				1
		7				7
		9		13		22
6						6
			6			6
35						59
						3
	2	1				4
41	14	38	6	13	4	147

observations and Duellman (1970); dendrobatids from personal observations and Savage (1968); centrolenids from personal observations and McDiarmid (1975), and ranids from personal observations and Zweifel (1964*b*).

become desiccated or overcrowded as the pond dries (Heyer, McDiarmid, and Weigmann 1975). The microhylids, rhinophrynid, *Rana palmipes,* most *Bufo* (*coccifer, coniferus, haematiticus, holdridgei, luetkenii, melanochloris, periglenes,* and *valliceps*), some *Hyla* (*rufitela, loquax, microcephala, phlebodes, angustilineata, pseudopuma, boulengeri, eleaeochroa,* and *staufferi*), *Phrynohyas venulosa,* and some *Smilisca* (*baudinii, phaeota,* and *puma*) use temporary ponds. Oviposition is during the wet season, and males call from or near the water. Detailed reproductive information for representatives of this breeding mode can be found in Stuart (1935, 1961), Taylor (1942), and Duellman (1960) for *Rhinophrynus dorsalis;* Novak and Robinson (1975) for *Bufo holdridgei;* Savage and Heyer (1969) and Duellman (1970) for hylids in general; and Zwiefel (1964*a*) and Pyburn (1967) for *Phrynohyas venulosa.*

A few species using this mode of reproduction presumably lay their eggs in streams. They include the three species of *Atelopus* (Bufonidae), *Rana warschewitschii* (Ranidae), *Smilisca sila,* and *S. sordida* (Hylidae). *Atelopus* breeds in the wet season, and the eggs are probably anchored to the undersides of rocks in the stream (Starrett 1967). These two species of *Smilisca* breed in the dry season when the stream volume and rate of flow are lowest (Duellman and Trueb 1966). *Atelopus* may call but do not chorus. They are territorial and pair before moving to the oviposition site (Sexton 1958; McDiarmid 1971), whereas *Smilisca* males form choruses or call in small groups (Duellman 1970; pers. obs.). The breeding habits of *R. warschewitschii* are not known in detail, but they often breed in the quiet backwaters of small stream or other marshy situations (pers. obs.).

Relatively few species of Costa Rican frogs breed in permanent ponds. Fish predation is likely to be intense (Scott and Starrett 1974), and permanent ponds are scarce in the country. Three species might be characterized as breeding more often in permanent than in temporary waters: *Bufo marinus, Rana vibicaria,* and highland *R. pipiens. Bufo marinus* has been studied in detail in Panama by Breder (1946) and by Zug and Zug (1979). They breed in many kinds of waters, most of which are permanent. In Costa Rica common breeding sites are the pools left behind by receding rivers (pers. obs.). The highland *Rana vibicaria* has been studied in Panama by Zwiefel (1964*b*).

Mode IB: Arboreal Water
A few species of Costa Rican tree frogs live their whole existence in tree canopies, breeding in tree holes and bromeliads. Two species of fringed-limbed *Hyla, fimbrimembra* and *miliaria,* are large (>100 mm in length) and very poorly known, and their breeding activity has not been recorded. Taylor (1952) took a specimen

from a water-filled tree cavity, and we assume that they breed in similar sites (see Savage 1980). *Anotheca spinosa* is another hylid that has been recorded as breeding in tree holes (Robinson 1961; Duellman 1970) and bromeliads (Taylor 1954). Their tadpoles are carnivorous, eating frog eggs and mosquito larvae (Taylor 1954). *Hyla zeteki* is a bromeliad breeder, and the tadpoles have highly modified mouthparts for eating frog eggs and possibly other tadpoles (Dunn 1937; Starrett 1960). A closely related species, *H. picadoi,* also breeds in bromeliads (Robinson 1977).

Mode IC: Constructed Basins
Males of *Hyla rosenbergi* usually construct mud basins where the females oviposit next to temporary ponds or streams, although in some circumstances eggs are laid in male territories that are in the shallow water at the edge of swamps (Breder 1946; Duellman 1970; pers. obs.). Breder (1946) offers an exceptionally detailed description and photographs of nests, tadpole development, and mating behavior.

Mode IIA: Eggs on Vegetation, Larvae in Water
The trend toward removing part of the amphibian life cycle from aquatic habitats starts with species that lay eggs out of water but whose tadpoles still develop in water. These species lay their eggs on vegetation over temporary ponds or streams, and the tadpoles hatch and drop into the water. Five species of *Agalychnis, Phyllomedusa lemur,* and *Hyla ebraccata* suspend their eggs over temporary ponds (Duellman 1970). Detailed breeding observations have been made on *Agalychnis callidryas* (Pyburn 1963, 1964, 1970; Duellman 1970), *A. annae* (Duellman 1963), and *A. spurrelli* (Boulenger 1913; Scott and Starrett 1974).

Hyla lancasteri and probably eight other species of *Hyla* (*debilis, legleri, pictipes, rivularis, rufioculis, tica, uranochroa,* and *xanthosticta*) and all centrolenids deposit eggs on vegetation over streams, into which the tadpoles fall after hatching. *H. lancasteri* eggs are deposited on the upper leaf surfaces (Trueb 1968). No parental care is known, and breeding is generally in the wet season, depending on the site. The thirteen species of Costa Rican centrolenids (*Centrolenella*) attach their egg clutches to foliage overhanging high-gradient streams. The greatly modified tadpoles fall into the swift current and bury themselves in the detritus and gravel on the stream bottom (pers. obs.). Males are territorial (McDiarmid and Adler 1974; Duellman and Savitsky 1976), and many guard their egg masses (McDiarmid 1975, 1978).

Mode IIB: Eggs in Foam Nest, Larvae in Water
Six species of Costa Rican leptodactylids construct foam nests and deposit their eggs in them, and the tadpoles

develop in temporary ponds. Heyer (1969) detected a definite trend toward terrestriality within the genus *Leptodactylus,* as suggested by the placement of the foam nest. The male uses his hind feet to whip up a mixture of air, water, mucus from the female, and semen (Rivero and Esteves 1969; Heyer and Rand 1977). The most aquatic forms float their nests on water (*Physalaemus pustulosus* [Breder 1946; Sexton and Ortleb 1966]. *Leptodactylus melanonotus* [Heyer 1976; pers. obs.], and *L. bolivianus* [Sexton 1962; pers. observ.]). The next step toward terrestriality is shown by forms that place their nests next to ponds or in burrows, depressions, or potholes that are likely to flood (*Leptodactylus pentadactylus* [Breder 1946; Vinton 1951; Rivero and Esteves 1969; pers. obs.]). A further step is seen in those *Leptodactylus* that place the foam nest in a burrow excavated by the male (*L. fragilis* [Dixon and Heyer 1968; Heyer 1970] and *L. poecilocheilus* [Dixon and Heyer 1968; Heyer 1969]). The latter group breeds before the heavy rains, and the tadpoles living in the nest are more advanced than other anuran tadpoles when the floods finally come (Heyer 1969).

Mode IIC: Eggs on Land, Larvae Carried to Water

The members of an entire family of frogs, the Dendrobatidae, lay their eggs on land and carry the tadpoles to water for development. One Costa Rican species, *Colostethus nubicola,* places its tadpoles in small streams, but the other species generally use tree holes, fallen palm petioles, leaf cups, and the leaf axils of bromeliads and aroids (Savage 1968; Silverstone 1975, 1976; pers. obs.).

Dendrobatids are diurnal and often very common. They have been studied frequently, both in captivity and in the wild. For recent general summaries of social and breeding behavior, see Silverstone (1975, 1976), Salthe and Mecham (1974), and Wells (1977a,b). In most species of dendrobatids, the males defend calling territories, but *Dendrobates auratus* is an apparent exception (Wells 1978). Dendrobatid mating takes place on land, usually without amplexus, and eggs are deposited in the litter or on low leaves. The eggs are tended, often by the male but sometimes by the female, and the tadpoles are taken onto the back of a parent. The parent carries the tadpoles for a varying number of days or even weeks and then deposits them in water for further development. Field studies of the territorial and breeding behavior of Costa Rican species include those on *Dendrobates auratus, D. granuliferus,* and *D. pumilio* (Dunn 1941; Eaton 1941; Breder 1946; Starrett 1960; Duellman 1966b; Kitasako 1967; Savage 1968; Goodman 1971a; Crump 1972; Bunnell 1973; Silverstone 1975; Wells 1978; Young 1979; Limerick 1980). *Colostethus* and *Phyllobates,* the other two Costa Rican genera, have received much less attention,

although Duellman (1967), Savage (1968), and Silverstone (1976) contain some information.

An intriguing question has arisen in dendrobatid studies. There is a possibility that adult frogs regularly monitor tadpoles in water and transfer them from one water source to another. Dunn (1941) discounted the idea, but Eaton's (1941) data show that when a tree hole was cleared of tadpoles, new ones "well past the hatching stage" would appear within a day. Eaton did not measure most of the tadpoles when they were taken from the water, but did so only after they had been in the laboratory for several days or weeks. One of us (Scott) watched a female *D. pumilio* visit sequentially almost all of the water cups in the leaf axils of a tank bromeliad. She was not carrying a tadpole, but she backed down into each cup, stayed a few seconds as if to give tadpoles a chance to climb on, then went on to the next cup. None of the leaf cups contained tadpoles.

Mode IIIA: Direct Development on Land

The direct development of large-yolked eggs in terrestrial nests is displayed by a number of common genera of Costa Rican amphibians. Presumably, all twenty-four species of plethodontid salamanders and the entire frog genus *Eleutherodactylus* (thirty-five species) lay small clutches of eggs on land. The embryos pass through a highly modified larval stage in the egg and hatch as tiny salamanders or froglets (Lynn 1942; Vial 1968; Starrett 1973; Houck 1977). The reproductive behavior of tropical salamanders has been studied in several species, but our knowledge of Costa Rican *Eleutherodactylus* reproduction is fragmentary at best. They do not congregate in breeding choruses like most other frogs, their breeding season is extended rather than concentrated, they are generally quite shy, and many species are nocturnal. It has been discovered that some bats are effective predators on many forest species of *Eleutherodactylus* (M. Tuttle, pers. comm.), which may be a reason for their shyness.

Mode IIIB: Viviparity

This last reproductive mode found in Costa Rican amphibians is viviparity. It occurs only in the caecilians, and all three species are viviparous. Eggs and larvae are retained in the oviduct. The larvae develop a special dentition for scraping and ingesting cells and secretions from the wall of the oviduct (Wake 1977).

THE EVOLUTION OF TERRESTRIALITY

A discussion of the evolution of the terrestrial trend in reproduction of Costa Rican amphibians can best be divided into two parts: one, with some hard data, on the adaptations necessary to accomplish the breeding mode and the second, almost entirely speculative, on the selective forces operating to produce these adaptations. A parallel discussion, with emphasis on South American frogs, is found in Lutz (1948).

Salthe (1969), Salthe and Duellman (1973), and Salthe and Mecham (1974) have summarized the egg and clutch size adaptations associated with different reproductive modes. A general criticism of these analyses is that "clutch size" is defined in practical terms as the number of eggs found in naturally deposited clusters. For most tropical species we do not know how often egg clusters are produced. Some species divide a single ovarian complement into several clusters (Duellman 1970; Pyburn 1970), some do not breed every year (Vial 1968), and others deposit a few eggs at regular intervals over an extended breeding season (Wells 1978). For these reasons the analyses do not reflect comparable degrees of reproductive effort between different species.

The cited authors formulated several hypotheses that are pertinent to our discussion (Salthe and Duellman 1973):

1. For salamanders and frogs of about the same size, those laying larger clutches lay smaller eggs.
2. Larger eggs produce larger hatchlings.
3. Larger eggs develop more slowly.
4. Larger eggs are associated with species whose larvae develop in streams and terrestrial sites.
5. There has been selection for increased clutch size in large frogs and for larger egg size in small frogs.
6. Because of points 4 and 5, small frogs are better at reproducing in ways novel to anurans.

Recently Crump and Kaplan (1979) tested some of these conclusions with a suite of Ecuadorian hylid frogs. Their results supported the hypothesis that frogs with more terrestrial breeding habits had larger eggs and smaller clutches than equivalent-sized frogs using aquatic breeding habitats.

Associated with the trend to produce larger eggs in nonpond environments are the changes in developmental rates. As we stated above, larger eggs develop more slowly (up to 3 weeks; pers. obs.), which automatically places more ecological emphasis on the egg stage of development. Slower egg development does not necessarily mean a longer total time between oviposition and metamorphosis; larger eggs produce larger tadpoles, which presumably have shorter larval periods. However, no studies have been made of the consequences of the trade-offs incurred by shifts in developmental rates for different life-history stages.

Shifts in emphasis in developmental rates and egg size and number are not the only ones seen in energy flow pathways between adult frogs and their offspring. Parental investment is measured not only in terms of egg and sperm production but also by the costs of mate attraction, increased exposure to predation, territorial defense,

nest production, and parental care. There are few data for the costs involved in the first four categories, but the fifth, parental care, has received a great deal of attention (Salthe and Mecham 1974; McDiarmid 1978).

Parental care is positively associated with terrestrial breeding in amphibians. Salthe and Mecham (1974) detected three major consequences of parental care: protection of eggs and larvae from predation; assurance of an oxygen supply to the eggs by manipulation; and a mechanism to provide a more suitable microhabitat, such as providing moisture to the eggs or moving tadpoles to the most favorable sites for development. All these factors appear to be operating among Costa Rican amphibians. Viewed in this context, parental care is an important accessory to a terrestrial life cycle. All species with documented parental care have smaller clutches than do close relatives lacking parental care (McDiarmid 1978). Whether these are two independent trends that are related through a third (increased terrestriality) or whether one trend causes the other is not clear, although McDiarmid (1978) believes that lowered fecundity is a preadaptation for parental care.

Nest-making is another clear adaptation leading to a more terrestrial breeding habitat. The foam nests of the leptodactylids and the mud basins of *Hyla rosenbergi* protect eggs and tadpoles from desiccation (Heyer 1969). *Leptodactylus fragilis* and *L. poecilocheilus* construct burrows in which they place their nests, with similar advantageous results.

Conspicuous tadpole adaptations are correlated with larval habitats and feeding modes. Starrett (1960, 1967, 1973) described many different types of Costa Rican tadpoles. Major selective forces appear to be associated with water type (stream, pond, bromeliad), position in the water column (interstitial, midwater, surface), substrate (mudbottom, rocky bottom), and diet (filter feeding, carnivory).

The trends toward terrestriality that we have examined are associated with selective pressures upon which we can only speculate. The main selective force appears to be an evolutionary effort to escape predation pressure on eggs and larvae. This pressure comes largely from fish (Heyer, McDiarmid, and Weigmann 1975). Frogs escape by using ephemeral aquatic habitats or terrestrial or arboreal nesting sites. In Costa Rica there are no native fish above about 1,500 m, and a whole radiation of stream-breeding hylids is found above this level (Savage and Heyer 1969). Most of the adaptations we have discussed are conducive to improving egg and larval survival in habitats that are not occupied by fish. The introduction of trout to Costa Rican upland streams is likely to menace their associated frog populations.

A selective regime that is largely unrelated to fish predation pressure is the special requirements imposed by stream habitats. Without special adaptations, eggs and tadpoles are poorly suited to life in a swift current. Thus, most stream-breeding frogs hang their eggs in trees, and many lay large-yolked eggs that produce large, strong tadpoles. The tadpoles themselves show special stream adaptations (Starrett 1960, 1967).

In summary, the "trend toward terrestriality" that we have discussed is driven not so much by selection for terrestriality per se as by selection for removing eggs and tadpoles from exposure to fish predation. Any water sources unoccupied by fish, or habitats in which tadpoles can hide, such as grass-filled marshes, are usually heavily used by frogs in Costa Rica. Some arboreal trends appear to be alternative adaptations to unfavorable limnological conditions such as strong stream flows.

Anuran Defense Adaptations

Tropical frogs often appear to be among the most defenseless of animals. They are small relative to other terrestrial vertebrates, many are rather slow moving, and they do not usually have teeth or claws suitable for self-defense. In lieu of more obvious structural and behavioral protection, amphibians have evolved an array of more subtle and passive defenses against predators.

TOXINS

One could generalize that all amphibians produce skin toxins. Many are not very potent, and their effects are not obvious, but several produce some of the most potent natural toxins known (Myers, Daly, and Malkin 1978).

The most common effects of skin toxins are the bad taste or other noxious results that serve to discourage or deter predators. Specific kinds of toxins are apparently restricted to certain taxonomic units with anurans. For instance, various species of toads (Bufonidae) have several identified toxins: atelopidtoxin, bufogenin, bufotenidine, and bufotoxin. These can cause hypertension, vasoconstriction, increased power in heartbeat, or hallucination; or they can directly poison the heart muscle. In the leptodactylid *Leptodactylus pentadactylus*, leptodactylin causes a neuromuscular block and a nicotinelike stimulation of the nervous system. South American *Physalaemus* skin toxins cause hypotension and vasocilation. Ranid skin toxins are hypotensive, and certain hylid toxins are hemolytic and hypotensive (Daly and Myers 1967; Habermehl 1974).

Some species of dendrobatids, as their common name "poison dart" frogs suggests, are probably the most toxic Costa Rican frogs. South American Indians used skin secretions from the more poisonous species to tip their arrows (Myers, Daly, and Malkin 1978). Batrachotoxin, found in the Costa Rican species *Phyllobates vittatus* and *P. lugubris,* blocks neuromuscular contraction and transmission (Albuquerque, Daly, and Witkop 1971). It also causes symptoms of muscle poisoning and respiratory paralysis and can cause death. *Dendrobates pumilio* and *D. auratus* secrete pumiliotoxin, which caused convulsions and death with subcutaneous injection in rats (Habermehl 1974). Myers, Daly, and Malkin (1978) reported that a specimen of *P. vittatus* touched on a human tongue caused numbness and a tightening of the throat. A snake (*Leimadophis*) was helpless for several hours after biting this species. These toxins seem to be readily absorbed by the mucosa of the mouth and throat, or by any porous skin, and cause respiratory difficulties. Contact with a cut or entrance into the circulatory system is also harmful and possibly lethal (Myers, Daly, and Malkin 1978). Apparently, in the family Dendrobatidae, the cryptic species in the genus *Colostethus* are relatively nontoxic, whereas members of *Dendrobates* are quite toxic and members of *Phyllobates* are very poisonous.

Several other Costa Rican frogs produce strong toxic symptoms in humans. The hylid *Phrynohyas venulosa* can produce sneezing in susceptible people in the same room, even without physical contact with the frog (pers. obs.). The toxin of this species can produce acute pain and local paralysis when in contact with mucous membranes or breaks in the skin (Janzen 1962). The two largest Costa Rican amphibians, *Bufo marinus* and *Leptodactylus pentadactylus,* both produce copious irritating skin secretions (Daly and Myers 1967; Habermehl 1974). *Bufo marinus* has muscular control over the paratoid gland; the toad can squeeze the gland and squirt the poison in a fine spray more than 30 cm (pers. obs.). This is why *B. marinus* can kill dogs and cats that pick this toad up in their mouths (Krakauer 1968). The small bufonid *Atelopus* is known to have powerful skin toxins, but they are not obvious during normal handling (Fuhrman, Fuhrman, and Mosher 1969).

Villa (1967, 1972) described defensive behavior in captive *Leptodactylus pentadactylus*. Individuals showed defensive behaviors including hissing, inflating the body, and raising of the hind legs with the snout near the ground. During this behavior a toxic skin secretion was produced that irritated open cuts and mucosa and caused sneezing.

Skin glands in tadpoles of some *Bufo* species and some hylids have noxious secretions, making them unpalatable (Wassersug 1973). In experiments in Costa Rica using human subjects, *Bufo marinus* tadpoles were found to have very distasteful skin, while tadpoles of *Smilisca phaeota, Hyla rufitela,* and *Colostethus nubicola* had distasteful bodies, perhaps partly because the gut contents were distasteful (Wassersug 1971). Myers, Daly, and Malkin (1978) found no batrachotoxin in tadpoles of a Colombian *Phyllobates* and found only traces in juvenile frogs. This suggests that in this species the toxins are formed in significant amounts only after metamorphosis.

357

Frog eggs can also be toxic. Licht (1967) recorded the deaths of two Indians who accidentally ate what were probably *Bufo marinus* eggs. Further studies with natural predators confirmed the hypothesis that the eggs of *B. marinus* were unpalatable compared with the eggs of several other anurans (Licht 1968, 1969).

COLORATION

Most amphibians are cryptically colored. They bear various shades and patterns of browns, greens, grays, and blacks, thus blending into the environment. Many cryptic species do not have potent skin toxins but depend on their coloration to make them less visible to predators. Some cryptic species, however, also have toxic defenses. *Phrynohyas venulosa,* for example, secretes a substance that can burn skin or mucous membranes (Janzen 1962). Most such species are sit-and-wait predators; being motionless much of the time, they further reduce their visibility. Many cryptic, nontoxic species are crepuscular or nocturnal, while the aposematic (conspicuous), toxic species are usually diurnal.

The species that have conspicuous colors (are aposematic) usually have strong toxins. The warning colors or contrasting patterns serve as a warning to predators, but they may also send an aggressive or courtship message to individuals of the same species. It is believed that birds, known to have color vision, are the main targets of the aposematic color signals. Wild birds react to warning colors in amphibians by avoiding toxic species (Brodie and Brodie 1980), and domestic fowl can learn to avoid dendrobatids (Cott 1904; Daly and Myers 1967; Kitasako 1967; Silverstone 1975).

Many frogs have "flash" colors that are assumed to serve a defensive function. Flash colors are bright colors, usually red, yellow, orange, or blue, sometimes with dark barring or mottling, on the surfaces of the hind legs and groin that are concealed when the frog is at rest. The resting frog is cryptic, but movement exposes a flash of bright color for a moment until the frog folds its legs again. This sudden change from procrypsis to a flash of color to procrypsis again is believed to confuse, startle, or misdirect a predator (Cott 1940). Like aposematic coloring, flash colors probably function against bird predators. Flash colors are seen in a wide variety of Costa Rican frogs, including four species of *Eleutheordactylus, Leptodactylus pentadactylus,* all five species of *Agalychnis,* three species of *Hyla,* and one species of *Rana.*

JUMPING ABILITY

Many authors have suggested that the unique saltatorial locomotion of frogs evolved as an escape mechanism (review in Inger 1962). Jumping has several advantages over the primitive salamanderlike walk. In dense grass-

lands or in low-shrub habitats, it is almost impossible to move very rapidly at or near ground level. Jumping is a much faster and more efficient mode of locomotion. The same applies to many riparian habitats. To this frog collector, the most elusive frogs are those that leap into a grass or vine tangle or jump from the shore into deep water.

Another likely advantage of saltatorial locomotion is that it leaves a discontinuous odor trail, which probably confounds the many snakes that are excellent scent followers.

Jumping is also a key frog adaptation in the exploitation of arboreal habitats. Flying, gliding, or leaping are the only methods of rapidly moving about in a tree canopy. The leaping ability of frogs enable them to use the discontinuous leaf and small twig substrate more effectively than any other vertebrate except birds. Some frogs are even able to glide (review in Scott and Starrett 1974). An important component of arboreal survival is rapid escape from predators, especially snakes.

VOICE

A few frogs emit a loud scream or squall when grabbed by a predator, especially a snake. Two Costa Rican species known to do this are *Leptodactylus pentadactylus* and *Rana pipiens* (Villa 1967; pers. obs.). Two escape opportunities may stem from this behavior. A mammalian predator could be startled enough to drop the frog. Another possibility is suggested by the observation that caimans are attracted to squalling *L. pentadactylus* (pers. obs.). If the caiman attacked the frog's captor, the frog might escape.

HOW TO OVERCOME ANURAN DEFENSES

Even the most effective anuran defense mechanisms can be circumvented by some predators. *Bufo marinus,* which has been known to lethally poison naive dogs and cats (Krakauer 1968), is eaten by opossums (*Didelphis* spp.), which open the toad's belly, where poison glands are scarce or absent, and eat the internal organs. Raccoons (*Procyon* spp.) do the same thing (pers. obs.).

Some toad-eating snakes are relatively immune to specific frog toxins compared with other species that do not ordinarily eat toads. Small doses of *Bufo marinus* venom killed snakes of the genera *Salvadora* and *Coluber,* but garter snakes (*Thamnophis sirtalis*) were not killed until the dose was tripled (Licht and Low 1968). Myers, Daly, and Malkin (1978) found that a common tropical frog-eating snake, *Leimadophis epinephalus,* was able to digest a juvenile *Phyllobates terribilis,* whose adults are the most toxic frogs known, but a presumably larger dose of toxin immobilized another snake of the same species for several hours. The mechanism by which snakes tolerate frog toxins is unknown, but an enlarged adrenal gland has been implicated in some species (Smith and White 1955).

Since amphibian toxins are generally concentrated in skin secretions, predators that avoid the skin can successfully feed on toxic frogs and tadpoles. Many invertebrate predators feed by puncturing their prey and sucking the body fluids (Wassersug 1973), and spiders and water bugs appear to be regular predators on Costa Rican frogs and tadpoles (pers. obs.).

Some tadpoles, including those of *Bufo marinus* and *Leptodactylus melanonotus,* are jet black and aggregate into dense clusters containing hundreds of individuals. The adaptive significance of this behavior is obscure. The aggregations are very conspicuous, and the tadpoles would be very vulnerable to predation except that, at least for *B. marinus,* they are unpalatable (Wassersug 1971, 1973).

The leaping ability of frogs is matched by a large radiation of dirunal sight-feeding snakes that eat mostly frogs. In Costa Rica, the majority (about thirty-five species) are forest-floor forms, but several (nine species) are arboreal.

Lizard Food and Feeding Habits

FEEDING HABITS

As a group, lizards are a highly successful line of reptilian evolution. Along with frogs, birds, and bats they share the distinction of being able to populate many diverse habitats with large numbers and many species of insectivorous forms. Lizards are often the commonest vertebrates in an area. Part of their success is almost certainly due to the fact that they are, in many habitats, the most effective terrestrial-arboreal predators on arthropods, a very abundant food resource.

Although most lizards feed primarily on arthropods, many species and even families have diverged into other feeding niches. A fair number of lizards are vegetarian, at least as adults. The related families Helodermatidae and Varanidae (with the exception of one species) are adapted to general carnivory; small species feed largely on insects, but large species take amphibians, other lizards, mammals, birds, and fish. Other lizard species are specialized for certain diets; for instance, one species of South American teiid feeds on aquatic snails.

The great majority of Costa Rican lizards eat arthropods, without specialization on any one taxon; there are no really carnivorous species like the tegus (*Tupinambis*) of South America or the varanid lizards (*Varanus*) of the Old World. Their diets differ between sites and seasons of the year because the types of arthropods available to them vary with habitat and season (Janzen and Schoener 1968; Hillman 1969; Sexton, Bauman, and Ortleb 1972; Fleming and Hooker 1975). Most lizards seem to feed opportunistically, attempting to catch most of the apparently potential prey they encounter. Generally, the sizes of prey items are positively correlated with the sizes (snout-vent length [SVL] or biomass) of the lizards. Individuals are limited by the maximum size they can capture and swallow, but larger individuals can also take smaller prey.

In Costa Rica the families taking arthropods exclusively are Teiidae, Gekkonidae, Anguidae, and probably Scincidae and Xantusiidae (Hillman 1969; Pough 1973; Duellman 1978). Although most species are opportunistic feeders on insects, spiders, and mites, one anguid, *Diploglossus monotropis,* is thought to specialize on land crabs (D. C. Robinson, pers. comm.). Members of the family Iguanidae are usually insectivorous, but the largest species, *Ctenosaura similis, Iguana iguana,* and the three species of *Basiliscus,* also eat vegetation (Taylor 1956; Montanucci 1968; Pough 1973; VanDevender 1978). *Ctenosaura* and *Basiliscus* are insectivorous as juveniles and more herbivorous as adults, while juvenile *Iguana* are generally herbivorous (pers. obs.). Plant parts eaten are fruits, buds, seeds, and leaves (Taylor 1956; Montanucci 1968). Adult *Basiliscus* may eat 25% to 50% vegetation, and large individuals also eat vertebrates and crustaceans (Montanucci 1968; VanDevender 1978).

Pough (1973) pointed out that iguanid and scincid lizards that weigh over 100 g are mainly herbivorous and those weighing less than 100 g are mainly insectivorous. The large lizards have a greater total energy requirement for body maintenance, but smaller lizards have a higher energy need per unit of body weight. Anthropod food is more abundant in small packages (insects) than in large ones, and there is more energy per unit of prey in animals than in plants. Plants also take longer to be digested and the percentage of assimilation is lower (Bennett and Dawson 1976). Small lizards are more adept at catching small, fast-moving prey. Compared with large lizards, they have a smaller body mass to move when pursuing prey and use less energy in doing so. Most lizards are not physiologically adapted to long pursuit times, since respiration quickly changes to the anaerobic pathway (Bennett and Licht 1972). Pursuit of small, fast-moving prey by large lizards is thus doubly inefficient. For large lizards it is often more efficient to eat plants, which require no energy for pursuit and are usually present in large quantities. Large lizards are also less vulnerable to predation and therefore they can spend more time basking in the sun. By doing so they can raise their body temperature and increase the otherwise slow rate of digestion of plant material.

FORAGING BEHAVIOR

For those lizards with insectivorous and carnivorous food habits, there are two main types of foraging strategies—sit-and-wait and active searching (Pianka 1966). Of the sit-and-wait predators, there are two patterns in Costa Rica, that shown by *Corytophanes cristatus* and that used by the species of *Anolis* and *Norops* (Iguanidae).

Corytophanes is a generally lethargic, cryptic species that eats large, slow-moving prey, mostly leipdopteran larvae, beetle larvae, and orthopterans, but not vegetation (Ream 1965; Andrews 1979). Individuals feed infrequently and eat few but relatively large items. Such large prey are not abundant in the habitat. This feeding strategy may have evolved as a means of predator avoidance. A cryptic species that spends little time foraging will reduce the risk of a predator's seeing individuals while they are moving (Andrews 1979).

Many anoles, *Anolis* and *Norops,* perch head downward on tree trunks and visually search for prey, usually in the leaf litter. When they see the movements of a prey item, they run from their perch and attempt to catch it. Furthermore, most of their hunting time is spent in searching and little in pursuit (Andrews 1971; Goodman 1971*b;* Scott et al. 1976). Goodman (1971*b*) found that forest anoles (e.g., *N. polylepis*) seem to rely on prey movements to locate prey, while the stream-dwelling *N. aquaticus* may not need such cues. Goodman believed that, perhaps since the latter species lives in a habitat with much moving water, it had to use some cue other than movement to locate food.

The anoles are generalized and opportunistic arthropod eaters (Rand 1967; Schoener 1968; Fleming and Hooker 1975), although Scott et al. (1976) found that males ate more ants and small insects because they spent more time on their perches than females. Subadults and females with oviducal eggs contain larger volumes of prey than males of the same size (Rand 1967; Schoener 1968; Scott et al. 1976; Stamps 1977). Taylor (1956) reported an 88 mm SVL *Norops capito* that was taken with a half-swallowed 50 mm SVL *Norops lemurinus* in its mouth.

Fleming and Hooker (1975) found that the food of *N. cupreus* in Guanacaste Province varied seasonally and with sex of the lizard. In the dry season, the mean prey size for males was greater than that for females, as was the range of prey sizes. The number of prey items eaten by the two sexes was similar. The mean prey size of females was greater in the wet season than in the dry season. In the dry season, both males and females ate more prey items than in the wet season.

Andrews and Asato (1977) studied the physiology and energy budget of Panamanian *Norops limifrons,* a sit-and-wait species. They found that, in the field, adult males had the lowest energy intake (63 cal/g/day), with immatures and adult females consuming considerably more food (90 and 124 cal/g/day, respectively). They attribute these differences to the increased energy demands of growth in immatures and egg production (one per 7 days) in females. A similar study has been done for one ac-

tively searching lizard species in Europe, although energy devoted to reproduction is not included (Avery 1971).

The active search strategy is found in species of such lizards as *Ameiva* and *Cnemidophorus* (Teiidae). They are opportunistic arthropod feeders, scrambling about in the litter, pushing their heads into the leaves and looking for food (Hillman 1969; pers. obs.). Hillman (1969) found that *A. festiva* and *A. quadrilineata* from the Osa Peninsula ate a few amphibians in addition to arthropods. These two species were broadly sympatric in his study area, and there was a great deal of overlap in prey taxa, but there were some differences owing to their feeding in different microhabitats. *Ameiva quadrilineata*, the smallest species, took significantly smaller prey than *A. festiva* and a third sympatric species, *A. leptophrys.*

Feeding strategies also place constraints on other aspects of the lizard's biology. For instance, lizards using the sit-and-wait strategy cannot thermoregulate as easily as lizards that are almost constantly on the move. They also use less energy, so they require less food. Because they cannot tolerate continuous exposure to the sun, they usually perch in the shade. As a result, sit-and-wait species tend to be thermal conformers, while active searchers usually thermoregulate to rather high temperatures. *Norops limifrons* in Panama, a sit-and-wait strategist, maintains a "normally active" temperature between 24° and 31° C, which is 1° to 2° C above ambient air temperature (Ballinger, Marion, and Sexton 1970), while foraging individuals of the three species of *Ameiva* (active searchers) studied by Hillman (1969) had relatively constant body temperatures between 37° and 38° C, which were 4° to 10° C higher than ambient temperatures.

Turtles and Crocodilians

The turtles of Costa Rica include both freshwater and marine forms. There are six species of marine turtles in two families, Cheloniidae and Dermochelyidae. There is a great deal of information on the Costa Rican population of the green turtle (*Chelonia mydas*), but very little is known about the hawksbill (*Eretmochelys imbricata*), loggerhead (*Caretta caretta*), olive ridley, (*Lepidochelys olivacea*), leatherback (*Dermochelys coriacea*) and Pacific green (*Chelonia agazzisii*) turtles.

The freshwater and terrestrial turtles of Costa Rica belong to three families: the snapping turtle, *Chelydra serpentina* (Chelydridae), the aquatic and terrestrial Emydidae, and the semiaquatic mud turtles, Kinosternidae. Little is known about the aquatic tropical snapper so it will not be discussed further, but the other groups will be discussed below.

The biology of the two species of crocodilians in Costa Rica is poorly known. The caiman (*Caiman crocodilus*) is a small (to 2.5 m) species that inhabits many interior lowland swamps and slow rivers. The crocodile (*Crocodylus acutus*) is a coastal species that was formerly common in mangrove swamps and coastal rivers. It is a large animal, with reliable records from Mexico of more than 4 m (Alvarez del Toro 1974).

SEA TURTLES

The green sea turtle that nests on the Caribbean (especially at Tortuguero, Limón Province, Costa Rica), is there only for the nesting period between June and October. The rest of the year the adults are at their feeding grounds, which include other parts of Costa Rica, the Gulf of Mexico, and parts of the western Caribbean. The population is characterized by the long migrations of 200 to 2,000 km between feeding grounds and nesting beaches (Carr and Giovannoli 1957; Carr and Ogren 1960; Carr and Hirth 1962; Carr, Ross, and Carr 1974; Carr, Carr, and Meglan 1978).

Mating occurs at the breeding area in the first half of the breeding season. The eggs that are fertilized in one season are laid 2 to 3 years later. From studies of tagged turtles it has been found that females return to a nest site near previous nest areas, and possibly near their hatching site. Individuals seem to be able to recognize a specific area of beach, but the method of discrimination is not well understood. Recognition may be visual, using distinct land features, whether recognizable by the turtle from far offshore or closer in.

Eggs are laid every 2 to 4 years, and females lay more than one clutch per season, perhaps up to five (Carr and Giovannoli 1957; Carr and Ogren 1960; Carr and Hirth 1962). Successive clutches are laid about 2 weeks apart. If a female nesting on Tortuguero is disturbed by a light, person, or noise, she will return to the ocean and attempt to nest later. Between clutches, the females remain in the general area, resting and sleeping in crevices or caves in cliff bases or under rock ledges (Carr, Ross, and Carr 1974). It is thought that they feed little or not at all between successive nestings, since there is little marine vegetation near the nest site. Adults are mainly herbivorous, while the young are mainly carnivorous (Carr and Ogren 1960).

Clutch size at Tortuguero is from 18 to 193 eggs ($\bar{x} = 100$, 406 clutches), and the incubation period is about 2 months. Reports of hatching success are from 50% to 83%. About 50% of those emerging from nests reach the water. In 1977, about 50% of nests at Tortuguero were destroyed by predators, mainly dogs, but also some coatis. Most young emerge at night when temperatures are most favorable, and those emerging during the day were eaten by vultures. Predation was greatest on nests farthest from the ocean, and beach erosion destroyed some nests nearer the water. The habit of long migration

and nesting in remote areas may have evolved to lessen egg predation. Predation by dogs is a recent development but is potentially very harmful if allowed to continue (Carr and Giovannoli 1957; Carr and Ogren 1960; Carr and Hirth 1962; Carr, Ross, and Carr 1974; Fowler 1979).

The loggerhead turtle is very similar to the green turtle in its reproductive habits. Eggs are laid every 2 to 3 years, and up to four clutches are laid every 12 to 19 days within a season. Females return to the same beach to nest within and between seasons. Individuals lay 48 to 159 eggs per clutch ($\bar{x} = 100$). If a female is interrupted during nesting, she will return on the same night or later to renest (Caldwell 1962; Kaufman 1971; Davis and Whiting 1977).

The hawksbill sea turtle is a circumtropical species that is associated with coral reefs and rocky shores. Carr, Hirth, and Ogren (1966) described nesting in Costa Rica. Hawksbills appear to nest earlier in the year than the green turtles. Also, in contrast to green turtles, which nest in concentrated colonies, hawksbill turtles, along with loggerhead and leatherback sea turtles, are usually solitary nesters. Nearly any tropical deep-sand beach free of human activity will be visited by nesting hawksbills (Carr, Hirth, and Ogren 1966). Formerly hawksbills were taken in larger numbers for the tortoise shell (*carey*), but the major threats now are meat and leather hunters and egg collectors.

Olive ridley sea turtles may nest singly, in small colonies, or in massive diurnal nestings, called *arribadas,* containing up to one hundred thousand females (Pritchard 1979). This behavior is restricted to a few beaches throughout the tropics, one of which is Santa Rosa National Park in Guanacaste Province, Costa Rica (Hughes and Richard 1974).

The leatherback turtle was studied at Tortuguero by Carr and Ogren (1959). They found that nesting females clustered in a small portion of the beach. Like the hawksbill, they nested before the green turtles that nested on the same beach. The general nesting pattern is similar to that of the green turtle. Four nests had between forty-five and eighty eggs with yolks.

FRESHWATER AND TERRESTRIAL TURTLES

The aquatic tropical slider, *Chrysemys ornata,* has a wide distribution in a broad range of habitats in tropical America. In Central America they occupy lowland waters, usually in permanent freshwater, especially larger, slow-moving rivers or tributaries with much submerged vegetation. Other important features of this species' habitat are basking sites and scattered open areas in adjacent forest where eggs are laid. Moll and Legler (1971) have carried out on this species the most intensive investigation yet done on a tropical freshwater turtle. Their

Panamanian studies should be directly applicable to Costa Rica, and the following paragraphs summarize their findings.

Adult *C. ornata* remain in sections of the river with much floating vegetation such as *Elodea*. Juveniles and hatchlings are found in backwaters and quieter areas. The turtles sleep in the daytime in a customary place on the edges of the floating vegetation mats. The food of adults is mostly aquatic and semiaquatic plants, with some animal material (about 17% by volume). Juveniles take about 19% animal matter by volume. Feeding is underwater and appears to be opportunistic.

Eggs are laid from January to May, in the dry season when rivers are lower and less likely to flood nests. Females may lay up to five clutches per season, with the number of clutches proportional to the size of the female. Nesting occurs at night in open areas that are exposed to sunlight for part of each day. The home ranges of females are different areas than the nesting sites. Migration to the sites occurs early in the dry season. It is not known how females select an area in which to nest, since sites are as far as 400 m from water. Clutch size is from nine to twenty-five eggs ($\bar{x} = 17.4$, from nineteen nests and nineteen dissections). The eggs hatch in May and June during the early rainy season, a pattern similar to that in other tropical reptiles. When the hatchlings are ready to emerge from the nest, the rain softens the nest plug, facilitating their exit. Food and cover are also more available at this time.

Predation on this species occurs mainly on eggs. A large proportion of nests are destroyed, principally by armadillos and the Panamanian teiid lizard *Ameiva ameiva*, but also by black rats, opossums, coatis, birds, dogs, swine, and humans. Fire ants prey on some hatchlings, and man is the greatest predator on adults. The female urinates on the completed nest, so the smell of the nest may be a means by which predators locate nests up to 2 to 3 days after oviposition.

The other emydid genus, *Rhinoclemys*, has three Costa Rican species. *Rhinoclemys funerea* is a larger (to 320 mm carapace length), flat, slider type of turtle found in wet Atlantic lowland rivers. Iverson (1975) describes the aquatic courtship of captives in Costa Rica, and Moll and Legler (1971) and Medem (1962) provide details of their life history. They leave the water to bask in the daytime and to feed at night. For this reason they are able to live in rivers without vegetation, unlike *C. ornata*. Their eggs are relatively large, with hard, brittle shells, and they are placed singly under leaf litter. No nest is dug, and they may breed at any time during the year (Medem 1962; Moll and Legler 1971; pers. obs.).

The other two species of *Rhinoclemys* are more terrestrial. A colorful red-striped form (*R. pulcherrima*) is found in the dry lowlands of Guanacaste Province in Costa Rica. During the wet season individuals can be found moving about in temporary marshes, fields, and woodlands. They disappear during the dry season (pers. obs.). Little else is known about their biology. The third Costa Rican species, *R. annulata*, is a terrestrial box-turtle-like species of the Atlantic lowlands. Mittermeir (1971) studied this species briefly in Panama. These turtles eat a wide variety of plant foods and apparently mate on land.

The family of mud turtles, Kinosternidae, is represented in Costa Rica by three species in the genus *Kinostetnon*. Some biological information is available for *K. leucostomum*, but we can assume that the other two species are similar. According to Moll and Legler (1971) and Medem (1962), this species is generally found in swamps, slow streams, and temporary ponds, although individuals may also travel overland. These turtles are omnivorous and, though aquatic snails often make up a large part of their diet, may feed on land (pers. obs.). One or two brittle eggs make up a clutch, which may be laid at any time. Eggs are placed under leaf litter or in shallow nests. *Kinosternon angustipons* differs in that it lays about four eggs per clutch (Legler 1966).

The life histories above demonstrate two reproductive patterns (Moll and Legler 1971). *Chrysemys ornata* exemplifies a generalized or north-temperate mode. This species has generally similar reproduction in temperate and tropical sites, with large clutches, relatively small egg size, seasonal egg production, several clutches per season, and a nest that is constructed in a particular habitat. This mode is successful in many habitats and is similar for most of the species in the family Emydidae. *Rhinoclemys* and *Kinosternon* have a more specialized or tropical mode of reproduction. The eggs are laid singly or in small clutches, are relatively large, and are produced continuously or nearly so, and there is no special nest construction or site. These features are adapted to a tropical climate, since reproduction is not limited to a few months of the year.

These two patterns can be viewed as different responses to selective pressure, perhaps predation. The small and scattered clutches laid by *Rhinoclemys* and *Kinosternon* may reduce the number of eggs destroyed by predators; the discovery of one egg would not mean the destruction of most of the offspring laid by a female. *Chrysemys* may avoid total loss of offspring by saturating an area with many nests containing large numbers of eggs (Moll and Legler 1971).

There are some differences between the tropical and temperate subspecies of *C. ornata*. Panamanian sliders produce larger eggs and larger and more clutches per season than does the temperate species *C. scripta*. This is a reversal of a trend common in many tropical vertebrates, including some birds, mammals, lizards, frogs, and other turtles. The reproductive season is two months longer in Panama than in temperate areas. Females of this species are larger in the tropics than outside, and fecundity is probably greater (Moll and Legler 1971).

CROCODILIANS

The spectacled caiman continues to be common in parts of wet lowland Costa Rica. Its biology has not been studied in Costa Rica, but Staton and Dixon (1975, 1977) provide information about the Venezuelan llanos and Alvarez del Toro (1974) describes Mexican populations. Caiman biology does not differ markedly from the crocodilian norm. The female scrapes vegetation into a pile to make a nest in which she buries twenty to thirty eggs. She (and sometimes a male) usually tends the nest for the incubation period of about 73 days. One or both parents may help the hatching young get out of the nest and may guard them for an indefinite period. Of thirty-two nests observed by Staton and Dixon (1977), 9% hatched; the others were destroyed by humans, cows, flooding, and large tegu lizards (*Tupinambis teguixin*). All but the last factor may be important in Costa Rica.

Almost nothing is known about Costa Rican crocodiles except their distribution. Natural history observations by Alvarez del Toro (1974) in Mexico are probably applicable. *Crocodylus* makes a nest that differs from that of caimans. Usually the crocodile digs a hole in sandy soil and deposits the eggs. Then the nest is covered and the sand packed down much like a marine turtle's nest. The female parent often tends the nest and helps the young emerge.

The social behavior of crocodilians is often mediated by acoustical signals, a mode of communication that is lacking in most other reptiles. The significance of most signals is not well established. The most common and strongest response is that of adults to calls given by young (Campbell 1973; Alvarez del Toro 1974; Garrick and Lang 1977; Garrick, Lang, and Herzog 1978; Staton 1978).

THE CONSERVATION OF MARINE TURTLES AND CROCODILIANS

The marine turtles and crocodilians of Costa Rica are not the only reptiles that are exploited by man, but human impacts are greatest on their populations. It is probably safe to say that their numbers are continually declining owing to harvest of eggs and adults for food, shells or skins. The major green turtle nesting beaches and one of the olive ridley beaches are well protected by the national park system, but egg poaching remains the rule in other areas, and all species of marine turtles except leatherbacks are taken in the ocean. Up until about 15 years ago, the crocodile was the only object of hide exploitation, but recent developments in processing the skins of caimans and sea turtles have led to their harvest also. Crocodiles are scarce along both coasts, except for a healthy protected population in Corcovado National Park on the Osa Peninsula. Caiman are more common, but numbers have recently decreased markedly in areas near human habitation.

Many authors have written of the plight of the esteemed green turtle, but perhaps none so eloquently as Archie Carr (1967). His efforts, and those of his colleagues have stimulated international support for marine turtle conservation, and nowhere has the response been more effective than in Costa Rica. The famous nesting aggregations in Tortugero and Playa Nancite are protected, and public sentiment is turning against turtle exploitation in other parts of the country. Unfortunately, crocodiles are not as easy to love as sea turtles (even though both shed real tears), and the future of *Crocodylus* is much less secure. We may never again see the huge 4 m animals that used to terrify the *campesinos* and eat their dogs. However, a dim light may be on the horizon, as represented by newborn juveniles in the estuarine waters of Corcovado National Park and Santa Rosa National Park (D. H. Janzen, pers. comm.).

Acknowledgments

We would like to thank all our field companions over the years in Costa Rica. Their help and the efforts of many others made this review possible. We also thank Rayann Robino for typing the various drafts and for maintaining quality control throughout.

*

Albuquerque, E. X.; Daly, J. W.; and Witkop, B. 1971. Batrachotoxin: Chemistry and pharmacology. *Science* 172:995–1002.

Alvarez del Toro, M. 1974. *Los crocodylia de México (estudio comparativo)*. México, D. F.: Instituto Mexicano Recursos Naturales Renovables, A.C.

Andrews, R. M. 1971. Structural habitat and time budget of a tropical *Anolis* lizard. *Ecology* 52:262–70.

———. 1979. The lizard *Corytophanes cristatus*: An extreme "sit-and-wait" predator. *Biotropica* 11:136–39.

Andrews, R. M., and Asato, T. 1977. Energy utilization of a tropical lizard. *Comp. Biochem. Physiol.* 58A: 57–62.

Avery, R. A. 1971. Estimates of food consumption by the lizard *Lacerta vivipara* Jacquin. *J. Anim. Ecol.* 40: 351–65.

Ballinger, R. E.; Marion, K. R.; and Sexton, O. J. 1970. Thermal ecology of the lizard, *Anolis limifrons* with comparative notes on three additional Panamanian anoles. *Ecology* 51:246–54.

Bennett, A. F., and Dawson, W. R. 1976. Metabolism. In *Biology of the Reptilia*, vol. 5, ed. C. Gans. London: Academic Press.

Bennett, A. F., and Licht, P. 1972. Anaerobic metabolism during activity in lizards. *J. Comp. Physiol.* 81: 277–88.

Boulenger, G. A. 1913. On a collection of batrachians and reptiles made by Dr. H. G. F. Spurrell, F. Z. S., in the Choco, Colombia. *Proc. Zool. Soc. London* 1913: 1019–38.

Breder, C. M., Jr. 1946. Amphibians and reptiles of the Río Chucunaque drainage, Darien, Panamá, with notes on their life histories and habits. *Bull. Am. Mus. Nat. Hist.* 86:375–436.

Brodie, E. D., Jr. and Brodie E. D., III. 1980. Differential avoidance of mimetic salamanders by free-ranging birds. *Science* 208:181–82.

Bunnell, P. 1973. Vocalizations in the territorial behavior of the frog *Dendrobates pumilis. Copeia* 1973:277–84.

Caldwell, D. K. 1962. Comments on the nesting behavior of Atlantic loggerhead sea turtles, based primarily on tagging returns. *Quart. J. Florida Acad. Sci.* 25: 287–302.

Campbell, H. W. 1973. Observations on the acoustic behavior of crocodilians. *Zoologica* 58:1–11.

Carr, A. F. 1967. *So excellente a fishe.* New York: Natural History Press.

Carr, A.; Carr, M. H.; and Meglan, A. B. 1978. The ecology and migration of sea turtles. 7. The west Caribbean green turtle colony. *Bull. Am. Mus. Nat. Hist.* 162:1–46.

Carr, A. F., and Giovannoli, L. 1957. The ecology and migrations of sea turtles. 2. Results of field work in Costa Rica. *Am. Mus. Nov.* 1835:1–32.

Carr, A. F., and Hirth, H. 1962. The ecology and migrations of sea turtles. 5. Comparative features of isolated green turtle colonies. *Am. Mus. Nov.* 2091:1–42.

Carr, A. F.; Hirth, H.; and Ogren, L. 1966. The ecology and migrations of sea turtles. 6. The hawksbill turtle in the Caribbean Sea. *Am. Mus. Nov.* 2248:1–29.

Carr, A. F., and Ogren, L. 1959. The ecology and migrations of sea turtles. 3. *Dermochelys* in Costa Rica. *Am. Mus. Nov.* 1958:1–29.

———. 1960. The ecology and migrations of sea turtles. 4. The green turtle in the Caribbean Sea. *Bull. Am. Mus. Nat. Hist.* 121:1–48.

Carr, A. F.; Ross, P.; and Carr, S. 1974. Internesting behavior of the green turtle, *Chelonia mydas,* at a mid-ocean island breeding ground. *Copeia* 1974: 703–6.

Cott, H. B. 1940. *Adaptive coloration in animals.* London: Methuen.

Crump, M. L. 1972. Territoriality and mating behavior in *Dendrobates granuliferus* (Anura: Dendrobatidae). *Herpetologica* 28:195–98.

———. 1974. Reproductive strategies in a tropical anuran community. *Misc. Pub. Mus. Nat. Hist. Univ. Kansas* 61:1–68.

Crump, M. L., and Kaplan, R. H. 1979. Clutch energy partitioning of tropical tree frogs (Hylidae). *Copeia* 1979:626–35.

Daly, J. W., and Myers, C. W. 1967. Toxicity of Panamanian poison frogs (*Dendrobates*): Some biological and chemical aspects. *Science* 156:970–73.

Davis, G. E., and Whiting, M. C. 1977. Loggerhead sea turtle nesting in Everglades National Park, Florida, USA. *Herpetologica* 33:18–28.

Dixon, J. R., and Heyer, W. R. 1968. Anuran succession in a temporary pond in Colima, México. Bull. *Southern California Acad. Sci.* 67:129–37.

Duellman, W. E. 1960. A distributional study of the amphibians of the Isthmus of Tehuantepec, México. *Pub. Mus. Nat. Hist. Univ. Kansas* 13:19–72.

———. 1963. A new species of tree frog, genus *Phyllomedusa,* from Costa Rica. *Rev. Biol. Trop.* 11:1–23.

———. 1966a. The Central American herpetofauna: An ecological perspective. *Copeia* 1966:700–719.

———. 1966b. Aggressive behavior in dendrobatid frogs. *Herpetologica* 22:217–21.

———. 1967. Social organization in the mating calls of some Neotropical anurans. *Am. Midl. Nat.* 77:156–63.

———. 1970. The hylid frogs of middle America. *Monogr. Mus. Nat. Hist. Univ. Kansas* 1:1–753.

———. 1978. The biology of an equatorial herpetofauna in Amazonian Ecuador. *Misc. Pub. Mus. Nat. Hist. Univ. Kansas* 65:1–352.

Duellman, W. E., and Savitsky, A. H. 1976. Aggressive behavior in a centrolenid frog, with comments on territoriality in anurans. *Herpetologica* 32:401–4.

Duellman, W. E., and Trueb, L. 1966. Neotropical hylid frogs, genus *Smilisca. Pub. Mus. Nat. Hist. Univ. Kans.* 17:281–375.

Dunn, E. R. 1937. The amphibian and reptilian fauna of bromeliads in Costa Rica and Panamá. *Copeia* 1937: 163–67.

———. 1941. Notes on *Dendrobates auratus. Copeia* 1941:88–93.

Eaton, T. 1941. Notes on the life history of *Dendrobates auratus. Copeia* 1941:93–95.

Fleming, T. H., and Hooker, R. S. 1975. *Anolis cupreus:* The response of a lizard to tropical seasonality. *Ecology* 56:1243–61.

Fowler, L. E. 1979. Hatching success and nest predation in the green sea turtle, *Chelonia mydas,* at Tortugero, Costa Rica. *Ecology* 60:946–55.

Fuhrman, F. A.; Fuhrman, G. J.; and Mosher, H. S. 1969. Toxin from skin of frogs of the genus *Atelopus:* Differentiation from dendrobatid toxins. *Science* 165: 1376–77.

Garrick, L. D., and Lang, J. W. 1977. Social signals and behaviors of adult alligators and crocodiles. *Am. Zool.* 17:225–39.

Garrick, L. D.; Lang, J. W.; and Herzog, H. A., Jr. 1978. Social signals of adult American alligators. *Bull. Am. Mus. Nat. Hist.* 160:153–92.

Goodman, D. E. 1971a. Territorial behavior in a Neotropical frog, *Dendrobates granuliferus. Copeia* 1971: 365–70.

———. 1971b. Differential selection among immobile prey among terrestrial and riparian lizards. *Am. Midl. Nat.* 86:217–19.

Habermehl, G. G. 1974. Venoms of amphibia. In *Chemical zoology,* vol. 9, *Amphibia and reptilia,* ed. M. Florkin and B. T. Scheer. New York: Academic Press.

Heyer, W. R. 1969. The adaptive ecology of the species groups of the genus *Leptodactylus* (Amphibia, Leptodactylidae). *Evolution* 23:421–28.

———. 1970. Studies on the genus *Leptodactylus* (Amphibia: Leptodactylidae). II. Diagnosis and distribution of the *Leptodactylus* of Costa Rica. *Rev. Biol. Trop.* 16:171–205.

———. 1976. Studies in larval amphibian habitat partitioning. *Smithsonian Contrib. Zool.* 242:1–27.

Heyer, W. R.; McDiarmid, R. W.; and Weigmann, D. L. 1975. Tadpoles, predation, and pond habitats in the tropics. *Biotropica* 7:100–111.

Heyer, W. R., and Rand, A. S. 1977. Foam nest construction in the leptodactylid frogs *Leptodactylus pentadactylus* and *Physalaemus pustulosus* (Amphibia, Anura, Leptodactylidae). *J. Herp.* 11:222–25.

Hillman, P. E. 1969. Habitat specificity in three sympatric species of *Ameiva* (Reptilia: Teiidae). *Ecology* 50:476–81.

Houck, L. D. 1977. Life history patterns and reproductive biology of Neotropical salamanders. In *The reproductive biology of amphibians,* ed. D. H. Taylor and S. I. Guttman. New York: Plenum Press.

Hughes, D. A., and Richard, J. D. 1974. The nesting of the Pacific ridley *Lepidochelys olivacea* on Playa Nancite, Costa Rica. *Marine Biol.* 24:97–107.

Inger, R. F. 1962. On the terrestrial origin of frogs. *Copeia* 1962:835–36.

Iverson, J. B. 1975. Notes on courtship in *Rhinoclemys funerea. J. Herp.* 9:249–50.

Janzen, D. H. 1962. Injury caused by toxic secretions of *Phrynohyas spilomma* Cope. *Copeia* 1962:651.

Janzen, D. H., and Schoener, T. W. 1968. Differences in insect abundance and diversity between wetter and drier sites during a tropical dry season. *Ecology* 49:96–110.

Kaufman, R. 1971. Studies on the loggerhead sea turtle, *Caretta caretta caretta* (Linné) in Colombia, South America. *Herpetologica* 31:323–26.

Kitasako, J. T. 1967. Observations on the biology of *Dendrobates pumilio* Schmidt and *Dendrobates auratus* Girard. M.S. thesis, University of Southern California, Los Angeles.

Krakauer, T. 1968. The ecology of the Neotropical toad, *Bufo marinus,* in south Florida. *Herpetologica* 24:214–21.

Legler, J. M. 1966. Notes on the natural history of a rare Central American turtle, *Kinosternon angustipons* Legler. *Herpetologica* 22:118–22.

Licht, L. E. 1967. Death following possible ingestion of toad eggs. *Toxicon* 5:141–42.

———. 1968. Unpalatability and toxicity of toad eggs. *Herpetologica* 24:93–98.

———. 1969. Palatability of Rana and Hyla eggs. *Am. Midl. Nat.* 82:296–98.

Licht, L. E., and Low, B. 1968. Cardiac response of snakes after ingestion of toad parotoid venom. *Copeia* 1968:547–51.

Limerick, S. 1980. Courtship and oviposition in the poison-arrow frog, *Dendrobates pumilio. Herpetologica* 35:69–71.

Lutz, B. 1948. Ontogenetic evolution in frogs. *Evolution* 2:29–39.

Lynn, W. C. 1942. The embryology of *Eleutherodactylus nubicola,* an anuran which has no tadpole stage. *Pub. Carnegie Inst. Washington* 541:27–62.

McDiarmid, R. W. 1971. Comparative morphology and evolution of frogs of the Neotropical genera *Atelopus, Dendrophryniseus, Melanophryniscus,* and *Oreophrynella. Sci. Bull Los Angeles County Mus. Nat. Hist.* 12:1–66.

———. 1975. Glass frog romance along a tropical stream. *Terra, Los Angeles County Mus.* 13:14–18.

———. 1978. Evolution of parental care in frogs. In *The development of behavior: Comparative and evolutionary aspects,* ed. G. M. Burghardt and M. Bekoff. New York: Garland STPM Press.

McDiarmid, R. W., and Adler, K. 1974. Notes on territorial and vocal behavior of Neotropical frogs of the genus *Centrolenella. Herpetologica* 30:75–78.

Medem, F. 1962. La distribución geográfica y ecología de los Crocodylia y Testudinata en el Departamento del Chocó. *Rev. Acad. Colombia Cienc. Exactas Fis. Nat.* 11:279–303.

Mittermeir, R. A. 1971. Notes on the behavior and ecology of *Rhinoclemys annulata* Gray. *Herpetologica* 27:485–88.

Moll, E. O., and Legler, J. M. 1971. The life history of a Neotropical slider turtle, *Pseudemys scripta* (Schoepff), in Panama. *Sci. Bull. Los Angeles County Mus. Nat. Hist.* 11:1–102.

Montanucci, R. R. 1968. Comparative dentition in four iguanid lizards. *Herpetologica* 24:305–15.

Myers, C. W.; Daly, J. W.; and Malkin, B. 1978. A dangerously toxic new frog (*Phyllobates*) used by Emberá Indians of western Colombia, with discussion of blowgun fabrication and dart poisoning. *Bull. Am. Mus. Nat. Hist.* 161:307–66.

Nelson, C. E. 1972. Systematic studies of the North American microhylid genus *Gastrophryne J. Herp.* 6:111–37.

Novak, R. M., and Robinson, D. C. 1975. Observations on the reproduction and ecology of the tropical montane toad, *Bufo holdridgei* Taylor in Costa Rica. *Rev. Biol. Trop.* 23:213–37.

Pianka, E. R. 1966. Convexity, desert lizards, and spatial heterogeneity. *Ecology* 47:1055–59.

Pough, F. H. 1973. Lizard energetics and diet. *Ecology* 54:836–44.

Pritchard, P. C. H. 1979. Taxonomy, evolution and zoogeography. In *Turtles: Perspectives and research,* ed. M. Harless and H. Morlock. New York: Wiley.

Pyburn, W. F. 1963. Observations on the life history of the treefrog, *Phyllomedusa callidryas* (Cope). *Texas J. Sci.* 15:155–70.

———. 1964. Breeding behavior of the leaf frog, *Phyllomedusa callidryas,* in southern Veracruz. *Year. Am. Phil. Soc.* 1964:291–94.

———. 1967. Breeding and larval development of the hylid frog *Phrynohyas spilomma* in southern Veracruz, México. *Herpetologica* 23:184–94.

———. 1970. Breeding behavior of the leaf-frogs *Phyllomedusa callidryas* and *Phyllomedusa dacnicolor* in México. *Copeia* 1970:209–18.

Rand, A. S. 1967. Ecology and social organization in the iguanid lizard *Anolis lineatopus. Proc. U.S. Nat. Mus.* 122:1–77.

Ream, C. 1965. Notes on the behavior and egg laying of *Corythopanes cristatus. Herpetologica* 20:239–42.

Rivero, J. A., and Esteves, A. E., 1969. Observations of the agonistic and breeding behavior of *Leptodactylus pentadactylus* and other amphibian species in Venezuela. *Breviora* 321:1–14.

Robinson, D. C. 1961. The identity of the tadpole of *Anotheca coronata* (Stejneger). *Copeia* 1961:495.

———. 1977. Herpetofauna bromelicola Costarricense y renacuajos de *Hyla picadoi* Dunn. In *Historia natural de Costa Rica,* ed. L. D. Gomez, San José: Museo Nacional de Costa Rica.

Salthe, S. N. 1969. Reproductive modes and the numbers and sizes of ova in the urodeles. *Am. Midl. Nat.* 81:467–90.

Salthe, S. N., and Duellman, W. E. 1973. Quantitative constraints associated with reproductive mode in anurans. In *Evolutionary biology of the anurans,* ed. J. L. Vial. Saint Louis: University of Missouri Press.

Salthe, S. N., and Mecham, J. S. 1974. Reproductive and courtship patterns. In *Physiology of the amphibia,* ed. B. Lofts, vol. 2. New York: Academic Press.

Savage, J. M. 1966. The origins and history of the Central American herpetofauna. *Copeia* 1966:719–60.

———. 1968. The dendrobatid frogs of Central America. *Copeia* 1968:745–76.

———. 1980. The tadpole of the Costa Rican fringe-limbed tree-frog, *Hyla fimbrimembra. Proc. Biol. Soc. Wash.* 93:1177–83.

Savage, J. M., and Heyer, W. R. 1969. The tree-frogs (family Hylidae) of Costa Rica: Diagnosis and distribution. *Rev. Biol. Trop.* 16:1–127.

Schoener, T. W. 1968. The *Anolis* lizards of Bimini: Resource partitioning in a complex fauna. *Ecology* 49:704–26.

Scott, N. J. 1976. The abundance and diversity of the herpetofaunas of tropical forest litter. *Biotropica* 8: 41–58.

Scott, N. J., Jr., and Starrett, A. 1974. An unusual breeding aggregation of frogs, with notes on the ecology of *Agalychnis spurrelli* (Anura: Hylidae). *Bull. Southern California Acad. Sci.* 73:86–94.

Scott, N. J., Jr.; Wilson, D. E.; Jones, C.; and Andrews, R. M. 1976. The choice of perch dimensions by lizards of the genus *Anolis* (Reptilia, Lacertilia, Iguanidae). *J. Herp.* 10:75–84.

Sexton, O. 1958. Observations on the life history of a Venezuelan frog, *Atelopus cruciger. Acta Biol. Venezuela* 2:235–42.

———. 1962. Apparent territorialism in *Leptodactylus insularum* Barbour. *Herpetologica* 18:212–14.

Sexton, O. J.; Bauman, J.; and Ortleb, E. 1972. Seasonal food habits of *Anolis limifrons. Ecology* 53: 182–86.

Sexton, O. J., and Ortleb, E. P. 1966. Some cues used by the leptodactylid frog, *Engystomops pustulosus,* in selection of the oviposition site. *Copeia* 1966:225–30.

Silverstone, P. A. 1975. A revision of the poison-arrow frogs of the genus *Dendrobates* Wagler. *Sci. Bull. Los Angeles County Mus. Nat. Hist.* 21:1–55.

———. 1976. A revision of the poison-arrow frogs of the genus *Phyllobates* Bibron in Sagra (family Dendrobatidae). *Sci. Bull. Los Angeles County Mus. Nat. Hist.* 27:1–53.

Smith, H. M., and White, F. N. 1955. Adrenal enlargement and its significance in the hognose snakes (*Heterodon*). *Herpetologica* 11:137–44.

Stamps, J. A. 1977. The relationship between resource partitioning, risk, and aggression in a tropical territorial lizard. *Ecology* 53:349–58.

Starrett, P. 1960. Descriptions of tadpoles of middle American frogs. *Misc. Pub. Mus. Zool. Univ. Michigan* 110:1–37.

———. 1967. Observations on the life history of frogs of the family Atelopodidae. *Herpetologica* 23: 195–204.

———. 1973. Evolutionary patterns in larval morphology. In *Evolutionary biology of the anurans: Contemporary research on major problems,* ed. J. L. Vial. Saint Louis: University of Missouri Press.

Staton, M. A. 1978. "Distress calls" of crocodilians—whom do they benefit? *Am. Nat.* 112:327–32.

Staton, M. A., and Dixon, J. R. 1975. Studies on the dry season biology of *Caiman crocodilus* from the Venezuelan llanos. *Mem. Soc. Cienc. Nat. La Salle* 35:237–65.

———. 1977. Breeding biology of the spectacled caiman, *Caiman crocodilus crocodilus,* in the Venezuelan llanos. *U.S. Fish Wildl. Serv. Wildl. Res. Rep.* 5:1–21.

Stuart, L. C. 1935. A contribution to a knowledge of the herpetology of a portion of the savannah region of central Petén, Guatemala. *Misc. Pub. Mus. Zool. Univ. Michigan* 29:1–56.

———. 1961. Some observations on the natural history of tadpoles of *Rhinophrynus dorsalis* Dumeril and Bibron. *Herpetologica* 17:73–79.

Taylor, E. H. 1942. Tadpoles of Mexican anura. *Univ. Kansas Sci. Bull.* 28:37–55.

———. 1952. A review of the frogs and toads of Costa Rica. *Univ. Kansas Sci. Bull.* 35:577–942.

———. 1954. Frog-egg-eating tadpoles of *Anotheca coronata* (Stejneger) (Satientia, Hylidae). *Univ. Kansas Sci. Bull.* 36:589–95.

———. 1956. A review of the lizards of Costa Rica. *Univ. Kansas Sci. Bull.* 38:3–322.

Trueb, L. 1968. Variation in the tree frog *Hyla lancasteri*. *Copeia* 1968:285–99.

VanDevender, R. W. 1978. Growth ecology of a tropical lizard, *Basiliscus basiliscus*. *Ecology* 59:1031–38.

Vial, J. L. 1968. The ecology of the tropical salamander. *Bolitoglossa subpalmata*, in Costa Rica. Rev. Biol. Trop. 15:13–115.

Villa, J. 1967. Comportamiento defensivo de la "rana tenero," *Leptodactylus pentadactylus*. *Rev. Biol. Trop.* 15:323–29.

———. 1972. *Anfibios de Nicaragua*. Managna: Instituto Geográfico Nacional, Banco Central de Nicaragua.

Vinton, K. W. 1951. Observations on the life history of *Leptodactylus pentadactylus*. *Herpetologica* 7:73–75.

Wake, D. B., and Lynch, J. F. 1976. The distribution, ecology, and evolutionary history of plethodontid salamanders in tropical America. *Sci. Bull. Los Angeles County Nat. Hist. Mus.* 25:1–65.

Wake, M. H. 1977. The reproductive biology of caecilians: An evolutionary perspective. In *The reproductive biology of amphibians*, ed. D. H. Taylor and S. I. Guttman. New York: Plenum Press.

Wassersug, R. 1971. On the comparative palatability of some dry season tadpoles from Costa Rica. *Am. Midl. Nat.* 86:101–9.

———. 1973. Aspects of social behavior in anuran larvae. In *Evolutionary biology of the anurans: Contemporary research on major problems*, ed. J. L. Vial. Saint Louis: University of Missouri Press.

Wells, K. D. 1977a. The courtship of frogs. In *The reproductive biology of amphibians*, ed. D. H. Taylor and S. I. Guttman. New York: Plenum Press.

———. 1977b. The social behavior of anuran amphibians. *Anim. Behav.* 25:666–93.

———. 1978. Courtship and parental behavior in a Panamanian poison-arrow frog (*Dendrobates auratus*). *Herpetologica* 34:148–55.

Young, A. M. 1979. Arboreal movement and tadpole-carrying behavior of *Dendrobates pumilio* Schmidt (Dendrobatidae) in northeastern Costa Rica. *Biotropica* 11:238–39.

Zug, G. R., and Zug, P. B. 1979. The marine toad, *Bufo marinus*: A natural history resumé of native populations. *Smithsonian Contrib. Zool.* 284:1–58.

Zweifel, R. G. 1964a. Life history of *Phrynohyas venulosa* (Salientia: Hylidae) in Panamá. *Copeia* 1964: 201–8.

———. 1964b. Distribution and life history of a Central American frog, *Rana vibicaria*. *Copeia* 1964: 300–308.

CHECKLIST OF REPTILES AND AMPHIBIANS

N. J. Scott, J. M. Savage, and D. C. Robinson

Taxon	La Selva	Osa	Cañas, Taboga	San José	Las Cruces	Cerro
Amphibia						
Gymnophiona						
Caecilidae						
Dermophis mexicanus				X		
D. parviceps		X		X	X	X
Gymnopis multiplicata	X		X			
Caudata						
Plethodontidae						
Bolitoglossa alvaradoi						
B. arborescandens						
B. cerroensis						X
B. colonnea	X	X		X		
B. epimela						
B. lignicolor		X				
B. robusta						X
B. sooyorum						
B. striatula						X
B. subpalmata						
B. sp. 1						
B. sp. 2						
Chiropterotriton diminuta						
C. picadoi				X		

Taxon	La Selva	Osa	Cañas, Taboga	San José	Las Cruces	Cerro
C. richardi						
Oedipina alfaroi						
O. altura						
O. carablanca						
O. collaris						
O. complex					X	
O. cyclocauda						
O. parvipes		X				
O. paucidentata						
O. poelzi						
O. pseudouniformis	X					
O. uniformis	X	X		X		
Anura						
Rhinophrynidae						
Rhinophrynus dorsalis			X			
Microhylidae						
Gastrophryne pictiventris	X					
Glossostoma aterrimum		X				
Hypopachus variolosus			X	X		
Leptodactylidae						
Eleutherodactylus altae	X					
E. biporcatus	X	X			X	
E. bufoniformis						
E. caryophyllaceus	X					
E. cerasinus	X					
E. cruentus	X	X			X	
E. moro						
E. pardalis					X	
E. ridens	X	X			X	
E. diastema	X	X				
E. hylaeformis						
E. vocator		X			X	
E. sp. 1						
E. crassidigitus	X					
E. fitzingeri	X	X	X			
E. longirostris		X			X	
E. sp. 2						
E. andi						
E. talamancae	X					
E. gaigei						
E. bransfordii	X	X	X		X	
E. gollmeri						
E. mimus	X					
E. noblei	X					
E. podiciferus						
E. melanostictus						X
E. rayo						
E. fleischmanni				X		X
E. punctariolus						X
E. rugulosus	X		X		X	
E. taurus		X				
E. angelicus						
E. escoses						
Leptodactylus bolivianus		X	X			
L. fragilis			X			

Taxon	La Selva	Osa	Cañas, Taboga	San José	Las Cruces	Cerro
L. melanonotus	X	X	X		X	
L. pentadactylus	X	X	X		X	
L. poecilochilus		X	X		X	
Physalaemus pustulosus		X	X			
Bufonidae						
Atelopus chiriquiensis						
A. senex						
A. varius				X	X	
Bufo coccifer			X	X		
B. coniferus	X	X			X	
B. fastidiosus						
B. haematiticus	X	X			X	
B. holdridgei						
B. leutkenii			X			
B. marinus	X	X	X	X	X	
B. melanochloris		X				
B. periglenes						
B. valliceps						
Crepidophryne epioticus						
Hylidae						
Agalychnis annae				X	X	
A. calcarifer	X					
A. callidryas	X	X				
A. saltator	X					
A. spurrelli		X				
Anotheca spinosa					X	
Hyla rufitela	X	X				
H. colymba						
H. rosenbergi		X				
H. lancasteri					X	
H. ebraccata	X	X			X	
H. loquax	X					
H. microcephala			X		X	
H. phlebodes	X					
H. fimbrimembra						
H. miliaria					X	
H. angustilineata						
H. pseudopuma				X	X	
H. boulengeri	X	X	X			
H. elaeochroa	X	X				
H. staufferi			X			
H. debilis						
H. legleri					X	
H. pictipes						X
H. rivularis						
H. rufioculis					X	
H. tica						
H. uranochroa						
H. xanthosticta						
H. picadoi						
H. zeteki						
Phrynohyas venulosa		X	X			
Phyllomedusa lemur						
Smilisca baudinii	X		X			
S. phaeota	X	X				

Taxon	La Selva	Osa	Cañas, Taboga	San José	Las Cruces	Cerro
S. puma	X					
S. sila		X				
S. sordida		X	X	X	X	
Dendrobatidae						
Colostethus nubicola		X			X	
C. talamancae		X				
Dendrobates auratus		X				
D. granuliferus		X				
D. pumilio	X					
Phyllobates lugubris	X					
P. vittatus		X				
Centrolenidae						
Centrolenella pulverata		X				
C. albomaculata	X	X			X	
C. euknemos						
C. granulosa		X				
C. ilex						
C. prosoblepon	X	X		X	X	
C. spinosa	X	X				
C. chirripoi						
C. columbiphyllum		X				
C. fleischmanni				X	X	
C. talamancae						
C. valerioi	X	X				
C. vireovittata						
Ranidae						
Rana palmipes	X		X			
R. pipiens	X		X	X		X
R. vibicaria						
R. warschewitschii	X			X	X	
Reptilia						
Testudinata						
Chelydridae						
Chelydra serpentina			X			
Kinosternidae						
Kinosternon angustipons	X					
K. leucostomum	X	X		X		
K. scorpioides			X	X		
Cheloniidae						
Caretta caretta						
Chelonia agassizii						
C. mydas						
Eretmochelys imbricata						
Lepidochelys olivacea						
Dermochelyidae						
Dermochelys coriacea						
Emydidae						
Chrysemys ornata		X				
Rhinoclemmys annulata	X					
R. funerea	X					
R. pulcherrima			X	X		
Squamata–Sauria						
Gekkonidae						
Coleonyx mitratus			X			
Gonatodes albogularis			X			

Taxon	La Selva	Osa	Cañas, Taboga	San José	Las Cruces	Cerro
Lepidoblepharis xanthostigma	X	X			X	
Phyllodactylus tuberculosus			X			
Sphaerodactylus millepunctatus						
S. homolepis	X					
S. lineolatus		X				
S. pacificus						
Thecadactylus rapicaudus	X	X				
Iguanidae						
Anolis chocorum						
A. cristatellus						
A. frenatus						
A. insignis		X			X	
A. microtus						
Basiliscus basiliscus		X	X		X	
B. plumifrons	X					
B. vittatus	X					
Corytophanes cristatus	X	X				
Ctenosaura similis		X	X			
Enyaliosaurus quinquecarinatus			Santa Rosa National Park			
Iguana iguana	X	X	X			
Norops altae						
N. aquaticus		X			X	
N. biporcatus	X	X			X	
N. capito	X	X			X	
N. carpenteri	X					
N. cupreus			X	X		
N. fungosus						
N. godmani						
N. humilis	X				X	
N. intermedius				X		
N. lemurinus	X				X	
N. limifrons	X	X				
N. lionotus	X					
N. pachypus						X
N. pentaprion	X	X	X			
N. polylepis		X			X	
N. sericeus			X			
N. townsendi						
N. tropidolepis						
N. vociferans						
N. woodi					X	
N. sp. 1						
Polychrus gutturosus	X					
Sceloporus malachiticus				X		X
S. squamosus						
S. variabilis			X			
Teiidae						
Ameiva festiva	X	X			X	
A. leptophrys		X				
A. quadrilineata	X	X				
A. undulata			X			
Anadia ocellata					X	
Bachia blairi		X				
Cnemidophorus deppii			X			
Gymnopthalmus speciosus			X			
Leposoma southi		X				

371

Taxon	La Selva	Osa	Cañas, Taboga	San José	Las Cruces	Cerro
Neusticurus apodemus		X				
Ptychoglossus plicatus					X	
Xantusiidae						
Lepidophyma flavimaculatum	X	X			X	
Scincidae						
Eumeces managuae			X			
Sphenomorphus cherriei	X	X	X		X	
Mabuya unimarginata	X	X	X		X	
Anguidae						
Celestus cyanochloris						
C. sp. 1	X					
Coloptychon rhombifer						
Diploglossus bilobatus	X					
D. monotropis						
Gerrhonotus monticolus						X
Squamata–Serpentes						
Anomalepidae						
Anomalepis mexicanus						
Helminthophis frontalis				X		
Liotyphlops albirostris						
Typhlopidae						
Typhlops costaricensis						
Leptotyphlopidae						
Leptotyphlops goudotii			X			
Boidae						
Boa constrictor	X	X	X			
Corallus annulatus						
C. hortulanus		X				
Epicrates cenchria			X			
Aniliidae						
Loxocemus bicolor			X			
Tropidophiidae						
Ungaliophis panamensis	X					
Colubridae						
Amastridium veliferum	X	X			X	
Chironius carinatus		X				
C. grandisquamis	X	X			X	
C. exoletus					X	
Clelia clelia	X	X	X		X	
C. scytalina						
Coluber mentovarius			X			
Coniophanes fissidens	X	X				
C. piceivittis			X			
Conophis lineatus			X			
C. nevermanni			X			
Dendrophidion nuchalis					X	
D. paucicarinatum				X		
D. percarinatum	X	X			X	
D. vinitor	X				X	
Dipsas articulata						
D. bicolor						
D. tenuissima						
Drymarchon corais		X	X			
Drymobius margaritiferus	X		X	X		
D. melanotropis	X				X	
D. rhombifer	X					

Taxon	La Selva	Osa	Cañas, Taboga	San José	Las Cruces	Cerro
Elaphe triaspis			X			
Enulius flavitorques			X			
E. sclateri	X					
Erythrolamprus bizonus			X	X		
E. mimus	X	X			X	
Geophis brachycephalus				X		
G. godmani						
G. hoffmanni		X		X	X	
G. ruthveni						
G. zeledoni						
Geophis sp. 1					X	
Hydromorphus concolor				X		
Imantodes cenchoa	X	X	X			
I. inornatus	X	X			X	
Lampropeltis triangulum			X		X	X
Leimadophis epinephalus	X			X	X	
Leptodeira annulata			X	X		
L. nigrofasciata			X			
L. rubicata		X				
L. septentrionalis	X	X			X	
Leptodrymus pulcherrimus			X			
Leptophis ahaetulla	X	X				
L. depressirostris	X					
L. mexicanus	X		X			
L. nebulosus	X					
L. riveti		X			X	
Mastigodryas melanolomus	X	X		X	X	
Ninia atrata						
N. maculata	X	X		X		
N. psephota						X
N. sebae			X			
Nothopsis	X	X				
Oxybelis aeneus		X	X			
O. brevirostris	X					
O. fulgidus			X			
Oxyrhopus petola	X	X				
Pliocercus euryzonus	X					
Pseustes poecilonotus	X	X				
Rhadinaea calligaster						X
R. decipiens	X					
R. decorata	X	X				
R. fulviceps		X				
R. godmani						X
R. guentheri	X	X				X
R. pachyura						
R. pulveriventris						
R. serperaster						
Rhinobothryum bovallii						
Scaphiodontophis venustissimus	X	X				
Scolecophis atrocinctus			X	X		
Sibon annulata	X					
S. anthracops			X			
S. argus						
S. dimidiata		X				
S. longifrenis						
S. nebulata	X	X				

Taxon	La Selva	Osa	Cañas, Taboga	San José	Las Cruces	Cerro
Spilotes pullatus	X	X	X			
Stenorrhina degenhardtii		X				
S. freminvillii			X			
Tantilla alticola			..		X	
T. annulata		X				
T. armillata			X			
T. reticulata						
T. ruficeps	X	X			X	
T. schistosa		X				
T. vermiformis			X			
Thamnophis marcianus						
T. proximus			X			
Tretanorphinus nigroluteus	X					
Trimetopon gracile						
T. pliolepis	X			X	X	
T. simile						
T. slevini						
T. viquezi						
Trimorphodon biscutatus			X			
Tripanurgos compressus		X				
Xenodon rabdocephalus	X	X			X	
Micruridae						
Micrurus alleni	X	X				
M. clarki						
M. mipartitus	X					
M. nigrocinctus	X	X	X			
Hydrophiidae						
Pelamis platurus						
Crotalidae						
Agkistrodon bilineatus			Santa Rosa National Park			
Bothrops asper	X	X				
B. godmani						
B. lateralis						
B. nasutus	X	X				
B. nigroviridis						X
B. nummifer					X	
B. ophryomegas			X			
B. picadoi						
B. schlegelii	X	X			X	
Crotalus durissus			X			
Lachesis muta	X	X				
Crocodilia						
Crocodylidae						
Caiman crocodilus	X	X	X			
Crocodylus acutus		X	X			

SPECIES ACCOUNTS

Agalychnis callidryas (Rana Calzonudo, Gaudy Leaf Frog)

N. J. Scott

Agalychnis callidryas (Hylidae) is the gaudiest frog in Central America (see fig. 8.1 for a similar species). It is a relatively large (to 70 mm) tree frog with large, webbed feet and dilated toe tips. In its most colorful form (like those at La Selva), the dorsum is bright leaf green, sometimes with round white spots, the throat and belly are creamy white, the hands and feet are orange, the anterior and posterior surfaces of the thigh are dark blue, the sides of the body are dark blue to purple with prominent ivory horizontal borders and vertical bars, and the iris of the eye is blood red (Duellman 1970). Most new frog "picture books" have at least one photograph of this spectacular species.

FIGURE 8.1. *Agalychnis saltator* adult in usual nocturnal sitting position (*a*) and in climbing position (*b*). Finca La Selva, Sarapiquí District, Costa Rica (photo, D. H. Janzen). This frog is similar to *Agalychnis callidryas*.

The distribution of *A. callidryas* is lowland Central America from southern Mexico to Panama near the Colombian border. It is absent from dry lowlands (Duellman 1970).

The breeding habits of *A. callidryas* have been studied most intensively by Pyburn (1963, 1970), and the general pattern is characteristic of most phyllomedusine hylids (*Agalychnis* and *Phyllomedusa* in Costa Rica). A male gives a single-noted "cluck" from trees or other vegetation overhanging temporary pools. A female approaches what seems to be a prechosen male, and they go into amplexus with the female carrying the male on her back. She then climbs down to the pool and evidently fills her bladder by absorption through the skin. The pair moves back up into the vegetation, where the female appears to select a leaf. She oviposits on the leaf, and the male fertilizes the eggs. Clutches vary in size; in two studies they averaged twenty-nine and forty-two eggs (Duellman 1963; Pyburn 1970). The female, with the male still on her back, climbs back down to the pond, refills her bladder, and repeats the process.

A female may lay three to five clutches in one night. The jelly surrounding the eggs imbibes the water from the female's bladder. If the female is not allowed to fill her bladder, the egg mass dries up and dies in a short time (Pyburn 1970). The colubrid snake *Leptodeira septentrionalis* is a common predator on the eggs of *A. callidryas* (Duellman 1958; Pyburn 1963).

Hatching occurs after about 5 days. The tadpoles fall into the pond, where they become midwater plankton feeders. Metamorphosis took place 79 days after hatching in a captive tadpole (Pyburn 1963). Adult *Agalychnis* live in tree canopies when not breeding and often spend the daytime hours in bromeliads or plastered to a green leaf.

*

Duellman, W. E. 1958. A monographic study of the colubrid snake genus *Leptodeira*. *Bull. Am. Mus. Nat. Hist.* 114:1–152.

———. 1963. Amphibians and reptiles of the rainforests of southern El Petén, Guatemala. *Pub. Mus. Nat. Hist. Univ. Kansas* 15:205–49.

———. 1970. The hylid frogs of Middle America. *Monogr. Mus. Nat. Hist. Univ. Kansas* 1:1–753.

Pyburn, W. F. 1963. Observations on the life history of the treefrog, *Phyllomedusa callidryas* (Cope). *Texas J. Sci.* 15:155–70.

———. 1970. Breeding behavior of the leaf-frogs *Phyllomedusa callidryas* and *Phyllomedusa dacnicolor* in Mexico. *Copeia* 1970:209–18.

Ameiva and *Cnemidophorus*
(Chisbalas, Macroteiid Lizards)

A. C. Echternacht

The forty genera and approximately two hundred species of the lizard family Teiidae are distributed in temperate, subtropical, and tropical regions from the United States through Middle America and the West Indies to about 40° S latitude in South America. Most genera are strictly tropical, but *Cnemidophorus* is widely distributed in the United States, and a few genera extend into temperate

South America. Eleven species belonging to eight genera occur in Costa Rica. Of these, six genera are represented by small, secretive lizards commonly known as microteiids. The remaining two genera, *Ameiva* Meyer and *Cnemidophorus* Wagler, are macroteiids and are among the most conspicuous of terrestrial vertebrates in Neotropical lowland (to 1,500 m) areas. These small to moderately large lizards are extremely active, are diurnal, and are important as predators of terrestrial arthropods and as prey for larger predators. Some species are abundant in open or second-growth situations such as along trails and roads, back of beaches, and in clearings, manmade and otherwise. Because of their broad geographic distribution, local abundance, and numerous instances of sympatry, macroteiids lend themselves especially well to a variety of types of ecological investigation. Of practical import is the observation that, where they occur near man, macroteiids are important reservoirs of *Salmonella* (Kournay, Myers, and Schneider 1970) and other organisms actually or potentially pathogenic to humans or domestic animals.

In body form, *Ameiva* (fig. 8.2) and *Cnemidophorus* are indistinguishable, but it is not difficult to identify species since they occur in a given area. The following descriptions of the four species of *Ameiva* and one of *Cnemidophorus* that occur in Costa Rica emphasize color and pattern characteristics useful in field identification and indicate maximum size attained. Geography can also be an important aid to identifying Costa Rican species. Sizes given are snout-vent lengths (SVL). Total lengths are not given because the tail is easily broken and regenerated at a shorter length than the original. Incidence of

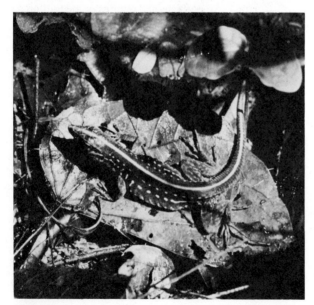

FIGURE 8.2. *Ameiva festiva festiva* male sunning on a fallen *Bauhinia* leaf on the floor of the rain forest. Finca La Selva, Sarapiquí District, Costa Rica (photo, D. H. Janzen).

tail breakage has been used as an indicator of predator pressure on lizard populations.

Cnemidophorus deppei. This lizard is easily identified by seven narrow cream-colored stripes on the black ground color of the dorsum. It is a small macroteiid, reaching maximum SVL of about 80 mm. The species ranges from Mexico to Costa Rica and is found in Costa Rica in Pacific coastal areas in Guanacaste and Puntarenas provinces to somewhere between Puntarenas and Quepos. *C. deppi* frequents sandy situations with sparse vegetation and is common in oceanfront dunes and upper reaches of beaches (Fitch 1973a). Definitely heliotherms, these lizards are active primarily on sunny days and retire to burrows when temperatures are relatively low or the sun obscured by clouds. They are most active in the morning. After warming, they are active foragers, thermoregulating by shuttling between shaded and nonshaded areas. As the temperature rises they become less active, and on a hot afternoon only young individuals may be evident. When active, *C. deppei* maintains a very high body temperature. Fitch (1973a) recorded body temperatures of 189 active lizards and found that most ranged between 29° and 42° C, 9° to 12° above ambient air temperatures. The activity threshold is about 26° C. Although some reproduction is evident throughout the year, there is geographic variation in intensity within Costa Rica. Fitch (1973a,b) found marked seasonality in a population at Playas del Coco; there is about a five-month period during the dry season (December–April) when relatively few gravid females are evident. Egg laying picks up in May and remains at a high level through October before tapering off. At Boca de Barranca the onset of the dry season brought only a slight decrease in egg production. Females produce an average of about three eggs per clutch and begin laying small clutches at 5–6 months. The interval between clutches and the incubation time are not known, but Fitch (1973a) estimates that a female productive throughout the breeding season could produce seventeen or more eggs per season if clutches are produced at one-month intervals.

Ameiva quadrilineata. The smallest of Costa Rica's *Ameiva*, this species reaches a maximum SVL of about 80 mm. It is characterized by four narrow cream or white stripes on the dorsum. A pair of these on each side bound a black dorsolateral field which, in large individuals, may contain lighter vermiculations. *Ameiva quadrilineata* occurs in the Caribbean coastal lowlands from southern Costa Rica into Panama and on the Pacific slope from about Quepos, Costa Rica, to the Azuero Peninsula in Panama. In Costa Rica, in addition to lowland coastal localities, its range extends up the valley of the Río General and Río Grande de Térraba to San Isidro del General. Ecologically, *A. quadrilineata* is the best-known species of the genus. Like *Cnemidophorus deppei* it is a beach lizard, but it also occurs inland in clearings in humid forest and is especially abundant in coconut groves. The ranges of *A. quadrilineata* and *C. deppei* may overlap along the coast northwest of Quepos, but the species seem largely allopatric and are ecologically quite similar. Favoring open areas, *A. quadrilineata* may occasionally be found in tree-fall clearings in deep forest and may actually invade forested areas by colonizing tree falls increasingly farther into the forest. Like *C. deppei*, *A. quadrilineata* is active only on sunny days, and activity is reduced after midday as temperatures rise, by overcast skies, and by lower temperatures. Hirth (1963), studying *A. quadrilineata* at Tortugero, Limón Province, obtained temperature records for 698 lizards and suggested that the ecological optimum was 37.6° C, with the normal activity range 34.6–40.0° C. He found the greatest activity at air temperatures of 29° to 30° C, with optimum substrate temperature 32.5° C. Thermoregulation is by shuttling. Hirth (1963), Smith (1968a,b) and Fitch (1973a,b) have studied the reproductive biology of *Ameiva quadrilineata*. All found reproduction generally acylic but with definite peaks associated with rainy seasons. Smith, working at Pandora, Limón Province, found that egg clutches averaged slightly more than two eggs, with laying occurring 17–21 days after ovulation.

Ameiva undulata. This moderately large (SVL to about 100 mm) teiid has the broadest range of any of the Middle American species, second only to *Ameiva ameiva* of Panama and South America in the genus. It ranges from Nayarit, Mexico, to northeastern Nicaragua on Atlantic slopes, with a population isolated on Islas del Maiz off the east coast of Nicaragua. In Costa Rica, *A. undulata* is found in Guanacaste Province and to about Quepos in Puntarenas Province. It also occurs on the Meseta Central. Throughout its range, *A. undulata* is found in forest or forest-edge situations or, in drier regions, in dense thickets and scrub (Echternacht 1968, 1971). In the absence of more heliophilic species such as those of *Cnemidophorus*, *A. undulata* may occupy more open habitats (see below). In Costa Rica, Fitch (1973a) found them in "leaf litter in open type of woodland, or woodland edge, or situations near to woodland" and "in xeric scrub and brush, in lowland swamp forest, gravelly edges of streams, in cafetal, banana groves, pineapple plantations, fields, pastures, along railroad tracks and roads, and in suburban yards and vacant lots." These lizards have a broad brownish or greenish middorsal field that may be bounded by narrow white or cream-colored stripes. Females usually have pronounced dark dorsolateral fields also bounded below by narrow light stripes, but males develop a lateral pattern of white or bluish bars extending down from the light stripes that border the middorsal field. Although *A. undulata* is more shade tolerant than either *C. deppei* or *A. quadrilineata*,

it still is a heliotherm and remains inactive on cool or overcast days. Fitch (1973a) found activity greatest between 0900 and noon on sunny days. Body temperatures of active lizards ranged from 29.6° to 40.5° C, but only one was below 33° C. Most captures were at air temperatures of 28° to 31° C. Reproduction is acyclic (Fitch 1973a) but affected by seasonal variation in precipitation. This is more pronounced in lowland areas (e.g., La Irma, Guanacaste Province) than on the Meseta Central (e.g., Las Pavas, San José Province). During the drier times of the year, adults are scarce, though juveniles remain active.

Ameiva leptophrys. This, the largest of the Costa Rican *Ameiva* (maximum SVL about 130 mm), has a range restricted to southwestern Costa Rica, the Pacific slopes of Panama west of the canal, and eastern Panama on both Caribbean and Pacific versants. It has not been collected in Colombia but is expected there. In Costa Rica it is abundant in the Palmar Norte–Osa Peninsula–Golfito area (Puntarenas Province) and has been collected at San Isidro del General (San José Province) and near La Julieta (Puntarenas Province). The lizard is very similar to *Ameiva undulata* unless one examines the dorsal head scales, which are greatly subdivided compared with the normal macroteiid pattern as evidenced by *A. undulata* (Echternacht 1971). Fortunately, the two species are largely allopatric. *Ameiva leptophrys* is a forest species (Hillman 1969; Echternacht 1971). In the vicinity of Palmar Norte (Echternacht 1971) *A. leptophrys* may be found basking in sun-flecked areas beneath dense, low vegetation. On the Osa Peninsula, Hillman (1969) found adults foraging most frequently in small clearings or along trails in forest and basking at the forest edge. Hillman also noted that the peak activity period for adults was midmorning, preceded by a period of basking; foraging declined toward midday. Newly hatched individuals were most active in foraging at midday. Hillman found sixteen foraging *A. leptophrys* to have a mean body temperature of 37.2° C. Nothing is known of the reproductive biology of *A. leptophrys*.

Ameiva festiva. This brightly colored lizard (fig. 8.2) ranges from Tabasco, Mexico, to Colombia on the Atlantic slopes and from Costa Rica to Colombia on the Pacific side. Two subspecies are present in Costa Rica. *Ameiva f. festiva* occurs primarily in the Caribbean lowlands except where it crosses the divide in the vicinity of Laguna de Arenal and Tilarán (Guanacaste Province). *Ameiva f. occidentalis* is found in southeastern Costa Rica, from San Isidro del General to Palmar Norte and in the lowlands of the Osa Peninsula and Golfito regions. Both subspecies are characterized by a well-developed white or bluish white vertebral stripe (which may be quite faded in large adult males). The Caribbean subspecies (*festiva*) has dark dorsolateral fields bordered dorsally and ventrally by a series of fine white dashes. The Pacific subspecies (*occidentalis*) lacks the dark dorsolateral fields but retains the uppermost of the fine white dashed lines that border the middorsal field in which the vertebral stripe lies. Additionally, the vertebral stripe in *A. f. festiva* either is straight-sided or has slightly undulating borders and is of uniform width the length of the back, whereas the vertebral stripe is broader and widens posteriorly as it becomes increasingly sinusoidal. Both subspecies are moderately large, reaching maximum SVL of about 120 mm. *Ameiva festiva* occupies habitats intermediate in degree of insolation to those of *A. leptophrys* and *A. quadrilineata*, both of which it is sympatric with. Hillman (1969) found *A. festiva* foraging most often at forest edge on ground partially covered with leaf litter. Greatest foraging activity occurred at midmorning. Twenty-one foraging *A. festiva* were found to have body temperatures averaging 37.7° C. Smith (1968a,b) found that reproduction is acyclic in this species, females producing three to four clutches averaging about 2.5 eggs each over the year at Pandora. Fitch (1973), sampling a variety of areas, supported Smith's findings.

Juvenile Costa Rican *Ameiva*, with the exception of *A. festiva* with its conspicuous vertebral stripe, are sometimes difficult to distinguish. All have a broad middorsal field and a dorsolateral field bounded above and below by narrow white or cream-colored stripes. Scale characteristics (Echternacht 1971) will allow unqualified identification, but merely knowing which species are in a given area and the ecological observations outlined above will narrow the choices considerably. Females retain the juvenile pattern throughout life, but in all species of *Ameiva* occurring in Costa Rica except *A. quadrilineata* the male pattern is altered ontogenetically. This usually means a loss or fading of stripes, increased mottling in middorsal, dorsolateral, and lateral fields, and, in *A. undulata*, the appearance of lateral bars. During the breeding season, or when males are reproductive, the ventral surface, normally white or cream-colored, may become bluish or, especially in *A. undulata* and *A. leptophrys*, salmon or coppery. Females of all species except *A. quadrilineata* may also develop this ventral coloration. The chin and neck regions of reproductive male *Ameiva* may become yellow, orange, or red. Reproductive male *Cnemidophorus deppei* are also characterized by a blue venter and they, along with *Ameiva festiva, A. undulata,* and *A. quadrilineata*, have brilliant blue tails as hatchlings and small juveniles.

The macroteiids of Costa Rica are all terrestrial insectivores, although all probably climb into low vegetation to forage occasionally. All are diurnal; the only record of nocturnal activity followed heavy rains that may have flooded the lizard from a burrow (Echternacht 1971). The lizards are not territorial, and adults of both

sexes may be found foraging with juveniles, although as a rule there are microhabitat differences between juveniles and adults. Macroteiids have a well-developed Jacobson's organ and a long, forked tongue. They feed not only on actively moving prey but on insect pupae and larvae dug from beneath shallow layers of soil or leaf litter. Most forage by moving slowly through an area, digging and probing in litter and under sticks and rubble, seemingly locating much of their prey by olfaction. Home ranges (where known) are surprisingly small given the locomotor abilities of these lizards (Hirth 1963; Fitch 1973a). As indicated, juvenile lizards tend to segregate from adults by microhabitat. Thus Echternacht (1968) found adult *A. undulata* in coconut groves back of beaches in northern Honduras and juveniles in dense grass at the beach edge of the grove. Hillman (1969) reports hatchling *A. leptophrys* foraging in low ground cover bordering a road and in the ecotone between forest and open areas, whereas adults foraged in small clearings in the forest itself.

As many as three species of macroteiid lizards may be found together in Costa Rica. In the Caribbean slope lowlands, *A. festiva* and *A. quadrilineata* often occur together, as they do in islands of Bocas del Toro off northwestern Panama. In southeastern Costa Rica *A. festiva* is sympatric with both *A. leptophrys* and *A. quadrilineata. Ameiva undulata* is sympatric with *Cnemidophorus deppei* in Guanacaste and along the northwestern coast of Puntarenas Province. At Quepos, *A. undulata* and *A. quadrilineata* are sympatric and, although collections are lacking, *A. undulata* and *A. leptophrys,* and *C. deppei* and *A. quadrilineata*, may be sympatric somewhere between Boca de Barranca and Quepos. Where sympatric, these macroteiids are ecologically segregated. Because *C. deppei* and *A. quadrilineata* seem to be ecological equivalents, documentation and description of sympatry is especially desirable. In general, where *Ameiva* and *Cnemidophorus* are sympatric, the former occupies more shaded areas, the latter more open. Fitch (1973a) observed this in Guanacaste for *A. undulata* and *C. deppei*, as did Echternacht (1968) for the same two species and for *A. undulata* and *Cnemidophorus lemniscatus* in northern Honduras. Where *Ameiva* occurs alone, as at Panajachél on Lake Atitlán in Guatemala, it (*undulata*) occupies all those parts of the habitat jointly utilized by both genera where sympatric (Echternacht 1971). The most thorough documentation of habitat partitioning by macroteiid lizards is that provided by Hillman (1969) reporting a study conducted on the Osa Peninsula of Costa Rica. He clearly demonstrated the ecological distinctions in the accounts of *A. festiva, A. leptophrys,* and *A. quadrilineata* given above and suggested that microgeographic allopatry was related to feeding behavior: "What they eat, where they eat, and when they eat." *Ameiva leptophrys* and *A. quadrilineata* overlap very little in any of these respects. *Ameiva festiva* overlaps both other species spatially but tends to forage later in the morning than *A. leptophrys* and to eat larger items than *A. quadrilineata*. Within the genus *Cnemidophorus*, Duellman (1965) and others have pointed to the size disparity often evident among sympatric pairs of species. This sort of separation of sympatric species along a size gradient is evident among teiid lizards in Costa Rica and is associated both with microhabitat partitioning and probably with differences in size of prey taken, although Hillman (1969) found no significant differences between sizes of prey items eaten by *A. leptophrys* and *A. festiva*. Hillman was, however, able to demonstrate that *A. quadrilineata* ate items significantly smaller than those eaten by the other two species.

*

Duellman, W. E. 1965. A biogeographic account of the herpetofauna of Michoacán, México. *Pub. Mus. Nat. Hist. Univ. Kansas* 15:627–709.

Echternacht, A. C. 1968. Distributional and ecological notes on some reptiles from northern Honduras. *Herpetologica* 24:151–58.

———. 1971. Middle American lizards of the genus *Ameiva* (Teiidae) with emphasis on geographic variation. *Misc. Pub. Mus. Nat. Hist. Univ. Kansas* 55:1–86.

Fitch, H. S. 1973*a*. A field study of Costa Rican lizards. *Univ. Kansas Sci. Bull.* 50:39–126.

———. 1973*b*. Population structure and survivorship in some Costa Rican lizards. *Occas. Pap. Mus. Nat. Hist. Univ. Kansas* 18:1–41

Hillman, P. E. 1969. Habitat specificity in three sympatric species of *Ameiva* (Reptilia: Teiidae). *Ecology* 50:476–81.

Hirth, H. F. 1963. The ecology of two lizards on a tropical beach. *Ecol. Monogr.* 33:83–112.

Kourany, M.; Myers, C. W.; and Schneider, C. R. 1970. Panamanian amphibians and reptiles as carriers of *Salmonella*. *Am. J. Trop. Med. Hyg.* 19:632–38.

Smith, R. E. 1968*a*. Experimental evidence for a gonadal-fat body relationship in two teiid lizards (*Ameiva festiva*, *Ameiva quadrilineata*). *Biol. Bull.* 134:325–31.

———. 1968*b*. Studies on reproduction in Costa Rican *Ameiva festiva* and *Ameiva quadrilineata* (Sauria: Teiidae). *Copeia* 1968:236–39.

Basiliscus basiliscus (Chisbala, Garrobo, Basilisk, Jesus Christ Lizard)

R. W. Van Devender

These relatively large lizards (fig. 8.3) are among the most interesting animals in Central America. Their resemblance to miniature dinosaurs and their ability to run

FIGURE 8.3. *Basiliscus basiliscus* large adult male (dead). Near Bagaces, Guanacaste Province, Costa Rica (photo, D. H. Janzen).

across water make basilisks noteworthy. They are common along most streams and bodies of water in the Pacific drainage of Costa Rica. They sometimes reach startling densities of about two hundred to four hundred lizards per hectare. Basilisks are a lowland species and rarely occur above about 1,000 m. They are common in Santa Rosa National Park, Corcovado National Park, and Paloverde. They are occasionally seen at San Vito and even around San José. Obviously they are relatively successful at coexisting with man.

Adult male basilisks have large crests on their heads, backs, and tails (fig. 8.3), making them look like living sailfin dinosaurs. The crests are supported by bony projections from the skull and vertebrae and may be up to 6 cm long. These lizards weigh 200–600 g and reach almost a meter in length. About three-quarters of the length is tail. Females are much smaller, rarely exceeding 300 g and 600 mm, and carry only a small crest on the back of the head. Basilisks are basically brown with darker cross bands and a light stripe along the lips and along the sides. The markings are more distinct in juveniles and are often obscured in adults, although some adult males take on a rich greenish cast after shedding.

The name Jesus Christ lizard refers to the animals' ability to run across the surface of streams or ponds. The image is strengthened because they do this in a bipedal position. The "secret" of walking on water is that the lizards move very quickly and have very large hind feet with flaps of skin along each toe, so that they can essentially skip across the water. This ability is best developed in young lizards and poorest in adult males. Smaller basilisks can run 10 to 20 m or more over the water without sinking, whereas adult males look more like motorboats if they have to do more than a few meters. Basilisks are alert, active lizards that use water-walking both in escaping predators and in feeding.

These lizards are diurnal; they eat almost anything that moves and some things that do not. Adults eat a wide variety of insects, other invertebrates (including shrimp and scorpions), small vertebrates (including lizards, snakes, fish, mammals, and birds), and some flowers and fruit (including *Ardisia, Muntingia, Cordia, Spondias,*

Manilkara, Psidium, Ficus, and *Sloanea).* Twigs and leaves are usually excluded from the diet. Juvenile lizards, although primarily insectivorous, sometimes catch and eat small fish. When *Iguana* and *Ctenosaura* eggs hatch in May, the hatchlings are the preferred food of all basilisks that can overcome the smaller lizards. The only predators that could pose a major threat to basilisks by day are raptors. By night, opossums (*Philander* and *Chironectes*) and some snakes catch the sleeping lizards. Basilisks minimize this threat by sleeping in vegetation overhanging water. When the vegetation is disturbed the basilisks jump into the water. Their long, sharp claws aid them in climbing.

The life history of this species has been studied at Finca La Pacifica near Cañas, Guanacaste (See Van Devender 1975, 1979 for more information). Females mature when they are about 18 months old and continue to grow throughout their lives. They produce clutches of two to eighteen eggs about five to eight times during a 10-month breeding season beginning at the end of the dry season. Smaller, younger females lay smaller clutches. After about 3 months the eggs hatch into 2 g lizards that can fend for themselves. The eggs are subject to flood loss, and most populations show some kind of age-class dominance. Hatchling survivorship is only about 15%, and adults have about a 40% chance of surviving to the next year. The oldest known wild basilisk was a male that was at least 7 years old, and many males live for 4, 5, or 6 years. Females probably do not survive so long. The adult males show a size-determined dominance hierarchy, and a young male may be 3–4 years old before really entering the main breeding population. In local situations with fewer large males, the waiting time is somewhat shorter. Since the testes begin to enlarge when males are about a year old and quickly reach mature size, young males may have opportunities for surreptitious matings before they achieve dominant status. These younger males are often attacked by larger males.

The genus *Basiliscus* contains four species distributed from Tamaulipas, Mexico, to western Venezuela, Ecuador, and Colombia (Peters and Donoso-Barros 1970; Maturana 1962). All four species are reported from Costa Rica. *Basiliscus basiliscus* has two subspecies: *B. b. basiliscus,* which ranges along the Pacific slope from Nicaragua to western Colombia and Ecuador, and *B. b. barbouri* Ruthven from western Venezuela and Santa Marta, Colombia. *Basiliscus vittatus* Wiegmann, the striped basilisk, occurs from Mexico to Colombia. It was studied at Tortugero, Costa Rica, by Hirth in 1963 and in Veracruz, Mexico, by Glidewell in 1974. It is smaller than the other species and seems more adapted to open situations like beaches. The male has a single large crest on the head and none on the body. The double-crested basilisk, *B. plumifrons* Cope, is the Caribbean analogue of

B. basiliscus, which it resembles in size and form. It differs in being bright green, having a red iris, and having two crests on the head. It also seems more predisposed to leave the vicinity of water. This species is relatively common at La Selva and ranges from Nicaragua to Panama in the Caribbean lowlands. The final species, *B. galeritus* Dumeril, is a problematic form in the Pacific drainage from southern Costa Rica to Colombia and Ecuador. It differs from the sympatric *B. basiliscus* in lacking a skin webbing between the dorsal rays that form the dorsal crest. It may be the juvenile of *B. basiliscus.*

*

Glidewell, J. R. 1974. The reproductive ecology of the striped basilisk, *Basiliscus vittatus* Wiegmann (Iguanidae) in southern Mexico. M.A. thesis, University of Texas at Arlington.

Hirth, H. F. 1963. The ecology of two lizards on a tropical beach. *Ecol. Monogr.* 33:83–112.

Maturana, H. R. 1962. A study of the species of the genus *Basiliscus. Bull. Mus. Comp. Zool., Harvard Univ.* 128:1–34.

Peters, J. A., and Donoso-Barros, R. 1970. *Catalogue of the Neotropical Squamata.* Part II. *Lizards and amphisbaenians.* U.S. National Museum Bulletin 297. Washington, D.C.: Smithsonian Institution Press.

Van Devender, R. W. 1975. The comparative demography of two local populations of the tropical lizard, *Basiliscus basiliscus.* Ph.D. diss., University of Michigan.

———. 1979. Growth ecology of a tropical lizard, *Basiliscus basilisus. Ecology* 59:1031–38.

———. 1982. Comparative demography of *Basiliscus basiliscus* (Sauria: Iguanidae). *Herpetologica,* in press.

Boa constrictor (Boa, Béquer, Boa Constrictor)

H. W. Greene

The boa constrictor (fig. 8.4) is a large, nonvenomous Neotropical member of the tropicopolitan family Boidae. It ranges from Sonora and Tamaulipas south along both coasts of Mexico, thence throughout much of Central and South America to Argentina and Paraguay. Geographic variation in this species has not been well studied, but eight subspecies are currently recognized (Lazell 1964; Peters and Orejas-Miranda 1969).

Boas are easily distinguished from other Neotropical snakes by the following combination of characters: shiny, smooth scales in fifty-five or more rows at midbody; no enlarged, platelike scales on sides or top of the head; and a distinct postorbital stripe on each side of the head. The color pattern consists of squarish, dark dorsal blotches on a light brown or gray background; these blotches are more distinct anteriorly and tend to form broad, irregular

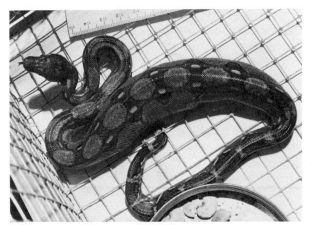

FIGURE 8.4. *Boa constrictor* 2–3 months old containing a newly eaten 39 g *Liomys salvini* mouse; boa weighed 50 g before eating the mouse. Santa Rosa National Park, Guanacaste Province, Costa Rica (photo, D. H. Janzen).

bands on the posterior part of the body and the tail. Young boas are usually more brightly marked than adults, and in some large individuals the pattern is very obscure. The color pattern is certainly cryptic, and Janzen (pers. comm.) has suggested that the red, yellow, and black markings on the tail might mimic a venomous coral snake. Like most other primitive snakes, boas have a pelvis and vestigial hind limbs. The latter are visible externally as clawlike "anal spurs" on either side of and slightly lateral to the vent. These apparently function during courtship, since males have been seen to stroke females with them (Mole and Urich 1894).

Boas inhabit a remarkable range of environments from sea level to 1,000 m, including wet and dry tropical forest, savanna, very dry thorn scrub, and cultivated fields (Martin 1958; Pope 1961; Scott 1969). Throughout much of this distribution they are crepuscular or nocturnal, and they usually are able to maintain preferred temperatures without basking. At the northern extreme of the range in western Mexico individuals do bask at times and may aggregate to reduce heat loss (Brattstrom 1965; Myres and Eells 1968; McGinnis and Moore 1969). Lazell (1964) reported "dens" of three to twelve boas on Dominica, but the function of these aggregations is not obvious. Boas that have fed recently prefer slightly higher temperatures until defecation occurs (Regal 1966).

Boas climb well, and young ones seem especially arboreal (Lazell 1964). Herpetologists often assume that these relatively heavy-bodied snakes are sit-and-wait predators instead of active searchers (e.g., Pianka 1974). Recent observations suggest instead that boas actively search for good places to sit and wait. Montgomery and Rand (1978) followed a 2.4 m, 11.3 kg adult in Panama with telemetry equipment; the snake moved from burrow

to burrow every 3–4 days, evidently waiting in each one for the residents to return. B. A. Dugan (pers. comm.) saw a boa about 2 m long capture a blue-gray tanager on Perico Island, Panama. The snake was suspended from a *Cecropia peltata* branch approximately 2 m above the ground and had been sighted regularly in the tree for one month. Tanagers feed on the inflorescences of *Cecropia,* and this observation is consistent with the idea that boas choose good sites to ambush prey.

There are general references to boas eating a variety of wild lizards, birds, and mammals as well as poultry and dogs (Alvarez del Toro 1972; Pope 1961). Items that have been recorded from individual snakes include teiid lizards (*Ameiva, Cnemidophorus, Tupinambis*), iguanid lizards (*Ctenosaura, Iguana*), a blue-gray tanager, an antbird, opossums (*Didelphis*), bats (*Artibeus jamaicensis, Desmodus rotundus*), spiny rats, *Rattus rattus,* agoutis (*Dasyprocta*), a juvenile tree porcupine (*Coendou rothschildi*), three young rabbits, young deer, coatis (*Nasua narica*), an ocelot, and mongoose (Beebe 1946; Bogert and Oliver 1945; Davis and Smith 1953; B. A. Dugan, pers. comm.; Janzen 1969; Lewis and Johnson 1956; Mole 1924; Mole and Urich 1894; Villa and Lopez 1966). An adult boa in Panama was evidently killed by an arboreal anteater (*Tamandua tetradactyla*) that it had partially swallowed (N. Smythe, pers. comm.).

Prey apparently is recognized by visual, thermal, and chemical cues (Burghardt 1970; Ulinski 1972; Gamow and Harris 1973). It is seized by a rapid forward movement of the snake's head. The mouth is opened wide during this strike, and the prey is impaled on the sharp, recurved teeth (see Frazzetta 1966 for a detailed mechanical analysis of the strike in *Python*). Simultaneously the snake lifts the prey free of the substrate and applies a constricting coil (Greene and Burghardt 1978). Constriction apparently ceases after the prey stops moving (Quesnel and Wehekind 1969; Greene, unpublished), then the snake locates the prey's head and swallows the animal whole.

Wild boas vary in temperament, but some are aggressive. They sometimes hiss loudly with the mouth partly opened and draw the head and neck into an S-shaped posture (Alvarez del Toro 1972, fig. 93); my experience is that this indicates a readiness to bite. Adult boas have numerous large teeth that can inflict serious wounds, so they should be approached and handled carefully.

Boas give birth to live young. Litters are recorded to contain twenty to sixty-four young, each approximately 0.5 m long. There is no known parental care. The events of the reproductive cycle vary considerably, perhaps geographically, but this has not been well studied. Mating has been reported from August to March and birth from March to August (Fitch 1970; Honegger 1970; Pope

1961). Sexual maturity evidently occurs at a length of 1.5–2 m, and the maximum length is between 5 and 6 m. A boa constrictor is known to have lived at least 38 years, 10 months in captivity (Bowler 1977).

Boa constrictors are threatened in some areas by habitat destruction and the pet trade, but otherwise they seem to do well in the vicinity of humans (Lazell 1964). A permit is currently required to import any member of the family Boidae into the United States. Boas are long-lived, among the largest carnivores in terms of adult weight, and relatively common in many parts of the New World tropics. They might be important top predators in some ecosystems, and it is unfortunate that we still know so little about their biology.

*

Alvarez del Toro, M. 1972. *Los reptiles de Chiapas.* Tuxtla Gutierrez: Instituto de Historia Natural de Chiapas.

Beebe, W. 1946. Field notes on the snakes of Kartabo, British Guiana and Caripito, Venezuela. *Zoologica* 31:11–52.

Bogert, C. M., and Oliver, J. A. 1945. A preliminary analysis of the herpetofauna of Sonora. *Bull. Am. Mus. Nat. Hist.* 83:297–426.

Bowler, J. K. 1977. Longevity of reptiles and amphibians in North American collections. *Soc. Study Rept. Amphib., Herp. Circ.* no. 6.

Brattstrom, B. H. 1965. Body temperatures of reptiles. *Am. Midl. Nat.* 73:376–422.

Burghardt, G. M. 1970. Chemical perception in reptiles. In *Communication by chemical signals,* ed. J. W. Johnson, Jr., D. G. Moulton, and A. Turk, pp. 241–308. New York: Appleton-Century-Crofts.

Davis, W. B., and Smith, H. M. 1953. Snakes of the Mexican state of Morelos. *Herpetologica* 8:133–43.

Fitch, H. S. 1970. Reproductive cycles in lizards and snakes. *Misc. Publ. Mus. Nat. Hist. Univ. Kansas* 52:1–247.

Frazzetta, T. H. 1966. Studies on the morphology and function of the skull of the Boidae (Serpentes). Part II. Morphology and function of the jaw apparatus in *Python sebae* and *Python molurus. J. Morph.* 118: 217–96.

Gamow, R. I., and Harris, J. F. 1973. The infrared receptors of snakes. *Sci. Am.* 228:94–100.

Greene, H. W., and Burghardt, G. M. 1978. Behavior and phylogeny: Constriction in ancient and modern snakes. *Science* 200:74–77

Honegger, R. E. 1970. Beitrag zur Fortpflanzungsbiologie von *Boa constrictor* und *Python reticulatus* (Reptilia, Boidae). *Salamandra* 6:73–79.

Janzen, D. H. 1969. Altruism by coatis in the face of predation by *Boa constrictor. J. Mammal.* 51:387–89.

Lazell, J. D. 1964. The Lesser Antillean representatives of *Bothrops* and *Constrictor. Bull. Mus. Comp. Zool., Harvard Univ.* 132:245–73.

Lewis, T. H., and Johnson, M. L. 1956. Notes on a herpetological collection from Sinaloa, Mexico. *Herpetologica* 12:277–80.

McGinnis, S. M., and Moore, R. G. 1969. Thermoregulation in the boa constrictor, *Boa constrictor. Herpetologica* 25:38–45.

Martin, P. S. 1958. A biogeography of reptiles and amphibians in the Gomez Farias region, Tamaulipas, Mexico. *Misc. Publ. Mus. Zool. Univ. Michigan,* no. 101.

Mole, R. R. 1924. The Trinidad snakes. *Proc. Zool. Soc. London* 1924:235–78.

Mole, R. R., and Urich, F. W. 1894. Biological notes upon some of the Ophidia of Trinidad, B.W.I., with a preliminary list of the species recorded from the island. *Proc. Zool. Soc. London* 1894:499–518.

Montgomery, G. G., and Rand, A. S. 1978. Movements, body temperature and hunting strategy of a *Boa constrictor. Copeia* 1978:532–33.

Myres, B. C., and Eells, M. M. 1968. Thermal aggregation in *Boa constrictor. Herpetologica* 24:61–66.

Peters, J. A., and Orejas-Miranda, B. 1969. *Catalogue of the Neotropical Squamata.* Part I. *Snakes.* U.S. National Museum Bulletin 297. Washington, D.C.: Smithsonian Institution Press.

Pianka, E. R. 1974. *Evolutionary ecology.* New York: Harper and Row.

Pope, C. H. 1961. *The giant snakes.* New York: Alfred A. Knopf.

Quesnel, V. C., and Wehekind, L. 1969. Observations on the constrictive phase of feeding behaviour in *Boa constrictor. J. Trinidad Field Nat. Club* 1969:12–13.

Regal, P. J. 1966. Thermophilic response following feeding in certain reptiles. *Copeia* 1966:588–90.

Scott, N. J. 1969. A zoogeographic analysis of the snakes of Costa Rica. Ph.D. diss., University of Southern California.

Swanson, P. L. 1950. The iguana, *Iguana iguana iguana. Herpetologica* 6:187–93.

Thomas, M. E. 1974. Bats as food source for *Boa constrictor. J. Herp.* 8:188.

Tschambers, B. 1949. Boa constrictor eats porcupine. *Herpetologica* 5:141.

Ulinski, P. S. 1972. Tongue movements in the common boa (*Constrictor constrictor*). *Anim. Behav.* 20: 373–82.

Villa, B., and Lopez, W. F. 1966. Cinco casos de predacion de pequeños vertebrados en murcielagos de Mexico. *Ann. Inst. Biol. Univ. Nat. Mexico.* 37:187–93.

Bolitoglossa subpalmata (Escorpiones, Salamandras, Mountain Salamander)

N. J. Scott

This salamander (Plethodontidae) (fig. 8.5) is restricted to higher elevations in the Cordilleras Central and Talamanca of Costa Rica. Although it is rarely found as low as 1,500 m, populations become abundant at elevations over 2,400 m. It is the best-studied species of tropical

FIGURE 8.5. *a,* Three adult *Bolitoglossa subpalmata* exposed by lifting a surface-level rotten log (note variation in color). *b,* adult *B. subpalmata. c,* As in *b.* Cerro de la Muerte (2,800 m), Costa Rica (photos, D. H. Janzen).

salamander, and most of this account is derived from the works of Vial (1966, 1968).

The only salamanders that have significantly penetrated the tropics anywhere in the world are a few genera of American forms belonging to a section of the family Plethodontidae that undergoes direct development in the egg. Three genera, *Bolitoglossa, Oedipina,* and *Chiropterotriton,* reach Costa Rica from the north; the first two reach Colombia and Ecuador in northwestern South America, but *Bolitoglossa* is the only northwestern genus with species widespread in South America (Wake and Lynch 1976).

Bolitoglossa subpalmata tends to be arboreal in the lower parts of its range, where it can be found in bromeliads, but individuals are also present on the ground under moss and liverworts. At higher elevations these salamanders become almost entirely terrestrial, taking refuge under surface debris such as rocks and logs (fig. 8.5). During dry periods they penetrate crevices and root tunnels in the soil. Populations are sparse at lower elevations, but at 3,000 m near the summit of the Cerro de la Muerte population densities may surpass nine thousand per hectare (Vial 1968).

Egg clutches in the high-elevation populations studied by Vial (1968) are deposited in cavities under well-

imbedded rocks and logs. Thirty-one clutches contained thirteen to thirty-eight eggs ($\bar{x}=23$). Usually an adult female was coiled around each clutch, but in four cases males were found instead. The adult occasionally rotated the eggs with its forelimbs and tail. Unattended clutches invariably died.

The larval stage is passed in the egg, and small salamanders hatch after an incubation period of 4 to 5 months. Growth is slow, averaging about 3 mm per year in both juveniles and adults. Sexual maturity is attained by the 6th year in males and the 12th year in females. Maximum ages probably approach 18 years (Vial 1968).

A notable feature of high elevation *Bolitoglossa subpalmata* populations is the striking polymorphism in color and pattern (Vial 1966). In six samples at 150 m elevational intervals along a highway, each population had a unique combination of chromatophore density and pattern. The differences are obvious and striking, and they are of the type that usually distinguishes full species in this genus. The evolutionary forces behind this kind of extreme polymorphism are unknown.

The adults feed at night on a wide variety of soil and litter-surface insects, which are out and active even at temperatures of 0–4° C at the highest elevations (D. H. Janzen, pers. comm.).

*

Vial, J. L. 1966. Variation in altitudinal populations of the salamander, *Bolitoglossa subpalmata,* on the Cerro de la Muerte, Costa Rica. *Rev. Biol. Trop.* 14:111–21.
———. 1968. The ecology of the tropical salamander, *Bolitoglossa subpalmata,* in Costa Rica. *Rev. Biol. Trop.* 15:13–115.
Wake, D. B., and Lynch, J. F. 1976. The distribution, ecology, and evolutionary history of plethodontid salamanders in tropical America. *Los Angeles County Nat. Hist. Mus. Sci. Bull.* 25:1–65.

Bothrops asper (Terciopelo, Fer-de-Lance)

N. J. Scott

This common large snake (reaching lengths of more than 2 m in Costa Rica) (Crotalidae) (fig. 8.6) is the most feared and dangerous in Central America and tropical Mexico. It is much more inclined to bite than other large vipers, which tend to retreat when approached (Picado T. 1976). Terciopelos produce many cubic centimeters of very toxic venom. In older literature the species is known as *Bothrops atrox.*

The young of *B. asper* tend to be arboreal. At this age they have a yellow tail tip that may serve to attract lizard and frog prey (Neill 1960). As they grow they become terrestrial, feeding on mammals, especially opossums, and occasionally birds (March 1928; Picado T. 1976).

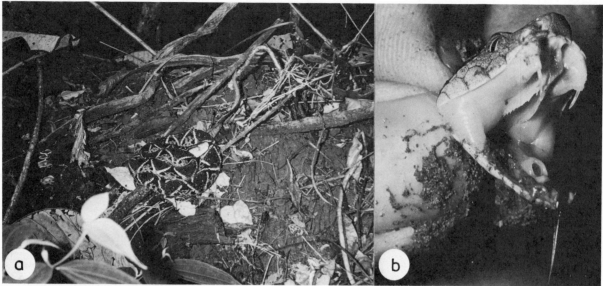

FIGURE 8.6. *Bothrops asper.* *a,* Adult 2 m in length coiled on forest floor, Rincón, Osa Peninsula, Costa Rica. *b,* Yearling juvenile with mouth open to show fangs and smaller teeth. Interior Corcovado National Park, Osa Peninsula, Costa Rica (photos, D. H. Janzen).

In Costa Rica terciopelos are abundant in lowland areas that receive more than about 2.5 m of rain per year, but they also occur along the major rivers in drier areas (Taylor et al. 1974). Overgrown fields are favorite habitats, although they may be found almost anywhere. Adults eat small mammals.

The young are born free living, and litters can be large, with as many as seventy-five young in Costa Rica.

Write or call R. Colwell, Department of Zoology, University of California, Berkeley, for information on what it is like to be bitten by a terciopelo.

*

March, D. D. H. 1928. Field notes on barba amarilla (*Bothrops atrox*). *Bull. Antivenin Inst. Am.* 1:92–97.

Neill, W. T. 1960. The caudal lure of various juvenile snakes. *Quart. J. Florida Acad. Sci.* 23:173–200.

Picado T., C. 1976. *Serpientes venenosas de Costa Rica.* 2d ed. San José: Editorial Universidad de Costa Rica–Editorial Costa Rica.

Taylor, R. T.; Flores, A.; Flores, G.; and Bolaños, R. 1974. Geographical distribution of Viperidae, Elapidae and Hydrophiidae in Costa Rica. *Rev. Biol. Trop.* 21:383–97.

Bothrops schlegelii (Oropél [Gold Morph], Bocaracá, Eyelash Viper, Palm Viper)

R. P. Seifert

This is the only lowland species of regularly arboreal *Bothrops* in Costa Rica (fig. 8.7). It is characterized by an enlarged flaplike supraocular scale that extends outward just above the eye, giving the eye a hooded appearance. For this reason the snake is commonly called the eyelash viper; its arboreal habitats give it an anternative common name, the palm viper. The function of the enlarged scale above the eye is unknown, although it has been suggested that it may help to protect the eye as the animal moves among vines and twigs in its arboreal habitat (Cohen and Myres 1970). The eyelash viper, which reaches a maximum length of less than 1 m (with an average adult length of around 50 cm), has a polychromatism unique among *Bothrops* species. Specimens include individuals with green, brown, rust, gray, or light blue ground color and diamond patterns of darker colors. In addition, there is a bright gold morph, usually with red flecks on the tips of a few scales. The gold morphs rarely have any patterning on the body and, according to the San Diego Zoo, are reported only from Costa Rica. The genetic basis for the polymorphism and the selective advantages of the various morphs are unknown. Litters from the same female are reported to include individuals of several different colors (Norman Scott, pers. comm.).

The eyelash viper is strictly arboreal, and specimens are usually collected while they are resting or sunning themselves on leaves, branches, or floral bracts. In captivity the snakes eat mice and frogs, and some young specimens will eat anoles (*Norops*). They will eat most species of frogs, but only at small sizes. *Hyla ebraccata* Cope is avoided (pers. obs.). While it is notoriously difficult to determine the life span of wild snakes, I estimate an "average" life span after first-year mortality at about 10 years, although one captive specimen has been kept for more than 16 years (Bowler 1974).

FIGURE 8.7. *Bothrops schlegelii. a,* Adult of the mottled morph stretches out to a neighboring branch. Finca La Selva, Sarapiquí District, Costa Rica. *b,* Adult of mottled morph perched on tree trunk 1 m above ground. Corcovado National Park, Osa Peninsula, Costa Rica (photos, D. H. Janzen).

Bothrops schlegelii is distributed from southern Mexico to Pacific Ecuador and the extreme northwest of Venezuela (Peters and Orejas-Miranda 1970). This snake represents the member of the arboreal *Bothrops* phyletic linage (including *B. schlegelii, B. nummifer* [Ruppell], *B. lateralis* [Peters], and *B. nigroviridis* [Peters] in Costa Rica) with the most primitive morphological characters and is the *Bothrops* species most closely related to the sister group from southeast Asia, *Trimeresurus* (Brattstrom 1964). *B. schlegelii* carries about 10 to 20 mg of a venom that, drop for drop, is more toxic to humans than most *Bothrops* in Costa Rica (Minton and Minton 1969). The arboreal habits of this snake mean that bites usually occur on the upper part of the body. Three to six deaths from *B. schlegelii* bites are reported annually in Costa Rica (Roger Bolanos, pers. comm.).

*

Bowler, J. K. 1977. Longevity of reptiles and amphibians in North American collections. *Soc. Study Rept. Amphil., Hertp. Cir.* no. 6.

Brattstrom, B. H. 1964. Evolution of the pit vipers. *Trans. San Diego Soc. Nat. Hist.* 13:185–268.

Cohen, A. C., and Myres, B. C. 1970. A function of the horns (supraocular scales) in the sidewinder rattlesnake, *Crotalus cerastes,* with comments on other horned snakes. *Copeia* 1970:574–75.

Minton, S. A., Jr., and Minton, M. R. 1969. *Venomous reptiles.* New York: Charles Scribner's Sons.

Peters, J. A., and Orejas-Miranda, B. 1970. *Catalogue of the Neotropical Squamata.* Part 1. *Snakes.* U.S. National Museum Bulletin 297. Washington, D.C.: Smithsonian Institution Press.

Bufo haematiticus (Sapo, Toad)

N. J. Scott

This true toad (Bufonidae) (fig. 8.8) is characteristic of low- and mid-elevation wet forests between Nicaragua

FIGURE 8.8. *Bufo haematiticus* juveniles from the forest floor. Rincón, Osa Peninsula, Costa Rica (photo, D. H. Janzen).

and Colombia. Unlike the more familiar members of the genus, *Bufo haematiticus* lacks obvious "warts" and has an apparently smooth skin. Like other toads, however, it does have paired parotoid glands in the dorsolateral skin of the neck region (Taylor 1952). These glands are inconspicuous because their borders blend in with the surrounding skin, but they secrete appreciable quantities of a viscous white poison when the toad is stressed.

This species congregates in pools left behind by forest streams and rivers to lay strings of eggs that hatch into tadpoles in the usual toad fashion. It spends the remainder of the year foraging for arthropods in the litter of the forest floor. It has been found calling from beneath loose boulders on the Río Reventazón (D. Robinson, pers. comm.).

*

Taylor, E. H. 1952. The frogs and toads of Costa Rica. *Univ. Kansas Sci. Bull.* 35:577–942.

Bufo marinus (Sapo Grande, Sapo, Giant Toad, Marine Toad)

G. Zug

The marine toad (fig. 8.9) is the largest lowland toad of tropical America (from southern Texas to central Brazil). Sapo grande is familiar to everyone because it has become a commensal of man and is now more common in and around human dwellings than in its natural habitats of savanna through open forest. In fact, closed-canopied rain forest appears to be an effective barrier to its long-distance dispersal. In Costa Rica the toad occurs in most open and semiopen habitats to about 2,000 m.

Adult marine toads range in body length from 90 to 200 mm (80 g to 1.2 kg)—most less than 130 mm. Adults and half-grown juveniles are easily recognized by the large ovate parotoid gland on each side above the tympanum (fig. 8.9). Juvenile and postmetamorphs are somewhat more difficult to identify but usually can be differentiated from other toads by regular rows of paravertebral tubercles. The tadpoles are small (10–25 mm total length); the body and tail are black or dark brown with a distinctive pale cream stripe along the lower edge of the caudal musculature. Sexually active adults are dimorphic. Females bear the juvenile mottled pattern of a dusky brown dorsal ground color with irregular blotches of beige and chocolate and usually a beige middorsal stripe. Males are a uniform cinnamon brown and are spiny; each wart is capped by one or more horny spines; the thumb is somewhat enlarged and darkly kerantinized.

These creatures are equal-opportunity eaters. If it is bite-sized and animate it is food, no matter how noxious, toxic, or biting/stinging. True bugs, daddy longlegs, millipedes, ants, wasps, and such, are taken with apparent impunity, although beetles and ants predominate. Marine

FIGURE 8.9. *Bufo marinus,* front foot lost in nature, white defensive secretion rich in toxins dripping down parotoid gland. Santa Rosa National Park, July 1980 (photo, D. H. Janzen).

toads eat small vertebrates, including juvenile marine toads, and have learned to eat dog and cat food set outside for family pets. One exotic population in Papua New Guinea (Zug, Lindgren, and Pippet 1975) was found to depend upon vegetable matter as a major food resource during times of low prey abundance.

The marine toad's commensal habits make it highly visible, hence presumably highly abundant. Some exotic populations do reach extreme densities (e.g., three hundred toads/hectare) around human habitations. Such densities are not known for native populations in commensal situations. Two seminatural populations in Panama were estimated at fifty to one hundred toads per hectare. Natural populations in savanna are probably ten to twenty-five toads per hectare at best, and rain-forest margin populations maximally are ten toads per hectare.

Marine toads are predominantly nocturnal, although the tadpoles and recent metamorphs have a large component of diurnal activity. During the day the toads remain sheltered beneath logs, rocks, roots, and such in small burrows. They begin to appear aboveground at dusk and in seminatural populations will be active for 2 or 3 hrs before disappearing for the night. On any given evening only a fraction of the population will be active— one-fourth to one-third on even the most ideal evenings. On the average a toad is active one evening out of three or four, and the pattern of activity is extremely variable.

Each toad appears to have several recognizable feeding stations, but on any given evening it will usually occupy only one. However, a shift can occur during a single evening, and on the next evening of activity the toad is most likely to appear at the new station. The shifting of feeding stations indicates that the toad is familiar with a fairly large forage area and uses landmarks to navigate in this area.

Activity is strongly influenced by daily and seasonal weather. The peak of foraging activity occurs in the early wet season and gradually declines throughout the wet season. There may be a minor rise at the beginning of the dry season, but the decline continues to a low at the end of the dry season. Within this general seasonal trend is a daily trend that shows increased activity with successive dry days following bouts of wet days in the midst of the wet season or the reverse for the dry seasons. These minitrends generally peak within 3 to 4 days after the change in weather pattern.

I am strongly impressed by the toad's sensitivity to the availability of water and speculate that its daily activity is greatly influenced by its needs for regulating its water economy. In spite of the marine toad's assumed impervious skin, it is highly susceptible to desiccation (at relative humidity of 75–80%, a 20 g toad reaches lethal water loss in 24 hr, a 100 g toad in 48 hr, and a 200 g toad in 72 hr (see Zug and Zug 1979, fig. 18). Thus desiccation during the dry season is potentially an important mortality factor.

The toxicity of parotoid secretion makes predation on late-term juveniles and adults unlikely or low. Birds, snakes, and small terrestrial mammals are likely to be the dominant predators on metamorphs and small juveniles. These life stages may suffer the highest mortality owing to predation. The jelly coat of the eggs is toxic (Licht 1968), and the skin of the tadpoles is distasteful (Wassersug 1971), so vertebrate predation is likely low. The intensity of invertebrate predation on the larval stage is unknown. Abiotic mortality (drying pools, etc.) may occasionally be extreme for the tadpoles.

Although the marine toad's reproduction has been assumed to be acyclic, such reproductive behavior has been demonstrated only for exotic populations. Native populations are largely confined to the seasonal tropics, and the reproduction of any population reflects the seasonality of its locale. Eggs are laid in the shallow margin of both permanent and temporary bodies of water—usually with little or no overhead canopy. A female will deposit from five thousand to twenty-five thousand eggs depending upon her size and health. Generally there is one major reproductive period at the junction of the dry and wet seasons; other minor peaks may occur at the end of the wet season or be initiated by heavy rains following an extended drought. Timing of reproduction seems to be such that metamorphosis occurs during periods of high humidity and prey abundance.

The growth of the toadlets is relatively rapid—0.65 mm/day. At this rate a toad would reach the size of sexual maturity (90–95 mm) in about 100 days. However, just as activity decreases with the progression of the wet season and the dry season, growth does likewise. Presumably, a toad requires one full year to reach the size of sexual maturity, although it may not actively breed until its second year. Male growth slows appreciably at sexual maturity. Female growth also slows at sexual maturity, although not as greatly as that of males. Furthermore, females continue to grow actively for 3 or 4 years after maturity but males apparently grow for only a single year. Thus adult females will tend to be larger than males.

*

Johnson, C. R. 1972. Thermal relations and daily variation in the thermal tolerance in *Bufo marinus*. *J. Herp.* 6:35–38.

Krakauer, T. 1968. The ecology of the Neotropical toad, *Bufo marinus*, in southern Florida. *Herpetologica* 24:214–21.

Licht, L. E. 1968. Unpalatability and toxicity of toad eggs. *Herpetologica* 24:93–98.

Wassersug, R. 1971. On the comparative palatability of some dry-season tadpoles from Costa Rica. *Am. Midl. Nat.* 86:101–9.

Zug, G. R.; Lindgren, E.; and Pippet, J. R. 1975. Distribution and ecology of the marine toad, *Bufo marinus*, in Papua New Guinea. *Pacific Sci.* 29:31–50.

Zug, G. R., and Zug, P. B. 1979. The marine toad, *Bufo marinus:* A natural history resumé of native populations. *Smithsonian Contrib. Zoo.* 284:1–58.

Caiman crocodilus (Caiman, Lagarto, Baba, Babilla, Cuajipalo, Cayman)

J. R. Dixon and M. A. Staton

This species (fig. 8.10) is one of the smallest of Western Hemisphere crocodilians and probably the most abundant in existence today. Adult males average 100 cm in snout-vent length, while females normally reach 80 cm. *Caiman crocodilus* ranges from southern Pacific Mexico south to Ecuador and from eastern Honduras east and south to the Amazon basin and central Brasil. In Costa Rica, caimans are found in both Atlantic and Pacific lowlands, occupying small creeks, ponds, playas, and occasionally brackish mangrove swamps and stormtide inner beach lowlands.

Ovarian development and courtship commence about 3 months before nesting (Staton and Dixon 1977). During courtship, adult males establish and patrol temporary aquatic territories. Two distinct tail displays, one perpendicular to the water's surface and one parallel, are frequent during this period. The latter seems to function in territoriality and courtship, since copulation has been seen only after this display.

Nesting periods are variable. For example, Chirivi-Gallego (1973) observed nesting toward the end of the dry season; Alvarez del Toro (1974) reports nesting toward the middle of the dry season; Staton and Dixon (1977) found nesting during the early wet season; and Medem (1958, 1960, 1962) observed nesting at all times other than the early wet season. Little is known of nesting in areas of permanent water.

The nest is a mound of materials immediately available in the nest area, such as grass, leaves, twigs, and soil. It

FIGURE 8.10. *Caiman crocodilus*, also commonly referred to as *Caiman sclerops*, is one of the most common and abundant crocodilians in Latin America (photo, M. A. Staton).

may be in flooded fields (eggs above water level), at water's edge, or 200 m or more from nearest water. Nests averaged 117 cm in length, 104 cm in width, and 44 cm in height in a study by Staton and Dixon (1977). Humidity and temperature reach levels outside the nest that would be lethal to developing embryos, but conditions vary little within the egg chamber. Staton and Dixon (1977) report average values of 90.5% relative humidity and 29.9° C inside the egg chamber.

Egg laying commences 2 to 6 days after nest construction begins. The smallest recorded nesting female measured 108 cm total length (Chirivi-Gallego 1973). A correlation between female size and either clutch or egg size, though suspected, has not been demonstrated. The size of eggs laid over a 3-month nesting period in the Venezuelan llanos during 1973 varied with date of laying (larger eggs generally produced earlier). In that study (Staton and Dixon 1977) eggs averaged 63.8 mm in length, 40.7 mm in width, and 59.9 g in weight. Assuming that larger eggs (and therefore larger hatchlings) represent an advantage during the first year of life of young caimans, a mechanism for the natural selection of fittest individuals seems evident.

Incubation lasts 73 to 75 days (Alvarez del Toro 1974; Staton and Dixon 1977). Hatchlings average 41 g in weight and 21 cm in total length. Vocalization of young within the eggs attracts adults and stimulates them to open the nest and release the hatchlings. While Staton and Dixon (1977) report only the female parent present at hatching, Alvarez del Toro (1974) saw parents of both sexes participate in nest opening and transfer the young to the nearest water.

Protection of the nest and young appears to be related to survival opportunities for the adult caiman concerned. During the intense dry season of the Venezuelan llanos, postnatal care lasted for a maximum of 4 months, after which females abandoned young to seek more permanent water (Staton and Dixon 1977). Postnatal care may last longer in areas of more permanent water. Young may remain together near the nest area for up to 18 months (Gorzula 1978).

Growth rates vary with food availability. For example, Gorzula (1978) noted that it took 6 years for individuals to reach 1 m in total length in parts of the Venezuelan llanos; in other areas, or in captivity, this length may be reached in 3 yeras (Blohm 1973; pers. obs.). Furthermore, Gorzula noted faster growth during wetter years in the llanos (accompanied by greater productivity and food availability).

Possible predators of young and juvenile *Caiman crocodilus* are white-necked herons, jabiru storks, wood storks, maguari storks, common egrets, anhingas, anacondas, raccoons, and possibly foxes. Eggs are preyed upon by foxes, tegu lizards, and man. Adults are preyed upon by large anacondas and man. Cannibalism has been noted (e.g., Staton and Dixon 1978). Mortality is high during the nesting phase and during the first few years of life.

Foods vary according to size and opportunity. Hatchlings and young feed primarily on aquatic insects. Older individuals subsist on a diet consisting mainly of fish and amphibians. Howler monkeys, capybaras, armadillos, and large birds have been eaten as carrion (Staton and Dixon 1978).

Caimans frequently bask along the banks of streams and ponds. The amount and temperature of the water, distance to water, available shade, and time of day play important roles in determining the amount of time spent basking, in the shade, or in the water. Body temperatures average 30° C (Staton and Dixon 1978). In some parts of the species' range, individuals are known to aestivate (Medem 1958) during the dry season.

*

Alvarez del Toro, M. 1974. *Los crocodylia de México.* Mexico: Instituto Mexicano Recursos Naturales Renovables, A. C.

Blohm, T. 1973. Convenencia de críar crocodilidos en Venezuela con fines económicos y para prevenir su extincion. Proc. Simposio Intl. sobre Fauna Silvestre y Pesca Fluvial y Lacustre Amazonica, Manaus, Brazil.

Chirivi-Gallego, H. 1973. Contribución al conocimiento de la babilla o yacare tinga (*Caiman crocodilus*) con notas acerca de su manejo y de otras especies de Crocodilia neotropicales. Proc Simposio Intl. sobre Fauna Silvestre y Pesca Fluvial y Lacustre Amazonica, Manaus, Brasil.

Gorzula, S. 1978. An ecological study of *Caiman crocodilus crocodilus* inhabiting savanna lagoons in the Venezuela llanos. *Oecologia* 35:21–34.

Medem, F. 1958. El conocimiento actual sobre la distribución geográfica y ecológica de los crocodylia en Colombia. *Rev. Univ. Nac. Colombia* 23:37–57.

———. 1960. Datos zoo-geográficos y ecológicos sobre los crocodylia y testudinata de los ríos Amazonas, Putumayo y Caqueta. *Caldasia* 8:341–51.

———. 1962. La distribución geográfica y ecológica de los crocodylia y testudinata en el departmento de Chocó. *Rev. Acad. Colombiana Cienc. Ex., Fis., Naturales* 11:279–303.

Staton, M., and Dixon, J. R. 1977. Breeding biology of the spectacled caiman, *Caiman crocodilus crocodilus*, in the Venezuelan llanos. *U.S.D.I. Fish Wildl. Serv. Wildl. Res. Rep.* 5:1–21.

———. 1978. Studies on the dry season biology of *Caiman crocodilus crocodilus* from the Venezuelan llanos. *Mem. Soc. Cienc. Nat. La Salle* 35 (1975):237–65.

Centrolenella fleischmanni (Ranita de Vidrio, Glass Frog)

R. W. McDiarmid

Frogs of the genus *Centrolenella* include about sixty-five species found in tropical moist forests of the New World from southern Mexico southward to Bolivia, Paraguay, and northern Argentina. They, together with *Centrolene geckoideum*, constitute the family Centrolenidae. Centrolenid frogs are Neotropical endemics and, like dendrobatids, are important components of most wet-forest assemblages. The family relationships are not well understood, but most herpetologists would ally them either with the Hylidae or the Leptodactylidae.

There are thirteen species of *Centrolenella* in Costa Rica. Their systematic relationships and distributions are discussed by Starrett and Savage (1973), who also present a key to Costa Rican species.

Centrolenid frogs are generally small (less than 50 mm) green arboreal species that are found along vegetated streams from sea level to nearly 3,800 m elevation. In many species the viscera and heart are visible through the skin, giving rise to the name "glass frog." All species for which data are available deposit their eggs on or beneath leaves overhanging streams (McDiarmid 1975, but there are errors in the figure captions). A few species occasionally attach their eggs to moss on branches. The eggs are enclosed in a gelatinous mass and may be deposited on the upper leaf surface, near the tip, or beneath the leaf. Those on the upper surface are usually dark (black or brown), are laid in a single layer, and have little protective jelly. Those put near the leaf tip may be dark or light and usually swell with water, increasing their total volume two to four times. As a result they become pendant and form a drip tip from the leaf. Eggs placed beneath the leaf are white or light green and have less jelly than the drip-tip types. Nonpigmented eggs that are exposed to direct sunlight suffer high mortality (McDiarmid, unpublished), which helps explain the pigmented nature of most of the clutches placed on the upper leaf surface. Also, the large jelly volume associated with the light-colored drip-tip types probably serves as a protective layer to prevent developmental abnormalities.

The eggs develop on the overhanging leaves for varying periods, from 8 to 20 or more days. The length of egg development on the leaf is more a reflection of local weather conditions than of variance in developmental times. Often clutches develop up to a point and then hatch during heavy rains. This facultative hatch serves to increase the probability that the tadpoles will reach the water when they drop off the leaf. This timing may also make the small tadpoles less visible to fish in the stream,

since water is often turbid during a heavy rain. Tadpoles dropped into a stream without the associated disturbance of raindrops on the water surface are quickly eaten by fish that respond to surface disturbance.

After a while the tadpoles become bright red and bury themselves in the decaying leaf litter and detritus that accumulates in slower parts of the stream. The bright color apparently is the result of an extensive network of surface capillaries and probably is associated with cutaneous respiration in this low-oxygen environment. Since the tadpoles are rarely seen, their bright colors apparently are not disadvantageous in terms of visibility to predators. The duration of larval life is unknown, but laboratory-reared tadpoles take several months to reach a size appropriate for metamorphosis (McDiarmid, unpublished). As they approach metamorphosis they begin to take on the characteristic adult coloration.

Adult males show varying degrees of territoriality depending on species and local densities. For most species, vocalization functions to space males and to attract females. The note-repetition rates are known to increase three to four times during male-male interactions (McDiarmid, unpublished). When vocal interactions fail to disperse potential male intruders, resident males frequently resort to physical defense. This male contact and defense has been described for *C. fleischmanni* and *C. valerioi* (McDiarmid and Adler 1974). Individual males may breed several times in a short period; nothing is known about female reproductive periodicity.

Parental care is another interesting aspect of the reproductive behavior of some species of *Centrolenella*. An ethocline from species lacking parental care to those with parental care exists in the *C. fleischmanni* group. In species with parental care the males are involved in egg attendance and guarding. In a comparison of two species, *C. colymbiphyllum* and *C. valerioi*, McDiarmid (1978) attributed the relatively higher survivorship of individual male *C. valerioi* offspring to the increased investment of males of *C. valerioi*, who spend 24 hr with their clutches, compared with male *C. colymbiphyllum*, who leave their clutches unattended during daylight. Predation by visual hunting predators, particularly wasps, accounted for most of the differences in survivorship of eggs and unhatched larvae between these two species.

The dorsal coloration of these two species also underscores the differences in parental behavior. *C. colymbiphyllum* is essentially a uniform green with small yellow dots. *C. valerioi* has a reticulate green pattern on a yellowish background. During the day an attending male *C. valerioi* is strikingly similar in appearance to his egg clutches. McDiarmid (1978) suggested that the dorsal coloration of *C. valerioi* evolved in response to its diurnal attendance at the egg clutch(es) in response to visually hunting diurnal predators. *C. colymbiphyllum* does not resemble its egg clutches, has the more typical diurnal behavior of frogs, and "sleeps" in the surrounding vegetation. As it gets dark, the male *C. colymbiphyllum* returns to the egg site and resumes calling.

Males of *Centrolenella fleischmanni* show varying degrees of fidelity to their call sites and in certain instances have been seen on or near their clutches several nights after they were laid. An interesting association between *C. fleischmanni* and a predaceous *Drosophila* has been studied by Villa (1977). In some situations predation by fly larvae may result in very high mortality for *C. fleischmanni* eggs. Considerably more work needs to be done on the behavioral and evolutionary responses of male *C. fleischmanni* to egg predators, especially to predation by flies.

*

McDiarmid, R. W. 1975. Glass frog romance along a tropical stream. *Terra Los Angeles County Mus.* 13:14–18.

————. 1978. Evolution of parental care in frogs. In *The development of behavior: Comparative and evolutionary aspects,* ed. G. M. Burghardt and M. Bekof, pp. 127–47. New York: Garland STPM Press.

McDiarmid, R. W., and Adler, K. 1974. Notes on territorial and vocal behavior of Neotropical frogs of the genus *Centrolenella*. *Herpetologica* 30:75–78.

Starrett, P. H., and Savage, J. M. 1973. The systematic status and distribution of Costa Rican glass-frogs, genus *Centrolenella* (family Centrolenidae), with description of a new species. *Bull. Southern California Acad. Sci.* 72:57–78.

Villa, J. 1977. A symbiotic relationship between frog (Amphibia, Anura, Centrolenidae) and fly larvae (Drosophilidae). *J. Herp.* 11:317–22.

Chelonia mydas (Tortuga, Tortuga Blanca, Green Turtle)

A. Carr

The sea turtles of the world (fig. 8.11, 8.19) belong to five genera, all represented in Costa Rica. Three of them—*Chelonia* (green turtle), *Eretmochelys* (hawksbill), and *Dermochelys* (leatherback)—occur on both the Pacific and the Caribbean coasts. *Lepidochelys* (ridley) forms huge breeding assemblages on Pacific beaches but is unknown on the Caribbean coast. The loggerhead (*Caretta*) is a nonbreeding visitant along the Caribbean shore, and though it probably strays into Pacific coastal waters is has not yet been recorded there.

The taxonomy of existing sea turtles is in an elementary state. *Caretta, Dermochelys,* and *Lepidochelys* each appears to be a circumtropical complex of partly isolated but intergrading forms. West Atlantic *Lepidochelys*

FIGURE 8.11. *Chelonia mydas,* adult female walking across beach sand. Tortuguero National Park, Costa Rica (photo, A. Carr).

kempi, which is essentially restricted to the Gulf of Mexico and Atlantic coasts of the United States, is specifically distinct from *L. olivacea,* which ranges widely in the Indo-Pacific, in West Africa, and along the Atlantic coasts of South America. The only distinct localized species of any marine turtle genus is the Australian flatback, *Chelonia depressa,* which ranges along the Queensland coast and through Torres Strait to northernmost western Australia. For the rest, *Chelonia* is a taxonomic mess, and Costa Rica is fortunate in housing the two relatively well-differentiated terminal forms of a world-circling loop of races that are the despair of taxonomists and zoogeographers.

Chelonia is easily identifiable by conformation and scale differences. There are four pairs of lateral laminae on the carapace, as in hawksbills, and only one pair of elongate and short prefrontals on the top of the head between the eyes, instead of two pair, as in the hawksbill. The fore flippers are very long, and the head is short and rounded—not narrow and bird-jawed as in the hawksbill. The average overall shell length of the Caribbean form is about 100 cm; the Pacific population is a little smaller. The most obvious character separating mature individuals of *C. agassizi* from the Pacific and *C. mydas* is the melanistic tendency of the former, in which the shell and upper soft parts are often deep black, and black pigmentation gives the plastron a bluish cast. The plastron of Caribbean *C. mydas* is usually uniform light lemon white; the upper soft parts are gray, and the carapace is tan or olive, sometimes rayed or mottled. Another trait that is variable but of use in distinguishing *C. mydas* and *C. agassizi* is the outline of the carapace. In *C. agassizi* the shell is deeper and more straight-sloped than that of *C. mydas,* which is usually lower and more evenly curved. If green turtles existed only in Costa Rica, the Atlantic and Pacific forms could easily be identified with zoological keys, and there would be no doubt that separate species are involved. As the situation is, one must make up one's own mind whether to call the Pacific black "green" turtle *C. agassizi* or *C. mydas agassizi,* because if one were to inspect the whole series of circumtropical populations from Puntarenas to Tortuguero the distinguishing features would be seen to overlap in confusing ways.

In the Caribbean there are only two sizable breeding aggregations of *Chelonia.* One occurs at Aves Island, 100 miles from Monserrat, the other at Tortuguero, Costa Rica. Green turtles of the Brazilian coast breed mostly at Ascension Island in the central equatorial Atlantic, and on the coast of Surinam. Smaller colonies nest elsewhere, and isolated nestings occur along suitable shores as far north as Florida.

Except for some observations of Cornelius (1976), little has been learned of the reproductive ecology of the Pacific population of *Chelonia* in Costa Rica. Tag recoveries suggest that some interchange occurs with stock in the Galápagos Islands (B. Pritchard, pers. comm.).

The nesting population at Tortuguero, 50 miles up the Caribbean coast from Puerto Limón, has been under continuous observation since 1955. A tagging program begun then has been resumed every season, and recoveries of tags on the nesting beach and at a distance from it have revealed a number of features of the life cycle (Carr, Carr, and Meylan, 1978).

The nesting season extends from early July into October, with the peak usually coming in the second half of August. Records show that a female may come ashore to lay eggs from one to seven times during her season at the breeding ground, the average being two or three. Meylan (1978) has shown that between nesting emergences the females remain in the vicinity of the nesting beach, moving back and forth along the shore between the bounding river mouths and not going far offshore.

Of more than seventeen thousand turtles tagged at Tortuguero, none has been recorded nesting on any other beach. This strongly suggests that the mature turtles are coming back to their natal shore to breed; but this cannot be proved because of the difficulty of marking the hatchlings by any lasting means. Once a female turtle begins her reproductive regimen, however, she faithfully returns to the 22 miles of the Tortuguero shore. Besides this tendency to go back to Costa Rica and seek out the section between Parismina and the mouth of Río Tortuguero, there is a statistically demonstrable tendency for

females to nest near their previous nest sites. Schulz (1975) found the Surinam colony to be somewhat less site-tenacious, although with a clear tendency to return to subsections of the 30-mile section of coast where his tagging is done.

The nesting behavior of all sea turtles is strikingly similar, though not identical. The nesting of the Tortuguero population was described by Carr and Ogren (1960).

No sea turtle population has been found to be composed of females that nest every year. The remigratory periodicity of the Costa Rican colony has been determined in some detail. Of some fourteen hundred remigrations that have been recorded at Tortuguero, only six occurred after one-year absences. Three years is the most frequent period, with two years next, and then four years. Longer intervals may occur, but these cannot be clearly detected because of the possibility of missed arrivals. A turtle is not locked into a steady remigratory rhythm. One season she may return after an absence of two years, the next time after three, then after two again, and so on. Neither the lack of one-year remigratory periods nor the causes of the modulation of period length are understood. They may, in part at least, reflect ecological conditions in the foraging habitat or along the migratory routes to the rookery. The search for the factors involved is an important obligation of future sea turtle research.

The Costa Rican green turtle is a good subject for such research, because its chief nesting and foraging grounds are both known. Tag returns show that although some turtles migrate to the Tortuguero breeding grounds from all through the western Caribbean, most Tortuguero turtles go to the Miskito Bank area of Nicaragua when they finish nesting. Miskito Bank is covered with extensive areas of submarine spermatophytes, making it one of the best feeding grounds in the world for *Chelonia.* Since primitive times, the Miskito Indians have exploited the turtle colony, and during the past century most of the green turtles that entered the United States market were brought from there by turtle schooners from Grand Cayman. Nietschmann (1979) described the intimate interaction between the Indians and the green turtle of the Miskitia. Mortimer (1976) has just completed a study of the feeding habits of the colony. Bjorndal (1979) studied their nutritional ecology, finding among other things that they digest cellulose as efficiently as cattle.

One of the wholly unexplained features of green turtle demography is the fluctuation in the breeding populations. This tendency is worldwide—wherever nesting colonies have been kept under observation, marked change has been noted from year to year in the numbers of nestings. Some observers attribute these puzzling changes to a breakdown in philopatry; that is, they suggest that nestings drop in some seasons because turtles go

391

somewhere else to lay that year. That explanation may have limited validity at some rookeries, but it certainly does not hold in Costa Rica. The Tortuguero nesting colony of 1979 was the smallest in twenty-four seasons; only 428 females nested on the 5-mile research section of the nesting shore. The next year, 1980, there were 3,192 arrivals, representing the biggest colony ever recorded at Tortuguero. A part of this fluctuation may be caused by congruent cycle shifts that either bring many turtles in early or cause them to prolong absences that routinely would have ended the season before. However, the increasing strength of recent peaks suggests that because of the protection the colony has received during the past twenty years in Costa Rica and during the past five years in Nicaragua a small real increase in total population may have occured.

Important gaps remain in what is known of the ecology of the green turtle. The life cycle involves a series of developmental and periodic shifts in habitat, and not much has been learned about the habits of the animal in any of these beyond what tagging reveals. When the young turtles hatch, they swim seaward and are lost to view for about a year. Some probably get into sargassum rafts, although how prevalent this is, or how long they stay there, is unknown (Carr and Meylan 1983). At weights of 0.5 kg or so they begin to reappear in inshore waters, moving from one locality to another as increasing size brings changes in feeding habits. At weights of around 40 kg Caribbean green turtles appear to take up residence in or around grass flats. On reaching weights of about 60 kg their migratory breeding regimen begins.

The worst blank places in the knowledge of sea turtle biology are our ignorance of the "lost year" ecology of the hatchling; the routes and guidance mechanisms of the migratory travel; and the age at sexual maturity and span of sexual longevity. Courtship, mating, and the ecology of both males and females in the internesting habitat also require more attention. These gaps not only are scientifically distressing but also hinder efforts to give the species the effective protection that will be required if the steady decline of most of its populations is to be controlled.

*

Bjorndal, K. A. 1979. Cellulose digestion and volatile fatty acid production in the green turtle, *Chelonia mydas*. *Comp. Biochem. Physiol.* 63A:127–33.

Carr, A. F.; Carr, M. H.; and Meylan, A. B. 1978. The ecology and migrations of sea turtles. 7. The West Caribbean green turtle colony. *Bull. Am. Mus. Nat. Hist.* 162:1–46.

Carr, A. F., and Meylan, A. B. 1983. Evidence of passive migration of green turtle hatchlings in Sargassum. *Copeia,* in press.

Carr, A. F., and Ogren, L. 1960. The ecology and migrations of sea turtles. 4. The green turtle in the Caribbean Sea. *Bull. Am. Mus. Nat. Hist.* 121:1–48.

Cornelius, S. E. 1976. Marine turtle nesting activity at Playa Naranjo, Costa Rica. *Brenesia* 8:1–27.

Meylan, A. B. 1978. The behavioral ecology of the West Caribbean green turtle (*Chelonia mydas*) in the internesting habitat. M.S. thesis, University of Florida.

Mortimer, J. A. 1976. Observations on the feeding ecology of the green turtle, *Chelonia mydas,* in the western Caribbean. M.S. thesis, University of Florida.

Nietschmann, B. 1979. Ecological change, inflation, and migration in the far western Caribbean. *Geograph. Rev.* 69:1–24.

Schulz, J. P. 1975. Sea turtles nesting in Surinam. *Zool. Verhand., Rijksmuseum Nat. Hist. Leiden* 143: 1–144.

Clelia clelia (Zopilota, Musarana)

N. J. Scott

Clelia clelia (Colubridae) is found in the tropical lowlands of southern Mexico and Central and South America. In Costa Rica it may be found in all but the driest lowlands. A very similar smaller species (*C. scytalina*) is found at higher elevations. Adults are strong, large (to 2.5 m) black or gray snakes that usually forage at night. The juveniles are bright red with black heads and yellow collars, but by the time the snakes are 1 m long the red and white has been largely obscured by black pigment.

The musurana feeds most commonly on other snakes, even the deadly terciopelo (*Bothrops asper*), although it sometimes eats large lizards and mammals. In Brazil a campaign was started in the 1930s to raise musuranas and to release them as viper-control agents. The impracticalities of the undertaking soon terminated the project, but campesinos throughout Latin America know and appreciate *Clelia* perhaps more than any other snake species.

Clelia is one of the few snakes that possess grooved fangs associated with venom glands on the rear of the upper jaw but that also constrict their prey. The fangs and venom are employed in feeding, but I have never known a specimen to bite in defense. The problems of holding strong, slippery prey while chewing and allowing the slow-acting venom to take effect were presumably the evolutionary forces that selected for the unusual combination of constriction and envenomation.

Conophis lineatus (Guarda Camino)

N. J. Scott

Conophis (Colubridae) is a genus of medium-sized (to 125 cm), racerlike snakes endemic to the dry lowlands of Middle America. These snakes are found in the daytime on the forest floor, below second-growth vegetation of various ages, and in open pasture and roadsides. As the name implies, the head is cone-shaped and scarcely differentiated from the body. *Conophis lineatus* (fig. 8.12) is one of the two Costa Rican species of *Conophis,* and it is common in the dry northwest and the Meseta Central; it also occurs in second growth in Corcovado National Park (D. H. Janzen, pers. comm.). This fast striped snake bites fiercely when grabbed. The long fangs on the rear of its upper jaw slash the skin of prey or captor and introduce a strong venom. Its bites cause pain, local swelling, and hematoma, and serum oozes from the slashes. The symptoms may persist as long as two days (Johanbocke 1974; Wellman 1963). The wound may bleed freely for an hour or more, suggesting an anticoagulant action of the venom (D. H. Janzen, pers. comm.). The bite is more venomous to humans than that of any other Costa Rican snake except the corals, vipers, or sea snake.

This snake may be encountered at midday as it actively forages along the ground for lizards (especially *Cnemidophorus*) and the eggs of ground-nesting birds such as the ground cuckoo and doves. The longitudinal gray white stripes against the dark gray brown background blend well with grass litter. In captivity *Conophis* also eats frogs, small mammals, and snakes (Wellman 1963; pers. obs.).

*

Johanbocke, M. M. 1974. Effects of a bite from *Conophis lineatus* (Squamata: Colubridae). *Bull. Phil. Herp. Soc.* 22:39.
Wellman, J. 1963. A revision of snakes of the genus *Conophis* (family Colubridae) from Middle America. *Publ. Mus. Nat. Hist. Univ. Kansas* 15:251–95.

FIGURE 8.12. *Conophis lineatus,* 56 cm total length. Adult from roadside herbaceous vegetation. Santa Rosa National Park, December 1979 (photo, D. H. Janzen).

Crotalus durissus (Cascabel, Tropical Rattlesnake)

N. J. Scott

This species (Crotalidae) (fig. 8.13) and its close relatives are the only rattlesnakes found in tropical America. The color pattern of the group is characterized by a pair of longitudinal stripes on the neck that give way to diamonds on the body and by a dark, usually black, tail. This species ranges in the dry lowlands and middle elevations from southern Mexico to Brazil and Paraguay, with zoogeographically interesting gaps in Panama and northern Brazil (Hoge 1966; Klauber 1972). In Costa Rica it occurs in forest and open country in the dry northwestern parts and a few relict areas on the Meseta Central (Taylor et al. 1974; Picado T. 1976). It is a large snake, growing to 1.8 m on a diet composed largely of mammals and (in Costa Rica) large lizards (Picado T. 1976). It bears live young, as do all rattlesnakes. Young

FIGURE 8.13. *Crotalus durissus,* 43 cm long, 2 months old. Santa Rosa National Park, July 1980 (photo, D. H. Janzen).

appear at the beginning of the rainy season in Santa Rosa National Park (D. H. Janzen, pers. comm.).

The tropical rattlesnake produces a powerful venom with a stronger neurotoxic component than is usual in North American rattlesnakes (Klauber 1972). March (1928) vividly describes the blindness, paralysis, and suffocation characteristically found in persons bitten by tropical rattlesnakes in Honduras.

In Central America this rattlesnake is often reluctant to use its rattles, although they are well developed. It is an aggressive snake when aroused, raising its head well off of the ground and even attacking at times (March 1928; Picado T. 1976). It is resistant to its own venom (D. H. Janzen, pers. comm.).

*

Hoge, A. R. 1966. Preliminary account on Neotropical Crotalinae (Serpentes: Viperidae). *Mem. Inst. Butantan* 32(1965):109–84.

Klauber, L. M. 1972. *Rattlesnakes: Their habits, life histories, and influence on mankind.* 2 vols. 2d ed. Berkeley: University of California Press.

March, D. D. H. 1928. 45. Field notes on the Neotropical rattlesnake (*Crotalus terrificus*). *Bull. Antivenin Inst. Am.* 2:55–63.

Picado T., C. 1976. *Serpientes venenosas de Costa Rica.* 2d ed. San José: Editorial Universidad de Costa Rica–Editoral Costa Rica.

Taylor, R. T.; Flores, A.; Flores, G.; and Bolaños, R. 1974. Geographical distribution of Viperidae, Elapidae and Hydrophiidae in Costa Rica. *Rev. Biol. Trop.* 21:383–97.

Ctenosaura similis (Garrobo, Iguana Negra, Ctenosaur)

H. S. Fitch and J. Hackforth-Jones

The ctenosaur (garrobo, iguana negra) (fig. 8.14) is a large iguanid lizard that ranges from southern Mexico to Panama. Closely related allopatric species occur over much of Mexico. The flesh is edible; it is generally preferred over that of the iguana (*Iguana iguana*) and is credited with medicinal properties, especially as a cure for impotence. Thousands of ctenosaurs are sold each year in the *mercados* of several dozen Middle American cities, and countless others are captured and eaten by *campesinos* throughout most of its range.

The color pattern is cryptic. It is subject to local, individual, sexual, and ontogenetic variation, and fairly rapid change is possible, through lightening or darkening, according to temperature and activity. Adults are marked with broad, poorly defined transverse dark bands (usually four on the body) on a tan ground color (fig. 8.14*b*). The bands tend to be split middorsally by lighter areas. The limbs are similarly banded, and the tail is pale

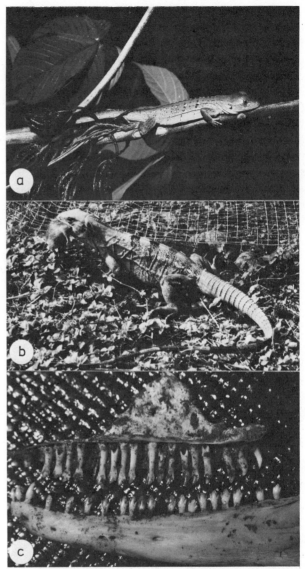

FIGURE 8.14. *Ctenosaura similis. a,* One-month-old, 6 cm snout-vent lizard sleeping on vegetation at night. *b,* Three-year-old, 32 cm snout-vent wild adult that has just captured a free-running 90 g *Sigmodon hispidus. c, Top,* inside view of upper mandible of adult, snout to right; *bottom,* outside view of lower mandible of adult, snout to left. Santa Rosa National Park, June 1980 (photos, D. H. Janzen).

tan. The dorsal surface may have spots of dull red or orange, especially in the breeding season. On the body the scalation is fine and granular, but there is a dorsal crest of enlarged, sickle-shaped scales up to 12 mm in old males, much shorter and flattened in females. The tail has whorls of large spiny scales and serves as a weapon of defense. There is a transverse fold of skin on the throat. In 893 adults, males averaged 345 mm (239–489) and feamles 276 mm (204–347) in snout-vent length, with mean weights of 1,034 g and 575 g. The males have relatively broader heads, more massive jaw musculature, and more elongate muzzles than females. The pleurodont teeth are large, slightly recurved, and caniniform in front; those of the posterior two-thirds of the tooth row are smaller and tricuspidate (fig. 8.14c).

Ctenosaurs are easily distinguished from iguanas, in that iguanas have a large scale on the side of the head slightly below and behind the rear angle of the lower jaw, have greener coloration and longer tails, and are found only in the moistest riparian sites in deciduous forest habitats. In Costa Rica, ctenosaurs occur throughout the deciduous and semievergreen forests of lowland Guanacaste Province and Puntarenas Province, and in the beach-edge vegetation along the entire Pacific coast, even at the wettest sites (e.g., Corcovado National Park). As mentioned below, they are generally associated with drier habitats and low forest and scrublands over most of their range. In Guanacaste Province, however, in those areas where substantial forest remains (e.g., Santa Rosa National Park), even the largest adults are highly arboreal as well as terrestrial. They roost at night in tree hollows as much as 20 m off the ground, climb far out into flimsy tree crowns to forage, and when chased, are as likely to climb a tree as to run off across the ground.

Adult ctenosaurs are heliothermic. They emerge from shelter only when the sun is shining and do not remain out long when the sky becomes overcast. Body temperature of 36° to 37° C is preferred and is maintained by behavioral thermoregulation. When they are out, ctenosaurs spend most of their time basking. At relatively low temperatures they sprawl on the substrate with maximum surface exposed to sunshine. During warming, successive postures typically involve facing away from sun, raising the head, raising the forequarters, and orienting with body held erect against a supporting object that shields it from sunshine except for the head or forequarters.

Ctenosaurs are adaptable and occur in varied habitats including margins of lowland rain forest, vacant city lots and gardens, cemeteries, and road edges bordering cultivated fields. The preferred habitat is xeric open woodland, especially where there are rock outcrops and boulders or an abundance of dead wood with logs and standing hollow snags. Each lizard centers its activity on a shelter, which is most often a ground burrow but may be a tree cavity or even a hollow fence post. The lizards excavate their own burrows. They are strong diggers, aided by their heavy, sharp curved claws. Burrows are often situated beneath boulders or tree roots, where they are protected from digging predators. Well-situated burrows last for many years and may be used by a succession of individuals. Typically the burrows are flat-bottomed, wider than high, and arched above. They are wide enough to permit the lizard to turn around. The tunnels are winding, and some are branched. Some are not much

over 1 m long. Some burrows, remote from the lizard's center of activity, are used for escape in an emergency but are not used regularly. Ctenosaur burrows provide shelter for many other kinds of animals, including mammals, snakes, other lizards, and assorted invertebrates. An elevated perch near the shelter is required for basking and display. About 22 m is a typical radius for the animal's normal activities, but adults range more widely than yearlings, and males range farther than females.

Ctenosaurs are territorial, with each individual defending its shelter and perch and adjacent areas. However, defense does not ordinarily involve the entire home range. Territorial aggression varies seasonally and is much more developed in males than in females. Firstyear young show mutual aggression and territorial spacing, but they do not challenge adults. Male and female may associate amicably as a consort pair sharing the same shelter and perch. Such associations are ephemeral, and after a period of days the male usually wanders away to find another female, since there are usually several within his range. At high population densities there is much overlapping of areas; there are many subordinate individuals that do not defend territories except against smaller and weaker opponents, and a sort of social hierarchy prevails. Actual fighting is infrequent. The stereotyped bobbing display serves to assert territorial tenure and to threaten potential rivals. The display is speciesspecific but fairly typical of those that occur in iguanids in general. It consists of ten to twelve head bobs with changing rate and amplitude. The first bob is performed slowly; the head is raised to the maximum possible height then lowered more rapidly, and there are several lower and faster bobs followed by several short, quick upward jerks of the head.

Ctenosaurs are primarily vegetarian. In the rainy season, when succulant growth is abundant, food is easily obtained, and the lizards are not highly selective, cropping low vegetation. They may damage cultivated crops, such as beans, in the early stages of growth. In the dry season, when food is much scarcer, flowering and fruiting trees become important sources. Individuals may make unusually long trips to such trees, and several ctenosaurs may gather to feed in the same tree. Among others, flowers of *Tabebuia rosea* and *T. ochracea* and fruits of *Spondias purpurea* are important dry-season foods. In general the vegetation taken is tender and nutritious, low in fiber and high in protein. Ctenosaurs are predators at times and have been recorded as feeding on a molossid bat, rodents (*Oryzomys, Sigmodon, Scotinomys*), lizards (skink, *Cnemidophorus, Sceloporus*) and lizard eggs, frogs, young chicks and other small birds, and a variety of insects and spiders. Also, adult ctenosaurs have been found to contain eggs of their own species in their digestive tracts, and once the tail of an immature ctenosaur was found, indicating cannibalism of sorts. The young take a relatively high proportion of animal food, and some have been found with their stomachs crammed with insects such as grasshoppers, but even hatchlings take some vegetation.

Ctenosaurs ordinarily attain sexual maturity late in their second year at a snout-vent length a little over 200 mm. There is a single annual clutch, and each female produces eggs. This is one of the most productive of lizards. Clutch size is strongly related to body size and age, with from twelve to eighty-eight eggs per clutch. Second-year primiparas average about twenty-two eggs per clutch, but the largest females average about seventy. Clutches averaged forty-three in a random sample of sixty-nine females. Breeding may begin in December and extends through January and part of February. Abdominal fat bodies are prominent in both sexes at this time of year and are usually 6–7% of body weight in reproductive females. Ovulation is concentrated at about mid-February, and egg laying occurs about 5 weeks later. Oviducal eggs averaged about 22% (16–40%) of total female weight. The clutch occupies much of the body cavity, and females may feed little or not at all during the late stages of internal egg development. The eggs are laid in burrows in open, sunny places, and several females (up to five) may oviposit in the same burrow system, but with each clutch in a separate chamber, a widened pocket with fine, damp earth as an incubation medium. Three nest burrows ranged from 11 m to 22 m in total length, with tunnels 0.20–0.36 m below the ground surface, winding in a complex pattern with loops and dead ends.

Hatching occurs from April into July. In northwestern Costa Rica it is concentrated in May, after the first heavy rains end the dry season. Hatchlings are 48–58 mm in snout-vent length and weigh 3.5–4.5 g. They are strikingly different from adults in appearance and behavior. At some times and places, at least, the hatchlings are pale tan with cryptic markings of darker brown reticulations. At first they run on the ground in open places. They are light and slender, exceedingly active, swift, and alert. They are much more slender than adults, with short heads and attenuated tails (220% snout-vent length vs. 150% in larger adults). They are nomadic and depend on speed and agility rather than on specific shelters for escape from danger. Some apparently are bright green when they hatch, and tan-colored individuals soon turn green, matching the verdant vegetation that springs up at the beginning of the rainy season. These bright green juveniles assume scansorial habits, usually climbing on low trees and bushes (fig. 8.14a). They are much less wary than adults and can usually be approached within a few meters. Their density is rapidly reduced by predators, including various large snakes (notably *Trimorphodon biscutatus*), hawks, jays, and perhaps small carnivores such as skunks and raccoons. Growth is rapid at first, with a daily increment of as much as 0.6 mm, but it slows to half that rate before the end of the first year. At an age of 4 months, young have approximately doubled their length at hatching, and they have quadrupled it by the time they reach adolescence late in the second year. Even then they are less than half the maximum snout-vent length of adults. Although longevity is unknown, it seems that adults may survive for many years, continuing to grow slowly.

*

Fitch, H. S., and Henderson, R. W. 1978. Ecology and exploitation of *Ctenosaura similis*. *Univ. Kansas Sci. Bull.* 51:483–500.

Rand, A. S. 1978. Reptilian arboreal folivores. In *The ecology of arboreal folivores,* ed. G. G. Montgomery, pp. 115–22. Washington, D.C.: Smithsonian Institution Press.

Dendrobates granuliferus and *Dendrobates pumilio* (Ranita Roja, Rana Venenosa, Poison Dart Frogs)

M. L. Crump

Dendrobates granuliferus and *Dendrobates pumilio* are small, red diurnal frogs of the family Dendrobatidae with allopatric geographic distributions. *Dendrobates granuliferus* is confined to Costa Rica, where it occurs from sea level to 700 m, in lowland forests of the Golfo Dulce region of the Pacific coast (Silverstone 1975). Populations of *D. pumilio* are found at elevations from sea level to 960 m; the species' range extends from lowland forests of the Caribbean drainage of Central America, from northern Nicaragua through Costa Rica to western Panama (Silverstone 1975). The black and bright green *Dendrobates auratus* (fig. 8.15) is common on the forest floor in Corcovado National Park.

The two species described herein are closely related and belong to the "pumilio group" as defined by Silverstone (1975). Although both species are red in dorsal color, they are saily distinguished by skin texture and by venter and hind-limb coloration. *Dendrobates granuliferus* is the slightly smaller species (snout-vent length of adults to 22 mm) and has a strongly granular dorsum; the dorsum is red, without black flecks or spots, and the limbs and venter are green or blue green, with black spots on the dorsal surface of the hind limbs. *Dendrobates pumilio* is a slightly larger frog (snout-vent length of adults to 24 mm) with a smooth or only slightly granular red dorsum; the dorsal pattern is extremely variable geographically, some individuals being uniformly red and others having black dots or spots on the dorsum. The limbs and venter of *D. pumilio* are either red or partly or entirely blue or black. In both species the male has a

FIGURE 8.15. *Dendrobates auratus,* young adult (black with bright green markings), on grass blades. August 1980, Sirena, Corcovado National Park, Osa Peninsula, Costa Rica (photo, D. H. Janzen). This frog is similar in life form to *Dendrobates granuliferus* and *D. pumilio.*

darkly pigmented gular vocal sac, whereas the female's throat region is red.

The common name of these frogs is "poison arrow frogs," or more correctly "poison dart frogs." The name stems from the fact that the Chocó Indians of western Colombia use the alkaloid poisons secreted from dendrobatid skin glands for poisoning their blowgun darts. Neither *D. granuliferus* nor *D. pumilio* has been documented to be used in this manner; their toxins are much less potent than those of *Phyllobates,* the genus used by the Indians for poisoning darts (Myers, Daly, and Malkin 1978). For a discussion of the chemical composition of these skin toxins see Myers and Daly (1976). The combination of the bright coloration and the toxicity of the skin of dendrobatids suggests that these frogs are classic examples of aposematic coloration. One explanation given for these adaptations relates to the foraging strategy of these diurnal frogs. Most species feed primarily on ants and termites. Because their prey items are small and the frogs must expend much time and energy foraging, they are potentially exposed to high predation pressure. Thus, toxic skin and warning coloration may have evolved as antipredator mechanisms.

The vocalizations of *D. granuliferus* and *D. pumilio* are very similar and have been described as "insect-like buzzes" and "insect-like chirps" (Savage 1968). For an extensive analysis of spectrograms for the two species see Myers and Daly (1976). Goodman (1971) and Crump

(1972) studied vocalization of *D. granuliferus* on the Osa Peninsula. They found that males called during daylight hours, from sites 0.1–2 m above the ground—tree trunks, limbs, stems, logs, and leaves. The elevated sites presumably allow the calls to be heard at greater distances. When calling, males raise the anterior portion of the body and hold the forelimbs nearly vertical. Crump (1972) found that nearest-neighbor distances for seventeen calling males ranged from 3.1 to 4.8 m; most males called consistently from one site during the 5 days of observation and defended their calling territories by a combination of physical combat and vocalization. Aggressive behavior includes both belly-to-belly grasps and amplexus type grasps (both inguinal and axillary); during much of the encounters, the frogs emit a sporadic buzz call. Male vocalization is also used in attracting females and plays an integral role in the mating sequence, during which the male calls and leads the female to an appropriate oviposition site (Crump 1972). Vocalization has also been studied in *D. pumilio* (Bunnell 1973). Bunnell reported that males distribute themselves uniformly within suitable habitat at an interindividual distance of 2–3 m. Individual calling sites remained constant for a least a week and were maintained by vocalizations. The call serves as an effective eistance advertising mechanism, since individuals respond to intruding males by changing the rate and temporal patterning of their own calls. As in *D. granuliferus,* male *D. pumilio* reinforce territorial defense by attack and physical combat. Bunnell noted no difference between the vocalization given when a female approached a male and the apparent territorial call.

Reproduction in *Dendrobates* involves deposition of eggs on land in moist situations, with subsequent carrying of the tadpoles to water on the dorsum of an adult. Amplexus is absent from all members of the genus studied so far. Oviposition in *D. granuliferus* has been observed by Crump (1972) on the Osa Peninsula. Once a male has attracted a female by calling, he scouts ahead for an appropriate oviposition site and she follows. When she lags behind, he stops and calls softly, waiting for her to catch up. Tactile courtship behavior consists of the female's rubbing the male's head and chin with her head. The two frogs eventually position themselves vent to vent, facing away from each other. Presumably, as the female releases the eggs, the male releases sperm. Clutch size of four pairs observed in the field ranged from three to four ($\bar{x} = 3.5$). Only the females have been reported to carry tadpoles (Wells 1977). Courtship and mating in *D. pumilio* is similar to that in *D. granuliferus,* but involves fewer tactile interactions. Limerick (1980) reported the first field observations of courtship and oviposition in *D. pumilio;* these observations were made at Finca La Selva, in Heredia Province. Females approach calling males and follow them to appropriate oviposition sites (usually dry, curled leaves or dry leaves covered by other leaves, on the ground). The male deposits sperm on a leaf; after the male moves off the spot, the female deposits eggs in the same place. Clutch size ranges from three to five eggs ($\bar{x} = 3.5, N = 11$). Seven days after oviposition, Limerick saw a female pick up a single tadpole and carry it away, presumably to an aquatic development site. In captivity, both males and females carry the tadpoles to water (Wells 1977, from S. Rand, pers. comm.; Crump, pers. obs.). Clutch size of captive pairs ranges from six to sixteen eggs (Oertter 1953).

Recently a fascinating discovery concerning the reproductive behavior of *D. pumilio* was made with captive individuals. Weygoldt (1980) reported that in addition to attending the eggs and transporting the larvae to water, the female attends the tadpoles and provides them with unfertilized, nutritive eggs. As the female approaches the water-filled bromeliad, the tadpole signals its presence by stiffening its tail and vibrating it rapidly, producing conspicuous circular movements in the water. The female then deposits an unfertilized egg, which the tadpole eats by bitting a hole in the jelly capsule and sucking out the contents. The female provides a tadpole with from seven to eleven eggs, at intervals ranging from 1 to 9 days. This is the *only* documented case in which a vertebrate regularly produces nutritive eggs and brings them to free-living offspring. The behavior has been confirmed by another report for *D. pumilio* from Panama (Graeff and Schulte 1980). How widespread this behavior is among the dendrobatids (or anurans in general) is anybody's guess. We need *many* more detailed field observations concerning courtship and parental care behavior for the poison dart frogs.

*

Bunnell, P. 1973. Vocalizations in the territorial behavior of the frog *Dendrobates pumilio. Copeia* 1973:277–84.

Crump, M. L. 1972. Territoriality and mating behavior in *Dendrobates granuliferus* (Anura: Dendrobatidae). *Herpetologica* 28:195–98.

Goodman, D. E. 1971. Territorial behavior in a Neotropical frog, *Dendrobates granuliferus. Copeia* 1971: 365–70.

Graeff, D., and Schulte, R. 1980. Neue Erkenntnisse zur Brutbiologie von *Dendrobates pumilio. Herpetofauna* 2:17–22.

Limerick, S. 1980. Courtship behavior and oviposition of the poison-arrow frog *Dendrobates pumilio. Herpetologica* 26:69–71.

Myers, C. W., and Daly, J. W. 1976. Preliminary evaluation of skin toxins and vocalizations in taxonomic and evolutionary studies of poison-dart frogs (Dendrobatidae). *Bull. Am. Mus. Nat. Hist.* 157:175–262.

Myers, C. W.; Daly, J. W.; and Malkin, B. 1978. A dangerously toxic new frog (*Phylloabtes*) used by Embera Indians of western Colombia, with discussion of blowgun fabrication and dart poisoning. *Bull. Am. Mus. Nat. Histo.* 161:307–66.

Oertter, J. 1953. Nochmals *Dendrobates typographicus:* Das Erdbeerfröschchen. *Aquar. Terrar. Z.* 6:260–62.

Savage, J. M. 1968. The dendrobatid frogs of Central America. *Copeia* 1968:745–76.

Silverstone, P. A. 1975. A revision of the poison-arrow frogs of the genus *Dendrobates* Wagler. *Nat. Hist. Mus. Los Angeles County Sci. Bull.* 21:1–55.

Wells, K. D. 1977. The courtship of frogs. In *The reproductive biology of amphibians,* ed. D. H. Taylor and S. I. Guttman, pp. 233–62. New York: Plenum.

Weygoldt, P. 1980. Complex brood care and reproductive behavior in captive poison-arrow frogs, *Dendrobates pumilio* O. Schmidt. *Behav. Ecol. Sociobiol.* 7: 329–32.

Drymarchon corais (Zopilota, Indigo)

N. J. Scott

This widespread species (fig. 8.16) is found associated with riverbeds, swamps, and seasonal marshes throughout lowland tropical America. Two disjunct populations

FIGURE 8.16. *Drymarchon corais* disappears into shadows on rocky creek bed; visible portion is 1 m long, with posterior half black and anterior half dirty beige. March 1980, Río Poza Salada, Santa Rosa National Park, Costa Rica (photo, D. H. Janzen).

occur in east Texas and in Florida-Georgia. In Costa Rica the species may be found almost anywhere below 1,000 m elevation. This impressive beige to brown snake may reach 4.5 m in length and has a short lateral diagonal dark bar just behind the head. It is diurnal, a racerlike terrestrial and aquatic hunter. It may also climb low bushes.

The food habits of the indigo are more catholic than those of probably any other snake in Costa Rica. Any kind of vertebrate may be taken, including fish, eggs, small turtles, snakes, lizards, frogs, mammals, and birds. It has no venom and it does not constrict; it depends on its unusually strong jaws to subdue prey. Large adults are commonly encountered weaving a thorough ground-covering apparent search pattern over rock-strewn dry riverbeds in Santa Rosa National Park. Investigating each crevice and holding its head close to the soil, the snake gives the appearance of looking for odor-cues to prey.

Eleutherodactylus bransfordii (Rana)

N. J. Scott

Eleutherodactylus bransfordii (Leptodactylidae) is a small (maximum 30 mm) frog living at low and mid elevations of Costa Rica, Nicaragua, and Panama in forests that receive more than about 1.8 m of rain annually (Savage and Emerson 1970). At most sites it is the commonest amphibian in the forest litter (Scott 1976). It appears to forage during the day, but it breeds at night (pers. obs.).

In common with other members of the genus, *E. bransfordii* lays eggs in moist terrestrial sites. The embryos go through the tadpole stage in the egg and hatch as tiny froglets.

Surprisingly little is known about the details of the biology of *E. bransfordii*. Limerick (1976) studied their food habits and found that they were generalized arthropod predators. Of their food items 39% were ants and mites, and beetles, spiders, homoptera, and insect larvae made up another 35%. Collembola were common in the litter, but they were not often eaten. She found that prey size increased with jaw width. Little else is known about what is perhaps the commonest frog in Costa Rica.

Eleutherodactylus bransfordii displays a polychromatism of color, pattern, and skin texture that has caused it to be described seven different times (Savage and Emerson 1970). The polymorphism is apparently the result of a complex of genes and alleles that result in an almost infinite number of morphotypes. Some of the color and skin ridge patterns are usually correlated, but other characters vary independently. Frogs showing most of the range of possible skin and color characters can be found at any one site.

Savage and Emerson (1970) consider the situation a clear example of balanced polymorphism. They could not correlate morph frequencies with any environmental variable. They conclude that the mosaic of colors and textures produced on the forest floor by leaf litter and patchy sunlight ephemerally selects for a wide variety of phenotypes depending on microhabitat, season, and a host of other variables. Clearly the opportunity exists for a long-term experimental study that should shed light on a complex evolutionary pattern.

At higher elevations, *Eleutherodactylus podiciferus* occupies the same habitats as *E. bransfordii* does at lower elevations, and it displays a similar range of individual variation (D. Robinson, pers. comm.).

*

Limerick, S. 1976. Dietary differences of two sympatric Costa Rican frogs. M.S. thesis, University of Southern California, Los Angeles.

Savage, J. M., and Emerson, S. B. 1970. Central American frogs allied to *Eleutherodactylus bransfordii* (Cope): A problem of polymorphism. *Copeia* 1970: 623–44.

Scott, N. J., Jr. 1976. The abundance and diversity of the herpetofaunas of tropical forest litter. *Biotropica* 8: 41–58.

Eleutherodactylus diastema (Martillito, Tink Frog)

N. J. Scott

In any low- and mid-elevation Costa Rican wet forest, on a damp night, the sharp *tink!* calls of *Eleutherodactylus diastema* (Leptodactylidae) are usually the most prominent sound. The sheer energy of the call when heard at close range is doubly impressive when, after a long and frustrating search, one finds that the caller is a tiny frog less than 25 mm long. The males seem to establish fixed calling sites hidden in bromeliads or leaf trash in small trees or understory shrubs. There is a suggestion of organized call sequences in this frog (D. Robinson, pers. comm.).

Little is known about the details of the biology of this common frog. Taylor (1955) found several egg clutches in bromeliads, and a single female may lay up to ten eggs, each one 4 mm in diameter. As in all other members of the genus, the eggs hatch directly into tiny frogs.

These frogs are very agile on their stubby legs (Taylor 1955), and they can either jump or run like mice. Color-pattern polymorphism is present in this species, though not to the degree that is in some other *Eleutherodactylus* such as *E. bransfordi*. *E. diastema* belongs to a species group whose taxonomy is still highly unsatisfactory.

*

Taylor, E. H. 1955. Additions to the known herpetological fauna of Costa Rica, with comments on other species. No. II. *Univ. Kansas Sci. Bull.* 37: 499–575.

Gymnopis multiplicata, Dermophis mexicanus, and *Dermophis parviceps* (Soldas, Suelda con Suelda, Dos Cabezas, Caecilians)

M. H. Wake

Three species of elongate, limbless, tailless burrowing amphibians, the caecilians (Amphibia: Gymnophiona), occur in Costa Rica. *Dermophis mexicanus* (fig. 8.17) is found on the Atlantic slope, *D. parviceps* on the Pacific and Atlantic slopes of central and southern Costa Rica, and *Gymnopis multiplicata* throughout the country, except at higher elevations. *Gymnopis* can be distinguished externally from *Dermophis* by the position of its tentacle, just anterior to the eye (halfway between eye and nostril in *Dermophis*) and by having its eyes not visible, for they are covered by bone (in *Dermophis* the eyes are distinct dark structures covered only by skin). *Dermophis mexicanus* is distinguished from *D. parviceps* by its much larger size and its greater number of annular folds about the body.

The species are tropical lowland to premontane in distribution, from sea level to 1,400 m in Costa Rica. They are found in meadows and forests under logs and rocks, occasionally under the bark of downed logs during the

FIGURE 8.17. *Dermophis mexicanus,* 330 mm total length. Specimen collected near San Marcos, Departamento San Marcos, Guatemala; typical of members of the species that occur in Costa Rica as well (photo, M. H. Wake).

dry season, burrowed into soil, under leaf litter, and in piles of rotting coffee hulls, manure piles, and similar warm, moist habitats. Daytime collecting on the Osa Peninsula required that one clear the leaf litter and soil from between the buttresses of trees to a depth of 45 to 60 cm before finding them. They do emerge to the surface frequently at night during rain, presumably to forage. They have been collected under such conditions by herpetologists visiting Costa Rica and "running the roads" to collect snakes.

Gut analyses of these species show that the diet is composed of a variety of invertebrates, including, in order of frequency, several species of earthworms, termites, coleopteran and hemipteran larvae, and occasional larger prey, such as 60 to 80 mm dermapteran and orthopteran instars. There is some variation according to local prey abundance. Moll and Smith (1967) reported that a large (417 mm total length) *D. mexicanus* in Chiapas had eaten two lizards, a 56 mm SVL *Ameiva undulata parva* and a 35 mm SVL *Anolis dollfusianus,* and they debated whether this apparently unique record of vertebrate prey meant that the lizards had been dead when eaten. It is probable, though not demonstrated by my data, that individuals of *D. mexicanus* eat small snakes, such as the burrowing, worm-eating *Geophis* that occurs in microsympatry in some areas. The diet of these species, then, is composed largely of ground-dwelling or burrowing prey. Like other amphibians, these species appear to be opportunitist feeders, consuming prey in accord with their abundance, and with larger animals able to consume fewer but larger prey items. The primary predators on the caecilians are snakes, particularly coral snakes, and occasionally birds.

Gymnopis and *Dermophis,* and caecilians generally, have a number of adaptations correlated with the morphological "constraints" associated with their acquisition of the burrowing habit. Their bodies are long, with the vent nearly terminal. They move in a controlled modified sine-wave fashion by a complex pattern of contractions of body wall and vertebral musculature. They burrow into the ground by digging and pivoting movements of the head, working against the partially coiled rear part of the body held stationary on the ground to provide resistance. They may also follow root channels and cracks between rocks and logs. The skin is co-ossified to the skull in these burrowing forms. As with many amphibians, the skin contains numerous glands, some of which secrete a material toxic to other species of vertebrates; however, it obviously does not repel all potential predators. Another general characteristic is that only the right lung is developed in these species and it is elongate, similar to the condition in snakes.

A structure unique to caecilians among vertebrates can be observed in operation in living *Gymnopis* and *Der-*

mophis. The pair of tentacles, whose position has been alluded to as a generically distinguishing feature, are chemosensory structures that conduct airborne particles to the olfactory epithelium. The animals continually extend and withdraw the tentacles in order to "sense" the environment. Further, the tentacles are moved and lubricated by muscles, nerves, and glands that are associated with the eyes in all other vertebrates. The evolutionary modification that resulted in a "new" structure, but that used structural material already available, is of particular interest in assessing caecilian evolutionary biology.

Gymnopis multiplicata and *Dermophis mexicanus* are known to be live-bearers, and *D. parviceps* is presumed to be so. Sperm transfer for reproduction is effected by the insertion of the everted rear part of the cloaca of the male into the vent of the female, and internal fertilization then takes place. Nothing is known of mate selection or courtship. The developing eggs are retained in the oviducts of the female. The embryos exhaust the supply of yolk before they emerge from the egg membrane. This occurs at 10–15 mm total length in both species. When the embryos hatch in the oviducts, they begin feeding on material secreted by oviducal glands, thus effecting a nonplacental mode of maternal nutrition or viviparity. The fetuses have a species-specific dentition that they lose at birth, acquiring the monocuspid adult dentition typical of these species. The fetal teeth are used to scrape the oviduct lining and to stimulate its secretory activity. The fetal teeth in *G. multiplicata* are biconvex and topped with a row of small spikes of enamel; those of *D. mexicanus* are spoon-shaped, with a double (early in development) or single medial spike. Litter size in *G. multiplicata* is two to ten; in *D. mexicanus* it is two to sixteen. Young are born at 100–120 mm total length in *G. multiplicata* and 110–51 mm in *D. mexicanus*. Reproductive females are usually between 300 and 400 mm in total length. Over a dozen 120 mm young in a 350 mm female, all deriving their nutrition from the secretions of her oviducal epithelium, pose a considerable physiological demand on the female!

The three species of caecilians constitute a large, biologically interesting, and ecologically important component of the extensive ground-litter fauna of Costa Rica. A number of aspects of their biology make them particularly appropriate for study by evolutionary biologists.

*

Moll, E. O., and Smith, H. M. 1967. Lizards in the diet of an American caecilian. *Nat. Hist. Misc. Chicago Acad. Sci.* 187:1–2.

Savage, J. M., and Wake, M. H. 1972. Geographic variation and systematics of Middle American caecilians, genera *Dermophis* and *Gymnopis*. *Copeia* 1972: 680–95.

Taylor, E. H. 1968. *The caecilians of the world: A taxonomic review.* Lawrence: University of Kansas Press.

Wake, M. H. 1977. The reproductive biology of caecilians: An evolutionary perspective. In *The reproductive biology of amphibians,* ed. D. H. Taylor and S. I. Guttman, pp. 73–101. New York: Plenum.

———. 1980. Reproduction, growth, and population structure of the Central American caecilian *Dermophis mexicanus*. Herpetologica 35:244–56.

Hyla boulengeri (Ranita de Boulenger, Boulenger's Hyla)

N. J. Scott

Hyla boulengeri (Hylidae) has been chosen as a representative hylid frog, of which there are about thirty-nine species in Costa Rica (Savage and Heyer 1969). It has a modal life history that can serve as a model for most species in the family.

The adult frogs are rather strange-looking (Duellman 1970; Villa 1972), with rough skins and long snouts. They are also somewhat flattened, enabling them to squeeze into their daylight retreats in wood crevices or bromeliads. In common with most other hylids, they have large adhesive toe disks that enable them to climb about on leaves and branches.

The distribution of *H. boulengeri* is typical of several Costa Rican amphibians and reptiles. Its range encompasses the lowlands of Nicaragua, Costa Rica, Panama, and the Pacific coasts of Colombia and Ecuador (Duellman 1970).

Males congregate on stumps, small trees, and shrubbery over shallow temporary ponds. Their call is a single low-pitched, catlike *meow!* that is repeated at irregular intervals. Calling males can be found in almost every month. Eggs are deposited in a mass in the water. The tadpoles are rather bizarre, with short, deep bodies and tails. The oral denticles around the beak are exceptionally long, curved, and pointed (León 1969). Judging from the tadpoles' morphology, I suspect they are midwater nekton feeders. The adults eat insects.

*

Duellman, W. E. 1970. The hylid frogs of Middle America. *Monogr. Mus. Nat. Hist. Univ. Kansas* 1:1–753.

León, J. R. 1969. The systematics of the frogs of the *Hyla rubra* group in Middle America. *Pub. Mus. Nat. Hist. Univ. Kansas* 18:505–45.

Savage, J. M., and Heyer, W. R. 1969. The tree-frogs (family Hylidae) of Costa Rica: Diagnosis and distribution. *Rev. Biol. Trop.* 16:1–127.

Villa, J. 1972. *Anfibios de Nicaragua.* Managua: Institución Geográfico Nacional, Banco Central de Nicaragua.

Imantodes cenchoa (Bejuquilla, Chunk-headed Snake)

N. J. Scott

Morphologically, *Imantodes cenchoa* (Colubridae) (fig. 8.18) is one of the more bizarre snakes. This large-scaled snake is less than 1 m long and is very slender. Its neck is especially thin, but the head is relatively wide and blocky. The body is laterally compressed, and the mid-dorsal scale row is conspicuously enlarged. The pupils of its bulging eyes are vertically elliptical like a cat's. Such obvious characters are unusual in snakes, a group that is generally inclined toward more subtle adaptations.

Many of the adaptations have evolved to facilitate existence in a special arboreal habitat—that of the outer small twigs and leaves of shrubs and trees. In this fragile habitat the snake forages at night on small frogs that perch on leaves or small lizards that sleep on twigs. With enlarged vertebral scales, body shaped like an I-beam, and internal vertebral modifications, *Imantodes* can easily bridge gaps in the vegetation up to one-half its length.

FIGURE 8.18. *Imantodes cenchoa,* adult. Santa Rosa National Park, July 1980 (photo, D. H. Janzen).

The thin neck deliberately projects the head out to the tips of branches and leaves without startling its prey. During the day, *Imantodes* hides in bromeliads or other arboreal refuges (Henderson and Nickerson 1976).

A less obvious adaptation correlated with the attenuated body form is the low egg clutch size, which ranged from one to three in thirteen females from all parts of the range (Zug, Hedges, and Sunkel 1979). It is not known whether a single female lays more than one clutch a year. In South American samples a year-long breeding season is suspected, but seasonal breeding is probably the rule in areas with marked wet-dry seasons. Growth rates were about 3.5 mm a week for immature snakes.

There are two forms of *I. cenchoa* in Costa Rica. In wet low- and mid-elevation forests, a relatively dark-colored snake with few blotches and greatly enlarged vertebral scales is found, commonly in bromeliads. A quite different pale snake with many blotches and only slightly enlarged vertebrals occurs in dry lowlands. This form has been called *I. gemmistratus,* but the two types intergrade in narrow contact zones on the Pacific slopes of the Cordillera de Guanacaste, on the Meseta Central, and in the region of Parrita on the Pacific coast. *I. cenchoa* is found from southern Mexico to Bolivia and Paraguay.

*

Henderson, R. W., and Nickerson, M. A. 1976. Observations on the behavioral ecology of three species of *Imantodes* (Reptilia, Serpentes, Colubridae). *J. Herp.* 10:205–10.

Taylor, E. H. 1951. A brief review of the snakes of Costa Rica. *Univ. Kansas Sci. Bull.* 34:1–188.

Zug, G. R.; Hedges, S. B.; and Sunkel, S. 1979. Variation in reproductive parameters of three Neotropical snakes, *Coniophanes fissidens, Dipsas catesbyi,* and *Imantodes cenchoa. Smithsonian Contrib. Zool.* 300: 1–20.

Lepidochelys olivacea (Lora, Carpintera, Pacific Ridley Sea Turtle)

S. E. Cornelius

The Pacific or olive ridley (fig. 8.19) is probably the most abundant of the seven currently recognized species of sea turtles. However, they have been consistently neglected until this decade, are frequently misidentified, and are at present the least understood.

The olive ridley is widely distributed in circumtropical seas. It appears to be most abundant in the eastern Pacific Ocean, where it extends from Chile to California. In the estern Pacific it ranges north to Japan and into the Indian Ocean. In the Atlantic Ocean it is commonly known only along the Gulf of Guinea (Africa) and in northeastern

FIGURE 8.19. *Lepidochelys olivacea. a,* Arribada of nesting turtles at Playa Nancite, Santa Rosa National Park. *b,* Adult female digging nest at Playa Nancite, Santa Rosa National Park (photos, S. E. Cornelius).

South America. Major nesting beaches have been identified in the Mexican states of Jalisco, Guererro, and Oaxaca, the Nicoya Peninsula of Costa Rica, the Guianas of South America, the Indian state of Madras, Sri Lanka, Malaysia, the Arabian Peninsula, and the Eritrean coast of the Red Sea.

This ridley and its severely endangered congener, *L. kempi* of the Gulf of Mexico, are the smallest sea turtles. Females are known to mature at a carapace length of about 55 cm. This is thought to take between 7 and 9 years in both sexes. Mature female ridleys of Pacific Middle America average 63 cm in carapace length and slightly more than 40 kg in weight. Those from the Guianas are significantly larger. Data on growth rates are scarce, but it appears that juveniles increase carapace length by about 5 cm per year (Carr and Caldwell 1958).

The genus *Lepidochelys* is characterized by five or more pairs of costal scutes on the carapace, four inframarginal plates between carapace and plastron, and two pairs of prefrontal scales between the eyes on top of the head. In addition, the ridleys possess a series of pores between the inframarginals, the function of which is unknown.

The two ridleys are distinguished from each other by the presence of only five pairs of costal scutes in *L. kempi* as opposed to a highly polymorphic condition in *L. olivacea.* At Santa Rosa National Park about 51% of adult females exhibit six pairs. The scutation of the remaining ones are distributed among at least fourteen other arrangements, with 13% of these exhibiting five pairs. The olive ridley has a lighter (in color), higher, and relatively narrower carapace than Kemp's ridley. There are also certain cranial differences. Whether any of these differences rank at the specific level is questioned by some investigators.

Ridleys appear to prefer coastal areas, but large groups have been seen in the open ocean. Deraniyagala (1939) felt that they were more of bottom dwellers than others and frequented the shallow water between reef and shoreline of Indo-Pacific islands. In fact, very little is known of the habits of all sea turtles away from the nesting beaches where they have been observed and studied the most.

Food habits of olive ridleys are not well known. Early reports stated that their diet consisted primarily of vegetation. It seems likely, considering the frequent open ocean observations of ridleys and the few cursory examinations of stomach contents, that fish, mollusks, echinoderms, jellyfish, and especially pelagic crabs are important food items.

The phenomenon of synchronized mass nesting, where several thousand turtles emerge together, is peculiar to the ridleys. Two sites of such activity, called *arribadas* or *salidas* in Latin America, are known on the Pacific coast of Costa Rica. At Playa Nancite in Santa Rosa National Park the species goes by the name "carpintera." This name is used at least as far south as Playas del Coco. At Playa Ostional, approximately 100 km south of Nancite, it is known as "lora." At both of these 1,300 m long beaches, as many as 120,000 individuals have been estimated to nest over 4- to 8-day periods from July to December (Hughes and Richard 1974). There are also reports of sizable mass nesting efforts during the dry-season months of January, February, and March, with smaller but still impressive arribadas occurring during April, May, and June. It appears that the olive ridley has an unusually long nesting season, possibly extending the year around, as may be the case with the green turtle (*Chelonia mydas*) in the eastern Pacific (Cornelius 1975, 1976).

Local lore throughout the range of the ridleys is surprisingly consistent. The fleets are supposed to arrive during the last quarter moon, with a strong onshore wind and on a rising tide. However, attempts to relate the occurrence of arribadas to environmental parameters have not been successful. In two separate studies, one of which included a coordinated effort between Nancite and Ostional, no external factors could be shown to trigger the emergences, and no relationship existed between the timing of arrivals at the two beaches (Hughes and Richard 1974; Robinson and Cornelius, unpublished).

Arribadas at Ostional take place at about 2-week intervals. Similar interarribada periods occur at Nancite during July and August, but these lengthen to 3½ to 4 weeks from September to November. The unpredictable nature of arribadas and the difficulty of correlating their occurrence with any known environmental factor suggest that they may be triggered by a pheromone (Hughes and Richard 1974).

Nearly 99% of the olive ridleys that use Playa Nancite during the peak nesting season are involved in arribadas. However, solitary nesters can usually be observed every night. Their behavior is stereotyped and well documented. They generally prefer a fairly level beach free of flotsam above the high-water spring tide line. When nesting alone, ridleys are not nearly as selective as green turtles, although a steep sand embankment, the upper beach vegetation line, an estuary, or temporary tidal or freshwater impoundment will usually cause them to "half-moon" or return promptly to the ocean without nesting. During the march up the beach ridleys plow through the sand with their noses, implying that olfactory sensing may play a role in beach recognition or site selection on the beach.

The egg-laying process takes approximately 50 min. Half that time is spent in actual construction of the nest cavity and deposition of the eggs. The cavity is roughly flask-shaped and about 40–50 cm deep. When the hind flippers can no longer remove any sand, oviposition commences, with eggs dropping singly and sometimes two or three simultaneously. The average clutch size is 120 eggs. After depositing the eggs the turtle spends up to 10 min filling in the nest cavity and tamping the sand firmly with the hind flippers. The nest is concealed by scattering sand with all four flippers. At any stage in the laying process after excavation of the nest cavity, the turtle may be disturbed or removed from the site and this nesting behavior will not be significantly altered. The return trip to the water is normally made in haste, but again the head is held low with the snout sometimes touching the sand.

During mass emergences, nesting behavior is altered somewhat. Each wave of emerging turtles shows complete indifference to lights and other disturbances that usually send solitary nesters retreating to the surf. The turtles also are not deterred by such obstacles as driftwood, vegetation, or estuarine seepage.

Many healthy females make several emergences, both in a single night and sometimes over two or three nights before finally nesting. Turtles with deformed, amputated, or paralyzed limbs and thus unable to successfully nest are frequent sights, especially toward the end of the arribada. This makes it even more difficult to estimate the size of the arribada. Many of the late nesters inadvertantly excavate previously deposited eggs. Approximately 30% of all eggs are destroyed during the same arribada or a subsequent one that may occur before the 50-day indubation period has elapsed.

Eggs that escape arribada-related disinterment are subject to great losses at some beaches as a result of human activities and domestic animals. The eggs are gathered by local people both for their own use and as a commercial venture. Popular demand is based on the mistaken belief that turtle eggs possess aphrodisiac qualities.

Natural predators of eggs in Costa Rica include coyotes (*Canis latrans*), raccoons (*Procyon* spp.), opossums (*Didelphis marsupialis*), and coatis (*Nasua narica*). Two species of vultures (*Coragyps atratus* and *Cathartes aura*) and two species of crabs (*Geocarcinus quadratus* and *Ocypode occidentalis*) are the chief predators on hatchlings while they are on the beach. Magnificent frigate birds (*Fregata magnificens*) are extremely efficient at snatching up hatchlings both on the open beach and after they reach the water. Sharks are more active within the surf zone while hatchlings are emerging, and it is likely that a host of other aquatic predators await the young turtles, including other turtles. Ridley hatchlings have been found in the stomachs of leatherback turtles (*Dermochelys coriacea*), for example (Pritchard 1971).

As with other sea turtles, essentially nothing is known of the life history of ridleys after the hatchlings leave the nesting beach. They most certainly are pelagic and are transported by currents until they are at least a year old. Whether they return as adults to their natal beaches and, if so, how this is accomplished remains a mystery.

The conservation outlook for the olive ridley is not as encouraging as their impressive numbers at nesting beaches implies. The very behavior that makes this species so awe-inspiring may contribute to its demise. Recurrent massing of hundreds of thousands of turtles at a few accessible beaches has permitted intensive human exploitation throughout its range. In 1968 alone, Mexican fishermen harvested more than a million turtles for the leather trade. Since then, fishery authorities of that country have enacted an artificial hatchery program and quota system in an attempt to manage the resource. Yearly decreases in numbers of females returning to the principal Mexican beaches have not been encouraging, and these populations may already have reached a critical level.

Until recently, ridleys nesting in Costa Rica were thought to be fairly safe, assuming they were distinct from those populations in Mexico. During the late 1970s massive commercial exploitation of nonnesting olive ridleys developed in Ecuador, and preliminary estimates indicate the annual harvest is greater than that which currently exists in Mexico. Both Mexican and Costa Rican tagged ridleys have been captured in the nearshore waters off Ecuador, suggesting that a significant portion of the eastern Pacific population spends the nonnesting season there.

Although no organized ridley turtle fishery exists in Costa Rica at present, such exploitation has occurred in the past and may redevelop if the Mexican beaches are unable to supply the lucrative turtle products trade. The development of the Ecuadorean fishery compounds the vulnerability of the Costa Rican nesting population.

*

Bustard, R. 1972. *Sea turtles: Their natural history and conservation*. New York: Taplinger.

Carr, A. F. 1952. *Handbook of the turtles*. Ithaca: Cornell University Press.

Carr, A. F., and Caldwell, D. K. 1958. The problem of the Atlantic ridley turtle in 1958. *Rev. Biol. Trop.* 6:245–62.

Cornelius, S. E. 1975. Marine turtle mortalities along the Pacific coast of Costa Rica. *Copeia* 1975:186–87.

———. 1976. Marine turtle nesting activity at Playa Naranjo, Costa Rica. *Brenesia* 8:1–27.

Deraniyagala, P. E. P. 1939. Tetrapod reptiles of Ceylon. *Columbo Mus. Publ.*, pp. 1–421.

Hughes, D., and Richard, J. 1974. The nesting of the Pacific ridley turtle (*Lepidochelys olivacea*) on Playa Nancite, Costa Rica. *Mar. Biol.* 24:97–107.

Marquez, R.; Villanueva, A.; and Peñaflores, C. 1976. Sinopsis de datos biologicos sobre la tortuga golfina, *Lepidochelys olivacea* (Eschscholtz, 1829). INP sinopsis sobre la pesca no. 2, SAST-Tortuga Golfina 5, 21 (07), 016,01.

Pritchard, P. C. H. 1969. Sea turtles of the Guianas. *Bull. Florida St. Mus. Biol. Sci.* 13:85–140.

———. 1971. *The leatherback or leathery turtle Dermochelys coriacea*. IUCN Monograph no. 1. Morges: IUCN.

Rebel, T. P., ed. 1974. *Sea turtles and the turtle industry of the West Indies, Florida, and the Gulf of Mexico*. Miami: University of Miami Press.

Richard, J., and Hughes, D. 1972. Some observations of sea turtle nesting activity in Costa Rica. *Mar. Biol.* 16:297–309.

Leptodactylus pentadactylus (Rana Ternero, Smoky Frog)

N. J. Scott

This large frog (fig. 8.20) is second in size only to the marine toad (*Bufo marinus*) in Costa Rica, reaching a length of at least 160 mm (Taylor 1952). It inhabits dry and wet lowland and intermediate elevation forests, where adults live in rock crevices or in burrows in the forest floor, frequently in riparian situations. They forage around the mouth of the burrow and use it for escape.

FIGURE 8.20. *Leptodactylus pentadactylus*, adult. Corcovado National Park, Osa Peninsula, Costa Rica (photo, G. Stevens).

Adult food habits are poorly known, but the frogs are aggressive and can eat snakes up to 500 mm long. They are probably important forest floor predators on smaller frogs.

All *Leptodactylus* build foam nests in which the eggs are laid. In *L. pentadactylus*, nests may include 2–7 liters of foam. They are placed in dry hollows in streambeds or other seasonally flooded sites or next to small ephemeral pools (Breder 1946). Tadpoles of this species showed the greatest resistance to desiccation of seven sympatric anuran species studied by Valerio (1971). They are effective predators on other tadpoles and frog eggs (Heyer 1970; Heyer, McDiarmid, and Wiegmann 1975), but they can grow and metamorphose while feeding on plant material (Vinton 1951).

In some areas adult frogs emit loud squalls when captured. This noise is extremely attractive to caimans (*Caiman crocodilus*, pers. obs.). Apparently the captured frog attracts large predators that may attack the frog's captor.

Adult *L. pentadactylus* secrete skin toxins that are highly irritating to mucous membranes and cuts in the collector's skin (Villa 1969).

The breeding call is a loud *whorup* repeated every 5–10 sec. It has been described by Breder (1946), Fouquette (1960), Villa (1969, 1972), and Heyer (1979). The males develop stout thumb spines and (in some areas) chest spines during the breeding season. Presumably these help the male hold the female in amplexus.

*

Breder, C. M., Jr. 1946. Amphibians and reptiles of the Río Chucumaque drainage, Darien, Panamá, with notes on their life histories and habits. *Bull. Mus. Nat. Hist.* 86:375–436.

Fouquette, M. J. 1960. Call structure in frogs of the family Leptodactylidae. *Texas J. Sci.* 12:201–15.

Heyer, W. R. 1970. Studies on the genus *Leptodactylus* (Amphibia: Leptodactylidae). II. Diagnosis and distribution of the *Leptodactylus* of Costa Rica. *Rev. Biol. Trop.* 16:171–205.

———. 1979. Systematics of the *pentadactylus* species group of the frog genus *Leptodactylus* (Amphibia: Leptodactylidae). *Smithsonian Contrib. Zool.* 301:1–43.

Heyer, W. R.; McDiarmid, R. W.; and Weigmann, D. L. 1975. Tadpoles, predation and pond habitats in the tropics. *Biotropica* 7:100–111.

Taylor, E. H. 1952. The frogs and toads of Costa Rica. *Univ. Kansas Sci. Bull.* 35:577–942.

Valerio, D. C. 1971. Ability of some tropical tadpoles to survive without water. *Copeia* 1971:364–65.

Villa, J. 1969. Comportamiento defensivo de la "Rana ternero," *Leptodactylus pentadactylus*. *Rev. Biol. Trop.* 15:323–29.

———. 1972. *Anfibios de Nicaragua*. Managua: Instituto Geográfico Nacional, Banco Central de Nicaragua.

Vinton, K. W. 1951. Observations on the life history of *Leptodactylus pentadactylus*. *Herpetologica* 7:73–75.

Leptotyphlops goudotii (Culebra Gusano, Worm Snake, Blind Snake)

N. J. Scott

The snakes of the family Leptotyphlopidae have rudimentary eyes that do not form an image and may not even be light sensitive. This species is widespread throughout the drier parts of the Neotropics; in Costa Rica it is common in Guanacaste Province, northern Puntarenas Province, and the Meseta Central. It is sometimes found on the ground surface during the dry season, but ordinarily it lives under rocks and logs or in deeper burrows.

There have been no ecological studies of this species, but a congener (*L. dulcis*) has been studied in the southwestern United States. This species is a commensal with ants and termites, feeding on workers, larvae, pupae, and other soft-bodied arthropods. Sometimes the snakes eat the entire prey item, but on other occasions they apparently suck out the body contents, leaving a hollow shell (Smith 1957; Reid and Lott 1963; Punzo 1974). Their jaws are highly modified for their specialized feeding habits, and they are unique among snakes in that they have teeth only in the lower jaw (List 1966).

The United States species has also developed a striking behavioral pattern that enables it to coexist with its hosts. When newly introduced into an ant colony, the snake is generally attacked. It then elevates the free margins of its scales, forming a barrier similar to the surface of a pine cone, and secretes a repellent substance. The ants eventually cease their attacks as the snake acquires the colony odor, and the scales are lowered to form the normal slick,

low-friction body surface (Gehlbach, Watkins, and Reno 1968). The snake can also follow ant pheromone trails (Watkins, Gehlbach, and Baldridge 1967).

The Costa Rican species probably has similar habits. Occasionally the snakes aggregate into small colonies where they may be accompanied by another small fossorial snake, *Enulius flavitorques*, that specializes in feeding on small reptile eggs.

*

Gehlbach, F. R.; Watkins, J. F., II; and Reno, H. W. 1968. Blind snake defensive behavior elicited by ant attacks. *Bioscience* 18:784–85.

List, J. C. 1966. Comparative osteology of the snake families Typhlopidae and Leptotyphlopidae. *Illinois Biol. Monogr.* 36:1–112.

Punzo, F. 1974. Comparative analysis of the feeding habits of two species of Arizona blind snakes, *Leptotyphlops h. humilis* and *Leptotyphlops d. dulcis*. *J. Herp.* 8:153–56.

Reid, J. R., and Lott, T. E. 1963. Feeding of *Leptotyphylops dulcis dulcis* (Baird and Girard). *Herpetologica* 19:141–42.

Smith, H. M. 1957. Curious feeding habit of a blind snake, *Leptotyphlops*. *Herpetologica* 13:102.

Watkins, J.; Gehlbach, F.; and Baldridge, R. S. 1967. Ability of the blind snake, *Leptotyphlops dulcis*, to follow pheromone trails of army ants *Neivamyrmex nigrescens* and *N. opacithorax*. *Southwest. Nat.* 12:455–62.

Micrurus nigrocinctus (Corál, Coral Snake, Coralillo)

H. W. Greene and R. L. Seib

There are approximately fifty species of highly venomous New World coral snakes (fig. 8.21), distributed from the southeastern and southwestern United States to Argentina (Roze 1967; Peters and Orejas-Miranda 1969). The three genera (*Leptomicrurus, Micruroides, Micrurus*) have classically been placed in the Elapidae with cobras, kraits, mambas, and their relatives. However, recent morphological studies (Savitzky 1978) suggest that they might be more closely related to several genera of "mildly venomous" South American colubrids.

Snakes of the genus *Micrurus* have elongate bodies, small heads, short tails, fifteen rows of smooth dorsal scales, and two scales (rather than three) on each side of the snout between the eye and the nostril. The color pattern is usually some combination of red, black, and yellow, or white bands. Most species, including *M. nigrocinctus*, rarely if ever exceed 1 m in total length.

Four species of *Micrurus* occur in Costa Rica (Savage and Vial 1974). *M. mipartitus* is bicolored (black with

FIGURE 8.21. *Micrurus nigrocinctus,* adult on forest floor litter. Llorona, Corcovado National Park, Osa Peninsula, Costa Rica (photo, D. H. Janzen).

bands of white, pink, or red) and occurs on both sides of Costa Rica (D. Robinson, pers. comm.). Three species are tricolored, at least ventrally, with a repeated banded pattern of red-yellow-black-yellow-red; they can be distinguished by the arrangement of black on the head scales. *M. clarki* has the parietals (two large scales medial and posterior to the eyes) covered by an extension of the black head coloration; it occurs in Panama, and there is a single specimen available from an unspecified locality in Costa Rica. *M. alleni* has a linear extension of the black head color along the suture between the two parietal scales. Adults of this species from the Pacific uplands near the Panamanian border are entirely black dorsally but retain the tricolored ventral pattern; adults of *M. alleni* from the Atlantic versant of Costa Rica are tricolored dorsally. *M. nigrocintus* (fig. 8.21), the common coral snake of Costa Rica, occurs at low and moderate elevations throughout the country. In this species the black head cap ends near the posterior border of the eyes, and the parietal scales are mainly yellow or white.

As a group, coral snakes occupy a variety of habitats at low and moderate elevations, from deserts in the southwestern United States and northern Mexico to dry and wet forests in the tropics (Roze 1967; Savage and Vial 1974). There are numerous reports of diurnal and nocturnal activity (Greene and McDiarmid 1981). Very little is known about their population biology. Presumably all species lay eggs, and it is possible that the females guard their clutches (Campbell 1973).

The diet of coral snakes typically consists of elongate vertebrates, including synbranchid eels, caecilians, lizards, amphisbaenians, and other snakes (Alvarez del Toro 1972; Greene 1973*a*). Specific items recorded from twenty-eight *M. nigrocinctus* are one caecilian, two reptile eggs, four lizards, and twenty-two snakes (Schmidt 1932; Swanson, 1945; Smith and Grant 1958; Landy et al 1966; Greene 1973*a;* Seib, unpublished). The snake prey included three *Adelphicos,* five *Geophis,* and five

Ninia, all common forest litter inhabitants that feed largely on earthworms (Greene 1975; Seib, 1978, 1980.).

Field and laboratory observations on several species (including *M. nigrocinctus*) demonstrate that coral snakes forage by crawling slowly and poking their heads under surface litter (Greene 1973*a*). Prey is recognized by chemical and perhaps visual cues, seized with a quick forward movement, and held until immobilized. Coral snakes have a hollow fang at the anterior end of each maxillary bone that conducts venom; numerous solid teeth in the upper and lower jaws are used for holding and swallowing prey. Prey are typically swallowed headfirst, and the overlapping scales of reptiles are used to locate the anterior end before ingestion (Greene 1976).

Coral snakes often exhibit a spectacular defensive display when disturbed, including some or all of the following components (Gehlbach 1972; Greene 1973*b*): the body is flattened and erratically snapped back and forth; the head is alternately hidden and swung from side to side with the mouth open, and any object that is contacted is bitten; the tail is coiled, elevated, and waved about; and the contents of the cloaca are discharged. Coral snakes are difficult to handle safely because of their smooth scales, small heads, and indistinct necks. The venom usually has a neurotoxic effect on mammals, and several human fatalities are on record (Minton and Minton 1969). In some cases there is apparently no venom injected (T. Papenfuss, pers. comm.), perhaps because it is expended during the defensive display, but even a brief bite should be considered potentially very serious.

The possibility that the bright colors of *Micrurus* are aposematic and that some presumably less dangerous species of colubrids are mimics has been widely debated, usually on the basis of erroneous assumptions (Hecht and Marien 1956; Mertens 1956, 1957; Wickler 1968; Gehlbach 1972; Greene and Pyburn 1973; Grobman 1978). Presumed mimics in Costa Rica include colubrids of the genera *Dipsas, Erythrolamprus, Lampropeltis, Leimadophis, Oxyrhopus, Pliocercus, Rhinobothrium, Scaphiodontophis, Scolecophis, Sibon,* and *Tantilla* (Savage and Vial 1974); a caterpillar (*Pseudosphinx tetrio*); and a turtle (*Rhinoclemmys pulcherrima*) (Janzen 1980). Recent studies (Greene and McDiarmid 1981) permit several conclusions. (1) Brightly banded patterns are probably cryptic in some contexts (Thayer 1909; Jackson, Ingram, and Campbell 1976; Pough 1977). (2) Venomous coral snakes are capable of killing large animals, but there are several records of successful predation on *Micrurus* (Smith 1969). (3) The meaning of the brightly banded pattern need not be learned by a predator, and Smith (1975, 1977) demonstrated innate avoidance of coral snake patterns by two species of birds.

(4) There is parallel geographic color pattern variation among several presumed models and mimics, even extending to bizarre and highly localized variants. (5) Most colubrids involved in these presumptive mimicry systems are also venomous; they possess a Duvernoy's gland (Taub 1967) and enlarged, sometimes grooved posterior maxillary teeth. Among Middle American genera, the bite of *Erythrolamprus* is known to produce symptoms in humans (Picado 1931), and a bite from a *Pliocercus* caused severe pain and swelling (Seib 1980). In summary, it is very likely that the color patterns of some or all of these snakes are aposematic, and that some form of mimicry exists. Additional field observations and more experimental studies using natural predators are needed to clarify the exact nature of the relationships.

The antiserum for *Micrurus* made by Instituto Clodomiro Picado in Costa Rica is ineffective for *Micrurus mipartitus* (D. Robinson, pers. comm.).

*

Alvarez del Toro, M. 1972. *Los reptiles de Chiapas*. Tuxtla Gutierrez: Instituto de Historia Natural de Chiapas.

Campbell, J. A. 1973. A captive hatching of *Micrurus fulvius tenere* (Serpentes, Elapidae). *J. Herp.* 7: 312–15.

Gehlbach, F. R. 1972. Coral snake mimicry reconsidered: The strategy of self-mimicry. *Forma et Functio* 5:311–20.

Greene, H. W. 1973*a*. The food habits and feeding behavior of New World coral snakes. M.A. thesis, University of Texas at Arlington.

———. 1973*b*. Defensive tail display in snakes and amphisbaenians. *J. Herp.* 7:143–61.

———. 1975. Ecological observations on the red coffee snake, *Ninia sebae*, in southern Veracruz, Mexico. *Am. Midl. Nat.* 93:478–84.

———. 1976. Scale overlap, a directional sign stimulus for prey ingestion by ophiophagous snakes. *Z. Tierpsychol.* 41:113–20.

Greene, H. W., and McDiarmid, R. W. 1981. Coral snake mimicry: Does it occur? *Science* 213:1207–12.

Greene, H. W., and Pyburn, W. F. 1973. Comments on aposematism and mimicry among coral snakes. *Biologist* 55:144–48.

Grobman, A. B. 1978. An alternative solution to the coral snake mimic problem. *J. Herp.* 12:1–11.

Hecht, M. K., and Marien, D. 1956. The coral snake mimicry problem: A reinterpretation. *J. Morph.* 98: 335–65.

Jackson, J. F.; Ingram, W., III; and Campbell, H. W. 1976. The dorsal pigmentation pattern of snakes as an antipredator strategy: A multivariate approach. *Am. Nat.* 110:1029–53.

Janzen, D. H. 1980. Two potential coral snake mimics in a tropical deciduous forest. *Biotropica* 12:77–78.

Landy, M. J.; Langebartel, D. A.; Moll, E. O.; and Smith, H. M. 1966. A collection of snakes from Volcan Tacana, Chiapas, Mexico. *J. Ohio Herp. Soc.* 5:93–101.

Mertens, R. 1956. Das Problem der Mimikry bei Korallenschlangen. *Zool. Jahrb.* (*Syst.*) 84:541–76.

———. 1957. Gibt es Mimikry bei Korallenschlangen? *Natur Volk* 87:56–66.

Minton, S. A., and Minton, M. R. 1969. *Venomous reptiles*. New York: Charles Scribner's Sons.

Peters, J. A., and Orejas-Miranda, B. 1969. *Catalogue of the Neotropical Squamata*. Part I. *Snakes*. U.S. National Museum Bulletin Washington, D.C.: Smithsonian Institution Press.

Picado, C. 1931. *Serpientes venenosas de Costa Rica*. San José.

Pough, F. H. 1977. Multiple cryptic effects of crossbanded and ringed patterns of snakes. *Copeia* 1977: 834–36.

Roze, J. A. 1967. A checklist of the New World venomous coral snakes (Elapidae) with descriptions of new forms. *Am. Mus. Novitates,* no. 2287.

Savage, J. M., and Vial, J. L. 1974. The venomous coral snakes (genus *Micrurus*) of Costa Rica. *Rev. Biol. Trop.* 21:295–349.

Savitzky, A. H. 1978. The origin of the New World proteroglyphous snakes and its bearing on the study of venom delivery systems in snakes. Ph.D. diss., University of Kansas.

Schmidt, K. P. 1932. Stomach contents of some American coral snakes, with the description of a new species of *Geophis*. *Copeia* 1932:6–9.

Seib, R. L. 1978. Implications of similarity in patterns of snake species diversity in coffee fincas of Guatemala and Panama. Paper presented at Am. Soc. Ichthyol. Herpetol. Meeting, Tempe, Arizona (abstract).

———. 1980. Human envenomation from the bite of an aglyphous false coral snake, *Pliocercus elapoides* (Serpentes: Colubidae). *Toxicon* 18:399–401.

Smith, H. M., and Grant, C. 1958. New and noteworthy snakes from Panama. *Herpetologica* 14:207–15.

Smith, N. G. 1969. Avian predation on coral snakes. *Copeia* 1969:402–4.

Smith, S. M. 1975. Innate recognition of coral snake pattern by a possible avian predator. *Science* 187: 759–60.

———. 1977. Coral-snake pattern recognition and stimulus generalization by naive great kiskadees (Aves: Tyrannidae). *Nature* 265:535–36.

Swanson, P. L. 1945. Herpetological notes from Panama. *Copeia* 1945:210–16.

Taub, A. M. 1967. Comparative histological studies on Duvernoy's gland of colubrid snakes. *Bull. Am. Mus. Nat. Hist.* 138:1–50.

Thayer, G. H. 1909. *Concealing coloration in the animal kingdom*. New York.

Wickler, W. 1968. *Mimicry in plants and animals*. New York: McGraw-Hill.

Norops polylepis (Lagartija, Anole, Anolis Lizard)

R. M. Andrews

This small arboreal lizard (*Anolis polylepis* of older literature) is found in low- and middle-elevation rain forests of southwestern Costa Rica. This species is sexually dimorphic in body size; males reach a maximum snout-vent length of 53 mm, and females reach a maximum snout-vent length of 48 mm (and see fig. 8.22). Males are easily distinguished from females by the presence of a solid orange throat fan or dewlap (fig. 8.22*a*). The body color of most individuals is a solid or blotchy brown, but some females have a distinct middorsal white stripe or series of diamond-shaped figures. Individuals are usually found perching on understory vegetation in shaded habitats. *Norops polylepis* is the most commonly encountered of the seven species of *Norops* reported for southwestern Costa Rica. Population densities vary, but with experience a person can expect to find six to ten individuals per hour of search time. On the Osa Peninsula near Rincón, a 1,000 m^2 area that was regularly censused from mid-May to mid-July had a resident population that ranged from twenty-six to thirty-one individuals. The other anoles that are sympatric with *N. polylepis* are seen much less often because of their low population densities or because they live high in the forest canopy.

Reproductive activity appears to be correlated with rainfall. Although females lay eggs year round, the proportion of females with oviducal eggs is less during the dry season than during the wet season. Females that were repeatedly caught and palped during the dry season laid an egg every 2 weeks. Judging from the results of studies on similar-sized species elsewhere in Central America, the rate of oviposition may increase to one egg per week during the wet season. Behavioral observations indicate a marked increase in courtship and copulation at the onset of the wet season (May–June). This upswing in reproductive activity results in a pulse in the number of juveniles in the population in August and September; the lag results from a roughly 50-day incubation period. Newly hatched individuals are about 19 mm in snout-vent length and grow rapidly, becoming sexually mature in 3–4 months at a snout-vent length of 39 mm. Mark-recapture studies indicate that the population probably turns over every year.

FIGURE 8.22. *a,* Two male *Norops sericeus* (*Anolis sericeus* of older literature) display at each other; dewlap is yellow with a blue spot in the middle. *b,* Male (*on left*) and female *Norops cupreus* (*Anolis cupreus* of old) during copulation. (*a* and *b,* June 1980, Santa Rosa National Park, Costa Rica) (photos, D. H. Janzen). These anoles are similar to *N. polylepis*.

Norops polylepis individuals are highly territorial. However, the function of territoriality is different for adult males and adult females. Males defend large areas against intrusion by other males. Territory sizes may be as large as 65 m^2 but average about 30 m^2. During territorial interactions the dewlap is repeatedly extended, and the head and body are bobbed up and down in patterns typical of the species. These displays are used to advertise the presence of a resident male and are often exchanged by two males, each from its own territory. Intrusion by one male into the territory of another results in the escalation of aggressive behavior, which ranges from stereotyped displays to biting and chasing. The resident is usually successful in driving the intruder away. The territory of an adult male includes the territories of one to three adult females. Thus the function of territoriality in males appears to be maintenance of exclusive access to females. On the other hand, female territories, averaging about 7 m^2, serve entirely for feeding. The importance of females as a limiting resource for males is indicated by the fact that small sexually mature males are not associated with females. Furthermore, a large adult male will shift his territorial boundaries to include those of neighboring females within a day after the neighboring male disappears. Juveniles are also territorial, but their territories do not overlap with those of other individuals.

Norops lizards can be characterized by the structural characteristics of their perch sites. Thus, ecologists distinguish the structural habitats of anoles as trunk-ground, canopy, and so forth. *Norops polylepis* is called a shrub-ground species because individuals typically perch less than 2 m above the ground on shrubs and on the stems of small trees. The attention of foraging individuals is focused toward the leaf litter surface where most food items are located. Adult male *N. polylepis* are usually seen on higher perches than are adult females. This difference in structural habitat is related to the time and activity budgets of the two sexes. Adult males spend more than half of their active day interacting with other males. High perches are used for this activity, probably because high perches make good vantage points. However, when males are feeding or courting females they use much lower perches. In contrast to the activities of males, adult females may spend as much as 90% of their active day in scanning their surroundings for food. Low perches are used for this activity.

Like most anoles, *N. polylepis* is a sit-and-wait predator on invertebrates. Prey are relatively large; more than 50% of items eaten are 5 mm or more in length. Palatable soft-bodied insects such as the larvae of lepidopterans, crickets and other orthopterans, and cockroaches make up the bulk of their diets. A preference for large prey is associated with low feeding rates; about once an hour individuals leave their perches and dash out to capture some arthropod.

Norops polylepis serve as prey for many species in higher trophic levels. Because of their small size and exposed perches, individuals are eaten by a diversity of predators. Motmots and trogons are conspicuous bird predators on anoles, and many species of snakes, especially the vine snakes, eat them as well. Two sympatric lizards, *Norops capito* and *Corytophanes cristatus,* occasionally prey upon *N. polylepis.* More surprisingly, anoles also fall prey to large invertebrates. Both mantids and predaceous katydids have been seen eating juvenile *N. polylepis.*

*

Andrews, R. M. 1971*a*. Structural habitat and time budget of a tropical *Anolis* lizard. *Ecology* 52:262–70.
———. 1971*b*. Food resource utilization in some tropical lizards. Ph.D. thesis, University of Kansas.
Hertz, P. E. 1975. Thermal passivity of a tropical forest lizard, *Anolis polylepis*. *J. Herp*. 8:32–327.
Taylor, E. H. 1956. A review of the lizards of Costa Rica. *Univ. Kansas Sci. Bull*. 38:1–322.

Oxybelis aeneus (Bejuquillo, Vine Snake)

N. J. Scott

Oxybelis aeneus (fig. 8.23) has one of the largest distributions of any Neotropical snake, ranging in dry habitats from southern Arizona and Tamaulipas, Mexico, to central Bolivia and southeastern Brazil (Keiser 1974). Adults are long (2 m) and very slender, and the snout is drawn out into a blunt point.

This snake is aboreal and is primarily a lizard feeder. It has mild venom and large rear fangs and, if allowed to chew, can cause local swelling and blistering (Crimmins 1937). It is not usually inclined to bite.

The gray to brown snakes are relatively common in second-growth vegetation in Guanacaste. They simulate vines very closely, and their commonest defense is to remain frozen with the tongue extended, depending on their camouflage to protect them. When discovered, they have an impressive open-mouth bluff display where they show the unusual black lining of the mouth and strike without biting hard. They sometimes pass the dry season in a somewhat quiescent state in hollow trees and other moist places (Santa Rosa National Park, D. H. Janzen, pers. comm.).

*

Crimmins, M. L. 1937. A case of *Oxybelis* poisoning in man. *Copeia* 1937:233.

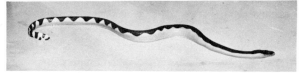

FIGURE 8.24. *Pelamis platurus,* adult, black markings above, yellow below. September 1970, Gulfo Dulce, Costa Rica (photo, H. K. Voris).

FIGURE 8.23. *Oxybelis aeneus. a,* Adult climbing through forest understory shrub. *b,* Dorsal side of adult head. *c,* Threat display by adult; interior of mouth is dark blue black. Llorona, Corcovado National Park, Osa Peninsula, Costa Rica (photos, D. H. Janzen).

Keiser, E. D., Jr. 1974. A systematic study of the Neotropical vine snake *Oxybelis aeneus* (Wagler). *Bull. Texas Mem. Mus.* 22:1–51.

Pelamis platurus (Culebra del Mar, Pelagic Sea Snake)

H. K. Voris

Along the Pacific Ocean beaches of Costa Rica one sometimes encounters stranded pelagic sea snakes. All sea snakes have oarlike tails and neurotoxic venom. They are related to the terrestrial cobras and coral snakes.

Pelamis (fig. 8.24) is a monotypic genus with a huge but discontinuous geographic range extending from the east coast of Africa to the west coast of Central America. These snakes are mainly tropical, and surface water temperatures below 20° C apparently restrict the species'

range to the north and south (Dunson and Ehlert 1971). *Pelamis* is the only sea snake (Hydrophiidae) of the fifty known species that is truly pelagic in habits. It lives near or at the surface in deep water, usually 1–20 km from shore. To a large extent the snakes drift passively and are often found concentrated in large numbers in drift lines or slicks (Kropach 1971). These drift lines consist of bands of debris at the surface 3–6 m in width and often many kilometers in length. Physical factors such as wind, waves, and temperature fronts form and maintain these slicks. The debris forms shelter for small fish and invertebrates, and larger fish aggregate near the slicks to feed. *Pelamis* feeds on a variety of small pelagic fish that gather under the snakes in the drift lines (Klawe 1964; Kropach 1975; Voris 1972). Their feeding behavior is specialized to these circumstances. When feeding, the snake swims slowly backward at the surface with its mouth slightly open. Small fish line up underneath the snake and move along under it, gradually falling back toward its head. *Pelamis* strikes laterally and somewhat underneath itself from this position (Pickwell 1972). Venom apparently immobilizes the prey in less than a minute, and the fish is then usually swallowed head first.

Pelamis is sometimes called the yellow-bellied sea snake because of its typical coloration: yellow below with a dark longitudinal dorsal stripe. However, numerous color varieties have been observed and have attracted a great deal of interest (Smith 1926; Visser 1967; Kropach 1975). They range from nearly all black to entirely yellow. Partial extensions of black into the yellow frequently produce a band effect posteriorly. The extremes are not necessarily "freaks of nature." For example, in September 1970 several researchers and I collected 268 specimens of *Pelamis* in the mouth of the Golfo Dulce, Costa Rica, and 3% of these snakes were the all-yellow variety. The function of the color pattern in *Pelamis* could be countershading or possibly disruptive coloration, but Kropach (1975) has made a fairly convincing case for warning coloration. Some data exist that indicate that the highly venomous snakes are conspicuous to their natural predators (large fish) and are avoided by them.

The movements of *Pelamis,* and any other sea snake for that matter, are poorly understood. A mark and recapture project in the Bay of Panama produced only one certain recapture from 961 snakes that were marked and released. Seasonal differences in the local abundance of *Pelamis* seem to occur, and there is evidence that movements may be both extensive and complex (Kropach 1975).

Living in a habitat with no rough surfaces for scraping off skin when shedding, a shedding *Pelamis* ties itself in a simple knot and then pulls its body through it, leaving the skin behind (D. Robinson, pers. comm.).

*

Dunson, W. A., and Ehlert, G. W. 1971. Effects of temperature, salinity and surface water flow on distribution of the sea snake *Pelamis. Limn. Oceanogr.* 16: 845–53.

Klawe, W. L. 1964. Food of the black-and-yellow sea snake. *Pelamis platurus,* from Ecuadorian coastal waters. *Copeia* 4:712–13.

Kropach, C. 1971. Sea snake (*Pelamis platurus*) aggregations on slicks in Panama. *Herpetologica* 27: 131–35.

———. 1975. The yellow-bellied sea snake, *Pelamis,* in the eastern Pacific. In *The biology of sea snakes,* ed. W. A. Dunson. Baltimore: University Park Press.

Pickwell, G. W. 1972. The venomous sea snakes. *Fauna* 4:17–32.

Smith, M. A. 1926. *The monograph of the sea-snakes (Hydrophiidae).* London: Oxford University Press.

Visser, J. 1967. Color varieties, brood size and food of South African *Pelamis platurus* (Ophidia: Hydrophiidae). *Copeia* 1:219.

Voris, H. K. 1972. The role of sea snakes (Hydrophiidae) in the trophic structure of coastal ocean communities. *J. Mar. Biol. Assoc. India* 14:429–42.

FIGURE 8.25. Foam-covered egg mass of *Physalaemus pustulosus* (white sphere in lower right) at edge of drying puddle in lava rock creek bed. Río Guapote, Santa Rosa National Park, Costa Rica, May 1980 (photo, D. H. Janzen).

Physalaemus pustulosus (Rana, Sapito Túngara, Foam Toad, Mud-puddle Frog)

A. S. Rand

Physalaemus pustulosus, the Central American mud-puddle frog (fig. 8.25), ranges from Mexico through Central America and into northern South America; its congeners are South American. It occurs in the lowlands to moderate elevations, avoiding both very dry and very wet areas.

In Costa Rica, Savage (1976) records it from the Pacific lowlands but not elsewhere. It occurs at San Vito, Rincón de Osa, and Cañas, Taboga, but not at La Selva, San Jośe, or Cerro de la Muerte (Robinson, 1971). I did not hear it at Llorona or Sirena (Corcovado National Park) in August 1978.

Most observations reported here were made on Panamanian populations, and those in Costa Rica may behave differently.

P. pustulosus is a small frog, about 25 to 35 cm long. It is brown and rough skinned, toadlike in shape and general appearance, but lacks the distinctive parotoid poison glands. It is distinctive in having a dermal tarsal tubercle. This genus belongs to the family Leptodactylidae, which is quite close to the toads and a dominant family in the Neotropics and Australia. Its members are very diverse in form and behavior; the group of genera to which *P. pustulosus* belongs all build foam nests, and the group includes the large, familiar frog *Leptodactylus pentadactylus* (Lynch 1970).

P. pustulosus is terrestrial, living among the leaf litter in forest, in second growth, and in scrub pasture, agricultural land, and gardens. It is nocturnal in its breeding and probably in other activities as well. Unlike *Dendrobates, Colostethus,* and *Bufo typhonius,* with which it commonly occurs in Panama, it is only occasionally seen by day and is never found sleeping at night. Like all small frogs it is insectivorous, and unlike many is not an ant specialist (M. Ryan, pers. comm.). At Santa Rosa National Park it is diurnally active on the leaf litter in the rainy season.

These frogs lack conspicuous poison glands and are not warningly colored; rather, they are highly cryptic when not breeding. They are frequently eaten by snakes (e.g., *Leptodeira*). toads (*B. marinus*), the frog *Leptodactylus pentadactylus*, *Philander* opossums, and bats (*Trachops cirrhosus*) at the breeding ponds and probably by other predators as well.

They breed throughout the year in Panama if suitable sites are available. Sometimes they may aestivate during the dry season; Duellman (1965) found several buried 25 cm deep in a stream bank in Mexico. Maximum breeding activity occurs just after the first rains and is minimal during the dry season. Breeding is slowed by a drought period during the wet season and stimulated by flooding rains at any time of year, though little breeding occurs during very heavy rainstorms. The maximum activity is seen just after the first heavy rains of the wet season, usually in April, probably because females have been inhibited from breeding during the dry season and most are ready to lay when the rains come. The population is then synchronized, and all breed together. Females lay subsequent clutches as soon as their eggs are ready, then the population quickly desynchronizes and one sees a few nests made every night.

Davidson and Hough (1969) maintained a laboratory colony of *P. pustulosus* in New York. They report that with unlimited food a female could produce clutches at 6-week intervals.

They also provide information on growth rate; frogs were able to breed for the first time at a minimum of 2–3 months after metamorphosis and at a size of half to two-thirds that of an average adult.

Tadpoles in pans on Barro Colorado Island, Panama, metamorphose in about 4 weeks, but with a great variance. The rainy season on Barro Colorado Island lasts from about mid-April until mid-December, 8 to 9 months. It seems possible that *P. pustulosus* might have two or three generations a year. However, at this point nothing is known about growth, maturation, or mortality rates under natural conditions, and Davidson and Hough's figures should be treated with caution.

Breeding takes place in a wide variety of places; running streams and permanent large bodies of water are rarely used, but almost any sort of small accumulation of water may be selected. Puddles, potholes, water caught in big pods, tapir tracks, or between tree roots, overflow pools along streams, and pools formed by drying streams are all natural nest sites; drains, ditches, road ruts, tank tracks, shell holes, footprints, and a wide variety of other

artificial sites have all been used. Enamel trays set out for them in the laboratory clearing on Barro Colorado Island were quickly found and persistently used, even though the frogs had to climb several inches up the side to enter the tray.

Both males and females are attracted to the calls of males, but it is not clear how the first male finds a new breeding site or what cues he uses to recognize a good one. It is probably not only smell; clean trays with fresh water are selected, and cement pools that have had water continuously for months also are used. Nor is it only topography; pools along streams at the bottom of valleys are used, as are pools on ridge tops and tractor ruts in level fields. Nor is it only vegetation; clean developing trays, densely grass-grown roadside ditches, and a small cement pond full of *Hydrilla* have all been used. Several factors in combination may be involved, but the question of how the first male finds a pond remains open.

Males call at the breeding site, usually inflated and floating on the water and commonly hidden among emergent vegetation.

In a chorus there are males that call persistently and start the chorus after a pause; other males that answer but seldom initiate a chorus; and still others that do not call at all. Some evenings a chorus may have a rigid organization with a single initiating male and the others calling in a fixed order (Brattstrom and Yarnell 1968). Other evenings the order is more variable and several frogs may initiate (M. Ryan, pers. comm.).

The call repertoire consists of: (1) a series of "clucks," which are release calls given by a male when another male attempts amplexus and to which the amplexing male responds by releasing the clucking male. (2) A "glug" call given by an inflated male when he is suddenly startled and rapidly deflates and dives; this has no apparent interspecific communication function but may occasionally startle a predator. (3) A "mew," an agnostic call given by a male when he is interacting with another male. It is frequently associated with the calling male turning to face away from the other male and backing toward him kicking and mewing. Males are not territorial because they do not defend a fixed area, but they do maintain interindividual distances through these aggressive interactions. (4) The mating call of *P. pustulosus* is one of the most complicated described for a frog. It has several forms. The simplest is given by a male calling alone and is a "whine," a glissando falling in frequency from about 700 to 500 Hz and decreasing in loudness. It is about 0.5 sec long. It is repeated more or less regularly at about 2-sec intervals. If a soloing male hears the call of a second male he may change his call by adding at the end of the whine, a "chuck." The chuck is a short, harsh sound with maximum energy of about 2 KHz. If the second male is close, or if several other males call, a calling male is likely to add two chucks to his whine. One can induce these changes in a male's calls with appropriate tape recordings, simulating differences in distance by varying loudness and differences in numbers of frogs by varying the time between calls, because in a chorus each frog generally maintains about a 2-sec interval between his calls.

One sometimes hears, in a natural chorus, calls with three chucks. I could not consistently elicit a three-chuck call with a tape stimulus. But, when I watched a pond, I heard that three-chuck and occasional four-chuck calls were produced when a calling male saw another frog move close to him. Three-chuck calls were frequently followed by an attempt to amplex with the moving frog. If the amplexed frog was a male, he clucked and was released; if the amplexed frog was a female the pair remained in amplexus and a nest was eventually built. Wooden models of frogs manipulated near a calling male elicited three-chuck calls, demonstrating that a visual component was involved.

A female ready to oviposit will approach a tape recorder that is playing either a whine or a whine with chucks, but not the chucks alone. Given a choice between a whine and whine with chucks, she chooses the whine with chucks.

Why does a male ever give less than the most attractive call?

It is striking that the whine call has the characteristics of a sound that is hard to locate, while the chucks have those that make a sound easy to localize. I suggest that the male gives a call that is hard to locate when he is alone, because any female ready to mate will eventually find him and he is less likely to be found by a predator hunting by sound. Jaeger (1976) reports a *Bufo marinus* using *P. pustulosus* calls to locate a *Physalaemus* chorus and then eating several of the males. A. Jaslow (pers. comm.) reports that both *B. marinus* and *Leptodactylus pentadactylus* seem to use calls to find calling male *P. pustulosus*. M. Ryan, R. Tuttle, and C. Rand (pers. comm.) have demonstrated with playback experiments that the carnivorous bat *Trachops cirrhosus* prefers a more complex call. Where more males are calling together there is greater competition for mates. When mate competition is high each male is willing to risk more from predation and to give a more easily locatable call.

A female ready to mate approaches a calling male; he does not attempt amplexus until she is within a few centimeters.

M. Ryan (pers. comm.) reports that larger males in a chorus are more likely to mate than are smaller males and that females choose larger males on the basis of their lower-pitched mating calls.

Calling begins at dusk and usually slows down by 2200, though sometimes a chorus may continue until dawn. Most pairs are formed in the early evening by 2100 or 2200, and nests are made during the night after the chorus dies down, occasionally on the following night.

Once a male has amplexed a receptive female the pair usually leaves the calling site, moving at least a short distance. This reduces the chances of their being found by a predator who has been attracted to the highly locatable calls frequently associated with a pair formation. Hopping and swimming, the female carries the male to a nesting spot, usually at the edge of the pool where the male was calling. Sexton and Ortleb (1966) showed that a pair preferred to place its nest against a vertical wall arising from a platform a couple of cm below the water's surface to either a slanting wall, a wall or platform alone, or a wall with a deeper platform. No observations have been made on how a perferred site is found or recognized.

Frequently nests are placed next to one another. However, this placement is most likely to be result of the behavior of several females and not the result of multiple matings by a single male as has been suggested (Brattstrom and Yarnell 1968; Rand 1957). Sometimes one sees two or even more pairs making nests simultaneously in the same spot. Twice M. Ryan (pers. comm.) saw three females start construction with their cloacas in juxtaposition. Nest building was filmed and described by Heyer and Rand (1977). Usually a nest-building pair floats in the water, frequently with the female's front feet just touching bottom. In making the nest, which takes half an hour to an hour, occasionally longer, the female repeatedly produces a combination of eggs and jelly that the male picks up with his hind feet from her vent, fertilizes, and whips into foam. He beats air into the jelly with rapid alternate strokes of his hind legs to form a fist-sized foam mass (fig. 8.25). The glistening white foam, with one hundred to two hundred white eggs embedded, floats high on the water and usually is stuck to either the side of the pool or adjacent vegetation. The eggs hatch in a day and a half or two days. If the nest is still floating, the tadpoles wriggle down through the liquefying foam and into the water below. If the nest has been stranded by falling water levels, the tadpoles collect under the nest, where they may survive for up to 5 days. The floating white nest may serve several functions. Its color is reflectant and may keep egg temperature down; evaporation from the foam would act in the same direction. Measurements by Ryan did not detect these effects. The eggs are above the surface of the water and so less susceptible to drying from small and temporary changes in water level. They are held in an oxygen-rich environment compared with the depths of the water on which it floats. The foam protects the eggs against small predators such as ants and tadpoles (M. Ryan, pers. comm.), and perhaps also against bacteria and fungi. Which of these are true and which are evolutionarily important is still unclear.

The tadpoles are mottled brown, cryptic against the bottom, where they usually spend the day. They are nocturnal (Heyer, McDiarmid, and Weigman 1975), feeding on detritus and sometimes the floating eggs of *Hyla creptians* (A. Jaslow, pers. comm.). They are eaten by *Leptodactylus pentadactylus* tadpoles, dragonfly nymphs (Heyer and Muedeking 1976), and probably other small predators. Fish and macrobrachium shrimps take them eagerly in aquariums. They are not distasteful to man (Wassersug 1971). The tadpoles develop to metamorphosis in 4 to 6 weeks and transform into frogs 5–7 mm long.

It has been argued (Heyer 1975; Wassersug 1974) that the basic frog-tadpole life cycle evolved to exploit the burst of production in the relatively predator-free temporary pools that form with the coming of the rains in the seasonal tropics. Though by no means the "primitive" frog, *Physalaemus pustulosus* does exploit the temporary pools in the lowland tropics, and its behavior and ecology are best understood in the context of adaptation to this environment.

*

Brattstrom, B. H., and Yarnell, R. M. 1968. Aggressive behavior in two species of leptodactylid frogs. *Herpetologica* 24:222–28.

Davidson, Eric, H., and Hough, Barbara R. 1969. Synchronous oogenesis in *Engystomops pustulosus*, a Neotropic anuran suitable for laboratory studies: Localization in the embryo of RNA synthesized at the Lampbrush stage. *J. Exp. Zool.* 172:25–48.

Duellman, W. E. 1965. *Engystomops pustulosus*. *Pub. Mus. Nat. Hist. Univ. Kansas* 15:577–614.

Heyer, W. Ronald. 1975. A preliminary analysis of the intergeneric relationships of the frog family Leptodactylidae. *Smithsonian Contrib. Zool.*, no. 99.

Heyer, W. Ronald; McDiarmid, Roy W.; and Weigmann, D. L. 1975. Tadpoles, predation and pond habitats in the tropics. *Biotropica* 7:100–11.

Heyer, W. Ronald, and Muedeking, Miriam H. 1976. Notes on tadpoles as prey for naiads and turtles. *J. Washington Acad. Sci.* 66:235–39.

Heyer, W. Ronald, and Rand, A. Stanley. 1977. Foam nest construction in the leptodactylid frogs *Leptodactylus pentadactylus* and *Physalaemus pustulosus* (Amphibia, Anura, Leptodactylidae). *J. Herp.* 11:225–28.

Jaeger, R. G. 1976. A possible prey-call window in anuran auditory perception. *Copeia* 4:833–34.

Lynch, John D. 1970. Systematic status of the American leptodactylid frog genera *Engystomops*, *Eupemphix* and *Physalaemus*. *Copeia* 3:488–96.

Rand, A. S. 1957. Notes on amphibians and reptiles from El Salvador. *Fieldiana, Zool.* 34:505–34.

Robinson, D. R. 1971. Check list of Costa Rican Amphibia and Reptilia. In *The book: Data, keys, illustrations and descriptions*, ed. C. E. Schnell. Ciudad Universitaria: Organization for Tropical Studies.

Savage, Jay M. 1976. *A preliminary handlist of the herpetofauna of Costa Rica.* 2d ed. San José: Editorial Universidad de Costa Rica.

Sexton, O. J., and Ortleb, E. P. 1966. Some cues used by the leptodactylid frog, *Engystomops pustulosus*, in the selection of the oviposition site. *Copeia* 2:225–30.

Wassersug, R. J. 1971. On the comparative palatability of some dry-season tadpoles from Costa Rica. *Am. Midl. Nat.* 86:101–9.

———. 1974. Evolution of anuran life cycles. *Science* 185:377–78.

Rana palmipes (Rana, Web-footed Frog)

D. C. Robinson

In spite of its broad distribution, from low elevations in southern Veracruz and the Isthmus of Tehuantepec, Mexico, to the Amazon basin of northern Brazil, surprisingly little has been published on this species. It is equally surprising, and refreshing, that it has not been broken up into innumerable subspecies.

Although somewhat larger, reaching 110 mm snout-vent length, the species is reminiscent of the green frog, *Rana clamitans*, in general appearance. As suggested by the specific epithet, the toes are fully webbed. The dorsal surface of the tibia bears longitudinal glands unique among the Costa Rican species of *Rana*. *Rana maculata* is a species found in Nicaragua not far from the Costa Rican Pacific border. It has a light stripe on the upper lip and lacks the tibial glands. This species should be watched for in Guanacaste.

Rana palmipes prefers quiet water and usually stays near the edge, leaping into the water and hiding on the bottom or under bordering vegetation when startled. Like most species of *Rana*, it is active both day and night. Greding (1976) described the call of specimens in the lake on the grounds of CATIE, Turrialba, as consisting of " 'grunts,' each lasting about 0.2 sec. . . . Grunts are separated by intervals of 2.0–11. sec. of silence." He provides audiospectrograms. Food items reported by Noble (1918) include fish and juveniles of the same species.

The tadpole, at least in Nicaragua (Villa 1972), may be distinguished from those of *R. pipiens* and *R. warschewitschii*, sympatric species, by its having four upper and four lower labial tooth rows. It reaches 60–70 mm total length, with metamorphosis occurring at a snout-vent length of 28.1–30.6 mm. Volpe and Harvey (1958) described and illustrated three stages of the developing larvae. Breder (1946) stated that in Panama "the tadpoles of *Rana palmipes* appeared to feed on the newly laid eggs of *Bufo* near Yavisa on March 10. At least they scraped in feeding attitude along the jelly-like strings which were too new to have accumulated much detritus."

Savage (1966) supplied a map of the distribution of this species in Mexico and Central America. In Costa Rica it is found on both the Atlantic and the Pacific lowlands and hence is not sympatric with *Rana vibicaria,* the fourth Costa Rican species, which is found only at high altitudes. The investigation by Zweifel (1964) of this latter species could be used as a model for a comparative study of *R. palmipes.*

*

Breder, C. M., Jr. 1946. Amphibians and reptiles of the Rio Chucunaque drainage, Darien, Panama, with notes on their life histories and habits. *Bull. Am. Mus. Nat. Hist.* 86:375–436.

Greding, E. J., Jr. 1976. Call of the tropical American frog *Rana palmipes* Spix (Amphibia, Anura, Ranidae). *J. Herp.* 10:263–64.

Noble, G. K. 1918. The amphibians and reptiles collected by the American Museum expedition to Nicaragua in 1916. *Bull. Am. Mus. Nat. Hist.* 38:311–47.

Savage, J. M. 1966. The origins and history of the Central American herpetofauna. *Copeia* 4:719–66.

Villa, J. 1972. *Anfibios de Nicaragua.* Managua: Colección Fauna Nacional, Instituto Geográfico Nacional y Banco Central de Nicaragua.

Volpe, E. P., and Harvey, S. M. 1958. Hybridization and larval development in *Rana palmipes* Spix. *Copeia* 3:197–207.

Zweifel, R. G. 1964. Distribution and life history of the Central American frog, *Rana vibicaria. Copeia* 2:300–308.

Rhadinaea decorata (Culebra)

N. J. Scott

This pretty little snake (Colubridae) is a common inhabitant of the wet lowland forest floor in eastern Mexico, Central America, and northwestern South America. It is a diurnal frog-eater that seldom reaches 400 mm total length (Myers 1974). There are seven other species in the genus in Costa Rica that play similar roles in wet forests at all elevations. Other small snakes that have similar habits are members of the genera *Coniophanes, Mastigodryas, Dendrophidion,* and *Pliocercus.* Their principal prey are probably frogs of the genus *Eleutherodactylus.*

The biology of *R. decorata* and its allies is virtually unknown. Several of them, like *R. decorata,* have bright red bellies. They are oviparous.

*

Myers, C. W. 1974. The systematics of *Rhadinae* (Colubridae), a genus of New World snakes. *Bull. Am. Mus. Nat. Hist.* 153:1–262.

Rhinoclemmys annulata (Tortuga Parda Terrestre, Jicote, Jicotea, Brown Land Turtle)

C. H. Ernst

This diurnal, terrestrial turtle is a rain-forest resident on the Caribbean lowlands of Costa Rica and also follows the gallery forests onto the highlands to over 1,500 m elevation.

Adults may grow to 20 cm in carapace length. The high carapace is usually flattened across the vertebrals and is extremely variable in color and pattern, ranging from totally black to dark brown with orange pleural and vertebral blotches to tan with yellow on the pleurals and vertebrals. The pleural blotches often consist of radiations from the dorsal-posterior corner. The vertebral keel is usually yellow. (This variation reminds one of the similar situation is eastern box turtles, *Terrapene carolina,* of North America; it provides good concealment among the dried leaves and vegetation on the forest floor.) The unhinged plastron is well developed, upturned anteriorly and notched posteriorly; it is black or dark brown with a yellow border and may have a yellow midseam. The snout projects slightly, and there is a wide yellow or reddish stripe running from the orbit at a slight angle to the nape. Another stripe runs from the lower posterior orbit to the tympanum, where it meets a similar stripe from the upper jaw. There is also a stripe from the upper anterior orbit to the tip of the snout. The yellow chin may be mottled with very small dark spots. The toes are unwebbed, and the forelimbs have large yellowish scales with dark stripes of wide black spots.

Males have concave plastrons and longer tails with the vent beyond the carapace margin; females have flat plastrons and shorter tails with the vent beneath the carapace.

Rhinoclemmys annulata is herbivorous, feeding on ferns, shrubs, and various seedlings. Mittermeier (1971) listed the following food plants: ferns—*Tectaria incisa, T. eurylobi, Adiantum* sp.; tall shrub seedlings—*Hybanthus prunifolius, Pavonia rosea, Faramea occidentalis, Stylogyne* sp., *Xylosma* sp.; shrub seedlings—*Alseis blackiana, Psychotria limonenus, Acalypha diversifolia;* vines—*Philodendron* sp., *Hiraea* sp., *Selaginella arthritica;* seedlings—Bignoniaceae. Fruits such as bananas and papaya are also relished.

Most activity (i.e., foraging or movements) occurs during the morning hours (0700–1200). The turtles are also very active immediately after heavy rains, when they can be found marching along paths and roads. When not active, they scoop out forms in fallen leaves or retreat beneath tangled vines or among root masses. They often enter pools of water to cool off. One specimen was collected with a leech (*Placobdella*?) attached, and ticks

(*Ambylomma sabanerae, A. crassum,* and *A. humerlae*) may heavily infest them.

Few observations have been made on the reproductive habits of *R. annulata*. There are conflicting reports about whether it actually digs a nest cavity or just hides the eggs under leaf litter. The egg-laying period is unknown, and courtship has not been described. Apparently only one or two ellipsoidal eggs are laid at one time.

This turtle, though fairly common in many areas, is practically unknown, and studies of its ecological and behavioral parameters are needed.

*

Ernst, C. H. 1978. A revision of the Neotropical turtle genus *Callopsis* (Testudines: Emydidae: Batagurinae). *Herpetologica* 34:113–34.

Ernst, C. H., and Ernst, E. M. 1977. 1977. Ectoparasites associated with Neotropical turtles of the genus *Callopsis* (Testudines: Emydidae: Batagurinae). *Biotropica* 9:139–42.

Medem, F. 1956. Informe sobre reptiles Colombianos I. Noticia sobre el primer hallazgo de la tortuga *Geoemyda annulata* (Gray) en Colombia. *Caldasia* 7:317–25.

———. 1962. La distribución geográfica y ecología de los Crocodylia y Testudinata en el Departamento del Chocó. *Rev. Acad. Colombiana Cienci. Exactos Fis. Nat., Bogota* 11:279–303.

Mittermeier, R. A. 1971. Notes on the behavior and ecology of *Rhinoclemys annulata* Gray. *Herpetologica* 27:485–88.

Rhinoclemmys funerea (Tortuga Negra del Río, Jicote, Black River Turtle)

C. H. Ernst

This large aquatic turtle (carapace length to 32 cm) (fig. 8.26) inhabits the Caribbean drainage of Costa Rica. Its preferred habitats include marshes, swamps, ponds, streams, and rivers in humid forested areas. There it can often be seen basking on partially submerged logs.

Adults have a high, somewhat domed, dark brown to black carapace, but some yellow occurs on the pleurals of the juvenile shell. The unhinged plastron is well developed, upturned anteriorly, and notched posteriorly; it is black with yellow seam borders and a wide yellow midseam. The head is black with a wide lateral yellow stripe above the tympanum. Two narrower stripes run from the orbit and the corner of the mouth to the tympanum. The snout protrudes slightly, and there are large black spots on the yellow lower jaw and chin. The toes are strongly webbed, and the skin of the forelimbs is black with yellow vermiculations.

Males have concave plastrons and longer tails with the vent posterior to the carapace margin; females have flat plastrons and shorter tails with the vent beneath the carapace.

FIGURE 8.26. *Rhinoclemmys funerea,* adult. Costa Rica, 1980 (rule 15 cm in length) (Escuela de Biología, Universidad de Costa Rica, D. C. Robinson; photo, D. H. Janzen).

In the wild these turtles are highly herbivorous, feeding on a variety of fruits, grasses, and broad-leaved plants; but in captivity they accepted meats. They often forage on land at night and consequently are sometimes parasitized by the tick *Ambylomma sabanerae*.

Both sexes attain sexual maturity at approximately 20 cm plastron length (Moll and Legler 1971). Spermatogenesis occurs from April through August, and corpora lutea or oviducal eggs are present in females from April through July. During courtship the male chases the female in the water, and when she slows or stops he swims to her side, presents his extended head and neck, and rapidly vibrates his head in the sagittal plane (Iverson 1975). Ovipositing occurs one to four times a season, with clutches averaging three eggs. The nesting act has not been recorded. Eggs incubated at 20–35° C by Moll and Legler (1971) hatched in 98 to 104 days.

As can be seen, relatively little is known of this turtle's behavior or ecology.

*

Ernst, C. H. 1978. A revision of the Neotropical turtle genus *Callopsis* (Testudines: Emydidae: Batagurinae). *Herpetologica* 34:113–34.

Ernst, C. H., and Ernst, E. M. 1977. Ectoparasites associated with Neotropical turtles of the genus *Callopsis* (Testudines: Emydidae: Batagurinae). *Biotropica* 9:139–42.

Iverson, J. B. 1975. Notes on courtship in *Rhinoclemys funerea*. *J. Herp.* 9:249–50.

Moll, E. O., and Legler, J. M. 1971. The life history of a Neotropical slider turtle, *Pseudemys scripta* (Schoepff), in Panama. *Bull. Los Angeles County Mus. Nat. Hist.* 11:1–102.

Rhinoclemmys pulcherrima (Tortuga Roja, Red Turtle)

C. H. Ernst

The Costa Rican subspecies of red turtle, *Rhinoclemmys pulcherrima manni* (Dunn), is one of the most beautiful of the world's turtles. Its high-domed carapace (length to 23 cm) has a gaudy pattern of orangish red, yellow, and black ocelli on each pleural, and there are similarly colored concentrics on each vertebral (fig. 8.27a). This pattern tends to break up the outline of the turtle, and the colors help camouflage it among forest vegetation; this is especially important for concealing the defenseless young. The unhinged plastron (fig. 8.27b) is well developed and notched posteriorly; it is yellow with a narrow to wide central dark blotch, and the seams are often dark-bordered. The head (fig. 8.27c) is brown to greenish and contains a series of bright orange red stripes: (1) a median stripe running forward between the orbits to the dorsal tip of the snout where it meets two other stripes, one from each orbit, to form a prefrontal arrow (the lateral stripes may extend through the orbit to the nape, and any of these stripes may be discontinuous); (2) a stripe running posteriorly from below the nostrils along the upper jaw to the tympanum; (3) a stripe running from each nostril to the corresponding orbit; and (4) several stripes (usually two or three) from the orbit to the tympanum. The yellow lower jaw and chin may have dark ocelli. The toes are only slightly webbed, and the forelimbs are covered with large red or yellow scales with rows of black spots.

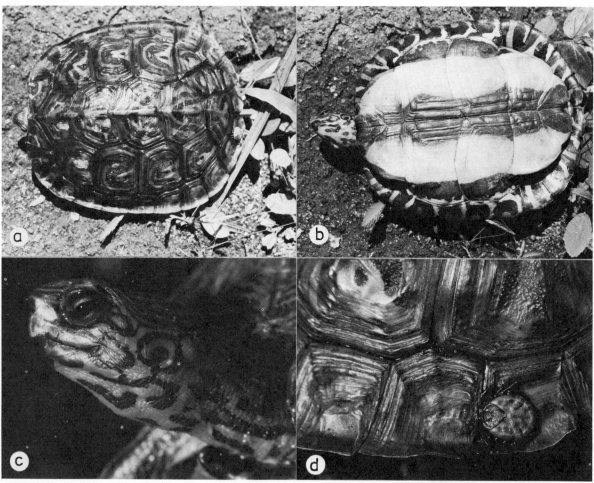

FIGURE 8.27. *Rhinoclemmys pulcherrima. a,* Dorsal view of adult. *b,* Ventral view of adult, margins of carapace strongly marked with yellow bands against a black spot with a red center. *c,* Head marked with yellow, red, and black. *d,* Tick feeding between dorsal scutes. Santa Rosa National Park, June 1980 (photos, D. H. Janzen).

Males have concave plastrons and longer tails with the vent beyond the carapace margin; females are larger, with flat plastrons slightly upturned anteriorly and shorter tails with the vent beneath the carapace rim.

Rhinoclemmys pulcherrima occurs in Pacific Costa Rica southward to the vicinity of San José. Over most of the range it is a lowland species. Originally it was probably an inhabitant of moist woodlands or scrublands, but now it is common in cleared areas, especially those close to streams, where it occupies gallery forests. The red turtle seems to prefer moist situations and has been observed wading and swimming in streams and rain pools, especially during the dry season. It is very active after rains, when many can be found walking through the fields and along roads. Conversely, it has been found up to 1 km from water, but in such cases it usually seeks out moist vegetation.

In their terrestrial habitat these turtles come in contact with ticks and are often infested (fig. 8.27*d*). Both *Amblyomma sabanerae* and *A. dissimile* have been recorded.

In nature, *R. pulcherrima* is probably an omnivore, but with stronger preferences toward plant foods. The wild foods have not been recorded, but captives readily eat a variety of domestic fruits and vegetables, earthworms, fish, beef strips, and canned dog food. When given a choice, they usually choose plant foods over meats.

Reproductive habits in the wild have not been recorded, but Christensen (1975) has published some observations on captive Guatemalan *R. p. incisa*. He reports that their courtship is not spectacular, consisting only of a rather direct approach by the male. His turtles laid four clutches of three to five eggs each from September through December. The eggs were incubated at 65–85°F, and some young hatched from 30 January to 17 March. (Duration of incubation was 115–86 days.) The hatchlings first showed a preference for green leaves and small insects, but within a few weeks they were accepting nearly everything eaten by adults.

It can be seen that very little has been reported on this common Costa Rican turtle. A thorough study would certainly be rewarding.

Janzen (1980) has hypothesized that *R. pulcherrima* is a Batesian mimic of the coral snake (*Micrurus nigrocinctus*), which is common in its deciduous forest habitat. The proposed mimicry is based on the brilliant red, yellow, and black concentric rings on the backs of juveniles and on the relatively persistent red, yellow, and black banding along the margin of the underside of the turtle and on the upper side of the plastron where it projects out under the turtle's head.

*

Christensen, R. M. 1975. Breeding Central American wood turtles. *Chelonia* 2:8–10.

Ernst, C. H. 1978. A revision of the Neotropical turtle genus *Callopsis* (Testudines: Emydidae: Batagurinae). *Herpetologica* 34:113–34.

Ernst, C. H., and Ernst, E. M. 1977. Ectoparasites associated with Neotropical turtles of the genus *Callopsis* (Testudines: Emydidae: Batagurinae). *Biotropica* 9: 139–42.

Janzen, D. H. 1980. Two potential coral snake mimics in a tropical deciduous forest. *Biotropica,* 12:77–78.

Mertens, R. 1952. Die Amphibien und Reptilien von El Salvador. *Abh. Senckenberg Naturforsch. Ges.* 487: 1–120.

Rhinophrynus dorsalis (Alma de Vaca, Sapo Borracho, Mexican Burrowing Toad)

M. S. Foster and R. W. McDiarmid

This interesting frog (fig. 8.28) is the only living member of the family Rhinophrynidae, from which two other species are known in the fossil record. It is widely distributed in the Pacific lowlands from near the mouth of the Río Balsas, Michoacán, Mexico, south to northwestern Costa Rica and on the Gulf and Caribbean coasts from southern Texas to northern Nicaragua (Fouguette 1969; Duellman 1971). In Costa Rica it is found on the Nicoya Peninsula and in the adjacent lowlands of Guanacaste Province south to Caldera near Puntarenas. It is most common in subtropical and tropical dry forest habitats characterized by distinct wet and dry seasons. It inhabits forest but most frequently is encountered in pastures, cultivated fields, roadside ditches, and other open areas during periods of heavy rain.

FIGURE 8.28. *Rhinophrynus dorsalis,* blackish purple with orange markings, collected while calling. Santa Rosa National Park, 10 May 1980 (photo, D. H. Janzen).

The body form of these frogs is unusual, having sometimes been described as an amorphous mass or blob of jelly. Snout-vent lengths of adults range from 50 to 88 mm ($\bar{x}$ = 60–65 mm) with females generally larger than males (Fouquette 1969). The head is somewhat cone-shaped with no distinct neck region; the eyes are very small with movable lids and can only be described as beady. The frogs have short, fat legs and an extremely loose-skinned, pliable body which they can inflate markedly, greatly increasing body size and forming a more or less rigid structure. The noticeably smooth skin varies from shades of dark gray and maroon brown to dark brown dorsally with pale yellow to red orange markings that usually include a vertebral stripe and irregular spots or splotches. Ventrally the frogs are uniform gray.

When aboveground, the frogs generally walk with their legs splayed out to the sides. They appear a bit clumsy, with their stomachs more or less touching the ground, but if disturbed they can hop quite respectably and despite their build may jump 15 cm or more. The species is fossorial, and individuals burrow hind-end first by means of large keratinized digging tubercles located on each hallux and on the adjacent metatarsals (Fouquette 1969). The legs may be used alternately or simultaneously for digging. As the frog burrows into mud, it gradually turns in the hole, entering the ground in corkscrew fashion. Dirt is thrown up in irregular folds around the opening, but the animal's wiggling and turning cause the hole to collapse and the sides to cave in toward the center and cover the opening once the frog is beneath the surface. Frogs have been located 7–15 cm beneath the surface during the wet season but undoubtedly go deeper in the dry season, when they often are found under the bases of fence posts (Foster and McDiarmid, n.d.). Underground, the frog makes a small, round chamber more or less equivalent in diameter to its length. Inside the chamber it inflates its body, so tightly wedging itself inside that it cannot be dislodged unless one wall of the chamber is completely removed.

How long frogs may occupy a chamber at any time is not known, though during the rainy season it may be as little as one day, with individuals coming up at night, presumably to feed (the diet consists of a variety of insects, especially ants). Other individuals have been recorded occupying burrows for up to a month before moving (Foster and McDiarmid, n.d.), though in captivity they have stayed buried for as long as 2 years without feeding (Fouquette and Rossman 1963). Once buried, the frogs dry quickly (though the soil may remain moist); the skin usually is *completely* dry to the touch when an individual is dug up or emerges, and it may be caked with dirt. Although the skin is highly glandular and copious amounts of a sticky white material are secreted when the frog is disturbed, no evidence of this material or any parchmentlike covering has been noted in buried individuals. This secretion may serve as a defense mechanism, since it causes a severe allergic reaction in some humans and has been known to rot cloth "snake" bags, despite frequent washings, after a week to 10 days. Frogs dug up after passing several to many days in burrows often release several milliliters of urine immediately on removal. They may rub their bodies in it to moisten at least the ventral surface and sometimes more of the body. Immediately upon being removed from the burrow, the frogs are alert and move about actively.

Breeding among individuals in a population is highly synchronized and seems to coincide with the first rain of the season heavy enough to fill the ponds in which the frogs breed. The ponds used in Guanacaste, Costa Rica, usually fill in late May or early June and persist through the wet season, though the frogs breed only once in late May or early June, and all tadpoles usually have metamorphosed by the latter part of July (Foster and McDiarmid, n.d.). Occasionally the population is divided, each part breeding once in conjunction with heavy rains a few days to a few weeks apart. Though breeding usually occurs only once in the population, individuals begin activity with the first heavy rains, and occasional animals may be found at that time. Most of these move toward the breeding ponds, where they burrow again until conditions are appropriate for reproduction. In anticipation of that, males may be heard calling from their underground chambers on afternoons of heavy rain. When the appropriate breeding night arrives, the frogs move rapidly toward the ponds. Often males begin calling from land as they approach the pond. They usually enter the water immediately and sit half submerged in the shallows calling; or, inflating their bodies, they may call while floating like balloons over the deeper parts of the pond with legs outstretched. The call is extremely loud and is best described as a long-drawn-out whoop with a rising inflection at the end. Large choruses of calling *Rhinophrynus* are deafening and may be heard for several kilometers. Early in the evening, most males approach the pond alone. By 2130 or so, as many as 80% of the frogs approaching the pond are already in amplexus, the male being carried along on the back of the female. Amplexus is pelvic. Both the male and the female are submerged for egg laying, during which the eggs are extruded one at a time but with six to twelve following each other in rapid succession and rapidly sinking to the bottom (Foster and McDiarmid, n.d.). Though initially separate, the eggs shortly become very sticky on the surface, and adjacent eggs may adhere to each other to form clumps. Clutch size is extremely variable and may range from two to eight thousand.

The eggs hatch after several days, releasing larvae that are broad and deep with broad, flat heads. Their most characteristic feature is a wide, slitlike mouth that extends across the entire front of the head and is bordered by a series of barbels (Orton 1943). They are blackish above and iridescent silvery gold below. Within the pond the tadpoles aggregate into schools that vary in size from about 10 cm in diameter to more than a meter across. Spacing and movements of individuals within the schools vary considerably (Stuart 1961; Foster and McDiarmid, n.d.). In some the tadpoles are regularly arrayed, moving together in a single direction in a coordinated fashion. In others the individuals "boil," describing a circular path downward in the center of the school and upward at its periphery. The tadpoles are filter feeders that strain algae and detritus from the water. Under certain conditions of high density they also may be cannibalistic (Starrett 1960; Foster and McDiarmid, n.d.). The tadpoles are preyed upon heavily by both vertebrates (e.g., *Kinosternon scorpioides, Podiceps dominicus, Jacana spinosa, Pitangus sulphuratus,* several species of herons, *Synbranchus marmoratus,* etc.) and invertebrates (naiads, larvae or adult odonates, belostomatids, hydrophilids, dytiscids, etc.). Both development time and size at metamorphosis vary markedly according to water temperature and other conditions in the pond. Metamorphosis is approximately simultaneous in all tadpoles in a population, and froglets leave the pond en masse (Foster and McDiarmid, n.d.) much as has been described for species of *Scaphiopus* (Neil 1957; Bragg 1965). Newly metamorphosed froglets are pigmented black, though small spots on the snout and a vertebral line often are visible. Froglets may walk, but they more often hop, being able to cover 10–12 cm in a single leap. When they leave the water the tail is still obvious, but the froglets are able to burrow immediately, simply folding the tail over the dorsal surface of the body. True to their schooling habit, they have been found in aggregations some 2 weeks or more after leaving the pond (Foster and McDiarmid, n.d.).

*

Bragg, A. N. 1965. *Gnomes of the night: The spadefoot toads.* Philadelphia: University of Pennsylvania Press.

Duellman, W. E. 1971. The burrowing toad, *Rhinophrynus dorsalis,* on the Caribbean lowlands of Central America. *Herpetologica* 27:55–56.

Foster, M. S., and McDiarmid, R. W. n.d. The reproductive ecology and behavior of *Rhinophrynus dorsalis* in northwestern Costa Rica, in preparation.

Fouquette, M. J., Jr. 1969. Rhinophrynidae, *Rhinophrynus, R. dorsalis. Cat. Am. Amphib. Rept.,* 78.1–78.2

Fouquette, M. J., Jr., and Rossman, D. A. 1963. Noteworthy records of Mexican amphibians and reptiles in the Florida State Museum and the Texas Natural History Collection. *Herpetologica* 19:185–201.

Neill, W. T. 1957. Notes on metamorphic and breeding aggregations of the eastern spadefoot, *Scaphiopus holbrooki* (Harlan). *Herpetologica* 13:185–87.

Orton, G. 1943. The tadpole of *Rhinophrynus dorsalis. Occ. Pap. Mus. Zool. Univ. Michigan* 472:1–7.

Starrett, P. 1960. Descriptions of tadpoles of Middle American frogs. *Misc. Publ. Mus. Zool. Univ. Michigan* 110:1–37.

Stuart, L. C. 1961. Some observations on the natural history of tadpoles of *Rhinophrynus dorsalis* Dumeril and Bibron. *Herpetologica* 17:73–79.

Sceloporus malachiticus (Lagartija Espinosa, Spiny Lizard)

D. C. Robinson

This is the southernmost representative of the large group of spiny lizards, iguanids found throughout temperate North America, south to and including Panama. There are some ninety-five species in the genus, three of which reach Costa Rica. *Sceloporus malachiticus* may be readily distinguished from *S. squamosus* and *S. variabilis,* which are themselves very similar, by size (*S. malachiticus* larger), color (green or dark as opposed to striped and tan), or vertical range (600 m and above in Costa Rica). The species is found from Veracruz and Chiapas, Mexico, to Panama, and the nominate subspecies is found from Guatemala to Panama.

A young specimen living in the patio of my house showed considerable metachrosis as a function of temperature (or light?), being invariably dark, almost black, in the early morning hours and malachite green at noon. Here is a chance for investigation. This individual, at the altitude of San José, slept clinging vertically, several inches off the ground, on the base of an elephant ear plant (Araceae). Although at higher altitudes (e.g., Cerro Asunción, Cerro de la Muerte) the species tends to be terrestrial, it is commonly seen on rooftops and walls around San José. On a rooftop it will remain in one spot for a while, apparently searching for insects and occasionally catching them within its visual acuity range, then will suddenly run to another spot a few meters away and repeat the process. Del Toro (1960) gives the food as insects, whereas an unpublished student report lists insects, especially bees, as well as leaves, young shoots of chayote (a type of squash), coffee flowers, and ripe coffee beans, from which the author asserts that they extract the sweet juice. He also states that no species of *Sceloporus* in Costa Rica was observed to eat ants. These observations merit corroboration. Reznick, Sexton, and Mantis (1981) have investigated initial prey preferences of neonate and inexperienced individuals of this species and demonstrated an innate avoidance of an aposematic prey similar to a species sympatric with the lizards.

Sceloporus malachiticus, unlike many other species of the genus, is viviparous. Marion and Sexton (1971) studied the reproductive cycle in Costa Rica and reported "an annual ovarian cycle, leading to one brood of young. . . . Embryos were carried for a considerable length of time, with the majority being born in the early dry season during late January and February. . . . Number of embryos was strongly correlated to female size, and the average of all lizards collected was six young. Young females mature around 65 mm snout-vent length." Viviparity (ovoviviparity preferred by some) is common in squamatans from high latitudes or altitudes and is presumably an adaptation whereby the basking behavior of the gravid female assures adequate temperatures for embryonic development. Ovulation occurs in September. It is not known whether temperature preferences or requirements vary seasonally with respect to reproductive cycle, nor do we know the exact role of metachrosis in temperature regulation. Information on basking temperatures of the two sexes during the gravid season is desirable.

The following occurrence, near Jardín de Dota, suggests a predator. We were trying to catch a specimen of *S. malachiticus* on a bank. It escaped to the entrance of a hole but entered only at the latest possible moment. On removing it seconds later, we found it dead and then, with considerably more care, we extracted a *Bothrops godmani*.

Greenberg (1977) published a paper on *S. cyanogenys,* another viviparous species, which includes a "behavior inventory." This study should certainly be consulted by anyone interested in the behavior of *S. malachiticus.*

*

Del Toro, M. A. 1960. *Reptiles de Chiapas.* Tuxtla Gutiérrez, Mexico: Institutio de Historia Natural de Chiapas.

Greenberg, N. 1977. An ethogram of the blue spiny lizard, *Sceloporus cyanogenys* (Reptilia, Lacertilia, Iguanidae). *J. Herp.* 11:177–95.

Marion, K. R., and Sexton, O. J. 1971. The reproductive cycle of the lizard *Sceloporus malachiticus* in Costa Rica. *Coepia* 1971:517–26.

Reznick, D.; Sexton, O. J.; and Mantis, C. 1981. Initial prey preferences in the lizard *Sceloporus malachiticus*. *Coepia* 1981:681–86.

Sphenomorphus cherriei (Escincela Parda, Skink)

H. S. Fitch

This small lizard is a typical skink, having the head, body, and tail elongated and the limbs small and weak (see fig. 8.29 for a skink). Some technical scincid charac-

FIGURE 8.29. Adult skink, *Mabuya unimarginata,* life-size. Santa Rosa National Park, July 1980 (photo, D. H. Janzen). This animal is similar in aspect to *Sphenomorphus cherriei.*

ters are: dentition pleurodont (that is, having the teeth set on the inner margin of the jawbone), temporal arch present on side of skull (but partly covered over by a posterior extension of the postfrontal bone), pupil of eye round, six cervical vertebrae, osteoderms present (these are minute bony plates, one underlying each scale), providing, in effect, a light armor like chain mail and conferring considerable protection against small predators.

Within the large family Scincidae, cosmopolitan in the warmer parts of the world, *S. cherriei* belongs to the subfamily Lygosominae, along with a host of other species. All but a few of these occur in the Old World tropics. The lygosomines are of special interest in showing an evolutionary trend toward subterranean habits and loss of limbs, perhaps paralleling the early ancestors of the snakes in this regard. There are lygosomines at every stage, from those that are "lacertiform" (fairly typical lizards, with well-developed limbs, capable of running and even climbing) to those that are "serpentiform" with bodies slender and elongate and limbs absent. Lygosomines usually live where there is dense ground cover, and in locomotion the walking movements of the limbs are supplemented by lateral undulatory movements of the body. Ground objects along the skink's course do not impede its progress but are used to brace against as the lizard pushes its body forward by wriggling movements. When the animal is moving slowly, as in searching for food, progress may be mainly by walking, with some dragging of the body and tail, but in a dash for shelter an alarmed skink may progress by rapid wriggling movements with little assistance from the limbs. In lygosomines that live in dense grass, leaf litter, loose soil, or other heavy cover, the evolutionary trend has been for the body to become progressively longer and the wriggling movements more effective in locomotion, with accompanying reduction in limbs. As the limbs become smaller the number of toes is reduced. Finally the limbs themselves are lost, but internally the snakelike skink differs from a true snake in retaining well-developed pectoral and pelvic girdles and in many other structures.

Typical lizards differ from snakes in having eyelids,

but lygosomine skinks have evolved in the direction of a snakelike eye. In the large genus *Leiolopisma* eyelids are present, and as in other lizards it is the lower lid that covers the eye. This lower lid has at its center a transparent window through which the skink may see out even with its eyes shut. Through further evolution the genus *Ablepharus* has developed a snakelike eye—permanently open and covered with a transparent brille. *S. cherriei* has in the past usually been assigned to the large genus *Leiolopisma* or the closely related *Scincella*, but unlike the skinks of those genera it has the primitive type of lower eyelid, with scaly covering and no window.

Other morphological characters pertaining to the skull bones and the scalation of the head also indicate that relationships of *S. cherriei* are with the genus *Sphenomorphus* rather than with *Leiolopisma* or *Scincella*. This poses a zoogeographical riddle because the many other *Sphenomorphus* species are confined to Southeast Asia, Indonesia, Australia, and Melanesia.

S. cherriei is not readily mistaken for any other kind of lizard that shares its range. The dorsal surface is bronze brown with a satiny sheen, with numerous black specks that are noticeable only on close inspection. The sides are darker than the dorsum. A black stripe on each side begins behind the nostril, passes across the eye and temporal region and neck, and becomes diffuse on the side of the body. There is a pale cream-colored line below the eye, extending posteriorly onto the side of the body, where it fades. The ventral surface is yellow on the body and tail base, grading into gray farther along the tail. The scales are smooth and rhomboidal and arranged in regular rows, sixty-two to seventy dorsally from the occiput to the end of the body (averaging a few more in females than in males) and thirty or thirty-two rows around the body. Snout-vent length in adults ranges from 48 to 66 mm (average 54.6). Although females attain a slightly larger maximum size, the average is just the same in males and females—an unusual relationship. In most skinks, for instance, females are larger than males. There are average differences in proportions. The male has a relatively broader head, and the base of the tail is slightly swollen (as it lodges the hemipenes). Also, there is a difference in relative limb length. If the hind limb is extended forward along the side and the forelimb extended backward, the toe tips usually overlap slightly in adult males but usually fail by a narrow margin to overlap in adult females. In individuals with intact tails the tail is from 1½ to 1⅔ times the snout-vent length. The relative tail length averages somewhat greater in males than females and is greater in adults than in juveniles.

The geographic range extends from Tabasco in southern Mexico south through most of Central America and into Panama. *S. cherriei* occurs in a variety of climates at low and medium altitudes but chiefly in humid lowlands with a rain-forest type of vegetation. It thrives best in forest edge and disturbed situations, rather than in primary rain forest. It perhaps attains maximum densities in cacao groves; at least it is much more easily seen and captured there than in more natural situations. The shade and heavy leaf litter provide some of the main requirements.

Activity is strictly diurnal and is concentrated during a few hours of the daily cycle. It usually reaches a peak about midmorning, when air has warmed to the preferred level. The skinks are active mainly at environmental temperatures between 23° and 27° C, and their body temperatures usually approximate their surroundings but tend to be a little higher. Like other forest lizards, these are not habitual baskers, but they may rest for a few moments in patches of sunlight, thereby rapidly raising body temperature above that of the air and substrate. Usually at such times only part of the body is exposed to sunshine. In fact, the lizards tend to keep under cover whether resting or moving. Body temperatures during activity are usually 25–27° C. During the heat of midday the skinks usually retire to shelter and are not in evidence. There is a second daily peak of activity about midafternoon, but it is minor compared with the morning peak. Perhaps it consists of the minority of lizards that have failed to obtain a stomachful of food in the course of their morning foraging.

Food consists mostly of small arthropods. A great variety of insects are taken, including many larvae and pupae. Like other skinks, these are olfaction-oriented and can find and recognize prey even if it is immobile. The protrusible forked tongue serves for constant testing of the substrate and conveys olfactory sensations to Jacobson's organ in the palate. Prey is taken only within a certain size range. It is swallowed whole (after being crushed in the jaws, beaten against the ground, or both, which sometimes results in knocking off appendages). Ingesting the prey whole imposes an upper limit on the size of objects taken. However, relatively large food objects are preferred, and a full stomach may contain only one or a few items. Large adults are able to swallow hatchlings, and cannibalism may aid in the maintenance of stable populations.

S. cherriei is oviparous, whereas viviparity seems to be the most frequent mode of reproduction in the Old World species of *Sphenomorphus*. The egg clutch is small, with only one to three eggs; two is the most frequent number. Larger females tend to lay more eggs per clutch than smaller ones and also may produce clutches oftener. Ovarian follicles grow slowly over periods of weeks. In the humid Caribbean lowlands there is reproduction throughout the year, but probably its level is influenced by the amount and distribution of rainfall. For instance, at Turrialba, where the climate is cooler and dryer than in the adjacent lowlands, egg laying comes to a halt in November and does not resume until April. It is not known how many clutches a female may produce in the course of a year. Natural nests have not been described. In the damp leaf litter where the lizards live, the nest burrows excavated by most lizards for their eggs seem superfluous, and perhaps the eggs are dropped separately without the female's digging a burrow for them.

Hatchlings of *S. cherriei* are relatively large; with a snout-vent length of 22 mm, they are about 40% of adult length. Few reptiles have a higher ratio of hatchling to adult length, and in some it is much lower. The young make their most rapid growth in their first month. By the time they are 7 months old they have attained a snout-vent length of 48 mm, the minimum size for sexual maturity, and females may have enlarging ovarian follicles. Additional time is required for the eggs to mature and be laid, and for several weeks of incubation. Average generation time may be about a year. Population turnover is fairly rapid, and no marked individuals have been recaptured after intervals longer than 7 months.

Natural enemies of *S. cherriei* are numerous and varied. Snakes may be most important and probably include most species that co-occur with the skink, but not the largest or smallest kinds or some others adapted to specialized diets other than lizards. Among mammals such predators as the coati (*Nasua narica*), armadillo (*Dasypus novemcinctus*), and opossum (*Didelphis marsupialis*) are surely important. Larger lizards also eat them; in one instance an anole (*Anolis lemurinus*) that was captured had swallowed a skink except for the tail, which still protruded from the anole's mouth. Birds also must be important predators, although no specific records are at hand. More than raptors, such ground-foraging birds as tinamous, curasows, guans, and even robins might take them frequently. Also, the larger kinds of frogs and toads that forage on the forest floor must eat them at least occasionally.

The body armor of osteoderms is effective only against the smallest natural enemies. Otherwise the skinks must depend on their elusive jerky movements and the dense cover in their chosen habitat to escape predators. The tail often serves as an effective escape mechanism through autotomy. Caudal vertebrae other than those near to the body have transverse fracture planes across the middle of their centra, and the tail breaks easily if the skink is grasped by it. The broken-off tail wiggles vigorously at first and often diverts the attention of a predator for the instant it takes the stub-tailed skink to reach shelter. The high incidence of regenerated tails (often with several regenerated segments) among older and larger individuals attests to the effectiveness of autotomy as an escape mechanism.

Also, the tail functions in balance and locomotion. The skink's elusiveness is due to its ability to make quick turns and to dodge rather than to actual fleetness. These maneuvers are accomplished partly with the aid of the tail. With a flip of the heavy tail an excited skink can instantly spin around through an arc of 180° and dart away in a new direction. In leaf litter such sudden changes in direction are effective in deceiving a predator, and the skink may escape and hide without actually traveling more than a few centimeters. Still another function of the tail is storage of fat. Usually the tail is plump and rounded and accounts for a substantial part of the total weight. Obviously loss of the tail through autotomy involves serious loss of stored energy and of agility in locomotion.

At times when conditions are not favorable for activity the skinks work their way beneath the layer of surface litter and rest at ground level, hidden and insulated. There is no den and no regular home base. An almost infinite number of hiding places are available, but the lizards do tend to stay within a small familiar area or home range. For forty-four instances in which individuals marked and released were recaptured after substantial intervals, the average distance moved was 13.4 m. If this distance is considered to represent a home-range radius, the home range would cover a circular area of 417 m². However, female movements averaged longer than male movements; the six longest movements were all made by females. The twenty-nine female movements indicate an average home range of 476 m² whereas fifteen male movements indicate home ranges of only 295 m². *S. cherriei* hence differs from most other lizards whose spatial relations have been studied, and in fact from vertebrates in general, in that females wander more widely than males.

In summary, *S. cherriei* is of ecological significance because it attains high biomass for a secondary consumer, and it is in turn a food source for larger predators. However, because of its secretive habits, most details of its reproduction, population dynamics, and interactions with community associates remain poorly known. Large-scale studies of natural populations need to be conducted, and effective live traps or pitfalls need to be devised to capture the animals, alive and unharmed, in sufficient numbers. Food habits need to be investigated by collecting large numbers of stomachs and identifying their contents by comparison with reference material. Also, supplementary observations are needed on confined individuals tested with a variety of potential prey animals, to determine the limitations imposed by size, by sematic colors and displays, and by noxious secretions. Details of reproduction, such as the usual interval between clutches and usual incubation period, are best learned from individuals maintained in laboratory colonies. Finally, the relationships of *S. cherriei* to Old World species of *Sphenomorphus* and related genera, and to other New World lygosomines, need to be reexamined.

Fitch, H. S. 1973. A field study of Costa Rican lizards. *Univ. Kansas Sci. Bull.* 50:39–126.

Greer, A. E. 1974. The generic relationships of the scincid lizard genus *Leiolopisma* and its relatives. *Australian J. Zool.,* suppl. ser. 31:1–67.

Taylor, E. H. 1956. A review of the lizards of Costa Rica. *Univ. Kansas Sci. Bull.* 38, pt. 1:1–322.

9 MAMMALS

INTRODUCTION

D. H. Janzen and D. E. Wilson

The contemporary mammalian fauna of Costa Rica (Goodwin 1946) is not exceptional either in the species it contains or in its ecological diversity when compared with the fauna of the rest of Central America or even tropical lowland Mexico. Almost all Costa Rican mammals have ranges encompassing Central America, and many extend into South and North America. Although this essay is focused on Costa Rica, it has wider application.

The wild mammals that have been studied most intensively in Costa Rica include the frugivorous bat *Carollia perspicillata* (Heithaus and Fleming 1978), vampire bat, *Desmodus rotundus* (Turner 1975), disk-winged bat, *Thyroptera tricolor* (Findley and Wilson 1974; Wilson and Findley 1977), howler monkey, *Alouatta palliata* (Glander 1975), and pocket mice, *Liomys salvini* and *Heteromys desmarestianus* (Fleming 1974, 1977a,b; Fleming and Brown 1975; Vandermeer 1979; Janzen 1982b,c; Bonoff and Janzen 1980; Hallwachs and Janzen 1983). As a group, bats have received the most attention (Brown 1968; Gardner, Laval, and Wilson 1970; Gardner and Wilson 1971; LaVal 1970, 1977; Fleming, Hooper, and Wilson 1972; Fleming, Heithaus, and Sawyer 1977; Mares and Wilson 1971; Howell and Burch 1974; Heithaus, Opler, and Baker 1974; Heithaus, Fleming, and Opler 1975; Bradbury and Vehrencamp 1976a,b, 1977a,b; LaVal and Fitch 1977; Vehrencamp, Stiles, and Bradbury 1977), and large mammals the least (Janzen 1981a,b, 1982a). Free-ranging cows and horses are grossly understudied in view of their ease of observation, contemporary ecological importance, and similarity to the large Pleistocene herbivores that once influenced Costa Rican vegetation (Janzen and Martin 1982).

Except in the national parks, all large and many small Costa Rican wild mammal populations are subjected to extreme hunting pressure or habitat destruction. Only now are large-mammal densities in the national parks beginning to recover following intensive hunting and competition from livestock for the past one hundred to two hundred years. A reliable informant told Franklin Chaves, the director of Santa Rosa National Park, that in 1947–49 he shot thirty-six tapirs in the bottomlands of the area when it was not yet a park; a Nicaraguan hunter with dogs is rumored to have shot sixteen jaguars and mountain lions in the same area in one year during the mid-1960s.

Fortunately, a rapidly spreading enlightenment of the Costa Rican populace is alleviating the hunting pressure and is resulting in the preservation of substantial pieces

Front view of skull of adult paca (*Cuniculus paca*). This 10 kg nocturnal forest-floor rodent lives in burrows and hollow logs in the daytime. If disturbed, it growls like a dog; the enlarged rugose cheekbones serve as resonating chambers, magnifying the sound. Santa Rosa National Park, Costa Rica (photo, D. H. Janzen).

426

of habitat as well. Costa Rica has set aside no fewer than twenty-four national parks and reserves, totaling 2,093 km^2 (4.1% of the country) in the past nineteen years (Bonilla 1979). However, in the unprotected portions of Costa Rica there are several subtle aspects of local mammal extinction and population reduction that are poorly understood. In most habitats, many species still exist as widely scattered individuals, transients from more protected areas, or individuals that have adjusted to new diets. However, their interactions with indigenous food sources and types, with other mammals, and with conspecifics have been heterogeneously interrupted, extinguished, or distorted to a largely unknowable degree. Rapidly changing selective pressures have resulted in ecological and behavioral repertoires containing indecipherable mixtures of historical constraints and environmental demands. Great care is needed, for example, in interpreting the adaptive nature of the behavior of bats such as *Artibeus, Glossophaga,* and *Carollia* in relation to the flower-fruit-insect cycles in the brushy cow pastures and woodlots of lowland Guanacaste. However, the rotting of large crops of guapinol fruits (*Hymenaea courbaril*) below trees isolated in pasture fencerows is no great ecological puzzle, for the agoutis (*Dasyprocta punctata*) that eat these fruits have been gone from these pastures for two hundred years. In short, as with other organisms, mammal-mammal and mammal-nonmammal interactions become extinct before the participants do. This is especially conspicuous in the interaction-rich habitats of Costa Rica (Janzen 1974; Janzen and Martin 1982).

Although systematists have been contributing to our knowledge of Central American mammalogy for well over one hundred years, it is only in the past twenty years that ecologists have begun asking questions and providing partial answers. We have chosen to orient this essay around a number of such ecological questions, even though speculation may have to serve in lieu of proof.

How Diverse Is the Costa Rican Mammal Fauna?

Simpson (1964) found that mammal species richness per unit area increases from Canada through Panama. Subsequently, Fleming (1973a) and Wilson (1974) independently analyzed the same species-richness gradient and found that, if bats are deleted from the analysis, the number of mammal species per unit area remains roughly the same from the central United States to Panama. In short, the increase in species richness with decreasing latitude is attributable almost solely to an increase in the number of bat species. Furthermore, the increase in bat species diversity is primarily due to the large numbers of noninsectivorous species. Frugivores, nectarivores, fish eaters, blood feeders, and carnivores are essentially nonexistent in temperate regions but are all well represented

in the Costa Rican fauna. However, a recent analysis of the same gradient (McCoy and Connor 1980) suggests that, if the unit areas studied are larger, other mammal species richness does increase as lattitude decreases.

Marsupials are also reasonably diverse in Costa Rica. The Virginia opossum, *Didelphis virginiana,* has Guanacaste as the southern limit of its range. Its more tropical relative, *Didelphis marsupialis,* is found throughout the country (Gardner 1973). These two species are primarily large terrestrial scavengers. There are two medium-sized scansorial omnivores, the four-eyed opossums, *Philander opossum* and *Metachirus nudicaudatus.* Morphologically, *Metachirus* appears to be better adapted for an arboreal existence, with its long limbs and longer tail. The most arboreal marsupial is the woolly opossum, *Caluromys derbianus.* This beautiful little animal is also omnivorous. Three species of small mouse opossums, genus *Marmosa,* are found on the ground and in the undergrowth. They are somewhat shrewlike in appearance and are probably ecological equivalents of insectivores. The most strikingly different marsupial is a water opossum, *Chironectes minimus.* These animals can be seen foraging in small streams throughout the country at lower elevations, and as recently as ten years ago we encountered them in the stream on the campus of the University of Costa Rica in San José.

The order Insectivora is poorly represented in the tropics. Only three species of shrews (*Cryptotis*) occur in Costa Rica, and they are restricted to the interior highlands.

As many as ten species of monkeys and apes can occur sympatrically in a West African rain forest (Booth 1956; Gartlan and Struhsaker 1972), including five species of small prosimians (Charles-Dominique 1974). Wilson has seen three species of prosimians in the same vine tangle in Cameroon. Of the sixteen genera and approximately fifty species of New World monkeys (Mittermeier and Coimbra-Filho 1977), only four occur in Costa Rica. One of these, the squirrel monkey, *Saimiri oerstedii,* is restricted to the Pacific lowlands in the southern part of the country. Capuchins (*Cebus capucinus*) are insectivorous but feed opportunistically on a variety of other things. Spider monkeys (*Ateles geoffroyi*) are wide-ranging aerial acrobats that essentially trapline fruiting trees. Howler monkeys (*Alouatta palliata*), the most conspicuous of the primate fauna, are noisy, sedentary canopy browsers that feed on leaves and fruit. Primate species richness increases rapidly to the south, culminating in Amazonian Brazil, where twenty-two species are listed from an area of 250,000 km^2 (Mittermeier and Coimbra-Filho 1977).

Of the three species of rabbits in Costa Rica, only one (*Sylvilagus brasiliensis*) is wide-ranging. Another has the southern limit of its range in Guanacaste, and the third is a highland endemic.

Although a few square kilometers of desert in the southwestern United States or northern Mexico may have twenty or more species of rodents (Findley et al. 1975), even the most species-rich Costa Rican rain forest contains only about fourteen. This figure is almost equaled by habitat-rich areas of eastern deciduous forest in the United States (Fleming 1973b). Santa Rosa National Park, a mixture of grassland, deciduous forest, rocky ridges, and evergreen riparian forest, boasts only two caviomorphs (agouti and paca), a porcupine (*Coendou mexicanum*), a squirrel (*Sciurus variegatoides*), two rice rats (*Oryzomys*), a climbing rat (*Ototylomys phyllotis*), a spiny pocket mouse (*Liomys salvini*), and a cotton rat (*Sigmodon hispidus*), for a total of nine species (Bonoff and Janzen 1980). Temperate-zone boreal coniferous forests may contain up to ten sciurids (Findley et al. 1975), and Old World tropical rain forests may have as many as nine (Emmons 1975) to twenty-tree (Muul and Liat 1979). All of Costa Rica has only five species of squirrels, and three is the maximum in any one forest.

Pocket gophers (*Macrogeomys*) are represented by only four species, all restricted endemics. Heteromyids, most diverse in arid-temperate and subtropical regions, in Costa Rica are limited to *Heteromys desmarestianus* in wet forests and *Liomys salvini* in dry forests. Although twenty-eight species of cricetine rodents have been recorded from Costa Rica, virtually none are widespread and abundant. The greatest diversity is found in the genus *Oryzomys*, with at least ten species. Several of these ten are arboreal, as are *Tylomys, Ototylomys,* and *Nyctomys.* Aquatic mice are represented by two species of *Rheomys.* Costa Rican *Reithrodontomys* (seven species) are mostly restricted highland forms, as are the two *Peromyscus* species. *Scotinomys* are highland mice that are active during the day and that make audible vocalizations.

Costa Rica, like other Neotropical countries, seems to have a depauperate marine mammal fauna. The lack of pinnipeds is not surprising, since they are essentially restricted to temperate and arctic waters (which is probably a reflection of the greater fish abundance in northern near-shore waters). The only exceptions are a population of sea lions (*Zalophus californianus*) on the Galápagos and monk seals in Hawaii and the Mediterranean. The Caribbean monk seal, *Monachus tropicalis,* once occurred on islands off the coast of Honduras but is now extinct (Kenyon 1977). Monk seals are a classic example of large, majestic animals that are incapable of adjusting to man's domination of the environment.

Table 9.1 lists the species of cetaceans that might be expected to occur in Costa Rican waters (J. G. Mead, pers. comm.). Only seven species are recorded from its coastal waters, and two more from nearby Panama.

A viable population of bottle-nosed dolphins (*Tursiops truncatus*) appears to exist in the Caribbean. In October

TABLE 9.1 Marine Mammals Expected in Costa Rican Waters

Scientific Name	Common Name
Tursiops truncatus	Bottle-nose dolphin
Stenella attenuata [a]	Spotted dolphin
S. longirostris [a]	Spinner dolphin
S. coeruleoalbus [a]	Striped dolphin
Delphinus delphis [a]	Common dolphin
Steno bredenesis	Rough-toothed dolphin
Lagenodelphis hosei	Fraser's dolphin
Feresa attenuata	Pygmy killer whale
Peponocephala electra [a]	Melon-headed whale
Lagenorhynchus obliquidens	Pacific white-sided dolphin
Globicephala macrorhyncha	Pilot whale
Pseudorca crassidens	False killer whale
Orcinus orca [c]	Killer whale
Grampus griseus [a]	Risso's dolphin
Physeter catodon [a]	Sperm whale
Kogia simus	Dwarf sperm whale
K. breviceps	Pygmy sperm whale
Ziphius cavirostris [b]	Cuvier's beaked whale
Mesoplodon densirostris	Blainville's beaked whale
M. ginkgodens	Gingko-toothed beaked whale
M. carlhubbsi [c]	Hubb's beaked whale
Megaptera novaeanglia [b]	Humpback whale
Balaenoptera acutorostrata	Minke whale
B. physalus	Fin whale
B. edeni	Bryde's whale
B. borealis [c]	Sei whale
B. musculus [c]	Blue whale
Eubalaena glacialis [c]	Right whale

[a] Recorded from Costa Rica.
[b] Recorded from Panama.
[c] Rare possibility.

1976 a mass stranding of more than two hundred melon-headed whales (*Peponocephala electra*) occurred at Playa Tambor, Ballena Bay, on the Nicoya Peninsula. Wilson visited the site and salvaged material for further study, including stomachs containing squid beaks and small fish parts, indicating that the animals had recently fed. The reasons for such mass strandings of apparently healthy animals remain unknown. This species is an apparently widespread pelagic form about which little is known. A similar stranding of about five hundred of these animals occurred in Japan in 1965 (Nishiwaki and Norris 1966).

Bats, edentates, carnivores, and artiodactyls will be discussed in later sections, which focus on the particular ecological problems faced by each. To summarize, the Costa Rican mammalian checklist contains two hundred species, half of which are bats. The fauna is probably not at the equilibrium species number that could be supported by the habitat diversity present before human intervention. The question of human intervention, to be discussed in more detail in a later section, is probably more ancient and complex than previously thought.

How Do Tropical Mammals Cope with Seasonal Stress?

The climatic rigors of winter have played a large role in shaping ecological responses of extratropical mammals to stressful seasons. The primary problem in these areas is coping with superabundant food supplies during part of the year and greatly reduced or nonexistent resources during another. The two most striking adaptations of this seasonality are hibernation and migration.

In Costa Rica, temperatures in any one zone vary only slightly through the year, and food resources for most mammals are probably little affected by this variation. Moisture regimes are far more variable, and seasonal rainfall patterns undoubtedly affect some kinds of mammals. For most of these animals the time of stress is the dry season, especially in areas like Guanacaste, which has a pronounced five-month dry season. Responses to the dry season are varied, but dormancy is not a viable alternative for tropical mammals for several reasons:

1. Even if a Costa Rican mammal could go dormant for the dry season, its predators and parasites would not, because their food source (the dormant mammal) would still be available. Snakes and other vertebrates adapted to seeking prey in subterranean or intralog burrows would find dormant mammals easy prey. Army ants (*Eciton* spp.) and fire ants (*Solenopsis* spp.) would probably quickly consume a dormant mouse or bat. Poikilothermic ectoparasites would undoubtedly greatly increase their population sizes if released from the normal cleaning and preening exercises of an active host. These are problems not faced by a chilled marmot in a snow-covered burrow in Colorado—winter is on its side, even if some warm-blooded vertebrates are still active in the winter.

2. Dormancy requires stored food reserves, and the warmer the temperatures, the more reserves required per day (e.g., see Janzen and Wilson 1974). It may be physically impossible for a mammal of a given size to carry enough fat to survive an extended period of dormancy at tropical temperatures. This may be why some populations of temperate-zone bats actually migrate northward in search of cold hibernacula, and why lowland Mexican *Myotis velifer* moves into the highlands to hibernate (Villa-R. 1966). McNab (1973) postulated that vampire bats cannot handle more northern climates because they cannot accumulate enough fat to hibernate.

3. Fat accumulation depends on resources being pulsed in such a way that an overabundance is available immediately before the stressful season. Insect densities are highest at the beginning of the tropical rainy season and lowest at the end of the rainy season when insectivorous mammals would need the most food for fat deposition. Although more variable, fruit resources show roughly the same pattern, and most fruits are so nutrient-poor as to make fat deposition physiologically difficult.

Seeds are available during the dry season, but a lull in seed availability occurs at the beginning of the rainy season, a time when massive downpours might render subterranean sites unsuitable for prolonged occupancy. Herbivorous mammals have abundant available resources at the end of the rainy season, but they probably also suffer less shortage during the dry season than it appears, since riparian refugia retain substantial amounts of leafy vegetation.

Some tropical mammals do accumulate fat and use it as a reserve for stressful seasons. Camels, fat-tailed sheep, Brahma cattle, and steatopygous humans are examples. A Brahma bull can live through a 3-month east African dry season largely by metabolizing the fat in its hump, and the camel's legendary ability to survive in the desert may be largely due to the fat stores in its hump. It is probably not an accident that the fat is stored in a lump rather than being spread as a warm coat just under the skin.

4. Highland areas with cooler temperatures might alleviate some of the problems associated with tropical dormancy, especially during the rainy season when week-long periods of little or no insolation or insect activity are common. However, only facultative heterotherms such as some bats are known to undergo periods of torpor in such situations. McNab (1969) found most Neotropical bats he tested, including *Artibeus jamaicensis*, to be homeothermic (constant deep body temperature) endotherms. In constrast, Studier and Wilson (1970) found many tropical species, including *A. jamaicensis* and the other species studied by McNab (1969), to be highly variable in thermoregulatory capabilities; most species showed patterns chacteristic of nonhomeothermic endotherms. Recently, Studier and Wilson (1979) showed that these differences are a result of length of time in captivity. *Artibeus jamaicensis* are heterothermic when first captured and quickly become homeothermic in captivity. They suggested that thermoregulation is dependent on the nutritional state of these animals. In the wild, *A. jamaicensis* feeds on fruits that vary seasonally in abundance from scarce to plentiful; individual bats may undergo a natural period of diel torpor, whereas animals kept with free access to food may never go torpid as long as the food supply is constant and plentiful.

Food storage in bulk achieves the accumulation of reserves for a future stressful period while avoiding the problems associated with dormancy. However, hoarding of seeds or other resources, a common practice among many northern heteromyids and sciurids, is uncommon among Costa Rican mammals. *Heteromys desmarestianus* hoards seeds in the rain forest at Finca La Selva (Vandermeer 1979), and *Liomys salvini* does the same in the deciduous forests of Guanacaste (Fleming and Brown 1975). However, both belong to a hoarding family (Heteromyidae) that probably evolved the behavior in desert habitats. They are the only heteromyids in a small-rodent fauna of forty-five species. Furthermore, they probably lose a much higher fraction of their hoarded seeds to fungi (Janzen 1979) than do their desert-dwelling relatives and probably depend less on caches than on daily harvesting of new seeds (Fleming 1977*b*). Certainly, a much smaller proportion of the seeds found in any Costa Rican habitat can be cached in the soil without high losses to fungi and germination than is true with seeds in more northern or more arid areas.

Actually, the stress of a tropical dry season probably is considerably less than that of a northern winter. Food resources may be lowered or changed, but for most mammals they are not eliminated. Many kinds of specialized food resources are available continuously throughout the year. Termites and ants are available for anteaters (though they vary in quantity and quality with season), vertebrate blood is available for vampire bats, and fish are available to fish-eating bats (*Noctilio leporinus*).

Mammals with less restricted diets sometimes switch food resources seasonally. Rodents that feed on seeds in the dry season may become more insectivorous during the rainy season or may take some combination of fruits, buds, flowers, and leaves. *Micronycteris hirsuta,* a bat that forages by foliage gleaning large insects during most of the year, switches to a variety of understory fruits during the dry season (Wilson 1971*b*). Often, food scarcity in one area may be synchronized with food abundance in other areas. Insect populations on open hillsides are high during the wet season, but very low during the dry season; in adajacent shady riparian habitats, however, insects are abundant during the dry season (Janzen 1973).

Some Costa Rican mammals, like other animals, undoubtedly migrate(d) locally to escape seasonal effects. In areas of deciduous forest traversed by strips of evergreen vegetation along ever-flowing rivers (e.g., ríos Cañas, Corobici, Tempisque, and Potrero, which flow from the volcanic cordillera across Guanacaste to the sea), howler monkeys spread out over the deciduous forest during the rainy season and retreat to the riparian vegetation during the dry season. When there was still forest (and river) at the Ministerio de Agricultura y Ganadería field station on Finca Taboga (1965–70), we saw them lined up perhaps one troop per 0.5 km or less along the Río Higueron in March. It seems likely that the frugivorous and nectarivorous bats that show up in profusion at certain species of trees in flower and fruit in Guanacaste (*Hymenaea courbaril, Crescentia alata, Bauhinia ungulata* and *B. pauletia, Anacardium excelsum, Spondias mombin, Brosimum alicastrum, Piper* spp., *Andira inermis,* and *Ficus* spp.) may move up to tens of kilometers to where stands or populations of these trees are in fruit. Tapirs and peccaries reputedly move into the

Raphia taedigera palm swamp around Laguna de Corcovado in Corcovado National Park in the dry season when the palm fruits are falling.

Why Are So Many Costa Rican Carnivores Frugivorous?

The Costa Rican Carnivora comprise six felids, two canids, six procyonids, and seven mustelids. All except the otter (*Lutra longicaudus*) and mountain lion (*Felis concolor*) are known or alleged to consume large amounts of fruit. When offered bananas, eggs, and meat in a bowl in Santa Rosa National Park, wild hooded skunks (*Mephitis macroura*) take the banana as often as any of the other items. Coyote (*Canis latrans*) feces at Santa Rosa are full of seeds of species such as *Chomelia spinosa, Cissus rhombifolia, Alibertia edulis, Manilkara zapota, Ficus* spp., and *Genipa americana*. Tayra (*Eira barbara*) and raccoon (*Procyon lotor*) feces are regularly full of the seeds of a variety of species. Coatis (*Nasua narica*), kinkajous (*Potos flavus*), and olingos (*Bassaricyon sumichrasti*) are widely known as frugivores; coatis even swallow whole fruits as large as *Spondias mombin* (2–3 cm long, 1.5–2 cm diameter) and defecate the nuts whole. Because these animals lack complex stomachs or digestive ceca, all are probably dispersal agents that rarely digest seeds, and we suspect that they carry them for less than 72 h. They are likely to gulp them down with little chewing of the fruit, and therefore fragile seeds that would be ground up by an herbivore's molars may survive the trip through the digestive system of a carnivore. Carnivores often swallow large seeds that a browser would spit out. Whether they are "good" or "bad" dispersal agents, of course, depends on the biology of the plant.

That carnivores should easily become ripe-fruit eaters (but not folivores or green-fruit or seed predators) probably centers on the fact that animal-dispersed ripe fruits are evolutionarily designed to be eaten by vertebrates such as birds, bats, monkeys, tapirs, horses, and agoutis. Given the general similarities of vertebrate digestive systems, it is likely that by producing a fruit that can be eaten by a specific dispersal agent, the fruit becomes edible to many other species as well. Furthermore, part of designing a "good" fruit is not only putting sugars, vitamins, proteins, and lipids in as a reward, but putting them in cellular containers from which they are easily extracted by the correct animals. Because Carnivora have alimentary tracts evolved for extracting nutrients from nearly maximally digestible tissues (compare the ease of digesting a kilo of flesh and fat with the difficulty of digesting a kilo of twigs and leaves), certain kinds of fruits should be the closest thing available to the food believed to be eaten originally by carnivores.

Of course we can turn the question around and note that if the multitude of tree species whose fruits are eaten by Costa Rican (and other tropical) Carnivora grew in southern Canada, perhaps the northern carnivores would be just as frugivorous as their tropical relatives. Certainly temperate-zone bears, foxes, raccoons, and coyotes eat some species of juicy or fleshy fruits when encountered. Perhaps the "Carnivora" are misnamed; although they obviously have specialized traits for catching and eating prey animals, they may always have been highly frugivorous.

An adjunct of increased frugivory among the carnivores is an increase in the number of arboreal forms. The gray fox (*Urocyon cinereoargenteus*) and tayra (*Eira barbara*) regularly forage in trees. All the procyonids are arboreal to some degree, and kinkajous and olingos are entirely so. All the cats also exhibit arboreality to some extent, though we do not know where they get the fruits (e.g., *Manilkara zapota*) whose seeds appear in their dung.

Why Do Rat Trappers Become Bat Netters in the Tropics?

The first quarter of this century spanned a period of intense work on the description of the rodent fauna of temperate North America. Mammalogists of this time, such as C. Hart Merriam, Vernon Bailey, Edgar Mearns, E. A. Goldman, and E. W. Nelson, were primarily systematists with a keen eye for natural history. The diversity of the rodent fauna and their relative ease of capture led to a period of descriptive ecological studies during the second quarter of this century. The past thirty years have seen a blossoming of studies dealing with population dynamics and community ecology.

During the first half of the century, work on bats was essentially limited to systematics and anecdotal life-history tidbits. The difficulty of studying nocturnal, volant animals was alleviated somewhat by the discovery that bats could be captured in Japanese mist nets, which had been used for some time to capture birds.

Although early naturalists managed to secure a surprisingly large number of forms of Neotropical bats, they often had only single specimens, which were sent to European museums for description by systematists. These early naturalists were aware of but confused about some of the unusual adaptations of Neotropical bats — witness the number of generic names given to frugivorous species that were mistakenly thought to be vampires (*Vampyrum, Vampyrops, Vampyressa, Vampyriscus, Vampyrodes*).

The age of mist netting was already here by the time mammalogists began attempting ecological studies of tropical animals. Students interested in studying small-mammal ecology in the tropics found a rather depauperate rodent fauna that was much more difficult to sample than its temperate-zone counterpart, and an incredibly diverse and interesting bat fauna that could be readily sampled by mist netting.

Although mist nets opened many new paths of inquiry, they are by no means a perfect sampling technique. Bats are not randomly distributed in the air space, so nets have to be placed where the bats are most likely to encounter them — near roosts, across flyways, over watering areas, or around food sources. Nets are most commonly placed at ground level, so species that routinely fly over or in the forest canopy are less likely to be captured. Many species, especially insectivores, have highly sophisticated echolocation systems that are capable of detecting the nets. Almost all species can learn the location of a net and subsequently avoid it. Often predators are attracted to a net full of noisy bats, and many an opossum has obtained an easy meal from nets that are not closely watched. Students not accustomed to working with bats are easily bitten while trying to extract bats from nets, and the chance of getting rabies from such a bite, though slight, is worrisome to many people.

In spite of these problems, the use of mist nets has furthered knowledge of the Costa Rican bat fauna. That fauna comprises nine families, fifty-two genera, and 103 species. Comparable figures for the United States are four, fifteen, and forty. Ecologically, the diversity is even more striking, because all the United States species are insectivorous, with the exception of a few fruit and nectar feeders that migrate into the extreme southwestern part of the country during the summer. The Costa Rican fauna includes roughly forty-three insectivores, twenty-five frugivores, eleven nectarivores, three blood feeders, two carnivores, one fish eater, and eighteen that feed on some combination of the above. Actually, as details of food habits become better known, an increasing number of these species are relegated to the last category (Gardner 1977).

The most common foraging technique for bats throughout the world is aerial insectivory (Wilson 1973*a*). These bats, including Costa Rican members of the families Emballonuridae, Mormoopidae, Natalidae, Furipteridae, Thyropteridae, Vespertilionidae, and Molossidae, have highly evolved echolocation systems that allow them to pursue and capture insects on the wing (Novick 1977). More is known about social organization and foraging in emballonurid bats than perhaps any other bat group in Costa Rica, thanks to the excellent work of Bradbury and Vehrencamp (1976*a,b*, 1977*a,b*). They studied five species (*Rhynchonycteris naso, Saccopteryx leptura, Saccopteryx bilineata, Balantiopteryx plicata,* and *Peropteryx kappleri*) that divide food resources by a combination of prey size and habitat partitioning. The smaller species tended to forage in groups, whereas the larger ones foraged solitarily; all shifted their foraging areas in response to seasonally changing patterns of insect abundance. Small groups of two to ten bats were the rule of *S. leptura* and *P. kappleri*, five to fifty for *R. naso* and *S. bilineata*, and large colonies with hundreds of individuals for *B. plicata*.

Rhynchonycteris naso is one of the smallest (4.5 g) of Costa Rican bats and has unique roosting sites on exposed tree trunks or cliffs, usually adjacent to waterways. The roosting individuals are spaced 2 to 4 cm apart, often in a vertical column. They are cryptically marked with grizzled gray pelage broken by white zigzag lines, and when disturbed they fly off to another of the three to six roost sites used by each colony. The colony maintains a foraging range over the adjacent waterway and socially subdivides the area. Adult breeding females forage together in the center of the range, while younger, nonbreeding females and males forage on the periphery and defend the territory against conspecifics from other colonies. The colonies are composed of roughly equal numbers of males and females, but a dominance hierarchy may exist among the males.

Saccopteryx bilineata was the first bat species in which a social organization based on harem formation was clearly documented and described (Bradbury and Emmons 1974). Males defend territories, often between the buttresses of large trees. Each territory of about 2 m² contains one to eight females. The males have an elaborate repertoire of vocal, visual, and olfactory displays, which they perform regularly at the roosting site.

The family Mormoopidae is a Neotropical endemic, so closely related to the Phyllostomidae that it was formerly considered a subfamily of it (Smith 1972). These bats, represented in Costa Rica by four species of the genus *Pteronotus*, have long been a favorite subject for echolocation studies (Novick 1977), owing in part to their highly specialized, high-intensity systems that combine constant-frequency and frequency-modulated pulses.

The families Natalidae, Furipteridae, and Thyropteridae are also endemic to the Neotropics. *Thyroptera*, the disk-winged bat, is uniquely adapted for roosting in rolled *Heliconia* leaves by adhering to the inner surfaces with suction disks on the wrists and ankles (Findley and Wilson 1974; Wilson and Findley 1977) These small (4 g) bats form colonies of one to nine individuals of mixed sexes and ages, at a density of about four colonies per hectare on the Osa Peninsula. The colonies are socially cohesive, and because of the ephemeral nature of the roost sites each bat must move to a new leaf of the appropriate size (diameter of opening 50 to 100 mm) every few days.

The family Vespertilionidae is cosmopolitan and provides most of the members of temperate-zone bat faunas. Although Costa Rica has twelve species, they are rarely encountered, probably owing to some combination of low numbers and difficulty of capture in mist nets. Half the Costa Rican species belong to the genus *Myotis*, which has about sixty species worldwide and is the most widely distributed genus of mammal other than *Homo*. The two species of *Lasiurus* are migratory but are so little studied in Costa Rica that we do not know if resident populations also exist. All Costa Rican vespertilionids are aerial insectivores, and most forage in or below the canopy in forested areas.

Free-tailed bats (Molossidae) are also aerial insectivores. They are specialized for fast, high-altitude flight (Findley, Studier, and Wilson 1972) and regularly forage over the forest canopy or above watercourses. Most of the eleven Costa Rican species are rarely encountered, although some species of molossids are commonly found roosting in attics. Although none have been the subject of intensive study in Costa Rica, the Mexican free-tailed bat, *Tadarida brasiliensis,* is a migratory species that has been studied extensively in the United States and intensively at Carlsbad Caverns (Constantine 1967; Geluso, Altenbach, and Wilson 1976; Wilson, Geluso, and Altenbach 1978; Altenbach, Geluso, and Wilson 1979).

The other common foraging pattern for insectivorous bats is foliage gleaning, in which large insects are picked off foliage or the ground. Many members of the phyllostomid subfamily Phyllostominae also feed in this manner. All of these bats possess a suite of morphological characters in common including large ears and short, broad wings. They are capable of slow, highly maneuverable locomotion through the foliage, but how they differentiate between insects and the substrate is unknown.

The two species of noctilionid bats, *Noctilio albiventris* and *N. leporinus,* have foraging patterns that may include some combination of aerial insectivory and foliage gleaning. *Noctilio albiventris* forages along solitary beats about 1 m above the surface of watercourses. The bats appear to be catching insects mainly from the air, but their enlarged hind feet suggest that they may occasionally take insects or small fish from the water surface. *Macrophyllum macrophyllum,* a phyllostomine, forages in similar areas and may do the same (Gardner 1977). The fishing bat, *N. leporinus,* has carried this behavior a step further and specializes in plucking small fish off or from near the water surface. It forages over fresh and salt water.

Other phyllostomines have evolved a similar behavior in foraging over land. *Tonatia* and *Mimon* foliage glean large insects but may occasionally take small vertebrates such as lizards. *Trachops cirrhosus* also foliage gleans but appears to be specialized for capturing frogs from the forest floor (M. Tuttle, pers. comm.). The next logical step is seen in the carnivores, including *Phyllostomus hastatus, Chrotopterus auritus,* and especially *Vampyrum spectrum*. Vehrencamp, Stiles, and Bradbury (1977) radio tracked *V. spectrum* foraging in deciduous woodlands in Guanacaste. The bats' primary prey was sleeping birds, and the authors speculated that olfaction might be used in locating the prey. The bats appeared to focus on birds sleeping in the vegetation rather than in holes, and they took birds weighing 20 to 150 g. Many of the prey items either roosted communally or had a strong odor.

The final major foraging type is found in the vampire bats, family Desmodontidae, of which there are three in Costa Rica. The common vampire, *Desmodus rotundus,* has received the most attention (McNab 1973; Turner 1975). Although probably originally adapted to feed on large wild mammals such as deer, tapir, and peccaries, vampire bats have found a plentiful new source of food in man's livestock. Turner's (1975) study at La Pacifica in Guanacaste outlines basic details of their life history and documents prey preferences that include calves and estrous females, and even swiss over brahma cattle. These preferences were probably due to the increased exposure of the preferred types while sleeping but may also have to do with blood chemistry.

Desmodus shows a variety of interesting adaptations for its unique mode of life, including locomotory abilities on the ground that are unmatched by other bats (Altenbach 1979). These bats have highly developed senses of olfaction (Schmidt 1973) and vision (Chase 1972) but only a low-intensity echolocation system (Novick 1977). The dentition is highly specialized; the incisors are enlarged for scooping out a small piece of flesh, and the cheek teeth are almost vestigial (Phillips, Grimes, and Forman 1977). The saliva contains anticoagulants that keep the blood flowing once a bite is made (DiSanto 1960). The digestive tract is modified to deal with large quantities of blood (15 ml per day), which is low in carbohydrates and fat but high in protein. This causes rapid excretion of highly concentrated urine after the bats have returned to the roost and concomitant water-balance problems (McFarland and Wimsatt 1969).

Vampire bats are a problem to livestock producers, owing both to direct effects of blood loss on the animals and to indirect complications such as infection from the bites and disease potential, especially paralytic rabies. Rabies-control programs have been undertaken in many Latin American countries, and these normally include destruction of vampire populations. Thus man has given vampire bats a double dose of environmental determinism—first by introducing livestock that caused vampire populations to increase greatly and then by controlling selected populations because they interfere with man's activities. In a captive colony at the Cincinnati Zoological Gardens, Mills (1980) observed colony mates feeding a female, which had recently given birth, by carrying blood from a bowl and then regurgitating it. On one occasion when the baby bat was a few weeks old but still nursing, the mother regurgitated blood herself and allowed the baby to feed from her mouth.

Diaemus youngii, a close relative of *Desmodus,* feeds primarily on birds (Sazima and Uieda 1980). These bats are adept at sneaking along the underside of a branch to a roosting bird, biting it on the toe or leg, and feeding.

This species seems to be rare in Costa Rica, although specimens have been taken at Finca La Pacifica in Guanacaste (Gardner, Laval, and Wilson 1970) and at Santa Rosa National Park (T. Fleming, pers. comm.).

The third species of vampire bat, *Diphylla ecaudata,* is also rare in Costa Rica, although it is known from the Osa Peninsula (Starrett 1976) and we have taken specimens at Finca Palo Verde in Guanacaste. This species also feeds on bird blood (Gardner 1977).

Frugivorous species in Costa Rica belong primarily to the phyllostomid subfamilies Stenodermatinae and Carolliinae. Most of these species roost in small groups or solitarily in the foliage. Some species modify roosting sites by cutting leaves to make tents. Included here are *Uroderma bilobatum, Artibeus jamaicensis, Artibeus phaeotis, A. watsoni,* and *Ectophylla alba* (Foster and Timm 1976). *Ectophylla alba* is one of the few species that is nearly all white. These tiny bats roost in small groups on the underside of *Heliconia* leaves, which they modify into tents by cutting holes along both sides of the midrib (Timm and Mortimer 1976). They have an unusual layer of subcutaneous melanin covering the skull that may provide some of the protection that would be supplied by darker skin (Gardner and Wilson 1971).

Artibeus jamaicensis is among the better studied of Neotropical bats (Morrison 1978a,b, 1979; Janzen et al. 1976; Fleming 1971). These bats are particularly fond of figs, and much of their natural history has been worked out on fig-rich Barro Colorado Island in Panama. Males defend harems of four to eleven in tree hollows. Morrison (1978a) used radio tracking to follow their nightly routine of flying to a fig tree, plucking a fruit, and flying up to several hundred meters away to hang up and eat it. They then return for another, taking up to ten figs a night by this pattern. A feeding roost can be recognized by the pile of chewed fragments of figs that accumulates underneath. We have seen areas on Barro Colorado where the ground was littered with such piles over many square meters. These bats eat more figs than they need for caloric reasons, and they produce urine that is extremely dilute compared with that of most mammals (E. H. Studier, pers. comm.). This suggests that they may be processing extra fruit to obtain sufficient quantities of some trace mineral or other necessary nutrient that is in short supply, such as salt or protein. It is a mystery why they fly far from the fruit tree to eat the fruit.

The subfamily Carolliinae has one genus, *Carollia,* with four species in Costa Rica. *Carollia perspicillata* has been the subject of intensive studies of foraging behavior at Santa Rosa National Park (Heithaus and Fleming 1978). These bats tend to roost in colonies of more than one hundred individuals in small caves, although some individuals roost in hollow trees or solitarily in the vegetation. From these day roosts, the bats fly an average 1.6 km to feeding areas, and they average another 1.5 km in moving back and forth between two to six such feeding areas. *Piper* spp. compose over 50% of the diet, and night roosts are usually 30–40 m from food plants. The bats average thirty to forty trips a night between food source and night roost. This pattern is not unlike that described for *Artibeus jamaicensis* in feeding on figs (Morrison 1978a), except that *Artibeus* makes fewer trips with larger fruits over longer distances (and see Janzen et al. 1976).

Nectarivorous bats in Costa Rica belong primarily to the phyllostomid subfamily Glossophaginae. These bats, with characteristically elongated rostra and tongues and reduced dentition, hover in front of flowers to feed on nectar and pollen. The most common species throughout the country is *Glossophaga soricina,* a second-growth forest species that feeds on fruit and occasional insects as well as nectar (Howell and Burch 1974; Gardner 1977). At least one phyllostomine, *Phyllostomus discolor,* also feeds heavily on nectar and pollen (Gardner 1977). Heithaus, Fleming, and Opler (1975) found considerable amounts of pollen on the frugivorous species *Artibeus jamaicensis, A. lituratus, A. phaeotis, Sturnira lilium,* and *Carollia perspicillata.* Their data suggest seasonal shifts between frugivory in the wet season and nectarivory in the dry season. Heithaus, Opler, and Baker (1974) contrasted the visitation patterns of the large *Phyllostomus discolor* and small *Glossophaga soricina* to *Bauhinia pauletia* patches at Finca La Pacifica. Individuals of *Phyllostomus discolor* forage in groups, grasp branches high on the plant and pull the flowers down, drain the nectar well, and seem to concentrate on *Bauhinia.* Individuals of *Glossophaga soricina* forage singly, hover in front of both high and low flowers, take small amounts of nectar, and seem to be less specialized on *Bauhinia.*

This diversity of resource use in bats makes it possible to compare and contrast faunas from different parts of the world. Analytical zoogeographers normally do this by comparing overlap values calculated on the basis of taxa shared between regions (Simpson 1964; Wilson 1974). This type of analysis shows the Neotropical bat fauna to be most closely related to the Nearctic one, a finding that is not surprising, since the common worldwide pattern is for contiguous areas to be most alike (Wilson 1973a). However, a similar analysis based on trophic diversity yields the ecologically more satisfying finding that the Neotropical fauna is most like the Australian, Oriental, and Ethiopian ones and least like the Nearctic and Palearctic ones (Wilson 1973a).

This trophic diversity of bats is correlated with a number of morphological features. One of the more interesting correlations is between food habits or foraging type and brain size (Eisenberg and Wilson 1979). The lowest brain/body weight ratios are found in the aerial insectivores and the highest in frugivores and nec-

tarivores. Foliage gleaners, fishing and vampire bats, and carnivores are somewhat intermediate in brain size.

Aerial insectivores have brains almost as small as those of extant primitive members of the order Insectivora. Presumably, bats evolved from terrestrial insectivores, and brain-size modifications have accompanied shifts in foraging behaviors and food habits. Perhaps foraging for flying insects can be accomplished by a fairly stereotyped behavioral pattern based heavily on echolocation. Fruit-feeders, on the other hand, may require larger brains to integrate inputs from a variety of sensory modalities used in locating and feeding on seasonally pulsed, localized food resources. They not only must know where to find food today, but must census the habitat well enough to know where to find it tomorrow and next week as well. The same process has been postulated for orangutans (Hrdy and Bennett 1979).

These correlations cut across phylogenetic lines in such a way as to make parallelism unlikely. Costa Rican phyllostomids have brain/body-weight ratios comparable to those of Old World pteropodids, or flying foxes, which also feed on fruit and nectar. Similarly, the low ratios seen in New World aerial insectivores are found in endemic Old World groups as well.

Before leaving the bats, we should briefly discuss some of the interesting demographic patterns that are beginning to surface. Small terrestrial mammals tend to reach sexual maturity in a few months, and they have large litters, short gestation periods, several litters per year and live for only a year or two. In contrast, most bats require several months to a year to reach sexual maturity, have gestation periods of 2–6 months, have one offspring per litter, often have only one or two litters per year, and may live up to 30 years (Keen and Hitchcock 1980).

Reproductive patterns of Costa Rican bats show four basic patterns that may be thought of as a continuum (Wilson 1973b). The basic types of cycle for temperate-zone species is to produce only one litter per year at a time when food resources are plentiful. This pattern is seen in many insectivorous species in Costa Rica (Wilson and Findley 1971; Mares and Wilson 1971; Fleming, Hooper, and Wilson 1972; Bradbury and Vehrencamp 1977b). These bats tend to time reproductive events so that the young are weaned at the time of maximum food availability (usually early in the rainy season).

Most frugivorous and nectarivorous species have two litters per year (Wilson 1979). Some insectivorous species may have this pattern if they are inhabitats that have more stable food resources (Bradbury and Vehrencamp 1977b). The typical pattern in the frugivorous and nectarivorous species is to wean the first young at the beginning of the rainy season, undergo postpartum estrus, and wean a second young later in the rainy season. A period of sexual diapause then follows. This usually lasts for a few months, and then the cycle begins again. An interesting variation on this pattern is seen in *Artibeus jamaicensis* (Fleming 1971). These bats undergo postpartum estrus after the second litter, but the implanted blastocyst develops very slowly through the end of the rainy season until the dry season. Then development accelerates, and the young bat is ready for weaning at the normal time the first litter of the year is weaned in other bat species.

Myotis nigricans, a small insectivorous vespertilionid, has the third pattern, seasonal polyestry. Up to three litters are produced in succession each year, with a short sexual diapause at the end of the rainy season (Wilson and Findley 1970; Wilson 1971*a*).

The fourth pattern, aseasonal polyestry, is found in vampires, *Desmodus rotundus* (Wilson 1979). These bats enjoy a relatively stable food source, and in most areas they tend to reproduce throughout the year. However, the long gestation period (6–7 months) and lactation period (3–9 months) may mean that individual females are producing fewer than two young per year anyway (Schmidt and Manske 1973).

In short, bat reproductive cycles seem to be strongly influenced by food availability, which is in turn strongly correlated with seasonal rainfall patterns. Most evidence suggests that reproduction patterns are directed toward weaning young at the most favorable times, and that the stresses of gestation and lactation are less critical than might otherwise be supposed (Fleming, Hooper, and Wilson 1972; Bradbury and Vehrencamp 1977*b;* Wilson 1979).

What Is Especially Tropical about the Costa Rican Mammalian Fauna?

Monkeys, anteaters, sloths, and noninsectivorous bats are the ecologically unique tropical mammals found in Costa Rica. Small Costa Rican rodents do not seem to be different in any major way from extratropical counterparts. Agoutis and pacas might seem to be candidates, but their large size, small litters, extensive parental care, and great longevity are to some degree paralleled by temperate-zone rodents such as beavers and porcupines. Armadillos, peccaries, frugivorous procyonids, and marsupials all range well into extratropical habitats. Aside from a slight tendency toward the increased frugivory already discussed, tropical carnivores are rather unexceptional.

ANTEATERS

Mammals that largely eat ants and termites are found around the world in the tropics, and rarely outside (cf. Bequaert 1922) (though bears approximate this dietary habit with ants at certain times of year). Each major type of anteater—echidnas, pangolins, aardvark, aardwolf, anteaters—is probably independently evolved. They are all nearly toothless, have long sticky tongues, and have large digging claws on powerful feet. Anteaters are probably missing from the extratropical regions because of the absence of large termite colonies (Y. Lubin, pers. comm.) and because large ant colonies are generally inaccessible during the winter.

The three Costa Rican anteaters are distinctive. The giant anteater (*Myrmecophaga tridactyla*) is a large (20 kg) terrestrial forest dweller. Tamanduas (*Tamandua mexicana*) are medium-sized and scansorial. They are the anteaters most frequently encountered in Costa Rica and are equally at home on the ground or in trees. The smallest species, the silky anteater (*Cyclopes didactylus*), is almost totally arboreal and is rarely seen.

SLOTHS

The two species of sloths are *Bradypus variegatus,* the three-toed sloth, and *Choloepus hoffmani,* the two-toed sloth. Both are highly specialized for a low intake rate of highly indigestible food, namely mature leaves of forest trees. Sloths use fewer resources per day than most mammals and have a suite of corresponding characteristics such as their proverbial lethargic behavior, long interdefecation periods, and variable, nearly poikilothermic, body temperature (Goffart 1971; Montgomery and Sunquist 1978).

Bradypus is more commonly seen because it is active during the day, whereas *Choloepus* is nocturnal and spends the daylight hours asleep, often in dense masses of leaves (Montgomery and Sunquist 1978). Both have exceptionally thick fur. *Bradypus* occurs at a density of 8.5 per hectare on Barro Colorado Island, a very high density for a Neotropical large mammal (Montgomery and Sunquist 1975). Each animal occupies a home range of less than 2 ha and may use fifty trees of up to thirty species, feeding on mature and young leaves. Food passage is so slow that rates must be measured in days rather than hours. Sloths descend from the canopy about once a week to defecate. Although analyses are unavailable, sloth feces probably contain a highly concentrated residue of indigestible secondary compounds (lignins, tannins, etc.).

Mother sloths carry the young for a few months after weaning, giving them the opportunity to learn individual trees. Then the mother disperses, leaving the home range to the offspring. This unqiue dispersal system probably minimizes intraspecific fighting over food (Montgomery and Sunquist 1978).

Although sloths do not occur in the Old World, the arboreal folivore habit occurs in a variety of primates, and in Australia it is seen in koalas and phalangerids. The absence of sloths from the temperate zone may be due to thermoregulatory problems that are also shaped by their food habits.

435

MONKEYS

The four species of Costa Rican monkeys were discussed earlier. Primates are another group essentially restricted to the tropics, and their absence from the temperate zone is not really surprising. Humans are the only contemporary primates that do conspicuously well in many extratropical habitats, and they are obviously using more than their own flesh and blood to deal with these habitats. One of humanity's truly unique traits is the propensity and ability to store and dispense large stores of food for the bad season. It is tempting to argue that northern winters would be just too hard on arboreal monkeys in terms of exposure, food availability, and predator avoidance. However, it should be noted that there is a lightly subsidized population of howler monkeys apparently surviving in a deciduous French woodland. Although the vine-free northern forests might appear to be poor substrate, monkeys seem to move quite well in tropical forests poor in vine entanglement. We suspect that the lack of year-round food availability would be the real problem for an arboreal extratropical primate. A very fat monkey might make it through a northern winter, but its arboreal mobility would be severely reduced, and sheltering sites would be very scarce.

For all the mammals discussed above it is obvious that no single trait is keeping them out of extratropical habitats, nor is there any single habitat characteristic that is an absolute barrier. For example, all the mammal groups discussed show the ability in some of their species or populations to withstand some cold or desiccation. Competition with other animals is a commonly suggested explanation of why they are missing from extratropical habitats. Whether direct, indirect, or diffuse in nature, the question of competition is simply unexplored.

To turn this question around, we also note that there are a number of extratropical mammals that do not range into the tropics in general and Costa Rica specifically. Bears are missing, and it is easy to blame their absence on an absence of large pulses of highly edible food types (big acorn crops, salmon runs, blueberry crops, winter-killed deer, etc.). The social cursorial carnivores seem to require much greater big game populations than now occur in Costa Rican forests. The social rodents (beaver, muskrats, marmots, prairie dogs) seem to lack large natural stands of highly edible plants (though capybaras are fair analogues to beaver and muskrats). The same may be said of the large cervids. However, if the Pleistocene megafauna had not disappeared it is possible that they would have helped keep more grassland open, thereby generating habitat for themselves and smaller grassland forms.

What Happened to the Pleistocene Megafauna?
There are several reasons to believe that the fauna of large mammals that ranged over North America from ten

to sixty thousand years ago was also present in Costa Rican forests. First there are Pleistocene horse fossils (*Equus fraternus*) from a variety of Costa Rican sites, including Guanacaste Province (L. Gómez, pers. comm.), where contemporary horses do very well. The same applies to gomphotheres (Snarskis, Gamboa, and Fonseca 1977; L. Gómez, pers. comm.). There is even a single ground sloth record from the San Carlos region of northern Costa Rica (L. Gómez, pers. comm.). If those animals were present, it is possible that some of their carnivorous and herbivorous associates were also present. Second, Venezuela and Mexico contain many more fossils of these groups, including sites of kills by ancient humans (Bryan et al. 1978). Judging from the very broad habitat ranges of contemporary large mammals in Africa, it is likely that animals that occurred in southern North America and northern South America also occurred in Costa Rica. Third, horses and cattle maintain solid breeding populations, even when left much to themselves, in a variety of Costa Rican habitats (including nearly pure forest in Corcovado National Park and Guanacaste).

Assuming that the big mammals were here, where did they go? There is no reason to believe that all of Costa Rica underwent any dramatic climate change ten thousand years ago. Martin (1973) postulated that Pleistocene hunters, rapidly descending on a naive set of large mammals, quickly extinguished the species that were slow to learn and whose traits were especially vulnerable to human hunting methods. The scarcity of fossil beds in the tropics make this type of speculation difficult to substantiate. However, part of the problem is that the tropics seem to be generally unsuitable for fossil preservation. A dead horse or cow on the rain-forest floor is represented by nothing but a skull in less than a year, and only the teeth remain after that. The same applies to larger mammals in deciduous forest, once the rainy season comes. One of us (Janzen) has observed that nothing but teeth and skull fragments were left of an elephant 7 months after it died in a Cameroon rain forest; only natural scavengers processed it. At a similar site an elephant 2 years after death had only the decomposing molars remaining. The wet tropics are notoriously poor sites for animal preservation as fossils, and observing the high speed of decomposition on land or in water makes it obvious why.

Why do we care? Certainly extinctions of animals occur all the time, and this change is an integral part of the evolutionary process. However, it seems possible that the "natural" habitats studied today in Costa Rica have undergone ten thousand years of ecological adjustments among the surviving fauna and flora, but many of the possible evolutionary changes have not yet occurred. The habitats should be liberally sprinkled with anachronisms, such as sizable crops of big-seeded large fleshy fruits that are not consumed by the contemporary mammals. Also,

436

spines and other mechanical and chemical defenses of vegetative parts are widespread, but from what are they protecting the plants (Janzen and Martin 1982)? For example, the large fruits of *Enterolobium cyclocarpum*, *Pithecellobium saman*, *Hymenaea courbaril*, *Annona purpurea*, *Sapranthus palanga*, *Cassia grandis*, *Acacia farnesiana*, *Crescentia alata*, and *Guazuma ulmifolia* are only part of the Guanacaste species that are eaten by horses and cattle and probably were originally dispersed by the Pleistocene megafauna. These plants probably have different distributions and densities among habitats now that their major dispersal agents are missing. In fact, a mixed grassland-forest, populated by range cattle and horses, is probably a more "natural" habitat for these plants than the pre-Columbian pure forest habitats being protected by Costa Rican parks.

How Good Are Costa Rican Mammals as Seed Dispersers?

Seed dispersal by Costa Rican mammals appears rather simple. Mammals eat fruits and spit or defecate the seeds elsewhere, or they carry the seeds off to eat later (cache and scatter hoard) but for various reasons do not eat them. However, to illustrate the deceptive nature of this simplistic view, a few of the high points of an ongoing study of horses, spiny pocket mice, and guanacaste seeds in Santa Rosa National Park are mentioned below.

Horses avidly eat the newly fallen fruits of the guanacaste tree (*Enterolobium cyclocarpum*), and the ungerminated seeds appear in the dung (Janzen 1981c). These later germinate to produce healthy seedlings. However, when the horse is chewing the fruits, it spits out 40–60% of the seeds (Janzen 1981b). Some of these seeds have been nicked by the horse's molars; this raises the immediate germination percentage upon contact with moist soil from about 3% to 10–15% for most seed crops. However, the spit seeds are left below the parent tree, where their almost certain fate is to be eaten by spiny pocket mice (*Liomys salvini*) if the tree is growing in forest. Beginning on the second day after the seeds are swallowed, a very small percentage of the seeds appear each day in the dung until about day 10–15, depending on the horse. Then, after weeks, occasional further seeds appear. The seeds in the dung are in three states. About 90% are ungerminated and do not germinate if placed in water; they are alive but unscarified. About 1–3% of the seeds are soft, just beginning to germinate, and still alive; they produce seedlings growing out of the dung (their fate to be determined by habitat, season, dung-beetle activity, and microsite exposure of the dung). An equal percentage of the defecated seeds are soft, recently germinated, and killed by the horse's digestive processes. The bulk of the seeds swallowed by horses never appear in the dung, and it appears that they are either digested or remain (in the cecum?) for many months. Seed-coat fragments occur frequently in the dung, but indigestible buttons used as controls remained in the horse for months.

As implied above, defecation in dung of even some guanacaste seeds does not mean that the horse is a "good" guanacaste seed disperser. When horse dung with guanacaste seeds in it is left in Santa Rosa National Park deciduous forest, the spiny pocket mice find it in 1–2 nights and eat the seeds. The rate at which they find dung-free seeds is substantially less. However, if the dung is dropped in open grassland several hundred meters or more from forest, seeds placed in it germinate unmolested (though the seedlings are on occasion eaten by *Sigmodon hispidus*). We do not as yet know the fate of these guanacaste seedlings in open grassland, but fire and dry-season desiccation must take a heavy toll. When cattle consume guanacaste fruits, they spit out fewer than 5% of the seeds and pass nearly all the rest undamaged and ungerminated within 10 days; as many as half of these seeds may appear in the dung on day 4–5. The tapir (*Tapirus bairdii*) eats many fewer guanacaste fruits, spits about as many seeds as do horses, digests at least 70% of the seeds it swallows, but defecates in water (Janzen 1981a). By doing the latter it not only places the seeds in a *Liomys*-free habitat, but substantially increases the chance that the seedling will end up on a relatively competition-free and water-rich gravel bar or riverbank (a habitat often occupied by guanacaste trees).

If there are no large mammals present to eat the newly fallen guanacaste fruits, they lie indehiscent through the remaining 1–2 months of the dry season and then rot open during the first 2 months of the rainy season. In grassland, the seeds simply become part of the soil seed bank and occasionally germinate in later years as the hard seed coat is scarified by soil chemical reactions. In forest the pods are opened by the resident *Liomys* population and the seeds are taken off to an underground burrow (though some are eaten on the spot). If they happen to be just starting to germinate, they are peeled of their seed coats and eaten directly. In the laboratory, an adult mouse can maintain its body weight on a pure diet of about 10–13 germinating seeds per day for at least a month (Hallwachs and Janzen 1983). If ungerminated, some are eaten directly by chewing off the seed coat at one end and gnawing through the extremely hard seed contents; a mouse can maintain its body weight on a pure diet of about 6–7 such seeds per day, again for a month. A highly variable number of the hard seeds are also notched at an end, in one to four places; these germinate immediately when placed in water or moist soil, and the mouse then eats them (W. Hallwachs, pers. comm.). What we do not yet know is the fate of guanacaste seeds that the mouse caches below ground but then loses because it dies or cannot relocate them.

As mentioned earlier, spiny pocket mice are avid collectors of guanacaste seeds (as well as other species of

437

seeds) from horse dung (Janzen 1982*b,c*). If forty piles of dung (a normal adult horse dung pat is about 1.5 kg) are placed out in the forest with twenty guanacaste seeds buried in the center of each, it is normal for the *Liomys* in the upland forests of Santa Rosa National Park to get all the seeds the first night. The size of the dung pat has little effect; twenty to five hundred seeds buried in the center of as much as 15 kg of horse dung are 99–100% discovered and removed the first or second night. Cattle dung, a more liquid and more caustic substrate, sometimes retains its seeds as long as 4 days in the face of active *Liomys* seed harvesting. Guanacaste seeds placed in the same forest, but without dung associated, sometimes remain as long as a week before they are removed. In certain circumstances horse dung is a more effective trap bait than oatmeal or peanut butter, though for this to occur, there must have been seed-enriched horse dung in the area previously.

All seed-eating and frugivorous mammals probably function as seed dispersers for some species of Costa Rican plant. However, there are many variables peculiar to the seed and the animal. Fruits of *Spondias mombin* are eaten whole by coatis, spider monkeys, and howler monkeys; the large nuts are defecated within 1–2 days. Horses and a captive tapir, however, avidly chew the fruit pulp off the nut and spit it out (below the parent tree in nature). Agoutis also eat the pulp and then sometimes bury the nuts (Smythe 1978).

Many animals eat figs, and it appears that the seeds are generally too small to be ground up. *Artibeus* bats are champion fig eaters (Morrison 1978*a;* Janzen 1979), but their seed dispersal is complex. They carry a fig from the parent tree to a feeding roost tens of meters away (and see their similar treatment of Guanacaste *Andira* fruits, Janzen et al. 1976) and bite pieces out of the fig wall and inner seed-floret mix. After chewing this mix and pressing out the juices, they spit it out as a pellet. These pellets may accumulate by the hundreds below a single bat's feeding roost, and each contains an average of about one viable seed (the remaining seeds are empty shells, since fig wasps long ago emerged from them). However, while feeding on the fig, the bat is somehow removing a small number of only viable seeds along with the juices. These come out in the feces, and a single fecal load may contain as many as fifty of these good seeds. These fecal pellets are dropped in widely scattered areas on the vegetation and ground, as well as at the feeding roost.

After collecting dung of many species of Costa Rican mammals in many habitats, we are left with the general impression that mammals generate widely scattered, diffuse seed shadows, but that these often contain intense small peaks and contour lines (e.g., 55,000 *Piper auritum* seeds below one bat feeding roost in Corcovado National Park; Janzen 1978*a*). It is commonplace to come upon a pile of monkey feces containing several hundred seeds of *Genipa americana, Chomelia spinosa,* or *Alibertia edulis* in Santa Rosa National Park. On the other hand, we suspect that there is much greater seed mortality by mammalian dispersal agents than generally realized. Peccaries almost never pass entire seeds and are adept at cracking those that require as much as several hundred pounds pressure to break (e.g., Janzen and Higgins 1979; Kiltie 1979). Tapir dung almost never contains viable seeds, but seed coat fragments are common in it. Deer customarily spit out all seeds except the very smallest. Even mice such as *Oryzomys, Sigmodon,* and *Liomys* ground up the minute seeds in such fruits as *Muntingia calabura* and *Ficus* spp. as well as defecating some whole seeds (W. Hallwachs, pers. comm.).

In interpreting mammal dispersal of seeds, extreme caution must be used for two other reasons. First, as implied above in the interaction of mammals with guanacaste seeds, the detailed site of seed defecation matters, as does the fact that the seeds are marked with a conspicuous odor flag for a while after defecation. Second, many mammals eat seeds while still in the milk stage and are thus seed predators rather than dispersers. Monkeys and squirrels are heavy offenders. Further, in addition to killing seeds directly, when they pick immature fruits and eat some of the seeds, the remaining seeds often die even if untouched.

What Are the Special Costa Rican Challenges to a Mammal?

With respect to the gross traits of the physical environment, Costa Rica is about as hospitable as any tropical country. Snow has never been recorded there. Although nighttime temperatures may drop as low as −3° C on the tops of the taller mountain ranges, the coldest daylight temperatures are in the range of 5–15° C. These extremes do not appear to be much of an instantaneous challenge for a warm-blooded animal. However, the impact of a physical environmental challenge, such as a drop in temperature, is also a function of the temperature regime in which the animal normally lives. It may well be that apparently small temperature extremes encountered by a Costa Rican mammal in moving over elevational gradients, extremes that seem minor to those of us accustomed to extratropical fluctuations, are severe challenges (Janzen 1967).

Although Costa Rica has (had) extensive areas of deciduous forest, these differ strongly from similar deciduous forest in Mexico and Venezuela in that the lowlands of Guanacaste are crossed at frequent intervals by everflowing rivers off the Pacific slopes of the volcanoes. These linear oases are dry-season sites of mammal concentration of water, shade, fruit and foliage, and animal prey. During the Pleistocene this riparian vegetation probably experienced the same heavy usage as is currently experienced by riparian vegetation in eastern Africa during the dry season. Of course the dry season means a shortage of water for most mammals and thereby restricts their movements, but the challenge is not as severe as it would be if moist habitats were not nearby and if certain remnants of the rainy season did not persist. There are tree holes with drinking water (Glander 1978), many trees with juicy fruits (based on the groundwater supply accumulated during the rains), and local springs and surfacings of underground streams. One such waterhole in Santa Rosa National Park contains a volume of about 8 liters of water at any one time and is daily visited by several deer, five to fifteen coatis, five to fifteen peccaries, two to five agoutis, five to twenty white-faced monkeys, and numerous birds.

On the other hand, the frequent rainy season rains undoubtedly render many underground cavities inhospitable for mammal nests and sleeping sites. Logs and dead standing trees rot rapidly and are often waterlogged. Dry cavities, especially large ones, are probably in short supply in many areas.

In contrast to the physical environment, there are a number of fairly drastic biotic challenges to a Costa Rican mammal in comparison with, for example, those faced in the eastern deciduous forests of North America. Ants are probably one of the worst. Both army ants and various solenopsines (e.g., *Solenopsis* fire ants) are killers of live-trapped small rodents in rain-forest sites and may be a major source of nestling mortality for those that nest on, in, or near the ground. Even arboreal nesting will not help mammals escape the climbing army ants such as *Eciton burchelli*. Ants are quick to occupy small carcasses (Cornaby 1974) and probably keep small carnivores away. Snakes are of course a predation threat to small and medium-sized mammals in all forests, but Costa Rican forests contain a much greater array of sizes and foraging types of snakes than do extratropical forests. Boa constrictors take animals as large as coatis (e.g., Janzen 1970), and the large vipers take animals agouti-sized and smaller. Whether predation pressure by birds and predaceous mammals is more intense in a Costa Rican forest than in an extratropical forest is unknown. Although the tropics are often thought of as more "disease-ridden" for humans and their livestock, there is no compelling natural-history information that we know of to indicate that this is also true for Costa Rican wild mammals. There has never been a comparative survey of the parasites or diseases of animals found in both northern and Costa Rican habitats.

It is tempting to suggest that food for herbivores is generally less edible in Costa Rica forests than in extratropical ones, but this generalization is probably too broad to be useful (or true). The large northern coniferous and fagaceous forests produce highly edible seed crops compared with the mix of secondary-compound-rich seeds found on the floor of a tropical forest. However, it is hard to compare these forests because of the highly pulsed nature of the northern seeds as compared with the more uniform production of tropical seeds (Janzen 1971, 1978b). There are certainly a large number of species of foliage that large browsing herbivores reject in tropical forests (e.g., Janzen 1982a; Glander 1975), but northern forests likewise have species of plants consistently rejected by deer, elk, moose, and such. Perhaps after we have much more browsing data for tropical tapirs, horses, peccaries, and white-tailed deer we will be able to make a more reliable statement.

ACKNOWLEDGMENTS
This study was supported by NSF DEB 77-04889 (Janzen) and the United States Fish and Wildlife Service (Wilson). The manuscript was constructively criticized by W. Hallwachs, M. A. Bogan, and A. L. Gardner.

*

Altenbach, J. S. 1979. *Locomotor morphology of the vampire bat, Desmodus votundus.* Special publication 6, American Society of Mammalogists.

Altenbach, J. S.; Geluso, K. N.; and Wilson, D. E. 1979. Population size of *Tadarida brasiliensis* at Carlsbad Caverns in 1973. In *Biological investigations in the Guadalupe Mountains National Park, Texas,* pp. 341–48. United States National Park Service Proceedings and Transactions, no. 4.

Bequaert, J. 1922. Ants in their diverse relations to the plant world. *Bull. Am. Mus. Nat. Hist.* 45:333–584.

Bonilla, A. 1979. Servicio de Parques Nacionales. *Ascona Bul.* 5:5–6.

Bonoff, M. B., and Janzen, D. H. 1980. Small terrestrial rodents in 11 habitats in Santa Rosa National Park, Costa Rica. *Brenesia* 17:163–74.

Booth, A. H. 1956. The distribution of primates in the Gold Coast. *J. W. Afr. Sci. Ass.* 2:122–33.

Bradbury, J. W., and Emmons, L. 1974. Social organization of some Trinidad bats. I. Emballonuridae. *Z. Tierpsychol.* 36:137–83.

Bradbury, J. W., and Vehrencamp, S. L. 1976a. Social organization and foraging in emballonurid bats. I. Field studies. *Behav. Ecol. Sociobiol.* 1:337–81.

———. 1976b. Social behavior and foraging in emballonurid bats. II. A model for the determination of group size. *Behav. Ecol. Sociobiol.* 1:383–404.

———. 1977a. Social organization and foraging in emballonurid bats. III. Mating systems. *Behav. Ecol. Sociobiol.* 2:1–17.

———. 1977b. Social organization and foraging in emballonurid bats. IV. Parental investment patterns. *Behav. Ecol. Sociobiol.* 2:19–29.

Brown, J. H. 1968. Activity patterns of some Neotropical bats. *J. Mamm.* 49:754–57.

Bryan, A. L.; Casamiquela, R. M.; Cruxent, J. M.; Gruhn, R.; and Ochsenius, C. 1978. An El Jobo mastodon kill at Taima-taima, Venezuela. *Science* 100: 1275–77.

Charles-Dominique, P. 1974. Ecology and feeding behavior of five sympatric lorisids in Gabon. In *Prosimian biology,* ed. R. D. Martin, G. A. Doyle, and A. C. Walker, pp. 131–50. London: Duckworth.

Chase, J. 1972. Role of vision in echolocating bats. Ph.D. diss., Indiana University.

Constantine, D. B. 1967. Activity patterns of the Mexican free-tailed bat. *University of New Mexico Publications in Biology* 7:1–79.

Cornaby, B. W. 1974. Carrion reduction by animals in contrasting tropical habitats. *Biotropica* 6:51–63.

DiSanto, P. E. 1960. Anatomy and histochemistry of the salivary glands of the vampire bat *Desmodus rotundus murinus. J. Morphol.* 106:301–35.

Eisenberg, J. F., and Wilson, D. E. 1979. Relative brain size and feeding strategies in the chiroptera. *Evolution* 32:740–51.

Emmons, L. 1975. Ecology and behavior of African rainforest squirrels. Ph.D. diss., Cornell University.

Findley, J. S.; Studier, E. H.; and Wilson, D. E. 1972. Morphologic properties of bat wings. *J. Mamm.* 53: 429–44.

Findley, J. S., and Wilson, D. E. 1974. Observations on the Neotropical disk-winged bat, *Thyroptera tricolor* Spix. *J. Mamm.* 55:562–71.

Findley, J. S.; Harris, A. H.; Wilson, D. E.; and Jones, C. 1975. *Mammals of New Mexico.* Albuquerque: University of New Mexico Press.

Fleming, T. H. 1971. *Artibeus jamaicensis,* delayed embryonic development in a Neotropical bat. *Science* 171:402–4.

———. 1973a. Numbers of mammal species in North and Central American forest communities. *Ecology* 54:555–63.

———. 1973b. The number of rodent species in two Costa Rican forests. *J. Mamm.* 54:518–21.

———. 1974. The population ecology of two species of Costa Rican heteromyid rodents. *Ecology* 55: 493–510.

———. 1977a. Growth and development of two species of tropical heteromyid rodents. *Am. Mid. Nat.* 98:109–23

———. 1977b. Response of two species of tropical heteromyid rodents to reduced food and water availability. *J. Mamm.* 58:102–6.

Fleming, T. H., and Brown, G. J. 1975. An experimental analysis of seed hoarding and burrowing behavior in two species of Costa Rican heteromyid rodents. *J. Mamm.* 56:301–15.

Fleming, T. H.; Heithaus, E. R.; and Sawyer, W. B. 1977. An experimental analysis of the food location behavior of frugivorous bats. *Ecology* 58:619–27.

Fleming, T. H.; Hooper, E. T., and Wilson, D. W. 1972. Three Central American bat communities: Structure, reproductive cycles, and movement patterns. *Ecology* 53:555–69.

Foster, M. S., and Timm, R. M. 1976. Tent-making by *Artibeus jamaicensis* (Chiroptera: Phyllostomatidae) with comments on plants used by bats for tents. *Biotropica* 8:265–69.

Gardner, A. L. 1973. *The systematics of the genus Didelphis (Marsupialia: Didelphidae) in North and Middle America.* Special Publications of the Museum, Lubbock: Texas Tech Univeristy.

———. 1977. Feeding habits. In *Biology of bats of the New World family Phyllostomatidae,* part 2, ed. R. J. Baker, J. K. Jones, Jr., and D. C. Carter, pp. 293–350. Special Publications of the Museum. Lubbock: Texas Tech University.

Gardner, A. L.; Laval, R. K.; and Wilson, D. E. 1970. The distributional status of some Costa Rican bats. *J. Mamm.* 51:712–29.

Gardner, A. L., and Wilson, D. E. 1971. A melanized subcutaneous covering of the cranial musculature in the phyllostomid bat, *Ectophylla alba. J. Mamm.* 52:854–55.

Gartlan, J. S., and Struhsaker, T. T. 1972. Polyspecific associations and niche separation of rainforest anthropoids in Cameroon, West Africa. *J. Zool.* 168: 221–66.

Geluso, K. N.; Altenbach, J. S.; and Wilson, D. E. 1976. Bat mortality: Pesticide poisoning and migratory stress. *Science* 194:184–86.

Glander, K. E. 1975. Habitat and resource utilization: An ecological view of social organization in mantled howler monkeys. Ph.D. diss., University of Chicago.

———. 1978. Drinking from arboreal water sources by mantled howling monkeys (*Alouatta palliata* Gray). *Folia Primat.* 29:206–17.

Goffart, M. 1971. *Form and function in the sloth.* Oxford: Pergamon Press.

Goodwin, G. G. 1946. Mammals of Costa Rica. Bull. Am. Mus. Nat. Hist. 87:275–458.

Hallwachs, W., and Janzen, D. H. 1983. *Enterolobium cyclocarpum* seeds as food for Costa Rican *Liomys salvini* (Heteromyidae). *Brenesia,* in press.

Heithaus, E. R., and Fleming, T. H. 1978. Foraging movements of a frugivorous bat, *Carollia perspicillata* (Phyllostomatidae). *Ecol. Monogr.* 48:127–43.

Heithaus, E. R.; Fleming, T. H.; and Opler, P. A. 1975. Foraging patterns and resource utilization in seven species of bats in a seasonal tropical forest. *Ecology* 56:841–54.

Heithaus, E. R.; Opler, P. A.; and Baker, H. G. 1974. Bat activity and pollination of *Bauhinia pauletia:* Plant-pollinator coevolution. *Ecology* 55:412–19.

Howell, D. J., and Burch, D. 1974. Food habits of some Costa Rican bats. *Rev. Biol. Trop.* 21:281–94.

Hrdy, S. B., and Bennett, W. 1979. The fig connection. *Harvard Mag.* 82:25–30.

Janzen, D. H. 1967. Why mountain passes are higher in the tropics. *Am. Nat.* 101:233–49.

———. 1970. Altruism by coatis in the face of predation by *Boa constrictor. J. Mamm.* 51:387–89.

———. 1971. Seed predation by animals. *Ann. Rev. Ecol. Systm.* 2:465–92.

———. 1973. Sweep samples of tropical foliage insects: Effect of seasons, vegetation types, elevation, time of day, and insularity. *Ecology* 54:687–708.

———. 1974. The deflowering of Central America. *Nat. Hist.* 83:48–53.

———. 1977. Why fruits rot, seeds mold, and meat spoils. *Am. Nat.* 111:691–713.

———. 1978a. The size of a local peak in a seed shadoe. *Biotropica* 10:78.

———. 1978b. Seeding patterns of tropical trees. In *Tropical trees as living systems,* ed. P. B. Tomlinson and M. H. Zimmerman, pp. 83–128. New York: Cambridge University Press.

———. 1979. How to be a fig. *Ann. Rev. Ecol. Syst.* 10:13–51.

———. 1981a. Digestive seed predation by a Costa Rican Baird's tapir. *Biotropica* 13 (suppl.):59–63.

———. 1981b. Seed swallowing by Costa Rican range horses. *Ecology* 62:587–92.

———. 1981c. *Enterolobium cyclocarpum* seed passage rate and survival in horses, Costa Rican Pleistocene seed dispersal agents. *Ecology* 62:593–601.

———. 1982a. Wild plant acceptability to a captive Costa Rican Baird's tapir. *Brenesia,* in press.

———. 1982b. Attraction of *Liomys* mice to horse dung and the extinction of this response. *Anim. Behav.* 30:483–89.

———. 1982c. Removal of seeds from horse dung by tropical rodents: Influence of habitat and amount of dung. *Ecology* 63:1887–1900.

Janzen, D. H., and Higgins, M. L. 1979. How hard are *Enterolobium cyclocarpum* (Leguminosae) seeds? *Brenesia* 16:61–67.

Janzen, D. H., and Martin, P. S. 1982. Neotropical anachronisms: Fruits the gomphotheres ate. *Science* 215:19–27.

Janzen, D. H.; Miller, G. A.; Hackforth-Jones, J.; Pond, C. M.; Hooper, K.; and Janos, D. P. 1976. Two Costa Rican bat-generated seed shadows of *Andira inermis* (Leguminosae). *Ecology* 57:1068–75.

Janzen, D. H., and Wilson, D. E. 1974. The cost of being dormant in the tropics. *Biotropica* 6:260–63.

Keen, R., and Hitchcock, H. B. 1980. Survival and longevity of the little brown bat (*Myotis lucifugus*) in southeastern Ontario. *J. Mamm.* 61:1–7.

Kenyon, K. W. 1977. Caribbean monk seal extinct. *J. Mamm.* 58:97–98.

Kiltie, R. A. 1979. Seed predation and group size in rain forest peccaries. Ph.D. diss., Princeton University.

LaVal, R. K. 1970. Banding returns and activity periods of some Costa Rican bats. *Southwest. Nat.* 15:1–10.

———. 1977. Notes on some Costa Rican bats. *Brenesia* 10/11:77–83.

LaVal, R. K., and Fitch, H. S. 1977. Structure, move-

ments and reproduction in three Costa Rican bat communities. *Occas. Pap. Mus. Nat. Hist., Univ. Kansas.* 69:1–28.

McCoy, E. D., and Connor, E. F. 1980. Latitudinal gradients in the species diversity of North American mammals. *Evolution* 34:193–203.

McFarland, W. N., and Wimsatt, W. A. 1969. Renal function and its relation to the ecology of the vampire bat, *Desmodus rotundus. Comp. Biochem. Physiol.* 28:985–1006.

McNab, B. K. 1969. The economics of temperature regulation in Neotropical bats. *Comp. Biochem. Physiol.* 31:227–68.

———. 1973. Energetics and the distribution of vampires. *J. Mamm.* 54:131–44.

Mares, M. A., and Wilson, D. E. 1971. Bat reproduction during the Costa Rican dry season. *Bioscience* 21:471–77.

Martin, P. S. 1973. The discovery of America. *Science* 179:969–74.

Mills, R. S. 1980. Parturition and social interaction among captive vampire bats, *Desmodus rotundus. J. Mamm.* 61:336–37.

Mittermeier, R. A., and Coimbra-Filho, A. F. 1977. Primate conservation in Brazilian Amazonia. In *Primate conservation*, ed. H.S.H. Prince Rainier III and G. H. Bourne, pp. 117–66. New York: Academic Press.

Montgomery, G. G., and Sunquist, M. E. 1975. Impact of sloths on Neotropical forest energy flow and nutrient cycling. In *Tropical ecological systems: Trends in terrestrial and aquatic research,* ed. F. B. Golley and E. Medina, pp. 69–98. New York: Springer-Verlag.

———. 1978. Habitat selection and use by two-toed and three-toed sloths. In *The ecology of arboreal folivores,* ed. G. G. Montgomery, pp. 329–60. Washington, D.C.: Smithsonian Institution Press.

Morrison, D. W. 1978a. Foraging ecology and energetics of the frugivorous bat *Artibeus jamaicensis. Ecology* 59:716–23.

———. 1978b. Lunar phobia in a Neotropical fruit bat *Artibeus jamaicensis* (Chiroptera: Phyllostomidae). *Anim. Behav.* 26:852–55.

Muul, I., and Liat, L. B. 1979. Comparative morphology, food habits, and ecology of some Malaysian arboreal rodents. In *The ecology of arboreal folivores,* ed. G. G. Montgomery, pp. 361–68. Washington, D.C.: Smithsonian Institution Press.

Nishiwaki, M., and Norris, K. S. 1966. A new genus, *Peponocephala* for the odontocate cetacean species *Electra electra. Sci. Rept. Whales Res. Inst., Tokyo* 20:95–100.

Novick, A. 1977. Acoustic orientation. In *Biology of bats,* vol. 3, ed. W. A. Wimsatt, pp. 73–286. New York: Academic Press.

Phillips, C. J.; Grimes, G. W.; and Forman, G. L. 1977. Oral biology. In *Biology of bats of the New World family Phyllostomatidae,* part 2, ed. R. J. Baker, J. K. Jones, Jr., and D. C. Carter, Special Publication of the

Museum, no. 13. Lubbock: Texas Tech University.

Pond, C. M. 1978. Morphological aspects and the ecological significance of fat distribution in wild vertebrates. *Ann. Rev. Ecol. Syst.* 9:519–70.

Sazima, I., and Uieda, W. 1980. Feeding behavior of the white-winged vampire bat, *Diaemus youngii,* on poultry. *J. Mamm.* 61:102–4.

Schmidt, U. 1973. Olfactory threshold and odour discrimination of the vampire bat (*Desmodus rotundus*). *Period. Biol.* 75:89–92.

Schmidt, U., and Manske, U. 1973. Die Jugendentwicklung der vampirfledermäuse (*Desmodus rotundus*). *Z. Säugetierk.* 38:14–33.

Simpson, G. G. 1964. Species density of North American recent mammals. *Systm. Zool.* 13:57–73.

Smith, J. D. 1972. Systematics of the chiropteran family Mormoopidae. *Misc. Publ. Mus. Nat. Hist. Univ. Kansas* 56:1–132.

Smythe, N. 1978. The natural history of the Central American agouti (*Daryprocta punctata*). *Smithsonian Contrib. Zool.* no. 257.

Snarskis, M. J., Gamboa, H.; and Fonseca, O. 1977. El mastodonte de Tibas, Costa Rica. *Vinculos* 3:1–12.

Starrett, A. 1976. Comments on bats newly recorded from Costa Rica. *Contrib. Sci., Los Angeles County Mus. Nat. Hist.* 277:1–5.

Studier, E. H., and Wilson, D. E. 1970. Thermoregulation in some Neotropical bats. *Comp. Biochem. Physiol.* 34:251–62.

———. 1979. Effects of captivity on thermoregulation and metabolism in *Artibeus jamaicensis* (Chiroptera: Phyllostomatidae). *Comp. Biochem. Physiol.* 62A: 347–50.

Timm, R. M., and Mortimer, J. 1976. Selection of roost sites by Honduran white bats, *Ectophylla alba* (Chiroptera: Phyllostomatidae). *Ecology* 57:385–89.

Turner, D. C. 1975. *The vampire bat.* Baltimore: Johns Hopkins University Press.

Vandermeer, J. H. 1979. Hoarding behavior of captive *Heteromys desmaretianus* (Rodentia) on the fruits of *Welfia georgii,* a rainforest dominant palm in Costa Rica. *Brenesia* 16:107–16.

Vehrencamp, S. L.; Stiles, F. G.; and Bradbury, J. W. 1977. Observations on the foraging behavior and avian prey of the Neotropical carnivorous bat, *Vampyrum spectrum. J. Mamm.* 58:469–78.

Villa-R., B. 1966. *Los murciélagos de México.* Mexico, D.F.: Instituto de Biología, Universidad Nacional Autonomo de México.

Wilson, D. E. 1971a. Ecology of *Myotis nigricans* (Mammalia: Chiroptera) on Barro Colorado Island, Panama Canal Zone. *J. Zool.* 163:1–13.

———. 1971b. Food habits of *Micronycteris hirsuta* (Chiroptera: Phyllostomidae). *Mammalia* 35:107–10.

Wilson, D. E. 1973a. Bat faunas: A trophic comparison. *Syst. Zool.* 22:14–29.

———. 1973b. Reproduction in Neotropical bats. *Period. Biol.* 75:215–17.

———. 1979. Reproductive patterns. In *Biology of bats of the New World family Phyllostomatidae,* part 3, ed. R. J. Baker, J. K. Jones, Jr., and D. C. Carter, pp. 317–78. Special Publications of the Museum, no. 16. Lubbock: Texas Tech University.

Wilson, D. E., and Findley, J. S. 1970. Reproductive cycles of a Neotropical insectivorous bat, *Myotis nigricans. Nature* 225:1155.

———. 1971. Spermatogenesis in some Neotropical species of *Myotis. J. Mamm.* 52:420–26.

———. 1977. *Thyroptera tricolor. Mamm. Species,* no. 71.

Wilson, D. E.; Geluso, K. N.; and Altenbach, J. S. 1978. The ontogeny of fat deposition in *Tadarida brasiliensis. Proc. 4th Int. Bat Res. Conf., Kenya Nat. Acad. Adv. Arts Sci. Nairobi,* pp. 15–20.

Wilson, J. W., III. 1974. Analytical zoogeography of North American mammals. *Evolution* 28:124–40.

CHECKLIST OF MAMMALS

D. E. Wilson

This checklist is organized by sites frequently visited by biologists, but to the best of our knowledge (D. E. Wilson and D. H. Janzen) contains all the terrestrial mammal species known for Costa Rica, except for the manatee at Tortuguero National Park on the Caribbean coast (pp. 498–500).

"La Selva" refers to the vicinity of Puerto Viejo de Sarapiquí, in the Atlantic coastal lowlands of interior Heredia Province. "Osa" refers to the vicinity of Rincón in the head of the Golfo Dulce and Corcovado National Park, both on the Osa Peninsula in the southwestern coastal lowlands. "Guanacaste" refers to the deciduous forest and accompanying riparian vegetation from northern Puntarenas Province through Guanacaste Province (including the Nicoya Peninsual) below about 400 m

elevation. "San José" refers to the Meseta Central with its small farms and urban sprawl (900–1,200 m elevation). "San Vito" refers to the vicinity of San Vito de Java and Finca Las Cruces about 8 km to the south, at an elevation of 900 to 1,800 m on the Pacific face of the Talamanca Cordillera just north of the Panamanian border. "Cerro de la Muerte" refers to the regenerating brush (commonly misnamed "páramo") following clearing and wide-spaced fires on Cerro de la Muerte and Cerro Asunción along the Pan American Highway between Cartago and San Isidro del General, and the oak forests and pastures around Pensión La Georgina and Villa Mills (2,800–3,300 m elevation). "Monteverde" refers to the evergreen forest and accompanying pastures and fields around Santa Elena, Monteverde, and the Monteverde Forest Reserve at 1,500–1,900 m elevation on the Pacific slope of the Guanacaste Cordillera (Puntarenas Province).

X = positively identified observation or collection of species;
E = species to be expected at site on basis of its known occurrence in similar or contiguous areas.

Taxon	La Selva	Osa	Guanacaste	San José	San Vito	Cerro de la Muerte	Monteverde
Marsupialia							
Didelphidae							
Didelphis marsupialis	X	X	X	X	X	—	X
D. virginiana	—	—	X	—	—	—	E
Chironectes minimus	E	X	X	X	E	—	E
Philander opossum	X	X	X	X	X	—	X
Marmosa alstoni	E	X	E	X	—	—	E
M. mexicana	—	X	—	—	X	—	—
M. robinsoni	—	E	—	—	—	—	—
Caluromys derbianus	X	X	X	X	E	—	X
Metachirus nudicaudatus	E	X	E	—	—	—	—
Insectivora							
Soricidae							
Cryptotis gracilis	—	—	—	—	—	X	X
C. nigrescens	—	—	—	X	—	X	—
C. parva	—	—	—	X	—	—	X
Chiroptera							
Emballonuridae							
Balantiopteryx plicata	—	—	X	—	—	—	—
Saccopteryx bilineata	X	X	X	E	—	—	—
S. canescens	—	—	—	—	—	—	—
S. leptura	X	X	X	—	—	—	—
Peropteryx kappleri	X	E	X	X	—	—	—
P. macrotis	E	X	X	X	—	—	—
Cormura brevirostris	X	X	—	—	—	—	—
Rhynchonycteris naso	X	X	X	—	—	—	—
Centronycteris maximiliani	X	X	—	—	—	—	—
Diclidurus virgo	E	X	E	X	—	—	—
Cyttarops alecto	X	E	—	—	—	—	—
Noctilionidae							
Noctilio albiventris	X	E	X	—	—	—	—
N. leporinus	X	X	X	—	—	—	—

Taxon	La Selva	Osa	Guanacaste	San José	San Vito	Cerro de la Muerte	Monteverde
Mormoopidae							
Pteronotus davyi	E	E	X	E	—	—	—
P. gymnonotus	E	X	X	—	—	—	X
P. parnelli	X	X	X	X	X	—	X
P. personatus	E	X	X	E	—	—	—
Phyllostomidae							
Phyllostominae							
Micronycteris brachyotis	X	E	X	—	—	—	—
M. hirsuta	X	X	X	—	X	—	E
M. nicefori	X	—	X	—	—	—	—
M. megalotis	X	X	X	—	E	E	X
M. minuta	X	E	X	X	—	—	—
M. schmidtorum	X	E	X	X	—	—	—
M. sylvestris	—	E	X	—	—	—	—
Barticonycteris daviesi	X	—	—	—	—	—	—
Tonatia bidens	X	X	E	—	—	—	—
T. minuta	X	X	E	—	—	—	—
T. sylvicola	X	E	X	—	—	—	—
Macrophyllum macrophyllum	X	X	X	—	—	—	—
Lonchorhina aurita	E	E	X	—	X	—	—
Mimon cozumelae	X	E	E	—	—	—	—
M. crenulatum	X	E	—	—	—	—	—
Trachops cirrhosus	X	X	X	—	—	—	X
Phylloderma stenops	X	—	—	—	—	—	—
Phyllostomus discolor	X	X	X	X	X	—	E
P. hastatus	X	X	X	E	X	—	—
Chrotopterus auritus	E	E	X	E	—	—	—
Vampyrum spectrum	X	X	X	—	—	—	X
Glossophaginae							
Glossophaga alticola	—	—	X	—	—	—	—
G. comissarisi	X	X	X	X	X	—	X
G. soricina	X	X	X	X	X	—	X
Lonchophylla mordax	E	X	—	E	X	—	—
L. robusta	X	X	—	E	X	—	—
Anoura cultrata	—	—	—	X	X	E	X
A. geoffroyi	—	—	—	E	X	X	X
A. werckleae	—	—	—	—	E	X	—
Choeroniscus godmani	X	—	X	X	—	—	X
Hylonycteris underwoodi	X	E	X	E	X	E	X
Lychonycteris obscura	X	—	—	X	—	—	
Carolliinae							
Carollia brevicauda	X	X	X	X	X	—	X
C. castanea	X	X	X	—	—	—	—
C. perspicillata	X	X	X	X	X	E	—
C. subrufa			X				
Stenodermatinae							
Vampyrops helleri	X	X	X	X	X	—	—
V. vittatus	—	—	—	X	X	—	X
Vampyrodes major	X	X	E	—	—	—	—
Uroderma bilobatum	X	X	X	X	X	—	—
Artibeus aztecus	—	—	—	—	X	X	X
A. jamaicensis	X	X	X	X	X	E	X
A. lituratus	X	X	X	X	X	E	X
A. phaeotis	X	X	X	—	X	—	—
A. toltecus	—	—	X	X	X	—	X
A. watsoni	X	X	X	X	X	—	—

Taxon	La Selva	Osa	Guanacaste	San José	San Vito	Cerro de la Muerte	Monteverde
Enchisthenes hartii	E	X	E	X	X	—	X
Vampyressa nymphaea	X	E	—	—	—	—	—
V. pusilla	X	X	—	X	X	—	—
Ectophylla alba	X	E	—	—	—	—	—
Mesophylla macconnellii	—	—	—	—	E	—	—
Chiroderma salvini	—	E	E	—	X	—	—
C. villosum	X	X	X	X	X	—	E
Sturnira lilium	X	X	X	X	X	—	X
S. ludovici	X	—	—	E	X	X	X
S. mordax	—	—	—	E	X	—	X
Centurio senex	E	X	X	X	—	—	—
Desmodontinae							
Desmodus rotundus	X	X	X	X	X	E	E
Diaemus youngii	E	E	X	—	—	—	—
Diphylla ecaudata	E	X	X	E	—	—	—
Natalidae							
Natalus stramineus	—	—	X	—	—	—	—
Furipteridae							
Furipterus horrens	X	E	—	—	—	—	—
Thyropteridae							
Thyroptera tricolor	X	X	E	—	E	—	X
Vespertilionidae							
Myotis albescens	X	E	X	—	—	—	—
M. elegans	X	—	X	—	—	—	—
M. keaysi	X	X	X	E	E	E	X
M. nigricans	X	X	X	X	X	X	X
M. oxyotus	—	—	—	E	E	X	X
M. riparius	X	E	X	E	—	—	X
Rhogeessa tumida	X	X	X	X	—	—	—
Eptesicus andinus	X	X	—	X	X	X	X
E. furinalis	X	E	X	X	E	—	—
E. fuscus	X	—	E	X	E	—	—
Lasiurus borealis	E	E	X	X	E	E	—
L. ega	E	X	E	X	E	—	X
Molossidae							
Molossops greenhalli	E	E	X	X	—	—	—
Tadarida brasiliensis	E	E	E	X	—	—	—
Molossus ater	X	X	X	X	—	—	—
M. bondae	X	E	E	E	—	—	—
M. molossus	E	E	X	E	E	—	—
M. pretiosus	E	E	X	E	—	—	—
M. sinaloae	X	X	E	X	—	—	—
Eumops auripendulus	E	X	E	—	—	—	—
E. glaucinus	E	E	E	X	—	—	—
E. hansae	—	E	—	—	—	—	—
E. perotis	—	—	X	—	—	—	—
Primates							
Cebidae							
Saimiri oerstedii	—	X	—	—	—		
Alouatta palliata	X	X	X	E	E	—	X
Ateles geoffroyi	X	X	X	—	E	—	X
Cebus capucinus	X	X	X	X	X	—	X
Hominidae							
Homo sapiens	X	X	X	X	X	X	X

445

Taxon	La Selva	Osa	Guanacaste	San José	San Vito	Cerro de la Muerte	Monteverde
Edentata							
Myrmecophagidae							
Myrmecophaga tridactyla	—	E	—	—	—	—	
Tamandua mexicana	X	X	X	X	—	—	X
Cyclopes didactylus	E	X	—	E	—	—	—
Bradypodidae							
Bradipus variegatus	E	X	X	X	E	—	X
Choloepus hoffmani	X	X	X	X	E	—	
Dasypodidae							
Cabassous centralis	E	E	X	E	—	—	X
Dasypus novemcinctus	X	E	X	E	E	—	X
Lagomorpha							
Leporidae							
Sylvilagus brasiliensis	X	X	E	X	—	—	X
S. dicei					X	X	
S. floridanus	—	—	X	—	—	—	—
Rodentia							
Sciuridae							
Sciurus granatensis	X	X	—	X	X	E	—
S. deppei	X	X	X	—	—	—	X
S. variegatoides	X	E	X	X	—	—	X
Syntheosciurus brochus	—	—	—	—	—	—	—
Microsciurus alfari	X	X	—	—	X	—	X
Geomyidae							
Orthogeomys cavator	—	E	—	—	—	—	—
O. cherriei	E	—	—	—	—	—	E
O. heterodus	—	—	—	X	—	X	—
O. underwoodi	—	—	—	—	—	—	—
Heteromyidae							
Liomys salvini	—	—	X	X	—	—	—
Heteromys desmarestianus	X	X	—	X	X	—	X
H. oresterus	—	—	—	—	—	—	—
Erethizontidae							
Coendou mexicanum	X	E	X	X	—	X	X
Dasyproctidae							
Agouti paca	X	X	X	—	—	—	X
Dasyprocta punctata	X	X	X	X	E	—	X
Echimyidae							
Hoplomys gymnurus	X	X	X	—	—	—	—
Proechimys semispinosus	X	X	X	—	—	—	—
Muridae							
Oryzomys albigularis	X	—	—	X	—	X	—
O. alfari	X	—	—	—	—	—	—
O. alfaroi	—	—	X	—	E	—	—
O. aphrastus	—	—	—	—	—	—	—
O. bombycinus	X	—	—	—	—	—	—
O. caliginosus	X	X	—	X	—	—	—
O. capito	—	X	—	—	—	—	—
O. concolor	—	—	—	—	—	—	—
O. fulvescens	E	E	X	X	E	X	—
O. palustris	—	X	X	—	—	—	—
Tylomys watsoni	—	X	—	—	—	—	X
Ototylomys phyllotis	—	X	X	X	—	—	—
Nyctomys sumichrasti	X	X	—	—	—	—	X

Taxon	La Selva	Osa	Guanacaste	San José	San Vito	Cerro de la Muerte	Monteverde
Zygodontomys brevicauda	—	X	—	—	X	—	—
Sigmodon hispidus	—	X	X	X	—	—	X
Rheomys hartmanni	—	—	—	—	—	X	—
R. underwoodi	—	—	—	—	—	—	E
Peromyscus mexicanus	—	—	—	—	—	—	—
P. nudipes	—	—	X	X	X	X	X
Scotinomys teguina	—	—	—	—	E	—	X
S. xerampelinus	—	—	—	—	—	X	—
Reithrodontomys brevirostris	—	—	—	—	—	—	—
R. creper	—	—	—	X	—	X	E
R. gracilis	—	—	X	—	—	—	—
R. mexicanus	—	—	—	X	E	—	X
R. paradoxus	—	—	—	—	—	—	—
R. rodriquezi	—	—	—	—	—	—	—
R. sumichrasti	—	—	—	X	—	E	—
Mus musculus (introduced)	Possible almost anywhere—not always close to human buildings						
Rattus rattus (introduced)	Possible almost anywhere—not always close to human buildings						
R. norvegicus (introduced)	Possible almost anywhere—more associated with towns, fincas, etc.						

Carnivora
  Canidae

Taxon	La Selva	Osa	Guanacaste	San José	San Vito	Cerro de la Muerte	Monteverde
Canis latrans	—	—	X	X	—	E	E
Urocyon cinereoargentus	—	X	X	X	E	—	X

  Mustelidae

Taxon	La Selva	Osa	Guanacaste	San José	San Vito	Cerro de la Muerte	Monteverde
Mustela frenata	X	—	E	X	E	X	X
Eira barbara	X	X	X	—	X	—	X
Gallictis vittata	X	X	X	—	—	—	—
Spilogale putorius	—	—	X	X	—	—	—
Conepatus semistriatus	E	X	X	X	—	—	X
Lutra longicaudus	X	X	X	X	—	—	—
Mephitis macroura	—	—	X	—	—	—	—

  Procyonidae

Taxon	La Selva	Osa	Guanacaste	San José	San Vito	Cerro de la Muerte	Monteverde
Procyon cancrivorus	—	X	E	—	E	—	—
P. lotor	E	X	X	X	X	—	X
Nasua narica	X	X	X	E	—	E	X
Potos flavus	X	X	X	—	X	—	X
Bassaricyon gabbii	E	E	—	—	—	—	X
Bassariscus sumichrasti	—	E	E	X	—	—	—

  Felidae

Taxon	La Selva	Osa	Guanacaste	San José	San Vito	Cerro de la Muerte	Monteverde
Felis concolor	—	X	X	—	—	E	X
F. onca	X	X	X	E	E	E	X
F. pardalis	E	X	X	E	E	E	X
F. tigrina	—	E	—	—	—	E	—
F. wiedi	E	X	X	—	E	—	X
F. yaguaroundi	E	X	X	X	E	—	X

Artiodactyla
  Tayassuidae

Taxon	La Selva	Osa	Guanacaste	San José	San Vito	Cerro de la Muerte	Monteverde
Tayassu pecari	X	X	X	—	—	—	—
Dicotyles tajacu	X	X	X	—	—	—	X

  Cervidae

Taxon	La Selva	Osa	Guanacaste	San José	San Vito	Cerro de la Muerte	Monteverde
Odocoileus virginianus	—	X	X	—	—	—	X
Mazama americana	E	X	—	—	—	E	X

Perissodactyla
  Tapiridae

Taxon	La Selva	Osa	Guanacaste	San José	San Vito	Cerro de la Muerte	Monteverde
Tapirus bairdii	X	X	X	—	—	X	X

SPECIES ACCOUNTS
Alouatta palliata (Congo, Howling Monkey, Howler Monkey)

K. E. Glander

This large New World primate is best known for the stentorian vocalizations of the adult males (fig. 9.1a) These loud calls can be heard for more than 1 km in dense forests and are often given at sunrise and sunset as well as in response to such stimuli as people, airplanes, rain, thunder, and other howlers. The vocalizations are believed to be a spacing mechanism (Jolly 1972), and they may also serve as a means of communication within a social group (Jones 1978).

An adult male Costa Rican howler weighs 6 to 7 kg. Adult female howlers (fig. 9.1b) weigh 4 to 5 kg. Adults are black with brown or blond saddles and have long guard hairs on their flanks. These guard hairs give them their common name, mantled howling monkeys. At birth infants weight about 0.4 kg and are silver to golden brown. They acquire the adult pelage by 12 weeks of age and begin to move away from their mothers about the same time.

FIGURE 9.1 *Alouatta palliata. a,* Adult male. Barro Colorado Island, Panama (photo, J. H. Kaufmann). *b,* Adult female with juvenile. Finca La Pacifica, near Cañas, Guanacaste Province, Costa Rica (photo, K. E. Glander).

Female mantled howling monkeys become sexually active when they are about 36 months old and have their first infant at between 40 and 46 months of age (Glander 1981). Before impregnation the females experience a regular estrous cycle averaging 16 days, demonstrate sex skin changes, and participate in multiple matings. Gestation takes 6 months; births have been scattered in some years and clustered in others. The interval between births averaged 23 months, and lactation may last 18 months. (Glander 1980)

Mantled howler groups usually consist of several adult males, several adult females, and associated juveniles and infants. The average group size for La Pacifica howler groups is eleven animals (Glander 1975), with eighteen the average for Barro Colorado groups (Carpenter 1934). Linear dominance hierarchies exist, with all adult males being dominant to all females (Glander 1975). Rank and age are negatively correlated—that is, the youngest adult of either sex occupies the alpha position for that sex (Jones 1978; Glander, pers. obs.). Both juvenile males and females usually leave their maternal group (Glander 1980). The males leave earlier than the females (15 to 36 months compared with 24 to 40 months).

Howling monkeys are considered to be leaf-eaters (Jolly 1972). Indeed, during a one-year study leaves made up 63.6% of the diet of Costa Rican howlers (Glander 1975). Fruit and flowers composed 30.7%. More specifically, the average yearly diet consisted of 19.4% mature leaves, 44.2% new leaves, 12.5% fruit, 18.2% flowers, and 5.7% petioles and pulvinus (Glander 1975). It is important to separate mature and new leaves as dietary items because they are very different types of food. Compared with mature leaves, new leaves are short-term occurrences, contain more water, less fiber, and fewer secondary compounds, and require more time to harvest (Glander 1981).

Yearly averages for ingested tree parts, such as those above, mask a great deal of variability in the daily diet. Howlers are extremely selective, ingesting certain tree parts from certain tree species. For example, the study group ate new leaves of *Andira inermis, Ficus glabrata,* and *Hymenaea courbaril* but never ate mature leaves from any of these tree species. In some cases they ate the mature leaves of certain individual trees but not the mature leaves from other trees of the same species (*Gliricidia sepium, Bursera simaruba*) (Glander 1975). The mature leaves of *Andira inermis, F. glabrata,* and *H. courbaril* all contained condensed tannins, while the new leaves of these tree species contained either no tannins or hydrolysable tannins (Glander 1981). A similar situation occurred within a tree species. Mature leaves of *G. sepium* and *B. simaruba* that were ingested contained either no tannins or hydrolysable tannins, while those that were not eaten contained condensed tannins. In addition, mature leaves that were not eaten contained alkaloids, while those that were eaten did not contain alkaloids (Glander 1981).

Nutritional analyses show that mature leaves that were eaten contained significantly more protein, more methioine, and less fiber than those that were not eaten (Glander 1981). Further, mature leaves that were eaten did not differ significantly from new leaves that were ingested.

It appears that the study group was selecting an optimal diet, at last in terms of maximizing total protein and certain essential amino acids while minimizing the intake of fiber and plant secondary compounds (Glander 1981). Faced with a wide variety of mature leaves (ninety-six tree species were present in the 9.9 ha home range of one group of howlers) the howlers can and do select the best items available (in terms of highest nutrients and lowest content of secondary compounds). Phenophase availability changes throughout the year, and this is reflected in the daily diet composition. The study group preferred new leaves and flowers to mature leaves. Thus, during the late dry and early wet seasons when these phenophases are available new leaves and flowers may constitute 100% of daily diet. Similarily, during the late wet season fruit and mature leaves make up the bulk of the diet.

Alouatta palliata commonly inhabits both lowland and montane forests (up to 2,500 m) from southern Mexico to northwestern South America (Napier and Napier 1967). In Costa Rica they are the last remaining nonhuman primates in many relict patches of forest.

*

Carpenter, C. R. 1934. A field study of the behavior and social relations of howling monkeys (*Alouatta palliata*). *Comp. Psychol. Monogr.* 10:1–168.

Glander, K. E. 1975. Habitat and resource utilization: An ecological view of social organization in mantled howling monkeys. Ph.D. diss., University of Chicago.

———. 1980. Reproduction and population growth in free-ranging mantled howling monkeys. *Am. J. Phys. Anth.* 53:25–36.

———. 1981. Feeding patterns in mantled howling monkeys. In *Foraging behavior: Ecological, ethological, and psychological approaches,* ed. A. C. Kamil and T. D. Sargent, pp. 231–57. New York: Garland Press.

Jolly, A. 1972. *The evolution of primate behavior.* New York: Macmillan.

Jones, C. 1978. Aspects of reproductive behavior in the mantled howler monkey. Ph.D. diss., Cornell University.

Napier, J. R., and Napier, P. H. 1967. *A handbook of living primates.* London: Academic Press.

Artibeus jamaicensis (Murciélago Frutero Jamaicano, Jamaican Fruit Bat)

D. W. Morrison

The Jamaican fruit bat (fig. 9.2*a*) is one of the most commonly mist-netted bats in Central America. Adults are stout bodied, weighing about 50 g, with a wingspan of 40 cm (forearm 58–65 mm). Found in both wet and dry forests from Mexico to Brazil, these bats occasionally take pollen and insects (Heithaus, Fleming, and Opler 1975) but feed primarily on the fruits of large trees (Gardner 1977). Of 131 fecal samples collected from mist-netted *Artibeus jamaicensis* in Panama (Bonaccorso 1975), 104 contained *Ficus* spp. (figs), 11 *Calophyllum longifolium,* 8 *Quararibea asterolepis,* 6 *Spondias mombin,* 5 *Cecropia* spp., 2 *Dipteryx panamensis,* and 2 *Piper* spp. Unlike the smaller fruit bat *Carollia perspicillata, A. jamaicensis* only rarely takes *Piper* spp. or other widely

FIGURE 9.2. *Artibeus jamaicensis. a,* Adult bat. Finca La Pacifica, near Cañas, Guanacaste Province, Costa Rica. *b,* Ground beneath a presumed *Artibeus* feeding roost, littered with wads of chewed fig (e.g., dry lump in lower right with fig wasp exit hole in seed) and intact seed-rich feces (e.g., moist "rope" of intact seeds in upper right). Santa Rosa National Park, Guanacaste Province, Costa Rica (photos, D. H. Janzen).

scattered subcanopy fruits. While in flight the bats pluck fruits from the fruiting tree (Jimbo and Schwassman 1967) and use their well-developed chest and jaw muscles and long canines to carry even large fruits (e.g., 12 g *Andira inermis*) to feeding roosts (fig. 9.2*b*) from 25 m to over 200 m away (Janzen et al. 1976; Morrison 1978*a*). *Artibeus jamaicensis* emits relatively low-intensity echolocation cries (as do other phyllostomid or "leaf-nosed" bats) and probably makes use of its large eyes and complex internal nasal structures for orientation and food finding.

Radio-tracking observations of foraging *A. jamaicensis* revealed that distances from day roosts to food trees vary greatly (0.2 to 10 km) depending on the density and distribution of ripe fruit trees (Morrison 1978*a,b*). Regular feeding flights and infrequent, prolonged flights in search of trees about to ripen are timed to avoid bright moonlight. On nights one week before and after full moon, individuals suspend foraging completely and return to their day roosts for the 1–7 h of the night when the moon is highest. This "lunar phobia" (and the use of tree hollows as day roosts) may have evolved to reduce losses to visually oriented predators like owls and opossums (Morrison 1978*c*).

An individual of *A. jamaicensis* feeding on figs carries away more than its own weight in fruit each night, based on counts of feeding passes made by radio-tagged bats (Morrison 1978*a*). At the feeding roost the bat holds the fruit between its forearms and bites off small pieces of the rind, which it then sucks dry and spits out as pellets. Many of the seeds are swallowed, and apparently most of these are passed unharmed in the feces (fig. 9.2*b*).

Females have a postpartem estrus and undergo two pregnancies per year in rapid succession. In Panama the ova fertilized during the March–April birth peak produce a second birth peak about four months later. The ova fertilized during this second estrus implant in the uterus as blastocysts, but further development is suspended for 2.5 months (Fleming 1971). Although a number of other fruit bats are seasonally biestrous, only *A. jamaicensis* is known to have delayed embryonic development. Perhaps fortuitously, the period of delay coincides with the annual lean season for *Ficus* fruits in Panama (Morrison 1978*a*).

Mark-recapture records (Handley 1978) indicate that only 40% of the *A. jamaicensis* newborns survive their first year. The survival rate of adults is roughly 60% per year and does not change much with age. About 3% reach the age of 6 years.

During the day *A. jamaicensis* roosts in caves, foliage, and hollow trees. Foliage roosts are used by solitary males or occasionally by two or three male and subadult bats. Hole roosts contain three to eleven females, their nursing or recently weaned young (in season), and invariably only one adult male (Morrison 1979). Infrared ob-

servations on radio-tagged harems revealed that hole roosts are vigorously defended (Morrison and Hagen-Morrison, n.d.). During the breeding season harem males do an extraordinary amount of "patrol" flying (investigating, chasing, escorting) in the vicinity of the day roost. To feed, harem males carry each fruit back to near the day roost, sometimes commuting more than 1.5 km (round trip) for each fruit. Harem males averaged over 3 h in flight per night, twice the time spent by females and nonharem males.

Certain observations suggest that *A. jamaicensis* forages in small groups: (1) Clustered arrival times at mist nets have been reported for this species in Mexico (Dalquest 1953) and Costa Rica (Heithaus, Fleming, and Opler 1975). (2) While being removed from a mist net, individuals frequently give a distress call (a prolonged series of yips) that can attract several more *A. jamaicensis* (but also other fruit bat species). In Panama, however, the members of three radio-tagged harems foraged independently (Morrison and Hagen-Morrison, n.d.). Although harem females sometimes fed from the same fruit tree in the course of a night, they did not travel together, nor did they roost near each other while feeding. Nevertheless, group foraging may occur in situations where fruiting trees are more widely dispersed (Ward and Zahavi 1973).

*

Bonaccorso, F. J. 1975. Foraging and reproductive ecology of a community of bats in Panama. Ph.D. diss., University of Florida.

Dalquest, W. W. 1953. Mammals of the Mexican state of San Luis Potosí. *Louisiana State Univ. Biol. Sci. Ser.* 1:1–229.

Fleming, T. H. 1971. *Artibeus jamaicensis:* Delayed embryonic development in a Neotropical bat. *Science* 171:402–4.

Fleming, T. H.; Heithaus, E. R.; and Sawyer, W. B. 1977. An experimental analysis of food location behavior of a frugivorous bat. *Ecology* 58:619–27.

Fleming, T. H.; Hooper, E. T.; and Wilson, D. E. 1972. Three Central American bat communities: Structure, reproductive cycles, and movement patterns. *Ecology* 53:555–69.

Gardner, A. L. 1977. Feeding habits. In *Biology of bats of the New World Phyllostomatidae*, ed. R. J. Baker, J. K. Jones, Jr., and D. C. Carter, pp. 293–350. *Spec. Publications of the Museum*, no. 13. Lubbock: Texas Tech University.

Handley, C. O., Jr. 1978. BCI Bat Project: A five year report. Mimeographed.

Heithaus, E. R.; Fleming, T. H.; and Opler, P. A. 1975. Foraging patterns and resource utilization of seven species of bats in a seasonal tropical forest. *Ecology* 56:841–54.

Janzen, D. H.; Miller, G. A.; Hackforth-Jones, J.; Pond, C. M.; Hooper, K.; and Janos, D. P. 1976. Two Costa

Rican bat-generated seed shadows of *Andira inermis* (Leguminosae). *Ecology* 57:1068–75.

Jimbo, S., and Schwassman, H. O. 1967. Feeding behavior and daily emergence pattern of *Artibeus jamaicensis*. *Atas Simp. Biota Amazonica* 5:239–53.

Morrison, D. W. 1978*a*. Foraging ecology and energetics of the frugivorous bat *Artibeus jamaicensis*. *Ecology* 59:716–23.

———. 1978*b*. Influence of habitat on the foraging distances of the fruit bat *Artibeus jamaicensis*. *J. Mamm.* 59:622–24.

———. 1978*c*. Lunar phobia in a Neotropical fruit bat, *Artibeus jamaicensis*. *Anim. Behav.* 26:852–55.

———. 1979. Apparent male defense of tree hollows in the bat *Artibeus jamaicensis*. *J. Mamm.* 60:11–15.

Morrison, D. W., and Hagen-Morrison, S. n.d. Economics of harem defense by a Neotropical bat. In review.

Ward, P., and Zahavi, A. 1973. The importance of certain assemblages of birds as "information-centres" for food finding. *Ibis* 115:517–34.

Ateles geoffroyi (Mono Araña, Mono Colorado, Spider Monkey)

J. F. Eisenberg

The spider monkey genus *Ateles* has a range from southern Tamaulipas in Mexico to the Mato Grosso in Brazil. Kellogg and Goldman (1944) divided the genus *Ateles* into four species. Hershkovitz (1972) suggested that only one specific name for *Ateles* is valid (*Ateles paniscus*). Given the morphological and chromosomal variation within the genus and our imperfect knowledge of the history of primate distributions in the northern Neotropics, I feel it is premature to conclude that only one species exists. Rather, for the purposes of this discussion, I will consider that the Central American spider monkeys may be conveniently subsumed under the definition proposed by Kellogg and Goldman for the species *A. geoffroyi* (fig. 9.3).

There are nine described subspecies of *Ateles geoffroyi* based upon variation in coat color. All species of *A. geoffroyi* when adult show dark fur on the dorsal sides of the forearms and on the dorsal aspect of the hind limbs from the knee to the heel. The color of the ventrum, back, shoulders, and tail varies greatly, from blond in the subspecies *A. g. ornatus* to almost black in *A. g. pan*. Within Costa Rica two subspecies are generally encountered, *A. g. ornatus* in the north and *A. g. panamensis* (fig. 9.3) in the south. *A. panamensis* is a much darker animal, with the dorsal trunk characteristically reddish brown and the hind limbs, tail, and forelimbs black. The cap and the shoulders are also black. The natal coat varies from all black in *A. g. panamensis* to blond in *A. g. ornatus*.

FIGURE 9.3. *Ateles geoffroyi*, adult female with juvenile in an *Ochroma lagopus* tree. Barro Colorado Island, Panama (photo, J. F. Eisenberg).

Ateles geoffroyi is abundant in Santa Rosa National Park and was studied there by Freese (1976). The numbers of *Ateles geoffroyi* have been greatly reduced over most of its former range in Central America. This has resulted both from land clearing and from hunting. Hunting monkeys for food can vary a great deal depending on which part of Central America one resides in. Local custom may actually prohibit eating monkey flesh, but in many parts of Central America monkeys are actively sought as food. Since *Ateles geoffroyi* is one of the largest New World species, it is vulnerable to hunting, and those who eat monkey flesh claim its quality is very high.

Adult *Ateles geoffroyi* may attain a total length of more than 1.28 m. Head and body length ranges from 0.42 to 0.59 m, and the tail greatly exceeds the head and body length, averaging about 0.75 m. Adults may weigh more than 8 kg. There is little sexual dimorphism, but adult males tend to be slightly heavier than adult females and have a greater head and body length. The tail of the female is proportionately larger than the tail of the male.

The spider monkey is diurnally active and is noted for its extreme specialization for an arboreal way of life. It moves rapidly through the trees, brachiating with its forelimbs and using its tail as an assist during locomotion.

The form of its brachiation is not completely homologous to that shown by the gibbon. The body proportions of the spider monkey have given it its common name, since the limbs are long and slender. The tail is fully prehensile and can support the entire weight of the animal.

The gestation period in the spider monkey is approximately 225 days. Intervals between births can range from 2 to 3 years. Presumably lactation demands during the first year of the infant's life induce a lactation anestrus, and the female generally will not begin to cycle again until weaning is completed.

At birth the young animal weighs approximately 500 g. It remains in intimate association with the mother for the first 3 months of life. Initially it is carried ventrally and, at about 1.5 to 2 months of age it begins to ride dorsally on the mother's body. The young will continue to suckle from the mother until it is almost 1 year of age, although at this age it has begun to take considerable solid food. The weaning process is gradual, with solid foods being taken from about 3 months of age on. The age of weaning is probably in part a function of the nutritional condition of the female and the young. Since the female produces only a single young and the inter-birth interval is variable and extended, the reproductive rate of *Ateles* in the wild is very low. Thus wild populations of *Ateles* are slow to recover from any form of hunting. It appears that the genus *Ateles* is very sensitive to human perturbation of the habitat, and it may be among the first primate species to decline with severe disturbance.

The most extensive studies on feeding have been conducted by Hladik and Hladik (1969) with *Ateles geoffroyi* in Panama and by Klein (1972) with *Ateles belzebuth* in Colombia. *Ateles* is primarily a frugivore and feeds with great selectivity at moderate to extreme heights in mature forests. *Ateles geoffroyi* can consume up to 20% of its annual diet in the form of young leaves. Leaves are no doubt taken at certain seasons of the year as a means of increasing plant protein in its diet. Hladik and Hladik (1969), Carpenter (1935), and Eisenberg and Kuehn (1966) provide food lists from field observations for *Ateles geoffroyi*. Klein (1972) provides similar data for *Ateles belzebuth* in Colombia. The Hladiks note that *Ateles* can be an important dispersal agent for *Trichilia* and *Ficus* seeds. These seeds will germinate after passing through the digestive tract.

Freese (1976) indicates that the most frequently encountered group size for *Ateles geoffroyi* is two animals. This in no way gives an accurate indication of the total troop size, however, because *Ateles* troops tend to fractionate into numerous subgroups so that only when they assemble at specific feeding sites or at sleeping trees can the whole troop be accurately censused. This tendency for fractionation of troops was noted as early as 1935 by Carpenter. The subgroups of an *Ateles* troop do not neces-sarily recombine into the same social unit at sleeping trees at the conclusion of the day's activity. Furthermore, there is a tendency for unisexual subgroup formation where groups of adult and subadult males move independently of smaller female units. There are indications in the literature that in some circumstances an *Ateles* group may exhibit a simplified troop structure containing one adult male, several females, and their offspring. Freese (1976) has noted such troop structures during censusing in Costa Rica, and Durham (1975) has developed evidence for both unimale and multimale troops of *Ateles paniscus* in Peru. He notes that the unimale condition is typically shown by smaller troops that utilize habitats at high elevations. Nevertheless, at moderate carrying capacities it is apparent that the total troop of *Ateles* for a given area consists of several adult males, juvenile males, and adult females and their dependent offspring. This troop may assemble at various times at feeding trees and sleeping trees, but the predominant tendency is for the troop to fractionate into small subgroups that forage independently. Loud, long calls may be employed in coordinating subgroup movement patterns. These long calls can promote assembly of troop members over a considerable distance, especially when encounters with other neighboring troops are taking place. Long calls could serve the purpose of assembly as well as proclaiming the occupancy of an area (see Eisenberg 1976).

A total troop for *Ateles geoffroyi*, when it is assembled in one place, may consist of about twenty animals. The home range of such a troop in a large part depends on the carrying capacity of the habitat, but troop home ranges of 2.5 to 4 km^2 would not be unreasonable. The density of *Ateles* generally is low compared with that for howler monkeys and *Cebus* monkeys. Freese (1976) reported a density of six to nine per square kilometer in Santa Rosa National Park.

Ateles has a complex communication system that integrates vocalizations, facial expressions, body postures, and chemical signals. Marking behavior by adult males involves spreading secretions from the chest gland on branches or foliage. The vocal repertoire is extraordinarily complex, and the use of intergrading vocal signals is commonplace. Discrete vocalization patterns specific to defined situations are also discernible. Barking frequently accompanies mobbing responses to terrestrial predators or invaders. Long calls of at least two types are used to coordinate movements and are employed during intertroop encounters. The social dynamics of *Ateles geoffroyi* has been studied in Panama by Dare (1974) and by Eisenberg and Kuehn (1966). Communication in the genus *Ateles* has been reviewed by Eisenberg (1976).

*

Carpenter, C. R. 1935. Behavior of red spider monkeys in Panama. *J. Mamm.* 16:171–80.

Dare, R. 1974. The social behavior and ecology of spider monkeys *Ateles geoffroyi* on Barro Colorado Island. Ph.D. diss., University of Oregon.

Durham, N. M. 1975. Some ecological, distributional, and group behavioral features of Atelinae in southern Peru, with comments on interspecific relations. In *Ninth International Congress of Anthropological and Ethnological Sciences,* in manuscript.

Eisenberg, J. F. 1976. Communication mechanisms and social integration in the black spider monkey, *Ateles fusciceps robustus,* and related species. *Smithsonian Contrib. Zool.* no. 213.

Eisenberg, J. F., and Kuehn, R. E. 1966. The behavior of *Ateles geoffroyi* and related species. *Smithsonian Misc. Coll.* 151:1–63.

Freese, C. 1976. Censusing *Alouatta palliata, Ateles geoffroyi* and *Cebus capucinus* in the Costa Rican dry forest. In *Distribution and abundance of Neotropical primates,* ed. R. W. Thorington and P. G. Heltne. Washington, D.C.: National Academy of Sciences.

Hershkovitz, P. 1972. The recent mammals of the Neotropical region: A zoogeographic and ecological review. In *Evolution, mammals and southern continents,* ed. Keast, Erk, and Glass, pp. 311–432. Albany: State University of New York Press.

Hladik, A., and Hladik, C. M. 1969. Rapports trophiques entre vegetation et primates dans la forêt de Barro Colorado (Panama). *Terre et Vie* 23:25–117.

Kellog, R., and Goldman, E. A. 1944. Review of the spider monkeys. *Proc. U.S. Nat. Mus.* 96:1–45.

Klein, L. L. 1972. The ecology and social organization of the spider monkey, *Ateles belzebuth.* Ph.D. diss., University of California, Berkeley.

FIGURE 9.4. *Bradypus variegatus,* adult female with young (between her and tree). Barro Colorado Island, Panama (photo, G. G. Montgromery).

Bradypus variegatus (Perezoso de Tres Dedos, Three-toed Sloth)

G. G. Montgomery

The three-toed sloth (fig. 9.4) is legendary for its slow movement and for the untrue supposition that it feeds exclusively on the leaves of *Cecropia* trees. This medium-sized mammal is perhaps the most important vertebrate primary consumer in the canopy of moist Neotropical forests. There are fewer than six species of *Bradypus* distributed in lowland moist forests from Honduras to northern Argentina and Paraguay (Wetzel 1980; Wetzel and Dias de Avila-Pires 1980; Walker 1975). *Bradypus variegatus,* which occurs in Costa Rica and Panama (Wetzel and Kock 1973), has been the subject of intensive field studies on Barro Colorado Island in the Panama Canal Zone since 1970 (Sunquist and Montgomery 1973; Montgomery and Sunquist 1974, 1975, 1978).

The myth of the relationship between three-toed sloths and *Cecropia* trees arises because three-toed sloths are very difficult to see in most of the kinds of trees they use. *Cecropia* and a very few other tree species are excep-

tions, and most casual sightings of three-toed sloths are in these trees. *Cecropia* trees have an open growth form and large leaves that grow near the ends of the branches; thus a sloth in a *Cecropia* tree is relatively easy to see. Perhaps the best way to find a three-toed sloth is to look into each *Cecropia* tree that you pass. However, sloths in the study on Barro Colorado Island used at least ninety-six other species of trees (Montgomery and Sunquist 1975), and in most of those species they were almost invisible even after they had been precisely radio located (Montgomery, Cochran, and Sunquist 1973). Some of the sloths were never found in *Cecropia* trees, and others used them only seasonally (Montgomery and Sunquist 1978).

Three-toed sloths are arboreal mammals that live, feed, and reproduce many meters above the forest floor near the upper levels of the forest canopy. They feed almost entirely on leaves, using a large ruminantlike stomach and long intestinal tract to aid in digesting this energy-rich but relatively indigestible foodstuff (Parra 1973; Bauchop 1978). Some mix of the kind of leaves taken as food is probably necessary (Freeland and Janzen 1974), and an arboreal folivore probably must change from tree to tree to obtain a mixed diet, even though there may be several species of lianas in the crowns of some trees (Montgomery and Sunquist 1978). Early reports that sloths spend essentially their entire lifetime in a single tree are not true, and a three-toed sloth moves from tree to tree on average about once every 1.5 days (Sunquist and Montgomery 1973) by passing between tree crowns, often using pathways formed by lianas that interlace the crowns. To descend to the ground each time they changed from tree to tree would be very wasteful of the sloths' energy.

Why, then do sloths descend to void their urine and feces? The answer to this is not yet clear. What is known is that the sloth accumulates urine and feces for about a week (Montgomery and Sunquist, 1975), then descends to the forest floor and, using its stubby tail, digs a slight depression in the forest floor, voids the feces into this depression, urinates over it, and covers the feces with leaves with a stereotyped movement of the hind legs as it begins to climb back to the forest canopy. The entire process of descending to the forest floor, defecating, and returning to the canopy usually takes less than 30 min. During this period the sloth is exposed to terrestrial predators, other mammalian predators that hunt in trees, and avian predators that hunt below the canopy surface. The selective forces that promote and maintain this behavior must be strong. The only tenable hypothesis advanced to date is that slow decomposition of sloth feces at the bases of trees an individual sloth tends to reuse promotes differential growth of the leaves of those trees and might provide the sloth with a more constant or higher-quality food supply (Montgomery and Sunquist 1975). This hypothesis badly wants testing.

A number of kinds of arthropods live as adults on three-toed sloths, and deposit eggs on sloth dung when the sloth defecates on the forest floor. Waage and Montgomery (1976) showed that the life cycle of the pyralid moths, so-called sloth moths, begins when eggs are deposited on sloth dung by a gravid female that presumably leaves her sloth while it defecates and oviposits on the dung. The larvae feed on dung and pupate in silken tubes among the dung pellets. Newly emerged adults fly up into the canopy and find a sloth. Beetles of at least three genera have a similar life cycle (Waage and Best 1980), and individual sloths may carry nine hundred or more beetles. At least three species of mites also live on sloths and utilize sloth dung in their reproductive cycles.

Three-toed sloths live at high population densities in forests in Panama. Census results indicate that there are five to eight three-toed sloths per hectare (Montgomery and Sunquist 1975, 1978). Three-toed sloths are relatively large, and their commonness allows them to make a substantial contribution to the biomass of primary consumers in the forest canopy (Montgomery and Sunquist 1975; Eisenberg and Thorington 1973). The censuses were done by measuring the rate at which piles of feces were deposited on the forest floor by sloths living above small study plots. It would be instructive to have similar censuses of sloths in forests in other parts of the Neotropics.

The metabolic rate of three-toed sloths is approximately half what might be expected for a mammal of like size (4–7 kg). They have a correspondingly low rate of food passage, measured in days whereas in other ruminant and ruminantlike animals it is measured in hours (Parra 1978). The three-toed sloth may be viewed as a compromise among being large enough to move about in treetops, with a large gut to store and process large quantities of relatively indigestible food, and being light enough not to break the branches and lianas on which it must move to feed on leaves. To maximize body size while attempting to minimize body weight, the sloth has sacrificed muscle mass. The ratio of muscle to skeletal and supportive tissue is much lower than in a terrestrial mammal of comparable size (Grand 1978). A part of the weight gained by reducing muscle mass is taken up by the large gut for storage and passage of food. Gut capacity of three-toed sloths is approximately 30% of their total body weight (Goffart 1971).

To conserve energy gained from the relatively energy-poor diet, three-toed sloths have a heavy fur coat that provides insulation. While resting, they use body postures that tend to conserve heat. In part the slow rate of digestion and food passage is related to the fact that their body temperature drops almost to ambient temperature each night and is raised to a more normal mammalian temperature only when the animals bask in sunlight during the day (Montgomery and Sunquist 1978; McNab 1978).

A major predator on three-toed sloths, the harpy eagle, takes advantage of the circumstance that sloths go into sunlight in the tops of trees to thermoregulate and snatches them off the branches while in flight (Retting 1978).

Even though three-toed sloths eat less than might be expected on the basis of their body size, because of their low rate of metabolism (McNab 1978; Nagy and Montgomery 1980) and the fact that their rate of food passage and digestion is slow (Montgomery and Sunquist 1978), they are important primary consumers, cropping about 2% of the total annual leaf production in the forests of central Panama. Cropping of leaves by an individual sloth is reasonably selective, and each genealogy of sloth has a modal tree species that it tends to use and crop more heavily than other tree species (Montgomery and Sunquist 1975, 1978). Modal tree species differ among the different genealogies of sloths, so that the total impact of the sloths living in an area is spread among a number of tree and liana species.

Three-toed sloths reach sexual maturity at relatively great age for their body size, reproduce slowly, live for a long time, and suffer relatively low rates of mortality after they have survived social weaning and reached adulthood (Montgomery 1980). Sloths marked on Barro Colorado Island as adults have lived for 6 to 8 years after being marked, thus they are known to be at least 9 to 11 years of age. We suspect that they may live 20 to 30 years in the wild.

Both males and females reach sexual maturity at about 3 years of age. Adult males are characterized by a patch of shorter hair on their backs that is colored pale to bright yellow, with a dorsoventral black stripe through the center. Adult females lack such a marking. It is essentially impossible to distinguish the sexes of young and juvenile sloths externally because there are no external genitalia.

Adult females produce one young per year, spending half the year pregnant and the other half carrying and caring for their dependent young (Montgomery and Sunquist 1978). We have estimated the gestation period as 6 months. Young sloths nurse for about 6 weeks after they are born, but they begin eating leaves when they are 2 weeks old, first by licking fragments of leaves from the mother's lips and then by eating from leaves that the mother is eating. For a total of about 5.5 months, the female sloth carries her young (fig. 9.4) everywhere she goes, and young and mother are never separated. If the young loses its grip on the female and falls, she ignores its distress calls (Montgomery and Sunquist 1974) and behaves as if she cannot find it or is unwilling to search for it (Beebe 1926).

The young sloth feeds on leaves during the time it is being nutritionally weaned, and during the next 4.5 months while it rides on the mother before it is socially weaned (Montgomery and Sunquist 1978). These leaves are from the trees and lianas the mother feeds on. In this way the mother sloth teaches her young the location of the trees on her home range space and gives it food preferences for the species of trees and lianas from which the mother feeds. At an age of about 6 months, the mother sloth very abruptly socially weans her young by moving away from it. The young inherits the set of trees on the mother's home-range space, and for the next 6 months the mother uses a different set of trees on an adjacent home-range space. The mother thus has a two-part home range, one part used for rearing young and the other part used while she is without dependent young and is pregnant. Mortality of young sloths following social weaning is relatively high, and it is probably rare that two successive young will occupy the same portion of the mother's home range space, although the mother moves back into the same area with the birth of each succeeding young.

This system of rearing young leads to genealogies of sloths that have food preferences separate in part from those of other genealogies living in the same areas (Montgomery and Sunquist 1978). Three-toed sloths' home ranges overlap freely, and, though sloths of different genealogies may live in approximately the same areas, the differences in food preferences lead them to tend to use different species of trees within those areas. There is some tendency as well for them to use different individual trees of species that are shared as food and resting places.

*

Bauchop, T. 1978. Digestion of leaves in vertebrate arboreal folivores. In *The ecology of arboreal folivores,* ed. G. G. Montgomery, pp. 193–204. Washington, D.C.: Smithsonian Institution Press.

Beebe, W. 1926. The three-toed sloth *Bradypus cuculliger cuculliger* Wagler. *Zoologica* 7:1–67.

Eisenberg, J. F., and Thorington, R. W., 1973. A preliminary analysis of a Neotropical mammal fauna. *Biotropica* 5:150–61.

Freeland, W. J., and Janzen, D. H. 1974. Strategies in herbivory by mammals: The role of plant secondary compounds. *Am. Nat.* 108:269–89.

Goffart, M. 1971. *Function and form in the sloth.* New York: Pergamon Press.

Grand, T. I. 1978. Adaptations of tissue and limb segments to facilitate moving and feeding in arboreal folivores. In *The ecology of arboreal folivores,* ed. G. G. Montgomery, pp. 231–41. Washington, D.C.: Smithsonian Institution Press.

McNab, B. K. 1978. Energetics of arboreal folivores: Physiological problems and ecological consequences of feeding on an ubiquitous food supply. In *The ecology of arboreal folivores,* ed. G. G. Montgomery, pp. 153–62. Washington, D.C.: Smithsonian Institution Press.

Montgomery, G. G. 1980. Socio-ecology of Xenarthra (= Edentata): Parental investment by extreme K-strategists. In *Mammalian behavior,* ed. J. F. Eisenberg et al. Special Publication. American Society of Mammalogists, in press.

Montgomery, G. G.; Cochran, W. W.; and Sunquist, M. E. 1973. Radio-locating arboreal vertebrates in tropical forest. *J. Wildl. Mgmt.* 37:426–28.

Montgomery, G. G., and Sunquist, M. E. 1974. Contact-distress calls of young sloths. *J. Mamm.* 55:211–13.

———. 1975. Impact of sloths on Neotropical energy flow and nutrient cycling. In *Ecological studies,* vol. 2, ed. F. B. Golley and E. Medina, pp. 69–98. New York: Springer-Verlag.

———. 1978. Habitat selection and use by two-toed and three-toed sloths. In *The ecology of arboreal folivores,* ed. G. G. Montgomery, pp. 329–59. Washington, D.C.: Smithsonian Institution Press.

Nagy, K. A., and Montgomery, G. G. 1980. Field metabolic rate, water flux and food consumption in three-toed sloths (*Bradypus variegatus*). *J. Mamm.* 61: 465–72.

Parra, R. 1978. Comparison of foregut and hindgut fermentation in herbivores. In *The ecology of arboreal folivores,* ed. G. G. Montgomery, pp. 205–29. Washington, D.C.: Smithsonian Institution Press.

Retting, N. L. 1978. Breeding behavior of the harpy eagle (*Harpia harpyja*) *Auk* 95:629–43.

Sunquist, M. E., and Montgomery, G. G. 1973. Activity patterns and rates of movement of two-toed and three-toed sloths. In *The ecology of arboreal folivores,* ed. G. G. Montgomery, pp. 329–59. Washington, D.C.: Smithsonian Institution Press.

Waage, J. K., and Best, R. M. 1980. Arthropod associates of sloths. In *The evolution and ecology of sloths, anteaters and armadillos (Mammalia: Xenarthra = Edentata),* ed. G. G. Montgomery. Washington, D.C.: Smithsonian Institution Press.

Waage, J. K., and Montgomery, G. G. 1976. *Cryptoses cholopei:* A coprophagous moth that lives on a sloth. *Science* 193:157–58.

Walker, E. P. 1975. *Mammals of the world.* 3d ed., vol. 1 (rev. J. L. Paradiso). Baltimore: Johns Hopkins University Press.

Wetzel, R. M. 1980. The identification and distribution of recent Xenarthra (= Edentata). In *The evolution and ecology of sloths, anteaters and armadillos (Mammalia: Xenarthra = Edentata),* ed. G. G. Montgomery. Washington, D.C.: Smithsonian Institution Press.

Wetzel, R. M., and Dias de Avila-Pires, F. 1980. Identification and distribution of the recent sloths of Brazil (Edentata). *Rev. Brasil. Biol.* 40:831–36.

Wetzel, R. M., and Kock, D. 1973. The identity of *Bradypus variegatus* Schinz (Mammalia: Edentata). *Proc. Bio. Soc. Washington* 86:25–33.

Canis latrans (Coyote)

D. H. Janzen

Coyotes (Canidae) are found throughout the Guanacaste lowlands, in both forest and pasture habitats. They give the distinct impression of being totally natural there, but then, so do feral range cows. However, I see no reason to suspect that they are recent invaders following extensive clearing of forest, since they are found throughout the deciduous forests at Santa Rosa National Park. Coyotes range from Canada to Costa Rica, and old Guanacaste residents have been seeing coyotes for at least seventy years.

The Guanacaste coyotes have not been weighed but appear to me to be about 70% of the weight of adults in the western United States. Their hair seems shorter but is the same gray beige yellow color as that of United States coyotes, and their tail hairs are as long and dense. The only other native canid in Guanacaste is the gray fox (*Urocyon cinereoargenteus*). This is easily distinguished from the coyote by the fox's gray color and tiny size. Adult gray foxes at Santa Rosa appear to be about the size of a large rabbit.

Coyotes are often seen early in the morning while scavenging road kills along the highway from Liberia to

FIGURE 9.5. *Canis latrans,* adult scavenging a road-killed rabbit. May 1977, Guanacaste Province, Costa Rica (photo, D. H. Janzen).

La Cruz (fig. 9.5). I have observed them eating road-killed rabbits, ctenosaur lizards, snakes, owls, and small rodents, but it appears that they reject tamanduas and vultures. In captivity, Guanacaste coyotes are extremely omnivorous, eating all kinds of commercial meat, table scraps, and domestic fruits. Coyote feces in Santa Rosa National Park contain rabbit, agouti, and small rodent fur, lizard scales, and seeds. *Liomys salvini* and *Sigmodon hispidus* fur is often present in the scats, but in March *S. hispidus* fur easily makes up 90% of the scat volume. *Manilkara zapota, Mastichodendron capriri, Alibertia edulis* and *Ficus* seeds pass through the gut without digestion, and scats in January almost always contain some of these seeds. I have seen coyotes apparently eating carrion from the carcass of a dead cow. They visit water holes during the dry season and are encountered foraging in dense forest as well as in pastures. I have seen them digging into marine turtle nests on Playa Nancite at Santa Rosa.

Young Guanacaste coyotes tame very easily. A wild-caught adult brought to Finca La Pacifica was confined on a 5 m chain by the main house. It was fed there and exposed to house dogs and numerous visitors. Within 5 months it was as tame as a somewhat nervous dog, had developed a slight bark, begged for attention by rubbing against my leg, wagged its tail when petted, and greatly enjoyed having its back scratched. When it escaped about a year later, it returned to the house on its own accord on numerous occasions, though it eventually disappeared.

I have seen no sign of dog-coyote hybrids in Guanacaste. Coyotes howl at night at the main headquarters of Santa Rosa at least during June, November–December, and March. At least four to six animals are often involved in a chorus and may be scattered over an area several hundred meters on a side.

*

Fox, M. W. 1975. The wild canids: Their systematics, behavioral ecology and evolution. New York: Van Nostrand Reinhold.

Janzen, D. H. 1976. The depression of reptile biomass by large herbivores. *Am. Nat.* 110:371–440.

Carollia perspicillata (Murciélago Candelaro, Lesser Short-tailed Fruit Bat)

T. H. Fleming

This abundant phyllostomatid bat (fig. 9.6a) occurs throughout the tropical parts of Central and South America from sea level to about 1,000 m elevation. It sometimes occurs along with one or two congeners (*C. castanea, C. brevicauda,* and *C. subrufa*), from which it can be distinguished by size (forearm length usually 42 mm or greater) and dental characteristics (see Pine 1972). Its pelage is usually brown or gray, but some populations, such as at Santa Rosa National Park, contain bright orange individuals, probably as a result of the bleaching action of ammonia fumes in poorly ventilated caves. Adults weigh 18–22 g, and this species is not sexually dimorphic in weight.

C. perspicillata is a gregarious bat that often lives in caves containing tens to hundreds of individuals; it also roosts in a variety of other places, including hollow trees, culverts, wells, and the underside of bridges. Colonies contain mixtures of both sexes and different age classes. This is a harem-forming bat, but details of its social system have not been sudied in nature (see Porter 1978 for laboratory observations).

In Costa Rica and Panama there are two annual birth periods, one toward the end of the dry season (March or April) and another in the middle of the wet season (July or August) (Fleming, Heithaus, and Sawyer 1972). Some females give birth to a single young twice a year. Females carry young babies with them when they forage at night but leave larger babies in the day roost.

C. perspicillata is primarily a frugivorous bat but also visits flowers, presumably for nectar, in the dry season. Its diet has been carefully documented at Finca La Pacifica and Santa Rosa National Park in Costa Rica (Heithaus, Fleming, and Opler 1975; Fleming, Heithaus, and Sawyer 1977; Heithaus and Fleming 1978). When available (mostly in the wet season), its preferred fruit is infructescences of various *Piper* species (Piperaceae), which it grabs in flight before returning to a night roost to strip the pulp and seeds corn-on-the-cob style. Fruit relocation experiments show that *C. perspicillata* uses a constantly active search image to find ripe *Piper* fruits. In addition to *Piper* spp., it also eats fruits of *Cecropia*

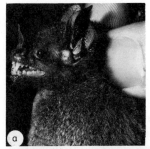

FIGURE 9.6. *Carollia perspicillata. a,* Adult bat. Hacienda Palo Verde, Guanacaste Province, Costa Rica. *b,* Cave floor beneath sleeping roost deeply littered with defecated seeds of *Cecropia* (rugose elongate ovals) and *Muntingia calabura* (monospecific patches of very small light-colored seeds) and dropped seeds of *Acacia collinsii* (oval in upper right) and *Annona reticulata* (largest seed at top); note lygaeid bugs that are feeding on seeds (lower left). Santa Rosa National Park, Guanacaste Province, Costa Rica (photos, D. H. Janzen).

peltata, Chlorophora tinctoria, Solanum hazenii, Muntingia calabura, and, in the dry season, *Karwinskia calderoni* and *Ficus ovalis* at Santa Rosa. In the dry season it visits flowers of *Ceiba pentandra, Manilkara zapota, Crescentia* spp., *Pseudobombax septinatum,* and other species in Guanacaste. To judge from the high frequency of mixed species "pollen loads," it often visits several flower species in succession at La Pacifica.

The foraging behavior of *C. perspcillata* has been studied using radiotelemetry at Santa Rosa National Park (Heithaus and Fleming 1978 and unpublished data). In the wet season most individuals forage within 1.5 km of their day roost and consistently visit one to four feeding areas for extended periods of time (several weeks). On any given night, an individual usually visits two of its feeding areas and "shuttles" between them every 1–2 h; this "shuttle" rate is reduced on moonlit nights and when ripe *Piper* fruits are available. Within the feeding areas fruits are taken from trees or shrubs and eaten in night roosts—bowers of vegetation 30–60 m from the fruit source. Since seeds pass very rapidly through *C. perspicillata* (in ≤ 20 min), most seeds are deposited quite close to the parent plant. In the wet season *C. perspicillata*'s total nightly flight distance is about 5 km.

Many aspects of *C. perspicillata*'s dry-season foraging behavior are similar to those in the wet season with one important difference: flight distances are one and a half to two times as great then owing to the patchier distribution of food. Also, in the dry season individuals are more likely to return to the day roost for an hour or more after feeding for a while than they are in the wet season. The reason for this difference is not currently known. In both seasons, individuals sometimes leave their usual feeding spots, apparently to "scout out" potential feeding areas. Individuals gradually "phase out" old feeding areas when changing foraging locations.

Sex, reproductive condition, and probably social status play important roles in determining where individuals choose to feed. In general, males feed closer to the day roost than females, and the heaviest males (harem masters?) feed closest to the roost (Jamieson 1977; Heithaus and Fleming 1978). Pregnant females tend to feed in areas richer in *Piper* than do other sex-reproductive combinations.

Very little is known about the physiological ecology of *C. perspicillata*. Using captive animals in Panama, Studier and Wilson (1970) found that individuals of this species varied considerably in their ability to maintain a high constant body temperature when exposed to gradually lowering ambient temperatures. Some individuals went into torpor, whereas a lactating female remained homeothermic. At Santa Rosa, individuals forage every night regardless of weather conditions. Counts of fresh fruits under night roosts indicate that individuals eat most of the pulp (and pass most of the seeds) of up to thirty-five *Piper amalago* fruits (whose wet weight is about 1.6 g) in one night.

Because of its abundance, *C. perspicillata* is one of the major seed dispersers in tropical forests. It is more common in second growth than in primary forest and thus is an important disseminator of the seeds of early successional plants. In addition to its seed-dispersal activities, it also visits, and presumably pollinates, a number of tropical trees. Its major enemies include various owls, the carnivorous bat *Vampyrum spectrum,* opossums, and snakes.

*

Fleming, T. H.; Heithaus, E. R.; and Sawyer, W. B. 1977. An experimental analysis of the food location behavior of frugivorous bats. *Ecology* 58:619–28.

Fleming, T. H.; Hooper, E. T.; and Wilson, D. E. 1972. Three Central American bat communities: Structure, reproductive cycles, and movement patterns. *Ecology* 53:555–69.

Heithaus, E. R., and Fleming, T. H. 1978. Foraging movements of a frugivorous bat, *Carollia perspicillata* (Phyllostomatidae). *Ecol. Monogr.* 48:127–43.

Heithaus, E. R.; Fleming, T. H.; and Opler, P. A. 1975. Foraging patterns and resource utilization in seven species of bats in a seasonal tropical forest. *Ecology* 56:841–54.

Jamieson, R. W. 1977. Foraging behavior of *Carollia perspicillata,* a Neotropical frugivorous bat. M.S. thesis, University of Missouri–Saint Louis.

Pine, R. H. 1972. The bats of the genus *Carollia. Texas A&M Agric. Expt. Sta. Tech. Monogr.* no. 8.

Porter, F. L. 1978. Roosting patterns and social behavior in captive *Carollia perspicillata. J. Mamm.* 59: 627–30.

Studier, E. H., and Wilson, D. E. 1970. Thermoregulation in some Neotropical bats. *Comp. Biochem. Physiol.* 34:251–62.

Cebus capucinus (Mono Cara Blanca, White-faced Capuchin)

C. H. Freese

Cebus capucinus (fig. 9.7) is a diurnal, arboreal, prehensile-tailed primate of the family Cebidae. There are four species in the genus *Cebus,* but *capucinus* is the only one in Central America, its range extending from Belize to extreme northern Colombia.

Female capuchins give birth to singletons at 1–2-year intervals. Data from Santa Rosa National Park in Costa Rica and Barro Colorado Island in Panama indicate that most births occur during the dry season (December to early April) (C. Freese, pers. obs.; Oppenheimer 1969). Young achieve locomotory independence at 5–6 months of age, and sexual maturity is reached in 3–4 years by females and probably by males (Oppenheimer 1968; Hamlett 1939). Adult *C. capucinus* weigh 2.5–3.5 kg, with males somewhat larger than females. The body is black except for the white shoulders, upper chest, and face (fig. 9.7).

C. capucinus inhabit wet lowland forest on the Caribbean coast of Central America and deciduous dry forest on the Pacific coast, and they range up to an altitude of at least 1,500 m in Costa Rica and Panama (C. Freese, pers. obs.; Goodwin 1946) and 2,000 m in Colombia (Hernandez-Camacho and Cooper 1976). They will forage in young secondary growth as well as in mature forest, and occasionally they are found in mangrove forest (Freese 1976a). On rare occasions one may even see individuals traveling across a Guanacaste savanna.

All *Cebus* are omnivorous, most of their diet consisting of fruits and, in lesser quantity, insects. The diet of *C. capucinus* on Barro Colorado Island contains by weight an estimated 20% animal prey (especially insects), 65% fruit, and 15% green plant material (Hladik and Hladik 1969; Oppenheimer 1968). In Santa Rosa National Park the proportion of insect foraging to total foraging time varied from 30% during the dry season to 51% early in the wet season when there was an abun-

FIGURE 9.7. *Cebus capucinus,* adult male in profile. Santa Rosa National Park (photo, C. H. Freese).

dance of insect larvae (Freese 1977). Other plant parts, particularly new branch growth and flowers, are occasionally important, and small vertebrates are eaten rarely. In some areas capuchins are well known for their propensity to raid agricultural crops, especially corn (Jimenez 1970).

Fruits are usually ripe when eaten, and capuchins often test for ripeness by smelling, biting, or squeezing them. Some hard fruits are pounded on branches or rocks to soften them or to knock out seeds. Among fleshy fruits the fruit is seldom swallowed whole; instead, it is chewed to obtain the juices or fleshing covering and then spit out. In Santa Rosa this is true of all fruits with sizable pits (e.g., *Spondias mombin* and *Bunchosia* [?] sp.), and of most other types of fruit (e.g., *Ficus* spp. and *Manilkara zapota*). In some species (e.g., *Bursera simaruba* and *Muntingia calabura*) only the dried seeds are extracted and eaten. Flowers (e.g., *M. zapota* in Santa Rosa and *Clitoria arborescens* in Panama) are chewed and spit out, and the same appears to be true of new stem growth (e.g., *B. simaruba* in Santa Rosa and *Gustavia superba* on Barro Colorado Island) (Freese 1977; Oppenheimer 1968).

C. capucinus on Barro Colorado Island ate the fruit of approximately ninety-five plant species and the branch growth, buds, and various flower parts of twenty-four species during a long-term study (Oppenheimer 1968). During a shorter study at Santa Rosa National Park products from forty-two species of plants were eaten or at least tasted (Freese 1977). In both Santa Rosa and Barro Colorado, individuals ate an average of five to seven plant species per day. However, at Santa Rosa the most utilized plant species each week represented an average 48% of observed plant feeding time, and the two species most utilized accounted for 65% (Freese and Oppenheimer 1981).

Insects commonly eaten include Lepidoptera larvae, ants, cicadas and grasshoppers, spittle bugs, and various species of Coleoptera (Freese 1976*b,* 1977; Oppenheimer 1968). During the dry season in Santa Rosa the capuchins ate many adult insects (e.g., cicadas and swollen-thorn acacia ants), but in the wet season Lepidoptera larvae became a common prey. Among the vertebrates or vertebrate products eaten by *C. capucinus* are included birds' eggs, young birds, nestling squirrels, and small anolis lizards. Also, an adult male was once seen to attack a 1.7 m iguana and break off and eat 30–40 cm of its tail (Baldwin and Baldwin 1972). To round out this eclectic diet, *C. capucinus* has been reported to feed on oysters at low tide (Dampier 1697, cited by Hill 1960; Hernandez-Camacho and Cooper 1976, citing pers. comm. from C. R. Carpenter).

Capuchins forage over the entire vertical range of their habitat, from the forest floor to the top of the canopy. While foraging for insects, the members of a *C. capucinus* troop often spread out over an area more than 200 m in diameter. Even a large fruiting tree seldom contains most of the troop members simultaneously. When foraging for insects they search through dead leaves and the undersides of green leaves, rip off dead bark, roll over logs, split hollow vines vines and thorns, and generally dig into anything that may harbor insects.

Capuchins may be important agents of seed dispersal for some tree species. For example, on Barro Colorado Island it was estimated that one troop of *C. capucinus* dispersed more than 300,000 tiny seeds of *Miconia argentata* each day, or 150,000 seeds per hectare per year. Two-thirds of the seeds that had passed through the gut of the capuchins germinated, a germination rate equal to that of uneaten seeds, but defecated seeds germinated 10 days sooner. Data for some species, such as *Trichilia cepo,* indicated that seeds that passed through the gut of *C. capucinus* had a higher germination rate than uneaten seeds (Hladik and Hladik 1969).

C. capucinus affect their vegetative environment in other ways. The pruning of *G. superba* by *C. capucinus* increases its branching, which in the long run may result in greater fruit production from those trees (Oppenheimer and Lang 1969). Similar results might be expected from the extensive pruning and defoliation in Santa Rosa during October and November of *B. simaruba,* the seeds of which are a major food for capuchins in March and April. However, how is fruit production affected by the loss of so much photosynthetic material? Also, the eating of *M. zapota* flowers by capuchins in May in Santa Rosa may reduce the future supply of fruit from this species in December and January.

Predation on insects by *C. capucinus* must significantly reduce insect damage to some plant species. For example, on Barro Colorado Island the eggs of the bruchid beetle *Amblycerus centralis* are deposited on the fruits of *Apeiba membranacea,* but *C. capucinus* monkeys meticulously remove the grubs from most of the fruits, thus probably reducing seed destruction (Oppenheimer 1968). But insect predation may be destructive to some plants. When the capuchins of Santa Rosa preyed on the swollen-thorn acacia ants (primarily *Pseudomyrmex belti*), they did so by ripping off branches and opening thorns with their teeth. This often resulted in extensive physical destruction of the acacia, loss of the ant colony, and subsequent death of the plant (Freese 1976*b*).

Beside obtaining moisture from fruit and other foods, capuchins drink water directly. If it is available, *C. capucinus* drinks water from tree holes, but during the dry season in Santa Rosa, when all tree holes were dry, a troop drank at least once and often twice each day from a ground spring (Freese 1978).

Travel and foraging constitute approximately 70–80% of the capuchins' daytime activity in Santa Rosa and on Barro Colorado, with most of the remaining time spent in rest. The monkeys begin to feed almost immediately after leaving the sleeping trees about dawn, peaks in rest tend to occur around midday, and a surge in feeding again occurs in the late afternoon. A *C. capucinus* troop in Santa Rosa was estimated to travel an average of 2 km per day, seldom going less than 1 km or more than 3 km in one day.

The observed home ranges of *C. capucinus* troops fall between 0.5 and 1.0 km². Territorial defense between troops occurs, but at least in some cases there is considerable home-range overlap. The population density of *C. capucinus* has been estimated at eighteen to twenty-four per km² on Barro Colorado (Oppenheimer 1968) and five to seven per km² in Santa Rosa (Freese 1976*a*), although at Santa Rosa their numbers may have exceeded thirty animals per km² if only the more mature forest in the park is considered.

Predators on capuchins include humans and probably large raptors, boa constrictors, and felids.

*

Baldwin, J. D., and Baldwin, J. I. 1972. The ecology and behavior of squirrel monkeys (*Saimiri oerstedi*) in a natural forest in western Panama. *Folia Primat.* 18:161–84.

Dampier, W. 1697. *A voyage round the world.* (Cited by Hill 1960.)

Freese, C. H. 1976*a*. Censusing *Alouatta palliata, Ateles geoffroyi,* and *Cebus capucinus* in the Costa Rican dry forest. In *Neotropical primates: Field studies and conservation,* ed. R. W. Thorington, Jr., and P. G. Heltne, pp. 4–9. Washington, D.C.: National Academy of Sciences.

———. 1976*b*. Predation on swollen-thorn acacia ants by white-faced monkeys *Cebus capucinus. Biotropica* 8:278–81.

———. 1977. Food habits of white-faced capuchins (*Cebus capucinus*) in Santa Rosa National Park, Costa Rica. *Brenesia* 10/11:43–56.

———. 1978. Behavior of white-faced capuchins at a dry-season waterhole. *Primates* 19:275–86.

Freese, C. H., and Oppenheimer, J. R. 1981. The capuchin monkeys, genus *Cebus.* In *Ecology and Behavior of New World Primates,* ed. R. A. Mittermeier and A. F. Coimbra-Filho. Rio de Janeiro: Academia Brasileira de Ciencas.

Goodwin, G. G. 1946. Mammals of Costa Rica. *Bull. Am. Mus. Nat. Hist.* 87:275–458.

Hamlett, H. W. D. 1939. Reproduction in American monkeys. I. Estrous cycle, ovulation and menstruation in *Cebus. Anat. Rec.* 73:171–87.

Hernandez-Camacho, J., and Cooper, R. W. 1976. The non-human primates of Colombia. In *Neotropical primates: Field studies and conservation,* ed. R. W. Thorington, Jr., and P. G. Heltne, pp. 35–69. Washington, D.C.: National Academy of Sciences.

Hill, W. C. O. 1960. *Primates: Comparative anatomy and taxonomy.* Vol. 4. *Cebidae.* Part A. Edinburgh: University Press.

Hladik, A., and Hladik, C. M. 1969. Rapports tropiques entre végétation et primates dans la forêt de Barro Colorado (Panama). *Terre et Vie* 1:25–117.

Jimenez, J. J. 1970. Condición económica de los monos en Costa Rica. *O'Bios* 2:21–40.

Oppenheimer, J. R. 1968. Behavior and ecology of the white-faced monkey, *Cebus capucinus,* on Barro Colorado Island, C.Z. Ph.D. diss., University of Illinois, Urbana.

———. 1969. Changes in forehead patterns and group composition of the white-faced monkey (*Cebus capucinus*). In *Proceedings of the Second International Congress of Primatologists,* 1:36–42. Basel: Karger.

Oppenheimer, J. R., and Lang, G. E. 1969. *Cebus* monkeys: Effect on branching of *Gustavia* trees. *Science* 165:187–88.

Coendou mexicanum (Puercoespín, Prehensile-tailed Porcupine)

D. H. Janzen

Coendou mexicanum (fig. 9.8*a*) is the spiniest of the Costa Rican rodents and has stiff, barbed detachable body hairs (quills) (fig. 9.8*b*) much like those of the North American porcupine (*Erethizon dorsatum*). However, whereas the North American porcupine has a broad tail densely covered with hair and long quills (also used as a prop, like that of a woodpecker, when cutting bark off large trunks), the tail of *C. mexicanum* is thin, with hairs and spines only at the base. The terminal 10–15 cm

FIGURE 9.8. *Coendou mexicanum. a,* Old adult. Finca La Pacifica, near Cañas, Guanacaste Province, Costa Rica. *b,* Hind foot of road kill, with its own quills stuck into bare sole; quill/hair ratio is normal for this species. *c,* Tail of road kill showing naturally bare area on prehensile tail. Guanacaste Province, Costa Rica (photos, D. H. Janzen).

Panama and is apparently not sympatric with the North American porcupine in any area.

In Guanacaste the easiest way to find a prehensil-tailed porcupine is to look inside the base of large hollow trees in the forest for accumulations of the unique fecal pellets—flattened ovoids about 2 cm long and 1 cm wide. The food material within is very finely ground and does not contain intact seeds or large wood fragments. Many liters of these pellets accumulate in the trees that *C. mexicanum* uses for diurnal resting places. The animal roosts high in the hollow trunk during the day (and may on occasion be heard doing interior decorating with its incisors). At night it forages, but it often returns to the same hollow tree day after day. I have found two adult porcupines in the same cavity (November). The cavity has a very rank, musky odor. If its tail can be grabbed, the porcupine can be pulled out without much struggle. No study has been made of the wild food. In captivity, *C. mexicanum* readily eats table scraps, garden vegetables, and commercial fruits. It holds fruit in its front paws when feeding, much as a squirrel does. The molars are very similar to those of an agouti, and the surface appears to be irregular enough for breaking and grinding seeds and rough woody foliage.

I have found three porcupines dead at the end of March in dry riverbeds in Santa Rosa National Park, apparently killed by disease or starvation. A semitame margay (*Felis wiedii*) was released in Santa Rosa in June (1978) and several days later came into the dining hall with porcupine quills firmly imbedded in its face and neck. *C. mexicanum* quills have been found in the feces of a large felid in Costa Rica (Vaughan 1980). When attacked manually, *C. mexicanum* will bite, roll into a ball, or try to run away. There is no indication that it tries to hit the attacker with a portion of the body rich in quills (in strong contrast to the North American porcupine).

*

Vaughan, C. 1980. Predation of *Coendou mexicanus* by large Felidae. *Brenesia.* 18:368.

Cyclopes didactylus (Tapacara, Serafin de Platanar, Silky Anteater)

G. G. Montgomery

The best way to find a silky anteater (fig. 9.9) in the wild is to look up into clumps of small-diameter lianas within 10 m of the forest floor for something that resembles a golden tennis ball. You might thus see a silky anteater sleeping in the curled position it assumes to conserve body heat while it rests with lowered body temperature during daylight hours (Montgomery and Nagy, n.d.).

of the tail is largely naked and can curl strongly around small branches (fig. 9.8c), even allowing the animal to hang by its tail alone. I suspect that this difference between the two porcupines relates in great part to the former species' being a bark eater, while the latter species browses twigs and eats fruits and seeds, which requires it to move in the flimsy part of the tree crown. *C. mexicanum* has an exceptionally large, soft, inflated-appearing nose. Healthy adults weigh 4–6 kg and are therefore only about one-quarter the weight of North American porcupines in Michigan and Minnesota.

C. mexicanum is found throughout the lowlands of Costa Rica, though it is seen most often in Guanacaste deciduous forest. This is probably because the crowns of trees are lower and visibility is better there than in evergreen rain forests. The species ranges from Mexico to

FIGURE 9.9. *Cyclopes didactylus,* adult female walking upright on thin branch. Costa Rica (Servicio de Parques Nacionales de Costa Rica; photo, D. H. Janzen).

The silky anteater is the smallest of the four species of New World anteaters (Mammalia: Xenarthra: Myrmecophagidae). The monospecific genus *Cyclopes* occurs in moist forests from southern Mexico to Bolivia and Brazil (Wetzel 1980). Walker (1975) indicates that the body length, exclusive of the 178 to 203 mm prehensile tail, is 153 to 178 mm. However, in a sample of eleven adults measured on Barro Colorado Island in Panama, tail lengths ranged between 170 and 225 mm and total lengths between 355 and 440 mm; average body weight for the eleven adults was 223 g (range 155 to 275 g). Banded and golden anteaters (*Tamandua mexicana* and *T. tetradactyla*) weigh about 4 kg, and giant anteaters (*Myrmecophaga tridactyla*) weigh about 30 kg.

The silky anteater is strictly nocturnal (Sunquist and Montgomery 1973; Montgomery 1980*c*), almost completely arboreal, and, except for occasional contact between mothers and their young, solitary.

The hind foot is the key to the way silky anteaters move about and feed. *Cyclopes* moves and feeds on a substrate consisting mostly of small lianas and branches in the trees (usually about the size of a lead pencil). The hind foot is highly modified, permitting the animal to grip with its hind foot placed crosswise on the small stem with the foot pointed in either direction. Each front foot of the silky anteater, as in all New World anteaters (Taylor 1980), bears a large, sharp, pointed claw that is used both for defense and for opening holes in stems and lianas through which the anteater can feed on ants living inside.

When climbing, the anteater grasps small stems with its hind feet and uses its prehensile tail for balance. The animal can hang by its prehensile tail but probably does so rarely, except when it slips and falls. As the anteater walks along horizontal branches (fig. 9.9) and lianas, it trails the prehensil tail behind, wrapped partly around the stem, in position to support the animal if it falls.

When the silky anteater feeds, its body stands perpendicular to the direction of the small stem. It grasps the liana stem or small branch with hind feet turned in opposite directions. In this way it grips the stem tightly and maintains torque and balance without using the front feet. It then bends over and inserts its large, sharp foreclaw into the stem to open a slit in it. It holds this slit open with the foreclaw and inserts its long, mobile tongue. Ants and ant brood are drawn into the mouth with the tongue. Once the anteater has taken ants from that location, it moves down the stem or branch and repeats the procedure.

Silky anteaters on Barro Colorado Island fed entirely on ants, consuming about three thousand each day (seven hundred to five thousand each day depending on the age and sex of the anteater). Termites and other invertebrates were very rarely (one of fifteen thousand food items) found in samples of stomach contents and fecal material (Montgomery 1980*b*). Each sample of stomach contents and feces contained about eighteen species of ants, but the bulk of the ants in any one sample were from only one or two species. For each silky anteater, the species of ant that formed most of the daily food supply was relatively consistent from day to day, and there was relatively great consistency in the ant species that formed the predominant part of the diet among silky anteaters with adjacent territories. However, because not all anteaters fed from the same substrate, there was a tendency for each stomach and fecal sample to contain some ants that were exclusive to that sample. Important ants in the diets of silky anteaters were those of the genera *Crematogaster, Solenopsis, Camponotus,* and *Zacryptocerus.*

Silky anteaters have a harem-territory social system in which the territory of each male includes the territories of approximately three adult females (Montgomery 1980*c*). The females' territories are exclusive with respect to other females, but the male moves freely through them. The territories of both males and females are relatively large for a small mammal, perhaps in part because the food supply is dispersed and ants are well able to defend themselves against the depredations of these anteaters.

Silky anteaters bear single young and, as in the other anteater genera, invest considerable time and energy in caring for them (Montgomery 1980*a*). Until they are about one-third the mother's body weight, the young nurse; at that size they begin to eat ants on their own. The young is not carried by the mother during her nocturnal foraging but is left in the tree where the mother spent the day. Young are left alone for about 8 h each night.

The young begins to feed on ants when it is about one-third the size of the mother. For at least the next 6 weeks, until it is about two-thirds her size, it is fed milk and also forages for ants near where the mother has left it for the night. Before the mother changes her daily rest location, which she does almost every night, she returns to the young before dawn and carries it to the new location. The mother and young spend the day together, inactive, in a shaded rest site among the lianas that is relatively secure and protected.

When the young is approximately half the weight of the mother, it abruptly leaves her home range and disperses in a straight line cross-country, eventually finding a place where it will try to establish a new home range of its own. The mother then becomes pregnant again, probably producing at least two young every year.

Population densities of the silky anteater are relatively low, and they have relatively large home ranges for their size and for the amount of food potentially available to them (Montgomery 1980c). They consume only a small proportion of the available food, taking an estimated 0.5% or less of the ants on their home range each day. They move about almost continuously throughout the night, traveling approximately one thousand body lengths (less tail), and forage through the crowns of twenty or more trees each night. Their pattern of feeding is probably much like that of the other New World anteaters, in which each feeding bout is of short duration and the anteaters take only a small proportion of the available ants from each colony (Montgomery and Lubin 1977), covering a large number of ant colonies during each feeding period. This apparent foraging strategy of cropping a continuously renewed food supply occurs in large part because the ants have a variety of ways to defend themselves against anteaters, including dispersed colonies, biting and stinging soldiers, and nests built in relatively inaccessible places (Lubin, Young, and Montgomery 1977; Lubin and Montgomery 1981).

Silky anteaters apparently live quite close to the energetic limits for an animal using ants as a food supply. Each day they expend energy approximately equal to the maximum amount available from the ants they take in, they have lowered metabolic rates and body temperatures during the day while they rest, and they conserve heat by a thick insulating coat of fur (Montgomery and Nagy, n.d.).

*

Lubin, Y. D., and Montgomery, G. G. 1981. Defenses of *Nasutitermes* termites (Isoptera, Termitidae) against *Tamandua* anteaters (Edentata, Myrmecophagidae). *Biotropica* 13:66–76.

Lubin, Y. D.; Young, O. P.; and Montgomery, G. G. 1977. Food resources of anteaters (Edentata: Myrmecophagidae). I. A year's census of arboreal nests of ants and termites of Barro Colorado Island, Panama Canal Zone, *Biotropica* 9:26–34.

Montgomery, G. G. 1980a. Socio-ecology of Xenarthra (= Edentata): Parental investment by extreme K-strategists. In *Mammalian behavior*, ed. J. F. Eisenberg et al. Special Publication. American Society of Mammologists, in press.

———. 1980b. Impact of mammalian anteaters (*Cyclopes, Tamandua*) on arboreal ant populations. In *The evolution and ecology of sloths, anteaters and armadillos (Mammalia: Xenarthra = Edentata)*, ed. G. G. Montgomery. Washington, D.C.: Smithsonian Institution Press.

———. 1980c. Home-range spaces, movement patterns, and foraging strategies of the four species of Neotropical anteaters (Myrmecophagidae). In *The evolution and ecology of sloths, anteaters and armadillos (Mammalia: Xenarthra = Edentata)*, ed. G. G. Montgomery. Washington, D.C.: Smithsonian Institution Press.

Montgomery, G. G., and Lubin, Y. D. 1977. Prey influences on the movements of Neotropical anteaters. In *Proceedings of the 1975 Predator Symposium,* ed. R. L. Phillips, and C. J. Jonkel. Missoula: Montana Forest and Conservation Experiment Station, School of Forestry, University of Montana.

Montgomery, G. G., and Nagy, K. L. n.d. Energetics of free-living silky anteaters (*Cyclopes*). In manuscript.

Sunquist, M. E., and Montgomery, G. G. 1973. Activity pattern of a translocated silky anteater (*Cyclopes didactylus*). *J. Mamm.* 54:782.

Taylor, B. K. 1980. Functional anatomy of the forelimb of anteaters. In *The evolution and ecology of sloths, anteaters and armadillos (Mammalia: Xenarthra = Edentata)*, ed. G. G. Montgomery. Washington, D.C.: Smithsonian Institution Press.

Walker, E. P. 1975. *Mammals of the world.* 3d ed., vol. 1 (rev. J. L. Paradiso). Baltimore: Johns Hopkins University Press.

Wetzel, R. M. 1980. The identification and distribution of recent Xenarthra (= Edentata). In *The evolution and ecology of sloths, anteaters and armadillos (Mammalia: Xenarthra = Edentata)*, ed. G. G. Montgomery. Washington, D.C.: Smithsonian Institution Press.

Dasyprocta punctata and *Agouti paca* (Guatusa, Cherenga, Agouti, Tepezcuintle, Paca)

N. Smythe

The most commonly encountered diurnal mammal in the low- to middle-elevation rain forest between southern Mexico and northern Argentina is the agouti (*Dasyprocta* spp.) (fig. 9.10a,b). Agoutis are caviomorph (New World hystricomorph) rodents, relatives of guinea pigs, chinchillas, coypus, capybaras, and their sympatric cousin the paca (*Agouti paca*). The nocturnal pacas (fig.

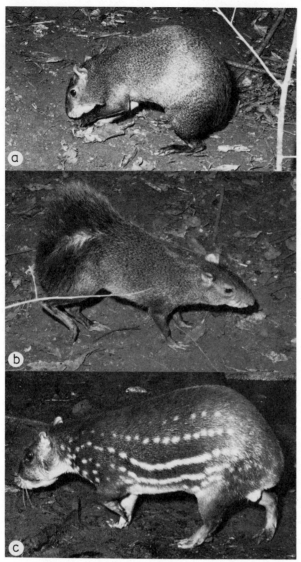

FIGURE 9.10. *a, Dasyprocta punctata,* adult placing a leaf over a seed it has buried. *b, Dasyprocta punctata,* adult with rump hair erected. *c, Agouti paca,* adult male; note everted anal glands. Barro Colorado Island, Panama (photos, N. Smythe).

9.10*c*) are somewhat larger than agoutis and almost twice the average weight and are brown with horizontal rows of cream-colored spots along the flanks. Both species are favorite game animals throughout their range, the paca being preferred for its excellent meat and freedom from odor.

Agoutis and pacas exhibit many characteristics reminiscent of some primitive ungulates (agoutis are, for example, very similar in general appearance to *Hyracotherium,* especially in such features as the legs). They are both primarily seminivore-frugivores, although the agouti can more easily penetrate extremely hard seed coats. This, and other differences between the two spe-

cies, are reflected by the differences in their activity patterns. The agouti sits on its haunches to eat, elevating its head to watch for potential predators and, incidentally, freeing the forepaws, which can then be used to manipulate hard seeds. This ability permits it to concentrate gnawing at a chosen spot. Although pacas do sometimes eat hard seeds, they have much greater difficulty.

Agoutis run as their primary means to escape predators. Pacas, although they can run surprisingly fast for short distances, effectively escape in the extreme darkness of the forest night by leaping away from the source of disturbance and "freezing": staying absolutely motionless for as long as 45 min. The lack of the need to run means that pacas can store food as fat, whereas the agoutis' solution to seasonal scarcity is to bury seeds during times of plenty and dig them up later. These seeds cannot be stored in a single cache, however, since they would then be an exploitable food source for peccaries (*Tayassu tajacu*). So agoutis bury seeds in a dispersed pattern and, since they must bury a surplus because of the uncertainty of retrieval, act as important dispersers of their food plant propagules. Pacas like to eat in the darkest possible place, and they carry fruits and seeds to sheltered feeding spots. In this way they may also disperse a few seeds, but far less efficiently than agoutis.

Young caviomorphs are all born in a very advanced state. Baby agoutis are born in one of their mother's habitual sleeping spots, usually single but occasionally in pairs. At dawn of their first day the mother leads them to possible nest sites—holes that are impregnable to coatis (*Nasua narica*), tayras (*Eira barbara*), or other possible enemies—and the young select a suitable site, furnishing it with leaves and twigs. The mother, also being unable to enter the nest, calls the baby to feed each morning and evening. Before it is allowed to suckle, she stimulates it to urinate and defecate by licking its perineum, then ingests all the products. This removes the odors of the young animal from the nest site, presumably making it less noticeable to potential predators. It also probably reinforces the odor bond between the young animal and its mother.

Odor forms an important mode of communication for agoutis. They make habitual trails, feeding and sleeping spots, and other objects within their 2–3-ha home range by dragging the perineum across an object, thus rubbing it with the paired, evertible anal glands. It is interesting that pacas also possess these glands, and they are everted under similar conditions (e.g., during aggressive encounters), but pacas do not use olfactory communication nearly as much as agoutis and never mark in the same way. Males of both species, in common with many other caviomorphs, mark prospective mates by spraying them with urine during a very active courtship ritual.

The fighting behavior of the two species is interesting

to compare. Agoutis usually move out of the way of any other agouti that walks directly toward them. A pursuing animal may try to bite the fleeing one on the rump, which in agoutis is covered with long hair that can be erected, usually in flight situations, and presumably protects the rump from the bites of a pursuing conspecific or potential predator. Occasionally two agoutis of the same sex will run toward one another, leap high into the air a moment before meeting, and lash out at one another with their powerful hind legs, sometimes severely wounding one another.

Pacas do not run from one another, but stand head to head and slash at one another with their large incisors. They do not possess lengthened hair on the rump, but the integument of the entire back consists of thick connective tissue overlain by extremely fragile skin. This skin tears and slips over the connective tissue with surprising ease, presumably making it very difficult for a potential predator or an aggressor to maintain a hold on its victim. Pacas, particularly adult males, have greatly inflated zygomatic bones that probably aid in the fighting by increasing the mass of the skull and also act as resonators to amplify sounds made both vocally and by grinding the jugal teeth together. These sounds may be used in social communication, but their chief function is in attempted intimidation of potential predators. In the extreme dark of the forest floor, it is difficult to believe that a 10-kg animal could make such an ominous sound.

During flight from predators, agoutis utter repeated high-pitched alarm barks. Young animals have a much lower threshold for this activity than do adults and will often rush off barking at the slightest disturbance. Agoutis that are being chased by, for example, a jaguaroundi (*Felis yagouaroundi*) or a domestic dog run in circles but will not leave the small home range. This behavior, in conjunction with their strong odor, makes them easy prey for human hunters and dogs, a combination that, even without firearms, can eliminate entire local populations of agoutis.

The only canid that has evolved in the humid Neotropics is the now very rare *Speothos venaticus,* the bush dog. It is nocturnal (presumably the temperature/humidity regime of the rain forest makes it impossible for a cursorial predator to adequately cool itself in the daytime) and is purported to specialize in pacas as prey items. Pacas have evolved a special defense, probably in response to *Speothos:* they run to bodies of water, jump in, and are said to be able to remain immersed for a considerable time. This behavior has enabled pacas to survive in many areas, for instance in riparian forests, where the adjacent upland forest has been cleared. However, perhaps owing to their nocturnal foraging behavior, pacas sometimes persist in tiny fragments of remnant vegetation among altered agricultural lands; for example,

pacas are occasionally seen in the suburbs of San José, where they are reputed to live among small patches of trees in unused gardens (D. Janzen, pers. comm.).

In Costa Rica, agoutis and pacas are common in relatively undisturbed forest to elevations of at least 2,000 m, and they range from the driest deciduous forests (e.g., Santa Rosa National Park) to the wettest forests; both species are even found foraging for seeds on mangrove forest floors when the tide is out. However, as measured by frequency of encounter in the forest, their local density varies enormously from year to year, and at least some of this is clearly due to local variation in annual seed crop production by forest trees (D. Janzen, pers. comm.).

*

Kleiman, D. G.; Eisenberg, J. F.; and Maliniak, E. 1979. Reproductive parameters and productivity of caviomorph rodents. In *Vertebrate ecology in the northern Neotropics,* ed. J. F. Eisenberg, pp. 173–83. Washington, D.C.: Smithsonian Institution Press.
Smythe, N. 1978. The natural history of the Central American agouti (*Dasyprocta punctata*). *Smithsonian Contrib. Zool.* 257:1–52.

Dasypus novemcinctus (Cusuco, Armadillo)

R. M. Wetzel

The nine-banded armadillo (fig. 9.11) presents a problem because of the inconsistency of its vernacular and scientific names. The movable bands more frequently number eight in the northern (Central America to Oklahoma) and southern (Argentina and Paraguay) parts of its range. These bands, if counted along the middle of the back, vary from seven to ten, with a mean of nine occurring most frequently in middle and northern South America, a region that includes the type locality, Pernambuco, Brazil.

The armadillo's body is encased dorsally by a carapace of dermal bone (scutes) overlain with epidermal scales. The flexible carapace is divided into a scapular shield, followed by a series of eight or nine movable bands, and terminates in a pelvic shield. The tail is long and slender, encircled by rings of armor on the proximal two-thirds. The top of the head is covered with a plate of scutes; the nose is long and slightly upturned; ears are prominent, hairless, and set close together. Tiny, peglike teeth vary from seven to nine on each side of the upper and lower jaws; incisors and canines are lacking. Hair is sparse on the carapace, occurring between the bands, but is somewhat more prominent on the underside. The carapace is dark, with yellowish scales more numerous laterally. Scales are round or in rosette patterns on the shoulder and pelvic shields but triangular on the movable bands. The

465

FIGURE 9.11. *Dasypus novemcinctus,* adult male at peak of characteristic leap-hop used to escape the grasp of a potential predator. March 1980, Santa Rosa National Park, Costa Rica (photo, D. H. Janzen).

forefoot has four toes and the hind foot five; all toes are heavily clawed. The female has one pair of pectoral and one pair of inguinal mammaries. Measurements of adults, Texas to Argentina, are length of head and body, 384–573 mm; length of tail (not a dependable measurement, since the slender tip is often broken), 276–430 mm; length of ear (from notch), 35–57 mm; weight, 2.9–8 kg.

Little has been reported on the ecology, behavior, and natural history of this species outside the United States (see summary, Wetzel and Mondolfi 1979). Copulation is said to occur with the female lying on her back. In the southern United States breeding occurs in July or August, but implantation is delayed for 3–4 months. Embryonic growth of 120 days begins in November, and four precocial young are born in early spring. The quadruplets result from division of a single fertilized ovum, so all are of the same sex and "identical." The question can be raised whether the embryonic "diapause" may be an adaptation to the reversed seasons of the United States and thus perhaps is reduced in Central America and absent in South America. Polyembryony is restricted to the long-nosed armadillos, genus *Dasypus,* one or two young being the rule in the other eight genera of armadillos. Sexual maturity is usually reached in a year, and the life-span is about four years.

Finding food can involve a lengthy, snuffling search with frequent rootings into the ground. The armadillo's diet is predominantly insects and larvae but also includes fruits, berries, fungi, snails, slugs, earthworms, millipedes, centipedes, and small vertebrates. Because of the armadillo's weak mandible and reduced dentition, its diet is confined to relatively soft or small food items. In a Texas study, beetles formed 42% of the total volume of food; forty thousand ants of three species were taken in one meal by one armadillo; and 126 of 169 armadillo stomachs contained termites (Kalmbach 1944).

The armadillo is a powerful digger; in loose soil it can disappear within a few minutes. Studies in Florida have found burrows up to 8 m long and 2 m deep; it is evidently a wide-ranging animal with a minimum home range of 5.7 ha (Layne 1976; Layne and Glover 1977). Burrows may contain a large amount of nesting material, and armadillos have been observed carrying vegetation for bedding by holding the grass with the forelegs while hopping on the hind legs (Eisenberg 1961). This bipedalism is also a feature of other armadillos and anteaters of the order Edentata.

Although armadillos are adapted to the tropical and subtropical climates in which they evolved, they do have some temperature-regulatory mechanisms. The species' body temperature is relatively low for a mammal but fairly constant within the range of temperatures of its environment. Adaptations to heat include an initial low metabolic rate, vasodilation, panting, and returning to the burrow during the heat of the day. Although armadillos cannot survive in areas with long, severe winter freezes, some adjustments to cold include vasoconstriction, shivering, and huddling in nesting material in the burrow. Escape behavior is often preceded by sitting upright on the haunches, listening, and sampling the air for scent, followed by a headlong dash through the underbrush. When its escape cover includes cacti or spiny bromeliads, the armadillo's armor gives it considerable advantage over its predators. If it cannot reach a burrow and capture is at hand, an upward leap, sometimes of over 1 m, is a common surprise maneuver.

Population levels of the armadillo, whether by season, long-range cycles, or habitat, are not known. They occur in a wide variety of habitats, from cloud forest, moist montane, and lowland tropical rain forest to grassland and thorn scrub forest. One estimate of numbers of tropical mammals suggests that armadillos may be second only to sloths in abundance in tropical rain forests (Eisenberg and Thorington 1973).

The naked-tailed armadillo, *Cabassous centralis* (Miller), is the only other armadillo that reaches as far north as Costa Rica. Unique in lacking bony scutes on the tail, it is a small (mean length of head and body, 341 mm), fossorial armadillo with a short tail (mean length, 154 mm), short, rounded ears (mean length from ventral notch, 33 mm), a rounded carapace with about eleven movable bands, rectangular scutes, and large crescent-shaped claws on the third, fourth, and fifth front toes. Its diet is chiefly termites, and its tunnels have been frequently found in or near termite colonies (Wetzel 1980).

*

Eisenberg, J. F. 1961. Observations on the nest building behavior of armadillos. *Proc. Zool. Soc. London* 137:322–24.

Eisenberg, J. F., and Thorington, R. W. 1973. A preliminary analysis of a Neotropical mammal fauna. *Biotropica* 5:150–61.

Kalmbach, E. R. 1944. *The armadillo: Its relation to agriculture and game.* Austin, Texas: Game, Fish and Oyster Commission.

Layne, J. N. 1976. The armadillo, one of Florida's oddest animals. *Florida Nat.* 49:8–12.

Layne, J. N., and Gover, D. 1977. Home range of the armadillo in Florida. *J. Mamm.* 58:411–13.

Talmage, R. V., and Buchanan, G. D. 1954. The armadillo (*Dasypus novemcinctus*): A review of its natural history, ecology, anatomy and reproductive physiology. *Rice Inst. Pamph. Monogr. Biol.* 41:1–135.

Wetzel, R. M. 1980. Revision of the naked-tailed armadillos, genus *Cabassous* McMurtrie. *Ann. Carnegie Mus. Nat. Hist.* 49:323–57.

Wetzel, R. M., and Mondolfi, E. 1979. In *Vertebrate ecology in the northern Neotropics*, ed. J. F. Eisenberg, pp. 43–63. Washington, D.C.: Smithsonian Institution Press.

Desmodus rotundus (Vampiro, Vampire Bat)

D. C. Turner

Of the three genera of true hematophagous vampire bats, each containing one species, *Desmodus* is by far the most abundant throughout its geographic range, which stretches from northern Mexico through Argentina. *Desmodus rotundus,* the common vampire bat (fig. 9.12), feeds exclusively on the blood of vertebrates. It is highly mobile, capable of walking, running, and hopping as well as flying. This bat is quick to react to disturbances; the selective advantage of agility to an animal that can feed on prey ten thousand times its size is obvious.

The vampire is capable of olfactory orientation (Schmidt and Greenhall 1971) but has large eyes and better visual acuity than other chiropterans (Chase 1972). It uses low-intensity calls for echolocation, best suited for the detection of large objects. Which sense, or which combination of sensory modalities, actually is used to find prey is not yet known.

The superior incisors (fig. 9.12) of the vampire are razor sharp and are used to remove a small (ca. 3 mm) piece of flesh from the prey. A number of studies have demonstrated the presence of anticoagulant or fibrinolytic activities of the saliva. The feeding bite as opposed to the aggressive bite of *Desmodus* is painless (D. Turner, pers. exp.), and the vampire laps blood flowing from the wound site (capillary action, not suction, is involved). A fresh wound on a prey animal can easily be identified

FIGURE 9.12. *Desmodus rotundus,* adult face and dentition. Finca La Pacifica, near Cañas, Guanacaste Province, Costa Rica (photo, D. H. Janzen).

from the dripping blood. A captive vampire will ingest about 15 ml of blood per day, this meal being singularly high in protein and low in fats and carbohydrates.

Presumably *Desmodus* experienced a population explosion when domestic animals were brought to the New World. These afforded the vampires a more accessible and more plentiful supply of blood than did the native wildlife. Today, serological tests of blood meals from *Desmodus* in Mexico, Trinidad, and Costa Rica (Greenhall 1970; Schmidt, Greenhall, and Lopez-Forment 1970; Turner 1975) indicate a nearly complete switch to domestic animals, particularly cattle, horses, and poultry. Turner's (1975) study indicated strong prey preferences even within domestic cattle, which were partly related to the degree of exposure within herds at night.

On its foraging flights, the vampire avoids moonlit periods. Presumably it hunts alone or, at most, in small groups. Upon locating a prey animal, it lands either directly on its body or on the ground, especially if the prey is bedded down. It bites cattle at various places on the body, but quite often on the neck. The prey either shows no reaction or, for example, shakes its head, temporarily displacing the bat. But the vampires are persistent. After feeding the bats may fly to a temporary roost or return directly to the diurnal roost. A number of vampires have been seen feeding successively from the same wound, and aggressive threats are not uncommon in this situation.

Often *Desmodus* utilizes riverbeds as flyways, and its foraging range is small relative to those of other bat species (ca. 2 km on either side of rivers in Turner's 1975 study). Efficiency at finding and feeding on prey is fairly high, with a mean foraging time of about 2–3 h on any given night.

Vampires roost communally during the day in tree hollows, abandoned wells, caves, and such. Their roosts are easily distinguishable from those used exclusively by other bat species by the potent ammonia odor and by the dark orange, viscous "goo" (their excreta) on the roost walls and floor. When *Desmodus* shares roosts with other bat species, they are often found in the uppermost, most secluded areas. Both sexes roost together, and roost turnover for individuals can be very high when a number of potential roosts exist close by; but vampires have also been reported to use the same roost over long periods. Self-grooming and social grooming in the roost are common.

Although pregnant vampires can be netted in any month of the year, Turner's (1975) data suggest higher pregnancy rates for the wet season in northern Costa Rica, and this may be related to prey availability. Females can be captured that are both pregnant and lactating, indicating a postpartum estrous. In captivity, mothers feed young vampires blood from their mouths at 3 months of age, and juveniles visit prey with their mothers at 5 to 6 months of age (Schmidt and Manske 1973).

Through their unique feeding habits, vampires can transmit a number of diseases, the most serious, of course, being paralytic rabies. Annual losses in domestic stock from vampire-transmitted rabies virus are estimated at over $100 million throughout Central and South America. *Desmodus* is known to survive the virus itself, and infection rates appear to be low in naturally occurring populations.

*

Chase, J. 1972. Role of vision in echolocating bats. Ph.D. diss., Indiana University.

Greenhall, A. M. 1970. The use of a precipitin test to determine host preferences of the vampire bats, *Desmodus rotundus* and *Diaemus youngi*. *Bijdrag. Dierk.* 40:36–39.

Schmidt, U., and Greenhall, A. M. 1971. Untersuchungen zur geruchlichen Orientierung der Vampirfledermäuse (*Desmodus rotundus*). *Z. Vergl. Physiol.* 74:217–26.

Schmidt, U.; Greenhall, A. M.; and Lopez-Forment, W. 1970. Vampire bat control in Mexico. *Bijdrag. Dierk.* 40:74–76.

Schmidt, U., and Manske, U. 1973. Die Jugendentwicklung der Vampirfledermäuse (*Desmodus rotundus*). *Z. Säugetierk.* 38:14–33.

Turner, D. C. 1975. *The vampire bat: A field study in behavior and ecology.* Baltimore: Johns Hopkins University Press.

Didelphis marsupialis (Raposa, Zarigüeya, Zorro Pelón, Zorra Mochila, Opossum)

A. L. Gardner

Adults of *Didelphis marsupialis*, the largest marsupial in Costa Rica, approach 1 m in total length, of which the tail is about half. Very large adults may exceed 5 kg, but most weigh considerably less (0.8–2.5 kg.). The two color phases (gray and black) may be equally common, although the gray phase usually predominates. The fur is dense, with the guard hairs long and coarse. The lower legs are black. The sides of the head, snout, and underparts are paler than the rest of the body and may be stained yellowish to orange, presumably by secretions from midventral chest glands. The cheek is dark; individual hairs are pale basally, usually dusky tipped, and often tinged yellowish. The ears are bare, white-tipped in young but all black in subadults and adults. The tail is prehensile, thickly haired at its base (proximal 10%); the bare portion is black on the proximal half or more, with the rest white. Each foot bears five well-developed toes; the opposable, thumblike hallux is the largest. Females bear a pouch.

Normal dentition is fifty teeth: incisors, 5/4; canines, 1/1; premolars, 3/3; molars, 4/4 on each side. The only deciduous teeth are the last upper premolars. Teeth are fully erupted by 10 months of age. Greatest length of skull varies from 90 to 125 mm in adults. Opossums apparently grow throughout life, and males are consistently larger than females of equivalent age. Much of the differential in size between the sexes is due to the demands of reproduction (principally lactation), which diverts energy from growth processes in the female.

Cheek color is the easiest character to use when distinguishing *D. marsupialis* from its northern sympatric and similar-sized congener *D. virginiana* (Virginia opossum). The all-white-cheeked *D. virginiana* (fig. 9.13), while uncommon in Costa Rica, may be expanding its range and has been found as far south as Cañas.

Didelphis marsupialis is found countrywide below 1,500 m but is rare or absent at higher elevations. This nondiscriminating omnivore forages at night, usually along watercourses, and eats just about anything edible it encounters. Some have been found with their stomachs filled with coffee beans. *Didelphis*, among New World mammals, perhaps comes closest to being a commensal of man. In many areas the opossum's acquired dependence on refuse dumps as food sources concentrates the animals close to human habitations, where they also prey on poultry and fruit crops. Individuals are solitary except when breeding and do not defend territories. Opossums often travel more than 1 km per night. Den

FIGURE 9.13. *Didelphis virginiana*, adult male (*on right*) with long canines (females have short canines), and two juveniles; these animals are very similar to *Didelphis marsupialis*, except that they have white to creamy white facial cheeks whereas the cheeks of *D. marsupialis* are tan to brown. June 1980, Santa Rosa National Park, Costa Rica (rule is 12 in long) (photo, D. H. Janzen).

sites include caves, rock crevices, hollow logs and trees, and abandoned dens of other mammals. Because the female has a pouch and carries her young, she is not restricted to fixed dens or nests during any time of the year.

Costa Rican *D. marsupialis* probably has two litters per year, with birth peaks in February and July and no reproductive activity between October and late December. Gestation is 12–13 days. Many more young are born (about twenty) that can be accommodated in the pouch (average number of teats is nine), and the average number of pouch young approximates six. After its journey from vulva to pouch, each young firmly attaches to a nipple, where it will remain for at least 60 days. Young are weaned at about 100 days of age. Females are reproductively mature at 7 months; spring-born females may breed during their first year.

Mortality is highest among newly weaned young. Predators include owls, snakes, and most mammalian carnivores. Opossums are well known for the variety and number of parasites they harbor; however, rates of loss to parasitism and disease are not known. They are highly resistant to crotalid venom. Whereas opossums are often

killed by humans to keep them from damaging poultry and fruit crops, many more are killed by vehicles.

The flesh of *D. marsupialis* is usually considered unpalatable, and they are not hunted for food. These opossums rarely put on appreciable amounts of body fat, in contrast to *D. virginiana*, which can become extremely fat and is often hunted for food.

"Playing possum," a death-feigning response to strong threat, is not as common in *D. marsupialis* as it is in *D. virginiana*. Stereotyped bluff behavior includes gaping and hissing while slowly moving the head from side to side and shifting weight from one front foot to the other. This behavior may be accompanied by lunging toward the threat and biting. When aroused, *D. marsupialis* may respond by growling, hissing, flailing the tip of the tail, and (in males) snapping the canines together.

The opossums are capable climbers and spend considerable time foraging in vegetation.

Eira barbara (Tolumuco, Tayra)

D. H. Janzen

This chocolate brown to black mustelid (also called *Tayra barbara* in older literature) is found throughout Costa Rica below about 2,000 m elevation and ranges from central Mexico to tropical southern South America. An adult (fig. 9.14*a*) weighs about 5 kg and looks like a thin-haired, lanky, very large mink with a long and long-haired tail. The body hair is very short and the skin is darkly pigmented beneath the hair. The feet are not webbed, and they look like long-clawed mink feet. The dentition is like that of a mink or otter (fig. 9.14*b*).

Tayras are terrestrial and arboreal foragers but do not search in water (as do grison and otters). I have seen them up to 20 m off the ground in the crowns of large deciduous forest trees at Santa Rosa National Park, and I saw one walk down the straight, clean bole from a crown of a 40 m tree in Corcovado National Park. I watched one chase an adult agouti on a dirt road for at least 50 m (Rincón, Osa Peninsula, 1965), but the rodent outran it. When foraging on the forest floor they are very inquisitive, appearing to visually and olfactorily examine many crevices and holes. However, the two I watched for extended periods did not catch litter insects, and were not nearly as disruptive of the litter as are coatis. Tayras give the impression of searching for large prey items (presumably birds nests, carrion, lizards, fruit, or eggs). An adult was seen to pick up a 500-g ripe sapotaceous fruit on the forest floor and carry it away after making an aggressive display to the observer (Corcovado National Park). Tayras forage throughout the day, and in captivity they are active in the daytime and sleep at night.

In captivity they are highly omnivorous, eating eggs, chicken and goat meat and bones, papayas, pineapples,

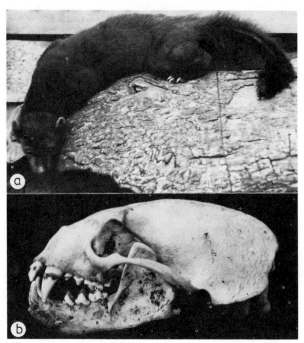

FIGURE 9.14. *Eira barbara, a,* Captive adult. Finca La Pacifica, near Cañas, Guanacaste Province, Costa Rica. *b,* Skull of adult. Finca La Selva, Sarapiquí District, Costa Rica (photos, D. H. Janzen).

bananas, bread, and other table scraps. A large scat deposit in Santa Rosa, at the den described below, contained agouti fur, rabbit fur, and seeds of at least six species of fruit (including seeds of *Manilkara zapota, Ficus* spp., *Ardisia revoluta,* and *Alibertia edulis*). I suspect that their diet is very similar to that of raccoons, coyotes, and small cats.

A tayra den at Santa Rosa had a 12-cm diameter entrance hole to a cavity of about 10 liters volume under the base of a standing *Manilkara zapota* tree. The tree was about 30 m up a steep hill in broken deciduous forest above the Río Guapote, a seasonal creek through the uplands of the park. A large scat pile decorated a rock about 30 cm from the entrance. On 5 May (last month of the dry season) the den contained a large adult female and three half-sized tayras. They ran out of the den one by one (adult first) while I stood several meters away.

If caught very young, tayras become very tame. They make poor pets, however, since they are very restless, nip strangers, and have a strong mustelid odor.

*

Ewer, R. F. 1973. *The carnivores.* London: Weidenfeld and Nicolson.

Felis onca (Tigre, Jaguar)

C. B. Koford

This largest of Central American carnivores, an endangered species, was once fairly common in coastal mangroves, lowland savannas, and wet and dry shrublands and forests up to about 1,000 m elevation. But because of its conspicuous tracks, the high value of its pelt, its reputation as a stock killer, and its vulnerability to hound pursuit and still hunting, this cat is now rare except in parts of large unhunted reserves. It occurs in Tortuguero National Park, Santa Rosa National Park, Corcovado National Park, Río Macho Forest Preserve (?), and lower levels of Cordillera Talamanca. Even where vegetation type seems uniform, the distribution is patchy. Its tracks (fig. 9.15*b*) are now very abundant at Corcovado, and sightings are occasional.

Adult males weigh 50–100 kg, females a third less. The ground color is yellowish brown dorsally, white ventrally, and the animals are black spotted all over, the spots on the sides forming open "mariposas," some with contained dots (not in the leopard). Possibly there are a few of the black pelage phase in Costa Rica. The tail is short, less than half the length of the head and body. The head, shoulders, and forefeet are massive for grasping prey.

Jaguars are rarely seen in daylight, but occasionally one suns on a cliff or log. They scratch tree trunks, but it is not sure that they urine mark objects or make territorial scratches on the ground. They are fairly aquatic and easily swim rivers, small lakes, and straits between mangrove islets. They favor damp sites such as streambeds in gallery forests, where footprints often reveal jaguars' presence, approximate size, and travels. At any season, jaguars of either sex may roar at night. Some hunters

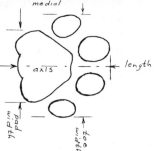

b

FIGURE 9.15. *Felis wiedii. a,* adult. Costa Rica (photo, D. H. Janzen). *b,* Suggested method of measuring cat footprint (forefoot) (drawing, C. Koford).

470

elicit responses with vocal imitations or by jerking on a waxed cord fixed to the skin head of a gourd drum.

Although jaguars seem to prefer peccaries as prey, they also take monkeys, agoutis, deer, birds, fish, lizards, turtles, and other animals. In Surinam they take sea turtles on nesting beaches. Mud tracks reveal feeding on dead fish, alligators, iguanas, and other carrion left by receding waters. On occasion, a jaguar returning at night to finish up a carcass will meet the lamp beam and shotgun blast of a waiting hunter. Sometimes a jaguar kills a cow, pig, goat, dog, or other domestic beast. Most ranchers say that a tigre usually kills only one animal and eats it before hunting again, wheras a puma (*F. concolor*) may kill several livestock and eat only one. The kill is usually made with a bite at the nape, the canines breaking the prey's neck or penetrating its skull. The ribs are eaten, not just stripped of flesh. A jaguar seems not to avoid the scent of man, and one may follow a man walking a trail. Although unprovoked attacks on man are rare, in Panama a jaguar recently charged a man who was carrying a bag of trapped birds.

In forest reserves the average density of adult jaguars is roughly one per 100 km^2 at any one time. Annual home ranges are probably several hundred km^2 for males, less for females. Single vagrants, mostly young males, may occur far from the normal zones of residence and breeding. The season of births probably varies regionally. Gestation is about 3 months, and the usual litter is two. Apparently males take no part in raising the young, which may accompany the mother for a year. Females reach sexual maturity at about 3 years of age and do not breed in successive years if their young survive.

As in most cats, footprints are characterized by unequal size of the four toes, with the next-to-medial toe longest and the outer toe smallest; heel pad with three posterior lobes and two angular anterior corners; width of forefoot print greater than its length (of hind foot, equal or narrower); and no claw marks. The strongly clawed thumb rarely rouches ground. In shallow dust the forefoot strack may measure 100 mm or more across the toes. Pumas (*F. concolor*) have smaller feet with slightly more elongate toes. Domestic dog prints can be large, but the central pair of toes are of the same size and shape and often show claw marks, and the outer pair of toes are symmetrical; the heel pad's posterior margin forms a smooth curve, and the anterior apex is rounded. In all these carnivores, at a fast walk the print of the hindfoot falls a few inches ahead of the print of the forefoot. The best single footprint measurement is the width of the hind foot pad. Often one can recognize individual cats by the size and shape of their footprints. For the record, photograph the tracks vertically, with cross-lighting to show detail and a millimeter scale alongside the prints; or, better, cast the print in melted candle wax or in plaster.

Although export and internal commerce in wildlife products have long been prohibited in Costa Rica, there was considerable smuggling of skins to Nicaragua (for later legal export) in the early 1970s, when the hunter price for a dried skin was about $200. But recently, some former hunters told Mrs. Hagnauer of La Pacifica Zoo that they had quit the trade (uneconomic? risky?). Sport hunting of jaguars is still permitted under license (true in 1978), but it has essentially ceased because of lack of skilled guides and trained dogs, and the fact that spotted cat trophies cannot be imported to the United States.

The main threat to the remaining jaguars in Central America is the clearing of forest for crops and grazing. When roads penetrate a primitive zone, the jaguar and white-lipped peccary (*Tayassu pecari*) are the first large mammals to disappear. And jaguars seem to be poor colonizers of cutover lands or new areas regardless of the abundance of prey there.

In the literature, the scientific name is also given as *Leo onca* (L.), technically most valid, or the outdated *Panthera onca* for subgrouping convenience. Jaguars range from northern Mexico to northern Argentina. The puma has much greater ecological and geographic range and occurs along with jaguars throughout Costa Rica.

*

Koford, C. B. 1976. Latin American cats: Economic values and future prospects. In *The world's cats*, vol. 3, pt. 1, pp. 79–88.

Felis wiedii (Tigrillo, Caucel, Margay)

C. B. Koford

This endangered spotted cat (fig. 9.15*a*) was formerly widespread in thick woods from coastal lowlands to interior mountains. Because of the small size of its pelt, it has not been hunted as intensively as the ocelot (*F. pardalis*), yet it is now rare because much of its habitat has been cleared and replaced by banana groves and pastures. Margays shun open country and occur in forested watershed reserves, to above 3,000 m elevation, throughout Costa Rica. Their tracks are abundant in many habitats in Corcovado National Park and Santa Rosa National Park.

Adults are the size of a large house cat, weighing 3 to 5 kg, with a somewhat bushy tail well over half the length of head and body. Forefeet and hind feet are about the same size, up to 50 mm across the toes (track of a 1.2 kg immature was 35 mm wide). The larger ocelot has big forefeet and a shortish tail. As in no other Neotropical cats, the hair of the back of the head and nape slants forward in the margay and ocelot. Both have open spots outlined in black, but in the ocelot the lateral spots tend to be joined to form long bands a few centimeters wide. There are occasional black individuals. The smaller, rarer *F. tigrina* has closed spots and has been taken above 3,000 m in southern Costa Rica.

An agile climber and jumper, the margay is the most arboreal of Neotropical cats. Ocelots also climb well, and both may sleep in trees and nest in hollows. Margays probably feed on monkeys, large and small rodents, birds, lizards, and insects; occasionally they raid chicken coops. Captives may pluck birds before eating them and will eat figs. At Santa Rosa National Park, a semitame individual attacked a porcupine and was thoroughly punctured with quills in the face and neck (D. Janzen, pers. comm.).

Both the ocelot and the margay mark branches and objects with sprayed urine, which forms black deposits, and they may show their clenched teeth when nosing urine. Apparently the margay is more nocturnal and more solitary than the ocelot, which is occasionally seen in pairs and can live peaceably in captive groups. Both cats are hunted at night with shotgun and lamp, but steel foothold traps are also used.

Ocelots and margays breed poorly in captivity, but L. Hagnauer (Finca La Pacifica) has reared a number of both by careful manipulation of the timing of proximity of males and females and offspring. They are probably sexually mature at 2 years of age. Gestation takes about 12 weeks, and the usual litter is one or two young. The breeding season varies with environment; in Chiapas births occur from March to June (Alvarez del Toro 1977).

The margay ranges from Mexico to northern Argentina. In the literature it is sometimes listed under the genus *Leopardus* or included as part of *Margay tigrina*.

*

Alvarez del Toro, M. 1977. *Los mamíferos de Chiapas.*

Glossophaga soricina (Murciélago Lengualarga, Nectar Bat)

D. J. Howell

Glossophaga soricina (fig. 9.16) belongs to the subfamily Glossophaginae, a group with the misleading name nectar-feeding bats. By karyotypic and behavioral (acoustic) evidence, the subfamily seems not to be a natural one (Baker 1967; Howell 1974). Members of *Glossophaga* show closer alliance with *Phyllostomus* than with other members of the subfamily (who share important traits with *Carollia*).

These leaf-nosed bats are small (weight 8–13 g, forearm < 42 mm, wingspan averaging 275 mm) and grayish brown. The rostrum is elongate and houses a long extensible tongue (fig. 9.16) with filiform papillae at the tip. The ears are rather short and blunt, the eyes relatively large. The broad, highly cambered wings allow slow and delicate movement through dense vegetation. These bats can hover for a few moments when feeding from flowers or gleaning moths.

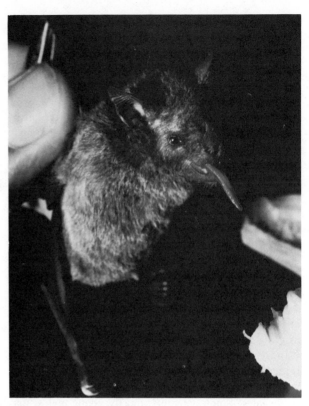

FIGURE 9.16. *Glossophaga soricina*, adult licking banana with tongue two-thirds extended. July 1980 Santa Rosa National Park, Costa Rica (L. Herbst; photo, D. H. Janzen).

In accord with its omnivorous diet, *Glossophaga* is the most generalized bat in the glossophagine subfamily: the tail and interfemoral membrane are much reduced compared with the full membranes and long tails of most insectivorous bats but are not as diminished as in other glossophagines. The teeth number thirty-four, including 2/2 well-developed incisors and 3/3 molars. More committed nectar feeders within the subfamily have fewer teeth owing to missing incisors or molars or both. The ability of *Glossophaga* to resolve small targets with sonar is better than that of its nectar-feeding relatives (Howell 1974), although sounds produced may be a hundred to a thousand times less intense than in insectivorous bats. The sounds are loosely frequency modulated and may include several harmonics (Griffin and Novick 1955). This spreading of the sound energy over a broad band, coupled with low intensity, may account for the bats' reluctance to fly during fog. At San Vito during foggy hours, glossophagine net capture markedly diminishes.

Members of *Glossophaga* are opportunistic feeders (Alvarez and Gonzales Quintero 1970; Howell 1974; Howell and Burch 1974), utilizing flowers, fruits, and insects. During the rainy season, Lepidoptera compose the bulk of the diet, which may also include fruits. Of the fruits, *Muntingia* (Elaeocarpaceae) is a favorite. *Musa* (Musaceae) and *Acnistes* (Solanaceae) are heavily fed

472

upon in cultivated stands. Many of the moths eaten may be gleaned from these fruits or from surrounding vegetation. Pollen is a minor dietary item during rainy months, though *Crescentia* (Bignoniaceae) is taken where available. During the profuse bloom of chiropterophilous plants in the dry season (especially February and March), *Glossophaga* may rely primarily on nectar and pollen. Legumes like *Inga* and *Hymenaea* and a variety of white- or purple-flowered bombacaceous trees are visited. *Glossophaga* does not eat anthers; while the bats drink nectar, pollen adheres to the general body surface. Glossophagine hairs possess a specialized divaricate scale structure that aids in pollen collection (Howell and Hodgkin 1976). Much of this pollen is groomed from the fur and ingested.

G. soricina have a preference for tropical dry habitats (Holdridge et al. 1971), disturbed sites, and dry stream beds. These areas are richest in chiropterophilous trees; bat-pollinated species are often among the dominants (Howell 1982). Mean recapture distance of six bats from ninety-six banded in one study was 358 m (Fleming, Hooper, and Wilson 1972). Compared with the ranges of several other phyllostomids (frugivores), this figure suggests a relatively large home range.

Where these bats occur in wet forests (e.g., La Selva) they may trapline (Fleming, Hooper, and Wilson 1972), making individual or group visits to a regular pattern of flowers or trees. This behavior may depend on abundance and distribution of food, since they seem not to trapline in dry forest (La Pacifica) (Baker, Cruden, and Baker 1971).

Being small and usually homeothermic, *Glossophaga* has a high resting metabolism. Like hummingbirds, glossophagines exhibit flight metabolism 10–14 × standard metabolic rate (Howell 1979). By Thomas's (1975) power equation $P = 58.4 \ m^{-0.21}$, *Glossophaga soricina* flight should cost about 1.54 watts or 1.32 kcal/bat/h. Such high-activity metabolism suggests that research relating energetics to foraging style might be fruitful.

Although most tropical bats do not enter deep torpor as do many temperate bats, *Glossophaga soricina* may, in certain circumstances, lower its normal resting body temperature (approximately 37° C) by a few degrees. At body temperatures of 34.9° C they exhibit the slow movement and inability to fly that characterize torpor. Rasweiler (1973) found this phenomenon in the laboratory during a heating failure and also when bats were sealed in their cave for 24 h and thus deprived of food. Even this slight degree of facultative heterothermy would save substantial energy, but to what degree it is employed in natural situations is unknown. In view of the broad diet and relatively constant yearly temperatures in tropical caves, one wonders whether *Glossophaga* ever face food

shortages or cold spells. The behavior may be useful on rainy nights and bears investigation. Specimens of *Glossophaga* I have observed over the past thirteen years in diurnal roosts are ever alert and ready to fly.

The bats are highly gregarious; clustering serves to reduce evaporative water loss for each cluster member and allows each bat to maintain a higher and less variable body temperature than that of individual bats forced to hang singly in the same microenvironment (Howell 1976). The compactness of clustering may correlate with ambient temperature or with time since last feeding.

Despite their obvious sociality, little attention has been paid to these bats' behavior. Glossophagines have a highly developed olfactory epithelium and a well-innervated vomeronasal apparatus (Jacobson's organ) (Mann 1963; Bhatnagar and Kallen 1974). This latter may function during mating and other social activities. There is only slight sexual dimorphism (Walker 1975; Villa-R. 1966), males being somewhat larger, in contrast to the usual condition in bats. Females exhibit menstruation; ovulation and mating may be biannual in Central America with birth peaks in April–June and December–February (Fleming et al. 1972). Females usually segregate into maternity colonies during these times. One young is born, feet first, in each season. It clings to its mother with recurved milk teeth, nursing for approximately 1 month before it can fly. The milk of *Glossophaga* has been reported to contain much less energy than the milk of other glossophagines (Jenness and Studier 1976). How the young bats make the transition from milk to adult food is not known.

Glossophaga, like most bats, has no specialized predators. Occasionally opportunistic hawks appear during the "dinner flight" exodus and manage to catch a few. Destruction of habitat and other activities of man (including biology) may be the most serious threat to their populations. Vertebrate ecology courses often include bat studies. Since bats constitute the main mammalian biomass of the tropics, these projects are failure-proof in the sense that specimens are always obtained. However, one study alone killed 217 *Glossophaga soricina* for studies of dietary habits. Of these, only thirty-eight bats' stomachs contained any food. Such studies are repeated almost yearly. Bats macerate their food thoroughly; from the time the bolus passes the mouth until it is reduced to feces, the taxonomically identifiable parts of the diet remain the same. Scales of Lepidoptera, sclerids of fruit pulp, and pollen grains and seeds are unaffected by digestion and pass intact. Since bats are prone to defecate upon being handled, condensed samples of the diet can be obtained without killing the animals.

The hundreds of alcohol-preserved specimens on deposit with the Universidad de Costa Rica might be used for projects, thus conserving dwindling bat populations.

473

That *Glossophaga soricina* is an important pollinator and disperser of tropical plants and that disturbed populations have so little reproductive "bounce-back" ability dictate that scientific studies extract as much information as possible from living bats and utilize any sacrificed animals to the utmost.

If specimens of *Glossophaga* are to be maintained in captivity, it is important that their diet include at least 10% protein and that it be presented in a way that prevents bats from wallowing or splashing the food on their fur. Protein inadequacy and food drying on the fur both cause fur loss, which in turn leads to thermal and osmotic stress.

*

Alvarez, T., and Gonzales Quintero, L. 1970. Análisis polinico del contenido gástrico de murciélagos Glossophaginae de Mexico. *Anal. Esc. Nac. Cienc. Biol.* 18:1–77.

Baker, H.; Cruden, R.; and Baker, I. 1971. Minor parasitism in pollination biology and its community function: The case of *Ceiba acuminata*. *Biol. Sci.* 21: 1127–29.

Baker, R. J. 1967. Karyotypes of bats of the family Phyllostomidae and their taxonomic implications. *Southwest. Nat.* 12:407–28.

Bhatnagar, K., and Kallen, F. C. 1974. Cribriform plate of ethmoid, olfactory bulb and olfactory acuity in forty species of bats. *J. Morph.* 142:71–90.

Fleming, T.; Hooper, E. T.; and Wilson, D. 1972. Three Central American bat communities: Structure, reproductive cycles and movement patterns. *Ecology* 53:555–69.

Griffin, D., and Novick, A. 1955. Acoustic orientation of Neotropical bats. *J. Exp. Biol.* 130:251–300.

Holdridge, L. R.; Grenke, W. C.; Hatheway, W. H.; Liang, T.; and Tosi, J. A., Jr. 1971. *Forest environments in tropical life zones.* New York: Pergamon Press.

Howell, D. J. 1974. Feeding and acoustic behavior in glossophagine bats. *J. Mamm.* 55:263–76.

————. 1976. Weight loss and temperature regulation in clustered versus individual *Glossophaga soricina*. *Comp. Biochem. Physiol.* 53:197–99.

————. 1979. Flock foraging in nectar-feeding bats: Advantages to the bats and to the host plants. *Am. Nat.,* in press.

Howell, D. J., and Burch, P. 1974. Food habits of some Costa Rican bats. *Rev. Biol. Trop.* 21:281–94.

Howell, D. J., and Hodgkin, R. C. 1976. Feeding adaptations in the hairs and tongues of nectar-feeding bats. *J. Morph.* 148:329–36.

Jenness, R., and Studier, E. 1976. Lactation and milk in biology of the New World family Phyllostomidae. Part 1. *Spec. Publ. Mus., Texas Tech. Univ.* 10:201–18.

Mann, G. 1963. The rhinencephalon of Chiroptera. *Invest. Zool. Chil.* 9:1–93.

Rasweiler, J. J. 1973. Care and management of the long-tongued bat, *Glossophaga soricina* (Chiroptera, Phyllostomatidae), in the laboratory with observations on estivation induced by food deprivation. *J. Mamm.* 54:391–404.

Thomas, S. 1975. Metabolism during flight in two species of bats, *Phyllostomus hastatus* and *Pteropus-gouldii*. *J. Exp. Biol.* 63:273–93.

Villa-R., B. 1966. *Los murciélagos de México.* Mexico, D. F.: Instituto de Biologia, Universidad Nacional Autonomo de México.

Walker, E. 1975. *Mammals of the world.* 3d ed., vol. 1. Baltimore: Johns Hopkins University Press.

Heteromys desmarestianus (Ratón Semiespinosa, Spiny Pocket Mouse)

T. H. Fleming

This locally common heteromyid rodent (fig. 9.17) is usually found at medium to high elevations from southern Mexico to eastern Panama but occurs near sea level along the Caribbean coast in Costa Rica and Panama and on the wet Osa Peninsula in Costa Rica. Its usual habitat is montane or tropical rain forest. It can be distinguished from sympatric Costa Rican rodents by its size, spiny pelage, and white venter but dark forelimbs.

H. desmarestianus is sexually dimorphic with adult males weighing about one-third more than females (83 g vs. 62 g). It has external, fur-lined cheek pouches and is quadrupedal. Its tail is about 20% longer than its head

FIGURE 9.17. *Heteromys desmarestianus,* an abundant seed-eating rodent of wet tropical forest. Finca La Selva, Sarapiquí District, Costa Rica (photo, T. H. Fleming).

and body length, and Eisenberg (1963) reports that it is a good climber. Like *Liomys salvini,* sexually active males have greatly enlarged scrotal testes and epididymides.

The population ecology of this spiny pocket mouse has been studied in detail at Finca La Selva by Fleming (1974a). It is primarily a granivore and eats seeds of the palms *Welfia georgii* and *Socratea durissima* as well as those of other species. Individuals also occasionally nibble on the toxic seeds of *Pentaclethra macroloba* but cannot survive on such a diet. Population density fluctuates from about ten to eighteen mice per hectare within years but is relatively stable between years. The reproductive season lasts at least 10 months, but most females and some adult males become reproductively inactive during extended dry periods (the opposite of *L. salvini*). Females produce up to five litters of 3.1 young per year; the interval between successive pregnancies is usually 2 months or longer. Females mature at an age of about 8 months, males at about 9 months. Juvenile and adult survivorship is high (annual probability of survival is greater than 20%, and some animals live at least 20–30 months).

Selected aspects of the behavior of *H. desmarestianus* have been studied by Fleming (1974b) and Fleming and Brown (1975). In social organization, this spiny pocket mouse is more tolerant of conspecifics than is *L. salvini,* and dominance relationships are less size-dependent than in its dry forest counterpart. Individual home ranges are relatively small (range, 0.08–0.20 ha) and overlap extensively within and between sexes and age classes. *H. desmarestianus* is not as intense a burrower as *L. salvini* and occasionally places its nests above ground in hollow logs. It is an intensive seed hoarder and stores seeds in or near its nest as well as in caches around its home range.

Compared with *L. salvini, H. desmarestianus* has less ability to withstand food and water deprivation (Fleming 1977). On a reduced diet of husked sunflower seeds (2% of average adult weight per day), individuals lose about 2.6% of their initial weight each day and die by the time they have lost about 20% of their weight. Food-deprived animals do not undergo torpor. Without free water, they lose weight rapidly and die after 2 or more days of deprivation.

H. desmarestianus is a "key industry" animal in the wet forest and plays a functional role similar to that of *L. salvini* in the dry tropical forest. Reflecting a different suite of abiotic and biotic selective pressures in the wet forest, its demographic, behavioral, and physiological characteristics contrast sharply with those of *L. salvini.* It is more K-selected, is socially more tolerant of conspecifics, and is less tolerant of food and water deprivation.

*

Eisenberg, J. F. 1963. The behavior of heteromyid rodents. *Univ. California Publ. Zool.* 69:1–100.

Fleming, T. H. 1974a. The population ecology of two species of Costa Rican heteromyid rodents. *Ecology* 55:493–510.

———. 1974b. Social organization in two species of Costa Rican heteromyid rodents. *J. Mamm.* 55: 543–61.

———. 1977. Response of two species of tropical heteromyid rodents to reduced food and water availability. *J. Mamm.* 58:102–6.

Fleming, T. H., and Brown, G. J. 1975. An experimental analysis of seed hoarding and burrowing behavior in two species of Costa Rican heteromyid rodents. *J. Mamm.* 56:301–15.

Liomys salvini (Ratón Semiespinosa, Guardafiesta, Spiny Pocket Mouse)

T. H. Fleming

This common heteromyid rodent (fig. 9.18) occurs in the dry tropical lowland forests of the Pacific coast of Middle America from Oaxaca, Mexico, to central Costa Rica. It also occurs extensively along the Pacific slopes of Central American mountains to altitudes of 1,200–1,500 m near San José. It can be distinguished from sympatric Costa Rican rodents by its size, spiny pelage, and white venter and forelimbs.

L. salvini is sexually dimorphic in weight. Adult males weigh about one-third more than females (51 g vs. 39 g). It has external, fur-lined cheek pouches in which it carries seeds and other food, nesting material, and sometimes small babies. It is quadrupedal (unlike its desert-dwelling relatives *Dipodomys* and *Microdipodops*), and its tail is only slightly longer than its head and body length. Eisenberg (1963) reports that *Liomys* is a clumsy climber. Sexually active males have greatly enlarged scrotal testes and epididymides.

The population ecology of this spiny pocket mouse has been studied in detail at Finca La Pacifica by Fleming (1974a). Its diet includes seeds and insects. In the dry season seeds of *Cochlospermum vitifolium* are an important part of its diet. Population density fluctuates within years owing to a seasonal reproductive cycle but is relatively stable (at two to nine mice per hectare) between years. The reproductive season (January to about mid-June) corresponds to the dry and early wet seasons. Females produce one or two litters of about 3.8 young annually; females born early in the breeding season sometimes mature quickly enough to produce one litter before the season is over. Males are sexually mature at about 6 months of age. Turnover rate in the population is relatively high, so that each year-class dominates the population for only one year. A few individuals live to be 15–18 months old.

FIGURE 9.18. *Liomys salvini,* an abundant seed-eating rodent of dry tropical forests. Finca La Pacifica, near Cañas, Guanacaste Province, Costa Rica (photo, T. H. Fleming).

Several aspects of the behavior of *L. salvini* have been studied by Fleming (1974*b*) and Fleming and Brown (1975). Regarding social organization, Eisenberg (1963) postulated that species of *Liomys* should be less social (dispersed into individual, defended home ranges) than species of the other genus of tropical heteromyids, *Heteromys*. In support of this hypothesis, pairwise encounters in a neutral arena indicate that members of the same sex are relatively intolerant, with larger individuals generally being dominant over smaller ones. In dry forest the mice occupy overlapping home ranges averaging about 0.20 ha and place their nests in burrow systems. The home ranges of young of the year tend to be separate from those of adults. Before the onset of breeding, large males tend to be surrounded by more potential mates than smaller males, and their survivorship is higher than that of other males during the breeding season.

L. salvini shares two behavioral traits with its northern relatives: it is an intense burrower and a seed hoarder. Individuals utilize, and presumably construct, several complex burrow systems in their home ranges. They cache seeds in special chambers within their burrows and also in shallow pits around their home range. Although they are primarily seed predators, they undoubtedly forget the locations of some of the seeds they hoard and thereby also function as seed dispersers.

Two aspects of the physiology of *L. salvini* have been examined: its ability to withstand food and water deprivation and its ability to undergo torpor (a trait found in many temperate heteromyids) (Fleming 1977). When their food ration is reduced to 1.7 g of husked sunflower seeds per day (0.9% of average adult weight), individuals lose weight at a daily rate of 2.6% but can easily withstand a 20% weight reduction without becoming seriously weakened. Individuals do not utilize torpor to conserve energy under a restricted food regime. When deprived of drinking water, individuals lose about 3.4% of their weight per day, but they can survive at least 1 week without free water. Their rate of weight loss on this regime is higher than that of desert-dwelling heteromyids but lower than that of desert cricetine rodents.

L. salvini is a "key industry" animal in the dry tropical forest, where it is usually the most common terrestrial small mammal. It serves as prey for a number of carnivorous mammals, birds, and snakes and in turn preys on the seeds of a variety of tropical plants as well as on larval and adult insects. Its demographic, behavioral, and physiological adaptations offer interesting contrasts with its wet-forest counterpart *Heteromys desmarestianus* and its northern desert-dwelling relatives.

An ongoing study of seed predation by *L. salvini* in Santa Rosa National Park (W. Hallwachs and D. Janzen, pers. comm.) has found considerably higher densities of *L. salvini* in the park forests in 1979 than that calculated by Fleming for La Pacifica. At these densities, this seed-specialists mouse may have a major influence on the survival of many species of seeds on the forest floor. The best-studied case so far is the fate of *Enterolobium cyclocarpum* seeds (guanacaste: Leguminosae), and this interaction is probably representative of the interactions between *Liomys* and many other species of seeds. Where *Liomys* occurs, all or almost all of artificially or naturally fallen *Enterolobium* seeds are carried off within a few nights. Laboratory feeding studies show that *Liomys* can survive for months and gain weight on a pure diet of germinating *Enterolobium* seeds, even though the seeds contain a protease inhibitor and two uncommon amino acids and are fatally toxic, unless boiled, to the other common rodent of the park, *Sigmodon hispidus*. A pure diet of the very hard, dry, and ungerminated seeds (with drinking water) is not as healthful, however; two of nine *Liomys* on this diet died within the first 4 days. The survivors lost weight at the beginning of the diet and had not regained all of it even after 30 days. However, the mouse has some behavioral control over the quality of its diet. By cutting notches through the seed coats with their incisors, individuals of *Liomys* on the hard-seed diet scarify a number of seeds in addition to the ones they eat. These seeds soften and readily germinate into better-quality food on the moist soil in *Liomys* burrows during the rainy season. The survival of *Enterolobium* seeds in *Liomys* habitats may depend very much on the mouse's behavior after seed caching and on the depth of the storage chambers in natural *Liomys* burrows.

*

Eisenberg, J. F. 1963. The behavior of heteromyid rodents. *Univ. California Publ. Zool.* 69:1–100.

Fleming, T. H. 1974*a*. The population ecology of two species of Costa Rican heteromyid rodents. *Ecology* 55:493–510.

———. 1974*b*. Social organization in two species of Costa Rican heteromyid rodents. *J. Mamm.* 55:543–61.

———. 1977. Response of two species of tropical heteromyid rodents to reduced food and water availability. *J. Mamm.* 58:102–6.

Fleming, T. H., and Brown, G. J. 1975 An experimental analysis of seed hoarding and burrowing behavior in two species of Costa Rican heteromyid rodents. *J. Mamm.* 56:301–15.

Myotis nigricans (Murciélago Pardo, Black Myotis)

D. E. Wilson

The genus *Myotis* (family Vespertilionidae) contains about eighty species, six of which are known from Costa Rica. The general appearance of *M. nigricans* is much like that of other small New World species of the genus. The length of head and body is 40–50 mm; tail, 35–45; and forearm, 30–40; weight is 3–5 g. The color varies from bone brown to cinnamon above, and pale to dark brown below. The fur on the back is somewhat silky, not woolly, and is usually 4–5 mm long.

In general, the distribution corresponds to the entire Neotropical region, from the southern edge of the Mexican plateau to just below the Tropic of Capricorn. Known elevational range is from sea level to 3,150 m. The species occurs in virtually every tropical and sub-tropical forest association, as well as in areas of savanna and scrub. There is no fossil record.

These bats roost most commonly in the attics of buildings and in hollow trees. Studies on thermoregulation revealed that body temperatures vary directly with ambient temperatures from 2.8° to 28.3° C, with body temperatures 0.9° to 5.3° above ambient temperatures. The bats exhibit torpor when cooled and recover upon warming. Pregnant females show no evidence of homeothermy (Studier and Wilson 1971).

Myotis nigricans has a unique reproductive cycle (Wilson and Findley 1970; Myers 1977). In Panama, under a seasonal regime comparable to that in many parts of Costa Rica, fertilization and implantation occur in late December and early January. The gestation period is approximately 60 days, and the first parturition peak occurs in February. This is followed by postpartum estrus and repetitions of the cycle resulting in birth peaks in April–May and in August. The third peak is followed by a period of declining reproductive activity until late December, when a new annual cycle begins. This cycle seems to be correlated with a seasonal food supply (insects) such that no young bats are weaned during the dry season (January–March) when insects are relatively scarce. The first birth peak results in a maximum number of young bats being weaned in April, coinciding with the onset of the rainy season and the concomitant insect bloom. Copulation ceases in September and resumes in December.

Males undergo a spermatogenic cycle similar to the female cycle outlined above. Spermatogenesis slows or stops during September, October, and November, and no sperm storage occurs. However, individuals of *M. nigricans* from Mexico more closely resemble temperate-zone bats in their reproductive condition at certain times of the year (Wilson and Findley 1971).

Young remain attached to their mothers for the first 2 or 3 days, then are left behind in large groups when the mothers go to feed at night. Mothers seek out their own young, either by smell or by sound, upon returning to the roost. Mortality rates are high for young bats owing to predation, diseases, and parasitism. Adult weight is reached by week 2 after birth, and flight begins in week 3, though young are not proficient flyers until week 4 or 5. Adult proportions and measurements are gained by week 5 or 6; molt to adult pelage and fusion of epiphyses of the long bones to the diaphyses occurs between weeks 8 and 13, rendering the young externally indistinguishable from adults. Weaning occurs at about week 5 or 6, and dispersal from the roost comes at any time thereafter (Wilson 1971). Males become reproductively active at weeks 15–17, and females probably somewhat later. Some individuals of *M. nigricans* are known to live for at least 7 years in the wild (Wilson and Tyson 1970).

In a colony of one thousand individuals living in an attic on Barro Colorado Island, adult females outnumbered males by two to one, possibly owing to differential dispersal. Numerous outlying roosts of subadult males suggested territoriality of a sort, with new roosts formed by males, who in turn attract females.

Predators may include a variety of mammals (opossums, cats, other bats) snakes, and arthropods (cockroaches, spiders). Homing studies (Wilson and Findley 1972) demonstrated that some individuals of *M. nigricans* were capable of returning to the roost from 50 km within 2 days. The results suggested that they were familiar with an area having a radius of about 13 km.

Myotis nigricans is an aerial insectivore, and lepidopteran scales have been found in fecal samples. Alberto Cadena found plant remains in the stomach of a specimen from Costa Rica (pers. comm.), but no other incidence of noninsect food has been found.

In general these bats become active at sunset, and all individuals that can fly leave the roost within an hour of sunset, except during heavy rains. They return to the roost during the hour before sunrise, and some use the same general area, if not the exact spot, of the roost day after day. They remain lethargic until midmorning, when the roost begins to warm. In Panama they responded to high midday roost temperatures by moving down the walls to the floor and splitting the original tight clusters into small groups and solitary individuals. They cannot survive temperatures above 42° C for more than 2 h. *Myotis nigricans* tends to roost in large clusters composed of females and young, with the males separate and solitary. The presence of a few adult males in the clusters suggests a social hierarchy of some sort such as harem formation.

*

LaVal, R. K. 1973. A revision of the Neotropical bats of the genus *Myotis*. *Nat. Hist. Mus. Los Angeles County Sci. Bull.* 15:1–54.

Mares, M. A., and Wilson, D. E. 1971. Bat reproduction during the Costa Rican dry season. *BioScience* 21: 471–77.

Myers, P. 1977. Patterns of reproduction of four species of vespertilionid bats in Paraguay. *Univ. California Publ. Zool.* 107:1–41.

Studier, E. H., and Wilson, D. E. 1971. Thermoregulation in some Neotropical bats. *Comp. Biochem. Physiol.* 34:251–62.

Wilson, D. E. 1971. Ecology of *Myotis nigricans* (Mammalia: Chiroptera) on Barro Colorado Island, Panama Canal Zone. *J. Zool.* 163:1–13.

Wilson, D. E., and Findley, J. S. 1970. Reproductive cycle of a Neotropical insectivorous bat, *Myotis nigricans*. *Nature* 225:1155.

———. 1971. Spermatogenesis in some Neotropical species of *Myotis*. *J. Mamm.* 52:420–26.

———. 1972. Randomness in bat homing. *Am. Nat.* 106:418–24.

Wilson, D. E., and LaVal, R. K. 1974. *Myotis nigricans*. *Mamm. Species* no. 39:1–3.

Wilson, D. E., and Tyson, E. L. 1970. Longevity records for *Artibeus jamaicensis* and *Myotis nigricans*. *J. Mamm.* 51:203.

Nasua narica (Pizote, Coati)

J. H. Kaufmann

The most diurnal and social member of the raccoon family (Procyonidae), the coati (fig. 9.19) is flexible and opportunistic in its behavior and inhabits a wide geographic and ecological range (Kaufmann 1962). *Nasua narica* breeds from southeastern Arizona and southwestern New Mexico (Kaufmann, Lanning, and Poole 1976) south through Panama. *Nasua nasua* occupies South America from Colombia to Argentina, and the smaller *Nasua* (or *Nasuella*) *olivacea* is a rare denizen of the high Andes in Venezuela, Colombia, and Ecuador. Within its range the coati occupies every wooded habitat from temperate oak and pine forests up to 3,000 m to lowland tropical rain forests, and it occasionally ranges into deserts and savannas.

A slender, faintly ringed tail as long as the body, often carried erect, and a mobile snout that extends well beyond the lower jaw are the coati's most conspicuous features. Adult males weigh about 6 kg, with a total length of 1,100 to 1,200 mm and a tail of 500 to 600 mm. Females are about 10% smaller. The coat color ranges from dark brown to reddish and even yellowish. Light-tipped guard hairs form a pale wash over the shoulders, and the tip of the snout and broken eye-rings are whitish. Color is independent of sex or age and may change in the same individual from molt to molt. At home both on the ground and at the top of the tallest trees, coatis have

FIGURE 9.19. *Nasua narica*, adult. Panama (photo, J. H. Kaufmann).

strong claws on the toes of their plantigrade feet. Sharper and more curved than the foreclaws, the rear claws are used more in climbing. Coatis descend tree trunks headfirst like squirrels, make tree-to-tree crossings on slender limbs 30 m or more above the ground, and sometimes walk upside down suspended below lianas. The tail is not prehensile but serves well as a balancing rod.

Coatis are truly omnivorous, eating a wide variety of whatever fruits and animals are seasonally abundant in their locality. In tropical forests they feed primarily on forest litter invertebrates most of the year, but they switch mainly to fruit when certain trees such as almendro (*Dipteryx*), fig (*Ficus*), and hogplum (*Spondias*) produce large crops. They also catch a few vertebrates, mostly lizards and mice, and Smythe (1970) suggested that the larger males may specialize more on vertebrate prey. Most of the coati's invertebrate prey—insects, spiders, millipedes, snails—is taken from low vegetation, found by nosing through the leaf litter, or obtained from small pits dug with the forepaws. The strong, blunt foreclaws are used to rip apart rotten logs and stumps and to dig lizards and tarantulas from burrows up to 1 m deep. Most food is located through the extremely sensitive olfactory sense.

Primarily diurnal, coatis in undisturbed tropical habitats retire for the night to one of several roost trees and descend again at dawn to begin the day's foraging. In Arizona they use rocky ledges and dens. In populated areas of tropical America where they are hunted for food by humans, coatis have become more nocturnal.

Confusion over the coati's social organization is reflected in the names given to them by both aborigines and scientists. "Coati" is derived from the Tupian Indian dialect of South America and refers to the species generally. "Coati-mundi" refers specifically to solitary coatis but has been generally misused in English to refer to all coatis. Solitary and social coatis were originally named as separate species (*N. solitaria* and *N. sociabilis*) in South America, and many of the common names still used in tropical America perpetuate the confusion.

We now know that adult males are solitary, whereas females and males less than 2 years old live in bands. These loosely organized bands, with from about four to twenty members each, are based on the family unit of a female and her young of the previous two years. A typical band includes several such units, plus perhaps a nonbreeding female or two. There is no apparent dominance order, except that the juveniles, because of the active support of their mothers, often dominate adults and subadults. Mutual grooming among band members is common, but there is little other cooperation, and active competition for food is the rule. Isolated observations of food sharing, apparent leadership, nest sharing (James

Russell, pers. comm.), and possible altruism during an attack by a predator (Janzen 1970) have been reported from the field. Smith (1977) described an instance of a captive female, who had eaten her own litter a month earlier, helping to care for another female's litter. It is believed that all or most of the females in a band are probably related, making coatis an excellent species in which to study possible kin selection. This would require a longitudinal study of marked individuals for many years so that the genetic relationships among all members of a band are known.

Males voluntarily leave the bands when they become sexually mature. Mutual hostility usually marks encounters between solitary males, but actual fights are rare except in the mating period. Members of bands usually drive off adult males when they meet, but meetings between bands are more amicable.

Coatis have a single annual breeding season. On Barro Colorado Island in Panama the mating period lasts for about 1 month early in the dry season (January or February). At this time one adult male joins each band and stays with it during the entire mating period. He is completely subordinate to the females in the band. He grooms with them and sleeps in the same roost tree on most nights; copulation takes place in the trees, chiefly at night. Other solitary males, mostly younger ones without bands of their own, often approach the bands of estrous females, but they are usually resisted by the females and are attacked and driven off by the adult male accompanying the band.

The gestation period is 10 to 11 weeks, and litters in Panama are born in April or May. In Arizona mating occurs in April, and the young are born in June. About a week before the young are born, the pregnant females individually leave the band and build tree nests. The young are born in the nests and stay there for about 5 weeks. During this time the mothers divide their time between caring for their young and foraging alone for their own food. The nonbreeders in the band apparently remain more or less together, although the maturing males are becoming more independent as the time when they will leave the band approaches. When the new young are able to run and climb well enough to keep up with the others, they are brought to the ground and the band reunites.

The bands have undefended, overlapping home ranges of 30 to 50 ha in tropical forests, though they may cover 200 to 300 ha in the arid canyons of the southwestern United States. Within each home range is a core area that is used constantly throughout the year; the peripheral areas of the ranges are visited only intermittently except when certain preferred fruits are available. The core areas do not overlap, and they thus qualify as "territories" according to Pitelka's definition of an area of more or less exclusive use. Adult males wander at times over a larger area than the bands but are also more inclined to localize near a particularly good food source.

Adult coatis are apparently preyed on by few animals other than man, but potential predators, especially on the young, include boas, raptors, cats, and tayras. More important in population control are such diseases as canine distemper and rabies. Population crashes have been noted in both Panama and Arizona. Grooming helps to control external parasites such as ticks, but occasionally coatis harbor botfly larvae beneath the skin. Coatis may compete for food with birds such as parrots and doves and with mammals such as armadillos, squirrels, peccaries, and monkeys.

*

Janzen, D. H. 1970. Altruism by coatis in the face of predation by *Boa constrictor. J. Mamm.* 51:387–89.

Kaufmann, J. H. 1962. Ecology and social behavior of the coati, *Nasua narica*, on Barro Colorado Island, Panama. *Univ. California Publ. Zool.* 60:95–222.

Kaufmann, J. H.; Lanning, D. V.; and Poole, S. E. 1976. Current status and distribution of the coati in the United States. *J. Mamm.* 57:621–37.

Smith, H. J. 1977. Social behavior of the coati (*Nasua narica*) in captivity. Ph.D. diss., University of Arizona.

Smythe, N. 1970. The adaptive value of the social organization of the coati (*Nasua narica*). *J. Mamm.* 51:818–20.

Noctilio leporinus (Murciélago Pescador, Fishing Bulldog Bat)

C. Brandon

The fishing bulldog bat, *Noctilio leporinus* (fig. 9.20), is found in lowland areas on mainland Central and South

FIGURE 9.20. *Noctilio leporinus* immediately after gaffing food (a grasshopper) from the water surface in the laboratory (photo, C. Brandon and S. Altenbach).

America and the Greater and Lesser Antilles. The mainland range is from about 27° north latitude to 30° south latitude. It is found in areas where it has access to open bodies of fresh or salt water where fish may be caught. This bat often roosts in hollow trees or in buildings.

Noctilio is a relatively large bat with a mass of about 60 to 90 g and a wingspan of up to 60 cm. The greatly enlarged hind feet used for gaffing fish are one of its most distinctive characteristics. The face of this bat is bulldoglike, with narrow, pointed ears and very small eyes. The dorsal surface of the body varies from dark brown to light orange with a whitish middorsal stripe. The variation is apparently due to environmental factors such as wear or ammonia bleaching in the roost. The ventral surface is generally a lighter grayish white. *Noctilio* has long, pointed wings with a high aspect ratio (about 8). This type of wing is usually seen in bats that have many internal adaptations for strong, efficient flight (such as the molossids). *Noctilio* completely lacks these internal adaptations and probably developed long wings because of the obstacle-free environment in which it forages.

The diet of *Noctilio* consists primarily of fish but also includes insects and crustaceans picked up from the water surface and insects caught in the air. The bat fishes over relatively still water (ponds, slow-moving rivers, pools, and bays) by flying close to the surface of the water in fairly straight passes with the feet occasionally dipping into the water. On some of these dips it gaffs small fish with its greatly enlarged feet. Experimental work and high-speed photography have revealed many details of the fishing process (fig. 9.20). The bats can detect very small objects breaking the water surface or the presence of a small upwelling or ripple in the water, assumed to be caused by a small fish. These clues to the presence of a fish are detected solely by the bat's acute sonar. When it detects one of these indications, the bat swings its feet into the path of the target and dips one or both feet into the water for a distance of 10 to 20 cm (occasionally 1 m). Each foot sweeps a path 3 to 4 cm wide, and if the target spotted with the sonar was a fish it is often gaffed by the large claws. The bat then transfers the fish to its mouth and usually finds a place to hang upside down and eat it before continuing to fish (a fish carried in the mouth blocks the normal path for sonar emission, making echolocation difficult). Sometimes it chews the fish and pushes it into its cheek pouches on the wing so that fishing is not interrupted.

Noctilio is easy to keep in captivity (compared with most bats). Within a day or two of capture it will spontaneously learn to eat from a dish of fish or mealworms placed in the cage. Taming is also rapid, and within a few days the bats can be held in the hand without trying to escape. Gloves should be used, however, until one is familiar with handling the bats, because of the rather large canines and powerful jaws. These bats are also easy to train for experimental work. They quickly learn to do a variety of tasks. *Noctilio* has been kept in captivity for several years.

Noctilio leporinus belongs to the family Noctilionidae, which contains one other species, *Noctilio albiventris*. *N. albiventris* is smaller than *N. leporinus*, with a mass of 30–40 g and a wingspan of about 40–45 cm. The foot is proportionally smaller than that of *N. leporinus*. *N. albiventris* feeds primarily on insects caught on the wing or from the surface of a body of water. Its dipping for insects on water is similar to the foraging of *N. leporinus*. *N. albiventris* probably fishes occasionally, and it has fished in the laboratory. Although the phylogenetic relationships of the family Noctilionidae have been in dispute, recent karyotypic studies have indicated that they are most closely related to the Mormoopidae within the Phyllostomatoidea.

*

Bloedel, P. 1955. Hunting methods of fish-eating bats, particularly *Noctilio leporinus*. *J. Mamm.* 36:390–99.

Davis, W. 1973. Geographic variation in the fishing bat, *Noctilio leporinus*. *J. Mamm.* 54:862–74.

Patton, J., and Baker, R. 1978. Chromosomal homology and the evolution of phyllostomatoid bats. *System. Zool.* 27:449–62.

Suthers, R. 1965. Acoustic orientation by fish-catching bats. *J. Exp. Zool.* 158:319–42.

Suthers, R., and Fattu, J. 1973. Fishing behaviour and acoustic orientation by the bat (*Noctilio labialis*). *Anim. Behav.* 21:61–66.

Odocoileus virginianus (Venado, Venado Cola Blanca, White-tailed Deer)

D. H. Janzen

When not hunted, white-tailed deer (Cervidae) (fig. 9.21) become common and conspicuous along forest edges in Guanacaste Province. In the 1940s, when white-tailed deer skins were in demand for fine leather, the annual Guanacaste harvest was ten to forty thousand animals, and deer meat was cheaper than beef and was standard diet for hunters' dogs (Franklin Chaves, pers. comm.). Continuous hunting pressure coupled with nearly complete elimination of forest stands in Guanacaste made the white-tailed deer rare by the late 1960s, and it is now a protected animal. Population comeback is very slow, except in Santa Rosa National Park, where the population now undoubtedly contains many hundreds of animals. At Santa Rosa, a day's walk on dry-season trails is guaranteed to yield five to fifteen deer sightings, and there are many places where one can rely on encountering a deer.

FIGURE 9.21. *Odocoileus virginianus*, adult female. Guanacaste Province, Costa Rica (photo, D. H. Janzen).

Guanacaste white-tailed deer are the same species as the white-tailed deer of the United States and Canada, and the population is continuous from Costa Rica north, in the deciduous forest lowlands (or their remnants) of the Pacific coastal plain. It appears that white-tails do not range through the rain forest of the southern Pacific lowlands of Costa Rica and into northern Panama rain forest, but I suspect that with the ever-greater clearing of the forest there will shortly be a corridor of fields and edges all the way from Quepos (Puntarenas Province) to the Boquete-David area that will be occupied by whitetails (and thereby connect the Guanacaste population with the Pacific coast of Panama). There are somewhat questionable sightings of white-tailed deer from the Atlantic lowlands of Costa Rica, but I am not confident that the observers knew how to distinguish white-tailed deer from the smaller and more red rain-forest brocket deer (*Mazama americana*). White-tailed deer occur to at least 2,200 m elevation in Costa Rica on the Pacific side (Monteverde) and undoubtedly will become members of the disturbed forest habitat from this elevation down on the Atlantic side as more forest is destroyed. *O. virginianus* ranges well into northern South America, and it may be common in grassland-forest mixes (e.g., Eisenberg, O'Connell, and August 1979).

Costa Rican whitetails appear to me to be about half to two-thirds the body weight of Minnesota–Michigan deer. A healthy male with three tines on its antlers weighed about 30 kg. The males have small antlers; even a four-tined rack weighs about one-quarter that of a four-tined Minnesota rack. I suspect that a shortage of calcium-rich food, as well as the smaller body weight of the fighting males, is responsible. Males are in velvet from December through April or even May in the Guanacaste lowlands. In Santa Rosa, small shrubs stripped of their bark by males cleaning antlers and practicing fighting are encountered in February–June. The Santa Rosa rutting season appears to fall between July and November. Shed antlers disintegrate within months, helped along by generous gnawing by small rodents. I have seen spotted small fawns in February and May–July, though by July they are nearly half the size of adults. One female at Santa Rosa was being followed by two fawns.

At Santa Rosa, white-tailed deer are browsers of dicot twigs and leaves and harvesters of fallen fruit, just as in the United States. During the first half of the rainy season they forage (among other places) along the forest-grassland interface, browsing sucker shoots and low branches. Favorite foods are the large leaf blades of *Cochlospermum vitifolium* (they conspicuously leave the leaf petioles behind) and the large compound leaves of *Spondias mombin, S. radlkoferi,* and *S. purpurea.* At Finca La Pacifica the captive deer accept a few leaves of a wide variety of native species (*Malvaviscus arboreus* being a favorite) but emphatically reject a number of species as well. In the large deer pen it is conspicuous that, no matter how hungry, the deer will not browse the leaves off the *Stemmadenia* and *Rauwolfia* (Apocynaceae) shrubs growing there. In strong contrast to tapir and peccary feces from the Santa Rosa habitat, whitetail deer feces consist of extremely finely milled material. The feces of white-tailed deer can be distinguished from those of all other Guanacaste mammals in that they constitute a cluster of twenty to fifty hard 1.5–2 cm diameter irregular spheroids scattered over a few hundred square centimeters.

Santa Rosa whitetails eat fallen acorns (*Quercus oleoides*), panamá seeds (*Sterculia apetala*), guacimo fruits (*Guazuma ulmifolia*), figs (*Ficus* spp.), and nance fruits (*Byrsonima crassifolia*). I suspect that they eat many other species of fruits as well. However, deer feces never contain seeds (except an occasional fig seed), and I suspect that they are always either ground up (e.g., the first three species listed above) or spit out when chewing cud (e.g., *B. crassifolia*).

The only study published of the diet of "tropical" white-tailed deer concerns those in La Michilía Reserve in Durango, Mexico. The vegetation is essentially that of a southwestern United States montane mixed oak-conifer forest, and the deer ate the same sorts of browse as they do in the United States (Gallina, Maury, and Serrano 1978). However, the relevant information to Guanacaste is that for the La Michilía deer the foliage of *Phoradendron, Pithecellobium,* and *Quercus* was among the most frequently eaten. This may help to explain why, for example, the two very common *Phoradendron* (parasitic shrubs in the Loranthaceae) at Santa Rosa occur only above about 2 m height on their host plants even though there are numerous apparently susceptible branches lower down.

White-tailed deer at Santa Rosa use the white tail flag just as they do in the United States. I get the impression that if a deer one is approaching thinks it has not been seen, it sneaks off with its tail held tightly down. If it thinks it has been seen, it bounds off with its tail held up as a white flag. If not pursued, it stops running after a few meters and continues to walk off, often browsing on the way. At Santa Rosa a mountain lion (*Felis concolor*) was observed to chase a newly released adult female white-tailed deer from the center of a horse pasture to the edge (about 80 m), apparently killing it just inside the tall brush at the pasture edge (1700, December 1979).

*

Eisenberg, J. F.; O'Connell, M. A.; and August, P. V. 1979. Density, productivity, and distribution of mammals in two Venezuelan habitats. In *Vertebrate ecology in the northern Neotropics,* ed. J. F. Eisenberg, pp. 187–207. Washington, D.C.: Smithsonian Institution Press.

Gallina, S.; Maury, E.; and Serrano, V. 1978. Hábitos alimenticios del venado cola blanca (*Odocoileus virginianus* Rafinesque) en la reserva La Michilía, estado de Durango. In *Reservas de la biosfera en el Estado de Durango,* ed. G. Halffter, pp. 57–108. Publication 4. Mexico, D. F.: Instituto de Ecología, A. C.

Oryzomys caliginosus (Ratón Pardo, Ratón Arrocero Pardo, Costa Rican Dusky Rice Rat)

A. L. Gardner

A medium-sized rice rat chatacterized by dark color and a tail shorter than the combined length of head and body, *Oryzomys caliginosus* (fig. 9.22) is a common rodent of the central and southern Middle American province. The

FIGURE 9.22. *Oryzomys caliginosus,* adult. La Llorona, Corcovado National Park, Osa Peninsula, Costa Rica (photo, D. H. Janzen).

species ranges from the Mosquito lowlands of Honduras southward through the Pacific lowlands of Ecuador. Usually common in disturbed forest habitats below 1,000 m along the Caribbean versant and adjacent lowlands of Costa Rica, *O. caliginosus* also occurs in appropriate habitats on the Pacific lowlands south of the Guanacaste region.

The predominately black fur contains a mixture of yellowish and red hairs, imparting a reddish hue to an otherwise dark color pattern. The dorsum and venter are essentially the same color except that the underparts of some specimens appear decidedly redder or yellower. The skin of the ears, feet, and sparsely haired tail is blackish. The scaled epidermis of the upper surface of the feet (particularly the hind feet) is visible through the hair. The tail averages shortest (43% of total length) among species of Costa Rican *Oryzomys.* The pollex bears a nail (as in other oryzomyines); digital bristles on the hind feet are weakly developed and do not extend beyond the ends of the claws.

Males and females are approximately the same size. Average external measurements (mm) of seven male and nine female adults from Costa Rica are: total length, 218 (195–237); tail, 93.5 (79–105); hind foot, 27 (25–28); ear, 16.4 (15–18). The average weight (g) of five adult males was 44 (42–68.5); that of six adult females, 55.5 (46–72). The lightest adult female (46 g) was neither lactating nor pregnant; the other females showed evidence of reproductive activity.

Little is known about reproduction in *O. caliginosus.* Fleming (1970) reported pregnant or lactating females in May, July, August, and November from an Atlantic lowland forest site in Panama. Finding nonreproductive females in Janauary, March, and April prompted him to suggest that *O. caliginosus* might give birth during the wet season instead of the dry season. However, my field notes and information on specimen labels of animals from eastern Costa Rica and Panama indicate pregnant or lactating females in February, March, and August. Adult females noted to be in nonreproductive condition were recorded in January, March, and April.

Goodwin's (1946) rather general statement on reproduction for all *Oryzomys* (p. 399), "From three to seven young are produced at birth, four or five being the usual number. There is no definite breeding season" was repeated by Asdell (1964) as specific for *O. caliginosus.* Nevertheless, the embryo count in eleven pregnant *O. caliginosus* from the Caribbean lowlands of Costa Rica and Panama averaged 3.5. (median = 4; range, 1–6). One of these from Costa Rica was both pregnant and lactating when captured, indicating postpartum estrus. Length of gestation is unknown.

The testes of an adult male caught in August each

measured 7 by 12 mm. The epididymides were swollen, indicating reproductive activity.

The diet of *O. caliginosus* in the field is unknown. The few stomachs I have examined contained white, finely chewed plant material mixed with a few insects.

An ongoing study on *O. caliginosus* from Corcovado National Park (W. Hallwachs, pers. comm.) found in laboratory feeding that two adult specimens of *O. caliginosus* were the most eager and thorough insect eaters of the four species compared (*O. caliginosus, O. palustris, Sigmodon hispidus, Liomys salvini*). One specimen of *O. caliginosus* ate 105 bruchid beetles (*Caryedes brasiliensis*) in the 3-h period. This was 11% of the animal's 47-g body weight. The same animal consumed most of a 4-g cicada and a 2-g dung beetle (*Dichotomius colonicus*) in one meal. Insects were eagerly eaten any time of day or night. Of the seeds and fruits offered, *O. caliginosus* avoided or ate little of those known or suspected to be rich in toxic secondary compounds (especially legume seeds) and readily ate those fruit and seed parts highly edible to humans (e.g., fruit pulp and seeds of *Ficus* spp., *Terminalia catappa, Passiflora foetida,* and fruit pulp of *Hymenaea courbaril*). Though the specimens were healthy and powerful adults, they showed no inclination to chew through hard nuts or even to extract *Terminalia catappa* seeds from fractured nut cases. On the other hand, they would chase down and quickly catch even the most agile butterflies and moths released into their cage.

Live-trapping results at Cariari, Costa Rica (ca. 100 m), during 1966–67 indicated that *O. caliginosus* occupies a variety of agricultural and disturbed-forest habitats. The topography in the vicinity of Cariari is of low releif; the region is a broad alluvial plain cut by numerous streams and the Río Tortuguero. Overgrown cornfields and abandoned banana groves yielded the highest numbers and forest habitats the lowest. *Oryzomys caliginosus* was the second most common rodent encountered (37 of 140 terrestrial rodents caught) and was exceeded only by *Heteromys desmarestianus* (73 of 140). Associated rodents trapped were *Oryzomys bombycinus* (4), Oryzomys (*Sigmodontomys*) *alfari* (5), *Proechimys semispinosus* (12), *Hoplomys gymnurus* (7), and *Rattus rattus* (2).

Rodents caught in the vicinity of Pacuare, Costa Rica (ca. 400 m), were *Oryzomys caliginosus* (8), *Oryzomys alfari* (1), *Heteromys desmarestianus* (6), and *Peromyscus nudipes* (10). Pacuare is in a river valley that has steep rocky slopes rising about 500 m above the river terraces. All but one specimen of *O. caliginosus* (caught in a riverside cane thicket) were taken in overgrown pastures and in brushy, vine-covered vegetation at the bottom of the slopes.

Nest sites are likely to be in leaves and other debris associated with logs, buttresses of large trees, and the bases of matas of bananas.

Oryzomys caliginosus is microtine or akodont in form. The species so closely resembles *Akodon aerosus* of South America that the two are often misidentified in the field. Small dark-colored rodents (e.g., species of *Akodon* and *Scotinomys*) tend to be behaviorly similar in that they live in habitats where the lower vegetation and ground cover are comparatively dense, have insectivorous habits, and are at least partially diurnal. *Oryzomys caliginosus* seems to fit each of these categories; some of the specimens from Cariari were caught during the day.

KEY TO COSTA RICAN SPECIES OF *ORYZOMYS* (BASED ON EXTERNAL CHARACTERS)

1. Hind foot without prominent digital bristles; generally occurring below 1,000 m 2
   2. Tail shorter than head and body; color blackish; body size medium to small; hind foot less than 29 mm . . . . *O. Caliginosus*
   2′. Tail equal to or longer than head and body; color reddish to yellowish brown; body medium-sized to large; hind foot greater than 29 mm 3
      3. Pelage color yellowish to buffy brown; hind foot narrow, white above; tail equal to length of head and body (includes *O. cousei*). . . . .*O. palustris*
      3′. Pelage color darker, usually reddish brown; hind foot broad, brown above; tail longer than head and body (known in the literature as *Nectomys alfari*) . . . . *O. alfari*
1′. Hind foot with conspicuous digital bristles (often extending beyond claws); occurring from sea level to páramo 4
   4. Hind foot short and broad; plantar tubercles pale and large; ears clothed externally with tawny hairs not contrasting with color of head . . . .*O. concolor*
   4′. Hind foot long and narrow; plantar tubercles dark and small; ears clothed externally with blackish hairs contrasting with color of head 5
      5. Body size large; hind foot 33 mm or longer; occurring above 1,200 m. 6
         6. Hind foot less than 40 mm and clothed above with whitish to pale brown hairs; occurring from Volcán Irazú through the Cordillera Talamanca into western Panama (also known in the literature as *O. albigularis*) . . . .*O. devius*
         6′. Hind foot 40 mm and clothed above with dark brown hairs; known only from type locality (San Joaquin de Dota) . . . . *O. aphrastus*
      5′. Body medium-sized to small; hind foot shorter than 33 mm 7

7. Supraorbital vibrissae long (usually over 45 mm) .... *O. bombycinus*
7'. Supraorbital vibrissae shorter (less than 40 mm) 8
8. Pelage conspicuously short and crisp .... *O. alfaroi.*
8'. Pelage long and lax 9
9. Body small (approximately house-mouse size); tail longer than head and body; hind foot shorter than 23 mm .... *O. fulvescens*
9'. Body medium-sized; tail approximately equal to length of head and body; hind foot longer than 28 mm .... *O. talamancae*

*

Asdell, S. A. 1964. *Patterns of mammalian reproduction,* 2d ed. Ithaca, N.Y.: Comstock.

Fleming, T. H. 1970. Notes on the rodent faunas of two Panamanian forests. *J. Mamm.* 51:473–90.

Godwin, G. G. 1946. Mammals of Costa Rica. *Bull. Am. Mus. Nat. Hist.* 87:275–458.

Procyon lotor (Mapache, Raccoon)

G. C. Sanderson

The raccoon (*Procyon lotor*) (fig. 9.23) ranges across the North American continent, except in parts of the Rocky Mountains, from well into Canada to as far south as Panama. The Costa Rican raccoon (*P. l. crassidens* Hollister) is also found in Nicaragua, Salvador, and perhaps Honduras and western Panama. The isthmian raccoon (*P. l. pumilus* Miller) is the race found in most of Panama (Goldman 1950, p. 70). The southern distribution of this form is in doubt.

Both Goldman (1950, p. 24) and Hall and Kelson (1959, p. 885) list seven species and twenty-five sub-

FIGURE 9.23. *Procyon lotor,* subadult foraging in stream. Hacienda Palo Verde, Guanacaste Province, Costa Rica (photo, D. H. Janzen).

species, all in the *P. lotor* group, in the subgenus *Procyon* and one (crab-eating raccoon) in the subgenus *Euprocyon.* However, Koopman, Hecht, and Ledecky-Janeck (1957) and McKinley (1959) indicate that the Bahama raccoon (*P. maynardi*) found on New Providence Island probably resulted from introductions of the mainland form (*P. lotor*). Koopman, Hecht, and Ledecky-Janeck (1957, p. 164) consider the Bahama raccoon as *P. l. maynardi.* One wonders if further study may change the status from species to subspecies of the other named island species in the Subgenus *Procyon* recognized by Goldman (1950) and Hall and Kelson (1959).

In North America, raccoon populations had declined to low levels by the 1930s. A continentwide population explosion began with the 1943 breeding season (Sanderson 1951a,b; Keefe 1953). The rapid increase in numbers continued into the late 1940s, and high population levels have been maintained since that time. It is conservatively estimated that there are fifteen to twenty times as many raccoons today as there were in the 1930s. With the increase in numbers, raccoons extended their ranges to include areas where they were absent or rare during the 1930s: for example, sandy prairies in Illinois, desert areas, and coastal marshes. In addition, they extended their range many miles to the north in Canada (Sowls 1949; Mann and Gunn 1956). The raccoon is at present reported so far north in Canada that native Indians have no name for it.

In Costa Rica raccoons are very common in the habitats immediately behind the beaches of both coasts and are occasionally encountered near lowland rivers and marshes well in from the sea. In marine areas they join with the other vertebrates to raid sea turtle nests for eggs.

The black face mask and the ringed tail are typical of the raccoon (*P. lotor*), and these two characteristics are even shared with the crab-eating raccoon (*P. cancrivorus*). The ranges of these two species overlap in Panama and in southern Costa Rica. The two species can be readily distinguished by the usual backward direction of the fur on the nape of *P. lotor,* whereas the hair on the nape of the crab-eating raccoon grows forward. Underfur is absent in the crab-eating raccoon, and the thighs and forearms are black. The Costa Rican raccoon has underfur and grayish forearms and thighs. The patterns of the mask and ringed tail are visible even in pale brown and partially albino raccoons.

Both forms typically have six mammae, but eight have been observed. The mammae of *P. lotor* remain tiny and unpigmented and difficult to locate in the underfur until the female ovulates (Sanderson and Nalbandov 1973). After ovulation the mammae enlarge and do not return to the virgin state. Mammae of raccoons that have ovulated may be unpigmented, slightly pigmented, or solid black, and they vary considerably in length among individuals.

The reasons for these variations are not known, but they are not related to whether the female has been psuedo-pregnant or pregnant or whether she has nursed young.

Raccoons in the northern states in Canada have dense underfur and long guard hairs. Typically the guard hairs become shorter and the underfur less dense in raccoons found to the south. Pelts from raccoons taken in the southern states are known in the fur trade as "hair" pelts. Raccoons taken farther north tend to be darker than the paler raccoons found in southern coastal areas and in the desert. However, Goldman (1950, p. 69) says of the Costa Rican raccoon, "One of the darkest known forms of the group."

Northern raccoons also typically weigh more the farther north they are taken. During twenty-three hunting and trapping seasons (November–January of 1955–56 through 1977–78) I weighed nearly 10,500 raccoons from west-central Illinois. Adult males averaged 16.3 lb, parous females, 14 lb, and all raccoons, 12.3 lb. Among these raccoons, the heaviest individuals were two adult males that weighed 26.5 lb each. The average body lengths of raccoons from this area were 623 mm for adult males, 591 mm for parous females, and 576 mm for all raccoons. No weights were found for Costa Rican raccoons; however, Goldman (1950, p. 70) reports body lengths for two adult males of this race from Nicaragua at 630 and 640 mm. Adult males of these body lengths would average about 16.5 lb during the hunting and trapping season in west-central Illinois. It is doubtful if the two Nicaraguan raccoons weighed this much, because the Illinois raccoons would typically have 5–6 lb of fat at this season; a condition probably not found in the Nicaraguan raccoons. In Alabama, Johnson (1970, p. 31) reported that 277 adult males averaged 9.5 lb and 174 adult females, 8.1 lb. The largest raccoon he reported was an adult male weighing 19.4 lb.

Raccoons do not hibernate, but during cold periods in the northern states they remain in their dens for several days at a time. During these periods they seem to need water more than food and may come out of the den to eat snow or lick ice. During periods of extreme cold, raccoons of all sexes and ages often den together. It is not unusual to find from three to a dozen or more raccoons denned together in a large tree den. Groups numbering in the twenties and thirties have been found denned together in barns and other buildings. The larger groups consist of all sexes and ages, but the groups of three to five are usually a female and her young.

Raccoons have a keen sense of hearing. The sense of sight is perhaps less well developed than the sense of hearing, and the sense of smell is not as keen as hearing and sight. The raccoon's sense of touch is highly developed; the animal often searches for food in water, then eats what it captures without looking at it or without obviously smelling it.

Observations indicate that raccoons have backup systems in reserve when one system fails. In Missouri I once caught an adult male raccoon with both front legs off just below the elbows. This animal was in a tree den about 5 m off the ground in midwinter. Although he was not as fat as the average adult male in the same area, he was in reasonably good condition. I examined a young-of-the-year raccoon, which had been blind from birth, that was brought into an Iowa furhouse in December. Again, this animal was not excessively fat (young-of-the-year raccoons usually have less body fat than adult males and nulliparous females), but it was in fair condition.

The one thing that most people "know" about the raccoons is wrong. This "known fact" is that they always wash their food. Not true! I have not observed wild raccoons "washing" their food before eating it, although a tame raccoon allowed to capture wild animals for food will sometimes "wash" them before eating. "Washing" is a trait of captive raccoons, but many captives pick food from the feeding dish and place it directly in the mouth with no intermediate steps. Even those captives that apparently wash their food are in fact feeling it. Perhaps dipping something (food or an unfamiliar item such as a nail or marble) in water makes the palms of the raccoon's "hands" more sensitive. In any case, captive raccoons often "wash" unfamiliar items without benefit of water. Studied have shown highly developed nerves in the hands of the raccoon.

J. H. Kaufmann (pers. comm.) offers the following comments on "washing" of food by raccoons: "The raccoon's Latin name 'lotor' means 'the washer' and refers to its familiar habit of dousing food in water before eating it. A critical evaluation of the evidence, however, reveals that only captives douse their food, and that this behavior has nothing to do with cleanliness or moistening the food (Lyall-Watson 1963). Clean foods and dirty, wet and dry, are all doused with equal frequency. Dabbling is the fixed motor pattern used in searching for aquatic prey in the wild, and washing food is simply a substitute for this normal behavior which has no other outlet in captivity. G. Ewer has even suggested that raccoons may enjoy their monotonous captive diet more if they go through the motions of catching it first."

Although a carnivore by classification, the raccoon is perhaps the most omnivorous animal in North America by choice of food. The raccoon's love for sweet corn in the "milk" stage is well known; however, throughout the corn belt, corn is the number one food of raccoons during the fall and winter. Raccoons are also fond of crayfish, fish, mussels, earthworms, insects (both larvae and adults), birds and birds' eggs, small mammals, wild grapes, persimmons, pokeberries, acorns, and most other wild fruits and nuts. In fact, raccoons will feed on most any animal matter, either fresh or carrion, and most fruits and seeds. They seldom eat uncooked fruits that are highly acid (such as tomatoes and citrus fruits) and do not usually feed on uncooked carrots, potatoes, and similar root crops.

Along seacoasts raccoons feed on crabs and a wide variety of other marine organisms, and, although they are usually nocturnal, along the seacoast raccoons come out to feed when the tide is out regardless of the time. Although most raccoons live near water, in sandy areas in Illinois they may live a mile or more from water. In Florida raccoons lick dew or dig shallow wells in the sand to get rainwater that is lying on top of the heavier salt water when no other fresh water is available.

In Costa Rica the raccoons probably follow the same feeding patterns as raccoons in other areas; those along the seacoast feed on marine organisms, and those away from the seacoast feed on animals they can catch or find dead and on most available edible fruits and seeds.

In captivity raccoons do well for extended periods on a diet of dry dog food. "Checkers" or pellets are preferable to meal because less food is wasted. A number of individuals who have given me pet raccoons reported that their animals would eat only graham crackers, marshmallows, ice cream, scrambled eggs, or some other single food item. By the third day all raccoons in my cages were eating dry dog food.

As with other aspects of the biology of the raccoon, little or nothing is published about the reproduction of the Costa Rican raccoon. Sanderson and Nalbandov (1973) provide a detailed report on reproduction of the raccoon in Illinois. Most adult male raccoons in Illinois are sexually active from about October through May. Most, but not all, juvenile males become sexually active 2–3 months later than the adults. Although males may be found with sperm during all months, a single individual was never found to be sexually active throughout the year. In central Illinois most mating occurs during mid-February, and most young are born in mid-April. The gestation period is 63 days.

Johnson (1970, p. 43) reports that the mean conception date in Alabama is 17 April and the mean birth date for litters is 18 June—about 2 months later than in Illinois. Johnson (1970, p. 45) found fetuses from May through August, and from weights of eye lenses he estimated birth dates to range from March through September. If young nurse as long in the south as they do in the north and remain with their mothers as they do in the north, there is not enough time for a female to rear two litters in one year.

Female raccoons are spontaneous ovulators and always undergo pregnancy or pseudopregnancy after ovulation. Pseudopregnancy lasts approximately as long as pregnancy in the raccoon. After ovulation, mammae in females enlarge and may become pigmented. Mammae do not return to the preovulatory condition. In the central United States and to the north, females rear only one litter each year. If, however, a female is only pseudopregnant or loses her first litter at or near birth, she may ovulate a second time (and may become pregnant) in the same year. By the time these second matings occur, most adult males are no longer sexually active. Thus, yearling males probably sire most second litters. In Illinois about half of the yearling females breed. If a yearling female does not breed at about the same time as the adult females, she does not mate until her second year. Thus nulliparous (as determined by preovulatory mammae) adult females killed during the hunting and trapping season in Illinois are animals that failed to ovulate as yearlings.

Captive females that become pseudopregnant often undergo extreme changes in behavior. A gentle pet may become a vicious animal impossible to handle without special equipment.

Litter sizes in Illinois range from one to seven and average 3.5. Other studies have shown average litter sizes of 2.4 in Maryland, 1.9 in coastal North Carolina, 5.0 in New York, and 2.6 in Alabama. At birth young raccoons are blind and have little fur, and the face mask and rings on the tail are barely visible as pigment on the skin. Young raccoons, called cubs, open their eyes at 18–23 days of age. If the female moves the young, she carries them individually by the nape of the neck as a cat does. The young depend exclusively on milk for about 10 weeks, at which time they leave the den and begin to travel with their mother. The young are weaned by about the 15th or 16th week but usually travel with the female and den with her until the breeding season the next spring (Sanderson 1970).

*

Goldman, E. A. 1950. Raccoons of North and Middle America. *North American Fauna* no. 60.

Hall, E. R., and Kelson, K. R. 1959. *The mammals of North America*. Vol. 2. New York: Ronald Press.

Johnson, A. S. 1970. Biology of the raccoon (*Procyon lotor varius*) Nelson and Goldman in Alabama. *Auburn Univ. Agric. Exp. Sta. Bull.* no. 402.

Keefe, J. 1953. Knee deep in coons. *Missouri Conserv.* 14:10–11.

Koopman, K. F.; Hecht, M. K.; and Ledecky-Janeck, E. 1957. Notes on the mammals of the Bahamas with special reference to the bats. *J. Mamm.* 38:164–74.

Lyall-Watson, M. 1963. A critical re-examination of food "washing" in the raccoon (*Procyon lotor* Linn.). *Proc. Zool. Soc. London* 141:371–93.

McKinley, D. 1959. Historical note on the Bahama raccoon. *J. Mamm.* 40:248–49.

Mann, S. A., and Gunn, J. 1956. Raccoons in Saskatchewan. *Blue Jay* 14:27.

Sanderson, G. C. 1951a. Breeding habits and a history of the Missouri raccoon population from 1941 to 1948. *North American Wildl. Conf. Trans.* 16:445–60.

———. 1951b. The status of the raccoon in Iowa for the past twenty years as revealed by fur reports. *Iowa Acad. Sci.* 58:527–31.

————. 1970. The raccoon. In *Alive in the wild,* ed. Victor H. Cahalane, pp. 92–97. Englewood Cliffs, N.J.: Prentice-Hall.

Sanderson, G. C., and Nalbandov, A. V. 1973. The reproductive cycle of the raccoon in Illinois. *Illinois Nat. Hist. Surv. Bull.* 31:29–85.

Sowls, L. K. 1949. Notes on the raccoon (*Procyon lotor hirtus*) in Manitoba. *J. Mamm.* 30:313–14.

Saccopteryx bilineata (Murciélago de Saco, Sac-wing Bat)

J. Bradbury

This little bat is one of the more commonly encountered species in Costa Rica. It occurs in most lowland habitats including the drier forests of Guanacaste. In the latter sites, colonies are found roosting in the lower and more illuminated sections of hollow riparian forest trees. In wet forest they frequent the buttress cavities of large *Ceiba* trees as well as tree hollows. They may also be found in cliff cracks and the outer reaches of caves. The genus is immediately recognizable through its small size, its peculiar roosting posture in which the feet obtain purchase on vertical surfaces while the anterior portions of the body are rotated out from the surface, and its dark fur with two parallel white wavy lines running along the back. *S. bilineata* is easily confused with the sympatric *S. leptura.* The former species is larger (7–9 g), lives in larger colonies (five to fifty animals, although solitary males may be encountered), and favors cavities as roosts. The latter species is smaller (5–6 g), lives in small colonies (one to nine animals in dry forest and one to five animals in wet forest), and prefers to roost in exposed tree boles or the undersurface of large tree limbs. A third species, *Rhynchonycteris naso,* lives in large colonies on tree boles or cliff faces, but is nearly always within 30 m of running water. It is also smaller (4–5 g) and has tan grizzled fur.

Saccopteryx bilineata is highly social. Colonies at the day roosts are always divided into contiguous territories defended by one adult male each. Females are distributed unequally among male territories, generating harems of from one to nine females per male. This social structure is maintained by a repertoire of stereotyped signals that are relatively easy to observe in the field. At dawn, returning males land in their territories at the roost and begin to sing long and complicated songs that are audible to humans. As females return, and at various times during the day, males fly from the roost surface in a short loop and hover before roosting females. While hovering, the male opens two glands in the antebrachial membrane of the wing and wafts a scent at the female with his wing beats. The secretion is easily detectable by man. The male also vocalizes during the "hovers" with a stereo-typed sequence of chirps, and the female may respond with a vocalization. Males may move to a territorial boundary while on the roost surface and shake their opened wing glands at males or females in adjacent territories. Neighboring males may engage in "scent fights" for long periods at a common boundary.

While males are relatively philopatric at the roost, females shift frequently between harems and between colonies. Major changes in colony and harem size seem to correlate with major seasonal changes. Although males display at all times of year, copulation is limited to a short period in late rainy season, and parturition is highly synchronous with the onset of the rains in May. Females have only a single young each year. (This is to be contrasted with sympatric *S. leptura,* which may produce young in May and again in October–November.)

These bats are entirely insectivorous. They leave the day roosts before it is totally dark and forage under the canopy in the forest adjacent to the roosts. As it grows darker, they fly to current foraging areas that may be as much as 300 m from the day roost. The species is opportunistic in that it tends to feed for 3–10-week periods within a given habitat type as the underlying plants go through major phenological activity periods. Thus in Guanacaste they may feed successively over the river on one side of the riparian forest, then over the other side of the riparian forest in dry season, and then move between a series of patches of deciduous forest as each goes through leaf flush and insect levels rise in the wet season. Individual colonies appear to have nonoverlapping annual foraging ranges. Within an area currently used by a colony, each female has her own foraging beat, and females currently roosting with a given harem male tend to have adjacent beats. The foraging range of each harem male overlaps those of his current harem females. Thus the social structure at the roost appears to be mapped directly on the foraging grounds. Females that shift harems or roosts shift foraging sites accordingly.

Predation on these small bats appears to be low. They do not avoid flight in moonlight as do some larger bat species. At the roost they are exceedingly wary, they do not go torpid during the day, and they have excellent vision even at moderately strong light levels. When disturbed at the roost they will either drop into darker cavities or fly quickly to another site nearby. Most mortality of adults appears to occur during the second half of the dry season, when insect abundance is lower and body weights may drop to 17% of wet-season values. Annual survival for adults is about 78% at all sites studied (Costa Rica, Trinidad, and Panama).

Parental care is undertaken only by females. Young are never left at the roost at night, but are carried by their mothers to individual hiding sites where they are left while the mother forages. Youngsters can fly at 2 weeks but typically suckle for several months. During this period, stomachs of young will contain both milk and insects. Dispersal occurs in August and September when young are about 3 months old. While nearly all females emigrate from their parental colonies (and typically out of the study areas), up to 50% of the young males attempt to establish territories near or within their parental colonies. A few males even remain in a "crypto" condition within their parental harem and may ascent to harem ownership when their presumed fathers die.

*

Bradbury, J., and Emmons, L. 1974. Social organization in some Trinidad bats. 1. Emballonuridae. *Z. Tierpsych*. 36:137–83.

Bradbury, J., and Vehrencamp, S. 1976. Social organization and foraging in emballonurid bats. 1. Field studies. *Behav. Ecol. Sociobiol*. 1:337–81. (Three additional papers derived from data in the 1976 paper above followed in the same journal. Cf. *Behav. Ecol. Sociobiol*. 1:383–404; 2:1–17; 2:19–29.)

Sciurus granatensis (Ardilla Roja, Ardilla Chisa, Red-tailed Squirrel)

L. R. Heaney

The red-tailed squirrel (fig. 9.24) is currently the only Neotropical sciurid for which more than minimal ecological data are available. It is a common species in some parts of Costa Rica, which includes the northern edge of its range; it is widespread and extremely variable mor-

FIGURE 9.24. *Sciurus granatensis,* adult. Sirena, Corcovado National Park, Osa Peninsula, Costa Rica (photo, D. H. Janzen).

phologically in northern South America. Most of the following data are from squirrels at a single study site in Panama (Heaney and Thorington 1978; Glanz et al. 1981).

Adult females average 465 g, and males are slightly smaller. Adult females have nonoverlapping home ranges varying from ⅓ to 1 ha, whereas males overlap with each other and with females and have home ranges from 1 to 4 ha. Accordingly, food habits vary between the sexes. Both prefer large fruit and especially hard-shelled seeds of palms and some legumes. Males move freely from one large fruiting tree to another and thus rarely eat anything other than the most preferred foods. Females are restricted to eating whatever is available in their home ranges; they often eat young leaves, soft fruit, flowers, and bark. Females frequently cache palm nuts and rely on them during periods of low food availability; males rarely cache nuts, but they eat those cached by females. Nuts are scatter hoarded by the squirrels. The same nuts are parasitized by the larvae of bruchid beetles. When squirrels are at high densities, most nuts are cached, and few are damaged by bruchids. When squirrel densities are low, as they generally are in Costa Rica, bruchids may damage more than half the nuts. However, the number of cached nuts eaten later by the squirrels is high, so that the net rate of seed loss is higher where the squirrels are present.

S. granatensis may produce two or three litters per year, averaging two young per litter. Mating activity is especially conspicuous during the dry season. Matings take place during a mating chase, in which four to eight males follow a female for 3–4 h, usually in the morning. Sometimes a single male establishes dominance and keeps other males several meters from the female, but equally often no male remains dominant. There is usually a single very brief (10 sec) copulation. The female seems able to choose the male she mates with (using deception to evade a dominant male if necessary); there is evidence that females prefer males they know well—that is, males who pass through the females' home ranges often. Nests are usually in tree hollows. Gestation is roughly 44 days, and lactation continues for 8–10 weeks. Dispersal distance of young is variable, with females sometimes occupying a corner of the mother's original home range and other young moving at least 1 km. Observed percentages of young in the population vary annually from 28% to 56%. Maximum local densities are eight to ten per hectare, with "good" densities closer to two per hectare; they can maintain populations with densities under 0.2 per hectare.

As the common name implies, *S. granatensis* has a rusty-red tail, often with a black tip, and short, coarse, reddish brown fur on the dorsum, and a light rusty venter. Another common squirrel in Costa Rica is *Sciurus varie-*

gatoides, a larger squirrel with longer fur. The tail is grizzled. Some populations have a prominent brown patch on the back, with light-colored sides; other populations have a grizzled appearance with a rusty color on the limbs. There is usually a prominent white postauricular patch. This species occurs in relatively drier, more open, or more disturbed habitat than *S. granatensis* but is often sympatric. They reportedly are territorial; their presence is often obvious because of the leaf nests they make in the tops of trees, much like those made by squirrels in the United States.

S. deppei is smaller than *S. granatensis; S. deppei* has a dark, narrow tail, brown body with an orangish belly, and small, light postauricular patches. This species prefers dense vegetation and is reportedly more terrestrial than the preceding two species. *Microsciurus alfari,* a pygmy squirrel, also occurs in Costa Rica, mostly at higher elevations; they are a nondescript brown and much smaller than any of the foregoing species. *Syntheosciurus poasensis* is known in Costa Rica for only one specimen taken in cloud forest on Volcán Poás.

*

Glanz, W. E.; Thorington, R. W.; Madden, J.; and Heaney, L. R. 1981. Seasonal food use and demographic trends in *Sciurus granatensis.* In *Seasonality of Neotropical rain forest environments,* ed. E. Leigh. Washington, D.C.: Smithsonian Institution Press, in press.
Heaney, L. R., and Thorington, R. W., Jr. 1978. Ecology of Neotropical red-tailed squirrels, *Sciurus granatensis,* in the Panama Canal Zone. *J. Mamm.* 59: 846–51.

Sigmodon hispidus (Rata Algodonera Hispida, Hispid Cotton Rat)

R. H. Baker

Cotton rats of the genus *Sigmodon* are dominant grass-eating and runway-making rodents in most grassy or grassy/brushy habitats of south temperate to tropical North and Central America. In this region cotton rats inhabit environments and play a community role somewhat similar to those of voles of the genus *Microtus* in north temperate and boreal parts of the continent (Baker 1969). Although the fossil record is sparse (Martin 1974), cotton rats probably originated no later than Pliocene times in tropical America (Hooper 1949), either in a South American (Hershkovitz 1966) or a Central American pastoral habitat (Baker 1969), perhaps from a grass-eating cricetine (phyllotine) ancestor (Hershkovitz 1962).

The genus contains at least seven species (Baker and Shump 1978; Zimmerman 1970); speciation is greatest in the Mexican area. The ubiquitous hispid cotton rat enjoys the most extensive distribution, occurring in selected open land of southern North and Central America, although populations in Costa Rica and other Central American countries may ultimately prove to be specifically separate from the wide-ranging *S. hispidus* (A. S. Ahl, pers. comm.; Bowers 1971; Dalby and Lillevik 1969; Johnson et al 1972; Zimmerman 1970). Although different cotton rats are able to thrive in similar grassy habitats, one species tends to dominate or possibly exclude the other when two species occur in the same area (Petersen 1973).

A typical adult cotton rat (fig. 9.25) is medium-sized, approximately 250–300 mm long (from nose to tip of tail), and weighs 100–200 g (Jiménez 1971, 1972). The body is heavyset, and the head is relatively small. The tail is shorter than the head and body, thick and tapering, sparsely haired, and annulated. The ears are rounded and partly obscured by long fur growing at their anterior basal edges. The legs are short and the feet are large. The pelage is short, appressed, and rather coarse. The molar teeth have high crowns and flat surfaces with long S-shaped folds surrounded by thick layers of enamel. The cotton rat's dentition and alimentary canal are both adapted for masticating and digesting harsh, grit-covered grasses and forbs plus seeds, fruits, insects, and other edibles (Fleming 1970). Cotton rats are highly productive (Fleming 1970); the gestation period is approximately 27 days (Meyer and Meyer 1944); litters may contain as many as twelve young, although laboratory litters of Costa Rican animals averaged only 2.8 (Bowdre 1971). The young are able to breed at 40–50 days of age (Odum 1955). Cotton rats harbor diseases and parasites important to man and domestic animals, compete for pasture grasses with domestic livestock, and damage cultivated crops, including rice, cotton, and maize. Cotton rats have also been used in biomedical studies (Meyer and Meyer 1944) and as bioassay test animals (Underhill 1973).

Hispid cotton rats are most active during daylight hours. They prefer grasslands or mixed grass and brush areas (Fleming 1970; Goertz 1964). Although originally at home on native prairie lands, at woodland edges, and along swamp and stream borders, the hispid cotton rat has readily moved into cleared forest lands, other disturbed habitats, and stands of grasses and forbs introduced as the result of human settlement. In some areas severe overgrazing and clean-farming practices have reduced or excluded cotton rat populations. The rodents move at ground level by following trails that they construct through the grassy and sometimes brushy cover. If the grass stems are dense, the rodents make their trails by clipping off the vegetation at ground level and keeping these trails cleared and even somewhat worndown through frequent use. Assorted terrestrial vertebrates, in-

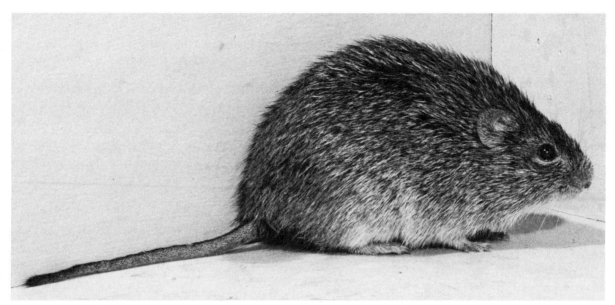

FIGURE 9.25. *Sigmodon hispidus* (hispid cotton rat); note heavy, short body, hairy ears, beady eyes, blunt nose, grizzled fur, and thick, sparsely haired tail (photo, R. H. Baker).

cluding other small mammals, take advantage of these trails as means of moving around.

Since overhead grasses may obscure these runs, an observer may be obliged to get down on hands and knees and part the grassy cover to view this rodent sign. Other prominent evidences of cotton rat activity along these runways include cylindrical fecal pellets (perhaps 6 mm long) often in piles (latrines), and grass clippings. These clippings, usually 15–30 mm long, are frequently in piles, resulting from the rat's habit of clipping basal sections of grass leaves to bring the tender growing tips of the plants down near ground level. The degree of freshness of these piles of cuttings is an indication of the current use being made of the runway systems. Cotton rats are efficient diggers and will excavate tunnels, often 1–3 m long. These underground runs may be just under the grass roots and may join surface passageways at each end.

Burrows containing nests, sometimes under shrub or tree roots, may be used as nurseries (Strecker 1929). However, cotton rat nests (for both nurturing young and refuge) are also constructed aboveground at bases of clumps of grass, adjacent to surface trails, and situated in well-drained areas or set in slight depressions with bordering ridges to reduce chances of flooding. On the Osa Peninsula in Costa Rica, Dawson and Lang (1973) found nests and nest entrances oriented to the southeast and northwest sides of grass clumps. They also noted that nest construction (coarse grass on the outside and fine grass on the inside of the roof area) helped keep out rain and effectively insulated the nest from high temperatures (also see Shump 1978).

In Costa Rica the hispid cotton rat is widespread from sea level to medium elevations (as at San José) in moderately grazed pasturage, in cultivated and fallow areas and their borders, and at swamp and marsh borders. The Organization for Tropical Studies Handbook for 1971 lists hispid cotton rats as occurring at Osa, Cañas, and San José. Near Rincón on the Osa Peninsula, Dawson and Land (1973) found cotton rats abundant in heavy grass (mostly *Paspalum* sp.) adjacent to an airstrip servicing the Tropical Science Center. Fleming (1973) reported them at La Pacifica but not at La Selva. At Lagos Lindora just west of Santa Ana, in the central highlands, hispid cotton rats were live trapped in tall, moderately grazed pasture grass growing on heavy black soil. Surface runways were obscure at this site, perhaps because of the wide spacing of the grass stems allowing free movement of the rodents at ground level. In its preferred habitat, the presence of the hispid cotton rat not only is made conspicuous because of its surface runways, latrines, and piles of grass cuttings, but this species may actually make up a major segment of the small mammal biomass in the area. Studies concerning its behavioral ecology, its relationships to other small mammals, its major enemies, and other aspects of its biology in Costa Rica not only will add to our knowledge of a small mammal important in tropical ecosystems but will also provide data useful for comparison with existing knowledge about cotton rats in the south temperate United States.

An ongoing study of the *S. hispidus* in Santa Rosa National Park (W. Hallwachs and D. Janzen, pers.

comm.) has made it clear that the hispid cotton rat is abundant in abandoned pastures covered with grass, herbs, and brush and also occurs in clearings (tree falls, old burns) inside the forest. The cotton rat and *Liomys salvini* (spiny pocket mouse: Heteromyidae) are the two most abundant species of rodents in the park; *Liomys* is mainly a forest mouse, but it also occurs in brushy grass and at the edges of forest clearings. Traps set in a pasture abandoned for a year and a half caught many more cotton rats in March 1980 (mid dry season) than in November 1979 (late rainy season) and also caught a number of small individuals (probably juveniles). This is surprising if cotton rats are largely foliage eaters, since leafy vegetation is very scarce in the second half of the dry season. An indication of high cotton-rat density at Santa Rosa, besides the rustlings and occasional sightings of cotton rats, is the large percentage of *Acrocomia vinifera* (Palmae) nuts cleaned of their sweet pulp by rodents beneath trees in open grassy pastureland. All coyote dung found in the park in March 1980 was rich in cotton-rat hair. Preliminary feeding studies of fruits, seeds, and insects suggest that individuals of *S. hispidus* are generally willing fruit eaters, moderate insect eaters (most will accept cryptic insects, but usually not in large quantites), and very choosy when it comes to seeds. *Liomys,* in contrast, seems to be a seed specialist that will eat some insects and fruits but with much less interest. *Sigmodon hispidus* is not an ideal animal for trapping or laboratory use. The rats chew vigorously and effectively on doors and triggers when live trapped, so galvanized steel traps are recommended. They also have an unusually strong, rank odor that must be washed from the trap between trapping bouts. In cages they are timid, frighten easily, and often do not calm down to laboratory life even after months of handling.

*

Baker, R. H. 1969. Cotton rats of the *Sigmodon fulviventer* group (Rodentia: Muridae). In Contributions in mammalogy, ed. J. K. Jones, pp. 177–232. *Misc. Publ. Mus. Nat. Hist., Univ. Kansas* 51:1–428.

Baker, R. H., and Shump, K. A., Jr. 1978. *Sigmodon fulviventer. Mamm. Species,* no. 94:1–4.

Bowdre, L. P. 1971. Litter size in *Sigmodon hispidus. Southwest. Nat.* 16:126–28.

Bowers, J. R. 1971. Resting metabolic rate in the cotton rat *Sigmodon. Physiol. Zool.* 44:137–48.

Dalby, P. L., and Lillevik, H. A. 1969. Taxonomic analysis of electrophoretic blood serum patterns in the cotton rat, *Sigmodon. Mich. State Univ. Publ. Mus., Biol. Ser.* 4:65–104.

Dawson, G. A., and Lang, J. W. 1973. The functional significance of nest building by a Neotropical rodent (*Sigmodon hispidus*). *Am. Midl. Nat.* 89:503–9.

Fleming, T. H. 1970. Notes on the rodent faunas of two Panamanian forests. *J. Mamm.* 51:473–90.

———. 1973. The number of rodent species in two Costa Rican forests. *J. Mamm.* 54:518–21.

Goertz, J. W. 1964. The influence of habitat quality upon density of cotton rat populations. *Ecol. Mono.* 34:359–81.

Hershkovitz, P. 1962. Evolution of Neotropical cricetine rodents (Muridae) with special reference to the phyllotine group. *Fieldiana: Zool.* 46:1–524.

———. 1966. Mice, land bridges and Latin American faunal interchange. In *Ectoparasites of Panama,* ed. R. L. Wenzel and V. J. Tipton, pp. 725–51. Chicago: Field Museum of Natural History.

Hooper, E. T. 1949. Faunal relationships of Recent North American rodents. *Univ. Mich. Mus. Zool. Misc. Publ.* 72:1–28.

Jiménez, J. J. 1971. Comparative post-natal growth in five species of the genus *Sigmodon.* I. External morphological character relationships. *Rev. Biol. Trop.* 19:133–48.

———. 1972. Comparative post-natal growth in five species of the genus *Sigmodon.* II. Cranial character relationships. *Rev. Biol. Trop.* 20:5–27.

Johnson, W. E.; Selander, R. K.; Smith, M. H.; and Kim, Y. J. 1972. Biochemical genetics of sibling species of the cotton rat (*Sigmodon*). In *Studies in genetics, VII,* pp. 297–305. University of Texas Publication no. 7213. Austin: University of Texas Press.

Martin, R. A. 1974. Fossil mammals from the Coleman IIA fauna, Sumpter County. In *Pleistocene mammals in Florida,* ed. S. D. Webb, pp. 35–100. Gainsville: University of Florida Press.

Meyer, B. J., and Meyer, R. K. 1944. Growth and reproduction of the cotton rat *Sigmodon hispidus hispidus* under laboratory conditions. *J. Mamm.* 25:107–27.

Odum, E. P. 1955. An eleven year history of a *Sigmodon* population. *J. Mamm.* 36:368–78.

Petersen, M. K. 1973. Interactions between the cotton rats, *Sigmodon fulviventer* and *S. hispidus. Am. Midl. Nat.* 90:319–33.

Shump, K. A., Jr. 1978. Ecological importance of nest construction in the hispid cotton rat (*Sigmodon hispidus*). *Am. Midl. Nat.* 100:103–15.

Strecker, J. K. 1929. Notes on the Texas cotton and Attwater woodrats in Texas. *J. Mamm.* 10:216–20.

Underhill, A. 1973. Use of Neotropical rodents in protein efficiency studies. *Lab. Anim Sci.* 23:499–503.

Zimmerman, E. G. 1970. Karyology, systematics and chromosomal evolution in the rodent genus, *Sigmodon, Mich. State Univ. Publ. Mus. Biol. Ser.* 4:385–454.

Silvilagus floridanus (Conejo, Cottontail Rabbit)

J. A. Chapman

The eastern cottontail rabbit (fig. 9.26) is a medium-sized lagomorph, tan to reddish brown in color. Its average

FIGURE 9.26. *Sylvilagus floridanus. a,* Adult in deciduous forest during the dry season (center of photograph, facing to the right). May 1980, Santa Rosa National Park, Costa Rica (photo, D. H. Janzen), *b,* Study skins of adults from Maryland, United States (photo, J. A. Chapman).

length is between 400 and 435 mm, and its weight ranges from 1,000 to 1,500 g. It is unique among the rabbits of the world in that it inhabits such diverse areas, occurring over broad geographic provinces from Canada into Central and South America. The cottontail is generally thought of as a mammal of farmlands, fields, and hedgerows; however, historically it occurred in natural glades and woodlands as well as deserts, swamps, prairies, hardwood forests, rain forests, and boreal forests (Chapman, Hockman, and Ojeda C. 1980).

The ability of this species to utilize diverse habitats has long intrigued wildlife biologists. Among the cottontail's adaptations is its ability to obtain water from vegetation. Thus, from the coldest arctic to the hottest desert, water usually is not a limiting factor. The only noticeable habitat requirement appears to be abundant shrubby vegetation. The cottontail's diet is composed entirely of plants.

Unlike other members of the Lagomorpha, which occupy very discrete ranges and habitats, the eastern cottontail occurs sympatrically with many other rabbits. Its range overlaps those of six other species of *Sylvilagus* and six species of *Lepus*. No other rabbit or hare occurs

sympatrically with so many other leporids. Recent studies have shown that widely separated populations of *S. floridanus* have a very different genetic makeup, which may account for the species' ability to occupy different habitats (Chapman and Morgan 1973).

Because the eastern cottontail is such an important game animal in North America, providing millions of hours of sport each year, the species has been widely introduced. These introductions have greatly altered the genetic composition of the eastern cottontail in North America, resulting in an integrade form capable of utilizing even more varied habitats and altered ecosystems (Chapman and Morgan 1973).

The eastern cottontail is one of the more fecund lagomorphs, producing larger litter sizes and more litters than other rabbits. Under ideal conditions this species may produce as many as twenty-five young per year in five to seven litters (Chapman, Harman, and Samuel 1977). During the breeding season, cottontails become very combative, and the females often are kicked and bitten repeatedly during the breeding process. Fights occur between males, who are often aggressive, since most of the breeding is done by a few dominant males within the area. Cottontails may begin breeding when they are only 3 months old. Nearly all the animals in a population die or are killed by predators in their first year of life.

The eastern cottontail's home range varies in size according to the habitat it occupies, but is generally 2–5 ha. In some situations these rabbits may reach densities of more than fifteen per hectare.

Cottontails are known to be occasional carriers of certain diseases dangerous to man, such as tularemia and Rocky Mountain spotted fever. Because of this there has been considerable concern over the past widespread introduction of cottontails to "replenish" low populations. This practice is now being discontinued since it is no longer considered ecologically sound.

Lagomorphs have a number of interesting behavioral characteristics. One such behavior is "freezing" when in imminent danger, for example, when a predator is about to strike. This often occurs after the rabbit has been pursued for some distance. The white tail of the cottontail, which the predator was so intently fixed on, suddenly is lowered and disappears from sight, leaving the pursuer disoriented. This may aid the eastern cottontail in escaping.

Another behavior exhibited by all cottontails is the reingestion of fecal material, termed coprophagy. Other animals, such as some rodents, also exhibit this behavior. The reingestion of certain pellets, produced only at certain times during the day, allows the rabbit to obtain essential vitamins that are not assimilated through the one-time ingestion of its food because they are produced by microbes low in the gastrointestinal tract.

Many lagomorphs thrive in man's environment—literally in man's backyard. In adapting to habitat alternations, the eastern cottontail has proved to be a hardy species. An urban hedgerow or weed patch affords this rabbit all the protection and food it needs. It can establish a nest for its young on a front lawn or near a busy city thoroughfare. Owing to its proximity to man, the cottontail is a very important mammal. However, it can be a significant crop depredator in some parts of its range. Because of this rabbit's importance as a game and pest species, it has been studied more than any other lagomorph.

In Costa Rica, cottontail rabbits occur in a wide variety of forest-edge habitats. In the regenerating burns on the top of the Cerro de la Muerte (2,800–3,200 m elevation), rabbit droppings are the only common vertebrate feces. Rabbits are occasionally seen sitting on the road shoulder at night next to the regenerating rain forest near Puerto Viejo de Sarapiquí at 50–80 m elevation. Rabbits are common around the historical center and main administration buildings (open grassy areas) as well as in the grass-forest mixes of the strongly deciduous forests at Santa Rosa National Park. Rabbit fur is occasionally found in coyote scats at this site. Although no weights are available, the Santa Rosa conttontails appear to weigh about half as much as adult cottontails from the north-central United States (D. Janzen, pers. comm.).

*

Chapman, J. A.; Harman, A. L.; and Samuel, D. E. 1977. Reproductive and physiological cycles in the cottontail complex in western Maryland and nearby West Virginia. *Wildl. Monogr.* 56:1–73.

Chapman, J. A.; Hockman, J. G.; and Ojeda C., M. M. 1980. *Sylvilagus floridanus. Mamm. Species* 136:1–8.

Chapman, J. A., and Morgan, R. P. 1973. Systematic status of the cottontail complex in western Maryland and nearby West Virginia. *Wildl. Monogr.* 36:1–54.

Tamandua mexicana (Oso Jaceta, Hormiguero, Tamandua, Banded Anteater, Lesser Anteater)

Y. D. Lubin

The banded or lesser anteater, *Tamandua mexicana* (fig. 9.27*a*) weighs 4–6 kg and is common in low- and mid-elevation habitats throughout central and northern South America. South and east of the Andes it is replaced by *T. tetradactyla,* which is somewhat different from *T. mexicana* morphologically (Wetzel 1975) but similar in its ecology and behavior. *T. mexicana* throughout its range is golden to brown with a black V across the back (like a vest worn backward, fig. 9.27*c*).

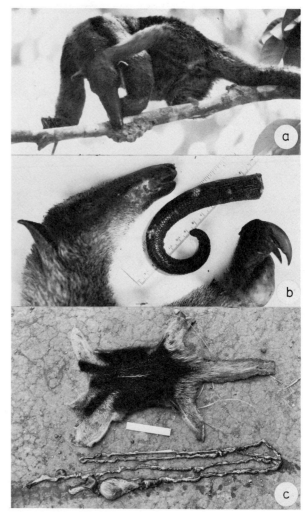

FIGURE 9.27. *Tamandua mexicana. a,* Adult scratching violently after attacking a nest of *Azteca* ants. Panama (photo, Y. Lubin). *b,* Head and end of prehensile tail. *c,* Color pattern and gastrointestinal tract (*b* and *c,* near Liberia, Guanacaste Province, Costa Rica, W. Hallwachs; photos, D. H. Janzen).

Tamandua can be thought of as the archetypal edentate anteater—it has a strong set of foreclaws (fig. 9.27*b*) for opening up wood and nests of ants and termites; a long, saliva-covered tongue with (microscopic) backward-pointing projections; a thick-walled, muscular stomach for crushing the hard chitinous exoskeletons of ants; and a prehensile tail (fig. 9.27*b*) for balance and arboreal movement.

Both species of *Tamandua* move both in the trees and on the ground (scansorial). They are active during the day or night, or both, depending on the individual. We radio tracked fifteen individuals of *T. mexicana* on Barro Colorado Island, Panama (Montgomery and Lubin 1977), and no two animals had the same activity pattern.

494

Individuals also differed in their degree of arboreality — some spent more time in trees and others more time on the ground.

This individuality is also reflected in the diet of *Tamandua*. *Tamandua* takes both ants and termites and very rarely bees (G. Otis and M. Winston, pers. comm., found *T. mexicana* attacking nests of Africanized honeybees in French Guiana). The percentages of ants and termites in the diet varies between individuals, with an average of about 40% ants (range 5–93%) for *T. mexicana* (based on counts from samples taken from stomach contents from twenty-eight anteaters). Anteaters that spent more time in trees tended to take more ants in the diet, while terrestrial individuals ate more termites. There is also a seasonal component to this variability; one radio-marked anteater that ate primarily ants switched to attacking nests of *Nasutitermes* and other termites during the transition from dry to wet season, when developing reproductives were present in the nests (Lubin and Montgomery 1981; see also section on *Nasutitermes* termites).

Tamandua takes a broad range of species of ants and termites, but they are by no means grazing in a nonselective fashion. Some types of ants, for example, were noticeably absent from the diet of *T. mexicana* or taken only very rarely; ponerine ants have a severe and painful sting, particularly the larger species; army ants (Dorylinae) such as *Eciton* and *Labidus* sting and bite and were rarely attacked; leaf-cutting ants (Attini, Myrmycinae) are spiny and may be unpalatable. It appears that the chemical defenses of most Formicinae (e.g., *Camponotus*), Dolichoderinae (e.g., *Azteca* and *Monacis*), and Myrmicinae (e.g., *Crematogaster, Pheidole*) are less effective against anteaters. Such defenses may "work" to reduce the level of predation on a given nest (by a build-up of unpalatability beyond the threshold level) and force the anteater into a strategy of cropping from many locations. This is undoubtedly the case with predation on *Nasutitermes* termites: the nasute soldiers are distasteful and successfully repel anteaters from nests (where the concentration of soldiers is high). Instead, anteaters take *Nasutitermes* primarily from dead wood and feeding aggregations away from the nest and therefore do rather little large-scale damage to the colony (Lubin and Montgomery 1981).

Tamandua has a single young at a time. Reproduction on Barro Colorado Island does not appear to be seasonal. The young remains with the female until it is nearly half her size. When the mother moves from one den site to another (in hollow trees, logs, or holes in the ground), the young rides on her back. She often moves the young at the beginning of an activity period and again at the end. During these movements she stops frequently to feed, and the young gets off and feeds alongside her. In this way the young may be taught about both diet and home range. Aside from mother-young interacitons and mating, *Tamandua* is solitary.

Tamandua uses distinct pathways, both arboreal and terrestrial, returning along the same routes repeatedly and often attacking the same colonies repeatedly. Home ranges are large, approximately 75 ha for *T. mexicana* on Barro Colorado and about 350 ha for *T. tetradactyla* in wooded savanna (llanos) habitat in central Venezuela. There is some overlap of home ranges, but the details of this are not clear.

The other two species of Neotropical anteaters might be considered modifications or variations on the archetypal anteater theme. The giant anteater, *Myrmecophaga tridactyla* L., now rare in Central America, weighs 25–30 kg, is strictly terrestrial, and specializes almost entirely on soil- and wood-nesting ants (especially *Camponotus, Pheidole,* and *Solenopsis*). Giant anteaters are common in the llanos of Venezuela, where they have large, overlapping home ranges (ca. 2,500 ha), but they have also been reported in forested areas such as the lowland wet tropical forests of Bocas del Toro, Panama (R. Cooke, pers. comm.) and of the Osa Peninsula, Costa Rica (D. H. Janzen, pers. comm.).

The little silky anteater, *Cyclopes didactylus,* weighs about 300 g, is strictly arboreal and nocturnal, and specializes entirely on tiny ants taken from nests inside hollow twigs and lianas (especially the Cephalotini and *Crematogaster*). *Cyclopes* is highly specialized for movement at night in small vines: the hind foot is padlike and opposable (like the foot of a chameleon), the tail is strongly prehensile, and the eyes are large compared with those of other species of anteaters (which hunt entirely by scent). Silky anteaters are probably not uncommon in lowland forest and secondary growth areas of Central and South America, but they are so difficult to see that they are considered very rare. We radio tracked seventeen silky anteaters on Barro Colorado Island in a period of six months. Silky anteaters have nonoverlapping home ranges of 5–10 ha. An individual silky anteater eats about six thousand ants per day.

*

Lubin, Y. D., and Montgomery, G. G. 1981. Defenses of *Nasutitermes* termites (Isoptera, Termitidae) against *Tamandua* anteaters (Edentata, Myrmecophagidae). *Biotropica* 13:66–76.

Montgomery, G. G., and Lubin, Y. D. 1977. Prey influences on movements of Neotropical anteaters. In *Proceedings of the 1975 Predator Symposium,* ed. R. L. Phillips and C. Jonkel, pp. 103–31. Missoula: Montana Forest and Conservation Experiment Station, University of Montana.

Wetzel, R. M. 1975. The species of *Tamandua* Gray (Edentata, Myrmecophagidae). *Proc. Biol. Soc. Washington* 88:95–112.

Tapirus bairdii (Danto, Danta, Baird's Tapir)

D. H. Janzen

This endangered species (fig. 9.28) is the largest contemporary indigenous terrestrial mammal in Central America. Before it was hunted with guns, it was common and ranged through all habitats from mangrove swamps, rain forest and deciduous forest to the bamboo thickets at 3,500 m in the Talamanca mountains. At present it is found only in areas where hunting is restricted or difficult, and in these areas (national parks, by and large) it is probably below normal density owing to past hunting. There are at least twenty to fifty in Santa Rosa National Park and probably one hundred to three hundred in Corcovado National Park.

An adult wild tapir weighs 150–300 kg and has short (1–3 cm long), sparse black hair over a black skin 1–3 cm thick. The skin on the back is so thick that it feels like a leathery, inflexible shell. Until 4–8 months of age, juveniles are brown with white spots and stripes. A tapir is stocky, with short powerful legs, but in the forest it can run as fast as a man. On the hind foot, a central large toe is flanked by two large toes and one small toe. The front foot has three large toes. When the foot is withdrawn from mud or other soft substrates, the flexible toes swing together, allowing easy and silent withdrawal from the larger hole made by the sinking splayed-out foot. The tail is very short and serves no obvious function other than to cover the anus. The upper lip is extremely flexible, long, and somewhat extensible; it is easy to imagine that it is

FIGURE 9.28. *Tapirus bairdii,* adult male. Guanacaste Province, Costa Rica (W. and L. Hagnauer, Finca La Pacifica, near Cañas, Guanacaste, Costa Rica; photo, D. H. Janzen).

the evolutionary forerunner of a trunk like that of an elephant. It is used, albeit not so dextrously as is the trunk of an elephant, for shoveling food into the mouth and plucking leaves from branches that the tongue and teeth cannot reach.

Dicot leaves, twigs, fruits, and some seeds appear to constitute the normal diet. Leafy material is coarsely chewed between the very strongly dentate molars, which show little wear even in old animals unless the animal lives in a sandy habitat. Soft fruit is chewed and mushed against the strongly and broadly ridged palate as well as between the molars. A chewing tapir may smash seeds that it takes up to 300–500 pounds of pressure to break (e.g., seeds of *Enterolobium cyclocarpum*), but hard and large seeds usually are not broken but rather are spit out or swallowed. The huge seeds of *Raphia taedigera* are reputed to be swallowed and passed whole by tapirs in Corcovado National Park. Hard seeds (e.g., those of *E. cyclocarpum*) are digested through a poorly understood process of delayed passage through the gut that probably involves germination of the seed.

The captive adult male tapir that was at Finca La Pacifica (Cañas, Guanacaste Province) was extremely particular, quantitatively and qualitatively, about what it ate. It usually rejected plants by odor or, more rarely, by tasting. On one occasion it vomited or coughed up aroid leaves a few seconds after eating them. It rejected at least 300 species of native broad-leaved plants and accepted another 150. With acceptable plants it ate different small quantities of each species before ceasing for that feeding bout. For example, it rejected the foliage of most woody legumes; it ate six species of Convolvulaceae vines and rejected three others; it ate eighty to two hundred mature *Guazuma ulmifolia* fruits in each of many consecutive feeding bouts. Wild food for tapirs appears not to be superabundant. A very large fraction of the vegetation in undisturbed forest is made up of species that the captive tapir refused to eat. Some of its favorite foods (e.g., *Alibertia edulis* foliage) are rare where tapirs occur in apparently normal numbers and common where tapirs have been eliminated. This suggests that the food scarcity may be in part generated by tapir browsing.

In the wild, apparently because they are still suffering the psychological effects of hunting, Costa Rican tapirs are very shy and wary. Their vision is poor, but their hearing and sense of smell are excellent. They run off ponderously if startled but can also sneak away without a sound. I have encountered tapirs feeding during night and day. In the deciduous forests of Santa Rosa National Park they seem to concentrate near water holes during the dry season. Whether this is for drinking water or defecation is unclear, since they seem to "want" badly to defecate in water. If water is not available (or inappropriate?) they will repeatedly defecate on the same site on dry land, as has been observed in Chirripó National Park. Tapir feces look like horse dung but contain much larger chips of woody twigs.

Juveniles (one per female) appear to accompany mothers for as much as a year after birth, until they reach what appears to be about two-thirds of the mother's weight. Mothers are reputed to attack humans that threaten their young. Tapirs make conspicuous trails in the forest, but they also pass through areas with no trails. They are usually seen one or two at a time, with no tendency to form herds. The corraled tapir at Finca La Pacifica had the same ticks and fungal diseases as do horses, and it died of a respiratory disease. It had no sign of torsalo infection (warble-fly infection), despite large numbers of these fly larvae in cattle in nearby pastures. It was very affectionate toward humans willing to scratch or rub its belly, armpits, or underchin. It tried to bite people who tried to ride it. With its front feet, it climbed readily up the corral side to get at withheld food.

In lowland South America there is a second common Neotropical species of tapir (*Tapirus terrestris*); its distribution overlaps that of *T. bairdii* in northwestern South America. In the mountains of South America there is a smaller, more furry tapir (*Tapirus roulini*). The only other extant tapir (*Tapirus indicus*) is black and white and is found in peninsular Malaysia. Fossil tapir remains have been found on all large land masses except Australia.

*

Janzen, D. H. 1981a. Digestive seed predation by a Costa Rican Baird's tapir. *Biotropica* 13 (suppl.): 59–63.

———. 1981b. Guanacaste tree seed-swallowing by Costa Rican range horses. *Ecology* 62:587–92.

———. 1981c. *Enterolobium cyclocarpum* seed passage rate and survival in horses, Costa Rican Pleistocene seed dispersal agents. *Ecology* 62:593–601.

———. 1982. Wild plant acceptability to a captive Costa Rican Baird's tapir. *Brenesia,* in press.

Terwilliger, V. J. 1978. Natural history of Baird's tapir on Barro Colorado Island, Panama Canal Zone. *Biotropica* 10:211–20.

Tayassu tajacu (Saino, Collared Peccary)

L. K. Sowls

This hoglike mammal (fig. 9.29) has one of the largest ranges of all North American ungulates. It is found as far north as Arizona, New Mexico, and Texas. In the Southern Hemisphere it occurs as far south as the Río Plata in Argentina. In this vast area it lives in a wide variety of habitats, showing great adaptability. Thus, in spite of persistent hunting for food and for the valuable hide,

FIGURE 9.29. *Tayassu tajacu* herd at a South American bait station (photo, L. K. Sowles).

which is marketable, this versatile mammal is still found in fair numbers in many parts of its range. It occurs in tropical rain forest, tropical deciduous forest, semidesert country, and scrub forests. In some agricultural areas peccaries raid farmers' crops.

There is considerable evidence that the northern animals are considerably larger than those farther south. There is a scarcity of published information on the size of animals from Latin America. In Arizona, where the species is larger, a sample of adult animals weighed 13.6–27.2 kg and was 45.7–55.9 cm high at the shoulders and 88.9–96.5 cm long (Sowls 1978).

The hair is coarse and long, measuring up to 15.2 cm on the back. The body is generally grayish to black. The white collar, from which it gets its name, is conspicuous. The collared peccary has only one dewclaw on each hind foot, and the feet are very small. Young animals at birth are reddish brown. As they grow older the color gradually changes to grayish black. A large scent gland that secretes an odoriferous liquid is on the back, about 12 to 15 cm from the base of a very short tail.

The collared peccary is highly social, traveling in herds of from three to more than thirty, which bed down in groups to keep warm. Friendly animals indulge in mutual rubbing, especially when meeting. One rubs the side of its head against the scent gland of the other animal, and the other reciprocates. Within the herd there is a regular dominance order that decreases serious fights. Vocalizations include a loud bark or alarm note, aggressive grumblings (especially when peccaries are feeding close together), tooth chattering as an aggressive threat, and a "purring" sound that is heard in all very young animals and most older ones. Aggressive actions include frontal encounters (Schweinsburg 1971; Schweinsburg and Sowls 1972; Sowls 1974).

The collared peccary inhabits a wide variety of habitats from virgin forest to scrubby timbered areas to desert areas. It eats a wide variety of foods including roots, tubers, bulbs, fruits, and rhizomes of a great many plants. In desert areas it may eat the pads or cladophylls of prickly pear. In areas of oak-woodland it eats acorns. In some areas it raids settlers' fields and eats maize, melons, squash, and beans (Leopold 1959; Langer 1979; Eddy 1961; Knipe 1958).

In Arizona and Texas most young are born in June, July, and August, the most favorable time of the year for vegetation after the summer rains (Jennings and Harris 1953; Low 1970; Sowls 1966). The gestation period varies from 142 to 148 days (Sowls 1961).

In Costa Rica collared peccaries range from sea level to at least 2,000 m elevation. The usual group size is two to fifteen animals. In the deciduous forest at Santa Rosa National Park, newborn young are encountered in May, 1–3 weeks after the rainy season begins. If taken from the adults, these young acclimate to humans almost instantaneously and make good house pets if one can tolerate their odor and aggressive foraging behavior. Adults can be kept in a corral together even if derived from different herds, provided they are kept physically (but not visually and olfactorily) separated for several months before merger. Costa Rican collared peccaries eat insects and small vertebrates (dead and alive) as well as plant matter. In Santa Rosa, fruits of *Ficus*, *Enterolobium cyclocarpum*, *Manilkara zapota*, *Hymenaea courbaril*, *Guazuma ulmifolia*, *Quercus oleoides*, *Brosimum alicastrum*, and other species are eaten, but in all cases except the figs the seeds are broken by molar action and therefore these animals are acting not as seed dispersers but as seed predators. During the dry season in deciduous forest, collared peccaries make daily trips to the same water hole, usually in the early morning. If water is scarce, there are numerous aggressive encounters at the water hole, but not all animals that arrive drink even when the opportunity is available. In the rainy season at Santa Rosa, collared peccaries browse large amounts of leafy foliage (e.g., *Ipomoea digitata*, *Guazuma ulmifolia*, *Luehea* spp.), and in captivity they will eat small portions of foliage of hundreds of species of native plants (D. Janzen, pers. comm.).

*

Eddy, T. A. 1961. Foods and feeding patterns of the collared peccary in southern Arizona. *J. Wildl. Mgt.* 25:248–57.

Jennings, W. D., and Harris, J. T. 1953. *The collared peccary in Texas*. Report no. 2. Austin: Texas Game and Fish Commission.

Knipe, T. 1958. *The javalina in Arizona*. Wildlife Bulletin no. 2. Tucson: Arizona Game and Fish Department.

Langer, P. 1979. Adaptational significance of the forestomach of the collared peccary, *Dicotyles tajacu* (L. 1758) (Mammalia: Artiodactyla). *Mammalia* 43: 235–45.

Leopold, A. S. 1959. *Wildlife of Mexico: The game birds and mammals*. Berkeley and Los Angeles: University of California Press.

Low, W. A. 1970. The influence of aridity on reproduction of the collared peccary (*Dicotyles tajacu*, Linn.) in Texas. Ph.D. diss., University of British Columbia.

Schweinsburg, R. E. 1971. The home range, movements and herd integrity of the collared peccary. *J. Wildl. Mgt.* 35:344–60.

Schweinsburg, R. E.; and Sowls, L. K. 1972. Aggressive behavior and related phenomenon in the collared peccary. *Z. Tiespsychol.* 30:132–45.

Sowls, L. K. 1961. Gestation period of the collared peccary. *J. Mamm.* 42:425–26.

———. 1966. Reproduction in the collared peccary (*Tayassu tajacu*) In *Comparative biology of reproduction in mammals*, ed. I. W. Rolands, pp. 155–72. London: Zoological Society.

———. 1974. Social behavior of the collared peccary *Dicotyles tajacu* L. In *The behavior of ungulates and its relation to management*, ed. V. Geist and F. Walther, 1:144–65. IUCN New Series, Publication 24. Morges, Switzerland: IUCN.

———. 1978. Collared peccary. In *Big game of North America: Ecology and Management*, ed. J. L. Schmidt and D. L. Gilbert, pp. 191–205. Philadelphia: Wildlife Management Institute and Stackpole.

Trichechus manatus (Manati, West Indian Manatee)

S. Ligon

The West Indian manatee (fig. 9.30) is a large (2.5–4 m, 200–600 kg) herbivorous marine mammal in the order Sirenia. It inhabits rivers, estuaries, and coasts in the tropical and subtropical regions of the New World Atlantic from Florida to the northern coast of Brazil. Manatees cannot tolerate low temperatures, and many have been killed during cold snaps (15–21° C) in Florida. In Costa Rica, manatees formerly were found in Sarapiquí, San Juan, Colorado, and San Carlos rivers (Frantzius 1869). Currently they are rare in Costa Rica, but with patience they can be seen in Tortuguero National Park. This species is now endangered as a result of heavy exploitation in the past. Manatees were taken for their meat, oil, and hides. The Miskito Indians of Costa Rica formerly hunted them regularly (Frantzius 1869). Today, threats are collisions with motorboats and barges, occasional illegal hunting, and herbicides that are often used on aquatic plants eaten by manatees. Manatees are legally protected in Costa Rica.

T. manatus is fusiform, and the head blends into the body with little or no suggestion of a neck. The muzzle angles downward to the large, fleshy lip pads that hang laterally over the sides of the mouth. These are covered

FIGURE 9.30. *Trichechus manatus* (drawings from photographs, S. Ligon).

with short, coarse bristles and are extremely flexible, being used to grasp vegetation that is tucked into the rear of the mouth where the grinding teeth are situated. Manatees are one of the few mammals that replace molars by migration from the back of the jaw. Semicircular nostrils, at the angle of the snout, are slowly raised above the water surface for breathing. The eyes are small, round, brown, and lashless, closing with a sphincter action. External pinnae are absent. Manatees are somewhat farsighted (Hartman 1979) but appear to have exceptional acoustic sensitivity. Flattened nails are present on the dorsal surface of the paddlelike flippers. These forelimbs are flexible and are used for "walking" on the substrate, scratching, and moving food to the mouth. Hind limbs are absent, and the body tapers posteriorly to a large, horizontally flattened spatulate tail. It is the vertical

water. Cruising animals move along at 4–10 km/h, but over short distances (100 m) fleeing manatees have been clocked at 25 km/h (Hartman 1979). Skin color varies from gray to brown, and the skin finely wrinkled all over. Short, unpigmented hairs are scattered sparsely over the body, and algal growths, barnacles, and skin incrustations often cover the skin.

Manatees are wholly herbivorous and feed on a variety of submerged, natant, and emergent vegetation. In Puerto Rico and Nicaragua, *Panicum molle* and *P. jumentorum* are reportedly favorites (Barrett 1935). Also eaten in fresh water are *Hydrilla, Myriophyllum, Ceratophyllum, Elodea, Typha, Cabomba,* and other species. The saltwater diet includes the sea grasses *Thalassia, Syringodium, Halophila,* and *Diplanthera.* That manatees will consume water hyacinth (*Eichornia crassipes*) has brought them to attention as a potential source of control of this prolific and troublesome weed, which chokes canals and inland waterways throughout the tropics.

Manatees appear to be arythmical, with no specific daily patterns (Hartman 1979). They generally feed from 6–8 h daily and rest from 2–12 h daily, usually doing both in short bouts. When resting or feeding, only the snout is exposed while breathing. Average submergence time is 4–5 min. Manatees are usually silent, and the squeaks and chirps heard under water appear to be impulsive rather than communicative. Cows and calves, however, do maintain vocal contact (Hartman 1979). Defecation is nearly continuous, and flatulence is very common; rising bubbles are a good field sign of manatees.

T. manatus is mildly social (Reynolds 1979), and while in groups individuals do exhibit social facilitation. Manatees have been observed playing in groups, chasing, bumping, and kissing. Males engage in homosexual activities (Hartman 1979). The only agonistic encounters thus far observed have been bumping and pushing between bulls in pursuit of estrous females (Hartman 1979). Associations are ephemeral and not based on age or sex. The only lasting relationship (1–2 years) is that between a cow and her calf (Hartman 1979).

The West Indian manatee breeds throughout the year. Gestation period is probably 385–400 days (Hartman 1979). Suckling occurs at the two axillary teats, under water. Longevity in the wild is unknown for this species, but a captive in Florida was maintained as an adult for 23 years (Anonymous 1973).

Parasites reported for this manatee are: trematodes, *Chiochis fabaceus* and *Opisthotrema cochleotrema;* nematodes, *Plicalolabia hagenbecki;* and copepods, *Harpacticus pulex* (Husar 1977). There is no documentation of predation on the West Indian manatee by any animal other than man.

*

Anonymous. 1973. Baby Snooks eats and performs, but problem continues. *Tampa Tribune,* 8 March.

Barrett, O. W. 1935. Notes concerning manatees and dugongs. *J. Mamm.* 16:216–20.

Frantzius, A. von. 1869. Die Säugethiere Costaricas. *Archiv. Naturgesch.* (Berlin) 35:247–325.

Hartman, D. S. 1979. *Ecology and behavior of the manatee (Trichechus manatus) in Florida.* Special Publication no. 5. American Society of Mammalogists.

Husar, S. L. 1977. The West Indian manatee (*Trichechus manatus*). *U.S. Fish Wildl. Serv., Wildl. Res. Rept.* 7:1–22.

Reynolds, J. E. 1979. The semisocial manatee. *Review,* June, pp. 93–96.

Vampyrum spectrum (Vampiro Falso, False Vampire Bat)

J. Bradbury

Vampyrum spectrum is the largest bat in the New World. It is an imposing animal with adult weights of up to 200 g and a wingspan approaching 80 cm. The species is the extreme in a series of phyllostominine bats that share a similar physiognomy and a dietary bias for larger prey. All have large complete pinnae, canidlike muzzles, and elongate nose leaves. Smaller forms such as *Micronycteris* feed on insects or insects plus fruit, intermediate forms such as *Trachops* and *Chrotopterus* mix larger insects with small vertebrates such as lizards, and the large *Vampyrum* favors substantial vertebrates such as birds, rodents, and other bats. The jaws of *Vampyrum* are strikingly endowed with large canine teeth and a row of carnassiallike shearing molars; the skull bears a pronounced sagittal crest to anchor the powerful jaw muscles. Were it not to have a nose leaf, this bat could easily be taken for a small dog in head form.

The scientific name is a misnomer. Early explorers hearing tales of vampire bats simply assumed that the largest and most fierce-looking species must be "the" vampire. One reported that individuals of *Vampyrum* fanned their victims to sleep with their large wings, and another suggested that the nose leaf and associated structures were suction devices used to remove blood. Both suggestions were clearly speculation, since the true vampires (*Desmodus, Diaemus,* and *Diphylla*) do not fan their victims and lap blood instead of suck it.

Vampyrum spectrum roosts in groups of up to five in the dark upper reaches of hollow trees. Most other bat species avoid these trees, with the exception of *Saccopteryx bilineata,* which may roost near the tree opening. The few groups that have been captured appear to consist of one adult pair and their recent young. One such group in Guanacaste consisted of the two adults, one suckling pup, one half-grown male, and one nearly adult-sized female that had not yet bred. In the roost the bats form a contact cluster. They appear to be highly social, and group composition may remain stable for long periods. When disturbed in the roost, the whole group emits a soft chittering sound. This noise is characteristic of the species and constitutes a good marker for the presence of *Vampyrum* in a given hollow tree. Captive groups have demonstrated a wide variety of social signals. Animals separated from their group, for example, for foraging, are greeted on their return to the roost by an interlocking of mouths much like that found in wolves. A rapid high piping accompanied by vibration of the closed wings is a contagious behavior that seems to agitate the whole group. Bats leaving a roost to feed often emit a loud screech as they depart and repeat it several times while in flight. The function of this sound is unclear, since the bats appear to forage singly.

As noted above, these bats are carnivorous. Most reports of stomach, feces, or roost-litter analyses agree that birds, rodents, and other bats are the major constituents of the diet. Some fruit and insects may be taken on occasion, but this appears to be rare. One long-term study on the remains of prey brought back to a roost in Guanacaste showed a heavy bias for nonpasserine birds such as anis, doves, parakeets, motmots, and trogons. Most of these prey are either fairly smelly or roost in groups at night. Some of the species taken match the bats in weight. This same study suggested that not all bats feed every night, that a foraging *Vampyrum* can sometimes fill its stomach within an hour after leaving the roost, and that the bats do not necessarily forage at great distances from the roost. It also showed that although the suckling pup in the study group was left behind in the roost, it was always "guarded" by one adult or subadult member of the group. Some evidence of provisioning by the adult male of a captive pair was observed in Trinidad, and this may be a common behavior in this species. It would certainly account for the presence of prey remains in the floor of the roost: these are quantitatively insufficient to account for the energy needs of all the bats in the group but are substantial enough to warrant some explanation. Since not all prey eaten are brought back to the roost, provisioning of youngsters (and the baby-sitter) seems a distinct possibility. It is clear that these bats have complex family lives that may show many parallels with other mammalian carnivores such as canids.

Vampyrum occurs over a wide range of the American tropics but is never dense. This is presumably a function of its status as a large carnivore. This sparse dispersion has been exacerbated in recent years by museum skin collectors, pet fanciers, and careless field biologists who will not leave the bats alone. Trinidad and Costa Rica are two sites in which *Vampyrum* roosts are now kept secret for fear that some small museum will feel the need to complete its skin collection at the expense of the remnant populations. Fieldworkers are encouraged to observe and enjoy these large bats, but unnecessary disturbance and collecting should be avoided whenever possible.

*

Casebeer, R. S.; Linsky, B. S.; and Nelson, C. 1963. The phyllostomid bats, *Ectophylla alba* and *Vampyrum spectrum,* in Costa Rica. *J. Mamm.* 44:186–89.

Goodwin, G. G., and Greenhall, A. M. 1961. A review of the bats of Trinidad and Tobago. *Bull. Am. Mus. Nat. Hist.* 122:191–301.

Greenhall, A. M. 1968. Notes on the behavior of the false vampire bat. *J. Mamm.* 49:337–40.

Peterson, R. L., and Kirmse, P. 1969. Notes on *Vampyrum spectrum,* the false vampire bat, in Panama. *Can. J. Zool.* 47:140–45.

Vehrencamp, S.; Stiles, F. G.; and Bradbury, J. 1977. Observations on the foraging behavior and avian prey of the Neotropical carnivorous bat, *Vampyrum spectrum. J. Mamm.* 58:469–78.

10 BIRDS

INTRODUCTION

F. G. Stiles

Costa Rica is fortunate among Latin American countries in having an avifauna that is both extremely rich (over 820 species, more than all of North America) and relatively well studied. The taxonomy and distribution of Costa Rican birds are well known owing to the efforts of a long series of investigators, beginning a century ago with von Frantzius and continuing with Lawrence, Zeledón, Cherrie, Carriker, Ridgway, Alfaro, and Austin Smith, through Slud and several recent workers, often connected with the Organization for Tropical Studies (OTS). For many years the Museo Nacional de Costa Rica was a major center of Neotropical ornithology, and a famous bird collection was amassed through the efforts of Zeledón, Carmiol, Underwood, Cooper, Endre, and others. The long series of breeding-biology and natural-history studies of Costa Rican birds by Skutch are unparalleled in the New World tropics and provide a starting point and stimulus for modern studies of ecology and behavior. Largely through the work of MacArthur and his co-workers and followers, studies on tropical birds continue to occupy a key place in our attempts to understand tropical communities. We are learning to ask more realistic questions, but few general and well-documented

answers are available as yet. With its fine national parks and growing research establishment, Costa Rica is an increasingly appropriate place to seek many of these answers.

This essay attempts to paint a broad outline of the ecology and evolution of the Costa Rican avifauna, with particular attention to new approaches and open questions. The discussion of classification and origins of the avifauna will serve to establish a common vocabulary at the outset. Then I will discuss how the avifauna is put together in time and space, with particular reference to various aspects of community organization. I will not treat population phenomena such as social systems, behavioral repertoires, or exploitation systems in any detail, since many of these topics will be covered in the ecological life histories of representative species. I hope this essay will help to stimulate and orient meaningful research on the birds of Costa Rica.

Composition and Affinities of the Avifauna

MAJOR TAXONOMIC GROUPS AND THEIR RELATIONSHIPS

Table 10.1 provides a quick sketch of the Costa Rican avifauna by families. The first large group of families, from Tinamidae through Rynchopidae, includes the large land birds (tinamous, chickenlike or galliform birds, vul-

Dorsal view of central tail feathers of an adult female great curassow (*Crax rubra*). Imagine the developmental process that produces the white bands across the rust background quite independently of the morphological development of the feather. Santa Rosa National Park, Costa Rica (photo, D. H. Janzen).

502

TABLE 10.1. Taxonomic and Ecological Survey of Costa Rican Birds

Family	Spp.[a]	BV/R[b]	PR[c]	NBV/R[d]	Representative Common Names	Ecological, Behavioral, Morphological Characteristics[e]
Tinamidae	5		5		Tinamous	Terrestrial, poor fliers; fallen fruits and seeds
Podicepedidae	2		2		Grebes	Freshwater divers; fish, aquatic insects
Procellariidae	7			7	Shearwaters, petrels	Pelagic; fish, squid; come to land only to nest
Hydrobatidae	5			5	Storm-petrels	Pelagic; mostly plankton feeders
Pelecanidae	2		1	1	Pelicans	Coastal (mostly); large; dive for fish; huge bill
Sulidae	4		1	3	Boobies	Coastal or pelagic; dive for fish or squid
Phalacrocoracidae	1		1		Cormorants	Fresh or salt water; pursue fish underwater
Anhingidae	1		1		Anhingas	Fresh water; pursue fish underwater; long neck, bill
Fregatidae	1			1	Frigatebirds	Marine soaring birds; swoop to surface, rob other birds
Phaethontidae	1			1	Tropicbirds	Marine; ternlike; plunge for fish, squid
Ardeidae	18		11	11	Herons, egrets	Long-legged waders; aquatic insects and vertebrates
Ciconiidae	2		2		Storks	Long-legged waders; large; heavy bill; mostly fish
Threskiornithidae	4				Ibises, spoonbills	Long-legged waders; curved or spatulate bill; fish, invertebrates
Anatidae	15		5	10	Ducks	Surface swimmers, some dive; plant matter, some insects, fish
Cathartidae	4		4		Vultures	Large, soaring carrion feeders
Accipitridae	36	2	28	8	Hawks, kites, eagles	Predators; soar or ambush in vegetation; strong bill, feet
Falconidae	12		9	3	Falcons, caracaras	High-speed predators, thicket hunters; wasp or carrion feeders
Pandionidae	1			1	Osprey	Dive for fish; coast or large rivers
Cracidae	5		5		Guans, chachalacas	Medium to large; mostly arboreal; fruits and seeds
Phasianidae	8		8		Quail, wood-partridge	Smaller; mostly terrestrial; fruits and seeds
Rallidae	13		11	2	Rails, gallinules	Marsh-dwelling swimmers and stalkers; aquatic invertebrates
Aramidae	1		1		Limpkin	Large wading snail-eaters; marshes
Heliornithidae	1		1		Sungrebe	Surface swimmers; streams and sloughs; insects from vegetation
Eurypygidae	1		1		Sunbittern	Stream- and swamp-edge waders, rock hoppers
Jacanidae	1		1		Jacanas	Marshes; walk on vegetation; insects, invertebrates
Haematopodidae	1		1 ?	1	Oystercatchers	Seashore, mud flats; mollusk feeders; scissors bill
Charadriidae	7		2	6	Plovers	Seashore, mud flats; peck-and-pursue predators; invertebrates
Scolopacidae	28			28	Sandpipers	Seashore, mud flats, fresh water; peck or probe; invertebrates
Phalaropodidae	3			3	Phalaropes	Fresh or water; surface feeders for tiny invertebrates
Recurvirostridae	2		1	1–2	Avocets, stilts	Long-legged, slender-billed waders
Burhinidae	1		1		Thickknees	Largely cursorial savanna dwellers
Stercorariidae	4			4	Skuas, jaegers	Gull-like, mostly pelagic predators and robbers

TABLE 10.1. Continued

Family	Spp.[a]	BV/R[b]	PR[c]	NBV/R[d]	Representative Common Names	Ecological, Behavioral, Morphological Characteristics[e]
Laridae	18	1		17	Gulls, terns	Seashore; omnivores and predators, or dive for fish
Rynchopidae	1			1	Skimmers	Skim water surface for fish
Columbidae	24		24	2	Pigeons, doves	Terrestrial or arboreal; strong fliers; fruits, seeds
Psittacidae	16		16		Macaws, parrots	Strong-billed arboreal frugivores; strong fliers; highly social
Cuculidae	10		8	2	Cuckoos, anis	Slender, long-tailed insectivores; some parasitic or highly social
Strigidae	16		14	2	Owls	Nocturnal or crepuscular predators; forest or savanna
Tytonidae	1		1		Barn owls	Highly nocturnal predators; open country, cities
Nyctibiidae	2		2		Potoos	Nocturnal; large insectivores; perch on stubs
Caprimulgidae	9		7	2	Nightjars, nighthawks	Nocturnal or crepuscular; sally for insects, or aerial pursuers
Apodidae	11		8	3	Swifts	Extremely aerial insectivores; rarely alight
Trochilidae	51		50	1	Hummingbirds	Small hovering nectarivores; also insects, spiders
Trogonidae	10		10		Trogons, quetzal	Thick-billed frugivores; also sit-and-wait predators
Alcedinidae	6		5	1	Kingfisher	Mostly freshwater; dive from perch for fish
Momotidae	6		6		Motmots	Strong-billed sit-and-wait predators, frugivores; racket tail
Galbulidae	2		2		Jacamars	Sally for insects, lizards, etc.; long or strong bills, metallic plummage
Bucconidae	5		5		Puffbirds	Fluffy, big-headed, strong-billed; sit-and-wait predators
Capitonidae	2		2		Barbets	Large-billed frugivors or insectivores; solitary or social
Ramphastidae	6		6		Toucans	Huge-billed, social frugivors and nest predators; arboreal
Picidae	16		15	1	Woodpeckers, piculets	Strong-billed, wood-drilling insectivores, also fruit

PASSERINES—ORDER PASSERIFORMES

Family	Spp.[a]	BV/R[b]	PR[c]	NBV/R[d]	Representative Common Names	Ecological, Behavioral, Morphological Characteristics[e]
Dendrocolaptidae	16		16		Woodcreepers	Slender, mostly long-billed trunk gleaners
Furnariidae	18		18		Foliage gleaners, leaf-tossers	Arboreal or terrestrial, rummage in foliage, epiphytes for insects
Formicariidae	29		29		Antbirds	Strong-billed insectivores; arboreal or terrestrial; some follow army ants
Rhinocryptidae	1		1		Tapaculos	Terrestrial; thicket-dwelling small insectivores
Cotingidae	19		19	1	Cotingas, tityras, etc.	Broad-billed; arboreal frugivores or insectivores
Pipridae	9		9		Manakins	Small, stubby frugivores; notable male display
Oxyruncidae	1		1		Sharpbill	Rare, canopy of subtropical forest; frugivores
Tyrannidae	75	3	60	13	Flycatchers, tyrannulets, kingbirds	Insectivores or frugivores; sally or glean; strong, often hooked bill

TABLE 10.1.   Continued

Family	Spp.[a]	BV/R[b]	PR[c]	NBV/R[d]	Representative Common Names	Ecological, Behavioral, Morphological Characteristics[e]
Hirundinidae	11		4	8	Martins, swallows	Aerial insectivores
Corvidae	5		5		Jays	Omnivores; strong bills, feet; highly social
Cinclidae	1		1		Dippers	Subtropical white-water streams; feed at water's edge; sometimes swim
Troglodytidae	23		23		Wrens	Noisy; insectivorous thicket dwellers; many highly social
Mimidae	1			1	Catbird	Inconspicuous thicket dwellers; insects and fruit
Turdidae	15		11	4	Thrushes, robins, solitaires	Canopy, understory, or open areas; fruit, invertebrates; notable songsters
Sylviidae	4		4		Gnatcatchers, gnatwrens	Small insectivores (gleaners); canopy or thickets
Bombycillidae	3		2	1	Silky-flycatchers waxwings	Flocking frugivores; mostly in canopy
Vireonidae	16	1	8	7	Vireos	Small, strong-billed leaf gleaners and frugivores
Parulidae	48		12	36	Warblers	Small, fine-billed (most); glean or sally; insects, some nectar and fruit
Icteridae	19	1	14	4	Orioles, caciques, blackbirds	Sharp-billed, various sizes; insectivores or omnivores; variety of social systems
Zeledoniidae	1		1		Wrenthrush	Small highland thicket dwellers
Coerebidae	7		7		Honeycreepers	Small, sharp-billed omnivores or nectarivores
Thraupidae	45		42	3	Tanagers	Frugivores or omnivores; often colorful; many heavy-billed
Fringillidae	49		46	4	Grosbeaks, finches, sparrows	Conical-billed seed or fruit eaters
Ploceidae	1		1		Old World sparrows	Conical-billed urban ominvores and granivores

[a] Number of species in family from Costa Rica.

[b] Breeding visitants and residents: present in Costa Rica only to breed, then leave.

[c] Permanent residents: present year-round, including breeding.

[d] Nonbreeding residents and visitants: present for part or even all of year (usually young birds) but do not breed; includes mostly northern migrants. This and the preceding two columns may add up to more than the total number of species, because some species occur in more than one category (often different subspecies)

[e] Representative ecological, behavioral, or morphological features of the family as represented in Costa Rica.

tures, and diurnal birds of prey) and water birds (all the rest). Most of these families have long fossil records and cosmopolitan or pantropical contemporary distributions. Exceptions are the sun bittern and limpkin, specialized offshoots of the widespread order Gruiformes (cranes, rails, etc.). The Cathartidae and Cracidae are at present restricted to the New World, but fossils may indicate wider distributions in the past. The tinamous are peculiar, considered by some to be closest to the large flightless "ratite" birds (ostrich, rhea, etc.) and by others to be closest to the Galliformes; they are sometimes considered the most primitive of living birds.

Families of the next group, Columbidae through Picidae, are often called the "higher nonpasserines." Most are cosmopolitan or pantropical, but there is also a sizable contingent of New World endemics (hummingbirds, motmots, potoos, jacamars, puffbirds, toucans). Of these, only the first have invaded North America north of Mexico. The other families include mainly specialized insectivores or frugivores or both: many are sit-and-wait predators taking large insects, small vertebrates, and sometimes fruit. Analogous ecological types occur in the Old World tropics, but not in the temperate zones.

The remainder of the families are in the huge order Passeriformes, the perching birds or "passerines," which includes more than half the living species of birds. This order has evidently undergone a major adaptive radiation very recently and is presumably evolving rapidly at present; morphological divergence within the order is relatively slight, and the relationships of many families and genera remain controversial. (Owing to their small size, the passerines also have a meager fossil record, and many groups may be older than supposed.)

Classification of the passerines at the family level has heretofore laid undue emphasis on a single character, the morphology of the syrinx—the organ of sound production (another name for the passerines is "songbirds"). The families Dendrocolaptidae through Tyrannidae have a simpler, supposedly more "primitive" syrinx and are collectively called the "suboscines"; the remaining families feature a more elaborate syrinx and constitute the supposedly more advanced "oscines." Conventional wisdom has it that the evolutionary history of the Passeriformes has consisted largely of the replacement of the primitive suboscines by the advanced oscines over most of the world. This interpretation has recently been challenged on both morphological and ecological grounds. The suboscines turn out to have an advanced or derived middle-ear apparatus; the oscine arrangement follows the general avian pattern (Feduccia 1977). In South America there is no evidence that suboscines are declining, even in the face of human influences or unusual weather (Willis 1976). These authors suggest that oscines and suboscines represent separate evolutionary lines that have evolved different morphological adaptions for producing and receiving sounds, perhaps in relation to the supposed original habitats of each group: the interior of tropical forest for the suboscines, nonforest (or canopy?) habitats for oscines. Certainly the acoustic features of these habitats differ (Morton 1975).

Except for two small paleotropical families of debatable affinities, the suboscines are a New World group, and only the Tyrannidae extend well into North America. Among the Costa Rican oscines, the families Hirundinidae through Bombycillidae, plus the Ploceidae and some of the heterogeneous family Fringillidae, are most diverse in the Old World (except for the wrens and Mimidae). The remainder, Vireonidae through the rest of the Fringillidae, are all closely related and represent the ma-

jor oscine radiation in the New World. They are collectively called the "nine-primaried oscines" (most birds have ten primary feathers per wing; the vireos do also, but the tenth primary is very small). As has been intimated, the Fringillidae constitute a diverse group including nine- and ten-primaried contingents, possibly with New and Old World origins. Seed-eating birds in general are thought to have radiated very recently, since grasses became abundant only in the Pliocene.

AFFINITIES OF RESIDENTS AND MIGRANTS

As a first step toward an ecological division of the Costa Rican avifauna, we might separate the permanent residents from the migrants and visitants. There are striking differences between water birds and land birds, oscines and suboscines, with regard to migration (table 10.2). The great majority of Costa Rica's water birds are migratory: most of the freshwater avifauna (ducks, herons, etc.) and shorebirds and their relatives (sandpipers, plovers, gulls, terns, etc.) breed in North America, while the marine birds (petrels, shearwaters, pelicans, frigatebirds, etc.) breed in such far-flung places as Cape Horn, Peru, New Zealand, the Galápagos, Panama, Baja California, and Alaska. In some groups, notably the herons, a small population may breed in Costa Rica (cf. Leber 1980), but a much larger population breeds in North America and spends the northern winter in the tropics. Most of the migratory freshwater avifauna (except the ducks) and many shorebirds, gulls, and terns maintain year-round populations in Costa Rica, but those birds present during the northern summer are nonbreeders, mostly yearlings. Many of these species are notably slow to mature (many herons, gulls, etc.), or they breed in hazardous areas like the Arctic tundra (shorebirds, jaegers, etc.). Thus the breeding success of young, inexperienced birds would probably be low in any case, and they would gain little by going north their first spring.

Among the land birds, only a handful of nonpasserines

TABLE 10.2. Patterns of Seasonal Occurrence in Different Taxonomic and Ecological Groups of Costa Rican Birds

Group	Permanent Resident Only	Breeding Resident Only	Resident and Migrant Populations	Nonbreeding Migrant or Visitant Only	Nonbreeding Summer Population	Total Species
Water birds	39	1	14+	96	40+	150
Land birds: nonpasserines	229	2	9	18	0	258
Land birds: suboscines	151	3	2	11	0	167
Land birds: oscines	172	1	3	69	0	245
Totals	592	7	28	193	40+	820 Total avifauna
		627 Total breeding avifauna		221 Total migrant avifauna		

NOTE: Figures are numbers of species.

are migrants, though some of their migrations are spectacular (e.g., *Buteo* hawks, vultures). The flycatchers include the only long-distance migrants among the suboscines: virtually all the flycatchers breeding in eastern and central North America reach Costa Rica in their migrations. Among the oscines, numerous species migrate, including most warblers and swallows. Unlike the water birds, the land bird migrants do not maintain a year-round presence in Costa Rica: first-year birds migrate north with older birds and are fully capable of breeding. However, many land bird migrants spend 6 or 7 months on their tropical wintering grounds—far longer than on their breeding territories in the north. Also, the great majority also have close relatives resident in the tropics: there is no taxonomic gap between resident and migrant land birds (Stiles 1979*a*). The major exception is the Parulidae, where most species and several whole genera are migratory. However, this family is thought to have originated in Central America, adopted the migratory habit early, and speciated extensively in the Pleistocene, as glacial and interglacial periods produced contractions and expansions of the breeding range (Mayr 1946; Mengel 1964). These arguments suggest that it is incorrect to consider at least the land bird migrants an "alien" element superimposed upon a tropical "endemic" avifauna: both are integral parts of the Costa Rican avifauna.

Zoogeography of Costa Rican Birds

HISTORICAL CONSIDERATIONS

It is now generally agreed that there was continuous land extending from North America through at least northern Nicaragua all through the Tertiary; that by the middle Miocene, land was continuous as far as central Panama; and that the last seaway separating Central and South America was closed at the end of the Pliocene (review in Howell 1969). The area from southern Mexico through northern Nicaragua has been called "nuclear Central America" or "tropical North America," since it was essentially a tropical peninsula of North America during the Tertiary and was the supposed center of origin of such groups as the wrens, motmots, and warblers, as well as the center of the New World radiation of the jays (Mayr 1946; Howell 1969).

The geological history of the area south of "nuclear Central America" is less well established. During most of the Tertiary, southern Central America was an island arc traversed by up to three major seaways, though apparently no single seaway existed continuously through the entire Tertiary; a continuous land bridge between North and South America may even have existed briefly during the Eocene (cf. Haffer 1974). By all accounts the region was tectonically unstable through the Tertiary, but lack of a single permanent water barrier permitted at least intermittent avifaunal exchange during this time. This made possible the early arrivals and extensive secondary radiations in South America of such Holarctic groups as the thrushes and swallows; conversely, the breeding insectivorous birds of North America are nearly all of Neotropical (including Central America) derivation (Snow 1978). The uplift of the Andes at the end of the Pliocene greatly restricted faunal interchange between Central America and Amazonia; modern Central American species of recent derivation have their closest affinities with the "trans-Andean" avifaunas north and west of these mountains (Haffer 1974).

The present-day Costa Rica–Chiriquí highlands, a volcanic island arc in the Oligocene, were uplifted into a single mountain range in the Miocene; another uplift at the start of the Pleistocene gave these highlands their present form (review in Wolf 1976). Intermittently isolated by seaways to the north and south in the Tertiary, these highlands became a major center of avian speciation and differentiation. In the Pleistocene, there were glaciers in the highest part of the Cordillera de Talamanca, and páramo vegetation probably occurred down to 2,000 m or even lower (Wolf 1976). During glacial periods tropical lowland forest was probably restricted to a few major patches or "refugia." In southern Central America, such refugia were probably in the Golfo Dulce region, near the Caribbean coast of Nicaragua or Costa Rica or both, and in the Darien of Panama (Haffer 1974; Muller 1973). These forests expanded in the warmer, wetter interglacial periods; the recurring isolation and rejoining of such refugia doubtless promoted speciation in birds and other groups (Haffer 1974).

CONTEMPORARY DISTRIBUTION PATTERNS

In his geographical summary of the resident avifauna of Costa Rica, Slud (1964) recognized four major "avifaunal zones," roughly corresponding to major geographic subdivisions of the country: the northern Pacific lowlands, the southern Pacific lowlands, the Caribbean lowlands, and the Costa Rica–Chiriquí highlands.

The most distinctive lowland avifauna is that of the northern Pacific lowlands—the tropical dry (and moist) forest. This "Guanacaste" avifauna is actually the southernmost segment of the Central American dry-forest avifauna, which extends north along the Pacific coast to Sonora, Mexico, and reaches its maximum diversity from about Oaxaca through El Salvador. It is the smallest Costa Rican lowland avifauna, sharing rather few species with other sectors of the country. Those species shared between the dry forest and more humid life zones usually occur in open or disturbed areas in the latter, but in forest in the former (e.g., *Todirostrum cinereum* and *sylvia*). Dry-forest species may therefore spread into more humid areas with deforestation, as has occurred over the Meseta Central.

The major bird habitats of this zone are tropical deciduous forest, evergreen riparian forest, and savanna that is maintained by burning. In the Tempisque basin an extensive system of seasonal swamps and lagoons (at present being rapidly drained) supports the richest freshwater avifauna in Central America. During the severe 6–7-month dry season, virtually all trees (except in riparian situations) lose their leaves, and many flower; many bodies of water dry up, and some kinds of bird food (many insects, some fruits) decrease in abundance (cf. Janzen and Schoener 1968). Dry-forest birds (and water birds) cope with these changes by shifts in habitat or diet or both, or by migration. This zone has several species of breeding migrants that "winter" in South America, as well as the largest contingent of wintering northern migrants of any region in Costa Rica (table 10.2). A number of species move to riparian situations during the dry season, then reoccupy the dry forest with the rains (e.g., *Thamnophilus doliatus*).

Given their overall similarities in climate, habitats, and avifauna, the Caribbean and southern Pacific lowlands can be considered together (cf. Muller 1973). The major habitat type is tropical wet or "rain" forest, whose evergreen character reflects the relatively short and mild dry season. The avifuana of this zone shows much stronger South American affinities than does that of Guanacaste, with such Neotropical groups as the antbirds, jacamars, toucans, and tanagers well represented (Howell 1969).

Along the Caribbean slope of Central America, tropical evergreen forest extends nearly continuously from northern Colombia to southeastern Mexico. In general the avifauna becomes progressively more depauperate, and the South American element more diluted with Central American endemics and species of northern affinities, as one moves along the isthmus, even without obvious habitat discontinuities. Several species barely reach Costa Rica (e.g., *Dysithamnus puncticeps*), others drop out at about the latitude of Limón (e.g., *Pionus menstruus*) or fail to reach Nicaragua (e.g., *Myiornis atricapillus*). Most of the "rain-forest" species in the Costa Rican avifauna extend southeastward to northwestern South America, but a few are Central American representatives of southern genera (e.g., *Phloeoceastes (Campephilus) guatemalensis, Aphanotriccus capitalis*) that evidently differentiated in the Pleistocene forest refugia (Muller 1973).

On the Pacific slope, tropical wet forest occurs (or did, until recently) only from the Parrita area south to western Chiriquí, Panama. Drier forests and savannas to the north and south, and the Cordillera de Talamanca on the east, isolate this area from the main body of tropical wet forest on the Caribbean slope. This isolation probably dates back to the Pleistocene refugia and is reflected in the avifauna: many sedentary tropical species common on the Atlantic slope (antbirds, tanagers, motmots, toucans, etc.) do not occur in the Golfo Dulce forests. Their places in the avifauna may be taken by endemic species or subspecies (e.g., *Thryothorus semibadius* replaces *T. nigricapillus; Thamnophilus bridgesi* replaces *T. punctatus*), or by middle-elevation species that extend to the lowlands here but not on the Atlantic slope (e.g., *Dysithamnus mentalis, Momotus momota*). A number of Atlantic species have no obvious replacements (e.g., *Phaenostictus mcleannani, Mitrospingus cassinii*), and the total avifauna of the Golfo Dulce area is smaller (table 10.3). There are also fewer wintering northern migrants, reflecting the region's relative isolation from the major migration routes along the Caribbean coast. Comparative autecological studies in the Caribbean and Golfo Dulce lowlands offer numerous opportunities for testing concepts like ecological equivalence and competitive release.

The General-Térraba region includes a small but interesting "subzone" of the Pacific southwest avifauna. This

TABLE 10.3. Avifaunal Characteristics and Levels of Endemism: Northeastern Costa Rica Compared with Golfo Dulce Region

	Golfo Dulce	Northeastern Costa Rica
Permanent resident water birds	22	18
Permanent resident land birds	216[a]	235[a]
Breeding residents	3	1
Winter resident land birds	29	32
Migrant land birds from North America	27	35
Altitudinal migrants	3	14
Endemic species	8	0
Endemic subspecies	10	0
Species at northern limit of range	10	18
Total	365	385

NOTE: The Golfo Dulce area includes the Palmar-Coto area and the Osa Peninsula; by northeastern Costa Rica is meant the area between La Selva and Tortuguero: the Llanuras de Tortuguero and the Llanuras de Sarapiquí. These areas are of approximately the same size (ca. 2,500 km²).

[a] Excludes mangrove specialists.

landlocked region gets less rainfall, especially during the dry season, than surrounding areas owing to the rain shadows cast by the Cordillera de Talamanca and the coast ranges. Scrub and savanna (whether anthropogenic or not remains controversial) have persisted in this region for a long time, and several South American savanna birds (e.g., *Synallaxis albescens, Emberizoides herbicola*) reach their northern limits here. Deforestation in the Golfo Dulce lowlands has also permitted several other southern open-country species to invade this area, where they have increased rapidly (e.g., *Milvago chimachima;* cf. Kiff 1975; Skutch 1971).

The Costa Rica–Chiriquí highlands form a well-defined avifaunal unit. Some fifty species and seventy-five subspecies, well over half of the avifauna, are endemic to these highlands (Slud 1964). In general, the level of endemism is higher in passerines than in non-passerines (except hummingbirds); not surprisingly, it is also higher in obligate high-elevation species than in species with wide altitudinal ranges (Wolf 1976). Overall avifaunal affinities are with South America: about three times as many species reach their northern, as opposed to southern, limits here (Slud 1964). However, geographic affinities of the avifauna shift with altitude. The rich cloud-forest avifauna of lower and middle elevations is almost exclusively South American in derivation, but the proportion of species with southern affinities (sensu Howell 1969) drops sharply at high elevations. Many tropical groups like antbirds, puffbirds, and manakins hardly enter the mountains at all, or extend only to middle elevations. At the highest elevations, the avifauna consists mainly of oscines and other species of widely distributed groups or with clearly northern affinities (e.g., *Junco vulcani, Melanerpes formicivorus,* etc.). Evidently the rich páramo avifauna of the Andes has not successfully colonized these highlands. The northern groups, on the other hand, doubtless arrived during a cool glacial interlude and remained as relict populations, progressively retreating to higher elevations with the warmer postglacial periods.

ALTITUDINAL DISTRIBUTIONS

For the most part it is difficult to define altitudinal belts or zones in the Costa Rican highland avifauna. Patterns of altitudinal replacement of congeners vary between genera and often do not coincide (fig. 10.1). This doubtless reflects that different groups are responding to different aspects of the habitat, which may change at different rates or in different places along an altitudinal transect. For instance, as one ascends the Cordillera de Talamanca, the forest canopy becomes dominated by oaks and the understory by bamboos—but these changes may occur gradually or suddenly, or at different elevations or slope exposures. *Catharus frantzii* is rather abruptly replaced by *C. gracilirostris* as the understory becomes dominated

by bamboo. However, the wood-wren *Henicorhina leucophrys* occurs abundantly from middle elevations well up into the bamboo zone, being replaced by *Thryorchilus browni* only at the highest elevations. Some canopy species are affected by other habitat parameters, such as the volume and kind of epiphytic growth (e.g., many Furnariidae).

Such complex and subtle patterns of avifaunal turnover were also found by Terborgh (1971) and Terborgh and Weske (1975) along an altitudinal transect in the Andes. They eventually concluded that several factors, notably interspecific competition, were important in limiting bird distributions altitudinally. Some altitudinal replacement patterns of congeners in the Costa Rican avifauna also suggest competition (fig. 10.1), but direct evidence is lacking. In other cases (e.g., *Tangara*), several species appear to be responding similarly, perhaps to discontinuously varying habitat parameters. The elevation band 600–1,400 m on the Caribbean slope is notable for the number of species restricted to it: several *Tangara* species and the tanager *Buthraupis,* the flycatcher *Phylloscartes,* several hummingbirds, and so forth. The wettest cloud forests occur at these elevations, and this vegetation has a notably rich avifauna in the Andes also (Terborgh 1977).

HABITAT RELATIONS AND DISTRIBUTION

A tropical forest contains several structural habitat types: forest canopy, forest interior, forest edge, and "nonforest," as related to the position and orientation of the foliage-air interface (fig. 10.2; Stiles 1979*a*). Natural light gaps and edges are an integral part of the dynamics of the forest itself, and many plants and animals require such situations to persist in forested areas (Stiles 1975; Schemske and Brokaw 1981; Hartshorn 1978). Natural light gaps vary greatly in size and permanence, from small tree falls through larger tree-fall gaps and streamsides, to extensive areas along rivers that are maintained in early successional stages by periodic floods. Many species now considered "second-growth" or "scrub" birds were limited to such riparian habitats in the past (Terborgh and Weske 1969). Given the dynamic, mosaic nature of the forest, I do not think it logical to restrict the term "forest birds" to those species found only in the interior of mature-phase forest (sensu Hartshorn 1978, 1980), as has been done by several authors (e.g., Slud 1964; Terborgh 1977). Conversely, to me the term "nonforest" bird should be restricted to those species requiring extensive areas where the foliage-air interface is close to the ground. With the deforestation and habitat changes wrought by man, these species are at present expanding their population sizes and distributions explosively—something that has not been taken into account in studies of their ecology and social systems (e.g., Pulliam 1973).

ELEVATION IN METERS

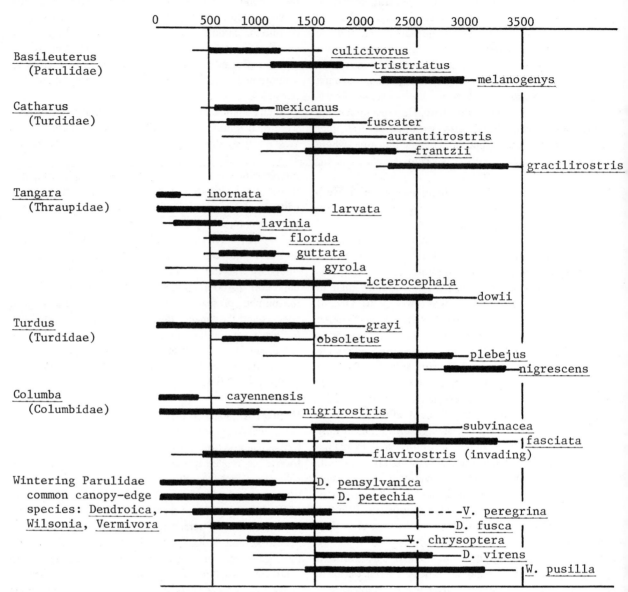

FIGURE 10.1 Elevation ranges of members of certain bird genera on the Atlantic slope of Costa Rica.

The transient, heterogeneous, and unpredictable nature of many light-gap habitats must have placed many of their birds under selective pressures very different from those affecting species of the adjacent forest interior. High mobility, flexibility in behavior or social systems, and high reproductive rates might have been important attributes of species continually required to "hopscotch" to new light gaps as the old ones grew up. Many such species (including most "nonforest" or "second-growth" types) occur over very wide altitudinal or humidity ranges (e.g., *Turdus grayi*, sea level to 1,800 m, in both wet and dry life zones). These species are often able to cross considerable expanses of forest: one can mist-net *Sporophila* seed eaters inside solid forest, but not ant thrushes in pastures.

By contrast, birds of the forest interior lived in an essentially continuous habitat until quite recently. There was probably little selection for dispersal ability per se: the sedentariness of forest birds and their reluctance to cross light gaps are proverbial (e.g., Willis 1974). Most such species tend to have small clutch sizes and to suffer intense nest predation (Skutch 1966; Cody 1966). The populations of forest birds are thus more liable to suffer local extinction or interruptions in gene flow (MacArthur 1972), leading to local differentiation and sometimes speciation (e.g., Diamond 1973). Most forest-interior birds and some canopy species are thus narrowly restricted in their ecological or geographic ranges. In effect, they are "life-zone specific," whereas the "habitat-specific" nonforest species can occupy their preferred

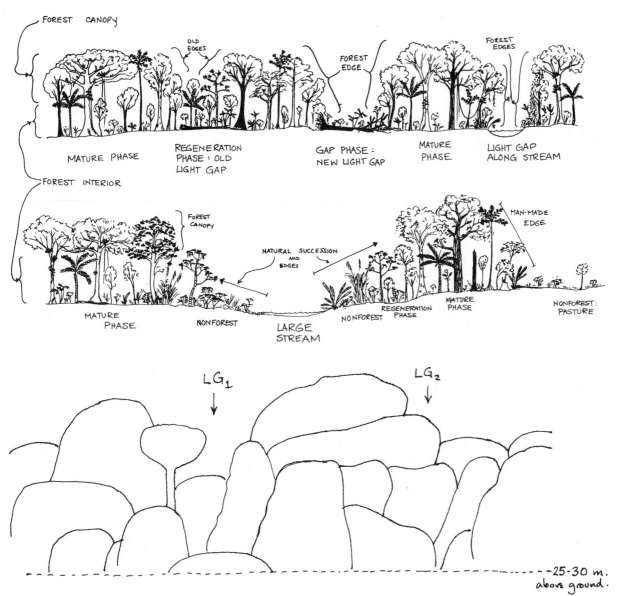

FIGURE 10.2. *a*, The forest mosaic: kinds of avian habitats. *b*, Configuration of the forest canopy at Finca La Selva, as seen from a platform 30 m aboveground, looking northeast. Note the presence of a sizable light gap of fairly recent for-mation (LG_1) and, in the foreground at right, an older gap now in the advanced regeneration phase (LG_2). Note also the amount of vertical "edge" habitat present in the canopy itself.

habitat or foliage configuration over a wide range of life zones. Many water birds are also "habitat specific" in this sense. The difference was brought home to me some years ago in a short visit to Colombia: more than 75% of the open-country and scrub birds I saw, but only about a third of the forest birds, occur in comparable habitats in Costa Rica.

Distributional gaps are by no means an exclusive property of forest birds, however. Historical patterns of hab-itat expansion and contraction are responsible in many cases, such as the relict populations of northern birds on high mountains. Another case is the savanna oriole *Icterus chrysater,* which at present skips Costa Rica in its

distribution but probably occurred here in the cooler, drier glacial periods when savannas were more extensive (Muller 1973). The presence of a similar, possibly com-peting congener may be responsible for some gaps—for example, the small flycatcher *Ornithion semiflavum,* which occurs in extreme northeastern and southwestern Costa Rica but is replaced by *O. brunneicapillum* over the rest of the Caribbean slope. Nevertheless, when a major distributional gap occurs in essentially continuous habitat with no obvious intervening competitor, the bird in ques-tion usually inhabits forest—for example, *Automolus ru-biginosus* (not recorded between central Nicaragua and southern Costa Rica). Common and accessible at San

511

TABLE 10.4.   Taxonomic Affinities of Permanent and Winter Resident Land Birds in Several Costa Rican Localities

	Tortu-guero (T)	La Selva (LS)	Virgen del Socorro (VS)	Muñeco (M)	Cerro Chom-pipe (CC)	Villa Mills[a] (VM)	Osa[b] (O)	Santa Rosa (SR)	Palo Verde (PV)	San Vito (SV)	Monte-verde[c] (MV)	San José (SJ)
Slope and elevation[d]	C, 5	C, 100	C, 900	C, 1,600	C, 2,250	D, 3,000	P, 100	P, 150	P, 20	P, 1,150	P, 1,500	P, 1,150
Permanent residents												
Nonpasserines	75	96	64	42	24	17	98	67	61	70	63	23
Suboscines	59	73	62	39	18	7	61	30	29	64	37	10
Oscines	56	66	76	52	32	24	57	33	31	72	47	32
Winter residents												
Nonpasserines	2	3	2	3	3	1	3	5	7	1	4	1
Suboscines	3	5	2	1	0	0	3	5	4	3	1	2
Oscines	24	24	20	10	6	2	23	26	26	23	13	24
Breeding residents												
All groups	1	1	1	1	0	0	3	5	5	3	3	3
Total resident land birds												
All groups	220	268	227	147	83	51	248	171	163	236	168	95

[a] Includes area below timberline, down to Villa Mills road camp.

[b] Excluding mangrove specialists and species restricted to elevations over 200 m.

[c] From the top of the community to the continental divide.

[d] C = Caribbean slope; P = Pacific slope; D = on the continental divide. Elevations are given in meters (mean for each locality).

Vito, this species might well repay further study in this regard.

Costa Rican Bird Communities

Many studies of tropical bird communities have been undertaken to compare these with temperate-zone communities, often to try to explain some aspect of "tropical species diversity." My concern here is with Costa Rican bird communities per se, but I shall make many passing references to tropical–temperate zone comparisons in this and the following sections. Good reviews of this subject have been written by Karr (1971, 1975).

TRENDS IN SPECIES NUMBERS

Two kinds of data have been used in evaluating the species richness and diversity of Central American bird communities: species lists derived from long-term qualitative observations (Slud 1960; Stiles 1979a), and short- or long-term quantitative censuses of small study plots (Orians 1969; Karr 1971). The former studies are more likely to include representative cross sections of the habitats locally available, especially as regards the dynamic habitat mosaic of tropical forests; but such data permit only limited statistical analyses. The second technique yields more quantitative data, allowing calculation of species diversity if questions of status can be resolved. However, no such study has yet evaluated avian use of the total forest habitat; most have dealt with a single small plot in mature-phase forest for each locality. Concepts like "rareness" can be defined precisely in such studies but lose biological meaning except in the sense of "use of the study plot" (e.g., Karr 1977). A third technique, used by

Pearson (1975) to study Amazonian bird communities, is to record species along lengthy transects through a representative habitat spectrum, where each species is rated according to its "detectability" (Emlen 1971). This method, combined with a dynamic habitat classification, may yield the best data on bird community structure. Valuable short-term studies could deal with avian utilization of different kinds of light gaps or phases of forest regeneration (cf. Hartshorn 1978). Mist netting has often been used to supplement various observational methods, but problems remain in equating the two kinds of data (cf. Karr 1971). Finally, no highly quantitative long-term study has yet taken adquate account of the effect of wintering migrants or other seasonal residents.

Species lists from various localities permit several conclusions concerning variations in bird communities with altitude and humidity (table 10.4, fig. 10.3). Numbers of permanent and winter resident species decline more or less linearly with altitude in the humid life zones of both slopes of Costa Rica. (I consider a species resident if it regularly spends 3 months or more per year at a site.) Several explanations for this trend have been proposed, mostly relating to the inverse relation between temperature and altitude. Decreases with altitude occur in primary productivity, insect biomass, abundances of

FIGURE 10.3. Numbers of resident taxa at various Costa Rican localities (land birds). The localities are: LS = Finca La Selva; O = Osa Peninsula; VS = Virgin del Socorro; SV = San Vito; MV = Monteverde; M = Muñeco; CC = Cerro Chompipe; VM = Villa Mills; SR = Santa Rosa National Park; PV = Palo Verde; SJ = San José; T = Tortuguero National Park.

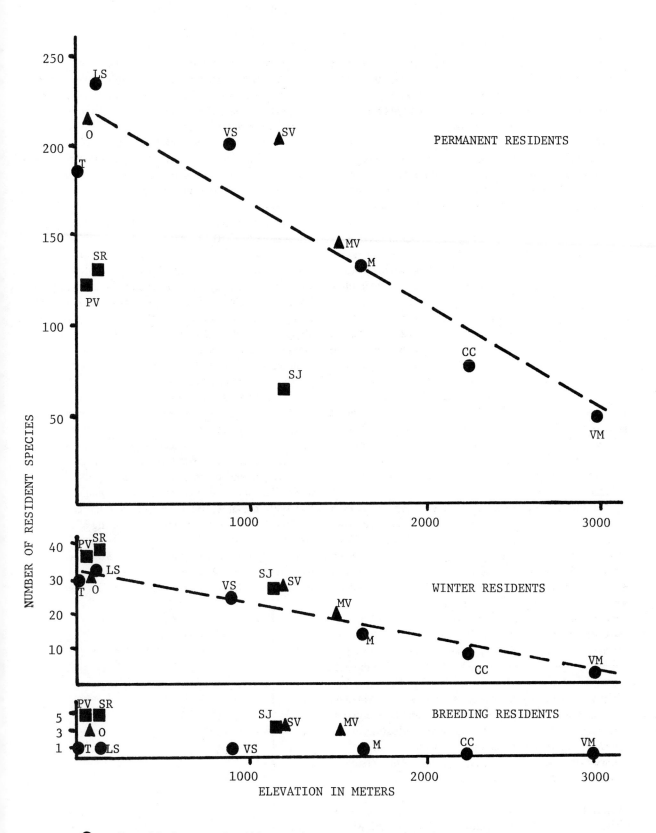

PERMANENT RESIDENTS

WINTER RESIDENTS

BREEDING RESIDENTS

NUMBER OF RESIDENT SPECIES

ELEVATION IN METERS

● – Localities on Caribbean slope or continental divide

■ – Humid localities on Pacific slope

▲ – Dry localities on Pacific slope

large or nocturnal insects and small herps, and average leaf size; wind increases with altitude (Orians 1969). Among birds, suboscines decrease most rapidly with altitude, followed by nonpasserines; oscines predominate at the highest altitudes (table 10.4).

This trend is not entirely smooth, however. The greatest number of species occurs not at sea level (Tortuguero) but toward where the lowlands meet the foothills of the Cordillera Central (La Selva). Also, a pronounced "shoulder" exists at lower middle elevations, at the lower edge of the cool, wet "cloud" forest (ca. 1,000–1,200 m). Janzen (1973) reported a peak of insect density and (in primary vegetation) species richness at these elevations. He ascribed this to a higher harvestable primary productivity at these elevations, owing to lower plant maintenance costs on cool nights. This might apply to the La Selva–Tortuguero bird comparison as well: nights at La Selva are definitely cooler. However, highland species at the lower end of their altitudinal distributions also occur at La Selva but not at Tortuguero (e.g., *Xiphorhynchus erythropygius*); some species such as ground foragers find their habitat restricted at Tortuguero. A similar decline in species richness with altitude was found in the Peruvian Andes by Terborgh (1977). He also reported a peak in bird diversity and biomass at lower middle elevations, but only with respect to mist-net data; it is not clear how comparable this peak is with that found by Janzen (1973) in insects.

The Osa Peninsula has fewer resident land birds than does La Selva, reflecting its isolation from both zoogeographic source areas and major migration routes from North America. The two Guanacaste sites have considerably fewer permanent residents and more seasonal residents than the wet lowland areas. This probably reflects the extreme seasonality in rainfall, leaf fall, flowering, and fruiting of the tropical dry forest itself. San Vito also has a strong wet-dry seasonality and a rich seasonal avifauna, but the dry season is ameliorated by frequent morning fogs; the forest there is evergreen, and the avifauna is rather more like that of humid life zones. San José is climatically intermediate between San Vito and Guanacaste. Its original forest was probably evergreen, but many of the dominant trees, native and exotic, in the present man-altered landscape are deciduous in the dry season; the avifauna is largely a depauperate version of that of Guanacaste.

PATTERNS OF HABITAT USE

The simplified habitat classification of figure 10.2 will be used to assess trends in habitat use by Costa Rican birds. Rather few birds are restricted to one of the four foliage types; the mode is two. The mean number of foliage categories occupied increases with altitude for both permanent and winter residents, though the minima for both

groups occur at Virgen del Socorro (fig. 10.4). Winter residents tend to occupy slightly more foliage categories than do permanent residents, but this difference largely disappears if only the oscines are considered among the latter (most winter residents are oscines). Foliage use by fall migrants is broader and does not increase with altitude. At this time one often sees migrants (e.g., *Vermivora peregrina*) accompanying mixed-species flocks inside forest, whereas during winter residence these species are found only at the foliage-air interface.

At all localities the greatest number of species occur at forest edge (fig. 10.5), where the foliage-air interface is strongly inclined and direct sunlight strikes a wide vertical range of foliage. Such edges occur at light gaps of various types and often are marked by thickets at ground level and tangles or festoons of vines higher up. Most canopy species follow the foliage-air interface down along such edges, often giving the misleading impression that they are birds of the edge per se (given the difficulty of detecting them in the canopy for an observer on the ground, which is particularly problematic for many winter resident passerines that vocalize little at this season) (cf. Greenberg 1981*b*). Moreover, there is a great deal of vertical or strongly inclined "edge" within the canopy itself, owing to the heterogeneity of forms and heights of trees (fig. 10.2*b*): the edge formed at light gaps is more like a downward extension of the canopy itself to these birds. This also explains why the two foliage categories that share the most species are canopy and edge (Stiles 1979*a*). Another group of species occuring at edges consists of nonforest birds that follow the foliage-air interface upward (e.g., *Ramphocelus passerinii*, which will use the canopy adjacent to an edge but not in solid mature-phase forest). A minority of species seem to pre-

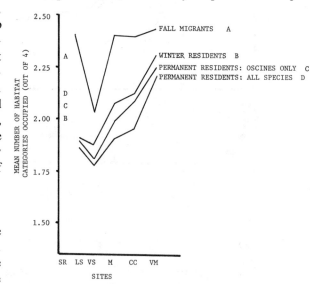

FIGURE 10.4. Mean number of foliage habitats occupied (out of four) by land birds at six Costa Rican sites.

fer the edge per se (e.g., *Thryothorus nigricapillus* or leks of *Phaethornis superciliosus,* in thickets). Food plants of *Phaethornis* and many other hummingbirds are most abundant at light gaps and edges (Stiles 1975).

In humid life zones, the numbers of species using forest interior and canopy are fairly similar, with fewer nonforest species. In the dry forest (Santa Rosa) there are more nonforest than forest interior species, reflecting both the extent of savannas there and the fact that in the dry season the forest interior effectively ceases to exist except in riparian habitats.

In humid localities the winter residents generally occur relatively more in nonforest habitats than do the permanent residents as a whole (fig. 10.5). This largely reflects taxonomic affinities: most forest-interior residents are suboscines, while the winter residents are mostly oscines. Permanent and winter-resident oscines are much more similar in foliage use (Stiles 1979*a;* Greenberg 1981*b*). At Santa Rosa, on the other hand, there are few forest-interior suboscines. Here the winter-resident oscines are a prominent element of the forest-interior avifauna.

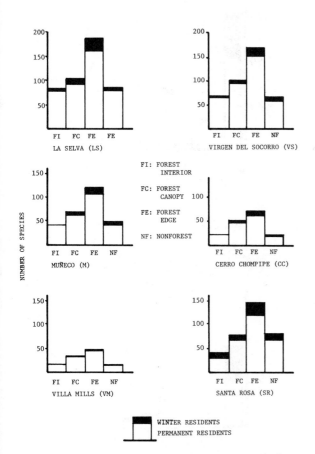

FI: FOREST INTERIOR
FC: FOREST CANOPY
FE: FOREST EDGE
NF: NONFOREST

WINTER RESIDENTS
PERMANENT RESIDENTS

FIGURE 10.5 Numbers of species of permanent and winter resident land birds occupying different habitats in six Costa Rican localities. See figure 10.3 for locations and elevations of different sites.

The degree of horizontal habitat selection may also differ between wet- and dry-forest birds. Orians (1969) recorded similar numbers of bird species in wet-season censuses of small plots in mature-phase wet and dry forests. The wet-forest plots thus had a much lower proportion (ca. 50%) of the total "forest" avifauna of their respective regions than did the dry-forest plots (ca. 90%). Taking into account the mosaic nature of tropical forest succession, it seems likely that different species might specialize on gap (e.g., *Grallaria fulviventris*), regeneration (e.g., *Myrmeciza exsul*), or mature (e.g., *Grallaria perspicillatus*) phases. Such specialization should be greater in tropical wet forests, since differences between phases largely are obliterated during the dry season in the deciduous dry forest. Since Orians's plot contained mostly or entirely mature-phase forest, with no major light gaps, it is not surprising that he found only about half the "forest" avifauna there, given the high species richness of edges and light gaps (fig. 10.5). Special foraging substrates, such as palms and bromeliads, are also more common in tropical wet forests, enhancing the possibility of habitat selection and also species richness relative to dry forests. The increase in species richness between secondary and primary Amazonian habitats with similar foliage profiles was ascribed by Terborgh and Weske (1969) largely to increased availability of such substrates in the latter. This is also a difference between wet-tropical and temperate-zone forests (Orians 1969).

Finer vertical habitat stratification in tropical forests than in temperate zone forests has been implicated as a major cause of higher bird species diversity in the former (MacArthur, Recher, and Cody 1966). In mature-phase tropical wet forest, many birds apparently do show strong preferences for certain strata. Generally, vertical foraging range is directly proportional to mean foraging height: canopy species forage over the widest range of heights; understory or ground species forage over the narrowest (Karr 1971; Pearson 1977). Taxonomic composition changes as well: antbirds and furnariids are the dominant foliage-gleaning element in the understory; flycatchers and oscines predominate in the canopy. These differences are much less pronounced in seasonally deciduous forest, whether in the dry tropics or in the temperate zone. Moreover, such stratification often breaks down at light gaps and edges. The consensus now is that increased vertical stratification is a relatively minor component of high tropical species diversity (Orians 1969; Karr 1971).

TROPHIC STRUCTURE AND FORAGING GUILDS

Because of the variety of food items eaten by tropical birds and the often unsuspected degree of polyphagy among them, it is not easy to derive a simple classification of food habits. Figure 10.6 gives the simplest scheme I could devise covering all major food

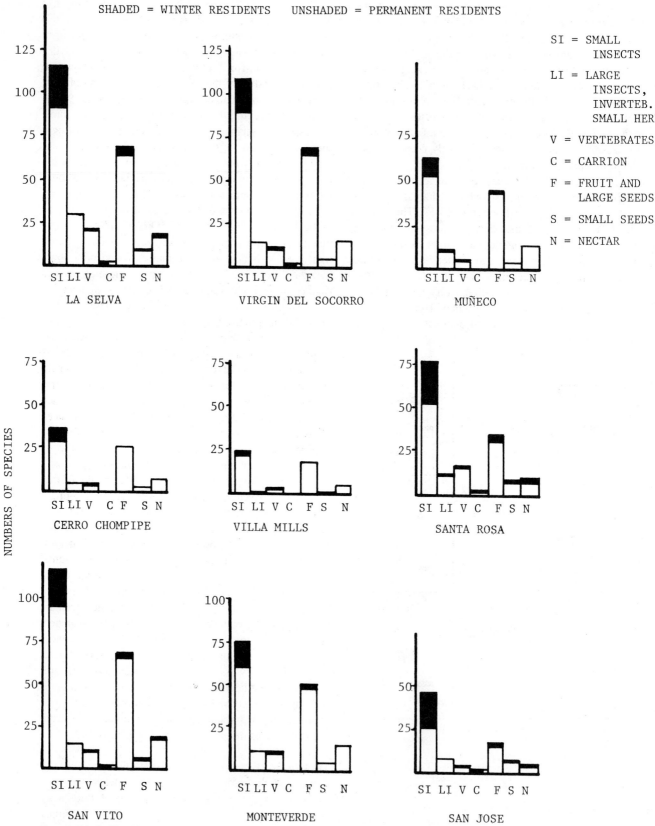

FIGURE 10.6. Number of resident bird species exploiting different food resources at nine Costa Rican sites.

516

types. Many species were placed half in one category, half in another; I preferred this to a broad "omnivore" category that would lump such odd bedfellows as hummingbirds and jays (e.g., Karr 1971). Neither can I consider frugivores, nectarivores, and insectivores to be even remotely independent categories, as did Terborgh (1977). All avian nectarivores require small arthropods as a protein source. Trogons, jays, motmots, some cotingas and flycatchers, and so forth, take both large insects and fruit, and a host of small flycatchers and oscines take small insects and fruit. Even large raptors often take large insects as well as vertebrates, and virtually all species taking large insects also take small herps. Large and small insects are usually taken by different foraging techniques: sit-and-wait "ambushing" for the former, active searching for the latter (Fitzpatrick 1980). A corresponding separation for large and small fruits might also be justified on theoretical grounds (McKey 1975; Howe and Estabrook 1977). I did not make this separation because too many intermediate or indeterminate fruit types exist, and the same bird species may provide different "quality" dispersal for different fruits (e.g., toucans at *Virola* and *Casearia;* cf. Howe 1977; Howe and Vande Kerckhove 1981).

Within these limitations, several conclusions can be drawn regarding how food habits of bird communities vary with altitude and humidity (figs. 10.6, 10.7). In humid life zones, small insects are exploited by nearly the same proportion of the avifauna at all altitudes, but the proportion of species taking large insects drops sharply as altitude increases. Carrion and vertebrate feeders also decline with altitude among the permanent residents, whereas nectarivores and frugivores increase slightly. However, the increase in frugivores is among the small, relatively unspecialized species like thrushes and tanagers; larger and more specialized species (toucans, barbets, cotingas; sensu Snow 1981) become much rarer at very high elevations. The proportion of seed eaters changes little with altitude, though the small doves of lower altitudes are replaced by oscines higher up. Dry lowland forest has relatively fewer frugivores and large-insect feeders; many nectarivores and frugivores are highly seasonal in occurrence (Wolf 1970; Morton 1977). Santa Rosa also has more graminivores and vertebrate feeders than wet forest, reflecting the prevalence of savanna with its abundant grasses and good hunting conditions for many raptors.

Most winter residents in humid life zones take small insects, but several are at least partly frugivorous (e.g., several warblers, thrushes) or nectarivorous (some warblers, orioles). Most groups decline with altitude, but vertebrate eaters increase somewhat. In tropical dry forest there are more winter residents exploiting vertebrates, seeds, and nectar than in tropical wet forest, and a con-

siderably higher proportion of the small-insect feeders in the community are winter residents (fig. 10.6).

Taxonomically related species exploiting a given type of food in a similar way (e.g., insectivorous foliage-gleaning birds) are said to compose a foraging guild (Root 1967). A critical aspect of tropical community diversity is the kinds of mechanisms that permit coexistence of the various potentially competing members of such guilds, since tropical guilds often have more members than their temperate-zone counterparts. Many studies have dealt with such morphological aspects of this problem as can be quantified in museum skins (ratios of bill lengths, body sizes, etc.). However, such morphological features evidently differ in importance in different guilds (Schoener 1965) and in any case provide only an indirect indication of the behavioral mechanisms really crucial to such coexistence—and these must be studied in the field. Many supposedly sympatric congeners in tropical forest rarely meet because of different microhabitat preferences (e.g., *Hylophilus* spp., *Todirostrum* spp.); others prefer different foraging substrates (e.g., *Myrmotherula axillaris* and *fulviventris*). Other aspects of morphology may reflect important differences in foraging behavior and food choice (e.g., wing-disk loading, rictal bristles, tail size, and other bill dimensions in small flycatchers; T. W. Sherry, pers. comm.).

The nectar feeders are probably the tropical guild that has been studied in most detail, at least in Central America. Differences in bill morphology, body size, and perhaps wing-disk loading affect foraging energetics and flower choice. Different foraging strategies, often characteristic of certain species or age-sex categories, may represent responses to typical dispersion patterns of preferred food plants. Resource division is further enhanced by interference mechanisms like feeding territoriality and interspecific dominance hierarchies, as well as by different microhabitat preferences and seasonal movements among otherwise similar forms (Wolf 1970; Wolf, Stiles, and Hainsworth 1976; Feinsinger 1976; Stiles 1975, 1979b, 1980).

Among frugivorous birds, potential for resource partitioning is provided by the variety of sizes, textures, nutrient contents, and degrees of accessibility of different fruits. Different fruits trees often attract very different sets of foragers that do different things with the fruit and are dependent upon it to different degrees (Snow 1971; Howe 1977; Ricklefs 1977). Interference competition is realtively unimportant among frugivores, since fruit sources generally provide either superabundant food or daily amounts too small to be worth defending (Snow 1971; Leck 1972; McKey 1975). No Neotropical frugivore guild has yet been analyzed in detail, but, as in nectarivores, the coexistence of many species probably is

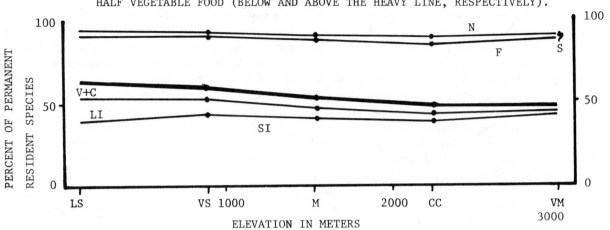

A. CHANGES IN PERCENTAGES (OF PERMANENT RESIDENT BIRD SPECIES) EXPLOITING DIFFERENT RESOURCES WITH ALTITUDE; NOTE SHIFT FROM MOSTLY ANIMAL FOOD TO HALF VEGETABLE FOOD (BELOW AND ABOVE THE HEAVY LINE, RESPECTIVELY).

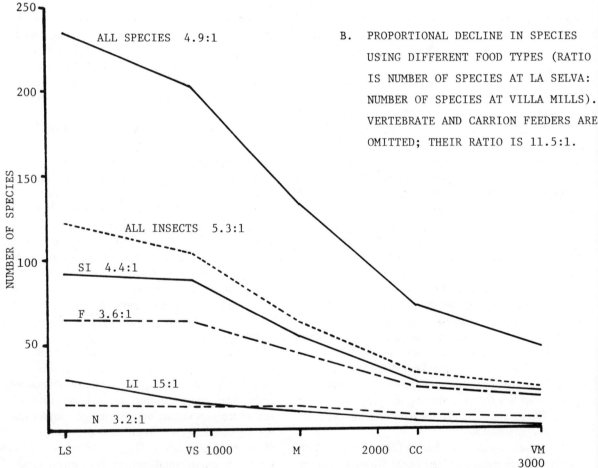

B. PROPORTIONAL DECLINE IN SPECIES USING DIFFERENT FOOD TYPES (RATIO IS NUMBER OF SPECIES AT LA SELVA: NUMBER OF SPECIES AT VILLA MILLS). VERTEBRATE AND CARRION FEEDERS ARE OMITTED; THEIR RATIO IS 11.5:1.

FIGURE 10.7. Changes in numbers of species exploiting different food resources along an altitudinal gradient: the Caribbean slope of Costa Rica (abbreviations of food types as in fig. 10.6; of localities as in fig. 10.3).

promoted by a complex interplay between the behavior and morphology of the birds and the qualitative and quantitative properties of their resource base. Quantitative, detailed observations of birds' visits to fruiting trees (e.g., Howe 1977; Kantak 1981; McDiarmid, Ricklefs, and Foster 1977) are still very much needed.

The availability of more types of resources at levels sufficient to permit specialization on them was proposed as a major component of the higher bird species diversity of the wet tropics (than the temperate zone) by Orians (1969). Nectar, large insects/small herps, and fruit are prominent among these "new" resources. The spectrum of food items within each of these resource types is itself broad enough to permit diverse behavioral and morphological specializations enhancing coexistence. Karr (1975) has calculated that fully 70% of the difference in bird species diversity between Illinois and wet lowland Panama forests is due to the greater range of resources and foraging opportunities in Panama.

Seasonal Patterns in the Costa Rican Avifauna

Each year a bird must face two and sometimes three major demands upon its time and energy, beyond those of self-maintenance: breeding, molt, and (for some species) seasonal movements of varying extent. Breeding is probably most critical from the viewpoint of natural selection, as well as being most expensive energetically. Molt is probably considerably less costly, but it must be accomplished regularly to maintain optimal capacities for flight, thermoregulation, and perhaps breeding (if a special nuptial plumage exists). Seasonal movements vary from long-distance migrations of thousands of kilometers to local habitat shifts, with energy expenditures varying proportionally.

CLIMATE AND RESOURCE AVAILABILITY

Ultimately, seasonal and geographic patterns of resource availability are crucial to the scheduling of energy demands in a bird's annual cycle. At high latitudes the regularity and large amplitude of day length and associated temperature cycles both place strict temporal constraints on, and provide reliable proximal cues to, the timing of resource availability to birds. These factors cycle at much lower amplitudes if at all in tropical habitats, where rainfall is the prime determinant of seasonal patterns. However, rainfall patterns vary both from place to place and from year to year at the same place. A given amount of rain may have different effects in different localities or upon different resources at the same locality. Thus patterns of resource availability and avian annual cycles within Costa Rica show a degree of spatial and temporal variation far exceeding that at higher latitudes. My approach to organizing this variation will be to construct a hypothetical "average" lowland Costa Rican lo-

cality, complete with rainfall and resource patterns and avian annual cycles, and then to discuss deviations from this idealized picture at real localities for which some data exist. For my hypothetical locality I have relied heavily on the information given by Skutch (1950, 1957, 1960, 1969), Karr (1976), and Snow (1965b), as well as data accumulated by many observers associated with OTS and my own data, gathered over a ten-year period. However, I emphasize that for no Costa Rican locality have quantitative data been gathered simultaneously on rainfall, resources for birds, and annual cycles of the entire avifauna.

The rainfall pattern at my hypothetical locality (fig. 10.8a) shows a broad pattern typical of Costa Rica: the driest months are February–March, and the rainy season has two peaks separated by a veranillo. The length and severity of the dry season and the timing and relative magnitudes of the two rainfall peaks, and of the veranillo, vary considerably from place to place. Mean monthly temperature varies by only about 2° C during the year, with higher temperatures during the dry season and veranillo and the lowest ones around the end of the rains.

The patterns of resource availability are given in figure 10.8b. Leaf fall occurs mainly early in the dry season, leaf flushing mostly at the start of the rains. Flowering peaks early in the dry season and again in the early wet season, then declines to very low levels by the end of the rains; there may be a slight resurgence in the veranillo. Fruiting shows a broad peak through the early to mid-rainy season and a secondary peak about the start of the dry season. Species producing large-seeded, nutritious fruit mostly flower in the dry season and fruit early in the wet season; succulent small-seeded fruits are less markedly seasonal (Smythe 1979) but still show a wet-season peak. The dry-season fruiting peak contains a mixture of fruit types. The middle of the wet season is the time of greatest seed abundance (specifically, fresh seeds of the grasses that sprouted with the rains). Insect abundance shows a small peak in the dry season, largely coinciding with the peak of flowering, and a much larger peak early in the rainy season, when soft, relatively nontoxic young leaves are most abundant. I infer a small secondary peak or shoulder in the veranillo and a minimum of insect abundance at the end of the rains, in part from the minimum of flowering and bird activity at these times. One point deserves emphasis: I hypothesize that variations in resource levels within the dry and wet seasons may be as great as differences between seasons. Comparing a single sample from dry and wet seasons may give a very incomplete or misleading idea of the annual variation in any given parameter or resource.

Different Costa Rican localities will present variations on this general theme with respect to both climate and resources, but for the most part the same relationships

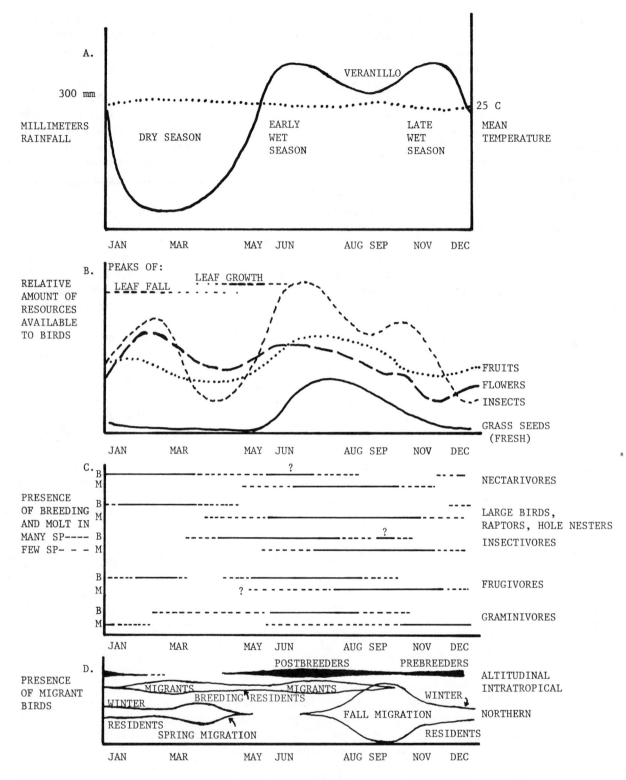

FIGURE 10.8. Hypothesized rainfall regime, resource distributions, and annual cycles of birds of an idealized lowland Costa Rican locality.

520

between the two should prevail. Thus insects might be more abundant during a short, mild dry season than during a long, severe one, especially toward the end (Janzen 1973). I also expect that the longer the rainy season, the heavier the later rains, or the weaker the veranillo, the more pronounced should be the decline in flowering (and perhaps insects) toward the end of the rains (cf. Stiles 1978a). At middle elevations the dry season is often less severe or is ameliorated by clouds and fog; some resources, such as insects, thus may fluctuate more irregularly (Buskirk and Buskirk 1976). At high elevations the cold rains and driving mists of the wet season probably depress insect activity so that insects might be more available to birds in the dry season. However, flowers and perhaps fruits may show less extreme seasonal variation (Wolf, Stiles, and Hainsworth 1976; Wolf 1976). Resource levels vary less inside forest than in more open areas owing to the buffering effect of the vegetation (Karr 1976).

Another "resource" to be considered is the weather itself. The dry season has many more hours of sunlight and, especially on the Pacific slope, high winds. These winds may make flight and foraging easier for some birds (e.g., large soaring species) but not for others (e.g., small aerial insectivores). On the other hand, heavy rains can limit the time available for foraging by some birds (Foster 1974); hard, cold rain at high elevations can also diminish thermal insulation and strain energy reserves, especially for young birds (Skutch 1950). Hard rain can damage some nests and flood ground nests. For many water birds, changes in water levels of marshes, ponds, and streams are the most important aspect of rainfall seasonality. Rises in water level can increase nesting and foraging habitat; falling water levels may concentrate prey (e.g., small fish) and increase foraging efficiency.

BREEDING AND MOLTING SEASONS
For most of our hypothetical avifauna, breeding seasons are fairly closely tied to the availability of critical resources (fig. 10.8c). Thus nectar feeders breed primarily during the first flowering peak, with a few (often different) species also breeding during the second, when different flowers are available (Stiles 1980). Insectivores, the largest single group of the avifauna, tend to breed from about the start of the rains through their first peak; a smaller peak of territorial activity and song (and probably breeding, at least at some sites) occurs about September–October. Most frugivores, especially small species like manakins, breed slightly later, in the early to middle rainy season. Large specialized frugivores may breed earlier if specific fruits (e.g., Lauraceae) are available (Snow and Snow 1964; Snow 1977). Graminivores fall into two groups: those that apparently require fresh grass

seeds and some insects (e.g., seed eaters), and those that require only dry grass and weed seeds (e.g., ground doves). The latter may start to breed early in the dry season and continue well into the wet, whereas the former tend to nest only in the middle to late wet season.

The diverse group of birds called "large birds, raptors, hole nesters, etc." seem rather more tied to the weather than to any specific resource for their dry-season nesting. In raptors, large water birds, and so on, both parents forage, often leaving the downy young untended in exposed nests where they would be highly vulnerable to heavy rains. By the time the rainy season comes these young will be well grown, and food supplies will then be increasing. For crepuscular feeders like owls and nightjars, the clear weather at dusk during the dry season may be especially critical energetically (Skutch 1950); nightjars are also ground nesters. There is no satisfactory explanation of why practically all hole nesters, of diverse food habits (parrots, toucans, woodpeckers, trogons, etc.), nest in the dry season. I strongly suspect that the nest microclimate is responsible: many of these birds do not remove the feces of the young from the nest, and during the wet season fungus and molds may be injurious to the young; such organisms are much less abundant during the dry season. For riverbank nesters like kingfishers, the lower water levels of the dry season are obviously important to nest safety as well.

In areas with severe dry seasons (e.g., Guanacaste), the breeding seasons of most small birds are shorter and more closely tied to the rains; in areas with shorter, milder dry seasons (e.g., La Selva), breeding seasons tend to be longer and less well defined, with more small birds (e.g., many tanagers) starting to breed in the dry season. Nesting seasons in forest tend to be longer and less sharply defined than those in open areas. As one climbs in altitude, the nesting season tends to become progressively earlier for many groups of birds, especially insectivores and small frugivores. The peak of breeding for the avifauna as a whole is March or April on the Cerro, May at La Selva. This doubtless reflects weather conditions as well as specific resource levels (see above).

In birds, the greatest energy demands of the nesting effort come when the young are well grown but not yet feeding themselves—about the time they leave the nest. For this period to coincide with the peak of resource availability, the nesting effort must begin earlier, often when resources are still scarce. For lack of other reliable proximate cues, rainfall itself often provides the stimulus for breeding in many small birds. The increase in cloudy weather or the first showers as the dry season ends may trigger breeding of many insectivorous passerines weeks before the insects required actually appear. Given the variability in rainfall patterns, there are often differences

521

of several weeks or even months in initiation of breeding from one year to the next (Skutch 1950; Snow and Snow 1964), a range of variation impossible at high latitudes.

Another feature of tropical breeding seasons is their length, often 4–6 months or even more. Long breeding seasons may be important in allowing ample opportunities for renesting, especially following a nesting failure. Nesting success of tropical birds is often far below that of birds of the temperate zone, primarily owing to higher nest predation (Skutch 1976; Ricklefs 1969). Especially in tropical forest, the probability of a given nest's being successful is only one in five or six for many species (Skutch 1966). This should tend to select against investing too much energy in any one nest: tropical birds, especially in forest, tend to have smaller clutches of eggs than do their temperate-zone counterparts (review by Cody 1966). Rather, given the enhanced possibilities for renesting (Snow and Snow 1964), many tropical birds apparently invest in any one nesting attempt the least energy (eggs) possible that would still yield a selectively acceptable return in offspring produced should the nesting be successful (see also Willis 1974).

Nearly all the birds of our hypothetical avifauna molt in the second half of the year (fig. 10.8c). For birds in general, a complete molt usually follows quickly upon breeding; thus the energy demands of the two are satisfied sequentially before resources become scarce. Molting seasons of individuals and populations of tropical birds tend to be more regular than breeding seasons, suggesting different sorts of physiological control mechanisms (Snow and Snow 1964; Stiles and Wolf 1974). A more flexible, opportunistic breeding seasonality and a more rigidly programmed molting season set the stage for possible overlap, which has been found in a number of Costa Rican birds and can reflect various ecological causes (Foster 1975). Regular molt breeding overlap is less frequent and may involve a very slow molt to minimize simultaneous energy expenditures, as in the hummingbird *Phaethornis superciliosus* (Stiles and Wolf 1974). The more usual situation is for molt to be arrested should a new breeding attempt be initiated, especially in females (review in Payne 1973). For many species of Costa Rican birds, this is most likely should a breeding attempt be initiated late in the year, for instance, if propitious conditions were to appear with the veranillo.

SEASONAL MOVEMENTS AND MIGRATIONS
Seasonal population movements often provide the only practical way of avoiding periods of scarcity or bad weather in some habitats or geographic regions, exploiting rich but transient resources in others, or both. I estimate that at least half of the Costa Rican avifauna shows some degree of seasonal movment. The most obvious and spectacular cases are birds that leave the areas where they have resided for up to 6–7 months for breeding areas in North America, taking advantage of the enormous burst of summer productivity at high latitudes. In a few species this pattern is displaced southward, and they migrate from "wintering" areas in South America to breed in Central America, especially on the Pacific slope. Within Costa Rica, many species also show pronounced seasonal movements, the most striking of which are movements by many water birds related to changing water levels, and the altitudinal migrations of many land birds. At least fifty to seventy-five species undertake at least partial altitudinal migrations, and this may be an underestimate, since movements of many forest birds remain poorly known. Perhaps even more widespread, but even less well documented, are major habitat shifts within a local region. For example, several hummingbirds at La Selva regularly shift from forest canopy or understory to second growth at certain seasons, following the flowering of certain food plants (Stiles 1978a, 1979b, 1980).

The usual pattern of altitudinal migration in Costa Rica is for birds to move upslope during the dry season to breed and to move downslope during the wet season, thereby avoiding the heaviest rains at high elevations. Such species may appreciably enrich some lowland avifaunas during the rainy season (fig. 10.8d, table 10.3). The number of altitudinal migrants is highest at middle elevations, but the proportion of breeding species that migrates altitudinally varies directly with altitude (fig. 10.9). A majority of the known altitudinal migrants are frugivorous or nectarivorous, including many hummingbirds and oscines and some flycatchers and cotingas.

In numerical terms, the land birds breeding in North America represent an ecologically very significant part of

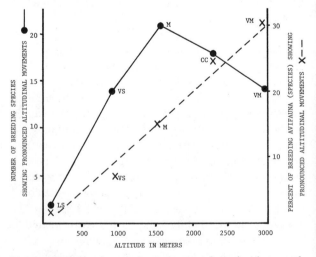

FIGURE 10.9 Numbers and percentages of species that are altitudinal migrants among the breeding avifaunas of several localities on the Caribbean slope of Costa Rica (abbreviations for localities as in fig. 10.3).

the Costa Rican avifauna. During fall migrations in September and October, the biomass of small insectivorous and frugivorous birds may be increased severalfold in some localities (fig. 10.8*d*), especially along the Caribbean coast, where the heaviest migratory waves pass. By mid-November, most northern migrants remaining in Costa Rica are winter residents that will not depart until the following March or April. Spring migration is much more rapid and largely confined to a narrow front along the coast; most inland localities do not experience a really large pulse of northbound migrants (fig. 10.8*d*). For one thing, natural mortality over the winter has reduced the number of birds migrating. All told, migratory land birds are present in numbers for all but 3–4 months of the year.

The effect of these long-distance migrants upon the resident avifauna has been a controversial subject (see Morton and Keast 1979 for various viewpoints). Most breeding by the resident avifauna, at least at lower elevations, occurs precisely during the period when the migrants are absent. However, this could be a reflection either of the normal seasonal rhythm of weather and resource availability of tropical habitats (fig. 10.8*b*), or of a release from competition by the migrants. No convincing evidence of niche expansion by residents as the migrants leave has yet been found; indeed, with resources on the increase in any case, one would hardly be expected. Slud (1960) noted that the migrants exploited habitats and resources that were not heavily used by residents. Now the time for a resident to expand its ecological range into this "migrant niche" would be during and following the breeding season, as populations increase and young birds are learning to forage. However, any tendency in this direction should swiftly be checked by the enormous influx of all migrants at this time and the resultant exploitation competition. The winter residents remaining after the flood of fall migrants has passed do indeed seem to complement the permanent residents ecologically, but they are in no sense an avifauna apart. Many of these species, strictly insectivorous on their breeding grounds, adopt more "tropical" customs of frugivory and nectarivory during their stay in Costa Rica (e.g., some warblers, orioles); others establish territories (some warblers, perhaps others), form flocks (buntings, some warblers), or even join tropical mixed-species flocks (a few warblers; e.g., Tramer and Kemp 1979; Greenberg 1981*a,b*).

In many water-bird groups, especially the Charadriiformes, the influence of the migrants is even more pervasive. Most Costa Rican shorebirds breed at high latitudes; owing to the short period available for breeding there, the peak of spring migration is later and that of fall migration earlier (April–May and August–September, respectively) than those of land birds (fig. 10.8*d*). Furthermore, sizable nonbreeding populations of many spe-

cies remain in Costa Rica all summer (table 10.2). Thus it is not surprising that Costa Rica has only two or three species of breeding shorebirds and one breeding tern, and that these are ecologically distinct from virtually all the migrants, which are resident for up to 8–9 months of the year in favorable habitat. As in the land birds, both resident and migrant taxa must be considered intergral parts of the Costa Rican avifauna.

Avian Social Systems in Costa Rica
This section treats the kinds of social units (number of members and their relationships) and the dispersion of these units. My objective is to present a general ecological framework for viewing social avian organizations in Costa Rica: detailed descriptions of the social systems of many species are given in the section on ecological life histories.

SOCIAL ORGANIZATIONS FOR BREEDING AND MAINTENANCE
It is often impossible to specify *the* social system of a species: many birds vary their social organization seasonally. Consider a familiar example, a typical migratory warbler (Parulidae) breeding in, say, Michigan and wintering in Costa Rica. Arriving on the breeding grounds in May, males stake out breeding territories and attract females by conspicuous singing. The breeding pairs occupy and defend these territories for perhaps 2 months; then follows a variable period of irregular wandering, perhaps as a family group, until in early September many birds gather into flocks for fall migration. Arriving in Costa Rica in early October, the warblers establish individual territories or home ranges that they occupy for 5–6 months until flocks again form for spring migration. Different social systems thus occur during the breeding, migratory, and nonbreeding or "maintenance" periods; one may recognize still another during the postbreeding period. Even if both members survive, pairs from one year do not necessarily reform in the next: there need be no lasting social bonds between individuals.

For birds resident year-round in a tropical region the situation may be rather different. The less extreme fluctuations in weather and resources may permit year-round occupation of a territory or home range and promote lasting associations between individuals (in pairs, flocks, etc.). One might thus expect the difference between breeding and maintenance social systems to be less pronounced in these birds than in long-distance migrants. Pairing for life is not unusual in many Costa Rican passerines (e.g., Willis 1966), and birds may also form other long-term associations as well. Postbreeding family groups may be maintained into the following breeding season, when the younger birds may help their parents in nesting chores (Skutch 1976; Lawton and Guindon 1981). Territories may be held year-round by pairs or groups, notably in insectivorous species like wrens and antbirds; frugivores and nectarivores, as well as some insectivores, may occupy the same home range all year, the precise pattern of occupation depending upon resource distribution (cf. Skutch 1957, 1960, 1969; Willis 1966; Stiles and Wolf 1979). The breeding social system may simply be superimposed upon the maintenance system. For instance, large *Columba* pigeons forage all year in wide-ranging flocks and may nest in loose colonies; breeding parents presumably alternate nesting chores and foraging with the flocks. Somewhat similar systems may occur in aerial feeders like swifts and swallows. Hermit hummingbirds trapline dispersed flowers all year, but when they are breeding their foraging routes start and end at the nest or lek territory (cf. Stiles and Wolf 1979). Several species participate in mixed-species flocks (see below) during breeding only when such flocks traverse their breeding territories (Buskirk et al. 1972).

The wider variety of available resources and the advantages of long-term residence for exploiting them, coupled with the spatiotemporal heterogeneity of tropical habitats, might favor evolution of a greater variety of social systems among tropical birds than among birds of higher latitudes. Attempting to quantify such a difference, Karr (1971) recognized three "territory" types: "classical" all-purpose territories; overlapping home ranges where dominance was often related to distance from the nest site (cf. Willis 1966); and "large territories or home ranges traversed irregularly." He concluded that the third type of "territory" was more common in tropical (Panama) than temperate-zone (Illinois) habitats, and more common in forest than in open habitats in Panama. However, he compared only breeding systems in Illinois with a mixture of breeding and maintenance systems in Panama, and he did not try to include the nature of the social units (individuals, pairs, flocks, etc.) in his analysis. Active territorial advertisement is not compressed into a short time span by tropical residents, who can thus employ less conspicuous and more subtle and varied means of defense; therefore it is often very difficult to distinguish territories in these birds, especially within a small study area.

Given these problems, it may be more meaningful to compare avifaunas with respect to the types of social units present. Here the distinction between breeding and maintenance social systems is crucial. A far greater variety of social units is present in breeding birds of tropical habitats than in temperate-zone birds. Whereas few of the latter breed in units other than the pair, in tropical birds many kinds of breeding units are represented: individuals (females nesting alone), permanent or transitory pairs, cohesive family groups, or larger flocks of related or unrelated individuals. Such complex social systems as helpers at the nest, compound clutching, and communal nesting are essentially restricted to resident tropical and subtropical birds, and in most cases they arise naturally from flock associations of the maintenance social system. Interestingly, single-species and multispecies flocks are not uncommon as nonbreeding social organizations among high-latitude birds (e.g., Morse 1970). The kinds of social units present in Michigan and Costa Rican avifaunas are much more similar in December than in June. Moreover, the northern birds spend more time each year in these more diverse maintenance systems than they do as breeding pairs. Long-distance migrants that breed in Costa Rica do so without exception as simple pairs. Altitudinal migrants within Costa Rica also tend to uphold the notion that long-term residence promotes complex social relations: practically all such species either pair for breeding or lack a strong pair bond (hummingbirds, bellbird, etc.). All of this implies that quantitative comparison of tropical and temperate-zone avifaunas with respect to social systems is considerably less straightforward than has previously been assumed.

Breeding social systems of Costa Rican birds are often strongly influenced by patterns of resource distribution and exploitation. Solitary nesting occurs mostly in nectarivores (hummingbirds) and frugivores (manakins, cotingas, some flycatchers, etc.), whose food is relatively abundant, stationary, and easily located, thereby reducing the time required for foraging, permitting the female to feed herself and her nestlings without aid (Morton 1973; Snow 1965a, 1971). The "emancipated" males in these species may form leks, which intensify sexual selection and may help females find males. Hummingbirds seem to show two divergent breeding systems based upon resource availability to males, with rather few intermediates. Males of socially dominant species hold territories at nectar-rich flowers that serve to attract females, who may choose males on the basis of territory (flower) quality; leks may form when species are unable to defend rich flowers because of subordinate social status or because defendable flowers are not present (Wolf and Sitles 1970; Stiles and Wolf 1979). At the other end of the scale, the most complex breeding systems are shown by insectivores and omnivores (anis, jays), though many frugivores and others that forage in family groups or flocks breed in these units: birds other than the breeding pair become helpers at the nest. Overall, the commonest breeding unit in the Costa Rican avifauna is still probably the unaided pair, especially in groups that must spend much time searching individually for active or concealed prey, such as small insectivores, raptors, piscivores, and other water birds. Intraspecific gregariousness is of little use to such species in foraging, though they may associate with mixed-species flocks.

FLOCKING IN COSTA RICAN BIRDS

The size, complexity, and frequency of mixed-species flocks (also called interspecies, multispecies, or heterospecific flocks or parties) in Neotropical avifaunas has always impressed temperate-zone observers. Enhanced foraging efficiency and more effective predator detection have been advanced as advantages accruing to birds in such flocks. Often considered mutually exclusive, the two hypotheses are actually complementary, as the following analyses show.

An ambitious attempt to evaluate avian social organizations in the Monteverde forest avifauna was made by Buskirk (1976; see also Powell 1979), who found that the species most likely to form or join flocks were active arboreal foragers, presumably the most vulnerable to (avian) predators. Flocking species typically moving in single- and in mixed-species flocks tended to exploit clumped and dispersed resources, respectively. Solitary foraging was the rule among terrestrial and "sit-and-wait" foragers and hummingbirds, all species with reduced vulnerability to predation. In table 10.5 I extended Buskirk's analysis to compare birds of different localities, food habits, and taxonomic affinities, choosing for comparison with Monteverde a highland (Villa Mills) locality and a lowland (La Selva) locality for which I

have fairly comprehensive information on social systems. I wanted specifically to compare the proportions of "nonsocial" birds (found most often in pairs or solitary) and "social" birds (characteristically found in groups or flocks), and among the social species to compare those intraspecifically gregarious only with those found regularly in mixed-species flocks. Among the latter, a few species at each site are both intraspecifically and interspecifically gregarious: these are the "nuclei" about which mixed-species flocks form (e.g., *Hylophilus* vireos and *Myrmotherula* at antwrens at La Selva, *Basileuterus* warblers and *Chlorospingus* tanagers in the highlands). A larger and more variable number of intraspecifically nonsocial species tend to join and follow these "nuclear species" and are usually called "attendant" species (cf. Moynihan 1962; Buskirk et al. 1972). Differences between sites in numbers of interspecifically gregarious species reflect mostly variation in numbers of attendant species. A subsidiary objective of this analysis was to test the oft-voiced subjective opinion that mixed-species flocks are more prevalent at middle elevations (e.g., Karr 1971).

Participation in mixed-species flocks clearly in influenced by taxonomic affinities among resident species (table 10.5). Most nonpasserines are nonsocial, with so-

TABLE 10.5.   Inter- and Intraspecific Gregariousness in the Social Systems of Different Taxonomic and Ecological Groups of Birds at Three Costa Rican Localities

	La Selva				Monteverde[a]				Villa Mills			
	All Species		Social Species		All Species		Social Species		All Species		Social Species	
	A	B	C	D	A	B	C	D	A	B	C	D
Taxonomic												
Nonpasserines	69	27	23	4	18	9	6	3	11	6	6	0
Suboscines	40	33	9	24	11	13	1	12	4	3	0	3
Oscines	26	40	20	20	8	20	8	12	11	13	4	9
Diet[b]												
Fruit/large seeds	23	42	30	12	9	15	9	6	6	12	7	5
Large insects/small herps	19	11	3	8	3	0	0	0	1	0	0	0
Small insects	49	43	18	25	13	25	6	19	11	10	3	7
Nectar	15	1	0	1	7	1	0	1	5	0	0	0
Vertebrates and carrion	23	0	0	0	5	0	0	0	2	0	0	0
Small seeds	6	3	2	1	0	1	0	1	1	0	0	0
Foraging												
Aerial	4	6	4	2	0	2	2	0	0	1	1	0
Active arboreal	70	75	36	39	14	37	12	25	11	20	8	12
Active terrestrial	22	14	10	4	12	3	1	2	9	1	1	0
Sentinel	39	5	2	3	11	0	0	0	6	0	0	0
Total	135	100	52	48	37	42	15	27	26	22	10	12
Winter residents	27	5	2	3	3	6	0	6	2	1	0	1

NOTE: A = solitary, pairs; B = social: interspecifically or intraspecifically gregarious; C = intraspecifically gregarious only; D = interspecifically gregarious irrespective of whether intraspecifically gregarious.
[a] Modified from Buskirk 1976.
[b] Diet types assigned as in figures 10.6 and 10.7.

cial species mostly only intraspecifically gregarious. Among suboscines, the proportion of social species is highest at Monteverde; at all elevations, most social suboscines join mixed-species flocks, usually as attendants. Most oscines are gregarious at all sites, and at higher elevations most of these are interspecifically so. Regarding diet, among frugivores at all elevations the prevalent social system is single-species flocks, though a fair proportion of species are solitary and may form leks. Flocks may increase the efficiency of locating widely scattered but rich fruit sources, and the typical movement pattern of long stops followed by long direct flights is ill suited to the foraging of insectivorous attendants (Buskirk 1976). Species taking small insects constitute the largest diet group; at high and low elevations about half the species are social, but at Monteverde two-thirds are. The mid-elevation peak in interspecifically gregarious foragers, and hence in mixed-species flocks, is a real phenomenon and moreover is due mainly to the high proportion of small insectivores that are attendants. Large insect feeders attend mixed-species flocks regularly only at La Selva, apparently taking advantage of the commotion caused by flock members, which may disturb suitable prey hidden in vegetation. Other diet groups contain virtually all nonsocial foragers.

I adopted Buskirk's foraging categories with these modifications: I have added a category for aerial feeders, and I prefer to consider small hover gleaners (e.g., many small Tyrannidae) as "active arboreal" rather than "sentinel" (sit-and-wait) foragers (cf. Fitzpatrick 1980). Also, I have included some species that forage near the ground in dense forest understory in the "active terrestrial" rather than "active arboreal" category. As Buskirk found, the latter is the only large group with a majority of social species, and it includes most of the interspecifically gregarious species at all sites. This is in spite of including the solitary-foraging hummingbirds, which I favor, since they are by no means without predators, at least at La Selva (Stiles 1978c). Active terrestrial and sentinel species are overwhelmingly nonsocial; aerial feeders are mostly social, perhaps reflecting colonial nesting habits or wide-ranging foraging that might otherwise impede social interactions.

Most of the winter residents are nonsocial except at middle elevations, where a majority of species are attendants of mixed-species flocks. These species have no need to form social bonds leading to reproduction at this time—mates would be unable to maintain contact in large (and mostly nocturnal) migratory flocks. Thus an individualistic social system might best spread these predominantly small, insectivorous or omnivorous birds in accordance with resource levels. Winter residents forming single-species flocks usually take predominantly

nectar, fruits, or seeds (e.g., *Vermivora peregrina*, *Passerina cyanea*). The higher development of mixed-species flocks is reflected in the fact that some common species (e.g., *Wilsonia pusilla*) regularly accompany such flocks at Monteverde (Buskirk 1976) but not, for example, at Villa Mills.

Birds in Costa Rican Ecosystems

The ecological roles of consumer organisms like birds in complex ecosystems can be viewed at several levels. The systems approach to energy flow indicates that the proportion of the productivity of temperate-zone grassland and forest ecosystems that is channeled through birds is energetically insignificant (Wiens and Innis 1974; Holmes and Sturges 1975). This conclusion doubtless applies to tropical systems as well, since total existence energy of the avifauna bears about the same relation to total annual ecosystem productivity (Karr 1975). Another potentially important role for birds is as biological control agents for herbivorous insects and rodents. Evidence that birds do fulfill such a role is at best inconsistent in simple, high-latitude ecosystems and is nonexistent for tropical ecosystems, where anecdotal accounts suggest, if anything, the contrary (D. H. Janzen, pers. comm.).

However, birds do play an extremely important role in Neotropical ecosystems as dispersal agents for the fruits, and to a lesser extent as pollinators of the flowers, of the dominant angiosperms. Indeed, the rise of the angiosperms to dominance of the world's richest floras has been causally linked to the evolution of birds as high-quality, long-distance dispersers (Regal 1977). For example, 49% of the tree species of La Selva have fruits dispersed primarily or exclusively by birds (Hartshorn 1979). These trees range from pioneer (e.g., *Cecropia*) to mature-phase species (e.g., *Virola, Protium*) and include most of the canopy species that require light gaps for seedling establishment (Hartshorn 1979). Birds may thus play a major role in maintaining the spatial heterogeneity and diversity of the forest itself, permitting trees to colonize light gaps at some distance from the seed source— and thereby also to escape some seed predation (Janzen 1970) although some birds are primarily seed predators (e.g., Higgins 1979). Bird-dispersed trees and shrubs are also abundant in forest understory, notably among the palms, Rubiaceae, and melastomes. Such important colonizers of light gaps and second growth as large monocot herbs like *Heliconia* and shrubs and small trees like *Hamelia, Neea, Rubus,* and *Miconia* are bird-dispersed. The crux of the bird/fruit interaction involves coadaptations of the size, energy and nutrient content, renewal rate, and abundance of the fruit and the nutritional needs, morphology, and behavior of the birds (Snow 1965*a,b,*

1971; Morton 1973; McKey 1975; Howe 1977; Howe and Estabrook 1977; Skutch 1980; Howe and Vande Kerckhove 1979).

Birds are also important pollinators of some segments of tropical vegetation. In Costa Rica, bird pollination is common among epiphytes (bromeliads, ericads, gesneriads, etc.) and among plants of light gaps and second growth (*Heliconia,* many Acanthaceae, Rubiaceae, Lobeliaceae, etc.). The major avian pollinators of the New World, the hummingbirds, come in three basic "models" that differ in morphology and behavior. The hermits are traplining foragers with long, curved bills; the "typical" hummingbirds have shorter, straight bills and a variety of foraging behaviors featuring territoriality at nectar-rich flowers in many species. Finally, a number of very small, short-billed nonhermits visit mostly small flowers with little nectar, otherwise visited regularly by insects. Morphological and caloric coadaptations between flowers and different "models" of hummingbirds are discussed by Snow and Snow (1972) and Stiles (1975, 1978a,b). Interestingly, very few canopy trees in Costa Rican forests are bird pollinated, and those few are adapted for passerine nectarivores like orioles that tend to travel in groups: the individualistic hummingbirds would quickly parcel such trees up into individual feeding territories and severely reduce cross-pollinations (Wolf and Stiles 1970; Stiles 1978b, 1981).

Given the possibility of year-round ecological interactions between birds and plants in tropical communities, the influence of their coevolutionary interactions should be more pervasive in structuring these communities than those at higher latitudes. Most of the foraging opportunities available to tropical but not temperate-zone birds have arisen through bird/plant coevolution. I submit that a major factor permitting this diversification has been the greater time available for coevolution in the tropics—time measured not in years but in the proportion of each year during which such ecological interactions are possible, during which birds and plants are exposed to the same environmental conditions and during which coadapted responses can be selected for. Migratory birds and "resident" plants at high latitudes come under totally different selective pressures in their respective winter homes; resident northern birds must remain active while plants are dormant. The numbers and positions of high-latitude birds and plants relative to one another in the spring, as the "selection period" begins, are the result of different and independent events during the winter. In the lowland wet tropics there are few or no such "time-outs"; continuous reciprocal selection can refine coadaptations within and between bird and plant communities. The local community is therefore the framework within which such selective pressures should act. Sympatric sets of plants sharing pollinators or dispersers, or birds sharing flowers or fruits, should present a diverse array of coadaptations such that resource loss through competition is minimized on the average. Moreover, given the spatial heterogeneity and year-to-year variability of tropical habitats and climate, such coadaptive solutions might often vary from one community to the next. Owing to the less severe temporal constraints on phenological events in the tropics, we might also expect more interlocality variation in plant and bird annual cycles here than in temperate regions. This in turn might help explain the notoriously patchy distributions of many tropical species. Clearly, we need more data on the phenology of tropical plant and animal communities from different localities within a region to evaluate these hypotheses.

The great mobility of birds is central to their key role in the dynamics of Neotropical forests, and also to their responsiveness to alteration and fragmentation of this forest by man. Large tracts of forest are required to maintain complex bird communities, many of whose species depend for their survival on the spatial heterogeneity of the forest. Conversely, many forest plants depend upon birds for access to suitable habitat within the forest mosaic. Isolation of a patch of forest is followed by an exponential decline in bird species that is inversely related to the area of the forest patch (Diamond 1972). Barro Colorado Island, a small forest reserve in Panama, has been losing species at a rate close to that predicted by theory since its isolation by Gatún Lake about sixty years ago (Willis 1974; Terborgh 1974). Eventually, loss of some plant species dependent upon these birds will follow, setting up a positive feedback that will eventually yield a very depauperate community, such as has seemingly occurred on Isla del Caño off the Osa Peninsula, a land-bridge island apparently isolated since the Pleistocene. Here a structurally diverse but floristically impoverished forest supports eight to ten resident bird species in an area of nearly 3 km^2.

The best long-term hope for Costa Rica's avifauna as a whole is the system of national parks. Costa Rica is making a courageous and costly attempt to protect sufficiently large areas of natural habitat to preserve most of its singularly rich biota. However, there is a critical shortage of ecological expertise in many areas, and at this time a number of key areas (e.g., the Osa highlands, the lower cloud forests on the Caribbean slope) remain outside the park system. Foreign scientists can make a contribution by using Costa Rica's national parks in their research whenever feasible, and in any case by making the techniques and results of work done in Costa Rica freely available to local students, scientists, and administrators. A key subject for continued monitoring is the avifauna: birds are more sensitive to habitat compression, isolation, and alteration than perhaps any other group of organisms, and over time they will provide as good a test as any of the effectiveness of parks and reserves in preserving tropical species richness.

*

Buskirk, R. E., and Buskirk, W. H. 1976. Changes in arthropod abundance in a highland Costa Rican rain forest. *Am. Midl. Nat.* 95:288–98.

Buskirk, W. H. 1976. Social systems in a tropical forest avifauna. *Am. Nat.* 110:293–310.

Buskirk, W. H., Powell, G. V. N.; Wittenberger, J. F.; and Powell, T. U. 1972. Interspecific bird flocks in tropical highland Panama. *Auk* 89:612–24.

Cody, M. L. 1966. A general theory of clutch size. *Evolution* 20:174–94.

Diamond, J. 1972. Biogeographic kinetics: Estimation of relaxation times for avifaunas of southwest Pacific islands. *Proc. Nat. Acad. Sci. U.S.* 69:3199–3203.

———. 1973. Distributional ecology of New Guinea birds. *Science* 179:759–69.

Emlen, J. T. 1971. Population densities of birds derived from transect counts. *Auk* 88:323–42.

Feduccia, A. 1977. A model for the evolution of perching birds. *Syst. Zool.* 26:19–31.

Feinsinger, P. 1976. Organization of a tropical guild of nectarivorous birds. *Ecol. Mongr.* 46:257–91.

Fitzpatrick, J. W. 1980. Foraging behavior of Neotropical tyrant flycatchers. *Condor* 82:43–57.

Foster, M. S. 1974. Rain, feeding behavior, and clutch size in tropical birds. *Auk* 91:722–26.

———. 1975. The overlap of molt and breeding in some tropical birds. *Condor* 77:304–14.

Greenberg, R. 1981a. Frugivory in migrant wood warblers. *Biotropica* 13:315–23.

———. 1981b. Abundance and seasonality of forest canopy birds. *Biotropica* 13:241–51.

Haffer, J. 1974. Avian speciation in tropical South America. *Publ. Nuttall Ornithol. Club,* no. 14.

Hartshorn, G. S. 1978. Tree falls and tropical forest dynamics. In *Tropical trees as living systems,* ed. P. B. Tomlinson and M. H. Zimmermann, pp. 617–38. Cambridge: Cambridge University Press.

———. 1980. Neotropical forest dynamics. *Biotropica* 12 (suppl.):23–31.

Higgins, M. L. 1979. Intensity of seed predation on *Brosimum utile* by mealy parrots. *Biotropica* 11:80.

Holmes, R. T., and Sturges, F. W. 1975. Bird community dynamics and energetics in a northern hardwoods ecosystem. *J. Anim. Ecol.* 44:175–200.

Howe, H. F. 1977. Bird activity and seed dispersal of a tropical wet forest tree. *Ecology* 58:539–50.

Howe, H. F., and Estabrook, G. F. 1977. On intraspecific competition for avian dispersers in tropical trees. *Am. Nat.* 111:817–32.

Howe, H. F., and Vande Kerckhove, G. A. 1979. Fecundity and seed dispersal of a tropical tree. *Ecology* 60:180–89.

———. 1981. Removal of wild nutmeg (*Virola surinamensis*) crops by birds. *Ecology* 62:1093–1106.

Howell, T. R. 1969. Avian distribution in Central America. *Auk* 86:293–326.

Janzen, D. H. 1970. Herbivores and the number of tree species in tropical forests. *Am. Nat.* 104:501–28.

———. 1973. Sweep samples of tropical foliage insects: Effects of seasons, vegetation types, elevation, time of day, and insularity. *Ecology* 54:687–708.

Janzen, D. H., and Schoener, T. W. 1968. Differences in insect abundance and diversity between wetter and drier sites during a tropical dry season. *Ecology* 49:96–110.

Kantak, G. E. 1981. Temporal feeding patterns of some tropical frugivores. *Condor* 83:185–87.

Karr, J. R. 1971. Structure of avian communities in selected Panama and Illinois habitats. *Ecol. Monogr.* 41:207–33.

———. 1975. Production, energy pathways, and community diversity in tropical forest birds. In *Tropical ecological systems: Trends in terrestrial and aquatic research,* ed. F. B. Golley and E. Medina, pp. 161–76. Ecological studies, vol. 2. New York: Springer-Verlag.

———. 1976. Seasonality, resource availability, and community diversity in tropical bird communities. *Am. Nat.* 110:973–94.

———. 1977. Ecological correlates of rarity in a tropical forest bird community. *Auk* 94:240–47.

Kiff, L. F. 1975. Notes on southwestern Costa Rican birds. *Condor* 77:101–3.

Lawton, M. F., and Guindon, C. F. 1981. Flock composition, breeding success, and learning in the brown jay. *Condor* 83:27–33.

Leber, K. 1980. Habitat utilization in a tropical heronry. *Brenesia* 17:97–136.

Leck, C. F. 1972. Seasonal changes in feeding pressures of fruit- and nectar-eating birds in Panama. *Condor* 74:54–60.

MacArthur, R. H. 1972. *Geographical ecology.* New York: Harper and Row.

MacArthur, R. H.; Recher, H.; and Cody, M. L. 1966. On the relation between habitat selection and species diversity. *Am. Nat.* 101:377–85.

McDiarmid, R. W.; Ricklefs, R. E.; and Foster, M. S. 1977. Dispersal of *Stemmadenia donnell-smithii* (Apocynaceae) by birds. *Biotropica* 9:9–25.

McKey, D. 1975. The ecology of coevolved seed dispersal systems. In *Coevolution of animals and plants,* ed. L. E. Gilbert and P. H. Raven, pp. 159–91. Austin: University of Texas Press.

Mayr, E. 1946. History of the North American bird faunas. *Wilson Bull.* 58:1–68.

———. 1964. Inferences concerning the Tertiary American bird faunas. *Proc. Nat. Acad. Sci. U.S.* 51:280–88.

Mengel, R. M. 1964. The probable history of species formation in some northern wood warblers (Parulidae). *Living Bird* 2:9–43.

Morse, D. H. 1970. Ecological aspects of some mixed-species foraging flocks of birds. *Ecol. Monogr.* 40:119–68.

Morton, E. S. 1973. On the evolutionary advantages and disadvantages of fruit eating in tropical birds. *Am. Nat.* 107:8–22.

———. 1975. Ecological sources of selection on avian sounds. *Am. Nat.* 109:17–33.

———. 1977. Intratropical migration of the yellow-green vireo and piratic flycatcher. *Auk* 94:97–106.

Morton, E. S., and Keast, A., eds. 1979. *Migrant birds in the New World tropics.* Washington, D.C.: Smithsonian Institution Press.

Moynihan, M. 1962. The organization and possible evolution of some mixed-species flocks of Neotropical birds. *Smithsonian Misc. Coll.* 143:1–140.

Muller, P. 1973. Dispersal centers for terrestrial vertebrates in the Neotropical realm. *Biogeographica* 2:1–244.

Orians, G. H. 1969. The number of bird species in some tropical forests. *Ecology* 50:783–801.

Payne, R. B. 1973. Patterns and control of molt. In *Avian biology,* ed. D. S. Farner and J. R. King, 2:103–55. New York: Academic Press.

Pearson, D. L. 1975. The relation of foliage complexity to ecological diversity of three Amazonian bird communities. *Condor* 77:453–66.

———. 1977. Ecological relationships of small antbirds in Amazonian bird communities. *Auk* 94:283–92.

Powell, G. V. N. 1979. Structure and dynamics of interspecific flocks in a Neotropical mid-elevation forest. *Auk* 96:375–90.

Pulliam, H. R. 1973. Comparative feeding ecology of a tropical grassland finch (*Tiaria olivacea*). Ecology 54:284–99.

Regal, P. 1977. Ecology and evolution of flowering plant dominance. *Science* 196:622–29.

Ricklefs, R. E. 1969. An analysis of nesting mortality in passerine birds. *Smithsonian Contrib. Zool.,* no. 9.

———. 1977. A discriminant function analysis of assemblages of fruit-eating birds in Central America. *Condor* 79:228–31.

Root, R. 1967. The niche exploitation pattern of the blue-grey gnatcatcher. *Ecol. Monogr.* 37:317–50.

Schemske, D. W., and Brokaw, N. 1981. Treefalls and the distribution of understory birds in a tropical forest. *Ecology* 62:938–45.

Schoener, T. W. 1965. The evolution of bill size differences among sympatric congeneric species of birds. *Evolution* 19:189–213.

———. 1971. Large-billed insectivorous birds: A precipitous diversity gradient. *Condor* 73:154–61.

Skutch, A. F. 1950. The nesting seasons of Central American birds in relation to climate and food supply. *Ibis* 92:185–222.

———. 1957, 1960, 1969. *Life histories of Central American birds.* Pacific Coast Avifauna, nos. 31, 34, 35. Berkeley: Cooper Ornithological Society.

———. 1966. A breeding bird census and nesting success in Central America. *Ibis* 108:1–16.

———. 1971. *A naturalist in Costa Rica.* Gainesville: University of Florida Press.

———. 1976. *Parent birds and their young.* Austin: University of Texas Press.

———. 1980. Arils as food of tropical american birds. *Condor* 82:31–42.

Slud, P. 1960. The birds of Finca "La Selva," a tropical wet forest locality. *Bull. Am. Mus. Nat. Hist.* 121:49–148.

———. 1964. The birds of Costa Rica: Distribution and ecology. *Bull. Am. Mus. Nat. Hist.* 128:1–430.

Smythe, N. 1970. Relationships between fruiting seasons and seed dispersal methods in a Neotropical forest. *Am. Nat.* 104:25–35.

Snow, B. K. 1977. Territorial behavior and courtship of the male three-wattled bellbird. *Auk* 94:623–45.

Snow, B. K., and Snow, D. W. 1972. Feeding niches of hummingbirds in a Trinidad valley. *J. Anim. Ecol.* 41:471–85.

Snow, D. W. 1965a. The evolution of manakin displays. *Proc. Thirteenth Int. Ornith. Congr.,* pp. 553–61.

———. 1965b. A possible selective factor in the evolution of fruiting seasons in tropical forest. *Oikos* 15:274–81.

———. 1971. Evolutionary aspects of fruit-eating by birds. *Ibis* 113:194–202.

———. 1978. Relationships between the European and African avifaunas. *Bird Study* 25:134–48.

Snow, D. W. 1981. Tropical frugivorous birds and their food plants: A world survey. *Biotropica* 13:1–14.

Snow, D. W., and Snow, B. K. 1964. Breeding seasons and annual cycles of Trinidad landbirds. *Zoologica* 49:1–39.

Stiles, F. G. 1975. Ecology, flowering phenology, and hummingbird pollination of some Costa Rican *Heliconia* species. *Ecology* 56:285–301.

———. 1978a. Temporal organization of flowering among the hummingbird foodplants of a tropical wet forest. *Biotropica* 10:194–210.

———. 1978b. Ecological and evolutionary implications of bird pollination. *Am. Zool.* 18:715–29.

———. 1978c. Possible specialization for hummingbird-hunting in the tiny hawk. *Auk* 95:550–53.

———. 1979a. The volutionary implications of habitat relations between permanent and winter resident landbirds in Costa Rica. In *Migrant birds in the New World tropics.* ed. E. S. Morton and A. Keast. Washington, D.C.: Smithsonian Institution Press.

———. 1979b. El ciclo anual en una comunidad coadaptada de colibries y flores en el bosque tropical muy húmedo de Costa Rica. *Rev. Biol. Trop.* 27:75–101.

———. 1980. The annual cycle in a tropical wet forest hummingbird community. *Ibis* 122:322–43.

———. 1981. Geographical aspects of bird-flower coevolution, with special reference to Central America. *Ann. Missouri Bot. Gard.* 68:323–51.

Stiles, F. G., and Wolf, L. L. 1974. A possible circannual molt rhythm in a tropical hummingbird. *Am. Nat.* 108:341–54.

———. 1979. The ecology and evolution of a lek mating system in the long-tailed hermit hummingbird. *Am. Ornithol. Union Monogr.*, no. 27.

Terborgh, J. 1971. Distribution on environmental gradients: Theory and a preliminary interpretation of distributional patterns in the avifauna of the Cordillera Vilcabamba, Peru. *Ecology* 52:23–40.

———. 1974. Faunal equilibria and the design of wildlife preserves. In *Tropical ecological systems: Trends in terrestrial and aquatic research,* ed. F. B. Golley and E. Medina, pp. 340–48. Ecological Studies, vol. 2. New York: Springer-Verlag.

———. 1977. Bird species diversity along an Andean elevational gradient. *Ecology* 58:1007–19.

Terborgh, J., and Weske, J. 1969. Colonization of secondary habitats by Peruvian birds. *Ecology* 50: 765–82.

———. 1975. The role of competition in the distribution of Andean birds. *Ecology* 56:562–76.

Tramer, E. J., and Kemp. T. R. 1979. Diet-correlated variation in social behavior of wintering Tennessee warblers. *Auk* 96:186–87.

Wiens, J. A., and Innis, G. S. 1974. Estimation of energy flow in bird communities: A population bioenergetics model. *Ecology* 55:730–46.

Willis, E. O. 1966. The behavior of bicolored antbirds. *Univ. California Publ. Zool.* 79:1–132.

———. 1974. Populations and local extinctions of birds on Barro Colorado Island, Panama. *Ecol. Monogr.* 44:153–59.

———. 1976. Effects of a cold wave on an Amazonian avifauna in the upper Paraguay drainage, southern Matto Grosso, and suggestions on oscine-suboscine relationships. *Acta Amaz.* 6:379–94.

Willson, M. F.; Anderson, S. H.; and Murray, B. G. 1973. Tropical and temperate bird species diversity: Within- and between-habitat comparisons. *Caribbean J. Sci.* 13:81–90.

Wolf, L. L. 1970. The impact of seasonal flowering on the biology of some tropical hummingbirds. *Condor* 72:1–14.

———. 1976. The avifauna of the Cerro de la Muerte region, Costa Rica. *Am. Mus. Nat. Hist. Novitates,* no. 2606.

Wolf, L. L., and Stiles, F. G. 1970. The evolution of pair cooperation in a tropical hummingbird. *Auk* 87: 467–91.

Wolf, L. L.; Stiles, F. G.; and Hainsworth, F. R. 1976. The ecological organization of a tropical highland hummingbird community. *J. Anim. Ecol.* 32:349–79.

CHECKLIST OF BIRDS

F. G. Stiles

This list gives an approximate idea of the status, abundance, and habitat preference of all bird species recorded to date at the sites most frequently visited by OTS courses, with the following qualifications:

1. The list for the Osa Peninsula refers to the peninsula as a whole, not just Corcovado National Park. However, virtually all the species listed, with the exception of certain water birds, can be expected to occur in Corcovado.

2. The San José–Universidad de Costa Rica area is included, since many students have their first experience with tropical birds in these areas.

3. Tortuguero is not included, since its avifauna is essentially a subset of that of La Selva, with the addition of certain water birds.

4. The list for Las Cruces also includes the area around San Vito, especially the scrub and marshes near the airport (since virtually everyone arriving or departing San Vito by air has an hour or two to kill there).

5. The list for La Selva also includes the Puerto Viejo area and the low-lying, grassy marshes across the Río Puerto Viejo.

Because of the obvious space limitations, only a very general idea of abundance and local distribution can be given. Thus, the habitats in which a bird is most commonly found are listed, and the abundance and status statements refer *to those habitats*—which might be widespread or very localized. For instance, the Chiriquí yellowthroat (*Geothlypis chiriquensis*) is common in grassy marshes around the San Vito airport—but is not found elsewhere in the area. The mourning warbler (*Oporornis philadelphicus*) is a very common winter resident in scrubby areas near these same marshes but is rather uncommon in low scrub elsewhere (including Las Cruces "proper"). Also, the status of a bird may vary from one habitat to the next: the *Sporophila* seedeaters might be classed as permanent residents in young second growth and as short-term visitors in forest. Many species may have "dual status" in any case—for example, many northern migrants occur both as transients and as winter residents. In such cases, only the category of longest-term residence (n instead of t, p instead of n, etc.) will be given as a rule; but it should be obvious that, as more transitory individuals come and go, abundance will vary.

In the lists that follow, the Latin name of the species is followed by a series of symbols and abbreviations. These are as follows:

* Long-distance migrant; breeds north of Costa Rica (usually in North America)
** Long-distance intratropical migrant: breeds in Central America, winters farther south.
*** Long-distance migrant breeding south of Costa Rica (chiefly certain marine species).
+ Migrations or pronounced seasonal movements within Costa Rica; these are primarily altitudinal for land birds and related to the rains and changes in water level for water birds.
° Individuals forage daily over a very wide range, often traversing several habitats or even life zones (large soaring birds, swifts, some swallows, some frugivores, etc.).
( ) Part of the population is relatively sedentary, part is migratory—as in species with resident and migrant subspecies, like the western wood pewee (*Contopus sordidulus*). This symbol also indicates variation in the degree of altitudinal migration between individuals, in different years, etc.

Under the column for each site, three kinds of data are listed for each species present; (maximum) abundance, status, and preferred habitat(s). The abbreviations are as follows:

Abundance

A Abundant; many can be recorded daily.
C Common; one or a few are recorded daily.
U Uncommon; one or a few seen at frequent intervals, usually not daily.
R Rare; seen regularly at longer intervals, in small numbers.
O Occasional; seen sporadically; usually at long intervals, in small numbers (but also applies to occasional flock "invasions").
X Accidental; five or fewer records to date.

Status

p Permanent resident; breeds in the area (presumably), can be seen at any time of year. Includes wide-ranging species that can appear daily but may breed at some distance, within Costa Rica (e.g., swifts, vultures).
n Nonbreeding resident; present for periods of several months (even year-round in some shorebirds, etc.) but breeds far from Costa Rica (northern migrants) or well outside the site in question (tropical species that range over wide areas seasonally but not daily).
b Breeding resident; breeds in the area, then leaves (altitudinal, intratropical, or water-bird migrants).
v Visitant; present in the area for relatively short periods; normally a bird out of its usual range or habitat.
t Transient migrant; a species that *only* occurs in the area during a long-distance migration.

? Status uncertain.

Preferred habitats

1. Aquatic
   a. Offshore marine: largely pelagic birds that do not use the shore per se and appear on land only when sick or starving.
   b. Shoreline—including sandy beach and rocky shores.
   c. Mangroves.
   d. Large streams, rivers.
   e. Ponds, lakes, lagoons (including large temporary puddles and ponds).
   f. Marshes.
   g. Forest streams and swamps.
   h. Mud flats and salinas (salt flats).
2. Aerial—ranging widely above various habitats; not particularly associated with any terrestrial vegetation formation (swifts, vultures, transient long-distance migrants, etc.).
3. Open habitats or heavily altered habitats.
   a. Savanna, grassland, pastures.
   b. Young second growth or low scrub.
   c. Agricultural land.
   d. Human habitations: urban and suburban, around buildings, etc.
   e. Páramo (Cerro de la Muerte).
4. Wooded habitats.
   a. Forest interior.
   b. Forest canopy.
   c. Forest edge, including light gaps of various types.
   d. Old second growth (with a more or less distinct "canopy" stratum).
   e. Tree plantations (cacao, pejibaye, etc.); tree-lined gardens, arboretums, etc.
   f. Riverine or gallery forest; tall riparian vegetation.

These abbreviations are always given in the following sequence: abundance, status, and habitat: capital letter, lower-case letter, then number(s) followed in most cases by one or more lower-case letters. Thus, for *Tinamus major* at La Selva; Cp4a: a common permanent resident in forest interior. For *Crypturellus soui* at La Selva: Cp3b4d: common permanent resident in young and old second growth, etc.

I wish to emphasize that these lists are neither final nor complete. In an area where deforestation and other man-generated habitat alterations are proceeding ever more rapidly, the avifauna will inevitably reflect these changes—new species invade, others die out locally. For this reason, I would be grateful to learn of any additions or corrections to the above lists, including changes in abundance. These data will be helpful in keeping tabs on Costa Rica's rich and changing avifauna.

Bird Species	La Selva and Vicinity	Osa Peninsula	Palo Verde	Santa Rosa	Las Cruces and Vicinity	Monte-verde	Universidad de Costa Rica, San José	Villa Mills
Tinamus major	Cp4a	Cp4a			Up4a			
Nothocercus bonapartei						Up4a		Xv?4a
Crypturellus soui	Cp3b4d	Cp3b4d			Cp3b4d			
C. boucardi	Up4a							
C. cinnamomeus			Cp4a	Cp4a				
Podiceps dominicus [+]	Xvld	Upld	Cble	Cble	Cplef			
Podilymbus podiceps [+]			Cble	Uble	Rp?lef			
Procellaria parkinsoni [**]								
Puffinus pacificus [**]		Xvlab						
P. tenuirostris [**]								
P. griseus [**]				Ovla				
P. lherminieri [***]								
Pterodroma hasitata [***]								
P. phaeopygia [***]								
Oceanites oceanicus [**]								
Oceanodroma tethys [***]								
O. leucorhoa [*]								
O. melania [*]								
Halocyptena microsoma [*]				Ovla				
Phaethon aethereus [***]		Rv?la		Ovla				
Pelecanus erythrorhynchos [*]			Xvle					
P. occidentalis [(***)°]		Unlbc		Cnlab				
Sula nebouxii [*]		Rvlab						
S. dactylatra [***]		Xlab						
S. sula [***]								
S. leucogaster		Cblab		Cp?lab				
Phalacrocorax olivaceus [+]	Upld	Cplbd	Cnle	Cnlbce	Rv?lef		Xv2	
Anhinga anhinga [(+)°]	Rvld	Uplde	Cblde	Rnlde				
Fregata magnificens [°]	Xv2	Cnlab2	Rv2	Cnlab2		Xv2		
Ardea herodias [* +]	Rvld	Unlbf	Unlf	Rnlb–d				
Butorides virescens [(*)]	Upldf	Cplc–f	Cblf	Uplbcd	Cplde		Rvld	
B. striatus								
Florida caerulea [* +]	Cnld	Cnlb–d	Cnlc–f	Cnlb–e	Rvlef			
Dichromanassa rufescens [*]		Rnlh						
Casmerodius albus [(*) +]	Rnld	Unlb–f	Abnlc–f	Unlb–3	Rvlef			
Egretta thula [* +]	Rnld	Rnlbdh	Cnlc–f	Unlb–e				
Bubulcus ibis [(*) +]	An,p?3a	Cp?3ac	Ap?3alf	Up?3a	Cv3a	Cn3a	Un3a	
Hydranassa tricolor [* +]	Ovld	Rnlfh	Unlc–f	Rnlb–d				
Agamia agami	Rplg	Rplg						
Nycticorax nycticorax [(*) +]	Ovld		Cnb?;df					
Nyctanassa violacea [(*)]	Ov,b?ld	Cp?lcd	Up?l–d	Up?lbc				
Tigrisoma lineatum	Rplg							
T. fasciatum								
T. mexicanum		Uplc–f	Upldf	Rplcdf				
Ixobrychus exilis [(*) +]	Xvlf	Rn?lf	Up?lf					
Botaurus lentiginosus [*]								
B. pinnatus [+]			Rp?lf					
Cochlearius cochlearius [(*)]	Ov?ld	Rvde	Abp?ld–f	Ovlcdf				
Mycteria americana [+°]	Xv2	Rvde	Abp?ld–f	Ovledf				
Jabiru mycteria [+°]			Up?ld–f					
Mesembrinibus cayennensis	Uplg							
Eudocimus albus [+]		Unbch	Cp?lc–f	Cnlb–e				
Plegadis falcinellus [* +]			Unlef					
P. chihi [*]								
Ajaia ajaja [+]		Unb–d	Ablef	Unlc–e				
Dendrocygna viduata [+]			Uble					
D. bicolor [+]			Clbe					
D. autumnalis [+]	Ovlde		Abp?lef	Un?lde				
Cairina moschata [+]	Op?ldg	Rplcd	Cp?lf	Rv?lc–e				
Anas acuta [* +]			Cnle					
A. platyrhynchos [*]								
A. cyanoptera [*]			Onlef					
A. discors [* +]	Rnlf	Unlef	Anlef	Utlde	Rtle		Rtle	
A. clypeata [* +]			Cnlef					
A. americana [* +]			Cnlef					
Aythya collaris [* +]			Cnle					
A. marila [*]								

Bird Species	La Selva and Vicinity	Osa Peninsula	Palo Verde	Santa Rosa	Las Cruces and Vicinity	Monte-verde	Universidad de Costa Rica, San José	Villa Mills
A. affinis *+			Un1e					
Oxyura dominica +			Ub1f	Rb1ef				
Sarcoramphus papa	Rp2	Cp2	Up2	Up2	Ov2	Rp?2		
Coragyps atratus°	Ap2	Ap2	Ap2	Ap2	Ap2	Cp2	Ap2	Rv2
Cathartes burrovianus +		Ovlf	Rn?lf					
C. aura (*)°	Ap,n2	Ap2	Apn2	Apn2	Ap2	Cp?2	Cpn2	Xv2
Elanus leucurus	Cp3ac	Cp3ac	Up3ac	Up3a	Cp3ab	Rp3a	Up3ab	
Elanoides forficatus ***°	Ubv2	Ub2		Rt2	Ub2	Cb24b		Rv2
Leptodon cayanensis	Op?4c	Up4bc	Up4bc	Up4bcf				
Chondrohierax uncinatus	Xv4c		Ov?4f					
Harpagus bidentatus	Up4bc	Up4bc	Rp?4b	Up4bc	Up4bc	Up4bc		
Ictinia mississipiensis *	Ot2							
I. plumbea **	Rv2	Rv2	Rvlcd	Cblc4bc				
Rostrhamus sociabilis +		Ovlef	Cplef					
Accipiter bicolor	Rp4a	Rp4a			Up4a–c	Up4bcd		
A. cooperii *					Rn4c	Ot2	On3e	
A. superciliosus	Rp4cd	Rp4ad						
A. striatus *				Rt3a	Ot3ab	Un3a4c	Rtn3ab	
Heterospizias meridionalis								
Buteo albicaudatus			Rp?3a	Rp3a				
B. jamaicensis (*)°	Xt2					Up23a		Cp23e4c
B. albonotatus		Rp4c	Uplf	Rp3a4c				
B. swainsoni *	At2	Ut2	Ut23a	Ct2	Ut2	Ct2	Rt2	Ct2
B. platypterus *	At,n2,4c	C5n2,4cd	Cn4bc	Atn24bc	Ctn24cd	An3a2	Utn3ab2	
B. magnirostris	Op?3b	Cp3ab	Cp3a4bc	Cp3a4bc				
B. brachyurus (*)	Ot2	Rt2		Utn23a4c				
B. nitidus	Xv4c	Up4c	Up4bc	Cp4bc				
Parabuteo unicinctus			Cp3a4c	Up3a4c				
Leucopternis albicollis	Up24b	Cp24b			Rp24b	Up24b		
L. semiplumbea	Up4ace							
L. princeps °(+)	Xv2				Ov24b	Cp24b		Xv2
Busarellus nigricollis		Upld						
Buteogallus anthracinus	Rp?4c	Aplbc	Cplcd	Aplbc4c				
B. urubitinga		Up4bc	Rplf4bc	Up4bc	Ov?4bc			
Harpyhaliaetus solitarius		Rp24b				Xv2		
Morphnus guianensis								
Harpia harpyja		Rp24b				Xv4b		
Spizastur melanoleucus	Op?2,4b	Rp24b						
Spizaetus ornatus	Ov2,4b	Rp24b		Xv2		Rv?24b		Xv2
S. tyrannus	Up2,4b	Up24b						Xt2
Circus cyaneus *	Otlf3a		Rvlf					
Geranospiza caerulescens	Rp4bc3	Rp4abc	Rp4b	Up4f				
Pandion haliaetus	Unld	Cnlb–e	Unlde	Cnlbc			Ot2	
Herpetotheres cachinnans	Up4bce	Cp4bc	Cp3a4bc	Cp3a4bc				
Micrastur semitorquatus	Ov4ac	Up4ab	Up4a–c	Up4a–c	Rp?4a–c	Rp4abc		
M. mirandollei	Rp4ac3							
M. ruficollis	Up4ad	Up4abd			Up4abd	Cp4ace		
Daptrius americanus	Op?4c	Up4bc						
Milvago chimachima		Up4cd						
Polyborus plancus		Up4c	Cp3a4c	Cp3a4c				
Falco peregrinus *	Ot2	Otlb	Unlef	Rtlbe			Ot2	
F. deiroleucus								
F. rufigularis	Rpldrc	Cp4ce						
F. columbarius *				Xtlb			Xt2	
F. sparverius *	Rt3a	On3a	Un3a	Un3a	Rn3ab	Cn3a	Un3a	
Crax rubra	Rp4a	Up4ab	Rp4bc	Up4a–c	Op4ab			
Penelope purpurascens	Up4bce	Up4bc	Up4bf	Up4bcf	Rp4b	Up4bc		
Ortalis vetula				Up3a4bc				
O. cinereiceps	Up3b	Rp?4d						
Chamaepetes unicolor						Cp4ab		Rp4ab
Dendrortyx leucophrys								
Colinus leucopogon			Up3a	Ap3ab			Up3ab	
C. cristatus								
Odontophorus gujanensis		Up4a						
O. erythrops	Rp4a							
O. leucolaemus						Cp4ac		
O. guttatus (+)	Ov4a				Up4ac			Rp4a

533

Bird Species	La Selva and Vicinity	Osa Peninsula	Palo Verde	Santa Rosa	Las Cruces and Vicinity	Monte-verde	Universidad de Costa Rica, San José	Villa Mills
Rhynchortyx cinctus								
Aramus guarauna[(+)]	Xvld	Ovldf	Aplf	Ovlef				
Pardirallus maculatus[(*)]			Uplf					
Amaurolimnas concolor	Uplg	Rplg4d						
Aramides cajanea	Ullg4ad	Uplcg	Up4flc	Uplc4f	Cp4alg			
A. axillaris								
Porzana carolina[*]			Unlf	Rtlf				
P. flaviventer			Ublf					
Micropygia schomburgkii								
Laterallus jamaicensis								
L. albigularis	Aplf3b	Aplf3b			Aplf3b			
L. ruber								
Gallinula chloropus	Xvlf		Cblef		Uplef			
Porphyrula martinica		Upldf	Cblf		Cplef			
Fulica americana[*]			Anle					
Heliornis fulica	Upldg	Cpld						
Eurypyga helias	Rp?ldg				Rv?ldg	Rvld		
Jacana spinosa[(+)]	Cplf	Cpldf	Ablef	Up?lef	Cp?lef			
Haematopus palliatus[(*)]		Up?lb		Up?lb				
Pluvialis squatarola[*]		Unlbh	Unlcd	Unlbch				
P. dominica					Rt3a			
Charadrius semipalmatus[*]		Cnlbh	Cnlcd	Cnlch				
C. alexandrinus[*]				Rtlb				
C. collaris[+]		Up?lb		Up?lbh				
C. vociferus[*(+)]	Utn3a		Cnlh3a				Un3a	Xvle
C. wilsonia[(**)(+)]		Cnlbh		Cp?lceh				
Bartramia longicauda			Rtlf					
Numenius phaeopus[*]		Cnlbch	Unlcd	Unlbch				
N. americanus[*]								
Limosa haemastica[*]								
L. fedoa[*]		Otlh						
Tringa flavipes[*]		Rnld	Unlef	Unld–f				
T. melanoleuca[*]	Xtld	Unld	Rnlef	Rtld–f				
T. solitaria[*(+)]	Rnlf	Unld–f	Unlf	Utld–f	Unlef		Utle	
Actitis macularia[*]	Anld	Anlb–f	Anlc–f	Cnlbf	Cnldef		Cnlde	
Catoptrophorus semipalmatus[*]		Clbch	Unlcd	Cnlbceh				
Heteroscelus incanus[*]		Ctlb						
Aphriza virgata[*]		Rtlb						
Arenaria interpres[*]		Unlbh		Unlbh				
Limnodromus griseus[*]		Rnlbh	Unlefh	Unlbeh				
L. scolopaceus[*]			Utlf					
Capella gallinago[*(+)]			Cnlf	Utnlef			Unlf3a	Xtld
Calidris canutus[*]		Rtlbh						
C. alba[*]	Anlb		Anlb					
C. pusilla[*]		Unlb	Rnlb	Unlbeh				
C. mauri[*]		Cnlbh	Rnlh	Cnlbeh				
C. minutilla[*]		Unlbh	Unlh	Cnlbeh			Rtlde	
C. fuscicollis[*]								
C. bairdii[*]								
C. melanotos[* +]		Rtlf	Utlfh	Rtlef			Ut3ale	
C. alpina[*]		Xvlh						
Micropalama himantopus[*]		Rtlef	Rtf					
Tryngites subruficollis[*]								
Philomachus pugnax[*]								
Himantopus mexicanus[(*)(+)]		Rvlfh	Cplf	Unleh				
Recurvirostra americana[*]								
Steganopus tricolor[*]								
Phalaropus fulicarius[*]								
Lobipes lobatus[*]		Rtla		Utla				
Burhinus bistriatus			Cp3a	Cp3a				
Catharacta skua[**]								
Stercorarius pomarinus[*]		Otla						
S. parasiticus[*]								
S. longicaudus[*]								
Larus delawarensis[*]								
L. argentatus[*]								
L. atricilla[*]		Cnlb	Unlde	Rvlb				
L. pipixcan[*]		Ctlb2	Utlde	Utlde2				

Bird Species	La Selva and Vicinity	Osa Peninsula	Palo Verde	Santa Rosa	Las Cruces and Vicinity	Monte-verde	Universidad de Costa Rica, San José	Villa Mills
L. philadelphia*		Xvlb						
Xema sabini*								
Chlidonias nigra*		Unlab		Cnlab				
Gelochelidon nilotica*		Rvlb	Rvlde					
Hydroprogne caspia*								
Sterna hirundo*		Utnlb		Uvlab				
S. forsteri								
S. anaethetus**				Cbla				
S. fuscata***		Xvla						
S. albifrons*		Rtlb						
Thalasseus maximus**		Uvlb		Unlab				
T. elegans*		Ovlb		Rvlab				
T. sandvicensis*		Uvlb		Unlab				
Gygis alba***								
Anous stolidus*		Rtnlab						
Rynchops niger*,***		Xtvlb						
Columba livia							Ap3d	
C. flavirostris°	Rv3abc	Ov?3a	Up3a4c	Cp3a4c		Ap3a4c	Rp3abd	
C. cayennensis°	Rv3ac?	Cplc3a						
C. fasciata+°					Rv4bce	Cp4bc		Ap4bc
C. speciosa	Up4bce				Rp?4bcd			
C. nigrirostris	Ap4bcde	Ap4b–e			Ap4bcd			
C. subvinacea*						Cp?4b		Ub4b
Zenaida macroura(*)	Xv3a		Un3a	Un3a			Rp?3ab	
Z. asiatica(*)			Cp3a4c	Cp3a4c				
Scardafella inca.			Ap3a4c	Ap3a4c			Up3ab	
Columbina passerina			Ap3a	Ap3a4c			Up3ab	
C. minuta				Rp?3a				
C. talpacoti	Ap3abc	Ap3a–c			Ap3ab			
Claravis pretiosa	Cp3ab	Cp3ab	Up3a4c	Rp4c–f	Cp3b4cd			
C. mondetoura								Rp?3b4c
Leptotila verreauxi	Xv3b	Cp3b4d	Ap4acf	Ap4acf	Cp3b4d	Cp3b4d	Ap3b4c–e	
L. plumbeiceps								
L. cassinii	Ap4cde	A4c–e			Ap4acd			
Geotrygon veraguensis	Up4ad							
G. lawrencii								
G. costaricensis						Up4a		Rv4ac
G. violacea								
G. montana	Ov4ad	Up4a			Up4ad	Up4a		
G. linearis						Op4a		
Ara ambigua+*	Up?n?4b					Rv4b		
A. macao°		Ap4bc	Up4bc	Rp4bf				
Aratinga finschi+°	Ap3a	Cp4cd			Cp24b–e	Up?4bcd	Am4b–e	
A. astec	Cp4bcde							
A. canicularis			Ap4bc	Ap4bc				
Pyrrhura hoffmanni+°						Rv4bcd		Cp24bcd
Bolborhynchus lineola+°						Rv?4bc		Cp24bcd
Brotogeris jugularis	Up?3ab	Cp3a4be	Ap4bc3a	Ap3a4b–f	Cp4b–e	Un4bc	Ov4bc	
Touit dilectissima+°								Rv4d
Pionopsitta haematotis	Cp4be	Cp4b–e			Up4b–e	Cp4bc		
Pionus menstruus								
P. senilis°	Ap4bce	Ap4b–e			Ap4b–e		Rv3c4b–e	
Amazona albifrons°			Ap3a4bc	Ap3a4bc				
A. autumnalis°	Cp4be	Up			Cp4bce	Up?4bc		
A. ochrocephala°		Xv3a	Up3a4bc	Up3a4bc				
A. farinosa°	Cp4be	Ap4bce			Up4bc			
Coccyzus erythropthalmus*	Rt3b	Rt3b		Rt3b4c			Rt3b	
C. americanus*	Rt3b	Rt3b	Rt4c	Rt3b4c			Rt3b	
C. minor*?		Ub?lc3b	Ub?lc4ac		Cblc4ac			
Piaya cayana	Cp3b–e	Cp4b–e	Cp4bc	Cp4bc	Cp4b–e	Cp4b–e	Up3b4b–e	
Crotophaga ani		Cp3ac			Ap3ab			
C. sulcirostris	Ap3ab		Ap3ab	Cp3ab		Cp3a	Cp3ab	
Tapera naevia	Up?3a	Ap3a–c			Cp3ab		Up3b	
Morococcyx erythropygius			Cp3ab4c	Cp3ab4c				
Dromococcyx phasianellus				Op?3b4c				
Neomorphus geoffroyi	Op4a							
Tyto alba	Up3ac	Up3ac	Cp3a	Cp3a	Up3a	Rp3a	Cp3a–d	
Otus guatemalae	Up4a							

Bird Species	La Selva and Vicinity	Osa Peninsula	Palo Verde	Santa Rosa	Las Cruces and Vicinity	Monte-verde	Universidad de Costa Rica, San José	Villa Mills
O. cooperi			Up4ac	Cp4acf				
O. choliba							Cp4de	
O. clarkii						Up4ba		Up4ab
Lophostrix cristata	Op?4ad	Rp?4ad		Op4cf				
Speotyto cunicularia								
Bubo virginianus								
Pulsatrix perspicillata	Up4ace	Up4ace	Cp4bc	Cp4bc		Up4ace		
Glaucidium minutissimum	Up4bce							
G. jardinii								Rp4b
G. brasilianum			Ap3a4bc	Ap3a4bc			Cp4cde	
Ciccaba virgata	Cp4cde	Up4b–e			Cp4b–e	Cp4b–e		
C. nigrolineata	Rp4b							
Rhinoptynx clamator			Up3ab4c					
Asio flammeus*								
Aegolius ridgwayi								Op4ab
Nyctibius grandis	Up4b	U–Rp4b						
Lurocalis semitorquatus	Cp4bc	Up3b4c						
Chordeiles acutipennis(*)		Up?3ba	Cplf3a	Cplbf3a				
C. minor(*)	Rt2	Rtv3a	Ut23a	Utp?3a				
Nyctidromus albicollis	Ap3ab	Ap3ab	Ap3a4c	Ap3a4c	Ap3a4c	Up3a4c	Up?3b4de	
Caprimulgus carolinensis*	Rn4bc	Rn4bc					Rt2	
C. rufus								
C. vociferus			On4ac	On4acf				
C. saturatus						Rp?4bc		Cp4bc
C. cayennensis		Xv?3a		Rb?3a				
Streptoprocne zonaris°	Up2	Up2	Uv2	Uv2	Cp2	Cp2	Uv3	Ov2
Chaetura pelagica*	Ot2	Rt2					Rt2	
C. vauxi°				Xv2	Cp2	Ap2	Up2	Rv2
C. cinereiventris	Ap2							
C. spinicauda°		Ap2			Cp2			
Cypseloides rutilus°					Up?2	Up2	Rv2	
C. cherriei								
C. cryptus								
C. niger(*)°	Ot?2	Uv2			Rn–v2	Rv2	Otv2	
Panyptila sanctihieronymi**?	Xv2							
P. cayennensis°	Up2	Cp2			Rp?2	Up2		
Doryfera ludovicae						Xv4c		
Glaucis aenea	Cp3b	Cp3b						
Threnetes ruckeri	Cp4acd	Cpracd						
Phaethornis guy(+)	Ov4ac				Ap4acd	Ap4acde		
P. superciliosus	Ap4acd	Ap4acd						
P. longuemareus	Ap4acd	Ap4acd	Up4af	Cp4af	Ap4acd	Up4acd		
Eutoxeres aquila(+)	Up4ac	Up4ac			Up4acd			
Phaeochroa cuvierii+	Ov4c	Cplc	Rb?lc4c	Ub?lc4c	Up4ce			
Campylopterus hemileucurus					Cp4acde	Cp4acde	Ov4cd	
Florisuga mellivora+	Cp4a–e	Ap4a–e						
Colibri delphinae+	Xv4c				Xv4c	Xv4c		
C. thalassinus+					Up4cd	Ab3b4ce	Rv3b4cd	
Anthracothorax prevostii(+)			Cb3a4c	Ub3a4c				
Klais guimeti	Cp4b–e	Cp4a–d			Up4b–e			
Lophornis delattrei								
L. helenae+	Rv?4bc						Xv3b	
L. adorabilis		Uplc3b4c		Rp?3b4c				
Popelairia conversii(+)	Ov4bc							
Chlorostilbon canivetii		Cp3b	Cp3b4ac	Cp3b4ac	Cp3b	Cp3b	Rp3b	
Thalurania furcata(+)	Ap4a–e	Cp4a–e			Cp4a–e			
Panterpe insignis						Ap4bc		Ap4bcd
Hylocharis eliciae	Rv4d	Up4bcd	Up4bf	Cp4abf		Up3b4cd	Xv3b	
Amazilia candida		Xv?						
A. amabilis	Cp4cde							
A. decora		Ap4cde			Cp3b4c–e			
A. boucardi		Cplc						
A. cyanifrons								
A. cyanura	Xv3b							
A. saucerrottei			Ap4a–c	Ap4a–d		Up3b4c	Ap3bd4c–e	
A. edward					Up3b4cd			
A. rutila			Ap4a–d	Ap4a–d				
A. tzacatl	Ap3b	Ap3b	Up4ac	Up4cf	Ap3bcf	Cp3bd	Ap3bd4c–e	

Bird Species	La Selva and Vicinity	Osa Peninsula	Palo Verde	Santa Rosa	Las Cruces and Vicinity	Monteverde	Universidad de Costa Rica, San José	Villa Mills
Eupherusa eximia					Rv?4e	Cp4abcd		Xv4c
E. nigriventris								
Elvira chionura					Cp4acde			
E. cupreiceps						Ap4acde		
Microchera albocoronata [+]	Un4bce							
Chalybura urochrysia	Cp4acde							
Lampornis hemileucus						Xv4bc		
L. calolaema					Up4a–e	Ap4a–e	Xv3b4cd	
L. castaneoventris					Rv4c			Rv4c
Heliodoxa jacula					Cp4acd	Up4acd		
Eugenes fulgens [(+)]						Xv4c		Cp3be4ac
Heliothryx barroti	Up4bce	Up4bce			Up4b–e			
Heliomaster constantii			Cp4bc	Cp4bc		Up4ce	Rp4cd	
H. longirostris	Rp4be	Up4bce			Cp4bce			
Philodice bryantae					Rv?3b	Cp3b4ce		
Archilochus colubris [*]	Xv3b	Un3b	Cn3b4bc	Cn3b4b–d		Un3b4c	Rt3bd	
Selasphorus flammula [+]								Ab3be4cd
S. simoni [+]								
S. scintilla [+]					Up?3b4c	Rv3brcd	Rv3b4cd	
Pharomachrus mocinno [+]						Cp4bc		Rp?4b
Trogon massena	Cp4b–e	Cp4b–e			Cp4b–e			
T. clathratus	Rp4b							
T. bairdi		Cp4b–e			Cp4b–e			
T. melanocephalus			Cp4bc	Cp4bc				
T. elegans			Up4b	Up4bf				
T. collaris [+]					Xv4b	Rv4b		Xv4b
T. aurantiiventris						Cp4bcd		
T. rufus	Cp4acd	Cp4acd			Cp4acd			
T. violaceus	Cp4de	Up4de	Up4bf	Up4bf	Cp4de			
Ceryle torquata [°]	Upld	Cplbd	Upld	Cplcde				
C. alcyon [*]	Rnld	Unlbde	Unlde	Cnlbde				
Chloroceryle amazona	Upld	Upld						
C. americana	Cpldg	Cplbde	Uplde	Cplde	Uplde	Rvld		
C. inda	Rp?lg							
C. aenea	Uplg	Uplg	Uplg	Upldg				
Hylomanes momotula								
Electron platyrhynchum	Cp4bcd							
E. carinatum								
Eumomota superciliosa [+]			Cp4ac	Cp?4ac				
Baryphthengus martii	Cp4bcd							
Momotus momota		Up4ad	Up4a	Cp4af	Ap4cde	Cp4ad	Cp4acde	
Galbula ruficauda	Cp4celg	Cp4cld			Upld4c	Rvld		
Jacamerops aurea	Rp4b							
Notharchus macrorhynchos	Rp?4bc	Up4bc	Up3a4bc	Up4bcf				
N. tectus	Up4bce							
Malacoptila panamensis	Cp4acde	Cp4acd			Up4acd			
Micromonacha lanceolata								
Monasa morphoeus	Ap4bce							
Eubucco bourcierii					Rv4bc			
Semnornis frantzii						Cp4bc		
Aulacorhynchus prasinus [(+)]	Xv4c				Xv4bc	Ap4b–e		
Pteroglossus torquatus	Ap4b–e		Rp4bf	Up4bcf			Xv4bc	
P. frantzii		Cp4b–e			Up4b–e			
Selenidera spectabilis [+]	Rv?4bc							
Ramphastos sulfuratus [°]	Apb–e			Rp4f		Up4b–e		
R. swainsonii [°]	Ap4b–e	Ap4b–e			Xv4bc			
Picumnus olivaceus		Up3b4d			Up3b4d			
Piculus rubiginosus					Up4b–e	Up4b–e		
P. simplex	Up4be	Up4be			Rp?4be			
Celeus castaneus	Up4be							
C. loricatus	Up4be							
Dryocopus lineatus	Up4cd	Up4cd	Up4bc	Up4bc	Cp4bcd	Rp4cd		
Campephilus guatemalensis	Cp4b–e	Cp4b–e	Up4bcf	Up4bcf	Cp4b–e			
Melanerpes formicivorus								Up4bc
Centurus hoffmanni			Ap4bcf	Ap4bcf		Cp4cd	Ap4b–e	
C. rubricapillus		Cp4cd			Ap4cde			
C. pucherani	Ap4b–e							
C. chrysauchen		Cp4b–e			Up4bc			

Bird Species	La Selva and Vicinity	Osa Peninsula	Palo Verde	Santa Rosa	Las Cruces and Vicinity	Monte-verde	Universidad de Costa Rica, San José	Villa Mills
Sphyrapicus varius[*]			Xv4c			Rn4cd	Rn4cd	
Veniliornis fumigatus	Rp4cd				Up4cde	Cp4abcd		
V. kirkii		Rp4bcd						
Dendrocopus villosus						Up4b–e		Cp4bcd
Dendrocincla fuliginosa	Up4ac							
D. anabatina		Cp4acde			Cp4acde			
D. homochroa			Up4a	Up4af	Up4ac	Up4acd		
Deconychura longicauda	Xv4a	Up4ac						
Sittasomus griseicapillus			Up4b	Cp4abf	Cp4abc	Cp4b–e		
Glyphorhynchus spirurus	Ap4a–e	Ap4a–e			Cp4a–e	Rv4bce		
Xiphocolaptes promeropirhynchus						Ov4bc		
Dendrocolaptes certhia	Cp4a–e	Cp4a–e	Up4ab	Up4abf	Cp4a–e	Up4a–e		
D. picumnus								
Xiphorhynchus guttatus	Cp4cde	Cp4cde			Rp?4cde			
X. flavigaster			Op4b	Up4bcf				
X. lachrymosus	Cp4abce	Cp4abce						
X. erythropygius	Up4b	Up4b			Cp4a–e	Cp4b–e		
Lepidocolaptes souleyetii	Cp4cde	Cp4cde	Cp4a–c	Cp4a–cf	Cp4cde	Up4cde		
L. affinis								Rn4abc
Campylorhamphus pusillus		Up4bc			Up4bc	Rp?4abc		
Synallaxis albescens		Up3ab			Cp3ab			
S. brachyura	Cp3b	Cp3b			Up3b			
Cranioleuca erythrops					Up4bc	Cp4bce		
Margarornis rubiginosus						Ap4bcd		Cp4bcd
Premnoplex brunnescens					Cp4a–c	Cp4a–e		
Pseudocolaptes lawrencii						Rp?4bc		Up4bcd
Hyloctistes subulatus	Up4ab	Up4ab			Rp?4bc			
Syndactyla subalaris					Ov4ab	Up4acd		
Anabacerthia striaticollis					Xv4ab	Rp4bcd		
Philydor rufus								
Automolus rubiginosus					Up4acd	Xv?4a		
A. ochrolaemus	Cp4acd	Cp4acd			Cp4acde			
Thripadectes rufobrunneus						Up4b–e		Xv4a
Xenops rutilans					Up4bce			
X. minutus	Rp4ce	Cp4bce	Up4ab		Cp4a–e			
Sclerurus albigularis						Up4a		
S. mexicanus					Ov?4a			
S. guatemalensis	Up4a	Up4a			Up4ad			
Cymbilaimus lineatus	Up4cde							
Taraba major	C3b	Cp3b			Up3b			
Thamnophilus doliatus	Ov?3b		Up4af	Cp4af				
T. bridgesi		Ap4acde			Cp4ab–e			
T. punctatus	Ap4acde							
Thamnistes anabatinus	Rp?4bc	Up4bce			Cp4b–e			
Dysithamnus mentalis [+]	Xv4a	Up4a			Cp4ac	Up4acd		
D. striaticeps	Cp4ac							
D. puncticeps								
Myrmotherula fulviventris	Ap4ac							
M. axillaris	Cp4a							
M. schisticolor		Cp4a			Cp4ac	Up4ac		
Microrhopias quixensis	Ap4cde	Ap4acde			Cp4cde			
Terenura callinota								
Cercomacra tyrannina	Cp4cd	Cp4cd			Cp3b4cd			
Gymnocichla nudiceps	Rp4cd	Up4cd						
Myrmeciza exsul	Ap4acd	Ap4acd			Up4acde			
M. laemosticta								
M. immaculata [+]	Xv4a					Rv4a		
Formicarius analis	Cp4ac	Cp4acd			Cp4acd	Up4a		
F. nigricapillus								
F. rufipectus								
Gymnopithys bicolor	Up4ac	Up4acd			Up4a			
Hylophylax naevioides	Up4ac			Rp4f				
Phaenostictus mcleannani	Up4a							
Pittasoma michleri								
Grallaricula flavirostris					Rp4a			
Grallaria guatimalensis						Rp4a		
G. fulviventris	Cp4cd							
G. perspicillata	Cp4a	Cp4a						
Scytalopus argentifrons								Cp4a

Bird Species	La Selva and Vicinity	Osa Peninsula	Palo Verde	Santa Rosa	Las Cruces and Vicinity	Monteverde	Universidad de Costa Rica, San José	Villa Mills
Piprites griseiceps	Rp4ac							
Pipra coronata		Ap4acd			Up4acd			
P. mentalis	Cp4acd	Cp4acd			Rp?4acd			
P. pipra								
Chiroxiphia linearis			Ap4af	Ap4af			Rp4a	
C. lanceolata								
Corapipo altera [+]	Uv4acd	Up4ac			Ap4acde			
Manacus aurantiacus		Up4cd						
M. candei	Ap4cd							
Schiffornis turdinus	Ov?4a	Cp4a			Up4a			
Cotinga amabilis°								
C. ridgwayi°		Up4bc			Up4bc			
Carpodectes nitidus°	Up?4bce							
C. antoniae°[+]		Uplc4bc						
Attila spadiceus	Ap4b–e	Ap4b–e	Ap4bc	Ap4bcf	Cp4b–e	Cp4a–e	Ov4a–e	
Laniocera rufescens	Rp4bc							
Rhytipterna holerythra	Cp4bce	Cp4bce			Up4bcd			
Lipaugus unirufus	Cp4bc	Ap4bc			Cp4bc			
Pachyramphus versicolor						Rv?4bc		Xv4b
P. cinnamomeus	Ap4cde	Cplc						
P. polychopterus	Cp4de	Cp4de			Cp4cde			
P. albogriseus								
Platypsaris aglaiae	Xv4c		Up4fc	Up4bcf				
Tityra semifasciata	Cp4b–e	Cp4b–e	Cp4bc	Cp4bcdf	Cp4b–e	Cp4b–e	Rp4b–e	
T. inquisitor	Up4b–e	Up4b–e	Rp4b	Up4bf	Rp4b–e			
Querula purpurata	Cp4bce							
Cephalopterus glabricollis [+]	Rv4ab					Rv4b		
Procnias tricarunculata [+]	Rv4be		Rv4b			Ab4bce		Xv4b
Sayornis nigricans						Rvld	Rpld	
Colonia colonus	Ap4bce							
Muscivora forficata [*]			An3alf	Un3a			Cn3ad	
M. tyrannus [(**)]			Xvlf					
Tyrannus tyrannus [*]	Ut4cde	Ct4b–e	Ct3a4bc	Ut3b4bce	Ut4bce	Ut4b–3		
T. verticalis [*]								
T. melancholicus	Cp3bc		Aplf3a	Cp3a4c	Ap3a–d4e	Up3ad	Cp3ad4e	
T. dominicensis [*]								
Legatus leucophaius [**]	Ub3a4e	Cb3a4ce	Ub3a4c	Cb3a4bc	Cb3ab4c	Rt3b4d	Ub4b–e	
Myiodynastes luteiventris [**]	Ut4ce	Ut4ce	Cb4bc	Cb4bcf	Cb4b–e	Cb4bce	Ub4b–e	
M. maculatus [(**)]	Xv4c	Up?4bce	Up?4b	Cp?4bcf				
M. hemichrysus						Cp4bc		
Megarhynchus pitangua	Ap4b–e	Ap4b–e	Ap4bcf	Ap4bcf	Cp4b–e	Cp4b–e	Cp4b–e	
Conopias parva	Ap4bc							
Myiozetetes similis	Cpldeb	Aplbc3b	Apldf4c	Aplcd4c	Ap3ab4de	Cp3abd	Up3bd4d	
M. granadensis	Ap3b4cde	Ap3b4cd			Ap4cde			
Pitangus sulphuratus	Cpld3a	Rp?lb3a	Apldf3a	Aplcd3a4c			Cp3adld	
Myiarchus crinitus [*]	Cn4bcd	Cn4b–e	Cn4bce	Cn4bcf	Un4b–e	Rtn?4bc	Utn4c–e	
M. cinerascens [*]								
M. nuttingi			Up4b–e	Up4bcd				
M. tyrannulus			Ap4b–e	Uplc4b–f				
M. panamensis		Cplc						
M. tuberculifer	Up4cde	Cp4b–e	Cp4bcdf	Cp4bcdf	Cp4b–e	Cp4b–e	Up4b–e	
Contopus borealis [*]	Rt4ce	Ut3a4c	Ut4bc	Ut4bcf	Ut4b–e	Ct4ce	Ut4ce	Ut4c
C. virens [*]	Atn4ce	Ct3a4bc	Ct4bc3a	Ct3a4bc	Ct3a4bc	At4c–e	At4c–e	Xt4c
C. sordidulus [(*)+]	Rt4ce	Rt4bc		Rt4c	Ut4c	Rtv4c–e	Rt4c–e	
C. cinereus	Cp3ab	Up3ab	Up3a4c	Up3ab4c			Up3b	
C. lugubris						Cp4c–e		
C. ochraceus								Rp4cd
Empidonax flaviventris [*]	Cn4ad	Cn4acd	Cn4ac	Cnracf	Cn4acde		Ctn3b4c–e	
E. virescens [*]	Ut4cde						Rt3b4c–e	
E. albigularis	Rp?3b							
E. traillii [*]	Rt?3b	Rt3b		Rn?3b4c			Rt3b	
E. alnorum [*]	Un3b4d	Ct3b4c	Cn4ac	Cn4ac	Un3b4c		Ct3b4c–e	
E. minimus [*]	Ot4de	Rt4cd				Ot3b	Ot3b4d	
E. flavescens [(+)]					Up4b–e	Cp4b–e		Xv4c
E. atriceps [(+)]								Cp4bcd
Mitrephanes phaeocercus					Up4b–e	Ap4b–e		
Terenotriccus erythrurus	Cp4acde	Cp4acd			Cp4acde			
Aphanotriccus capitalis	Up4de							
Myiobius sulphureipygius	Up4ace	Cp4acd			Up4ace			

539

Bird Species	La Selva and Vicinity	Osa Peninsula	Palo Verde	Santa Rosa	Las Cruces and Vicinity	Monteverde	Universidad de Costa Rica, San José	Villa Mills
M. atricaudus		Up3b			Rp3b4c			
Myiophobus fasciatus					Up3b			
Onychorhynchus mexicanus	Rplg4e		Up4f	Up4f				
Platyrinchus mystaceus						Cp4ad	Cp4ad	
P. cancrominus			Rp?4f	Rp?4af				
P. coronatus	Cp4a	Cp4a						
Tolmomyias sulphurescens	Up4d	Cp4cd	Ap4bcf	Ap4bcf	Cp4cde			
T. assimilis	Cp4bce							
Rhynchocyclus brevirostris	Up4ae	Up4acd		Rp4af	Cp4ace	Cp4acd		
Todirostrum nigriceps	Ap4bce							
T. cinereum	Cp3b	Cp3b4d	Ap4bc	Ap3b4bc	Ap3b4de	Up3b4d	Up3b4d	
T. sylvia	Up3b	Up3b	Up4af	Up4af				
Oncostoma cinereigulare	Cp4cd	Cp4cd	Up4af	Up4af				
Lophotriccus pileatus		Cp4ac			Up4acd	Up4ac		
Myiornis atricapillus	Ap4bce							
Phylloscartes superciliaris								
Capsiempis flaveola	Cp3b	Cp3b			Up3b			
Serpophaga cinerea						Ovld		
Elaenia flavogaster	Up3ab	Cp3ab	Up3b4c	Cp3bd4c	Cp3b4cde	Cp3b4c	Cp3b4cd	
E. chiriquensis [+]		Up3b			Up3b			
E. frantzii [+]					Rv3b4c	Cp4b–e	Rv3b4d	Ab4bcd
Myiopagis viridicata		Rp?lc4c	Cp4bc	Cp4bcf	Up?4cde			
Sublegatus arenarum		Rp?lc						
Camptostoma imberbe			Cp4bc	Cp4bcf				
C. obsoletum		Up4bcd			Up4cde			
Tyranniscus vilissimus [(+)]	Ap4b–e	Cp4b–e			Ap4b–e	Ap4b–e	Rv4bd	Uvb?4bcd
Tyrannulus elatus					Xv3b4c			
Acrochordopus zeledoni						Xv4bc		
Ornithion semiflavum		Cp4bcd			Up4bcde			
O. brunneicapillum	Cp4bce							
Leptopogon superciliaris					Cp4acd			
L. amaurocephalus	Ov4de							
Mionectes olivaceus [+]	Un4ad				Up4ace	Cp4acd		
M. oleaginea	Ap4acde	Ap4acde			Cp4acde			
Oxyruncus cristatus								
Progne subis[*]							Ot2	
P. chalybea[°]	Up3a	Cp3ab	Cp3alf	Cplc3a	Cp23a4c			
P. tapera[**]							Xt2	
Petrochelidon pyrrhonota[*]	Ut3a2	Ct3a2	Ut3a	Ct3a	Rt2		Ut2	
Hirundo rustica[*]	Atn3a2	Cn3a	An3a	An3a	Ut2	Ov3a	Atn23a	Xt2
Stelgidopteryx ruficollis[(*)]	Apnld3a	Cpnld3ab	Cpnlf3a	Cpnld3a	Ap3ab	Cp3a	Ctp23a	Xt2
Notiochelidon cyanoleuca[°]					Ap23abd	Cp23c	Ap23d	Cp2
Riparia riparia[*]	Rt3a2	Ut23a	Unlf3a	Ut3a	Rt2		Ut2	
Tachycineta bicolor[*]			Rn3a				Rt2	
T. albilinea	Apld	Cpldef	Apldf	Cplcdf				
T. thalassina[*]								
Calocitta formosa			Ap4bcf	Ap4bcf				
Psilorhinus morio[°]	Up3b					Cp3a4ce	Cp3a4b–e	
Cyanocorax affinis								
Cyanolyca cucullata						Up4ac		
C. argentigula								Rp4ab
Cinclus mexicanus						Ovld		
Cistothorus platensis								
Campylorhynchus zonatus	Cp4cde							
C. rufinucha			Ap4bc	Ap4bcf				
Thryothorus modestus		Ap3b		Up4cd	Cp3b	Cp3b	Cp3b4cd	
T. zeledoni	Rp3b							
T. rufalbus			Aup4af	cp4af		Cp4ad		
T. thoracicus	Ap4cde							
T. nigricapillus	Apld4cd							
T. semibadius		Apld4cd			Cp4cd			
T. pleurostictus			Ap4acd	Cp4acdf				
T. atrogularis	Up4d							
T. fasciatoventris		Cp4d						
T. maculipectus								
T. rutilus					Cp3b4cde			

Bird Species	La Selva and Vicinity	Osa Peninsula	Palo Verde	Santa Rosa	Las Cruces and Vicinity	Monte-verde	Universidad de Costa Rica, San José	Villa Mills
Troglodytes musculus	Up3d	Cp3d	Up3d	Up3d	Ap3ad	Ap3ad	Ap3abd	
T. ochraceus					Up3bc	Cp4bce		Ov4bc
Thryorchilus browni								Cp4acd
Henicorhina leucosticta	Ap4ac				Gp4ace			
H. leucophrys					Up4ac	Ap4acd		Up4a
Salpinctes obsoletus								
Microcerculus luscinia		Cp4ad			Up4ad			
M. philomela	Up4a							
Cyphorhinus phaeocephalus	Up4a							
Dumetella carolinensis*	Un3b						Ut3b	
Turdus albicollis+					Cp4a–e	Cp4a–c		
T. grayi	Cp3a–d	Cp3a–d	Cp4bc3d	Cp3d4bcf	Cp3bd	Cp3ad4d	Ap3bd4de	
T. obsoletus+								
T. plebejus*					Up?4bcd	Ap4b–e	Rv4cde	Cb4bc
T. nigrescens								Ap3bce
Myadestes melanops(+)	Xv4c				Rp?4bce	Cp4bce		Ub4bc
Hylocichla mustelina*	Ctn4acd	Un4acd	Un4af	Un4af	Un4acd	Up4ac	Un4ade	
Catharus ustulatus*	At3b4de	Ct3b4de	Ct4abc	Ctn4acf	Ct4cde	Ct3b4cd	At3b4cd	Rt3b4c
C. minimus*	At3b4de	Ut3b4d	Rt4a	Rt4ac		Ut3b4d	Ut3b4cd	
C. fuscescens*	Rt3b4c						Ot3b4d	
C. mexicanus						Cp4a		
C. fuscater						Cp4a		
C. frantzii						Cp4ac		
C. aurantiirostris					Cp4cd	Cp4acd	Cp4acde	
C. gracilirostris								Ap3a4a–d
Polioptila albiloris			Ap4bc	Ap4bc				
P. plumbea	Ap4bce	Cp4bce	Cp4bcf	Cp4bcf	Cp4bce			
Ramphocaenus melanurus	Cp4cd	Cp4cd	Cp4ac	Cp4ac	Cp4acd			
Microbates cinereiventris	Cp4a							
Bombycilla cedrorum*			Rv4bc	Ov4ce		Rv4ce	Rv4ce	Ov4c
Ptilogonys caudatus(+)							Ov4ce	Ap3b4bc
Phainoptila melanoxantha						Up4bce		Up3b4bc
Cyclarhis gujanensis					Up4b–e	Cp4bce	Cp4bce	
Smaragdolanius pulchellus	Ap4bce	Ap4bce			Cp4bce	Up4bc		
Vireo pallens								
V. carmioli+								Cp4bc
V. flavifrons*	Cn4b–e	Cn4b–e	Cn4bc	Cn4bc	Cn4b–e	Un4bce	Cn4b–e	
V. solitarius*			Xn?4c			Xv4d		Xv4d
V. griseus*								
V. olivaceus*	At4b–e	Ut4b–e	Ut4bc	Ct4bc	Ut4b–e	Ct4b–e	At4b–e	
V. altiloquus*								
V. flavoviridis**	Utn4cd	Utb?4cd	Ab4bc	Ab4bc	Ab4b–e	Ub4cde	Cb4b–e	
V. philadelphicus*	Un4cde	Cn4c–e	Cn4bc	Cn4bc	Cn4c–e	Un4cde	Cn4b–e	
V. gilvus*								
V. leucophrys(+)						Cp4bce		
Hylophilus flavipes		Up3ab						
H. ochraceiceps	Cp4a	Cp4a			Cp4ad			
H. decurtatus	Ap4b–e	Ap4b–e	Ap4bcf	Ap4bcf	Ap4b–e	Ap4b–e		
Diglossa plumbea						Cp4bce		Ap3b4bcd
Chlorophanes spiza	Up4bce				Cp4b–e			
Cyanerpes cyaneus		Cp4bcd	Cp4bc	Cp4bcf	Cp4b–e			
C. lucidus	Cp4bce	Ap4bce			Up4bce			
Dacnis cayana	Up4bce	Cp4bce			Up4b–e			
D. venusta+	Rv4bce	Up4bc			Up4bce	Cp4bc		
Coereba flaveola	Cp3b	Ap3b4b–e			Ap3b4b–e	Cp3b4b–e		
Mniotilta varia*	Un4cde	Un4c–e	Un4b	Un4bf	Un4cde	Un4c–e	Un4c–e	
Protonotaria citrea*	Ut3b	Cn1c3b	Cn1cd	Cn1cd	Rn1d3b		Un1d3b	
Helmitheros vermivorus*	Ot3b4d	On4d	On4af	Rn4af	Xt4c	Rn4acd	Rt3b4d	
Vermivora chrysoptera*	Un4cde	Un4cde	Rt4bc	Ut4bcf	Cn4b–e	Cn4acde	Utn4acd	
V. celata*								
V. pinus*	Ot?3b				Rn?4ce			
V. peregrina*	Ctn3b4ce	An3b4c–e	An4bcf	An4bcf	An3b4b–e	Un3b4c–e	An4b–e	Rn4bc
V. gutturalis								Cp4bcd
Parula america*						Xn4cd		
P. pitiayumi					Cp4bce	Up4bce		
Dendroica petechia*	Cn3ab	Cn3ab	An3abc	An3ab4bc	An3abd	Un3bd	An3bd	

541

Bird Species	La Selva and Vicinity	Osa Peninsula	Palo Verde	Santa Rosa	Las Cruces and Vicinity	Monte-verde	Universidad de Costa Rica, San José	Villa Mills
D. erithachorides		Aplc	Cplc	Uplc				
D. magnolia*	Rn3b4bd	Rn4cd		Rt4f				
D. tigrina*					Rn4c		Rn4ce	
D. caerulescens*					Xn4e			
D. coronata*	Ov3b	Rn4d3b					Xv3b	
D. townsendi*						Un4cde		
D. virens*	Rt4bce			Ut4bf	Cn4b–e	Cn4b–e	Otn4b–e	Un4bc
D. occidentalis*					Xv4c			
D. cerulea*	Ct4bce			Rt4f	Rt4b–e	Rt4bce		
D. fusca*	Ct4bce	Ut4bce		Rt4bf	Cn4bce	Un4b–e	Ct4b–e	
D. dominica*								
D. pennsylvanica*	An4b–e	An4b–e	Cn4bc	Cn4bcf	An4b–e	Up4b–e	Cn3b4b–e	
D. castanea*	Un4b–e	Un4b–e	Rn4bc	Rn4bcf	Un4b–e		Ut4b–e	
D. striata*			Xv4c					
D. pinus*							Xt4bc	
D. discolor*								
Seiurus aurocapillus*	Cn4cd	Cn4cd	Cn4ac	Cn4acf	Cn	Un4acd	Un4ade	
S. noveboracensis*	Cnldg	Cnlb–e	Cnldeg	Anlcdg	Unldeg	Rtld	Cnld	
S. motacilla*	Unlg	Rtlg			Unlg	Rnldg	Rtldg	
Oporornis formosus*	Cn4acd	Cn4acd	Rn4af	Un4af	Un4acd	Cn4acd	Cn4de	
O. philadelphia*	Ctn?3b	Cn3b	Rt3b	Un3b4c	Cn3b		Ctn3b	
O. tolmiei*	Ot3b						Rn3b4d	
Geothlypis trichas*	Xt?3b		Unlf	Rtldf	Cnlf			
G. chiriquensis					Cplef			
G. semiflava	Cp3b							
G. poliocephala	Cp3ab	Cp3ab	Cp3a	Cp3ab	Cp3ab	Up3ab	Up3ab	
Icteria virens*	Un3b	Rn3b4d					Ot3b	
Wilsonia citrina*	Rn3b4c						Rt3b4d	
W. pusilla*	Ct3b4cd	Ut4cde		Rt4bc	Cn4acde	An3b4a–e	Cn3b4d	An3b4a–e
W. canadensis*	At4bcde	Ct4acde	Ut4af	Ct4a–e	Ct4bcde	Ut4cd	At3b4b–e	
Setophaga ruticilla*	Ut4b–e	Utn?4bce	Rn4bc	Un4bcf	Un4b–e	Rt4b–e	Ut4b–e	
Myioborus miniatus					Cp4a–e	Ap4a–e	Rv4bc	Xv4c
M. torquatus(+)						Cp4bce		Cp4bc
Basileuterus tristriatus					Up4a	Cp4a		
B. culicivorus					Cp4ad	Cp4ad		
B. melanogenys								Up4ac
B. rufifrons			Cp4abc	Cp4a–df	Up?4d		Cp4b–e	
Phaeothlypis fulvicauda	Cpldg	Cpldg			Uplg			
Zeledonia coronata						Cp3b4acd		Cp3b4ac
Zarhynchus wagleri	Up4b–e	Rp4b–e			Up4bce	Rv4bc		
Gymnostinops montezumae	Ap4b–e						Uv24cd	
Cacicus uropygialis	Ap4bce	Ap4b–e						
Amblycercus holosericeus	Cp4d	Cp4d			Cp3b4d			Cp?3b
Scaphidura oryzivora	Rp?4bce	Up3b4cd			Rb?3b4c			
Molothrus aeneus+	Up?3a	Cp3a	Cp3a	Cp3a	Up3ab	Rv3a	Cp3acd	
Quiscalus mexicanus	Xv3a	Cplc3d	Aplcd	Cp3alc			Up3ac	
Q. nicaraguensis(+)								
Icterus spurius*	Un3b4de	Un3b4d	Un4bc	Un4bc	Un4cde		Un3b4cd	
I. prosthemelas	Up3b4de							
I. mesomelas	Rp4d							
I. pectoralis			Rp4bcd	Up4bcd				
I. galbula*	Ctn?3b4c–e	Cn3b4cd	Cn4bc	An4bcf	Cn4b–e	Un4cd	Cn4b–e	
I. pustulatus			Ap4bc	Cp3b4bc				
Agelaius phoeniceus(+)			Aplcdf					
Xanthocephalus xanthocephalus*			Xvlf					
Leistes militaris*								
Sturnella magna	Cp3a		Cp3a	Cp3ab	Ap3ab	Ap3a	Cp3ab	
Dolichonyx oryzivorus*				Xt3a				
Chlorophonia occipitalis(+)					Cp4bce	Cp4bce		Up4bc
Euphonia elegantissima					Rp4bce	Rp?4bcd		
E. anneae(+)						Up4bce		
E. minuta	Up4bce	Cp4bce			Up4b–e			
E. affinis			Ap4bcf	Ap4bcf				
E. luteicapilla	Cp4e	Cp4e			Cp4cde			
E. laniirostris		Up4cde			Up4cde			
E. hirundinacea			Up4bf	Up4bf		Up4cd		
E. gouldi	Ap4a–f							
E. imitans		Cp4bcde			Up4b–e			

Bird Species	La Selva and Vicinity	Osa Peninsula	Palo Verde	Santa Rosa	Las Cruces and Vicinity	Monte-verde	Universidad de Costa Rica, San José	Villa Mills
Tangara florida								
T. guttata					Up4b–e			
T. icterocephala [(+)]	Uv4bc	Up4bce			Ap4b–e	Ap4b–e		
T. larvata	Ap3b4d	Cp3b4d			Ap4c–e			
T. inornata	Cp4d–f							
T. gyrola [(+)]	Xv4c	Cp4bce			Cp4b–e			
T. lavinia								
T. dowii [+]						Cp4bce		Un4bc
Buthraupis arcaei								
Thraupis episcopus	Cp3bd	Cp3bd	Cp3bd	Cp3bd	Ap3bd	Cp3bd	Ap3bd	
T. palmarum	Up3b4d	Cp3b4cd		Up?3d4c	Ap3bd4de		Up3b4cd	
Ramphocelus passerinii	Ap3b4d	Ap3b4d			Ap3b4d			
Phlogothraupis sanguinolenta	Up3b4d							
Piranga rubra [*]	Cn4b–e	Cn4b–e	Cn4bcf	Cn4bcf	Cn4b–e	Un4b–e	Un4b–e	Xv4bc
P. flava [(+)]		Cp4bc				Up4bce		
P. olivacea [*]	Ut4bce	Ut4bce	Ut4bc	Ct4bc	Ut4b–e	Ut4cd	Ut4c–e	
P. leucoptera [(+)]					Up4b–e	Up4bce		
P. ludoviciana [*]			Cn4bc	Cn4bc			Rt3b4c–e	
P. bidentata					Up4c–e		Up4b–e	
Chlorothraupis carmioli	Ap4abf							
Habia rubica		Xv4a			Cp4ad			
H. fuscicauda	Cp4bcd							
H. atrimaxillaris		Cp4ac						
Lanio leucothorax	Rp4b	Cp4b						
Tachyphonus rufus	Cp3b							
T. luctuosus	Up4bcd	Cp4bce			Cp4b–e			
T. delatrii	Cp4ac							
Heterospingus rubrifrons								
Eucometis penicillata		Cp4acd	Up4af	Cp4af	Up4acd			
Mitrospingus cassinii	Ap4cd							
Rhodinocichla rosea								
Chrysothlypis chrysomelas								
Chlorospingus ophthalmicus					Ap3b4a–e	Ap3b4a–e		
C. pileatus						Cp4a–e		Ap3b4af
C. canigularis								
Saltator atriceps	Cp4cde							
S. maximus	Ap3b4de	Ap3b4d			Ap3b4c–e	Cp3b4cd	Rp4de	
S. coerulescens	Xv?3b						Ap3b4de	
S. albicollis					Cp3b4c–e			
Caryothraustes poliogaster	Ap4cde					Rv4cd		
Pitylus grossus	Cp4bce							
Pheucticus tibialis [(+)]	Xv4c					Cp4bcd		Xvab
P. ludovicianus [*]	Ut3b4c–e	Un4c–e	Un4bc	Cn4bcf	Cn4c–e	Un4cde	Ctn4b–e	
P. melanocephalus [*]								
Guiraca caerulea [(*)]			Up3ab	Up3ab			Rp3b	
Cyanocompsa cyanoides	Ap4bcd	Ap4bcd			Cp4acd			
Passerina cyanea [*]	Un3b		Un3ab	Un3ab	Un3ab		Cn3ab	
Tiaris olivacea	Cp3abc				Ap3abc	Ap3ab	Up3abc	
Spiza americana [*]		At3ab	Ut3ac	Rt3ab			Ut3abc	
Sporophila schistacea [+?]		Ov3b						
S. torqueola	Up3ab	Up3b	Cp3ab	Cp3ab			Up3b	
S. aurita	Ap3abc	Ap3abc4d			Ap3abc4d			
S. nigricollis [+]		Cp?3ab			Up?3ab		Xv3b	
S. minuta [*]					Up3ab			
Amaurospiza concolor								
Oryzoborus nuttingi	Uplf3b							
O. funereus	Cp3b	Cp3ab						
Volatinia jacarina	Cp3ab	Cp3ab	Cp3a–c	Cp3ab	Cp3ab		Cp3ab	
Carduelis xanthogaster [(+)]								Rp?4bc
C. psaltria					Up3b4cde		Rv3ab	
Sicalis luteola								
Spodiornis rusticus [+]						Rp?4c		Xv3b
Acanthidops bairdi [+]						Rv?4ce	Xv3b	Rn4bc3b
Pezopetes capitalis								Cp4ac
Pselliophorus tibialis [(+)]						Cp4acde		Cp?3b4ad
Atlapetes gutturalis					Cp3b4d	Cp3acd	Cp4acde	
A. brunneinucha					Up4ac	Cp4ac		
A. torquatus					Cp4acd			

543

Bird Species	La Selva and Vicinity	Osa Peninsula	Palo Verde	Santa Rosa	Las Cruces and Vicinity	Monte-verde	Universidad de Costa Rica, San José	Villa Mills
Lysurus crassirostris						Up4ac		
Arremon aurantiirostris	Ap4acd	Cp4acd			Cp4acd			
Arremonops rufivirgatus			Cp4ac	Cp4acf				
A. conirostris	Ap3ab	Ap3ab			Ap3b			
Melozone biarcuatum							Cp34bcde	
M. leucotis						Cp4cd	Up4acde	
Ammodramus savannarum[+]				Ov?3a				
Aimophila ruficauda			Ap3ab	Ap3ab				
A. rufescens[+?]								
A. botterii[+?]								
Junco vulcani								Cp3be
*Spizella passerina**[*]							Xv3b	
Zonotrichia capensis					Ap3a–d	Ap3abd	Ap3abd	Ap3bd
*Melospiza lincolnii**[*]						On3b		
Emberizoides herbicola								
Passer domesticus							Ap3d	

SPECIES ACCOUNTS

Actitis macularis (Andarrios Maculado, Spotted Sandpiper)

J. G. Strauch, Jr.

The spotted sandpiper breeds in North America from about the northern limit of trees south to southern portions of the United States. It winters from the southern limit of its breeding range south to Argentina and Peru. Migrant and wintering birds are common in Costa Rica from the coast inland to higher elevations. The species is regularly found in a variety of habitats, including ocean beaches, mangrove swamps, mud flats, and inland streams, pools, and meadows.

In winter the species is grayish olive brown above, white below, with a gray wash on the sides of the neck and upper breast. A few fall individuals and many spring birds can be found with the small round black spots on the white undersurface characteristic of the breeding plumage. In any plumage the species is easily recognized by its behavior. When standing it teeters almost continuously. It flies with stiff, slightly bowed wings in a shallow, rapid flutter.

Spotted sandpipers are not gregarious, although loose flocks are occasionally reported during migration. Generally only a few birds are seen at one time. During the winter individuals appear to set up feeding territories along strips of shoreline that they defend vigorously against conspecifics. Slud (1964) reports that aggressive interactions increase in the spring.

Spotted sandpipers feed by pecking at prey like tringine sandpipers, never probing like calidridine sandpipers. Their prey consists of a variety of insects and other invertebrates. In addition to taking prey from the substrate or vegetation, they often pluck close-flying prey from the air and may occasionally jump into the water to capture floating prey. They swim well and may even dive into the water to escape predators (Palmer 1967).

Many observations have suggested that females defend breeding territories and court males, but only recently has the species been shown to be polyandrous. In independent studies Hays (1973) and Oring and Knudson (1973) found that about half the females observed laid clutches for more than one male. Oring and Knudson suggest that polyandry evolved in this species as a response to high predation rates. Evidence for this was found by Maxson and Oring (1980). The evolution of polyandry in arctic and tropical birds is discussed by Jenni (1974).

*

Hays, H. 1973. Polyandry in the spotted snadpiper. *Living Bird* 11:43–57.

Jenni, D. A. 1974. Evolution of polyandry in birds. *Am. Zool.* 14:129–44.

Maxson, S. J., and Oring, L. W. 1980. Breeding season time and energy budgets of the polyandrous spotted sandpiper. *Behaviour* 74:200–263.

Oring, L. W., and Knudson, M. L. 1973. Monogamy and polyandry in the spotted sandpiper. *Living Bird* 11:59–73.

Palmer, R. S. 1967. Species accounts. In *The shorebirds of North America,* ed. G. D. Stout, pp. 212–43. New York: Viking Press.

Slud, P. 1964. The birds of Costa Rica: Distribution and Ecology. *Bull. Am. Mus. Nat. Hist.* 128:1–430.

Agelaius phoeniceus (Tordo Sargento, Red-winged Blackbird)

G. H. Orians

This familiar species (fig. 10.10), the most abundant breeding songbird in marshes throughout North America,

FIGURE 10.10. *Agelaius phoeniceus,* adult male in breeding plumage, United States (photo, G. H. Orians).

extends as a resident species in the marshes of Central America south to northern Costa Rica. Migrant redwings from North America move as far south as central Mexico in the winter but do not reach the breeding areas of Central American birds. South of northern Costa Rica there are no marsh-nesting blackbirds until eastern Panama, where red-breasted meadowlarks are encountered. There are several breeding species of *Agelaius* in the marshes of tropical and temperate South America, but none of these has a social organization like that of the redwing. Breeding populations of redwings are found in the marshes of the Tempisque basin in Guanacaste and along the Río Frío near the outlet of Lake Nicaragua. In Guanacaste, where they have been studied most intensively, redwings breed in seasonally flooded marshes that fill with water at the beginning of the rainy season in May and remain wet until December or January. Central American populations of redwings are quite variable, especially in female plumage, probably because they exist in rather isolated populations between which there is little interchange.

The social organization and behavior of Costa Rican redwings are very similar to those of northern birds. Territories, within which several females build nests, are defended by adult males. Females incubate eggs and feed nestlings unassisted by the males. Territories are sporadically visited during the dry season, but defense is not intense until May, when the rains begin. Breeding begins as soon as the growth of new vegetation is sufficient to support nests and extends until September. Large flocks of molting birds can be seen in October and November.

Breeding redwings in Guanacaste feed their young primarily upon invertebrates such as orthopterans, lepidopteran larvae, and spiders that live in marsh vegetation but do not have aquatic larval stages. This is in marked contrast to the resources supporting breeding of temperate redwings, where dragonflies, damselflies, and flies with aquatic larval stages dominate the diet of nestlings. There are emergences of these insects in tropical marshes, but they occur mostly at night when they are unavailable to foraging blackbirds. Emergences of aquatic insects in temperate marshes occur primarily during the day.

Territories of redwings in Costa Rica average from 1,000 to 2,400 m^2, depending upon the marshes, with a range from about 500 to over 4,000 m^2. Hence their territories are two to four times as large as those of redwings in most areas of North America. As is typical of tropical birds, redwings in Costa Rica have small clutches, averaging about 2.5 eggs, compared with over 4 eggs per clutch at high latitudes. Nestling growth rates are slower, and nest predation rates, primarily owing to snakes, are higher than in temperate latitudes. Female redwings in Costa Rica bring one prey item to their nests on each trip compared with an average of fifteen to twenty per trip in temperate marshes. This difference is apparently due to the fact that tropical prey must be pursued and often extracted from hiding places with gaping movements of the bill, a foraging technique incompatible with holding more than one prey item at a time. In contrast, temperate prey, mostly recently emerged from the water, are readily captured even if other prey are already held in the bill.

Though Costa Rican redwings deliver fewer prey items to their young per hour than their temperate relatives, there is no evidence that rates of visitation to nests are reduced to avoid predation. Females fly conspicuously to and from their nests, often chattering as they leave, behavior that does not suggest caution in the presence of potential predators. Instead, low feeding rates appear to be caused by the difficulty of capturing prey in tropical marshes and the need to return to the nest with each prey item captured. In addition, foraging tropical redwings have much shorter days than are encountered at high latitudes in May and June when young are in the nests.

The future of redwing populations in Costa Rica is uncertain. Many of the marshes in Guanacaste where they breed are being drained and converted to fields for rice and other crops. A few redwings persist along drainage ditches in these areas, but whether they will be successful enough to sustain the species is questionable. Many areas that supported large breeding populations in 1966–67 had been drained by 1972.

*

Orians, G. H. 1973. The red-winged blackbird in tropical marshes. *Condor* 75:28–42.

———. 1980. *Some adaptations of marsh-nesting blackbirds.* Princeton Monographs in Population Biology. Princeton: Princeton University Press.

Antbirds (Hormigueros, various genera)

E. Willis

Perhaps the following will serve as basis for antbird (formicariid) (fig. 10.11) accounts in lowland forests from Honduras to northern Argentina and for ovenbirds (furnariids) anywhere in the uplands:

"Look, class! Do you see that little dark bird? *There,* hopping in the dark green foliage! Didn't *anybody* see it?" Never mind. To see an antbird or ovenbird you have to return to the tropical rain forest alone or at most with your partner and stop when you see one move. You will soon learn that, by contorting, you can watch a bird behind several layers of foliage even with binoculars. The bird may even come out into sight and flit about in some characteristic foraging pattern after it stops its alarm behavior, perhaps with its mate or another species. It may be following army ants (*Eciton burchelli* or black, tiny *Labidus praedator*) to capture flushed arthropods or, more likely, flitting or clambering in a mixed-species foraging flock that will scold you and flee. Take notes on calls, behavior, distribution of white and rusty on the confederate gray plumage (rusty or brown in many females and in furnariids or woodcreepers), and you may find you have been the first of the class to have seen fasciated antshrikes (*Cymbilaimus lineatus*) or striped woodhaunters (*Hyloctistes subulatus*). Study them carefully, for the next person to check the exact place where you saw them will surely come up with barred antshrikes or streak-breasted treehunters (*Thripadectes rufobrunneus*) doing practically the same thing.

Fire back that antbirds and ovenbirds are well known to be very diverse in Neotropical forests and to have subtle differences in foraging, plumage, and calls (Skutch 1969). Cite that of thirty to forty antbirds species that occur sympatrically in moister Amazonian forests (fewer into dry or open regions, northward, southward, or in mountains), one can in the same flock find six little warblerlike "antwrens" stacked up at different levels: one *Myrmotherula* next to the ground, another 2 m up (*M. axillaris,* replacing all other species in Costa Rica), a third 5 m up, a fourth 10–15 m up, a *Herpsilochmus* in the subcanopy, and a *Terenura* in the canopy. A fifth *Myrmotherula* (*M. fulviventris* in Costa Rica) will be 5–10 m up checking dead instead of live leaves like the rest—perhaps trying to become a furnariid. A sixth tiny one will join at forest edges or in viny places, a seventh and sometimes an eighth in wet places. Not only that, but a vireo (*Hylophilus ochraceiceps,* also in Costa Rica) may be mimicking females of all the other species 5–10 m up. Dense foliage may have another antwren (*Microrhopias quixensis,* also in Costa Rica) at those levels. There will be a couple of larger *Thamnomanes* antshrikes sallying to foliage amid the activity like little flycatchers, one 2 m up and the other higher; two or more antshrikes (*Thamnophilus,* etc.) will be pecking larger prey at various levels; and a few larger antbirds (*Myrmeciza,* etc., like *M. exsul* in Costa Rica) will be hopping near the ground with or away from the flock. Many other birds, including flycatchers and furnariids or woodcreepers, may increase species totals to fifty in a single flock (Willis 1977). Recent studies in Peru (Charles Munn) and Panama show that different species in the flock often have the same territories, leading to brief wars when one flock passes another. Some birds seem to catch prey flushed by others, while others can stick their heads into rolled-up leaves

FIGURE 10.11. Antbirds. *a, Gymnocichla nudiceps,* adult female. Finca La Selva, Sarapiquí District, Costa Rica. *b, Phaenostictus mcleannani,* adult. Costa Rica. Both birds have bright blue featherless areas around the eyes (photos, F. G. Stiles).

only if other species of open foraging keep the lookout (Willis 1972).

The flock may pass but leave an entirely different ant-following flock (Willis and Oniki 1978), often composed of large antbirds like the Costa Rican ocellated antbird (*Phaenostictus mcleannani*) preempting the center, medium ones like the Costa Rican bicolored antbird (*Gymnopithys bicolor*) fussing at the edges, and small ones like the Costa Rican spotted antbird (*Hylophylax naevioides*) sneaking peripherally; at edges or in wet forests there will be another medium species (like the Costa Rican bare-crowned antbird, *Gymnocichla nudiceps*); and in northern Amazonia little white-plumed antbirds (*Pithys albifrons*) add to the confusion by infiltrating daringly, suffering billions of attacks yearly, only (defying competitive exclusion) to become speedier than the "roadrunner." Actually, roadrunners may be present in the form of ground cuckoos (*Neomorphus geoffroyi* in Costa Rica) at the edges of the ant raid. In addition there will be various woodcreepers using large trunks, and one (*Dendrocincla merula*, not in Costa Rica) right among antbirds on slender saplings, it clinging vertically and they crosswise. A tanager or two (in Costa Rica, gray-headed tanagers, *Eucometis penicillata* or ant-tanagers, *Habia fuscicauda* or *H. atrixaxillaris*) may take horizontal perches. Many amateur ant followers may wedge in at the edges; in depauperate forests there will be only amateurs. You can further point out that compared with the Amazon even the best Costa Rican forests are extremely depauperate in antbirds (because of all those North American migrants part of the year?) and that barred antshrikes were there only because dry or cut-up Costa Rican forests lose nearly everything.

In the highlands there will be a low formicariid/furnariid ratio in mixed flocks or with whatever ants exist. (The ants are slow and rare in cool regions. One can count woodcreepers as trunk-climbing furnariids, since ant-following ovenbirds are few.) The basic foraging difference between furnariids and formicariids is that the former appear to be nearsighted, the latter only moderately so. Furnariids love to rummage in nearby dense leaves and vines; formicariids like a bit more open foliage and sally short distances as well as glean from nearby surfaces. Furnariid success in the highlands may be attributable to epiphytes cluttering the area and hindering the jumpy antbirds as well.

*

Skutch, A. F. 1969. *Life histories of Central American birds.* Pacific Coast Avifauna, no. 35. Berkeley: Cooper Ornithological Society.

Willis, E. O. 1972. The behavior of spotted antbirds. *A.O.U. Monogr.*, no. 10.

———. 1977. Lista preliminar das aves da parte nor-oeste e áreas vizinhas da Reserva Ducke, Amazonas, Brasil. *Rev. Brasil. Biol.* 37:585–601.

Willis, E. O., and Oniki, Y. 1978. Birds and army ants. *Ann. Rev. Syst. Ecol.* 9:243–63.

Ara macao (Lapa, Scarlet Macaw)

D. H. Janzen

The scarlet macaw (*Ara macao*) (fig. 10.12a) ranges from Mexico to central South America and is the only macaw on the Pacific side of Costa Rica. It is seen only rarely on the Caribbean side of Costa Rica, which is occupied by the largely green buffon's macaw (*Ara ambigua*). Although an occasional pair of scarlet macaws or a single bird is seen as high as 1,000 m elevation on the Pacific side of Costa Rica, the species is basically a lowland forest inhabitant. While it was probably a common member of all forests on the Pacific side of Costa

FIGURE 10.12. *Ara macao. a,* Adult male and female captives. Costa Rica. *b,* Flock of fourteen adults shortly after being chased out of a *Terminalia catappa* tree in which they were preying on nearly mature seeds. Llorona, Corcovado National Park, Osa Peninsula, Costa Rica, August 1979 (photos, D. H. Janzen).

Rica, at present it is common enough to be seen regularly only in the forested parts of the upper Golfo de Nicoya (e.g., Palo Verde National Park) and the Osa Peninsula (e.g., Corcovado National Park). The birds are most commonly observed flying overhead, calling raucously and very loudly; their long, trailing tail feathers and short psittacid wings on a large body make it impossible to confuse them with other birds. There appears to be only one nesting pair that lives in the evergreen lowland forests of Santa Rosa National Park (this pair has not been seen to venture into the upland deciduous forests of the park). On the coast in Corcovado National Park as many as forty scarlet macaws may be seen at one time (fig. 10.12b), and there are at least two hundred in the park (probably many more).

Macaws are the largest Neotropical parrots, and the scarlet macaw is medium-sized. Its bright red orange plumage with touches of blue and yellow does not vary between the sexes or with developmental stage (once the bird is out flying). In captivity it does not talk especially well, but it will learn to clearly say individual words and short sentences. Scarlet macaws take to captivity as well as do the smaller parrots, but they tend to become vicious, largely because they are so powerful that their owners overreact when bitten. In captivity they eat a wide variety of table scraps and are particularly fond of nuts, cooked meat, chicken bones, sunflower seeds, corn on the cob, rice, and tortillas. They are not heavily frugivorous (neither are most parrots). They breed well in captivity, but this requires large flight cages, nest boxes, isolation from disturbance, and extreme patience (T. Small and R. Small, pers. comm.).

Scarlet macaws nest in holes in tall, thick living or dead trees. The five nests I have observed were all 30 m or more from the ground. The entrance holes were in vertical surfaces and ranged from 10 to 30 cm in all dimensions. An adult macaw is often visible just inside the entrance of an occupied nest hole, and it receives food from its mate without the other entering. Before the nesting season (at least April through July in Corcovado National Park) pairs, triplets, and larger groups are often seen clambering about over the upper trunks of large dead trees, appearing to be investigating and squabbling over holes and crevices.

Macaws can often be seen flying high and for distances of many kilometers over the rain forest at Corcovado National Park, and there is no doubt that they range very far for food. A favorite food is the nearly ripe seeds of *Terminalia catappa* (Combretaceae). The almond-sized and -shaped seeds are embedded in an extremely tough and fibrous nut inside a fleshy green fruit. The macaw cuts big chips out of the fruit wall with the sharp edge of its scoop-shaped lower mandible until it hits the nut, then simply cuts through its wall like a pair of very strong clippers. A flock of ten scarlet macaws will litter the ground below a beach-edge *T. catappa* with as many as three hundred cut-open fruits in an hour of foraging (10–30% of the fruits are picked and then dropped relatively intact through sloppiness or active rejection).

In Corcovado National Park macaws also cut open the nearly ripe fruits and remove the seeds of various species of Sapotaceae, and in Santa Rosa National Park they are the only predators on the nearly mature seeds of *Hura crepitans* (Euphorbiaceae). While in captivity scarlet macaws manipulate and split up to eat even very small seeds (e.g., sorghum, apple seeds, large fig seeds). It is my impression that they concentrate on the large-seeded species of trees in nature. There is no hint that they ever act as seed dispersers rather than seed predators. Feeding scarlet macaws are often very hard to locate from below, because their red color is much less evident in silhouette than when viewed in the incident sunlight, and because they can be extremely quiet when feeding. Although bird books often describe them as feeding on "fruits," in fact all my feeding observations in Costa Rica indicate that they rarely if ever eat "fruit" but rather are extracting full-sized but usually not-quite-mature seeds, which they dice crudely and swallow.

*

Forshaw, J. M. 1973. *Parrots of the world*. Garden City, N.Y.: Doubleday.

Brotogeris jugularis (Perico, Orange-chinned Parakeet)

D. H. Janzen

The orange-chinned parakeet (fig. 10.13a,c) ranges from southern Mexico to northern South America and is one of the most common psittacids from 500 m to sea level on the Pacific coastal plain of Costa Rica. It is one of the smallest parrots in Costa Rica but may occur in flocks of as many as fifty to one hundred individuals. Bright green but with an orange patch just under its lower bill, it is easily distinguished from all other Costa Rican psittacids. This bird is almost always seen as a member of a flock, but when the flock is at rest most if not all the birds seem to be paired with a nearby bird. At flight, at rest, and when in a tree full of fruit, there is nearly constant chatter, and when the birds are not in flight there are many apparent altercations. The flight of individuals is very rapid and erratic, with both the individual birds and the flock often changing direction.

These parrots nest during the first half of the dry season in both Guanacaste and Corcovado National Park. They occupy woodpecker holes in dead trees (or living *Scheelea* palm trunks), and the nest may be as little as 3 m off the ground to as high as 45 m. They commonly use large

FIGURE 10.13. *Brotogeris jugularis*. *a,* Captive adult. Guanacaste Province, Costa Rica. *b,* Bill of adult male. *c,* Freshly killed adult male with wings spread to approximate degree used during flight. *d,* Gizzard of adult male, sliced open to expose hundreds of fragments of seed coats of *Ficus* seeds (*upper*); intestine sliced open to expose mash of seed contents and fruit pulp. *b–d,* Santa Rosa National Park, Guanacaste Province, Costa Rica (photos, D. H. Janzen).

trees that were left when the forest was cleared for a field or pasture and may nest in holes in *Nasutitermes* nests on occasion (Power 1967). The young are fledged by the end of the dry season.

At least until very recently, juveniles were often brought into Costa Rican markets to be sold as household pets (this trade now seems largely confined to the slightly larger *Aratinga canicularis*). They make very affectionate and inquisitive pets, become attached to or pointedly antagonistic toward particular humans, and remain healthy on a diet of table scraps, meat, and birdseed. They do not talk at all well, but they will eventually learn words and may whistle quite clearly. If a pair is raised together, they will become attached to each other and less interested in humans, as is commonly the case with parrots.

Brotogeris jugularis is a seed predator in nature. For example, in Santa Rosa National Park it is a major predator on the seeds of *Bombacopsis quinatum* in late March and April. The bird perches on a thick twig near the nearly ripe 10-cm-long woody capsule (which will later dehisce to release wind-dispersed seeds), rips it open, and removes the large seeds one at a time, biting them into pieces and swallowing them. It customarily removes 10–50% of the seeds, and the fruit stops development (it is usually aborted) so that there is a 100% loss to the tree from that fruit. Since a large tree may produce one hundred to one thousand capsules, and since a bird may go

549

through three to ten in a morning, it is evident that a flock of fifty orange-chinned parakeets may wreak havoc with a *Bombacopsis* seed crop. The flocks do appear, however, to move frequently from tree to tree, rather than staying in one tree until they have eaten all the capsules. It is clear that certain fruits are easier for them to get to than others, and there are probably other reasons for moving. There is much "follow-the-leader" where one bird leaves the tree chattering and flies to another crown, to be followed by numerous other birds from the first crown. There are a number of species of trees in the Santa Rosa forest that have seeds and fruits that appear ideally suited for seed predation by *B. gularis* but are ignored (by other parrots as well): for example, *Cochlospermum vitifolium*, *Ateleia herbert-smithii*, *Plumeria rubra*, *Bursera simaruba*, and *Cedrela odorata*. I presume this immunity is due to chemical defenses in the seeds.

When a small-fruited (e.g., *Ficus ovalis*) fig fruits, large flocks of orange-chinned parakeets are regular visitors (Janzen 1981). For example, at the *Ficus ovalis* next to the Casona at Santa Rosa, they arrive at dawn and feed intensively until shortly before noon, then arrive again in late afternoon and feed until nearly dark. The birds clamber through the foliage, pick off ripe and ripening (reddening) figs, and take one or two scoop-shaped bites out of each fig before dropping it. They work so fast that it appears they must be swallowing material whole, and since these parrots do not have gravel in their gizzards, it seemed that they might well be dispersal agents for this tiny-seeded fig (the seeds are 1–2 mm diameter). I therefore shot one of the birds at 1300 while it was resting in the fig tree after spending all morning filling up on fig contents. The crop contained about 3,050 broken good seeds mixed with fruit pulp and about 350 apparently intact seeds that on closer inspection were found to be cracked. The gizzard contained 171 apparently intact seeds, at least 90% of which were cracked, and the seed coats from an estimated 1,575 seeds (fig. 10.13*d*). The intestines contained no whole seeds, but there were a very few seed-coat fragments (fig. 10.13*d*). Nowhere in the gastrointestinal tract were there seeds from which the fig wasps had exited—seeds that on average constitute about 55% of the seeds in a fig (Janzen 1979). Below the fig tree there were two kinds of fecal splats on foliage. One kind was a thin smear of fine particulate matter with small fig seed-coat fragments, and the other was a dense paste of intact seeds, wasp-exited seeds, and fig fibers. I interpret the above observations to mean that the orange-chinned parakeet quickly manipulates the contents of the bite out of a fig, so as to pick out the good seeds and crack each between the lower and upper bill (fig. 10.13*b*) before swallowing it. The seed coats in the gizzard are used to grind the cracked seeds, with most of the seed contents being passed down the intestine for absorption. When the

gizzard is full of indigestible seed coats, these are released down the intestine as a wad of fairly rapidly moving material. The fecal splats that contain intact seeds are from the frugivorous bats that frequent this tree at night. In short, the orange-chinned parakeet is nothing but a seed predator on this tree.

*

Forshaw, J. M. 1973. *Parrots of the world*. Garden City, N.Y.: Doubleday.

Janzen, D. H. 1979. How many babies do figs pay for babies? *Biotropica* 11:48–50.

———. 1981. *Ficus ovalis* seed predation by an orange-chinned parakeet (*Brotogeris jugularis*). *Auk* 98: 841–44.

Power, D. M. 1967. Epigamic and reproductive behaviour of orange-chinned parakeets in captivity. *Condor* 69:28–41.

Bubulcus ibis (Garcilla Bueyera, Cattle Egret)

D. E. Gladstone

The cattle egret (Ardeidae) (fig. 10.14) is the common white heron that is found accompanying cattle in pastures throughout the tropics. Its ubiquitous presence is surprising in that it arrived in the New World from Africa only about 1877. It was first sighted in Surinam and since has spread throughout large sections of eastern and central North America, northern South America, and Central America (Palmer 1962). In the Old World it is found throughout large areas of Africa, Mediterranean Europe, and Near East, India, and Australasia.

Cattle egrets are the smallest white herons found in the New World, standing only 19–21 in tall. They are distinct from snowy egrets (*Egretta thula*) and the white phase (immature) of little blue herons (*Florida caerulea*) in that both those species are larger (25–29 in tall) and have longer necks. Snowy egrets have distinctive yellow feet, and little blue herons have dark bills. Cattle egret legs and feet are black, and the bill can vary from yellow to orange (it turns bright red in breeding season). Cattle egrets also sometimes have orange buff patches on the crown, back, and breast; however, this trait is extremely variable, and its absence does not indicate that the bird is not a cattle egret. Like most ardeids, the sexes are monomorphic in plumage characteristics. It has been reported that males are slightly larger than females, but there is no easy method of distinguishing the sexes in the field.

Cattle egrets tend to nest in multispecies colonies with other herons, ibises, cormorants, anhingas, and other birds. They nest in many vegetation types from just a few centimeters off the ground to high up in trees. Colonies are usually near water. In Costa Rica, large colonies

FIGURE 10.14. *a, Bubulcus ibis* flock flushed from where it was feeding near the legs of cattle. Finca Taboga, Guanacaste, Costa Rica. *b,* Night roost of *B. ibis* near Puntarenas, Costa Rica (photos, D. H. Janzen).

Unlike all other New World herons, cattle egrets are primarily terrestrial feeders. While they perform a number of solo feeding behaviors typical of herons in general (Kushlan 1976), it is their use of other animals, now primarily cattle, as insect beaters that distinguishes them from other herons. In most of the reports of stomach contents, grasshoppers were the primary prey item (spiders, frogs, fish, and small birds were also reported; Jenni 1969). The egrets follow cattle and prey on the insects disturbed by their movements. Dinsmore (1973) made a series of paired comparisons of egrets foraging alone and with cattle. He found that they captured significantly more prey and took significantly fewer steps (his estimate of effort) when foraging within 3 m of cattle. It has been reported that the birds detick the cattle, but this has been discounted by several authors owing to the lack of ticks in egret stomachs. When cattle are absent, the egrets can serve as beaters for each other (by hopping, sometimes with leapfrog feeding; Gladstone 1977).

*

Dinsmore, J. J. 1973. Foraging success of cattle egrets, *Bubulcus ibis*. *Am. Midl. Nat.* 89:242–46.

Gladstone, D. E. 1977. Leap-frog feeding in the great egret. *Auk* 94:596–98.

———. 1979. Promiscuity in monogamous colonial birds. *Am. Nat.* 114:545–57.

Jenni, D. A. 1969 A study of the ecology of four species of herons during the breeding season at Lake Alice, Alachua County, Florida. *Ecol. Monogr.* 39:245–70.

Kushlan, J. A. 1976. Feeding behavior of North American herons. *Auk* 93:86–94.

Lack, D. 1968. *Ecological adaptations for breeding in birds.* London: Methuen.

Lancaster, D. A. 1970. Breeding behavior of the cattle egret in Colombia. *Living Bird* 9:167–94.

Palmer, R. A., ed. 1962. *Handbook of North American birds.* Vol. 1. New Haven: Yale University Press.

Siegfried, W. R. 1978. Habitat and modern range expansion of the cattle egret. In *Wading birds,* ed. A. Sprunt, IV, J. C. Ogden, and S. Wickler, pp. 315–24. Washington, D.C.: National Audubon Society.

occur in the Tempisque basin (Isla Pájaras: twenty to thirty thousand pairs), Laguna Caño Negro, and probably on various islands in the Golfo de Nicoya. Nesting commences with the rainy season and may extend into the beginning of the next dry season. At the start of the breeding season, males defend areas of branch that frequently later become the sites of their nests. After the male attracts a female and initiates a pair bond, both egrets build the nest from twigs or reeds, depending on the available vegetation. Nests from previous years are frequently reused. Nest materials are frequently stolen by other birds in the heronry, so it is common for one bird (usually the male) to gather the nest material while the other incorporates it into the nest. Cattle egrets are considered monogamous (Lack 1968) but have been reported to behave promiscuously (Gladstone 1979). Clutch size varies with location, usually ranging from two to six eggs per nest. Eggs are usually laid (and hatch) at about 2-day intervals so that there is always a succession of sizes of young in the nest. The youngest chicks are most frequently preyed upon or starve in a bad food year (predators on eggs or young include fish crows, boat-tailed grackles, purple gallinules, herring gulls, and rat snakes). Both parents share fairly equally in incubation and in bringing food to the young. I know of no reports where single parents have successfully raised young. Young begin to fly at about 40–50 days old and fledge at about 60 days.

Buteo magnirostris (Gavilán Chapulinero, Roadside Hawk)

F. G. Stiles and D. H. Janzen

The roadside hawk (fig. 10.15) is a small, chunky hawk (14–16 in. long, 250–300 g) with medium-length, rounded wings and tail. It is brownish gray above, becoming dull gray on the head and breast; the throat is whitish, and the belly and thighs are creamy white, barred with pale brownish or rust. The tail is dusky banded with pale brownish or rust; there is a conspicuous

FIGURE 10.15. *Buteo magnirostris,* adult. June 1980, Santa Rosa National Park, Guanacaste Province, Costa Rica (K. Innes; photo, D. H. Janzen).

patch of rufous in the primaries and secondaries. The eye is pale yellow, the cere and feet are bright yellow orange, and the bill is blackish. Immatures are brown above and whitish below streaked with brown; their eyes are brownish, their cere and legs duller yellow. Immatures are often extremely similar to those of two other *Buteo* hawks: *B. nitidus* (gray hawk) and *B. platypterus* (broad-winged hawk) but can be distinguished by their smaller size and thighs barred closely with rust.

The roadside hawk is a very sedentary bird and has been divided into numerous subspecies in its large range from Mexico to Argentina. In Costa Rica the species is abundant in Guanacaste, fairly common on the southern Pacific slope, and uncommon on the Atlantic slope. It occurs mostly in the lowlands but may be found up to about 1,200 m locally; it is rare on the Meseta Central (ca. 1,000–1,200 m). It is a bird of savannas, pastures, and second growth and very much deserves its vernacular name: it is often seen perched sluggishly on horizontal tree branches and stubs, or on fence posts along roads or tracks.

The usual hunting tactic of the roadside hawk is to drop from a low perch (typically 2–5 m) onto its prey, which includes mostly large insects (e.g., tettigoniid or acridid grasshoppers, large beetles, and moths) and small vertebrates (mostly lizards, some snakes and rodents, very rarely birds). We have seen it take 1–18-month-old ctenosaurs (*Ctenosaura similis*) as prey in Guanacaste, and Janzen saw one catch and kill a 1-m *Conophis lineatus* snake crossing closely cropped grass at Sirena, Corcovado National Park. It also takes still-twitching small vertebrates struck by passing cars, but it will not eat carrion. Its diet probably varies seasonally, including more vertebrates in the dry season (when visibility is enhanced) and large insects in the wet season (when these are more abundant). Unlike other *Buteo* hawks, roadside hawks soar rather seldom and then only to circle briefly; they never soar high in the air as do so many of their congeners. After periods of rain they often pose with wings and tail spread in the early morning sun as do vultures and anis.

Under most conditions the roadside hawk is a "tame," sluggish bird that can often be approached closely. When disturbed or excited, it is most likely to give a petulant or angry-sounding *kreeyaaahr* scream that instantly identifies it. In the breeding season, presumably during courtship, birds may give an excited-sounding, nasal barking *keh-keh-keh-keh*. The bird nests in the dry season (January or February to April or May), placing its small platform of sticks and debris at medium heights in trees in savanna or at woodland edges. The usual clutch is two eggs, dull white, speckled and washed with brown. Incubation and nestling periods are not known; fledglings have been encountered in Santa Rosa National Park in May.

The roadside hawk has undoubtedly increased in abundance in recent years owing to deforestation. It is one of the few native raptors that prefers to ply its trade in a cornfield or pasture rather than a forest. In recent years it has increased in abundance in the Sarapiquí region owing to the increasing deforestation south of La Selva.

On the Pacific slope, especially in Guanacaste, the roadside hawk coexists with the slightly larger gray hawk (*B. nitidus*). This species is slate gray above and finely barred gray and white below, with dark brown eyes. It is more numerous in areas of broken woodland and gallery forest and seems much more active and alert than the roadside hawk. It also eats relatively more vertebrates, including birds and rodents, though its staple is probably lizards. It also soars frequently, though usually not very high.

*

Wetmore, A. 1965. The birds of the Republic of Panamá, part 1. *Smithsonian Misc. Coll.,* vol. 150.

Butorides virescens (Garcilla Verde, Green Heron)

F. G. Stiles

The green heron (fig. 10.16) is the most widespread water bird in Costa Rica, where it occurs both as a permanent resident and as a migrant and winter resident. Although they do not occur in dense concentrations as do many other herons, green herons may be found virtually

FIGURE 10.16. *Butorides virescens*. Costa Rica (photo, F. G. Stiles).

anywhere that dense vegetation adjoins shallow, still or slow-flowing water. The birds are usually seen singly; often one flushes from the water's edge with a characteristic harsh *skwok* or *skow* and flies to thick vegetation, from which it peers out at the observer, raising and lowering its bushy crest and pumping its short tail, appearing furiously insulted at being so disturbed.

B. virescens is a small (ca. 200 g), rather short-necked heron with a glossy greenish black crest, chestnut maroon sides of the head and neck, white throat and ventral neck strip, gray belly, and dark bronzy greenish back and wings, the wing coverts scaled with buff. The eye is pale yellow, the bill is yellowish brown, and the feet and legs are bright yellow or orange (conspicuous in flight). Breeding adults have "frosty" gray-tipped elongate back plumes acquired in a partial molt shortly before the breeding season. Immatures are streaked with brown and white over the neck and underparts. There is no sexual dichromatism, but males average slightly larger. In southeastern Costa Rica and adjacent Panama a melanistic phase occurs, in which much or all of the plumage is a deep chocolate brown. The resident race *B. v. maculatus* averages smaller and slightly brighter than the migrant *B. v. virescens*. The green heron ranges from extreme southern Canada to central Panama; the northern populations are migratory, the southern ones resident. In central Panama it overlaps with the similar but gray-necked *B. striatus*, which occurs south to Paraguay. The occurrence of buff-necked birds in *B. striatus* has been interpreted as evidence of hybridization of *B. striatus* and *B. virescens*, but such birds also occur in South American populations that never come into contact with *B. virescens*. There is a single isolated record of *B. striatus* for Costa Rica.

In Costa Rica, green herons breed from sea level through lower middle elevations (e.g., locally on the Meseta Central) but are most abundant in the lowlands, especially on the Pacific slope. Northern migrants and winter residents seem most abundant on the northern Caribbean slope (to judge from seasonal changes in green heron abundance between Tortuguero and Limón). Migrants arrive along the Atlantic coast in September. They apparently migrate at night, usually singly, in contrast to most of the larger herons; at dusk in September and early October one can observe these herons flying up out of thick, marshy second growth near Cahuita, circling, and heading off southward. There is little information available on the northward migration in spring.

Green herons forage singly, usually standing still for long periods at the water's edge, neck drawn up and often extended, and beak pointed obliquely downward, waiting in ambush for small fish, frogs, or aquatic insects. When such prey comes within range, they seize it with a lightning stab of the bill. Sometimes the birds walk slowly in shallow water, especially in dense marsh vegetation; but they are always ambushers and do not actively pursue prey. They are remarkably agile in moving through thick, tangled vegetation.

Green herons breed either as solitary pairs or in loose colonies where populations are dense (as in some mangrove areas or extensive swamps). The main breeding season seems to be from about April or May through August or September, but earlier and later nestings are known. The nest is a flimsy, messy-looking platform of interlaced sticks, placed 1–5 m up in a tree or other vegetation overhanging water (or sometimes lower in dense reedbeds, etc.). In Costa Rica the usual clutch is two eggs, occasionally three, but up to six eggs have been found in a nest at Palo Verde, perhaps owing to laying by more than one female (F. Chaves, pers. comm.). The eggs are pale bluish green, with slightly rough shells. When an observer is near a nest containing eggs or small young, the adults fly about uttering a loud, squalling *kwaaaawh!* possibly a distraction display. Little is known about incubation and nestling periods of resident green herons; for nominate *B. virescens*, incubation requires 19–21 days, and the young leave the nest at about 2–3 weeks of age, are flying by about 3.5 weeks, and achieve independence within another 2 weeks or so. Older preflying young may scramble about in the nest tree with surprising agility if disturbed or frightened. The clutch size of northern populations is larger (usually four or five eggs) than in resident tropical *B. virescens*, but in general the biology of this species seems to vary remarkably little over its extensive range. Ecologically distinct from its mostly larger and more social relatives, the green heron's most striking feature is its ability to adapt to virtually all sorts of aquatic habitats, while its foraging tactics are effective at capturing almost any fairly small and slow-moving aquatic creature.

*

Palmer, R. S., ed. 1962. *Handbook of North American birds*. Vol. 1. New Haven: Yale University Press.

Slud, P. 1964. The birds of Costa Rica: Distribution and ecology. *Bull. Am. Mus. Nat. Hist.* 128:1–430.

Wetmore, A. 1965. The birds of the Republic of Panamá, part 1. *Smithsonian Misc. Coll.*, vol. 150.

Cairina moschata (Pato Real Aliblanco, Pato Real, Muscovy Duck)

E. G. Bolen

This large Neotropical duck (fig. 10.17) belongs to the tribe Cairinini (perching ducks) of the subfamily Anatinae (true ducks) in the family Anatidae. It thus is related to the wood duck (*Aix sponsa*), a species perhaps more familiar to North Americans. Both species have considerable amounts of metallic plumage, although the overall coloration of the muscovy is dark and more uniform than the showy plumage of the wood duck. The wild stock is the immediate progenitor of the common farmyard muscovy, which exhibits more highly variable coloration, including a white form or a mixture of white, green, and black or gray plumage.

Muscovies are found exclusively in the New World; the two other species of *Cairina* are exclusively Old World (Hartlaub's duck, *C. hartlaubi*, of Africa and the white-winged wood duck, *C. scutulata*, of Malaysia and portions of the East Indies). The range of muscovies extends from Mexico south through Central America to Peru on the west and to Uruguay and casually into northern Argentina on the east. In Mexico the species is known vernacularly as "pato real." There are no recognized races within its distribution.

Phillips (1922, p. 58) summarized records for Costa Rica, where the species was then regarded as "extremely common." Specific sites include the Gulf of Nicoya and La Palma, Miravalles, and Guanacaste; muscovies seem

FIGURE 10.17. *Cairina moschata,* adult male, stuffed (photo, E. Bolen).

more abundant on the Pacific side in Guanacaste and, indeed, in all of Central America.

Muscovies exhibit considerable sexual size dimorphism; males (1,990–4,000 g) are much larger than females (1,100–1,470 g) and have face patches of bare skin with caruncles posterior to the bill. Otherwise there are no pronounced sexual differences in their plumage.

Under field conditions, muscovies can be identified by their large size, chunky appearance, and dark coloration. A white patch on the upper wing coverts and the white under the wing offer a contrast to the dark green body plumage (which may appear black). The amount of white on the upper wing coverts may be age related; older birds allegedly have a larger white patch than do younger ones, although this distinction lacks supporting data from adult birds of known age. Muscovy ducks can be separated from the black-bellied whistling duck (*Dendrocygna autumnalis*), another tropical species common in Central America, in several ways: both have white wing patches, but on muscovies this marking does not extend as far toward the wing tip as it does on the black-bellied whistling duck; muscovies are dark, whereas whistling ducks are light brown with black abdominal plumage; the legs and feet of muscovies do not extend beyond the tail in flight, whereas this heronlike feature is prominent in whistling ducks; whistling ducks frequently call with their peculiar shrill vocalization (muscovies are usually silent); the legs and feet of muscovies are dark, whereas those of black-bellied whistling ducks are coral pink (appearing light colored at a distance); and muscovies are strong, swift fliers despite their large size (whistling ducks have a more labored wingbeat and less direct movement).

Unfortunately, there have been few detailed field studies of the muscovy's life history, and the synthesis that follows is compiled largely from general references (e.g., Delacour 1959) that may be somewhat inaccurate and are certainly incomplete. However, Rangel Woodyard (1982) recently investigated some aspects of muscovy ecology in Mexico.

Their habitat is primarily lowland forest where streams and lagoons are common. These requirements limit the Central American populations to coastal areas (in Mexico they are absent in portions of the Yucatan where surface water is lacking).

Johnsgard (1975, p. 166) noted that there is little indication of migratory behavior among muscovies except for responses to the dry seasons, when the birds move into coastal swamps and lagoons.

Muscovies are cavity nesters (as are black-bellied whistling ducks) and select sites as high as 15–20 m in trees with suitable hollows. Clutches consist of about eight eggs, although larger sets resulting from compound nesting (dump nesting) occur; incubation is relatively long (35 days) based on observations of domestic stock.

Muscovies and black-bellied whistling ducks are sympatric in much of the Neotropics and were observed perching together in Dutch Guiana (now Surinam) by Haverschmidt (1947). One may assume a priori that niches for these species are well defined where they have long coexisted and that interspecific competition for nest cavities is largely precluded. However, nest boxes erected for muscovies in Mexico received 11% utilization by muscovies the first year they were available, with another 11% used jointly by muscovies and black-bellied whistling ducks (mixed clutches); 56% of the boxes were used exclusively by black-bellied whistling ducks. All the muscovy nests hatched successfully, whereas only half of the mixed clutches were successful; 90% of the whistling duck clutches hatched (Rangel Woodyard 1982). Unfortunately, no method now exists to construct species-specific nest boxes, and mixed clutches may remain commonplace where these species are sympatric (nest boxes constructed with small entrances allow access only to whistling ducks, but those with entrances large enough for muscovies can be used by both species). Further, no site-specific differences in nesting habitat are known, so that the location of the nest boxes does not favor either species. Nonetheless, given the rapid destruction of riparian forests in much of Latin America, a nest box program for muscovies and black-bellied whistling ducks offers some potential for management.

Pair bonds are typically short in the perching ducks, and Johnsgard (1965, 1975) reported that their promiscuous mating is virtually the only time "pairs" are established. Fischer et al. (1982) found that the aggressive displays between males involved vigorous head bobbing, erected crests, lateral tail shaking, and partial elevation of the wings; about 90% of the displays ended at this stage. A second pattern continued in 10% of the encounters when the males turned to face each other and initiated vertical hovering flights 1–3 m in height; these flights were repeated two to six times before one of the males yielded and fled. Daily flights occur in the morning and evening, and the midday is spent loafing at the water's edge. At night muscovies roost gregariously in trees, perhaps in unisexual groupings.

Few detailed food habits studies have been published for muscovy ducks, but they are believed to eat a variety of foods. In addition to cultivated crops, particularly corn, there is mention of such diverse foods as small fish, insects (including termites), the seeds of various water plants, and even small reptiles. In Mexico, Rangel Woodyard (1982) compared muscovy diets from two areas with different ecological settings. In Tamaulipas, where grain crops are common, corn constituted the entire diet from May to August, whereas in the marshlands of Veracruz the seeds of waterlily (Nymphaea spp.) and mangrove (Avicennia nitida) made up 66% of the muscovy diet, with the balance composed of animal matter (represented by diverse orders of invertebrates but primarily Dipera and Coleoptera). The parasite loads in muscovies from the two areas reflected these differences in food habits; those birds feeding more heavily on invertebrates were infected with more helminths than those feeding on waste corn.

Likewise, the breeding season of muscovies is diverse. Reports from Mexico and from Central and South America record either enlarged gonads or nesting in December, February, May, July, and October, suggesting either that regional conditions stimulating breeding vary considerably or that there is no set breeding season in this species. The latter may be the case; whereas the reports above include the spring and winter months, females examined in El Salvador during January, February, and April were not breeding.

Little is known about the losses of muscovies, although one might assume that their eggs are taken by arboreal mammals and snakes. Johnsgard (1975, p. 166) speculates that adult males may suffer relatively little natural mortality because of their large size and strength. Phillips (1926, p. 305), quoting other observers from British Guiana (now Guyana), reported that ducklings and even adult birds are taken by tiger-fish and alligators; cats also may prey on muscovies.

The status of wild muscovies is uncertain. Most published reports mention that overhunting is serious and, coupled with habitat destruction, has diminished populations. Phillips (1922, p. 60) described the ease with which males are killed; a female is tied to a peg as a decoy, and the birds from the surrounding area are then flushed. Since the drakes are both numerous and aggressive, they fly over the living decoy and easily present themselves to the waiting hunter; sometimes fifty drakes can be killed in one day using such a decoy. Leopold (1959, pp. 167–68) noted that their flesh is excellent table fare; this and their large size make muscovies an attractive species for both native and visiting hunters. Their habits, too, may lend them to overexploitation; Wetmore (1926, p. 70) remarked that the birds, when disturbed, fly only a few yards and then alight en masse on large tree limbs. Their daily routine is quite habitual and a knowledgeable hunter can easily kill muscovies from appropriately located blinds (Saunders, Holloway, and Handley 1950, p. 27). Further, muscovies fly relatively close to the ground, although Saunders and his co-workers cite reports of wariness at the slightest sound or movement. Finally, native peoples commonly take muscovy eggs, either for food or more commonly to initiate domestic stocks. The latter practice, of course, not only reduces the native population (there are no studies of renesting) but also contributes to inbreeding and the production of a much-altered gene pool. In Brazil, for example, few barnyard ducks lack traces of muscovy lineage (Mitchell 1957, p. 57).

*

Delacour, J. 1959. *Waterfowl of the world.* Vol. 3. London: Country Life.

Fischer, D. H.; Sanchez, J.; McCoy, M.; and Bolen, E. G. 1982. Aggressive displays of male muscovy ducks. *Brenesia,* in press.

Haverschmidt, F. 1947. Field notes on the black-bellied tree duck in Dutch Guiana. *Wilson Bull.* 59:209.

Johnsgard, P. A. 1965. *Handbook of waterfowl behavior.* Ithaca: Cornell University Press.

⸻. 1975. *Waterfowl of North America.* Bloomington: Indiana University Press.

Leopold, A. S. 1959. *Wildlife of Mexico: The game birds and mammals.* Berkeley: University of California Press.

Mitchell, M. M. 1957. *Observations on birds of southeastern Brazil.* Toronto: University of Toronto Press.

Phillips, J. C. 1922. *A natural history of the ducks.* Vol. 1. Boston: Houghton Mifflin.

⸻. 1926. *A natural history of the ducks.* Vol. 4. Boston: Houghton Mifflin.

Rangel Woodyard, E. 1982. Some aspects in the ecology of muscovy ducks in Mexico. M.S. thesis, Texas Tech University.

Saunders, G. B.; Holloway, A. D.; and Handley, C. O. 1950. *A fish and wildlife survey of Guatemala.* Special Scientific Report 5. Washington, D.C.: U.S. Fish and Wildlife Service.

Wetmore, A. 1926. Observations on the birds of Argentina, Paraguay, Uruguay, and Chile. *U.S. Nat. Mus. Bull.* no. 133.

Calidris alba (Playerito Arenero, Sanderling)

J. G. Strauch, Jr.

This pale sandpiper is commonly found in small flocks on marine beaches throughout Central America following the waves like a clockwork toy. The sanderling is a holarctic breeding species that in the New World winters as far south as Tierra del Fuego. In the summer it is found inland, breeding on dry, often stony tundra. During migration it is found throughout North America, but south of there it is found mainly on marine shores, as it is in the winter.

Though it is one of the most common sandpipers in Costa Rica during migration, fewer birds are found in the winter (Slud 1964). A few nonbreeding brids may be found in the summer.

Its pale color, distinctive white wing stripe, and slightly larger size readily distinguish the sanderling from all other small species of calidridine sandpipers, sometimes collectively called "peeps." During migration a few individuals may show traces of the bright rufous breeding plumage on head and breast. This is the only sandpiper that lacks a hind toe. The lack of a hallux appears to be correlated with the species' use of hard substrates.

On mud flats it may often be found feeding with several other species of shorebirds, but it is usually the only small sandpiper feeding on hard sand beaches. On mud flats it takes a variety of invertebrates. On sandy beaches it usually feeds along the surf, where it gets mainly crustaceans, or along driftlines, where it takes insects and crustaceans. It feeds either by pecking at the surface of the substrate or, more commonly, by probing beneath the surface like other calidridine sandpipers. In California wintering sanderlings were found to maximize their foraging efficiency by switching feeding sites from ocean beaches to harbor sand flats with the tide (Connors et al. 1981). Quantitative information on its diet in Central America is unavailable. Feeding birds are usually very tame and can be easily approached and observed.

Although they are similar in appearance, the calidridine sandpipers show considerable diversity of behavior. Four types of mating systems have been identified: monogamous, serially polygamous, polygynous, and promiscuous (Pitelka, Holmes, and MacLean 1974). Parmelee (1970) and Parmelee and Payne (1973) report that in the Canadian arctic sanderlings have a serially polygamous mating system in which a female lays a clutch, then abandons it to the care of the male. Depending on local conditions, she may lay a second clutch, which either she or a second male incubates. On the other hand, Pienkowski and Green (1976) found that in Greenland the species is monogamous, with both members of a pair incubating and caring for the young. It is not clear whether these differences represent true population differences or inadequate observations from the different regions.

Eleven other species of calidridine snadpipers have been recorded in Costa Rica. Five of these—correlimos semipalmado, semipalmated sandpiper (*C. pusillus*); correlimos occidental, western sandpiper (*C. mauri*); correlimos menudo, least sandpiper, (*C. minutilla*); correlimos de Baird, Baird's sandpiper (*C. bairdii*); and correlimos pectoral, pectoral sandpiper (*C. melanotos*)—are regular and may occur in moderate to large numbers (Slud 1964). There are few records for the other species, but some of them may be of regular occurrence (Stiles and Smith 1977).

*

Connors, P. G.; Myers, J. P.; Connors, C. S. W.; and Pitelka, F. A. 1981. Interhabitat movements by sanderlings in relation to foraging profitability and the tidal cycle. *Auk* 98:49–64.

Parmelee, D. F. 1970. Breeding behavior of the sanderling in the Canadian high arctic. *Living Bird* 9:97–146.

Parmelee, D. F., and Payne, R. B. 1973. On multiple broods and the breeding strategy of arctic sanderlings, *Ibis* 115:218–26.

Pienkowski, M. W., and Green, G. H. 1976. Breeding biology of sanderlings in north-west Greenland. *Brit. Birds* 69:165–77.

Pitelka, F. A.; Holmes, R. T.; and MacLean, S. F., Jr. 1974. Ecology and evolution of social organization in Arctic sandpipers. *Am. Zool.* 14:185–204.

Slud, P. 1964. The birds of Costa Rica: Distribution and Ecology. *Bull. Am. Mus. Nat. Hist.* 128:1–430.

Stiles, F. G., and Smith, S. M. 1977. New information on Costa Rican waterbirds. *Condor* 79:91–97.

Calidris mauri (Correlimos Occidental, Western Sandpiper)

S. M. Smith

The western sandpiper (fig. 10.18) is an abundant migrant in Costa Rica. Recorded primarily from the two seacoasts, it is most common along the Pacific, where flocks of many hundreds can be found from August through April.

This is a bird of sand and mud beaches, where flocks probe for small invertebrates. At high tide it can often be found resting and feeding in salt ponds or "salinas."

The western sandpiper is a small black-legged "peep." Its bill averages longer (20.2–28.8 mm) than in other peeps and usually droops slightly at the tip. In the hand it can be told from all but semipalmated sandpipers (*C. pusilla*) by the partially webbed toes; the semipalmated sandpiper has a shorter, straight bill (15.1–23.9 mm). The wings when folded do not extend beyond the tail. As in most peeps, the rump is dark with some white on each side, and there is an indistinct wing stripe. Winter plumage is medium gray above, white below, with faint streaking on the breast. In breeding plumage the crown, ear coverts, and scapulars are bright rufous, and the breast is heavily streaked with brown.

Although technically migrants (the species does not breed in Costa Rica), small flocks of western sandpipers can be found throughout the summer in favorable habitats such as salinas along the Pacific coast. Little is known about the age or sex of these summering birds; they deserve further study.

Banded migrant and overwintering individuals have been recaptured repeatedly, indicating a high degree of

FIGURE 10.18. *Calidris mauri,* adult female. 18 April 1975, Costa Rica (photo, F. G. Stiles).

site fidelity. There is also some indication that individuals banded together are found together in subsequent years, perhaps indicating that mated pairs remain together in the nonbreeding season.

*

Prater, A. J.; Marchant, J. H.; and Vuorinen, J. 1977. *Guide to the identification and ageing of holarctic waders*. Tring, Herts, England: Maund and Iravine.

Smith, S. M., and Stiles, F. G. 1979. Banding studies of migrant shorebirds in northwestern Costa Rica. *Stud. Avian Biol.* 2:41–47.

Campephilus guatemalensis (Carpintero Pico de Plata, Flint-billed or Pale-billed Woodpecker)

L. L. Short

This is the largest of the Costa Rican woodpeckers, weighing 200 to 300 g, with wings 170 to 210 mm, and it is also the most specialized for excavating insects from the bark of trees. Some of the other Costa Rican woodpeckers perform superficial tapping, or glean for food, and species of *Melanerpes* even eat much fruit. *Campephilus guatemalensis* frequents lowland forest up to about 1,800 m elevation (locally) but prefers moist forest edges, clearing, and riparian forest. It also can be found in woodland patches of savannas and moist sections of dry tropical forests and woodlands. Flint-billed woodpeckers are black and white with a pale horny or yellowish bill. Males are red over the entire head and crest, and females have a black-and-red crest. White stripes extend from the sides of the neck to the upper back. The upper breast is black, but the lower breast to abdomen is barred black and brown. Immatures are browner, less constrastingly marked, and have darkish bills. Adults have buffy to yellow eyes; immatures are gray- or brown-eyed.

557

Like all true woodpeckers, the flint-bill perches mainly or entirely parallel to the tree trunk or branch, moving—usually upward—close to the surface of the bark.

The long bill of this woodpecker is straight, strongly chisel-tipped, broad across the nostrils, and somewhat flattened. Its tail is particularly stiffened and strong, especially the four central feathers, which are appressed against the bark in its movements and foraging. Along with the strong feet, toes, and claws, the tail holds the bird in place and counteracts forces of pecking and of perching. The woodpeckers feed at all heights in trees but prefer trunks and large branches, where they dig deep into the bark or deliver sidewise blows in scaling bark from dead trees. Sometimes they work over low stumps and fallen logs. Their food largely is beetle larvae of the families Cerambycidae and Scarabeidae, which they also feed to the young. They occasionally take fruit and berries. Detailed studies of their diet are unavailable and remain to be accomplished.

The loud but sporadic bursts of excavating, which draw attention to the woodpecker, must be distinguished from its drumming, a signal for communication (Short 1982). In most woodpeckers this is a regular, often species-specific series of taps with its own rhythm. The flint-bill and its relatives of the genus *Campephilus* (*Campephilus* replaces the old generic name *Phloeoceastes*), drum with a special one-two cadence, a double "bump-bump," or drum tap, repeated at intervals. No other Costa Rican species drums in this way. Softer, longer drumming may be associated with a nest site (Skutch 1969). Vocal signals include a rattling call and a rapid *heh-heh-heh* (Slud 1964, p. 195), as well as low notes of members of a pair when close together and a loud high bleating call of begging young.

The somewhat similarly colored, but smaller lineated woodpecker, picamadero barbirrayado (*Dryocopus lineatus*), always shows a full black (female) or red (male) malar stripe or "moustach"; its cheeks are black (versus red), and there is a white stripe between the cheek and moustache that connects with the white neck and back stripes (in the flint-bill the sides of the face in both sexes are red, the white neck stripe starting only at the back of the head). It feeds largely on ants, digging deep pits into decayed trees or stubs, or it may scale bark from trees. The lineated woodpecker uses a long series of taps as a drumming signal, and a long *wik-wik-wik* call is its chief vocalization (Short 1982). Its habitat is similar, but it more often feeds in lone trees in pastures or savannas. Interactions may occur with the flint-billed woodpecker and should be sought by interested observers.

The flint-billed woodpecker excavates a nesting cavity in a large tree and breeds between August and December (juvenile specimens known through February). Both sexes excavate and incubate the two eggs, the male incubating alone at night as is typical of woodpeckers. They incubate for long periods. Changeovers are accompanied by crest-raising displays and a whining note (Skutch 1969). The incubation period is not known precisely, nor is it known how long the young stay in the nest. Both adults bring insect larvae to the young, carried in the bill (not regurgitated). After fledging it is probable that the young remain with the adults for several months. Molt follows the breeding period. Each bird is thought to require its own roosting cavity, and such holes are excavated by independent young and, whenever needed, by adults.

The paired birds tend to remain together throughout the year, and they wander about a large territory, the dimensions of which have not been established.

These and other woodpeckers help to regulate populations of insects that may build up and cause serious damage to forests. The various sympatric species of woodpeckers tend to have separate modes of feeding and to show regular size variation (Short 1978). At each size there may be two or more species that forage differently, one excavating to a greater extent, the other perhaps probing and pecking more frequently. Sometimes there is habitat exclusion, usually among similar-sized, related species that forage similarly. There are sixteen Costa Rican woodpeckers (one a migrant from North America), and they exhibit size differences, various habitat preferences, and diversity of foraging techniques much like those found among thirteen sympatric woodpeckers in Malayan lowland forests (Short 1978). Details of these differences remain to be worked out in Costa Rican woodpeckers, although some aspects of altitudinal and habitat restrictions are known (Slud 1964).

*

Short, L. L. 1978. Sympatry of woodpeckers of lowland Malayan forest. *Biotropica* 10:122–33.

———. 1982. Woodpeckers of the world. *Delaware Mus. Nat. Hist.,* in press.

Skutch, A. 1969. *Life histories of Central American birds.* Pacific Coast Avifauna, no. 35. Berkeley: Cooper Ornithological Society.

Slud, P. 1964. The birds of Costa Rica: Distribution and Ecology. *Bull. Am. Mus. Nat. Hist.* 128:1–430.

Campylorhynchus rufinucha (Soterrey Matraquero, Rufous-naped Wren)

R. H. Wiley

This large, arboreal wren (fig. 10.19*a*) inhabits the Pacific coastal lowlands of Central America from Guanacaste Province and northern Puntarenas Province in Costa Rica northward into Mexico. Its resonant vocalizations, often produced by two or more individuals si-

FIGURE 10.19. *Campylorhynchus rufinucha. a,* Adult, *b,* Family group at nest in ant-acacia (*Acacia collinsii*). Hacienda Palo Verde, Guanacaste Province, Costa Rica (photos, F. G. Stiles).

multaneously, and its bulky nests, used as dormitories, make it one of the conspicuous birds in this area. The species exemplifies two features of many tropical insectivorous birds: year-round territoriality and coordinated duets by mated pairs. The genus includes about twelve species, one or another of which occupies virtually every terrestrial habitat from the southwestern United States (the cactus wren, *C. brunneicapillus*) to southern Brazil and Bolivia. These species include a complete spectrum of variation in sociality. In some species pairs occupy territories in the breeding season; in others large groups (as many as fifteen wrens) occupy breeding territories. In the latter case one pair produces the eggs, although all members of the group feed and defend the young. *C. rufinucha* exemplifies the pattern of isolated pairs, while a less-abundant species, the band-backed wren, *C. zonatus,* which occurs at La Selva, exemplifies the pattern of "helpers at the nest."

Rufous-naped wrens are easily identified by cream-colored underparts, a bold eye stripe, and bright rufous and black bars on the back. The sexes are identical in plumage.

These birds defend territories throughout the year in areas with scattered trees or columnar cacti—for in-

stance, in openings or along edges of dry forest, along fencerows, or in trees scattered in pastures. With a little patience an observer can follow them for long periods. They spend most of the day foraging for small arthropods in the foliage of bushes and trees from 1 m aboveground to the tops of the tallest trees. Unlike most wrens, they rarely feed on the ground. While foraging, they search actively through dense foliage by constantly hopping from twig to twig and flying 2–5 m at intervals. To judge from other species in the genus, territories are likely to be largely exclusive (used only by the territory residents) and crisscrossed several times in the course of a day by the foraging wrens. The resident wrens in a territory usually remain within 1–5 m of each other while feeding. Detailed study of a congeneric species revealed, however, that proximity of individuals conferred no advantage in foraging (Rabenold and Christensen 1979).

Rufous-naped wrens, like all members of the genus, construct bulky, unkempt nests that serve as dormitories throughout the year as well as nests for rearing young during the breeding season. Their nests have a complete roof and a concealed entrance on one side. From the outside the nest looks like a disorganized wad of grass some 20 cm in diameter, but inside it contains a deep, neatly lined pocket. The thick walls provide thermal insulation for the internal chamber (Ricklefs and Hainsworth 1969). Rufous-naped wrens frequently place their nests in full view in the branches of a columnar cactus or in the top of a swollen-thorn acacia with ants. The ants, which habituate to the presence of the nest in the tree and do not disturb the birds inside, presumably protect the nest from climbing predators such as snakes and small mammals (Skutch 1960; Janzen 1969).

During the breeding season at the start of the rains in May, June, and July, the pair of wrens in each territory builds a new nest for the eggs. The clutch size is usually four or five. While the female incubates, the male sleeps at night in a separate nest. The young wrens remain with their parents in family groups (fig. 10.19*b*) for most of their first year but, according to the available information, leave their parents before the following breeding season (Skutch 1960; Selander 1964). Students in OTS courses have reported small family groups of rufous-naped wrens in February in Guanacaste Province. On the other hand, four territories in November 1978 at Palo Verde had only pairs in residence. It is not known whether these pairs had failed to breed successfully or whether their young had left within the first 4 or 5 months after fledging. It also remains uncertain whether pairs can rear more than one brood in a year. In the cactus wren and certain South American members of this genus, a minority of pairs do succeed in rearing at least two broods in a year. In this case members of the first brood help to feed members of the second brood (Anderson and Anderson

1973). In other species in this genus, young normally remain in their natal group longer than one year and help to feed the young reared in this territory in subsequent years.

Most species in the genus *Campylorhynchus* perform remarkable duets (two birds coordinating vocalizations) and choruses (three or more birds vocalizing together). The duets of rufous-naped wrens in Costa Rica are unmistakable: they include short harsh notes, abrupt doublets consisting of two notes on different pitches, and nasal whistles that slur downward. Usually duetting partners are no more than 1–2 m apart, although sometimes pairs will duet when separated by much greater distances. Each duet consists of a repeated cadence. The partners sometimes contribute different notes to the cadences but evidently sometimes sing the same pattern in unison. Pairs have several such cadences in their repertoire. Cadences of neighboring pairs often differ. However, no accurate information is available about the number of cadences in the repertoires of pairs or about the extent to which neighboring pairs share cadences. In addition, single birds, probably of either sex to judge by other members of the genus, sometimes sing these cadences or similar cadences alone. These duets probably serve to advertise the pair's territory. Duetting is particularly frequent during the first hour after the wrens leave their nest about sunrise. Neighboring pairs often answer each other's duets. In other species in the genus, tape recordings of duets, when played back to a pair or group in its territory, evoke immediate approach and duetting by the resident pair. Pairs can recognize the cadences of their neighbors; they respond much more strongly to cadences from strange individuals that they have never heard before (Wiley and Wiley 1977). In all these respects the duets of *Campylorhynchus* wrens resemble the territorial songs of many other birds in which the male alone sings.

After the first hour of activity following sunrise, pairs of rufous-naped wrens often remain silent for long periods. It is often necessary to wait for a pair to duet before they can be located. At close range one can hear several other vocalizations used by a pair for communication. These calls presumably help them maintain contact during active foraging in dense foliage.

The band-backed wren, *C. zonatus,* occurs in areas of high rainfall on the Caribbean slope and coastal plain in Costa Rica, from sea level to about 1,400 m elevation. This species prefers the edges of tall forests and scattered trees in openings; it occurs around the buildings at La Selva. These wrens glean small anthropods from the foliage of trees, bushes, and epiphytes, often high aboveground. Their duets and choruses, consisting of loud, harsh notes in strongly rhymthical cadences, are the most conspicuous indication of their presence. Band-backed

wrens build their unkempt nests in dense foliage or epiphytes in isolated trees at a height of 2–30 m. They live in stable social groups of as many as eleven birds throughout the year (Skutch 1960). During the breeding season all members of the group help to feed the young, as well as to build nests and defend the territory. Young wrens probably remain in their natal group and help feed the young reared in the territory in subsequent years.

*

Anderson, A. H., and Anderson, A. 1973. *The cactus wren*. Tucson: University of Arizona Press.

Janzen, D. H. 1969. Birds and the ant × acacia interaction in Central America, with notes on birds and other myrmecophytes. *Condor* 17:240–56.

Rabenold, K. N., and Christensen, C. 1979. Ecological effects of aggregation for a social wren. *Behav. Ecol. Sociobiol.* 6:39–44.

Ricklefs, R. E., and Hainsworth, F. R. 1969. Temperature regulation in nestling cactus wrens: The nest environment. *Condor* 71:32–37.

Selander, R. K. 1964. Speciation in wrens of the genus *Campylorhynchus*. *Univ. California Publ. Zool.* 74: 1–259.

Skutch, A. F. 1960. *Life histories of Central American birds*. Pacific Coast Avifauna, no. 34. Berkeley: Cooper Ornithological Society.

Wiley, R. H., and Wiley, M. S. 1977. Recognition of neighbors' duets by stripe-backed wrens *Campylorhynchus nuchalis*. *Behaviour* 62:10–34.

Cathartes aura (Zopilote Cabecirrojo, Turkey Vulture)

F. G. Stiles and D. H. Janzen

Vultures are among the most conspicuous birds in rural Costa Rica, and of the four species present the turkey vulture (*Cathartes aura*) (fig. 10.20*a*) is the most widespread. Turkey vultures breed from southern Canada to Tierra del Fuego. The North American populations are migratory, wintering south to southern Brazil; with Swainson's and broad-winged hawks (*Buteo swainsoni* and *B. platypus*), turkey vultures form spectacular migratory flocks, often of hundreds of birds. These flocks climb circling in thermals, and then the birds glide for several miles, gradually losing altitude until they encounter another thermal that permits them to ascend again. In this way they can cover many miles with hardly a flap of their wings. At night such migratory flocks often descend en masse to festoon the trees over a considerable area. One such flock that descended on 20 September 1972 across the river from La Selva numbered about five hundred birds. As the sun rose after a rainy night and most

FIGURE 10.20. *a, Cathartes aura,* soaring. *b,* Black vultures (*Coragyps atratus*) waiting on the beach for a dead wave-washed tapir. Sirena, Corcovado National Park, Osa Peninsula, Costa Rica (photo, D. H. Janzen).

of the birds oriented toward it, spreading their wings to dry, the scene resembled a witches' sabbath.

Turkey vultures are dull black to brownish black birds with relatively long, narrow wings and tails. When in flight, they are easily distinguished from most other hawks and vultures by a gray undersides to the flight feathers (contrasting with the body and wing tips.) Their flight is distinctive: they can soar in the lightest breeze, their wings usually held well above the horizontal, teetering from side to side but rarely flapping (see Parrott 1971 and Pennycuick 1971 for analysis of vulture flight). The heads of adult birds are reddish, those of young birds blackish. Birds of the resident race *C. a. ruficollis* can be distinguished from those of the migrant race *C. a. meridionalis* by a whitish band across the bare skin of the nape. Nearly all birds seen in Costa Rica during the northern summer show this mark, and *C. a. ruficollis* is probably the only subspecies breeding in the country. There is no appreciable sexual dimorphism in size or color in turkey vultures: adult average about 1,400 g in weight and 65–70 cm in length, with a wingspan of 1.5–1.75 mm.

Turkey vultures are fairly common up to 1,500–2,000 m, and they are seen regularly to about 2,500 m and occasionally to 3,000 m. At one place or another the turkey vulture is sympatric with one to three other species of vultures and one hawk that acts like a vulture. The commonest of these is the black vulture (*Coragyps atratus*) (fig. 10.20*b*), a shorter, stockier bird (ca. 55–60 cm; wingspan 1.25–1.5 m) (cf. McHargue 1981) that is nevertheless heavier than the turkey vulture (1,500–1,700 g) and dominant to it at carcasses. Black vultures have short tails and shorter, broader wings that are all black beneath with a whitish blotch near the wing tip; their flight is heavier than that of the turkey vulture, with more frequent flapping and soaring on horizontal wings. The spectacular king vulture (*Sarcoramphus papa*) is half again the size of a black vulture but similar in build; adults have white body feathers, black flight feathers, and luridly colored naked heads (red, blue, orange, purple, etc.); immatures are black and require several years to attain adult plumage. The yellow-headed vulture (*Cathartes burrovianus*) is essentially a smaller, browner version of the turkey vulture with an orange yellow and purplish head (weight ca. 950–1,050 g) and occurs locally in wet, marshy savannas. The caracara (*Caracara plancus*) is smaller yet and distinctively marked (fig. 10.21); it is a hawk that scavenges extensively from carcasses as well as taking lizards, insects, and other small prey.

As a group the vultures offer interesting contrasts in foraging and social dominance. There is abundant experimental and morphological evidence that turkey vultures can locate food by smell (Stager 1964). We have observed turkey vultures feeding upon carrion as small as dead agoutis, boas, and kinkajous below the closed canopy of rain forest. In an OTS project many years ago in Guanacaste, turkey vultures found rotting ctenosaurs buried beneath piles of brush in open pastures. Morphological evidence (Stager 1964) suggests that king vultures, but *not* black vultures, can also find food by smell; we have seen king vultures find carcasses of agoutis,

FIGURE 10.21. *Caracara plancus* feeding on a dead Virginia opossum. Santa Rosa National Park, Guanacaste Province, Costa Rica (photo, D. H. Janzen).

snakes, peccaries, and sloths below thick rain-forest canopy. In Corcovado National Park a king vulture found a dead sloth that had been wrapped in a plastic bag and buried about 5 cm deep in the forest floor litter. The black vulture, on the other hand, appears to hunt carcasses strictly by sight, often cued by the behavior of turkeys or kings to arrive at carcasses not easily visible. Once a carcass is found, black vultures begin arriving very rapidly. They are dominant to turkey vultures and can force them to leave the carcass until the black vultures are satiated. Large numbers of black vultures can sometimes force even a king vulture from a carcass (D. Janzen, pers. obs.), although usually king vultures dominate black vultures and force them to make way. However, when there is a lot of food (several dead cows in one place) as many as fifty black, ten turkey, and ten king vultures may be seen feeding side by side (D. Janzen, pers. obs. in Corcovado).

Because of their subordinate status, turkey vultures are usually excluded from large or medium-sized carcasses once black vultures or king vultures arrive; they often must depend on being the first to find a carcass, and they make their living mostly off small carcasses that they can finish before black vultures arrive. Their foraging behavior is ideally suited to this; in contrast to high-soaring black vultures, turkey vultures quarter an area systematically, usually keeping fairly low over the ground. This tactic enables them to smell even small carcasses and descend upon them quickly. Individuals forage independently, and although they may cue on each other to find carcasses, rarely do more than three or four gather at any one small carcass. Black vultures tend to exploit mostly large carcasses, and numbers build up rapidly around rich food sources like slaughterhouses and dumps. Black vultures are common in towns and cities in many parts of Costa Rica and perform at least as much of the Sanitation Department's chores as do its human members. Density of turkey vultures in an area tends to be low but fairly constant. At Corcovado National Park, after the settlers left, their cattle remained for another year, and many died. In addition to turkey vultures and king vultures drawn from the surrounding forest, there were hundreds of black vultures within a few kilometers of Sirena. Now, with no cattle present, there is only an occasional black vulture seen along the beach (where they forage for sea-turtle nests and hatchlings as they do on other Costa Rican beaches), but turkey vultures and king vultures are still commonly encountered on carrion inside the forest canopy.

King vultures and black vultures, but not turkey vultures, are also reported to kill their own food at least occasionally—although their lack of talons means that prey must be very small, weak, or moribund.

Turkey vultures and king vultures are (or at least were

originally) largely or entirely forest-inhabiting in Central America, although both occur now in open country—the turkey vulture perhaps more than in forest at present. The biology of the yellow-headed vulture has never been studied in detail, and it would be extremely interesting to see how it coexists with the turkey vulture, since in sites where the yellow-headed vulture occurs the turkey vulture is also abundant.

Turkey vultures nest in large holes in trees, hollow logs, caves, deadfalls, and other such places. No nest is built. The two eggs are much more oblong than those of the hawks, dull whitish in color, heavily splotched with brown. Incubation requires about 40 days, and the young leave the nest at about 2 months of age. Just as juvenile African vultures require bone and other nonmeat parts of a carcass for development (Janzen 1976), we suspect that turkey vultures feed their offspring more than just meat torn from carcasses.

Vultures must either have digestive systems that process food very thoroughly before it gets to absorptive surfaces or have a physiology very resistant to the amines and other bacterial toxins produced by rotting meat (Janzen 1977), or both. Anthrax and hog cholera bacteria are destroyed by passing through the turkey vulture's digestive system. While vultures are rumored to transmit hoof-and-mouth disease (aftosa), because they feed on carcasses of animals killed by this disease, the rumor is unsubstantiated, and the process is quite unlikely, since the digestive system of a vulture would probably kill the disease organism and since vultures do not normally come in contact with living, healthy cattle. It is rumored among fishermen that vultures can digest brass fishhooks. Vultures are not indiscriminant consumers of rotting meat, and they take fresh meat eagerly. When fish intestines filled with ethanol were mixed with unadulterated fish intestines, the adulterated tissues were left behind by frantically feeding Mexican black and turkey vultures (D. Janzen, pers. obs.).

*

Janzen, D. H. 1976. The depression of reptile biomass by large herbivores. *Am. Nat.* 110:371–400.
———. 1977. Why fruits rot, seeds mold, and meat spoils. *Am. Nat.* 111:691–713.
McHargue, L. A. 1981. Black vulture nesting, behavior, and growth. *Auk* 98:182–85.
Parrot, G. C. 1971. Aerodynamics of gliding flight of a black vulture *Coragyps atratus*. *J. Exp. Biol.* 53:363–74.
Pennycuick, C. J. 1971. Gliding flight of the white-backed vulture *Gyps africanus*. *J. Exp. Biol.* 55:13–38.
Stager, K. E. 1964. The role of olfaction in food location by the turkey vulture and other cathartids. *Contrib. Sci. Los Angeles County Mus.* 81:1–63.

Chiroxiphia linearis (Saltanix Colilargo, Toledo, Long-tailed Manakin)

M. S. Foster

This highly dimorphic, lek-breeding species extends down the Pacific side of Central America from southern Mexico (Oaxaca and Chiapas) to central Costa Rica. In Costa Rica it is most common in the dry northwestern part of the country but spreads in decreasing numbers through the Meseta Central east to Juan Viñas and south into the Dota region. It occupies both tropical dry forest and tropical and subtropical moist forest, frequenting thickets and open vine tangles as well as middle-level trees. These birds are almost exclusively frugivorous, and one can usually find them feeding commonly on fruits of such species as *Ardisia revoluta, Cecropia peltata, Cocoloba caracasana, Muntingia calabura, Psychotria* spp., *Trema micrantha,* and *Trichilia cuneata,* to name a few.

Adult males are very brightly colored, their crimson red crowns, light blue backs and shoulders, and orange legs and feet contrasting sharply with the rest of the body, which is uniform black. Their exotic appearance is enhanced by the two elongated central rectrices (tail feathers) that extend beyond the rest of the tail for a distance about twice the length of the body. Compared with males, the females are rather dull (fig. 10.22a), being olive green above and slightly paler green below, though they too have orange legs and feet. The central rectrices are only slightly elongated in the female, and some individuals have a limited red crown. Young males resemble females initially, acquiring the adult male pattern over a period of 3–4 years. With each successive molt, they look more like adult males and less like females, exhibiting a mixture of blue, red, black, and green feathers.

Males of this species engage in communal reproductive displays, that is, displays requiring the participation of more than one individual (Foster 1977). These displays are performed on an exploded lek or arena that consists of a number of courts, each owned, but not actively defended, by a pair of adult males (rarely three). The courts are not contiguous, and male couples maintain auditory, rather than visual, contact. The communal displays include the frequently repeated *toledo* vocalization given synchronously by two males of a pair. This call apparently advertises the presence of the males at the display area and attracts females. When a female arrives, the birds move to one of several low display perches in their court. These perches, defended from use by other males, usually consist of a horizontal vine with associated accessory perches. Here the males jointly perform a coordinated jump display. Most commonly it takes one of

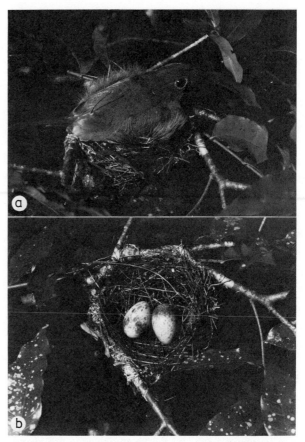

FIGURE 10.22. *Chiroxiphia linearis. a,* Adult female on nest at night. *b,* Nest after female has flown off. June 1980, Santa Rosa National Park, Guanacaste Province, Costa Rica (photos, D. H. Janzen).

two forms. In the up-down variant, the males are perpendicular to the display perch, facing a female on an adjacent perch. In a coordinated fashion they alternately jump into the air. In the cartwheel variant the males are parallel to the display perch, facing the female perched at one end. Their coordinated alternate jumps now describe a vertical circle with the anterior bird moving backward to the spot originally occupied by the other male while the latter individual moves foward to assume the position originally occupied by the first. Both the female and the males become visibly excited during these sequences, which vary in length but may include as many as one hundred jumps. Each jump in the display is accompanied by a wheezy *buzzee* call. The birds are very sensitive to any type of disturbance, and displays are continually interrupted and reinitiated. Finally, when the display is finished—this is signaled with a single high-pitched note given by the dominant male (see below)—one male executes a solo precopulatory display for the female, who is usually on the display perch at this time. He changes perches, describing a horizontal circle (to several meters in diameter) around her, going from perch to perch to perch with a very slow kind of floating flight that Slud has (1957) correctly likened to the flight of the blue morpho butterfly (*Morpho* sp.). If this display is successful, copulation ensues, and the female leaves to rear the young by herself.

The association of the paired males persists from one to several years (Foster 1977) and is in every way analogous to a male-female pair bond except for the absence of copulation. Partners usually display only with each other. Normally they occupy a single court for an entire reproductive season or from year to year, though the association represents a real attachment of the males to each other rather than common attachment to a given site. One male is dominant throughout the association and performs all copulations with any females attracted to the court. The males do not appear to be kin related or altruistic. Rather, the system seems to be maintained by selection operating at the level of the individual. The subordinate member of a pair presumably is far more likely to assume dominance on a court after the loss of his partner and thus to eventually be reproductively successful than is a solitary male (Foster 1977).

The reproductive season lasts from about March through September in Costa Rica (Foster 1976). The nests, built only by the female and placed without regard to the court where copulation occurred, are shallow cups suspended from forks in small trees (fig. 10.22*b*) Clutch size is one or two, and the beige tan eggs are heavily marked with medium to dark brown spots. The young are fed at least partly on fruit.

*

Foster, M. S. 1976. Nesting biology of the long-tailed manakin. *Wilson Bull.* 88:400–420.

———. 1977. Odd couples in manakins: A study of social organization and cooperative breeding in *Chiroxiphia linearis. Am. Nat.* 111:845–53.

Slud, P. 1957. The song and dance of the long-tailed manakin, *Chiroxiphia linearis, Auk* 74:333–39.

Chloroceryle americana (Martín Pescador Verde, Green Kingfisher)

J. V. Remsen, Jr.

The green kingfisher (fig. 10.23) inhabits wooded shorelines of streams and lakes from southern Texas to central Argentina. Within this range, this 7-in kingfisher may be found in a wide variety of climates and habitats, from sea level to 2,500 m and from rain forests to deserts. In Costa Rica the species is common in the lowlands on both slopes but rarely occurs higher than the Central Plateau. The essential components of suitable habitat seem to be rather simple: slow-moving or nonmoving permanent

FIGURE 10.23. *Chloroceryle americana,* adult. Hacienda Palo Verde, Guanacaste Province, Costa Rica (photo, F. G. Stiles).

fresh water bordered by low, brushy growth for hunting perches. In small streams in humid lowland tropical forests where the canopy closes overhead, shading the water most of the time, the green kingfisher is replaced by a smaller congener, the pygmy, or least kingfisher (*C. aenea*) or by a larger congener, the green-and-rufous kingfisher (*C. inda*), or both. Open, sunny shorelines are usually shared with larger congeners, the amazon kingfisher (*C. amazona*) and the ringed kingfisher (*Ceryle torquata*), one of the largest kingfishers in the world.

Prey items, exclusively small fishes and aquatic invertebrates, are obtained by plunging headfirst into the water and capturing them between the mandibles on impact. Most prey is captured within a few centimeters of the water surface; no underwater pursuit is involved. Hunting perches range in height from 1 to 5 m (mean about 1.5 m) and are seldom more than a meter back from the waterline. Prey length is slightly but significantly correlated with the height of the hunting perch from which the prey was captured. Occasionally a green kingfisher may hover briefly above the water before plunging. The angle of the dive (angle between average flight path from perch to entry point and water) ranges from 90° down to 15°, but smaller angles are never observed. Apparently reflection and refraction distort target images too severely for successful strikes at angles lower than 15°. Within this range of dive angles, there is no significant relationship between angle and success rate. Prey items range from 8 to 80 mm in length, but populations studied where all four other Neotropical kingfishers were present showed a much narrower range and variance. Perhaps populations at the periphery of this species range, where they are sympatric with only one other kingfisher (ringed), will show the greatest range and variance in prey size.

After a dive, the kingfisher leaves the water as soon as possible. Prey items are taken to a nearby perch and swallowed headfirst. Large prey are beaten against a branch before they are swallowed. The length of time prey is manipulated and beaten before swallowing is strongly correlated with prey size. Subsequent hunting perches usually overlook "fresh" patches of water undisturbed by the previous dive. Only 30% of the dive attempts are successful. Aborted dives are also frequently observed, in which the kingfisher pulls out of the dive before entering the water.

Green kingfishers are monogamous and highly territorial. Mates seem to become intolerant of one another during the nonbreeding season. Densities average about three birds per km of shoreline and are positively correlated with density of small surface fishes and, to some extent, with availability of suitable hunting perches.

Nesting tunnels are excavated in steep dirt banks, usually bordering a river or stream. The two forward-facing toes of all kingfishers are partially fused, presumably an adaptation to aid in pushing soil behind the bird as it digs and chisels its way forward with the bill. In the nest-excavating season, bills may be rather blunt from the abrasion of digging. The specific nest-site requirements with respect to height above water, distance below rim of bank, slope of bank, soil texture, proximity to water, and so forth, have never been quantified. The tunnel, usually less than 1 m in length, leads horizontally to a slightly enlarged chamber in which three to six white eggs are placed on bare dirt without nest material.

No full study of the nesting biology of this common and widespread species has been published. We do know that incubation is shared by the sexes (the female's share is much larger) and that the young take at least 21 days to fledge. If we assume that this species follows patterns shown by other kingfishers, young are fed larger and larger fish as they grow. The length of time a fledged juvenile remains dependent on its parents is unknown. Before learning to fish for themselves, juveniles "capture" floating leaves and sticks in rather sloppy, hesitant plunges, retrieve them from the water, and thrash them vigorously against a branch. Some birds make the transition from inanimate objects to live fish in one morning, although these prey may be much smaller than those normally captured by adults.

*

Bent, A. C. 1940. Life histories of North American cuckoos, goat-suckers, hummingbirds, and their allies. *Bull. U.S. Nat. Mus.*, no. 176.

Betts, B. J., and Betts, D. L. 1977. The relation of hunting site changes to hunting success in green herons and green kingfishers. *Condor* 79:269–71.

Remsen, J. V., Jr. 1978. Geographical ecology of Neotropical kingfishers. Ph.D. diss., University of California, Berkeley.

Slud, P. 1964. The birds of Costa Rica. *Bull. Am. Mus. Nat. Hist.* 128:1–430.

For other Neotropical kingfishers see:

Skutch, A. F. 1957. Life history of the Amazon kingfisher. *Condor* 59:217–29.

———. 1972. Ringed kingfisher. In Studies of tropical American birds. *Publ. Nuttall Ornithol. Club* 10: 88–101.

Cochlearius cochlearius (Pico-Inchara, Chocuaco, Cuaca, Boat-billed Heron)

D. W. Mock

The boat-billed heron (fig. 10.24*a*) is an aberrant night heron (family Ardeidae) whose bill is much wider (fig. 10.24*b*) than the thin, rapierlike bills of all other herons. Although it was described more than two centuries ago (Brisson 1760), rather little is known about the evolutionary and ecological significance of this strange bill. Because the bird is highly nocturnal—apparently more so than any of its relatives—direct field observations of feeding behavior are difficult. In Costa Rica, the boatbill is widely distributed through the lowlands on both coasts, wherever trees adjoin and overhang slow-moving or still water. They nest in colonies and roost gregariously, so they are found mostly in local concentrations within larger expanses of favorable habitat. They are abundant, for example, in the forested margins of the Río Sirena estuary at Corcovado National Park.

Originally, the boatbill was split off taxonomically as a separate, monotypic family, the Cochleariidae. Modern authors, however, place it near or among the night herons that it closely resembles. Cracraft (1967) argued that most of the distinctive features used to set it apart constitute a single adaptive complex; the broad bill and its supporting structures. After a careful examination of skeletal features, Payne and Risley (1976) concluded that the "postcranial skeleton is very like that of *N. nycticorax* [black-crowned night heron] and the similarity indicates that *Cochlearius* is a night heron with a special feeding apparatus."

Taxonomy aside, most scientific interest in this species centers on the bill's function, an issue that is far from settled. Most, but not all, authors believe it must be a feeding adaptation whose peculiar form reflects a peculiar niche. Wetmore (1965) reported seeing boatbills us-

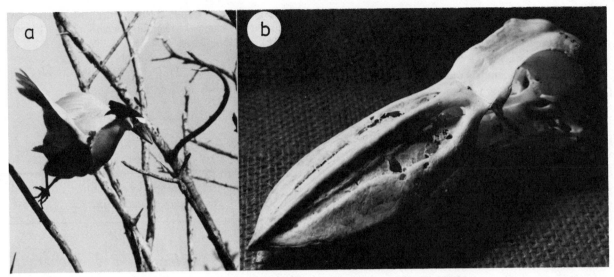

FIGURE 10.24. *Cochlearius cochlearius. a,* Adult starting to fly. *b,* Skull (photos, D. W. Mock).

ing their bills as "scoops" rather than as spears (the typical heron thrust). Mock (1975) hypothesized that special feeding techniques might be related to extremely low light levels: breeding in Mexico is apparently triggered by the onset of the rainy season (Dickerman and Juarez 1971), which also produces solid cloud cover for very dark nights. Temporally associated with this deepened nocturnal darkness is a great influx of shrimp and small fish into the rain-flooded brackish lagoons where the boatbills nest and feed. To take advantage of the ephemeral superabundance of food, the boatbills must be able to find prey in near total darkness. Mock (1975) reasoned that vision might play a reduced role in prey location and that the bird's very large eyes probably enable it to move about. He went on to propose that the bill might be especially touch-sensitive and therefore suited for locating prey tactilely. The bill's width would presumably aid such groping captures by substantially increasing the capture surface. In a second speculation, he proposed that such a broad bill opened rapidly would create a partial vacuum, drawing water and prey into the mouth. Unfortunately, none of these behavioral tricks could be observed in the field. Later, anatomical study did not reveal specialized proprioceptors on the margins of the bill (as exist, for example, in wood storks but which are not essential for tactolocation). So, while touch-feeding remains a possibility, it now seems less likely. Other potential ways of finding the prey include the use of acoustic cues and, perhaps, very faint visible reflections. When one wades through these shallow lagoons at night, hundreds of tiny splashes can be heard all around: unfortunately, little is known of the behavior of the prey species and their surface activities at night.

Whatever the method for locating the prey (visual, acoustic, and/or tactile), the extra width of the bill proba-bly serves to compensate for the accuracy sacrificed when grabbing in the dark. It has been compared to a "catcher's mitt" (Mock 1975).

Most recently, Biderman and Dickerman (1978) sought to test the touch-feeding hypothesis by observing boatbills with a special night-vision device. They gathered 16.5 h of direct observations of feeding behavior, but not during the rainy season (that is, not during the darkest time of the year and not when the temporary superabundance of prey is being exploited). It is interesting that the prey catching they observed was visually directed and no different from that of other night herons foraging in the same area.

We are left with at least three possible explanations. The first, apparently favored by Biderman and Dickerman (1978), is that the bill is specialized for something *other* than hunting. Citing descriptions of unusually loud bill-snap displays performed during courtship (in Mock 1976), they suggest that sound production may have been the *primary* selection factor. A second explanation would be that boatbills hunt pretty much like other night herons (that is, visually) but are active at darker times of the night—and season. The extra bill width would be a simple compensation for the strike's inaccuracy. A third choice is that the bill's unique potential is realized only during the rainy season, when ecological changes make food temporarily superabundant but not available to the "typical" night herons. By whatever means the prey is located under these especially dark conditions, the extra bill width could make capture efficient enough for economical exploitation.

Obviously, we need direct observations of boat-billed herons hunting under the darkest possible conditions (presumably using night-vision devices during the rainy season). Stomach-content diet studies from a variety of habitats are also needed. Finally, research on the nocturnal activities of their principal prey animals (e.g., *Dormitator latifrons*, *Pennaeus vannamei*, and *Macrobrachium* spp. in Mexico) would be extremely useful.

*

Biderman, J. O., and Dickerman, R. W. 1978. Feeding behavior and food habits of the boat-billed heron (*Cochlearius cochlearius*). *Biotropica* 10:33–37.

Brisson, M. J. 1760. *Ornithologia* 1:48, 5:506.

Cracraft, J. 1967. On the systematic position of the boat-billed heron. *Auk* 84:529–33.

Dickerman, R. W., and Juarez, L. C. 1971. Nesting studies of the boat-billed heron *Cochlearius cochlearius* at San Blas, Nayarit, Mexico. *Ardea* 59: 1–16.

Mock, D. W. 1975. Feeding methods of the boat-billed heron: A deductive hypothesis. *Auk* 92:590–92.

———. 1976. Social behavior of the boat-billed heron. *Living Bird* 14:185–214.

Payne, R. B., and Risley, C. J. 1976. Systematics and evolutionary relationships among the herons (Ardeidae). *Misc. Publ. Mus. Zool. Univ. Michigan*, no. 150.

Wetmore, A. 1965. The birds of the Republic of Panamá, part 1. Tinamidae to Rynchopidae. *Smithsonian Misc. Publ.*, vol. 150.

FIGURE 10.25. *Coereba flaveola*, adult. Panama (drawing, C. F. Leck).

Coereba flaveola (Reinita Mielera, Cazadorcita, Picaflor, Bananaquit)

C. F. Leck

This widespread species (fig. 10.25) is the best-known member of a small group of nectar-feeding birds that were formerly recognized as a single Neotropical family, Coerebidae, whose species are now often divided between wood warblers and tanagers. The bananaquit is a resident species from southern Mexico to Argentina and on almost all the islands of the West Indies (except Cuba). Often it is one of the most common or abundant local birds. Throughout its range there is considerable geographic variation (with thirty-five subspecies) both in plumage (e.g., there is a black melanic form on some of the Lesser Antilles) and in song. In Costa Rica it occurs throughout except the tropical dry forest and the higher montane elevations. In the lowlands, it is most numerous in semiopen or shrubby areas; at middle elevations it is most often found in forest canopy and edge situations.

The head, wings, and upperparts are black, with a white superciliary streak (over the eye); the rump is yellow, the throat is gray, and the rest of underparts are yellow (the female is paler than the male). The sharply pointed black bill is slightly decurved. Immatures are like adults but much duller and with a yellowish superciliary streak. Males weight is about 10 g and females about 9 g.

The bananaquit feeds mainly on nectar, from a large variety of flowers, especially large trees such as *Erythrina leonotis* and *Symphonia*. It also visits vines and herbaceous plants, including garden ornamentals (e.g., *Hibiscus*, *Allamanda*). For larger flowers it often "robs" the flower of its nectar by piercing a hole through the *base* of the corolla and thus not aiding in pollen dispersal. I have found that one can census the percentage of flowers so visited by simple inspection for bananaquit holes, even for flowers on the forest floor beneath taller trees. In competitive encounters at nectar resources this species can be dominant over sympatric hummingbirds (Leck 1973).

In addition to nectar feeding, bananaquits also feed at fruits (sucking the pulp or swallowing small pieces) and take insects (including larvae of Lepidoptera, Araneida, Coleoptera, Hemiptera, Homoptera, and Hymenoptera). Both Skutch and I have also seen them take the protein corpuscles (Müllerian bodies) from *Cecropia* trees, and Skutch believes they are an important part of the diet.

Near houses the bananaquit is often quite tame and will readily feed at tables, taking sweet liquids or sugar directly.

The birds sing throughout the year, with a wheezy series of high-pitched squeaks (several seconds' duration). Most pairs have several clutches in the year. The breeding can be in any month, but peaks are evident at certain seasons (at El General in Costa Rica the period from June through November is favored). In many areas of their range breeding appears synchronized with flowering peaks. Courtship involves a simple bowing and bobbing display, with yellow rump feathers raised. Both parents build the distinctive domed nest that is suspended

2 to 10 m above the ground. The well-woven nest is made of grass, narrow leaves, and twigs (in the nonbreeding season adults also construct separate roosting nests for sleeping; these are smaller and less well made). The clutch is usually two (rarely three) light buff eggs (color can vary). Only the female incubates (12–14 days), and young are fledged 2 to 3 weeks after hatching. I have noticed the fledged birds with bright red corners to their gape (mouth), apparently a feeding signal for the parents.

*

Leck, C. F. 1973. Dominance relationships in nectar-feeding birds at St. Croix. *Auk* 90:431–32.

Skutch, A. F. 1954. Bananaquit. In *Life histories of Central American birds*, pp. 404–20. Pacific Coast Avifauna, no. 31. Berkeley: Cooper Ornithological Society.

Columbina talpacoti (Tortolita Colorada, Palomita, Tortolita Rojiza, Ruddy Ground Dove)

A. F. Skutch

The male of this small dove is mostly cinnamon rufous, more pinkish on the underparts, with bluish gray crown and hindhead and prominent bars and spots of black on the wings. The female is much browner and grayer, with similar wing marks. The species ranges from northern Mexico to northern Argentina. In Costa Rica it is found from the lowlands of both coasts up to about 1,100 m. In this country it prefers clearings in regions where the natural vegetation is heavy, humid forest, so that it is most common on the Caribbean side and from the head of the Golfo de Nicoya southward on the Pacific side. In more arid country where Inca doves (*Scardafella inca*) abound, as through much of Guanacaste, it is replaced by the common ground dove (*Columbina passerina*), and in intermediate climates the two related species occur together.

Although it perches, roosts, and nests in trees and shrubbery (fig. 10.26), the ruddy ground dove appears to forage wholly on the ground, where it gathers seeds and probably also small invertebrates. It thrives best in regions of lush vegetation, yet it prefers to hunt over fairly open ground, as in pastures, cultivated fields, plantations of coffee or bananas, dooryards, and the barer areas of thickets. As one travels down the Térraba valley on the Inter-American Highway, a constant succession of these doves rises from the road in front of the approaching car. Dozens of individuals may scatter as one walks through a weedy field, but ruddy ground doves do not travel in flocks like some larger pigeons.

This dove's call, given by both sexes, is of two syllables and often sounds like *kitty-woo*. Sometimes a male

FIGURE 10.26. *Columbina talpacoti*, nest and nestlings on the top of a bunch of green bananas. Costa Rica (photo, A. F. Skutch).

and female remain for many minutes perching in contact, at intervals preening one another's feathers.

In the valley of El General, ruddy ground doves nest from January to September, most freely from February to June. In other regions, as in Surinam, nests with eggs have been found in every month, but chiefly in the two annual dry seasons. The nest is built in a tree, shrub, or stout forb, occasionally on an old nest of some other bird or on a bunch of green bananas hanging in a plantation, where the upturned "fingers" of the topmost "hand" offer a secure support (fig. 10.26). Sites range from about 30 cm to 9 m above the ground, but most nests are 1.2 to 2.4 m up. The nest is a firm, though slight and shallow, saucerlike structure, sometimes hardly more than a slightly concave platform. It is made of straws, weed stems, and fine twigs and lined with bits of dry grass and rootlets. It is built in the usual pigeon manner, with the female sitting on the growing nest to receive and arrange the pieces her mate gathers from the ground, one at a time, and lays in front of her while he stands on her back. In her absence he may bring a few pieces and arrange them himself. Two to 4 days suffice to complete the slight structure.

The set almost invariably consists of two plain white eggs, and the first is kept covered, by the parents' sitting alternately, for most of the interval of more than 25 h before the second is laid. Thereafter the male commonly incubates during one long session that lasts about 7 h through the middle of the day, the female all the rest of the time. The incubation period is from somewhat less than 12 to about 13 days. The blind, pink hatchlings are thinly covered with the short, buffy, hairlike natal down typical of pigeons. They are fed by both parents with regurgitated food, which at first is doubtless (as in other pigeons) largely milk secreted from the crop, but as days pass it contains increasing amounts of newly gathered solid items.

The young develop so rapidly that, if disturbed, they can fly weakly from the nest when only 9 days old, but they do not leave spontaneously until 12 to 14 days of age, when they fly strongly but alight clumsily. They may return to their heavily soiled nest to be brooded by their mother for 1 or 2 additional nights. The old nest may be used for a second brood. Twenty-one nests contained forty eggs, of which twenty hatched, producing eight fledglings from five nests. Thus, 20% of the eggs, and 24% of the nests, yielded at least one flying young.

*

Haverschmidt, F. 1953. Notes on the life history of *Columbigallina talpacoti* in Surinam. *Condor* 55:21–25.

Skutch, A. F. 1956. Life history of the ruddy ground-dove. *Condor* 58:188–205.

Wetmore, A. 1968. The birds of the Republic of Panamá, part 2. *Smithsonian Misc. Coll.*, Vol. 150.

Crax rubra (Pavón Grande, Pavón, Granadera, Great Curassow)

D. Amadon

The great curassow (*Crax rubra*) is the northernmost of seven closely related allopatric or parapatric species of curassows, which form a superspecies. Its range extends in humid forest at low or medium elevations from eastern Mexico south through Middle America into Colombia and Ecuador, west of the Andes. In Costa Rica curassows occur in deciduous and humid forests from the lowlands through lower middle elevations on both slopes. The other six species of the group are entirely South American in distribution.

The male of the great curassow (fig. 10.27a) is black above, slightly glossed with green, and pure white below; there is a large bright yellow, unfeathered knob or "caruncle" on the forehead. A further adornment is a crest of forward-curved feathers that runs the length of the crown. The female (fig. 10.27b) is very different — mostly brown, barred with blackish and white on head, wings, and tail — quite handsome, but protectively colored. There are two color phases; in one of them reddish tints prevail; from such a bird comes the species name

FIGURE 10.27. *Crax rubra. a,* Adult captive male. *b,* Adult captive female. Flores, Guatemala (photos, D. H. Janzen).

rubra. The hens lack the bill knob but have the crest, in this sex laced with white.

Curassows are large birds, as big as a hen turkey but more slender. They stalk about on the forest floor, feeding mostly on fallen fruit, tree seeds, and large insects. Sometimes they fly up into the trees to feed, and it is there, sometimes 10 to 12 m up, that they build their rather small nests. Only two eggs are laid, white with very rough shells. The downy chicks are clad in dense down, attractively patterned. From the first the chicks prefer to climb about in dense vegetation rather than coming to the ground; within a very few days they can fly short distances. At night the hen roosts on a tree limb, a chick sheltered under each wing. The birds are strictly monogamous. The male curassow helps lead his family about, and if danger threatens he utters a high-pitched whining whistle. At other times the pair keep in touch by low-pitched grunting sounds. The song of the male is an extremely low-pitched but far-carrying patterned series of notes, which may be imitated by humming with the mouth closed. The windpipe of curassows is variously modified, presumably to aid in producing this remarkable song, which they usually utter from high in a tree.

Despite their low rate of reproduction, curassows are probably long-lived — at any rate in some areas of remote forest they are the commonest large bird. But they are threatened not only by the destruction of humid and deciduous tropical forest — a worldwide curse — but by their palatability. As soon as a tract of forest is opened, the settlers, often protein-starved—hunt down and shoot the curassows. The outlook for the survival of these birds is bleak, except in large forest preserves (e.g., a good population remains in Corcovado, but La Selva is too small). In captivity curassows are somewhat difficult to breed and must be protected from frost.

Curassows are one of three divisions of the family Cracidae—the other two being the guans and the chachalacas, both smaller in size and more arboreal. This is a very distinct family of gallinaceous birds. It is the most arboreal of the order. No hybrids with other families are known.

*

Delacour, J., and Amadon, D. 1973. *Curassows and related birds*. New York: American Museum of Natural History.

Crotophaga sulcirostris (Garrapatero Piquiestriado, Tijo, Groove-billed Ani)

S. L. Vehrencamp

The groove-billed ani (*Crotophaga sulcirostris*) is a conspicuous and common bird occurring throughout the lowland and mid-elevation regions of Costa Rica. Because it prefers open, man-made habitats and is a typical "fence-post sitter," it can be readily observed while driving in a car. It is a member of the cuckoo family (Cuculidae), a group characterized by some of the most bizarre breeding systems found in birds (brood parasitism, communal nesting, polyandry). There are two other members of the genus, the smooth-billed ani (*C. ani*) and the greater ani (*C. major*). All three species occur in the Neotropics and are similar in appearance and social behavior (Davis 1940, 1941; Skutch 1959; Köster 1971).

The groove-billed ani is a medium-sized bird (70 g) with glossy black plumage, a long, loose tail, and a crested bill. It is primarily a terrestrial forager, taking insects such as Orthoptera, Lepidoptera larvae, and Coleoptera; it occasionally takes fruit during the dry season. Anis can frequently be seen foraging near cattle, which flush up insects and significantly improve the foraging success of the birds (Smith 1971). Flight is slow and laborious, and the birds prefer to hop to the tops of trees and glide to more distant areas. They typically call in flight, giving the *ti-jo* call for which Costa Ricans name the bird. This species occurs in virtually every type of habitat in Costa Rica except forests, mangrove swamps, and the cool highlands. They are most abundant in marshes and secondary growth, but they also occur in savannas, pastures, orchards, and other agricultural areas.

Breeding occurs during the wettest months of the year,

when grass growth is greatest and insect food is abundant. On the eastern coastal slopes, where rain falls during most months, nests can be found at all times of the year. In seasonal areas such as Guanacaste, breeding is restricted to the rainy season. The nests are large, bulky open-cup structures lined with green leaves (fig. 10.28). They may be situated quite low in thorny scrub vegetation (e.g., *Mimosa pigra*) or high in trees (ant-acacias, *Chlorophora*, *Guazuma*, or *Citrus* spp.) The eggs are turquoise blue covered by a chalky white calcium layer. They are extremely large for the size of the bird (11 g, or 17% of the body weight of the female). Incubation begins when the last egg is laid and lasts about 13 days. The nestlings are altricial and are fed soft-bodied insects. They grow extremely rapidly and can jump out of the nest when 6 days old. They are volant at 17 days and independent of adult feeding at about 6 weeks. The juveniles remain in close association with the adults for 9 to 12 months and become sexually mature as yearlings.

The most interesting aspect of the ani's biology is its communal breeding system. The birds typically live and breed in groups ranging from two to eight adults. The entire group defends a common territory for breeding and feeding. These territories will be defended year-round if food is available, and group composition remains relatively stable. Groups typically consist of equal numbers of males and females that pair off during breeding. A single nest is constructed, and each female deposits four to eight eggs to form a communal clutch. All group members contribute toward incubation and nestling feeding. Anis appear extremely social and cohesive, roosting, and sleeping in close contact and frequently engaging in allogrooming.

This rosy picture is somewhat diminished when one looks more closely at the specific costs and benefits of group nesting for each individual in the group. Individuals differ greatly in the number of eggs they get into the nest and in the amount of time and effort they expend in incubation and nestling care (Vehrencamp 1977). Some females roll others' eggs out of the nest in a pattern that greatly benefits the female that commences laying last. Last-laying females also incubate and feed nestlings *less* often than the other females. The behavior of last-laying females is reminiscent of the brood parasite breeding strategy. These females are usually the oldest females in the group, and it is argued that an intrasexual dominance hierarchy within the group determines the behavior and relative reproductive success of the different females. Males also do not contribute equally to the communal clutch. Presumably, egg ownership is skewed in the same way as for females if pairing is indeed as monogamous as it appears. Incubation effort and nestling care are also very different for males, but in this case the male with the most eggs in the nest provides the greatest amount of

FIGURE 10.28. *a, Crotophaga sulcirostris,* communal nest about 1 m above ground, lined with fresh green leaves of *Pithecellobium lanceolatum.* Finca Taboga, near Cañas, Guanacaste Province, Costa Rica. *b, Crotophaga ani. c, C. ani* in flight. Corcovado National Park, Osa Peninsula, Costa Rica (photos, D. H. Janzen).

work. If fact, the male mated to the oldest (last-laying) female performs the majority of the diurnal incubation and all of the nocturnal incubation. This male appears to be behaviorally dominant in all interactions within the group, and therefore it is presumed that an intrasexual dominance hierarchy also determines the behavior and ultimate reproductive success and survival of the males in the group.

The question therefore arises, What is the advantage of group nesting, especially for the less successful (subordinate) members of the group? Vehrencamp (1978) attempted to test several popular hypotheses for the possible advantages of group nesting: that groups have better territories than pairs; that groups have higher overall reproductive success than pairs owing to better predator protection, better foraging efficiency, or more rapid renesting; and that adult survival is higher in groups. The following conclusions emerged:

1. Large groups (three or more pairs) were found to occur primarily in secondary growth and marsh portions of the study area; single pairs and small groups occurred in the pastureland. Vegetation cover, territory size, and nest height differed significantly in these two habitats, but food abundance during the breeding season was similar. Overall bird density was five times higher in the marsh habitat than in the pasture.

2. Overall nest predation rates were similar in the two habitats. Groups in the pasture had significantly lower predation rates than pairs, but there was no significant difference in predation rates between groups and pairs in the marsh.

3. The fraction of nestlings raised to independence was similar for the two habitats. Groups in the pasture were less successful in raising nestlings than were pairs, but there was no significant difference in juveniles raised per pair for large and small groups in the marsh.

4. In both habitats, pairs were more likely to attempt second broods than were groups. Second broods were much more frequent in the pasture than in the marsh.

5. Annual reproductive success (juveniles/pair/year) was the same for all commonly occurring group sizes within each habitat but was higher in the pasture than in the marsh because of the high frequency of second broods.

6. In the pasture, male and female survival chances were similar, but in the marsh adult survival was considerably higher for females and subordinate males than for dominant males. The source of adult mortality appeared to be nest predators. It was suggested that a high rate of nocturnal nest predation on low marsh nests benefits females and subordinate males at the expense of the dominant male. In the pasture, nest predators on the isolated tree nests may more commonly be diurnal, leading to high risks for all birds. Therefore, females and subordinate males increase their survival chances and their lifetime fitness by breeding in groups in the marsh habitat. Alpha males breeding in the marsh also benefit from the group situation via the egg skew effect created by female egg tossing if they can mate with the dominant female.

The communal nesting strategy is a complex one, with different rewards and costs for individual group members depending on their sex and status in the group and on the type of habitat in which they are nesting.

*

Davis, D. E. 1940. Social nesting habits of smooth-billed ani. *Auk* 57:179–218.

———. 1941. Social nesting habits of *Crotophaga major. Auk* 58:179–83.

Köster, F. 1971. Zum Nistverhalten des Ani. *Bonn Zool. Beit.* 22:4–27.

Skutch, A. F. 1959. Life history of the groove-billed ani. *Auk* 76:281–317.

Smith, S. M. 1971. The relationship of grazing cattle to foraging rates in anis. *Auk* 88:876–80.

Vehrencamp. S. L. 1977. Relative fecundity and parental effort in communally nesting anis, *Crotophaga sulcirostris. Science* 197:403–5.

———. 1978. The adaptive significance of communal nesting in groove-billed anis (*Crotophaga sulcirostris*). *Behav. Ecol. Sociobiol.* 4:1–33.

Crypturellus cinnamomeus (Tinamú Canelo, Gongolona, Gallina de Monte, Rufescent Tinamou)

D. A. Lancaster

Five species of tinamous occur from central Mexico through Panama. Costa Rica is the only country that has them all. The highland tinamou, *Nothocercus bonapartei*, occurs in high mountains the length of the country. The great tinamou, *Tinamus major*, prefers the humid forests on both slopes of the Cordillera throughout Costa Rica. The slaty-breasted tinamou, *Crypturellus boucardi*, like-wise prefers the humid forests but is restricted to the northeastern lowlands. The little tinamou, *C. soui*, can be found in fairly dense second growth and thickets up to about 1,000 m on both slopes. The rufescent tinamou, *C. cinnamomeus* (fig. 10.29), inhabits mostly the drier woodlands. Although these preferences can be stated, considerable overlap occurs, and even the great tinamou may be found sometimes in the fairly dense, low second growth that is the most common habitat for *C. soui*.

The rufescent tinamou seldom is found in the deep, tall wet forests. Rather, the forest edge, the dense scrub, and regenerating second-growth woods all are home to *C. cinnamomeus*.

The geographic range of *C. cinnamomeus* extends from central Mexico (the northernmost species of tin-amou) south to western Costa Rica. Here the species can be found in the tropical dry forest from about sea level to the lower elevations of the Cordillera de Guanacaste and the Cordillera de Tilarán.

The tinamous are as terrestrial as any group of birds inhabiting the various kinds of heavily vegetated habitats in Central America. The rufescent, or thicket, tinamou is one of the most common of the five species of tinamous that occur in Central America and Costa Rica. When speaking of tinamous, however, the application of "com-mon" is strictly relative. When tinamous are not breed-ing, one can walk the rain forests for days and not catch a glimpse of them. Even during the breeding season they are much more often heard than seen.

At this time of year its plaintive whistled call can be heard throughout the day, but most frequently in the early and late hours and occasionally at night. The melancholy whistled call—lasting only 1–1.5 sec—usually consists of a single mournful, resonant whistle, either a single long-drawn-out note or a note with a "dip" in the middle.

Even a glimpse of the rufescent tinamou will probably give away its identity; tinamous are very chunky-bodied, with relatively long necks and small heads, and appear almost tailless. *C. cinnamomeus* is a medium-sized bird, larger than any of the quail. Its rusty brown plumage is not highly patterned, but there is fine black barring on the

FIGURE 10.29. *Crypturellus cinnamomeus*, adult. Near Playa Coco, Guanacaste Province, Costa Rica (L. Wolf; photo, D. H. Janzen).

back. The bill is black, the throat is white, and the legs are coral red. The flesh has a greenish color but is good to eat.

Secretive in habits, this tinamou is most often seen solitarily. During the dry season its presence may be noted by the rustling of leaves caused by the bird's foot-steps or by the sweeping action of its bill as it searches beneath leaves for food. Unlike many gallinaceous birds, tinamous do not scratch for food with their feet.

Tinamous' diets are rather catholic. The rufescent tin-amou spends its life on the ground feeding mostly on a wide variety of seeds and fruits that fall to the ground during the year; but lepidoteran larvae, beetles, ants, and termites also contribute to the diet of these birds.

The rufescent tinamou constructs no nest (fig. 10.30). Its glossy, unmarked purplish pink eggs are laid directly on the ground between the buttresses of a tree or at the base of a log. Only the males incubate, and they do so for a period probably similar to that found for *C. boucardi*—16 days. The clutch size is variable, usually numbering two to seven eggs. The newly hatched young are highly precocial and leave the nest soon after hatching.

Like other tinamous, the rufescent tinamou is reluctant

FIGURE 10.30. *Crypturellus cinnamomeus,* nest site with seven pale lavender eggs shortly after male has fled. Near Bagaces, Guanacaste Province, Costa Rica, March 1977 (photo, D. H. Janzen).

to fly and usually does so only when hard pressed by a predator. For protection it relies heavily on crypticity, both in plumage and in behavior. It will move stealthily away when the danger is still some yards off, or it will freeze, becoming immobile until the predator has passed or is nearly upon it. Only then will the tinamou take to the air. Its flight in these circumstances is very loud and powerful but poorly controlled; it does not fly long distances, sometimes only 30 yards or less.

The rufescent tinamou is one species that should do well in spite of hunting pressure, which is considerable, for these birds readily move into second growth as it replaces taller forests that have been cut for *milpas* or timber.

*

Blake, E. R. 1977. *Manual of Neotropical birds.* Vol. 1. Chicago: University of Chicago Press.

Lancaster, D. A. 1964. Life history of the Boucard tinamou in British Honduras, part 1. Distribution and general behavior. *Condor* 66:165–81.

———. 1964. Life history of the Boucard tinamou in British Honduras, part 2. Breeding biology. *Condor* 66:253–76.

Leopold, A. S. 1959. *Wildlife of Mexico.* Berkeley and Los Angeles: University of California Press.

Slud, P. 1964. The birds of Costa Rica: Distribution and ecology. *Bull. Am. Mus. Nat. Hist.* 128:1–430.

Cyanocorax morio (Urraca Parda, Piapia, Brown Jay)

M. F. Lawton

The most homely of the Neotropical jays, the brown jay has neither crest nor gaudy plumage to distinguish it. However, it is a large, noisy, conspicuous bird, not shy of man, and consequently easy to study. It is widespread in disturbed habitats from the Río Grande Valley of Mexico to the Bocas del Toro mountains of northern Panama. In recent years its range has been expanding north into Texas and south into central Panama.

Although it was originally described in 1829 (*Pica morio* Wagler), its taxonomic status is still not well understood. From a genus (*Psilorhinus*) composed of two species (*P. mexicanus* and *P. morio*), the bird has been demoted first to a monotypic genus (*P. morio*) and most recently to a subgenus of the *Cyanocorax* jays. In lowland Costa Rica brown jays occasionally flock with magpie jays (*Cyanocorax* [*Calocitta*] *formosa*), and in Mexico a hybrid of these two forms has been collected (Pitelka, Selander, and Del Torro 1956).

Like a number of their congeners, at birth brown jays have yellow eye rings, bills, legs, and feet. As the birds age these soft parts darken in idiosyncratic patterns, making it possible to identify and roughly age individuals without trapping and color banding. Information on population structure and dynamics can therefore be gathered in a relatively short time, unusual in avian populations.

Brown jays live in flocks with apparently stable membership throughout the year. The birds prefer disturbed habitat, and their home ranges comprise a mosaic of pastures, windbreaks, old fields, and banana patches. Flocks of six to ten birds utilize 3–5 ha home ranges, defending a territory within the home range only while breeding.

Like most corvids, brown jays are omnivorous and forage in a variety of habitats. Flocks move as a group between habitats (e.g., from pasture to windbreak), but birds forage individually. When widely dispersed or in areas of low visibility, they maintain contact vocally.

The jays forage at all levels and display a wide variety of foraging techniques. When feeding on insects, birds will flake bark from limbs or prod into the decaying wood of fallen logs. They are adept at catching flying insects, often flying convoluted loops after their prey. At times they perch on snags and make sudden, flycatcherlike sallies after flying insects. While foraging near the forest floor, the jays will often investigate the undersides of leaves, taking spiders and pupae when found.

Although in the cool mountains where they have been most closely watched they rarely approach standing water, occasionally the jays have been observed sipping from epiphytic bromeliads. They probably get most of their water from fruits, of which they take a wide variety, both wild and domestic, throughout the year. Their occasional practice of looting the nests of other species, and their regular marauding in cornfields and orchards, have earned brown jays a bad name in Costa Rica.

The aspect of the biology of the brown jay that has received the most attention is its breeding behavior. As

Skutch (1935, 1960) reported, brown jays are cooperative breeders with helpers at the nest. Recently a long-term study has been conducted in Monteverde (Lawton 1979; Lawton and Guindon 1981), a dairy-farming community at about 1,500 m elevation in the Cordillera de Tilarán in northern Costa Rica. Some of the findings of that study are at remarkable variance with those reported by Skutch and may, in part, be due to geographic variation between the populations studied. The student is urged to read Skutch's pioneering accounts.

In Monteverde the breeding season occurs during the dry-season months of January to May. During the courtship and nest-building months of January and February the climate is dominated by the Atlantic trade winds that sweep across the community, often driving a cold, stinging mist before them. These storms, called *temporales,* persist from 4 to 8 days and appear to complicate nest-site selection. Indeed, the effect of the temporales on nest sites was abundantly demonstrated in 1978, when in mid-April an unusually late temporale swept hurricane-force winds through the community. Ten of twelve nests under observation at that time were destroyed by the winds.

As the dry season progresses, the build-up of warm air on the Pacific slope begins to stall the trade winds, and the strength and frequency of the temporales abate. It is during the calm months of March through May that eggs are laid and nestlings hatched and reared.

Nests are generally constructed by the flock's oldest members, usually a single pair. Younger flock members help build and will occasionally sit on the nest, but their efforts are irregular. In flocks compoased entirely of birds 1 and 2 years old, nest building is a protracted affair that may last up to 3 months.

Nests are almost invariably built in isolated trees in pastures. Site selection may be a response to predation pressure; in the few instances when nests were built in windbreaks, the nests invariably suffered predation. Surprisingly, in two years only one of more than thirty nests built in isolated trees failed owing to predation.

During the protracted period between the completion of a nest and egg laying, females spend increasing amounts of time sitting on their nests, giving a distinctive whine call that can be heard for a quarter of a mile. (This bizarre behavior, not yet fully understood, makes finding nests ridiculously easy and is a trait one would assume would attract the attention of every conceivable predator. That it does not result in the annihilation of the species is one of nature's unsolved mysteries.) Often, more than one female flock member will call simultaneously, one on the nest, another nearby. In the interim before egg laying, it is not unusual for several flock members—in one case five in one day—to take turns sitting on the nest.

Egg laying and egg ownership within flocks are among the most poorly understood, if crucial, aspects of brown jay breeding behavior. In some nests more than one egg per day appears, clear indication that more than one female has contributed to the clutch. How frequently this occurs is unknown. That the average clutch in Monteverde (4.5) is close to twice that reported by Skutch suggests that it is not uncommon.

There is great interflock variability in incubation and brooding behavior. In one flock where more than one female was definitely known to have laid eggs, more than two hundred hours of observation showed that only one bird incubated and brooded. On the other hand, in a flock where egg ownership was unclear, but where it was obvious that birds were tossing each other's eggs out of the nest, three birds shared the duties of incubation and brooding. At none of sixteen flocks observed over a two-year period, however, was there evidence that only one pair participated in courtship, copulation, egg laying, incubation and brooding. These observations suggest that in this population there are multiple pathways to breeding status, and that intraflock competition for breeding status occurs.

All flock members feed nestlings. However, there are great differences between individuals in how much food they deliver and when they deliver it. Quantitative description and analysis of nestling care is presented elsewhere (Lawton, n.d.) and suggests that inter- and intraflock differences are the result of flock composition, history, and probable breeding status of the individual.

*

Lawton, M. F. 1979. The breeding behavior of the brown jay in Monteverde: A variable mating system. In manuscript.

———. n.d. Nestling care among brown jays: Inter- and intra-flock comparisons. In preparation.

Lawton, M. F., and Guindon, C. F. 1981. Flock composition, breeding success and learning among brown jays (*Cyanocorax* [*Psilorhinus*] *morio*). *Condor* 83:27–33.

Pitelka, F. A.; Selander, R. K.; and Del Torro, M. A. 1956. A hybrid jay from Chiapas, Mexico. *Condor* 58:98–106.

Skutch, A. F. 1935. Helpers at the nest. *Auk* 52:257–73.

———. 1960. *Life histories of Central American birds.* Pacific Coast Avifauna, no. 34. Berkeley: Cooper Ornithological Society.

Cypseloides rutilus (Vencejo Cuellicastaño, Golondrina, Chestnut-collared Swift)

C. T. Collins

The chestnut-collared swift (*Cypseloides rutilus*) occurs widely from Mexico to Peru and Bolivia as well as eastward to Trinidad. Within Costa Rica it is more commonly associated with the central highlands region and mountain slopes but is also at times recorded throughout the lowlands (Slud 1964). This in part reflects the incredible mobility of swifts. The approximately seventy-eight species in this family are among the most aerial of birds, catching nearly all their food on the wing and, in some cases, spending the night aloft as well as copulating on the wing. They range in size from the diminutive pygmy palm swift (*Micropanyptila furcata*) of Venezuela, which may weigh only 6–7 g, up to several giants, including the white-naped swift (*Streptoprocne semicollaris*) of western Mexico, which approaches 180–200 g body weight. At 20.2 g (Collins 1968), the chestnut-collared swift is one of the six medium to small swifts that coexist in Costa Rica.

Few swifts have sexual differences in plumage coloration as is typical of chestnut-collared swifts. In this case the male has a complete collar of chestnut brown that expands ventrally to include most of the upper breast and throat. Females typically lack all chestnut coloration but on occasion have a partial collar or nape band, and rarely a full collar. Juveniles, contrary to several published accounts, all have a partial collar and distinctive chestnut edges to many of the crown and nape feathers. The chestnut coloration is not usually seen in the field unless the observer is lucky enough to be above the swifts or can otherwise view them against a dark background; in silhouette little other than a black shape can be seen. Even then their distinctively narrower and uniformly tapered wings and longer tail will serve to separate them from the several species of *Chaetura* swifts with which they frequently occur. Only size, a very poor character for swifts high overhead, would likely be of any use in separating them from the two other similar-sized species of *Cypseloides*, *C. cherriei* at 23 g and *C. cryptus* at 30 g.

The swifts of the genera *Cypseloides* and *Streptoprocne* form the distinctive subfamily Cypseloidinae. They all show a distinct affinity for water and waterfalls as an essential ingredient of their nesting/roosting ecology. The larger species actually nest on mossy ledges behind waterfalls, at times dashing through films or torrents of water to reach their damp, dark sanctuary. The smaller species tend to build a nest of moss, ferns, and similar plant material on a dark rock surface over a pool of water or in the spray zone around small waterfalls. Perhaps as a constraint imposed by this nest site, clutch sizes are small, two for *C. rutilus,* and the nestling period approaches 40 days. Growth of the young is slower than for a similar-sized species of *Chaetura* (Collins 1968), and the young develop a distinctive downlike nestling covering, consisting of adult semiplumes that grow in early, as an aid to nestling thermoregulation in this cool envi-

ronment (Collins 1963). These nest and roost sites seem to be less accessible to predators, and nest success is greater than for some other swifts. Adult survival is also very high (83%; Collins 1974), and some individuals most certainly reach ages of 20–25 years or more.

Like other swifts, the chestnut-collared swift spends nearly all the daylight hours on the wing, where it captures most or all of its food from the abundant arthropods that make up a form of aerial plankton. The birds take a wide array of types and sizes of insects and, like other swifts, probably take ballooning spiders when available. For *C. rutilus* the maximum prey size seems to be about 10 mm in length (Collins 1968). Larger swifts seem to take larger prey items. This may well be the basis of a form of resource partitioning. Shifts in preferred feeding zones are also quite likely among species taking similar-sized food items. This topic is currently under study (Collins, in prep., Hespenheide 1971, 1975, in prep.) and should do much to clarify the problems of coexistence in an aerial environment. For an update on the spot-fronted swift, *C. cherriei,* see Collins (1970).

Although their mobility makes swifts at time frustrating subjects for study, much is still to be learned about them, particularly in Costa Rica.

*

Collins, C. T. 1963. The "downy" nestling plumage of swifts of the genus *Cypseloides*. *Condor* 65:324–28.
———. 1968. The comparative biology of two species of swifts in Trinidad, West Indies. *Bull. Florida State Mus.* 11:257–320.
———. 1974. Survival rate of the chestnut-collared swift. *Western Bird Bander* 49:10–13.
———. 1980. The biology of the spot-fronted swift in Venezuela. *Am. Birds* 34:852–55.
Hespenheide, H. A. 1971. Food preference and the extent of overlap in some insectivorous birds, with special reference to the Tyrannidae. *Ibis* 113:59–72.
———. 1975. Selective predation by two swifts and a swallow in Central America. *Ibis* 117:82–99.
Slud, P. 1964. The birds of Costa Rica: Distribution and Ecology. *Bull. Am. Mus. Nat. Hist.* 128:1–430.

Dendroica petechia (Reinita Amarilla, Cazadorcita, Mangrove Warbler, Yellow Warbler)

H. Wagner

The yellow warbler, or mangrove warbler (fig. 10.31) as the tropical races are called, is a rarity among migratory species. Some of the geographical races are migratory, leaving the tropics to breed in the north temperate zone; many of the geographical races are yearround tropical residents. The tropical residents are found exclusively in

FIGURE 10.31. *Dendroica petechia,* adult. Costa Rica (photo, F. G. Stiles).

mangrove swamps except on islands, where, presumably, release from competitive pressures enables the birds to exist in many different habitats. On Cozumel Island, off the Yucatan Peninsula, the resident yellow warbler is found in all habitats *except* mangroves. The migrants are found in mangrove swamps to some extent but are also found in most other tropical habitats, especially in secondary growth and semiarid woodland. They are not found in the forest interior. In some localities, both the yellow warbler and the mangrove warbler are found in the mangroves. Sometimes either one or the other occurs but not both. The yellow warbler is found in Costa Rica from mid-August through mid-May.

The yellow warbler represents a taxonomic problem. There are three well-defined groups of races (sometimes considered two or three species): the northern migratory *D. p. aestum* group with all-yellow heads; the chestnut-headed, resident *D. p. enthachorides* group (true mangrove warblers); and the similarly resident, more or less rufous-faced *D. p. petechia* group (golden warblers) of the West Indies, the Galápagos, and Isla del Coco. Certainly the two forms in Costa Rica (resident mangroves and migrant yellows) are ecologically different species (Slud 1964). In Costa Rica, migrant yellow warblers are common from the lowlands to middle elevations on both slopes; they prefer low scrub and open areas with scattered trees and shrubs. Mangrove warblers are common in mangrove swamps the length of the Pacific slope, and very locally on the Caribbean slope.

The range of the mangrove warbler coincides to a large extent with the range of mangroves in the New World. It does not extend to the east farther than Venezuela, however. The species is found in the Galápagos Islands, throughout much of the West Indies, Florida, and as far north as the mangroves extend in the Gulf of California and the Gulf of Mexico. The yellow warbler breeds over most of North America, up into Alaska.

Both the yellow warbler and the mangrove warbler are primarily insectivorous, gleaning insects from the bark, foliage, and roots of trees and shrubs. On occasion they snap up flying insects, often hovering in place for several seconds. They are also seen foraging on the mud in mangrove swamps at low tide.

Distinctive plumage differences between the mangrove warbler and the yellow warbler occur only in the adult males. The male mangrove warbler has a chestnut hood or cap and streakings on the breast and belly; the male yellow warbler has only the chestnut streaking. Female mangrove warblers are distinguishable, at least in Costa Rica, by the rufous tinge to the crown and face. Mangrove warblers are also larger than yellow warblers (11–12 g vs. 8–10 g).

Both the yellow warbler and the mangrove warbler are territorial year-round. In the nonbreeding season, their territories contain only a single bird, male or female. Although females and immature males may defend their own territories in the nonbreeding season, they often join mixed-species flocks. Some northern races of the yellow are particularly dull in plumage in the immature and rarely hold territories. It is postulated (Morton 1976) that, because they arrive later in the year owing to a longer migratory path, it is more profitable for those individuals to remain unrecognized by conspecific territory holders and thereby avoid aggression than it would be to establish a marginal territory.

The mangrove warbler breeds from April through July. The nest, a compact cup, is usually placed in the fork of a shrub or tree. It is made of vegetable fibers and fine grasses and lined with plant down and hair. The species can recognize alien—in this case, cowbird—eggs in its nest. The yellow warbler builds a new nest directly on top of the old, burying the contents of the first. Three- and four-layered nests have been found. The number of eggs laid is two to five, and eggs are greenish white with brown splotching. Incubation starts when the last egg is laid and lasts 11 to 12 days. The fledglings leave the nest 8 to 10 days after hatching—unless disturbed. The nestlings are fed insects by both parents, and this continues after fledging until the young are self-sufficient.

Mortality in small birds such as the mangrove warbler is very high at the egg, nestling, and fledgling stages owing to predation from ants, snakes, and other bird species. Adult mortality is much lower, but the hazards of migration may be a significant factor in the mortality of the adult yellow warbler.

*

Morton, E. S. 1976. The adaptive significance of dull coloration in yellow warblers. *Condor* 78:423.
Slud, P. 1964. The birds of Costa Rica: Distribution and ecology. *Bull. Am. Mus. Nat. Hist.* 128:1–430.

Eumomota superciliosa (Pajaro Bobo, Momoto Cejiceleste, Turquoise-browed Motmot)

S. M. Smith

The turquoise-browed motmot (fig. 10.32) is among the most beautiful of Costa Rican birds. Among its more striking features are the wide turquoise "brow" stripe, the typical motmot black mask outlined below with turquoise, the black throat streak bordered with turquoise, and the two long back-curved, racket-tipped central tail feathers. The head and breast are olive green, the belly is buff, and the back is rich chestnut. This is a relatively small motmot, weighing approximately 60–65 g.

Turquoise-browed motmots reach the southern limit of their range in Costa Rica, where they are restricted to the tropical dry forest of Guanacaste and northern Puntarenas. Here they are found in arid open country and forest edges, often conspicuously perched on telephone wires or even fence posts along roads. When alarmed, they swing their tails from side to side like pendulums, a behavior pattern typical of many motmots. They have a dipping flight pattern.

Being in the same avian order as kingfishers, turquoise-browed motmots nest in burrows in the earth, especially in stream banks and road cuts. Their tunnels are often 1.5 m or more in length. Both sexes share in excavation, incubation, and feeding of young. Clutches are generally three or four eggs. The young are altricial and do not leave the burrow until almost 4 weeks after hatching, usually about July. They remain dependent on their parents for at least another 4 weeks.

Calls of this species are many and varied. Perhaps the most commonly heard call is a simple *honk,* vaguely similar to a distant train whistle. Another common call, often given by more than one bird, can be written *ka-wukawuk* and is generally given repeatedly, often in chorus. This call is most often heard at dawn or dusk.

Turquoise-browed motmots have long, powerful beaks, and besides eating many large insects and spiders they often catch small reptiles such as lizards and snakes. Hand-reared inexperienced young birds have been shown to avoid wooden sticks painted with a generalized coral snake pattern; apparently this species does not have to learn to avoid this potentially lethal "prey."

Although the typical adult central tail feathers have bare shafts between the base and the racket tips, these feathers do not grow this way. Instead there is at first a complete blade, although the barbs to be lost are shorter, and more loosely attached, than the permanent barbs at either end of the feather. Although I often watched my hand-reared motmots preening their tail feathers, I never saw them remove these central barbs this way; rather, they simply brushed them off against the branches in their cage in normal flight. I suspect they are lost in wild birds in the same manner.

*

Orejuela, J. E. 1977. Comparative biology of turquoise-browed and blue-crowned motmots in the Yucatan Peninsual, Mexico. *Living Bird* 16:193–208.

Skutch, A. F. 1947. Life history of the turquoise-browed motmot. *Auk* 64:201–17.

Smith, S. M. 1975. Innate recognition of coral snake pattern by a possible avian predator. *Science* 187:759–60.

———. 1977. The behavior and vocalizations of young turquoise-browed motmots. *Biotropica* 9:127–30.

FIGURE 10.32. *Eumomota superciliosa,* adult with fully developed tail feathers. Guanacaste Province, Costa Rica (photo, F. G. Stiles).

Fregata magnificens (Rabihorcado Magno, Tijereta, Tijerilla, Magnificent Frigatebird)

R. W. Schreiber

The frigatebirds (fig. 10.33) are an exclusively marine pantropical family. Two species are restricted to individual islands (*Fregata andrewsi* to Christmas Island, Indian Ocean, and *F. aquila* to Ascension Island, central Atlantic). *F. magnificens* (magnificent frigatebird) is widely distributed in the Caribbean, the Gulf of Mexico, several locations in the Atlantic, the Pacific coast between Baja California and Peru, and the Galápagos. *F. minor* (great

FIGURE 10.33. *Fregata magnificens,* adult with wings slightly cocked downward to begin dive (photo, R. W. Schreiber).

frigate) is sympatric with *F. magnificens* on the Galápagos and is found throughout the tropical Pacific and Indian oceans, often also sympatrically with *F. ariel* (lesser frigate) on about half their breeding sites, although *F. minor* extends somewhat farther north. Data on breeding locations, timing of nesting, and isolating mechanisms are needed.

In Costa Rica the magnificent frigatebird is apparently a nonbreeding visitant present in good numbers year-round. The species is exceedingly abundant around Puntarenas (where adult males make up 70–90% of the population) and on the Golfo de Nicoya (still a preponderance of males); many roost on Cabo Blanco (sometimes up to 30% or more females). In general, frigatebirds are more abundant on the Pacific than on the Caribbean coast.

The family is a closely knit group; all members have extremely small tarsi and feet. All are basically black with some white in the breast, primarily in females and juveniles, who also have white heads. Rufous is present in the young of some species. The ballooning red gular pouch of the displaying males indicates courtship activity. The family is adapted to highly specialized feeding by snatching flying fish and squid from the water surface. They never naturally enter the water. Various species weigh between 800 and 1,700 g, extremely light for a bird with a 2 m wingspan, and the wing loading is lower than in any other known bird. The wings are long and pointed and the tail is deeply forked, giving the characteristic flight profile. The coracoid and furcula are fused to the sternum, the only such instance in birds. Field identification of the various species is often very difficult, and the major isolating mechanisms between the species are bill size, eye-ring color, and behavior.

While population size of most species is unknown, probably five hundred thousand pairs of *F. magnificens* make it the most abundant species, although individual colonies of any species rarely contain more than ten thousand pairs. Only ten thousand total *F. aquila* and fewer than one thousand pairs of *F. andrewsi* exist. Habitat destruction and man-introduced cats, rats, pigs, and so on cause severe population problems.

Frigatebirds nest in bushes, and consistent winds seem to be important in nest-site selection, since they have difficulty in landing and in becoming airborne. They rarely spend extended periods in the air but prefer to roost for the night, although at times they are found far from land. The migration patterns are unknown for most species, but the central Pacific *F. ariel* moves downwind to the western Pacific during the first years of life before returning to its nesting islands. Nests are in colonies that form around displaying males. The nest is jealously guarded by both males and females, who share incubation duties, although the male gathers the nesting material and the female does the building. The single egg is large but fragile and requires about 55 days of incubation. The slow-growing nestlings are dependent on their parents for 6 months, then after fledging they return nightly and are fed primarily by the female for up to 14 months more—among the longest dependence periods known in birds. The breeding strategy needs documentation, but males may be breeding once a year and females only every second year. Males are considerably smaller than females. Most mortality of young occurs during the nestling stage or as the young are acquiring independence. Frigatebirds and other marine species are adapted to an erratic "boom or bust" food availability with their deferred maturity (onset of breeding at 5 to 8 years), long life-span (probably 40 years or more), and low reproductive potential. All aspects of the breeding cycle need further elicidation.

Frigatebirds have a spectacular habit of parasitizing other birds for food (kleptoparasitism), but the role of this feeding method in the total feeding regime needs investigation. Differences exist in the level of kleptoparasitism in different species and between the ages and sexes in different locations. Frigates also assume a "sunning" posture whose function is totally unknown but that is probably related to thermoregulation.

*

Harrington, B. A.; Schreiber, R. W.; and Woolfenden, G. E. 1972. The distribution of male and female magnificent frigatebirds, *Fregata magnificens,* along the Gulf coast of Florida. *Am. Birds* 26:927–31.

Nelson, J. B. 1976. The breeding biology of frigatebirds: *A comparative review. Living Bird* 14:113–55. (This "review" contains a great deal of inaccurate data with much speculation and should not be viewed as the definitive statement on the family.)

Sibley, F. C., and Clapp, R. B. 1967. Distribution and dispersal of central Pacific lesser frigatebirds *Fregata ariel. Ibis* 109:328–37.

Stiles, F. G., and Smith, S. M. 1977. New information on Costa Rican waterbirds. *Condor* 79:90–97.

Galbula ruficauda (Jacamar Rabirrufo, Gorrión de Montaña, Rufous-tailed Jacamar)

T. W. Sherry

The rufous-tailed jacamar (*Galbula ruficauda,* Galbulidae) is one reason bird watchers go to the Neotropics. Its brilliant, iridescent blue green head, back, and central tail feathers, long and uptilted bill, and spectacular insect pursuits in open habitats have gained the bird more notice in the literature than most other tropical birds. It is rich rufous on the breast, belly, and outer two pairs of tail feathers; the throat is either white (male) or light rufous (female). Skutch (1963) describes jacamars as "electrified with a high voltage." "Imagine," he said, "a small, glittering hummingbird enlarged to the size of a starling with no loss of daintiness or brilliance."

Skutch (1963) and Slud (1964) both describe the habitat and distribution of *Galbula ruficauda* in Costa Rica. It is primarily a lowland bird, reaching to about 1,000 m elevation on both Atlantic and Pacific slopes, but it does not occur in northern Guanacaste Province. It is found in forested regions but prefers tangles, cutover woodland borders, dense streamside thickets, and thickety second growth near or within forest. Skutch (1963) indicates that it likes little-disturbed forest in the Pacific southwest of the country. Whether its habitat preferences are related more to foraging behavior or nesting requirements is not known (see below).

Phylogenetically the status of jacamars is uncertain. They are generally considered closely related to puffbirds (Bucconidae), and both families are placed in the order Piciformes (with toucans, barbets, and woodpeckers, for example), but both jacamars and puffbirds may be more closely related to Coraciiformes (motmots, todies, kingfishers, and Old World bee-eaters) on the basis of eggwhite protein similarity (Sibley and Ahlquist 1972). *Galbula ruficauda* belongs to the *G. galbula* superspecies comprising five parapatric species, and Costa Rican birds belong to the (variably) black-chinned subspecies, *G. r. melanogenia* (Haffer 1974). As a whole the family contains eight genera and seventeen species, thirteen of which belong to superspecies complexes, thus indicating fairly recent, Pleistocene, radiation of the family at the

species level (Haffer 1974). The only other Costa Rican jacamar, *Jacamerops aurea,* is monotypic. It is quite different from *Galbula,* being larger (66.8 g, $N = 3$, vs. 27 g, $N = 14$, for *Galbula;* Sherry, unpub. data), a forest bird, and widespread through much of the Neotropics, though rare throughout. *Jacamerops* has a shorter, wider, and more decurved bill than *Galbula.*

Prey selection merits some discussion because of the unusual morphology and spectacular foraging flights of *Galbula.* One cannot fail to notice its occasional dashes after such butterflies as a *Morpho.* A more detailed account and review of prey selection, morphology, and foraging behavior in jacamars is forthcoming (Sherry, in prep.; and Sherry and DeVries, in prep.). Typically the rufous-tailed jacamar sallies after flying insects in often acrobatic pursuits, and a bird tends to return to a temporarily favored perch before subsequent sallies (Skutch 1937, 1963; Slud 1964). What is less widely appreciated is its regular snatching of prey from vegetation (Sherry, in prep.). I have also seen it trooping with antwren flocks in primary forest understory in the Caribbean lowlands of Costa Rica. But *Galbula* is best typified as a forest-edge predator on large, soft-bodied, and agile insects—Lepidoptera, Odonata, and some Hymenoptera and Diptera. Several morphological characteristics are probably related to this pursuit of insects: relatively narrow and long wings, and a tail that is long and fully developed for agility in flight (see account of ruddy-tailed flycatcher, *Terenotriccus erythrurus*).

The long jacamar bill, which looks better suited to opening letters than catching insects, is its most distinctive morphological characteristic. Three hypotheses have been advanced for bill length and shape: (1) It is primarily adapted to handle venomous Hymenoptera (Fry 1970*b*). The bill length would keep stinging insects away from the face and provide leverage for beating insects against the perch. (2) Mechanically, the tips of a bill can move more rapidly, for a given muscle force, through an arc the greater the radius (bill length) of the arc, thus facilitating capture of agile insects while in flight (Lederer 1975). (3) Skutch (1963) has stressed the importance of Lepidoptera and Odonata in the jacamar diet, implying the adaptiveness of the bill in capturing and handling such long-bodied, long-winged prey. A long bill would thus serve to reach past the insect's wings and secure it by the body. These three hypotheses are not mutually exclusive. The flimsiness of the bill would make rapid movement easier but would prohibit use of prey that necessitate more massive, crushing bills (see account of nunbird, *Monasa morphoeus*).

Notes on the prey of *Galbula* are abundant, if fragmentary (Skutch 1937, 1963; Fry 1970*a,b;* Haverschmidt 1968; Burton 1976; Hespenheide, unpub.; Sherry, unpub.; and Remsen, pers. comm.). The birds take a variety of insect prey. A few Homoptera, Hemiptera, Diptera, Coleoptera, and adult Lepidoptera are consistently in the diet. Odonata and Hymenoptera often predominate. Whereas Fry has stressed the importance of Hymenoptera, particularly venomous types, in *Galbula* diets, Skutch has emphasized Odonata and Lepidoptera. I think the difference in emphasis stems not from work on different species in different geographic locations, but from different seasons of observation. Skutch reported on breeding jacamars that probably include more large forms—Lepidoptera and Odonata—in the diet for efficiency of transport to nestlings. Jacamars may schedule nesting to correspond with peak abundances of such items. Fry's (1970*b*) data show that nestlings were fed proportionately more Lepidoptera and Odonata than adults consumed. Odonata and Lepidoptera together dominated nestling diets at a nest I observed at Finca La Selva, Costa Rica, in May 1978, whereas I have rarely observed adults taking such prey outside the breeding season. In certain habitats or parts of the nesting cycle the birds do take many Hymenoptera such as euglossine bees, judging by the remains of such insects in nesting burrows (F. Stiles, pers. comm.).

Jacamars apparently do not randomly select Lepidoptera, though data are scarce. Skutch (1937, 1963) noted that they rarely if ever take heliconiine butterflies, presumably because they are unpalatable. I have seen the birds ignore these butterflies (or mimics) even when they flew right past. Two observations are relevant to the evolution of unpalatability in butterflies (Sherry and DeVries, in prep.): The nymphalid butterfly *Nessaea aglaura* was eaten once and rejected once by the adults at one nest; and an adult *Catagramma bugaba,* also a nymphalid, was still living when it was rejected by a jacamar that had caught it, allowing that its unpalatability could be detected and it could still live to reproduce—thus distastefulness could evolve via individual selection. *Morpho cypris* butterflies were successfully captured twice and missed twice, indicating that the jacamar can capture Lepidoptera that are among the best fliers, though with difficulty.

Several very interesting accounts treat jacamar equivalents or close competitors. Fry (1970*a,b*) argues that bee-eaters (Meropidae) are the Old World equivalents of Galbulidae on the basis of morphological and plumage convergence and extent of diet similarity. He also discusses the Meropidae in detail (Fry 1969). Burton (1976) compares and contrasts the foraging and diet in relation to morphology of the sympatric paradise jacamar (*Galbula dea*) and swallow-wing (*Chelidoptera tenebrosa,* Bucconidae) in Surinam, two species that are very similar ecologically.

Skutch (1937, 1963, 1968, and included references) discusses breeding and nesting biology in detail. Jacamars build their own burrow nests, generally in vertical or steeply inclined banks or upturned root masses, but sometimes in termite nests as well. These upturned root masses are an important site for jacamars in flat areas in Costa Rica, and the tree-fall gap created provides a good foraging site (F. Stiles, pers. comm.). They nest solitarily in 0.3–0.5 m-long burrows that they sometimes reuse in subsequent breeding efforts. In Central America eggs are generally produced from March to June. Skutch has observed two- and three-egg clutches in Costa Rica and four-egg clutches in Guatemala and Venezuela; F. Stiles (pers. comm.) has also observed three- and four-egg clutches in Costa Rica. The 19–23-day incubation period is long for similar-sized piciforms but about right for burrow-nesting coraciiforms. The nestling period is 18–26 days for *G. ruficauda,* and some evidence suggests that the duration of the nestling period depends on local ecological conditions, time of year, or both (Skutch 1963). Nestlings call persistently from the nest after about 6 days of age, but this apparently does not affect nest predation, since the major (mammalian) predators do not cue on the sounds of the nestlings (Skutch 1963).

Plumage dimorphism has aided study of sexual reproductive roles. Skutch (1963) observed that both sexes incubate and feed nestlings, but that females incubate at night. Skutch also observed differences in nestling-feeding behavior of the adults. Males delivered food more often and consistently hunted nearer the nest than females. I observed precisely this pattern at a nest at Finca La Selva, Costa Rica; the female at this nest also tended to return with larger items (Odonata) than the male. Why the male tends to stay nearer the nest than the female, if this is a consistent pattern, is not known.

*

Burton, P. J. K. 1976. Feeding behavior in the paradise jacamar and the swallow-wing. *Living Bird* 15: 223–38.

Fry, C. H. 1969. The recognition and treatment of venomous and non-venomous insects by small bee-eaters. *Ibis* 111:23–29.

———. 1970*a*. Convergence between jacamars and bee-eaters. *Ibis* 112:257–59.

———. 1970*b*. Ecological distribution of birds in northeastern Mato Grosso State, Brazil. *An. Acad. Brasil. Ciênc.* 42:275–318.

Haffer, J. 1974. Avian speciation in tropical South America. *Publ. Nuttall Ornithol. Club* 14:1–390.

Haverschmidt, F. 1968. *Birds of Surinam.* London: Oliver and Boyd.

Lederer, R. J. 1975. Bill size, food size, and forces of insectivorous birds. *Auk* 92:385–87.

Sibley, C. G., and Ahlquist, J. E. 1972. A comparative study of the egg white proteins of non-passerine birds. *Bull. Peabody Mus. Nat. Hist.* 39:1–276.

Skutch, A. F. 1937. Life history of the black-chinned jacamar. *Auk* 54:135–46.

———. 1963. Life history of the rufous-tailed jacamar *Galbula ruficauda* in Costa Rica. *Ibis* 105:354–68.

———. 1968. The nesting of some Venezuelan birds. *Condor* 70:66–82.

Slud, P. 1964. The birds of Costa Rica: Distribution and ecology. *Bull. Am. Mus. Nat. Hist.* 128:1–430.

Geotrygon montana (Paloma-perdiz Rojiza, Ruddy Quail Dove)

A. F. Skutch

The fifteen species of quail doves of the genus *Geotrygon* are stout, quaillike, terrestrial pigeons of tropical American woodlands. The most widespread and successful of these pigeons is the ruddy quail dove (fig. 10.34), which ranges through humid forests from southeastern Mexico to Bolivia and Paraguay and occurs also in the Greater Antilles—one of the few small terrestrial birds these islands share with the tropical American mainland. In Costa Rica it is found from the lowlands of the Caribbean and southern Pacific up to about 1,100 m. The male is largely rufous chestnut; the female is more brownish and olive.

One most frequently sees these doves walking over the leaf-strewn ground in the deep shade of forest undergrowth, with heads nodding and bills inclined strongly downward. They may try to escape detection by walking rapidly into concealing vegetation or, if alarmed, fly low until lost amid the trees. They are capable of long, sustained flight, which they occasionally use to cross clearings. With the destruction of ancient forests they adapt to tall second growth, and they may even emerge to forage

FIGURE 10.34. *Geotrygon montana,* suspended (dying) by foot where it is caught in an axillary fork of a climbing vine. Finca La Selva, Sarapiquí District, Costa Rica (photo, A. Cry).

on bare, shady ground in dooryards, especially while light is dim. Their food is fallen berries, seeds, and small invertebrates, all gathered from the ground.

The quail-dove's call is a low, moaning *cooo,* heard chiefly from March to June. It is delivered from the ground or from a perch, rarely as much as 7 m up, and may be continued for many minutes at the rate of about twenty calls per minute. The quail dove's *cooo* is easily confused with that of the gray-chested dove (*Leptotila cassinii*), which inhabits the same woodlands but enters clearings and light thickets much more frequently than the quail-dove does. Ruddy quail doves are found singly or in pairs, never in flocks.

In the valley of El General, quail doves lay eggs from February to August, and the height of the breeding season is from April to July, when the forest is wet from frequent rains. For its nest, which may be as low as 45 cm and is rarely as high as 3 m, the quail dove selects almost anything able to support such a slight, loose construction. A favorite site is the broad surface of a fallen palm frond that has lodged horizontally amid the undergrowth. Often the doves build more securely on the thick, clustered, living leaves of an aroid, fern, or bromeliad growing on a trunk or rock. Frequently they choose the top of a low, decaying stump or the interlacing branches of shrubs and tangles of vines. The slightly concave platform is composed of dead twigs and petioles, covered with small leaves that may be green or brown. Additional leaves are brought while incubation is in progress.

Like most, but by no means all, members of the pigeon family, quail doves lay two eggs. Unlike most pigeons' eggs, these are more or less buffy, without markings. Apparently correlated with this less conspicuous coloration, the first egg is left uncovered much of the time until the second is laid, about midday more than 24 h later. (Many pigeons sit over their first white egg during this interval.) The quail doves incubate according to the widespread pigeon pattern, with the male taking one long daytime session lasting 8 or 9 h and the female sitting from mid- or late afternoon until her mate replaces her next morning. Accordingly, they change over only twice daily. The incubation period of only 11 days is exceptionally short for pigeons, many species of which take 2 weeks or more to hatch their eggs.

The nestlings are fed in the usual pigeon manner, by regurgitation from the crop. At first, while still sightless, they are usually fed singly; but after their eyes open they insert their bills on opposite sides of the parent's mouth and receive their food simultaneously. As they grow older, the number of meals per day decreases, but each apparently becomes more copious. The nestlings' development is so rapid that they remain on the nest only 10 days, at which age they fly strongly. If disturbed, they may jump to the ground and walk steadily away when only 8 days old. A month after their departure, the parents may refurbish the old nest and lay again.

Among the adaptations that make ruddy quail doves highly successful inhabitants of predator-infested tropical forests are the buffy (rather than white) eggs, in a small, inconspicuous nest that they keep clean by swallowing empty shells and all droppings (rather exceptional among pigeons), and the extremely short incubation and nestling periods. The parents' often prolonged distraction displays, or "injury feigning," may lure enemies away from eggs or young. Nevertheless, of seventeen nests of known outcome, only five, or 29.4%, were successful.

*

Skutch, A. F. 1949. Life history of the ruddy quail-dove. *Condor* 51:3–19.

Wetmore, A. 1968. The birds of the Republic of Panamá, part 2. *Smithsonian Misc. Coll.*, vol. 150.

Herpetotheres cachinnans (Guaco, Laughing Falcon)

A. F. Skutch

Plumage and voice make this stout, short-winged, long-tailed hawk (fig. 10.35) exceptionally easy to recognize. In both sexes the dorsal plumage and wings are dark brown, and the blackish tail is crossed by four or five broad white bands. The notably large head and all the underparts are white or nearly so, except for the broad black mask that covers the cheeks and extends to the hindhead. The vernacular name "guaco" is a good rendition of its loud, far-carrying call, which sounds like *wah-*

FIGURE 10.35. *Herpetotheres cachinnans,* with downy nestling in a hollow high in a great trunk of a forest tree. Costa Rica (drawing, A. F. Skutch).

co, wah-co, usually repeated many times, in a "hollow" voice that seems mysterious, especially when heard at night, as it frequently is. (This call is sometimes confused with that of the collared forest-falcon, *Micrastur semitorquatus,* which is rather similar in tone but different in phrasing.) Less frequently heard, because much fainter, is the rapid *ha-ha-ha* that sounds like subdued human laughter. Other notes sound like *how-how-how, haw-haw,* and *wac-wac;* and low throaty notes are heard at close range.

The laughing falcon is found in wet forests and arid woodlands from northern Mexico to northern Argentina. In Central America it ranges from both coasts up to (rarely) about 1,800 m. A rather sluggish, slow-flying bird, it is often seen at the forest edge or in a clearing, perching conspicuously on a stub or branch. Where it has not been persecuted, it often permits one to watch it as long as one wishes. From such a high lookout, it scrutinizes the thicket or grass below for the snakes that are, with rare exceptions, its only food. Spying one, the falcon suddenly drops with great force and seizes it. The captor's first act is to bite off the serpent's head, a wise precaution, since coral snakes and other venomous species are included in its prey. Occasionally it drops upon a snake too big to be overpowered and hastily retreats. Usually, however, it rises with its decapitated victim and carries it lengthwise in its talons to devour it on a high perch, or perhaps takes it to its nest. Rarely, the falcon catches a small rodent.

The few available nesting records suggest that the guaco prefers a large hollow, high in a great tree (fig. 10.35), but in regions where such sites are not available it will occupy a hole in a cliff or the very bulky open nest built by a hawk or caracara. Apparently the guaco lays a single large egg, densely mottled with shades of brown.

Following a laughing falcon that was carrying a snake, I discovered an eyrie in a hollow about 30 m up in a huge tree at the forest's edge, in the valley of El General. In it was a single nestling, covered with buffy down, that already had a black mask like those of its parents. All day one of them, probably the female, guarded it, either standing in the cavity or watching from a nearby branch. Each morning and evening the other parent brought a decapitated snake and delivered it to his mate, who draped it over a high bough while the two joined in a prolonged loud duet that seemed like a hymn of victory. Often after a long delay, the mother shared the snake's flesh with her nestling. One afternoon a tayra (*Eira barbara*) climbed up the long trunk; before I could chase the big, black weasel away, it killed the nestling. However, I drove it off before it ate its victim. Returning to her nest after an interval, the parent, who had helplessly watched the mammal ascend to her nest, devoured her offspring before her mate returned with the evening snake.

This falcon benefits all the smaller birds by eating the snakes that prey so heavily upon their nests, and aids man by killing venomous serpents.

*

Skutch, A. F. 1971. *A naturalist in Costa Rica.* Gainesville: University of Florida Press.
Wetmore, A. 1965. The birds of the Republic of Panamá, part 1. *Smithsonian Misc. Coll.,* vol. 150.

Iridoprocne albilinea (Golondrina Lomiblanca, Golondrina, Mangrove Swallow)

R. Ricklefs

The mangrove swallow is a small (13–16 g) member of the *Tachycineta-Iridoprocne* group of swallows, of which representatives in the United States are *I. bicolor* (tree swallow) and *T. thalassina* (violet-green swallow). The mangrove swallow is distributed throughout coastal lowlands of Central America, from Sonora and Tamaulipas in Mexico to eastern Panama. An isolated population occurs in northwestern Peru.

Mangrove swallows forage in open areas, usually just above the surfaces of lakes, larger rivers, and bays, occasionally over marshes and open meadows, and rarely over the canopies of forests bordering major waterways. The swallows eat small flying insects, all of which they take on the wing. The bulk of the diet probably consists of adults of insect species with aquatic larvae. But the stomachs of two individuals collected by Henry Hespenheide in Guanacaste, Costa Rica, in July 1968 contained flying ants, other Hymenoptera, Homoptera, and beetles, in approximately that order of abundance.

Mangrove swallows breed during the dry season and into the transition between dry and wet seasons. In central Panama, eggs are laid between January and April, and young may be fed into July. The onset of breeding is marked by the breaking up of flocks of swallows, normally four to several dozen individuals. The swallows apparently are monogamous. Pairs defend nest sites and possibly extensive feeding territories. Nests are widely spaced. They are often situated in holes or crevices in trees or stumps emerging from water, but at present nests are commonly located in various artificial structures, such as buildings and power poles, when they are available. Mangrove swallows readily take to nesting boxes.

The normal clutch is three to five eggs, incubation lasts 16 days, and the young remain in the nest for between 3 and 4 weeks. Nesting success apparently depends on food availability, which may increase as the season progresses. Young reared late in the breeding season in Panama in 1968 were much heavier than those in earlier broods that year.

The foraging rate of the adults is sensitive to the thermal environment, particularly humidity and solar radiation. On hot, sunny, humid afternoons the adults fly about 50% of the time, compared with nearly 100% shortly after dawn and before dusk. Apparently flight is limited by the rate of evaporative cooling.

Observations of one pair of swallows at Barro Colorado Island, Panama Canal Zone, suggested that adults subdivided their feeding area according to the disposition of the food captured. When they were feeding their young, the adults fed close to the nest. When foraging for themselves, they restricted their activities to areas 200–300 m from the nest.

After fledging, the young remain within the parents' nest area for up to 20–25 days and are fed, at a gradually decreasing rate, for at least 10–15 days. If the first brood is reared successfully, a second clutch may follow about a month after the first young fledge (a total nest cycle of 70 days). Probably no more than two broods are raised.

After the end of the breeding season, mangrove swallows congregate in small flocks. They do not migrate long distances, but there is no information on the extent of local dispersal during the nonbreeding season. The proximate and ultimate factors that stimulate the onset and end of the breeding season are not known.

Few species of birds exploit the aerial habitat in which the mangrove swallows forage. Flycatchers feed closer to the shore, and most consume larger prey. Martins fly higher above the surface and probably take larger prey. Dragonflies and swallows may compete for food in some areas; swallows and wasps may compete for nesting sites. Predators possibly include accipiters. Both snakes and mammals may gain access to some nests.

*

Ricklefs, R. E. 1971. Foraging behavior of mangrove swallows at Barro Colorado Island. *Auk* 88:635–51.
———. 1976. Growth of birds in the humid, New World tropics. *Ibis* 118:179–207.

Jacana spinosa (Jacana Centroamericana, Mulita, Cirujano, Gallito de Agua, Northern Jacana)

D. A. Jenni

Wherever one finds floating aquatic vegetation in Costa Rica, on lakes, marshes, reservoirs, or along streams, one is apt to find the northern or American jacana breeding (fig. 10.36). When walking, the coffee brown body and blackish neck and head color are sometimes amazingly cryptic. Bright yellow patches—bill, carpal spurs, and a wattle on the forehead—interrupt the crypsis. When a jacana extends its wings in display or flight

FIGURE 10.36. *Jacana spinosa*, with wings outstretched. Turrialba, Costa Rica (photo, T. Mace).

it reveals brilliant yellow (sometimes lime yellow) primary and secondary feathers. These flash colors make the birds suddenly conspicuous and are analogous to the flash colors of grasshopper wings. Although they occur on floating aquatic vegetation throughout Costa Rica, they nest in greatest numbers in seasonally flooded areas in Guanacaste. In Guanacaste and other strongly biseasonal localities the jacanas breed during the rainy season after water levels have begun to rise (Jenni 1982). When water levels remain fairly constant year-round, they may breed in any month, as at the pond at CATIE (IICA) near Turrialba (Jenni and Collier 1972). Even where they breed year-round there are definite, but temporally irregular, peaks in breeding activity. These peaks, unlike those in Guanacaste, are not obviously controlled by rainfall patterns.

All species in this circumtropical family (Jacanidae) have greatly elongated toes as an adaptation for walking, feeding, and breeding on floating aquatic plants. The nest, built over water, is a simple platform made of whatever vegetation is available near the site. Stems and leaves are simply gathered and compacted; there are no complex weaving movements. Although nest-building movements are conspicuous, the nest itself ranges from a very slight accumulation to a modest pile of aquatic plants. In some sites with little floating vegetation, the area for a meter or more around the nest may be cleared of vegetation, making the nest temporarily conspicuous. Clutch size is four. Nest loss is extremely high; in some years 100% of first nests are lost. Purple gallinules rob jacana nests, and rising water levels coupled with unstable floating nests apparently cause many losses, but most losses are unexplained.

Jacanas have a reversal of the typical avian sex roles. Males perform all functional nest building, incubation, and direct care of the young. Males sometimes pick chicks up beneath their wings, especially during heavy rainfall (Jenni and Betts 1978). Females perform some nest-building movements (apparently for display purposes only) and occasionally "stand guard" in the vicinity of the chicks while males feed elsewhere. The precocial young are never fed by adults but tend to feed faster when accompanied by a male. Abandoned young chicks starve. Adults provide important antipredatory services by defending chicks from purple gallinules, turtles, caimans, and humans. Antipredatory behavior includes loud, strident vocalizations. Most displays are accompanied by conspicuous vocalizations (Jenni, Gambs, and Betts 1974).

Jacanas are often found feeding in flooded sugarcane fields, in pastures, and in grasslands away from suitable breeding habitats. At Turrialba there are often as many nonbreeding adult-plumaged birds roosting on the lake and feeding in nearby grasslands (including a soccer field) as there are breeding birds present on the lake. Jacanas feed primarily on insects gleaned from the surface of the vegetation, but they frequently feed on ovules of water lilies.

The four eggs are laid at a rate of one per day (approximately every 24.5 to 25 h), and effective incubation, approximately 28 days, does not begin until the clutch is complete. Females often start laying replacement or second clutches as soon as 7 to 10 days after completing first clutches. The minimum interclutch interval recorded is 4 days. The eggs are quite small ($\bar{x} = 7.9$ g) compared with the weight of breeding females ($\bar{x} = 160.9$ g), which average nearly 75% heavier than breeding males ($\bar{x} = 91.4$ g). Larger female size, thought to be an adaptation for increased clutch production in face of high egg loss, is also probably an evolutionary result of intensive female intrasexual competition. Females dominate males in most social situations. The departure of invading females in response to the displays of a territorial male is probably because the male display simultaneously communicates his paired status.

The polyandrous mating system of the northern jacana is the best-known example of simultaneous polyandry (Jenni 1974). Each male defends a small breeding-feeding territory from which he excludes all other males.

Each female defends the territories of from one to four adjacent males against all conspecific intruders, including neighboring male(s) with whom she has simultaneous bonds. Although initial establishment of polyandrous relationships sometimes occurs sequentially in Guanacaste, the bonds between a female and her males persist through the breeding season. At Turrialba the bonds persist indefinitely or until individuals are replaced. In other avian polyandrous systems, females typically abandon first males, who incubate and raise chicks by themselves. In the northern jacana the females do not abandon males after laying for them but continue to consort with them all and to monitor activities in their territories.

Females provide replacement clutches, perform guard duty, and attack potential predators as necessary. Pair bonds are retained, and females may provide second clutches for males when chicks reach 12 to 16 weeks of age. The polyandrous system is based on female-female interactions. Males form pair bonds by behaving subordinately toward whichever female is able to exclude all other females from his territory. The number of males per female varies seasonally, annually, locally, and in response to changes in quality of habitat as reflected in male territory size. At Turrialba the long-term average is 2.3 males per female, although there are almost always one or more monagamous females present. In Guanacaste the ratio increases from 1 at the beginning of the breeding season to as high as 2.5 males per female before vegetation becomes too dense for further observation.

Although males sometimes incubate eggs and raise chicks that are their unquestioned genetic offspring, paternity is often uncertain. Females may copulate with as many as four different males within a single hour. Evidence suggests that some females copulate more often with the male who receives the clutch than with other males. Although paternity is not guaranteed for polyandrous males, there is almost always some probability that that male has fathered the chicks. Copulation is conspicuous. Mounts last as long as a minute or more, but cloacal contact lasts only 2 or 3 sec.

Because nesting, hatching, and fledgling rates are so low, it has not been possible to test adequately either the hypothesis that females with more males succeed in raising more young than females with fewer males (female advantage hypothesis) or the hypothesis that males who "share" their female with other males raise more young than monogamous males (male advantage hypothesis). That number of males per female is a proximal consequence of female-female interaction and that males play no role in determining whether monogamous or polyandrous females occupy their territory argue against the male-advantage hypothesis. There is no evidence to support the hypothesis that polyandry in the northern jacana is a consequence of a skewed sex ratio.

585

Costa Rica is the southern limit of range of the northern jacana. The southern jacana (*J. jacana*) occurs from central Panama through South America. The southern form (also called wattled jacana or, in Panama, black jacana) appears to be the ecological equivalent of the northern form and, although it is poorly known, appears very similar in behavior and social organization (Osborne and Bourne 1977). In Panama the jacanas are black, but birds from the southernmost parts of the range are light coffee brown, similar to the northern jacana. The southern and northern forms overlap along the Pacific slope of western Panama and extreme southern Costa Rica. Though there are few jacanas in the area, there is evidence that the two species may interbreed (Betts 1973). However, supposed hybrids could be immatures of the southern form. This problem remains unstudied, and the status of jacanas in this region is unresolved.

Two jacanas occur in Africa. There is one in India and southern Asia, which overlaps with the pheasant-tailed jacana (*Hydrophasianus chirurgus*), which ranges as far north as Peking. There is another species in northern Australia.

*

Betts, B. J. 1973. A possible hybrid wattled jacana × northern jacana in Costa Rica. *Auk* 90:687–89.

Jenni, D. A. 1974. Evolution of polyandry in birds. *Am. Zool.* 14:129–44.

———. 1982. Comparison of territory establishment in seasonal and permanent breeding populations of the American jacana, *Jacana spinosa. Ecology,* in press.

Jenni, D. A., and Betts, B. J. 1978. Sex differences in nest construction, incubation, and parental behaviour in the polyandrous American jacana (*Jacana spinosa*). *Anim. Behav.* 26:207–18.

Jenni, D. A., and Collier, G. 1972. Polyandry in the American jacana (*Jacana spinosa*). *Auk* 89:742–65.

Jenni, D. A.; Gambs, R. D.; and Betts, B. J. 1974. Acoustic behavior of the northern jacana. *Living Bird* 13:193–210.

Osborne, D. R., and Bourne, G. R. 1977. Breeding behavior and food habits of the wattled jacana. *Condor* 79:98–105.

Mionectes oleaginea (Mosqueitero Ojenido, Tontillo, Ochre-bellied Flycatcher)

T. W. Sherry

Skutch (1960) aptly describes the nondescript plumage of the ochre-bellied flycatcher (*Mionectes oleaginea,* Tyrannidae). The bird is essentially olive green with a peculiar ochre yellow lower breast and abdomen. It is easily distinguished, however, by its habit of twitching one wing at a time above its back. Tyrannidae in general are noted for a spectacular adaptive radiation during the long period when South America was isolated from other continents (Keast 1972). Though there are many omnivorous "flycatchers," the ochre-belly is a particularly unusual product of that radiation, being largely frugivorous (see below). Meyer de Schauensee (1966) lists three species of *Pipromorpha* and two of *Mionectes,* though Traylor (1977) has placed the ochre-belly and other former *Pipromorpha* into *Mionectes.*

One encounters the ochre-bellied flycatcher in deep forest, thinned woodland and borders, and out into adjacent clearings when fruit is available (Skutch 1960; Slud 1964). In Amazonia, where it is widely sympatric with its congener *M. macconnelli,* however, *M. oleaginea* rarely occurs inside primary forest (Willis, Wechsler, and Oniki 1978). The ochre-belly ranges from southern Mexico to Peru, Bolivia, and Brazil and is found on Trinidad and Tobago (Meyer de Schauensee 1966). In Costa Rica it occurs widely from the lowlands of both coasts to about 1,500 m elevation (Slud 1964), but the center of abundance is the lowlands. Within forest it occurs in the understory, except when occasionally accompanying a mixed-species bird flock to higher levels (Slud 1964). Ochre-bellies generally remain solitary.

Though mainly a frugivore, the ochre-belly eats some insects (Skutch 1960; Haverschmidt 1968; Hespenheide, unpub. data). *M. oleaginea* eats a variety of fruits: mistletoe (Loranthaceae), *Zanthoxylum, Alchornea,* and *Siparuna* (Skutch 1960); *Faramea, Heliconia, Cephaelis,* some Araliaceae, some Araceae, some Palmae (F. Stiles, pers. comm.); and *Clusia* and Melastomataceae (Sherry, unpub. data). Correspondingly, the ochre-belly's bill is not flat like that of most flycatchers but is about as deep as it is wide. The rictal bristles that characterize most insectivorous flycatchers (see account, e.g., of *Terenotriccus erythrurus,* the ruddy-tailed flycatcher) are absent in the ochre-belly.

Ochre-bellies are less like most flycatchers than like such birds as manakins (Pipridae) and hummingbirds (Trochilidae) in the complete liberation of males from parental duties. These birds depend largely upon fruit and nectar, resources that are easily found and gathered by females alone. Both Skutch (1976) and Willis, Wechsler, and Oniki (1978) argue that heavy nest predation in some tropical frugivores/nectarivores has selected for females to drive males away from nest sites. Males could also compete with females for foods near the nest sites (Willis, Wechsler, and Oniki 1978). Especially if their resources are not defendable, the males thus "liberated" would best increase their fitness through self-advertisement (Emlen and Oring 1977; Bradbury 1981). Solitary males display for females up to 7 months of the year (March–September in Central America) in a "court," 10–30 m in diameter, using many perches, usually within

15 m of the ground (Skutch 1960). Females attracted to the unmusical, repetitious songs of males mate, then depart to raise young alone; the mating system is promiscuous.

"Exploded leks," an intermediate situation in the evolution of leks (Bradbury 1981), best describe the dispersion of male ochre-bellied flycatchers. Males display in ways similar to lekking species, and though they occasionally form leks locally (I have observed at least six males displaying within about 0.5 ha at Finca La Selva, Costa Rica; see also Willis, Wechsler, and Oniki 1978), they are often widely enough dispersed to be out of earshot of each other. Male liberation from nesting duties is a necessary but not sufficient condition for lek formation and maintenance (Bradbury 1979). Geometrically, males should virtually never *benefit* from displaying communally (i.e., on leks); only female dispersion, particularly large home ranges, should make clumping the best available strategy for males, since females would prefer males to be clumped (Bradbury 1979). The ecological factors determining female home-range size—for example, fruit dispersion and abundance—are not known but are presumably variable, since male dispersion is locally variable. Ochre-bellies are monomorphic sexually, perhaps because the sexual selection that would operate on a lek is largely absent (Emlen and Oring 1977).

Skutch (1960) describes nesting and breeding in detail. Females build pear-shaped nests that hang (0–4 m high) from a vine, branchlet, or aerial root. Nests are almost always along a stream, and they usually touch or are very near to a solid support such as a tree or mossy bank. In Central America the nest is frequently camouflaged with bright green mosses or liverworts; *M. macconnelli* builds nests that are similar to those of *M. oleaginea* except for the camouflage (Willis, Wechsler, and Oniki 1978). Females are shy around the nest. The 19–21-day incubation period is similar to that of other flycatchers with relatively safe (hanging and/or streamside) nest sites. Clutch size is 2.7 in *M. oleaginea* (N = 23; Skutch 1976) and 3 in *M. macconnelli* (N = 9; Willis, Wechsler, and Oniki 1978)—high in both cases for species with hanging nests. Females feed nestlings by regurgitation. The extent of insectivory while females are producing eggs and feeding young is unknown, but the growth rate of *M. macconnelli* nestlings is slow for the family (Willis, Wechsler, and Oniki 1978), suggesting less insectivory and more frugivory relative to other flycatcher species.

In Costa Rica *Mionectes olivaceus* is essentially a middle-elevation analogue of *M. oleaginea*, except that the former regularly migrates to the lowlands during the nonbreeding season (F. Stiles, pers. comm.). *M. olivaceus* is perhaps more insectivorous than *M. oleaginea* but takes many small fruits as well (e.g., *Trema*, Melastomataceae, *Heliconia*, and *Urera*—F. G. Stiles, pers.

comm.). It flocks more than the ochre-belly. Its nesting habits are similar to those of *M. oleaginea*, but it may be monogamous on the basis of observations of both sexes at a nest site (F. G. Stiles, pers. comm.).

Snow and Snow (1979) have published an excellent article independently treating the natural history and social system of the ochre-bellied flycatcher in Trinidad. Their more detailed study is largely complementary to and consistent with my account here.

*

Bradbury, J. W. 1981. The evolution of leks. In *Natural selection and social behavior,* ed. R. D. Alexander and D. Tinkle, pp. 138–69. New York: Chiron Press.

Emlen, S. T., and Oring, L. W. 1977. Ecology, sexual selection, and the evolution of mating systems. *Science* 197:215–23.

Haverschmidt, F. 1968. *Birds of Surinam.* London: Oliver and Boyd.

Keast, A. 1972. Ecological opportunities and dominant families, as illustrated by the Neotropical Tyrannidae (Aves). *Evol. Biol.* 5:229–77.

Meyer de Schauensee, R. 1966. *The species of birds of South America and their distribution.* Philadelphia: Livingston.

Skutch, A. 1960. *Life histories of Central American birds: Families Vireonidae, Sylviidae, Turdidae, Troglodytidae, Paridae, Corvidae, Hirundinidae and Tyrannidae.* Pacific Coast Avifauna, no. 34. Berkeley: Cooper Ornithological Society.

———. 1976. *Parent birds and their young.* Austin: University of Texas Press.

Slud, P. 1964. The birds of Costa Rica: Distribution and ecology. *Bull. Am. Mus. Nat. Hist.* 128:1–430.

Snow, B. K., and Snow, D. W. 1979. The ochre-bellied flycatcher and the evolution of lek behavior. *Condor* 81:286–92.

Traylor, M. A., Jr. 1977. A classification of the tyrant flycatchers (Tyrannidae). *Bull. Mus. Comp. Zool.* 148:129–84.

Willis, E. O.; Wechsler, D.; and Oniki, Y. 1978. On behavior and nesting of McConnell's flycatcher (*Pipromorpha macconnelli*): Does female rejection lead to male promiscuity? *Auk* 95:1–8.

Monasa morphoeus (Monja Cariblanca, Julío, White-fronted Nunbird)

T. W. Sherry

The white-fronted nunbird (*Monasa morphoeus*) is a distinctive and conspicuous member of the Costa Rican avifauna. As early as 1863, Bates noted in his *Naturalist on the River Amazons* how social and active were nunbirds by contrast with other puffbirds (Bucconidae), which are characterized by a "dull inactive temperament." *M. morphoeus* has an essentially uniform gray body with white facial bristles around the bill (hence "nunbird") and a conspicuously large, coral-red bill.

Nunbirds and the closely related jacamars belong to the order Piciformes, as do woodpeckers, toucans, and barbets, though some authorities consider puffbirds and jacamars more closely related to Coraciiformes (see discussion of rufous-tailed jacamar, *Galbula ruficauda*). Like essentially all puffbirds, nunbirds birds are strictly carnivorous, "sit-and-wait" predators on insects and small vertebrates. Such sit-and-wait predators are limited to lowland tropics (Orians 1969; Croxall 1977), and the puffbirds are Neotropical. The Bucconidae include ten genera, and *Monasa* includes four species (Meyer de Schauensee 1966). Most puffbird genera are built on the same body plan as *Monasa:* large-headed, stout-billed, and heavy-bodied. The swallow-wing (*Chelidoptera tenebrosa*), however, is distinctive (it occurs only in South America; see Burton 1976 for discussion of its foraging behavior, food preferences, and morphology). In addition to *Monasa,* Costa Rica has puffbirds in the genera *Malacoptila, Northarchus,* and *Micromonacha.*

The white-fronted nunbird is one of the larger puffbirds, weighing just over 100 g. It not only is social, occurring in groups of up to ten or more individuals, but is also fairly tame and often very vocal. The posture is upright, and the tail is often flicked backward, then slowly reset at a vertical position, especially when the bird is excited. Nunbirds are forest-based and come to the ground in open areas (Slud 1964). They range from southeastern Honduras to Bolivia and southeastern Brazil, from lowlands to just over 300 m in Costa Rica (Slud 1964), though I have seen them up to 750 m elevation on Cerro Pirre, Darien Province, Panama.

Nunbird prey selection and prey handling are discussed by Sherry and McDade (1982). In general, nunbirds seem best adapted to preying on Orthoptera up to about 6 g mass, though they include a variety of insects in their diets. Orthoptera are relatively easy to catch and hold, and nunbirds can "handle" them about as easily as any prey, though the birds may require up to 12 min continuous handling before swallowing the prey. Although most prey are snatched from vegetation while the birds are in flight, they readily take flying insects. I have observed them capture larval Lepidoptera, Coleoptera, and a variety of Orthoptera (phasmatids, tetigoniids, blatids, gryllids, and mantids) in the wild. In experimental situations they have eaten Neuroptera (corydalids), Homoptera (fulgorids), Hemiptera (pentatomids), and vertebrates (*Anolis* lizard). Skutch (1972) has seen them feed additionally on odonates, spiders, millipedes, and small frogs. Thus nunbirds consume a broad range of foods but few agile prey. Of prey offered them in experiments, nunbirds have rejected some Coleoptera for presumed physical reasons (cerambycids, scarabs, elaterids, and the enormous buprestid *Euchroma gigantea*) and chemical reasons (?) (passalids); Orthoptera for physical reasons (large size alone in tetigoniids) and chemical reasons (aposematic—or mimetic—phasmatid and acridid). A large (3-g) cicada successfully escaped a pursuing nunbird three times because the bird could not hold onto it. On the other hand, nunbirds consumed aposematic pentatomids, fulgorids, and Lepidoptera larvae, all of which were clearly distasteful to them on the basis of long handling times and extensive bill-wiping behavior. One nunbird took four such fulgorids (*Enchophora sanguinea*) in quick succession, and so one cannot claim these events were "mistakes." Clearly, unpalatability is not an all-or-none phenomenon; there is probably some predator that can or will consume just about any prey item. Nunbirds probably have difficulty catching some prey (Lepidoptera, Diptera), and they cannot extract from the vegetation some insects that they could otherwise handle (big-legged Orthoptera). Thus the factors that affect prey selection are diverse, and insects use a diverse array of defenses against birds such as nunbirds: size and shape, strength of limbs, hardness and roundness, sudden clicks and stridulations, noxious chemicals or imitation of insects with undesirable characteristics, evasive flight, and protective coloration, among others.

Many Orthoptera have sharp spines, strong jaws, and various horny protuberances. One can best understand some morphological characteristics of nunbirds in the context of handling such prey items once they are caught. The bill is massive and much deeper than wide, especially toward the tip. Much time is spent crushing prey and whacking it against the perch until it is soft enough to swallow. Nunbirds and many puffbirds have big heads and hook-tipped bills for crushing and holding prey. Handling times for different prey individuals of the same size and taxon are similar, and when body shape is controlled, handling time is an increasing but power function of prey mass. Most if not all puffbirds have elaborate development of stiffened bristles all around the bill, and these almost certainly protect soft parts of the head from heavily armed or otherwise noxious insects. The long nunbird bill may help the bird extract or snatch prey from the vegetation or may help it hold onto large insects during handling bouts. In summary, the evidence on prey selection and handling implicates a complex coevolutionary relationship involving an array of behavioral and morphological traits of both predator and prey.

An important defense of large insects is, of course, to remain motionless and hidden, and a tactic of sit-and-wait predators is to wait for these insects to move and so reveal themselves. I have seen a nunbird fly directly to a tree trunk from about 20 m distant and pick off a brown tetigoniid in well-shaded forest. It is sometimes difficult, however, for insects to remain motionless when a large flock of birds or a swarm of army ants moves through an area. Nunbirds almost always travel with large mixed-species bird flocks containing caciques (*Cacicus uropygialis*), woodcreepers (*Xiphorhynchus lacrymosus*, e.g.), cinnamon woodpeckers (*Celeus loricatus*), rufous pihas (*Lipaugus unirufus*), rufous mourners (*Rhytipterna holerythra*), and various *Trogon* species. The beating function, in which flock members inadvertently reveal insects, is likely an important attraction to nunbirds (see also Charnov, Orians, and Hyatt 1976). Nunbirds briefly follow army ants when swarms are encountered, capturing the large insect prey fleeing the ants. I have also watched a solitary ant cause an orthopteran to move a leg, thus prompting a nunbird to attack. Are solitary ants abundant enough in the vegetation to disclose various arthropods and thus facilitate the sit-and-wait foraging strategy of some tropical birds?

Although I hypothesize that nunbirds benefit from the beating action of bird flocks in revealing insect prey, there is evidence that joining a flock also reduces the chance of predation on adult birds. I have observed several instances of dozens of birds simultaneously scrambling beneath the trees, usually in response to a sharp call of one or a few flock members. I have not, however, identified a predator in these instances. The evolution of alarm calls is theoretically straightforward in many tropical mixed-species bird flocks, since most participating species are represented by at least two individuals that probably are genetically related. Morse (1977) reviews explanations for heterospecific flock formation.

Skutch (1972) was the first person to describe nunbird nesting behavior, which remains little studied otherwise. What he observed helps explain their spectacular social behavior. Groups of birds ("helpers at the nest") aid the adults in feeding young, and perhaps in nest defense. Skutch observed cases in which three, four, and five adults fed nestlings, and adults usually came to a given nest simultaneously. Nestlings almost always come to the burrow mouth to get food, often in response to calls of the adults. Nestlings are generally quiet, but they call more and are less prudent at the burrow entrance when hungry—for example, during particularly rainy weather (Skutch 1972). The nest itself is usually constructed by burrowing 1–1.5 m at an angle in level or somewhat sloping ground within primary forest. I have watched birds building a nest in December and have seen recently fledged young in May. Skutch reports birds fledging in late April and May after an approximately 30-day nestling period. F. Stiles (pers. comm.) reports two two-nestling broods. Molt is postnuptial and probably lasts several months. Most birds I have handled in October were molting.

The ultimate ecological factors favoring the particular social system of nunbirds are not known. The variety of social behaviors and great range of vocalizations probably are related to the cooperation within the presumed family groups during the nesting season and throughout the year (Brown 1978 reviews the topic of cooperative breeding by birds). Slud (1964) and Skutch (1972) have described many vocalizations and a spectacular display involving coordinated "barking" or "gobbling" for up to 15 min at a time by birds lined up on one or a few branches. This display is probably territorial in function (though see Skutch 1972), and its frequency appears to increase between October and December, a time of year when resurgence in song activity occurs in many birds (F. Stiles, pers. comm.). The display is intensely emotional, and birds stream to the location of the bird initiating the calls. The social life of nunbirds, which might help educate young recruits about the home terrain, predators, and social behavior, might also help them learn what foods to take or avoid and how to handle them. Skutch (1972) reports young nunbirds repeatedly practicing foraging by flying up to an adult and snatching prey from its bill. Skutch did not see young birds forage on their own for at least a month after fledging.

Activity of their mixed-species bird flocks affects many aspects of nunbird life, including, I believe, their somewhat greater activity levels relative to other puffbirds. On many occasions nunbirds ceased taking choice prey items during my experiments and left when the flock left. Thus nunbird home ranges may be related to flock home ranges, at least outside the breeding season. I have observed what appeared to be the same flock of nunbirds repeatedly visit the Finca La Selva (Sarapiquí lowlands) Arboretum every day and sometimes more frequently. Thus a flock seems to occupy a fairly specific home range and to revisit parts of it at frequent intervals. The daily cycle can be relaxed. Birds intersperse social displays and even siestas between more active feeding bouts. In October I have seen birds flopped down in the grass in a sunny spot with wings spread out—obviously sunning (Skutch 1972; L. McDade, pers. comm.).

*

Brown, J. L. 1978. Avian communal breeding systems. *Ann. Rev. Ecol. Syst.* 9:123–55.

Burton, P. J. K. 1976. Feeding behavior in the paradise jacamar and the swallow-wing. *Living Bird* 15: 223–38.

Charnov, E. L.; Orians, G. H.; and Hyatt, K. 1976. Ecological implications of resource depression. *Am. Nat.* 110:247–59.

Croxall, J. P. 1977. Feeding behavior and ecology of New Guinea rainforest insectivorous passerines. *Ibis* 119:113–46.

Meyer de Schauensee, R. 1966. *The species of birds of South America and their distribution*. Philadelphia: Livingston.

Morse, D. H. 1977. Feeding behavior and predator avoidance in heterospecific groups. *BioScience* 27: 332–39.

Orians, G. H. 1969. The number of bird species in some tropical forests. *Ecology* 50:783–97.

Sherry, T. W., and McDade, L. A. 1982. Prey selection and handling in two Neotropical hover-gleaning birds. *Ecology,* in press.

Skutch, A. 1972. Studies of tropical American birds. *Publ. Nuttall Ornithol. Club* 10:1–228.

Slud, P. 1964. The birds of Costa Rica: Distribution and ecology. *Bull. Am. Mus. Nat. Hist.* 128:1–430.

Nyctidromus albicollis (Pochocuate, Chatacabras Campestre, Cuyeo, Cuiejo, Pauraque)

E. P. Edwards

The pauraque, a member of the family Caprimulgidae, is distributed from southern Texas through Middle America and northern South America (and Trinidad) to northwestern Peru (west of the Andes) and to northeastern Argentina (east of the Andes). It seems to be by far the most abundant caprimulgid in many parts of Mexico and Central America. It is widespread and abundant in Costa Rica, occurring in savanna, open woodland, brushland, woodland edge, farmland, and openings in humid forest, throughout the country at elevations from sea level to about 3,000 m above sea level. It is particularly abundant in partly open country, such as open brushland with some grass and some bare ground, or in open, rather arid, low thorny woodland, or along the edges of such areas; but is also very common where forests or woodlands have been cleared or partly cleared for agriculture.

The species appears not to be migratory even in the northern portion of its breeding range. Wintering individuals often move into dense thickets during the nonbreeding season, however, particularly where the winters are relatively cold. It is not known to hibernate in winter, as does one of its close relatives, the poor-will.

Considerably larger than most other New World caprimulgids, approximately 24 cm in length, the pauraque nonetheless seems a typical member of the family. Although cryptically colored and patterned, with most of its plumage mottled, barred, and speckled black, brown, gray, and buff, the male pauraque has a sharply contrasting broad white bar on each wing and a large white patch on each side of the tail at the tip. The patches on wing and tail are hidden unless the wings are extended and the tail spread, but they flash conspicuously when the birds flies or performs a distraction display. The female is similar to the male except that the bar on the wing is narrower and the pale patch on the tail is very much smaller and usually mostly buff. The overall plumage

tone in the species ranges from a gray phase to a brown phase, with a full range of intermediate individuals, apparently distributed in a way that cannot be related to geographic variation. The pauraque has long, pointed wings, a rather long, slightly rounded tail, and a very large mouth (fig. 10.37), but relatively tiny bill. It has longer legs than its close relatives and at times will walk or even run a short distance.

The pauraque is nocturnal, calling persistently on moonlight nights during the breeding season and flying up from the ground or from a perch on a rock or log to

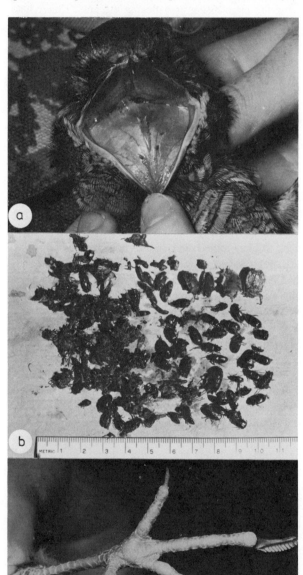

FIGURE 10.37. *Nyctidromus albicollis. a,* Adult with mouth open. *b,* Gizzard contents including pentatomid stink bugs and many small black carabid beetles. *c,* Foot with highly modified toe that may be used to comb the hairs around the mouth. Santa Rosa National Park, Guanacaste Province, Costa Rica (photos, D. H. Janzen).

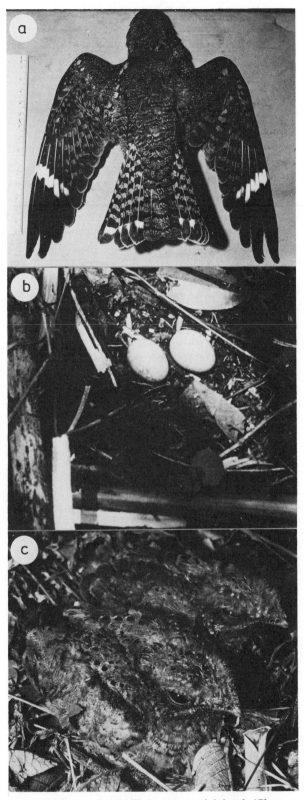

capture night-flying insects such as beetles and moths. Wetmore (1968) wrote that the "capacho feeds extensively on beetles, particularly on scarabaeids, but including others, as passalids, cerambycids, elaterids, and curculionids" (and see fig. 10.37).

More than most other tropical caprimulgids, except possibly the nighthawks (fig. 10.38) (at least partly because it is so abundant), the pauraque is to be encountered in the daytime as well, when it may be frightened from its resting place to flutter up and away, in erratic flight, a few feet above the ground, then drop back to a place of concealment 15 to 20 m or so from where it flew up. A careful observer may occasionally be able to see the bird on the ground by noting where a bird has landed after being disturbed, but more frequently the bird will fly again before it can be found, and after two or three such incidents in succession it will be completely lost.

In mid-April the pauraque is much in evidence (because of its loud and persistent calling) in the mixed farmland and scrubby open woodland of Guanacaste. It is almost equally notable in the wet pastures and fields and forest edge in the vicinity of Finca La Selva. On favorable nights, usually when the moon is nearly full, and especially shortly after dark and shortly before dawn, from several to many can be heard calling persistently, at various distances from the listener. The call can be heard from a half-mile to a mile or more on a still night. Wetmore (1968) writing about the pauraque in Panama, notes that "on some occasions at dawn in January at La Jagua the chorus from all sides has been a truly amazing volume of sound." In southeastern Mexico in 1947 "during the bright moonlight nights of April 1 to 5 Pauraques were calling in great numbers on the Monserrate Plateau" (Edwards and Lea 1955). Typically represented as *per-wee-oo* or *cu-wheer* or *cuh-cuh-cuh-wheer,* the call sounds more like *per-zhee-oo* or *per-zhee-er* in the vicinity of Hacienda La Pacifica in Guanacaste.

At such times the birds move out from under dense cover of shrubs or trees or thickets and perch on bare ground or rocks or fallen branches or trunks in open spaces where they can see their insect prey readily and can effectively fly up to capture the passing insects. Probably the pauraque, like the poor-will, which has it eyes set high on its head, can see insects straight overhead without moving its head from a horizontal position. Frequently the pauraque can be observed on a dirt road or trail at night, and when seen in the light of a flashlight or automobile headlights its eyes glow orange or orange red. In such circumstances an observer can often ap-

FIGURE 10.38. *a,* Road-killed common nighthawk (*Chordeiles minor*); this bird is similar to *Nyctidromus albicollis* but is much more aerial, has longer pointed wings, has a shorter tail, and has white across the tail. *b,* Two-egg "nest" of *Nyctidromus albicollis* on forest floor. *c,* Chicks of *N.* *albicollis* on forest floor (they were accompanied by a parent pauraque engaged in a frantic broken-wing act). Santa Rosa National Park, Guanacaste Province, Costa Rica (photos, D. H. Janzen).

591

proach to within a few feet of a pauraque or with care may even capture it in the hand. On occasion an observer may see it in its feeding flight, a fluttering flight a few feet up into the air and then down again to the take-off point or nearby (Alvarez del Toro 1971). When seen by artificial light at night the bird usually appears pale gray or tan, but even then the white wing patches and tail patches of the male flash conspicuously if the bird flies.

The nest is merely a slight depression (or less) in a bare space on the ground (fig. 10.38), near, or often directly under, the outer branches of a shrub or small, shrubby tree. The normal clutch of eggs is two; these are basically pinkish or buffy, usually mottled, spotted, or blotched with pale reddish brown or cinnamon. The male and female incubate in turn during the daytime, spending as much as 2 to 3 h on the eggs at each turn. Skutch (in Bent 1940) reported that only the female was observed to incubate at night. Both sexes brood the young birds as well. When an incubating or brooding adult is frightened from the nest it will flutter away only a few meters to a place of concealment, or it may on occasion perform a distraction display (fig. 10.38). Slud (1964) noted such a distraction display "only in the brightly white-patterned males. If incubating, the male flits as though injured and flaps helplessly on the ground. If brooding, it crawls as though hugging the ground on half-bent legs and half-opened, flipper-like wings, flops about with spread wings, and makes a froglike gargle, all to draw attention to itself. The baby birds sit immobilized even when touched and do not occur in the same spot on successive days."

Skutch (in Bent 1940) has observed that the parents will move eggs back to their original position if they have been displaced a short distance, in contrast to the behavior attributed to some caprimulgids of moving eggs *away* from the original nest site when the bird is disturbed at the nest. The young birds (fig. 10.38) are fed at night as one might expect, and presumably both male and female bring food to the young. The young birds seem able to walk with greater facility than can most other caprimulgids, and chicks only 2 or 3 days old have been observed to clamber several meters from the nest site to be fed, on an occasion when the parent did not return directly to the nest (Skutch, in Bent 1940).

*

Alvarez del Toro, M. 1971. *Las aves de Chiapas.* Chiapas, Mexico: Gobierno del Estado de Chiapas, Tuxtla Gutiérrez.

Bent, A. C. 1940. Life histories of North American cuckoos, goatsuckers, hummingbirds and their allies. *U.S. Nat. Mus. Bull.,* no. 176.

Edwards, E. P., and Lea, R. B. 1955. Birds of the Monserrate area, Chiapas, Mexico. *Condor* 57:31–54.

Slud, P. 1964. The birds of Costa Rica: Distribution and ecology. *Bull. Am. Mus. Nat. Hist.* 128:1–430.

Wetmore, A. 1968. The birds of the Republic of Panamá, part 2. Columbidae (Pigeons) to Picidae (Woodpeckers). *Smithsonian Misc. Coll.* vol. 150.

Otus choliba (Sorococa, Estucurú, Tropical Screech Owl)

S. M. Smith

The tropical screech owl (fig. 10.39) is one of the most common owls in Costa Rica. It is found primarily on the Meseta Central and nearby mountains and has apparently not been recorded much below 700 m. This owl frequents semiopen areas such as coffee plantations, pastures, and forest edges. It is strictly nocturnal and primarily insectivorous, eating large grasshoppers and katydids as well as beetles and moths. I have seen tropical screech owls feeding on insects at a street light on the University of Costa Rica campus.

This is a small owl species, with ear tufts and lemon yellow irises. Its most distinctive markings are a lightish facial disk prominently rimmed with black and white underparts marked uniformly with a clear-cut herring-

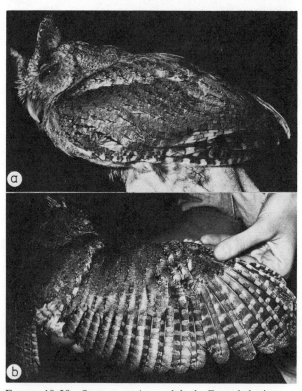

FIGURE 10.39. *Otus cooperi. a,* adult. *b,* Extended wing. Santa Rosa National Park, Guanacaste Province, Costa Rica (photos, D. H. Janzen). This owl is similar to *Otus choliba* but is less heavily streaked, and *O. choliba* has a heavier black margin to the facial disk.

bone pattern (each feather has a dark central line with three or more cross bars). The head (except for the facial disks), back, wings, and tail are brown mottled and barred with golden buff, and the scapulars are tipped with white, giving a white line along each side above the wing. The bill is light horn color; the legs are feathered to the base (not the tips) of the toes. The ear tufts in an undisturbed tropical screech owl are usually very inconspicuous, but when the owl is alarmed the ear tufts become prominent.

Because they are so nocturnal, tropical screech owls are more commonly heard than seen. Their voices are frequently heard in residential areas around the edges of cities like San José. Their most common call is a low trill, usually followed by two or more *toos: prrr pu pu*. Less freqeuntly, a loud laugh is given, usually in flight.

Little is known of their nesting in Costa Rica. Nests are typically in cavities in trees; eggs are white and round. The young are brooded for about a week and fledge when they are approximately 30 days old (Thomas 1977). In Costa Rica the young fledge about March.

*

Thomas, B. T. 1977. Tropical screech owl nest defense behavior and nestling growth rate. *Wilson Bull.* 89: 609–12.

Panterpe insignis (Colibri Garganta de Fuego, Fiery-throated Hummingbird)

F. G. Stiles

This bold and strikingly beautiful hummingbird is endemic to the Costa Rica–Chiriquí highlands, from the Cordillera de Tilarán to Volcán Chiriquí. On the Cordillera Central and the Cordillera de Talamanca *Panterpe* occurs abundantly from about 2,500 m up to timberline in oak forests and adjacent habitats. At the northern extreme of its range above Monteverde, it is common in cloud forest at 1,600–1,800 m. The monotypic genus *Panterpe* may be allied to the Andean genus *Metallura* (R. Ortiz, pers. comm.); if so, the fiery-throated hummingbird is unusual among high-elevation Costa Rican birds in having South American affinities.

In the field, *Panterpe* usually appears as a glossy green hummingbird of medium size (5–6 g) with a dark blue tail and a slender, straight (ca. 20 mm) bill. The bird's brilliant iridescent colors are visible only at close range in good light, and from a point above and in front of the bird. These colors include a patch of violet blue on the chest, a brilliant blue crown set off by velvety black on the sides and back of the head, and a glittering coppery orange throat and breast. At close range a small white spot is visible behind the eye. Females are distinctly

smaller than males but scarcely less brilliant in color. *Panterpe* is also an exceedingly noisy hummingbird, giving a variety of high-pitched chirps, twitters, and squeals, mostly with a rather liquid quality; there seems to be no true song. A curious buzzing note is given in sexual encounters, preceding and during copulation.

Panterpe is also notable as the fiercest hummer of the highlands. In interspecific interference competition for feeding rights at nectar-rich flowers, *Panterpe* wins consistently over its highland neighbors, the larger *Eugenes fulgens* (8–10 g), the similar-sized *Colibri thalassinus* (ca. 5 g), and the tiny *Selasphorus flammula* (2.5 g). Its alpha position in the dominance hierarchy gives *Panterpe* the ability to control nectar-rich patches of any flower for which its medium-length bill gives access to the nectar. Outside the breeding season females as well as males are able to defend feeding territories against other hummingbirds.

Panterpe visits a wide variety of flowers on the Cerro de la Muerte, about ten to fifteen species in any given month. It has a strong preference for epiphytic ericads like *Macleania*, *Cavendishia*, and *Satyrium* and the bromeliad *Thecophyllum* (*Vriesia*) *orosiense*. Other favorite flowers include *Fuchsia* spp., certain ericads (*Vaccinium*, *Gaultheria*), *Tropaeolum*, and *Salvia* spp. When more highly preferred flowers are scarce, *Panterpe* will visit *Centropogon valerii*, *Miconia* sp., and *Rubus* spp. Access to some flowers with long corolla tubes normally visited only by *Eugenes* (bill 30–37 mm) is provided by *Diglossa plumbea*, the slaty flower-piercer. This small (10 g) passerine grasps a flower with its hooked upper mandible, pierces it with the needle-sharp lower mandible, and inserts its tongue through the hole to extract the nectar. *Panterpe* may follow a *Diglossa* from flower to flower of the long-tubed *Centropogon talamancensis*, using the *Diglossa* holes to extract nectar; a *Panterpe* may occasionally even defend a clump of *Diglossa*-pierced *Centropogon* against its legitimate pollinator, *Eugenes*. Like other hummingbirds, *Panterpe* has at best indifferent success in defending its own territories against individuals of *Diglossa*, which are usually furtive and persistent, keeping to the densest part of the plants where the hummers cannot get at them. Other competitors for nectar, against which *Panterpe*'s aggressiveness does not avail, are arthropods, the large bee *Bombus ephippiatus*, and two species of *Rhinoseius* mites. *Bombus* may pierce long-tubed flowers as does *Diglossa*, sometimes easing access for *Panterpe;* it is a major nectar competitor at flowers like *Gaiadendron* and *Vaccinium*. Occasionally *Panterpe* may evict a bee bodily from its territory, but male *Eugenes* feeding at *Cirsium* are past masters of such tactics, often seizing the bee and literally throwing it out (an operation aided by their long bill). The *Rhinoseius* mites live on the nectaries of various flower species, where they often become very abundant. When a hummingbird inserts its bill into the flower, mites may hop aboard and move quickly to the bird's nostrils, where they are transported to another flower.

Panterpe provides an excellent illustration of the importance of food supply in determining the breeding season. Most birds on the Cerro de la Muerte, including hummingbirds, breed during the dry season. However, *Panterpe* breeds in close association with the flowering of the nectar-rich ericad *Macleania glabra,* which usually occurs sometime between late July and November, the coldest, wettest, nastiest time of year. Such close flowering-breeding associations are not unusual in hummingbirds and their flowers. The nest of *Panterpe* is a sturdy felted cup of tree-fern scales, plant down, and moss, decorated on the outside with moss and lichens, the whole held together with spiderwebs. The nest site is usually protected—under an overhang, in the lee of dense vegetation, and so on. As in all hummingbirds, the clutch consists of two elliptical white eggs. Incubation and nestling periods are unknown.

Panterpe is typical of a number of dominant, aggressive species in which the males hold territories at rich clumps of flowers during the breeding season. The quantity and quality of flowers a male controls are a major part of his ability to attract females and mate. Since most *Macleania* is localized in large clumps, males controlling several such clumps will be better able to attract females. This is particularly so in *Panterpe*, where unlike most hummingbirds a pair bond of sorts is formed. Males will allow particular females access to flowers in their territory that they defend against all other hummers but do not themselves use; such females nest near the territory of the male and presumably copulate with him. Thus the female gains a "guaranteed" food source, the male is "guaranteed" paternity. The number of females with which a male can so associate obviously depends on how much *Macleania* he can control, above his own requirements for self-maintenance. The male takes no direct part in the nesting attempt itself; indeed, there is no reliable report of direct male aid in any hummingbird.

Panterpe plays a decisive role in organizing the hummingbird community at high elevations in Costa Rica. Being both behaviorally dominant and broad-niched, *Panterpe* affects the foraging niches of all other species present. *Colibri* is effectively relegated to a flower that *Panterpe* uses only when its preferred flowers are scarce (*Centropogon valerii*); when *Panterpe* turns to this flower (often May–July), *Colibri* leaves the area. *Eugenes* is mostly restricted to long-tubed flowers that *Panterpe* cannot exploit efficiently; it also occurs in the understory, whereas *Panterpe* is most abundant in the canopy in undisturbed forest. *Eugenes* is, in effect, a high-elevation hermit equivalent (no true hermits occur above 2,000 m

in Costa Rica), females and often males visiting widely scattered flowers. *Selasphorus* is restricted to low-nectar flowers, or clumps of nectar-rich flowers that are too small to be defended by *Panterpe*. Its foraging niche is very broad, since in general it "takes what is left over."

*

Colwell, R. K. 1973. Competition and coexistence in a simple tropical community. *Am. Nat.* 107:737–60.

Colwell, R. K.; Betts, B. J.; Bunnell, P.; Carpenter, F. L.; and Feinsinger, P. 1974. Competition for nectar of *Centropogon valerii* by the hummingbird *Colibri thalassinus* and the flower-piercer *Diglossa plumbea,* and its ecological implications. *Condor* 76:447–52.

Wolf, L. L. 1969. Female territoriality in a tropical hummingbird. *Auk* 86:490–504.

Wolf, L. L., and Stiles, F. G. 1970. Evolution of pair cooperation in a tropical hummingbird. *Evolution* 24:759–73.

Wolf, L. L.; Stiles, F. G.; and Hainsworth, F. R. 1976. Ecological organization of a tropical highland hummingbird community. *J. Anim. Ecol.* 45:349–79.

Pelecanus occidentalis (Pelicano Pardo, Buchón, Alcatraz, Brown Pelican)

R. W. Schreiber and M. B. McCoy

The brown pelican (*Pelecanus occidentalis*) (fig. 10.40) is one of the best-known most popular birds of the Western Hemisphere. Large size, graceful flight, and an easily caricatured shape contribute to making pelicans popular attractions along warm marine coasts from North Carolina south to northern Brazil, where the muddy waters of the Orinoco evidently have prevented the species from spreading southward. Along the Pacific coast, brown pelicans range from southern British Columbia to southern Chile. Several races have been described in this extensive range; *P. o. carolinensis* is the form found along both coasts of Costa Rica (Blake 1977). The large Humboldt current form, *P. o. thagus,* is sometimes considered a distinct species.

In Costa Rica brown pelicans are common to abundant year-round on the Pacific coast, especially in the Golfo de Nicoya and along the Guanacaste coast. A single breeding colony is known, on Isla Guayabo in the Golfo de Nicoya. This colony was estimated to contain 150–200 breeding pairs in 1972 (Stiles and Smith 1977), but more recent and exhaustive censuses in 1979 indicate 480–500 pairs (McCoy, unpub. data). Even so, peak numbers and evident migratory flocks or concentrations of pelicans in September–October and April–May suggest that a good proportion of Costa Rican pelicans are migrants from the much larger colonies in the Gulfo de Panamá (Stiles and Smith 1977). On the Atlantic coast brown pelicans are far less numerous, with small concentrations likely to be

FIGURE 10.40. *Pelecanus occidentalis. a,* Two adults. *b,* Adult with two downy young on nest (photos, R. W. Schreiber and M. B. McCoy).

found at river mouths and estuaries. There are no known pelican breeding colonies on the Atlantic coast of Costa Rica.

Pelican populations in several parts of the United States showed drastic declines in the 1960s and early 1970s (Schreiber and Delong 1969; Schreiber and Risebrough 1972). Contamination by chlorinated hydrocarbons appears to be the major cause of these declines. The major sources of these substances in the environment are pesticides like DDT or Endrin, or their breakdown products (e.g., DDE), which persist and retain their toxicity long after application. Chlorinated hydrocarbons like DDE interfere with calcium deposition in the eggshell, resulting in thin-shelled eggs that may break before incubation can be completed; the direct relation between DDE and eggshell thinning has been overwhelmingly documented (Blus et al. 1976). The brown pelican is officially listed as endangered by the United States Department of the Interior, and its plight was a major factor in producing the ban on DDT use in 1972. Since that time, DDT contamination and eggshell thinning have decreased in most areas, and the pelican is showing

marked signs of recovering its successful reproductive status (Anderson et al. 1975; Schreiber 1979*a*).

The concern for the pelicans' welfare in the United States has led to several intensive studies of its breeding biology there and in Baja California. However, very little is known of the reproductive success of brown pelicans elsewhere in their extensive range. Data on numbers of birds, location of nesting and roosting/loafing areas, age-class composition of the population, and timing of the nesting season should be collected. There is cause for grave concern regarding the future of the Costa Rican pelican population: the Isla Guayabo breeding colony is being exposed to ever-increasing levels of pesticide contamination owing to the continuing sharp increase in rice and cotton cultivation in the Tempisque basin. Importation of chlorinated insecticides in 1978 was 283,000 kg; of that 45,000 was DDT (of concentration 75%) (data from Ministry of Agriculture, San José).

The Isla Guayabo colony is only now receiving scientific study, and any census-type data on pelican populations or observations of marked birds (such as can be collected by OTS groups at, say, Playas del Coco) could be valuable in enabling us to monitor population trends and distribution.

Adult brown pelicans weigh 2–5 kg, with males averaging heavier than females and having longer wings and bills. It takes 3–5 years to attain the full adult plumage: black brown below, silvery or brown above (appearing pale brown from a distance), the head either white or yellow and neck black or white depending on season of the year. Young birds have white bellies and all brown or tan heads, necks, backs, and wings. Flight feathers are probably molted once a year, but the head and neck undergo a more complex series of plumage changes that are not fully understood. In adults, complicated changes in colors of plumage and soft parts (bill, pouch, and iris) are synchronized with the breeding cycle; a bird with bright yellow head feathers, reddish bill, and white or black neck is breeding or soon will begin. The feathers fade and wear through the nesting cycle, to be replaced later by fresh plumage.

As in all Pelecaniformes, the young enter the throats of the adults to force them to regurgitate. Males and females share chick-raising duties equally. Nestlings require 10–12 weeks to fledge. Eggs are laid asynchronously, normally three to a clutch, and incubation lasts 30 days.

The brown pelican is the only member of the family Pelecanidae that is strictly marine and the only species that dives for fish; the other species are found primarily inland and feed in communal groups. The nesting season is highly variable, and in tropical areas nesting may occur year-round (Palmer 1962; Schreiber 1980). Young are less successful than adults in diving to catch fish, but with time they become more skilled at the complicated technique (Orians 1969; Schreiber, Woolfenden, and Curtsinger 1975).

We made four monthly visits (from February to May 1979) to the pelican nesting colony on Isla Guayabo to determine reproductive success and status. The island consists of about 3 ha of stratified sedimentary rock jutting upward to about 35 m from the Golfo de Nicoya and is more or less flat topped with almost perpendicular cliffs on all sides. It is 8 km southwest of Puntarenas and is under the protection of the National Park Service as a biological reserve. The soil is well developed, and the vegetative cover is dense, consisting mostly of grass, tall annual forbs, and a large spiny shrub of the family Malvaceae that covers one third to one half of the island's area.

This plant grows in five distinct dense patches on the island to heights of 1–4 m, and it is in the tops and lower edges of this spiny, dense growth that the pelicans nest. The higher, larger, and less accessible parts of these patches are occupied first, and as space diminishes lower areas are selected, down to 1 m. Nests are distributed 1–2 m apart throughout the shrubby growth (pecking distance between two sitting adults).

On each visit we counted as many of the nests as possible on foot and from the top of a single palm tree situated centrally on the island. The fate of 48 selected nests was also followed on the first two visits.

On the first visit we observed 430 nests, with an estimated 490 total nests initiated. In the early morning, (0600), while both adults were still at the nest, we counted 765 adults from the palm, which corresponded nicely to the 380 nests visible from the tree. Of the nests seen from the tree 25 already had chicks, and the chicks of 3 nests were already close to fledging. However, most of the nests were starting the third week of incubation. No subadults (1–2 years) were observed in or near the colony during any of the four visits.

The average number of eggs per nest in the 48 selected nests on the last visit was 2.42, with the majority containing three eggs. Because these nests were lower, therefore younger, this value may be an underestimate, since egg laying may not have been fully completed. The 13 nests with chicks contained an average of 2.08 per nest, with most containing three.

Six weeks later on the second visit the number of chicks per nest had dropped to 1.41 in these same nests, (48) with a desertion rate of 16.7%. Most were 4 weeks old and contained two chicks per nest. In the large northern patch of nesting vegetation we counted 251 chicks in 149 nests (1.68 per nest). Between the first and second visits a large, unexplained number of nests disappeared.

Because of nest disappearance and chick mobility, we counted only total numbers of chicks on the third and fourth visits. We counted a total of 506 chicks for all areas on the third visit. Strangely, very low mortality occurred in the north section between the second and third visits (251 down to 248), which could be attributed to an error in observation.

During the fourth visit we counted 188 chicks in all areas excluding the northern patch or section. This lower figure (down from 258) cannot be attributed solely to mortality, since many chicks had fledged.

The high nesting levels encountered in this year compared with 1972 data (Stiles and Smith 1977) again show the variability between years that has been observed in all other colonies and attributed to fluctuating nutrient levels in the sea (Schreiber 1979a). At peak nest levels observed on the first visit there still seemed to be enough room in the vegetation for 20–25% more nests.

Plenty of nests contained three eggs, and no crushed eggs were found on the ground or in any nests. In fact, several fallen eggs were found intact on the ground. The last chick to hatch usually died first, and heavy mortality hit the remaining chicks from 3 through 6 weeks of age owing to falls and strangulations in the dense brush. If a chick reached 6 weeks of age, it seemed to have a good chance of fledging. No forms of avian predation were observed, although large lizards and snakes are present and may be a factor. Disturbance by humans remains slight owing to the difficulty of access, but other factors such as entanglement in fishing line are not well understood; however, two frigate birds (*Fregata magnificens*) fell victim to this fate on the island during the study.

Temperatures pose another problem to the eggs and young—bare chicks in this colony—since March is the hottest month of the year, with midday temperatures of 36–40° C. The adults protect the eggs and young while sitting on the nest. Adults constantly pant rapidly through partially opened beaks, which flutters their gular pouches, blowing air over the numerous blood vessels in the thin skin (Schreiber 1977). This thermoregulation is enhanced by the bird's positioning the beak and pouch away from the sun, using the head and neck as a shield. As the sun moves along its path the birds rotate their bodies clockwise bit by bit, thus always facing away from the sun. What an impressive sight to see several hundred birds perfectly aligned in the same direction! When an adult is relieved by its mate it heads straight for the water, splashing upon landing and stabbing its beak into the water several times apparently to wet the dried skin of the pouch. We saw panting in week-old chicks, and adults begin both aspects of thermoregulation about 1.5 h after sunup.

Adult presence at the nest declined steadily as the season progressed, until by the fourth visit we saw virtually no adults in the vegetation; they came near only to feed the young and then left. The young became progressively darker in color, grew less noisy, and seemed to remain near their nest site for a time even when able to fly, but it was not possible to determine how many birds did this or for how long.

Up to the third visit (six weeks after the major hatch) the overall chick production was about 1.18 young per nest initiated (506/430), which may be close to normal production in other colonies (Schreiber 1979b). Several eggs were collected from three-egg nests to determine concentrations of chlorinated hydrocarbons. The present data suggest that the colony at this time is doing fairly well; however, close monitoring should be continued, since these insecticides are still entering the country at an alarming rate from the United States and United States companies in Europe.

On the last visit, seventeen chicks were color-banded with red leg bands and blue plastic leg streamers. Any reports of marked birds in any part of the country would be greatly appreciated, since we need to learn more about distribution and migration. A more intensive marking program is planned for following years.

*

Anderson, O. W., et al. 1975. Brown pelicans: Improved reproduction off the southern California coast. *Science* 190:806–8.

Blake, E. R. 1977. *Manual of Neotropical birds*. Chicago: University of Chicago Press.

Blus, L. J., et al. 1976. Residues of organochlorines and heavy metals in tissues and eggs of brown pelicans, 1969–1973. *Pest. Monit. J.* 11:40–53.

Orians, G. H. 1969. Age and hunting success in the brown pelican (*Pelecanus occidentalis*). *Anim. Behav.* 17:316–19.

Palmer, R. S. 1962. *Handbook of North American birds*. New Haven: Yale University Press.

Schreiber, R. W. 1976. Growth and development of nestling brown pelicans. *Bird Band.* 47:19–39.

———. 1977. Maintenance behavior and communication in the brown pelican. *AOU Monogr.* 22:1–78.

———. 1979a. The brown pelican: An endangered species? *BioScience* 30:742–47.

———. 1979b. Reproductive performance of the eastern brown pelican. *Contrib. Sci., Nat. Hist. Museum, Los Angeles County* 317:1–43.

———. 1980. Nesting chronology of the eastern brown pelican. *Auk* 97:491–508.

Schreiber, R. W., and Delong, R. L. 1969. Brown pelican status in California. *Audubon Field Notes* 23:57–59.

Schreiber, R. W., and Risebrough, R. W. 1972. Studies of the brown pelican. *Wilson Bull.* 84:119–35.

Schreiber, R. W.; Woolfenden, G. E.; and Curtsinger, W. E. 1975. Prey capture by the brown pelican. *Auk* 92:649–54.

Stiles, F. G., and Smith. S. M. 1977. New information on Costa Rican waterbirds. *Condor* 79:91–97.

Phaethornis superciliosus (Ermitaño Colilargo, Gorrión, Long-tailed Hermit)

F. G. Stiles

Walking through wet lowland forest, one is from time to time accosted by a rather dull-colored hummingbird (fig. 10.41) with a long, curved bill; the bird will approach to within a meter or less and submit one to a detailed inspection from several angles, then suddenly dash off into the understory with a shrill squeak. Such curiosity toward humans is widespread among the members of the subfamily Phaethorninae, called hermits because they tend to wander widely and singly through the forest understory. The long-tailed hermit, *Phaethornis superciliosus,* is one of the commonest (and most inveterately curious) of the hermits throughout the wet Caribbean and southern Pacific lowlands of Costa Rica. It is a typical hermit in many respects: long curved bill (35–40 mm), dull colors (bronzy greenish above, brownish gray below, with conspicuous paler stripes behind and below the eye and down the throat), reduced sexual dimorphism (males average larger than females but are identical in color), foraging (long-distance traplining), and social system (males form courtship assemblies or leks during the breeding season). At the same time, its annual cycle demonstrates some extremely interesting adaptations to strong and variable seasonal rhythms of flower availability.

P. superciliosus is a medium-sized hermit (about 6 g) whose most conspicuous plumage feature is the greatly elongated (65–75 mm) white-tipped central rectrices. The bird also possesses an orange mouth lining that, together with the facial stripes, produces a striking pattern when the bill is opened. Among the most widespread of hermits, *P. superciliosus* ranges from southern Mexico to Amazonian Brazil. It is always a bird of forest understory, forest edge and light gaps, and old second growth. Above 500–800 m elevation it is abruptly replaced by the green hermit, *P. guy,* of similar size and habits.

In the wet lowlands *P. superciliosus* coexists with up to four other hermit species and eight to ten members of the subfamily Trochilinae, the "typical hummingbirds" or "nonhermits," which mostly have shorter, straight bills. All hermits are traplining foragers that do not defend feeding territories at flowers. The nonhermits employ a variety of foraging tactics, and at least males of some

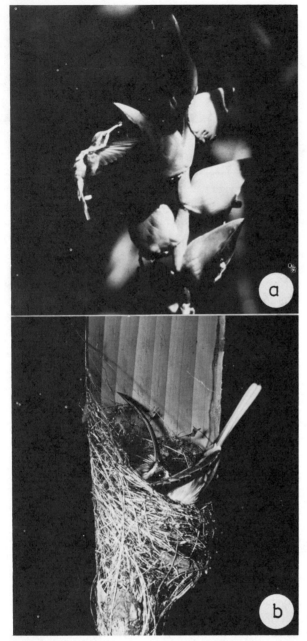

FIGURE 10.41. *Phaethornis superciliosus. a,* Adult male visiting flower of *Heliconia.* Finca La Selva, Sarapiquí District, Costa Rica (photo, F. G. Stiles). *b,* Adult on nest with eggs. Corcovado National Park, Costa Rica (photo, D. H. Janzen).

species are regularly territorial at nectar-rich flowers. For many flowers, visitation patterns are thus mediated by interference competition within and between species. Among nonhermits, interspecific dominance hierarchies are related to size (body weight), but even rather large hermits like *P. superciliosus* can be excluded from flowers defended by smaller (4–5 g) but more aggressive nonhermits. The survival of hermits in such a system re-

quires the existence of numerous flowers that cannot be profitably exploited by nonhermits owing to their long, curved corollas and scattered distributions. The different species of hermits coexist because of differences in flower choice and specificity, habitat preferences, and lengths of foraging routes. At Finca La Selva, traplines of male *P. superciliosus* may extend to 1 km from leks, although 300–500 m seems more typical. The most frequently visited flowers are species of *Heliconia* (especially *H. pogonantha* at La Selva), *Costus, Aphelandra, Malvaviscus, Passiflora vitifolia,* and so forth. The diet also includes numerous small spiders, chiefly orb-weavers, and insects gleaned from their webs or less often from foliage. Typically birds will pause briefly for spider-hunting as they trapline nectar sources.

The most striking behavioral feature of *P. superciliosus* is the male courtship assemblies or leks, which typically contain about a dozen (range three to twenty-five) males. Leks are located in areas of dense thickets, usually along streams that serve as flyways and as habitat for important food plants. Each male on a lek defends a small territory in dense understory vegetation. The foci of lek activity are the three to six song perches in each territory, where the male spends most of his lek time advertising his presence with a monotonously repeated, single-note song. Challenges of one male by another, and male-female interactions, are initiated with visual and vocal displays centered on the song perches. Because of the density of the vegetation, even adjacent males are generally unable to see each other; the song provides the main means of communication on the lek. Each male on the lek appears to know the location of the regularly used song perches of all the other males.

The lekking season of *P. superciliosus* at La Selva commences when *Heliconia pogonantha* attains good bloom, between late November and January: most males arrive on the lek within a week or two of one another. Lek activity is very intense through May or June; between late June and August the old males gradually leave the lek, their places often being taken by young males a few months old. These birds probably cannot fertilize females, but their chances of obtaining a lek territory the following season are greatly enhanced by the experience they gain as immatures. As flowering at La Selva declines from August to November, all lek activity drops drastically by late August, effectively ceasing by late September. Nesting by females occupies nearly the same 8–9-month span as lekking by males: roughly from December or January through August, with a peak in the dry season. Very few nests succeed between September and November, when flowers are scarce. Survivorship of lek males averages 90% or better during the long lekking season but drops to about 50–60% during this period of flower scarcity; up to 80% of the annual mortality occurs in the month of November alone. Birds weigh less in this month and have low or declining fat reserves.

As in all hummingbirds, the female *P. superciliosus* builds the nest, lays and incubates the eggs, and feeds the young with no aid from the male: indeed, such "emancipation" of the male from the nesting effort is thought to be a prerequisite for the evolution of leks. The nest is a compact cup of plant fiber, held together and attached with spiderwebs to the underside of the tip of a palm leaf or a strip of a banana or *Heliconia* leaf. A loose, dangling "tail" including bits of dead leaves and such gives the nest the appearance of a piece of hanging trash. Although such a nest site is perfectly protected from rain and might seem virtually predator-proof, 75–80% of all nests fail, usually owing to predation. Incubation of the two elliptical white eggs requires 17–18 days, and the young do not leave the nest until 22–27 days of age; the female feeds the young for perhaps another week or two after they fledge. Thus a successful nesting requires at least two months. Probably a female can raise no more than three broods in a season, and owing to frequent nest failures one or two is more likely. Evidence from other hummingbird species suggests that a female whose nest fails will promptly start another; the long breeding season thus permits many attempts.

Given the high annual mortality, a long breeding season is obviously important in permitting *P. superciliosus* to exist at La Selva. The breeding season is effectively lengthened by the regular overlap of molt and reproduction in at least some individuals. This is facilitated by a very slow molt (ca. 4 months) that spreads the energy demand over a long period. Studies on marked birds indicate that each individual molts at almost exactly the same time each year, but that different birds may be up to 6–8 months out of phase. Data from young birds followed through 1–2 years indicate that the molt cycle is somehow started or keyed at about the time of hatching; whether the cycle is a true free-running circannual rhythm or must be reset annually remains to be seen. However, its ecological effect is to provide for regular feather renewal— especially important for a humming-bird—and flexibility in breeding schedules, to take advantage of the year-to-year variability in flowering seasons. Males can molt and be fully active on the lek simultaneously; females may interrupt a molt for a breeding attempt, an indication that breeding is energetically more costly for females. Such a system of scheduling annual energy demands (a fixed molting season, a more variable breeding season) may be widespread in tropical birds.

*

Skutch, A. F. 1964. Life histories of hermit hummingbirds. *Auk* 81:5–25.

Snow, D. W., and Snow, B. K. 1964. Breeding seasons and annual cycles of Trinidad land-birds. *Zoologica* 49:1–39.

Stiles, F. G. 1975. Ecology, flowering phenology, and hummingbird pollination of some Costa Rican *Heliconia* species. *Ecology* 56:285–301.

Stiles, F. G., and Wolf, L. L. 1974. A possible circannual molt rhythm in a tropical hummingbird. *Am. Nat.* 108:341–54.

———. 1979. The ecology and evolution of a lek mating system in the long-tailed hermit hummingbird. *Am. Ornithol. Union Monogr.*, no. 27.

Pharomachrus mocinno (Quetzal)

A. LaBastille

The quetzal, one of the most beautiful birds in Central America, is the national bird of Guatemala (fig. 10.42). The graceful, shy trogon (Trogonidae) appears on that country's unit of currency (one quetzal equals one dollar) and on its shield, stamps, and flag. In Costa Rica the bird is less popular, yet still admired.

The species covers a 1,000-mile range, at elevations roughly from 1,500 to 2,500 m, although there is one record of close to 3,200 m in Guatemala. In Costa Rica it occurs locally as low as 1,300 m or as high as 3,000 m. The center of the range is about 1,500–2,500 m. The northern subspecies (*Pharomachrus mocinno mocinno*) occurs from southern Mexico to Honduras and northwestern Nicaragua, and the southern subspecies (*P. m. costaricensis*) is found from extreme southern Nicaragua to western Panama. The bird is endangered in nearly every country owing to destruction of the cloud-forest habitat.

FIGURE 10.42. *Pharomachrus mocinno. a,* Adult male perched at nest entrance in side of large tree in forest understory. *b,* Nestling (photos, N. Wheelwright).

The common name, quetzal, is derived from *quetzalli,* an early Aztec word for the birds' tail feathers, also meaning "precious" or "beautiful." The Latin genus name translates from Greek as "long mantle," referring to the male's flowing tail coverts. Also called the resplendent trogon, this small, pigeon-sized bird (35 cm) sports a meter-long tail, short head crest, and carmine red breast in the males. The head, back, and wing coverts of both sexes are a vivid emerald green. Females are generally duller, show less red, and have no long tail plumes. The shimmering green plumage blends well with wet foliage and offers excellent camouflage under rainy conditions in the forest canopy.

Seen at magnification of 10,000 times, the feather of a quetzal is not green at all; it is brown. The composition is one of tiny brown packets of melanin spaced approximately 5,400 Ängstroms apart. The wave length of green light is in this range; therefore, the physical phenomenon of interference makes light hitting the feather reflect green.

A bird of the canopy, the quetzal is quite wary. When it surveys the surroundings, it sits with the red parts facing away from any suspected intruder or danger. The bird may sit motionless for long periods, only occasionally turning its head slowly from side to side. When threatened or suspicious, the quetzal's alarm call is a harsh *weec-weec,* montonous and grating. The sound is accompanied by a quick flick of the tail feathers opened fanlike every second. The species is most active during courtship, when the males may launch into spiraling skyward flights, then plummet back to the canopy with their long tail feathers rippling behind. Courtship chasing through the trees is also common.

The breeding season occurs between March and June. Paired birds dig at rotten tree stumps and snags, usually deepening and enlarging holes made by woodpeckers, toucans, or other animals. Their beaks and claws are not strong enough to penetrate live wood. Most nest holes are found at a height of 10 m and measure roughly 10 by 10 by 30 cm. Two eggs constitute the normal clutch. They are light blue and measure approximately 39 by 32 mm. Both parents share in nest making, incubation, and care of young (fig. 10.42). Normally they divide the day into two shifts each.

The average quetzal territory (the defended area) is judged to be about 350 m radius around the nest tree, with vertical dimensions of from 4 m to above the canopy. The males begin a round of territorial calling at dawn until midmorning, then again at dusk. This call is a sharp, two-toned, melodious whistle, repeated every 8 to 10 min. The home range (feeding area held during nesting season) occupies approximately 6 to 10 ha in the top third of the forest canopy. Quetzals come lower during the nesting period because they depend upon finding dead and decaying tree stubs in which to carve out their nest holes; however, the birds have never been observed on or near the ground.

Their diet is chiefly fruits such as wild figs and avocados, insects, and small frogs and lizards. It is presumed that quetzals obtain their drinking water from food or use water held in the bases of bromeliads.

Nest trees appear to be the major *direct* natural limiting factor for quetzal survival in the wild. There is often a scarcity of trees with wood soft enough to permit nest excavation. Those trees that are right are usually in the last stages of decay before falling. They are susceptible to damage by earthquakes, heavy rains soaking into the wood, wind, and other climatic factors.

Human activity resulting in habitat destruction is the chief *indirect* factor affecting the birds. In Central America, large tracts of cloud forest are being cleared for cattle pasture, agriculture, or cut-and-burn shifting agriculture by native farmers. Often their fires escape and burn uncontrolled for weeks. In addition, cloud forests are being logged for tropical timbers, roof shingles, firewood, and charcoal. There is a steady trend by private plantation owners of clearing mountain and volcano slopes. They plant coffee, tea, cardamom, spices, nuts, quinine, and semitemperate vegetables. In many places the line of cultivation is already at an altitude of 1,500 to 2,000 m. Predictably, the loss of trees and topsoil causes long-range damage to the watershed and water table. Humans, domestic animals, wildlife, and fish living at lower levels may find streams and springs diminishing and floods increasing owing to removal of protective cover from that "giant sponge"—the cloud forest—above.

Another minor danger to quetzals comes from natives who trade illegally in skins, feathers, and live specimens. They try to earn extra money by selling quetzals and hunt them with blowguns, old shotguns, rifles, and traps.

In recent years a few quetzal reserves have been established in Central America. In Costa Rica the birds are protected on Volcán Poás, Braulio Carrillo, and Chirripó National parks and at Monteverde Forest Preserve. In Guatemala the private reserve on Volcán Atitlan has placed sixteen articifial nest boxes in the cloud forest in an attempt to encourage reproduction of resident birds. There is also a private Quetzal Biotopo reserve near Cabán under the control of the University of San Carlos. A system of cloud forest parks extending from Mexico through Panama is desperately needed to protect this unique ecosystem and this beautiful bird before both are gone.

*

Bowes, A. L. 1969. The quetzal, fabulous bird of Mayaland. *Nat. Geograph,* 135:140–50.

Bowes, A. L., and Allen, D. G. 1969. Biology and conservation of the quetzal. *Biol. Conserv.* 1:297–306.

Kern, J. 1968. Quest for the quetzal. *Audubon* 70:20–29.

LaBastille, A. 1973. Establishment of a quetzal cloud-forest reserve in Guatemala. *Biol. Conserv.* 5:60–62.

———. 1974. Use of artificial nest boxes by quetzals in Guatemala. *Biol. Conserv.*, vol. 6.

———. 1976. A question of quetzals. *Anim. King.* 78:18–24.

———. 1976. The quetzal. *Tier,* 4–7 January, p. 53.

LaBastille, A.; Allen, D. G.; and Durrell, L. W. 1972. Behavior and feather structure of the quetzal. *Auk* 89:339–48.

Ridgway, R. 1911. The birds of North and Middle America, part 5. *U.S. Nat. Mus. Bull.,* no. 50.

Skutch, A. 1944. Life history of the quetzal. *Condor* 46:213–35.

Premnoplex brunnescens (Subipalo Moteado, Spotted Barbtail)

G. V. N. Powell

The spotted barbtail (*Premnoplex brunnescens*), a member of the passerine family Furnariidae (ovenbirds), is a small bird (15 g) with rich brown upperparts and olive brown underparts heavily spotted with buff. Barbtails inhabit middle-elevation forest (above 800 m) between Costa Rica and Bolivia. They forage as a typical tree-creeping species, moving up trunks and larger branches probing arthropods from bark crevices and among epiphytes. *Premnoplex* is shy, quick to retreat to cover in response to any disturbance. Its presence is most frequently detected by sharp, staccato warning notes given singly in response to threatening stimuli. Like many montane Neotropical species, barbtails apparently pair for life and maintain territories throughout the year. Average territory size in lower montane wet forest in Costa Rica (Monteverde, 1,500 m) is about 2 ha. Resident birds regularly range beyond their territory boundaries, trespassing onto adjacent territories. Overlap of home ranges is extensive, and territorial defense, particularly against neighboring conspecifics, is frequent. Agonistic behavior is primarily restricted to threats and supplantings, but when trespassers are slow to retreat, physical fighting may follow. Threat behavior is interesting, since it is specialized for a bird that predominantly perches on vertical stalks and therefore has little flexibility in body movements and orientations. A threatening bird extends both wings fully straight behind its back until they are parallel and almost touching. At the same time it spreads the tail and braces it against the substrate and raises its crown feathers. These displays are sequenced with bursts of loud staccato notes given either singly or in rapid succession.

Barbtails breed between March and June, the breeding season for most middle-elevation insectivorous species.

Their nests are hollow moss structures built into moss-covered tree nooks or attached to tangles of vines. The nest cup is reached via a narrow entrance tunnel. Two young are generally produced from successful nests. Fledglings remain with their parents up to 2 months and then become a floating population occupying habitat that is infrequently used by territorial conspecifics. Whenever young birds are encountered by territorial birds they are chased from the area.

Premnoplex is a consistent participant in understory mixed-species flocks. In Costa Rica, *Basileuterus* (Parulidae) and *Chlorospingus* (Thraupidae) are the principal nuclei of understory mixed flocks in higher-elevation forests. At Monteverde pairs of *Premnoplex* follow *Basileuterus* families for extended periods (109 ± 95 min). Their propensity to follow flocks varies throughout the year, ranging from 40% in breeding season to 90% during nonbreeding season. Examination of their territorial configurations suggests that *Premnoplex* territories are aligned to be congruent with the territories of *Basileuterus*. This enables *Premnoplex* to remain with the same family of warblers without encountering neighboring territories. The congruency reduces the frequency of agonistic encounters with adjacent conspecifics and minimizes the likelihood that birds will be excluded from a mixed flock because it crosses into a new *Premnoplex* territory.

*

Buskirk, W. H. 1972. Ecology of bird flocks in a tropical forest. Ph.D. diss., University of California, Davis.

Skutch, A. 1967. *Life histories of Central American highland birds,* ed. R. A. Porter, Jr. Publication no. 7. Cambridge, Mass.: Nuttall Ornithological Club.

Quiscalus mexicanus (Zanate, Great-tailed Grackle)

K. A. Arnold

The great-tailed grackle, *Quiscalus mexicanus* (fig. 10.43), is a member of the Pan-American songbird family the Icteridae. The species, recognized in 1961 as distinct from the North American boat-tailed grackle, *Q. major,* ranges from Colombia through Middle America to the south United States from California to western Louisiana. In the past twenty-five years, the species has spread northward to Kansas, Illinois, and Indiana and through the river valleys of Arizona to California. It is a permanent resident in most of its range but migrates from the northern part of its United States range into milder climates during the winter.

This bird, like many other icterids, is colonial and strongly sexually dimorphic. The male is both more col-

FIGURE 10.43. *Quiscalus mexicanus* adult male (photo, K. A. Arnold).

orful and larger, averaging about 50% more by weight. Males are frequently polygamous. The colonies are usually built near human habitation. It is likely that the recent northward spread resulted from this strong association with humans.

In Texas males establish territories in late March and early April, although great-tails have initiated nesting as early as February. The peak of egg laying occurs in late April and early May, with the peak for nestlings in mid-May and the peak for fledging in late May. Nesting may extend into mid-July.

Although the male defends a territory and will join a mobbing action against an intruder in the colony, it is the female that builds the nest, incubates the eggs, and feeds and broods the young. The nests are bulky, woven structures, usually placed in upright forks of trees in the top meter of the canopy. Although constructed mostly of grass, man-made materials such as string and paper strips are frequently incorporated. In Texas a female lays two to six eggs, with a mode of three. Renesting occurs only when a clutch or nest is lost. Incubation lasts about 13 days, and the nestling period is also about 13 days. As with many passerines, reproductive success ranges from 45% to 60%. Sex ratio of chicks hatched is about 50:50, but males are greatly reduced in number the first year after hatching. Females enter the breeding population in the first season after hatching. However, the first-year males, as with many other icterids, are not involved in breeding.

After fledging, the young remain with the female for several weeks, sometimes as long as 10 weeks. These family units are probably the basis for the establishment of roosts as several families coalesce into a loose aggre-gation, both for daytime foraging and for nighttime roosting. These roosts are frequently problems to human communities, although this is usually at a nuisance level.

Great-tails are opportunistic feeders. Studies in Texas show that they typically feed on insects, including large numbers of orthopterans, but will turn to grains when insect populations are depressed. They consume small vertebrates and in South Texas may be a serious predator on the eggs and nestlings of white-winged doves. Their grain-eating habits cause conflict with man, especially when nonbreeding grackle flocks eat large numbers of newly planted seeds or emerging grain sprouts. Adult males usually forage in different areas from females and young, generally alone or in two or threes. Females and young often forage in flocks ranging from ten to several hundred, which probably reflects their greater agility in pursuing and capturing more agile insects; the large tail of the male is at times a hinderance to his movements.

From studies in Texas, great-tails are known to be migratory. This leads to the establishment of large roosts around urban centers. The birds abandon their small colonies in less populated situations and join neighboring colonies in summer and fall roosts. Thus these roosts may have populations drawn from several hundred square miles.

Males display before females both in the colonies and in adjoining open areas. Two or more males, even in the absence of females, will display the "head up" behavior. This occurs even outside the reproductive season. During the breeding season a male selects a well-exposed perch and performs with displays and loud, squeaky calls. One of the calls resembles the increasing whine of a motor just starting. When a female lands near a displaying male, the male responds with a "flutter chase" in which he circles the female with feathers erect, wings raised and fluttering, and gives a series of squeaky notes. If the female is receptive, a pair bond is established through continuation of the displays; otherwise the female departs.

In spite of conflicts with human populations, this conspicuous species continues to do well. It shows a dynamic population growth that probably will continue for many years.

*

Arnold, K. A., and Folse, L. J., Jr. 1977. Movements of the great-tailed grackle in Texas. *Wilson Bull.* 89: 602–8.

Davis, W. R., II, Arnold, K. A. 1972. Food habits of the great-tailed grackle in Brazos County, Texas. *Condor* 74:439–46.

Grotie, R. E., and Kroll, J. C. 1973. Growth rate and ontogeny of thermoregulation in nestling great-tailed grackles, *Cassidix mexicanus prosopidicola* (Icteridae). *Condor* 75:190–99.

Kok, O. B. 1971. Vocal behavior of the great-tailed grackle (*Quiscalus mexicanus prosopidicola*). *Condor* 73:348–63.

Pruitt, J. 1975. The return of the great-tailed grackle. *Am. Birds* 29:985–92.

Selander, R. K., and Giller, D. R. 1961. Analysis of sympatry of great-tailed and boat-tailed grackles. *Condor* 63:29–86.

Ramphastos swainsonii (Dios Tede, Toucan de Swainson, Chestnut-mandibled Toucan)

H. F. Howe

This is the largest toucan in Central America. It occurs in lowland and highland wet forests from Honduras to Ecuador; in Costa Rica it is most common in the wet forests of the Caribbean slope. Unlike its smaller congener *R. sulfuratus* Gould, the keel-billed toucan (fig. 10.44), the chestnut-mandible toucan is absent from the seasonal dry forest of Guanacaste. In its proper habitat, the large bird is one of the most conspicuous members of the avifauna.

Despite its size and abundance, the natural history of

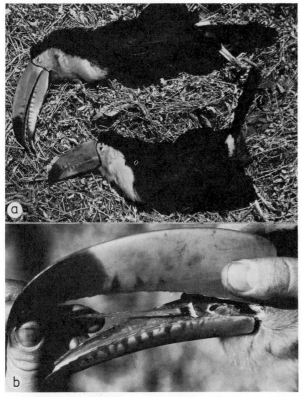

FIGURE 10.44. *Ramphastos sulphuratus. a,* Shot by rural hunter (note male with much larger bill). *b,* Bill with highly modified tongue. Tilarán, Guanacaste Province, Costa Rica (photos, D. H. Janzen).

the chestnut-mandibled toucan is poorly known. Females average a little less than 600 g, and males are approximately 70 g heavier (Howe 1977). Prominent brown-and-yellow bicolored bills are also dimorphic; with practice a naturalist can distinguish males from females by the large size of the male's bill. Otherwise the sexes look alike, with a black body, yellow bib, white rump, and red undertail coverts. Van Tyne (1929) and Skutch (1971) have studied a few nests, finding that the birds raise broods of two or three in natural tree cavities. Both sexes help care for the young. The piercing call of this species is one of the most striking sounds of the Neotropical wet forest, but the context in which it is given is not clear. Some birds call from fruiting trees; evidently this is a territorial display. But in March and April, and sometimes at other times of the year, congregations of up to twenty individuals—sometimes with keel-billed toucans included—create a noisy jumble of cries and creaks (from the smaller species) from prominent trees in the forest. The problem awaits the attention of an ethologist. The striking color patterns of both of the large Central American toucans may function in either courtship or intimidation, but not in humdrum daily affairs such as copulation, which takes less than 5 sec and is accompanied by a conspicuous lack of preliminaries.

Food is diverse, consisting of fruit and occasional animals. This toucan is one of the largest avian frugivores in the forest, and its choice of fruit is not restricted by size as much as in smaller birds. In Costa Rica and Panama I have seen the species eat the tiny seeds of *Cecropia* and *Ficus* (Moraceae), medium-sized berries, drupes, and arilloids of *Casearia* (Flacourtiaceae), *Sorocea* (Moraceae), *Protium* and *Tetragastris* (Burseraceae), *Faramea* (Rubiaceae), and bulky drupes and arilloids of *Virola* (Myristicaceae), *Beilschmiedia* (Lauraceae), and *Socratea* (Palmae), among many others. Small seeds are passed unharmed through the gut; large ones are retained in the crop for 5–30 min and regurgitated in viable condition. The bird utilizes only the edible fleshy part of the fruit. Although this bird eats many kinds of fruit, it seems to be most important as a dispersal agent at trees such as *Virola,* in which the edible aril is largely fat (more than 50%) and protein (more than 2.5%). At some heavily laden trees, toucans simply occupy portions of the crown and eat and regurgitate seeds in place, performing no dispersal function at all (Howe 1977). At other trees, such as the sugar-fruited *Tetragastris* tree in Panama, chestnut-mandibled toucans are conspicuous consumers but are actually insignificant as dispersal agents, since monkeys and other mammals remove far more seeds per visit (Howe 1980). The extent to which a bird is a dispersal agent or simply a fruit thief depends on the size of the crop, the palatability of the fruit, and the proportion of fruit taken to young in tree cavities. This toucan is an archetypal "fearless frugivore" and does not process fruit under cover of surrounding vegetation, as do many small birds. In addition to fruit, this bird opportunistically eats large insects and actively hunts for other animal food, such as birds' eggs, nestlings, and lizards. It usually stays in the canopy but it sometimes descends to the understory to feed at shrubs, or even to the forest floor to pursue small animals.

Very little is known for sure about the behavioral ecology of these birds, but extensive observations at fruiting trees have yielded some insights (Howe 1977, 1980). Males feed fruit to females, and the two sexes preen each other. Well after breeding stops, males defend portions of fruiting trees against all other frugivores except their mates, suggesting both "pair cooperation" and a stable mating bond. Males of a pair frequently arrive first at a fruiting tree and feed for a few moments before the female arrives. The male leaves for another tree of the same or a different species before the crop is depleted, and the female finishes what is left. Then she follows her mate. Since both sexes displace smaller frugivores, this visitation pattern allow pairs to dominate some food resources (e.g., *Virola sebifera,* a small tree) by "holding down" two trees at once. Displacement of other birds is usually accomplished by threat, but bill clashes between toucans occur. In only one instance have I seen a female actually attack a male and attempt to displace him from a fruiting tree; the male promptly drove her out. This suggests an advantage to large body or bill size. When fruit is abundant, toucans of one or both species travel in groups of three to eight. At such times, intra- and interspecific aggression is neglibible. Both sexes parasitize the ability of keel-billed toucans to find food. Frequently the larger birds arrive at a tree "on the tail" of a keel-billed toucan, drive the smaller bird out of the tree, and commence to eat. I have similarly seen chestnut-mandibled toucans discover and take over tree cavities used by the smaller birds for drinking and bathing, and I once witnessed a unique interaction in which the larger toucan captured an *Ameiva* lizard that was being chased across the forest floor by a keel-billed toucan. Obviously a great deal remains to be discovered about these spectacular birds.

*

Howe, H. F. 1977. Bird activity and seed dispersal of a tropical wet forest tree. *Ecology* 58:539–50.
———. 1980. Vertebrate destruction and dispersal of a superabundant tropical fruit. *Ecology* 61:944–59.
Skutch, A. F. 1971. Life history of the keel-billed toucan. *Auk* 88:381–424.
Van Tyne, J. 1929. The life history of the toucan *Ramphastos brevicarinatus*. *Misc. Publ. Zool. Univ. Michigan* 19:1–43.

Sporophila aurita (Espiguero Variable, Setillero de Laguna, Variable Seedeater)

F. G. Stiles

This small finch (10–12 g; females average slightly heavier) (fig. 10.45) is common in semiopen and secondary growth from southern Mexico to Peru. The common name refers to the variability in male plumage. In Costa Rica the Caribbean slope is occupied by the race *S. a. corvina,* with males entirely black except for a small white wing patch and wing linings. The Pacific race *S. a. aurita* has males largely black, but with white on the throat, neck, lower breast and belly, rump, and wings. The two forms meet and hybridize in central Panama. Females of both are essentially olive brown, paling to dull buff (*corvina*) or whitish (*aurita*) in the center of the belly. On both slopes of Costa Rica variable seedeaters are among the most abundant birds of humid lower elevations (to about 1,200–1,500 m locally) wherever the forest has been removed. They are often found with other species of small seed-eating birds (e.g., *Tiaris olivacea,* yellow-faced grassquit; *Volatinia jacarina,* blue-black grassquit; *Oryzoborus funereus,* thick-billed seed-finch; and other species of *Sporophila*). Members of the genus *Sporophila* may easily be distinguished from these other species by their heavy bills with rounded (not conical) silhouettes. Four other species of the genus occur in

FIGURE 10.45. *Sporophila aurita aurita,* adult male. December 1975, Costa Rica (photo, F. G. Stiles).

Costa Rica, at least two of which are actively expanding their range with deforestation. Males of the white-collared seedeater (*S. torqueola*) resemble those of *S. a aurita* but have much more white; females are buffy below, and both sexes have prominent wing bars. This species was formerly restricted mainly to Guanacaste and the Meseta Central (where it is still far more abundant than *S. a. aurita*) but can now be found throughout the lowlands, although less abundantly than *S. a. aurita* in most areas. The slate-colored (*S. schistacea*) and yellow-bellied (*S. nigricollis*) seedeaters occur in southwestern Costa Rica; the former is uncommon and local, the latter increasingly common and expanding its range onto the Meseta Central. The tiny ruddy-breasted seedeater (*S. minuta*) is a savanna species with a very patchy distribution and two centers of abundance: the palm savannas south of the Lago de Nicaragua, and those of the Térraba valley.

All *Sporophila* species have generally similar habits; outside the breeding season they commonly form flocks that may contain several species of seedeaters (not only *Sporophila* but often *Tiaris, Volatinia,* etc.). The main food for all species is seeds of panicoid grasses, but different species may prefer seeds at different stages of maturity (J. E. Sánchez, pers. comm.). Often, however, grass seeds seem superabundant, and the feeding of the different species appears to be identical. There may also be some habitat segregation, particularly toward the breeding season. *Sporophila* nests in bushes and small trees, while *Tiaris* and *Volatinia* usually prefer dense grass or forbs; *Oryzoborus* often nests in taller grass in wet meadows and marshes.

Males of *S. aurita* sing sporadically practically year-round, but most intensely toward the end of the dry season and into the rains, the principal breeding season. The song is a rambling medley of warbles, trills, and buzzy notes, rather like that of a goldfinch (*Spinus*) in effect and often very melodious. The main nesting season runs from about May or June through September in most areas of Costa Rica, corresponding with the period when the grasses whose growth was stimulated by the rains are ripening their seeds. The breeding season is longer and less well defined in areas without a strong dry season. The breeding system is monogamy; pairs defend the nest and its vicinity against other breeding birds but seem to permit foraging flocks to approach the nest more closely.

The nest of *S. aurita* is a loosely woven but sturdy, compact cup of rootlets and grass fibers, usually placed about 1–2 m up in a shrub or small tree. The usual clutch is two eggs, but sets of three are known and seem to be more common in the Caribbean race *S. a. corvina.* The eggs are pale bluish gray heavily speckled and blotched with brown. The female does practically all of the nest building, and only she incubates and broods the hatch-lings, but both male and female feed them. The incubation and nestling periods are both 12–13 days. Young are fed on both seeds and insects. Two broods are usually raised in a season. The annual molt of adults commences in September or October, continuing through December or early January (La Selva). Young males apparently pass their first year in a dull, femalelike plumage, which they begin to replace with the adult coloration starting about April or May: more data are needed on this point.

The variable seedeater is typical of a number of open-country or second-growth birds that have evidently benefited enormously from man's influence upon habitats in Central America. The original (pre-*Homo*) habitat of the species was doubtless the grassy swamps, open second growth, and scrub along the courses of large rivers, where periodic flooding prevents establishment of trees, as well as large light gaps caused by extensive blow-downs within forest; it probably was not a very abundant bird. In forested country, *S. aurita* still occupies these habitats, and it is able to cross extensive tracts of forest in search of good areas—as evidenced by the occasional capture of a *Sporophila* or two in mist nets set well inside virgin forest. However, man's deforestation of most of the Central American mainland has changed the seed-eater's world from patches and islands of good habitat in a sea of poor habitat (forest), to essentially a sea of good habitat with ever-shrinking patches and islands of bad. The accelerating pace of deforestation over the past few centuries has proabbly permitted birds like *Sporophila aurita* to sustain a nearly or quite exponential population growth for some time. This in turn may well have affected behavior, reproductive strategies, and so forth. It would be extremely interesting to compare the biology of a species like *S. aurita* in a typical disturbed area with that of a local population in a large expanse of primary habitat.

*

Pulliam, H. R. 1973. Comparative feeding ecology of a tropical grassland finch. *Ecology* 54:284–99.
Skutch, A. F. 1954. *Life histories of Central American birds.* Pacific Coast Avifuana, no. 31. Berkeley: Cooper Ornithological Society.
Slud, P. 1964. The birds of Costa Rica: Distribution and ecology. *Bull. Am. Mus. Nat. Hist.* 128:1–430.

Terenotriccus erythrurus (Mosqueitero Colirrufo, Tontillo, Ruddy-tailed Flycatcher)

T. W. Sherry

The ruddy-tailed flycatcher (*Terenotriccus erythrurus*, Tyrannidae) (fig. 10.46) is widespread in moist and wet-

FIGURE 10.46. *Terenotriccus erythrurus,* adult, showing rictal bristle configuration and size when bill is open. Costa Rica (drawn from photo, T. W. Sherry).

forested regions from southeastern Mexico to Central Brazil and Bolivia. It is conspicuous for a forest flycatcher because of its active, "flitty" foraging in lower and middle forest levels and because of its tameness. It is small (just over 7 g), and is bright rufous on the tail, contrasting with more gray olive on the upperparts and ochre below. Though it belongs to that infamous class of confusingly similar, tiny Neotropical flycatchers, it is distinct and not easily confused with other species. Not surprisingly, *Terenotriccus* is a monotypic genus (Meyer de Schauensee 1966).

The ruddy-tail is found in a variety of forest and old second-growth habitats in forested parts of Costa Rica from the lowlands up to about 1,400 m elevation (Slud 1964). At Finca La Selva it is found in almost any shaded habitat including old cacao plantations, the open arboretum, old second-growth, and primary forest and treefall gaps. It is more restricted in Pacific than Caribbean Central America, not extending north of the Gulf of Nicoya in Guanacaste Province (Skutch 1960; Slud 1964).

The bird has evoked little interest aside from Slud's (1964) brief distribution and song description and Skutch's (1960) brief natural history notes. Yet *Terenotriccus* is a very unusual species. It is very specialized in diet, even compared with tropical insectivores. It feeds largely on jumping Homoptera (71% Fulgoroidea and 23% Cercopoidea, based on nine stomachs examined, Sherry [ms.]; see also Haverschmidt 1968), and it may

provide clues to why some birds, particularly resident tropical ones, specialize more than others.

A comparative approach illuminates some of the bird's peculiar morphological traits in relation to its prey selection and foraging behavior (Sherry 1979b, and in prep.). It has as low a wing loading (total mass per wing area) as any resident tropical flycatcher I have studied. *Terenotriccus* frequently pursues insect prey acrobatically in variably (often poorly) lit microhabitats within tropical forest. Its wings are rounded like those of other forest pursuers, however, and not pointed like those of open-habitat pursuers. *Terenotriccus* also hovers, somewhat like a hummingbird, when searching for prey; and it flits at leaves and twigs to snatch small insects or knock them off the substrate before a pursuit. The bird has long, stiff rictal bristles that form a spectacular basket around the bill when it is open (fig. 10.46). The stiffness and configuration of the bristles when the bill is open argue that they serve a physical function—to catch or hold onto agile insect prey in poorly lit microhabitats. Finally, the ruddy-tail has a relatively long, full tail, as do other pursuers (see account of rufous-tailed jacamar, *Galbula ruficauda*). Such a full tail would improve agility in pursuing prey because of the additional surface area for braking, steering, or lifting the flying bird. *Terenotriccus* also has the large eyes typical of understory, rain-forest flycatchers.

Other "flycatchers" confirm the relationship of predation on fulgoroid Homoptera with predator morphology (low wing loading, well-developed tails, and rictal bristles) and predator behavior (acrobatic prey pursuit in poorly lit environments). The resident tropical sulfur-rumped flycatcher (*Myiobius barbatus*) frequents the same habitats in Costa Rica as the ruddy-tail, and both regularly occur with mixed-species antwren flocks, probably at least in part because the activity of flock members flushes insects from the vegetation (see account of the white-fronted nunbird, *Monasa morphoeus*). The American redstart (*Setophaga ruticilla*, Parulidae) migrates from the tropics and regularly preys on homoptera while breeding in the temperate zone (Sherry 1979a); it also preys regularly on fulgoroid Homoptera during migration (Sherry and Hespenheide, unpub. data). The blue-gray gnatcatcher (*Polioptila caerulea*, Sylviidae) is another temperate-zone, generalized insectivore like the American redstart; it uses occasional pursuit flights and includes substantial numbers of Homoptera in its diet (Root 1967).

The endemic genus *Nesotriccus* (Cocos Island Flycatcher, Tyrannidae) uses several techniques to capture a variety of insect types on its isolated, rain-forested island in the central-eastern Pacific (between Costa Rica and the Galápagos Islands). Yet fulgoroids, which are relatively abundant on the island (Sherry and Webster, unpub.

data), comprise 42–60% of the diet of *Nesotriccus*, which has wings and tail almost identical to those of *Terenotriccus* (Sherry, in prep.).

A number of families of fulgoroid Homoptera in forests are abundant, small, inconspicuous, and quick to leap from the substrate at the approach of a potential predator (e.g., insect net). The combination of behavioral and morphological traits of *Terenotriccus* suggest it has exploited the predictable predator-avoidance behavior of fulgoroids by becoming adapted to take the insects in flight after their initial hop from the substrate. It is possible that fulgoroids are a relatively abundant and safe group on which to specialize because of their ability to escape most bird (and lizard?) predators. *Terenotriccus* ignores many insects that it surely encounteres while foraging. Whether this is because of its specialized morphology or for "psychological" reasons is not known.

How the geographical distribution of the ruddy-tail is related to seasonality and abundance of Fulgoroidea is not clear either. The birds do not occur in forests with a very marked dry season, but they do occur on Barro Colorado Island, Panama, where fulgoroids undergo marked seasonality in relation to the 3-month dry season (Wolda 1977). It is not known whether *Terenotriccus* broadens its diet under conditions of prey scarcity (if such occurs), for example, during a severe dry season. In summary, I hypothesize that the apparent success of *Terenotriccus*, judged by abundance and geographical range, is related to the abundance and predictability of fulgoroids and the bird's ability to catch them.

Skutch (1960) provides all of what information exists on breeding in the ruddy-tail. The song is a lispy, two-syllable call in which either the first or the second syllable is emphasized (see also Slud 1964), and a dawn song consists of these notes strung together. Nests are hanging, pyriform structures suspended 1.5–4 m above the ground from drooping twigs, dangling vines, or palm fronds. The female alone builds the nest and may take 20 days or more to do so. Females also incubate and feed the young without the aid of the male. This degree of male liberation is somewhat unusual in insectivores, more like the norm in frugivores and nectarivores. Clutch size is two eggs ($n = 2$). The incubation period is extremely long— 22 days or more—like that of other forest flycatchers with hanging nests (*Myiobius* and *Onychorhynchus*, e.g.). Presumably long incubation periods (whatever the advantages) would be permitted by relatively safe nesting sites, just as long nestling periods are permitted (Morton 1973), but little is known of the advantages or disadvantages of long nestling/incubation periods of tropical insectivores.

Terenotriccus is generally encountered solitarily during much of the year, but groups of two or three birds, presumably family groups, are encountered for months after the breeding period (Sherry, unpub. data). Immediately after fledging, family groups are very cohesive, and young are often observed packed together along a branch while resting, as in some other flycatchers (e.g., *Myiornis* and *Empidonax;* Sherry, pers. obs.). The young are very noisy at such times, but they fly well, and so predation on them may not be as important as the need to be fed by an adult.

*

Haverschmidt, F. 1968. *Birds of Surinam*. London: Oliver and Boyd.

Meyer de Schauensee, R. 1966. *The species of birds of South America and their distribution*. Philadelphia: Livingston.

Morton, E. S. 1973. On the evolutionary advantages and disadvantages of fruit eating in birds. *Am. Nat.* 107: 8–22.

Root, R. H. 1967. The niche-exploitation pattern of the blue-gray gnatcatcher. *Ecol. Monogr.* 37:317–50.

Sherry, T. W. 1979*a*. Competitive interactions and adaptive strategies of American redstarts and least flycatchers in a northern hardwoods forest. *Auk* 96: 265–83.

———. 1979*b*. Specialization on fulgoroid Homoptera in Neotropical flycatchers. Abstract, Forty-ninth Annual Meeting, Cooper Ornithological Society.

Skutch, A. 1960. *Life histories of Central American birds: Families Vireonidae, Sylviidae, Turdidae, Troglodytidae, Paridae, Corvidae, Hirundinidae and Tyrannidae*. Pacific Coast Avifauna, no. 34. Berkeley: Cooper Ornithological Society.

Slud, P. 1964. The birds of Costa Rica: Distribution and ecology. *Bull. Am. Mus. Nat. Hist.* 128:1–430.

Wolda, H. 1977. Fluctuations in abundance of some Homoptera in a Neotropical forest. *Geo-Eco-Trop.* 3:229–57.

Thamnophilus doliatus (Batara Barreteado, Barred Antshrike)

E. O. Willis

Nobody, not even Skutch (1969), knows much about this little zebra-striped bird (males; females are rusty) anywhere in its vast range from Mexico to Argentina. Yet it was one of the first antbirds I saw, in British Honduran second growth, and one of the most recent, in second-growth edges of arboreal caatinga on the São Francisco River of eastern Brazil. It seems to like the scrappy little remnants of vegetation man often leaves in the tropics, and perhaps it will still be here to study in the distant future. The barred antshrike is the only antbird in most of the tropical dry forest, its center of abundance in Costa Rica; darker zebra-striped antshrikes tend to replace it in wetter scrub (e.g., *Cymbilaimus lineatus* in the Caribbean lowlands). It is a common forest bird on large Coiba

Island off the south coast of Panama, where most other birds are absent despite a former connection to the mainland. Those with a mathematical bent may enjoy comparing the size of Coiba with national parks in Costa Rica and estimating how long it could be until only barred antshrikes live in them.

Although the canopy on Coiba is structurally like scrub, this is true of forest canopy on the mainland too (image yourself in Amazonia at flood season, floating among the treetops as if crossing a bushy pasture for sea cows). The barred antshrike's success in habitats as diverse as Coiba forest and Brazilian caatinga seems related instead to local absence of competing species; Diamond (1975) would call it a "supertramp," absent from any habitat that holds many species. Does it exclude birds from such places, or does it do well only where easily captured arthropods are unexploited by others? The latter seems more likely: not competition but opportunity. The related slaty antshrike (*Thamnophilus punctatus*) has done well on Barro Colorado Island in central Panama after loss of many forest insectivores, and its success seems due to its foraging from the ground nearly to the canopy as well as searching for a wide variety of arthropods in many places (Oniki 1975). In the Amazon it becomes a bird of sandy or dry woodlands, not quite as depauperate as those in which barred antshrikes live. Barred antshrikes have even heavier hooked beaks, are slightly larger, forage in an even larger variety of habitats (normally in dense thickets), and are capable of using the canopy of Coiba though they normally forage near the ground. It is likely that their slow hopping and peering are energetically efficient where branches and insects are common. They are not especially prolific at nesting, since they and many other antshrikes lay two eggs (three at times; Marchant 1960) in cup nests in low forks, nest repeatedly over long nesting seasons (Snow and Snow 1964), and molt during or between nestings. Males and females incubate and care for nestlings and fledglings, as in most antbirds; immatures leave parents after an unknown period, probably about a month as in Panamanian slaty antshrikes. The nest is not well concealed, except by dense foliage, and may be poorly suited to environments with many predators; but slaty antshrikes survive well despite 90% loss in fairly well-concealed nests on Barro Colorado.

Foraging in barred antshrikes should be variable, and they may learn well like some northern birds, if they use all the insects taken by a wide variety of forest species. More likely, they take only easily located insects. The song—a series of grunts ending in a nasal snarl, and easily mistaken for that of several other antshrikes (including the slaty antshrike)—is much the same from Mexico to Brazil and probably is not learned. The same may be true for their weird whining and cawing calls.

The success of barred antshrikes around humans may be temporary. Even if future wars or nuclear accidents do not create radioactive areas that must be left as parks, European forest birds have in some cases moved into human areas. The European blackbird (*Turdus merula*), once a shy denizen of black-mud swamps, now loves lawns. Wood pigeons (*Columba palumbus*) do better in city parks than in the best forests of Poland. Some Neotropical birds may yet move into human-created scrub, increasing diversity but ousting barred antshrikes and other specialists in low diversity.

*

Diamond, J. M. 1975. Assembly of species communities. In *Ecology and evolution of communities,* ed. M. L. Cody and J. M. Diamond, pp. 342–444. Cambridge: Belknap Press, Harvard University.

Marchant, S. 1960. The breeding of some S.W. Ecuadorian birds. *Ibis* 102:349–82.

Oniki, Y. 1975. The behavior and ecology of slaty antshrikes (*Thamnophilus punctatus*) on Barro Colorado Island, Panama Canal Zone. *An. Acad. Brasil. Ciênc.* 47:477–515.

Skutch, A. F. 1969. Barred antshrike. In *Life histories of Central American birds,* pp. 191–96. Pacific Coast Avifauna, no. 35. Berkeley: Cooper Ornithological Society.

Snow, D. W., and Snow, B. K. 1964. Breeding seasons and annual cycles of Trinidad land-birds. *Zoologica* 47:65–104.

Todirostrum cinereum (Espatulilla Común, Pechita, Tontilla, Common Tody-Flycatcher)

T. W. Sherry

Its pale yellow irises peering out of a black face and crown lend the common tody-flycatcher (*Todirostrum cinereum,* Tyrannidae) a stern look (fig. 10.47). This contrasts sharply with its periodic bursts of wagging its tail above its back and side-stepping along a branch while intently watching a potential victim. Its gray black head, grading to a gray green back and tail, contrasts with bright yellow underparts. The wing feathers are yellow margined, and the outer tail feathers have pale yellow tips. The flat, spatulate bill is exceptionally long for the size of the bird.

As Skutch (1960) notes, its acquaintance is easily made: it ranges extensively in open country from southern Mexico to Bolivia and eastern Brazil, forages actively, and calls frequently. In Costa Rica *T. cinereum* occupies a range of habitats in generally open country, including forest borders, new second growth, margins of shaded streams within open country, pastures with

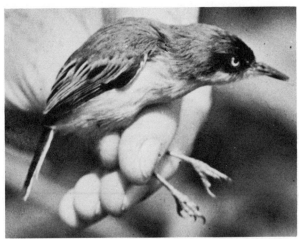

FIGURE 10.47. *Todirostrum cinereum*. Costa Rica (photo, F. G. Stiles).

shrubs, and suburban yards; but it does not occur in suitable habitats within heavily forested regions (Slud 1964; pers. obs.). It occurs in the seasonally dry parts of Guanacaste Province but prefers wetter regions from the lowlands to about 1,500 m elevation. It is the most widespread of all fourteen species in the genus but curiously does not occur in much of Amazonia, perhaps because of competitive exclusion by *T. maculatum* (Fitzpatrick 1976).

Some genera of tyrannids are distinctive and monotrypic, but *Todirostrum* and related genera were involved in repeated speciation during the Pleistocene, presumably because fluctuations in the extent of forest and nonforest habitats during wet and dry periods repeatedly isolated populations in refugia (Fitzpatrick 1976). Fitzpatrick has derived hypothetical speciation scenarios for much of the genus from present-day distribution and ecology. *T. cinereum* accordingly became isolated from *T. maculatum* perhaps two "dry" periods ago. The two species are now well differentiated but appear to exclude each other over a broad contact zone because of ecological similarity (see above).

Bright plumage color and small size of tody-flycatchers have evoked comparison with wood-warblers (Parulidae). Most wood-warblers, however, glean arthropods on foot and search actively for relatively immobile prey. Tody-flycatchers, by contrast, forage primarily by dashing suddenly in flight to snatch arthropods from vegetation (Haverschmidt 1955; Skutch 1960; Slud 1964; Fitzpatrick 1976, 1980). This behavior allows tody-flycatchers to surprise attack relatively wary prey and to snatch prey from substrates that are more difficult for gleaning birds to reach. Diptera, among the most wary and agile of flying insects, are the recurrent element in *Todirostrum* diets, although a diverse array of arthropods are consumed (brief notes in Haverschmidt 1955, 1968).

The "surprise-attack syndrome" of *Todirostrum* species, particularly *T. nigriceps* of the Caribbean lowland forests of Costa Rica, explains how a variety of morphological characteristics likely function. A small body mass (6.2 g for both *T. cinereum* and *T. nigriceps*) may be accelerated more rapidly from zero velocity by a given force from the wings. Small, rounded wings (*Todirostrum* wing loading, or total body mass per wing area, is large relative to other flycatchers) can accelerate a bird rapidly by allowing a high wingbeat frequency (Greenewalt 1975). The small wings and tail of *Todirostrum* species would preclude adept flight maneuverability (see discussion of wing and tail morphology in *Terenotriccus erythrurus*, this volume) but would decrease induced drag and thus facilitate acceleration from a resting position. Long tarsi and well-developed leg musculature of *Todirostrum* species would make it easier to leap into flight, thus giving a higher rate of acceleration from zero velocity. One of the most remarkable *Todirostrum* characteristics, a disproportionately long and spatulate (flat) bill, would serve to snatch soft-bodied prey such as Diptera from leaf surfaces at high attack speeds. The convergence of *Todirostrum* with the true "todies" (a family of brightly colored insectivores endemic to the Greater Antilles — see Kepler 1977) provides the best evidence for my interpretation of the surprise-attack syndrome. The two groups have independently evolved the foregoing syndrome of morphological characteristics, and both groups capture large numbers of Diptera using identical foraging behavior.

Among sympatric *Todirostrum*, species are thought to segregate by habitat (Slud 1960; J. Fitzpatrick, pers. comm.). In the Sarapiquí lowlands (Caribbean) of Costa Rica, *T. cinereum* is in open habitats; *T. sylvia* is restricted to dense young second-growth, overgrown pasture (and forest canopy —F. G. Stiles, pers. comm.); and *T. nigriceps* is high in trees at the pasture/forest interface (Slud 1960; Sherry, unpub. data). The black-capped pygmy-tyrant (*Myiornis atricapillus*) is another ambush predator related to the tody-flycatchers. Its wings and tail and its foraging behavior and height characteristics are very similar to those of *T. nigriceps*, and it becomes much more abundant than *T. nigriceps* going from edge to primary forest habitats (Sherry, unpub. data).

Tody-flycatchers build large (for their size) hanging nests that are "felted" rather than "woven" (Skutch 1976). The entrance and chamber are pushed into the side of the matted mass of dried grasses and fibers, usually under a projecting leaf (Skutch 1930, 1960, 1976; Haverschmidt 1955). Construction may require more than a month, but successive nests, in the case of nest failure, generally require less construction time (Skutch 1960). Nests that hang from slender vines and twigs should be safe from snakes and most mammalian predators; nonetheless, predation on nests is often high (Skutch 1960). Crested oropendolas (*Psarocolius decumanus*) probably prey upon *T. maculatum* nests (Haverschmidt 1955). An interesting difference among tody-flycatchers is the extent to which they construct their nests near the nests of stinging Hymenoptera: *T. sylvia* has never been reported to do so; *T. cinereum* rarely if ever does so in the Caribbean lowlands of Costa Rica but occasionally does so in Guanacaste Province; *T. maculatum* does so occasionally; and *T. nigriceps* almost always does so (Skutch 1930, 1960, 1972; Haverschmidt 1955; Sherry, unpub. data; F. Stiles, pers. comm.).

The sexes contribute nearly equally to nesting duties in all species studied, and males help build nests and feed nestlings while leaving incubation entirely to the females. Incubation lasts between 17 and 19 days, a long time compared with temperate flycatchers, but appropriate for tropical species with hanging nests (Skutch 1976). Nestling periods determined thus far are 17 or 18 days for *T. maculatum* and *T. cinereum* (Haverschmidt 1955, 1978) and 18–21 days for *T. sylvia* (Skutch 1972). Clutch sizes vary from 1.8 ($N = 11$) for *T. maculatum* in Surinam to 2.0 ($N = 7$) for *T. sylvia* (Skutch 1976) to 2.6 ($N = 16$) in Central American *T. cinereum* (Skutch 1976). Interestingly, *T. cinereum* has two-egg clutches ($N = 21$) in Surinam (Haverschmidt 1978). There are no data for *T. nigriceps*. How these clutch-size differences relate to ecological factors remains to be determined, but one might predict that the safety of the nest site, including the vegetative cover and proximity of Hymenoptera nests, should be related to clutch size within *Todirostrum*.

*

Fitzpatrick, J. W. 1976. Systematics and biogeography of the tyrannid genus *Todirostrum* and related genera (Aves). *Bull. Mus. Comp. Zool.* 147:435–63.

———. 1980. Foraging behavior of Neotropical tyrant flycatchers. *Condor* 82:43–57.

Greenewalt, C. H. 1975. The flight of birds. *Trans. Am. Phil. Soc.* 65:1–67.

Haverschmidt, F. 1955. Notes on the life-history of *Todirostrum maculatum* in Surinam. *Auk* 72:325–31.

———. 1968. *Birds of Surinam*. London: Oliver and Boyd.

———. 1978. The duration of parental care in the common tody-flycatcher. *Auk* 95:199.

Kepler, A. K. 1977. Comparative study of todies (Todidae): with emphasis on the Puerto Rican tody, *Todus mexicanus*. *Pub. Nuttall Ornithol. Club* 16:1–190.

Skutch, A. 1930. The habits and nesting activities of the northern tody-flycatcher in Panama. *Auk* 47:313–22.

———. 1960. *Life histories of Central American birds: Families Vireonidae, Sylviidae, Turdidae, Troglodytidae, Paridae, Corvidae, Hirundinidae and Tyrannidae*. Pacific Coast Avifauna, no. 34. Berkeley: Cooper Ornithological Society.

———. 1972. Studies of tropical American birds. *Publ. Nuttall Ornithol. Club* 10:1–228.

———. 1976. *Parent birds and their young*. Austin: University of Texas Press.

Slud, P. 1960. The birds of Finca "La Selva" Costa Rica: A tropical wet forest locality. *Bull. Am. Mus. Nat. Hist.* 121:49–148.

———. 1964. The birds of Costa Rica: Distribution and ecology. *Bull. Am. Mus. Nat. Hist.* 128:1–430.

Turdus grayi (Yiquirro, Clay-colored Robin)

E. S. Morton

The clay-colored robin (fig. 10.48) ranges from central Mexico to northern Colombia. It is the sole lowland *Turdus* throughout this range and is actively excluding other *Turdus* species up to 2,000 m wherever extensive forest clearing occurs. It is found in gardens, parks, lawns, and along the edges of savannas and river borders in forested regions. In Costa Rica it occurs throughout the lowlands and middle elevations in suitable habitat but is most abundant on the Meseta Central and in Guanacaste.

The sexes are identical in all plumages (brownish gray above, paler below), but juveniles have black spots on the breast and buff-spotted breast feathers and wing coverts. These buff-spotted wing coverts persist past the postjuvenile molt in June and July and permit aging until the first postnuptial molt in July–August of the next year. Eye color is brick red in adults, brown in first-year birds. The adult weight varies from 65 to 86 g, with females weighing 73–86 g (median, 80 g) and males 65–75 g (median, 68 g). The significance of heavier females is unknown.

The clay-colored robin closely resembles the American robin (*T. migratorius*) in size, foraging behavior, and breeding behavior. Like all *Turdus* species it is omnivorous, feeding on invertebrates found on the ground or

FIGURE 10.48. *Turdus grayi*, adult. Costa Rica (photo, F. G. Stiles).

within 3 cm under the surface as well as on fruit. Unlike the American robin, which is frugivorous during the non-breeding season, the clay-colored robin is dependent upon fruit for breeding. Ground foraging appears very like that of the American robin, a combination of hops and walks followed by stalls while the bird looks at the surrounding ground. It pecks worm castings, then does extensive digging with its bill. It also surveys the ground from low (1–3 m) perches during dry periods when earthworms are probably not attainable. Flycatching occurs rarely, usually during ant or termite mating swarms.

The start of breeding is exceedingly variable but is conspicuous. Males begin singing in dawn choruses about 2 weeks before egg laying begins. These choruses, and intermittent daytime singing bouts, persist throughout the breeding season, which lasts from 2 to 4 months. Populations only a few kilometers apart may differ by a few days to a month in the time breeding begins. In the Panama Canal Zone breeding begins about 2 weeks after the beginning of the dry season, and about 70% of breeding attempts are confined to this season. In other areas, particularly areas with more prolonged and severe dry seasons, breeding begins near the end of the dry period and lasts into the first quarter of the wet season. On the Meseta Central of Costa Rica, song begins in March, and eggs are laid in April or May; usually the rains have begun and earthworms and insects are abundant by the time the young fledge. The "Yiquirro" is prominent in local folklore: the campesinos say that during the period of intense song at the end of the dry season the birds are "calling the rain."

Food for raising young may not be the primary factor determining this species' breeding season (Morton 1971). Adults feed almost entirely on fruit while raising young on invertebrates (Morton 1973), and there fruit availability may determine the nesting season in some areas.

The nest is a mud-lined cup of moss and grass, often with epiphytes such as *Peperomia* inserted into the outer surface. The nest is lined with rootlets. Nests are placed in tree crotches, in forks of large branches, on palm leaves, and on windowsills and such, near houses. Two or three 6- to 8-g eggs are laid per clutch. They are blotched with tan and maroon on a light blue green background. Incubation begins with the laying of the second egg, resulting in asynchronous hatching and rapid starvation of small young during food stress. Hatching takes 13 days of incubation. The young fledge in about 13 days. They are fed invertebrates during the first 4 days and a mixture of fruit and insects from then until fledging. Postfledging parental care tapers off rapidly for a tropical passerine, and young are on their own in about 2 weeks. Fledging sizes vary greatly, and weights of 38 to 55 g have been recorded. Parents become very aggressive toward their own young when the adults start another breeding cycle. Up to three successful clutches in one breeding season have been recorded for a single pair.

Captive, hand-raised young underwent a complete postjuvenile molt except for the wing coverts about 4.5 months after fledging. The replacement of wing and tail feathers in this molt is unusual and may represent an adaptation to overcome starvationlike conditions during the nestling stage. They may fledge with wing feathers suitable for a 38-g bird but not economical for the adult size attained before the postjuvenile molt.

*

Morton, E. S. 1971. Nest predation affecting the breeding season of the clay-colored robin, a tropical song bird. *Science* 171:920–21.

———. 1973. On the evolutionary advantages and disadvantages of fruit eating in tropical birds. *Am. Nat.* 107:8–22.

Tyrannus melancholicus (Tirano Tropical, Pecho Amarillo, Tropical Kingbird)

J. W. Fitzpatrick

Among the largest of the tyrant flycatchers (Tyrannidae), this conspicuous species (fig. 10.49) is common from northern Mexico south throughout tropical Central and South America to Argentina. In Costa Rica it can be found in a variety of open habitats including forest borders, brushy clearings and second growth, marsh and river edges, scrub and thorn forest, suburbs and even cities. It is absent from dense forest and upper montane habitats. Tropical kingbirds are most common below 1,200 elevation, but they occur up to 2,000 m in nonforest situations, and they abound on utility wires around San José (e.g., Slud 1964).

The large size, solid gray head and throat, clear yellow belly, and deeply forked tail separate the tropical kingbird from the other common, yellow-bellied flycatchers that share its habitat, nearly all of which have contrasting black-and-white head patterns (e.g., *Pitangus sulphuratus, Megarhynchus pitangua, Myiozetetes similis, M. granadensis,* and *Conopias parva*). In Costa Rica the only other kingbird with yellow underparts is the western kingbird (*Tyrannus verticalis*), a rare winter visitor mainly to savanna areas in northern Guanacaste and the lower El General valley.

The common vocalizations of the tropical kingbird all include high-pitched, twittering syllables uttered in rapid succession: *Tee-tetetetete* or *pip-pip-piririree*. These are frequently given as members of a mated pair meet and greet each other on a perch, with wings fluttering and

FIGURE 10.49. *Tyrannus melancholicus,* adult perched and waiting for insects. Costa Rica (photo, F. G. Stiles).

tails spread (see Smith 1966). The dawn song, a characteristic of many tyrant flycatchers, is similar but is given with several introductory *tick*s. It is often the first bird sound heard as dawn approaches.

Tropical kingbirds almost invariably search for prey from exposed perches, including dead limbs, treetops, fence posts, and utility wires. Their diet largely consists of aerial insects captured during long, graceful sallies into the open air. Prey items tend to be large and easily identifiable, at least to order. They commonly include Odonata, Orthoptera, Hymenoptera, Coleoptera, and large Diptera (e.g., Hespenheide 1964; Ohlendorf 1974). They sometimes haunt areas of flowering shrubs to catch butterflies. Throughout its range, the tropical kingbird regularly supplements its insect diet with fruit, especially during seasonal abundance of mistletoe and large fruiting trees (e.g., *Ficus, Crematosperma, Didymopanax*).

The long, pointed wings, the wide and deeply forked tail, and the very short tarsi of kingbirds appear to be adaptations to their stereotyped "aerial hawking" foraging methods (Fitzpatrick 1978). Frequently, long sallies are accompanied by impressive aerial maneuvers as the prey attempts to escape, and the agility required for this is provided in part by the elongated outer tail feathers. This adaptation reaches an extreme in the two "scissor-tailed" kingbirds sometimes placed in the genus *Muscivora* (*Tyrannus forficatus* and *T. savana*).

As with other aerial hawking tyrannids (e.g., *Mitrephanes phaeocercus, Contopus* spp., *Colonia colonus*), tropical kingbirds frequently return many times in succession to a single favored perch (Fitzpatrick 1978). Their tendency to return to a perch is inversely proportional to the search time immediately preceding the sally. This indicates that they can to some extent measure the prey density surrounding a perch. Thus they often abandon perches at which prey appears with low frequency.

Permanently mated pairs of tropical kingbirds are territorial throughout the year (Smith 1966). In conjunction with the aerial hawking habit, their territories are small for a bird of their size (36–48 g). Often the home range consists of a few favored limbs or tree falls that provide good vantage points from which to watch for passing prey. Occasionally, however, birds from several territories will gather and feed together over a temporary swarm of large insects (e.g., termites or dragonflies).

Tropical kingbirds in Costa Rica nest from mid-March through June (Skutch 1954, 1960). They habitually raise only a single brood, although they may attempt many nests before they succeed in fledging young. The nest is a loose, bowl-shaped cup poorly concealed on an open limb of a bush or low tree. Often nests are placed near or over water. Tropical kingbirds frequently nest in conjunction with large colonies of caciques and oropendolas, a habit shared with many of the large yellow-bellied flycatchers. At least one member of the pair usually can be seen perched near or directly over the nest, and most foraging takes place near the nest site during breeding season. Incubation lasts about 15 days, and nestlings leave the nest about 18 days after hatching (Skutch 1960). Young kingbirds have rufous edges on the wing and tail feathers but otherwise resemble the adults.

The aggressive behavior of tropical kingbirds toward many larger bird species has been described by many authors (e.g., Slud 1964). This "mobbing" behavior is most commonly directed at open-country hawks, which kingbirds may pursue and strike for minutes on end until the predator leaves the area. Other nest predators, especially toucans and araçaris (*Ramphastos* and *Pteroglossus* spp.), also are victims of active mobbing by kingbirds.

In contrast to the aggressiveness of tropical kingbirds toward predators, this species rarely attacks other flycatchers. This is true despite the frequent occurrence of up to six potentially competing, large tyrannid species sharing the kingbird's open habitats. Ecologically, many of these relatives are more generalized and omnivorous than the kingbird, showing less dependence upon large aerial prey. In lowland Peru, tropical kingbirds have been found sharing an evening roost bush with four of these large tyrannid species. It is unknown whether this communal roosting occurs throughout the kingbird's range.

612

In Costa Rica, kingbirds may form large communal roosts with scissor-tailed flycatchers.

Recently it was discovered that the kingbird population occupying the northeastern coast of Mexico, previously thought to be a subspecies of *T. melancholicus,* actually represents a distinct species, *Tyrannus couchii.* The two sibling species coexist in southern Veracruz and the Yucatan Peninsula (Smith 1966; Traylor 1979).

Because it occurs in a wide range of habitats, showing a preference for open or disturbed sites, the tropical kingbird has almost certainly increased in abundance and geographic distribution in response to the clearing of forests by man. The species is common in any tropical settlement, living and nesting successfully even in the midst of South America's largest cities.

*

Fitzpatrick, J. W. 1978. Foraging behavior and adaptive radiation in the avian family Tyrannidae. Ph.D. diss., Princeton University.
———. 1980a. Foraging behavior of Neotropical tyrant flycatchers. *Condor* 82:43–57.
———. 1980b. Search strategies of tyrant flycatchers. *Anim. Behav.,* in press.
Hespenheide, H. A. 1964. Competition and the genus *Tyrannus. Wilson Bull.* 76:265–81.
Ohlendorf, H. M. 1974. Competitive relationships among kingbirds (*Tyrannus*) in trans-Pecos Texas. *Wilson Bull.* 86:357–73.
Skutch, A. F. 1954. Life history of the tropical kingbird. *Proc. Linn. Soc. N.Y.* 63–65:21–38.
———. 1960. *Life histories of Central American birds.* Pacific Coast Avifauna, no. 34. Berkeley: Cooper Ornithological Society.
Smith, W. J. 1966. Communications and relationships in the genus *Tyrannus. Publ. Nuttall Ornithol. Club,* no. 6.
Traylor, M. A. 1979. Two sibling species of *Tyrannus* (Tyrannidae). *Auk* 96:221–33.

Vermivora peregrina (Reinita Verdilla, Tennessee Warbler)

F. G. Stiles

This nondescript little warbler (fig. 10.50) is an extremely abundant winter resident over much of Costa Rica, especially the Pacific slope, where it regularly drives Christmas-vacation bird watchers frantic through its vague resemblance to a variety of equally inconspicuous little flycatchers, greenlets, and others. However, it is a sprightly little bird with interesting behavior that provides an excellent illustration of how a northern spruce-woods warbler can be transformed into a typical tropical resident by a few thousand miles of migration.

The Tennessee warbler is perhaps the least colorful

FIGURE 10.50 *Vermivora peregrina,* adult. Costa Rica (photo, F. G. Stiles).

member of the family Parulidae, which includes the largest contingent of migrant and winter resident land birds in Costa Rica. The winter or basic plumage, that most often seen in Costa Rica, consists of olive green upperparts and whitish underparts, the throat and breast sometimes suffused with dull yellow; males tend to be less yellow below, with the head more or less gray tinged. The only even remotely conspicuous field marks are pale eyebrows and a dark line through the eye. In breeding plumage, acquired by a partial molt just before or during spring migration, the underparts are whiter and the head is very gray, especially in males. The bill is very fine and sharp-pointed. Birds weigh about 8–9 g as winter residents (male are slightly heavier) but may weigh up to 12–13 with migratory fat deposits.

V. peregrina breeds in brushy, boggy areas of regenerating forest from Yukon and Montana to southern Ontario and Maine. It gleans insects from treetop foliage in early summer but places its nest on or near the ground; the clutch is five or six brown-speckled white eggs. After breeding the birds move about widely, often in scrub and second growth, where they take many berries as well as insects. The Tennessee warbler winters from southern Mexico through Central America to northern South America, but Costa Rica is at or near its center of abundance. A few Tennessee warblers arrive in Costa Rica as early as late September, but the species becomes abundant only in late October, making it one of the latest fall migrants to arrive in numbers. From then until mid-March or early April they apparently occupy limited home ranges; banding data from the Universidad de Costa Rica indicates that birds return year after year to the same wintering area. Following a period of premigratory wandering (and fattening), most *V. peregrina* depart for the north in mid- to late April; occasional late migrants may be seen into early May. Migration is mostly by night, but in periods of bad weather many birds migrate along the Caribbean coast by day, especially in fall; in the spring, flocks of Tennessee warblers and other warblers may stream through the treetops along the coast in early to midmorning.

The favorite winter habitats of Tennessee warblers include scrubby edges, second growth, semiopen areas, coffee plantations, and similar habitats, as well as the canopy and edges of the tropical dry forest (largely leafless at this season); the bird is very uncommon in the canopy of wet forest and does not occur inside closed forest (except occasionally during migration). The species has apparently increased greatly in this century, perhaps reflecting deforestation at both ends of its migratory path.

On the winter range, Tennessee warblers are almost always found in groups or small flocks, sometimes accompanied by other warblers. Uttering the high, thin *chip* and *tseep* that constitute virtually their entire winter vocabulary, the birds troop about between flowering and fruiting trees and shrubs. They avidly visit the flowers of trees like *Erythrina* spp., *Inga, Calliandra,* and banana, as well as those of the introduced *Eucalyptus* and *Callistemon*. They are also very fond of the nectar of the woody vine *Combretum,* and a common sight in Guanacaste is an orange-faced Tennessee warbler, its plumage stained with *Combretum* pollen. Occasionally individuals will try to defend parts or all of small flowering trees of *Combretum* vines, but more often they feed in flocks and simply "swamp out" more aggressive nectarivores like orioles and hummingbirds. On the Meseta Central one can often locate a large blooming poro (*Erythrina poeppigiana*) tree by the sound of the *tseep*ing swarm of Tennessee warblers (as well as tanagers, robins, orioles, and even woodpeckers) at its flowers.

Tennessee warblers also take a variety of small, soft fruits, being especially fond of those of *Trema* and *Urera,* and certain aroids and mistletoes. They also glean actively for insects in foliage, sometimes using their bills to pry open rolled dead leaves—a tactic especially common in various Icteridae and, among warblers, in their relative *Vermivora chrysoptera*.

In their generalized, gregarious behavior, Tennessee warblers seem to resemble certain small tropical tanagers and honeycreepers far more closely than they do most parulids. Even more striking is the resemblance to the Old World tropical family Zosteropidae, the white-eyes. Like most northern-breeding warblers, *V. peregrina* spends easily twice as long each year on its wintering grounds as on its breeding territory; it is an integral and functional member of the tropical bird community.

*

Alvarez del Toro, M. 1963. La enredadera cepillo, fuente de atracción para las aves. *Inst. Cienc. Art. Chiapas, Mex.* 1963:3–5.

Morton, E. S., and Keast, A., eds. 1979. *Migrant birds in the New World tropics.* Washington, D.C.: Smithsonian Institution Press. (A symposium with various papers pertinent to *V. peregrina* and other migrant warblers.)

Pough, F. H. 1949. *Audubon bird guide: Small land birds.* Garden City, N.Y.: Doubleday.

Slud, P. 1964. Birds of Costa Rica: Distribution and ecology. *Bull. Am. Mus. Nat. Hist.* 128:1–430.

Stiles, F. G. 1982. Ecological and evolutionary aspects of bird-flower coadaptations, *Proc. Seventeenth Int. Ornithol. Congr.,* in press.

Zarhynchus wagleri (Oropendola Cabelicastaña, Oropendola, Chestnut-headed Oropendola)

N. G. Smith

This species is a gregarious icterid (Icteridae: orioles, blackbirds, caciques, grackles, etc.) that nests in colonies from southern Mexico to western Ecuador (fig. 10.51). It is an omnivore but relies heavily on fruit, particularly outside the breeding season. The sexes are similar in coloration, being mostly black with a dull chestnut head, yellow outer tail feathers, and a chisellike ivory-colored beak. They are dissimilar in size (males, 35 cm; females, 27 cm), and males usually weigh twice as much as females (212 g vs. 110 g). Males fledge at twice the weight (175–85 g) of the females, and it has been shown that it requires twice as much energy to raise a male as a female. As a consequence, when food is scarce more males than females die in the nests, producing an average secondary sex ratio of about 3:1 in favor of the females.

Their long (56 cm) baglike nests are placed at the ends of branches, usually in an umbrella-shaped tree in a clearing or at the edge of humid forest. There may be as many as one hundred, or as few as four, but thirty to forty nests is the usual range. The number of nests reflects the number of females, for they alone build the nest (10–14 days), incubate the eggs (17 days), and feed the young until fledging (30–36 days). The sex ratio at the colonies is usually about 5:1, females dominating. Thus the mating system is promiscuous and peculiar in some ways. I have never seen copulation at a colony site, a situation very different from that of other promiscuous oropendolas. Males display with bows and gurglelike vocalizations toward females but never toward one another, and they never fight. There is no dominance hierarchy.

During the nonbreeding season (June–December), chestnut-headed oropendolas wander about in monospecific flocks seeking, in the main, fruiting trees. Nesting begins with the onset of the dry season (December) and may continue into the beginning of the rainy season (May–June). Three complete breeding cycles are possible during that period. Colonies are cohesive through time, and the colony sites are usually used by the same individuals year after year. Banding studies have shown that the amount of interchange of individuals between

FIGURE 10.51. *Zarhynchus wagleri. a,* Adult. *b,* Colony of nests high in a large tree. Panama (photos, N. G. Smith).

colonies is very small. Dialects in certain male vocalizations occur. Switching chicks between colonies of different dialects has shown that the dialects are learned. Colony cohesiveness is not complete, for every so often a group will bud off from the parent colony. In this way dialects spread—that is, they are not necessarily colony-site specific.

As in other oropendolas and caciques, the normal clutch is two. Breeding success is very low. Over a 10-year period, the average number of chicks fledged per nest was 0.40. But the adults are extremely long-lived. At one colony, five females that had been banded as chicks were actively building nests in 1977 at the age of 26. Although toucans, snakes, opossums and bats cause significant mortality to eggs and chicks, the chief source of mortality in most years is attack by botfly larvae (*Philornis* spp.). Adults of *Philornis* deposit eggs or living larvae directly on the chicks. Small chicks with more than ten bots (not uncommon) usually die, particularly if they are weak from lack of food. Not all colonies of oropendolas are subject to the same pressure from botflies. Oropendolas nesting in association with wasps (*Protopolybia pumila, Stelopolybia araeta, Polistes* spp., *Polybia* spp. etc.) and stingless but biting bees (*Trigona* spp.) suffer significantly lower rates of *Philornis* attack than do those nesting away from these insects. The exact nature of this protection is still unclear. Experiments have shown that the Hymenoptera detect botflies by odor and wing noise. The reaction of the bees and wasps was typical of the behavior wasps or stingless bees display toward the countless parasitoids that attempt to gain entrance to their nests. They behave as if *Philornis* flies were wasp/bee parasitoids, though they are not.

But not all oropendolas nest with wasps or bees, and while the rate of botfly infestation in much higher than in the wasp/bee colonies, it too varies to a significant extent. This variability results from a different form of parasitism—brood parasitism by the giant cowbird, *Scaphidura oryzivora,* an all-black icterid somewhat smaller than a female *Zarhynchus wagleri.* More oropendola chicks survive to fledging from nests having *one* or (if food is exceptionally abundant) two cowbird chicks than from those lacking cowbirds. This is because the cowbird chicks preen their nest mates and remove the eggs and larvae of the botflies. The host birds do not reciprocate.

Oropendolas from the two colony situations behave differently toward invading cowbirds and cowbirds' eggs. Oropendolas in colonies associated with bees or wasps chase female cowbirds and toss out a high percentage of the cowbird eggs. Oropendolas in colonies lacking wasps or bees are generally not upset by cowbirds and generally accept their eggs. Cross-fostering experiments over nine years have shown that this "discrimination versus nondiscrimination" behavior is learned, not inherited. But it is still unclear how they learn it. Nevertheless, the evolutionary significance of the correlation between the behavior of the oropendolas toward cowbirds in the two situations is clear. Over a ten-year period, the reproductive success rates of the

615

oropendolas in the two situations varied, with a slight advantage accruing to those nesting in association with the wasps or bees. This was also true of the cowbirds.

*

Chapman, F. 1930. The nesting habits of Wagler's oropendola on Barro Colorado Island. *Smithsonian Ann. Rept.* 1930:347–86.

Drury, W. H., Jr. 1962. Breeding activities, especially nest building, of the yellowtail (*Ostinops decumanus*) in Trinidad, West Indies, *Zoologica* 47:39–58.

Schafer, E. 1954. Les conotos. *Bonner Zoolog. Beitr.* 1957:1–151.

Skutch, A. F. 1954. *Life histories of Central American birds.* Pacific Coast Avifauna, no. 31. Berkeley: Cooper Ornithological Society.

Smith, N. G. 1968. The advantage of being parasitized. *Nature* 219:690–94.

———. 1978. Alternate responses by hosts to parasites which may be helpful or harmful. In *Encounter: The interface between populations,* ed. B. Nikol. New York: Academic Press.

———. 1982. Some evolutionary, ecological, and behavioral correlates of communal nesting by birds with wasps or bees. *Proc. Thirteenth Int. Ornithol. Congr. Berlin,* in press.

Zeledonia coronata (Zeledonia, Wrenthrush)

J. H. Hunt

The wrenthrush (fig. 10.52) is found only in forested highlands and mountain regions, particularly in habitats that are frequently fog covered and almost always wet. The species' distribution is restricted to Costa Rica and the Chiriquí highlands of western Panama. The bird is a resident in *Swallenochloa* and *Chusquea* bamboo thickets at 3,000 m elevation on Cerro de la Muerte, and it is common in the ridgetop cloud forest above Monteverde.

Wrenthrushes are monomorphic. They resemble the common slender-billed nightingale thrush, *Catharus gracilirostris,* in being olive backed and slaty gray below. Wrenthrushes, however, are somewhat chunkier than nightingale thrushes and have conspicuously shorter tails. The orange crown patch bordered by two black stripes is distinctive but not as conspicuous as one might think.

Wrenthrushes are usually seen on or near the ground. They flick their wings occasionally while hopping about, and they rarely fly (and only poorly when they do). They never cock the tail in a wrenlike attitude as some illustrations show. They almost always remain concealed in dense vegetation and so are frustratingly difficult to see.

The birds will become habituated, after several days, to the presence of a diligent observer who may then watch them more easily.

Vocalizations are the easiest means to locate and identify wrenthrushes. The call, a single syllable, is heard frequently and is distinctive. It is very similar to the call of *Catharus gracilirostris,* but it is about an octave higher and very thin in tone quality. It rises in frequency as it is sounded, and it might be phoneticized as an upwardly inflected *sseee*. A long series of calls, one every few seconds, is a common pattern of calling, though single calls are also commonly heard.

The song figures and phrasing resemble those of many vireos: variable polysyllabic phrases are regularly spaced at intervals of a few seconds. The song, sung by both sexes, has the same thin, high, squeaky tone quality as the call. Songs are heard much less frequently than calls and may be seasonally associated with nesting. Members of a mated pair of wrenthrushes can be heard to countersing and countercall. That is, the individuals will alternate sounding a call or, when singing, a song phrase such that the two birds produce a sequence of rather regularly spaced calls or song phrases. A call or song series lasting one-half hour is not unusual.

From March to July the birds are dispersed in pairs; no observations have been made in other months of the year. A pair maintains a relatively large all-purpose territory of perhaps 0.5 ha or more. Both sexes participate in territorial display by singing and calling regularly near boundaries with adjoining territories. Countersinging and countercalling between birds on adjacent territories can be noted, and such vocalizations are the probable mechanism of territory demarcation. On one occasion all four individuals of two neighboring pairs were heard in simultaneous countersinging.

Foraging wrenthrushes move, singly or together, at a slow pace along an irregular route that loops over much of the territory. The birds apparently feed largely on small lepidopteran larvae. Provision loads carried to nestlings were visibly all lepidopteran larvae, and adult stomach contents were a pea soup of vegetable matter such as would result from feeding on caterpillars.

Both sexes participate in nest building, though the female does most of the work. Construction takes a week or more. Nests are domed, with an opening in the side. The construction material is various mosses, which are tightly packed together. Nests are always concealed in a vertical-faced, moss-covered site such as a gulley side or a sharp irregularity in the steep slope of a hill. Nests are exceedingly difficult to find.

Two eggs are laid. The white or cream eggs are heavily patterned with small brown spots. The eggs are rather robust, not pointed, and are relatively large for the size

FIGURE 10.52. *Zeledonia coronata*. *a*, Nest in situ on the crest of a creek bank. Arrow indicates nest opening. Vegetation overhanging site has been cleared away. *b*, Nest after removal from the site. *c*, Eggs removed from the nest.

d, Nestlings between two adult males (females are similar). Nestlings are approximately 17 (*left*) and 15 (*right*) days old. Villa Mills, Cerro de la Muerte, Costa Rica (photos, J. H. Hunt).

of the adult bird. Length of the incubation period is unknown, but it probably approaches the long extreme for small songbirds. The nestling period is believed to be very long for a songbird—perhaps 18 days. Both members of a pair are believed to provision nestlings. Young nestlings have sparse gray down. Older nestlings acquire a juvenile plumage that is the same as the adult plumage except for the crown patch, which probably appears shortly after fledging.

Wrenthrushes are not known to be gregarious, either with conspecifics or with other species.

Taxonomic placement of wrenthrushes, whether as a monotypic family or not, is an issue that probably turns on the personal prejudices of the systematists who tackle the question. What is not at issue is that affinities of *Zeledonia* clearly lie with the New World nine-primaried oscines. *Zeledonia* also shares numerous life-history and ecological characteristics plus some morphological traits with the Central American parulid genera *Myioborus, Basileuterus,* and *Ergaticus,* and these four genera may form a close phyletic assemblage. However, the short tail, short rounded wings, reduced carina, and robust body distinguish *Zeledonia* from the warbler genera. Though these features of the wrenthrush may all be specific adaptations to the birds' preferred habitat and foraging behavior, they nonetheless cause the species to be distinctive. *Zeledonia coronata* will probably continue to receive special placement in most taxonomic treatments.

*

Hunt, J. H. 1971. A field study of the Wrenthrush, *Zeledonia coronata. Auk* 88:1–20.

Zonotrichia capensis (Comemaiz, Rufous-collared Sparrow)

S. M. Smith

This species, known variously as the rufous-collared sparrow, Andean sparrow, or chingolo sparrow, or by the local Costa Rican name "comemaiz," is among the most common and visible birds in Costa Rica (fig. 10.53). Abundant throughout the Meseta Central, it at present occupies a niche similar to that of house sparrows (*Passer domesticus*) in north temperate regions.

In all plumages there is a short but distinct crest. Adults have a black crown and a wide gray stripe above a narrower black eye line, forming a typical *Zonotrichia* striped head pattern. Between the striped head and the brown-streaked back is the distinctive wide rufous collar. Underparts are clear gray, with two black blotches on each side of the breast, often joined to give a "bow tie" appearance. There are two distinct white wingbars. Young birds are streaked both above and below, lack the bow tie, and have considerably less rufous on the collar, duller head stripes, and indistinct wing bars. In either plumage, sexes are similar.

While apparently absent at sea level, this species

FIGURE 10.53. *Zonotrichia capensis,* adult. Courtyard of the Museo National, San José, Costa Rica (photo, D. H. Janzen).

ranges from a few hundred meters up to the top of the highest mountains, especially in the central ranges. It is, for example, an abundant and conspicuous resident at Cerro de la Muerte.

Songs of this species can be heard throughout its range in any month of the year. A common song on the Meseta Central is a whistled *drink your teaaa,* but several song types are present in most populations. Handford and Nottebohm (1976) have claimed that song type varies with factors such as altitude.

Costa Rican populations are monogamous and strongly territorial and, at least on the Meseta Central, have a year-round breeding season. Nests are in a wide variety of locations: high in trees, in low bushes, on the ground below dense vegetation, and in crevices in cliffs or rock walls. The most common clutch size is three eggs. Only the female incubates, but both parents feed the young, which can remain dependent for several weeks after fledging. Although Wolf (1969) claimed to have found distinct peaks of breeding, I did not find similar peaks in a four-year study of marked birds on the Universidad de Costa Rica campus.

Because of the strong and permanent territorial system, most young birds must spend time as nonbreeding floaters before becoming territory owners. These floaters form a highly organized social system, the "underworld" (Smith 1978), in which for each territory there is a separate male and female dominance hierarchy of floaters. When an owner dies it is quickly replaced with that territory's dominant underworld member of the appropriate sex. Underworld birds are typically furtive, so independent juveniles are rarely seen. Sometimes, however, large aggregations of rufous-collared sparrows can be found. These groups are mostly young, somewhat streaked birds, are formed only in times of very high productivity and seldom last more than a month at most. I suspect they are made up of birds that have not yet found a place in the underworld system.

Recently house sparrows have invaded Costa Rica. The effects of this invasion on local rufous-collared sparrow populations remain to be seen.

*

Handord, P., and Nottebohm, F. 1976. Allozymic and morphological variation in population samples of rufous-collared sparrows, *Zonotrichia capensis,* in relation to vocal dialects. *Evolution* 30:802–17.

Slud, P. 1964. The birds of Costa Rica: Distribution and ecology. *Bull. Am. Mus. Nat. Hist.* 128:1–430.

Smith, S. M. 1978. The "underworld" in a territorial sparrow: Adaptive strategy for floaters. *Am. Nat.* 112:571–82.

Wolf, L. L. 1969. Breeding and molting periods in a Costa Rican population of the Andean sparrow. *Condor* 71:212–19.

11 INSECTS

INTRODUCTION

D. H. Janzen

Costa Rica—all of it—is a tropical country with a tropical insect fauna. However, the insect fauna of no one Costa Rican habitat is even approximately representative in its ecological and faunistic aspects. In Corcovado National Park (36,000 ha), there are at least 220 species of breeding butterflies exclusive of skippers (Hesperiidae), hairstreaks (Lycaenidae), and metalmarks (Riodinidae); in Chirripó National Park (43,700 ha), about 70 km north of Corcovado, the comparable number is about thirty species, with less than 5% in common between the two parks (P. DeVries, pers. comm.). Yes, Chirripó National Park is at 2,000–3,500 m elevation and Corcovado is at sea level; but the rain-forest-clothed Isla del Caño (320 ha) that lies about 17 km off the coast of Corcovado appears to have only about five species of breeding butterflies, all of which occur on the adjacent mainland. I found almost as much variation in the richness and density of insect species from eight hundred sweep samples of old fields and pastures of various histories, and in the adjacent deciduous forest, in Palo Verde Wildlife Refuge (in the Tempisque River delta, Guanacaste Province) (Janzen 1976a) as I found in the same size Costa Rican samples taken from sea level to 3,000 m elevation,

night and day, second growth and primary forest understory, rainy season and dry season, and evergreen and deciduous forest (Janzen 1973a). Given such variation, the reader must view all my generalizations below as limited, often site-specific and attention-focusing, rather than as definitive about the tropics or Costa Rica. Costa Rica (51,054 km^2), about the size of West Virginia, contains nearly as many habitat types as does North America, and generalizations covering all of Costa Rica have about as much applicability as do generalizations about the insect ecology of the entire United States or Canada (and see Munroe 1956).

Rather than try to illustrate all aspects of insect ecology with Costa Rican examples, and thereby mainly pronounce that we known next to nothing about the ecology of almost all Costa Rican insects, I have chosen to write short essays on some topics that have received attention or that catch the interest of the Costa Rican ecological traveler. I know of no collection of essays on the insect ecology of other tropical countries from which to draw extensive comparisons. However, the following books and large papers contain a wealth of information on many aspects of the ecology of tropical insects, including Costa Rican ones: Schneirla 1971; Weber 1972; Wille and Michener 1973; Owen 1971; Halffter and Matthews 1966; Y. Gillon 1971; D. Gillon 1971; Wilson 1971;

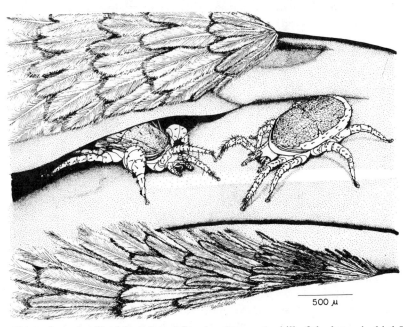

Rhinoseius colwelli adult male and female mites on the bill of the hummingbird *Eugenes fulgens*. The male is emerging from the nasal opening of the bird, whose bill is nearly one hundred times as long as the mite (drawing, S. Naeem).

Beeson 1941; Browne 1968; Mound and Waloff 1978; Wolda 1978a,b; Gray 1972.

Two areas of Costa Rican insect biology are accumulating information so rapidly that I am reluctant to try to extensively characterize them here: parasitoid biology and insect host plant interactions. Separate review papers dealing with them will appear in the not too distant future.

Why Do Moths Come to Lights?

On first arriving at a Costa Rican field station, people often see moths before any other insects; they display the puzzling behavior of coming to lights and roosting near them in a relatively inactive state (see Hienton 1974 and Weiss, Soraci, and McCoy 1941 for a review of the phenomenon). The more ultraviolet, the more moths. It is very unlikely that moths are attracted to light because light mimics a natural attractant. Rather, it is probable that light short-circuits a variety of physiological and behavioral systems and serendipitously results in moths arriving at lights, where a subset of them remain.

R. R. Baker, an English biologist who specializes in understanding the individual behavior of adult butterflies and moths with respect to migration and other collective movements, is developing an explanation that seems consistent with the patterns of moth attraction to lights in Costa Rica. He argues that the night-flying moth uses a distant point of light as a reference in flying from one place to another. Normally such points are distant (stars, moon), and by maintaining a somewhat constant angle to the light source, the moth gets where it wants to go. But if it chooses an artificial light and that light is close by, maintaining a constant angle to it will cause the moth to fly around it in an ever-tightening spiral until it arrives there. Finding itself in "daylight," it then roosts. See Robinson and Robinson (1950) for ideas and data that foreshadow this hypothesis. If Baker is correct, there are a number of important ecological correlates. Moths at lights are "attracted" only from relatively short distances (tens, not thousands, of meters); the smaller and more intense the light, the more moths should come (but the light would have to be enormous to win in competition with the moon); and, most important, moths must have cause to make geographically oriented flights. The latter implies that either they are migrating or they know in some sense the geographic location of larval host plants, adult nectar hosts, or good diurnal hiding spots rather than finding them solely through direct pursuit of chemical or visual cues; in short, they learn and remember. We do not expect even nocturnal caterpillars to be attracted to light. The collector's light mimics a distant landmark; one must thus be extremely careful in using the appearance of moths at lights as clues to moth ecology, just as in characterizing a town by the people passing through its plaza.

WHICH MOTHS DO NOT COME TO LIGHT?

The most conspicuous nonarrivals are diurnal species, such as the members of the Castniidae (large, colorful, very strong fliers along paths and streams in second growth). Members of the Pericopidae also often do not come to lights, and the more diurnal the pericopid species, the less common it is at lights. When diurnal fliers do come, pericopids such as *Pericopis separata* (apparent Müllerian mimics of butterflies that are attracted to light at Monteverde and Santa Rosa National Park) may leave shortly thereafter or fly about skittishly several meters from the bulb and leave if disturbed. Not only does Uraniidae have strongly diurnal members (e.g., the rainforest black-and-green *Urania fulgens*) that never come to lights, but its crepuscular and nocturnal members (e.g., *Sematura lunus* and *Coronidia orithea*) almost never come. Among the heavily diurnal Ctenuchidae and Sphingidae (e.g., *Aellopos* spp.), abundance at lights is generally much lower than the moths' abundance at flowers suggests it should be. In general, the more crepuscular small sphingids conform to this rule as well, though *Cautethia spuria* and *C. yucatana* (the smallest Costa Rican sphingids) are very common at lights yet also are frequent early-dawn visitors of Convolvulaceae (e.g., *Ipomoea trifida*, Santa Rosa National Park).

But a moth need not be a diurnal flier to be generally resistant to arriving at a light. Many species of medium-sized to large noctuids (e.g., the black witch, *Ascalapha odorata,* and many of its smaller relatives such as *Blosyris xylia*) come readily to rotten-fruit baits and are easily trapped in butterfly traps left up at night. However, they arrive at lights only very rarely. For example, when I was collecting moths all night in Santa Rosa National Park in May–July and November–December from a fluorescent light and a blacklight about 80 m from a butterfly trap baited with rotting fruit, fewer than ten individuals of only three species of these large noctuids came to the lights, while hundreds of individuals were collected in the trap or seen there. I have watched *Ascalapha odora* fly to a rotten fruit at night inside a fully lit house, feed, and then leave, apparently oblivious of the light. If one does come to a light, if often leaves if disturbed. Among the very small moths (especially those whose larvae are leaf, fruit, and seed miners), many species do not appear at lights. Many of these species do not fly long distances from their host plants, and therefore the light may have to be placed in many different microhabitats to obtain most of those in the area. On the other hand, they may neither be attracted to lights nor have cause to make flights based on orientation to lights. There undoubtedly are many species of large moths that are fully nocturnal in activities yet never appear at light. Those who take the time to rear moth larvae often rear species they have not seen at lights. However, the seasonality described in the next paragraph may also be in part responsible for this apparent unresponsiveness.

Many species of moths appear to arrive at light only during part of their adult phase. At Santa Rosa National Park it is commonplace to catch a number of species of adult sphingids visiting flowers in July (e.g., *Xylophanes, Enyo, Erinnyis,* and *Pachylioides* at *Stachytarpheta frantzii*), when the last time their species were seen at nearby lights was in late May and early June. The conspicuous white adults of two species of *Eulepidotis* (Noctuidae) were found abundantly in the foliage at night by flashlight in Santa Rosa National Park in June, yet they almost never came to the fluorescent lights and blacklights burning all night only 20 to 30 m away; in late December of the same year slightly worn individuals were common at the same lights (and were probably from the same cohort). That many species decrease their susceptibility to arriving at light with age is suggested by the preponderance of unworn and very fresh-appearing specimens at lights. This contrasts strongly with collections made from flowers, bait traps, and Malaise traps, where many specimens have tattered wing margins and extensive scale wear on the wings and thorax. A notable exception is the many individuals of large moths (Saturniidae and Sphingidae) with a distinctive deeply scalloped wing wear captured from lights at Monteverde. I suspect these are young individuals that have been fighting the high winds characteristic of this site.

Moths do not appear at lights with equal frequency at all times of night (e.g., Seifert 1974). Sphingids appear to have two peaks in arrival times: just after dark, and between 2300 and 0300. A light at Santa Rosa National Park may attract no sphingids before midnight and 10 to 30 after midnight, even at the dark of the moon. This is certainly not caused by simple inactivity by the moths during the first half of the night. In Corcovado National Park (Llorona) I collected five species of sphingids between 2100 and 2200, taking nectar from the fragrant white flowers of *Hedychium* (Zingiberaceae) about 100 m from a blacklight that attracted none of them. All these sphinx moth species come commonly to blacklights around midnight at Santa Rosa National Park. Saturniids also appear to arrive primarily during the second half of the night, and some such as *Hylesia lineata* have very strong peak periods of arrival. A light may attract one to three *H. lineata* males during most of the night and ten to forty during the last half-hour before dawn. Pyraustine pyralids, on the other hand, tend to arrive at the light in large numbers of species and individuals shortly after

dark, and almost no new ones appear after midnight. However, these moths may be found feeding actively at flowers between 0300 and 0500 along with the sphingids.

The sex ratios of moths at lights in Costa Rica, as elsewhere, deviate far from 1:1. Usually it is the males that are most abundant. Two data sets suggest that the male-imbalanced sex ratio is an attraction artifact. First, in both W. A. Haber's and my rearing records for hundreds of species of caterpillars found at Monteverde, Santa Rosa National Park, and the Cañas–Bagaces area, there is no hint of a badly imbalanced sex ratio. Second, during the July 1979 emergence of *Hylesia lineata* in Santa Rosa National Park, the sex ratio was 1:1 for more than three hundred adults emerging in the laboratory from reared caterpillars and wild-collected cocoons, but there were ten to fifteen males for each female at the lights every night for at least 2 weeks. The cause could be simple differential physiological susceptibility to lights (e.g., use of lights as landmarks) between the sexes, or it could be more extensive flight by males in search of females, which in turn would lead to their more frequently using the light as a landmark.

WHAT INTERFERES WITH ARRIVAL AT LIGHTS?
All other considerations aside, from Costa Rican rain forest to deciduous forest, from clear nights to rainy nights, there is conspicuously less arrival at lights by moths as the moon waxes. When the moon is full early in the evening but sets during the night, many more moths come after moonset than before. It is not clear that the absence of moths at lights on strongly moonlit nights means that there are fewer moths flying or that there are fewer adult moths available to arrive. For example, during the heavy emergence of *H. lineata* mentioned above, the laboratory emergences did not decline during the full moon (the moths emerge in midafternoon), but *H. lineata* at lights did decline during the full moon. Two casual explanations are commonplace among moth collectors. Some believe the moonlight interferes with light perception or use by the moths. This is consistent with Baker's hypothesis. Others suggest that moths do not fly in moonlight because it makes them more susceptible to predation by bats. I might add that bats probably catch most moths by sonar, and that it is well known among bat biologists that moonlight depresses the numbers of bats caught in nets. One could argue that this is caused by a depression in food density on moonlit nights, except that it applies to frugivorous and nectarivorous as well as insectivorous bats. It may also be easier to see nets in moonlight. Caprimulgid birds are visually oriented nocturnal aerial insect catchers that could also account for a depression in moth activity on moonlit nights, but I doubt that they are

generally common enough to generate an overall depression. Furthermore, they are not large enough (or fast enough, I suspect) to take the large sphinx moths, which are just as severely depressed in density at a light on moonlit nights as are little moths.

Looked at the other way round, cloudy, misty, and wind-free nights are correlated with the largest numbers of moths at lights. Costa Rican moths fly very well in the rain, and many struggle along even in a heavy downpour. It is tempting to suggest that in a light rain or mist they can fly quite free from bat predation directed by sonar. However, again this is a quite unrealistic hypothesis since a dense, low cloud cover with no mist or rain is often also associated with large numbers of moths at lights. Here one might hypothesize, in accordance with Baker, that the artificial light is the only orientation cue available.

It is noteworthy that the numbers of moths at lights is very high when artificial lights first appear in quantity at a site. Then, as the years pass, the moths often decline to near zero. When I first collected moths at the lights in Guanacaste in 1963 and 1965, the gas station lights in Cañas and Liberia were a rich source of sphingids, saturniids, and many small moths. Now, in the early 1980s, there is virtually nothing at these lights even at the best time of year. There are at least three possible causes. Over all these years, there could have been intense selection for moths that do not respond to city lights. This seems unlikely considering the minute fraction of the total Guanacaste moth fauna that would be in close contact with the lights of these and other towns. Second, the city could act as a huge light trap and essentially extirpate the moth fauna in its immediate vicinity. Again, local population flow should erase this effect. Third, the area of Guanacaste in original forest, heavily brushy pasture, and second-growth forest has easily been cut by half, if not more, since 1963–65. Around the towns and other light sources the area of woody vegetation has been reduced by at least 90%. I suspect that rather than moths' no longer being attracted to (confused by) lights, there are few if any moths left. While I have observed less closely, I believe I have seen the same thing in the vicinity of Puerto Viejo de Sarapiquí and Palmar Sur.

What Other Insects Come to Lights?

A highly heterogeneous array of other insect groups arrives at Costa Rican lights placed in the vicinity of insect-rich vegetation. In many ways this array is like that which arrives at an extratropical light. It is rich in numbers and poor in species of beetles in the Cerambycidae, Scarabaeidae, Carabidae, Meloidae, Dytiscidae, Hydrophilidae, Elateridae, and a variety of families with minute members (Scolytidae, Curculionidae, Staphylinidae, etc.). Some species of Tettigoniidae and Gryllidae are abundant while others, common and active nocturnally in nearby vegetation, rarely appear at the lights. The same applies to other vegetarian orders (e.g., most Hemiptera and Homoptera). Members of the Chrysopidae, Myrmeleontidae and Ascalaphidae (Neuroptera), and Mecoptera are common at lights yet are represented there by only a small subset of the species found in nearby vegetation at night. Like those found below the streetlights of a United States midwestern city, aquatic insects are abundant in the early and late rainy season (when moving from or to bodies of water) (e.g., Dytiscidae, Hydrophilidae, Megaloptera, Trichoptera, nymphuline pyralids, Belostomatidae); Ephemeroptera are characteristically scarce, but they are not a numerically prominent part of the Costa Rican aquatic fauna (see Stout and Vandermeer 1975). Hymenoptera are poorly represented except for certain common Ichneumonidae (e.g., *Thyreodon atriventris,* a sphingid parasite), *Megalopta* (a nocturnally foraging halictid bee; Janzen 1968a), the larger *Ptiloglossa* (a matinal and crepuscular foraging colletid bee, Janzen 1968c), and *Apoica* (a nocturnally foraging *Polistes* analogue) (but see Burbutis and Stewart 1979). If the light is near a stand of *Hymenaea courbaril* (guapinol, Leguminosae), lantern flies (*Fulgora laternaria*) may appear. An occasional butterfly or fly is attracted, but their scarcity clearly does not represent the populations from which they are drawn. Immatures are conspicuously absent at lights. In short, with a few notable exceptions (some Scarabaeidae and Tettigoniidae), the consistency and abundance of insects other than moths at Costa Rican lights does not lend support to the idea that their appearance, or lack of it, says much about the ecology of the animals in general. However, the patterns of heterogeneity described for moths also apply to the other insects that come to lights, again with some exceptions. For example, female dobson flies (*Corydalis* in the Megaloptera) at Santa Rosa National Park outnumber males at lights about thirty to one, and female dynastine scarabs are generally more abundant at Costa Rican lights than are males. Of course, none of these disparaging generalizations need be true for a particular species where it is found by other means that abundance at lights is proportional to some natural population trait.

Technology of Taking Moths at Lights

I and others collecting moths at lights in Costa Rica have found that the best return is obtained by hanging fluorescent and blacklight (bulb is white, light looks light blue) bulbs in front of white sheets hung on buildings or from ropes between trees in the forest. If wall current is not available, a 12-volt car battery will easily power two 15-watt bulbs all night. DC fluorescent fixture balast is available. Car battery rechargers will easily recharge a

12-volt battery from 110-volt wall current during daylight hours. The location and exposure of the light make a large difference in what species of moths come and in what numbers. The collector will have to experiment with respect to the groups of interest. In general, an ideal site is the side of a hill sheltered from the wind and facing across a narrow valley to a general forest canopy 50–200 m away, surrounded by irregular second-growth vegetation. Hilltops are particularly good for sphingids and some saturniids, while the upper edge of a cliff, at the same height as the adjacent forest canopy, is very good for small moths. A light on one side of a house in a forest may attract many moths on the same night when one on the opposite side attracts nearly nothing; the following night the catch may be reversed. In early December in Santa Rosa National Park, eighty-one species of pyraustine pyralids came to a pair of black and fluorescent lights one night, while only three were seen at an identical pair of lights 4 km away. Both sets of lights were exposed to forest and backed by grassland; all the species taken at the first set of lights were collected at some time during the year at the second set of lights.

We have no idea of the distance from which moths are attracted to lights. W. Haber (pers. comm.) suspects several kilometers or more; I suspect that 500 m is about the maximum distance, and the Baker hypothesis mentioned earlier suggests it is even less. Moths arrive at lights, and moths leave lights. For small moths, it is best to collect continually to get them all. Sphingids and saturniids usually stay several hours after arriving, but one cannot count on a sphingid that arrives at midnight still being there at 0500. Wind blows them off the sheet, they rouse and fly off at their own initiative, and they may be disturbed by arriving insects. Many fly to the light and then fly away without even landing. Some land on foliage up to 15 m from the light and never seem to approach more closely. If a light is repeatedly exposed at the same place, the local birds will learn to visit at dawn for breakfast. At night the lower parts of the sheet may be cleaned of moths by toads, skunks, and feral cats. Bats and caprimulgids often collect moths from the air in front of lights.

IN SUMMARY

Collecting moths at lights is a quick and efficient way to get a partial view of the species composition of the moth fauna of a habitat or region. To be more than this, it has to be coupled with rearing and other samples of density. Moths appear at light most frequently when newly emerged from the pupa (unworn), and males usually appear more often than do females. The absence of moths at light tells little about their actual abundance in the habitat, though it may corroborate other natural history information. Perhaps the worst potential ecological error in using data from lights in Costa Rica would be to conclude that the absence of moths at lights also means they are absent as food for carnivores, as pollinators, and as herbivores when larvae. A large pulse of sphingids at the lights could mean, for example, that there will be many pollinators available, that a large number of immigrants are about to leave the area, or that an intense emergence cue has been experienced by a large crop of dormant pupae gradually accumulated over many months of rainy season.

It seems safe to conclude that what we know of moths at Costa Rican lights is concordant with Baker's "landmark" hypothesis. Any landmark will be used to different degrees at different times by different animals. A nightly changing visual landmark may be very important to a male saturniid coursing the landscape for female pheromones, to a newly emerged sphingid searching for new nectar sources or oviposition hosts, or to an old adult migrating out as the dry season approaches. It may be of no interest to a female saturniid intent on tracking the odor of a particular species of shrub in vegetation at the right stage of succession, to a wise old sphinx moth that is reproductively dormant and knows the location of most nectar sources within several square kilometers, or to a pyralid that is using the full moon as its landmark. A moth may use a landmark to fly to its feeding area, and therefore be pulled into a light, but use its nose when it gets there and therefore ignore a light.

Do Costa Rican Insect Arrays Display Seasonality?
Every imaginable aspect of Costa Rican insect ecology has some or many seasonal components. The dominant seasonal influence is the regularly occurring long dry season (*verano;* later December through April or early May in Guanacaste, as little as a few weeks in February or March in the Caribbean lowlands, and 1–2 months in January–March on the Osa Peninsula). In addition, there is the irregularly occurring short dry season (*veranillo;* 0–6 weeks in June–August in Guanacaste). The first 2 months of the rainy season (*invierno*) are less intense, and the last 3 months of the rainy season (September–November) are more intense. Associated with these rainy and dry seasons are changes in soil moisture, flooding, windiness, wind direction, rain duration and intensity, cloudiness, fluctuation in temperature, average temperature, abundance and quality of carnivore prey and plant parts and species, vegetation shadiness, humidity, and other environmental traits. Costa Rican insects respond conspicuously to all these kinds of changes, just as do other tropical organisms (and see Wolda 1978*a,b;* Gray 1972; Y. Gillon 1971; D. Gillon 1971; Janzen 1967*a,b,* 1970, 1971*a,* 1973*a,* 1976*a,b,c,* 1978*a;* Schoener and

Janzen 1968; Janzen and Schoener 1968; Janzen and Wilson 1974; Janzen and Pond 1975; Dobzhansky and Pavan 1950).

Perhaps the most conspicuous, and most frustrating, aspect of understanding Costa Rican insect seasonality is that a response often is, or has the potential to be, a response to a variety of environmental events rather than to a single one such as omnipresent winter cold or a rain on desert dryness. Moisture is far more heterogeneously available in a rain forest or deciduous forest during the dry season than is warmth in the woods in Wisconsin in February. There certainly is no single factor responsible for *Phelypera distigma*'s (Curculionidae) producing one generation eating the leaves of *Guazuma ulmifolia* (Sterculiaceae) during about 20 days in June in Guanacaste and then sitting out the rest of the year as a sexually inactive adult (Janzen 1979*a*) hiding in leaf rolls and crevices. We know something of insect seasonality in only two of the many Costa Rican habitats—lowland rain forest (as exemplified by the Osa Peninsula and the Sarapiquí region) and lowland deciduous forest (as exemplified by Guanacaste Province below about 400 m elevation). I will discuss these habitats in detail and then add miscellaneous comments on a few others. Throughout I have tried to avoid the word "community" because it implies interactions and boundaries about which we know nothing.

A STRONGLY SEASONAL HABITAT

The lowlands of Guanacaste Province experience roughly 5 months of almost continuously windy, sunny weather during which no rain falls, followed by cloudy, rainy weather in which there is 1.5 to 2.5 m of rainfall and winds blow erratically, if at all. As the dry season comes on, the litter and soil dry at the surface, the area of green and shady vegetation shrinks to the riparian sites and scattered "evergreen" plant species, and the insects available as prey decline in density and become more heterogeneous. It is the "harsh" time of year for many insects; but just as the rainy season is the food-rich time for most herbivores and carnivores, the dry season is a food-rich time for seed predators and pollinators of woody plants (especially bees). The dry season ends much more abruptly than it begins; a convectional thunderstorm is finally dragged in off the Pacific Ocean and drenches a rather uniformly dry (by this time) soil. However, this beginning is often marked by false starts, and it may be as much as 3 weeks from the first rain until the soil is thoroughly drenched and plant leafing and stem elongation are fully under way. Being a farming species, we are most curious about how insects "pass the dry season," but I will also elaborate on how they deal with resource lows during the rainy season.

There are at least five commonly encountered ways that Guanacaste insects pass the dry season, and from one to all may be used by a given species: adult in reproductive diapause seeking a favorable microhabitat; dormant immature stage; adult migrating many kilometers; continuous low density breeding on a scarce resource; and normal population breeding and increase on a food available only during the dry season.

Very Local Movements by Adults in
Reproductive Diapause

During the dry season, the density and numbers of species of adult insects rise very conspicuously in moister sites such as marsh edges, river edges, north-facing slopes, groves of evergreen species of trees (e.g., *Hymenaea courbaril*, *Manilkara zapota*), deep, steep-sided dry creek beds, and cave entrances. Correspondingly, it falls in adjacent deciduous and sun-blasted vegetation. As the dry season progresses, the insect density in the moist sites declines, and by the end of April in the smaller refuges it may approach that of a dry hillside. The insects found in high numbers in local moist microhabitats are generally in reproductive diapause. Perhaps the most conspicuous example is *Eurema diara* (Pieridae). This flimsy little yellow, black, and white butterfly has several larval generations during the rainy season on herbaceous legumes. The last adults emerge in December and may be found sitting in loosely coherent groups of as many as several hundred on herbaceous vegetation in riparian or otherwise moist (or humid) microhabitats. Local migrations in December (Santa Rosa National Park) occur from uplands (300 m) toward the lowlands (sea level). Throughout the dry season they generally fly only when disturbed and do not visit flowers. With the onset of the rains, they mate and the ovaries become functional (O. Taylor, pers. comm.).

The leaf-eating weevil *Phelypera distigma*, mentioned earlier, is another such insect. I do not know whether it mates before or after the dry season, but individuals *in copulo* are encountered in June at the time of egg laying. This suggests that the female uses the dry season as a filter to remove "unfit" males. Adult harvestmen (Phalangida) and Erotylidae (pleasing fungus beetles) form aggregations of thousands of individuals in caves and hollow trees, where they passively wait out the dry season. Ithomiid and heliconiine adult butterfly populations may fall to well under 1% of their late rainy season density and be represented only by a few individuals in a few exceptionally moist pockets along a river drainage. From these microhabitats they spread out into upland vegetation with the oncoming rains (L. Gilbert, W. Benson, pers. comm.). The word reproductive "dormancy" might be more appropriate than reproductive "diapause" for the butterflies, since the mere provision of oviposition hosts might well cause immediate ovarial development. In the case of insects that feed on herbaceous species, it would be of great interest to see the results of offering green potted plants during the dry season. However, the weevil mentioned at the beginning of this paragraph is clearly in reproductive diapause, since young leaves of *Guazuma ulmifolia* are available in some places throughout the year yet are not oviposited on.

When Malaise traps are placed in a moist and shady creek bed and on an adjacent deciduous and dry hillside, documentation of local insect movements is easily obtained. In an ongoing study in Santa Rosa National Park, I am finding that adults of many species of insects are caught in the dry hillside trap during the rainy season and in the riparian trap during the dry season. This observation applies to major groups of insects as well as to species. While some of the seasonal movement may be by predators in pursuit of food (e.g., asilid fly adults moving to where the density of flying insects is highest or *Eciton burchelli* army ants moving to where there are the most litter insects), this cause probably does not apply to herbivorous insects whose larval host plants do not occur in the creek bed.

A major part of this movement is probably directed at conserving moisture by staying in a humid and shady site. Additionally, some insects take water directly from water holes. Density of social wasps and bees (*Polistes, Trigona*) in the riparian Malaise trap is greatly elevated during the dry season, and these and other Hymenoptera can be seen drinking at the minute water holes in large numbers. In the rainy season they are only rarely present in the riparian traps. The steepness of the humidity gradient from dry forest to a moist riverbed can be impressive. In an extreme case, the relative humidity at 1000 in May varied by thirty percentage points over 50 m, from the stream edge to the deciduous forest, and the air temperature varied by 6.2° C over the same transect on the side of the gorge below the COMELCO waterfall (near Bagaces); in the rainy season these differences were by and large obliterated (Janzen 1976c).

Moisture may also be obtained by direct consumption of foliage or prey that is inadequate for larval or ovarial development. Curculionid and chrysomelid beetles, and various Hemiptera, probably offer the best examples. For example, when the drying of creek beds and moist seepages leads to near cessation of new leaf production by *Heliconia latispatha* leaves, adults of *Cephaloeia* chrysomelid beetles are encountered heavily eating old leaves of *H. latispatha*. They are not mating at this time and are probably not laying eggs, but this food undoubtedly offers some moisture and perhaps calories to minimize dry-season reserve losses and desiccation. During dry-season lows in seeds and shoot tips, bugs of the Coreidae, Lygaeidae, and Pyrrhocoridae are often found sucking the body fluids out of dead insects, apparently as scavengers, not predators.

When the first rains occur, the exodus from moist and shady sites to the surrounding greening forest is dramatic. There are probably two major causes. First, in general the harvestable productivity in the heavily shaded forest understory should be the lowest of any microhabitat (aside from deep caves). Second, as mentioned earlier, the bulk of these species have their breeding-season food in other habitats. The phytophagous insects find their larval host plants producing new foliage in the hillside forest. The army ants (*Eciton burchelli*) apparently leave because their prey moves and because there is no longer a desiccation cost in the exposed areas. It is ironic that the evergreen trees in riparian sites, so valuable in producing dry-season shade, are generally useless as foliage food. *Hymenaea courbaril, Manilkara zapota, Sloanea terniflora, Ardisia revoluta, Ficus* spp., *Anacardium excelsum,* and so on, have very small herbivore loads compared with neighboring deciduous species (and see Stanton 1975). The adult bruchids that seek creekside moisture and shade in the dry season leave upward or outward to where the rainy-season flowers are found. There they obtain nectar and pollen on which to pass the seed-free rainy season.

Insects such as leaf-cutter ants (Attini), largely dependent on rainy-season vegetation but too sedentary to move easily, cannot be involved in the movements described here (not only do army ant colonies move into the creek beds during the dry season, but *Polistes* wasp colonies may even move the nest site near to the water). However, the workers may obtain moisture by cutting foliage largely for its value as a moisture source (G. Stevens, pers. comm.), change their foraging area from the relatively leafless hillsides to a more evergreen riparian site, if one is close enough, and forage at night. Just as when large folivorous vertebrates choose vegetation for its moisture content, such behavior makes host specificity extremely difficult to interpret. Equally difficult is the interpretation of the movements of carnivorous insects that are choosing prey according to water-balance needs rather than, or in addition to, caloric or protein harvest. Are the lizards and spiders so common in riparian sites in the dry season because that is the location of their prey or because of the higher humidity that makes less prey capture necessary?

Dormancy

Complete dormancy of various stages of insects, as commonly encountered with immature stages in northern latitudes, is not a conspicuous phenomenon in the dry season

625

(or rainy season) in tropical deciduous forest. There are, however, conspicuous exceptions such as ground-nesting insects like solitary bees, cicindelid beetles (Wille and Michener 1962), dung beetles, and moth pupae. I have postulated that this is so for reasons not unlike the reasons no tropical mammal is known to pass the dry (or other harsh) season in "hibernation" (Janzen 1973a; this volume, chap. 9). In short, the following things make complete dormancy in the dry season a poor way of waiting until larval food is again available: (a) The northern winter turns off or drives out many predators and parasitoids; in a tropical dry season many of these will not stop searching for food until they run out of it. Furthermore, active prey has a much greater chance of escaping than does a dormant egg, larva, pupa, or adult. (b) Since dry-season temperatures are as high as or higher (in soil, wood, and other solid substrates) than those of the rainy season, the dormant insect has to carry much more food reserve or be more competent at turning off its metabolism than would its northern counterpart (and see Janzen and Wilson 1974). (c) Water reserves are a problem analogous to that described above for food. (d) During the tropical severe dry season the active individual not only can avoid predators but can also actively seek water (and perhaps some nutrients). This should be especially important for those species that can use small amounts of water of a type highly unpredictable in exact location yet likely to occur (e.g., fallen fruit, dung, a newly dead carcass, a tree hole filled with water). (e) The beginning of the rainy season is highly unpredictable in its exact timing; an active adult insect can oviposit immediately on a new flush of leaves or other food source, whereas a dormant pupa has to receive eclosion cues, hatch, mature, mate, and then seek food plants. This timing will be of particular importance for those species feeding on rare plants, on plants whose leaves rapidly become unavailable through chemical changes, or on plants where there is strong competition over leaf or seed substrates as larval food.

There are, however, some conspicuous species that pass the Guanacaste dry season as dormant immatures. It appears that nearly all saturniids in Santa Rosa National Park pass the dry season as dormant pupae in the litter or soil (except for the pendant silk cocoons of *Rothschildia*) and use the moisture of the first rains as a hatching cue. They emerge, mate, do not feed, oviposit during a few days, and die. The second generation emerges about 2 months later (July–August) and repeats the process. However, the bulk of the pupae formed in October–November remain dormant until the beginning of the following rainy season. Some, however, such as *Eacles imperialis decoris* (the imperial moth), appear to have only the first generation and then remain as dormant pupae from August to May or June. A small number

of individuals of the bivoltine species (e.g., *Automeris, Rothschildia, Dysdaemonia, Dirphia*) appear to get the wrong signals and think it is July in November. They emerge but probably do not produce a successful third generation. At Santa Rosa National Park, *Hylesia lineata*, a tiny *Automeris*-like saturniid, offers an instructive deviation from the above generalizations. The entire population emerges from its pupae at the end of the rainy season (mid-November to early December) and mates. A female makes a ball of all her eggs and covers it with a thick beige felt of abdominal hairs. The ball hangs on a host plant branch. The eggs remain dormant in their conspicuous container and hatch 6 months later at the first rains. The larvae require about 2 months to develop, and the adults emerge about 3 weeks after pupating (in July). Again, the females make their arboreal egg masses (though often on leaf petioles as well as twigs). These then hatch in 2–3 weeks and produce the generation that again emerges at the end of the rainy season. Dry-season egg masses can sometimes be caused to hatch by repeated spraying with water (Janzen, unpub. data).

When the rains first start, the lights are often deluged with adult moths, beetles, and bugs, many of which must be adults newly emerged from pupae in response to wetting of the litter and soil. This has long been the classical explanation for this pulse of insects. However, in the case of many of the aquatic species, rather than emerging from pupae, they have emerged from concentrations of adults in small permanent bodies of water and are spreading out over the countryside to have one or more generations in temporary puddles, marshes, and streams. There is a smaller, but analogous, appearance of aquatic insects at lights at the end of the rainy season, which probably represents a return to permanent water bodies from drying temporary ones. Additionally, as will be discussed below, many of the adults appearing at lights at the beginning of the rainy season in Guanacaste may well be migrants from the higher elevation evergreen (and more moist) forest 5–30 km to the east.

Adult Migration

The deciduous forests of Costa Rica and Central America have no known migratory analogue to the monarch butterfly of higher latitudes. The *Danaus plexippus* population in Guanacaste is low in density and resident year-round over the province as a whole, though during the peak of the dry season it may be represented solely by adults and immatures in the more evergreen forests at 600–1,400 m elevation (e.g., Rincón National Park). However, there is circumstantial evidence for seasonal migration of Lepidoptera from the deciduous lowland forests to more highland sites (5–30 km away), with return at the beginning of the rainy season. For example, in the lowlands of Santa Rosa National Park, *Psychotria microdon* (Rubiaceae) is a common understory deciduous perennial shrublet. About the time of the first rains it puts out a new leaf crop, and seemingly out of nowhere appear numerous female *Xylophanes turbata* (Sphingidae) that lay enough eggs to create a very high density of large larvae. In 1978 and 1979 they defoliated all the *P. microdon* in many areas several hectares in extent. The caterpillars then pupated in the soil and litter and emerged about 2 weeks later. For a few days they were abundant at the lights, then they disappeared from the habitat. There was no second generation on the *P. microdon* leaves. However, throughout the year an occasional adult is taken at light at Monteverde (1,400 m elevation), and W. A. Haber has reared them there. It is possible that the adults are passing the 10 months between generations at Santa Rosa National Park as a few dormant pupae and a few long-lived flower-visiting adults in the deciduous forest. However, it seems more likely that they are passing this time as active adults in the cooler evergreen forests at higher elevation, where metabolic costs should be lower and predator intensity less, and perhaps even reproducing there. The same story can be told for *Aellopos titan*, a small diurnal sphingid whose larvae feed on leaves of various species of *Randia* in the Guanacaste lowlands. Haber (pers. comm.) suspects that a number of the lowland butterflies and sphingids seen passing through Monteverde are on their way from the Pacific to the Atlantic coast lowlands as part of seasonal movements. There is a small brown butterfly, *Eunica monima*, whose larvae eat the leaves of *Bursera simaruba* in Santa Rosa National Park. In June–July there is a single generation of this insect (during which it may be very abundant), followed by nearly complete disappearance of the adults for the rest of the year. However, enormous numbers of the adults have been seen in July high in the mountains at 1,000 m elevation on Volcán Rincón de la Vieja to the east, in an area where *B. simaruba* is absent (P. J. DeVries, pers. comm.). Do these butterflies return to the lowlands to oviposit in the following rainy season, or is this a case of explosive out-migration following the production of a very large dispersing population (as in the green page moth, *Urania fulgens*, Smith 1972)? The same question may be asked of the large white *Eurytides* swallowtail whose larvae feed on leaves of Annonaceae in Santa Rosa National Park.

Although it seems quite reasonable that seasonal long-distance in-country migration such as that postulated here for some large Lepidoptera may occur among other groups of insects, there have been no relevant studies. Other strong fliers, such as bees, are likely suspects.

Looked at the other way round, late in the rainy season a number of butterflies appear at Santa Rosa National Park that are thought of as being normal residents of the evergreen forests to the east. For example, throughout the year occasional morpho butterflies (*Morpho peleides*) are seen flying up a riverbed or taken in a bait trap in the park, but in November they are extremely common in riverbeds and other moist habitats. There is no larval generation of *M. peleides* in December–May; if these adults are to breed, they must do it elsewhere. This observation, and the occasional capture at lights in Santa Rosa National Park of a sphingid that is clearly a species of higher-elevation forests, brings to mind an ever-present aspect of an insect population in a highly seasonal site such as Guanacaste (or, as L. Gilbert points out, the north Mexicon-south Texas region). An insect species may be truly and permanently resident (e.g., various *Pseudomyrmex* acacia-ants); it may maintain a breeding population on most years with occasional extinctions followed by reinvasion from the nearby evergreen upper-elevation forest (e.g., *Rhinochenus* weevils in *Hymenaea courbaril* pods following a run of nonfruiting years); it may invade each year from a neighboring area and then be extinguished by the dry season irrespective of whether it had a breeding cycle (e.g., perhaps the clear-wing ithomiid *Itabalia* that appears occasionally in Santa Rosa National Park); or it may be absent and represented only by the occasional nonreproducing immigrant picked up in a sample before it dies a natural death.

Continuous Low-Density Breeding

By being somewhat plastic in their food demands, some insects maintain breeding populations throughout the dry season. Various species of *Dysdercus* bugs (Pyrrhocoridae) seem to move from feeding on the flowers and young fruits of malvaceous herbs and shrubs that reproduce in the rainy season (e.g., *Malvaviscus arboreus*, *Sida* spp., *Wissadula* spp.) to feeding on the seeds of various bombacaceous and sterculiaceous trees (*Bombacopsis*, *Sterculia*, *Ceiba*, *Pseudobombax*) in the dry season (e.g., Janzen 1972). While several bug species are involved and these bugs are notorious for feeding on food types on which they cannot reproduce, it appears safe to say that they breed during much of the year by using a variety of species of plants. In Santa Rosa National Park, the large and brightly colored red, yellow, and black larvae of the frangapani sphinx (*Pseudosphinx tetrio*) feed on the leaves of *Plumeria rubra* throughout the rainy season. Some are found feeding on even the very oldest leaf remnants on the trees in late December. Then, while some individuals pass the rainy season as dormant pupae or migrate out of the area, there are also larvae that develop while feeding on the large yellowish white flowers that are produced daily throughout much of the dry season by *P. rubra*. A leaf-cutter ant colony is clearly a large but highly subdivided arboreal folivore that feeds throughout the year in Guanacaste deciduous forests, but it takes quite different species of foliage during the dry season (G. Stevens and S. Hubbell, pers. comm.). It might not even be able to maintain its body weight or reproduce on what it takes in at that time, but it certainly is not dormant. Large army ant colonies (*Eciton, Labidus*) take quite different arrays of insect prey in the dry season and the wet season, both because of what is available and because of where they forage. I should note, however, that both leaf-cutter and army ants reproduce only once per year, so that their dry-season foraging is not analogous to that of a species that has continuous generations throughout the year.

The most continuously breeding species I know of in the Guanacaste lowlands are the acacia-ants, which appear to behave here just as I described for *Pseudomyrmex ferruginea* on *Acacia cornigera* in the lowlands of Veracruz, Mexico (Janzen 1966, 1967c), a habitat very similar to Guanacaste. Male and alate female pupae occur in all months in large colonies of all three species of Guanacaste *Pseudomyrmex* that fiercely defend a swollen-thorn acacia. Shortly after eclosion they leave the colony, and a mating swarm may be encountered in the top of a tree at the top of a hill before dawn any day of the year. The newly mated queens search for young or otherwise unoccupied ant-acacias at all times of year. This year-round search in a highly seasonal habitat is not surprising, since unoccupied seedlings and stunted saplings can be found at all times of year. Seeds germinate largely at the beginning of the rainy season (seeds of both *Acacia collinsii* and *A. cornigera* have by and large been dispersed by the time of the first rains), but some seedlings persist in an unoccupied state throughout the year. Since the unoccupied small plants produce occasional food bodies, and since even wind-blasted fully insolated leaf nectaries continue to make nectar, a founding queen can establish a colony in any month. Like the adult ant-acacias, the small plants do not drop all their foliage even in a severe dry season. The large plants may decrease the rate of new leaf production during the dry season, but the nectaries on old large leaves continue to function, and some large trees make a large number of leaves that are hardly anything more than petiolar and rachis supports for Beltian bodies. Clearly their function is feeding the ant colony in the dry season. The acacia-ant that is parasitic on this system, *Pseudomyrmex nigropilosa* (Janzen 1975), likewise breeds throughout the year, since trees for it to live in are becoming unoccupied throughout the year. This is especially so during the dry season, when large obligate acacia-ant colonies contract their territorial holdings. The *Azteca* ant colonies in Guanacaste *Cecropia* trees do not produce alates throughout the dry season even in riparian habitats. But even adult *Cecropia* trees do maintain a crop of tiny leaves with accompanying trichilia (source of the Müllerian food bodies; see Rickson 1971, 1973, 1976a,b; Marshall and Rickson

1973; Rickson and Denison 1975) even when the tree appears to be leafless.

I suspect that current vegetation disturbance patterns in Guanacaste have blurred a number of what would have been sharp breeding cycles among deciduous forest insects in largely unbroken forest. Much of Guanacaste vegetation is now forest edge and second growth. A trait of deciduous forest woody plants is that saplings, seedlings, and sucker shoots remain leafy and leaf-producing much longer into the dry season than do adults. For example, *Genipa americana* stands leafless from January through early May, but the suckers from an adjacent cut stump bear leaves throughout the dry season. For those species that normally have only a single generation on the young leaves of the new leaf crop of their host, such as *Phelypera distigma* on *Guazuma ulmifolia* (Janzen 1979a), the new leaves produced later in the rainy season on suckers from cut stumps and roadside saplings may be a site of later and abnormal generations if the insect has the cuing system to respond to their presence (as *P. distigma* apparently does not).

Dry-Season Breeders

For some insects, the Guanacaste dry season is the time of plenty—many solitary and social bees, fruit- and seed-drilling pyralid moth larvae, bruchid and weevil larvae, some tiger beetles (Cicindelidae), ant lions, and probably others. For these animals, part of the dry season and all of the rainy season is the harsh time of year in the sense that larval and oviposition sites are missing and dormancy may be difficult, as was discussed earlier.

Honeybee (*Apis mellifera*) colonies that were kept at La Colmena at Hacienda Palo Verde (now known as Refugio Rafael Rodriguez Lucas Caballero) illustrated well the fat-to-thin cycle for a social bee in the Guanacaste deciduous forest. These colonies had to be fed sugar (about 2 kg per month per hive) from May through October to keep them alive, yet they produced enough honey in December–April for two heavy-yield honey extractions. This may explain why honeybees have never become feral in Guanacaste even though there are a number of bee yards that could generate swarms (competition from ants and meliponid bees for nest site cavities may also contribute). There is a huge flush of species and individual flowering among woody plants during the Guanacaste dry season (Fournier and Salas 1966; Janzen 1967b; Frankie, Baker, and Opler 1974; Heithaus 1979a; Opler, Frankie, and Baker 1976), and this means a great deal of nectar and pollen food for both social and solitary bees. For example, carpenter bees (*Xylocopa* spp.) emerge from their pupal cells in May–June but remain in their tunnels as semiquiescent adults (males and females together) throughout the rainy season. They occasionally forage for nectar but spend much of many days in the "nest." As the dry-season flowering begins with the herbs at the end of the rainy season (e.g., *Crotalaria, Solanum, Centrosema, Ipomoea, Cassia, Canavalia*), these bees start gathering nectar and pollen in quantity and begin constructing new nests. Males are often seen hovering in apparent mate-seeking behavior at this time. By the middle to end of the dry season, it appears that most adults have died. The population continues as rapidly developing larvae and pupae that again hatch about the time of the first rains.

In Guanacaste there are hundreds of species of solitary bees that appear in the early dry season (e.g., Heithaus 1974, 1979*a,b*) from the underground cells where they have been waiting as prepupae since the end of the previous dry season. They collect pollen and nectar, construct and provision underground cells, and die. The number of generations per dry season is unknown but is probably only one. I suspect that they wait out the end of the dry season as prepupae rather than pupae because the former has a much lower surface area and should therefore be more resistant to desiccation. These solitary bees are accompanied at the flowers by five to nine species of social bees (*Trigona* and *Melipona*) (Heithaus 1974, 1979*a,b*; Johnson and Hubbell 1975; Hubbell and Johnson 1977). I suspect that these bee colonies suffer from the same wild fluctuations in food as do the honeybees described above, but they are able to survive because their individuals are smaller (and more numerous per unit colony weight), because they take a wider variety of food types (carrion, rotting fruit, pollen from grass and small herbs, all sizes of flowers, extrafloral nectaries, etc.), and because they have less biomass per colony. It is striking that as one moves from the deciduous forest to the Costa Rican rain forest, the number of social bee species rises slightly (and see Wille and Michener 1973), but the number of solitary bee species drops dramatically.

I should emphasize, however, that there are many plants that flower during the Guanacaste rainy season (especially herbs), and they are visited by bees (especially social bees and wasps, Megachilidae, and Halictidae) that are active and nesting during the dry season. *Ptiloglossa,* a large colletid bee that flies at dawn and earlier (e.g., Janzen 1968*b*), builds and provisions cells year-round, for example. The time from egg to adult is about 6–8 weeks, if I may generalize from specimens I reared in Veracruz in the same climate. A nest may be dug up in Guanacaste with cells of all stages and ages in it at any time of year. It is noteworthy, however, that many of the species that produce huge numbers of flowers at one time and attract enormous numbers of bees per plant (e.g., *Pterocarpus, Andira, Lonchocarpus, Tabebuia*) flower in the late rainy season or the first half of the dry season.

Most herbs and woody plants bear mature seeds some-time in the late rainy season or during the first half of the dry season. Just as for the seed-eating parrots and rodents, this is the time for the next generation of bruchid and weevil seed predators. In general these insects oviposit on the fruit when it is full sized but the seeds are still in the "milk stage"—soft, nutrient-rich, but not fully developed. The adult beetles tend to emerge from the seeds and fruits about the time the fruit crop is mature and dropping, or a bit before. Since most are quite prey specific (Janzen 1980*a*) and most of the prey species have relatively synchronized crops within and between crowns, these beetles usually have only one generation per year. The adults emerge very shortly after the larvae finish development and then move to local moist areas to pass the rest of the dry season. With the coming of the rains, the adults spread out through the vegetation and are found eating pollen and nectar in flowers.

An exception to this scenario is instructive. The *Cleogonus* weevils whose larvae develop in the fruits and seeds of *Andira inermis* emerge from the early rainy season fruits in May–June and burrow 20–40 cm into the ground to form a pupal cell (cf. Janzen et al. 1976). They remain there as prepupae through the rainy season and the following dry season, then pupate and emerge shortly after the soil is moistened by the next rainy season (this portion of the cycle can occur in a bucket of dirt). Such an emergence schedule would put the adult beetles right on the next fruit crop except that *A. inermis* trees fruit only every other year. The newly emerging weevils have to move until they locate another tree in fruit or wait another year as an active adult. Both events seem to occur (Janzen, unpub. data).

The numerous species of phyticine pyralid moth larvae that mine in deciduous forest fruits and seeds have phenologies very similar to those of the bruchids and seed-predator weevils. However, it appears that some of them may attack more species of plants than does the average seed-predator beetle, and thereby have more frequent generations. For example, it appears that the same larva mines the fruits and seeds of *Ateleia herbert-smithii* in December of some years at Santa Rosa National Park and annually mines the fruits of *Bauhinia ungulata* in the same habitat from January through March or even April. What the newly emerged and very delicate moths do to stay alive until the following December is a great mystery.

Some tiger beetles (Cicindelidae), being predaceous in open sandy habitats of the types exposed by dry-season shrinkage of Guanacaste rivers, remain dormant as adults in burrows through the rainy season and emerge to forage and produce larvae in the dry season (Wille and Michener 1962). Their relatives that forage on foliage and on shady forest paths, commonly encountered in Costa Rican rain forest, and their relatives that forage on Guanacaste ocean beaches do not display this type of seasonality. Ant lions (Myrmeleontidae) appear also to be dry-season active because of the physical conditions rather than food abundance (and see Simberloff et al. 1978). There is certainly a great deal more insect traffic across 10 cm² of bare dirt in the rainy season than in the dry season in Guanacaste, but during the rainy season ant lions are restricted to the dry soil below cliff and log overhangs. During the dry season they put their pitfall traps everywhere. There is a pulse of newly emerging adult ant lions toward the end of the rainy season. Whether they have been dormant since the previous dry season or represent the generation from sheltered sites during the rainy season is unknown. Again, as with tiger beetles, other closely related non-pitfall-constructing neuropterans (e.g., Ascelaphidae) breed during the rainy season.

The ways all these insects pass the rainy season illustrate its dangers. The above ground nesters do it as active adults. A carpenter bee in a hole in a tree has a chance of escape from ants, termites, and woodpeckers if active, but not if dormant. If a bruchid or weevil tried to sit out the rest of the dry season and all of the rainy season in the seed or fruit in which it developed, it would have little chance against vertebrate fruit and seed eaters and fungi and other decomposers. The soil nesters are better protected by dilution and mechanical protection; they sit it out underground. It is noteworthy that bee cell walls are impregnated with a variety of fungistatic compounds (S. Batra, pers. comm.) and the rainy-season-nesting *Ptiloglossa* bee even lines its cells with a tough layer of wax. The euglossines and bumblebees (*Bombus*) put their provisions and larvae in resin or wax cells that presumably are relatively impervious to rainy-season invasion by fungi and roots. Moth pupal cuticle must likewise be very resistant to fungi and roots. I suspect that weevils and tiger beetles that sit out the rainy season underground are likewise encased in some barrier to invasion.

A LESS CONSPICUOUSLY SEASONAL HABITAT

Insect activity dynamics in Costa Rican rain forests seem to often be centered on the details of sunny weather — how many hours a day, in the morning or afternoon, how many days consecutively, and so forth. My overall impression is that diurnal insect activity, as measured by adults present on the vegetation, reaches its annual low during the September–November peak in the rainy season. At this time there can be runs of as much as 2 weeks with heavy overcast and daily rain of many hours duration. The annual high seems to be February–March, when there are many hours and even days of sunny weather, the sunlight penetrates deep into the forest as sunflecks and as indirect scattered light, the litter dries somewhat, and height and bulk increment rates of second-growth vegetation seem highest. In the sweep

samples of rain-forest edge and understory near Rincón (inland side of the upper Osa Peninsula), foliage-inhabiting insects seemed to have the highest density and species richness during the dry-season samples (Janzen 1973a).

Philip DeVries offers the following characterization of the diurnal butterflies at Finca La Selva during July–December. When there is a run of several sunny days, the density builds up until it even approximates that seen during the first half of the rainy season at a place like Santa Rosa National Park. Then two days of rainy weather occur and the density falls very close to zero except for a few of the forest-floor satyrids. Then, when the next sunny day occurs, the density begins to slowly build back up as though somehow the previous set of adults had been eliminated by the rainy weather. While it is possible that the rain itself kills some adults, it is also likely that some starve to death or are taken by predators that would not have been able to catch them had they been warmer and therefore more alert and active.

Turning to the nocturnal moths, there is a early rainy season peak at lights (April–May) just as in Guanacaste, but it is less dramatic, and moths at lights do not disappear as thoroughly during the dry season as they do in Guanacaste. No saturniids are taken at the lights in Santa Rosa National Park during January–April, whereas as many as ten species may be taken at the lights at Finca La Selva during the same season (yet there are thirty species of saturniids known from Santa Rosa National Park and thirty-three from Finca La Selva). If I can assume that most of the foliage damage done in the Corcovado National Park rain forest is due to moth larvae (as seems to be the case in other Costa Rican forests), then there is clearly a peak in moth caterpillar density in late March and in April, during the first month of the rains. The new foliage dramatically acquires most of its annual damage during this brief period.

For specific plants and insect species the cycle of defoliation need not, however, match the clear seasonal periodicities of Guanacaste. At Corcovado National Park the *Mora megistosperma* stands change their leaves in early November (middle rainy season), and all the moth caterpillar (Pyralidae and Noctuidae) defoliation of the year occurs then. Peak damage to *Mora* seedlings in the rain forest at Llorona (Corcovado National Park) occurs in October–January.

The defoliation cycles of the understory *Pterocarpus* swamp spider lily (Janzen 1978b) (*Crinum erubescens*) by noctuid moth larvae (*Xanthopastis timais*) have several peaks a year and show no synchronization with season; different parts of the swamp at Llorona can even be on different parts of the cycle though they are only a few tens of meters apart.

There is no doubt that seasonality of insect activity in

Costa Rican lowland rain forest is blurry compared with that in Guanacaste deciduous forests, but it would be a large mistake to assume that rain forest populations cycle independent of the weather and consist of many overlapping generations. At Corcovado there is the time when the migrating uranid diurnal moths (*Urania fulgens*) appear (July–August). There is the time when no-see-ums (*Culicoides;* Ceratopogonidae) are horrible on the beaches (rainy season). The bembicid and sphecid wasps are busy digging holes and dragging in prey in sunny weather in March and are seen only on beach edges in the rainy season. Likewise, March is the time when the forest at night seems alive with newly molted adult tettigoniid grasshoppers. Strong periodicity in insect cycles is expected in the rain forest if for no other reason than there is strong periodicity in the plant cycles. Each plant has its characteristic time of flowering, fruiting, leaf flush, and senescence (e.g., Frankie, Baker, and Opler 1974). Yes, there are individuals out of synchrony, but not conspicuously more often than in deciduous forests. If you want to collect the larva of the pale green pyraustine pyralid (*Noorda esmeralda*) that mines the seeds of *Aspidosperma megalocarpon* or the weevil that mines its pods, you have to be on the Osa Peninsula in early August when the pods and seeds are shed. But, as implied above, only a few hundred meters away you can collect the larvae of *Xanthopastis tinais* from the stand of its lily host at any time of year.

The physical environment itself also generates periodicity in Costa Rican rain forest insects. It gets so hot and dry by the end of the dry season (March) at Finca La Selva and at Corcovado that fires can easily be set and maintained in second-growth vegetation and a good burn can be obtained for felled vegetation in a slash-and-burn agricultural cycle. As Stout (1978, 1979) showed for the creeks at Finca La Selva, the aquatic insects are pushed about both by backflooding of tributaries from the large rivers and by severe runoff from the forest floor during the peak rainy periods. At Corcovado National Park the rainy season winds, reaching tornado force at times, generate numerous and huge tree falls between May and August; I suspect that this is a peak oviposition time for wood-boring insects (Scolytidae, Cerambycidae, Buprestidae). When the rains start at the end of the dry season, there is a pulse of tree and large branch falls created by waterlogging of wood that has been gradually weakening over the past 1–3 months; again, this is a pulse of food for wood-boring insects. During the rainy season there are small puddles all over the rain-forest floor, in fallen fruits and leaves, flower and leaf bracts (e.g., Fish 1977; Seifert and Seifert 1979), and in cavities in trees. These contain many aquatic insects. Many of these seasonal pondlets dry up in the dry season; there is even a rain-forest dragonfly nymph (niad) on the Osa

Peninsula that is reputed to walk from puddle to puddle as they dry up. Even if there are flowers for nectar and pollen in the rainy season, they may have the food washed out of them, the pollen killed by rain (Jones 1967), and be inaccessible to flying insects. Not only can such a seasonal depression of pollinators influence their own future density, but it may lower the availability of seeds for seed predators and raise the amount of vegetative material for caterpillars at a later time in the yearly cycle.

OTHER HABITATS IN COSTA RICA

While we know next to nothing of the seasonality of insects in other Costa Rican habitats, they certainly are at least as seasonal as those in the lowland rain forest. W. A. Haber reports that there is a huge pulse of moths at the lights at Monteverde when the dry season breaks in April or early May. Windy nights are very poor for moth arrival at lights, and the Monteverde dry-season nights are often very windy. In collecting sphinx moth larvae from known hosts, Haber also finds an extreme low in November–December (late rainy season) and a high in May–August, just as is the case in Guanacaste (except that in Guanacaste the November low stays nearly at zero until the rains begin in May).

Moving up in elevation, even at 3,000 m on the Cerro de la Muerte there is a distinct and clear dry season of at least 3 months when it is dry enough to burn old second-growth vegetation as it stands (Janzen 1973c). Sweep samples of this vegetation in the dry season yield a variety of beetles, flies, and miscellaneous insects that are conspicuously lacking in rainy-season sweep samples (Janzen 1973a). On the Cerro, during the rainy season, the vegetation is generally wet even when the sky is clear, since direct insolation rarely lasts more than a few hours. On the other hand, the seasonality on the Cerro is not extreme enough to give it a proper summer and winter. Although it is warmer in the day and colder at night on the Cerro during the dry season than in the rainy season (Janzen 1967a), the slow rate of warming of waterlogged substrates and the generally low average temperature make living up there like living in a refrigerator, if the animal is confined to solid substrates. This is reflected in the total absence of insects that depend on substrate warmth, such as ants, termites, wood-boring beetles, and dung beetles. The outcome is that wood and dung decomposition, as well as litter decomposition, takes an extremely long time (Janzen 1973c).

The San Vito region, as represented by Finca Las Cruces (1,500 m), experiences a very distinct dry- and wet-season cycle. As on the Osa Peninsula, sweep samples of second growth found much higher densities of insects during the insolation-rich dry season than during the heavily overcast wet season (Janzen 1973a). Likewise, the dry season at Finca Las Cruces is the time for conspicuous butterfly activity, and Palmer (1977) found that tiger beetle larvae grew faster at this time (implying greater prey availability on the soil surface).

Costa Rica is a patchwork quilt of seasonal effects. One of the more dramatic is the area around Palmar Sur and Palmar Norte. In the coastal plain along the Río Térraba, where it flows past Palmar to the sea, the forest was evergreen rain forest before it was converted to a banana factory for United States consumers. Moving upstream, on the north-facing slopes along the south bank of the Río Térraba is semideciduous forest (remnants), with most of the deciduous species on the ridges and shoulders and most of the evergreens on the lower parts of the valleys that have tributaries to the Río Térraba. On the north bank of the Río Térraba, across the river, the south-facing slopes contained some truly deciduous forest with many species of trees characteristic of Guanacaste. All three of these habitats can be seen from one point in the lower Río Térraba valley.

Overlying the Costa Rican seasonality generated by amount and pattern of rainfall and insolation there is a third influence that must have an enormous direct and indirect effect on insects but is virtually unstudied. The trade winds blow continuously and hard (steady 5–15 miles an hour, gusts up to 50–60 mph) across much of Guanacaste, northern Puntarenas, and the Valle Central from late November through April. East-facing slopes may become absolutely deciduous while the accompanying west-facing slope is still moderately leafy. When they still had forest, the hills in the center of Finca Taboga (Estación Experimental MAG Enrique Jimenez Nuñez) south of Cañas offered particularly good examples. The drying effect of this wind is brought home vividly when one realizes that the largely wind-free coastal rain forests of Nigeria, with an evergreen canopy at 35–50 m height, are at the same elevation and receive the same amount of rainfall in the same pattern as the deciduous forests of Guanacaste with their canopy height of 10–30 m. These winds must also directly affect the insects. As W. A. Haber points out, the butterflies flying east from Guanacaste into the moist montane habitats must keep low in the valley bottoms and work their way up in the shelter of ridges running across the wind direction from the northwest.

What Sort of Pollinators Are Costa Rican Insects?
Good ones, when you consider the distances and speed over which many operate. The study of pollen donation and reception, in the guise of watching insects at flowers and wondering who might be the pollinator of this or that odd flower, has long attracted visitors to the tropics, and Costa Rica is no exception (as is amply demonstrated by the plethora of student reports on pollination in OTS

files). Yet, with all this attention, the folklore and facts accumulated until just a few years ago are amazingly sterile of conceptualization and facts that answer the real questions in tropical (and other) pollination biology: Over what distance and with what other parents does a plant exchange genetic information (pollen)? What combinations of pollen donation and seed production generate the highest fitness for a plant? What combination of seeds sired and seed crops cosired yields the highest fitness (and the converse for the seed-bearing tree)? Why does a plant potentially give up half of the genetic programming of its offspring? And so on. It is too easy to watch pretty flowers and amazing bees; there are very few good studies (e.g., Frankie, Opler, and Bawa 1976; Stiles 1975, 1977, 1979; Bawa 1974; Linhart 1973; Schlising 1970; Janzen 1971c, 1977a; Opler, Baker, and Frankie 1975).

The vast majority of Costa Rican higher plant species, excluding grasses and sedges (but see Soderstrom and Calderon 1971; Karr 1976; Pohl, Tiffany, and Karr 1979 for grass examples), are pollinated by insects. Birds and bats are conspicuous and spectacular pollinators of a relatively small number of species (e.g., Baker 1970; Howell 1979; Stiles 1975, 1977, 1979; Heithaus, Opler, and Baker 1974; Colwell 1973; Colwell et al. 1974; Feinsinger 1976; Feinsinger and Colwell 1978). Wind-pollinated nongrasses are suspected to occur: *Chlorophora tinctoria*, *Cecropia* spp., *Brosimum* spp., and *Trophis racemosa* in the Moraceae, *Quercus* spp. in the Fagaceae, and *Alnus* in the Betulaceae. The moraceous plants are a puzzle, and all seem to be in this category the world over except for figs (*Ficus;* cf. Janzen 1979b). The oaks and alders occur in pure stands or at least stands of low enough species richness that adjacent trees are often conspecifics. I suspect that wind pollination is probably the cheapest for the desired effect when conspecifics are very close together (and *Brosimum* and *Cecropia* often occur this way) but quickly becomes very ineffective with even small distances between conspecifics.

I wish I could discuss pollination by Costa Rican insects as an answer to each of the questions posed earlier, but the studies do not exist, and the miscellaneous data available cannot be structured in that same manner in this small space. Therefore I will briefly describe and discuss each of the insect pollination systems on which much time has been expended.

Self-Compatibility and Outcrossing Survey
It used to be reasoned that since tropical plant populations often have reproductive individuals tens to hundreds of meters apart, they are likely to be self-pollinated (e.g., Ashton 1969). However, various workers subsequently observing insects at tropical flowers, including Ashton, have come to feel that it is quite likely that animal-mediated pollen donation and reception is

sufficient at these distances to allow selection to generate and maintain self-incompatibility or substantial outcrossing even for self-compatible species. Bawa (1974) has also shown that 76% of a sample of 130 species of Guanacaste trees and large shrubs are in fact self-incompatible and is finding the same to be true for the rain forest at Finca La Selva. Obviously plants can get so widely separated in time and space that even highly direct animals cannot avoid generating a pollinator-limited system. Such distances should interspecifically vary for the plant life form, habitat, pollinators, season, degree of self-compatibility, value of outcrossing, and other pollination parameters. The maximum distances seem to be attainable by flowers pollinated by large, intelligent animals (birds, bats, sphingids, large bees in the Xylocopini, Euglossini, Colletidae) or very small ones like fig wasps attracted to what might best be called a plant interspecific pheromone (see below).

Keeping in mind the natural history of Costa Rican trees and their pollinators, there appear to be at least two major and nonmutually exclusive sets of selective forces that should generate obligatory outcrossing (or frequent outcrossing even if not obligatory).

1. Selection for specialization to maleness and femaleness (functional or morphological monoecy and dioecy) should be strongly associated with natural histories whereby a plant does best either with the annually cheaper behavior of donating much pollen to other plants or with the annually more expensive but intermittent behavior of occasionally making a fruit crop that is large enough to attract seed dispersers, satiate seed predators, efficiently use support structures, and so on. A tendency toward discreteness of sexual function (dioecy) should be favored by increasing reliability of (*a*) pollinator presence, (*b*) seasonal flowering cues, (*c*) conditions appropriate for flower and fruit development, and (*d*) conditions for resource harvest by adult plants, and by increasing difficulty for an individual to make a fruit or seed crop large enough to perform the necessary tasks. Insects, especially those that have moderately to extremely deliberate behavior in moving among numerous plants in a foraging bout, should be an especially important component of such a system. If some Finca La Selva rain-forest *Lecythis costaricensis* are to act as males while only the largest are to act as fruit-bearing females, the density (and proximity of individuals) as pollen donors may be substantially reduced. Only large bees with far from random foraging behavior (e.g., *Bombus,* euglossines, *Xylocopa*) will continue to function. The same applies to wild papayas growing as males and females in rain-forest clearings and pollinated by sphingids making their rounds. Especially if they are to be "mistake pollinated" (Baker 1976), the animal has to be intelligent enough and wide-ranging enough to be able to make a mistake.

2. Selection for outcrossing will be generated by any process that raises the value of being receptive to genetic information. One such process is the constantly changing set of competitive and trophic (predation and parasitization) challenges that face a tropical plant. The suite of herbivores, pathogens, seed predators, parasites, and others is constantly mutating, recombining, immigrating, and coming up with new combinations of abilities. The plant that isolates itself from the solutions found by its conspecifics is a dead lineage, by and large. The winter experienced by a northern pine or oak has probably not changed in the past 60 million years, nor has the good solution to its challenge; the biotic challenge to a rain-forest *Dipteryx panamensis* most decidedly has changed (even if by nothing more than the removal of gomphotheres as dispersal agents; Janzen and Martin 1982). In short, insects generate the problems for a tropical plant and also provide some of the answers in evolutionary time.

Large Long-Distance Fliers

Large bees and sphinx moths (Sphingidae) are conspicuous candidates for insects that readily move Costa Rican pollen hundreds to thousands of meters. Thanks to W. A. Haber's persistent inquiry in the Cañas and Monteverde region, the sphingids are beginning to reveal things long suspected. Haber finds them at lights at Monteverde with, for example, *Calliandra* pollen on their tongues when the nearest *Calliandra* patches are 10–15 km away. In his outdoor screen moth house he finds that adults have longevities exceeding 2 months and visit artificial flowers and oviposition hosts in a regular pattern, which it seems reasonable to view as a bonsai version of their free-world foraging and oviposition "trapline." Such a pattern of flower visitation, also suspected for the bees mentioned below, would provide high-quality pollination service for plants scattered among many hectares of flower-free vegetation. If the pollen is placed on different parts of the moth by different flowers (as again, Haber finds to be the case), one moth could simultaneously be a long-distance pollinator of several plant species. The plants visited (e.g., *Inga, Bauhinia, Luehea, Calliandra, Ipomoea, Alibertia, Plumeria, Brassavola, Psychotria, Carica, Posoqueria, Pachira, Bombacopsis, Cestrum,* etc.) are not evolutionarily passive participants. For example, Haber finds that one epiphytic cactus produced a strong odor from its buds for a number of nights before it opened and was then very intensely visited the night the flowers actually opened. Many of their flowers require that the insect have a long tongue to reach the nectar reward, are white and very visible at night (which is when they open), and are apparently not pollinated by other animals. See J. Beach's account of *Posoqueria* and W. A. Haber's accounts of *Luehea* and *Hylocereus* in this book.

As with bees, sphingids have the enigmatic behavior of not visiting all the flowers in a patch before moving on to another patch hundreds of meters away. For example, the small roadside patches of late rainy season *Ipomoea trifida* flowers in Santa Rosa National Park are visited before dawn by the smallest sphingids (*Enyo gorgon, Cautethia spuria, Perigonia lusca, Eupyrrhoglossum sagra*). The flowers are newly opened and full of nectar (occasional *Ptiloglossa* bees and skippers are the only other visitors at this hour), yet the moths characteristically visit single flowers at 1–2-m intervals and leave after visiting five to fifteen flowers. A patch of *I. trifida* regularly contains two hundred to five thousand flowers. Since many of the plants visited by these moths have the behavior of producing only a few flowers each night over many weeks or months (as is also the case with flowers visited by hummingbirds and large bees), and since these plants often produce grotesquely large floral displays when growing in the highly unnatural and competition-free habitat of roadsides and field/forest interfaces, it may well be that the apparent anomalous behavior of leaving behind resource-rich flowers represents the overlay of a fixed-action pattern on an anomalous resource.

One of the larger puzzles about sphingids relates to their apparent ability to move long distances. In Santa Rosa National Park there are certain times (June and November, especially) when no flowers of species known or suspected to be visited by sphingids are in bloom. Yet when the moths are taken at lights their honey crops are full of nectar. The implication is that they were captured while on a flight from more nectar-rich habitats; perhaps they even have the sexually or resource-pursuit segregated population structure hypothesized below for euglossine bees.

Large bees are a conspicuous part of the Costa Rican pollinator (or at least visitor) fauna. At 3,000 m elevation on the Cerro de la Muerte, *Bombus ephippiatus* queens (large, yellow-and-red) forage even in cloudy, misty weather, and the smaller black-and-yellow workers visit a somewhat different set of flowers in sunnier weather. In Corcovado National Park, from the tops of the 55 m tall yellow-flowered *Vochysia* crowns (April–May) to the ground-level scandent spiny *Solanum,* the big black *Bombus* gathers pollen and nectar and carries it to rainforest ground-level nests. Throughout the Costa Rican rain forests, female *Eulaema, Euglossa,* and *Eufriesia* (*Euplusia* of old; L. Kimsey, pers. comm.) are common nectar and pollen collectors from the tops of the tallest tree to ground level from a very diverse set of species (e.g., *Lecythis costaricensis, Dipteryx panamensis, Sickingia maxonii, Blakea* spp., *Stemmadenia* spp., *Mandavilla* spp., *Ipomoea* spp., *Cassia* spp., *Calathea* spp., *Canavalia* spp., *Centrosema* spp., etc.). In the Guanacaste deciduous forests, the genera listed above plus at least six species of large carpenter bees (*Xylocopa* and

related genera) (*a*) are prominent visitors to flowers with tubular anthers, from which they buzz the pollen (e.g., Michener, Winston, and Jander 1978) (*b*) display strong microhabitat preferences such as visiting a given species of flower more often the higher it is off the ground (e.g., Frankie and Coville 1979); (*c*) act like they are traplining plants in many genera; and (*d*) join the *Ptiloglossa* in foraging so early in the morning that one can only see the flowers move (e.g., *Ptiloglossa* on *Passiflora foetida;* Janzen 1968*b*). At Santa Rosa National Park, for example, the next largest *Xylocopa* begins the morning with nectar from *Gliricidia sepium* flowers, moves on to *Cassia biflora* and *Cochlospermum vitifolium* for pollen a bit later, and finishes up with nectar from *Encyclia cordigera* in the late afternoon after having visited (and probably pollinated) many other species of plants in between.

While the bees above all display some to many traplining traits (long adult life-spans, large size, behavioral plasticity in captivity, strong alertness to predators and awareness of the details of their surroundings, large eggs and few but elaborately constructed nest cells, long and powerful flight abilities, long to year-round flight seasons, knowledge of the location of even very few flowers), they also on occasion take advantage of mass-flowering plants simultaneously visited by swarms of halictid, anthophorid, megachilid, and apid bees (e.g., Heithaus 1979*a,b*). The latter species-rich and individual-rich families (especially in the Guanacaste dry season) may visit a single crown of a tree such as *Andira inermis, Lonchocarpus minimiflorus,* or *Dalbergia retusa* by the tens of thousands per day and clearly move pollen between flowers within the crown (and thereby heavily contaminate the stigmata of these self-infertile species). However, Frankie, Opler, and Bawa (1976) have shown that a small fraction of these bees move from tree to tree and can also provide outcrossing services. The movement may not only be through search for more or different pollen/nectar sources but also through harassment of females by large arrays of males in search of mates in each tree crown (G. Frankie, pers. comm.). We have no idea what fraction of the tens of thousands of seeds produced in a crop by one of these trees is pollinated by traplining bees as opposed to those that largely forage at mass-flowering plants. The mass flowerings of some trees (e.g., *Tabebuia ochracea*) are more heavily visited by the large "intelligent" bees, while others (e.g., *Pterocarpus rohrii*) are largely visited by other bees.

While generally not thought of in this context, the plants pollinated by medium-sized and large butterflies are probably also subject to much of the same system as that for large bees, sphingids, hummingbirds, and so on. Perhaps the most glaring example in Costa Rica is that of the array of nymphalid, hesperiid, papilionid, and pierid butterflies that regularly get their daily nectar from one of the two species of *Lantana* that are so common in Costa

Rican Pacific coastal brushy pastures, roadsides, riverbanks, and other deflected successional systems (and see Schemske's discussion of *Lantana* in this book). There must be at least thirty species of butterflies in Corcovado National Park and Santa Rosa National Park that heavily visit this nectar source (and many species are in common between the deciduous and rain-forest parks). They act as though they know where each flower-bearing bush is, and different species appear at predictable times of day. It seems that a visit to the pasture *Lantana* near its favorite set of *Passiflora* (oviposition sites) is a regular and scheduled event for a number of Corcovado National Park heliconiine butterflies. In Santa Rosa National Park there are forest swallowtails taking nectar from *Lantana camara* 1–3 km from the forest type in which they normally find their oviposition hosts. Where the two species of *Lantana* co-occur in Corcovado National Park, they are visited by two quite different arrays of butterflies (Schemske 1976). While *Lantana* may be contemptuously labeled a weedy species of perhaps little import to pre-Columbian forest, the same system appears to be operating with forest plants such as *Cordia panamensis, C. alba,* and *Cissus* spp. (and see Opler, Baker, and Frankie 1975). Finally, Gilbert feels that the system of interaction that he described for heliconiine butterflies traplining *Anguria* and *Gurania* cucurbits in Trinidad (Ehrlich and Gilbert 1973) is operating throughout the lowland to mid-elevation rain forests of Costa Rica and is especially well developed at Finca La Selva and Corcovado National Park.

The males of the euglossine genera mentioned earlier are perhaps the most flashy of the Costa Rican insect pollination systems. In short, we know that the males visit the long-lived flowers of about 2–3% of the species of Costa Rican orchids during the morning hours and remove chemicals from the flower parts by scraping with tarsal claws and brushes. The compounds are simple structures like eugenol, methyl salicylate, cineole, methyl cinnamate, and benzyl acetate, and they are transferred, via the midlegs, to grooves in the hind tibiae, where they are taken in by the bee. Norris Williams will shortly be telling us what they do with the chemicals; it is clear that none of the hypotheses about using the chemicals as longevity potions or to attract other males are tenable. It is also known that different species of bees are differentially attracted to pure and mixed compounds as well as to different species of orchids (some do not even come to any of the chemical baits that have been tried). When the bee visits, it rarely has a pollinarium glued to it at some relatively orchid-specific site (e.g., center of dorsum of thorax, frons, right front leg); when it then visits a stigma-bearing orchid of the appropriate species, the pollinium is plucked off. Since many orchids are self-fertile and readily make interspecific hybrids, it is believed that the specific behaviors of these euglossine bees are important in maintaining the distinctness of species boundaries as well as in conventional outcrossing functions (see Williams 1978 for a bibliography of this entire subject).

Chemical baiting of euglossines (Janzen et al. 1982) and data from marking of *Eulaema tropica* males at *Catasetum maculatum* flowers (Janzen 1981a) have led to a counterintuitive hypothesis about the population structure of euglossine bees, or at least those occupying a mixture of distinct habitats as represented by the deciduous forests of Santa Rosa National Park and its nearby montane evergreen forests. The important additions to the above summary of euglossine male natural history are that with chemical baits a number of species of males can be caught in an area where thorough collecting at flowers has never captured a female, and that these males may be carrying pollinaria from orchid species that do not occur in the habitat of the chemical baiting. Furthermore, males may be taken with chemical baits in habitats or regions of many square kilometers that lack nectar hosts for males or females in that season. Finally, in a mutualistic system involving many partners it is reasonable to expect participants that are parasitic on the system. With these observations in mind, I suggest that a usual euglossine bee population structure is that of the females occupying a set of geographically proximal habitats in which they nest, forage for nectar and pollen, and find their mates; all three needs may be met in the same or in quite different habitats, but they will be close to each other. The habitats need not interdigitate or be small, though it is probably to the female's economic advantage if they do. The suitability of Costa Rican habitats to meet these three needs will vary among seasons and habitats, and the carrying capacity for female euglossine bees may approach zero in some sites (it appears to be only about three at Santa Rosa National Park). Males, on the other hand, search for orchids (or a few other chemical-generating things like *Anthurium* and certain kinds of fungi), nectar hosts, and mates. There is no reason to expect the habitat of any but the last resource to overlap geographically with that of the female. For the viewpoint of a male that can range many kilometers in a few minutes and has no need to return to any fixed point in a widespread habitat type interdigitated with others (i.e., that habitat in which he finds receptive females), the best foraging pattern is likely to be to search broadly for orchids over an enormous area (many square kilometers), visit some more restricted (and likely different) area for flower nectar, and then fly to the area of female availability for some better portion of the day or week. We feel it is quite reasonable for the different sexes of birds and mammals to range through different habitats, and for different sexes of insects to range through different microhabitats (e.g., white male *Perhybris* conducting a complex lek high in the rain-forest canopy at Sirena (Corcovado National Park) while yellow-and-black-banded Batesian-mimic females flutter through the understory looking for *Capparis* on which to oviposit; P. DeVries, pers. comm.). It should not be surprising to find that euglossine bees do the same on a larger scale. We unconsciously assume that the bees' coming to baits is simply a distortion of their normal arrival at orchids they pollinate. However, a mutualistic system such as this can hardly avoid having a number of cheaters—bees that visit the orchids for chemicals yet are not correctly proportioned, sized, or behaved to pick up pollinaria. There is no selective pressure for the bee to evolutionarily mold its anatomy in this direction as long as other bee species are already carrying the pollen, and there is no selection to exclude such a bee until it becomes numerous enough that it actively deters the actual pollinators. Given these considerations, the question of carrying capacity of a site for euglossine bees becomes one of scale as well as biology, and one of total resources as well as number of species of euglossine-pollinated orchids.

Small Short-Distance Pollinators

In addition to the swarms of small bees mentioned above that visit mass-flowering legumes in the Guanacaste deciduous forests, there are a multitude of other relatively small insects that visit flowers and serve in some cases as pollinators (e.g., Rausher and Fowler 1979; Heithaus 1979a,b; Opler, Baker, and Frankie 1975). Flies, small moths, small beetles, and solitary and social wasps and butterflies offer thousands of species of nectar drinkers and pollen eaters to the sprays of small white-cream-yellow flowers prominent throughout the year in Costa Rican forests and understories. Palmae, Leguminosae, Flacourtiaceae, Anacardiaceae, Lauraceae, Compositae, Burseraceae, Melastomataceae, Polygonaceae, Simarubaceae, Boraginaceae, Dilleniaceae, Rubiaceae, Ebenaceae, Euphorbiaceae, Flacourtiaceae, Sapotaceae, Rhamnaceae, Verbenaceae, Araliaceae, Meliaceae, and Sapindaceae are just a few of the families that come immediately to mind with this type of pollination system. They may flower at night, in daytime, or both. The flowers blend together into a large landing platform, and the insect generally crawls or walks across many in moving from flower to flower. How these miscellaneous arrays of small insects manage to move pollen many hundreds of meters between, for example, the scattered large adults of *Enterolobium cyclocarpum* in Santa Rosa National Park (its millions of small white inflorescences apparently pollinated by small nocturnal moths and beetles; W. A. Haber, pers. comm.) is somewhat of a mystery. I suppose the insects could be viewed as an animated and somewhat directed wind.

It is clear that insect-insect interactions on these plants could be very important in either deterring or augmenting pollen exit and arrival (G. W. Frankie, pers. comm.). The highly territorial behavior by beetles on the flower spikes of *Cocoloba floribunda* (Rausher and Fowler 1979) and *Trigona*'s possessive exclusion of other bees from food sources, described by Hubbell and Johnson (1977) and Johnson and Hubbell (1975), must surely slow the contamination of pollinators with outgoing pollen (though this need not depress the fitness of the parent plant; Janzen 1977a). Bruchids plowing their way through mimosaceous legume anther fields often cause a pollen-gathering bee to leave that inflorescence. The male anthophorid bees popping in and out of the flowers in large arrays of Convolvulaceae (e.g., Schlising 1970; Real 1980) disturb skippers, bees, and wasps and probably increase the likelihood that they will move far enough to enter the flowers of another vine. Hummingbirds do the same (e.g., Primack and Howe 1975). Certain of these animals are likely to be much better pollinators than others. Stingless bees, very common at these and other flowers, are professional pollen scavengers, and few grains probably escape their body-cleaning in and out of the nest (yet they seem to be the sole pollinators of some palms and understory *Piper*). Many of the bruchids become covered with pollen but seem to move off the flower only to hide in the daylight and then move back onto the same inflorescences. I am surprised that many of these trees have not evolved the behavior of turning their flowering on and off at several-day intervals to raise the animal-mediated pollen flow in and out of their crowns.

Fig Pollination

Perhaps the most bizarre of all Costa Rican pollination systems is that displayed by some sixty-five species of figs (*Ficus*) (Burger 1977) in habitats ranging from mangrove edge at sea level to 2,500 m and through all degrees of seasonality. The general pollination system is as follows (see reviews in Janzen 1979b; Wiebes 1979). Each species of fig has its own species of pollinating fig wasp (Agaonidae). About the time the tree's branches are covered with tiny (0.5–1 cm diameter) green figs, thousands of these wasps appear out of the habitat, presumably attracted by a pheromone released by the tree (or the figs). One or more females enter the young fig by wiggling between a set of overlapping scales that occludes the hole (ostiole) in the apex of the fig. As the female does this, her body is stripped of antannae, wings, and probably much contaminant dirt and fungal spores. Once in the inner lacuna of the fig, which is lined with florets with receptive stigmata, she removes pollen from her pollen pockets and pollinates each of several hundred stigmata. She also attempts to oviposit down the style, and she lays an egg if she can reach the single-ovuled ovary (the florets have styles of various lengths). She and any others that have entered the fig die after oviposition, and the fig develops slowly for about a month, after which time the seeds are full-sized and the male wingless wasps begin to emerge from their ovarian containers. A male locates a female in a floret base, cuts into the cavity, inserts his abdomen to copulate, and then aids the female in leaving her floret. She then goes to the newly opened anthers, fills her pollen pockets, and leaves through the exit hole that the males cut in the wall of the still-green fig. She then flies off in search of another fig that is in a receptive state. In general, the fig ripening cycle is synchronized within but not between crowns. There are a number of parasites of the system. Small parasitic wasps oviposit through the walls of the fig into the already-parasitized ovary and, when newly emerged, leave through the exit hole cut by the agaonid males. Also, there are parasitic wasps apparently derived from pollinating agaonids. They enter through the ostiole and have pollen pockets, just as do the pollinating agaonids, but they do not carry pollen or oviposit. Additionally, several species of weevils and pyralid moth larvae develop inside the figs, grazing on the florets and developing seeds. Once the pollinators have left the hard green fig, it rapidly ripens and within a few days is taken by an animal or drops from the tree.

Figs are enigmatic in that *Ficus* tends to be among the most species-rich plant genera in each habitat that contains it. Their one-on-one pollination system may explain this in part. Since their pollinators are very specific, the different species do not compete for pollinators and therefore one of the barriers to intense species-packing has been removed. Figs are also unique in that, while they may be one of the most common trees in a forest from a forester's viewpoint, they are one of the rarest from a pollinator's viewpoint. If, for example there is one large adult per hectare, then on a given day there may be as few as one large adult per 365 hectares in just the right stage of pollinator reception. Finally, figs display perhaps most dramatically of all organisms the act of paying offspring (zygotes) in order to obtain outcrossing; somewhere between 20% and 80% of all fig babies in a fig crop are killed by the pollinating wasps and their parasitic associates (Janzen 1979*c*,*d*).

What Happens to the Insects on a Tropical Island?
Aside from rocky islets near shore, the few islands off Costa Rican shores (San Andres, Providencia, Isla del Caño, Cocos Island) offer very instructive entomological contrasts with the mainland.

Isla Providencia (Colombia)
Approximately 18 km^2 in area (13.21 N, 80.55 W), it has a gently contoured central rise to about 200 m elevation. 240 km off the Nicaraguan Caribbean coast (400 km from Costa Rica), this island has had nearly all its forest cut off, but much of the second growth has come back with only marginal use by cattle, plantations, and fields (in 1969—I have not been there since). The vegetation experiences at least 4 months of dry season (with occasional ocean rain squalls) and does not have sufficiently large drainage basins to generate year-round rivers. The plants are familiar Costa Rican mainland species with a dense input of introduced trees in the vicinity of the house sites scattered around the lower slopes of the central rise. Mangroves fringe the bays.

The most conspicuous insect occupant is the acacia-ant *Pseudomyrmex ferruginea,* which occupies *Acacia collinsii* exactly as it does on the Central American mainland. It seems very likely that the bird-dispersed seeds of *A. collinsii* got there first, followed by colonization by flying founding queens of *P. ferruginea* before the ant plant lost the traits hospitable to the ant. Judging from the low density of insects on the island (see below), I suspect that *A. collinsii* could survive as a breeding population on Providencia without its ant colonies. *P. ferruginea* is the most widely distributed acacia-ant (Tampico in northeastern Mexico to the Pacific coast of Colombia), but to the best of my knowledge it does not occur on any other island except those immediately offshore (e.g., off the coast of Yucatan). *P. ferruginea* could have colonized from Panama, Nicaragua, or points to the north. I doubt that it was introduced by man; it seems unlikely that nonbiologists would actively introduce an acacia-ant, and even if a founding queen landed on a ship, she would shed her wings and the trip ashore would be unlikely. The *Cecropia peltata* on Providencia has, on the other hand, arrived and stayed without its *Azteca* ants. As on the other Caribbean islands (Janzen 1973*b;* Rickson 1977), it has largely lost its ability to produce food bodies (through mutation or through introgression with *Cecropia* populations that had lost their ants on other islands).

Middle rainy season sweep samples in a variety of second-growth (old field) habitats on Providencia showed the same thing I found on Puerto Rico and adjacent smaller islands (Janzen 1973*a,* Allan et al. 1973). At the time of year when insect density should be highest, it is about the same level as in a Guanacaste old field at the peak of the dry season. Furthermore, the stage of succession on Providencia seemed to not make much difference—again, just as was the case in Puerto Rico. Isla del Caño displays the same paucity of insects (numbers as well as species) during both the rainy season and the dry season. It is evident that insectivorous animals have a much smaller resource base from which to harvest on these islands than in comparable habitats on the mainland. Perhaps associated with this (and with the lack of diurnal predators on vertebrates as well), the teiid *Ameiva* lizards on Providencia are primarily vegetarian, a behavior never displayed by their mainland relatives of equal size (Janzen 1973a).

The cause of insect depression in density on tropical islands is not self-evident, though several possibilities seem reasonable.

1. Whatever insects are to be present in the rainy season will have to be those that can make it through the dry season without using extensive riparian evergreen vegetation as a refuge. However, I might also note that islands that are moist even through the dry season (e.g., the higher and wetter portions of Puerto Rico) likewise do not have insect densities anything like those on the mainland.

2. Any kind of perturbation that generates local extinction will create lacunae in the island fauna because there are no sites from which reinoculation can easily occur. These lacunae should be filled by species that do not easily suffer local extirpation. These could well be species with slow population growth rates, because they put their resources into a small number of very competent offspring or because they use those rare types of resources that are not very susceptible to great fluctuation in abundance.

3. While insect density is generally low, two types of things are extraordinarily common. Predators in the form of ants, spiders, and carnivorous beetles seem to be generally at a high density throughout the year in most habitats (cf. Becker 1975). For example, single dead termites put out as bait on the litter surface at low elevations on Puerto Rico, on small offshore islands, and on Providencia and San Andres islands remain there 2–10 sec before they are picked up by scavenging ants, compared with 1–20 min in Costa Rican lowland mainland habitats. This predator array, adept at surviving periodic lows in food availability, may be very good at absorbing the beginnings of density pulses at the start of the rainy season. The other kind of insect that is common on these islands is what might be termed an "outbreak." A given species of chrysomelid beetle or, especially, Homoptera may be very abundant in one set of sweep samples and very rare or absent in those on another island or in another season on the same island. Closer examination of the host plants often reveals that during the time of abundance the foliage, shoot tips, and such, are being seriously defoliated at a level the plant cannot sustain. It would not be surprising to find that the set of insects in an island sample are drawn in major part from populations that are in boom-bust-reinvade cycles. If the species richness is low, as it should be for a variety of obvious reasons, this alone can work to generate a general low density of insects in most samples.

SAN ANDRES ISLAND (COLOMBIA)

Approximately 25 km² in area (south of Providencia), this nearly flat island (low limestone hills in some areas) is devoid of almost everything but coconut plantation understory and low old-field scrub. I believe the original vegetation is unknown. Much of what is there resembles the vegetation of abandoned lots in the suburbs of a coastal rain-forest town like Limón, Costa Rica. One set of sweep samples from this island, which I was only able to glance at, contained an exceptionally large number of grasshoppers but otherwise looked much like one taken in the same habitat (coconut palm understory) in Puerto Rico. It seems fair to say that there is not much point to examining the insect fauna of San Andres Island except perhaps during experiments on the outcome of invasions of known introductions.

ISLA DEL COCO (COSTA RICA)

About 520 km off the Pacific coast of Costa Rica, this small island has a fascinating insect fauna (there is only one resident butterfly, *Historis odius*). This fauna is currently being characterized by C. Hogue of the Los Angeles County Museum (Hogue and Miller 1980).

ISLA DEL CAÑO (COSTA RICA)

Approximately 320 ha in area (a rough triangle 3 km long and 2 km wide at the base), this heavily forested island lies about 17 km off the Pacific coast at the north end of Corcovado National Park and is part of that park (it is clearly visible from shore). In profile, it is a rock mesa about 100 m high dissected by small ever-flowing creeks running more or less radially to the beaches. The beaches are sand and rock and lack mangroves. The upland part of the island toward the coast appears to be clothed in undisturbed rain forest (but see below), while the triangle's apex clearly contains various ages of second growth (without cattle or equids) following clearing for old banana plantations, an aborted airstrip, and some cultivated areas. The slopes down to the sea are clothed by what appears to be undisturbed vegetation similar to that on the sea-facing cliffs of northern Corcovado National Park (especially just north of Llorona).

The insects of Isla del Caño display numerous cases of what is supposed to happen on islands. In short, compared with the adjacent mainland, species richness is very low, density of most populations is very low, a few species are very abundant, and carnivorous insects are less severely depressed than are herbivorous ones.

Defoliators

On the Corcovado National Park mainland, there are at least six species of *Heliconia,* and they support at least ten species of hispine chrysomelids eating their leaves and flower bracts. One, *Heliconia latispatha,* maintains a large breeding population on Isla del Caño, and its leaves are fed on by a small red *Cephaloleia,* the only one of the mainland *Heliconia* hispines that seems to have become established on the island. On the mainland this beetle feeds on flower bracts and leaves, but on the island it feeds on all parts of the plant (and see Seifert and Seifert 1979; Strong 1977). In November 1978 it was extremely common, with five to thirty adults per new rolled leaf; in March 1979, with many new rolled leaves in evidence, it was down to a density of less than one per rolled leaf. *Heliconia imbricata* has at least one plant on the island as well, but it is probably not a breeding population, and the usual rolled-leaf hispines are not present.

In November 1978 a leaf-mining (moth?) larva had done extensive damage to the old and new leaves of the only (and very common) epiphytic bromeliad on the island; all leaves were attacked and many were destroyed. In March 1979 there was no sign of the animal or its damage. Only four species of butterflies and two species of skippers appear to be common enough to be resident populations (some eighteen species have been captured, but only as one or two specimens). This is particularly startling considering that mainland Corcovado National Park must have more than 220 species of breeding butterflies exclusive of skippers, metalmarks, and hairstreaks (P. DeVries, pers. comm.). There appears to be no resident pierid, papilionid, heliconiine, or satyrid on Isla del Caño. Hundreds of mainland butterflies must surely be able to fly 17 km downwind, and there certainly is no evidence that either competitors or superior predators cause this faunal lacuna.

Using Malaise traps, general aerial collecting, sweeping, and beating the vegetation, I have been able to find fewer than five species of chrysomelid beetles, and even with the help of a blacklight (albeit only for two nights) only one species of scarab. One foliage-eating orthopteran, twenty-two species of moths (at lights and collected off foliage), and sixteen species of Homoptera/Hemiptera (general collecting, Malaise traps, sweeping) complete the faunal picture of foliage-eaters as a first approximation. Obviously, further collecting will turn up more, but this fauna is hardly 1% of what has been collected with the same amount of effort on the Corcovado National Park mainland.

The vegetation species richness of Isla del Caño is severely reduced compared with that of the mainland, and it is tempting to blame the inexplicable depression of defoliator density on this. The central plateau's "pristine" forest is almost entirely a tall evergreen canopy of *Brosimum utile, Calophyllum macrophyllum,* and *Hymenaea courbaril,* with scattered figs and Euphorbiaceae. Its understory is *Enallagma latifolia, Pentagonia gymnopoda, Brosimum utile* seedlings and saplings, and a few other treelets. The ocean-facing slopes are clothed with *Byrsonima crassifolia, Inga, Pseudobombax septinatum, Vismia baccifera, Hibiscus tiliaceus,* and a few other large woody plants found in the same habitat on the adjacent mainland. Where the forest was cleared now lie dense, often nearly monospecific, stands of *Trema micrantha,*

Pentagonia gymnopoda, Piper aequale, various Melastomaceae, and *Alibertia edulis,* with scattered individuals of *Costus comosus, C. villosissimus, Casearia, Ficus* spp., *Carapa slateri, Acalypha* and a few others. Two individual *Cecropia obtusifolia,* without their ants, have made it to the island but are certainly to be viewed as transients.

A person accustomed to working with the adjacent mainland vegetation will recognize this list as a curiously impoverished coastal flora, and I might add, a flora that is not known for supporting a large insect fauna even on the mainland. When I add that the central portion of Isla del Caño contains a nearly pure stand of *Brosimum utile,* and that the surface of the island appears to have been at one time almost entirely covered with Indian graves, it seems likely that in fact the flora is far from an island rain forest but rather is the remains of a *Brosimum* orchard planted by the Indians (the large seeds are one of the few rain-forest seeds that can be readily eaten by humans; they were eaten by indigenous peoples throughout Mexico and Central America and were probably strongly competed for with wild animals on the parrot-peccary-rodent-rich mainland). I suspect that with the original forest went the bulk of the original insect fauna that once occupied Isla del Caño.

Flower Visitors

With one exception, the bee fauna of Isla del Caño is terribly reduced. Only *Trigona fulviventris* represents the stingless bees, and it was likely brought there by humans rather than by rafting (L. Johnson, pers. comm.). One species of carpenter bee and several small halictids are the other flower visitors except for euglossines. However, *Euglossa* nests are commonly encountered in the forest understory, and *Pentagonia gymnopoda,* a rare but well-used nectar host for males and females of *Euglossa* on the mainland, is extremely common. But it is in baiting with chemicals that the extraordinary abundance of euglossine bees becomes evident (Janzen 1981*b*). On the mainland, baiting with cineole, benzyl acetate, eugenol, methyl cinnamate, and methyl salicylate at one site generates about twenty species of euglossines, including a few individuals each morning of *Euglossa hemichlora* at cineole and of *E. tridentata* at eugenol and cineole. Baiting with the same chemicals in November and March on the island brought well over a thousand bees per morning of *E. hemichlora* to eugenol, methyl salicylate, and methyl cinnamate and of *E. tridentata* to eugenol and cineole (with a few to methyl cinnamate and benzyl acetate). Additionally one *Eulaema meriana*-like bee and one other *Euglossa* came, but I suspect that these were transients from the mainland. These results are made even more spectacular by the fact that I can find no species of orchid on the island that is visited by euglossine bees.

The white tubular flowers of *Alibertia edulis* are probably pollinated by sphingids, and the *Inga* and *Pseudobombax* may be visited by this group as well; however, none have come to lights on the island. There are hummingbirds and some "hummingbird" flowers on the island (e.g., *Heliconia latispatha*).

Carnivorous Insects

There is one common mosquito on the island (*Wyeomyia*), and oddly enough it lives only in the forest on the plateau, where it makes life difficult for field biologists. I might add that nowhere on the adjacent mainland do mosquitoes approach the density of this one species on Isla del Caño. Presumably this is because on the island the usual larval predators are missing from the bromeliads or other small water units they breed in.

The ant fauna is at a high density, as on other islands, and many prominent mainland species are present (e.g., *Camponotus sericiventris*, *Ectatomma tuberculatum*, *E. ruidum*). However, army ants and leaf-cutter ants are not present (termites are), and the *Azteca* that occupy *Cecropia* had not colonized the two small *Cecropia* located to date. Only one social vespid (*Polistes* sp.) appears to be on the island, but it is very rare.

Insects at Carrion and Dung

Carcasses, discarded animal parts, and animal feces are nutrient-rich resources that rain down on all habitats the world over, but the patterns of input and uptake, and which animals are the agents, vary enormously with habitat and latitude. This pattern and its producers have received only a smattering of the attention they deserve, and the focus has almost never been on tropical-temperate comparisons (see Halffter and Matthews 1966; Cornaby 1974; Howden and Nealis 1975, 1978; Janzen 1976*b*, 1977*b;* Schubeck 1976; Bartholomew and Heinrich 1978; Klemperer 1978; Putman 1978; Heinrich and Bartholomew 1979; Miller and Peck 1979; Colwell 1969). Here I will just call attention to a few of the more glaring patterns, recognizing that the subject is ripe for extensive field experimentation.

When a road-killed medium-sized mammal (raccoon, porcupine, rabbit) is placed on the forest floor in a northern Michigan hardwood-coniferous forest, it is deluged with large flies and at least four species of large silphid beetles. There may be several hundred adult silphids plowing through the carcass for a week or more, the carcass and ground seethe with fly larvae, and the system is rampant with interactions of predators and prey, fungal parasitisms, and phoresy. In New Jersey, Schubeck (1976) found no fewer than seven species of silphids on fish and chicken carrion.

In Costa Rican lowland rain forest and deciduous forest, the story is grossly different. First, any dead vertebrate of small size is found in daytime by a vulture or at night by an opossum or other scavenger and reduced to bones and a bit of skin within 24 h. If the carcass is strongly caged so that the scavenging vertebrates cannot get at it, a few flies appear, and the carcass is quickly covered by ants and ant tumulus (and see Cornaby 1974). For example, mouse carcasses in live traps at Sirena, Corcovado National Park, will be seething with ants within a few hours after death. No carrion beetles appear at carcasses in the lowlands of Costa Rica, and even flies seem not to stand much of a chance. There is one species of silphid at Monteverde (1,500 m elevation) (S. B. Peck, pers. comm.), but as a general statement Silphidae are essentially absent from Costa Rican lowland beetle faunas (and it is easy to predict that they should be absent from other lowland tropical faunas as well). This leads to the observation that "Silphidae are a temperate-zone family"—which I feel should be converted to "Silphidae are poor competitors with tropical vultures and ants" or "Silphidae are specialists on large chunks of high-quality animal carrion that is unlikely to be harvested by other animals for a period of days to weeks."

Whether vertebrate carrion will be present long enough for a fly and beetle fauna to develop on it depends not only on the rate of removal of carcasses by vultures, mammalian scavengers, and ants, but also on the rate of input of carcasses. In African habitats, where at least for the Recent period the rate of large-mammal carcass input is substantially higher than in Central America, it is not surprising to find some lowland tropical insects that are competitive with the vertebrates in carcass scavenging. A snared diuker antelope that I observed in the Cameroon rain forest near Edea was already swarming with first-instar fly larvae at 0500 in the rain, though it had died during heavy rain between midnight and 0500. In the same forest, a 60 kg snared sitatunga antelope was reduced to bones, a wisp of skin, and many kilos of last-instar fly larvae in less than 72 h. These flies are competing with hyenas and forest vultures, and they have to be fast. There was of course a large Pleistocene mammal fauna in the Neotropics, Costa Rica included, and there undoubtedly was an insect fauna associated with its carcasses just as there is in Africa today. Some parts of what we see at present, such as the large carrion-burying scarabs in lowland tropical South America, are undoubtedly remnants of that fauna. I know of no study examining the degradation of horse-, tapir-, deer-sized carcasses in Central American forests, but the results should make very interesting comparison with African carrion reduction.

In short, if we wish to find a substantial fauna of professional carrion-reducing insects in Costa Rica, we must look in those places where there is naturally too little carrion to attract or sustain vultures (or their mammalian equivalents), and where ants do not do well. Hign-elevation forests fill the bill nicely, and that is where the Costa Rican silphids reside.

Small bits of carrion, such as moribund insects and vertebrate fragments dropped by predators in the canopy, are taken almost entirely by ants in Costa Rican lowland forests. The forest floor is a living sheet of open jaws waiting for prey or carcasses to fall from heaven. As I mentioned earlier, if dead termites are placed in long lines at 1 m intervals across the forest floor, they last about 1–20 min; if you watch closely, you see that virtually all are picked up by ants of a multitude of genera (*Camponotus, Solenopsis, Odontomachus, Neoponera, Ectatomma, Pseudomyrmex, Crematogaster, Pheidole,* etc.). It is the ant-poor areas of the world—Costa Rican mountain vegetation above 2,200 m, mangrove forest soil, white sand soil habitats—where these rates are substantially reduced and where one might expect other scavenger groups to be well developed.

While generated in a much more iteroparous manner than are essentially semelparous carcasses, vertebrate dung is also rich in nutrients and has a large specialist insect fauna associated. In contrast to carrion-feeding insects, there is no doubt that the species richness and complexity of arrivals at vertebrate dung increases in moving into the tropics. It is commonplace for a cow pat in England or Minnesota to have only one or two species of flies developing in it, whereas a Costa Rican cow pat may have a dozen or more. There are about seventy-five species of scarabaeine scarabs (the dung rollers and buriers) in the continental United States; thorough collection at a lowland Costa Rican rain-forest site will produce forty to sixty species (and see Howden and Nealis 1975). Even in the deciduous forests of Santa Rosa National Park as many as fifteen species of Scarabaeinae may be collected from a single pile of horse dung. Howden and Nealis's (1978) report of different sizes of dung beetles perching and foraging at different heights in the rain forest in Colombia is true for Costa Rica as well, but it has no temperate-zone counterpart. However, just as I expect dramatic differences in the carrion-insect interaction with increasing elevation in Costa Rica, dung-beetle interactions should also change. Just as ants, termites, and wood-boring beetles decline dramatically in density and species richness above about 2,200 m elevation on Costa Rican mountains and are essentially nonexistent above 3,000 m, dung beetles also drop out with elevation. Presumably the cause is the same—the wet soil substrate never warms up, even though the air may be warm on occasion. This has interesting effects— I know of a pile of rabbit dung that has been sitting at the same place apparently undisturbed for 3 years on Cerro de la Muerte; a pile of horse or cow dung may take 2 years to disappear in this habitat.

The density and diversity of dung-visiting scarabs, flies, and other insects at Costa Rican dung vary strongly with season in the deciduous forests and pastures of Santa Rosa National Park. For example, shortly after the first rains in May, a pile of horse dung will be essentially removed in 2–3 days by the combined action of six species of large dung beetles (*Dichotomius colonicus, D. centralis, D. yucatanus, Copris lugubris, Phaneus excelsus, P. wagneri*) and a host of smaller ones. By the end of July, the density of all six species has begun to taper off to the point that much of the pile remains, though it has been used. By November (last month of the rainy season), dung piles in pastures have only the occasional *Dichotomius colonicus,* and dung piles in forest have only *Dichotomius centralis*. By January (early dry season) dung beetles, except for some of the very smallest species (e.g., *Onthophagus hopfneri*), are gone. In March (middle of the dry season) there are no large dung beetles active in forest or grassland, and horse and cow dung simply mummifies in the drying sun and wind. When the rainy season begins, these resoaked piles of high-grade organic matter are degraded by fungi, aphodiine dung beetles, flies, and other litter organisms.

In addition to strong seasonal heterogeneity in dung-users' activity, there is strong local spatial heterogeneity in dung use in Costa Rican forests. In the small pastures cut out of the rain forest at Corcovado National Park, horse dung often sits and decays, showing no sign of dung-beetle activity except for a few very small species. In the rain forest only a few tens of meters away, a pile of fresh horse dung is overnight churned to a finely dissected mass by two large species of *Eurysternus* (at Llorona) and *Dichotomius colonicus* (at Sirena). At Santa Rosa National Park, at least 90% of the dung beetle biomass at horse dung in the forest in the middle rainy season is *Dichotomius centralis,* with an occasional individual of this medium-sized beetle at horse dung in pastures a few meters away; in the pasture, almost all the beetles are *Dichotomius colonicus, D. yucatanus,* and *Copris lugubris*. As the dry season comes on, almost all *D. centralis* are gone from the deciduous forest at a time (December) when there are still many individuals in the riparian evergreen forest only a few hundred meters away.

While it is well known among dung-beetle biologists that a large pile of dung may attract most of the species of dung beetles in a piece of vegetation, and that a trap baited with a small amount of human dung will likewise bring in nearly all species, it is clear that there are strong numerical differences among the beetles that arrive at the dung of different species of animals. Peccary dung at Santa Rosa National Park appears to attract almost nothing, while human dung in the same forest brings many species. *Deltochilum lobipes* is a very large dung beetle commonly encountered under mummified carcasses of vertebrates but very rarely taken at horse or cattle dung baits; it comes readily to human dung. While *Canthon cyanellus sallaei* is occasionally seen on monkey dung in the forest at Santa Rosa, it also makes feeding balls out of large arthropods such as dead millipedes. *Onthophagus hopfneri* is a minute species often found burying small portions of bird dung on the deciduous forest floor in the rainy season. Some rain-forest species appear to make their living collecting monkey dung off leaves high above the ground and then falling to the ground with the ball to bury it. G. Halffter (pers. comm.) notes that cow dung seems to be preferred over horse dung by many species of dung beetles, though this needs to be supported by numbers. I am very puzzled by the observation that tapir dung left on the sides of drying puddles at Santa Rosa appears to attract no dung beetles yet is very similar to horse dung except that it contains more large twigs.

In closing I should note that the interaction of insects at carrion and dung, and at other forms of decomposing materials such as fallen tree branches and trunks, differs qualitatively from that of most other consumer-resource pairs and therefore deserves some special study. It differs in that the opportunity for coevolution has been removed; what close fitting of the interaction exists must have come about through adjustment of the insect to the resource in contemporary and evolutionary time, without a corresponding evolutionary response by the resource. A thorough understanding of this kind of interaction may allow a factoring out of some of the noncoevolved interactions in systems that appear to be essentially coevolved (flower-insects, etc.).

ACKNOWLEDGMENTS
This study was supported by National Science Foundation grant DEB 77-04889.

*

Allan, J. D.; Barnthouse, L. W.; Prestbye, R. A.; and Strong, D. R. 1973. On foliage arthropod communities of Puerto Rican second growth vegetation. *Ecology* 54:628–32.

Ashton, P. S. 1969. Speciation among tropical forest trees: Some deductions in the light of recent evidence. *Biol. J. Linn. Soc.* 1:155–96.

Baker, H. G. 1970. Two cases of bat-pollination in Central America. *Rev. Biol. Trop.* 17:187–97.

———. 1976. "Mistake" pollination as a reproductive system, with special reference to the Caricaceae. In *Variation, breeding and conservation of tropical forest trees,* ed. J. Burley and B. T. Styles, pp. 161–69. London: Academic Press.

Bartholomew, G. A., and Heinrich, B. 1978. Endothermy in African dung beetles during flight, ball making, and ball rolling. *J. Exp. Biol.* 73:65–83.

Bawa, K. S. 1974. Breeding systems of tree species of a lowland tropical community. *Evolution* 28:85–92.

Becker, P. 1975. Island colonization by carnivorous and herbivorous Coleoptera. *J. Anim. Ecol.* 44:893–906.

Beeson, C. F. C. 1941. *The ecology and control of the forest insects of India and the neighboring countries.* Dehra Dun: Vasant Press.

Browne, F. G. 1968. *Pests and diseases of forest plantation trees.* Oxford: Clarendon Press.

Burbutis, P. P., and Stewart, J. A. 1979. Blacklight trap collecting of parasitic Hymenoptera. *Ent. News* 90:17–22.

Burger, W. 1977. Moraceae. *Fieldiana, Bot.* 40:94–215.

Colwell, R. K. 1969. Ecological specialization and species diversity of tropical and temperate arthropods. Ph.D. diss., University of Michigan, Ann Arbor.

———. 1973. Competition and coexistence in a simple tropical community. *Am. Nat.* 107:737–60.

Colwell, R. K.; Betts, B. J.; Bunnell, P.; Carpenter, F. L.; and Feinsinger, P. 1974. Competition for the nectar of *Centropogon valerii* by the hummingbird *Colibri thalassinus* and the flower-piercer *Diglossa plumbea,* and its evolutionary implications. *Condor* 76:447–52.

Cornaby, B. W. 1974. Carrion reduction by animals in contrasting tropical habitats. *Biotropica* 6:51–63.

Dobzhansky, T., and Pavan, C. 1950. Local and seasonal variation in relative frequency of species of *Drosophila* in Brazil. *J. Anim. Ecol.* 19:1–14.

Ehrlich, P. R., and Gilbert, L. E. 1973. Population structure and dynamics of the tropical butterfly *Heliconius ethilla. Biotropica* 5:69–82.

Feinsinger, P. 1976. Organization of a tropical guild of nectarivorous birds. *Ecol. Monogr.* 46:257–91.

Feinsinger, P., and Colwell, R. K. 1978. Community organization among Neotropical nectar-feeding birds. *Am. Zool.* 18:779–95.

Fish, D. 1977. An aquatic spittle bug (Homoptera: Cercopidae) from a *Heliconia* flower bract in southern Costa Rica. *Ent. News* 88:10–12.

Fournier, L. A., and Salas, S. 1966. Algunas observaciones sobre la dinámica de la floración en el bosque tropical húmedo de Villa Colón. *Rev. Biol. Trop.* 14:75–85.

Frankie, G. W.; Baker, H. G.; and Opler, P. A. 1974. Comparative phenological studies of trees in tropical wet and dry forests in the lowlands of Costa Rica. *J. Ecol.* 62:881–913.

Frankie, G. W., and Coville, R. 1979. An experimental study on the foraging behavior of selected solitary bee species in the Costa Rican dry forest. *J. Kansas Ent. Soc.* 52:591–602.

Frankie, G. W.; Opler, P. A.; and Bawa, K. S. 1976. Foraging behavior of solitary bees: Implications for outcrossing of a Neotropical forest tree species. *J. Ecol.* 64:1049–57.

Gillon, D. 1971. The effect of bush fire on the principal

pentatomid bugs (Hemiptera) of an Ivory Coast savanna. *Proc. Tall Timbers Fire Ecol. Conf.* no. 11, pp. 377–417.

Gillon, Y. 1971. The effect of bush fire on the principal acridid species of an Ivory Coast savanna. *Proc. Tall Timbers Fire Ecol. Conf.,* no. 11, pp. 419–71.

Gray, B. 1972. Economic tropical forest entomology. *Ann. Rev. Ent.* 17:313–54.

Halffter, G., and Matthews, E. G. 1966. The natural history of dung beetles of the subfamily Scarabaeinae (Coleoptera, Scarabaeidae). *Folia Entomol. Mex.* 12–14:1–312.

Heinrich, B., and Bartholomew, G. A. 1979. The ecology of the African dung beetle. *Sci. Am.* 241:146–56.

Heithaus, E. R. 1974. The role of plant-pollinator interactions in determining community structure. *Ann. Missouri Bot. Gard.* 61:675–91.

———. 1979a. Community structure of Neotropical flower-visiting bees and wasps: Diversity and phenology. *Ecology* 60:190–202.

———. 1979b. Flower visitation records and resource overlap of bees and wasps in northwest Costa Rica. *Brenesia* 16:9–52.

Heithaus, E. R.; Opler, P. A. and Baker, H. G. 1974. Bat-pollination in *Bauhinia pauletia. Ecology* 55:412–19.

Hienton, T. E. 1974. *Summary of investigations of electric insect traps.* Technical Bulletin 1498. Washington, D.C.: U.S. Department of Agriculture, Agricultural Research Service.

Hogue, C. L., and Miller, S. E. 1980. Entomofauna of Cocos Island, Costa Rica (including Arachnida and other terrestrial Arthropoda). First progress report on studies. Unpublished report distributed by the authors, Natural History Museum of Los Angeles County.

Howden, H. F., and Nealis, V. G. 1975. Effects of clearing in a tropical rain forest on the composition of the coprophagous scarab beetle fauna (Coleoptera). *Biotropica* 7:77–83.

———. 1978. Observations on height of perching in some tropical dung beetles (Scarabaeidae). *Biotropica* 10:43–46.

Howell, D. J. 1979. Flock foraging in nectar-eating bats: Advantages to the bats and to the host plants. *Am. Nat.* 114:23–49.

Hubbell, S. P. and Johnson, L. K. 1977. Competition and nest spacing in a tropical stingless bee community. *Ecology* 58:949–63.

Janzen, D. H. 1967a. Why mountain passes are higher in the tropics. *Am. Nat.* 101:233–49.

———. 1967b. Synchronization of sexual reproduction of trees with the dry season in Central America. *Evolution* 21:620–37.

———. 1967c. Interaction of the bull's horn acacia (*Acacia cornigera* L.) with an ant inhabitant (*Pseudomyrmex ferruginea* F. Smith) in eastern Mexico. *Univ. Kansas Sci. Bull.* 47:315–558.

———. 1968a. Notes on nesting and foraging behavior of *Megalopta* (Hymenoptera) in Costa Rica. *J. Kansas Ent. Soc.* 41:342–50.

———. 1968b. Reproductive behavior in the Passifloraceae and some of its pollinators in Central America. *Behavior* 32:33–48.

———. 1970. *Jacquinia pungens,* a heliophile from the understory of tropical deciduous forest. *Biotropica* 2:112–19.

———. 1971a. Escape of juvenile *Dioclea megacarpa* (Leguminosae) vines from predators in a deciduous tropical forest. *Am. Nat.* 105:97–112.

———. 1971b. The ecological significance of an arboreal nest of *Bombus pullatus* in Costa Rica. *J. Kansas Ent. Soc.* 44:210–16.

———. 1971c. Euglossine bees as long-distance pollinators of tropical plants. *Science* 171:203–5.

———. 1972. Escape in space by *Sterculia apetala* seeds from the bug *Dysdercus fasciatus* in a Costa Rican deciduous forest. *Ecology* 53:350–61.

———. 1973a. Sweep samples of tropical foliage insects: Effects of seasons, vegetation types, elevation, time of day, and insularity. *Ecology* 54:687–708.

———. 1973b. Dissolution of mutualism between *Cecropia* and its *Azteca* ants. *Biotropica* 5:15–28.

———. 1973c. Rate of regeneration after a tropical high elevation fire. *Biotropica* 5:117–22.

———. 1975. *Pseudomyrmex nigropilosa:* A parasite of a mutualism. *Science* 188:936–37.

———. 1976a. Sweep samples of tropical deciduous forest foliage-inhabiting insects: Seasonal changes and inter-field differences in adult bugs and beetles. *Rev. Biol. Trop.* 24:149–61.

———. 1976b. The depression of reptile biomass by large herbivores. *Am. Nat.* 110:371–400.

———. 1976c. The microclimate differences bewteen a deciduous forest and adjacent riparian forest in Guanacaste Province, Costa Rica. *Brenesia* 8:29–33.

———. 1977a. A note on optimal mate selection by plants. *Am. Nat.* 111:365–71.

———. 1977b. Why fruits rot, seeds mold, and meat spoils. *Am. Nat.* 111:691–713.

———. 1978a. Seeding patterns of tropical trees. In *Tropical trees as living systems,* ed. P. B. Tomlinson and M. H. Zimmerman, pp. 83–128. New York: Cambridge University Press.

———. 1978b. Description of a *Pterocarpus officinalis* (Leguminosae) monoculture in Corcovado National Park, Costa Rica. *Brenesia* 14/15:305–9.

———. 1979a. Natural history of *Phelypera distigma* (Boheman), Curculionidae, a Costa Rican defoliator of *Guazuma ulmifolia* Lam. (Sterculiaceae). *Brenesia* 16:213–19.

———. 1979b. How to be a fig. *Ann. Rev. Ecol. Syst.* 10:13–51.

———. 1979c. How many babies do figs pay for babies? *Biotropica* 11:48–50.

———. 1979d. How many parents do the wasps from a fig have? *Biotropica* 11:127–29.

———. 1980a. Specificity of seed-attacking beetles in the deciduous forests of Costa Rica. *J. Ecol.* 68: 929–52.

———. 1980b. Heterogeneity of potential food abundance for tropical small land birds. In *Migrant birds in the Neotropics,* ed. A. Keast and E. S. Morton, pp. 545–52. Washington, D.C.: Smithsonian Institution Press.

———. 1981a. Bee arrival at two Costa Rican female *Catasetum* orchid inflorescences, and a hypothesis on euglossine population structure. *Oikos* 36:177–83.

———. 1981b. Reduction in euglossine bee species richness on Isla del Caño, a Costa Rican offshore island. *Biotropica* 13:238–40.

Janzen, D. H.; DeVries, P. J.; Higgins, M. L.; and Kimsey, L. S. 1982. Seasonal and site variation in male euglossine bees arriving at chemical baits in a Costa Rican deciduous forest and rainforest. *Ecology* 63:66–74.

Janzen, D. H., and Martin, P. S. 1982. Neotropical anachronisms: The fruits the gomphotheres ate. *Science* 215:19–27.

Janzen, D. H.; Miller, G. A.; Hackforth-Jones, J.; Pond, C. M.; Hooper, K.; and Janos, D. P. 1976. Two Costa Rican bat-generated seed shadows of *Andira inermis* (Leguminosae). *Ecology* 56:1068–75.

Janzen, D. H., and Pond, C. M. 1975. A comparison, by sweep sampling, of the anthropod fauna of secondary vegetation in Michigan, England and Costa Rica. *Trans. Roy. Ent. Soc. London* 127:33–50.

Janzen, D. H., and Schoener, T. W. 1968. Differences in insect abundance and diversity between wetter and drier sites during a tropical dry season. *Ecology* 49: 96–110.

Janzen, D. H., and Wilson, D. E. 1974. The cost of being dormant in the tropics. *Biotropica* 6:260–62.

Johnson, L. K., and Hubbell, S. P. 1975. Contrasting foraging strategies and coexistence of two bee species on a single resource. *Ecology* 56:1398–1406.

Jones, C. E. 1967. Some evolutionary aspects of a water stress on flowering in the tropics. *Turrialba* 17: 188–90.

Karr, J. R. 1976. An association between a grass (*Paspalum virgatum*) and moths. *Biotropica* 8:284–85.

Klemperer, H. G. 1978. The repair of larval cells and other larval activities in *Geotrupes spiniger* Marsham and other species (Coleoptera, Scarabaeidae). *Ecol. Entomol.* 3:119–31.

Linhart, Y. B. 1973. Ecological and behavioral determinants of pollen dispersal in hummingbird pollinated *Heliconia*. *Am. Nat.* 107:511–23.

Marshall, J. J., and Rickson, F. R. 1973. Characterization of the D-glucan from the plastids of *Cecropia peltata* as a glycogen-type polysaccharide. *Carbohydrate Res.* 28:31–37.

Michener, C. D.; Winston, M. L.; and Jander, R. 1978. Pollen manipulation and related activities and structures in bees of the family Apidae. *Univ. Kansas Sci. Bull.* 51:575–601.

Miller, S. E., and Peck, S. B. 1979. Fossil carrion beetles of Pleistocene California asphalt deposits, with a synopsis of Holocene California Silphidae (Insecta: Coleoptera: Silphidae). *Trans. San Diego Soc. Nat. Hist.* 19:85–106.

Mound, L. A., and Waloff, N., eds. 1978. Diversity of insect faunas. *Symp. Roy. Ent. Soc. London* 9:1–204.

Munroe, E. 1956. Canada as an environment for insect life. *Canadian Ent.* 88:372–476.

Opler, P. A.; Baker, H. G.; and Frankie, G. W. 1975. Reproductive biology of some Costa Rican *Cordia* species (Boraginaceae). *Biotropica* 7:234–47.

Opler, P. A.; Frankie, G. W.; and Baker, H. G. 1976. Rainfall as a factor in the release, timing, and synchronization of anthesis by tropical trees and shrubs. *J. Biogeogr.* 3:231–36.

Owen, D. F. 1971. *Tropical butterflies.* Oxford: Clarendon Press.

Palmer, M. K. 1977. Natural history and population dynamics of *Pseudoxychila tarsalis* Bates (Coleoptera: Cicindelindae). Ph.D. diss., University of Michigan, Ann Arbor.

Pohl, R. W.; Tiffany, L. H.; and Karr, J. R. 1979. Probable source of fluid from spikelets of *Paspalum virgatum*. *Biotropica* 11:42.

Primack, R. B., and Howe, H. F. 1975. Interference competition between a hummingbird (*Amazilia tzactl*) and skipper butterflies (Hesperiidae). *Biotropica* 7: 55–58.

Putman, R. J. 1978. The role of carrion-frequenting arthropods in the decay process. *Ecol. Ent.* 3:133–39.

Rausher, M. D., and Fowler, N. L. 1979. Intersexual aggression and nectar defense in *Chauliognathus distinguendus* (Coleoptera: Cantharidae). *Biotropica* 11: 96–100.

Real, L. A. 1980. Nectar availability and bee-foraging on *Ipomoea* (Convolvulaceae). *Biotropica* 13(suppl.): 64–69.

Rickson, F. R. 1971. Glycogen plastids in Müllerian body cells of *Cecropia peltata*—a higher green plant. *Science* 173:344–47.

———. 1973. Review of glycogen plastid differentiation in Müllerian body cells of *Cecropia peltata*. *Ann. N.Y. Acad. Sci.* 210:104–14.

———. 1976a. Anatomical development of the leaf trichilium and Müllerian bodies of *Cecropia peltata* L. *Am. J. Bot.* 63:1266–71.

———. 1976b. Ultrastructure differentiation of the Müllerian body glycogen plastid of *Cecropia peltata* L. *Am. J. Bot.* 63:1272–79.

———. 1977. Progressive loss of ant-related traits of *Cecropia peltata* on selected Caribbean islands. *Am. J. Bot.* 64:585–95.

Rickson, F. R., and Denison, W. 1975. Ascomycete invasion of glycogen-rich Müllerian body tissue of *Cecropia obtusifolia* (Moraceae). *Mycologia* 67: 1043–47.

Robinson, H. S., and Robinson, P. J. M. 1950. Some notes on the observed behavior of Lepidoptera in flight in the vicinity of light-sources together with a description of a light trap designed to take entomological samples. *Ent. Gazette* 1:3–20.

Rockwood, L. L. 1973. The effect of defoliation on seed production of six Costa Rican tree species. *Ecology* 54:1363–69.

Schemske, D. W. 1976. Pollinator specificity in *Lantana camara* and *L. trifolia* (Verbenaceae). *Biotropica* 8:260–64.

Schlising, R. A. 1970. Sequence and timing of bee foraging in flowers of *Ipomoea* and *Aniseia* (Convolvulaceae). *Ecology* 51:1061–67.

Schneirla, T. C. 1971. *Army ants.* San Francisco: W. H. Freeman.

Schoener, T. W., and Janzen, D. H. 1968. Notes on environmental determinants of tropical versus temperate insect size patterns. *Am. Nat.* 102:207–24.

Schubeck, P. P. 1976. Carrion beetle response to poikilotherm and homeotherm carrion (Coleoptera: Silphidae). *Ent. News* 87:265–69.

Seifert, R. P. 1974. The Sphingidae of Turrialba, Costa Rica. *J. N.Y. Ent. Soc.* 82:45–56.

Seifert, R. P., and Seifert, F. H. 1979. Utilization of *Heliconia* (Musaceae) by the beetle *Xenarescus monocerus* (Oliver) (Chrysomelidae: Hispanae) in a Venezuelan forest. *Biotropica* 11:51–59.

Simberloff, D.; King, L.; Dillon, P.; Lowrie, S.; Lorence, D.; and Schilling, E. 1978. Holes in the doughnut theory: The dispersion of ant-lions. *Brenesia* 14–15:13–46.

Smith, N. G. 1972. Migrations of the day-flying moth *Urania* in Central and South America. *Carib. J. Sci.* 12:45–58.

Soderstrom, T. R., and Calderon, C. E. 1971. Insect pollination in tropical rainforest grasses. *Biotropica* 3:1–16.

Stanton, N. 1975. Herbivore pressure on two types of tropical forests. *Biotropica* 7:8–11.

Stiles, F. G. 1975. Ecology, flowering phenology, and hummingbird pollination of some Costa Rican *Heliconia* species. *Ecology* 56:285–301.

———. 1977. Co-adapted competitors: The flowering seasons of hummingbird-pollinated plants in a tropical forest. *Science* 198:1177–78.

———. 1979. Notes on the natural history of *Heliconia* (Musaceae) in Costa Rica. *Brenesia* 15 (suppl.): 151–80.

Stout, R. J. 1978. Migration of the aquatic hemipteran *Limnocoris insularis* (Naucoridae) in a tropical lowland stream (Costa Rica, Central America). *Brenesia* 14:1–11.

———. 1979. The effect of backflooding on the benthic invertebrate community in tropical streams. Ph.D. diss., University of Michigan.

Stout, R. J., and Vandermeer, J. 1975. Comparison of species richness for stream-inhabiting insects in tropical and mid-latitude streams. *Am. Nat.* 109: 263–80.

Strong, D. R. 1977. Rolled-leaf hispine beetles (Chryso-

melidae) and their Zingiberales host plants in Middle America. *Biotropica* 9:156–69.

Weber, N. A. 1972. Gardening ants: The attines. *Mem. Am. Phil. Soc.* 92:1–146.

Weiss, H. B.; Soraci, F. A.; and McCoy, E. E. 1941. Insect behavior to various wave lengths of light. *J. N.Y. Ent. Soc.* 51:117–31.

Wiebes, J. T. 1979. Co-evolution of figs and their insect pollinators. *Ann. Rev. Ecol. Syst.* 10:1–12.

Wille, A., and Michener, C. D. 1962. Inactividad estacional de *Megacephala sobrina* Dejean (Coleoptera, Cicindelidae). *Rev. Biol. Trop.* 10:161–65.

———. 1973. The nest architecture of stingless bees with special reference to those of Costa Rica (Hymenoptera: Apidae). 21 (suppl. 1):1–278.

Williams, N.J. 1978. A preliminary bibliography on euglossine bees and their relationships with orchids and other plants. *Selbyana* 2:345–55.

Wilson, E. O. 1971. *The insect societies.* Cambridge, Mass.: Belknap Press.

Wolda, H. 1978a. Fluctuations in abundance of tropical insects. *Am. Nat.* 112:1017–45.

———. 1978b. Seasonal fluctuations in rainfall, food and abundance of tropical insects. *J. Anim. Ecol.* 47:369–81.

CHECKLISTS OF INSECTS
Checklist of Sphingidae

W. A. Haber

Sphingid moths constitute a small, compact family of Macrolepidoptera. They belong to the suborder Frenatae, which is characterized by moths that have a frenulum or stiff bristle that holds the forewing and hind wing together in flight. The sphingidae are distinguished in keys by the hindwing venation: veins Rs and Sc are connected by a cross-vein (R_1) at about the middle of the discal cell (Borror and White 1970; Hodges 1971).

General shape is sufficient for recognizing most sphingids. The body is conically streamlined with a rounded head and a long, pointed abdomen. The forewings are long and narrow, but the hind wings are small, only about half as long as the forewings. Most have stout antennae with recurved tips. The body looks large for the size of the wings.

Apart from genitalia, sexes differ in that males are usually smaller than females and have narrower abdomens. In addition, within a species, the antennae of males look thicker because of rows of short setae. Sexual dimorphism in color pattern is rare in Sphingidae but occurs in *Erinnyis ello* and a few other species. In many of the smaller species, males have a "tail" formed of long, hairlike scales. The tail can be spread or folded like that of a bird. Often females lack the tail, and the abdomen ends in a point—for example, *Callionima, Enyo.*

Males have a small brush of white or cream scent scales folded into a slot on each side of the second abdominal segment. When a moth is held or disturbed, these scent scales are exposed, releasing a disagreeable odor. Males of a few species have additional scent brushes on the fore coxae (*Eumorpha*) or under a flap in the forewing (some *Enyo*). The scent scales probably function primarily in courtship and mating; however, the fetid odor of the abdominal brushes also suggests a possible defense against predators.

The life cycle of sphingids is fairly uniform. Eggs are laid singly on the undersides of host plant leaves. The eggs average about 1.5 mm long but vary among species from 1 to 3 mm. They are a little narrower than long and slightly flattened. Eggs of most species are shades of green (but occasionally yellow, blue green, or white) and lack macroscopic surface sculpturing. Eggs hatch in about 7–10 days.

Sphingid larvae are distinguished by having a horn on the eleventh abdominal segment (near the tip of the body). The horn may be stiff and covered with spines or setae as in *Manduca,* or soft and threadlike as in *Isognathus* and *Eumorpha*. In the latter genera the horn can be whipped back and forth or vibrated as a threat display. Some species lack the horn in the fifth instar (e.g., some *Eumorpha, Erinnyis*). Larvae are cylindrical or else have a prominent distension of the thoracic segments and first abdominal segment (*Eumorpha, Enyo*). Sphingids spend about 3 weeks to a month in the larval stage, passing through five instars.

Most larvae are cryptically colored. While green is predominant, many populations also contain brown color forms. Several species of *Xylophanes* change from green to chocolate brown in the last instar. A few species are remarkably snakelike—for example, *Xylophanes* and *Eumorpha*. One of the most dramatic of the snake mimics is *Hemeroplanes triptolemus*. At rest, the third and fourth instars of *H. triptolemus* resemble small green twigs, but when the larva is disturbed in turns its fore end upside down, expands the thorax, and assumes the shape and appearance of a vine snake (*Oxybelis*). The last instar is a formidable mimic of *Bothrops schlegelii*, an arboreal pit viper. The 12–15 cm long larvae of *Pseudosphinx tetrio* are ringed with yellow and black and have red heads, thereby producing the impression of a small coral snake (Janzen 1980).

Larvae have a wandering phase in which they leave the host plant to seek pupation sites. Most species pupate either a few centimeters underground or in a flimsy cocoon in leaf litter. *Madoryx oiclus* is unusual in that it spins a typical moth cocoon on tree trunks and incorporates bits of bark for camouflage.

A sphingid population usually feeds on one or a few species of plants locally, but different host-plant species are often used by distant populations. *Xylophanes germen* is exceptional in having fifteen species of larval hosts at Monteverde. While populations may be described as stenophagic, recorded hosts for the family have a broad taxonomic spread, including more than fifty families (Moss 1912, 1920; Hodges 1971; Harris 1972). Commonly used hosts include families of plants that produce white latex (Apocynaceae, Asclepiadaceae, Caricaceae, Euphorbiaceae, Moraceae) and those containing alkaloids in quantity (e.g., Rubiaceae, Solanaceae). Families with the most host records for Sphingidae are probably Apocynaceae, Rubiaceae, Solanaceae, and Vitaceae. Some of the more unusual hosts belong to Podocarpaceae, Pinaceae, Araceae, and Orchidaceae (Harris 1972).

Although many of the larval hosts are rich in toxic secondary compounds, I have seen no evidence that these poisons are sequestered as a predator defense. Overall colors of adults are mostly muted browns, grays, and greens, serving as camouflage while the moths rest during the day on tree trunks and among leaves. Many species do have flash and startle colors (red, orange, or yellow) on the hind wings or abdomen that may confuse predators long enough for the sphingid to escape. Some species strigilate (*Cocytius, Amplyterus, Protambulyx*), and *Amplyterus* and *Eumorpha* spp. in particular use sharp tibial spines to discourage predators.

Sphingids are well known as pollinators in the temperate zone, but they are perhaps more significant in the tropics, where they are the adapted pollinators of many trees, shrubs, and epiphytes (especially among Mimosaceae, Rubiaceae, Cactaceae, and Orchidaceae) (Haber and Frankie 1980a,b, and account of *Hylocereus costaricensis* in this volume). They are chiefly nocturnal feeders, and the white, tubular flowers they pollinate typically produce overpowering, gardenialike fragrances at night. The smaller species (e.g., *Enyo, Nyceryx, Perigonia*) often feed at dawn and dusk. About half a dozen Costa Rican species (*Aellopos, Eupyrrhoglossum*) are largely diurnal.

The sphingids are adroit fliers that can hover and fly backward and upside down. A sphinx moth can hover at a flower in a 40 km/h wind to suck nectar with its long, thin tongue. Tongue lengths vary among species, ranging from 10 mm in *Cautethia spuria* to 250 mm or more in *Neococytius cluentius* and *Amphimoea walkeri*. The long-tongued species are specialized for pollinating flowers with long, narrow tubes or spurs, such as *Crinum, Posoqueria, Hymenocallis, Lindenia, Hylocereus,* and *Epiphyllum*. However, these same moths sometimes feed on tiny composite flowers and orchids with shallow tubular corollas.

The family Sphingidae contains about one thousand known species (Carcasson 1976). About four hundred of these live in the New World. At least 121 species occur in Costa Rica, or 30% of the New World sphingid fauna. The entire United States and Canada have 115 species, and Alaska has only three (Hodges 1971). More generally, the pattern of sphingid species richness is weighted toward the wet tropics. South America, Africa, and tropical Asia each have about 260 species (Schreiber 1978; Carcasson 1976), or about 75% of the world total. Peru, with 13% of the land area of the United States, has 193 recorded species (Schreiber 1978).

The number of species that occur at single localities may be of more ecological interest. The checklists for Hacienda La Pacifica, Monteverde, and Turrialba result from thorough collections. La Pacifica (62 species) is situated in highly disturbed lowland, semideciduous forest (dry forest), Monteverde (73 species) includes extensive stands of mature, lower montane wet forest (cloud forest), and Turrialba (69 species) borders on premontane moist forest along the Río Reventazón (Seifert 1974). We have no thorough collections from lowland wet forest in Costa Rica, but it appears that wet forest habitats may contain 50–65% of the sphingid fauna of the country.

A majority of Costa Rican species have broad ranges that are almost continuous from Mexico to northern Argentina. *Xylophanes tersa* ranges from Canada to Argentina. Despite the reputation of sphingids as migrants and far fliers, a few species are endemic to Costa Rica (*Protambulyx xanthus, Sphinx biolleyi, Xylophanes jordani,* and *X. zurcheri*) (Cary 1951). The wide-ranging species often occupy a diversity of habitats within the country; the three primary divisions for sphingids are wet lowland, dry lowland, and mid-elevation forest. A minority of species are restricted to one of these habitats. For example, *Stolidoptera tachasara, Xylophanes germen, X. crotonis,* and *X. rhodina* are exclusively montane, while *Amphimoea walkeri, Protambulyx xanthus,* and *Xylophanes undata* have been found only in the wet lowlands. A few species are also characteristic of lowland dry forest, for example, *Ceratomia igualana, Erinnyis yucatana, Manduca barnesi,* and *Xylophanes turbata*.

The species checklist presented here is based primarily on collections of the author, R. P. Seifert, D. H. Janzen, and our colleagues during the 1970s, but I have included available published records as well (Godman and Salvin 1881; Cary 1951; Seifert 1967, 1974; Schreiber 1978). Undoubtedly, museum and private collections contain some unrecorded species. Recent collections continue to provide new records, and a few unidentified species are still in hand. Based on ranges of species occurring elsewhere in Central America, I estimate that the total for the country may be about 150 species.

ACKNOWLEDGMENTS

The following individuals contributed specimens, thereby adding to the locality records: Brian Bateson, Steve Bullock, Jim Crisp, Phil DeVries, Adrian Forsyth, Gordon Frankie, Benito Guindon, Carlos Guindon, Jenny Hackforth-Jones, Dan Janzen, Lucinda McDade, George Powell, and George Stevens. Most of the determinations were made by Ronald W. Hodges (United States National Museum) and Richard P. Seifert (George Washington University).

*

Borror, D. J., and White, R. E. 1970. *A field guide to the insects.* Boston: Houghton Mifflin.

Carcasson, R. H. 1976. *Revised catalogue of the African Sphingidae (Lepidoptera) with descriptions of the East African species.* 2d ed. London: E. W. Classey.

Cary, M. M. 1951. Distribution of Sphingidae (Lepidoptera: Heterocera) in the Antillean-Caribbean region. *Trans. Am. Ent. Soc.* 77:63–129.

Godman, F. C., and Salvin, O. 1881. *Biología Centrali-Americana: Heterocera.* 1:1–24, suppl., pp. 298–319.

Haber, W. A., and Frankie, G. W. 1980a. Pollination ecology of *Luehea* (Tiliaceae) in Costa Rica dry forest: Significance of adapted and non-adapted pollinators. Submitted.

———. 1980b. Community organization of sphingid pollination systems in a Costa Rican dry forest. In preparation.

Harris, P. 1972. Food-plant groups of the Semanophorinae (Lepidoptera: Sphingidae): A possible taxonomic tool. *Can. Ent.* 104:71–80.

Hodges, R. W. 1971. *The moths of America north of Mexico.* Fasc. 21. *Sphingoidea.* London: E. W. Classey and R. B. D. Publishers.

Janzen, D. H. 1980. Two potential coral snake mimics in a tropical deciduous forest. *Biotropica* 12:77–78.

Moss, A. M. 1912. On the Sphingidae of Peru. *Trans. Zool. Soc. London* 20:73–117.

———. 1920. Sphingidae of Para, Brazil. *Novit. Zool.* 27:333–423.

Schreiber, H. 1978. *Dispersal centres of Sphingidae (Lepidoptera) in the Neotropical region.* Biogeographica, vol. 10. Boston: Junk.

Seifert, R. P. 1967. A study of the Sphingidae (Lepidoptera) of Turrialba and San José with data from various other sites within Costa Rica. Report to Associated Colleges of the Midwest, 60 West Walton Street, Chicago, Ill., 60610.

———. 1974. The Sphingidae of Turrialba, Costa Rica. *J. N.Y. Ent. Soc.* 82:45–56.

Species	La Selva Field Station	Volcán Tenorio	CATIE, Turrialba	Monte-verde	Finca Las Cruces	Corcovado National Park	Santa Rosa National Park	Hacienda La Pacifica
Aellopos ceculus (Cram.)	x							
A. clavipes (R. and J.)				x			x	x
A. fadus (Cram.)				x			x	x
A. tantalus (L.)								
A. titan (Cram.)				x			x	x
Agrius cingulatus (F.)	x	x	x	x	x	x	x	x
Aleuron chloroptera (Perty)							x	
A. neglectum R. and J.								
Amphimoea walkeri (Bdv.)	x							
Amplyterus donysa (Drc.)				x	x			
A. gannascus (Stoll)	x	x	x	x	x	x	x	x
A. ypsilon R. and J.	x	x	x	x	x	x	x	
Callionima falcifera (Gehlen)	x	x	x	x			x	x
C. inuus (R. and J.)						x		
C. nomius (Wlk.)	x					x		
C. pan (Cram.)			x	x				
Cautethia spuria (Bdv.)			x	x			x	x
Cocytius antaeus (Dry.)		x	x	x				x
C. beelzebuth (Bdv.)		x	x	x				x
C. duponchel (Poey)	x	x	x	x	x	x	x	x
C. lucifer R. and J.				x			x	x
Dolbogene igualana (Schaus)							x	x
Enyo gorgon (Cram.)			x	x		x	x	x
E. lugubris (L.)		x	x	x		x	x	x
E. ocypete (L.)	x		x	x		x	x	x
E. taedium (Schaus)								
Erinnyis alope (Dry.)	x	x	x	x	x	x	x	x
E. crameri (Schaus)		x	x	x	x		x	x
E. domingonus (Butl.)[a]							x	
E. ello (L.)	x	x	x	x	x	x	x	x
E. lassauxii (Bdv.)		x	x	x			x	x
E. obscura (F.)		x	x	x			x	x
E. oenotrus (Cram.)	x	x	x	x			x	x
E. yucatana (Drc.)				x			x	x
Eumorpha anchemola (Cram.)	x	x	x	x	x	x	x	x
E. capronnieri (Bdv.)	x		x					
E. eacus (Cram.)								x
E. fasciata (Sulz.)	x	x	x				x	x
E. labruscae (L.)	x	x	x	x			x	x
E. obliqua (R. and J.)			x	x				
E. phorbas (Cram.)	x		x			x		
E. satellitia (L.)			x	x		x	x	x
E. triangulum (R. and J.)	x	x	x	x	x	x	x	
E. vitis (L.)	x	x		x		x	x	x
Eupyrrhoglossum sagra (Poey)	x			x		x	x	x
Hemeroplanes ornatus (Rothsch.)								
H. triptolemus (Cram.)			x				x	x
Hyles lineata (F.)				x			x	x
Isognathus rimosus (Grt.)			x	x			x	x
Madoryx oiclus (Cram.)			x	x		x	x	x
M. pluto (Cram.)			x	x	x	x		
Manduca albiplaga (Wlk.)	x					x		
M. barnesi (Clark)							x	x
M. corallina (Drc.)	x	x		x	x		x	x
M. dalica (Kby.)								

Species	La Selva Field Station	Volcán Tenorio	CATIE, Turrialba	Monte-verde	Finca Las Cruces	Corcovado National Park	Santa Rosa National Park	Hacienda La Pacifica
M. diffissa (Btl.)						X		
M. dilucida (Hy. Edw.)							X	X
M. florestan (Cram.)	X	X	X	X	X	X	X	X
M. hannibal (Cram.)		X	X			X		
M. lanuginosa (Hy. Edw.)							X	
M. lefeburei (Guer.)	X		X	X			X	X
M. lichenea (Burm.)			X					
M. lucetius (Stoll)								
M. muscosa (R. and J.)				X		X	X	X
M. occulta (R. and J.)	X	X	X	X			X	X
M. ochus (Klug)	X		X	X			X	X
M. pellenia (H.-S.)	X		X	X	X			
M. rustica (F.)	X	X	X	X	X	X	X	X
M. sesquiplex (Bdv.)								
M. sexta (L.)	X	X	X	X		X	X	X
Neococytius cluentius (Cram.)			X	X		X		X
Nyceryx coffeae (Wlk.)			X				X	X
N. eximia R. and J.			X	X				
N. magna (Fldr.)	X		X					
N. riscus (Schaus)				X			X	X
N. stuarti (Roths.)								X
N. tacita (Drc.)			X					
N. ericea (Drc.)				X				
Oryba achemenides Cram.	X							
O. kadeni (Schauf.)					X			
Pachygonia drucei R. and J.	X						X	
P. subhamata (Wlk.)				X				
Pachylia darceta Drc.	X		X		X	X		
P. ficus (L.)	X		X	X		X	X	X
P. syces (Hbn.)	X		X			X	X	X
Pachylioides resumens (Wlk.)	X		X	X		X	X	X
Perigonia lusca (F.)		X	X	X		X	X	X
P. stulta H.-S.			X	X				
Phryxus caicus (Cram.)							X	X
Protambulyx goeldii R. and J.								
P. strigilis (L.)	X	X	X	X	X	X	X	X
P. xanthus R. and J.	X							
Pseudosphinx tetrio (L.)		X	X	X			X	X
Sphinx biolleyi (Schaus)								
S. merops Bdv.	X		X	X			X	X
Stolidoptera tachasara (Drc.)				X				
Unzela japix (Cram.)						X	X	
U. pronoe (Drc.)	X					X		X
Xylophanes acrus R. and J.	X	X	X	X	X			
X. adalia (Drc.)								
X. amadis (Stoll)				X				
X. anubus (Cram.)	X	X	X	X		X	X	X
X. belti (Drc.)	X		X					
X. ceratomioides (G. and R.)	X	X	X	X	X	X	X	
X. chiron Dry.	X	X	X	X	X		X	X
X. crotonis (Wlk.)				X				
X. eumedon (Bdv.)								
X. germen (Schaus)				X				
X. guianensis (Rothsch.)						X		
X. hannemanni Closs				X				

Species	La Selva Field Station	Volcán Tenorio	CATIE, Turrialba	Monte-verde	Finca Las Cruces	Corcovado National Park	Santa Rosa National Park	Hacienda La Pacifica
X. jordani Clark				x				
X. libya (Drc.)	x	x	x	x		x		x
X. loelia (Drc.)	x	x	x			x	x	
X. maculator (Bdv.)				x			x	
X. neoptolemus (Stoll)			x	x	x			
X. pistacina (Bdv.)		x	x					
X. pluto (F.)	x	x	x	x		x	x	x
X. porcus (Hbn.)	x	x	x	x	x	x	x	x
X. rhodina R. and J.				x				
X. tersa (L.)	x	x	x	x		x	x	x
X. thyelia (L.)	x	x	x					
X. titana (Drc.)	x	x	x	x				
X. turbata (Hy. Edw.)							x	x
X. tyndarus (Bdv.)		x		x				
X. undata R. and J.	x	x				x		
X. zurcheri (Drc.)	x		x					

ª May be conspecific with *obscura* (Hodges 1971).

Checklist of Army Ants (Arrieras) (Formicidae: Ecitoninae)

C. W. Rettenmeyer

Following each species the symbols w, ♀, or ♂ refer to workers, queens, or males that are known from that species from any locality. Almost all species in the following list are known from fewer than five records.

Cheliomyrmex sp. w, ♂
> *Cheliomyrmex* occurs both north and south of Costa Rica, but no member of this genus has yet been reported from this country.

Eciton burchelli foreli Mayr, w, ♀, ♂
> This subspecies is apparently an Atlantic slope form, and the small workers have a yellow to orange gaster distinctly lighter than the thorax. It has been collected at Limón, Puerto Viejo, and La Selva (Heredia).

E. burchelli parvispinum Forel, w, ♀, ♂
> This subspecies is apparently a Pacific slope form, and the workers have a black to reddish gaster about the same color as the thorax. It has been collected at Cañas, Monteverde, Vara Blanca, Rincón (Osa Peninsula), and Palmar Sur.

E. dulcius crassinode Borgmeier, w, ♀

E. hamatum (F.), w, ♀, ♂
> The most common light brown to orange species.

E. jansoni Forel, ♂
> Probably the male of *E. dulcius crassinode*.

E. lucanoides conquistador Weber, w, ♀

E. mexicanum Roger, w, ♀, ♂

E. vagans (Olivier), w, ♀, ♂
> Two or three subspecies of *E. mexicanum* and *E. vagans* have been reported from Costa Rica.

Labidus caecus (Latreille), w, ♀, ♂

L. curvipes (Emery), ♂

L. praedator (F. Smith), w, ♀, ♂
> The most common small black to reddish black swarm raider with swarms usually 1–3 m wide.

L. spininodis (Emery), w

Neivamyrmex adnepos (Wheeler), w

N. alfaroi (Emery), w, ♀

N. antillanus (Forel), w

N. asper Borgmeier, w

N. compressinodis Borgmeier, w

N. diana (Forel), w, ♀, ♂

N. digitistipus Watkins, ♂

N. fumosus (Forel), ♂

N. gibbatus Borgmeier, w, ♀

N. halidayi (Shuckard), ♂

N. humilis (Borgmeier) w, ♀, ♂

N. impudens (Mann), w

N. klugi distans Borgmeier, ♂

N. longiscapus Borgmeier, ♂

N. macrodentatus (Mennozi), w

N. melsheimeri (Haldemann), ♂

N. opacithorax (Emery), w, ♀, ♂

N. pilosus mexicanus (F. Smith) w, ♀, ♂

N. pullus Borgmeier, ♂
> Not reported from Costa Rica but reported from north and south of this country.

N. spatulatus (Borgmeier), ♂

N. spinolai (Westwood), w, ♀, ♂

N. spoliator (Forel), ♂

N. sumichrasti (Norton), w

N. swainsoni (Shuckard), ♂

Nomamyrmex esenbecki wilsoni (Santschi), w, ♂

N. hartigi (Westwood), w, ♂

Checklist of Acridoid Grasshoppers (Chapulines)

H. F. Rowell

Within each subfamily, genera and species are listed alphabetically, rather than by tribe or other measure of relatedness.

Taxon	Locality					
	La Selva (Puerto Viejo)	Cerro de la Muerte	Rincón and Corcovado National Park (Osa Peninsula)	Las Cruces, San Vito	Monteverde (Tilarán)	La Pacifica, Palo Verde, and Santa Rosa National Park (Lowland Guanacaste)
Proscopiidae						
Proscopia septentrionalis			X			
Eumastacidae						
Eumastax dentata			X			
E. robertsi	X					
E. surda			X			
E. sp. indet. 1				X		
E. sp. indet. 2					X	
E. sp. indet. 3						X
Pyrgomorphidae						
Prosphena scudderi					X	?
Romaleidae						
Romaleinae						
Phaeoparia phrygana				X		
Chromacris colorata					X	X
C. trogon	X					
Legua crenulata	X					
Munatia decorata	?					
Procolpia lankesteri	X					
Taeniopoda maxima	X					
T. varipennis						X
Tropidacris cristata	X		X	X	X	X
Xyleus centralis						X
Genus nov., nr. *Pseudohisychius*			X			
Bactrophorinae						
Bactrophorus mirabilis			X			
Mezentia gibbera			X			
M. sp. indet.	X					
Caenolampis osae			X			
C. robertsi	X					
Nautia costaricensis			X			
N. flavosignata	X					
Rhicnoderma humile						X
Rh. olivaceum			?			
Rh. sp. indet. 1	X					
Rh. sp. indet. 2			X			
Rh. sp. indet. 3				X		

651

Taxon	Locality					
	La Selva (Puerto Viejo)	Cerro de la Muerte	Rincón and Corcovado National Park (Osa Peninsula)	Las Cruces, San Vito	Monteverde (Tilarán)	La Pacifica, Palo Verde, and Santa Rosa National Park (Lowland Guanacaste)
Rh. sp. indet. 4					X	
Taeniophora femorata			X			
T. panamae			X			
T. sp. nov.	X					
Zoumolampis bradleyi	X					
Acrididae						
Proctolabinae						
Adelotettix gigas	X					
Ampelophilus olivaceus			X	X		
Balachowskyacris olivaceus	X					
B. robertsi			X			
Drymacris nebulicola					X	
Drymophilacris bimaculata	X					
D. monteverdensis					X	
Kritacris arboricola	X					
Leioscapheus gracilicornis			X	X		
L. guapiles	X					
L. laselvae	X					
L. variegatus			X			
Paratela ovatipennis					X	
Tela neeavora	X					
Zosperamerus planus	X		X			
Z. virgatus	X		X			
Rhytidochrotinae						
Hylopedetes gemmeus					X	
H. nigrithorax				X		
H. surdus					X	
Scirtopaon dorsatus					X	
Leptysminae						
Guetaresia lankesteri	X					
Leptysma marginocollis						X
Stenacris fissicauda	X		X	X		X
S. xanthochlora						X
Stenopola dorsalis						X
S. punticeps			X			
Copiocerinae						
Copiocera harroweri			X			
C. specularis	X					
Ommatolampinae						
Abracris flavolineata	X		X	X	X	X
A. obliqua						X
Ateliacris annulicornis			X	X		
Leptalacris fastigiata					X	
Leptomerinthoprora flavovittatus	X					
L. modesta				X		

Taxon	Locality					
	La Selva (Puerto Viejo)	Cerro de la Muerte	Rincón and Corcovado National Park (Osa Peninsula)	Las Cruces, San Vito	Monteverde (Tilarán)	La Pacifica, Palo Verde, and Santa Rosa National Park (Lowland Guanacaste)
L. sp. indet.			X			
Microtylopteryx fusiformis	X				X	
M. hebardi	X					
M. talamancae				X		
Pseudanniceris nigrinervis	X		X			
Rhachicreagra drymocnemensis					X	
R. melanota					X	
R. nothra	X					
R. obsidian			?	X		
R. khayachrosa				X		
Vilerna aeneo-oculata				X		X
Genus, sp. nov. nr. *Pauracris*				X		
Genus, sp. nov. nr. *Tamnacris*	X					
Cyrtacantharidinae						
Schistocerca centralis						X
S. nitens	X		X	X	X	X
S. pallens						X
Melanoplinae						
Aidemona azteca				X		
Baeacris talamancensis		X				
Dichroplus morosus					X	
Oedipodinae						
Heliastis costaricensis						X
Lactista pellepidus						X
Acridinae						
Achurum sumichrasti					X	X
Amblytropidia auriventris			X	X		
A. costaricensis						X
Metaleptea brevicornis	X		X	X	X	X
Orphula pagana			X	X	X	X
Gomphocerinae						
Orphulella punctata	X		X	X	X	X
Rhammatocerus viatorius						X
Silvitettix biolleyi						X
S. communis			X	X		
S. maculata					X	
S. thalassinus						X
Total number of spp. at each locality	35	2	34	23	22	27

Total number of spp. in Costa Rica (to date)   146

Total number of spp. at all OTS sites combined   101

Checklist of Butterflies

P. J. DeVries

The ecology of butterflies in the tropics is relatively untouched. Here I discuss some aspects of the ecology of butterflies in Costa Rica and provide a bibliography for the beginning student.

Adult Biology

Butterflies (including skippers) are mostly diurnal. The greatest period of activity for adults is usually between 0800 and 1400. However, most species have peaks of activity at certain hours of the day. For example, butterflies in the riodinid genus *Euselasia* are active at the forest edge very early in the morning, and by 0900 they move to the forest canopy or within the forest, where they remain relatively inactive for the remainder of the day. Some male lycaenid butterflies (*Arcas, Thecla, Calycopis*) perch at a particular place at the same time every day (G. B. Small, pers. comm.). Different species have different perching times.

In general, female butterflies oviposit between about 1100 and 1300. The exceptions are species in habitats where there are few hours of sun each day, such as at high elevations. In these habitats females may oviposit any time of the day that there is sunshine.

Some butterflies are active at dawn and dusk. The best-known crepuscular butterflies are the brassolids (*Caligo, Opsiphanes*). There are a few hesperiids (*Celaenorrhinus, Bungalotis*) that are crepuscular, as well as one species of satyrid, *Manataria maculata*. There is one species known to be active at night, *Celaenorrhinus fritzgaertneri* (Hesperiidae). This medium-sized brown skipper spends the day gregariously in caves and hollow tree trunks (P. J. DeVries and J. Schul, unpub. data) during the dry season in the deciduous forest at Santa Rosa National Park. I suspect that other butterflies previously thought to be crepuscular will turn out to be nocturnal. For example, the brassolid *Narope cyllastros* comes to candlelight and blacklights long after sunset, as do some species of *Tagetes*.

SEASONALITY AND MIGRATION

Seasonal fluctuation of adult butterflies has not been studied in Costa Rica. Obvious fluctuations in numbers of adults are best observed in seasonal habitats like the dry forest in Guanacaste. For the more "stable" habitats (La Selva, Corcovado) the fluctuations are less extreme yet readily observable.

In general, June and July are the months of highest adult butterfly density in all habitats in Cost Rica, though the peak may not be very obvious in the rain-forest community. These months are the first third of the rainy season on the Pacific side of Costa Rica and contain a short dry spell on the Atlantic side of the country.

It is during these months on the Pacific side that there is a great abundance of butterfly larvae feeding on the newly produced foliage; some species have a generation on the new plant growth, followed by a migration of many individuals to the Atlantic side (e.g., *Eunica monima,* pers. obs.). There is an obvious rapid change in species composition as the wet season progresses. It appears that some of the species, migrant or nonmigrant, pass the dry season in Guanacaste as rare individuals in moist microhabitats and reproduce when the rains come in May (e.g., *Eunica monima, Eurema diara, Eurytides epidaus, Siproeta stelenes,* and *Smyrna blomfildia,* pers. obs.). At this time, such species are generally in reproductive diapause (O. Taylor, J. McKinnley, unpub. data).

In Costa Rica the best-known "butterfly" migrations are those of *Urania fulgens* (Uranidae), a day-flying moth (colipato verde) that behaves like a butterfly (Smith 1972). In some years its southward migration is composed of millions of individuals coming from Honduras and ending in Colombia, apparently increasing in numbers along the way. In the past I have seen mountain passes near Cerro de la Muerte so full of these migrating moths that the asphalt highway was slick with the bodies of moths killed by cars. Costa Rican butterflies known to migrate are *Ascia monuste, Phoebis agarithe, P. sennae* (Pieridae), *Eunica monima, Marpesia chiron* (Nymphalidae), and *Libytheana carinenta* (Libytheidae). Some of these species are known to migrate great distances and have been recorded from ships at sea. See Williams (1930) for a summary of recorded migrations.

In addition to these seemingly unidirectional migrations, ithomiids in Costa Rica are known to migrate up and down the mountains with changes in local weather conditions (pers. obs.) and with changes in the season (Haber 1977; F. G. Stiles, unpub. data). The postulated reasons for butterfly migrations include predation and parasitism and changes in host-plant quality and abundance (see Johnson 1978 and included references), but we lack a study on the natural history of a particular butterfly migrating.

ADULT FOOD

Since adult butterflies feed through a proboscis, the food must be in a liquid state before it can be taken up. Taking nectar from flowers is their most widespread manner of feeding. Baker (1975) has shown that nectars of butterfly-visited flowers tend to be high in free amino acids and sugars and therefore provide a higher-quality resource than if they had the sugar-rich nectar of bee flowers. Butterfly flowers tend to be red. *Lantana camara*

(Verbenaceae), *Asclepias curassavica* (Asclepidaceae), and *Hamelia patens* (Rubiaceae), for example, are heavily visited by nectar-feeding butterflies. The white flowers of *Cordia* spp. (Boraginaceae) are frequently visited by lycaenids and riodinids; Opler, Baker, and Frankie (1975) have shown that these butterflies are very important as pollinators of *Cordia*. Flower visitation for pollen has been well documented by L. Gilbert for *Heliconius* butterflies and *Anguria* and *Gurania* (Cucurbitaceae) flowers, and this behavior may occur in other genera of butterflies as well (DeVries 1979). Using pollen as a food resource is a highly specialized behavior and has been shown to have an enormous influence on the demography and ecology of the butterflies that perform it (Gilbert 1972; Dunlap-Pianka, Boggs, and Gilbert 1977).

Some butterflies never visit flowers but rely on rotting fruit, dung, carrion, and fungi as sources of food. The members of the nymphalid subfamily Charaxinae (*Prepona, Agrias, Anaea*) are almost never seen at flowers and are adept at locating small amounts of rotting fruits in the middle of the forest. Other non-flower-feeding nymphalids are *Hamadryas, Historis, Catonephele, Epiphile,* and *Eunica*. There are great differences in the attractiveness of various rotting foods to different species of butterflies. For example, I have used traps baited with fermenting bananas in habitats where there are many species of fruit feeders, yet only a small percentage visit the traps. I have taken some species of non-flower-feeding butterflies only on dog feces and have never seen them on any other occasion. To my knowledge there are no studies on food requirements or preferences of these non-flower-feeding butterflies in the Neotropics.

Feeding attractants are not always food. For example, Pliske (1975*a,b*) has shown that male ithomiids and danaids visit plants containing pyrrolizidine alkaloids (Boraginaceae and Compositae), which they use as precursors in their biosynthesis of mating pheromones. These are in turn used to generate multiple-species leks (Haber 1977). Some Costa Rican species of *Epidendrum* (Orchidaceae) may contain similar alkaloids as they also attract visits by male ithomiids (P. J. DeVries and C. Todzia, unpub. data). Male Papilionidae and Pieridae visit sand wet with water or urine to obtain sodium salts (Arms, Feeny, and Lederhouse 1974); these authors postulated that the salts are a necessary nutrient. Although this may be the case, in light of the recent work on chemicals used in sexual attraction, it may be that these males are getting a needed precursor for a mating pheromone.

Biology of Immatures
Butterfly larvae (caterpillars) are a mouth with chewing mandibles and a long body to house a long gut. Nearly all butterfly larvae are herbivores, and an individual gener-

ally takes only a very small fraction of the total biomass of a host plant. Some lycaenid larvae are predators on scale insects and ant larvae. Ehrlich and Raven (1965) have summarized host-plant data and have shown that related groups of butterflies feed on related plant taxa; they also coined the term coevolution to describe this phenomenon, which it almost certainly is not (D. H. Janzen, pers. comm.). Although the herbivore pressure that Costa Rican butterflies exert on their host plants is usually small compared with other insect herbivores, some have become major pests in crops (e.g., *Caligo* in banana plantations). *Heliconius* butterflies may exert selection pressure sufficient to influence leaf shape (Gilbert 1975). Although the host plants for many Neotropical butterfly genera are known, the bulk of the Costa Rican species are in need of detailed life history studies like those of Muyshondt (1976). The greatest gaps in knowledge of life histories are in the Lycaenidae, Riodinidae, and Hesperiidae.

Butterfly larvae may be either gregarious or solitary. Gregarious larvae are usually synchronous in their feeding, molts, pupation, and emergence. If molested, an aggregation of larvae reacts as a unit, which is thought to intensify defenses against predators and parasitoids. Solitary larvae have defenses such as crypsis, mimicry (e.g., of bird feces as in *Papilio*, flower buds and fruits as in lycaenids, or vegetation as in some pierids and satyrids), noxious chemicals, or leaf and silk houses. Frass chains made by the early instars appear to be characteristic of all Costa Rican Charaxinae (pers. obs.), which in later instars roll up leaves and live inside the rolls. Most lycaenid and riodinid larvae are tended by ants, as are aphids and other homopterans.

Most butterflies pupate off the host plant as single cryptic individuals. However some species, such as *Eumaeus minyas* (Lycaenidae), *Perute charops* (Pieridae), *Heliconius hewitsoni* (Nymphalidae), and *Melanis pixie* (Riodinidae), pupate gregariously in groups of up to fifty chrysalids, and adult emergence is simultaneous or occurs within a day or two. The females of some species of *Heliconius* butterflies mate while still in the chrysalis. The female inside the chrysalis emits a pheromone, and the male mates with her before she emerges.

The pupal stage has been badly neglected in ecological investigations and is an open field for studies of site, sociality, defenses, predation, rates, and so forth.

Habitats
In general it is difficult to speak of butterflies with respect to habitats. There are several zones where some genera and species are localized.

Pacific deciduous forest: obvious fluctuations in adult density throughout the year; some species characteristic

655

of Mexico reach their southern limit —for example, *Parides photinus, P. montezuma* (Papilionidae); generally species rich.

Pacific evergreen: characterized by the Osa Peninsula; very species rich (especially in riodinids and lycaenids); butterfly fauna characteristic of Panama, some South American species (e.g., *Heliconius hewitsoni, Papilio ascolius*); many of the ithomiid subspecies show a change to the southern forms.

Mid-elevation: both Atlantic and Pacific from about 500 to 1,600 m; a zone rich in species where there is a mixture of high- and low-elevation species.

High elevations: obviously very wet habitats, above 1,700 m to 3,000 m; few if any riodinids, a proliferation of satyrid genera with affinities to the South American Andes (e.g., *Lymanopoda, Oxeoschistus, Cyllopsis, Catyrginnis*); some endemics to above 2,600 m (e.g., *Catasticta cerberus*). Adults are specialists at living with very little sunshine per day.

Mountain passes: areas of mixtures of Atlantic and Pacific species; few hours of sun per day; some contain many endemic species (e.g., Bajo la Hondura, La Virgen del Socorro); ranges from 500 to over 1,500 m elevation.

Atlantic evergreen forest: very wet, very species rich; mixtures of Guatemalan and South American species, some endemics (e.g., *Dynamine ate, Perisama barnesi*).

Characterization of Butterfly Families in Costa Rica

The relationships of butterfly families and subfamilies, as conceived by Ehrlich's (1958) analysis of many characters, is portrayed in figure 11.1.

PAPILIONIDAE

Papilionidae are medium to moderately large butterflies with six walking legs, antennal clubs well developed, antennae with a distinctive gentle upward curve, and hind wings having tails in some species. The larvae all have eversible scent glands (osmeteria), and the chemicals they produce are believed to be defensive against predators and parasitoids. The osmeteria are everted from a pouch behind the head when the caterpillar is molested, and they are found only in papilionid larvae. The larvae have no spiny projections, are naked, and in some genera bear fleshy papillae. Colors vary from mottled brown yellow, mimicking bird feces, to bright red and white. The host plants in Costa Rica are Aristilochiaceae (*Battus, Parides*), Annonaceae (*Eurytides*), Rutaceae, Piperaceae, Lauraceae, Umbelliferae, and Hernandiaceae (*Papilio*).

All the species except those in the genus *Eurytides* are freqently seen feeding on flowers, especially those of *Lantana camara, Hamelia,* and *Stachytarpheta.* Species of *Eurytides* rarely visit flowers but on occasion are observed on the inflorescences of *Cordia* (Boraginaceae) and *Casearia* (Flacourtiaceae). The males of many spe-

cies are often seen drinking at puddles along with pierids and other puddling butterflies. The family occurs in all habitats in Costa Rica. Most species in the genus *Papilio, Battus,* and *Eurytides* fly in bright sunshine, whereas all the *Parides* species are forest butterflies that are seldom seen in the open.

PIERIDAE

Pieridae are small to medium-sized butterflies with six walking legs. Most of the species are white, yellow, or black, or some combination thereof. Some species are mimics of ithomiid, *Heliconius,* or danaid butterflies, but can be recognized by the six walking legs. The larvae are generally green and often have yellow or black bands or stripes. The head capsule of the larva is round, with surface granulations. The host plants in Costa Rica are Leguminosae, Capparidaceae, Cruciferae, Simaroubaceae, and Loranthaceae.

Most of the species of this family fly in open sunny areas; the mimetic species are forest insects. All species feed on flower nectar and are common along forest edges, trails, pastures, and gardens. The males of many species drink at puddles in large aggregations. All the species except the mimetic forest species fly very rapidly.

ITHOMIIDAE

Ithomiidae are small to medium-sized butterflies with four walking legs and elongate front wings. Most species have transparent or semiopaque wings, and many are striped in orange, black, and yellow. The antennae lack well-developed clubs, the head is small in relation to the body in most of the species (compare with *Heliconius*), and the males of all species have tufts of scent hairs arising from the upper side of the costa of the hind wing. All are forest butterflies that have a characteristic lazy flight with deep wingbeats. The larvae are naked and lack spines or hairs. Some genera have fleshy horizontal projections arising near the base of the prolegs. The larvae are a variety of colors, and colors vary at the generic level. They may be green, white with black and orange rings, dull gray with blue and red markings, and so on. Many of the larvae are cryptic while on the host plant. The host plants are in the Solanaceae and Apocynaceae.

Ithomiids are frequently seen feeding on flowers along forest edges, trails, and watercourses or in aggregations in the forest. These aggregations are multigeneric leks and tend to appear in the same site day after day. The males are attracted to dead plants of certain Boraginaceae (*Helitropium, Myosotis*) and certain composite flowers, where they extract precursors for mating pheromones, which are in turn used to generate the lek. Many of the species in Costa Rica migrate seasonally along an altitudinal gradient. All the species are considered distasteful to vertebrate predators and serve as models for Müllerian and Batesian mimicry complexes.

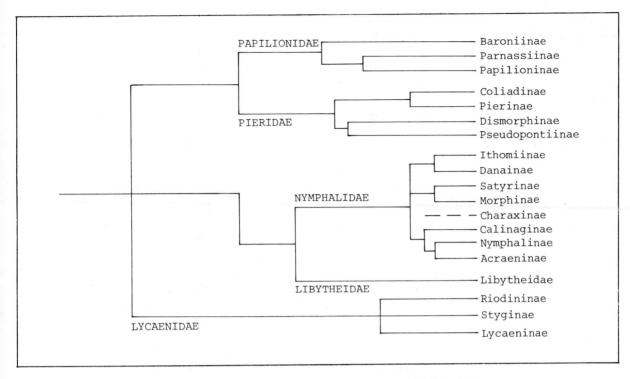

FIGURE 11.1. Relationships of the families and subfamilies of the butterflies (after Ehrlich 1958).

DANAIDAE

Danaidae are medium-sized butterflies that are dull orange or brown like the monarch butterfly or mimetically resemble ithomiids or heliconiids. The front wing apex is somewhat elongate, and they have four walking legs and short, fairly stout antennae. All but one Costa Rican species have white dots on the black thorax. Males of some species have abdominal "hair-pencils" that evert when the thorax is lightly pinched. The larvae are usually white with alternating rings of dark colors and bear two mobile whiplike papillae near the head. The host plants are Apocynaceae, Asclepiadaceae, Caricaceae, and Moraceae.

The Costa Rican species that look like monarch butterflies fly in open second-growth areas. The remaining species fly in the forest along watercourses, forest edges, and tree falls. The forest species are frequently encountered on the flowers of *Senecio* (Compositae), and the species of more open areas are found on the flowers of *Asclepias curassavica* (Asclepiadaceae) or *Lantana camara* (Verbenaceae).

Satyridae

Subfamily Brassolinae

Brassolinae are medium-sized to large butterflies with four walking legs. Most species have prominent ocelli (apparent vertebrate eye mimics) on the underside of the hind wing. The larvae are large and dull green or brown. The head capsule usually has a corona of stout clublike horns, the dorsal two being the largest. The last segment of the larva is split into a forked tail, and all the larvae are very cryptic when on the host plant. The host plants are in the Musaceae, Heliconiaceae, Marantaceae, Palmae, Bromeliaceae, and Gramineae (especially bamboos).

They are frequently seen at dawn or dusk, flying along watercourses, trails, or forests edge; they are active during the day only in the deep shade of the forest. None of the species feed on flower nectar, but all feed on sugar-rich rotting fruits or on sap flows from wounds in tree trunks.

Subfamily Satyrinae

Satyrinae are small to medium-sized butterflies, and most species are dull brown with the underside marked with small ocelli. They have four walking legs, and the base of the costal vein in the forewing is swollen like a bladder. The larvae are dull green or brown, usually with a forked tail, and the head capsule may be round and unadorned or bear two short, stout dorsal horns. All their larvae are very cryptic and lethargic on the host plant. The host plants are in the Gramineae, Cyperaceae, Palmae, Marantaceae, Heliconiaceae, and Selaginellaceae.

Nearly all species are forest understory inhabitants or fly in well-shaded areas. At high elevations they are most frequently encountered in or near bamboo thickets. None of the species feed on flower nectar, but all feed on sugar-rich rotting fruits, carrion, or sap flows that have been invaded by fungi. Some feed at decomposing fungi

657

on the forest floor. Very few species are brightly colored, and all but a few white or blue *Euptychia* are very cryptic.

Subfamily Morphinae

Morphinae are large, fast-flying blue butterflies, though one species is red on the underside and gray above and is seen gliding about in the forest canopy. The larvae are mottled bright red and yellow, the head capsule has a dense covering of erect hairs, and there are tufts of hair on the body. Larvae feed on Leguminosae in Costa Rica and are recorded on Erythroxylaceae, Gramineae (bamboos), and Menispermaceae in South America. Owing to the unusual larval morphology there is uncertainty about the systematic affinities of the morpho subfamily.

All Costa Rican species are forest butterflies. They are frequently seen along trails, watercourses, and forest edges, where they are conspicuous because of their brightly colored blue upper sides and multiocellated undersides.

NYMPHALIDAE

Subfamily Charaxinae

Charaxinae are medium-sized to large butterflies with a strong thorax and four walking legs. The antennae are stout and gradually thicken toward the apex. Most of the species are blue against a dark background on the upper side of the wings, but some are orange or brown with the underside of the wings being cryptic and mimicking a dead leaf. The larvae bear no spines but have fleshy warts or granulate bumps that may be brightly colored. The head capsule bears two stout dorsal horns or large granulate warts. The early-instar larvae make frass chains off the leaf edge, and some later instars roll leaves into cylinders in which they rest when not feeding. The host plants are Euphorbiaceae, Piperaceae, Leguminosae, Lauraceae, and Erythroxylaceae. Owing to the morphology of the larvae, pupae, and wing veins, some authors consider this group a separate family.

All the members of this large group of butterflies feed on sugar-rich fruit juices or sap flows or at animal carcasses. None of the species feed on flower nectar; all are forest butterflies that spend much of their time in the forest canopy when not feeding on fallen fruits. While on the ground or on tree trunks they are very difficult to see owing to the dead leaf coloration of the underside. When disturbed they fly rapidly upward to the canopy. Males are frequently observed to perch on subcanopy leaves in light gaps in the forest and to patrol small areas. There are a substantial number of species in Costa Rica that are known from a few specimens in museums. Very little is known about the natural history of most of the species.

Subfamily Apaturinae

Apaturinae are small to medium-sized butterflies with dimorphic sexes. The males have iridescent blue, green, or purple upper sides to the wings, while females have a large medial transverse white stripe on the upper side (resemble many species of *Adelpha*). Both sexes are pale white or yellowish on the underside. The larvae resemble those of satyrids and charaxines but differ in having a pair of branched horns on the head capsule. The larvae never have spines but are covered in a dense pile of short hairs. In Costa Rica none of the species have been reared.

These butterflies are most frequently encountered drinking at puddles, on riverbanks, or at water seepage on road cuts, but all the species are fast fliers and are difficult to catch while drinking. Occasionally they are encountered feeding on flower nectar of *Cordia* (Boraginaceae).

Subfamily Nymphalinae

Nymphalinae have four walking legs and well-developed antennal clubs that are often spatulate. This subfamily contains many patterns and wing shapes, as well as many sizes and color patterns. The larvae, though diverse in morphology, are all spiny. Some species bear branched spines all over the body. The head capsule may bear spines or may be naked, and the pupae usually bear spines as well. The larvae feed on many families and species of plants. Some important host-plant families are Euphorbiaceae, Passifloraceae, Acanthaceae, Compositae, Rubiaceae, Ulmaceae, Urticaceae, Sapindaceae, and Amaranthaceae.

This group of butterflies is found in all habitats, from open pastures to rain forest at high to low elevations. Also within this subfamily there is a large array of feeding behaviors by adults. They feed at flower nectar and pollen, fruits, and puddles. Mimicry systems are well developed in this group (though most are Batesian mimics except for *Heliconius*).

LIBYTHEIDAE

The Neotropics contains only one genus of Libytheidae; *Libytheana* is easily recognized by its very long, snout-like palpi. The larvae have not been reared in Costa Rica, but host-plant records from the rest of the world indicate that they feed on *Celtis* (Ulmaceae).

Adults are freqently encountered drinking at puddles along road cuts or in pastures. They exhibit a variable density from year to year and are known for their migratory habits in the southern United States.

LYCAENIDAE

These small butterflies often have threadlike tails on the hind wing underside margins that, when the animal is perched with its wings folded over its back, appear to be antennae on a head. Most of the Costa Rican species have iridescent blue upper sides. The males have four walking legs while the females have six, and both sexes usually perch on the top sides of leaves. The larvae are sluglike, usually uniform in color, and often mimic flower buds or fruits. They are tended by ants. There are many families of plants recorded as larval hosts, for example, Leguminosae, Anacardiaceae, Lauraceae, Rosaceae, and Fagaceae.

These butterflies are most frequently encountered on plants with tiny flowers (especially Boraginaceae), where they feed on flower nectar. Males of some of the species are known to have specific perching times during the course of a day and are faithful to their perch day after day. They may be found in almost all habitats in Costa Rica.

RIODINIDAE

These small butterflies have long, thin antennae and most species are beautifully colored with metallic gold or silver spots on the undersides. These butterflies usually perch on the undersides of leaves (see Lycaenidae) with the wings held horizontally. The larvae are similar to those of the lycaenids, but they often have forked head capsules and may even be hairy. The sides of the larvae are "skirted" ventrally (wider at the bottom than at the top) and these "skirts" are held tightly appressed to the substrate of the host plant. The larvae are usually tended by ants that feed on a visible "honey gland" on the dorsum. They feed on the leaf tissue of a great diversity of host plants (e.g., Costaceae, Margraviaceae, Leguminosae, Verbenaceae, Lecythidaceae, Lauraceae, Passifloraceae, Marantaceae, Orchidaceae, Euphorbiaceae, and Vouchysiaceae).

The butterflies are often encountered on flowers (especially Boraginaceae), where they feed on nectar. The bulk of the species are forest inhabitants, and few species occur above 1,400 m elevation in Costa Rica.

HESPERIIDAE

Hesperiidae are small to medium-sized butterflies; many are dull brown with white spotting, with or without tails on the hind wings, and some are metalically colored. The characteristic hooks on the tips of the antennae separate this family from all other diurnal lepidopterans. The larvae are naked, often brightly colored, and the head capsule is large and without spines (with a distinctive constricted neck). The larvae roll leaves in which they roost in the daytime, and they feed at night on a diversity of host plants. Some important ones are in the Gramineae, Palmae, Leguminosae, Piperaceae, Rutaceae, Myrtaceae, and Rubiaceae.

These butterflies are encountered in all habitats in Costa Rica. Some species have extraordinarily large geographic ranges. All feed on flower nectar, and it is common to encounter them feeding on fresh bird feces. Some of the species have very long probosces and are able to feed at flowers with long corolla tubes that are normally thought of as hummingbird or hawkmoth flowers.

Provisional Checklist
The following is a nearly complete list of the butterfly species of Costa Rica. The records are based on specimens of known Costa Rican origin that I have seen in the collections of the Museo Nacional de Costa Rica, United States National Museum, Carnegie Museum, Allyn Museum of Entomology, British Museum (Natural History), Museum of Comparative Zoology (Harvard), and the private collections of G. B. Small, P. A. Opler, K. Wolfe, D. H. Janzen, and F. G. Stiles. Additionally, I have included published records of Costa Rican butterflies from Seitz (1910–12), Godman and Salvin (1879–1901), Rothschild and Jordan (1906), and Fox (1968). The nomenclature follows that of these authors. At present (1980), synonymies and nomenclatorial details are under study by a project sponsored by the Smithsonian Institution. That work has not been published, but I have used some of the names of Nymphalidae to be published by G. Lamas in this project. The names in parentheses that follow the name used in this list are old synonyms commonly encountered in the literature. Satyridae, Lycaenidae, and Hesperiidae deserve special comment.

Satyridae: There is no satisfactory classification for the tribe Euptychini at present. M. Singer (pers. comm.) says there is disagreement between many of the Seitz names and the type specimens in the British Museum (Natural History). Caution should be used when referring to the names on the present list. I have followed the broad definition of "*Euptychia*" used by Seitz rather than splitting it into the many genera erected by Forster (1964) for this group (except for *Cyllopsis;* Miller 1974). The higher classification of the satyrids follows Miller (1968).

Lycaenidae: The taxonomy of this family is very poorly developed in the Neotropics. The broadly defined generic name "*Thecla*" is used because better-defined generic names are unavailable. The names on the list have been taken from published records in Godman and Salvin (1879–1901), Schaus (1913), Clench (1955), Field (1967a,b), and Nicolay (1971a,b), except for those species recorded from the San Vito area, which are based on specimens collected by G. Small and myself.

Hesperiidae: All the hesperiid names in this list have been taken from the Catalogs of the American Hesperiidae, volumes 1–4, by Evans (1951, 1952, 1953, 1955). His work is based on specimens in the British Museum (Natural History), and I have included only those species that Evans records from Costa Rica. The present hesperiid list is very incomplete and includes at most 50% of the Costa Rican species.

The symbols to the right of the species names indicate records from Costa Rican field sites frequented by OTS and related groups of biologists. The records are based on specimens collected by G. Small, D. Janzen, P. Opler, L. Gilbert, M. Singer, W. Haber, and myself. The families Lycaenidae, Riodinidae, and Hesperiidae are not included in the field site lists.

Authors of the field site lists are: La Selva, DeVries and Opler; San Vito, Small and DeVries; and Corcovado National Park, Santa Rosa National Park, Monteverde, Colonia Socorro, and Cerro de la Muerte, DeVries. H. K. Clench is the author of the riodinid list.

ACKNOWLEDGMENTS
I thank the following persons for support: H. Clench, W. Field, L. Gilbert, L. Gómez, D. Harvey, D. Janzen, G. Lamas, L. Miller, P. Opler, R. Silberglied, M. Singer, G. Small, F. G. Stiles, C. Todzia, R. Vane-Wright, and T. F. Waller.

And W. Hallwachs, who typed it.

*

Adams, M. 1973. Ecological zonation and the butterflies of the Sierra Nevada de Santa Marta, Colombia (Lepidoptera). *J. Nat. Hist.* 7:699–718.

Alexander, A. J. 1961. A study of the biology and behavior of the caterpillars and emerging butterflies of the subfamily Heliconiinae in Trinidad, West Indies. Part 1. Some aspects of larval behavior. *Zoologica* 46:1–24.

Arms, K.; Feeny, P.; and Lederhouse, R. C. 1974. Sodium: Stimulus for puddling behavior by tiger swallowtail butterflies, *Papilio glaucus*. *Science* 185:372–74.

Baker, H. G. 1975. Studies of nectar-constitution and pollinator-plant coevolution. In *Coevolution of animals and plants,* ed. L. E. Gilbert and P. R. Raven, pp. 100–140. Austin: University of Texas Press.

Benson, W. W. 1971. Evidence for the evolution of unpalatability through kin selection in the Heliconiinae (Lepidoptera). *Am. Nat.* 105:213–26.

———. 1972. Natural selection for Müllerian mimicry in *Heliconius erato* in Costa Rica. *Science* 176:936–39.

Brower, L. P., and Brower, J. V. Z. 1962. The relative abundance of model and mimic butterflies in natural populations of the *Battus philenor* mimicry complex. *Ecology* 43:154–58.

———. 1964. Birds, butterflies, and plant poisons: A study in ecological chemistry. *Zoologica* 49:137–59.

Brown, K. S., and Benson, W. W. 1974. Adaptive polymorphism associated with multiple Müllerian mimicry in *Heliconius numata*. *Biotropica* 6:205–28.

Brown, K. S.; Sheppard, P. M.; and Turner, J. R. G. 1974. Quaternary refugia in tropical America: Evidence from race formation in *Heliconius* butterflies. *Proc. Roy. Soc. London* 187:369–78.

Carpenter, G. D. H. 1941. The relative frequency of beak-marks on butterflies of different edibility to birds. *Proc. Zool. Soc. London* 3:223–30.

———. 1942. Observations and experiments in Africa by the late C. F. M. Swynnerton on wild birds eating butterflies and the preference shown. *Proc. Linn. Soc. London* 154:10–46.

Clench, H. K. 1955. A revised classification of the butterfly family Lycaenidae and its allies. *Ann. Carnegie Mus.* 16:261–74.

Collenette, C. L., and Talbot, G. 1928. Observations on the bionomics of the Lepidoptera of Matto Grosso, Brazil. *Trans. Ent. Soc. London* 76:391–416.

Cook, L. M.; Frank, K.; and Brower, L. P. 1971. Experiments on the demography of tropical butterflies. 1. Survival rate and density in two species of *Parides*. *Biotropica* 3:17–20.

DeVries, P. J. 1979. Pollen feeding in Costa Rican *Battus* and *Parides* butterflies (Papilionidae). *Biotropica* 11:237–38.

Downey, J. C. 1962. Host plant relations as data for butterfly classification. *Syst. Zool.* 11:150–59.

Dunlap-Pianka, H.; Boggs, C. L.; and Gilbert, L. E. 1977. Ovarian dynamics in heliconiine butterflies: Programmed senescence versus eternal youth. *Science* 197:487–90.

Ehrlich, P. R. 1958. The comparative morphology, phylogeny, and higher classification of the butterflies (Lepidoptera: Papilionidae). *Univ. Kansas Sci. Bull.* 39:305–70.

Ehrlich, P. R., and Gilbert, L. E. 1973. Population structure and dynamics of the tropical butterfly *Heliconius ethilla*. *Biotropica* 5:69–82.

Ehrlich, P. R., and Raven, P. H. 1965. Butterflies and plants: A study in coevolution. *Evolution* 18:586–608.

Emmel, T. C., and Leck, C. F. 1969. Seasonal changes in organization of tropical rain forest butterfly populations in Panama. *J. Res. Lepid.* 8:133–52.

Erickson, J. M., and Feeny, P. 1974. Sinigrin: A chemical barrier to the black swallowtail butterfly, *Papilio polyxenes*. *Ecology* 55:103–11.

Evans, W. H. 1951. Catalog of the American Hesperiidae in the British Museum. Part 1. Introduction and Pyrrhopyginae. *Brit. Mus. Publ. London*, pp. 1–92.

———. 1952. Catalog of the American Hesperiidae in the British Museum. Part 2. Pyrginae. *Brit. Mus. Publ. London*, pp. 1–178.

———. 1953. Catalog of the American Hesperiidae in the British Museum. Part 3. Pyrginae. *Brit. Mus. Publ. London*, pp. 1–232.

———. 1955. Catalog of the American Hesperiidae in the British Museum. Part 4. Hesperiinae and Megathyminae. *Brit. Mus. Pub. London*, pp. 1–499.

Feeny, P. 1975. Biochemical coevolution between plants and their insect herbivores. In *Coevolution of animals and plants,* ed. L. E. Gilbert and P. R. Raven, pp. 1–19. Austin: University of Texas Press.

Field, W. D. 1967a. Preliminary revision of the butterflies of the genus *Calycopis* Scudder (Lycaenidae: Theclinae). *Proc. U.S. Nat. Mus.,* vol. 119, no. 3552.

———. 1967b. Butterflies of the new genus *Calystryma* (Lycaenidae: Theclinae, Strymonini). *Proc. U.S. Nat. Mus.,* vol. 123, no. 3611.

Ford, E. B. 1945. *Butterflies*. London: Collins.

Forster, W. 1964. Beiträge zur Kenntnis der In-secktenfaun Boliviens. XIX. Lepidoptera III. Satyridae. *Veröff. Zool. Staatssaml. München,* 8:51–188.

Fox, R. M. 1968. Ithomiidae (Lepidoptera: Nymphaloidea) of Central America. *Trans. Am. Ent. Soc.* 94:155–208.

Gilbert, L. E. 1969. On the ecology of natural dispersal: *Dione moneta* in Texas (Nymphalidae). *J. Lep. Soc.* 23:177–85.

———. 1971. Butterfly-plant coevolution: Has *Passiflora adenopoda* won the selectional race with heliconiine butterflies? *Science* 172:585–86.

———. 1972. Pollen feeding and reproductive biology of *Heliconius* butterflies. *Proc. Nat. Acad. Sci.* 69:1403–7.

———. 1975. Ecological conseqeunces of coevolved mutualism between butterflies and plants. In *Coevolution of animals and plants,* ed. L. E. Gilbert and P. R. Raven, pp. 210–40. Austin: University of Texas Press.

Gilbert, L. E., and Singer, M. C. 1975. Butterfly ecology. *Ann. Rev. Ecol. Syst.* 6:365–97.

Godman, F. D., and Salvin, O. 1879–1901. *Biologia Centrali Americana Insecta: Lepidoptera-Rhopalocera.* London: R. H. Porter.

Haber, W. 1977. Evolutionary ecology of tropical mimetic butterflies (Lepidoptera: Ithominae). Ph.D. diss., University of Minnesota.

Hemming, F. 1967. The generic names of the butterflies and their type-species. *Bull. Brit. Mus. (Nat. Hist.), Ent.* 9(suppl.):1–509.

Johnson, C. G. 1978. *Migration and dispersal of insects by flight.* London: Methuen.

Krieger, R. I.; Feeny, P.; and Wilkinson, C. G. 1971. Detoxification enzymes in the guts of caterpillars: An evolutionary answer to plant defenses? *Science* 172:579–81.

Miller, L. D. 1968. The higher classification, phylogeny, and zoogeography of the Satyridae (Lepidoptera). *Mem. Am. Ent. Soc.* 24:1–174.

———. 1974. Revision of the Euptychiinae (Satyridae). 2. *Cyllopsis* R. Felder. *Bull. Allyn Mus.,* no. 20.

Muyshondt, A. 1976. Notes on the life cycle and natural history of butterflies of El Salvador. 7. *Archeoprepona demophon centralis* (Nymphalidae). *J. Lep. Soc.* 30:23–32.

Nicolay, S. S. 1971a. A revision of the genus *Arcas* with descriptions of new species (Lycaenidae, Strymonini). *J. Lep. Soc.* 25:87–108.

———. 1971b. A new genus of hairstreak from Central and South America (Lycaenidae, Theclinae). *J. Lep. Soc.* 25(suppl.) 1:1–39.

Norris, M. J. 1936. The feeding habits of the adult Lepidoptera Heteroneura. *Trans. Roy. Ent. Soc. London* 85:61–90.

Opler, P. A.; Baker, H. G.; and Frankie, G. W. 1975. Reproductive biology of some Costa Rican *Cordia* species (Boraginaceae). *Biotropica* 7:234–47.

Owen, D. F. 1971. *Tropical butterflies.* Oxford: Clarendon.

Owen, D. F., and Chanter, D. O. 1972. Species diversity and seasonal abundance in *Charaxes* butterflies (Nymphalidae). *J. Ent.,* ser. A, 46:135–43.

Papageorgis, C. 1974. The adaptive significance of wing coloration of mimetic Neotropical butterflies. Ph.D. diss., Princeton University.

Pliske, T. E. 1975a. Attraction of Lepidoptera to plants containing pyrrolizidine alkaloids. *Environ. Ent.* 4:455–73.

———. 1975b. Pollination of pyrrolizidine alkaloid-containing plants by male Lepidoptera. *Environ. Ent.* 4:474–79.

Ross, G. N. 1966. Life history studies on Mexican butterflies. 4. The ecology and ethology of *Anatole rossi,* a myrmecophilous metal mark (Lepidoptera: Riodinidae). *Ann. Ent. Soc. Am.* 59:985–1004.

Rothschild, W., and Jordan, K. 1906. A revision of the American papilios. *Nov. Zool.* 13:411–752.

Schaus, W. 1913. New species of Rhopalocera from Costa Rica. *Proc. Zool. Soc. London* 24:339–72.

Schemske, D. W. 1976. Pollinator specificity in *Lantana camara* and *L. trifolia* (Verbenaceae). *Biotropica* 8:260–64.

Scott, J. A. 1974. Mate-locating behavior of butterflies. *Am. Midl. Nat.* 91:103–16.

Seitz, A. 1910–12. *Die Grossschmetterlinge de Erde,* vol. 5, Stuttgart: Alfred Kernan.

Singer, M. C. 1972. Complex components of habitat suitability within a butterfly colony. *Science* 173:75–77.

Smiley, J. 1978a. Plant chemistry and the evolution of host specificity: Evidence from *Heliconius* and *Passiflora. Science* 201:745–47.

———. 1978b. The host-plant ecology of *Heliconius* butterflies in northeastern Costa Rica. Ph.D. diss., University of Texas.

Smith, N. G. 1972. Migrations of the day-flying moth *Urania* in Central and South America. *Carib. J. Sci.* 12:45–58.

Southwood, T. R. E. 1962. Migrations of terrestrial arthropods in relations to habitat. *Biol. Rev.* 37:171–214.

Stichel, H. 1910–11. Lepidoptera, Riodinidae. *Gen. Ins.,* fasc. 112A (1910), pp. 1–238; fasc. 112B (1911), pp. 239–452.

———. 1928. Lepidoptera, Nemeobiinae. *Tierreida,* Lieferung 51.

Swynnerton, C. F. M. 1926. An investigation into the defenses of the butterflies of the genus *Charaxes.* 3. *Int. Ent. Kongr.* 2:478–506.

Wagner, W. H., Jr. 1973. An orchid attractant for monarch butterflies (Danaidae). *J. Lep. Soc.* 27:192–96.

Watt, W. B.; Hoch, P. C.; and Mills, S. 1974. Nectar resource use by *Colias* butterflies: Chemical and visual aspects. *Oecologia* 14:353–74.

Williams, C. B. 1930. *The migration of butterflies.* Edinburgh: Oliver and Boyd.

Young, A. M. 1972. Community ecology of some rainforest butterflies. *Am. Midl. Nat.* 87:146–57.

	La Selva	San Vito	Corcovado National Park	Santa Rosa National Park	Monte-verde	Colonia del Socorro	La Montura	Cerro de la Muerte
Papilionidae								
Battus belus varus Kollar	X	X	X	X	X	X	X	
B. crassus Cramer	X		X					
B. loadamas rhipidius Rothschild & Jordan							X	
B. lycidas Cramer								
B. polydamas Linnaeus	X	X	X	X	X	X	X	
Parides arcas mylottes Bates	X	X	X	X	X	X	X	
P. childrenae Gray	X		X			X	X	
P. erithalion sadyattes Druce	X					X		
P. iphidamas Fabricius	X	X	X	X		X	X	
P. lycimenes Boisduval	X					X		
P. montezuma Westwood				X				
P. photinus Doubleday				X	X			
P. sessostris zestos Gray	X				X			
Eurytides agesilaus neosilaus Hopffer			X					
E. branchus Doubleday				X				
E. caliste olbius Rothschild & Jordan						X	X	
E. epidaus Doubleday				X				
E. euryleon clusoculis Butler	X		X		X	X	X	
E. ilus hostilius Felder								
E. lacandones Bates			X					
E. marchandi panamensis Oberthur	X		X			X	X	
E. orabilis Butler		X	X			X	X	
E. pausanias prasinus Rothschild & Jordan	X							
E. phaon Boisduval								
E. philolaus Guerin				X				
E. protesilaus dariensis Rothschild & Jordan			X			X	X	
Papilio anchisiades idaeus Fabricius	X	X	X	X	X	X	X	
P. androgeus epidarus Godman & Salvin		X	X	X				
P. ascolius zalates Godman & Salvin		X				X		
P. astylas pallas Gray								
P. birchalli Hewitson	X					X		
P. cleotas archytas Hopffer					X			X
P. cresphontes Linnaeus	X	X	X	X	X	X	X	
P. garamas syedra Godman & Salvin								X
P. isidorus chironis Rothschild & Jordan								
P. polyxenes stabilis Rothschild & Jordan		X			X			
P. rhodostictus Butler & Druce		X						
P. thoas nealcles Rothschild & Jordan	X	X	X	X		X		
P. torquatus tolmides Godman & Salvin								
P. victorinus vulneratus Butler					X	X		
Pieridae								
Dismorphinae								
Dismorphia amphiona praxinoe Doubleday	X	X	X			X		

	La Selva	San Vito	Corcovado National Park	Santa Rosa National Park	Monte-verde	Colonia del Socorro	La Montura	Cerro de la Muerte
D. crisia lubina Butler		X			X	X	X	
D. eunoe desine Hewitson					X	X	X	
D. lua costaricensis Schaus								
D. theucarilla fortunata Lucas	X	X				X		
D. zaela oreas Salvin						X	X	
D. zathoe pallidula Butler & Druce		X			X	X	X	
Enantia licina marion Godman & Salvin	X					X		
E. melite amalia Staudinger		X				X	X	
Lieinix cinarescens Salvin								X
L. nemesis Godman & Salvin		X			X	X	X	X
L. viridifascia Butler								X
Patia orise sorona Butler	X	X				X		
Pseudopieris Godman & Salvin								
P. nehemia Boisduval								
Pierinae								
Anteos clorinde Godart	X	X	X	X	X			
A. maerula Fabricius				X				
Aphrissa boisduvallii Felder			X	X				
A. statira Cramer	X	X	X	X				
A. trite Linnaeus	X	X						
Appias drusilla Cramer		X	X	X	X	X		
Archonias Huebner								
A. tereas approximata Butler		X				X		
Ascia josepha Godman & Salvin				X	X			
A. limona Schaus								
A. monuste Linnaeus	X	X	X	X	X	X	X	
Catasticta cerberus Godman & Salvin								X
C. flisa Herrich-Schäffer					X			X
C. nimbice bryson Godman & Salvin		X			X			X
C. prioneris hegemon Hopffer					X			X
C. sisamnus Fabricius		X			X			X
C. strigosa actinotis Butler								X
C. teutila Doubleday		X			X			X
C. theresa Butler								X
Colias cesonia Stoll	X	X	X	X	X	X		
Charonias eurytele Hewitson		X				X		
Eurema albula Cramer	X	X				X		
E. arbela Felder		X						
E. boisduvaliana Felder				X				
E. daira Felder	X	X	X	X	X	X		
E. dina Westwood				X				
E. elathia Cramer								
E. gratiosa Doubleday & Hewitson				X	X			
E. lisa Boisduval								X
E. mexicana Felder		X			X	X	X	X
E. nise Godart	X	X						
E. proterpia Fabricius		X	X	X	X	X		
E. salome Felder	X	X	X		X	X		
E. xanthoclora Kollar		X			X	X		
Hesperocharis costaricensis Bates								
H. crocea Bates								
H. graphites Bates								X
Itaballia caesia tenuicornis Butler & Druce		X			X	X	X	
I. demophile centralis Joicey & Talbot				X	X			

663

	La Selva	San Vito	Corcovado National Park	Santa Rosa National Park	Monte-verde	Colonia del Socorro	La Montura	Cerro de la Muerte
I. kiacha pisonis Hewitson								
Kricogonia lyside Godart				X				
Leodonta dysoni Doubleday		X			X	X	X	X
Leptophobia aripa Boisduval		X			X	X	X	X
Melete florinda Butler		X					X	
M. isandra Boisduval				X				
M. monstrosa Staudinger		X						
Perrhybris lypera Kollar	X							
P. pyrrha Fabricius	X		X					
Pereute charops Boisduval		X			X		X	X
P. cheops Staudinger								
Phoebis agarithe Boisdival	X		X	X				
P. argante Fabricius	X	X	X	X	X	X		
P. philea Linnaeus	X	X	X	X	X	X	X	
P. rurina Felder		X	X	X	X	X	X	
P. sennae Cramer	X	X	X	X		X		
Pieriballia mandella noctipennis Butler & Druce		X	X		X	X		
Nymphalidae								
Apaturinae								
Doxocopa callianira Menetries								
D. cherubina Felder		X				X		
D. clothilda Felder	X					X		
D. cyane Latreille		X				X		
D. excelsa Gillot								
D. laure Drury				X	X			
D. pavon Latreille	X	X		X		X		
D. plesaurina Butler & Druce								
D. zunilda felderi Godman & Salvin								
Charaxinae								
Agrias aedon rodriguezi Schaus							X	
A. amydon philatelica DeVries	X			X				
Archaeoprepona amphimachus amphiktion Fruhstorfer	X	X	X	X	X	X	X	
A. antimache gulina Fruhstorfer	X	X		X				
A. camilla Godman & Salvin	X							
A. demophon centralis Fruhstorfer		X	X	X	X			
A. meander mendax Bryk	X	X				X		
A. pheadra Godman & Salvin								
Prepona laertes octavia Fruhstorfer	X	X		X	X	X		
P. dexamenes Hopffer								
P. gnorima Bates		X						
P. deiphile lygia Fruhstorfer								
Siderone marthesia Cramer			X	X				
S. syntyche Hewitson								
Zaretis itys Cramer	X						X	
Z. ellops Menetries			X	X				
Z. callidryas Felder		X						
Hypna clytemnestra velox Butler	X	X	X			X		
Consul fabius cecrops Doubleday	X	X	X	X	X	X	X	
C. jansoni Salvin						X		
C. electra Westwood		X			X			
Anaea aieda Guerin-Meneville				X				
Fountainea nobilis peralta Hall								
F. eurypyle confusa Hall		X			X			

	La Selva	San Vito	Corcovado National Park	Santa Rosa National Park	Monteverde	Colonia del Socorro	La Montura	Cerro de la Muerte
F. ryphea Cramer								
F. glycerium Doubleday		X		X		X	X	
F. halice chrysophana Bates								
Memphis aureola Bates	X					X		
M. ambrosia Druce								
M. arginussa eubaena Boisduval	X	X			X	X		
M. artacaena Hewitson	X	X	X					
M. aulica Rober		X						
M. centralis Rober								
M. chaeronia indigotica Salvin		X				X		
M. elara Godman & Salvin		X						
M. forreri Godman & Salvin			X	X				
M. herbacea Butler & Druce								
M. lankesteri Hall								
M. laura kingi Miller	X							
M. lyceus Druce						X	X	
M. morvus boisduvali Comstock	X							
M. neidhopferi Rottgers, Escalante, & Coronado								
M. oenomais Boisduval	X	X	X					
M. orthesia Godman & Salvin	X							
M. pithyusa Felder	X	X		X	X	X		
M. proserpina Salvin								
M. xenocles Westwood	X	X				X		
M. beatrix Druce		X				X	X	
Colobura dirce Linnaeus	X	X	X	X	X	X	X	
C. dirceoides Sepp								
Historis acheronta Fabricius	X	X	X	X		X		
H. odius Fabricius	X	X	X	X	X	X		
Baeotus baeotus Doubleday & Hewitson	X							
Smyrna blomfildia datis Fruhstorfer	X	X	X	X	X			
Pycina zamba zelys Godman & Salvin					X		X	
Tigridia acesta Linnaeus	X	X	X			X	X	
Biblis hyperia Cramer			X	X				
Mestra amymone Menetries								
Hamadryas amphinome mexicana Lucas	X	X	X	X				
H. arethusa saurites Fruhstorfer	X	X	X	X		X		
H. arinome Godman & Salvin	X							
H. februa Huebner		X	X	X	X			
H. fornax fornacalia Fruhstorfer		X						
H. glauconome Bates				X				
H. iptheme Bates		X						
H. guatemalena Bates				X	X			
H. feronia ferinulenta Fruhstorfer	X	X	X			X		
Panacea lysimache Godman & Salvin								
Ectima lirissa rectifascia Butler	X				X			
Eunica alcmena Doubleday	X	X	X					
E. augusta Bates	X			X			X	
E. caresa Hewitson								
E. excelsa Godman & Salvin			X				X	
E. malvina Bates		X		X				
E. mira Godman & Salvin	X	X				X		
E. monima modesta Bates	X			X		X		

	La Selva	San Vito	Corcovado National Park	Santa Rosa National Park	Monte-verde	Colonia del Socorro	La Montura	Cerro de la Muerte
E. mygdonia Godart				X				
E. norica Hewitson		X					X	
E. pomona Godman & Salvin		X					X	
E. tatila coerula Godman & Salvin								
E. venusia Felder			X				X	
Myscelia ethusa pattenia Butler & Druce				X				
M. cyaniris Doubleday	X	X	X	X	X	X		
M. leucocyana Felder	X						X	
Marpesia alcibiades Staudinger								
M. berania Hewitson	X	X	X	X	X	X		
M. coresia Godart		X			X	X	X	X
M. chiron Fabricius	X	X	X	X	X	X		X
M. marcella Felder		X	X				X	
M. merops Doyere	X	X	X		X	X	X	X
M. petreus Bates	X	X	X	X	X			
Dynamine ate Godman & Salvin								
D. agacles Dalm		X						
D. dyonis Geyer								
D. chryseis Bates								
D. glauce Bates								
D. hoppi albicola Rober	X							
D. hecuba Schaus						X	X	
D. mylitta Cramer	X	X	X	X	X			
D. salpensa Felder	X		X					
D. sosthenes Hewitson								
D. thalassina Boisduval								
D. theseus Felder								
Temenis laothoe libera Fabricius	X	X	X	X	X	X		
T. pulchra Hewitson		X						
Epiphile adrasta Hewitson		X		X	X			
E. eriopis Hewitson							X	
E. grandis Butler								
E. orea plusios Godman & Salvin		X					X	
Pseudonica flavilla canthara Doubleday	X	X	X			X		
Catonephele chromis godmani Stichel							X	
C. numilia esite Felder	X	X	X					
C. nyctimus Westwood	X	X	X		X	X		
C. orites Stichel	X							
Nessaea aglaura Doubleday & Hewitson	X		X					
Haematera pyramus thysbe Doubleday & Hewitson								
Diaethria astala Guerin		X					X	X
D. eupepla Salvin & Godman		X					X	X
D. marchalli Guerin-Meneville	X	X	X		X	X	X	
Cyclogramma pandama Doubleday & Hewitson		X				X	X	X
Callicore anna Guerin								
C. atacama manova Fruhstorfer								
C. brome Boisduval								
C. bugaba Staudinger		X					X	
C. faustina Bates								
C. lyca aerias Godman & Salvin	X	X	X			X	X	

	La Selva	San Vito	Corcovado National Park	Santa Rosa National Park	Monte-verde	Colonia del Socorro	La Montura	Cerro de la Muerte
C. patelina Hewitson	X							
C. peralta Dillon								
C. pitheas Latreille				X				
C. texa titania Salvin		X		X				
Perisama barnesi Schaus							X	
Pyrrhogyra nearea Cramer				X				
P. edocla Doubleday & Hewitson		X				X	X	
P. crameri Aurivillius	X		X					
P. otolais Bates	X		X					
Adelpha basiloides Bates				X				
A. boetia oberthurii Boisduval		X						
A. boreas opheltes Fruhstorfer						X	X	
A. celerio Butler	X	X	X	X	X	X		
A. cocala lorzae Boisduval	X		X					
A. cytherea marcia Fruhstorfer	X	X	X			X		
A. demialba Butler					X	X	X	X
A. diocles Godman & Salvin								X
A. erotia delinita Fruhstorfer								
A. erymanthis Godman & Salvin						X		
A. felderi Boisduval								
A. fessonia Hewitson			X	X				
A. iphicla iphicleola Bates	X	X	X	X	X	X		
A. ixia leucas Fruhstorfer	X	X				X		
A. justina lacina Butler	X							
A. lerna aeolia Felder								
A. luceria Druce		X					X	X
A. leucopthalma mephestopheles Butler		X			X	X	X	
A. melanthe Bates	X	X	X	X	X	X		
A. naxia epiphicla Godman & Salvin								
A. salmoneus salmonides Hall								
A. tracta Butler		X			X	X	X	X
A. zalmona sophax Godman & Salvin						X	X	
A. zea paroeca Bates							X	
A. zina restricta Fruhstorfer						X	X	X
A. stilesiana DeVries & Chacon							X	
Hypanartia lethe Fabricius		X			X	X	X	
H. godmani Bates		X				X	X	X
H. arcaei Godman & Salvin							X	X
H. kefersteini Doubleday		X			X	X	X	X
Siproeta epaphus Latreille		X			X	X	X	
S. stelenes biplagiata Fruhstorfer	X	X	X	X	X	X		
S. superba euoe Fox & Forbes								
Anartia fatima Linnaeus	X	X	X	X	X	X		
A. jatrophae Linnaeus	X	X	X	X	X			
Vanessa cardui Linnaeus								X
V. virginiensis Drury		X					X	X
Hypolimnas misippus Linnaeus								
Chlosyne lacinia Geyer	X	X	X	X	X			
C. quetala Reakirt				X				
C. janais Drury				X				
C. hyperia Fabricius				X				
C. poecile Felder							X	
C. gaudialis Bates	X					X		
C. narva bonplandi Latreille	X	X	X			X		
C. melanarge Bates				X				

667

	La Selva	San Vito	Corcovado National Park	Santa Rosa National Park	Monte-verde	Colonia del Socorro	La Montura	Cerro de la Muerte
C. erodyle rubrigutta Rober								
Thessalia ezra Hewitson	X							
T. theona Menetries			X	X				
Phyciodes artonia diallus Godman & Salvin								
P. crithona Salvin								
P. fulviplaga Butler		X			X	X	X	
P. dracaena phlegias Godman & Salvin								
P. ardys Hewitson								
P. sosis Godman & Salvin								
P. otanes Hewitson								
P. frisia tulcis Bates			X	X				
Tritanassa eranites Hewitson		X				X		
T. myia griseobasalis Rober	X		X	X				
T. fulgora Godman & Salvin							X	X
T. cassiopea Godman & Salvin								X
T. dora Schaus								X
T. ofella Hewitson								
T. drusilla Bates								
Eresia anieta Hewitson	X	X	X			X		
E. nigrella niveonotis Butler & Druce							X	
E. phyllra nigripennis Salvin						X	X	
E. alsina Hewitson						X		
E. sestia coela Druce	X							
E. eunice mechanitis Godman & Salvin		X						
E. eutropia Hewitson	X	X				X		
E. clara Bates	X	X						
E. sticta Schaus						X	X	
E. poecilina Bates						X		
E. hera leucodesma Felder	X							
Microtia elva Bates				X				
Euptoetia claudina poasina Schaus								
E. hegesia hoffmani Comstock		X	X	X	X			
Philaethria dido Linnaeus	X	X	X			X		
Dione moneta poeyi Butler		X			X	X	X	X
D. juno Cramer		X		X				
Agraulis vanillae Linnaeus	X	X	X	X	X	X		
Dryadula phaetusa Linnaeus	X	X	X	X	X			
Dryas iulia moderata Riley	X	X	X	X	X	X		
Eueides procula vulgiformis Butler & Druce				X				
E. vibilia vialis Stichel			X					
E. lineata Salvin & Godman		X			X	X		
E. isabellae Cramer	X	X	X	X	X	X		
E. aliphera Godart	X	X	X					
E. lybia olympia Fabricius	X						X	
E. lybia lybioides Staudinger		X	X					
Heliconius doris Linnaeus	X	X	X			X		
H. ismenius telchinia Doubleday	X			X		X		
H. ismenius clarescens Butler		X	X	X				
H. hecale zuleika Hewitson	X	X	X	X	X	X	X	
H. melpomene rosina Bates								
H. cydno galanthus Bates	X			X		X	X	
H. cydno chioneus Bates								
H. pachinus Salvin		X	X					
H. erato petiverana Doubleday	X	X	X	X	X	X		
H. hecalesia formosus Bates		X	X		X	X	X	
H. sara sara Fabricius	X					X		

	La Selva	San Vito	Corcovado National Park	Santa Rosa National Park	Monte-verde	Colonia del Socorro	La Montura	Cerro de la Muerte
H. sara theudela Hewitson		X	X					
H. sapho leuce Doubleday	X							
H. eleuchia Hewitson						X	X	
H. charitonia Linnaeus	X	X	X	X	X	X	X	
H. clysonimus montanus Salvin		X		X	X	X	X	
Acraeinae								
Altinote leucomelas Bates		X			X	X	X	X
Actinote melampeplos Godman & Salvin		X						
A. guatemalena Bates	X							
A. anteas Doubleday		X			X	X		
A. lapitha Staudinger			X					
Ithomiidae								
Eutresis dilucida Staudinger		X					X	
E. hyperia theope Godman & Salvin		X			X		X	
Olyras crathis staudingeri Godman & Salvin					X		X	
O. insignis Salvin		X			X	X	X	
Tithorea harmonia helicaon Godman & Salvin				X				
I. tarricina pinthias Godman & Salvin	X	X	X		X	X		
Melinaea lilis imitata Bates	X					X		
M. scylax Salvin		X	X					
Thyridia psidii melantho Bates	X	X	X		X	X		
Mechanitis polymnia isthmia Bates	X	X	X	X	X	X	X	
M. lysimnia doryssus Bates	X	X	X	X	X	X	X	
M. menapis saturata Godman & Salvin		X			X	X	X	
Scada zibia xanthina Bates	X							
Napeogenes cranto paedaretus Godman & Salvin						X	X	
N. peridia hemisticta Schaus	X					X		
N. tolosa amara Godman	X	X	X		X	X		
Hypothyris euclea valore Haensch	X	X	X	X	X	X	X	
H. lycaste callispila Bates		X					X	
Ithomia bolivari Schaus	X							
I. celemia plaginota Butler & Druce			X					
I. diasa hippocrenis Bates	X							
I. heraldica Bates	X	X	X		X	X	X	
I. patilla Hewitson	X	X	X	X	X	X	X	
I. terra vulcana Haensch							X	
I. xenos Bates		X			X	X	X	X
Hyaliris excelsa decumena Godman & Salvin		X			X	X	X	
Aeria eurimedia agna Godman & Salvin	X		X					
Hyposcada virginiana evanides Haensch	X	X	X		X	X		
Oleria paula Weymer	X	X	X		X			
O. zea rubescens Butler & Druce		X			X	X	X	
O. vicina Salvin		X			X		X	X
O. zelica pagasa Druce	X	X	X			X		
Callithomia hezia Hewitson	X	X	X					
C. hydra megaleas Godman								
Ceratinia tutia dorilla Bates	X	X	X					

669

	La Selva	San Vito	Corcovado National Park	Santa Rosa National Park	Monteverde	Colonia del Socorro	La Montura	Cerro de la Muerte
Dircenna chiriquensis Haensch		X			X		X	X
D. euchytma Felder	X		X					
D. klugi Geyer		X			X	X	X	X
D. relata Butler & Druce		X			X	X	X	
Godyris zygia Godman & Salvin		X	X					
G. zavaleta caesiopicta Niepelt	X					X		
Greta polissena umbrana Haensch		X			X	X	X	
G. oto Hewitson		X			X	X	X	
G. nero Hewitson		X			X	X	X	X
G. andromica lyra Salvin		X			X	X	X	
G. annette Guerin		X			X	X	X	
Hypoleria cassotis Bates		X	X					
Pseudoscada utilla pusio Godman & Salvin	X							
P. lavinia troetschi Staudinger								
Episcada salvinia opleri Lamas		X			X		X	X
Pteronymia agalla obscurata Fabricius		X	X					
P. artena Hewitson		X			X	X	X	
P. tigranes Godman & Salvin						X	X	
P. cottyto Guerin-Meneville								
P. donata Haensch								
P. fulvescens Godman & Salvin					X	X		
P. fulvimargo Butler & Druce					X	X	X	
P. notilla Butler & Druce		X			X	X	X	
P. parva Salvin	X					X		
P. simplex Salvin		X			X	X	X	X
P. lonera Butler & Druce		X			X		X	
P. fumida Schaus								
Heterosais guilia cadra Godman & Salvin	X							
Danaidae								
Anetia thirza insignis Salvin		X			X		X	X
Ituna illione albescens Distant					X	X		
Lycorea cleobaea atergatis Doubleday	X	X		X	X	X	X	
Danaus plexippus Linnaeus	X	X	X	X	X	X	X	X
D. gilippus Linnaeus	X	X	X	X	X	X	X	X
D. eresimus montezuma Talbot	X		X	X	X			
Libytheidae								
Libytheana carinenta mexicana Michener	X	X		X				
Satyridae								
Brassolinae								
Brassolis isthmia Bates	X							
Caligo atreus Kollar	X	X	X	X		X		
C. eurilochus sulanus Frushstorfer	X	X	X			X		
C. illioneus Kollar	X							
C. memnon Felder		X	X	X	X	X		
Catoblepia josephus Godman & Salvin								
C. orgetorix championi Bristow	X							
C. xanthicles Godman & Salvin								
Dynastor darius stygianus Butler	X	X	X	X				
Eryphanis aesacus bulboculus Butler		X				X	X	

670

	La Selva	San Vito	Corcovado National Park	Santa Rosa National Park	Monte-verde	Colonia del Socorro	La Montura	Cerro de la Muerte
E. polyxena lycomedon Felder	X	X	X					
Opsiphanes cassina fabricii Boisduval	X	X	X	X	X			
O. cassiae castaneus Stichel		X						
O. invirae cuspidatus Stichel	X	X				X		
O. bogotanus Distant						X	X	
O. quiteria quirinus Godman & Salvin		X						
O. staudingeri Godman & Salvin							X	
O. tamarindi sikyon Fruhstorfer						X		
Morphinae								
Antirrhea miltiades Fabricius	X							
A. pterocopha Godman & Salvin						X	X	
A. tomasia Butler			X					
Caerois gertrutus Stichel	X		X					
Morpho amathonte Deyerolle	X	X	X			X	X	
M. cypris Westwood	X					X	X	
M. granadensis polybapta Butler	X							
M. peleides Kollar	X	X	X	X	X	X	X	
M. theseus Deyerolle	X	X	X		X	X	X	
Satyrinae								
Cyllopsis argentella Butler & Druce						X	X	X
C. hedemani Felder								
C. hilara Godman								
C. pephredo Godman								
C. rogersi Godman & Salvin						X	X	
C. vetones Godman & Salvin		X			X	X		
Haetera macleannania Bates								
Citherias menander Drury	X	X	X			X		
Dulcedo polita Hewitson	X							
Pierella helvina incanescens Godman & Salvin	X	X	X					
P. luna Fabricius	X	X	X					
Manataria maculata Hopffer	X			X	X	X	X	X
Oressinoma typhla Westwood & Hewitson						X	X	
Taygetis andromeda Cramer	X	X	X	X	X	X		
T. godmani Staudinger								
T. keneza Butler		X						
T. kerea Butler				X				
T. penelea Cramer								
T. mermeria excavata Butler			X	X				
T. salvini Staudinger	X							
T. rufomarginata Staudinger	X	X				X		
Pseudodebis zimri Butler	X							
Taygetina bang-hassi Weymer								
Euptychia agnata Schaus	X							
E. alcinoe Butler			X					
E. arnaea Fabricius	X	X	X					
E. calixta Butler		X			X	X	X	X
E. confusa Staudinger	X	X	X			X		
E. cyclops Butler							X	X
E. drymo Schaus								
E. gigas Butler		X			X	X		
E. gulnare Butler								
E. hermes Fabricius								
E. hesione Sulzer	X	X	X			X		

671

	La Selva	San Vito	Corcovado National Park	Santa Rosa National Park	Monte-verde	Colonia del Socorro	La Montura	Cerro de la Muerte
E. hilara Butler								
E. insolata Butler & Druce	X		X					
E. jesia Butler	X		X					
E. labe Butler	X	X	X			X		
E. libye Linnaeus	X	X	X	X	X	X		
E. lineata Godman & Salvin								
E. metaluca Boisduval	X	X	X			X		
E. mollis Staudinger								
E. mollina Huebner						X		
E. palladia Butler								
E. renata Cramer					X	X	X	
E. satyrina Bates		X	X		X	X	X	
E. terrestris Butler								
E. themis Butler				X	X			
E. tiessa Hewitson	X							
E. usitata Butler	X		X					
E. westwoodi Butler	X	X	X					
E. antonöe Cramer	X		X					
E. sp. 1	X	X	X			X		
E. sp. 2	X							
E. sp. 3			X					
Amphidecta pignerator Butler								
Dioriste cothon Salvin							X	
D. cothonides Grosse-Smith						X	X	
D. tauropolis Doubleday & Hewitson		X			X			
Drucina leonata Butler					X	X	X	X
Eretris hulda Butler & Druce								X
E. subrufescens Smith & Kirby								
E. suzannae DeVries					X	X	X	
Pedaliodes cremera Godman & Salvin								X
P. manis Felder		X						
P. perperna Hewitson						X	X	
P. pisonia dejecta Bates		X				X	X	X
P. triaria Godman & Salvin								X
Oxeoschistus euryphile Butler						X	X	
O. puerta submaculatus Butler & Druce					X	X		
Catargynnis dryadina Schaus								X
C. rogersi Godman & Salvin		X					X	X
Pronophila timanthes Salvin		X			X	X	X	X
Lymanopoda euopis Godman & Salvin								X

Lycaenidae
(NOTE: □ = San Vito)
Eumaeus minyas Huebner □
Theorema eumenia Hewitson □
Arcas imperialis Cramer
A. delphia Nicolay
A. splendor Nicolay
Evenus regalis Cramer
E. coronata Hewitson
Pseudolycaena damo Druce
Atlides inachus Cramer □
A. bacis Godman & Salvin
A. gaumeri Godman & Salvin
Panthiades battus jalan Reakirt

P. ochus Godman & Salvin □
Cycnus phaleros Linnaeus
Brangas caranus Cramer
Arawacus aetolus Sulzer □
A. sito Boisduval
Callophrys miserabilis Clench
C. goodsoni Clench
C. longula Hewitson □
C. herodotus Fabricius
C. pastor Butler & Druce
C. agricolor Butler & Druce
Chalybs janias Cramer
Iaspis talayra Hewitson
Rekoa meton Cramer

Parhassius m-album urraca Nicolay
P. orgia Hewitson
P. polibetes Cramer
P. jebus Godart
Oenomanus ortygnus Cramer
Erora aura Godman & Salvin
Tmolus echion Cramer
T. crolinus Butler & Druce
Calycopis xeneta Hewitson □
C. isobeon Butler & Druce
C. beon Cramer □
C. bactra Hewitson
C. susanna Field
C. drusilla Field
C. amplia Hewitson
Chlorostrymon telea Hewitson
C. simaethis Drury
Symbiopsis smalli Nicolay
Strymon yoyoa Reakirt □
S. melinus Huebner
Hemiargus huntingtoni hannoides Clench
H. isola Reakirt
H. hanno Stoll
H. ceranus zachaeina Butler & Druce
Celastrina pseudoargiolus gozora Boisduval
Leptotes cassius striata Edwards
Everes comyntas texana Chermock
Theritas mavors Huebner
"Thecla" telemus Cramer
T. augustula Butler & Druce
T. nepia Godman & Salvin
T. hisbon Godman & Salvin
T. hemon Cramer
T. oceia Godman & Salvin □
T. busa Godman & Salvin
T. perpenna Godman & Salvin
T. hyas Godman & Salvin
T. cadmus Felder □
T. petelina Hewitson
T. cyda Godman & Salvin
T. barajo Reakirt □
T. eunus Godman & Salvin
T. phaea Butler & Druce □
T. palegon Cramer
T. atena Hewitson
T. janthina Hewitson
T. cupentus Cramer
T. azurinus Butler & Druce
T. temesa Hewitson
T. mycon Godman & Salvin
T. ocrisia Hewitson
T. thales Fabricius □
T. keila Hewitson
T. tephraeus Huebner
T. leos Schaus
T. syncellus Cramer (= *bitias*)
T. syedra Hewitson
T. orcynia Hewitson
T. bassania Hewitson
T. coelicolor Butler & Druce
T. myrsina Hewitson
T. orcidia Hewitson
T. arza Hewitson □
T. paralus Godman & Salvin
T. eupopea Hewitson

T. heraclides Godman & Salvin
T. endela Hewitson
T. hesperitius Butler & Druce
T. autoclea Hewitson
T. denarius Butler & Druce
T. sethon Godman & Salvin □
T. camissa Hewitson □
T. charichlora Butler & Druce
T. clarina Hewitson
T. tamos Godman & Salvin
T. atrius Herrich-Schäffer
T. myron Godman & Salvin
T. lampetia Godman & Salvin
T. celmus Cramer
T. lollia Godman & Salvin
T. iambe Godman & Salvin
T. carnica Hewitson
T. tera Hewitson
T. hesychia Godman & Salvin
T. maevia Godman & Salvin
T. mathewi Hewitson
T. azia Hewitson
T. mulucha Hewitson
T. columela istapa Reakirt
T. cestri Reakirt
T. agra Hewitson
T. hypocrita Schaus
T. subflorens Schaus
T. melma Schaus
T. guapilia Schaus
T. amphrade Schaus
T. lisus Stoll □
T. crines Druce □
T. politus Druce □
T. gabatha Hewitson □
T. lycabas Fabricius □
T. minthe Godman & Salvin

Riodinidae
(NOTE: □ = San Vito)
Euselasia bettina Hewitson
E. aurantia Butler & Druce □
E. leucophyra Schaus
E. matuta Schaus
E. chrysippe Bates
E. regipennis Butler
E. sergia Godman & Salvin
E. mystica Schaus
E. procula Godman & Salvin
E. hieronymi Godman & Salvin □
E. inconspicua Godman & Salvin
E. leucon Schaus
E. argentea Hewitson
E. eucrates leucorrhoa Godman & Salvin □
E. portentosa Stichel
E. amphidecta Godman & Salvin
E. hypophaea Godman & Salvin
E. eubule Felder
E. midas crotopiades Stichel
E. aurantiaca Godman & Salvin
E. corduena anadema Stichel
Hades noctula Westwood □
Methone (= *Methonella*) *cecilia caduca* Stichel
M. chrysomela Butler □
Eurybia elvina Stichel

E. cyclopia Stichel
E. lamia fulgens Stichel
E. dardus unxia Godman & Salvin
E. patrona persona Staudinger
E. lycisca Doubleday, Westwood, & Hewitson □
Mesosemia grandis Druce □
M. gaudiolum Bates
M. albipuncta Schaus
M. telegone Boisduval
M. tetrica Stichel (= *methion* Godman & Salvin)
M. carissima Bates
M. cecropia Druce
M. calypso hesperina Butler
M. coelestis Godman & Salvin
M. cachiana Schaus
M. ephyne esperanza Schaus
M. asa Hewitson □
M. zonalis Godman & Salvin
Leucochimona leucogaea Godman & Salvin
L. lagora Herrich-Schäffer (= *molina* Godman & Salvin)
L. iphias Stichel
L. lepida Godman & Salvin
L. philemon polita Stichel
Peropthalma tullius Fabricius □
P. lasius Stichel
Hermathena oweni Schaus
H. candidata Hewitson
Voltinia radiata Godman & Salvin
Napaea eucharila picina Stichel □
N. theages Godman & Salvin □
Cremna umbra Boisduval
Ithomeis eulema imitatrix Godman & Salvin □
Brachyglenis esthema Felder
B. dodone Godman & Salvin □
B. dinora Bates
Chamaelimnas villagomes xanthotaenia Stichel
Lepricornis unicolor Godman & Salvin
L. strigosus Staudinger
Isapis agyrtus hera Godman & Salvin
Melanis crenitaenia Stichel
M. pixie Boisduval
M. sanguinea Stichel
M. iarbas melantho Menetries
M. sp. 1
Xenandra nigrivenata Schaus
Syrmatia aethiops Staudinger
Chorinea faunus bogota Saunders
Rhetus arcius thia Morisse
R. periander naevianus Stichel
R. dysonii Saunders □
Riodina barbouri Bates
Ancyluris cacica Felder
A. jurgensenii Saunders
A. inca Saunders □
Necyria beltiana Hewitson
N. ingaretha Hewitson
Notheme eumeus diadema Stichel
Monethe rudolphus Godman & Salvin
Lyropteryx lyra cleadas Druce
Uraneis ucubis Hewitson
Esthemopis clonia Felder
E. caeruleata Godman & Salvin
E. linearis Godman & Salvin
Mesenopsis melanchlora Godman & Salvin
Mesene phareus rubella Bates

M. mygdon Schaus
M. margaretta White □
M. leucopus Godman & Salvin
M. silaris Godman & Salvin
Phaenochitonia ignicauda Godman & Salvin
P. ignipicta Schaus
P. sagaris tyriotes Godman & Salvin
P. phoenicura Godman & Salvin
Pachythone philonis Hewitson
P. ignifer nigriciliata Schaus
P. gigas Godman & Salvin
Symmachia rubina Bates
S. accusatrix Westwood
S. leena Hewitson
S. probetor belti Godman & Salvin
S. tricolor hedemanni Felder
S. histrica Stichel
S. esclepia xypete Hewitson
Caria domitianus Fabricius
C. harmonia Godman & Salvin
C. rhacotis Godman & Salvin
C. lampeto Godman & Salvin
Chalodeta chaonitis Hewitson (doubtful)
Chimastrum argenteum Bates □
Baeotis zonata Felder
B. nesaea Godman & Salvin □
Argyrogramma holosticta Godman & Salvin □
A. sulphurea macularia Boisduval □
Anteros allectus Westwood
A. chrysophrastus roratus Godman & Salvin
A. formosus micon Druce
A. kupris Hewitson □
A. carausius Westwood
A. medusa Druce
A. renaldus indigator Stichel
A. sp. 1
Sarota chrysus Stoll
S. subtessellata Schaus
S. turrialbensis Schaus
S. gyas Cramer
S. myrtea Godman & Salvin
S. gamelia Godman & Salvin
S. psaros Godman & Salvin
Charis ausius Cramer
C. gynaea zama Bates
C. hermodora Felder
C. iris Staudinger
C. velutina Godman & Salvin □
C. irina Stichel
Calephelis fulmen Stichel
C. sixola McAlpine
C. costaricola Strand
C. browni McAlpine
C. schausi McAlpine
Nelone cadmeis Hewitson
Lasaia sessilis Schaus
L. agesilas Latreille
L. agesilas callaina Clench
L. oileus Godman
Calynda lusca venusta Godman & Salvin
C. hegias Felder
Emesis lucinda aurimna Boisduval
E. mandana Cramer
E. vulpina Godman & Salvin
E. fatima nobilata Stichel

E. tenedia Felder □
E. tegula Godman & Salvin
E. ocypore aethalia Bates
E. cypria paphia Felder □
E. vimena Schaus
Parnes nycteis Westwood
Apodemia multiplaga Schaus
A. walkeri Godman & Salvin
Audre (=*Hamearis*) *erostratus* Westwood
A. domina Bates
A. albina Felder
Metacharis cuparina victrix Hewitson
M. nigrella Bates
Cariomothis poeciloptera Godman & Salvin
Calospila (=*Polystichtis*) *luciana* Fabricius
C. cilissa Hewitson
C. pelarge Godman & Salvin
C. lasthenes Hewitson
C. sp. near *idmon* Godman & Salvin
C. sp. 2
Adelotypa (= *Echenais*) *eudocia* Godman & Salvin
A. densemaculata Hewitson
A. glauca Godman & Salvin
A. patronia Schaus
Calociasma icterica Godman & Salvin
C. lilina Butler
Catocyclotis aemulius adelina Butler
Nymula phylleus praeclara Bates
N. mycone Hewitson
N. velabrum Godman & Salvin
N. ethelinda nymphidioides Butler
N. nycteus Godman & Salvin
N. clearista Butler
Juditha (=*Peplia*) *molpe* Huebner
J. ipsea Godman & Salvin
J. dorilis Bates
Nymphidium haemostictum Godman & Salvin
N. chione onaeum Hewitson
N. ascolia Hewitson
N. lenocinium Schaus
Thisbe irenea belides Stichel
T. lycorias adelphina Godman & Salvin □
Lemonias (=*Anatole*) *agave* Godman & Salvin
Menander (=*Tharops*) *menander purpurata* Godman & Salvin
M. pretus picta Godman & Salvin
Pandemos palaeste salvator Stichel
P. godmani Dewitz
Orimba cyanea jansoni Butler
O. alcmaeon Hewitson
O. cleomedes Hewitson
Theope eudocia pulchralis Stichel
T. herta Godman & Salvin
T. barea Godman & Salvin
T. pedias isia Godman & Salvin
T. phineus Schaus
T. caenina Godman & Salvin
T. cratylus Godman & Salvin
T. virgilius Fabricius
T. diores Godman & Salvin
T. theustis Godman & Salvin
T. phaeo folia Godman & Salvin
T. basilea Bates
T. eleutho Godman & Salvin
T. thebais matuta Godman & Salvin
T. thestias decorata Godman & Salvin

T. sp. 1
Corrachia leucoplaga Schaus

Hesperiidae
Pyrrhopyginae
Pyrrhopyge phidias evansi Bell
P. zenodorus Godman & Salvin
P. creon Druce
P. aesculpatus Staudinger
P. cosyra Druce
P. maculosa erythrosticta Godman & Salvin
Elbella scylla dulcinea Plotz
E. patroba Hewitson
Mysoria barcastus ambigua Mabille & Boullet
M. thasus Stoll
Myscellus amystis hages Godman & Salvin
M. belti Godman & Salvin
M. pegasus perissadora Dyar
Passova gellias Godman & Salvin
Oxenetra hoppferi Staudinger

Pyrginae
Phocides polybius lilea Reakirt
P. distans licinus Plotz
P. thermus Mabille
P. pigmalion Cramer
P. urania vida Butler
Tarsoctenus corytus gaudialis Hewitson
Phanus vitreus Stoll
P. obscurior Kaye
P. marshallii Kirby
Udranomia orcinus Felder
Augiades crinisus Cramer
Hyalothyrus neleus pemphigargyra Mabille
Entheus matho Godman & Salvin
Proteides mercurius Fabricius
Epargyreus clarus Cramer
E. spina Evans
E. clavicornis orizaba Scudder
Polygonus leo Gmelin
P. manueli Bell & Comstock
Chioides catillus albofasciata Hewitson
C. catillius albius Evans
C. zilpa Butler
Aguna asander Hewitson
A. claxon Evans
A. aurunce Hewitson
A. coelus Stoll
Typhe danus undulatus Hewitson
T. ampyx Godman & Salvin
Polythrix octomaculata Sepp
P. asine Hewitson
P. caunus Herrich-Schäffer
P. metallescens Mabille
Chryspplectrum pernicious epicinia Butler & Druce
Codatractus carlos Evans
C. alcaeus Hewitson
C. bryaxis imaleana Butler
Ridens crison cachinnans Godman
R. biolleyi Mabille
Urbanus proteus Linnaeus
U. viterboana Ehrman
U. viterboana alva Evans
U. pronta Evans
U. esmeraldus Butler

U. pronus Evans
U. evona Evans
U. elmina Evans
U. esta Evans
U. acawoios Williams
U. dorantes Stoll
U. telemus Huebner
U. tanna Evans
U. simplicius Stoll
U. procne Plotz
U. doryssus Swainson
U. albimargo Mabille
U. chalco Huebner
Astraptes talus Cramer
A. fulgerator azul Reakirt
A. tucuti Williams
A. palliolum Druce
A. egregius Butler
A. phalaecus Godman & Salvin
A. apastus Cramer
A. enotrus Stoll
A. samson Evans
A. colossus helen Evans
A. alardus latia Evans
A. alector hoppferi Plotz
A. cretus cranna Evans
A. latimargo bifascia Herrich-Schäffer
A. chiriquensis Staudinger
A. galesus cassius Evans
A. anaphus anneta Evans
Autochton vectilucis Butler
A. neis Geyer
A. longipennis Plotz
A. zarex Huebner
A. bipunctatus Gmelin
Achalarus albociliatus Mabille
A. toxeus Plotz
Venada advena Mabille
Cabares potrillo Lucas
Dyscophellus phraxanor Hewitson
D. euribates Stoll
D. porcius Felder
D. ramusis ramon Evans
Nascus phintias Schaus
N. phocus Cramer
N. paulliniae Sepp
Porphrogenes probus Moschler
Ocyba calathana calanus Godman & Salvin
Orneates ageochus Hewitson
Celaenorrhinus monartus Plotz
C. fritzgaertneri variegatus Godman & Salvin
C. stalingsii Freeman
C. similis approximatus Williams & Bell
C. eligius Stoll
Spathilepia clonius Cramer
Cogia hippalus hiska Evans
C. calchas Herrich-Schäffer
Telemiades amphion fides Bell
Arteurotia tractapennis Butler & Druce
Eracon mnemon Schaus
Spioniades abreviata Mabille
Polytor polytor Prittwitz
Nisioniades bessus godma Evans
N. laurentina Williams & Bell
N. ephora Herrich-Schäffer

Pachyneuria licisca Plotz
Pellicia costimacula arina Evans
P. angra Evans
Morvina fissimacula Mabille
Cyclosemia anastomosis Mabille
C. herennius subcaerulea Schaus
Gorgopas chlorocephala Herrich-Schäffer
Bolla cylindus Godman & Salvin
B. cupreiceps Mabille
B. phylo pullata Mabille
B. brennus Godman & Salvin
B. eusebius Plotz
Staphylus vulgata Moschler
S. caribbea Williams & Bell
S. mazans ascalaphus Staudinger
S. azteca Scudder
S. vincula Plotz
S. evemerus Godman & Salvin
Diaeus lacaena varna Evans
Gorgythion begga pyralina Moschler
Ouleus cyrna Mabille
O. calavius Godman & Salvin
O. fredricus salvina Evans
Zera zera Butler
Z. phila hosta Evans
Z. hyacinthinus Mabille
Z. tetrastigma Sepp
Quadrus cerealis Stoll
Q. contubernalis Mabille
Q. lugubris Felder
Pythonides jovanius amaryllis Staudinger
P. herennius proxenus Godman & Salvin
Sostrata bifasciata nordica Evans
Paches loxuc zonula Mabille
P. polla Mabille
Atarnes sallei Felder
Potomanaxas hirta paphos Evans
P. thestia cranda Evans
P. latrea caliadne Godman & Salvin
Mylon lassia Hewitson
M. orsa Evans
M. salvia Evans
M. menippus Fabricius
M. cajus hera Evans
M. pelopidas Fabricius
M. jason Ehrman
Carrhenes fulvescens calidias Godman & Salvin
C. canescens Felder
C. callipetes meridensis Godman & Salvin
Xenophanes tryxus Stoll
Antigonus nearchus Latreille
A. erosus Huebner
A. corrosus Mabille
Anisochoria pedaliodina polysticta Mabille
Aethilla lavochrea Butler
Achlyodes bursirus heros Ehrman
A. thrasos Jung
A. selva Evans
Grais stigmaticus Mabille
Doberes anticus sobrinus Godman & Salvin
Timochares trifasciata Hewitson
Anastrus sempiternus Butler & Druce
A. tolimus Plotz
A. meliboea Godman & Salvin
A. obscurus nearis Moschler

Tosts platypterus Mabille
Ebrietas osyris Staudinger
E. anacreon Staudinger
E. evanidus Mabille
Cycloglypha thrasibulus Fabricius
C. tisias Godman & Salvin
Helias phalaenoides Evans
Camptoplerra theramenes Mabille
C. auxo Mabille
Theagenes albiplaga aegides Herrich-Schäffer
Chiomara asychis georgina Reakirt
C. mithrax Moschler
Gesta gesta invincius Butler & Druce
Erynnis zarucco funeralis Scudder & Burgess
E. tristus tatius Edwards
Pyrgus communis adepta Plotz
P. oileus Linnaeus
P. oileus orcus Stoll
Heliopetes macaira Reakirt
H. laviana Hewitson
H. arsalte Linnaeus
H. alana Reakirt

Hesperiinae
Dala pulchra Godman
D. octomaculata Godman
D. eryonas Hewitson
D. lalage lathea Schaus
D. faula lysis Schaus
Falga sircas Godman
Synapte silius Latreille
S. malitiosa pecta Evans
S. salenus Mabille
Zariaspes mys Huebner
Anthoptus epictetus Fabricius
Lento hermione Schaus
Corticea corticea Plotz
C. lysias Plotz
Molo mango Guenee
Racta apella Schaus
Apaustus gracilius Felder
Callimormus radiola Mabille
C. saturnus Herrich-Schäffer
C. juventus Scudder
Eutocus facilis Plotz
Virga xantho Schaus
Eprius veleda Godman
Mnasicles geta Godman
Methionopsis ina Plotz
Sodalia sodalis Butler
Thargella caura Plotz
Lucida lucia oebasus Godman
Phanes aletes Geyer
Monca telaca tyrtaeus Plotz
Nastra leucone Godman
N. insignis Plotz
Cymaenes tripunctata alumna Butler
C. laureolus Schaus
C. odilia trebius Mabille
Vehilius stictomenes illudens Mabille
V. inca Scudder
Mnasilus allubita Butler
Mnasinous patage Godman
Mnastheus chrysophrys Mabille
M. simplicissima Herrich-Schäffer

Moeris remus Fabricius
M. rita Evans
M. vopiscus Herrich-Schäffer
M. striga stroma Evans
Parphorus storax Mabille
P. oeagrus Godman
Papias sobrinus Schaus
P. phainis Godman
P. phaeomelas Geyer
P. dictys Godman
P. subcostula integra Mabille
P. nigrans Schaus
Cobalopsis latonia Schaus
C. nero Herrich-Schäffer
C. potaro Williams & Bell
Lerema lumina Herrich-Schäffer
L. assius Abbot & Smith
L. ancillaris liris Evans
Morys compta micythus Godman
M. gesia lyde Godman
Tigasis zalates Godman
T. nausiphanes Schaus
Vettius marcus Fabricius
V. coryna conka Evans
Paracarystus hypargyra Herrich-Schäffer
Turesis lucas Fabricius
T. theste Godman
Thoon mobius Mabille
Justinia phaetusa morda Evans
Eutychide complana Herrich-Schäffer
E. paria Plotz
E. candallariae Strand
Styriodes lyco Schaus
Dion gemmatus Butler & Druce
Enosis immaculata Hewitson
E. agularis infuscata Plotz
Vertica verticalis coatepeca Schaus
Argon argus Moschler
Megaleas syrna Godman & Salvin
Talides sergestus Cramer
T. alternata Bell
Synale synaxa Hewitson
Carystoides lebbaeus Hewitson
Carystina aurifer Godman & Salvin
Damas clavus Herrich-Schäffer
Lychnucoides saptine Godman & Salvin
Perichares philetes dolores Reakirt
P. deceptus Butler & Druce
Orses cynisca Swainson
Quinta cannae Herrich-Schäffer
Cynea anthracinus luctatius Schaus
C. irma Moschler
C. corisana Moschler
C. megalops Godman
C. cynea Hewitson
Decinea lucifer Huebner
Orthos gabina Godman
Conga chydaea Butler
Copaeodes minima Edwards
Polites vibex praeceps Scudder
Wallengrenia otho pustulata Geyer
Pompieus pompieus Latreille
Atalopedes campestris Boisduval
A. mesogramma Latreille
Buzyges idothea Godman

677

Poanes zabulon Boisduval & LeConte
P. rolla Mabillle
P. inimica Butler & Druce
Paratryone melane poa Evans
Mellana fieldi Bell
M. myron Godman
Halotus angellus Plotz
H. rica Bell
Euphyres conspicua Edwards
Metron chrysogastra Butler
Atrytonopsis ovinia zaovinia Dyar
Calpodes ethilus Stoll
Panoquina evadnes Stoll
Zenis jeba janka Evans
Tirynthia conflua Herrich-Schäffer
Nyctelius nyctelius Latreille
Thespieus dalman Latreille
T. macareus Herrich-Schäffer
T. aspernatus Draudt

Vaccera lacheres Godman
V. caniola Herrich-Schäffer
Oxynthes corusca Herrich-Schäffer
Niconiades xanthaphes Huebner
Aides dysoni Godman
Xeniades chalestra pteras Godman
Saliana triangularis Kaye
S. fusta Evans
S. esperi Evans
S. antonius Latreille
S. longirostris Sepp
S. salius Cramer
S. severus Mabille
Thracides phidon Cramer
Aroma aroma Hewitson

Megathyminae
Megathymus indecisa Butler & Druce

SPECIES ACCOUNTS
Acrocinus longimanus (Arlequín, Harlequin Beetle)

J. A. Chemsak

This cerambycid beetle (fig. 11.2) is conspicuous for its large size (43–75 mm) and elaborate harlequinlike pat-tern of black, yellowish, and reddish markings. It is further distinctive for the long sharp spines at the sides of the pronotum, the very long antennae, and the extremely elongate front legs of the males. These front legs are subject to allometric development, and in large individuals both tibiae and femora are considerably longer than the body. The species ranges from southern Mexico to South America and uses a variety of trees as host plants. Among these are a number of species of *Ficus, Lonchocarpus spruceanus, Artocarpus integrifolia, A. incisa, Guazuma ulmifolia, Chorisia speciosa, Caryocar brasiliensis, Enterolobium timbouva, Urostigma enorme, Castilla elastica, Chlorophora tinctoria, Brosimum alicastrum, B. paraense,* and *Parahancornia amapa.*

Females frequently select trees infested with bracket fungus (*Fomes* sp.) for oviposition. The coloration of the fungi provides an ideal camouflage for the beetles. Before oviposition, the female makes an incision about 20 mm wide and 8 mm deep in the bark. The egg-laying period lasts 2 to 3 days, and fifteen to twenty eggs are deposited. Upon hatching, the larvae begin to bore into the wood-forming galleries with a series of frass ejection holes. Larvae mature within 7 or 8 months and tunnel downward for about 12 cm, where they excavate a shallow pupal cell. The pupal cell, measuring 30–35 mm by 20 mm, is plugged at the outside opening by wood fibers. Pupation lasts about 4 months. Upon eclosion, the adult emerges through a fresh hole gnawed 40 to 8 cm above the entrance hole. The life cycle is annual, and adults are active in Costa Rica from about June to November.

Adults are diurnal but are reported as also being attracted to lights. They are strongly attracted to sap secreted by various trees, especially *Bagassa guianensis.* Mating occurs on the surface of a suitable host tree. In addition to being a secondary sexual characteristic utilized in mating, the very long front legs of the males are

FIGURE 11.2. *Acrocinus longimanus,* adult male perched on an 8 cm diameter tree trunk. August 1980, Sirena, Corcovado National Park, Osa Peninsula, Costa Rica (photo, D. H. Janzen).

reported to be useful in traversing the branches of the trees the beetles live in. This species is distinctive in serving as a host or carrier for pseudoscorpions, which are found under the elytra of the beetles.

Since the larvae bore subcortically around the trunks, the trees usually die when heavily infested. However, since perfectly healthy trees are seldom attacked, and since most of the trees used have little commercial value as timber, *Acrocinus* cannot be regarded as a serious pest.

*

Duffy, E. A. J. 1960. *A monograph of the immature stages of Neotropical timber beetles.* London: British Museum (Natural History).

Actinote leucomelas (Mariposa, Actinote)

D. J. Harvey

This species (fig. 11.3) ranges from Mexico to Panama. In Costa Rica it occurs between 400 and 1,800 m elevation on the Atlantic and Pacific sides. The sexes are dimorphic. Males are black, with blue iridescence on the upper surface of the wings and a yellow patch in the basal area of the forewing underside. Females are larger, with a yellow patch on the upper surface of the forewing and a striated pattern on the underside. The Acraeinae reach their greatest diversity in the Old World tropics and have only about fifty species in the New World. If the New World species warrant splitting into two genera, *Actinote* and *Altinote* (see Potts 1943), then *leucomelas* belongs in the latter.

The larval host plant in Costa Rica (San Vito and San José) is *Mikania* sp. (Compositae) (P. DeVries, pers. comm.). The yellow eggs are deposited in large clusters on the undersides of host-plant leaves, and they hatch simultaneously. The larvae, which are dark with many branched spines, feed gregariously. Pupation takes place singly, off the host plant. The pupae are chalky white with short black spines.

Adults are extremely common at times (particularly in September–December), presumably owing to mass emergences. They visit flowers, such as those of *Inga vera* (Leguminosae). Females approaching an *Inga* flower in the canopy are often "dive bombed" by males. Females close their wings and drop suddenly, presumably to avoid courting males. They will repeat this behavior until they reach a flower (P. DeVries, pers. comm.). Successful courtship has not been recorded for any New

FIGURE 11.3. *Altinote leucomelas. a,* Upper side of female. *b,* Underside of female. *c,* Upper side of male. *d,* Underside of male. Costa Rica (photos, P. J. DeVries).

World acraeine butterfly. In Old World *Acraea,* the male seizes the female on the wing, grasping her about the thorax or bases of the forewings with his legs. The pair falls struggling to the ground, where mating takes place (Marshall 1902, pp. 539–40). During mating, male acraeines deposit a conspicuous plug, known as a sphragis, on the ventral tip of the female's abdomen (see Eltringham 1912, pp. 7–9 and included references). This plug presumably prevents further matings (see Ehrlich and Ehrlich 1978).

Adults of *A. leucomelas* appear to be toxic. They fly weakly and resemble some aposematic ctenuchid moths. When the thorax is pinched, the butterfly releases a drop of yellowish brown fluid. Adults of some *Actinote* species release a foul odor when crushed (Müller 1878). Their bodies are rubbery and can withstand several pinchings (bird attacks?). They can remain alive for about 1 h in a fully charged cyanide jar. Old World *Acraea* are also relatively insensitive to cyanide (refs. in Eltringham 1912), and some actually secrete this compound (Rothschild 1976). It is not known whether *A. leucomelas* is cyanogenic. Adults may be afforded some protection against vertebrate predators by toxins derived from their larval host plants. Most *Actinote* species appear to be specialists on members of two tribes of the Compositae (Eupatoriae and Senecioniae). Both tribes contain pyrrolizidine alkaloids (Culvenor 1978), which are probably stored in some *Actinote* species. Several arctiid moths that feed on *Senecio* (Compositae) are known to store pyrrolizidine alkaloids from their host plants (Aplin and Rothschild 1971). Although captive mantids and some birds reject some species of *Acraea* (Marshall 1902), nothing is known about the acceptability of *A. leucomelas* to potential predators in the field.

*

Aplin, R. T., and Rothschild, M. 1971. Poisonous alkaloids in the body tissues of the garden tiger moth (*Arctia caja* L.) and the cinnabar moth (*Tyria* [= *Callimorpha*] *jacobaeae* L.) (Lepidoptera). In *Toxins of animal and plant origin,* ed. A. de Vries and K. Kochva. London: Gordon and Breach.

Culvenor, C. C. J. 1978. Pyrrolizidine alkaloids: Occurrence and systematic importance in angiosperms. *Bot. Notiser.* 131:473–86.

Ehrlich, P., and Ehrlich, A. 1978. Reproductive strategies in the butterflies. 1. Mating frequency, plugging, and egg number. *J. Kansas Ent. Soc.* 51:666–97.

Eltringham, H. 1912. A monograph of the African species of *Acraea* Fab., with a supplement on those of the Oriental region. *Trans. Ent. Soc. London* 1912:1–374.

Marshall, G. A. K. 1902. Five years observations and experiments (1896–1901) on the bionomics of South African insects, chiefly devoted to the investigation of mimicry and warning colours. *Trans. Ent. Soc. London* 1902:287–584.

Müller, F. 1878. Notes on Brazilian entomology. *Trans. Ent. Soc. London* 1878:211–23.

Potts, R. W. L. 1943. Systematic notes concerning American Acraeinae (Lepidoptera: Nymphalidae). *Pan-Pacific Ent.* 19:31–32.

Rothschild, M. 1976. *Acraea andromache* reared on an acyanogenic strain of *Passiflora coerulea* (note of an exhibit). *Proc. Roy. Ent. Soc. London* 40:35.

Aellopos titan (Cinta Blanca, White-banded Sphinxlet)

W. A. Haber and G. W. Frankie

Aellopos titan is a small diurnal sphingid (fig. 11.4) abundant at lowland and mid-elevation sites throughout Costa Rica (up to 1,600 m). Adults are easily recognized by the dark brown to black wings and body and the broad white band crossing the top of the abdomen at its base. Because of its flight, the moth is usually mistaken at first for a hummingbird. Close up, two lines of translucent white spots appear on the forewing along with a small black

FIGURE 11.4. *a, Aellopos fadus,* old female resting on a lump of dirt in dry riverbed at midday. *b,* Two color morphs of last-instar larvae of *Aellopos titan* (host, *Randia karstenii*). Both Santa Rosa National Park, Guanacaste, Costa Rica (photos, D. H. Janzen).

spot at the tip of the discal cell. Wingspan is 4–5 cm. The species ranges from New York to Rio de Janeiro.

Biologists often encounter this moth as it visits flowers of ornamental plants, for example, *Stachytarpheta jamaicensis* and *Duranta repens,* around hotels and field stations. In the wild (Guanacaste Province), *A. titan* commonly feeds on nectar from flowers of *Chomelia spinosa, Cnidoscolus urens, Randia spinosa, Erythroxylon havenense, Muntingia calabura, Genipa americana,* and *Calliandra tapirorum.* Its tongue length is only 15–20 mm, restricting it to short-tubed and unspecialized flowers.

Seasonally, the adults peak in abundance during June and July, but they also occur as late as October in wetter localities. Daily activity spans all the daylight hours (0500–1800), but it is concentrated in early to mid-morning and within an hour of sundown.

The life history of *Aellopos titan* may serve as an example for most species of Sphingidae. Females lay single eggs on the undersides of host-plant leaves. Eggs are oval and pale yellow green (1 × 1.5 mm). Larvae are cylindrical caterpillars that come in green or brown forms (polymorphic, dichromatic), and both types are cryptic. Development from egg to adult takes about 8 weeks. The mature larva burrows a few centimeters into the soil and pupates there inside a thin silk cocoon. Host-plant species are members of the genera *Genipa* and *Randia* (Rubiaceae). The adult moths feed on flowers of the larval host plants even though these flowers are not specially adapted to diurnal sphingids.

Students of tropical birds often state that *Aellopos titan* must be a mimic of the female adorable coquette (*Lophornis adorabilis*), a small Costa Rican hummingbird, because of the general similarity in appearance and the specific field mark of the white transverse band. However, mimicry between the two species is unlikely, since the bird occupies only about 0.01% of the range of the moth. It seems more likely that the hummingbird would be the mimic, or that it is an example of convergence. The moth does have a distinction that may be a defense mechanism: the abdomen is heavily sclerotized (Hodges 1971) and extremely slippery (because the scales are readily detached). A bird that catches one of these moths may find that eating it or even holding onto it is tricky. There is no indication that either larvae or adults are unpalatable. Primary defenses are camouflage for the larvae, and the hard, slippery body and incredible flying ability of the adult—they can fly upside down and backward at the same time and use the borders of a 3-by-5 card for a racetrack.

A few other species of diurnal sphingids occur in Costa Rica. Two of these are very much like *A. titan* (*Aellopos fadus* [fig. 11.4], *A. clavipes*). Another common diurnal and crepuscular species, *Eupyrrhoglossum sagra,* is brown with a bright yellow diagonal line across the hind wing and rows of yellow spots along the sides of the abdomen.

It is notable that species numbers of diurnal sphingids are much lower in the tropics than in the temperate zone, even though nocturnal sphingids are more species rich in the tropics. This trend may be related to the prominence of hummingbirds (a possible competitor for nectar) in the American tropics compared with temperate habitats.

Little, if anything, is known of foraging behavior, home ranges, or life-spans of these moths; however, marked individuals return to the same nectar sources for several days in succession.

*

Hodges, R. W. 1971. *The moths of America north of Mexico.* Fasc. 21. *Sphingoidea.* London: E. W. Classey.

Agrilus xanthonotus (Yellow-spotted Byttneria Borer)

H. A. Hespenheide

The stem-boring buprestid *Agrilus xanthonotus* is one of the most common members of its genus in Central America. In Costa Rica it is found in the driest parts of Guanacaste, the wettest parts of the Caribbean lowlands, and on the Meseta Central (for example, on the campus of the Universidad de Costa Rica), always in association with its host plant *Byttneria aculeata* Jacquin ("uña de gato") of the Sterculiaceae, in turn a common plant of second growth and forest edge. The genus *Agrilus* is the largest of its family in Costa Rica (at least seventy species), in Central America (six hundred species), and perhaps the largest genus of living organisms (several thousand species worldwide). The large number of species reflects the generally narrow host specificity of each and the success of the genus in dispersing to every continent and in exploiting woody angiosperms.

Agrilus xanthonotus is about 7 to 10 mm long and brighter or darker metallic blue, with three pairs of conspicuous yellow spots of pubescence on the elytra as well as some additional yellow pubescence on the underparts. Adults are usually found feeding on the youngest leaves of shoots of the scandent, thorny plant, often together with another, somewhat smaller stem-boring buprestid *Paragrilus aeraticollis* (black elytra, olive green pronotum) and chrysomelids. At least three other smaller and less strikingly marked species of *Agrilus* are associated with *Byttneria aculeata* in other parts of Central America (Mexico, Panama), especially in wetter areas, though I have not seen these in Costa Rica.

In addition to the stem-boring buprestids, the leaf-mining species *Pachyschelus communis* uses *Byttneria* throughout Costa Rica. The mine is serpentine, shows a

681

characteristic pattern in the deposition of the fecal material in the mine (two rows of spots), and terminates if successful in a disk-shaped pupal cell of silk. *Pachyschelus* is the largest genus of buprestid leaf-miners (30 of 135 species known from Costa Rica), although *P. communis,* despite its name, is less common than a couple of other species of the genus (e.g., *P. collaris* on species of the legume genus *Desmodium*). *P. communis* shares the leaves of *Byttneria* with at least five other miners in Costa Rica and Panama: three undetermined microlepidopterans, an agromyzid fly, and a hispid beetle (*Baliosus* nr. *ruber*).

In addition to the obligate herbivore fauna of *Byttneria,* characterized by *Agrilus xanthonotus* and *Pachyschelus communis,* there is another fauna that is focused on the foliar nectaries of the plant (Arbo 1972; Hespenheide 1982; Hilje 1980; review by Bentley 1977). Observations made by Tom Sherry and myself at Finca La Selva during March–April and November–December showed there are three major groups of species of insects visiting *Byttneria* nectaries: ants of more than twenty species (but primarily one species of *Ectatomma*) that station themselves at active nectaries and move relatively little; a group of flies, including members of the Richardiidae, that are continuously associated with a plant but move from leaf to leaf depending on their disturbance by ants or other visitors; and a set of more transient visitors that includes both smaller flies and a variety of parasitoid wasps, especially of the family Chalcididae. This last group of insects suggests that *Byttneria* functions as an "insectary plant" (Atsatt and O'Dowd 1976) and affects the insect and plant community about it, beyond serving as a host for its own herbivores. Hilje (1980) concluded from his study of the plant at several localities in Costa Rica that ants of the genera *Pheidole* and *Crematogaster* did not protect *Byttneria* against invertebrate herbivores and that vertebrate herbivores may have been more important in the evolution of the plant. Hespenheide (1982) concludes that protection of the plant by parasitoids may be more important than that by ants.

*

Arbo, M. M. 1972. Estructura y ontogenía de los nectarios foliares del genero *Byttneria* (Sterculiaceae). *Darwiniana* 17:104–58.

Atsatt, P. R., and O'Dowd, D. J. 1976. Plant defense guilds. *Science* 193:24–29.

Bentley, B. L. 1977. Extrafloral nectaries and protection by pugnacious bodyguards. *Ann. Rev. Ecol. Syst.* 8:407–27.

Hespenheide, H. A. 1982. Herbivores, ants, and visitors to extrafloral nectaries of *Byttneria aculeata* Jacquin (Sterculiaceae): How does the plant benefit? Manuscript.

Hilje, L. 1980. Apuntes acerca de la fauna asociada con *Byttneria aculeata* Jacq. (Sterculiaceae) en Costa Rica. *Brenesia* 17:175–78.

Anartia fatima (Cocinera, White-banded Fatima)

R. Silberglied

This extremely common butterfly of disturbed areas, easily recognized by the yellow or white vertical bands on the wings (fig. 11.5), is distributed from Mexico through Panama. Its larvae feed on a number of plants in the family Acanthaceae, especially the ubiquitous weed *Blechum brownei*. Adults can be seen taking nectar at many kinds of flowers, especially *Lantana*.

This species owes its abundance to extensive clearing and fresh second growth in reasonably moist areas. Its close relative *A. jatrophe* is generally found in drier sites, while species of the related genus *Siproeta* frequent tree falls and other small clearings. All these butterflies utilize the same larval food plants.

In any population of *Anartia fatima,* individuals with yellow bands and individuals with white bands will be found flying together. It had in the past been assumed (Emmel 1972, 1973) that this color-band difference represented a genetic polymorphism. Recent studies (Taylor 1973; Silberglied, Aiello, and Lamas 1980) reveal that

FIGURE 11.5. *Anartia fatima,* upper side (*top*) and underside (*bottom*). Costa Rica (photos, P. J. DeVries).

color is related to age. Males always have brilliant yellow bands upon eclosion, but with time the bands fade to white. In females the band is not necessarily yellow at eclosion but may be anywhere in the range from yellow through white. Female bands also fade to white in time. Because the color of the male bands is a direct reflection of age, it is easier to study the age structure of populations of this species than with most other butterflies.

Striped patterns of butterflies similar to *Anartia fatima* have frequently been called "disruptive," and presumably protect their bearers from visually-hunting predators. However, this hypothesis is not supported by experimental evidence (Silberglied, Aiello, and Windsor 1980).

Butterflies of the genus *Anartia* have been shown to be palatable to a wide array of predators, including amphibians, reptiles, birds, and mammals. They are also acceptable to spiders, mantids, and other predatory arthropods. For this reason as well as its local abundance, *Anartia* has commonly been used as a "control" butterfly in studies of unpalatability and mimicry.

Anartia butterflies show relatively little sexual dimorphism, so the sexes are rather difficult to differentiate when in flight. Males can generally be recognized because they seem to chase not only every other *Anartia* butterfly that comes within a few feet but also other species of butterflies, birds, and people. Females, which are slightly lighter in the dark areas of the wings, spend much of their time flitting at ground level seeking oviposition sites. In the hand, the sexes may be differentiated by carefully extruding the genitalia or by comparing the prothoracic legs; those of the female are bare at the tip and have small barbs, while the male forelegs are fully scaled.

Anartia fatima and its relatives are easily reared in the laboratory. Development requires about 5 to 6 weeks from egg to adult, depending on temperature and other conditions. Females will readily oviposit on sprigs of food plants in small screened cages. The larvae are dark in color and covered with small tubercules and setae that are not urticating; the head bears a pair of knobbed black horns called scoli. Larvae are extremely difficult to find under field conditions.

*

Emmel, Thomas C. 1972. Mate selection and balanced polymorphism in the tropical nymphalid butterfly, *Anartia fatima*. *Evolution* 26:96–107.
———. 1973. On the nature of polymorphism and mate selection phenomena in *Anartia fatima* (Lepidoptera: Nymphalidae). *Evolution* 27:164–65.
Silberglied, R. E.; Aiello, A.; and Lamas, G. 1980. Neotropical butterflies of the genus *Anartia*: Systematics, life histories and general biology (Lepidoptera, Nymphalidae). *Psyche* 86:219–60.
Silberglied, R. E.; Aiello, A.; and Windsor, D. M. 1980. Disruptive coloration in butterflies: Lack of support in *Anartia fatima*. *Science* 209: 617–19.
Taylor, O. R. 1973. A non-genetic "polymorphism" in *Anartia fatima* (Lepidoptera: Nymphalidae). *Evolution* 27:161–64.
Young, Allen M., and Stein D. Studies on the evolutionary biology of the Neotropical nymphalid butterfly *Anartia fatima* in Costa Rica. *Milwaukee Pub. Mus. Contrib. Biol. Geol.* 8:1–29.

Anthrax gideon (Mosca Abeja, Bee Fly)

M. K. Palmer

Larvae of this bombyliid fly (fig. 11.6) are ectoparasites of the larvae of *Pseudoxychila tarsalis* (Coleoptera: Cicindelidae) in Costa Rica (Palmer 1982). Although the taxonomy of this group is in question, this species probably occurs from southern Mexico to Argentina and Brazil, and it probably always parasitizes tiger-beetle larvae.

Adult flies are active during the dry season, and females may be seen on sunny days between about 0900 and 1500 ovipositing in beetle burrows. Females fly slowly about 6 cm from the surface of the banks where beetle burrows are situated; when she finds a suitable burrow, the female hovers in front of it and sometimes alights briefly at the entrance if no beetle is visible. To

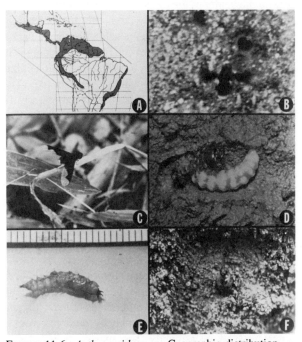

FIGURE 11.6. *Anthrax gideon. a,* Geographic distribution. *b,* Female hovering in front of tiger beetle hole while laying an egg. *c,* Female resting. *d,* Last-instar larva. *e,* Pupa. *f,* Pupal case at entrance of beetle burrow after eclosion of fly. Costa Rica (photos, M. Palmer).

683

oviposit, she hovers about 4–5 cm from the burrow and flips her abdomen quickly toward the hole once for each egg laid.

A. gideon females are quite specific about where they oviposit. Fewer than 1% of all eggs are laid on something other than *P. tarsalis* burrows. Females are also able to discriminate between occupied larval holes and empty ones: burrows into which fly eggs are laid are about twice as likely to be occupied by a larva as are burrows chosen at random. Flies apparently discriminate by sight alone, since they oviposit on artificial "burrows" stuffed with aluminum foil (to simulate the reflective surface of a beetle's head capsule) but will ignore such holes when they are empty. Flies also overwhelmingly preferred third-instar hosts to other stages (at least during most of the dry season), in both areas of Costa Rica that have been studied (San Vito and the "waterfall area" on the road to Puerto Viejo).

Female flies usually lay between one and five eggs per burrow. Eggs are whitish, are roughly spherical, and have a pebbly surface that appears to be sticky when the egg is first laid. Between 20% and 50% of the eggs land inside the burrow (depending on burrow size), and the rest stick to the soil surrounding the burrow. Since eggs collected from these edges did not hatch under a variety of laboratory conditions, it is hypothesized that direct contact with the beetle or its burrow is required for hatching.

Upon hatching, the fly larva attaches to its host, usually on the venter of the thorax but also around the dorsal "hump" of the abdomen. Fly larvae do not increase in size until the beetle larva has constructed the pupation chamber and sealed off its burrow. Hormonal changes in the host's body may trigger fly development at this point, and the fly consumes its host within a week or two. The pupal stage requires 24–28 days in the laboratory. In nature the puparial skin is shed at the host's burrow entrance when the adult fly emerges; adults remain near the burrow for about an hour hardening the exoskeleton before flying away. All males I have ever seen in nature were observed at this point in the life cycle (males have an all-black abdomen, whereas the female's abdomen has a white tip; the situation is exactly reversed in the temperate species *Anthrax analis,* which parasitizes several species of tiger beetles in the temperate zone).

Survivorship of *A. gideon* larvae was very low in the laboratory. Overall, 32% of beetle larvae in the field bear fly larvae (for third instars this value is 45%), but many of these beetles are able to rid themselves of parasites and become adults. Usually, only one fly emerges from a single host, but occasionally a host may yield two smaller flies. The maximum adult life-span is probably not over 3–4 weeks and may be much shorter (adults in captivity survived 6 days or less, and reports of 6–12 days for other species can be found in the literature). Adult food sources are not known, but if they feed at all (many species do not) it is probably on nectar.

*

Palmer, M. K. 1982. Biology and behavior of two species of *Anthrax* (Diptera: Bombyliidae), parasites of the larvae of tiger beetles (Coleoptera: Cicindelidae). *Ann. Ent. Soc. Amer.,* in press.

Apiomerus pictipes (Reduvio, Chinche Asesina, Assassin Bug)

L. K. Johnson

Assassin bugs (Hemiptera: Reduviidae) get their name because of the sudden death they deal their insect prey. There are thirty-one assassin-bug subfamilies, including the Apiomerinae, a New World group of diurnal bugs that await their prey on foliage and flowers. The genus *Apiomerus* has a generally tropical distribution, but species occur as far north and south as Canada and Argentina. *Apiomerus pictipes* Herrich-Schäffer, discussed here, is a common species, recorded from Colorado, New Mexico, Mexico, Central America, and Bogotá, Colombia.

In Costa Rica adults of *Apiomerus pictipes* (fig. 11.7a) are about 12–14 mm long, with a narrow head, large eyes, and a beak that folds underneath the head, the tip fitting into a stridulatory groove on the prosternum. The color pattern is variable. The head, the antennae, and the membranous regions of the forewings are black or brownish black; the thickened basal portion of the forewing is generally a contrasting shade of rust, orange, brown, gold, or red; the ferrugineous pronotum may be broadly banded in black; and the legs are quite variable, with patches that may be redder than the rest of the body. Overall the insect is anything from boldly patterned to blackish. The abdomen, triangular in cross section, has black and white bands and projects, shelflike, beyond the folded hemelytra on either side (fig. 11.7b). Females tend to be a little larger than males and to have a broader, deeper abdomen. The best way to sex them, however, is to inspect the ventral surface of the abdomen. In males it is glabrous, while in females it is densely covered with hairs, which become matted and sticky with resinous material. Species of the genus *Apiomerus* may be hard to tell apart and are best distinguished by an expert on the basis of genital characters.

Apiomerus pictipes is a sit-and-wait predator. In the tropical dry forest zone of Guanacaste Province the adults station themselves on flowering shrubs and forbs, particularly those in open areas, and wait for their insect prey. Plants chosen include *Wissadula, Cordia inermis, Baltimora recta, Ardisia revoluta,* and *Cassia biflora.* The movement of a flower visitor causes the bug to turn or

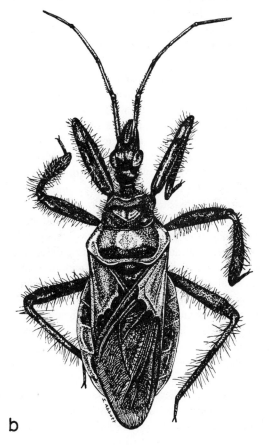

FIGURE 11.7. *Apiomerus pictipes. a,* Two adults on a *Quercus oleoides* tree in front of the tubular nest entrance of their *Trigona dorsalis* prey. The rim of the tube glistens with resin droplets collected by the bees; females of *A. pictipes* in particular may apply this resin to their raptorial front legs, making it easier for them to secure prey. The two bugs are facing one another aggressively. If neither backs away they may lift their forelegs in threat or even grapple briefly. Such aggressive encounters tend to space assassin bugs. Guanacaste Province, Costa Rica (photo, W. Loher). *b,* A dark female; the large eyes can detect prey up to 20 cm away (drawing, S. Abbott).

advance toward the intended victim and slowly, stiffly raise its forelegs. With lightning speed the bug then seizes the insect with its anterior legs and inserts its beak, injecting a proteolytic saliva that paralyzes almost instantly. If the prey has a hard cuticle, the bug may probe for a suitable insertion point, rotating the prey in its forelegs and poking with its stylets at various joints. The bug then sucks its victim for up to an hour or more, occasionally reinserting. A bug can walk around with prey impaled on its beak, with its raptorial appendages free to make other captures.

Prey can be detected by entirely visual means: when tiny paper objects are dangled in front of the bugs, they will raise their forelegs and even strike. Chemical senses may also be employed, as suggested by the way bugs sometimes touch the prey with their antennae before striking, and by the fact they will pick up dead but still moist insects and suck on them. All kinds of insect prey may be taken, including Orthoptera, other assassin bugs, and ants such as *Camponotus* and *Paracryptocerus*. *Trigona* bees are easily caught because they hover before landing, giving a bug ample time to get into striking position. Flies, on the other hand, are often missed because they move too fast. Even when a bug and a fly are placed together in a small closed container, the fly proves elusive. By the time the bug has turned toward the fly and assumed the striking position, the fly is anywhere but in its original spot, climbing the walls, zipping through the air, or walking over the bug's head.

Apiomerus pictipes waits for its prey at nonfloral as well as floral sites. Bugs will appear at fresh fecal material, oozing tree wounds where bees collect material for nest construction, and *Trigona* nest entrances. An advantage of such sites is that they provide sticky material that, when applied to the raptorial legs, aids in prey capture. *A. pictipes* uses glues such as honeydew, fecal material, and tree resin collected from the nest tube of *Trigona* bees or from the corbiculae of the bee victims themselves. The glue may be applied after a series of unsuccessful strikes, as in the case of a bug on a mound of horse feces. The bug struck at and missed eight sepsid flies. Then it dipped the tips of its front legs into the moist fecal material and spread the paste over the prothoracic legs by rubbing them against the mesothoracic legs. The bug then tried for a ninth fly and missed.

Both male and female bugs catch prey, but where several bugs at one site can be compared, it appears that females are better assassins. Females, needing protein for egg production, not only are more likely to try for prey, but are more likely to catch it.

It is not clear whether *Apiomerus pictipes* is aposematic and noxious or cryptic and tasty. The bugs' coloring varies, and they are conspicuous against some backgrounds and camouflaged against others. Ants find dead or dying specimens palatable, but live bugs may be bad-tasting or even dangerous to prey on. *A. pictipes* performs behaviors that can be construed as warnings: when alarmed, a bug will give off a distinct scent, and if seized it will often stridulate, jerking its head so as to rub its beak along the striae of the stridulatory furrow. The sound can be heard as a faint squeaking if the bug is held close to the ear. Assassin bugs should be held carefully, it must be emphasized, since they will defend themselves. The bite resembles the jab of a red-hot needle, and the experience is not one a would-be predator would care to repeat. At night the bugs seek shelter, crawling under the leaf litter or wedging themselves in tree crevices.

Mating takes place in the afternoon at feeding sites where bugs have accumulated and continues overnight in assorted crevices. The male initiates the process, apparently recognizing the female from a distance of several centimeters. His approach is careful, especially if she raises her forelegs in the predatory manner. When the male is within a centimeter or two he rushes her, couples, and twists back out of reach. A scuffle may ensue with the female evading copulation, and, rarely, the male is captured and eaten. Male success is greater if the female is sucking prey; overall only about two-thirds of the mating attempts result in copulation. During copulation the female remains upright, controls the locomotion of the pair, and captures prey.

Uncoupling is, if anything, more ticklish, since both parties risk cannibalism. The two bugs separate at dawn and back off, eyeing one another closely. Not only does the female sometimes kill the male, but the male has been observed to feed on the very female he went to such trouble to mate with.

Individual males will repeatedly attempt to mate until they succeed and will attempt to mate on successive days. Individual females have been known to mate at intervals as short as 2 days.

The eggs of *A. pictipes* are cylindrical objects with chorionic collars that are attached to the substrate at the narrow end in groups of eight to thirty-one. A given female may oviposit several clutches during the dry season in Guanacaste. One group of sixteen eggs was found in February on the side of a *Trigona fulviventris* nest tree where a dozen bugs caught a regular supply of bees; the other observed clutches were laid in captivity.

Among *Apiomerus* species, several functions have been found for the ventral abdominal hairs in females. The function in *A. crassipes* is thought to be tactile, enabling the female the determine the position of the egg group during and just after oviposition. In *A. flaviventris* the hairs hold glutinous plant materials that are applied to the eggs during oviposition to glue them down, prevent water loss, repel parasites, and provide sticky material for the nymphs to put on their mesothoracic legs so they can capture prey. The tactile function seems improbable for *A. pictipes,* since females put resin on their initially downy abdominal hairs, rendering them useless for sensory functions. Most likely the hairs in *A. pictipes* provide a storage site for glue. Whether the glue is used for the benefit of the eggs or nymphs has not been determined.

In captivity, the nymphs hatch in the morning. Hatching has not been observed in nature, but a group of hairy, reddish first instars was found in late March on the ground near the entrance of a *Trigona dorsalis* nest, where adults had earlier been seen. The nymphs were trying to catch tiny flies that arose from the leaf litter.

The relationship between *Apiomerus pictipes* and *Trigona* in the dry forest of Guanacaste is an imporant one. Up to two dozen bugs will aggregate at one nest in the dry season, preying on bees in such numbers that they sometimes destroy the colony. Particularly hard hit are colonies at the bases of trees and colonies that are near clearings or open fields. On the other hand, certain *Trigona* species are not victimized, namely those in which the defending bees mount a mass biting attack against large insects found at the entrance.

Since *Trigona fulviventris* and *T. dorsalis* are docile bees that nest at the bases of trees, it is not surprising that these species suffer heavy predation by *A. pictipes* in the dry season. The bugs at a *T. fulviventris* nest tree capture up to twenty workers per day as they enter and leave the nest. Predation rises to forty to eighty workers per day at *T. dorsalis* nests because of a maladaptive defense these bees possess. When one *T. dorsalis* is captured, the bee releases an alarm pheromone that attracts other workers, which hover in front of the pheromone source as well as in front of other strange insects around the entrance. This hovering behavior harasses small ants and drives them away, but it works very much to the advantage of the assassin bugs, which pick the hovering bees out of the air. Thus, in the case of *T. dorsalis,* when one bee is captured, several others are caught in the next few minutes. Over time, thousands of workers are killed, and in separate years two *Trigona dorsalis* colonies were observed to dwindle and die, while a fluffy pile of dead bodies mounted under the entrance.

There is some reason to believe that the intense relationship between *T. dorsalis* and *A. pictipes* is a recent phenomenon, since *T. dorsalis* is a forest bee and *A. pictipes* is an insect of open fields. In the past century, in Guanacaste, man has cleared away so many trees that the forest-field ecotone has become prominent.

Yet *Trigona* must have been prey of *A. pictipes* in evolutionary time as well, for the assassin bugs are attracted to *Trigona* pheromone. When a bee is captured and releases alarm pheromone, bugs emerge from crevices where the capture could not have been seen. When defending bees are alarmed during a nest raid, the number of assassin bugs at the nest rises quickly. When I catch bees with an insect net, a bug sometimes flies in and alights on me or the net; something that never happens unless I am catching *Trigona*. Assassin bugs are also attracted to the resource-marking and recruiting phero-mones of *Trigona* bees. Bugs land on sugar-water baits to which stingless bees have recruited and appear at aggre-gations of bees at resin and food sources. The presence of the bees themselves is not required for attraction, since bugs have flown in to pheromone-marked baits after an experiment was terminated and the bees chased away.

The responsiveness of *A. pictipes* to *Trigona* pher-omones (which promise a local abundance of prey) may have evolved out of an already close predator-prey re-lationship between diurnal reduviids and bees. Reduviids and bees seem to be predator and prey around the world. For example, *Apiomerus nigrolobus, A. flaviventris,* and *A. crassipes* (the "bee assassin") feed heavily on honey-bees; reduviids in Thailand prey on *Trigona;* and other reduviids mimic Central American *Trigona*. What is the advantage of bees as prey? Bees fly to given spots to find food and hover in front of flowers before landing, in-specting them for quality, conspecific marking pher-omones, or the characteristics they have learned to asso-ciate with food reward. When hovering, they can be caught by assassin bugs too slow to catch flies.

*

Champion, G. C. 1897. Insecta, Rhynchota, Hemiptera-Heteroptera. *Biol. Cent.-Am.* 2:1–416.

Jackson, J. F. 1973. Mimicry of *Trigona* bees by a redu-viid from British Honduras. *Florida Ent.* 56:200–202.

Miller, H. C. E. 1971. *The biology of the Heteroptera.* Hampton, Middlesex: E. W. Classey.

Stejskal, M. 1969. *Apiomerus crassipes,* parásito de las abejas *Apis mellifica* L. *Rev. Núcl. Monagas* 1:125–34.

Swadener, S. O., and Yonke, T. R. 1973. Immature stages and biology of *Apiomerus crassipes* (Hemiptera: Reduviidae). *Ann. Ent. Soc. Am.* 66:188–96.

Szerlip, S. L. 1971. Contributions to the biology and behavior of *Apiomerus flaviventris* Herrich-Schaeffer (Hemiptera: Reduviidae). M.A. thesis, Arizona State University.

Weaver, E. C.; Clarke, E. T.; and Weaver, N. (1975). Attractiveness of an assassin bug to stingless bees. *J. Kansas Ent. Soc.* 48:17–18.

Ascalapha odorata (Bruja Negra, Black Witch)

C. L. Hogue and D. H. Janzen

Common throughout the lowland to mid-elevation Neo-tropics, *Ascalapha odorata* (Noctuidae) (fig. 11.8) is oc-casionally attracted to house and street lights. It is a common nocturnal visitor to bananas and other rotting fruit baits and may be found high in the canopy at night

FIGURE 11.8. *Ascalapha odorata* adult perched at a black-light; notch out of lower left wing is typical bird damage (large beetles are Meloidae attracted to the same blacklight). July 1980, Santa Rosa National Park, Guanacaste Province, Costa Rica 1980, Santa Rosa National Park, Guanacaste Province, Costa Rica (photo, D. H. Janzen).

feeding at punctures in ripe fruits left by feeding verte-brates. During the daylight hours it is often flushed from below rocky overhangs, out of hollow trees, and from other shady roosting sites (where it roosts solitarily). Because of its large size and dark, batlike appearance, it often attracts attention and suspicion. It is regarded by the superstitious as a harbinger of death and is known in Mexico as "mariposa de la muerte" and "miquipapalotl" (Nahuatl: miqui, "death," "black"; *paplotl,* "moth"). On the Yucatan Peninsula its habit of entering houses is the basis of the Mayan name "x-mahan-nail" (*mahan,* "to borrow"; *nail,* "house"). It enters houses both to feed on fruit and to roost in the shade in the day.

The adults are somewhat variable in size but usually have a wingspan of about 15 cm. The females are slightly larger than the males and are recognizable by a generally lighter color and a contrasting white transverse band crossing the wings from anterior to posterior. The upper surfaces of the wings of both sexes are otherwise dark brown, with fine wavy or zigzag lines and conspicuous eye spots near the leading edge of the forewing (smaller) and at the posterior apex of the hind wing (larger and double). The body is an even dark brown and has no scale tufts. Another characteristic color feature is a violet iri-descent sheen that may be seen with oblique light; this is much more noticeable in the female because of the paler ground color.

The larva has been described a number of times. At maturity it is very large, attaining a length of more than 6 cm, and has rather stout proportions. It is widest at the fourth segment (first segment of the abdomen) and tapers abruptly posteriorly. The ground color is gray or gray brown, heavily mottled with black. There is a wide mid-dorsal longitudinal band of light gray that expands on the tenth body segment into a subtriangular area. There is also a broken, undulating lateral band through the spir-acles. The head is all black or may be brownish black dorsally.

Although there is one record from *Ficus carica* (Moraceae), larval food plants probably normally consist of various leguminous plants, of which the following have been observed: *Mora oleifera, Cassia fistula, Gymnocladus dioica* (Caesalpinaceae), *Acacia decurrens, Pithecellobium unguiscate,* and *Pithecellobium saman* (Mimosaceae). It probably feeds on many other genera. C. L. Hogue once reared larvae on the introduced *Acacia dealbata* in Los Angeles, but undersized adults were produced. The larvae feed during the night and rest during the day on tree bark, usually in depressions; the pattern is particularly cryptic in this microhabitat.

Pupation occurs in accumulations of leaves on the ground, in crotches between large branches, and in crevices in rotting dead branches.

A remarkable feature of this moth is its "migratory" habit. Every year in the United States, where it does not maintain a breeding population (with possible local exceptions in the extreme southern portions), it turns up in scattered localities. Specimens, usually worn males, appear regularly in Los Angeles, San Francisco, and even New York, Minneapolis, and southern Canada. Holland's moth book mentions a specimen taken in Colorado during a snowstorm on the Fourth of July! Most such occurrences are in the late summer and fall (August to October) and indicate a northward or radial movement from breeding areas in Mexico or possibly farther south. No experimental work has been done to determine migration paths. While such movements are traditionally called "migration" by entomologists, there is no evidence that the black witches caught in the northern United States are anything other than wanderers carried far beyond their normal habitat.

In lowland Costa Rica, adults of this moth are present throughout the year but are much more conspicuous during the wet months than the dry. Specimens fly about street lights in San José and sometimes decorate the interior of the band shell in Central Park in the rainy season. *A. odorata* appears at higher density at rotting fruit at ground level in Santa Rosa National Park than in the evergreen rain forest of Corcovado National Park (W. Hallwachs, pers. comm.).

During the dry season in the deciduous forests of Santa Rosa National Park, adults of *A. odorata* move into the shady dry creek beds, where many species of nearly evergreen trees keep the humidity up and the temperature down. The moths roost in dark crevices between large boulders and may come out at night to feed on fallen moist figs in the creek beds. These adults probably contribute substantially to the next generation on the new foliage when the rains come, but the sudden appearance of very fresh individuals at fruit bait at this time suggests that some pass the dry season in the pupal state. Their large size, general alertness in the daytime and at night, ability to fly rapidly the moment they are disturbed, body toughness, dry-season presence, and active search for high-quality adult food all suggest that black witches may have life-spans measured in months rather than weeks.

In common with many other noctuids that come readily at night to rotting fruit baits, the black witch may come in large numbers to fruit while rarely appearing at incandescent lights, fluorescent lights, or blacklights only a few tens of meters away. Adults may also fly into a well-lit house, ignoring the lights and flying directly to rotting bananas to feed. When finished or disturbed, such a moth may directly fly out of the well-lit microhabitat.

The species belongs to the owlet moth family (Noctuidae) and is placed in the Erebinae, one of the "quadrifid" subfamilies (with an apparently four-branched median vein in the hind wing) along with the underwing moths (*Catocala*) and the moth with the greatest wingspread of all moths in the world, *Thysania agrippina,* the "bird wing moth" or "white witch."

The species was known as *Erebus odora* in earlier literature and also recently as *Otosema odorata.*

*

Comstock, J. 1936. Notes on the early stages of *Erebus odora* L. (Lepidoptera). *Bull. California Acad. Sci.* 35:95–98.

Sala, F. 1959. Possible migration tendencies of *Erebus odora* and other similar species. *J. Lepid. Soc.* 13:65–66.

Atta cephalotes (Zompopas, Leaf-cutting Ants)

G. C. Stevens

Leaf-cutting ants (*Acromyrmex* and *Atta* species) (fig. 11.9) can be found in forests below about 2,000 m elevation throughout Costa Rica. The underground nests of *Atta cephalotes* can be seen as large bare areas with nest exits sometimes more than 50 m apart. These large nests can contain up to five million workers, ranging from the smallest minima (2 mm in length) to the largest soldier (up to 20 mm in length), with media workers (about 10 mm in length) being the most common to the casual observer. It is the media workers that do most of the leaf collection. The minima are mostly concerned with internal functions, as nurse ants and as tenders of the fungus gardens.

Leaf-cutting ants grow a fungus on the leaf material they collect. This fungus no longer has the ability to produce spores, making taxonomic placement of the adult form difficult if not impossible. The fungus is a basidiomycete, possibly *Leucocoprinus* (or *Leuco-*

FIGURE 11.9. *Atta cephalotes. a,* Worker ant carrying a 15 mm long very young fruit of *Lonchocarpus* back to the nest. *b,* Well-cleared trail across forest-floor litter, with ants carrying freshly cut pieces of leaves (note very small worker ant riding on leaf in center of photograph). Santa Rosa National Park, Guanacaste Province, Costa Rica (photos, D. H. Janzen).

agaricus) *gonogylophora* (Martin 1969). In the nests the fungus appears as a spongy, breadlike structure reaching a diameter of between 15 to 30 cm. Mature colonies may have several hundred of these fungus gardens with complex interconnecting tunnels between them.

Freshly cut plant parts are brought into the colony by foragers and delivered to minima workers that clean and scrape their surface. It is thought that this cleaning and removal of the cuticle speeds fungal growth and removes foreign fungi and bacteria. The minima workers then cut and chew the plant parts into small pieces while adding saliva and fecal material to form a sticky mass. This mass is then added to the fungus garden, and several tufts of fungal mycelia are placed on it. More fecal material is then added to the garden, and other ants continue to add fecal droplets from time to time. The fungus rapidly grows on the new substrate, and when it has become a dense mat the ants collect the swollen tips of the hyphae (gongylidia) as food (Quilan and Cherrett 1977, 1978; Weber 1966, 1972; Wilson 1971).

In laboratory cultures the ants' fungus does not do well in competition with other species of fungi and bacteria. When free nitrogen is added to the culture material, the growth rate of the fungus is increased. The fungus lacks a complete complement of proteolytic enzymes (Martin

and Martin, 1970*a,b;* Martin et al. 1975), and without these enzymes the fungus grows slowly on a medium without free nitrogen, as in freshly cut leaves where the nitrogen is tied up in polypeptides. The fungus obtains these proteolytic enzymes from the fecal material of the ants, which contains all twenty amino acids as well.

The coevolution of the fungus and the ant is even more complex. The gongylidae of the fungus collected by the ants is rich in proteolytic enzymes, and these enzymes are not available for digestion of plant material by the fungus until they are defecated by the ants (Boyd and Martin 1975). The digestive system of the ants has evolved so as not to break down these enzymes. The ants then are simply moving the fungal enzymes from areas in the garden where they are in excess to areas where they are in short supply.

To start a new colony, some of the fungus must be present as an inoculum. This small piece of fungus is carried in the buccal pouch of the founding queen when she leaves the colony on her mating flight. These flights occur about 30 min before dawn's first light on several consecutive nights at the beginning of the rainy season at Santa Rosa National Park. Virgin reproductives leave the colony in great numbers and fly high in the air to mate. One colony produces both males (fig. 11.10) and female reproductives simultaneously. The females are believed to mate from three to five times.

FIGURE 11.10. *Azteca* ants pin a male *Atta cephalotes* to a blacklight sheet where they are foraging for insect prey. May 1980, Santa Rosa National Park, Guanacaste Province, Costa Rica (photo, D. H. Janzen).

689

After the founding queen has mated she returns to the ground and begins to search for a place to start her nest. There seems to be higher survival among queens that dig their new nests near the bases of trees, possibly as a way of avoiding digging vertebrate predators. Mortality at this stage is almost 90%. The major causes of death is fungal attack. This is not the fungus that the queen carries with her, but a kind of fungus that is a threat to many insects and to which the queen is quite susceptible at this time since she has no workers to groom her.

After selecting a nest site, the young queen digs a narrow shaft 10 cm deep with a small chamber at the end. It is here that she starts her garden. She feeds the garden with her own eggs and excrement, and only after the garden is doing well will she attempt to raise workers. If the queen should lose the garden at this stage she will die, because she is unable to get more fungus to start another. The queen remains underground for the next 4–5 weeks without food or water. She tends the garden, moves as little as possible, and waits until her young mature. After 4–5 weeks the first workers appear, and they begin to clean her and care for the garden. At this stage the colony entrance looks like a small volcano about 8 cm across. As the number of workers increases they begin to collect leaves for the fungus. In 3 or 4 years the colony is as large as any of the mature colonies in the forest, although the production of reproductives may be less. There are reports of *Atta* colonies living for more than 20 years, but in Santa Rosa National Park it appears that they live no longer than 7 or 8 years.

Adult *Atta* colonies contribute to the nutrient cycling in the tropical dry forest, being one of the major movers of nutrients in the system (Lugo et al. 1973). Spent fungus that is disposed of outside the nest or old abandoned nests provide a food source for many scavenger insects and microorganisms.

Not all plant species in the forests of Santa Rosa National Park are collected by *Atta cephalotes,* but more than eighty species are taken in a one-year period (Hubbell et al., 1979). The complexities of the preferences of these ants is just beginning to be explored. At this time the chemistry of the plants in the area is still poorly known. The ants appear to be very specific in their plant collection, and they employ intense scouting at all times of the year.

There is evidence that individual ants seek out specific resources when they leave the colony. Marking and transfer experiments showed that individuals belonging to a trail with one resource remained faithful to it when given a choice between that resource and others. New resources are always processed cautiously at first, and only after some days will the new material be readily accepted by the foraging ants.

Hubbell et al. (1979) have also shown with marking experiments that the workers in a multitrail colony have the ability to move between trails and therefore are not locked onto one of the trail systems, or sides of a colony. How the workers are allocated between trails within a colony is unknown.

The working hypothesis in these studies is that the ants are in some way optimizing the growth rate of the fungus. This assumes that the colony fitness is related to the amount of fungus it can produce. Tests are now under way in the laboratory to determine if indeed the ants do select plant material that speeds or enhances the growth of the fungus. It has been suggested (Littledyke and Cherrett 1976) that the fungus is not the only source of food for the ants. Radioactive tracers in leaves rapidly appear in the mouth and guts of foraging ants. This suggests that the ants are eating plant juices, and the fungus could be used just to supply another carbon source, cellulose. If this were the case, possibly the ants are not dependent only on the growth rate of the fungus. There is some field evidence for this claim. Several times during the year (most commonly at the beginning of the rainy season) ants collect large numbers of leaf fragments and then do not incorporate them into the gardens. Possibly these leaves are collected only for the juices they contain. More careful studies of the number of reproductives produced given various foraging habits or environments need to be done.

*

Boyd, N. D., and Martin, M. M. 1975. Faecal proteases of the fungus growing ant, *Atta texana:* Their fungal origin and ecological significance. *J. Insect Physiol.* 21:1815–20.

Hubbell, S. P.; Stevens, G. C.; Wilson, B. R.; Hewitt, S.; Leaman, D. J.; Klahn, J; Roper, D.; and Budilier, S. 1979. Foraging behavior of the leaf-cutting ant, *Atta cephalotes* L. in a tropical dry forest of Guanacaste, Costa Rica. In preparation.

Littledyke, M., and Cherrett, J. M. 1976. Direct ingestion of plant sap from cut leaves by the leaf-cutter ants *Atta cephalotes* (L.) and *Acromyrmex octospinosus* (Reich.) (Formicidae, Attini). *Bull. Ent. Res.* 66: 205–17.

Logu, A. E.; Franworth, E. G.; Pool, D.; Jerez, P.; and Kaufman, G. 1973. The impact of the leaf-cutter ant *Atta colombica* on the energy flow of a tropical wet forest. *Ecology* 54:1292–1301.

Martin, M. M. 1969. The biochemical basis of the fungus–attine ant symbiosis. *Science* 169:16–20.

Martin, M. M.; Boyd, N. D.; Gieselmann, M. J.; and Silver, R. G. 1975. Activity of faecal fluid of a leaf-cutting ant toward plant cell wall polysaccharides. *J. Insect Physiol.* 21:1887–92.

Martin, M. M., and Martin, J. S. 1970a. The biochemical basis for the symbiosis between the ant *Atta colombica tonsipes* and its food fungus. *J. Insect Physiol.* 16:109–19.

———. 1970*b*. The presence of protease activity in the rectal fluid of attine ants. *J. Insect Physiol.* 16:227–32.

Quilan, R. J., and Cherrett, J. M. 1977. The role of substrate preparation in the symbiosis between the leaf-cutting ant *Acromyrmex octospinosus* (Reich.) and its food fungus. *Ecol. Ent.* 3:161–70.

———. 1978. Aspects of the symbiosis of the leaf-cutting ant *Acromyrmex octospinosus* (Reich.) and its food fungus. *Ecol. Ent.* 3:221–30.

Weber, N. A. 1966. The fungus-growing ants. *Science* 153:587–604.

———. 1972. *Gardening ants, the attines.* Philadelphia: American Philosophical Society.

Wilson, E. O. 1971. *The insect societies.* Cambridge: Harvard University Press.

Azteca (Hormiga Azteca, Azteca Ants, Cecropia Ants)

C. R. Carroll

Azteca is a genus in the Dolichoderinae, a subfamily of ants easily recognized by their characteristic odor (various methylated heptanones). The genus is found only in the New World tropics, where it is conspicuous as an aggressive member of the arboreal nesting ant community. Colonies of *Azteca* usually have polymorphic workers, with the majors having large heart-shaped heads. Many species in the genus are extremely difficult to separate unless reproductives are present. *Azteca* ants (fig. 11.10) seem to be largely restricted to those tree species that have hollow green nodes or stems, or trunks in which they can tend populations of several species of mealybugs (Pseudococcidae). The mealybugs provide the ants with sugar, several vitamins, and amino acids. In Costa Rica, stem- and trunk-nesting *Azteca* are commonly associated with the trees *Pithecellobium saman*, *Triplaris americana*, *Cocoloba caracasana*, *Terminalia lucida*, *Cordia alliodora*, and several species of *Cecropia*.

Occasionally *Azteca* construct external nests of carton, a material they make from plant fibers and secretions. South of Costa Rica, carton-nesting *Azteca* species are much more common and occasionally make extremely large nests. For example, in the north-central Amazon basin, *Azteca* species (probably *Azteca chartifex*) construct carton nests on the trunks of large forest trees. Occasionally these nests reach widths of 1 m and lengths of more than 2 m. In these regions the carton-nesting *Azteca* are the New World analogues of the Old World carton-nesting *Crematogaster* ants in the African wet tropics. These enormous colonies presumably have a great effect on local insect populations and therefore indi-

rectly on local plant populations as well, but this has not been investigated. All *Azteca* that live inside plant cavities use carton material to modify and partition their nests. It seems likely that the habit of building large external carton nests is simply an extreme extension of their general use of carton for nest modification.

Dennis Leston has frequently argued that tropical ant communities typically have a mosaic distribution of colony foraging areas that is determined by the presence of various aggressive species. In the Neotropics, species of *Azteca* contribute to such mosaic colony distributions by aggressively excluding many other species from nesting in the vicinity of their colonies. *Azteca* workers will cut into the stem nests of other species and destroy the contents even though they do not often take over the stem as part of their colony nest site. This aggressiveness can easily be verified with simple experiments. For example, I colonized ten artificial soda straw nests with complete colonies of the stem-nesting ant *Pseudomyrmex gracilis* and placed the nests within a 20-m radius of a large *Azteca* colony that was nesting in the trunk of a large *Cocoloba caracasana* tree. Within a week, *Azteca* workers were observed cutting into nine of the ten nests. Control straws without ants were ignored by *Azteca* workers. *Azteca* ants may even exclude mutualists from their host plants. For example, even though *Pseudomyrmex triplaridis* is an aggressive species that is obligatorily associated with the riparian tree *Triplaris americana*, it is displaced or prevented from entering young *Triplaris* when such trees occur near large *Azteca* colonies.

Although large colony size and aggressive behavior may be an advantage in displacing other, potentially competing, ants, there are disadvantages as well. Aggressive behavior represents a calorie drain on the colony with no immediate foraging payoff. Curiously, *Azteca* workers seldom rob the brood from other ants even when they have breached a nest and the brood are easily available. Large colony size coupled with aggressive behavior may result in more successful displacement of other ants, but the long-term caloric and nutrient return must be large if their strategy is to be successful. Since *Azteca* tend mealybugs for their sugary secretions, these ants have thereby secured a fraction of their caloric needs, and this undoubtedly subsidizes some of the energy cost of aggressive behavior.

In addition to the energy costs of large colony size and aggressive behavior, another potential disadvantage comes from nest predation. An *Azteca* colony represents a large resource for any animal that is capable of overcoming the colony defenses. Woodpeckers are important predators on *Azteca* colonies. In riparian sites in Guanacaste Province, the large woodpecker *Phloeoceastes guatemalensis* frequently destroys *Azteca* colonies that are nesting in small trees. For example, at one riparian locality *Azteca* colonies were attacked in eleven saplings of *Pithecellóbium saman* that ranged in height from 4 to 15 m. As many as 80% of previously occupied stems had been torn apart, and old scars indicated that the trees had been visited by woodpeckers in previous years as well. *Cecropia* trees in lowland sites have a mutualistic relationship with several species of *Azteca*. These trees commonly have one or more scars in each hollow internode section from woodpecker attacks. Colonies of other arboreal nesting species that have small colony subunits dispersed through the vegetation are less frequently attacked by woodpeckers. The reason is probably that these highly dispersed nests represent a resource that requires a large search effort for relatively small rewards. However, as alternative sources of food disappear for woodpeckers in the dry season of deciduous forests, attacks on stem-nesting ants increase. In the seasonally dry forests of Guanacaste Province there is a significant increase in the attack rate on stem-nesting ants in upland sites during the dry season. The attack rates in riparian forests do not change seasonally.

The high frequency of woodpecker attacks on large *Azteca* nests seems to have some consequences for the coexistence of other ant species with *Azteca*. In *Cordia alliodora* the hollow nodes may be frequently colonized by many different species of arboreal nesting ants. However, *Azteca* and the armored ant (a species of *Paracryptocerus*) are the most frequent inhabitants, and the ants are very likely obligatorily associated with the tree. In the upland forests of Guanacaste Province, approximately 30% of the green and living *Cordia* nodes contain *Paracryptocerus*, whereas in riparian forests and in the wet lowland forests of the Atlantic watershed the occupancy rate drops to less than 5%. In the latter two locations, *Azteca* ants occupy 23% of the *Cordia* nodes. They have a strong preference for the terminal young green nodes, and, although these nodes have more interior room and are good feeding sites for mealybugs, they are also the nodes that are most frequently opened by woodpeckers. At Finca La Selva it is difficult to find more than a few percent of the terminal nodes of large *Cordia* trees that have not been torn open by woodpeckers. Thus, while *Azteca* successfully controls the best nodes for mealybug nutrition, the result is increased predation by woodpeckers. To the extent that woodpeckers depress the colony growth rate and colony size of aggressive *Azteca* ants, coexistence with other ants that nest in more interior nodes should be favored. It is difficult to test this hypothesis in any rigorous manner, since it is almost impossible to find large *Cordia* trees that are free of substantial damage from woodpeckers.

Young *Azteca* queens seem to have a high mortality rate during the initial stages of colony founding. The frequency of young colonizing queens of both *Azteca* and *Paracryptocerus* follows the same seasonal pattern. In the dry forests of Guanacaste, for example, their peak abundance occurs during the first two months of the rainy season. Out of a sample collection of sixty-two young queens of *Azteca* and *Paracryptocerus* in *Cordia* nodes, the following percentages of living and dead queens were obtained. In Guanacaste, 25% of the *Azteca* queens were dead, and at Finca La Selva in the Atlantic lowlands 52% of the young *Azteca* queens were dead. Only living queens of *Paracryptocerus* were found. If most of the young queens that are released from a colony fail to successfully establish new colonies, then we might expect that *Azteca* colonies would compensate by producing large numbers of colonizing queens. This does not seem to be the case, since only 33% of *Cordia* nodes with *Azteca* contain winged queens, while 53% of such nodes with *Paracryptocerus* contain winged queens. This situation is similar to that of another common aggressive arboreal nesting ant in Costa Rica, *Crematogaster brevispinosa*. These ants also have a high extinction rate for new colonies, and yet colonies do not maximize the output of potential queens.

Compared with other ant species, highly aggressive species may have an unusually high mortality rate for small colonies. Perhaps the reason is that the food returned for each foraging effort per worker is unusually low and therefore small colonies of aggressive species are frequently outcompeted for food by other, more efficient species. If this is true, we would expect strong selection for the following traits. In general, aggressive species should allocate more energy and food to colony growth than to colony multiplication through queen production. In contrast to other ant species, we should expect to find that production of new queens is delayed until the colony approaches its maximum expected size. We would also expect to find strong selection for traits that minimize competitive overlap for food with other species. In the case of large colonies of aggressive species this is accomplished overtly by destroying the nests of other ant species. In the case of small colonies of aggressive species, minimizing food overlap is accomplished by tending mealybugs inside plant cavities. If mealybugs are not available, then the small worker force of incipient colonies must face strong diffuse competition from the colonies of other species in the vicinity. Thus the presence or absence of mealybugs at the stage of colony founding may be the most critical factor in colony survival and subsequent fitness.

*

Carroll, C. R. 1979. A comparative study of two ant faunas: The stem-nesting ant communities of Liberia,

West Africa, and Costa Rica, Central America. *Am. Nat.* 113:551–61.

Emery, C. 1894a. Estudios sobre las Hormigas de Costa Rica. *Ann. Mus. Costa Rica,* pp. 45–64.

―――. 1894b. Studio monografico sul genere *Azteca* Forel. *Mem. Acc. Bologna* 3:119–52.

Bittacus banksi (Bitacido, Bittacid, Hanging Fly)

G. W. Byers

Three genera of Bittacidae (Insecta: Mecoptera) occur in Costa Rica: *Bittacus, Kalobittacus,* and *Pazius.* The only fairly common species is *Bittacus banksi* Esben-Peterson, which has been found along the western coast of Mexico, in Yucatan, and in much of lowland Central America. The following comments pertain to Bittacidae generally because, of the nine species now known from Costa Rica (1980), six are still undescribed and unnamed. We have virtually no observations of the behavior of any species, almost no detailed habitat information, and no knowledge whatever of the immature forms of any Central American species.

Adult bittacids may be found in low, shaded, herbaceous growth or grasses but, unless hunted in these habitats, are most likely to be seen around lights at night. They are fairly large insects with long, slender abdomens, long legs, and four elongate, many-veined, often hyaline and iridescent wings. *Bittacus* includes the largest and most robust species, *B. banksi* (fig. 11.11) being about 22 mm in overall length with a wingspan of approximately 45 mm. At rest, *Bittacus* species fold the wings alongside the abdomen. The one known species of *Pazius* is large but more slender, about 25 mm long and 37 mm across the outspread wings. Species of *Kalobittacus* are only about 13 mm in length with a 32-mm wingspan; they rest with the wings held out to the sides. The legs terminate in a single large claw that with the last tarsal segment folds back against the more basal part of the tarsus to form a raptorial appendage. Occasionally bittacids are seen carrying insect prey grasped in one of the hind legs, since these legs are most frequently used in prey capture. The bittacid feeds by inserting its slender beak (a prolongation of the head, bearing scissorlike mandibles at its tip) into the prey organism and consuming the contents, leaving the hollow exoskeleton.

In flight, bittacids are slow and awkward, giving somewhat the impression of a large crane fly with an extra pair of wings. When not flying, the insects suspend themselves from a twig or the edge of a leaf, usually by means of the front and middle legs. When alarmed, they ordinarily fly only a few meters and come to rest in low vegetation (that is, they are not likely to fly up into trees that are shading their habitat). Males offer prey insects to females as a nuptial meal. They may also evert two pale-colored, rounded pheromone-dispersing vesicles from the back of the abdomen to attract females from distances up to several meters, then display the nuptial prey. *Kalobittacus* and *Pazius* are active mainly by day, while *Bittacus* is chiefly nocturnal and may ascend into the foliage of trees at night.

Larval bittacids, as far as is known, are terrestrial and saprophagous, feeding particularly on dead insects. They move only slowly along the ground surface in search of food and are occasionally collected in pitfall traps at night. They have somewhat the appearance of sordid-whitish caterpillars with branched, fleshy projections from most body segments. These projections are often encrusted with soil placed on them by the larvae.

Records of bittacids from Costa Rica are mainly from the Pacific lowlands, less often from montane environments. *Bittacus* and *Kalobittacus* probably occur throughout the country, but *Pazius* has so far been found only at Golfito (but ranges through Panama into northwestern South America). There are collection records for every month from May to September, with a distinct peak of abundance in July for all three genera. Readers are urged to record observations and collect specimens of these insects to the extent permitted, and to make these available to taxonomists of Mecoptera.

Blaberus giganteus (Cucaracha, Giant Cockroach, Giant Drummer, Cockroach of the Divine Face) and *Xestoblatta hamata* (Cucaracha)

C. Schal

The Blattaria are diverse behaviorally, ecologically, and physiologically, yet the higher classification is well established and the phylogenetic relationships are well worked out. Hence the group is amenable to comparative and evolutionary studies. Of the approximately four thousand described species of cockroaches, a very small percentage share man's domicile. The vast majority occur in the tropics, where in some habitats the most abundant species are undescribed (Fisk and Schal 1981). Like other animals and plants, they are experiencing range reduction and possibly extinction as man extends his range into the tropical forests.

I have chosen to present a comparative approach to two Costa Rican species. The reader should bear in mind that although the physiological and behavioral literature based on laboratory studies is rather large, field ecological data are sparse and limited to enclosed natural

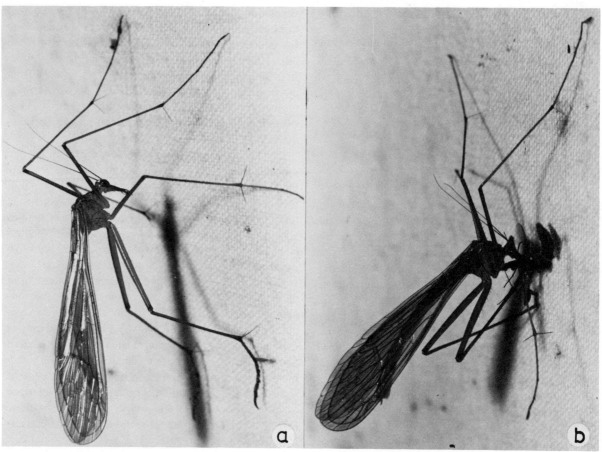

FIGURE 11.11. *Bittacus banksi. a,* Adult resting at blacklight; note fully extended hind tarsi.
b, Adult eating small fly caught at blacklight; note curled and grasping position of hind tarsi.
Santa Rosa National Park, Guanacaste Province, Costa Rica, June 1980 (photos, D. H. Janzen).

habitats such as caves, hollow trees, and decomposing logs.

Blaberus giganteus (= *B. colosseus*) is a large cockroach (fig. 11.12*a*) that has been widely collected in all seven provinces of Costa Rica. It and its close relative *Archimandrita* sp. are probably the largest Neotropical cockroaches by weight. *B. giganteus* is a nocturnal insect occasionally seen at lights. At the La Selva field station, and in La Pacifica and Santa Rosa in Guanacaste, it is commonly found in hollow trees, sharing the habitat with bats, opossums, and various arthropods. The cockroaches within the tree stratify vertically along micro-meteorological gradients. Small nymphs occur in the bat guano at the base of the tree. At night they are active aboveground in the exposed moist sections, but during the day they retreat to the drier, more protected portion of the substrate. They are adept at burrowing (Crawford and Cloudsley-Thompson 1971), a behavior that has important adaptive value in light of the common raids on such trees by army ants. Larger instars occur higher in the tree, and adults occupy perches above them. By day, both adults and large nymphs hide in crevices in the inner wall of the tree.

Males of *B. giganteus* exhibit an interesting behavior toward attractive odors. Males engage in escalated agonistic encounters and increase their searching along the floor of the cage when a sexually receptive, virgin female is introduced. This behavior may be related to the ecological stratification of the age classes. Since nymphs occur below the adult males, a newly ecdysed female will most probably approach males from below. Also, since oviposition occurs in the guano, postoviposition receptive females move upward from the base of the tree. The male enhances his chances of encountering receptive females by directing his search downward. Nothing is known about the diurnal variation in micro-meteorological profiles that may produce directional air flow to enhance chemical communication (as in forest habitats, Schal 1982; see below).

The social behavior of *B. giganteus* has been examined both in the laboratory and in the field (Gautier 1974*a,b*; pers. obs.). The social structure is plastic, describing a continuum between territoriality and hierarchy. At low densities, most males occupy perches without temporal or spatial changes in site occupancy. As the density increases and the number of preferred unoccupied sites

FIGURE 11.12. *a, Blaberus giganteus,* adults feeding. *b, Xestoblatta hamata,* adults copulating. Finca La Selva, Sarapiquí District, Costa Rica (photos, C. Schal).

decreases, a territorial/hierarchical system emerges, with more males meandering without site specificity. At even higher densities, males, females, and large nymphs clump together in preferred areas, leaving large regions unoccupied. Top-ranking males are distinguishable by their erect posture and aggressiveness.

Sexually receptive females passing near groups of males disrupt the territorial or hierarchical structure. Aggressive behavior is escalated, and males engage in hoarding, a combination of sexual displays directed at the female and agonistic acts directed at other males. Recent studies have attempted to delineate the male social system with regard to the ontogeny and physiological correlates of agonistic behavior. However, it is not known

695

whether hierarchies and territories in this species confer greater mating success on the dominant male, as in the cockroach *Nauphoeta cinerea* (Schal and Bell 1982*b*).

In contrast to *Blaberus, Xestoblatta hamata* (fig. 11.12*b*) is a forest-dwelling Costa Rican cockroach. It is similar in size and appearance to *Periplaneta americana* but is not known to occur outside tropical forests. Like the giant cockroach, this species exhibits age-class and sexual-height stratification (Schal 1982). Nymphs occur in the leaf litter. Adults migrate from the leaf litter to occupy nocturnal perches in the understory, then move back to the forest floor before sunrise. In an extensive study at the La Selva field station I found that males oriented to chemical signals (pheromones) emitted by females. Temperature and wind-profile data provide evidence for a vertical ascent of air in the forest understory. Thus directional transport of airborne pheromone molecules may explain the observed sexual stratification with males perching higher than females (Schal 1982).

Unlike *Blaberus,* an ovoviviparous cockroach that incubates about forty eggs internally for 60 days, the oviparous *Xestoblatta* female is an efficient reproductive machine, ovipositing approximately twenty-five eggs every 8 to 10 days. *Xestoblatta* females rely on two kinds of food resources in addition to an opportunisitc food habit that allows them to exploit "seasonal food" (fruits, seeds, flowers; *Blaberus* has a superabundant food resource in bat guano). One such food source is the shed bark of a legume, *Inga coruscans*. At La Selva, marked females return to shedding *Inga* trees at regular intervals that correlate well with early stages of the ovarian cycle immediately following oviposition. Chemical analysis of the sequestered materials indicates that the bark has low nitrogen and high lipid content. Hence, *Inga* may provide *Xestoblatta* females with energy reserves and materials to be used in vitellogenesis (providing the eggs with food reserves). These materials are acquired in the first 4 days after oviposition. At other stages in the ovarian cycle other foods are taken, depending on their chemical composition. Thus lipids are preferred early in the gonadotrophic cycle, then proteins are taken, and carbohydrates are selected before oviposition.

An important nitrogen source is provided by males. After copulation (on the 4th night of the ovarian cycle), the male empties the contents of his uricose accessory sex glands into his genital region. The female feeds on this material. Labeled uric acid injected into males is recovered in the female's eggs after mating; that is, paternal material is utilized for nymphal development (Schal and Bell 1982*a*). The quantity of uric acid taken by the female and sequestered in the eggs depends on the female's nutritional state. More male-derived uric acid is recovered from females on nitrogen-deficient diets than from females on high-protein diets (Schal and Bell 1982*a*).

Unlike most cockroaches, *Xestoblatta* females mate repeatedly during their adult life. The contribution of male urates to the female probably constituted an important factor in the evolution of this mating system.

Blaberus and *Xestoblatta* are very different in their ecological niches, mating systems, social structures, nutritional requirements, and morphology. The forests and plantations of Costa Rica include a large diversity of cockroaches: brightly colored wasp and beetle mimics, diurnally active species, acoustically communicating species, semiaquatic species in ephemeral bromeliad pools, species possessing noxious chemical defenses, others that share the nests of ants and termites, cave dwellers with antennae several times as long as their bodies, flat species well adapted for life under tree bark, and saltatory species that provide a serious challenge to the diverse forest herpetofauna that preys upon them. Reproductively, the cockroaches have oviparous, ovoviviparous, viviparous, and parthenogenic representatives, which fit well into ecological reproductive strategy classifications of r- and K-selected species.

*

Crawford, C. S.,and Cloudsley-Thompson, J. L. 1971. Concealment behavior of nymphs of *Blaberus giganteus* L. (Dictyoptera: Blattaria) in relation to their ecology. *Rev. Biol. Trop.* 18:53–61.

Fisk, F. W., and Schal, C. 1981. Notes on new species of epilamprine cockroaches from Costa Rica and Panama (Blattaria: Blaberidae). *Proc. Ent. Soc. Washington* 83:694–706.

Gautier, J. Y. 1974*a*. Processus de différenciation de l'organisation sociale chez quelques espèces de Blattes du genre *Blaberus:* Aspects écologiques et éthologiques. Doctoral diss., University of Rennes.

———. 1974*b*. Etude comparée de la distribution spatiale et temporelle des adultes de *Blaberus atropos* et *Blaberus colosseus* (Dictyoptères) dans quatre grottes de Trinidad. *Rev. Comp. Anim.* 9:237–58.

Schal, C. 1982. Intraspecific vertical stratification as a mate-finding mechanism in tropical cockroaches. *Science* 215:1405–7.

Schal, C., and Bell, W. J. 1982*a*. Ecological correlates of paternal investment of urates in a tropical cockroach. *Science,* in press.

———. 1982*b*. Determinants of dominant-subordinate interactions in males of the cockroach *Nauphoeta cinerea. Biology of Behavior,* in press.

Blastophaga and **Other Agaonidae**
(Avispita del Higo, Fig Wasp)
D. H. Janzen

Fig flowers (*Ficus* spp.) are pollinated by 1–2 mm long wasps in the Agaonidae (chalcidoid parasitic Hymenoptera). Agaonidae the world over are split into many genera (Wiebes 1979), but many Costa Rican agaonids are *Blastophaga*. A generalized life cycle for a *Blastophaga* (cf. Janzen 1979a) is that the female fig wasp flies to a particular species of *Ficus* at a time when it is bearing a crop of very small immature figs (called syconia in the fig literature). Each of these immature figs is a hollow sphere. The spheroidal syconium is really an invaginated compound receptacle thickly lined with hundreds of pistillate florets, each with a fully developed and receptive stigma. The female wasp enters through a natural hole (ostiole) in the distal end of the fig. However, the ostiole is densely plugged by overlapping scales (fig. 11.13b), and she has to push and weave her way through this plug. After she has entered, a second or third female that tries to enter sometimes dies stuck in the plug. In the process of entering, the successful wasp is stripped of her wings and probably most dirt, fungal spores, and bacterial contaminants. The pollen she carries is not removed because it is in two small pockets in her thorax. The tight plug of scales in the ostiole restricts entry to a small number of female wasps (though repeated entry sometimes wears a clear tunnel through the ostiole, allowing many females to enter; Janzen 1979b). After pollination and oviposition, the female dies in the syconium.

Once inside the syconium, she moves from stigma to stigma and pollinates each. It is assumed that a single pollen grain is used for each stigma. At the time of pollination, she also probes down the style with her ovipositor. If the style is short, she contacts the single-ovuled ovary and lays an egg at the side of the ovule. If the style is so long that she cannot reach the ovule, she lays no egg. However, these are relative statements, since an increase in the number of wasps in the syconium can lead to oviposition in almost every female floret. Some species of agaonids are parasites of the system, ovipositing in the above manner but not pollinating the flowers. They are therefore dependent on some other species of agaonid to pollinate the flowers in the young fig (a developing fig that is not pollinated is aborted by the parent). The agaonids and their parasites (see below) generally kill 30–80% of the ovules in a syconium, and therefore a syconium generally produces fifty to two hundred wasps (Janzen 1979c).

After about a month, the wingless male agaonids emerge from a small number of the florets and crawl or burrow through the tightly packed florets seeking out florets that contain female wasps. The male cuts a hole in the side of the floret and, inserting his extensible abdomen, copulates with the female inside. These males may also fight to the death with each other inside the fig, and in some species there are two quite different male morphs, one of which is specialized for fighting (Hamilton 1979). The newly mated females emerge (or are helped out of the floret) over a period of 1–2 days and go directly to the newly dehiscent anthers of the recently matured male florets, where they stuff their thoracic pockets with pollen. At this time the males, apparently in concert, cut an exit hole through the ostiole or wall of the fig and die, often falling out on the ground. The females walk out of the tunnel without damaging their wings and fly off in search of a tree with a new crop of young figs that have just become receptive to wasps, thereby completing the cycle. The fig then ripens within a few days and is eaten by vertebrates. The fruits consumed therefore have both intact and dead seeds (cf. Janzen 1979a).

If only one wasp enters a syconium, the resulting set of agaonids contains only brothers and sisters, so all mating is between sibs. The degree of relatedness of the wasps from one fig is relevant in understanding why the males cooperate in digging the tunnel through the side of the fig. However, there is a second powerful selective pressure for cooperation. If one male is not strong enough to do it, the others must cooperate or their mates will not escape, irrespective of the degree to which the males are related. The average number of agaonids to enter a syconium ranges from 1.5 to as high as 7 within a single fig tree's crop (syconia that do not receive a pollinating wasp are aborted by the fig tree, except for commercial fig varieties). The distribution of entering females among syconia is such that it appears that females avoid syconia that already have a wasp in them until most contain a wasp (Janzen 1979b).

The tight synchrony of syconium development within a fig tree crown is generally thought to prevent inbreeding by *Ficus*, since the emerging wasps must fly to another tree to find receptive syconia. However, it is unknown whether wild figs could produce fertile seeds with their own pollen if syconia of different ages were simultaneously present on one tree. Self-fertilization does seem possible in island populations lacking intra-crown synchrony of syconial development (Ramirez 1970), and in Santa Rosa National Park there are trees of *Ficus ovalis* that bear developing figs for about three months (June–August) (Janzen 1979c). In the latter case, at the time of emergence of the first generation of wasps, the same branches have receptive syconia with newly entering wasps. However, it is still possible that the emerging females have a behavioral response to fly long distances before being attracted to receptive figs, and that they therefore do not attempt self-pollination. One fig tree may produce several crops during a year, but they are separated by several months. It is assumed, but undemonstrated, that fig wasps live only a few days after leaving the fig.

Adult fig wasps are eaten by those predators that prey on all sorts of small insects (spiders, ants, dragonfly adults, flycatchers, swifts, swallows, Malaise traps).

697

FIGURE 11.13. *Blastophaga* and other Agaonidae. *a,* Ripe figs (*Ficus*) (dark) and ripening figs from which the fig wasps have emerged. *b,* Section through a fig showing ostiole (upper hole) and seeds from which fig wasps have emerged (seeds in center with small exit hole). *c,* Leafless fruit-bearing *Ficus cotinifolia* adult (note person in crown for scale). *d,* Fruit-bearing branches of tree shown in *c* (fruits at stage of having been pollinated about 1 week before). All at Santa Rosa National Park, Guanacaste, Costa Rica (photos, D. H. Janzen).

There is no evidence that the developing young syconia with their contained wasps are eaten by any animals. However, lygaeid bugs feed on figs on the parent tree as well as on the ground (cf. Slater 1972), and I suspect that they would puncture and suck the contents of ovaries with larvae as well as those without. While on the tree, the figs (fig. 11.13*a*) of many species are oviposited in by curculionid weevils (*Ceratopus* spp.). The weevil larvae burrow through the developing florets and generally destroy most of the florets by the time the fig falls. Nearly mature figs are also fed on by the larvae of several species of pyralid moths. Once they fall to the ground, figs are fed on by many animals. However, if the wasps have not left a fig by this time, they are destined to die in the unopened fig anyway (wasps in fallen figs usually mean that the males were unsuccessful in cutting an exit hole through the wall of the syconium).

Agaonids are parasitized by a number of genera of torymid wasps, which oviposit through the wall of the syconium while the agaonid larvae are developing inside. The females of these wasps are easily distinguished from agaonids because they generally have ovipositors much longer than their bodies so that they can penetrate the thick syconium walls. The parasites (parasitoids) exit through the hole made by the agaonid males, and there may be nearly as many individuals as agaonids. However, if there are too many parasitoids, there may not be enough agaonid males to cut the exit hole, since there are substantially more female than male agaonids produced in a fig.

Fig trees, and therefore fig wasps, are found from sea level to about 2,500 m elevation in Costa Rica (as in the rest of the tropics) and in all habitats except mangroves (they may even be there as small epiphytic shrubs, however). There is probably at least one species of pollinating agaonid for each species of fig in Costa Rica. Burger's (1977) monograph on Costa Rican figs lists about sixty-five species, and there are about nine hundred described species of figs in the world (and therefore at least approximately that many species of agaonids). Since each species of fig has its own species of pollinating agaonid, fig trees appear to be free of interspecific competition for pollinators. This may be a partial explanation for why there are generally more species in *Ficus*

than in any other tree genus in a given Costa Rican habitat (there are four to eight species of *Ficus* in most Costa Rican habitats).

Some core questions about fig wasps that remain unexplored are: What fraction of those arriving at a tree are of the proper pollinating species? How long do the females live after emerging from a syconium? How synchronous are crops within the crown and within the population, and how does this vary with habitat? What are the sibling relationships of the wasps from a fig? Can figs hybridize, and do they? An even more complex set of questions remains to be answered about figs themselves (Janzen 1979*a*).

*

Burger, W. 1977. Moraceae. *Fieldiana, Bot.* 40:94–215.

Hamilton, W. D. 1979. Wingless and fighting males in fig wasps and other insects. In *Reproduction, competition and selection in insects*, ed. M. S. Blum and N. A. Blum. New York: Academic Press.

Janzen, D. H. 1979*a*. How to be a fig. *Ann. Rev. Ecol. Syst.* 10:13–51.

———. 1979*b*. How many parents do the wasps from a fig have? *Biotropica* 11:127–29.

———. 1979*c*. How many babies do figs pay for babies? *Biotropica* 11:48–50.

Ramirez, W. 1970. Host specificity of fig wasps (Agaonidae). *Evolution* 24:680–91.

Slater, J. A. 1972. Lygaeid bugs (Hemiptera: Lygaeidae) as seed predators of figs. *Biotropica* 4:145–51.

Wiebes, J. T. 1979. Figs and their insect pollinators. *Ann. Rev. Ecol. Syst.* 10:1–12.

Bombus ephippiatus (Chiquizá de Montaña, Bumblebee)

R. Heithaus

This is the most common bee (fig. 11.14) at high altitudes in Costa Rica. It is especially abundant above the oak forests on Cerro de la Muerte. It may be found at altitudes over 3,400 m, or as low as 1,000 m. It also occurs in Panama and El Salvador (Bernhardt and Montalvo 1979), but the limits of distribution for this species are unknown. Like most other species of *Bombus, B. ephippiatus* is basically adapted to cool climates and is not found in lowland tropical habitats.

The workers are shaped like typical hairy bumblebees. They are basically black, with yellow hairs on the sides of the thorax and two longitudinal yellow stripes extending about half the length of the abdomen. There is much variation is size, with body lengths varying between 10 and 17 mm. Males resemble workers in color and size, but they may have some yellow on the face, just above the mandibles. Males also lack the pollen-carrying hairs that females have on their hind legs. Queens are quite unlike workers or males, and they might be mistaken for

FIGURE 11.14. *Bombus ephippiatus* queen. San Gerardo de Dota, Cerro de la Muerte, Costa Rica (2,450 m) (photo, D. H. Janzen).

a "new" species by a casual observer. They are twice the length and breadth of workers and have much more yellow and orange.

Workers may be encountered during all months of the year, and reproductives are found during most months. There is some seasonality to the production of reproductive castes, since queens and males were especially common during August on Cerro de la Muerte (Heithaus, unpub. data). Like most other bumblebees, *Bombus ephippiatus* is partially endothermic, so it is frequently active when other nectar-feeding insects are not foraging. This probably contributes to its great success in high-altitude habitats relative to other types of bees. On foggy days and early in the morning, workers may be found walking or resting on flowers.

This bee is the most abundant potential pollinator and the most effective pollinator for many species of plants in high-altitude habitats. On Cerro de la Muerte it visits nearly all the plants that are animal pollinated, including those that are "adapted" for pollination by hummingbirds or flies. Workers' choice of plants is largely correlated with flower abundance and with the amount of nectar produced per flower. Workers tend to visit only one or two species of flower even though the species is extremely broad in its feeding. There is some evidence that "flower constancy" is lower for individuals of *B. ephippiatus* than for temperate bumblebees (Heithaus, unpub. data). The major food plants for *B. ephippiatus* on Cerro de la Muerte are *Senecio oerestedianus, S. andicola, Cirsium subcoriaceum* (all Compositae), *Pernettya coriacea, P. prostrata* (Ericaceae), *Hypericum irazuense* (Hypericaceae), *Lobelia irazuensis* (Lobeliaceae), and

Myrrhidendron donnell-smithii (Umbelliferae). Hummingbirds and tachinid flies also use these flowers extensively. There have been no experimental studies demonstrating competition among these groups, but hummingbirds (*Eugenes fulgens*) show interference behaviors against *B. ephippiatus* workers. The birds chase workers from *Cirsium* flowers and have been seen to catch workers in their bills and fling them to the ground.

A few references given below provide an entry to the extensive work on the ecology of the genus *Bombus*. Very little work has been done on *Bombus ephippiatus*. Many interesting questions may be generated by studies of this "tropical" species in a genus of bees that has been successful primarily in temperate-zone habitats.

*

Bernhardt, P., and Montalvo, E. A. 1979. The pollination ecology of *Echeandia macrocarpa* (Liliaceae). *Brittonia* 31:64–71.

Heinrich, B. 1976a. Resource partitioning among some eusocial insects: Bumblebees. *Ecology* 57:874–89.

———. 1976b. The foraging specializations of individual bumblebees. *Ecol. Monogr.* 46:105–28.

Michener, C. D., and Amir, M. 1977. The seasonal cycle and habitat of a tropical bumblebee. *Pacific Insects* 17:237–40.

Richards, K. W. 1978. Nest selection by bumblebees (Hymenoptera: Apidae) in southern Alberta. *Canadian Ent.* 110:301–18.

Brentus anchorago (Bréntido, Brentid Beetle)

L. K. Johnson

The Brentidae (Coleoptera: Curculionoidea) are a family of weevils found in tropical and subtropical forests. Some species are myrmecophilous, but most of the approximately thirteen hundred species are wood-boring, with larvae that develop inside the wood of dead or dying host trees.

One of the most common and widespread Neotropical brentids is *Brentus anchorago* L. It ranges from southern Florida and Baja California, through Central America, into South America as far as Uruguay and Argentina. In Costa Rica it occurs in lowland dry forest and lowland wet forest, and at elevations up to 2,100 m on Volcán Irazú.

A preferred host tree in both Florida and Costa Rica is *Bursera simaruba* (Burseraceae). In Costa Rica it also occurs on *Bursera tomentosa,* on *Pseudobombax septinatum* (Bombacaceae), and on cut lumber; in Panama it breeds on *Cavanillesia platanifolia* (Bombacaceae); and in Paraguay it was reported from *Pentapanax warmiingiana* (Araliaceae). The adult weevils are frequently found in great numbers at densities up to four hundred per square meter.

Adults of *B. anchorago* are long and slender with elongate prorostra tipped by tiny mandibles. The cuticle is shiny and black with narrow yellow stripes running the length of the longitudinally grooved elytra. The size variation in the adults is perhaps unsurpassed in any other coleopteran, the females ranging from 8 to 27 mm in length and the males from 9 to 52 mm. Sexual dimorphism as in other brentids, is marked: the female is broader for her length, with a shorter, more downcurved rostrum, while the male has a long, straight rostrum, with the antennae nearer the tip (fig. 11.15a). *Brentus anchorago* differs from similar brentids in Costa Rica by being shinier and slimmer. The male, furthermore, can be distinguished by the pronounced indentation halfway along his prothorax (fig. 11.15b).

The life cycle begins when an ovipositing *B. anchorago* bores a small hole in the bare wood of a decaying tree with her mandibles, working the rostrum into the wood up to the depth of the antennal insertion. In the hole is deposited an elliptical, yolky egg that is 1–2 mm long depending on the size of the female. The larva that emerges is white and relatively slender, with a sclerotized head and minute thoracic legs. With sclerotized mandibles the larva chews itself a gallery below the cambium, where it presumably feeds on sap or fungal mycelia. The different larval galleries in *B. anchorago* are crowded close to one another but are not thought to come into contact. There are indications that larval life may last a year.

As adults, the beetles can survive for more than one breeding season. During the dry season in the Guanacaste deciduous forest they appear to undergo reproductive diapause. The adults support themselves during this period by feeding on sap or by visiting flowers. They will inset their rostra into flowers of *Cordia curassavica, Cordia inermis* (Boraginaceae), and *Casearia corymbosa* (Flacourtiaceae); and they occurred on *Calycophyllum candidissimum* (Rubiaceae) in numbers up to twenty to thirty per branch.

In April and May in southern Florida, which is the beginning of the wet season, adult weevils accumulate on *Bursera simaruba*. In Guanacaste they appear on rotting *Bursera* throughout the wet season. Healthy trees are not used, but the weevils arrive quickly at a fallen branch, suggesting they are attracted by chemical cues signaling the onset of decay. A *Bursera* log becomes less attractive as decay progresses, and by the time the wood is crumbly and the log is losing its shape, the weevils have left.

On the log the weevils live under loose bark and in holes made in the sapwood. Mating and oviposition take place by day on the exposed surfaces, provided the wood is not wet with rain or heated by direct rays of the noon sun. The male wanders about on the surface of the log. When he finds a drilling female he lays his rostrum across her and guards her, copulating for about 1 min at inter-

FIGURE 11.15. *Brentus anchorago. a,* Adults of both sexes 18 mm in length. The female (*left*) is broader, with a shorter and more downcurved rostrum, and the antennae are placed farther back from the tip of the rostrum to permit easier drilling of oviposition holes. The male (*right*) has a proportionately longer rostrum (drawing by S. Abbott). *b,* Long, shiny, and slim male. The narrowing midsection of the prothorax is typical of the species (photo, A. Forsyth). *c,* A medium-sized male mating with a large female that is pushing with a prothoracic leg at the snout of an intruding male. Costa Rica (photo, A. Forsyth).

vals, until the oviposition hole is prepared and the female begins laying.

Male rivalry occurs in this species and probably explains the elongate male snout. While guarding a female the male periodically sweeps his rostrum over her, twiddling his antennae. If in his sweeping he detects a second male snout, the two males begin fencing with their rostra. The smaller male is generally routed, since the longer rostrum has greater speed and leverage. If the two males are about the same length, the fight becomes more intricate. They stack themselves head-to-tail and nip at one another's genitalia with their tiny mandibles, while trying to protect their own genitalia with their hind tarsi. Disturbance by a rival is especially likely to occur during

copulation, at which time the resident male has fewer defenses (fig. 11.15*c*).

Females also fight one another. A given female will sometimes interrupt several other females engaged in reproductive activities. Frequently an attacking female will insert herself under the snout of a drilling female and push up, thereby extracting the driller from her oviposition hole. At this point a fight may ensue, with poking, swatting, or mutual genital nipping. As with the males, it is usually the smaller of the two weevils that eventually flees. The females do not appear to be fighting for the oviposition hole itself, although a hole takes a quarter of an hour or more to prepare. Rather, the females may be driving one another from suitable oviposition areas, in the manner sometimes observed for female hymenopterous parasitoids at trees filled with host larvae. The occurrence of aggressive behavior among females suggests the possibility of larval competition in *B. anchorago.*

Aggressive behavior is sometimes observed between the sexes as well. A male may swat a female trying to pry up the snout of the female he is guarding, or he may even attack one merely drilling in the vicinity of his female. A female, for her part, may behave aggressively toward an attendant male. Her first rejection tactic is to leave the hole she is drilling and begin walking. This makes it difficult for the male to remain in copulatory position on her slippery dorsum. If he stays in place, she may try to scrape him off by walking under the bark. Finally, the female may simply turn on the male and swat him. Females tend to reserve their rejection behaviors for males of their own size or smaller, but if a female has just oviposited, she tends to reject any display of male interest.

After a wet period the weevils teem with mites. The weevils try to scrape them off with their forelegs, but mites dislodged by scraping (or by weevil fighting) have little trouble clambering back onto their hosts. A more serious problem is predation. In Guanacaste *Anolis* lizards and *Phloeoceastes* woodpeckers feed on *B. anchorago,* the lizards hunting by stealth and the woodpeckers swooping down suddenly to snatch large individuals. Perhaps as a result of predation, the weevils studied during the course of one wet season got noticeably more wary at the approach of a human observer. Larger weevils were the most apt to retract under the bark, a pattern that became more pronounced with time, suggesting that large weevils with their larger eyes see danger better, and that they learn avoidance sooner, being the preferred target of large predators. A weevil may also freeze in response to the movement of a human observer, fall off the trunk if it is vertical, and "play dead." Such a weevil will remain motionless for a minute or two. The combination of reflex dropping and thanatosis is thought to confuse predators, but this awaits proof.

Ants, in contrast to the vertebrates, are inefficient predators of *B. anchorago*. Ants have trouble getting a purchase on the waxy bodies, and weevils walk away from them unharmed. Brentid slipperiness, incidentally, is best developed in those myrmecophilous species that are robbers of ants.

*

Beyer, G. 1904. A few notes on Brentidae. *J. N.Y. Ent. Soc.* 12:168–69.

Haedo Rossi, J. A. 1961. Bréntidos Argentinos (Brenthidae, Coleoptera). *Opera Lilloana* 6:1–317.

———. 1967. Bréntidos del Paraguay (Col. Brentidae). *Acta Zool. Lilloana* 22:157–83.

Johnson, L. K. 1982. Sexual selection in a brentid weevil. *Evolution,* in press.

Kleine, R. 1923. Neuere biologische Beobachtungen bei Brenthiden. *Deutsch. Ent. Zeitschr.* 1923:619–23.

———. 1927. Über die Brenthidenfauna von Costa Rica. *Stett. Ent. Zeit.* 88:288–96.

———. 1931. Die Biologie der Brenthidae. *Ent. Rdsch.* 48:149–53, 164–67, 173–76, 189–94.

———. 1933. Weitere biologische Mitteilungen über Brenthiden. *Ent. Rdsch.* 50:25–28, 49–50.

Sharp, D. 1895. Brenthidae. *Biol. Centr.-Amer.* 4:1–80.

Caligo memnon (Buhito Pardo, Caligo, Cream Owl Butterfly)

P. J. DeVries

This spectacular species of "owl" butterfly (fig. 11.16) ranges from Mexico to Colombia. In Costa Rica it inhabits forests, cafetales, and banana plantations from sea level to about 1,500 m elevation. Although it is found on both sides of the country, it is most abundant on the Pacific slope and appears to be unable to tolerate very wet areas like La Selva (pers. obs. in field and greenhouse). Adults have a wingspan of about 13 cm, being among the largest butterflies in the world. *C. memnon* (Satyridae: Brassolinae) is distinguished from similar species by its dull, blue gray color above with an ill-defined creamy yellow patch on the forewing upper side. The underside is mottled black and gray with two large "owl eyes" on the hind wing that are characteristic of the genus.

Host plants are *Musa sapientum* (Musaceae) and *Heliconia* spp. (Heliconiaceae). The mature larva is very large (11 cm long), may weigh up to 15 g, is light brown with fine brown striations along the dorsum, and has a stout forked tail. The head capsule is reddish with a dorsal evagination and a corona of stout horns. The chrysalis is light green to light brown and somewhat obovate, with the wing pads forming a small breast. The lethargic larvae feed gregariously and have an eversible gland anterior of the first set of legs that may act as a defense against ants. The larva of another species, *C.*

FIGURE 11.16. *Caligo memnon,* upper side (*top*) and underside (*bottom*). Costa Rica (photos, P. J. DeVries).

euriolochus, which also has this gland, was not attacked by a raiding swarm of *Eciton birchelli* (Formicidae) when placed in a raiding column (DeVries, unpub. data), perhaps owing to secretions from this gland.

Adults are crepuscular or are active during the day within the deep shade of the forest. If disturbed in the forest, they fly a short distance and then perch on the side of a vertical tree trunk displaying *one* of the "owl eyes," not both as illustrated in popular works. It has been suggested that these eyes mimic large vertebrate eyes (owls?) and act as a defense against predators. Another theory suggests that the eye spot set against the mottled pattern on the underside mimics a large distasteful tree frog that is found on the sides of trees (Strandling 1976). It is not uncommon to find adults with beak marks in the eyed portion of the hind wing, which makes me suspect that the eye spots may act as target areas for predators and allow the butterfly to escape with only a piece of wing

703

gone. Beak marks are very common in the eyed portions of satyrid butterflies, which appear to act as target areas (pers. obs.). Adults feed on a variety of rotting fruits: banana, mango, *Zapote* spp. (Sapotaceae), *Annona* spp. (Annonaceae), *Spondias* spp. (Anacardiaceae), pineapple, (Bromeliaceae), sap from wounds in trees and vines, fungi, dung, and carrion. They are not known to visit flowers, but I have one specimen from Santa Rosa National Park with a orchid pollinarium (probably *Epidendrum stamfordianum*) on the tip of the proboscis. This may be a common occurrence and would be overlooked unless the proboscis is uncoiled. In dry-forest habitats individuals are often found with heavy infestations of mites on the proboscis. Nothing is known about the biology of these mites and the butterflies they interact with. Caged magpie jays at La Pacifica readily ate adults, and I myself found no objectionable taste when I ate several. At times *C. memnon* can become a serious pest in banana plantations, and it has been the subject of biological control (Harrison 1962, 1964).

*

Harrison, J. O. 1962. The natural enemies of some banana pests in Costa Rica. *J. Econ. Ent.* 56:282–85.
———. 1964. Factors affecting the abundance of Lepidoptera in banana plantations. *Ecology* 45:508–19.
Strandling, D. J. 1976. The nature of the mimetic patterns of the brassolid genera, *Caligo,* and *Eryphanis.* *Ecol. Ent.* 1:135–38.

Callionima falcifera (Mancha de Plata, Silver-spotted Sphinx)

W. A. Haber and G. W. Frankie

This sphingid (fig. 11.17) is a common, widespread species that is likely to be encountered throughout Costa Rica except at very high elevations. Males are readily attracted to ultraviolet lights, but females rarely are. The adults are medium-sized (wingspan 6–7 cm) and very stout bodied. The ground color is red brown to charcoal gray with beige and darker brown markings. A shiny silver mark on the forewing in the shape of a whale with its tail in the air is a good field mark (although two rarer congeners have similar whale marks). The hind wings of both sexes are a rich red brown (fulvous). The female's abdomen tapers to a point, but that of the male ends in a brush of dense hairlike scales that expand laterally into a V-shaped tail (function unknown).

This species ranges from the southern United States through Central America. In South America it is replaced by a sibling species, *C. parce* (R. Seifert, pers. comm.). It is common in Costa Rica in both Atlantic and Pacific lowlands and reaches Monteverde and other mid-elevation sites. Adults can be found throughout the year even in the dry Pacific lowlands of Guanacaste Province.

FIGURE 11.17. *Callionima falcifera,* adult male perched at blacklight. June 1980, Santa Rosa National Park, Guanacaste Province, Costa Rica (photo, D. H. Janzen).

Adults are strictly nocturnal but may be observed visiting flowers shortly after dark (1830). They are active throughout the night, but nothing is known about the timing of nectar feeding, courtship and mating, and oviposition. *Callionima falcifera* has a very short tongue (for a sphingid) of 14–16 mm. It is thus adapted for visiting many species of nocturnal moth flowers with short tubes or open corollas with exposed nectar.

The host plants of the larvae are species of *Stemmadenia* (Apocynaceae), small to medium-sized trees with opposite shiny leaves and copious white sap rich in alkaloids. The fruit ("Huevo de caballo") is a dehiscing double pod packed with seeds that are individually coated with a bright red or orange aril attractive to birds. Eggs are laid singly beneath the leaves as in most species of hawkmoths. The pale green eggs are 1.5 × 1.3 mm.

Larvae occur in two distinct color forms: one is plain green, unmarked except for a white stripe on each side of the head; the second form is chocolate brown with a cream yellow saddle in the middle of the body. Larvae burrow into the soil to pupate.

Eggs require about 14 days to hatch; larvae complete development in another 2–3 weeks; and pupae last about 4 weeks, giving a generation time of 10 weeks. Generations are continuous and overlapping at Monteverde from May to November. As with most adult sphingids in Costa Rica, there are two peaks of abundance: May–June and September–October, corresponding to the two peaks in annual rainfall. In highly seasonal areas such as the Pacific lowlands some sphingids pass the dry season as pupae aestivating in the soil, while others probably emigrate to wetter habitats in the adjacent mountains or even to forests of the Atlantic drainage.

The cryptic adults are probably palatable to birds even though the larvae feed on plants rich in toxic alkaloids. The red brown color of the adults' hind wings may function as a startle color when the wings are flashed at a bird. When resting in the leaf litter of the forest, *C. falcifera* adults are virtually invisible unless they move. The gray and brown color forms of the adult may also function in forcing birds to maintain two search images.

The larvae have outstanding defenses in addition to camouflage. They squeak or stridulate when disturbed (a sound audible for about 30 cm), and they secrete noxious foam from glands behind the head on the first thoracic segment. The yellow foam has a bitter flavor, but it has not been analyzed. It may contain alkaloids collected from the host plant.

At present our knowledge of ecology and behavior of tropical sphingids is meager; however, because sphingids are a large and numerous component of the tropical fauna, it is certain that they involve significant relationships with plants, both as pollinators and as herbivores.

*

Hodges, R. W. 1971. *The moths of America north of Mexico*. Fasc. 21. *Sphingoidea*. London: E. W. Classey.

Calynda bicuspis (Palito Andando, Juanpalo, Guanacaste Stick Insect)

D. M. Windsor and A. Massey

Calynda bicuspis Stal. (fig. 11.18) is the only really common stick insect found in savanna habitats in the province of Guanacaste, Costa Rica. Rarely seen during the day, this large and conspicuous insect is easily spotted at night on many species of low shrubs. As evening ap-

FIGURE 11.18. *Calynda bicuspis,* adult female hanging below branch. Hacienda Palo Verde, near Bagaces, Guanacaste Province, Costa Rica (photo, D. H. Janzen).

proaches the insects abandon their motionless daytime postures and resume their usual activities—feeding and mating.

Nymphs and adults of both sexes occur in brown and green color phases with innumerable pattern variants. Both sexes are wingless as adults. The female abdomen terminates in a troughlike ovipositor used to flip eggs. Two appendages protrude from the end of the male abdomen, nonfunctional rods in immature males, sickle-shaped female claspers in mature males. Sexual maturity in females is not easily determined. An abdomen swollen by eggs is a sure sign of maturity, but not all adult females are swollen. Copulating females measured in the field were at least 12.5 cm long. The ovipositors of mature females usually extend at least 1 cm beyond the end of the abdomen.

Mature females of *Calynda* appear to continuously produce and disperse eggs, flipping each singly 1–2 m so that most eggs probably come to rest on the ground beneath the food plant on which the insect has just been feeding. Oviposition rates for captured females with food varied between one and twelve eggs per day. Most adults kept in culture lived for more than 6 months, and some individuals lived nearly a year.

Calynda eggs are remarkably seedlike in appearance: 1–2 mm in length, ovoidal, gray or brown, capped on one end, and striped longitudinally by the "micropylar plate." Hatching occurs any time between 70 and 150 days after oviposition. The first-instar nymphs are easily classified into one of two morphologies based on overall length; the short morph measures 11–12 mm, the long morph 15–17 mm. This does not appear to be a sexual dimorphism, since both males and females can be reared from either morph, nor does it relate to season of oviposition. Male nymphs appear to molt two fewer times than females, maturing 60–70 days after eclosion rather than the 90 days required by females.

While many phasmid species are noted for their parthenogenetic tendencies, *Calynda* appears to reproduce sexually. Nonmated females laid only sterile eggs, and males were at least as common as females in most immature size groups of the population. Reproductive males were nearly twice as abundant as mature females in an exhaustive census of *Calynda* in front of the Palo Verde field station during January 1979. Approximately 75% of all mature females discovered were *in copulo*. Much of the male population was clustered within 1 to 2 m of copulating females, suggesting rigorous competition between males for mates (Sivinski 1978). Once a male had successfully clasped a female it appeared he was unlikely to relinquish his position for several days, riding "piggyback" and even feeding from his position at the rear of the female. The hold of the male on the female's sixth and seventh abdominal segments is made even more secure by small, sharp hooks on the male's terminal abdominal segment that appear to dig into the female's intersegmental membranes. Mating was found to be assortative; that is, larger females tended to mate with larger males.

Phasmids are herbivores, and the literature that exists indicates that they tend to have specific plant preferences (Bedford 1978). *Calynda* appears exceptional in this regard, since we have recorded it feeding on at least a dozen different host plants and we suspect many more species could be added to the list. Favorite food plants include *Cassia biflora, Lonchocarpus minimiflorus, Indigofera* sp., *Guazuma ulmifolia, Mimosa pigra,* and *Gliricidia sepium. Calynda* was often observed browsing on the ant-acacia, *Acacia collinsii,* but never was it observed feeding on *A. farnesiana,* which has no ants.

Although *Calynda* appears active in all months of the year, abundance does appear to drop considerably by the end of the dry season, and only a few large adult females survive until the coming of the rains in late April or early May. *Calynda* is easily studied during the early dry season because the population becomes concentrated around the remaining islands of green vegetation. The population grows rapidly in the early months of the wet season, as evidenced by the abundance of immature individuals, but, individuals are dispersed and less apparent than in the early dry season.

*

Bedford, G. O. 1978. Biology and ecology of the Phasmatodea. *Ann. Rev. Ent.* 23:125–49.

Sivinski, J. 1978. Intrasexual aggression in the stick insects *Diapheromera veliei* and *D. covilleae* and sexual dimorphism in the Phasmatodea. *Psyche* 85:395–405.

Catasticta teutilla (Paracaída, Teutilla)

P. J. DeVries

This species (fig. 11.19) ranges from Mexico to Colombia; the genus is principally high-elevation Andean. In Costa Rica *C. teutilla* occurs in wet forest areas from 900 to 3,800 m elevation and is probably the most abundant *Catasticta* in Costa Rica. The sexes are dimorphic. Females have an orange stripe on the black base color of the upper side, males have white on black. Males of *C. teutilla* may be distinguished from the similar species *C. flisa* by having much more checkered yellow on the underside.

The host plant is a mistletoe, *Dendrophthora costaricensis* (Loranthaceae), a parasitic epiphyte of certain forest trees (DeVries, unpub. data). Eggs are laid in clusters of twenty to ninety eggs on the underside of the young leaves of the host plant, usually on the shoot apex. Larvae hatch simultaneously and are gregarious feeders. The larvae have a ground color of mottled green, are

FIGURE 11.19. *Catasticta teutilla. a,* Upper side of male (*left*) and female (*right*). *b,* Underside of male (*left*) and female (*right*). Costa Rica (photos, P. J. DeVries).

moderately hairy, and have a black head capsule and posterior segment that give the appearance of two heads. When molested, the larvae rear their heads up and exude a drop of dark greenish fluid from the mouth, which I assume is a defense. Pupation takes place off the host plant, on the bark of a tree, leaves, or lichens. The chrysalis is mottled black and green and looks like a bird turd. Adults emerge from the chrysalis in the morning.

Adults are actively foraging and courting during the sunny morning hours. Males perch in the tops of trees and shrubs and chase all butterflies that pass by. Ovipositing females are active from about 1000 till early afternoon, flying about solitary trees in pastures and along road cuts. The flight of both sexes is fluttery and erratic, similar to that of distasteful day-flying moths. It is not known whether *C. teutilla* is chemically protected. Adults visit the flowers of various composites, *Eupatorium* sp., melastomaceous shrubs, *Smilacina* sp. (Liliaceae), *Fuchsia* spp. (Onagraceae), *Symphonia* (Guttiferae), and *Inga* (Leguminosae).

The principal habitats in Costa Rica for *C. teutilla* are the high-elevation wet forests (Cerro de la Muerte, Talamanca, Volcán Irazú), where the mean number of sunny hours per day is very low, and very occasionally the species occurs in lower-elevation habitats (Turrialba, San José). That the adults are restricted in activity by the number of sunny hours per day raises the question how they deal with a spell of 2 weeks of cloudy and rainy weather, which is common in these habitats. In the morning hours adults perch on grass stems and bask in the sun, which I assume is to raise the body temperature to facilitate flight. In *Papilio polyxenes* (Papilionidae) the insects are unable to fly until they reach a critical body temperature (Rawlins and Lederhouse 1978), and I find the same true with *C. teutilla* early in the morning before the sun has warmed them.

*

Rawlins, J. E., and Lederhouse, R. C. 1978. The influence of environmental factors on roosting in the black swallowtail, *Papilio polyxenes asterius* Stoll (Papilionidae). *J. Lep. Soc.* 32:145–59.

Centris aethyctera and *C. fuscata* (Abejas Antofóridas, Anthophorid Bees)

G. W. Frankie, S. B. Vinson, and P. A. Opler

FIGURE 11.20. *Centris aethyctera* adult male perched on a leaf. Costa Rica (photo, G. W. Frankie).

Centris bees are important pollinators of many trees and lianas in the lowland dry forest in Costa Rica (Frankie and Coville 1979; Frankie, Opler, and Bawa 1976; Frankie et al. 1980). These bees, which are solitary in habit, are mostly active during the dry season (P. A. Opler, field collections). Two common species in this forest are *Centris aethyctera* (fig. 11.20) and *C. fuscata*.

Males and females of *C. aethyctera* are easily recognized by the repeating sequence of yellow, orange brown, and dark brown bands on the dorsal surface of the abdomen and the orange brown coloration on the ventral surface. (The sequence is best observed when the abdomen is fully extended.) The thoracic hairs are densely piled and buff colored. Both sexes average about 14 mm in length.

Males and females of *C. fuscata* have a solid red brown abdomen. The thoracic hairs are densely piled and light brown. Both sexes average about 14 mm in length. In the dry forest *C. fuscata* may be confused with *C. heithausii*, which is similar in size and coloration. However, *C. heithausii* may be separated from *C. fuscata* by its gray thoracic hairs. Also, females of *C. heithausii* tend to be larger than *C. fuscata* females by about 2 mm. Detailed descriptions of the above three *Centris* species can be found in Snelling (1974).

C. aethyctera and *C. fuscata* are both solitary ground-nesting species. Although little is known about the nesting biology of *C. fuscata*, considerable information is available on the nesting of *C. aethyctera* (Vinson and Frankie 1977).

Nests of *C. aethyctera* have been found in fully exposed sites in derived savanna and in patches of highly disturbed second-growth forest. Soils in these sites consist, respectively, of dark fine-particle clay and a mixture of sand and clay. The former soil is well known in Guanacaste Province, where it dries out and fractures into large blocks during the dry season and "disolves" into gumbo during the wet season.

Nest entrance holes are inconspicuous, having no turret or mound built around the openings. Excavated tunnels, which are unbranched and measure 0.9×1.1 cm in cross section, extend downward to a depth of 8 to 13 cm. Each contains four to seven linearly arranged, urn-shaped cells. In provisioned cells, the bottom portion is stocked with pollen and the upper portion with nectar. An elongate and slightly curved egg (0.4×0.99 cm) is deposited on the pollen beneath the nectar provision. Developing larvae apparently consume mostly nectar before utilizing the pollen. The uppermost cell, the last to be constructed, is only partially provisioned and contains no immatures of *C. aethyctera*. It is suspected that this false cell may represent an adaptation to confuse or distract parasitic bees of the genera *Mesoplia* and *Mesocheira*, several species of which are present in Guanacaste.

C. aethyctera nests only during the dry season, and apparently more than one generation of bees occurs each year.

Adults of *C. aethyctera* actively forage during December–April, while *C. fuscata* is restricted in its foraging to January–March (Frankie and Opler, field collections). Both bees visit a wide variety of plant species (mostly trees and to a lesser extent vines and lianas) for pollen or nectar or both. Examples of plant species commonly visited by both bees include the following: *Andira inermis, Byrsonima crassifolia, Cochlospermum vitifolium, Cydista heterophylla, Dalbergia retusa, Gliricidia sepium, Lonchocarpus costaricensis, Securidaca sylvestris, Tabebuia ochracea, T. impetiginosa,* and *T. rosea.*

C. aethyctera, C. fuscata and many other *Centris* species in the dry forest can be considered canopy-dwellers, since most of their foraging takes place there (Frankie and Coville 1979). This is due in part to the lack of suitable floral resources in the understory. A recent experimental study in Guanacaste indicated that when given

707

a choice between the same resource in the overstory and understory, most *Centris* still preferred overstory flowers (Frankie and Coville 1979). (Flowering individuals of the second-growth shrub *Cassia biflora* were transplanted to wooden boxes and positioned at the tops and bases of wooden towers 4.5 m in height in second-growth forest.) Interestingly, only *C. fuscata* and a few other *Centris* species showed any tendency to forage in the understory.

Males of *C. aethyctera* and *C. fuscata* are known to establish small territories in and around certain tree species during the morning. Once a territorial bee selects an appropriate site, it will regularly patrol around a central point; the patrolled area has a radius of 0.5–2 m. Most intruders will be vigorously pursued and examined at close range. Nonconspecifics and conspecific females will almost always be ignored once the initial examination has been made. However, encounter with a conspecific male results in a more vigorous interaction in which one individual is actively chased away. Territorial behavior apparently serves a mating function; but exactly how it aids mating is unclear, since apparent matings in trees have been observed only in rare instances (Frankie 1976; Frankie and Baker 1974; Frankie, Vinson, and Coville, in prep.).

In encounters between territorial bees and nonconspecifics as well as between conspecific females, the intruder usually is displaced to another side of the plant or completely excluded. Displacements of both types can easily be observed on small trees such as *Cochlospermum vitifolium*. It seems likely that displacements from a given tree increase the chances for outcrossing, since displaced bees usually visit at least a few flowers before being discovered (Frankie 1976; Frankie and Baker 1974; Frankie, in prep.).

*

Frankie, G. W. 1976. Pollination of widely dispersed trees by animals in Central America, with an emphasis on bee pollination systems. In *Tropical trees: Variation, breeding and conservation,* ed. J. Burley and B. T. Styles, pp. 151–59. London: Academic Press.

Frankie, G. W., and Baker, H. G. 1974. The importance of pollinator behavior in the reproductive biology of tropical trees. *An. Inst. Biol. Univ. Nal. Autón. México* 45, ser. Bot., 11:1–10.

Frankie, G. W., and Coville, R. 1979. An experimental study on the foraging behavior of selected solitary bee species in the Costa Rican dry forest. *J. Kansas Ent. Soc.* 52:591–602.

Frankie, G. W.; Haber, W. A.; Opler, P. A.; and Bawa, K. S. 1980. Characteristics and organization of the large bee pollination system in the Costa Rican dry forest. *Biotropica,* in review.

Frankie, G. W.; Opler, P. A.; and Bawa, K. S. 1976. Foraging behavior of solitary bees: Implications for outcrossing of a Neotropical forest tree species. *J. Ecol.* 64:1049–57.

Snelling, R. R. 1974. Notes on the distribution and taxonomy of some North American *Centris* (Hymenoptera: Anthophoridae). *Los Angeles County Mus. Contrib. Sci.* 259:1–41.

Vinson, S. B., and Frankie, G. W. 1977. Nests of *Centris aethyctera* (Hymenoptera: Apoidea: Anthophoridae) in the dry forest of Costa Rica. *J. Kansas Ent. Soc.* 50:301–11.

Chelobasis bicolor (Abejón de Platanillo, Rolled-leaf Hispine)

D. R. Strong

This beetle is a "rolled-leaf" hispine (fig. 11.21). The Hispinae are a subfamily of the coleopteran family Chrysomelidae (or Hispidae of the superfamily Chrysomelidae in older European literature). Chrysomelids are virtually all herbivorous. There are relatively few hispine species at high latitudes, and most mine into host tissues as larvae. In the New World tropics the number of hispine species is far greater, and both leaf-mining and surface-feeding larvae are common. The rolled-leaf hispines all have surface-feeding larvae. Actually, the rolled-leaf hispines are distinct morphologically from even other tropical, surface-feeding hispines. Adults are extremely flat, very waxy and, most interestingly, smooth (contra their name, *hisp,* "spine"). Larvae are extremely flat (fig. 11.21*a*), and do not look at all like most beetle larvae. Small individuals look like immature whiteflies (Aleyrodidae, Homoptera), and large rolled-leaf hispine larvae are reminiscent of water pennies (aquatic larvae of beetles in the family Psephenidae), common in streams of North America. The smooth adults and the odd morphology of larvae will probably qualify the rolled-leaf hispines as a new subfamily of chrysomelids when a morphological phylogeneticist "discovers" the group. Obviously the taxonomy of insects in the tropics is far behind that of groups like trees and vertebrates.

The rolled-leaf hispines are almost exclusively restricted to plants in the order Zingiberales, in the New World. The only known exception is an undescribed species that feeds and lives upon *Cyclanthus bipartatus* in both larval and adult stages. However, there are similar beetles, flat and with larvae like water pennies, on palms in the New World tropics. In the Old World tropics the restriction may not be as great, but from G. L. Gressitt's work we at least know that beetles similar to rolled-leaf hispines, with similar larvae, attack gingers in New Guinea.

In Central America all families in the Zingiberales support breeding populations of rolled-leaf hispines except the Musaceae (bananas and plantains), which are not native, and the Cannaceae. All genera of rolled-leaf hispines attack *Heliconia,* which is the only genus in the Heliconiaceae. Other families (Zingiberaceae = gingers,

FIGURE 11.21. Hispine chrysomelids. *a*, Larva of *Cephaloleia consanguinea* feeding on leaf surface of *Heliconia imbricata* (Finca La Selva, Sarapiquí District, Costa Rica). *b*, *Chelobasis bicolor*, feeds on *Heliconia latispatha* on the Pacific side of Costa Rica and on *Heliconia tortuosa* on the Atlantic side. *c*, *Cephaloleia instabilis*, feeds on *Heliconia latispatha* and *H. difficilis* on the Pacific side of Costa Rica. *d*, *Cephaloleia negripicta*, feeds on many species of *Heliconia* in most of Costa Rica. *e*, *Cephaloleia puncticollis*, feeds in flowers of *Heliconia imbricata* wherever this plant occurs in Costa Rica. *f*, *Cephaloleia vicina*, feeds on many species of *Heliconia* all over Costa Rica.

Costaceae, and Marantaceae) are attacked by only one genus of rolled-leaf hispines, *Cephaloleia*.

The genera of rolled-leaf hispines fall into two groups. The first group is *Cephaloleia*, the largest genus of these beetles, with about thirty biological species in Central America. At a single site all these species are usually distinguishable by adult size or color pattern or both. Host affiliation is also a useful taxonomic tool in the early stages of one's learning about these beetles. Among sites, there is great variation within rolled-leaf hispine species, and any judgments about systematics become much more subjective. The second group of genera comprises *Arescus, Nympharescus, Xenarescus,* and *Chelobasis*. Adults of species in this group are larger, thicker, and more polymorphic within sites than *Cephaloleia*.

In Central America, *Heliconia* has more species of rolled-leaf hispines than other zingibers. Although the formal taxonomy of *Heliconia* is at this time still un-published, Gary Stiles had discovered most distinct taxa in Costa Rica and has usable names for almost all of these. One does not need a formal taxonomy to begin work with these plants, because taxa are so morphologically distinct, especially within sites. The rolled-leaf hispines of *Heliconia* at low elevations in Costa Rica are given in table 11.1.

Adults of rolled-leaf hispines occur almost exclusively in the young, scroll-like rolled leaves of host plants. Rolled leaves are produced from the axil of the plant. At first only the tip of the young leaf protrudes from the axil, and at this early stage the interior of the leaf is not accessible to the beetles. After a period of days to weeks, depending upon species and season, the rolled leaf elongates far enough from the axil that the tip unfurls to expose the hollow interior. Leaves remain furled for several more days to a week after the tip has opened, and adult rolled-leaf hispines come and go from the scroll.

TABLE 11.1. Species Richness, Geographic Range, and Host Affiliations of the Rolled-leaf Hispine Genera of Tropical America

Rolled-leaf Hispine Tribes and Genera	Described Species[a]	Known Hosts	Known Geographic Range
Cephaloliini			
Cephaloleia	182 (65)	All families of Middle American Zingiberales except Cannaceae and Musaceae	All tropical America
Arescini			
Arescus	6 (0)	*Heliconia*	All tropical America
Xenarescus	1 (0)	*Heliconia*	Trinidad, Tobago, and northeastern South America
Chelobasis	4 (2)	*Heliconia*	All tropical America
Nympharescus	6 (0)	*Heliconia*	All tropical America Colombia, Ecuador, and Peru

SOURCE: The number of described species is taken from Uhmann (1957, 1964) cited in Strong 1977. Other information is from original field and museum experience.

[a] The figure outside parentheses for all tropical America, in parentheses the number of species known by Uhmann from Middle America.

Adults fly among rolled leaves. They do not frequently stay within a single scroll until it unfurls. There is much incoming and outgoing traffic, except in dry season, when the number of rolled leaves is very restricted. Even in rainy periods, large species of *Heliconia* produce rolled leaves infrequently; single stalks produce leaves only once every few months. Thus the number of rolled leaves in host populations is usually only a fraction of the number of stalks. This is not true in young host populations, composed of all young and rapidly growing plants.

Adults of most species of rolled-leaf hispines of *Heliconia* feed only from the rolled leaves. The exception in Central America is *Cephaloleia puncticollis* (small, wide, red or orange beetles), which feed and live within the bracts of *Heliconia* inflorescences during the flowering season (and see Seifert and Seifert 1979). *C. puncticollis* is replaced by *C. neglecta* in Venezuela and Trinidad. Not all *Heliconia* species are attacked by *C. puncticollis*, only those with erect inflorescences that collect water in the cup-shaped bracts. Species with pendant inflorescences have bracts that are dry inside and do not support larvae of *C. puncticollis*. During the flowerless season, *C. puncticollis* lives in and feeds from the rolled leaves of *Heliconia* just like other species.

Adult rolled-leaf hispines live a long time, and it is important not to collect them or disrupt their rolled leaves. Demographically, they are the elephants, whales, or redwoods of phytophagous insect life, and disturbances to their age distribution or population size are probably felt for a long time by a breeding unit. In one mark-recapture study, I recaptured two marked *Chelobasis perplexa* at La Selva 18 months after we had marked a group of twenty. The two recaptures were within 20 m of where the marked beetles had been released. It is difficult to do statistically adequate mark-recapture studies with rolled-leaf hispine adults because they are covered with a wax that makes it impossible for glue to stick. Marking dusts are cleaned off by the beetle within a few hours. The only long-term marking technique is branding, and this kills some beetles. When I have time and funds for long-term demographic studies, we will use tiny branding irons powered by batteries.

Eggs of all species are laid on wet, tender tissue of the host plant. Eggs are very flat and stick immovably to the host tissue. If not parasitized, eggs have direct development and hatch within 20 days; I have no evidence of egg diapause. A large fraction of eggs are parasitized by tiny chalcidid Hymenoptera, mostly in the families Eulophidae or Trichogrammatidae. Parasitized eggs turn black within hours after wasp oviposition. Unparasitized eggs are white. In a three-year study of egg survivorship of *Cephaloleia consanguinea*, a monophagous species of *H. imbricata*, between 35% and 50% of eggs laid were killed by parasitoids. Parasitoid pressure on *C. consanguinea* eggs at La Selva is constant. Additional, sporadic mortality comes from ants (*Crematogaster* sp.) Ants kill up to 20% of eggs remaining after parasitoid attack. It is interesting that army ants (Ecitonae) do not harm the *C. consanguinea* eggs even upon plants used for bivouacs.

Unparasitized eggs that have hatched are clear empty envelopes with a slit at one end from which the larvae have slid out. Nascent larvae are as flat as their eggs and have much the same oval shape. They begin to feed immediately after hatching. They scrape the pallisade layer from the host leaf by reciprocal movements of the ventrally facing mouth. Eye spots and the whole head are shielded beneath the dorsum of rolled-leaf hispine larvae. If you can see the mouth or eyes from above, or if the dorsum is not entire (if it has a break for an articulation for the head that can be seen from above) you have probably found a cassid larva (Chrysomelidae, Cassidinae = tortoise beetles). In tropical rain forests there are some species of cassids that do not have a frass covering, and these look a lot like rolled-leaf hispines.

Larvae stay out of sight. Some species (in *Chelobasis, Arescus,* and *Nympharescus*) live in and feed from rolled leaves. They slide between the wraps of the leaf scroll and usually feed from the bottom of the leaf, as opposed to adults, which feed from tissue that will become the top of the leaf. To feed after a rolled leaf unfurls, these larvae must either wait the several months until the stalk produces another leaf, feed on inflorescence bracts, or move to another stalk. Movement is very slow and usually only across *Heliconia* plants. A substantial proportion of larvae are hiding on stalks of plants at any one time. They move at night and ensconse themselves in hidden places during the day. Simple experiments indicate that larvae cannot sense rolled leaves even when they are very close. Once a larva of these genera is on or inside a rolled leaf, it does not leave until the leaf unfurls. Mortality during the search for rolled leaves is probably great owing to desiccation. Unlike eggs, however, larvae do not suffer much mortality from parasitism. In five years of collecting I have found fewer than ten larvae that have been parasitized. Tethered larvae used in experiments do not collect many parasitoids. The parasitoids of rolled-leaf hispid larvae are mainly flies.

The larvae of *Chelobasis, Arescus,* and *Nympharescus* develop extremely slowly. In experiments at La Selva, with *Chelobasis perplexa,* we estimated development of larvae that were kept constantly in fresh rolled leaves to be more than 8 months. Rolled leaves are rare to larvae, so the actual developmental period of the average larva in nature must be even longer than this. These larvae do not diapause; they move daily and will feed, albeit slowly, during every day of the long developmental period. *Chelobasis perplexa* has by far the longest developmental period of any chrysomelid known (Strong and Wang 1977).

Larvae of *Cephaloleia* species live on and feed from various places on the host plant. As already mentioned, *C. puncticollis* and *C. neglecta* lay eggs in upward-facing bracts of inflorescences, and larvae feed from the interior of these. *C. vicina* (affectionately known as "red neck")

is the most common and abundant rolled-leaf species in Central America, it also has the broadest tolerances — occurring in drier areas than other species. *C. vicina* larvae usually occur on the stalks of young *Heliconia* plants, near the ground beneath the leaf bases of the oldest leaves on the plant. *C. consanguinea* larvae live on the unfurled, mature leaves of *H. imbricata,* beneath detritus that has fallen from the canopy above. A semi-aquatic environment exists beneath this detritus (which is made up mostly of dead leaves and leaf pieces). After it rains, the tops of *H. imbricata* leaves dry, except beneath the detritus. Actually, there is an entire community beneath leaf debris fallen on *H. imbricata* leaves. Another hispid under the detritus is *Cheirispa dorsata.* It is reddish brown and sometimes has a black spot in the center of the elytra. Its larvae are flat but laterally legged. An unidentified solitary lepidopteran larva is also frequent under the detritus, as are two species of isopods, with assorted rarer species like crickets.

Rolled-leaf hispine pupae are found at various places on the plant. They are brown and are very similar morphologically to larvae. They are entirely immobile and stick tightly to the plant. The pupal phase usually lasts about 20 days or less, except during drought. In dry areas papae "oversummer," and adults emerge only after the first rains of the wet season. Pupae, like eggs, suffer tremendously from parasitoids. About 40% are killed in most censuses.

*

Seifert, R. P., and Seifert, F. H. 1979. Utilization of *Heliconia* (Musaceae) by the beetle *Xenarescus monocerus* (Oliver) (Chrysomelidae: Hispinae) in a Venezuelan forest. *Biotropica* 11:51–59.

Strong, D. R. 1977. Rolled-leaf hispine beetles (Chrysomelidae) and their Zingiberales host plants in Middle America. *Biotropica* 9:156–69.

———. 1977. Insect species richness: Hispine beetles of *Heliconia latispatha. Ecology* 58:573–82.

Strong, D. R., and Wang, M. D. 1977. Evolution of insect life histories and host plant chemistry: Hispine beetles on *Heliconia. Evolution* 31:854–62.

Climaciella brunnea (Avispa Mantíspida, Wasp Mantispid)

P. A. Opler

This large mimetic neuropteran (1.3–1.9 cm) (fig. 11.22) is a member of the Mantispidae, a family of predaceous lacewings. The genus *Climaciella* is thought to have three allopatric species ranging widely in Central America and the United States. *C. brunnea* ranges from the Pacific lowlands of Costa Rica to northern Mexico.

As can be seen from the figure, *Climaciella* has raptorial forelegs and captures prey in the same manner as

711

FIGURE 11.22. *Climaciella brunnea,* adult (large animal above stem). Guanacaste Province, Costa Rica (photo, P. A. Opler).

mantids and assassin bugs, that is, the "wait-and-snatch" capture method.

Mimicry in this insect is polymorphic and Batesian. In Costa Rica, five polistine wasps in two genera (*Polistes* and *Synoeca*) serve as models (Opler 1980). The mimicry expressed is as extreme as that reported by Clarke and Sheppard (1963, 1971, 1972) for *Papilio dardanus, P. memnon,* and *P. polytes,* in which females are polymorphic mimics of several distasteful swallowtail butterflies and males are of a monomorphic, nonmimetic "wild" type. *C. brunnea* surpasses these classic examples in at least two senses. Both sexes are always mimetic, and morph inheritance is at least partially sex-linked.

The five morphs, all of which may occur at a single site, mimic the following wasps and color patterns:

1. *Polistes instabilis* —yellow, red orange, and black, venter of abdomen black, with red brown wings.
2. *Polistes canadensis* —body completely red orange, with blue black wings.
3. *Polistes carnifex* —body primarily yellow with some red orange markings (no black), with yellow orange wings.
4. *Synoeca surinama* —body entirely black, with black wings.
5. *Polistes erythrocephalus* —similar to "surinama" morph, but head and portions of legs are red orange.

The "canadensis" morph is always female, and the "instabilis" morph, the most common morph in Costa Rica, is found in both sexes, although males predominate.

In Costa Rica the relative frequencies of different morphs vary from site to site, although the "instabilis" morph is always the most abundant. Although usually rare, these insects may sometimes congregate in large numbers during the late rainy season on plants that provide a combination of nectar (usually extrafloral) and abundant prey. Such aggregations have been found on the following plants in Costa Rica: *Ipomoea carnea* (Convolvulaceae) at Palo Verde, *Crotalaria incana* (Papilionoideae) at La Pacifica, *Crotalaria maypurensis* (Papilionoideae) at COMELCO Ranch, *Crotalaria pumila* (Papilionoideae) at Santa Rosa National Park headquarters, and *Indigofera suffruticosa* (Papilionoideae) at Santa Rosa hacienda.

Although the life-style of this species is unknown, it may have the following features, as extrapolated from reports on other mantispids (Batra 1972; Hoffman 1936; Hungerford 1936; Kuroko 1961; Smith 1934). Adults emerge in the late rainy season, whereupon mating and oviposition occur. Recently mated females have a whitish spermatophore protruding from the copulatory opening. Eggs have a long stalk and are cemented to leaves or stems in masses. Eggs hatch soon, and the fully legged larvae seek out protected places to pass the dry season. With the onset of the rainy season, the larvae seek out suitable hosts —spider egg cases or larval eusocial or social Hymenoptera. Upon locating the hosts, the larvae transform to an apodous parasitic form, then complete their development.

*

Batra, S. W. T. 1972. Notes on the behavior and ecology of the mantispid, *Climacellia brunnea occidentalis. J. Kansas Ent. Soc.* 45:334–40.

Clarke, C. A., and Sheppard, P. M. 1963. Interactions between major genes and polygenes in the determination of the mimetic patterns of *Papilio dardanus. Evolution* 17:404–13.

———. 1971. Further studies on the genetics of the mimetic butterfly *Papilio memnon* L. *Phil. Trans. Roy. Soc. London,* ser. B., *Biol. Sci.* 263:35–70.

———. 1972. The genetics of the mimetic butterfly *Papilio polytes* L. *Phil. Trans. Roy. Soc. London,* ser, B., *Biol. Sci.* 263:431–58.

Hoffman, C. H. 1936. Notes on *Climacellia brunnea* var. *occidentalis* Banks (Mantispidae—Neuroptera). *Bull. Brooklyn Ent. Soc.* 31:202–3.

Hungerford, H. B. 1936. The Mantispidae of the Douglas Lake, Michigan region, with some biological observations (Neuropt.). *Ent. News* 47:85–88.

Kuroko, H. 1961. On the eggs and first instar larvae of two species of Mantispidae. *Esakia* 3:25–31.

Opler, P. A. 1980. Mimetic polymorphism in *Climacellia brunnea* (Mantispidae, Neuroptera), a Neotropical lacewing. *Biotropica* 13:165–76.

Smith, R. C. 1934. Notes on the Neuroptera and Mecoptera of Kansas with keys for the identification of species. *J. Kansas Ent. Soc.* 7:120–45.

Culicoides (Purrujas, Biting Midges, Punkies, No-see-ums)

C. L. Hogue

Life near the coast, particularly in the vicinity of salt marshes, can be made utterly intolerable by these minute gnats that descend in clouds to bite. They favor the tender skin of the ears and neck but will ferociously attack any exposed area of the body. The bites are prone to form itching, oozing, painful lesions that are easily infected by scratching. In some sensitive individuals local large water-filled blebs develop at the site of the bite and general systemic reactions, including fever and malaise, may ensue.

The small size of these gnats, whose bite effects far exceed what one would expect from such miniscule creatures, has inspired a variety of vernacular names. In North America *Culicoides* are generally known as punkies or sand flies (the latter not to be confused with the *Phlebotomus* sand flies—family Psychodidae—responsible for leishmaniasis transmission) and "no-see-ums." Indeed, they are so small as to be almost invisible to the naked eye and can pass through ordinary sixteen-mesh wire screen and mosquito netting. In Costa Rica and most other parts of Hispanic America the common names purrujas and jejenes (with its variant spellings inhenes and ehenes) are used. Brazilians refer to these flies as maruims or polvorines, terms meaning "dust," another allusion to their minuteness.

Sand-fly annoyance is influenced by time of day, temperature, and wind. Most biting occurs on warm days and evenings when there is no air movement. So bad may their attacks be at such times that one's only salvation is to leave the area. Mosquito repellents have no real potency; only the native practice of building smoke fires seems to have much effect in discouraging these pests. It usually only is practical to minimize the problem by keeping the body well covered with clothing. The bites can be treated with antiobiotic salves to control infection; such salves should include a topical anesthetic to relieve the itching and so reduce the chances of introducing bacteria through scratching.

As with all hematophagous Diptera, only the females suck blood. Also, not all species of *Culicoides* bite man. The genus is cosmopolitan, but most species feed on the blood of other vertebrates. Some are even known to take the blood of invertebrates, including insects. In Costa Rica the worst offender is certainly the salt-marsh sand fly, *Culicoides furens*. This species is widely distributed along both coasts of tropical and subtropical North and South America.

This and many other pestiferous species breed in coastal marshes and swamps, often in association with black mangrove (*Avicennia*). More specifically, the larvae require areas of waterlogged sand mixed with humus above the flooding action of normal high tides. Shade seems also to be a prerequisite for proper development. The water saturating the breeding sites may be fresh or brackish. Larval food consists of organic detritus, yeasts, and algae. Some predaceous species feed on small invertebrates such as nematodes, rotifers, protozoans, and minute arthropods including insects. Other interesting nonbiting species of *Culicoides* develop in the water in land-crab holes and tree rot holes and in water that collects in bromeliad leaf bracts.

Culicoides larvae are 2–5 mm long and very slender and wormlike. The head capsule is yellow to brown, and the body is translucent whitish with some subcutaneous pigment in characteristic patterns on the thorax. There is a short neck segment (constricted portion of prothorax) followed by twelve approximately equal cylindrical body segments. Setae are minute, except the terminal one, and identification characters are subtle.

The larvae locomote between soil particles by serpentine gyrations; aquatic forms swim with quick eellike movements.

Pupae of the genus are roughly similar to those of mosquitoes in overall appearance. However, the abdomen is maintained in a more extended position and terminal swimming paddles are not present, being replaced by short spinelike projections. They are generally well pigmented and bear setae in definitive positions very useful in classification and identification. The latter are mostly borne on tubercles. Also of diagnostic value is the shape of the respiratory trumpet.

The medical importance of *Culicoides* is considerable and goes beyond the mere annoyance of their bites. An increasing number of species are being incriminated as vectors of organisms pathogenic to man and animals, and many others surely will be found to transmit disease. Some important parasites spread by punkies are the viruses of bluetongue in sheep, encephalitis in man and animals, and filarial worms (*Acanthocheilonema perstans, Mansonella,* and *Onchocerca*) in cattle and horses.

*

Atchley, W. R.; Wirth, W. W.; and Gaskins, C. T. 1975. *A bibliography and a keyword-in-context index of the Ceratopogonidae (Diptera) from 1758 to 1973.* Lubbock: Texas Tech Press.

Macfie, J. W. S. 1953. Ceratopogonidae from Costa Rica. *Beitr. Ent.* 3:95–105.

Dichotomius carolinus colonicus (Rueda Caca, Dung Beetle)

H. F. Howden

This dung-feeding nocturnal scarab beetle (fig. 11.23) occurs at low and middle elevations throughout most of

FIGURE 11.23. *Dichotomius carolinus colonicus*, adult (photo, H. F. Howden).

Halffter, G., and Matthews, E. G. 1966. The natural history of dung beetles of the subfamily Scarabaeinae (Coleoptera, Scarabaeidae). *Folia Ent. Mex.* 12–14: 1–312.

Howden, H. F., and Young, O. P. 1981. Panamanian Scarabaeinae: Taxonomy, distribution, and habits. *Contrib. Am. Ent. Inst.* 18:1–204.

Drymophilacris bimaculata (Saltamonte Oroverde, Chapulín Oroverde, Green-and-gold Solanum Grasshopper)

H. F. Rowell

This insect (fig. 11.24) is common at La Selva and throughout the forests of the San Carlos plains and the rest of the Caribbean lowlands. It is a typical representative of the acridid grasshoppers of tree-fall clearings and other light gaps in forest. This sort of habitat accounts for approximately 70% of the grasshopper species of the country. Typically such insects are flightless, brilliantly colored or conspicuously marked, and without the power of stridulation, and they are oligophagic or strictly monophagic feeders, accepting only one or a few species of plants as food.

D. bimaculata belongs to a subgroup of the subfamily Proctolabinae (family Acrididae) that feeds on the Solanaceae; this subgroup is confined to Costa Rica and Panama. The adult is about 2 cm long, green, with metallic gold head, prothorax, and genital region. The wings are reduced to small scales. The long antennae are black with white tips, the large protuberant eyes and the postocular stripe are black, and the posterior end of the male is black with two golden spots, giving the specific name. When the grasshopper sits on a horizontal surface, the anterior abdominal segments are the highest, giving a rather hunchbacked look. The male has inflated genital segments and big, black, inward-curving cerci. The larvae assume this coloration at the fourth of their six instars; before that they are jet black with bright orange head and prothorax, which is the color of a considerable assemblage of diverse insects found on Solanaceae, including chrysomelids, cercopids, cerambycids, and other taxa. Related and ecologically almost identical species include *D. monteverdensis* Descamps and Rowell 1978 and *Drymacris nebulicola* (Rehn 1929) at Monteverde. *Ampelophilus olivaceus* (Giglio-Tos 1897) from San Vito and the Osa Peninsula and *A. truncatus* (Rehn 1905) from the Meseta Central are also very similar, but they are basically green, red, and blue instead of being green, gold, and black and have somewhat less vestigial wings. They extend their acceptable food plants to include some Compositae genera.

D. bimaculata is typically found on species of *So-*

Central America (see Howden and Young 1981); the nominate species ranges into the southeastern portions of the United States. The species (or subspecies) is entirely black, *very* convex, with the anterior margin of the head abruptly rounded, and lacks "teeth." Individuals range from 22 to 30 mm in length, and large specimens, when bulk is considered, are the largest dung beetles in Costa Rica.

The species commonly feeds on cattle and horse droppings but is attracted to other types of dung including human feces. If the dung is not easily divided into fragments, the beetle digs a burrow at the edge of the dropping and carries a wad or ball of dung to the bottom of the burrow, often 15–40 cm in depth. Soil type and moisture influence the ease of digging, burrows usually being deeper in sandy soil. The dung taken into the burrow either may serve as adult food or may be formed into a brood mass containing a single large (10 cm), slightly elongate whitish egg. Details on burrows and brood balls can be found in Halffter and Matthews (1966, pp. 124–25). Development from egg to pupa takes approximately 2 months, with the new adults emerging during moist periods.

The adults do not belong to the "ball-rolling" group of scarabs, but if the dung is fairly firm (i.e., horse dung) an adult may push a piece of it away from the main dropping for a considerable distance before burying it. Adults begin activity at dusk and are frequently attracted to light. Along with many other species, can be collected by setting dung traps. The simplest trap is a can containing some dung, sunk to rim level in the ground.

*

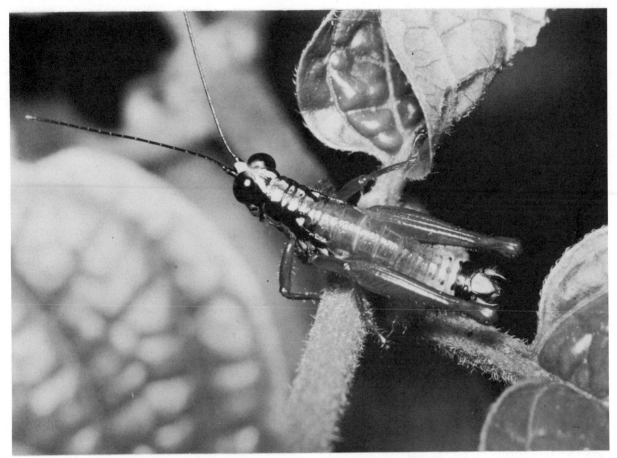

FIGURE 11.24. *Drymophilacris bimaculata*, adult male. Finca La Selva, Sarapiquí District, Costa Rica (photo, H. F. Rowell).

lanum, *Witheringia*, and *Cestrum* and is especially common on the spiny vine *Solanum siparunoides*. Apart from tree-fall clearings, it is conspicuous in the succession plots, in Arboretum 2, and around the edge of the pejebeyal at La Selva. The eggs of most acridids are laid in the ground, but the ovipositor valves of *Drymophilacris* are oddly shaped and very delicate, suggesting that it may use a plant or detritus substrate. All life stages are present year-round at La Selva, and the life cycle takes about 12 weeks. In spite of their bright coloration and the fact that most Solanaceae are filled with alkaloids poisonous to vertebrates, they do not seem to be distasteful or toxic to lizards, birds, ants, or mantises, and these potential predators build up no adverse response to them when fed on them under experimental conditions. Rather than being aposematic, the bright coloration seems to be used as a short-range intraspecific attractant and species identifier. Males appear to find their mates by first finding food plants, then searching them for conspecifics. The search is aided by the male's drumming on the plant stems with his back legs, which provokes an answering drumming by the female. They are extremely visual in their behavior and have to be approached with the sort of caution one would use to observe a bird. Males (often more than one) tend to stay with a female once they have found her, and both sexes follow each other around visually thereafter. The different species of the *Solanum* proctolabines have species-characteristic markings on the head and subgenital plate, forming "headlights" and "taillights" that seem to facilitate this behavior. Pairs sometimes stay together, often moving from plant to plant, for more than a week at a time. Copulation usually starts in the late afternoon and continues until early morning; molting also tends to take place at night.

Unlike most temperate grasshoppers, *Drymophilacris* and its relatives eat from the middle of a leaf rather than from the edge, producing central holes. They frequently cause considerable damage and may even kill off small plants. They require chemical cues found in *Solanum* leaves to elicit feeding: they will accept virtually anything smeared with crushed *Solanum* leaf but refuse neutral nutritive substances, like sweetened filter paper, without it. That is, their choice of food plant is governed by the phagostimulant chemicals, not phagorepellants.

715

This sort of behavior is typical of highly selective herbivores.

A major unsolved problem raised by this and similar flightless light-gap grasshopper species is dispersal to new habitats. Since they are monophags or oligophags, their food plants can never be easy to find in the high floristic diversity of the rain forest; further, succession in the light gap will eliminate their food plants within a few years and make it essential to find a new habitat. From the grasshopper's viewpoint, the forest is an archipelago of transient islands of suitable habitat. Flightlessness is not only characteristic of the Costa Rican species, but is convergently evolved over and over again in different taxa of light-gap grasshoppers throughout the world's rain forests —probably the situation is analogous to that of insects on oceanic islands, in that the ability to fly would tend to cause the insect to loose its food-plant "island" too easily. How long-term dispersal occurs is mysterious. No facultative winged forms are known; presumably individuals walk through the forest until they find a new spot. The species composition of the acridid fauna of forest light gaps is markedly variable, in a way which suggests that founder effects are important and that dispersal from gap and gap may be a limiting factor on the total species population.

Eciton burchelli and **Other Army Ants** (Hormiga Arriera, Army Ants)

C. W. Rettenmeyer

The Neotropical army ants (fig. 11.25) include about 150 species classified in five genera. Within their range extending from the southern United States to northern Argentina, army ants can be found in most habitats below about 2,000 m elevation. The number of species is highest in lowland forests without severe dry seasons, and in such moist forests there are typically four or five genera and about twenty species at any given locality.

Army ants are remarkably similar in their behavior and ecology and can be distinguished from other ants by the following features (Rettenmeyer 1963; Schneirla 1971). (1) Colonies are large, ranging from thirty thousand to more than one million. (2) The workers are polymorphic, and the largest individuals, called soldiers, are 9–14 mm long and possess large hook-shaped mandibles. The smallest individuals are about one-fifth the size of the soldiers and lack the excessively large mandibles. The differences in size and morphology of the adult workers are presumably due to differential food consumption as larvae. There are many inconspicuous species less than 5 mm long that lack distinct soldiers. (3) All species are almost exclusively carnivorous, feeding on arthropods and especially on other ants and social wasps. (4) The

ants forage in columns, running rapidly on long legs and carrying objects under their bodies. (5) Their eyes are reduced to a single facet or are absent, and they use chemical trails for orientation and for recruitment to prey. (6) Entire colonies migrate, often nightly when there is a larval brood, but a few species may stay in the same place for a few months. (7) Nests or bivouacs are clusters of hanging ants, usually subterranean but most frequently found inside hollow trees or logs or under objects. (8) At any given time the age of the entire brood is approximately the same (but the brood ranges greatly in size because of polymorphism). When larvae are predominant, the colony will probably emigrate that night; when there are only cocoons, the colony normally will not emigrate. (9) One queen is found in each colony (Rettenmeyer and Watkins 1978). (She should not be collected because the colony will die or fuse with another colony.) (10) Males, the only winged caste, are usually not present in a colony, but three hundred to three thousand are produced in some colonies, usually during the dry season or early rainy season. Males have large eyes and fly to lights.

Eciton burchelli (fig. 11.25) is the most famous of the New World army ants because of its spectacular raids (Rettenmeyer et al. 1982). Starting at dawn, the ants pour out of their bivouac, which is typically aboveground, under or in a log or tree. They spread across the ground around the bivouac but soon concentrate in one direction, generally away from their previous emigration route. The raiding party soon becomes fan-shaped, with one trunk column connecting with the nest. During the early hours of a raid, traffic is primarily away from the bivouac at a maximum rate of five to ten ants per second. That trunk column divides repeatedly as the ants get closer to the swarm front. It may take 1 or 2 h before much prey is brought back to the nest, and after 5 or 6 h the front may be 50 m or more from the bivouac. Much prey is kept in temporary caches along raid columns and will be returned to the nest later or carried to the new nest during the emigration.

Comparable to a wolf pack, but with fifty thousand miniature wolves, an army-ant swarm raid is the epitome of group predation. The swarm front, 3–15 m wide, advances across the forest floor driving most animals in front of it. Although neither larger nor stronger than many other ants they attack, the army ants are highly successful predators because of their large numbers and thorough coverage of the area. The army ants also have the fastest recruiting system known for any social insect and can recruit one hundred or more ants from a raid column to a food source within 1 min (Chadab and Rettenmeyer 1975). There is no evidence that army ants can detect their prey from a distance, and their searching is directed primarily by microtopography. The ants follow

FIGURE 11.25. *Eciton hamatum* soldiers and workers with full-grown larvae and one cocoon of a male or queen (*upper right*). The soldiers do not carry these larvae or cocoons even though their huge mandibles seem to be adapted for that purpose. Workers of *E. burchelli* are almost identical morphologically to these of *E. hamatum*, but those of *E. burchelli* have darker bodies and the soldiers' heads are not shiny (photo, C. W. Rettenmeyer).

logs or lianas and even go up to the tops of the tallest canopy trees.

Many arthropods are driven in front of the advancing swarm, and if they run or fly in the right direction they may successfully elude the ants. However, a single swarm raid may be accompanied by more than one thousand flies and a dozen or more antbirds that also present a threat to the escaping arthropods (Rettenmeyer 1961). The flies deposit eggs or larvae on escaping prey while avoiding the prey already caught by the ants. The antbirds also eat the escaping crickets, katydids, and other insects but do not eat the army ants (Willis and Oniki 1978). Any vertebrate that is not incapacitated will have no difficulty escaping the ants, but very rarely a small lizard or other vertebrate is killed by a swarm raid.

In addition to the large numbers of flies hovering or perched about the swarm raids, there are numerous arthropods other than army ants living in the colonies. These may be seen accompanying the raiding ants but are most numerous in the emigration columns. The most common but smallest species are abundant mites riding on the ants. There also are silverfish (Thysanura), rove beetles (Staphylinidae), histerid and limulodid beetles, and phorid flies. Some of these are predators on the ants, but most species do no measurable harm to their "host." By living in the ant colonies, these "guests" or "myrmecophiles" are provided with all their food and are protected from many predators and other environmental hazards. Among the most interesting guests are ant-mimicking wasps and staphylinids (Akre and Rettenmeyer 1966). The mimicry of their host is considered Wasmannian mimicry because the resemblance is probably the result of natural selection by the host (model) or some other intracolonial predator (Rettenmeyer 1970). It is unlikely that vertebrate predators could have caused the evolution of such mimicry by arthropods only 1–3 mm long.

Emigrations of *E. burchelli* start from midafternoon to early evening and may continue for 3–9 h depending upon the size of the colony, distance, terrain, and weather. Most emigrations are 50–70 m long. The queen stays inside the bivouac except during the nocturnal emigration, when she is typically accompanied by a retinue of numerous workers and soldiers (Rettenmeyer, Topoff, and Mirenda 1978). She usually emigrates after 90% of the colony has left the old bivouac. Many guests sometimes emigrate after all the ants have passed. Because army-ant queens never possess wings, army ants do not have the mating flights characteristic of other ants. A few new queens and up to three thousand males may be produced by large colonies during the dry season. The males fly from the parent colony within 2 weeks of their emergence, a few lucky ones will mate, and all will die

within about 3 weeks. A colony may divide into two, but no division into more than two colonies has been seen.

E. burchelli has two subspecies in Central America, which can look very different. Medium and small workers of *E. b. foreli* have a light orange abdomen (gaster) and a black head and thorax; the same size workers of *E. b. parvispinum* are entirely black to reddish black. The geographical ranges of the two subspecies are not well known, and both have been reported from the same locality in Costa Rica. Other species of *Eciton* range from yellow to dark red brown and black. All have stings and a distinctive army-ant odor as well as species-specific odors useful in field identification.

The basic behavior of all army ants is similar to that of *E. burchelli* with one major exception: all other army-ant species have smaller swarm raids or lack them completely. Most army ants have two or three narrow raid columns going in different directions from the bivouac. Since the advancing raid party is composed of only about fifty ants, large numbers of arthropods are not driven out by the raid front, and the "camp-following" birds and flies are absent. The few species of army ants having swarm raids are the most diverse in their diet, eating a wide range of arthropods in addition to ants. The column raiders specialize on ants but sometimes raid social wasps or termites. Because of the large numbers of species, colonies, and individuals, army ants are undoubtedly the most important predators on other ants.

*

Akre, R. D., and Rettenmeyer, C. W. 1966. Behavior of Staphylinidae associated with army ants (Formicidae: Ecitonini). *J. Kansas Ent. Soc.* 39:745–82.

Chadab, R., and Rettenmeyer, C. W. 1975. Mass recruitment by army ants. *Science* 188:1124–25.

Rettenmeyer, C. W. 1961. Observations on the biology and taxonomy of flies found over swarm raids of army ants. (Diptera: Tachinidae, Conopidae). *Univ. Kansas Sci. Bull.* 42:993–1066.

———. 1963. Behavioral studies of army ants. *Univ. Kansas Sci. Bull.* 44:281–465.

———. 1970. Insect mimicry. *Ann. Rev. Ent.* 15:43–74.

Rettenmeyer, C. W.; Chadab-Crepet, R.; Naumann, M. G.; and Morales, L. 1982. Comparative foraging by Neotropical army ants. *Proc. Simp. Int. Insectos Soc. Trop.* (Cocoyoc, Mexico, Nov. 1980), in press.

Rettenmeyer, C. W.; Topoff, H.; and Mirenda, J. 1978. Queen retinues of army ants. *Ann. Ent. Soc. Am.* 71:519–28.

Rettenmeyer, C. W., and Watkins, J. F., II. 1978. Polygyny and monogyny in army ants (Hymenoptera: Formicidae). *J. Kansas Ent. Soc.* 51:581–91.

Schneirla, T. C. 1971. *Army ants: A study in social organization.* San Francisco: Freeman.

Willis, E. O., and Oniki, Y. 1978. Birds and army ants. *Ann. Rev. Ecol. Syst.* 9:243–63.

Euchroma gigantea (Eucroma, Giant Metallic Ceiba Borer)

H. A. Hespenheide

Euchroma gigantea (fig. 11.26) lives up to its name in that it is both brightly colored and the largest member of the beetle family Buprestidae in the New World tropics. In fact, it is one of the largest relatively common beetles of any family, measuring between 5 and 6 cm long. The elytra are bright golden green, suffused in their central portions with a generous amount of red; the pronotum is metallic green with two large black spots, one on each side of the midline, rimmed with metallic red. Freshly emerged adults are covered with or soon develop a yellow waxy powder above and below that the beetle secretes only once. A number of other genera in the family also produce this characteristic efflorescence (white in some species), which is often mistaken for pollen, although only a small number of genera ever visit flowers.

Although the buprestid fauna of Costa Rica is incompletely known, *Euchroma* is among at least 110 species of seventeen genera whose larvae are borers in wood or stems. The family is typically thought of as wood borers, but more known species (135) are leaf miners in Costa Rica (see discussion under *Agrilus xanthonotus*), although collecting may have favored the latter group. Among the more common larger buprestids at tree falls, members of the genera *Chrysobothris* and *Actenodes* (about twenty species total) tend to predominate as family representatives in the large group of insects involved in the decomposition of the wood of trees. However, buprestids are probably less important overall than such beetle families as the Cerambycidae, Platypodidae, Cur-

culionidae (subfamilies Zygopinae and Cryptorrhynchinae), Brenthidae, and others.

The plant hosts of *Euchroma* are members of the family Bombacaceae. *Ceiba pentandra, Bombacopsis,* and *Pseudobombax* are genera and species on whose trunks I have seen or collected specimens. The abundance of the larval host plants undoubtedly contributes both to the beetle's relative commonness and to its wide distribution, since it has been recorded from Mexico to Argentina and in the Antilles. (Hubbell [1979] reports that adult *Euchroma* are a minor diet item of Tzeltal-Mayan Indians in Chiapas, Mexico, and are roasted before being eaten.) Adults can occasionally be seen flying in open areas or even sitting on the foliage of other plants but are most common on the trunks of living bombacaceous trees. In Panama I have seen an adult feeding at sap exuding from machete wounds on a *Bombacopsis*, but they are more frequently seen sitting on a trunk or walking up or down it.

As Opler, Southwood, Strong, and others have shown, more abundant plants tend to have larger faunas of associated herbivores. The wood-boring insect fauna of *Ceiba pentandra* is a large one. The activity at a large fallen *Ceiba* at Finca La Selva in November 1978 was considerable even though the tree had come down six months before (T. W. Sherry, pers. comm.). Besides an ovipositing female *Euchroma*, there was a large elaterid beetle of the genus *Chalcolepidius*, a large fly of the family Pantophthalmidae, and the zygopine weevil *Copturus montezumae*, as well as several smaller species and platypodids. Large pantophthalmid larvae were pushing sawdust out of tunnels probably dug for feeding on sap flow, and a variety of parasitoid Hymenoptera were ovipositing or searching along the bole and branches. Large predatory robberflies (Asilidae) of the genera *Andrenosoma* and *Pilica* patrolled the light gap for flying insect prey and probably laid eggs that would hatch as predators of wood-boring larvae, perhaps of *Euchroma*.

*

Hubbell, P. 1979. Adult beetles as food. *Coleop. Bull.* 33:91.

FIGURE 11.26. *Euchroma gigantea,* adult (colon coin is 28 mm diameter); inset, hind tarsus and ventral side of abdomen. Santa Rosa National Park, Guanacaste, Costa Rica (photos, D. H. Janzen).

Eulaema meriana (Chiquizá, Merian's Orchid Bee)

D. H. Janzen

Aside from *Trigona* stingless bees, the huge *Eulaema meriana* (Apidae: Euglossini) (fig. 11.27) bees are the most commonly observed species of bee in Costa Rican lowland rain-forest understory. Walk several kilometers of muddy forest trail on a sunny day at Finca La Selva, Corcovado National Park, or other intact lowland rain

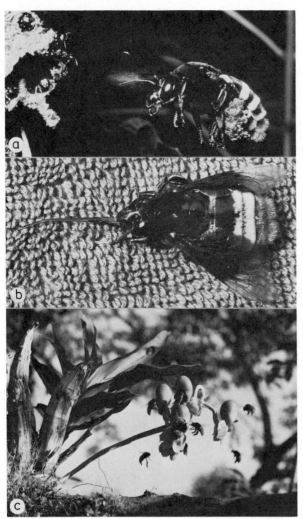

FIGURE 11.27. *Eulaema meriana. a,* Female hovering in front of *Crematogaster* carton nest while pilfering resins for nest construction (note hind corbiculae covered with resinous construction material). *b,* Male with tongue fully extended. *c, Eulaema polychroma* males visiting *Catesetum maculatum* orchid just as the males of *E. meriana* do in other parts of Costa Rica. *a* and *b,* Corcovado National Park, Osa Peninsula, Costa Rica. *c,* Santa Rosa National Park, Guanacaste Province, Costa Rica (photos, D. H. Janzen).

forest, and you are very likely to encounter a female chiquizá gathering mud from the trail to carry off on her pollen baskets and use for cell construction. The bee is basically furry black with wings that are dark at the base and light at the ends. The abdomen is ringed dorsally with a narrow cream yellow band, a wide cream yellow band, and a terminal reddish band; the last two bands are congruent. The bee has large and effective eyes and is likely to see you approaching before you see it. It will probably fly rapidly a few meters down the trail before reversing direction and coming back (curiosity?).

The female takes the mud she gathers to a cavity in the ground (e.g., an old rodent burrow) or low in a dead tree stump and builds clusters of clay cells, each about 2.5 cm long by 1.8 cm wide. Several females will work simultaneously in the same cavity on several cells. A nest may contain as many as thirty cells. Once the cell is constructed, the female provisions it with about 2 cc of pollen-nectar paste and lays a banana-shaped egg on its surface. In keeping with the life-style of other bees that put much effort into constructing a few cells, the egg is enormous—it may be as much as 1.4 cm long and 2 mm thick. The completed cell is then closed over with a carefully crafted clay cover, and there is no contact between parent and offspring until the new bee emerges several months later. Since it appears that *Eulaema* adults, like other large bees, may live as long as a year, there is the possibility of much parent-offspring interaction, and the several bees that simultaneously construct cells in a *Eulaema meriana* nest may be closely related.

Though mud is collected from the ground, pollen and nectar are collected from flowers at all levels in the forest—from *Calathea* only 1 m tall to the tops of 50-m trees like *Lecythis costaricensis*. Much indirect evidence, but no direct evidence, suggests that like other large tropical bees *E. meriana* females are quite familiar with the locations of many individual pollen and nectar sources that produce a small but regular number of flowers each day; the bees effectively visit these in a feeding route much like a trapline. *E. meriana* has been observed to take pollen from *Blakea, Solanum, Cassia,* and *Bixa* and very likely collects it from many other genera of plants. Nectar is collected from at least *Calathea, Costus, Lecythis, Mandavilla,* and *Centrosema* and probably many other species. However, nectar host records are confused because the males look just like the females and visit the same groups of plants when collecting nectar.

Male *E. meriana* are much more famous than are females. Along with other euglossine bees—*Euglossa, Exaerete, Eufriesia (Euplusia* of older literature)—they pollinate a set of Neotropical orchids (e.g., *Catasetum, Aspasia, Cycnoches, Gongora, Houlletia, Notylia, Sobralia*), which they visit to obtain chemicals that later end up in the mandibular glands (or at least slightly modified forms of them do; N. Williams, pers. comm.). Males of *E. meriana,* like other male euglossines, visit a particular subset of the total orchid-bee-pollinated orchids; furthermore, they can be attracted to a certain subset (cineole, benzyl acetate, methyl salicylate) of the chemicals that generally attract orchid bees.

Without the use of chemical baits (which will attract *E. meriana* in any lowland Costa Rican rain forest at any time of year), *E. meriana* males are most commonly observed in the forest understory flying a highly stereotyped "dance." A male flies up to a tree and grabs hold with its mandibles (as males do when they sleep at night on twigs); it holds the wings near the dorsal side of the body and buzzes them loudly several times in this position. It then drops off the tree and flies in front of the tree in a tight "figure eight" several meters across. It then flies to the tree and repeats the process. This may go on for hours, but the bee usually does not return to the same tree day after day. This behavior is usually observed in the midmorning hours in rain-forest understory (and is similar to that observed with other species of *Eulaema*). Sometimes more than one bee performs at a single site, and their flight paths may interweave. It is assumed that this dance is part of female attraction behavior or a mating display.

When *E. meriana,* again like other orchid bees (fig. 11.26c), visits an orchid, it scrapes very avidly with its front tarsi (and the brushes just behind them) at tissue somewhere in the orchid flower. It then backs off from the flower and, while hovering in flight, transfers the fluids from the plant to grooves in the hind tibiae. As this process is repeated, the bee becomes noticeably less cautious and its flight more "drunken"; some bees even become so disoriented that they temporarily cannot fly. Additionally, at its various (and progressively more drunken) trips into the flower, the bee may have a pollinarium (pollen sac) glued onto it (on thorax, legs, front of head, or other part). When it later visits another flower, the pollinaria are stripped off the bee by the stigma of the orchid. Different species of orchid-bee-pollinated orchids put the pollinarium on different parts of the bee and on different orchid bees. A *Catasetum* orchid visited by *E. meriana,* for example, may be visited by two or three species of *Eulaema* and four or five species of *Euglossa* simultaneously, but the pollinaria will generally be put on only one or two of these species, owing to their different sizes, shapes, and behaviors at the flower.

Orchid bees range from about where the Tropic of Cancer crosses Mexico south throughout the tropics of South America. *E. meriana* ranges from Guatemala through most of tropical South America below about 1,500 m elevation. It is very rare in deciduous forests, and the few *E. meriana* taken at chemical bait in very dry sites are probably wide-ranging transients or come from local populations associated with riparian evergreen vegetation. In most lowland Costa Rican rain-forest sites, if a set of chemical baits is put out, five to fifty individuals of *E. meriana* may arrive in the course of a morning.

As might be expected of a large aposematic bee whose females carry a very painful sting for self-defense when grabbed, there are a number of mimics of *E. meriana. E. meriana, E. bombiformis,* and *E. seabrai* form a Müllerian mimicry complex with much local variation in the Neotropics, and observations of "*E. meriana*" should normally be attributed to all three unless the bee was

captured and examined by a good bee taxonomist. All three occur in Costa Rica. All have an effective sting (females), and of course the males are Batesian mimics of the females. Additionally, there are beetles and large flies that are general to very specific Batesian mimics of *E. meriana* and the other members of its Müllerian ring. Furthermore, several species of *Eufriesia* (*Euplusia* of old) are also part of this Müllerian ring.

E. meriana is one of the four euglossine bees that has been attracted to baits on Isla del Caño just off the coast of Corcovado National Park; however, since only one individual came to the baits, I suspect it was a transient rather than part of a breeding population on the island.

In the past twenty years much work has been done on euglossine bees in Costa Rica and Panama, as well as in South America. Below I list some of the particularly relevant or recent papers, and I suggest that these be read and digested before anyone plans more fieldwork on euglossine bees.

*

Dodson, C. H.; Dressler, R. L.; Hills, H. G.; and Adams, R. M. 1969. Biologically active compounds in orchid fragrances. *Science* 164:1243–49.
Dressler, R. L. 1968. Pollination by euglossine bees. *Evolution* 22:202–10.
———. 1979. *Eulaema bombiformis, E. meriana,* and Müllerian mimicry in related species (Hymenoptera: Apidae). *Biotropica* 11:114–51.
Janzen, D. H. 1971. Euglossine bees as long-distance pollinators of tropical plants. *Science* 171:203–5.
———. 1981a. Bee arrival at two Costa Rican female *Catasetum* orchid inflorescences, and a hypothesis on euglossine population structure. *Oikos* 36:177–83.
———. 1981b. Reduction in euglossine bee species richness on a Costa Rican offshore island. *Biotropica* 13:238–40.
Janzen, D. H.; DeVries, P. J.; Higgins, M. L.; and Kimsey, L. S. 1981. Seasonal and site variation in Costa Rican euglossine bees at chemical baits in a deciduous forest and an evergreen forest. *Ecology* 63:66–74.
Williams, N. H. 1978. A preliminary bibliography on euglossine bees and their relationships with orchids and other plants. *Selbyana* 2:345–55.

Eulissus chalybaeus (Abejón Culebra, Green Rove Beetle)

D. H. Janzen

The Staphylinidae constitute a large and cosmopolitan family of predaceous (and scavenging) beetles with reduced elytra (forewings), elongate, supple bodies, and sinuous, fast movements; like snakes, the adults can move quickly through tangled substrate, litter, rotting fruit, and other semisolid materials in search of small insect prey. Large-animal dung is a habitat rich in insects, and horse and cow dung are no exceptions. Staphylinids are commonplace members of this microhabitat. In Guanacaste the most conspicuous is *Eulissus chalybaeus* (fig. 11.28). This staphylinid, a brilliant metallic green and about 2 cm in length, is a favorite "oh my" insect of collectors.

When a fresh horse pie is deposited in Santa Rosa National Park, within minutes one of these green beetles seems to fall out of the sky onto it (night or day). If four horse pies are put out in a wooded site over pitfall traps in an area of a few square meters, five to fifteen individuals of *E. chalybaeus* will arrive at them each night. Upon arriving, the beetle folds its long wings under its short elytra and wends its way down among the individual turds. There it awaits the arrival of the small- and medium-sized dung beetles (Scarabaeidae) that arrive shortly after. The primary prey in Santa Rosa at night are *Dichotomius yucatanus, Onthophagus championi,* and *Canthidium centralis.* The usual means of prey attack is to move under the scarab and grab it at the base of a leg or in the soft integument between the sclerites of the head and the thorax. The staphylinid chews its way into the beetle and consumes the soft inner parts. If the beetle is newly emerged (teneral) with soft sclerites, the staphylinid kills it much more rapidly than if it is a hard older beetle. There is no indication that *E. chalybaeus* follows the scarabs down their burrows.

In Santa Rosa, and probably elsewhere in Guanacaste, the smaller dung beetles are quite seasonal and have largely disappeared from the habitat by July to December, depending on the species. However, *E. chalybaeus* individuals are present at fresh livestock dung throughout the year, with a great increase in numbers with the coming of the rains (and dung beetles). It appears that a scarab's greatest chance of being eaten by a staphylinid is at the beginning and end of the scarab season, when the ratio of predator to prey is greatest. During peak scarab density there may be as many as a thousand scarabs in a dung pile with only one to seven staphylinids; one *E. chalybaeus* probably consumes one to four medium-sized scarabs per night.

This beetle is also found at carcasses and other sites rich in insects, and it undoubtedly preys on more than just dung-beetle adults. In the Corcovado rain forest, a different species of large mottled brown staphylinid appears to pose the same threat to dung beetles as does *E. chalybaeus* in Guanacaste.

Euptychia hermes (Nimfa Café de Zacate, Grass Nymph)

P. J. DeVries

According to the literature, this "species" (fig. 11.29) ranges from the northeastern United States throughout Central and South America. In Costa Rica it occurs from sea level to about 1,800 m elevation on both Atlantic and Pacific drainages and is the commonest satyrid butterfly. The term "species" is in quotation marks because there appear to be a number of taxa involved here. L. D. Miller (pers. comm.) informs me that it represents a number of genera and species. As a rule, there are usually two distinct phenotypes in a given habitat, and one of these phenotypes is noticeably less common. At high-elevation habitats like Volcán Santa Maria (Guanacaste), the slopes of Volcán Poás (Alajuela), and Volcán Barva (Heredia), there can be more than two phenotypes.

FIGURE 11.28. *a,* Lateral view of adult *Eulissus chalybaeus. b,* Frontal view of *a.* Santa Rosa National Park, Guanacaste, Costa Rica (photos, D. H. Janzen).

FIGURE 11.29. *Euptychia hermes,* underside. Costa Rica (photo, P. J. DeVries).

Adults are small (25–30 mm wingspread), dull brown, with a row of small ocelli on the outer margin of the hind wing. This row of ocelli is what is normally used to distinguish the "species."

The host plants are various species of grasses (Gramineae). The eggs are deposited singly on the host plant. The oviposition site may be a rock, a dead leaf, or the ground near the host plant. At times the ovipositing female will locate a host plant by landing on it, then fly above the host plant and "bomb" the egg to the ground from the air (M. Singer, pers. comm.). The larvae of this group are light green, with a small forked tail and a round, warty green head capsule. The larvae are nocturnal feeders and are extremely difficult to find during the day.

The adults occur in disturbed grassy areas like pasture and second growth, and in tree falls in the forest. One study (Emmel 1968) shows that populations tend to be sedentary during the Guanacaste dry season. Besides Emmel's superficial study, there are no other published studies on the adult biology of any Neotropical euptychiine that I am aware of. Adults are attacked by orobatid mites during the dry season in Guanacaste (Emmel 1968). I find that the small groups of *E. hermes* and other satyrids that congregate in river bottoms during the dry season in Santa Rosa National Park tend to be heavily infested with these mites. There is no information on the effect these mites have on *E. hermes* or any other satyrid. Adults of *E. hermes* do not feed on flowers, but rather on rotten fruits, dung, sap from tree wounds, and fungi.

*

Emmel, T. C. 1968. The population biology of the Neotropical satyrid butterfly, *Euptychia hermes.* 1. Interpopulation movement, ecology, and population sizes in lowland Costa Rica (dry season, 1966). *J. Res. Lep.* 7:153–65.

Eutrombicula (Coloradillas, Chiggers)

C. L. Hogue

Chiggers (fig. 11.30) are the subject of much conversation among persons who have ventured into disturbed scrub, bush, or second-growth forest margins in the humid tropics. These small (length less than 1 mm) mites may attach to the human skin to feed, causing persistent itching lesions that become inflamed and precipitate scratching bouts in the most restrained individual.

It is only the larval stage of this mite that bites. In its normal life cycle the larva attaches to a vertebrate (rarely invertebrate) host to feed on lymph and proteolyzed tissue. After engorging, during which process the body may swell many times in volume, it drops off permanently to continue development as a free-living mite, feeding on the eggs of soil-dwelling insects, and passes through one additional active nymphal stage before attaining adult-

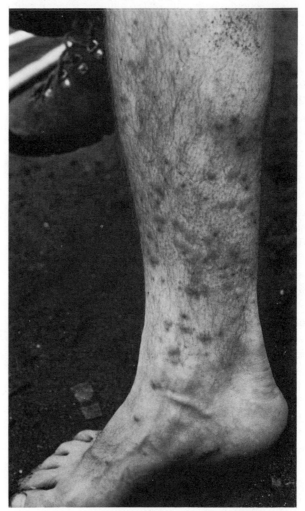

FIGURE 11.30. *Eutrombicula* "bites" on leg of hapless tourist. Sirena, Corcovado National Park, Osa Peninsula, Costa Rica (photo, D. H. Janzen).

hood. This developmental sequence also includes additiona quiescent phases when the mite does not feed and remains for a time within the detached, but not shed, skin of the previous active stage.

Adult mites are fairly large, frequently bright red, and covered densely with feathery hairs or setae. They are usually encountered just beneath the surface of the soil, in cracks, burrows, leaf litter, and humus or in decaying wood and logs where they actively seek out and devour the contents of other mites and insects, as well as their eggs. Reproduction is bisexual; to elicit insemination males deposit spermatophores (sperm packets) on the substratum, which females pick up with their genital suckers.

The chigger may be recognized from its appearance as well as from its tendency to ectoparasitism. As is typical of mite larvae, it has only six legs, instead of the eight possessed by later stages, and is often bright red, orange, yellow, or even white. Microscopically one can see its smooth spheroid body with spaced plumose setae. A pair of specialized setae or sensillae occur in the middle of a single, rectangular dorsal body plate (scutum), and these are either elongate and flagelliform or expanded and uniquely club-shaped. The mouthparts consist of a pair of heavy chelicerae and pair of palps which, together, give the anterior end the appearance of a head.

During feeding, the chelicerae pierce the skin and saliva is injected into the wound. The liquid of semidigested lymph and tissue is sucked up by the chigger, which then injects more saliva, repeating the process several times. The host tissue reacts by producing a tubelike core that continues to react with the mite's saliva and dissolve. It is the persistence of this core, called a stylostome, after the chigger drops off that causes the itching discomfort that lasts for many days and even weeks. Contrary to popular belief, the chigger does not burrow into the human skin; only the tips of the mouthparts are inserted.

Chiggers constitute a family of mites, Trombiculidae, containing nearly two thousand species throughout the world. It is those few species that normally parasitize reptiles that seem to cause an inordinate amount of allergic reaction when they accidentally attach to human skin. It appears to be the incompatability between the chigger's salivary enzymes and man's tissue chemistry that brings on the violent response. Rodent chiggers, or those normally on other mammals, generally cause little or no reaction when they accidentally bite man.

In Costa Rica three lizard chiggers belonging to the genus *Eutrombicula* are the most conspicuous for their attacks on humans: *E. batatas*, *E. goeldii*, and *E. alfreddugesi*. Numerous species in some twenty or more other genera seldom if ever attack *Homo sapiens*. In this country chiggers are not known to transmit human diseases, but in parts of Asia and the Pacific region they are responsible for a very serious chigger-borne rickettsiasis commonly known as "scrub typhus" or "tsutsugamushi fever."

The best protection from chiggers is wearing clothing tightly tucked in at the waist and boots. The mites like to squeeze into warm, compressed places, and this is why they are so often found attaching at the bra or belt lines and around the genitalia. When in chigger territory it is a good idea to check oneself over carefully at the end of the day, shower if possible, and physically remove any mites that are discovered. New bites should be sterilized with alcohol and likely will not cause any reaction. Lesions several days old should not be scratched; the itching and inflammation can be relieved with bite salves (use types containing surface-acting anesthetic).

Mosquito repellents have little effect against chiggers. The time-tested method of dusting nonwettable sulfur into the boots and pantlegs still appears to work best in discouraging their attacks.

In Costa Rica chiggers are usually called "colorados" or "coloradillas" in reference to their red color. Other common names in Latin America are "isangos" (Peru), "bêtes rouge" (Cayenne), and "mocuims" (Brazil).

The "chigger" should not be confused with another infamous tropical human ectoparasite, the "chigoe." The latter (also called "jigger") is a species of flea (*Tunga penetrans*) that habitually burrows in and around the toenails.

*

Brennan, J. M., and Yunker, C. E. 1966. The chiggers of Panama (Acarina: Trombiculidae). In *Ectoparasites of Panama*, ed. R. L. Wenzel and V. J. Tipton, pp. 221–66. Chicago: Field Museum of Natural History.

Johnston, D. E., and Wacker, R. R. 1967. Observations on postembryonic development in *Eutrombicula splendens* (Acariformes). *J. Med. Ent.* 4:306–10.

Michener, C. D. 1946. Observations on the habits and life history of a chigger mite, *Eutrombicula batatas* (Acarina, Trombiculinae). *Ann. Ent. Soc. Am.* 39:101–18.

Sasa, M. 1961. Biology of chiggers. *Ann. Rev. Ent.* 6:221–44.

Fidicina mannifera (Chicharra, Sundown Cicada)

A. M. Young

Cicadas (fig. 11.31), robust-bodied (12–40 mm long) hemimetabolous insects (Homoptera: Cicadidae), occur in both temperate and tropical regions. A subterranean nymphal stage sucks xylem juices (Cheung and Marshall 1973) from rootlets of woody and herbaceous plants, passing through several instars over a several-year period; the length of development depends upon species, locality, and a host of ecological factors. At maturity the

FIGURE 11.31. *Fidicina mannifera,* adult. Costa Rica (photo, A. M. Young).

nymph tunnels to the ground surface for the final molt. From a few to many individuals of a species emerge at the same spot, and such emergence sites are marked with discarded cast skins lying on the ground or clinging to plants. Adult emergences generally occur during cooler parts of the day or during the evening. Adults are short-lived, from a few weeks to a few months, although precise data on longevity are lacking for virtually all species. Adult cicadas suck juices from plants, and the males sing either synchronously in groups or as isolated individuals. Biologists believe the song serves as a courtship mechanism. Tropical regions have more cicada species than comparable areas of the temperate zone. For example,

although Costa Rica is only about the same area as West Virginia, it contains a greater number of cicada species than are found in all of the United States east of the Mississippi River. Although our understanding about such diversity of cicadas is at best rudimentary, recent studies in Costa Rica indicate that both temporal and spatial partitioning of the environment are key factors (Young 1980, and unpub. data). For example, in the lowland tropical rain-forest zone of northeastern Costa Rica some cicadas emerge in primary forest habitats while others emerge in secondary habitats. Within these habitats, some species experience peak emergence in the brief dry season, whereas others peak in abundance during the longer wet season. The mechanisms responsible for the timing of seasonal emergences in tropical cicadas have not been studied, though physiological effects of moisture and temperature on the nymphs probably are involved. Cicadas oviposit masses of oblong white eggs in living or dead branches and palm fronds (in some tropical species). Although adults are active in or near the forest canopy, oviposition in many tropical species takes place in the understory. Upon hatching, the nymphs drop to the ground and burrow into the surface. In Costa Rica, all species emerge each year—that is, they are annual species and none are periodical. This pattern might be true for other regions in the tropics, but no cicada has been studied over large regions. Thus the population structure of tropical cicadas is characterized by the occurrence of several overlapping generations of nymphs for a given species at a locality. Very little is known about the natural history of cicad nymphs. In the Costa Rican studies, nymphal casts are often abundant underneath individuals of certain tree species but absent underneath other nearby or adjacent tree species (Young 1980). Such patterns of spatial patchiness may reflect feeding sites of the nymphs.

In Costa Rica most cicadas are active in the forest canopy, and they are therefore difficult to observe although easy to hear. An exception is *Fidicina mannifera* (Fabricius), which is active lower down on the trunks of trees in primary forest. This widely distributed large (38 mm long; 1.3 gm dry weight) brownish cicada (fig. 11.29) is often seen sitting on the trunks of large forest trees, usually 2–3 m above the ground and higher, in lowland and foothill forests below 300 m elevation. Although it shares a large body size with two other Costa Rican cicadas, *Majeorona bovilla* Distant and *Quesada gigas* (Olivier), it is readily distinguishable from these species by these features: having a stout fuzzy body; having diffuse brown coloration in several wing cells; sitting and singing relatively low on tree trunks; and singing primarily at dusk and dawn. In lowland tropical wet forest areas such as Finca La Selva and Llorona, Corcovado National Park, the males of this big cicada are generally heard between 1745 and 1815, and it is quiet for the rest of the day. In patches of primary deciduous forest such as at Barranca and Santa Rosa National Park, the sound is heard intermittently throughout the day. Of the known thirteen genera and twenty-odd species of cicadas found in Costa Rica (Distant 1881; Young 1972, 1973, 1974, 1975, 1976, in prep.; T. E. Moore, pers. comm.), *F. mannifera* is unique in exhibiting only dawn-dusk singing at some localities. The song is a loud, low-pitched buzz with a sirenlike pattern of intensity. Generally a male sings only once on a tree, flying to many trees within an area. Males are heard in the same area over successive evenings. In Costa Rica, *F. mannifera* occurs on both the eastern and western slopes of the Central Cordillera and into the lowlands to the coasts (Young 1976; pers. obs.); this cicada is restricted by the availability of primary forest.

Field censuses of the discarded nymphal casts of *F. mannifera* in the primary forest at Finca La Selva indicate that this cicada emerges throughout most of the year, with a slight depression in rate in November and December. The large, shiny, chocolate brown cast nymphal skins of *F. mannifera* are often found hanging under the leaves of understory shrubs beneath large individuals of *Pentaclethra macroloba* (Willd.) Ktze. (Leguminosae) at Finca La Selva, and near individuals of allied genera in other regions. The typical range in the numbers of casts collected below a *P. macroloba* over the course of a year is one to forty-seven, based on a sample of twenty trees examined over four years (Young, in prep.). No explanation for the apparent association of the cicada with this tree species is available. The same trees have cast skins beneath them in different years, while other individuals in the same area may lack them.

*

Cheung, W. W. K., and Marshall, A. T. 1973. Water and ion regulation in cicadas in relation to xylem feeding. *J. Insect Physiol.* 19:1801–16.

Distant, W. L. 1881. Family Cicadidae. *Biol. Centr.-Am.* 48:16.

Young, A. M. 1972. Cicada ecology in a Costa Rican tropical rain forest. *Biotropica* 4:152–59.

———. 1973. Cicada populations on palms in tropical rain forest. *Principes* 17:3–9.

———. 1974. The population biology of Neotropical cicadas. 3. Behavioral natural history of *Pacarina* in Costa Rican grasslands. *Ent. News.* 85:239–56.

———. 1975. The population biology of Neotropical cicadas. 1. Emergences of *Procollina* and *Carineta* in a mountain forest. *Biotropica* 7:248–58.

———. 1976. Notes on the faunistic complexity of cicadas (Homoptera: Cicadidae) in northern Costa Rica. *Rev. Biol. Trop.* 24:267–79.

———. 1980. Habitat and seasonal relationships of some cicadas (Homoptera: Cicadidae) in central Costa Rica. *Am. Midl. Nat.* 103:155–66.

Fulgora laternaria (Machaca, Peanut-head Bug, Lantern Fly)

D. H. Janzen and C. L. Hogue

This large homopteran (fig. 11.32) is one of the best-known wild insects in Central America and northern South America because of the folk saying that if a girl is stung by a machaca, she must go to bed with her boyfriend within twenty-four hours or she will die. It is cited in almost every textbook as representative of Fulgoridae and as a representative tropical insect, both of which statements are quite false. In fact, lantern flies are harmless large fulgorid homopterans. They range from the tropical and the central Mexican lowlands well into South America. They are also famous among entomologists for the story originating in South America that the bulging frons is luminescent in the dark (Meriam, M.S. 1705. Metamorphosis Insectorum Surinamensis). Janzen has kept them live during the night and day, as have others, and never seen a hint of luminescence. On the other hand, if the array of eye spots found on the wings of

FIGURE 11.32. *Fulgora laternaria. a,* Adult perched on foliage displaying hind-wing eye spots after being molested (13-cm wingspan). *b,* Three adults in normal resting position on trunk of *Hymenaea courbaril.* Santa Rosa National Park, Guanacaste Province, Costa Rica, December 1979 (photos, D. H. Janzen).

butterflies, moths, other insects and on the hind wings of the machaca are functional in startling or warning small vertebrate predators, as seems reasonable though it is poorly documented, then the lizard head resemblance of the adult peanut-head bug (see Anonymous 1933) probably serves the same function. Alternatively, it may make the insect look like a small lizard to a bird or other predator that would not try to eat a lizard (for whatever reason).

The local common names given to this true bug reflect these ideas: "mariposa caiman" (Spanish, alligator butterfly), "cigarra vibora" (Spanish, serpent bug), "chicharra machaca" (Quechua, "cicada"-bore), "Jequiti-rana-boia" (Brazil, like an alligator), alligator-headed bug, and so on. The species is correctly named *laternaria* (Latinized from German for lantern, but the spelling *lanternaria* is often used), *phosphorea*, *candelaria*, *lampetis*, and *lucifera*. Some of these names actually represent valid species. The genus contains several that are difficult to separate. The literature indicates that at least two occur in Costa Rica.

Adult machacas are variously protected from vertebrate predators. First, they are almost always encountered sitting on large branches and trunks oriented along the length of the stem. Their gray-mottled, almost whitish wings perfectly match the bark of the plant on which they are almost always found; of at least one hundred adults encountered in the past five years in Santa Rosa National Park, only two were not sitting on the trunks of *Hymenaea courbaril* or guapinol. This coloration is usually not visible in museum specimens because it is due to a waxy surface layer that goes liquid in drying ovens, in the presence of paradichlorobenzene, and with age. Second, if the insect is observed closely, there is a resemblance to a vertebrate, as mentioned above. Third, if persistently bothered, a machaca may leap into flight and at that instant release a burst of a fetid odor that smells very much like a striped skunk. It then flies a short distaince to settle on another tree trunk. If pursued farther, it runs up the tree trunk out of reach. If grabbed or knocked to the ground, it then spreads its wings fully, displaying two enormous eyes on the hind wings. These eye spots are on a yellowish and brown mottled background and are reminiscent of the large eye spots on the undersides of *Caligo* butterfly hind wings. Finally, a disturbed machaca may rattle/drum its head against the tree trunk (P. J. DeVries, pers. comm.).

The adults are most abundant at Santa Rosa National Park in November–December (end of the rainy season), June (early rainy season), and July. If a blacklight is set in a guapinol grove in November it is likely to attract numerous males and females, and they occasionally appear at incandescent and fluorescent lights.

The nymphs have never been encountered in Costa Rica, but Janzen assumes that they feed on *H. courbaril* trees, probably high in the canopy or underground on the roots (see Hagmann, *Bol. Mus. Nac. Rio de Janeiro* 4:1 for immatures in Brazil). The adult proboscis is 15–20 mm long, suggesting that it penetrates the thick bark of a tree, probably guapinol. However, *F. laternaria* also occurs in the Caribbean rain forests of Costa Rica (e.g., Finca La Selva), and there is no native population of *H. courbaril* in this part of Costa Rica.

*

[Anonymous.] 1933. The alligator-like head and thorax of the tropical American *Laternaria laternaria*, L. (Fulgoridae, Homoptera). *Ent. Soc. London, Proc.* 7:68–70.

Haemagogus and Other Mosquitoes
(Zancudos, Blue Devils)

C. L. Hogue

Of all families of tropical insects, that of the mosquitoes (Culicidae) is the best known. This is because of their medical importance; mosquitoes act as biological vectors of numerous human afflictions, including those that have been the world's most prevalent (malaria) and virulent (yellow fever) arthropod-borne diseases.

All species require standing (or at most slow-moving) water habitats for larval and pupal development, the variety of which has contributed to the evolution of a world fauna of some three thousand species, 30% of which live in the Neotropics. There are probably more than two hundred species in Costa Rica. The greatest variety utilize so-called container habitats, that is, small, isolated collections of water off the ground, such as rainwater accumulations in bromeliad leaf axils, *Heliconia* flower bracts, tree rot holes, and bamboo stumps. These waters, which are often very rich in dissolved organic solutes, contrast with the more familiar, but less diverse, groundwater habitats, such as ponds, swamps, lake and stream margins, and bogs.

Some of the more conspicuous mosquito types likely to be encountered in Costa Rica are the following:

MALARIAL MOSQUITOES (*ANOPHELES*)
Throughout history malaria has been a health problem in Costa Rica no less than in other parts of Latin America. But, fortunately, as a result of intensive vector control programs and use of antimalarial drugs, the disease is now of only sporadic and local occurrence, principally in coastal areas.

Although about a dozen species of *Anopheles* occur in the country, several of which bite man and are capable of transmitting malaria, *A. albimanus* is the primary vector and the most common. It is a lowland and coastal species, breeding in various groundwater habitats, usually along well-vegetated stream margins and drainage ditches and in ponds and marshes. It shows a decided preference for full sunlight as well as for waters containing a rich growth of filamentous green algae.

The larvae of all *Anopheles* are easily distinguished from those of other mosquitoes by their resting posture, body parallel to the water surface (supported by dorsal stelliform groups of flattened hairs that spread by surface tension and fix the body to the film). In this position the larva feeds just below the surface by rotating its head 180° and working the mouth brushes dorsally. Adults also exhibit a characteristic position during feeding: when biting, the female holds her body at a steep angle relative to the skin ("stands on her head"). The main axis of the body in females of other genera is maintained nearly parallel to the substratum when they suck blood.

COMMON MOSQUITOES (*CULEX* AND *AEDES*)

Most mosquitoes encountered in Costa Rica will belong to these cosmopolitan genera. More than ninety species, with varied breeding and biting habits, are generally distributed throughout the country.

Culex quinquefasciatus (southern house mosquito) is the dominant urban pest on the Meseta Central (at least one to every hotel room!). Here it breeds in all sorts of water accumulations (usually very polluted) from small artificial containers (tin cans, barrels, plugged drainpipes) to groundwater (ditches, horse and cattle hoofprints, barnyard sloughs). *C. nigripalpus* resembles the foregoing species but occurs much more commonly in wild situations on the coastal plains. It also is more apt to bite during the daytime than *C. quinquefasciatus*, which normally feeds at night.

Another coastal species is *Aedes taeniorhynchus* (black salt-marsh mosquito) a widespread, decidedly anthropophilic mosquito found along both the Pacific (California to Peru) and the Atlantic (Massachusetts to Brazil) coastlines. It is adapted to brackish water, breeding in transient pools in mangroves and in salt marshes, and may develop very large populations, making such places extremely inhospitable. Females bite any time of the day, especially in the early evening after dusk, and may attack in droves. This is a smallish black mosquito with a distinct light band around the middle of the proboscis.

Those who must spend time where this and other mosquitoes are numerous should try to avoid bites. Medium-weight clothing gives the best protection (long-sleeved shirts and loose trousers), but repellents will help if applied frequently (every hour or so) to exposed skin and to clothes as well (especially where the cloth may be drawn tight over the skin when sitting or squatting—elbows, backs of legs, and your rear end). A mosquito bar (bed net) is a must where these pests are constant and in

known malarious areas. One should also employ prophylactic drugs religiously in the latter circumstance.

BLUE DEVILS (*HAEMAGOGUS*)

Biologists trying to remain quiet and immobile while performing field tasks in *Haemagogus* territory have given these steel blue, diurnal forest mosquitoes their derisive nickname. They are strongly attracted to man and indomitable in their attacks, during which they emit an irritating high-pitched whine. Their bites are also usually painful and have long-lasting aftereffects.

Haemagogus mosquitoes are characterized structurally by a body vestiture of broad, flat iridescent metallic body scales (reflecting blue, violet, gold, bronze, etc.) accompanied by a near absence of thoracic bristles. Breeding sites consist of tree holes and bamboo stumps or broken internodes, although immatures are occasionally found in other plant containers such as bromeliads and fallen fruits. The species are common in rain forests, open deciduous forests, and coastal mangrove associations.

This genus plays a primary role in the maintenance of reservoirs of sylvan or jungle yellow fever in Central and South America; *H. janthinomys* is considered the most important vector in Costa Rica but is probably less common that *H. equinus, H. iridicolor,* and *H. chalcospilans*.

GIANT MOSQUITOES (*TOXORHYNCHITES*)

The largest mosquitoes belong to this genus; females may attain a wing length of 8 mm. They are also recognized by their metallic blue, green, and silver colors. Fortunately they do not bite, the proboscis being recurved and adapted for liquid foods other than vertebrate blood.

The larvae are also monstrous; many grow to a body length of 20 mm or more. The head is squarish, and the mouth brushes are reduced to a series of heavy filaments used to grasp rather than filter. With these structures they catch and devour other aquatic invertebrates, especially the larvae of other mosquitoes. So voracious are they that biological control specialists once thought them the perfect answer to eradication of pest mosquitoes. However, attempts to employ them in this manner have never succeeded because of the low densities at which they invariably adjust their populations. Breeding sites consist of various containers, usually tree holes or bromeliad leaf axils.

CRABHOLE MOSQUITOES (*DEINOCERITES*)

This genus exhibits several biological features unusual for mosquitoes. As adults all its members (five species in Costa Rica) live and breed in the burrows of giant land crabs (*Cardisoma crassum* and *Ucides occidentalis* on the Pacific side, *C. guanhumi* and *U. cordatus* on the Atlantic). The association is obligatory, and the mosquitoes have evolved specific behavioral and physiological means for dealing with the special conditions prevailing in the habitat.

The larvae tolerate all extremes of water salinity. Populations of the same species have been found in burrow water ranging from a few parts per thousand salinity to more than forty parts per thousand (more concentrated than seawater). Individual larvae also tolerate severalfold daily changes in water salinity as it fluctuates with flooding from rain or underground tidal seepage.

Adults leave the burrow only to fly short distances to feed on bird, reptile, and, probably more rarely, mammal (including man) hosts (the food preferences are still mostly unstudied).

Courtship and mating do not involve the formation of a male swarm, as is usual for mosquitoes, but take place within the burrow as follows: males skate on the water with their nonplumose antennae held just above the surface. Probably by means of pheromones detected by sensillae on the antennae, the males locate female pupae, which they grasp and detain with the fore tarsal claws of one leg (greatly enlarged for the purpose). The pupa is held and guarded from the attentions of rival males (fought off with parries and thrusts from the hind legs) until the female emerges. The latter is immediately engaged in copulation, sometimes even before she completely escapes from the pupal skin, and pulled to the burrow wall, where insemination is completed. Thereafter the female is released to eventually feed and deposit her eggs singly on the sides of the burrow.

Note: In Costa Rica, mosquitoes are commonly referred to as "zancudos" (literally, "long-legged ones"), but "mosquito" is also often used. "Mosquita" is any small fly.

*

Adames, A. J. 1971. Mosquito studies (Diptera, Culicidae). 24. A revision of the crabhole mosquitoes of the genus *Deinocerites. Am. Ent. Inst., Contrib.* 7(2):1–154.

Arnell, J. H. 1973. Mosquito studies (Diptera, Culicidae). 32. A revision of the genus *Haemagogus. Am. Ent. Inst., Contrib.* 20(2):1–174.

Belkin, J. N.; Hogue, C. L.; Galindo, P.; Aitken, T. H. G.; Schick, R. X.; and Powder, W. A. 1965. Mosquito studies (Diptera, Culicidae). 2. Methods for the collection, rearing and preservation of mosquitoes. *Am. Ent. Inst., Contrib.* 1(2):19–78. (Spanish version, *Am. Ent. Inst., Contrib.* 1(2a):21–89.)

Horsfall, W. R. 1955. *Mosquitoes: Their bionomics and relation to disease.* New York: Ronald Press.

Kumm, H. W.; Komp, W. H. W.; and Ruíz, H. 1940. The mosquitoes of Costa Rica. *Am. J. Trop. Med.* 20:385–422.

Vargas, M. 1961. Algúnas observaciónes sobre los hábitos de *Anopheles (N.) albimanus* y *Anopheles (A.) punctimacula* adultos, en la localidad de Matapalo (Puntarenas) Costa Rica. *Rev. Biol. Trop.* 9:153–70.

Hamadryas februa (Soñadora Común, Calicó, Common Calico)

P. J. DeVries

This butterfly is widespread throughout Costa Rica and is probably the most common of the nine species of *Hamadryas* found there. *H. februa* (Nymphalidae) (fig. 11.33) may be distinguished from similar species by having the upper side mottled gray and two irregular brownish lines on the hind wing underside, one on each side of the line of ocelli. The sexes are monomorphic.

Host plants include the mildly urticating vines *Dalechampia heteromorpha* (Young 1974), *D. scandens, D. tiliafolia* (unpub. data), and other species of *Dalechampia* (Euphorbiaceae) (S. Armbruster, pers. comm.), which

FIGURE 11.33. *Hamadryas februa,* upper side (*top*) and underside (*bottom*). Costa Rica (photos, P. J. DeVries).

grow in second growth, forest edges, and tree falls. The eggs are laid singly on the leaves of the host plant, unlike other *Hamadryas* species that lay chains of eggs. The eggs are eaten by *Solenopsis* sp. ants (Formicidae) and by other *Hamadryas* larvae. The larvae are solitary feeders. The mature larva has a light green brown body with crosshatching across the back and a reddish brown head capsule with two knobbed horns. See Young (1974) for details of the early stages. The chrysalis varies from light green to brown and has two flattened horns arising from the head region, which is characteristic of all the *Hamadryas* pupae I have seen. In nature the chrysalis is very cryptic, resembling a curled leaf. Adults emerge in the morning.

Adults occur along forest edges and in light gaps in the forest. They do not visit flowers but feed on rotting fruits, carrion, dung, and mud. They perch head downward on tree trunks with the wings outspread against the substrate and are fairly cryptic in this position. These butterflies are "nervous" and fly from these perches on the tree trunks to chase other insects. They produce a crackling sound while flying, hence the common name "crackers." Some trees are heavily used for perches through time but are not maintained day-to-day by individuals (Ross 1963). It has been speculated that adults maintain a "home range" with regard to patchy host-plant distribution in Barranca, Puntarenas, Costa Rica (Young 1974), but there is little data to support this hypothesis, and it needs further study. My own mark-recapture data from bait traps show almost no recaptures in a given area over a 2-week period. Collenette (1928) suggests that adults of *Hamadryas* can hear, stating that a *H. februa* repeatedly responded to a clicking noise made by a small warbler. Although the crackling noise produced by adult *Hamadryas* butterflies has been known since Darwin's field trip on the *Beagle*, there is no satisfactory explanation for this behavior.

Experimental feeding of *Hamadryas* to caged magpie jays at La Pacifica showed that the jays readily ate them with no ill effects. In one instance I consecutively fed fifteen *H. februa* adults to the same jay with no ill effects. This suggests that *H. februa* adults do not sequester noxious compounds.

*

Collenette, C. L. 1928. An *Ageronia* responding to a noise made by birds. *Ent. Month. Mag.* 64:178–79.

Ross, G. N. 1963. Evidence for the lack of territoriality in two species of *Hamadryas* (Nymphalidae). *J. Res. Lep.* 2:241–46.

Young, A. M. 1974. On the biology of *Hamadryas februa* (Lepidoptera: Nymphalidae) in Guanacaste, Costa Rica. *Zeitschr. Ang. Ent.* 76:380–93.

Heliconius hecale (Hecale)

P. J. DeVries

Heliconius hecale (fig. 11.34) is distributed throughout Central and South America, having a number of races within this range. In Costa Rica it is the most widespread of all the *Heliconius* species, occurring from sea level to 1,700 m elevation on both Atlantic and Pacific slopes. *H.*

FIGURE 11.34. *Heliconius hecale*, adult male, upper side. Costa Rica (photo, P. J. DeVries).

hecale may be distinguished from *H. hecalesia*, a similar species, by the presence of at most two white or yellow spots on the black border of the hind-wing upper side. *H. hecalesia* always has three or four spots, and it tends to have a more elongate forewing apex. There are a number of forms of *H. hecale* in Costa Rica, one uncommon one having a yellow band across the hind wing and being essentially confined to northwest Guanacaste. The name *zuleika*, which is common in the older literature, is the subspecies name of the dominant form in Costa Rica. The sexes are monomorphic and are most easily distinguished when alive; the female is recognized by two glands everted from the tip of the abdomen, which give off a pungent smell.

The host plants are various species of *Passiflora* (Passifloraceae) that include: *P. vitifolia*, *P. oerstedi*, *P. auriculata*, *P. filipes*, and *P. platyloba*. Eggs are laid singly on the young leaves or tendrils of the host plant. As in most butterflies, eggs and young larvae are preyed upon by *Ectatomma* spp. and other predaceous ants. Ants are attracted to *Passiflora* by extrafloral nectaries that probably intensify predation of young larvae by ants compared with plants lacking extrafloral nectaries. Gilbert (1976) and Smiley (in prep.) have shown that host plant use by ovipositing *Heliconius* butterflies may be depressed by the presence of ants. Mature larvae of *H. hecale* are whitish with black spines and an orange head capsule, characteristic of the "silvaniform" *Heliconius* species of Brown and Mielke (1972). The chrysalis is light brown and spiny, with a row of reflective gold spots along the thorax and abdomen. For details concerning early stages see Young (1975).

Adult butterflies visit the flowers of *Anguria*, *Gurania* (Cucurbitaceae), *Cephaelis*, *Hamelia* (Rubiaceae), and *Lantana* (Verbenaceae) in the morning for pollen. The butterflies extract amino acids from the pollen (Gilbert 1972), thus increasing reproductive output and longevity (Dunlap-Pianka, Boggs, and Gilbert 1977). Adults roost gregariously, usually in the subcanopy of the forest, and return to the same roost nightly. Although a number of papers have been written on the subject of roosting *Heliconius* butterflies (Benson 1971; Carpenter 1933; Jones 1930; Moss 1933; Poulton 1933; Turner 1975; Young and Carolan 1976), there is still no satisfactory explanation for roosting behavior, and more research is needed. Adults occur in forest habitats and fly along forest edges, trails, and light gaps. Typical of the genus *Heliconius*, they have a lazy, conspicuous flight and are regarded as aposematic (Brower, Brower, and Collins 1963). *H. hecale* is part of a Müllerian mimicry complex in Costa Rica (and other countries) involving at least two species of Costa Rican ithomiid butterflies (*Tithorea tarricina* and *Callithomia hezia*), *Heliconius hecalesia*, and an unidentified day-flying pericopid moth. All of these Lepidoptera are regarded as distasteful to avian predators. My feeding experiments with caged magpie jays at La Pacifica show that the jays will eat *H. hecale* from Santa Rosa National Park without any immediately noticeable side effects.

*

Benson, W. W. 1971. Evidence of unpalatability through kin selection in the Heliconiinae (Nymphalidae). *Am. Nat.* 105:213–26.

Brower, L. P.; Brower, J. V. Z.; and Collins, C. T. 1963. Experimental studies with mimicry. 7. Relative palatability and Müllerian mimicry among Neotropical butterflies of the subfamily Heliconiinae. *Zoologica* 48:65–84.

Brown, K. S., Jr., and Mielke, O. H. 1972. The heliconians of Brazil (Lepidoptera: Nymphalidae). Part 2. Introduction and general comments with a supplementary revision of the tribe. *Zoologica* 57:1–40.

Carpenter, G. D. H. 1933. Gregarious resting habits of aposematic butterflies. *Proc. Ent. Soc. London* 8:110–11.

Dunlap-Pianka, H. C.; Boggs, L.; and Gilbert, L. E. 1977. Ovarian dynamics in heliconiine butterflies: Programmed senescence versus eternal youth. *Science* 197:487–90.

Gilbert, L. E. 1972. Pollen feeding and reproductive biology of *Heliconius* butterflies. *Proc. Nat. Acad. Sci., U.S.A.* 69:1403–7.

———. 1976. Development of theory in the analysis of insect-plant interactions. In *Analysis of ecological systems*, ed. D. J. Horn. Columbus: Ohio State University Press.

Jones, F. M. 1930. The sleeping heliconias of Florida. *Nat. Hist.* 30:635–44.

Moss, A. M. 1933. The gregarious sleeping habits of certain ithomiine and heliconiine butterflies in Brazil. *Proc. Roy. Ent. Soc. London* 7:66–67.

Poulton, E. B. 1933. The gregarious resting habits of danaine butterflies in Australia; also of heliconiine and ithomiine butterflies in tropical America. *Proc. Ent. Soc.* 7:64–67.

Turner, J. R. G. 1975. Communal roosting in relation to warning colour in two heliconiine butterflies (Nymphalidae). *J. Lep. Soc.* 29:221–26.

Young, A. M. 1975. Observations on the life-cycle of *Heliconius hecale zuleika* (Hewitson) in Costa Rica (Lep.: Nymphalidae). *Pan-Panific Ent.* 57:76–85.

Young, A. M., and Carolan, M. E. 1976. Daily instability of communal roosting in the Neotropical butterfly *Heliconius charitonius* (Lepidoptera: Nymphalidae: Heliconiinae). *J. Kansas Ent. Soc.* 49:346–59.

Historis odius (Orión)

P. J. DeVries

Historis odius (Nymphalidae) (fig. 11.35) ranges from the southern United States well into South America and is the only resident butterfly recorded from Isla del Coco, a Costa Rican island 300 miles off the coast of Ecuador. In Costa Rica it occurs in virtually all habitats from sea level up to 1,500 m elevation. The sexes are mono-

FIGURE 11.35. *Historis odius,* upper side (*top*) and underside (*bottom*). Costa Rica (photos, P. J. DeVries).

morphic. *H. odius* is distinguished from the similar species *H. acheronta* by not having tails on the hind wings and is generally larger.

The host plant is *Cecropia peltata* (Moraceae), a common, rapidly growing secondary-succession tree that at times is inhabited by *Azteca* spp. ants. Eggs are laid singly on the undersides of the leaves, usually on small plants (1–5 m tall). First-instar larvae build frass chains and rest on these when not feeding. These frass chains may extend 4 cm away from the leaf surface, and I assume they are used to keep the larvae away from the ants while allowing them to maintain the colony odor. The mature larva is about 7.5 cm long, mottled black, brown, orange, and blue, and has many branched spines along the back. Mature larvae rest on the vertical apical meristem of the host plant and are not molested by the ants. The chrysalis is light brown, has a single row of branched spines along the dorsum, and has two knobby horns on the head. When disturbed, the chrysalis wriggles like a fish out of water, thus the Costa Rican name *pescadito*.

Adults live in the forest and usually stay within the canopy unless feeding. They come to ground level to feed on the fallen fruits of *Ficus* spp. (Moraceae), *Genipa americana* (Rubiaceae), *Manilkara zapota* (Sapotaceae), *Spondias* spp., and mango (Anacardiaceae) or will feed on ripening fruits still in the canopy. They also feed on sap from tree wounds, carrion, and dung. *H. odius* is extremely good at finding small quantities of rotting fruit in the forest, which is typical of fruit-feeding butterflies. It appears to locate food by odor. Its behavior when trying to find a food item is a sailing flight that criss-crosses the general area of the food, and the insect usually perches several times before it actually locates the food and feeds. It does not feed on flowers and is an extremely fast and alert flier. Although not closely related, *H. odius* is highly convergent on the fruit-feeding charaxine nymphalids like *Prepona, Anaea,* and the Old World *Charaxes*. When not feeding the insects rest on tree trunks with their wings folded over their backs and mimic dead leaves. Females often rest on the trunks of *Cecropia* trees. Individuals are often found with large beak marks on their wings and magpie jays at La Pacifica ate them readily. I found them tasteless or flavored with the rotten bananas I had attracted them with.

Larval and pupal stages are attacked by parasitoid chalcid wasps, and a single chrysalis will produce about fifteen individual parasitoids.

Lasioglossum umbripenne (Abejita, Chupadora, Sweat Bee)

C. D. Michener

One of the major families of bees in the American tropics is the Halictidae, or sweat bees. One of the better-known species in the moist tropics is the Central American *L. umbripenne*. It is about 6 mm long, greenish black, and belongs to the large subgenus *Dialictus,* to which belong numerous species found in many different habitats. *L. umbripenne,* so far as is known, is found only in and near

forests. Its nesting behavior has been studied in the mountains northeast of Quepos and near Turrialba; it has also been observed nesting abundantly in the forests of the Osa Peninsula.

Nothing is known of the flower-visiting behavior of this bee. Probably, like its relatives, it uses a wide variety of different flowers, from which it collects pollen and nectar. It is therefore likely that it visits flowers of various forest trees, but it may also collect food from shrubs and herbaceous vegetation. Pollen and nectar are both used as food by the adults and also are stored as food for the larvae. The bees suck nectar out of the flowers with the probosis and carry it in the crop back to the nest. Pollen is ordinarily removed from the anthers with the help of the jaws and brushed up with the front tarsi, transferred to the middle legs, and thence to the large branched hairs that form the pollen-carrying scopa on the basal segments of the hind leg as well as in the vicinity of the thoracic-abdominal connection. In the scopa the pollen is carried back to the nest, where it is brushed out into a cell for use.

Although some halictids make horizontal burrows into earthen banks and others nest in rotten wood, this species usually nests in more or less horizontal ground, and the burrows go downward. The burrow entrance is constricted so that it can be rather efficiently plugged by the head or abdomen of a bee. Around the entrance, if the bees have been extending their nest recently and there has been no recent rain, one can see a pile of loose soil removed from the burrow. This is called the tumulus, and tumuli are often the most conspicuous evidence that the bee is present. The burrow itself is markedly larger in diameter than the entrance and extends downward in a rather irregular course, sometimes being branched. There are no special pots or cells for storing food for adult consumption. The only cells are brood cells, in each of which a young bee is reared. Each cell is an elongate oval excavation into the wall of the burrow. Its axis is nearly horizontal; it is beautifully shaped and smoothed on the inside, its upper surface a little more strongly concave than the lower surface. When the soil itself is so smooth as to be almost shining, the cell is lined with the waxlike secretion from Dufour's gland, possibly mixed with other glandular products. After being completed and lined, the cell is provisioned with pollen and nectar brought in from several foraging trips. The pollen is mixed with nectar and possibly secretions to form a semi-solid mass the shape of a flattened sphere that lies on the bottom of the cell. After the surface of this pollen ball has been smoothed, a bee lays a large, white, gently curved egg of top of the pollen ball. Then the cell is closed with earth. Although it may subsequently be opened "for inspection," food is not added. That is, the cells are mass provisioned, enough food being placed in a cell before the egg is laid to provide for the entire larval growth of one bee, which emerges as an adult a few weeks after egg laying. While young nests may be quite shallow, particularly during seasons when the soil is moist, older nests may attain depths of over a meter, with cells scattered along much of the deeper part of the burrow system.

Nests are started by single females burrowing into the gound. There appears to be some factor that causes such nest starts to be aggregated, so that over large areas there are no nests at all but in certain areas there may be hundreds or thousands in a limited space. The early progeny are mostly or entirely females and, while potentially egg layers, they are on the average smaller than the founding gynes. In nests with the latter, egg laying by the progeny is partly inhibited and they become workers. The workers do not mate; the eggs they lay, if they survive, become males. The result is a small eusocial colony, from two or three bees up to eighty bees, all females. Males, produced from time to time from unfertilized eggs, leave the nests almost as soon as they reach maturity and never return. Thus the colony consists entirely of females.

A curious difference in behavior exists between the two sites where the species has been studied. Northeast of Quepos the nests start at the beginning of the dry season and develop through the dry season (becoming larger and larger and growing at the same time), and most of the males as well as large females are produced late in the dry season. The large females mate and then disappear. The bees were not found anywhere during the wet season. Presumably the large fertilized females hide away somewhere during the wet season. In any event they appear again at the beginning of the following dry season and repeat the cycle. At Turrialba, on the other hand, although the study was not made through an entire year, it seems likely that the bees are active in the nests throughout the year and that nest construction and colony development are not synchronized as they are in the drier forest at Quepos. At Quepos queens are all larger than their workers, there being a size gap such that the castes can be recognized by size alone. At Turrialba, though queens are on the average larger than workers, the sizes of the castes overlap broadly. Studies of other populations of this species are much needed, particularly to see if intermediates between the Turrialba and Quepos populations can be found. There are no known morphological differences between these populations, although the seasonal differences and differences in caste sizes are striking.

*

Eickwort, G. C., and Eickwort, K. R. 1971. Aspects of the biology of Costa Rican halictine bees. 2. *Dialictus umbripennis* and adaptations of its caste structure to different climates. *J. Kansas Ent. Soc.* 44:343–73.

Wille, A., and Orozco, E. 1970. The life cycle and behavior of the social bee *Lasioglossum (Dialictus)* *umbripenne* (Hymenoptera: Halictidae). *Rev. Biol. Trop.* 17:199–245.

Limnocoris insularis (Chinche de Agua, Creeping Water Bug)

J. Stout

Most stream biologists working in mid-latitude streams are not acquainted with the family Naucoridae because most creeping water bugs are pantropical in their distribution. Further, most species occur in slow-moving streams or ponds. However, *Limnocoris insularis* (Hemiptera: Naucoridae), which is restricted to Central America, lives in fast-flowing small streams and rivers. Like many tropical species in this family, *L. insularis* is often locally abundant and dominates the macroinvertebrate benthic stream fauna. This small animal (6 mm long) is a voracious predator and is catholic in its choice of prey. Thus its numerical dominance probably affects the population density and distribution of potential invertebrate prey.

It takes approximately 2 months for *L. insularis* to mature from egg to adult. The process includes five instars. After maturation, adults can live up to at least 13 months. This life-cycle pattern is in stark contrast to the life cycles of many aquatic insects, where the nymphal or larval stages take much longer relative to the life-span of the adult. Studies at La Selva show that peak reproduction occurs during the dry season (April–June). Minor peaks can occur during unusually dry periods (October–November) at La Selva.

Limnocoris insularis individuals scurry along stream bottoms by walking around pebbles and rocks and by swimming in short bursts. If an individual encounters a prey such as a water penny or a free-living caddisfly larva, it will grasp it. While holding on with long tarsal claws at the apex of its raptorial front legs, the bug pierces the prey and sucks its fluids, using a hypodermiclike beak (fig. 11.36). Consuming one prey animal can take as long as 2 h. The skeleton of the hapless animal is then discarded. In spite of its ability to consume two or three prey items a day, *L. insularis* can exist without food for up to 1.5 months (laboratory data).

Most stream-living insects have been shown to have a net downstream movement pattern (Müller 1974; Otte 1971). Ostensibly, those animals recolonize upstream sites while in the areal, adult stage. In contrast, *L. insularis* moves actively against the current. These animals move upstream in both the nymphal and the adult stages (Stout 1978; in prep.). These tiny animals can travel upstream as fast as 30 m in 17 h. Their entire life cycle is aquatic, *and* the adults possess vestigial wings. If these animals did not move against the current, they could not colonize areas upstream of their initial locations. Until

733

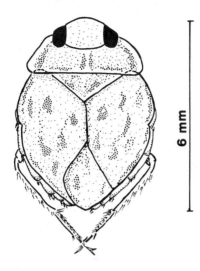

FIGURE 11.36. Adult *Limnocoris insularis*. Finca La Selva, Heredia, Costa Rica (drawing, J. Stout).

these facts were known for *L. insularis,* no one had reported that a stream-dwelling insect had a net upstream direction pattern during its complete life cycle.

At La Selva, *L. insularis* is found most commonly in the Quebrada El Surá—upward of thirty-five individuals have been taken from a kickscreen sample (dimensions 1.0 × 0.6 m). (See Usinger 1956 for collecting technique.) The animals clearly prefer riffle to pool areas along stream courses. Within riffles, they are most common where the heterogeneity in substrate particle sizes is high; that is, fewer animals occur in very fast water where large rocks predominate or among sites principally composed of sand and fine gravel.

The water bugs can be marked using Testor's dope (model airplane paint), allowing experimental manipulation and descriptive population studies to be done rather easily. The animals are air breathers and use the plastron method for breathing (see Thorpe 1950 for description); thus they can be handled out of water for extended periods. Unlike many aquatic insects, creeping water bugs can be easily manipulated. Caution is advised, since they hurt when they bite.

*

Müller, K. 1974. Stream drift as a chronobiological phenomenon in running water ecosystems. *Ann. Rev. Ecol. Syst.* 5:309–23.

Otte, C. 1971. Growth and population movements of *Potamophylax cingulatus* (Trichoptera) larvae in a South Swedish stream. *Oikos* 22:292–301.

Stout, J. 1978. Migration of the aquatic hemipteran *Limnocoris insularis* (Naucoridae) in a tropical lowland stream (Costa Rica, Central America). *Brenesia* 14:1–11.

Thorpe, W. H. 1950. Plastron respiration in aquatic insects. *Biol. Rev. Cambridge Phil. Soc.* 25:344–90.

Usinger, R. L. 1956. Aquatic hemiptera. In *Aquatic insects of California,* ed. R. L. Usinger, pp. 199–203. Berkeley: University of California Press.

Megaloprepus and *Mecistogaster* (Gallito Azul, Helicopter Damselfly)

J. Stout

Viewing a flying helicopter damselfly (fig. 11.37) is an amazing experience, even for a field-sophisticated entomologist. These pencil-thin animals first spread their long wings far apart, then each wing begins to beat slowly and independently from the beat frequency of the other wings, giving the animal an appearance of a windmill in slow motion. Adult helicopter damselflies (order Odonata) are among the longest of all insects, both in wingspan and in body length. Although they are large and fly very slowly, they are excellent maneuverers and avoid capture with disarming ease. Both nymphs and adults of the order are highly predaceous, and helicopter damselflies are no exception.

There are two genera of helicopter damselflies in Costa Rica, *Megaloprepus* and *Mecistogaster*. (Both genera are found from Mexico to Brazil.) *Megaloprepus* is the larger of the two and can be distinguished from *Mecistogaster* by dark purple blue bands on otherwise clear wings. Animals in this genus have the largest wingspan of all living Odonata, sometimes attaining a span of 190 mm. The long, slender abdomen is 102 mm in the male and 97 mm in the female. *Megaloprepus coerulatus* (the only species in Costa Rica) is usually found in the Atlantic and Pacific wet lowlands but has also been taken from near the Quebrada Java (a stream) at the Las Cruces field station.

FIGURE 11.37. *Mecistogaster* damselfly adult resting on a perch. Santa Rosa National Park, Guanacaste Province, Costa Rica, July 1980 (photo, D. H. Janzen).

The second genus, *Mecistogaster* (fig. 11.37), is also very large, having an abdominal length of 71 mm. It has yellow banding on the wings. Two species in this genus occur in Costa Rica, *M. modestus* and *M. ornatus.* Nymphs are found in tank bromeliads. The nymphs for these species were unknown until 1917 when P. P. Calvert discovered them in bromeliads taken from Cartago and from Juan Viñas. He noted than when ants of the species *Odontomachus hastatus* were found in bromeliads the chances were low that damselfly nymphs would also occur there (1917). Tank bromeliads are long and deep, and Calvert theorized that the abdominal length of adult females of this genus was an adaptation whereby females could lay eggs deep within the folds of bromeliad leaves. Not only do the adults use tank bromeliads as repositories for their young, but more recently they have been found using centers of cut and decomposing sugarcane stalks as oviposition sites (L. K. Gloyd, pers. comm.). In addition to being highly predaceous, nymphs of *M. modestus* are cannibalistic, as determined by stomach contents (Calvert 1917). To my knowledge, nymphs of *Megaloprepus coerulatus* have not yet been found, though Calvert (1923*a,b*) tried to find nymphs of this species for over a year.

Individuals of both genera specialize on spiders, taking spiders from under leaves or directly from orbs. The damselflies have a regular, methodical pattern to their hunt. It is in the seizing of orb-spinning spiders that their beautiful capture techniques become obvious. Apparently, the translucent ethereal wings and slender bodies are not discerned by the spider, allowing the damselfly to flutter in one spot a few feet away from the spider without making the spider move. With one flight burst, the damselfly attacks the spider, snips the succulent abdomen from its body, and eats it while letting most of the remaining parts fall to the ground or to the web.

Helicopter damselflies are very "skittish" and will generally fly directly up into the canopy if an attempt to capture them fails. However, they can be stalked if the observer is extremely cautious and stays at a distance of several meters. When one encounters these damselflies in the forest, the sight is awe-inspiring. Memories of prehistoric times when dragonflies and damselflies attained their greatest size flit through the mind of an odonatologist who sights the slow-beating helicopter wings as the damselflies lace through shafts of light above a tropical rain-forest floor.

*

Calvert, Philip P. 1917. *A year of Costa Rican natural history.* New York: Macmillan.

———. 1923*a*. Studies on Costa Rican Odonata. *Ent. News* 34:130–35.

———. 1923*b*. Studies on Costa Rican Odonata. 10. *Megaloprepus,* its distribution, variation, habits and food. *Ent. News* 34:168–74.

Megasoma elephas (Cornizuelo, Rhinoceros Beetle)

H. F. Howden

Megasoma elephas (fig. 11.38) is one of the largest scarabs in the subfamily Dynastinae (so-called rhinoceros beetles). Males of this species range from 55 to 80 mm in length and females from 54 to 82 mm (18–28 g fresh live weight, D. H. Janzen, pers. comm.). The head of the male is ornamented with a long, upward-curved, anteriorly projecting horn with a bifurcate apex; the pronotum

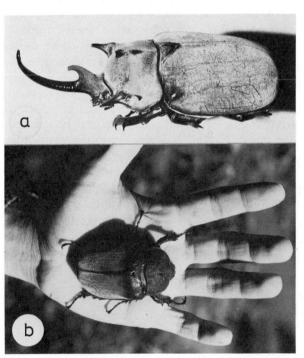

FIGURE 11.38. *Megasoma elephas. a,* Adult male. *b,* Adult female. Estacion Biología Los Tuxtlas, Veracruz, Mexico (photo, D. H. Janzen).

has a short conical horn on each side above the anterior angles. Females lack horns. The elytra and often other surfaces, particularly in males, are covered with a mat of fine hairs, appearing velvety. The sheer size and the fairly uniform brown to dark brown coloration are sufficient to identify the species. Only one other species of beetle that occurs in Costa Rica, *Dynastes hercules* L., is similar in size, but its elytra are usually mottled and dorsal hair is lacking. Also, the horns of the males are different, with *D. hercules* having a long anteriorly projecting, downward-curved pronotal horn. This extends forward over the head and is in opposition to the horn on the head, which extends forward and upward.

Megasoma elephas is found from southern Mexico through Central America to northern Colombia, then eastward into northern Venezuela.

The male horns in *Megasoma* are employed in fighting. Beebe (1949), in his book, *High Jungle,* indicates that males of *Megasoma* battle for the attention of females. This may be so, but in other genera males frequently fight apparently for a particular feeding site. This seems to be the most common cause for agonistic behavior between males.

Within the genus *Megasoma,* adults are apparently attracted to the natural sap flow of certain trees, but observations on this are sparse and whether it is a common occurrence remains unanswered. Larvae develop in large logs, and the time from egg to adult may be between 3 and 4 years. Because of the long time needed, large logs must be available, since the rate of decay in tropical forests is too fast to allow development in smaller logs or branches. Since this necessitates large tropical trees, the range of *Megasoma* in most localities appears to be limited to areas below 1,000 m where heavy forests occur.

If there is an endangered species list for tropical insects, *Megasoma elephas* should probably be included. The species apparently cannot survive in areas that are extensively cut over, a common occurrence in lowland tropical areas. Also, even selective cutting that takes out mature trees greatly diminishes the supply of large logs in the forest. In short, *Megasoma* primarily survives in lowland rain-forest areas that are not greatly disturbed. Since these areas have been greatly reduced in recent times, the beetle likewise has become a considerable rarity. An additional pressure put on its existence has been the recent upsurge in Europe of the use of showy insects as decoration. There is now a large market for spectacular insects, and *Megasoma* is undoubtedly a popular item. While collecting pressures contribute to the scarcity of *Megasoma,* the greatest danger is habitat destruction.

*

Beebe, C. W. 1949. *High jungle.* New York: Duell, Sloane and Pearce.

Hardy, A. R. 1972. A brief revision of the North and Central American species of *Megasoma* (Coleoptera: Scarabaeidae). *Can. Ent.* 104:765–77.

Melinaea lilis imitata (Melineas, Army Ant Butterfly)

C. C. Andrews

Melinaea lilis imitata (fig. 11.39) belongs to the subfamily Ithomiinae of the Nymphalidae. This butterfly is one of the largest ithomiines and has the yellow, black, and orange coloration characteristic of the "tiger-stripe"

FIGURE 11.39. *Melinaea lilis imitata. a,* Adult with wings folded over back (pen is 12 mm wide). *b,* Chrysalis. *c,* Last-instar larva. Finca La Selva, Sarapiquí District, Costa Rica (photos, C. Andrews).

mimicry complex. This complex includes a variety of ithomiines, heliconiines, danaines, and satyrids and even some moths.

M. lilis imitata ranges from Oaxaca, Mexico, to western Panama (Fox 1968). In Costa Rica the butterfly occurs predominately on the Caribbean side of the country in wet primary forests from sea level to about 1,200 m elevation. It is occasionally found in the Central Valley (San José area) and Pacific dry forest (P. J. DeVries, pers. comm.).

Ithomiine larvae in general feed on plants of the Solanaceae. I have discovered a host plant of *M. lilis imitata* (in Finca La Selva, Costa Rica) that is in the genus

Markea of the Solanaceae (unpub. data). These plants are epiphytic and are usually found 2–10 m above the ground on the sides of trees. *M. lilis imitata* has been observed ovipositing on the food plant, eggs and larvae collected from the host plant have been raised to maturity. To my knowledge, no other host-plant records for *M. lilis imitata* have been reported.

Before finding a suitable host plant for oviposition, a female butterfly flies through the forest alighting momentarily to "taste" various leaves with her tarsi. Usually the females are seen searching the vegetation between 2 and 10 m aboveground. Once she finds a suitable plant, the butterfly samples several of its leaves with her tarsi. She may occasionally stray over to a nearby plant and then return to the host plant. This process does not usually last more than 5 min before the butterfly crawls under the leaf and deposits a single egg. She may lay two or three eggs on a single plant, but the eggs are deposited singly on the leaves. The developmental period, from egg to adult, is about 30 days; 4 days are spent as an egg, 16 to 17 days in the larval stage, and 9 to 10 days in the pupal stage.

The larvae of *M. lilis imitata* are black-and-white striped, with an orange band behind the head capsule. Two dorsal tubercles project from behind the head capsule, which suggests affinities to the Danainae. These tubercles become quite long, up to 1.5 cm in the later instars, and may be important in protecting the caterpillars from parasites, since they flick and wave these tubercles when disturbed. The head capsule is black during the early instars but becomes black-and-white striped during the later instars. The pupae are mainly yellow with a sprinkling of black dots and lines.

Major sources of mortality for eggs of ithomiines in general are ants, species of *Trichogramma* wasps, and wasps of the family Scelionidae. Important predators and parasitoids of larvae are ants, spiders, Hemiptera, flies of the Tachinidae, and parasitic wasps of the Ichneumonidae, Chalcididae, and Braconidae (Haber 1978). To my knowledge, no parasitoids of the immature stages of *M. lilis imitata* have been reported.

Adult ithomiines have long been assumed to be distasteful to such predators as birds and to serve as mimetic models for both palatable and unpalatable butterflies (Müller 1879; Collenette and Talbot 1928; Brower, Brower, and Collins 1963). It is assumed that the distastefulness results from poisonous alkaloids that the larvae incorporate from the host plant (Brower and Brower 1964; Ehrlich and Raven 1965). Some ithomiine species have now been shown experimentally to be unpalatable and avoided by birds (Brower and Brower 1964; Haber 1978).

Ithomiines may frequently be found in large mixed-species groups. These aggregations are composed mainly of males (pers. obs.) and are formed gradually as males

perch and expose the scent scales on the upper surface of the hind wings. Other ithomiine butterflies, both males and females, are then attracted to the area (Haber 1978). These groups undoubtedly promote courtship, since matings and much courting behavior are seen in them. The aggregations are most active from about 1000 until 1400, and they may become quite large, containing fifty to one hundred individuals.

Adult ithomiines feed on a variety of flowers, as well as on bird droppings, insect remains, and fermenting fruit. Gilbert (1972) suggested that ithomiines may be using bird droppings as a source of nitrogen compounds to increase adult longevity. It has been speculated that the butterflies are using the uric acid in the droppings. Also likely is that the butterflies are obtaining amino acids from partly digested proteins. Gilbert (1972) has shown that some species of *Heliconius* butterflies collect pollen, from which they incorporate amino acids to augment egg production. He demonstrated that *Heliconius* butterflies fed pollen and sugar water laid five times as many eggs as those butterflies fed sugar water only. By exploiting a nitrogen resource as adults, *Heliconius* butterflies are able to live up to 6 months, as well as to produce eggs continuously. It is known that several species of ithomiines can live for a comparable period. From a mark-release study, Gilbert (1972) reports recaptures after 4 months on *Hypothyris euclea* and *Ithomia pellucida*. Recaptures are rare for many ithomiines, such as *M. lilis imitata*, because the animals travel great distances in short periods. This makes it difficult to estimate longevities in the field. For example, I recorded a recapture on another ithomiine, *Mechanitis polymnia*, in which the butterfly was recaptured 24 h later, 1 km from the point where it was released. Another recapture was recorded for this species in which the individual was recaptured 17 days later, 2 km from the site of marking. It may be that ithomiine butterflies can range 50 km or more during their life-spans.

Ray and Andrews (1980) report that the females of three ithomiine species, *Mechanitis polymnia isthmia*, *Mechanitis lysimnia doryssus*, and *Melinaea lilis imitata*, are frequently found in association with raiding swarms of the army ant *Eciton burchelli*. We proposed that the butterflies are attracted to the swarms as a means of exploiting the abundant droppings of the antbirds, which are also associated with *E. burchelli* raids. These butterfly species are often observed feeding on the bird droppings in the swarm vicinity. They are also seen searching the vegetation and investigating any small white spots that resemble bird droppings. Drummond (1976) was the first to report the association between ithomiines and *E. burchelli*. He reported seeing females of *M. polymnia isthmia* and *M. lysimnia doryssus* (formerly *M. isthmia isthmia* and *M. polymnia doryssus* respectively; see Brown 1977) following a raid of *E. burchelli* in Honduras. He did not observe the butterflies feeding on bird droppings and hypothesized that the swarm odor mimicked the courtship scent of the male ithomiines, which he assumed would attract only the females. Haber (1978) has shown, however, that both males and females are attracted to the courtship scent from the excised scent scales of the males. So Drummond's hypothesis does not really explain the absence of males. Young (1977) responded to Drummond by suggesting that the butterflies "were being 'fooled' by the swarm raid odors. The odors of decay associated with the swarm raid triggered food searching behavior by these butterflies, causing them to follow the army ants."

The observation that the butterflies are frequently found feeding on birds droppings at the army ant swarms suggests that they are not being "fooled" at all but derive benefit from following *E. burchelli* swarms. The preferential attraction of females to the ant swarms is probably due to their greater requirements for nitrogen compounds necessary in egg production.

*

Brower, L. P., and Brower, J. V. Z. 1964. Birds, butterflies and plant poisons: A study in ecological chemistry. *Zoologica* 49:137–59.

Brower, L. P.; Brower, J. V. Z.; and Collins, C. T. 1963. Experimental studies of mimicry. 7. Relative palatability and Müllerian mimicry among Neotropical butterflies of the subfamily Heliconiinae. *Zoologica* 48:65–84.

Brown, K. S. 1977. Geographical patterns of evolution in Neotropical Lepidoptera: Differentiation of the species of *Melinaea* and *Mechanitis* (Nymphalidae, Ithomiinae). *Syst. Ent.* 2:161–97.

Collenette, C. L., and Talbot, G. 1928. Observations on the bionomics of the Lepidoptera of Matto Grosso, Brasil. *Trans. Ent. Soc. London* 76:391–414.

Drummond, B. A. 1976. Butterflies associated with an army ant swarm raid in Honduras. *J. Lep. Soc.* 30:237.

Ehrlich, P. R., and Raven, P. H. 1965. Butterflies and plants: A study in coevolution. *Evolution* 18:586–608.

Fox, R. M. 1968. Ithomiidae (Lepidoptera: Nymphaloidea) of Central America. *Trans. Am. Ent. Soc.* 94:155–208.

Gilbert, L. E. 1972. Pollen feeding and reproductive biology of *Heliconius* butterflies. *PNAS* 69:1403–7.

Haber, W. A. 1978. Evolutionary ecology of tropical mimetic butterflies. (Lepidoptera: Ithomiinae). Ph.D. diss., University of Minnesota.

Müller, F. 1879. Ituna and Thyridia: A remarkable case of mimicry in butterflies. *Proc. Ent. Soc. London*, pp. xx–xxix. (Translation by Mr. Meldona from *Kosmos*, May 1879, p. 100.)

Ray, T. S., and Andrews, C. C. 1980. Antbutterflies: Butterflies that follow army ants to feed on antbird droppings. *Science* 210:1147–48.

Young, A. M. 1977. Butterflies associated with an army ant swarm raid in Honduras: The feeding hypothesis as an alternate explanation. *J. Lep. Soc.* 31:190.

Merobruchus columbinus (Gorgojo de Cenízero, Rain-tree Bruchid)

D. H. Janzen

This large bruchid beetle (fig. 11.40) is most apparent because of the 3–4 mm diameter holes it cuts when it emerges from the seeds and indehiscent pods of the large and common lowland deciduous forest tree *Pithecellobium saman* (cenízero). *M. columbinus* is a squat, beige cryptic beetle about 5 mm long, with the swollen hind femora characteristic of bruchids. It ranges from Mexico to northern South America; it is likely that it occurs throughout the native range of *P. saman* (however, the *P. saman* in the immediate vicinity of Palmar Norte appear to be indigenous yet lack *M. columbinus* seed predation). *P. saman* as an indigenous tree appears to be restricted to the highly seasonal lowlands of the Pacific coast. Where *P. saman* occurs on the Meseta Central, *M. columbinus* is also found.

About the time the immature fruits of *P. saman* enlarge

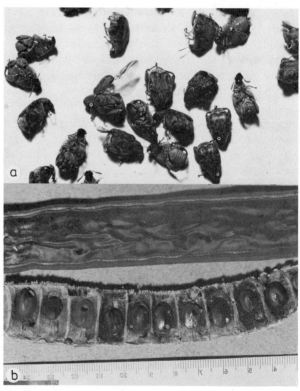

FIGURE 11.40. *Merobruchus columbinus. a,* Adult bruchids. *b,* Damage to seeds of *Pithecellobium saman.* Santa Rosa National Park, Guanacaste Province, Costa Rica (photos, D. H. Janzen).

to full size (December–January in the lowlands of Guanacaste; Janzen 1982) from minute fruit formed in the March–May flowering of the previous year, adult *M. columbinus* appear at the tree and glue ten to twenty single oval eggs on the glabrous pod surface. A beetle probably lays about fifty to one hundred eggs. A larva hatches within 1–2 weeks and bores through the green fruit until it enters a full-sized and nearly mature seed. There are only enough resources in a seed to mature one larva; all later entrants are apparently cannibalized by the first to enter. Within 2–3 weeks the larva has eaten all the seed contents and pupates. Before pupating, it cuts a circular groove in the seed coat. This disk is then cut or punched out by the newly eclosed adult after 1–2 weeks of pupation. The adult then cuts a hole of the same diameter through the wall of the maturing fruit. The beetles leave the pods about the time the pods are ready to fall from the tree, and therefore *M. columbinus* does not interact directly with the dispersal agents of *P. saman;* it is a predispersal seed predator. The intensity of seed predation can be most readily determined by X rays of the seeds or even the pods with the seeds still in them.

The beetle killed 43% of the seeds pooled from eighty-one seed crops in 1972 collected in Guanacaste (range 1–98% per crop; Janzen 1978). It is the primary predispersal seed predator of *P. saman,* though pods that lie under the tree for weeks are liable to have their seeds attacked by the more generalist bruchid *Stator limbatus.* *M. columbinus* attacks no other species of seed in Costa Rica.

There is no evidence of parasites of *M. columbinus* despite the enormous number of beetles and their larvae present at a tree each year. The newly emerging adults live free in the vegetation and may be collected in sweep samples and Malaise traps throughout the remainder of the dry season and nearly all of the wet season. They may feed on floral nectar (and pollen?), since they may be taken on flowers and at sugar baits, but there is no evidence of a second generation in the hard seeds in fallen pods. However, it is possible that some of the first beetles to emerge might produce a second generation in the crowns of the individuals that are late in the fruiting distribution. Adults of *M. columbinus* can fly, but the distances are unknown. Likewise, survivorship between seed crops is unstudied.

*

Janzen, D. H. 1978. Intensity of predation on *Pithecellobium saman* (Leguminosae) seeds by *Merobruchus columbinus* and *Stator limbatus* (Bruchidae) in Costa Rican deciduous forest. *Trop. Ecol.* 18:162–76.

———. 1982. Cenízero tree (Leguminosae: *Pithecellobium saman*) delayed fruit development in Costa Rican deciduous forests. *Am. J. Bot.* 69:1269–76.

Microstigmus comes (Avispa Colémbola, Collembola Wasp)

R. W. Matthews

Microstigmus wasps are tiny (4 mm long) amber-colored insects, completely nonaggressive toward people and notable primarily for their unique nests (fig. 11.41) and social behavior.

M. comes occupies a unique place in wasp natural history. A member of the pemphredonine subfamily of

FIGURE 11.41. *Microstigmus comes* nest attached to the underside of a *Crysophila guagara* palm frond; note the nest entrance. About the size of a spider egg sac, such nests were originally mistaken for them and the wasps were thought to be parasites of them. Females cooperate to gather and silk a single ball of material derived from the underside of fronds of the host palm. They mold this into a bag, then lower it on a silked petiole that is finally given the characteristic spiral. This nest construction behavior is without parallel in any other social insect. Rincón, Osa Peninsula, Costa Rica (photo, C. W. Rettenmeyer).

the large and diverse family Sphecidae (Bohart and Menke 1976), it is one of the very few members of this family to have achieved full sociality. Virtually all of the more than one thousand species of social wasps, such as *Polistes canadensis* (see species account in this book), belong to a different phyletic line, the Vespidae.

M. comes nests are found only in association with one of the commonest understory plants of the Osa Peninsula, the palm *Crysophila guagara* Allen (see species account in this book). They are constructed from waxy bloom gathered from the underside of the frond; careful examination—most easily accomplished under flashlight beam at night—reveals an oval or circular area about 10 cm in diameter surrounding the nest petiole, from which the wasps have scraped the waxy bloom. In a behavior completely unknown among other Hymenoptera, adult females of *M. comes* manufacture silk, secreted from glands in their abdomen and applied by a dense "brush" of setae situated ventrally on the last segment. This silk serves to bind the flocculent wax together, lines the cells and vestibule of the nest, and covers the double-coiled nest pedicel, giving it a slick, somewhat varnished appearance.

The single entrance is at the top of the pear-shaped nest bag where it joins the pedicel; rarely there is a double entrance. Pocketlike cells are clustered in the lower half of the bag, opening upward into a hollow vestibule that forms roughly the upper half of the nest interior. The number of cells ranges from one to eighteen, averaging 3.6 per nest.

Many nests contain two or more females (up to ten have been recorded from a single nest), whose pigmentation and ovarian development suggest that some are recently emerged, probably offspring of one of their nestmates. Males may be present as well—in an overall sex ratio very close to three females to one male—and apparently they cooperate in nest construction, maintenance, and defense. The presence of both sexes in the nest is itself a rare and noteworthy occurrence among the sphecid wasps.

Information obtained from dissection of all the females found in several nests suggests that one female in every nest dominates in oviposition. Such as reproductive division of labor is further indicated by the fact that each cell in a given nest will characteristically be at a different stage of development. Mature larvae of various ages are situated head-down in the cells, suspended from the cell rim by a prominent anal tubercle; they metamorphose into naked pupae. Complete development probably requires about 4 weeks.

Although females cooperate in prey gathering, only one cell is provisioned at a time, even when two or more females bring in prey simultaneously. Prey are springtails (Collembola), compressed into a compact food mass of thirty-one to fifty-eight individuals ($\bar{x} = 46$) representing several species of Entomobriidae and Sminthuridae. This species is a mass provisioner, laying a single egg in the cell only after the full complement of prey has been stocked as a mass glued to the cell side. Nothing is known of hunting behavior except that the prey are killed and transported back to the nest in the wasp's jaws.

Nests are attacked by a braconid wasp parasite, *Heterospilus microstigmi* Richards, which may sometimes be observed walking slowly over the outside of the nest bag. It normally oviposits through the nest to reach its host, upon which it feeds externally.

Although *M. comes* is the most common member of its genus in Costa Rica, at least three other species are known from the Osa Peninsula. One, *M. thripoctenus* Richards preys on thrips (Thysanoptera) and makes a nest of sawdust particles suspended by a long straight pedicel from a variety of plants (Matthews 1970). Additional species may be discovered when various habitats are carefully searched. For example, elsewhere other species nest in protected situations under rocks and the like; West-Eberhard (1977) discovered five new species within walking distance of her laboratory in Cali, Colombia, and she is preparing a taxonomic revision of the genus that will include more than fifty new species.

In summary, this little forest inhabitant is unique (1) for its pendant baglike nests formed from vegetative material, (2) for the ability of adult females to manufacture silk and use it in nest construction, and (3) for the presence of males who provide parental care. Furthermore, *M. comes* satisfies all three criteria for eusociality proposed by C. D. Michener and elaborated upon by Wilson (1971): reproductive division of labor, cooperative brood care, and overlap of generations. It is thus the only member of its family to have achieved full eusociality. Much remains to be learned about its behavior; for example, nothing is known of nest initiation, mating, or dispersal.

*

Bohart, R. M., and Menke, A. S. 1976. *Sphecid wasps of the world.* Berkeley: University of California Press.

Matthews, R. W. 1968a. Nesting biology of the social wasp *Microstigmus comes* (Hymenoptera: Sphecidae, Pemphredoninae). *Psyche* 75:23–45.

———. 1968b. *Microstigmus comes:* Sociality in a sphecid wasp. *Science* 160:787–88.

———. 1970. A new thrips-hunting *Microstigmus* from Costa Rica (Hymenoptera: Sphecidae, Pemphredoninae). *Psyche* 77:120–26.

Richards, O. W. 1972. The species of the South American wasps of the genus *Microstigmus* Ducke. *Trans. Roy. Ent. Soc. London* 124:123–48.

West-Eberhard, M. J. 1977. Morphology and behavior in the taxonomy of *Microstigmus* wasps. *Proc. Eighth Int. Congr. IUSSI, Wageningen, Netherlands,* pp. 123–25.

Wilson, E. O. 1971. *The insect societies*. Cambridge: Harvard University Press.

Morpho peleides (Celeste Común, Morfo, Morpho)

P. J. DeVries

THIS spectacular butterfly (fig. 11.42) ranges from Mexico to Colombia and is common in forests throughout Costa Rica from sea level to 1,400 m elevation. Adults have two forms. One form, almost completely iridescent blue above, is found principally on the Atlantic drainage. The other form has the blue above much reduced and occurs on the Pacific side from the city of Puntarenas south through Panama. One population near Villa Colón in the Meseta Central is nearly all brown above. *M. peleides* (Morphoidae) can be distinguished from the other *Morpho* species in Costa Rica by the dark chocolate ground color on the underside and by having pupillate eye spots on the underside.

FIGURE 11.42. *Morpho peleides,* upper side (*top*) and underside (*bottom*). Costa Rica (photos, P. J. DeVries).

The host plants include *Mucuna* spp., *Lonchocarpus* sp., *Machaerium* spp., and *Pterocarpus* sp. (Leguminosae) (Young and Muyshondt 1973). The dome-shaped eggs are laid singly on the underside of the host-plant leaves. Last-instar larvae attain a length of roughly 9 cm and are mottled red and yellow. The head capsule is densely hairy with reputedly urticating hairs. The chrysalis is light green, ovoid, and very similar to those of *Caligo* (Brassolidae). The time of development from egg to adult has been recorded at 115 days (Young and Muyshondt 1973).

Adults fly in the forest along road cuts, trails, and streams. Their flight is at times lazy, but they are extremely adept at avoiding butterfly nets. They appear to have flyways that are used by most individuals in a population, each using the same route as the previous one. Females are active during midday, flying amid the vegetation searching for oviposition sites. I have observed adults feeding on the fallen fruits of *Ficus* spp., *Brosimum* spp. (Moraceae), *Manilkara* sp., *Sapote* spp. (Sapotaceae), *Guazuma ulmifolia* (Sterculiaceae), *Mangifera indica, Spondias* spp. (Anacardiaceae), *Musa* sp. (Musaceae), *Theobroma cacao* (Sterculiaceae), mud, and carrion. For details of adult feeding behavior see Young (1975). Adults are often found with mites (orobatids?) on the proboscis (pers. obs.) Nothing is known about the biology of the mites and their effect (if any) on the butterflies. While on the ground feeding, the adults are extremely cryptic and flush abruptly from underfoot. For an explanation of the "flash and dazzle" theory of defense see Young (1971a). Young (1971b) records adults of *M. granadensis,* a very closely related species, roosting gregariously. This behavior is certainly worth investigating further and should be looked for in *M. peleides.* I have never seen this behavior in any of the *Morpho* species in Costa Rica. Adults are eaten by jacamars (Galbulidae) and large flycatchers (Tyrannidae). At times piles of *Morpho* wings are found under a jacamar perch in the forest. During the Guanacaste dry season in Santa Rosa National Park, adults exist at very low densities in the river bottoms and are very inactive. I do not know whether these adults live until the rains come and then reproduce or whether they are merely vestiges of a population that enters from elsewhere in the dry season.

*

Young, A. M. 1971a. Wing coloration and reflectance in *Morpho* butterflies as related to reproductive behavior and escape from avian predators. *Oecologia* 7:209–22.

———. 1971b. Notes on the gregarious roosting in tropical butterflies in the genus *Morpho. J. Lep. Soc.* 25:223–34.

———. 1975. Feeding behavior of *Morpho* butterflies in a seasonal tropical environment. *Rev. Biol. Trop.* 23:101–23.

Young, A. M. and Muyshondt, A. 1973. The biology of *Morpho peleides* in Central America. *Carib. J. Sci.* 13:1–49.

Myrmeleon (Hormiga León, Ant Lions)

M. S. McClure

Ant lions of the genus *Myrmeleon* are widely distributed throughout Costa Rica, having been reported from Guanacaste Province at Palo Verde (McClure 1976) and in Santa Rosa National Park (Wilson 1974), from Puntarenas Province on the Osa Peninsula (Wilson 1974), and from Limón Province at Tortuguero (Simberloff et al. 1978). They are generally more abundant in the lower rainfall areas, where suitable larval habitats (dry, loose-textured soil) are more available. In higher rainfall areas, larvae occur in the soil beneath rock overhangs, under slightly raised logs, and wherever they are protected from rains. The predaceous larvae of *Myrmeleon* remain at the bottom of conical pits that they construct in the soil (fig. 11.43), and feed upon ants and other small arthropods that slide into their traps.

The life cycle of the ant lion is longer than that of most insects because of the intermittent and quantitatively variable nature of the larval food supply. Thus, in a given locality there may be a considerable range of sizes among larvae that hatched at about the same time. The adult *Myrmeleon,* measuring 5 to 6 cm in length, is a delicate, elongate, thin-bodied insect with a relatively broad pronotum and a head with prominent compound eyes (fig. 11.44*b*). It resembles an adult damselfly except that it is softer-bodied, has longer, clubbed antennae, and has wings with quite different venation and tips that are pointed rather than rounded. Adult ant lions, predaceous on a variety of small arthropods, are crepuscular or nocturnal, resting during the day on low vegetation. These rather feeble fliers are easily captured near lights at night.

The imago lays her eggs singly in dry, loose soil. Shortly after hatching, the rough, squat, wedge-shaped larva (fig. 11.44*a*) begins its search for a suitable place to construct a pit. It plows backward across the terrain just beneath the substrate in a most irregular pattern of movements called "doodles" (fig. 11.43). Accordingly, the ant lion has often been referred to as the doodlebug. Once it finds a suitable location, the larva commences the formidable task of pit construction using a variety of morphological and behavioral specializations. Foremost among the morphological specializations are the oval-shaped, posteriorly tapered abdomen and flat head used for pushing and lifting sand during excavation of the pit. Metathoracic legs with fused tibia and tarsus and enlarged, forward-directed claws, together with a series of bristles on the body, also directed forward, enable the larva to move backward quickly through the soil or to anchor itself against forward movement.

An ant lion excavates a funnel-shaped pit, from 1 to 4 cm in diameter (fig. 11.43) by moving backward in a circle, using its oval abdomen as a plow and its flat head

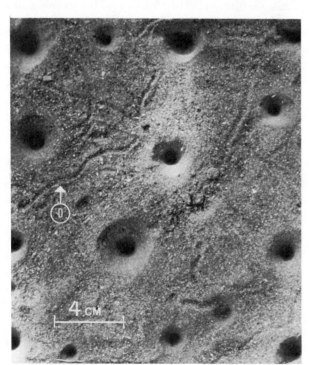

FIGURE 11.43. *Myrmeleon* ant lion larval pits and doodling trails (photo, M. S. McClure).

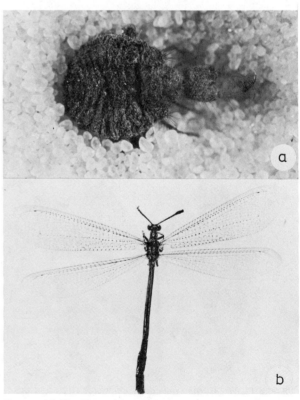

FIGURE 11.44. *Myrmeleon. a,* Larva on a sand background. *b,* Adult (photos, M. S. McClure).

as a shovel for flicking sand upward. The diameter of the finished pit is closely related to the size of the resident larva and the depth of the loose substrate into which the pit is dug. Regardless of the diameter of the pit, the angle by which the wall of the cone slopes upward from the base is similar for a given substrate (about 40°). Upon completion of its pit the larva remains motionless at the bottom, concealed beneath the soil. When an ant or other suitably small arthropod accidentally falls into the pit, the larva seizes it in long, piercing mandibles, sucks its body fluids, and then casts the remains from the pit with a flick of its head.

When fully grown, larvae of *Myrmeleon* measuring 10 to 12 mm spin spherical cocoons of sand and silk using a slender, fusiform spinneret at the tip of the abdomen. Completed cocoons measure 10 to 15 mm in diameter, males being slightly smaller than females. When ready to emerge the pupa slits the cocoon with its mandibles and pushes itself out and up to the surface of the soil by abdominal movements. Its skin then ruptures along the back, and the imago emerges, completing the cycle. The scant biological evidence available indicates that development of *Myrmeleon* from egg to imago normally requires at least 2 years. However, since larvae often fast or hibernate for extended periods, it is likely that 3 years or longer are required for larval development of some individuals. Larvae of various sizes and adults were abundant in February, during the dry season, at Palo Verde (Guanacaste Province) (McClure 1976), which indicates that developmental stages of *Myrmeleon* overlap extensively.

For decades naturalists throughout the world have been intrigued by the fascinating activities of pit-making ant lions. However, the bulk of the literature on *Myrmeleon* consists of descriptive accounts of doodling, pit constructing, and prey capturing behavior of larvae of temperate species. Of these numerous reports Topoff (1977) and Klein (1982) provides an especially detailed account of investigations into larval responses to various habitat conditions, including light, soil temperature, obstacles, and substrate texture, encountered during doodling and pit construction.

Research on tropical pit-making ant lions has centered on examining their feeding biology (Griffiths 1980*a*,*b*) including factors that affect dispersion and the spatial distribution of larvae. In his report on prey capture and competition in the ant lion, Wilson (1974) argued that natural selection should favor a larva that responds to food shortage by relocating its pit in such a way as to maximize prey capture and minimize intraspecific competition. He concluded that the ideal spatial distribution of pits that would achieve this end would be a "doughnut" configuration. Wilson claimed to show this "doughnut effect" in both natural and experimental populations of *Myrmeleon*. In subsequent experiments (McClure

1976) larval density was shown to have important effects on the spatial distribution of pits. Using nearest-neighbor analyses, I showed that ant-lion dispersion becomes increasingly regular as density increases, ultimately resulting in a uniform spatial arrangement at maximum density, with pits equidistant from one another. I argued that a uniform pattern of dispersion would maximize the distance between larvae and would therefore better optimize prey capture and reduce intraspecific competition than would be a "doughnut" configuration. Simberloff (1970) and Simberloff et al. (1978) question the validity of using neighbor analysis to determine the spacial configuration of pits and argue that ant-lion populations in nature and in the laboratory are not overdispersed and may be clumped. They suggest that of the various factors contributing to dispersion, sand-throwing during pit construction and cannibalism are more important than are food limitations. Further research on the bionomics and behavior of *Myrmeleon* ant lions is needed to determine the mechanisms involved in the dispersion of these fascinating pit-digging insects.

*

Griffiths, D. 1980*a*. The feeding biology of ant lion larvae: Prey capture, handling and utilization. *J. Anim. Ecol.* 49:99–125.

———. 1980*b*. The feeding biology of ant lion larvae: Growth and survival in *Morter obscurus*. *Oikos* 34: 364–70.

Klein, B. G. 1982. Pit construction by antlion larvae: Influence of soil illumination and soil temperature. *J. New York Ent. Soc.* 90:26–30.

McClure, M. S. 1976. Spatial distribution of pit-making ant lion larvae (Neuroptera: Myrmeleontidae): Density effects. *Biotropica* 8:179–83.

Simberloff, D. 1979. Nearest neighbor assessments of spatial configurations of circles rather than points. *Ecology* 60:679–85.

Simberloff, D.; King, L.; Dillon, P.; Lowrie, S.; Lorence, D.; and Schilling, E. 1978. Holes in the doughnut theory: The dispersion of ant-lions. *Brenesia* 14–15:13–46.

Topoff, H. 1977. The pit and the ant lion. *Nat. Hist.* 86:64–71.

Wilson, D. S. 1974. Prey capture and competition in the ant lion. *Biotropica* 6:187–93.

Nasutitermes (Comején, Hormiga Blanca, Nasute Termite, Arboreal Termite)

Y. D. Lubin

Nests of *Nasutitermes* termites (fig. 11.45) are common and conspicuous in lowland wet-forest and forest-edge habitats in Central America. These large, spherical dark brown or black nests (Thorne 1980) are generally arboreal. They are made of "carton"—wood that is chewed up by worker termites and cemented together with fecal "glue." The outer layer of carton is often soft, but it gets progressively harder toward the interior of the nest. Covered runways composed of the same substance lead from the nest to feeding sites in trees and in dead wood or leaves on the ground. The genus is widely distributed in the Neotropics, with many species occurring in Central America (Araujo 1970).

There are basically three castes in *Nasutitermes:* the reproductives and two sterile castes, the workers and the soldiers. Workers and soldiers may be males or females. Each colony generally has a single physogastric queen (fig. 11.46) and a king, though some nests are reported to have multiple queens. The sexual brood is produced seasonally. In the lowland monsoon forest on Barro Colorado Island, Panama nymphs with developing wing pads appear in nests at the end of the dry season (March). Swarming of winged adults occurs primarily in April and May after the first big rains of the wet season and may continue sporadically until August or September. Termites are hemimetabolous insects, and therefore all immature stages are technically "nymphs." Termite specialists, however, refer to immatures of reproductive castes as *nymphs* and to immatures of nonreproductive castes as *larvae.* Adult reproductives are also called imagoes, alates, or winged adults to distinguish them from neotenic reproductives that are derived from workers or nymphs with wing pads. Caste differentiation in termites is tremendously complex and poorly known.

Swarming and postflight behavior have not been stud-

ied in any of the Neotropical *Nasutitermes.* In the related genus *Trinervitermes* (a nasuti-termite from Africa), females alight and attract males to sex pheromones emitted from the tergal and/or sternal glands at the tip of the abdomen. The wings are shed in both sexes, and males follow the females "in tandem" in search of nesting sites, maintaining contact through tactile and olfactory stimuli (Leuthold 1975).

Pheromones play an important role in other kinds of communication in *Nasutitermes:* in orientation and in alarm and defense. Since worker termites are blind, orientation is entirely by means of chemical trails. The trail pheromone is produced in the sternal glands of workers and soldiers and elicits trail-following behavior in both of these castes (Stuart 1963). In *Trinervitermes* the sternal glands of soldiers are vestigial, while those of workers and alates are large and functional (Leuthold and Luscher 1974). Presumably trail pheromones are not of equal importance in all castes. Trails are laid in two contexts: to sources of food and to sites of disturbance. In the latter case, transmission of alarm through other pheromones or by tactile means is also involved.

Soldiers of *Nasutitermes,* the nasutes, are specialized for chemical defense: the head is elongated to form a snout or nasus (fig. 11.46) through which they squirt a strong-smelling, sticky secretion. The secretion is elaborated in the cephalic gland, which takes up most of the head capsule and contains volatile monterpenes (these give it the characteristic turpentinelike smell) and a low-molecular-weight component (Moore 1964; Vrkoc et al. 1973). The secretion gums up small arthropod predators and may also be toxic to them; it is both irritating and unpalatable to *Tamandua* anteaters (Edentata, Myrmecophagidae) (Lubin and Montgomery 1980).

The success of nasute soldiers in defense is due to their

FIGURE 11.45. *a, Nasutitermes* nest high on the trunk of a rain-forest tree (Corcovado National Park, Osa Peninsula, Costa Rica). *b, Nasutitermes* nest on a forest remnant tree in a cattle pasture (Potrerillos, Guanacaste, Costa Rica) (photos, D. H. Janzen).

FIGURE 11.46. *Nasutitermes* physogastric queen with nasutes' heads clearly visible against her yellow abdomen. Palmar Norte, Costa Rica (photo, D. H. Janzen).

numbers in the nest and their defensive behaviors. When a nest or covered runway of *N. corniger* (a common species found in Panama and Costa Rica) is breached, nasute soldiers rush out in large numbers while workers disappear within seconds into the trail or nest. Only after a few minutes do the workers return to repair the damage. The numbers of nasutes that emerge at breaks in carton nests is two to ten times the number emerging at breaks away from the nests (Lubin and Montgomery 1980). Predators that are repelled by nasute secretions (ants) or that find the nasutes distasteful (*Tamandua* anteaters) are thus prevented from attacking the nest.

Tamandua anteaters, in fact, avoid *Nasutitermes* carton nests where soldiers are present in large numbers, preferring to feed from concentrations of termites in dead wood away from the nest (Lubin and Montgomery 1980). Nests are attacked under special conditions: when they contain reproductives just before swarming, or when they contain ants. In both instances colonies may be less able to defend themselves (reduced soldier production), or anteaters may raise their tolerance level to nasute secretions in the face of a highly desirable food resource (lipid-rich reproductives).

Nasutes compose 12–20% of the total nest population in *N. corniger* (Lubin and Montgomery 1980). This is a large proportion compared with nonnasute species; for example, the mandibulate soldiers of *Microcerotermes exiguus*, a termitid with no apparent chemical defense system, form only about 2% of the population. The nasutes have no mandibles and must be fed by the workers, and thus they must represent a considerable energetic drain on the colony. Predation pressures of vertebrate predators, primarily anteaters, may be responsible for maintaining high proportions of nasutes in these colonies.

Major predators of *Nasutitermes* are *Tamandua* anteaters, several species of ants (including the termite specialists, *Termitopone*), *Anolis* lizards, and several reduviid bugs (Hemiptera) that specialize on *Nasutitermes* (e.g., *Salyavata variegata* in Panama). Swarming alates are taken by virtually every insect eater in the vicinity. Trogons, puffbirds, and parakeets hollow out nesting holes in *Nasutitermes* carton nests, causing considerable damage to the nests. Attacks by anteaters on carton nests of *Nasutitermes* and *Microcerotermes* on Barro Colorado Island accounted for some 20% of all observed damage to a sample of nests; the remaining damage was due to nesting birds and unknown causes (Lubin, Montgomery, and Young 1977). Ants of the genera *Azteca*, *Camponotus*, and *Monacis* will often usurp part of a *Nasutitermes* nest and may eventually cause the termites to abandon the nest.

*

Araujo, R. L. 1970. Termites of the Neotropical region. In *The biology of termites,* ed. K. Krishna and F. M. Weesner, pp. 527–76. New York: Academic Press.

Leuthold, R. H. 1975. Orientation mediated by pheromones in social insects. In *Pheromones and defensive secretions in social insects,* ed. C. Noirot, P. E. Howse, and G. Le Masne, pp. 197–211. Dijon: University of Dijon.

Leuthold, R. H., and Luscher, M. 1974. An unusual caste polymorphism of the sternal gland and its trail pheromone production in the termite *Trinervitermes bettonianus. Insectes Sociaux* 21:335–42.

Lubin, Y. D., and Montgomery, G. G. 1980. Defenses of *Nasutitermes* termites (Isoptera, Termitidae) against *Tamandua* anteaters (Edentata, Myrmecophagidae). *Biotropica* 13:66–76.

Lubin, Y. D.; Montgomery, G. G.; and Young, O. P. 1977. Food resources of anteaters (Edentata, Myrmecophagidae). 1. A year's census of arboreal nests of ants and termites on Barro Colorado Island. *Biotropica* 9:26–34.

Moore, B. P. 1964. Volatile terpenes from *Nasutitermes* soldiers (Isoptera, Termitidae). *J. Insect Physiol.* 10: 371–75.

Stuart, A. M. 1963. Origin of the trail in the termites *Nasutitermes corniger* (Motchulsky) and *Zootermopsis nevadensis* (Hagen), Isoptera. *Physiol. Zool.* 36: 69–84.

Thorne, B. L. 1980. Differences in nest architecture between the Neotropical arboreal termites *Nasutitermes corniger* and *Nasutitermes ephratae* (Isoptera: Termitadae). *Psyche* 87:235–43.

Vrkoc, J.; Ubik, K.; Dolejes, L.; and Hrdy, I. 1973. On the chemical composition of frontal gland secretions in termites of the genus *Nasutitermes. Acta Ent. Bohemoslov* 70:74–80.

Nephila clavipes (Araña de Oro, Golden Orb-Spider)

Y. D. Lubin

The largest of the orb-weaving spiders (family Araneidae) in the New World, *Nephila clavipes* females (fig. 11.47) weigh about 1 g and are about 2.5 cm long (body length). Orb webs of *Nephila* are easily recognized by their size (often 60 cm in diameter) and by the strong yellowish silk. *Nephila* silk is so strong that it was formerly used for gun sights (which require fine, durable threads), and silk from another species (*N. maculata*) is still used for fishing lures by coastal tribes in New Guinea.

The web of *Nephila* consists of an asymmetrical vertical orb with the hub near the top of the web, and a tangle of nonsticky threads—the barrier web—on one or both sides of the orb web (i.e., dorsal and/or ventral to the spider). The orb itself is constructed of nonsticky radii,

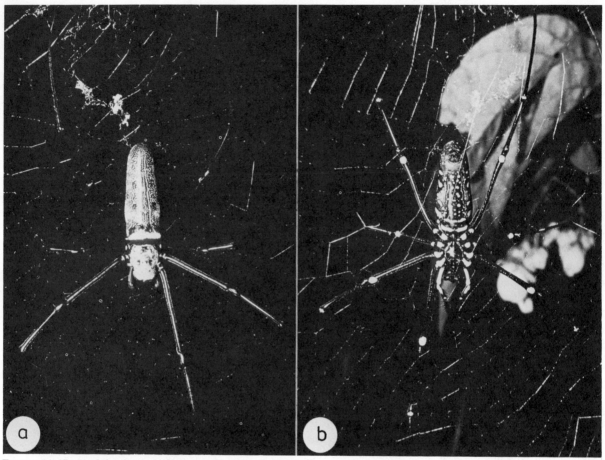

FIGURE 11.47. *Nephila clavipes,* adult female resting in web in forest understory.
a, Upper side. *b,* Underside. Sirena, Corcovado National Park, Osa Peninsula, Costa Rica
(photo, D. H. Janzen).

frame threads, and structural spiral and a viscid (sticky) spiral superimposed on the structural spiral. Unlike most other orb weavers, *Nephila* does not remove the structural spiral as she spins the sticky spiral, so that the finished orb web contains both these spiral elements. The entire web functions as a sticky trap for airborne insects. The spider sits at the hub, facing down, and monitors the web for vibrations set up by the impact of an insect on the web or by its struggling in the web.

Nephila immobilizes insects that become trapped in the orb web by biting them (Robinson and Mirick 1971), probably injecting venom and digestive enzymes with the bite. After the bite, the spider pulls the prey out of the web or cuts it out with the chelicerae and carries it back to the hub to feed. Large or bulky prey items are wrapped in silk before being transported to the hub (but after the initial bite). *Nephila* is active in prey capture both day and night and will take a wide variety of insects ranging from small dipterans to large scarab beetles and hawk-moths. Unlike many other orb weavers (e.g., *Argiope, Eriophora, Araneus*), *Nephila* does not attack insects ini-

tially by wrapping them in silk. This means that the struggling insect cannot be immobilized from a distance (by throwing silk over it); in the act of biting, the spider must come in direct contact with the insect and is therefore in some danger of being bitten, stung, kicked, or sprayed by the prey. Because of this, and indeed in spite of its size, *N. clavipes* is a "cowardly" spider and is unable to deal effectively with large or aggressive insects (e.g., large katydids or wasps) or with insects that have chemical defenses, such as pentatomid bugs and many ants (Robinson, Mirick, and Turner 1969).

Nephila clavipes is typically found in forest clearings and secondary-growth areas in a variety of lowland and mid-elevation habitats. When supporting structures are available, spiders will aggregate, often in groups of several hundred individuals. Individual webs are attached to one another by their frame threads and barrier webs. Aggregations of this type are a common sight on telephone and electric wires, radio towers, and bridges in Panama and Costa Rica. *N. clavipes* populations in lowland areas of Panama are highly seasonal, with two peaks of adults occurring in the early dry season (December–January) and early to middle rainy season (July–August) (Vollrath, n.d. *a;* Lubin 1978).

Males of *N. clavipes* are small, about one-tenth the weight of adult females. They mature in fewer instars than do the females (Vollrath, n.d. *b*). The males are variable in size, the ultimate size depending on the instar at which they mature (this may be under environmental and/or genetic control). Several adult males may live in the web of a single female, feeding on her prey. Aggressive interactions between males are common. Size may be important in determining the outcome of these interactions and ultimately the male's success in obtaining access to the female (Vollrath, n.d. *b*).

Webs of *Nephila* have numerous kleptoparasites associated with them. Theridiid spiders of the genus *Argyrodes* live in the webs of *Nephila* (and of other spiders as well), feeding on small insects that they remove directly from the orb web as well as on larger, predigested insects captured by the host (Vollrath 1980). *Argyrodes elevatus* may respond to vibrations set up by the host spider as it wraps the prey in the web, using these as cues to locate prey in the web (Vollrath 1979). Millichiid flies (*Phyllomyza*) feed on juices of *Nephila* prey that have been liquefied by the spider (Robinson and Robinson 1977). Pyralid moths and nematocerous flies sit on the nonsticky frame and barrier web threads and presumably gain protection from visually orienting predators (Robinson and Robinson 1975, 1976): emisinine bugs (Hemiptera), *Mischocyttarus* wasps, damselflies, and hummingbirds all steal prey from *Nephila* webs, though these cannot be considered true kleptoparasites (Vollrath 1980).

*

Lubin, Y. D. 1978. Seasonal abundance and diversity of web-building spiders in relation to habitat structure. *J. Arachnol.* 6:31–53.

Robinson, M. H., and Mirick, H. 1971. The predatory behavior of the golden-web spider *Nephila clavipes* (Araneae: Araneidae). *Psyche* 78:123–39.

Robinson, M. H.; Mirick, H.; and Turner, O. 1969. The predatory behavior of some araneid spiders and the origin of immobilization wrapping. *Psyche* 76:485–501.

Robinson, M. H., and Robinson, B. 1973. Ecology and behavior of the giant wood spider *Nephila maculata* (Fabricius) in New Guinea. *Smithsonian Contrib. Zool.* 149:1–76.

———. 1975. A tipulid associated with spider webs in Papua New Guinea. *Entomol. Month. Mag.* 112:1–3.

———. 1976. The ecology and behavior of *Nephila maculata:* A supplement. *Smithsonian Contrib. Zool.* 218:1–22.

———. 1977. Associations between flies and spiders: Bibiocommensalism and dipsoparasitism? *Psyche* 84:150–57.

Vollrath, F. 1979. Vibrations: Their signal function for a spider kleptoparasite. *Science* 205:1149–51.

———. 1980. Kleptoparasitism as opposed to kleptobiosis and commensalism. *Am. Nat.,* in press.

———. 1981. Behavior of the kleptoparasitic spider *Argyrodes elevatus* (Araneae, Theriddiidae). *Anim. Behav.,* in press.

———. n.d.*a.* Population dynamics of *Nephila clavipes*. In preparation.

———. n.d.*b.* Considerations of male size and sex-ratio in spiders. In preparation.

Nyssodesmus python (Milpies, Large Forest-floor Millipede)

I. L. Heisler

Nyssodesmus python (fig. 11.48) is a member of the millipede order Polydesmida, whose members possess twenty body segments, nineteen of which bear a pair of more-or-less horizontally oriented keels. In *N. python* the keels are large and the segments are relatively flat, giving these animals the appearance of overlong, very large isopods. Individuals are mostly dull whitish yellow except for a pair of dark brown longitudinal stripes extending along the sloping margins of the back. Females are 70–100 mm in length and 13–15 mm in greatest width. Males are smaller: 65–90 mm long and 12.5–14.5 mm wide. In males the first pair of legs on the seventh segment are modified into small curved "gonopods" that are used for sperm transfer. Taxonomic information on *N. python* and other Central American millipedes can be found in Loomis (1968) and Pocock (1910).

Nyssodesmus python (= *Platyrhacus bivurgatus* of older literature) occurs along the Caribbean slope of Costa Rica, but its exact range is unknown. It is very

FIGURE 11.48. *Nyssodesmus python* in copulo on forest floor. Finca La Selva, Sarapiquí District, Costa Rica (photo, D. H. Janzen).

abundant at La Selva and is found there almost exclusively in stands of *Heliconia imbricata* and in old cacao groves where the understory is uncut. Like other polydesmid millipedes, it appears to feed largely upon rotting wood. Millipedes possess a diversified gut flora that functions to release nutrients and reduce toxins in ingested plant materials (Sakwa 1974). Ecologically, they are important as decomposers. They also play an important role in the mineral cycle, since, unlike most other land arthropods, their exoskeletons contain large quantities of calcium salts in addition to chiton (Gist and Crossley 1975).

Very little is known about the natural history of tropical millipedes (see Causey 1943; Lewis 1974; Toye 1967). The general pattern of reproduction and development in the Polydesmida is as follows: the external genital openings (vulvae) of females are located ventrally in the connective membrane between the second and third segments. In males, the spermatic ducts open on or near the coxae of the second pair of legs. Before copulation, a male rolls the anterior portion of his body to bring his gonopods into contact with these openings, and in this manner transfers sperm to them. Copulation is venter-to-venter, and sperm is transferred by a series of thrusts of the gonopods into the female's vulvae. There it is stored in special receptacles until the time of oviposition.

Eggs are laid in small cavities in the soil, often constructed from frass. These hatch into seven-segmented, first-stadium juveniles that then pass through a series of juvenile stadia. At each molt new segments are added and legs appear on previously apodous segments. Molting takes place in chambers in the soil, also frequently constructed from frass.

In *Nyssodesmus python*, older juveniles resemble adults in shape but are unpigmented, are smaller, and possess fewer segments. Newly molted adults are soft and unpigmented; full pigmentation and calcification of the exoskeleton takes about a month. *N. python* also molts after reaching sexual maturity. The life-span of this species is not known but is probably more than a year and may be as much as several years.

Nearly all millipedes produce toxic chemicals used in defense against predators (Casnati et al. 1963). When disturbed, individuals of *Nyssodesmus python* roll up into a spiral, expel the contents of the hindgut, and release a liquid containing hydrogen cyanide and benzaldehyde. If expelled violently, this liquid can be sprayed as much as 30 cm. These behaviors, combined with their large size and rigid exoskeleton, seem to discourage most potential predators. The most likely sources of adult mortality are parasitism, desiccation, and traumatic injury, especially during the vulnerable molting periods.

The most obvious aspect of the behavior of *Nyssodesmus python* at La Selva is the "riding" of females by males after copulation. Year-round, most individuals are found in heterosexual pairs, with the male standing on the female's dorsum. Solitary females are uncommon and rarely remain unescorted more than 24 h. Males will ride females for up to 5 days and possibly much longer. They are not awaiting female receptivity, since copulation usually takes place within the first 6 h after encounter, and virtually all ridden females are receptive.

Sexual selection on males is the most likely explanation for the evolution of "riding" behavior in this species. Females remain receptive for prolonged periods and will mate with many males. Since sperm is not utilized until immediately before oviposition in millipedes, multiple matings by females can lead to competition among the sperm from different males for fertilization of a single clutch of eggs. In *N. python* it is likely that any gain in reproductive success experienced by a male who leaves a female after copulation in order to seek new mates is offset by greater losses owing to sperm competition from her subsequent matings. Solitary sexually active males generally remain so for longer periods than do solitary receptive females; hence a male's probability of remating is lower than a female's. Riding clearly reduces the likelihood that a female will mate with a new male. When a sexual competitor is present, a male in the riding position will flex the anterior segments of his body to force a female's head and anterior segments over her genital openings, making sexual access by an intruding male impossible. Females are probably unable to resist this forced flexion, since the muscles that produce dorsoflexion of the body are much larger than their antagonists.

Postcopulatory riding behavior has not been found in other millipede species. In *Nyssodesmus python* it probably results from a combination of exceptionally high population density and relatively nonseasonal breeding, both of which make extended receptivity and multiple mating by females more likely.

*

Casnati, G.; Nencini, G.; Quilico, A.; Pavan, M.; Ricca, A.; and Salvatori, T. 1963. The secretion of the myriapod *Polydesmus collaris collaris* (Koch.). *Experientia* 19:409–11.

Causey, N. B. 1943. Studies on the life history and the ecology of the hothouse millipede, *Orthomorpha gracilis* (C. L. Koch, 1847). *Am. Midl. Nat.* 29:670–82.

Gist, C. S., and Crossley, D. A., Jr. 1975. The litter arthropod community in a southern Appalachian hardwood forest: Numbers, biomass, and mineral element content. *Am. Midl. Nat.* 93:107–22.

Lewis, J. G. E. 1974. The ecology of centipedes and millipedes in northern Nigeria. *Symp. Zool. Soc. London* 32:423–31.

Loomis, H. G. 1968. *A checklist of the millipedes of Mexico and Central America.* Bulletin 266. Washington, D.C.: Smithsonian Institution Press.

Pocock, R. I. 1910. *Biologia Centrali-Americana, Insecta: Chilopoda and Diplopoda.* London: R. H. Porter.

Sakwa, W. N. 1974. A consideration of the chemical basis of food preference in millipedes. *Symp. Zool. Soc. London* 32:329–46.

Toye, S. A. 1967. Observations on the biology of three species of Nigerian millipedes. *J. Zool., London* 152:67–78.

Orophus conspersus (Esperanza, Bush Katydid)

D. C. F. Rentz

Orophus conspersus (fig. 11.49) and its relative *O. tessellatus* Saussure are two very common members of the tropical rain-forest community throughout Costa Rica. Both seem equally abundant, but perhaps *O. conspersus* has the edge. These insects are members of the Phaneropterinae—the bush katydids. They can be immediately recognized as such by checking the fore tibia.

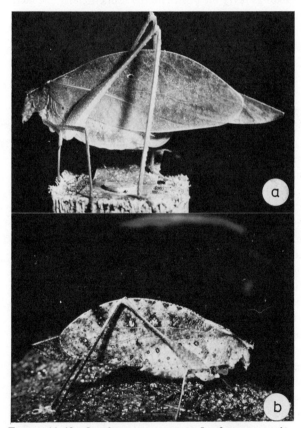

FIGURE 11.49. *Orophus conspersus. a,* Leaf-green morph, female. *b,* Dead-leaf morph, male. Finca La Selva, Sarapiquí District, Costa Rica (photos, D. C. F. Rentz).

Phaneropterines in the New World have an open, tambourinelike auditory structure. Other subfamilies of Tettigoniidae have an auditory structure with a bridge separating the inner and outer portions, which may be slitlike or rarely ovate.

O. conspersus is a leaflike insect. The forewings are ovate and angular; the hind wings, when folded at rest, protrude from beneath the forewings posteriorly. This species is usually greenish yellow or yellow brown. It is highly variable in color. The tegmina or forewings may have a few speckles or tessellations. Males and females are similar but easily distinguished. Males have a slightly modified stridulatory area on the dorsal surface of the forewing. It can be seen as a slightly swollen brownish vein positioned horizontally. The underside of this vein consists of a row of closely spaced pegs or lamellae that can be seen only under a microscope. The male lifts the tegmina slightly and rubs the stridulatory file across a modified vein (the scraper) on the opposite wing. This action creates the sound made by all tettigoniids (katydids). Females of some species are silent, but those of many species respond to the males' song by making a similar call by rubbing their wings together. Their call is usually much lower in intensity and involves the action of pegs on several veins of the forewing, which are moved across other pegs on the opposing forewing. The function of stridulation among tettigoniids is primarily to bring the sexes together. The structure and number of pegs in the stridulatory file is of considerable taxonomic value in that this structure reflects morphologically the uniqueness of the song of each species. Stridulation is a primary isolating mechanism in tettigoniids and is largely unstudied in the American tropics.

O. conspersus is the smaller of the two species that can be found sympatrically in most tropical lowland rain forests in Costa Rica. It averages for males 40 mm, females 44 mm in greatest length—front of head to tip of hind wings. *O. tessellatus* is a larger species, males averaging 53 mm and females 54 mm in total length. The fastigium of the vertex of *O. tessellatus* is low and weakly furrowed in *O. conspersus* but is much more prominent in *O. tessellatus* (Hebard 1927). The larger specimens of *O. conspersus* frequently are difficult to distinguish from the smaller ones of *O. tessellatus*. In general, *O. tessellatus* is a dark brown with most individuals resembling dark brown dead leaves. A small number may be greenish and some may be entirely green, but these are uncommon. Most individuals of *O. conspersus* are greenish, and I have never encountered any as dark brown as the darker ones of *O. tessellatus*.

Both species of *Orophus* are members of the forest understory. *O. tessellatus* is more likely to be found on the ground among dead leaves than up on bushes, where *O. conspersus* prefers to be. Both species appear to be nocturnal, and *O. conspersus* at La Selva and San Vito and on the Osa Peninsula appears to be the commonest species of tettigoniid along the trails at night. Most individuals perch exposed on leaf surfaces to a height of 2 m. Stridulation is sporadic, as for most forest tettigoniids (Rentz 1975).

The life cycle for both *Orophus* species appears to be continuous throughout the year, with a greater number of adults present during the wet season. Females have a peculiar laterally flattened ovipositor with serrated edges. Eggs are disk-shaped and extremely flattened. This evidence indicates that oviposition occurs between the layers of a single leaf. This has never been observed but would be interesting to see, since many species have host oviposition preferences and this might prove a very useful comparison between the two species. Once the eggs hatch the nymphs go through a number of instars (perhaps six to ten, but this is not known for certain) and eventually molt to maturity. Nymphs and adults are completely phytophagous and may prefer certain plants or perhaps certain parts of certain plants, such as leaves, flowers, pollen, or nectar. Nothing is known concerning the longevity of adults or the time taken for maturation.

Both species of *Orophus* have broad geographic distributions. *O. conspersus* is said to occur from Mexico to Darien, Panama, while *O. tessellatus* is known from Mexico to Ecuador. If modern-day taxonomic techniques, principally the use of recording data from calling males, were used to study these species, perhaps siblings and species complexes would be discovered.

*

Hebard, M. 1927. Studies in the Tettigoniidae of Panama (Orthoptera). *Trans. Am. Ent. Soc.* 53:79–156.

Rentz, D. C. 1975. Two new katydids of the genus *Melanonotus* from Costa Rica with comments on their life history strategies (Tettigoniidae: Pseudophyllinae). *Ent. News* 7, 8:129–40.

*Osmilia flavolineata** (Chapulín de Raya Amarilla, Yellow-lined Grasshopper)

H. F. Rowell

This is probably the most common and widely distributed acridid grasshopper (fig. 11.50) in the New World tropics, with a range from southern Mexico to Argentina. It belongs to the subfamily Ommatolampinae of the Acrididae. It is of medium size: males are up to 3.3. cm in length, females up to 4 cm. The wings are functional, and the insects fly readily. The general color is brown; the hindwings are pale yellow in Central America but pale blue farther south —in the past this was made the basis of a now-obsolete species distinction. The species is distinguished, especially in the male, by a conspicuous yel-

FIGURE 11.50. *Osmilia flavolineata**, adult. Finca Las Cruces, San Vito de Java, Costa Rica (photo, H. F. Rowell).

low stripe along the ventral edge of the hind femur and an oblique yellow line that runs from the point of insertion of the elytron on the pterothorax backward and downward to the base of the hind leg. This character provides the specific name. The larvae are cryptically colored, either green or brown; by analogy with other acridids, the polymorphism is probably influenced by genetic factors and also by environmental ones, of which the most influential are likely to be humidity and population density—crowding and relatively dry surroundings favor the brown morph. Superficially, the larva is very similar to that of *Schistocerca nitens,* which is often to be found in the same habitat. The larvae of *Osmilia* can be distinguished by an especially "flat-faced" appearance and by their slightly smaller size at all stages.

Osmilia looks and behaves much like a typical temperate-zone acridid, except that it does not stridulate. Ecologically it is of interest because of its tremendous success in dispersing to and colonizing disturbed habitats and because of its generalist feeding strategy, even in high-diversity forests (Rowell 1978). It is abundant in virtually all man-made habitats from suburban gardens through peasant fields to forest paths; it is very common around all OTS field stations and sometimes reaches tremendous densities in the La Selva Arboretum. It is also found commonly in habitats far from large-scale human activities, as for example in tree-fall clearings deep in forest, or in sand-dune vegation along Corocovado beach. It is apparently a typical "weedy species," virtually the only one in the whole Costa Rican acridid fauna of approximately 150 species.

So far no rigorous work has been carried out on the feeding habits of *Osmilia,* but preliminary observations show that it will accept a wide range of plants in captivity, and I have seen it eating at least ten different families of plants in the wild. This catholicity is unique among forest acridids (only *Schistocerca* and the big romaleid *Taeniopoda* approach it), and it would be of interest to examine its biochemical ability to handle plant secondary chemicals. The marked differences between the life-style of *Osmilia* and that of most Costa Rican grasshoppers, on the one hand, and the marked similarities between it and typical temperate-zone acridids on the other suggest that food-plant specialization is a critical feature of the natural history of most indigenous Costa Rican acridid species.

* Note added in press: the correct name for this grasshopper is now *Abracris flavolineata,* and it is so referred to in the checklist.

*

Rowell, H. F. 1978. Food plant specificity in Neotropical rain-forest acridids. *Ent. Exp. Appl.* 24:642–51.

Papilio cresphontes (Lechera, Papilio Grande, Giant Swallowtail)

P. J. DeVries

This species (fig. 11.51) ranges from Canada to Panama. In Costa Rica it occurs from sea level to about 800 m elevation on both Atlantic and Pacific drainages in secondary-succession habitats and in deciduous forest. *Papilio cresphontes* is sympatric with another species, *P. thoas*. These two species are extremely similar and can be told apart only in the hand. The most reliable character is a "notch" just above the claspers in the males of *P. cresphontes* that can be seen (with practice) or felt with the fingernail. *P. thoas* lacks this notch, making the dorsal side of the abdomen smooth all the way down to the end of the claspers. Another character, though less reliable, is the presence of dorsal yellow spot in the forewing cell in *P. thoas* that is absent in *P. cresphontes*. I am unable to tell the females of the two species apart except that *P. thoas* females oviposit on *Piper* spp. (Piperaceae).

Host plants include *Zanthoxylum* spp. and *Citrus* spp. (Rutaceae). The eggs are laid singly on the underside of the host-plant leaves. The larvae are mottled brown green with white blotches and mimic bird turds. When disturbed, the larvae everts the "stink horns" or osmeteria from just behind the head capsule. The osmeteria give off a "disagreeable" smell identified as isobutyric and 2-methyl butyric acid (Eisner et al, 1970) and are assumed to be a defense against predators. The osmeteria do not deter ovipositing parasitic Hymenoptera (pers. obs.), which attack a great number of the larvae in the field. The osmeteria are characteristic of all larvae in the Papilionidae. The chrysalis mimics a broken twig and is very cryptic. Pupation sites are apparently always on the sides of trees or branches, not on leaves.

Adults inhabit open areas, road cuts, and forest edges and are extremely fast, agile fliers. They are habitual flower visitors and flutter their wings while visiting flowers, as do other papilionids. They visit the flowers of *Lantana camara, Stachytarphta* spp. (Verbenaceae), *As-*

FIGURE 11.51. *Papilio cresphontes*. *a,* Upper side of male. *b,* Underside of male. Costa Rica (photos, P. J. DeVries).

clepias curassavica (Asclepiadaceae), *Helicteres guazumaefolia* (Sterculiaceae), *Malvaviscus* spp. (Malvaceae), *Delonix regia,* and *Caesalpinia pulcherrima* (Caesalpiniaceae). There is considerable overlap with pierid butterflies in the flowers visited. Males chase other butterflies for long distances and often have aerial dogfights with other males of *P. cresphontes*. The males visit wet sand and mud, apparently for sodium (Arms, Feeny, and Lederhouse 1974), which is thought to be a dietary supplement. It would not be surprising to find that they are gaining a chemical needed for courting females. Caged magpie jays at La Pacifica ate adult *P. cresphontes* readily without any ill effects. Adults are present throughout the year in Costa Rica.

*

Arms, K.; Feeny, P.; Lederhouse, R. 1974. Sodium: Stimulus for puddling behavior by tiger swallowtail butterflies, *Papilio glaucus*. *Science* 185:372–74.
Eisner, T.; Pliske, T. E.; Ileda, M.; Owen, D. F.; Vasquez, L.; Perez, H.; Franclemont, J. G.; and Meinwald, J. 1970. Defense mechanisms of arthropods.

27. Osmeterial secretions of papilionid caterpillars (*Baronia, Papilio, Eurytides*). *Ann. Ent. Soc. Am.* 63:914–15.

Paraponera clavata (Bala, Giant Tropical Ant)

D. H. Janzen and C. R. Carroll

This coal black ant is the largest in Central America. The workers are 16–22 mm long and solidly built; they look like giant editions of *Ectatomma ruidum* or *Ectatomma tuberculatum,* two other common and closely related widespread ponerine ants (Weber 1946). The huge workers of *P. clavata* are conspicuous foragers on the foliage of rain-forest understory in the Atlantic coastal lowlands of Costa Rica (up to about 500 m elevation) and are especially common at Finca La Selva near Puerto Viejo de Sarapiquí. They range from the Amazon basin to at least Atlantic coastal Nicaragua. Oddly, they are absent from the rain forests of the Pacific coast of Costa Rica.

Whereas *P. clavata* workers are seen on foliage and tree trunks during daylight hours (especially during the morning), the workers appear to forage primarily at night (Hermann 1975) and display a conspicuous nocturnal increase in activity in the laboratory (McCluskey and Brown 1972; McCluskey 1965). They forage high in the forest canopy as well as close to the ground, and workers are occasionally seen returning to the nest carrying medium-sized insects. These are probably killed with the mandibles and the very painful sting (cf. Hermann and Blum 1966; Hermann and Douglas 1976), but on the other hand the ants may simply be scavengers. In addition to insect prey, we have seen them guarding and collecting nectar from extrafloral petiolar nectaries of *Pentaclethra macroloba* seedlings and the extrafloral nectaries of *Costus* inflorescences. Workers are most commonly observed returning to the nest carrying nothing externally, or with a large drop of nectar between the mandibles. Young (1977) observed *P. clavata* apparently collecting fluids from the area of the red stripe on *Ochroma pyramidale* petioles (by biting into the plant tissue) and scraping tissue from the bases of *Eupatorium* leaf blades. All these observations occurred at Finca La Selva. There is no indication that *P. clavata* workers depart from the usual ponerine ant way of foraging for insect prey; they apparently walk about singly on the vegetation and do not recruit other workers to a food source.

On 6–8 August 1969 we excavated two nests of *P. clavata* at Finca La Selva, and we give the details here to obviate the need for further destructive sampling of the nests, which can be accomplished only with some human pain and the loss of a large animal. Each nest was at the base of a large tree in old disturbed forest immediately adjacent to primary forest (other nests were often encountered at the bases of *Pentaclethra macroloba* trees). The entrances were slightly raised, well-worn holes about 6 cm × 2 cm; the forest floor litter, moss, and *Selaginella* came to the entrance edges, and there was no excavated dirt (tumulus). Our excavation began early in the morning, and all ants returning to the nest were collected (the last returnees were taken between 1200 and 1500). Smooth-walled 2–3 cm diameter tunnels led downward and outward from the main entrance to the chambers.

Nest 1 had thirty-three chambers (deepest, 35 cm) and nest 2 had forty-three (deepest, 62 cm). The uppermost chambers were 7–10 cm below the surface. A representative chamber at 7 cm depth would have two to four more below it and 0.5 to 5 cm of dirt between it and the next in either vertical direction. The chambers were about 13–16 mm from floor to ceiling and 5–10 cm in roughly circular diameter. The floor was flat and smooth, but the ceiling was domed. Each chamber had two or three exits connected by 11–15 mm diameter tunnels with other chambers on the same level and other levels. In short, the nest architecture was a giant edition of that of *Ectatomma tuberculatum.*

As we started into the nest, about ten workers rushed out (all ants encountered in our excavations were collected). After we removed these, no more followed. As we dug down into more chambers, workers appeared in bursts of four to ten individuals with long intervals between when there were no attacking workers. Janzen was stung more frequently while picking up the brood scattered on the floor of a chamber; the worker would rush into the chamber from an as yet unseen entrance and pounce on his fingers or forceps. These waves of attack occured right down to the last chamber (containing the queen in both cases), but there was no evidence of a large attack organized at a level containing most of the workers in the colony. Disturbed workers release a heavy musky odor that could be smelled up to a meter from the excavation site; it may have been an alarm pheromone, or it could be a warning odor (olfactorily aposematic). The workers made a loud squeaking noise (again, aposematic?) even before they were picked up. Most chambers encountered were free of brood or eggs unless there was no further exit from the chamber because our excavation had cut its connections to other tunnels. Workers were moving the brood away from the site of excavation and were observed to pick up a large larva or cocoon and run out of the chamber with it rather than attack. In chambers that appeared not to have been disturbed, there were one to six eggs (about 1 mm in diameter and 2 mm long) and one to five small larvae and ten to thirty large larvae and cocoons.

In nest 2 the alates were scattered among the chambers, but they could well have run far from their usual place of residence. By the time the last chamber was excavated and the queen found, there were no more workers in the chambers. Neither dealate colony queen was physogastric (gaster distended with enlarged ovaries).

In addition to the dealate queen, nest 1 contained 708 workers, 211 unhatched worker cocoons, 68 eggs, 63 large larvae, 139 medium larvae, and 248 small larvae. Nest 2 contained 14 alate virgin queens, 12 alate males, 1,329 workers, 153 unhatched worker cocoons, 85 eggs, 71 large larvae, 72 medium larvae, and 90 small larvae. We have no reason to believe that these nests were other than representative mature colonies. At this time of year (August), alate (apparently newly mated) queens of *P. clavata* were occasionally encountered walking on the foliage, and males were taken at lights. McCluskey and Brown (1972) reported males of *P. clavata* at lights on Barro Colorado Island, Panama Canal Zone, in January. It would not be surprising to find that this ant produces sexual forms throughout the year.

Owing to its large size and the ease of marking individuals, this ant should be ideal for studies of individual ponerine ant foraging behavior where there is access to large tree crowns.

Several insects mimic *Paraponera*. For example, the cerambycid beetle *Acyphoderes sexualis* at rest resembles *Paraponera* and in flight resembles the wasp *Polybia rejecta* (Silberglied and Aiello 1976). Although *Paraponera* probably has few enemies, there is anecdotal evidence that fly parasites may be an important source of mortality. On three occasions, Carroll saw small flies (Diptera: Phoridae) hovering over the nest exits of *Paraponera* (Finca La Selva). In each case, when the fly hovered close to the nest exit, more than ten ants came rapidly out of the nest and went berserk trying to catch it. On two occasions we later killed the flies and dangled them in front of the nest exit, but the ants did not respond. The ants also did not respond to the presence of other small dead insects dangled in front of the nest exit, even though many ants passed within a few centimeters of the insects. Perhaps the ants are responding to the noise these flies make. However, in any case, since phorid flies are known to parasitize insects and since the response by *Paraponera* seems to be stereotyped, the situation seems worth investigating.

*

Hermann, H. R. 1975. Crepuscular and nocturnal activities of *Paraponera clavata* (Hymenoptera: Formicidae: Ponerinae). *Ent. News* 86:94–98.

Hermann, H. R., and Blum, M. S. 1966. The morphology and histology of the hymenopterous poison apparatus. 1. *Paraponera clavata* (Formicidae). *Ann. Ent. Soc. Am.* 59:397–407.

Hermann, H. R., and Douglas, M. 1976. Sensory structures on the venom apparatus of a primitive ant species (Hymenoptera: Formicidae). *Ann. Ent. Soc. Am.* 69: 681–86.

McCluskey, E. S. 1965. Circadian rhythms in male ants of five diverse species. *Science* 150:1037–39.

McCluskey, E. S. and Brown, W. L. 1972. Rhythms and other biology of the giant tropical ant *Paraponera*. *Psyche* 79:335–47.

Silberglied, R. E., and Aiello, A. 1976. Defensive adaptations of some Neotropical long-horned beetles (Coleoptera: Cerambycidae): Antennal spines, tergiversation, and double mimicry. *Psyche* 83:256–62.

Weber, N. A. 1946. Two common ponerine ants of possible economic significance, *Ectatomma tuberculatum* (Olivier) and *E. ruidum* Roger. *Proc. Ent. Soc. Washington* 48:1–16.

Young, A. M. 1977. Notes on the foraging of the giant tropical ant *Paraponera clavata* (Formicidae: Ponerinae) on two plants in tropical wet forest. *J. Georgia Ent. Soc.* 12:41–51.

Pelidnota punctulata (Comecornizuelo, Ant-Acacia Beetle)

D. H. Janzen and A. R. Hardy

In the deciduous forest lowlands of Costa Rica, adults of *Pelidnota punctulata* (fig. 11.52) are the most conspicuous and easily located ruteline scarabs. Close examination of several dozen ant-acacias (*Acacia cornigera, A. collinsii*) during the first half of the rainy season will usually reveal one to five of these 2.5 cm long hard, beige gray green shiny beetles clinging tightly to the small stems and petioles of dense leafy crowns. During the night these beetles feed on the tender young shoots of ant-acacias, and during the day they roost there. The

FIGURE 11.52. *Pelidnota punctulata* in its usual state of siege by the *Pseudomyrmex* ants occupying the *Acacia collinsii* it is feeding on. Santa Rosa National Park, Guanacaste Province, Costa Rica (photo, D. H. Janzen).

beetle ranges from the Tropic of Cancer in Mexico throughout the range of the ant-acacias to Colombia. The adult feeds only on the foliage of ant-acacias throughout this range. In years of fieldwork in their habitat, Janzen has seen them only on ant-acacia foliage. *P. punctulata* occurs on ant-acacias even in rain-forest habitats (e.g., on *Acacia allenii* in Corcovado National Park).

The adults are impervious to the biting and stinging attacks of the *Pseudomyrmex* acacia-ants. The ants try, but they cannot penetrate the heavy cuticle, except in the mouth. When an ant manages to insert its sting into the beetle's mouth, the beetle merely brushes it away and remains fixed in place on the plant. Adult *P. punctulata* are under nearly constant attack from the ants but show no fleeing response. On the other hand, if the equal-sized and otherwise very similar *P. punctata* is placed on an ant-acacia, it flies or drops from the plant as soon as it is attacked, a response generally displayed by insects that are not generally encountered on ant-acacias. It appears that *P. punctulata* has evolved a nonflight behavior for ants, which yields it an abundant source of green foliage and a safe diurnal roosting place; presumably it is much less often found by predaceous birds and insects when sleeping and feeding in the crown of an ant-acacia than it would be on foliage in general. However, its nonflight behavior would be functional only in a habitat where the only threat is an ant to which it is largely impervious.

Pelidnota contains more than one hundred tropical species, with twenty-six species in North and Central America and fifteen in Costa Rica. The very closely related *Plusiotis* (the bright metallic silver or gold, apple green, or yellow large scarabs that come to lights at places like Monteverde and San Vito) has twelve species in Costa Rica. It is likely that *Pelidnota* itself should be broken up into three genera, yielding four genera of quite similar beetles. However, *P. punctulata* is probably exceptional among them in being specific to one closely related group of plants for adult food. The larvae of all these beetles are associated with rotting logs, decaying root systems, and other soil surfaces rich in plant roots. They are white grubs that probably feed on fungi, rootlets, and rich organic soil. *Pelidnota punctata*, a species that ranges from the central United States at least to Costa Rica, has a 2-year life cycle in the United States.

Teneral adults (newly emerged from the pupal stage) of *P. punctulata* were found beneath a small log in Guanacaste just before the beginning of the rainy season (Hardy, pers. obs.). Immediately after the rains begin, these beetles are very common at fluorescent lights and blacklights placed in habitats rich in ant-acacias, and they continue to come to light sporadically, along with *P. punctata*, throughout the rainy season at Santa Rosa National Park.

*

Hardy, A. R. 1975. A revision of the genus *Pelidnota* of America north of Panama (Coleoptera: Scarabaeidae: Rutelinae). *Univ. California Publ. Ent.* 78:1–43.

Janzen, D. H. 1967. Interaction of the bull's horn acacia (*Acacia cornigera* L.) with an ant inhabitant (*Pseudomyrmex ferruginea* F. Smith) in eastern Mexico. *Univ. Kansas Sci. Bull.* 47:315–558.

Phoebis philea (Sulfúrea Quemada, Orange-barred Sulfur)

P. J. DeVries

This common species (fig. 11.53) ranges from the southern United States to southern Brazil. It is widespread in Costa Rica, occurring from sea level to about 1,400 m elevation. The sexes are dimorphic. The male is brillant yellow with a bright orange disk on the forewing upper side that is easily visible while flying. The female is more extensively orange on the hind wing and has dark spotted borders on both wings.

Host plants include *Cassia fruticosa*, *C. occidentalis*, and *Caesalpinia pulcherrima* (Caesalpiniaceae). These are trees that grow along forest edges or in second growth

FIGURE 11.53. *Phoebis philea*. *a*, Adult female. *b*, Adult male (photos, P. J. DeVries).

or that are planted as ornamentals. The eggs are laid singly on the underside of the host-plant leaf, although the same female may lay several individual eggs in succession on the same leaf. The egg is yellow and bullet shaped. The larvae are light green with minute black spotting along the back and are well camouflaged while on the host plant. The chrysalis is light green, at times pinkish, and has a bowed-out portion corresponding to the wing pads. This form of chrysalis is highly characteristic of a number of genera in the Pieridae.

Adults are very fast fliers and occur in open areas and second growth. They visit flowers of *Lantana camara, Stachytarpheta* spp. (Verbenaceae), *Turnera* spp. (Turneraceae), *Combretum farinosum* (Combretaceae), *Malvaviscus arboreus* (Malvaceae), and *Delonix regia* (Caesalpiniaceae). *P. philea* seems to overlap considerably with papilionid butterflies and hummingbirds in flower visitation. They are apparently very sensitive to red; I have commonly seen individuals that were flying along rapidly suddenly drop into the vegetation to visit a solitary red flower. Compared with other flower-visiting butterflies, *P. philea* appears to visit the uppermost flowers and then fly off to the next plant rather than visiting all the flowers on a plant. In addition to flowers, the males of *P. philea* visit wet sand and mud, probably to obtain sodium (Collenette and Talbot 1928; Arms, Feeny, and Lederhouse 1974). This general habit of many pierids has been known since Henry Bates was on the Amazon. Although there is no satisfactory answer to why they go to puddles, I suspect they may be getting some needed chemical for courting females, by analogy with male ithomiine butterflies getting pyrrolizidine alkaloids from Boraginaceae (Pliske 1975). The attractiveness of the sand may be enhanced by urinating on it and placing a dead *P. philea* or flat yellow leaf on it. Unlike other species of *Phoebis* (e.g., *P. sennae, P. argante*), which at times form huge aggregations on puddles, *P. philea* tends to visit puddles as solitary individuals.

The wing colors in *P. philea* are probably due to pteridines, as has been shown for other members of the family Pieridae (Harmsen 1966) and may play important roles in ultraviolet patterns.

*

Arms, K.; Feeny, P.; and Lederhouse, R. 1974. Sodium: Stimulus for puddling behavior by tiger swallowtail butterflies, *Papilio glaucus. Science* 185:372–74.

Collenette, C. L., and Talbot, G. 1928. Observations on the bionomics of the Lepidoptera of Matto Grosso, Brazil. *Trans. Ent. Soc. London* 76:391–416.

Harmsen, H. 1966. The excretory role of pteridines in insects. *J. Exp. Biol.* 25:1–13.

Pliske, T. E. 1975. Attraction of Lepidoptera to plants containing pyrrolizidine alkaloids. *Environ. Ent.* 4:455–73.

Pilica formidolosa (Mosca Asesina, Robber Fly)

E. M. Fisher

Pilica formidolosa (Walker) is a striking fly (fig. 11.54) 20 to 33 mm long, with a black body and a strongly contrasting red abdomen. Like all other members of the robber-fly family Asilidae, it is a predator that feeds exclusively on other arthropods. Its structural characteristics are well adapted for predation: long, stout legs terminating in sharp claws and covered with bristles; mouthparts formed into a sharply pointed proboscis; and very large, widely separated eyes, in front of which is a clump of bristles that serves to protect the eyes and antennae from the brief struggles of captured prey.

The numerous Neotropical species of *Pilica* and the related genera *Andrenosoma* and *Pogonosoma* all live in similar habitats, occupying fallen trees in forest clearings. *P. formidolosa* is widespread in Middle America, ranging from southern Mexico to eastern Panama. It is a characteristic inhabitant of light gaps in lowland evergreen and semideciduous forests, where the adult flies can be seen perching on newly fallen and older dead trees. Clearings are occupied by this (and related) species until emergent vegetation begins to overtop and shade the stems of the dead trees.

Studies done at Barro Colorado Island, Panama, indicate that the activity of *P. formidolosa* is closely regulated by the intensity of sunlight. These flies appear on the upper surfaces of the dead tree stems shortly after the areas are in direct sunlight—about 1000 in smaller light gaps within forests. In fair weather this species remains on the fallen trees until they are shaded over in late afternoon. During rainfall or on especially cool, overcast days, these flies perch on slender stems of living trees away from the clearings; they probably spend the night in these areas as well. Activity is greatest in the morning and the late afternoon; during the hottest hours of the day (ca. 1200–1400) the adults tend to rest in the shaded parts of the tree fall. They have limited tolerance for full sun-

FIGURE 11.54. *Pilica formidolosa* male perched on a rotten log. Panama (photo, E. M. Fisher).

light at any time of the day, however, and they can be seen to move into and out of the shade at frequent intervals—apparently to avoid overheating. This repositioning consists both of moving around the edges of the stem and of short flights—several meters—to adjacent stems.

Little is known concerning what tree species *P. formidolosa* prefers for perching sites. At Barro Colorado Island it generally was seen on relatively smooth-barked trees, of which the following have been identified: *Tachigalia versicolor, Enterolobium cyclocarpum, Prioria* sp., and *Inga* sp. (Fabaceae); *Tetragastris panamensis* (Burseraceae); and *Ceiba pentandra* (Bombacaceae).

Foraging behavior in *P. formidolosa* involves constant alertness while the adult is perched on top of a log. Nearly every insect flying nearby is noted visually, as indicated by the movements of the fly's head to maintain eye contact. Even insects as small as 5 mm long are detected at distances of 2 m. The fly also frequently shifts around, moving in semicircles to full circles, to watch for prey (and for predators, such as *Anolis* lizards moving down tree stems). When a potential prey item is sighted and passes close enough (within about 1 m is the usual attack distance), the robber fly chases it, attempting to grab it from behind. Only flying insects are attacked by *P. formidolosa*. An insect that it notices crawling on a tree stem nearby is treated in one of several ways: it may be ignored; the fly may watch it closely, even making an overflight of the other insect (if this initiates a flight by the insect, the robber fly will chase it immediately); the fly may move if the crawling insect is large and approaches too closely. The number of prey an individual of *P. formidolosa* catches is unknown, but the rate of capture is probably low. One fly was observed to make four unsuccessful chase flights at passing insects during a 35-min period. The European species *Andrenosoma bayardi* Séguy is estimated to take eight prey items per day and 360 per lifetime (Musso 1971).

The cues that cause *P. formidolosa* to attempt a prey capture probably are some combination of body size and flight speed of the prey species, as is the case generally in the Asilidae (Lavigne and Holland 1969; Hespenheide and Rubke 1978). That this fly does make some selection is evidenced by its prey items as observed at Barro Colorado Island. Fourteen insects, each a different species, were identified as *P. formidolosa* prey: eleven Hymenoptera, two Coleoptera, and one Diptera. They ranged from about 45% to 80% of the length of their individual captors and averaged about 60%. Of the Hymenoptera, five were Vespidae, two were Pompilidae, and one each were Sphecidae, Formicidae, and Ichneumonidae (an additional prey record, from Puerto Viejo, Heredia, Costa Rica, is of another pompilid). The captured individuals of the first three families of wasps were all females, each

of them therefore capable of stinging and killing their attackers if allowed to do so.

Robber flies are able to overcome such large and potentially dangerous insects by the actions of salivary and labial gland secretions, which they inject into the prey with the proboscis. These fluids—venom and proteolytic enzymes—kill the victim immediately. Internal tissues are then digested extraintestinally, and the fly sucks them up (Kahan 1964). A male *P. formidolosa* was seen to feed on a pompilid (*Priocnemella rufothorax* [Banks]) for 30 min, moving its proboscis to various parts of the wasp's body. To reposition the wasp, the fly manipulated it with its forelegs; otherwise the wasp was impaled soley on the fly's proboscis. The robber fly thus had full use of all its legs and moved around frequently. It flew back and forth across the tree-fall clearing on six occasions while feeding on the wasp (possibly in response to being annoyed by this observer). Nearly all of the predation was seen between 1000 and 1200; this is partly because these observations were made during the rainy season: afternoons were frequently "rained out."

Other types of behavior observed in *P. formidolosa* include grooming, agonistic interactions, and mating. Grooming is frequent, about every 5 min or so, throughout the day. It is of the "usual fly type" and consists of rubbing "cleaning pads" on the front legs over the eyes and antennae, then rubbing the legs together. These pads are made up of close-set rows of flattened bristles on the ventral surface of the tibiae. The hind tibiae have a similar set, and these are used to clean the wings—both surfaces—and the abdomen.

Although *P. formidolosa* is apparently nonterritorial (marked individuals were never seen again after being released at their capture site), individuals have been observed to chase other robber flies away from their perch areas. If an insect (including a related *Andrenosoma* sp.) lands within about 2 m of a perched *P. formidolosa,* the latter will generally fly over to "investigate" the newcomer, usually circling once close overhead. If this precipitates a flight by the other insect, the *Pilica* will chase it immediately; if the newcomer remains perched, it will be ignored. Such activity is probably a component of normal predatory behavior for this species.

What passes for courtship in *P. formidolosa* is very similar. If a male observes one of its kind perching nearby, it will watch it closely for a while—up to several minutes. It will then fly over to it and, if it is a receptive female, land directly on top of it. If the other fly is a nonreceptive female (or a male), it will usually fly up and meet the approaching male; they will make brief contact (interpreted as "grappling," since their legs apparently interlock momentarily) then part, and one or both will fly away. If the male has landed on a receptive partner, coupling is immediately accomplished, and the flies quickly turn around to face in opposite directions, attached end to end. Copulating flies were seen to stay together for as long as 20 min, often flying to new perches several times during mating, one leading the other (both using their wings). Although there may be some subtle, unobserved signaling between individuals of *P. formidolosa* before mating, this species definitely lacks the often elaborate and stereotypic courtship behavior that many other robber flies possess. Mating has been observed in the late morning and in the afternoon at 1300.

Andrenosoma spp. females oviposit in the entrances of beetle burrows. At Barro Colorado Island a gravid *Andrenosoma* sp. was seen to probe crevices and depressions of a fallen *Platypodium elegans* (Fabaceae) with her ovipositor, pausing at the deepest ones for up to 1 min; she encountered no beetle burrows during the 15 min of observation, and no deposited eggs were found. Oviposition has not been observed in the genus *Pilica*.

The immature stages of *Pilica* are also unknown, but they very likely share the habits of the temperate species of *Andrenosoma*, whose larvae live within the dead wood of the trees that the adults frequent. There they travel in Coleoptera burrows (especially Buprestidae and Cerambycidae), feeding on the larvae of these beetles. The duration of the larval stage is unknown. Pupation occurs near the periphery of the log, and the pupae eventually position themselves so their anterior ends project above the surface of the wood. The adults thus emerge directly to the exterior.

In Costa Rica and Panama, *P. formidolosa* coexists with other species of *Andrenosoma*, *Pilica*, and *Pogonosoma*. At Barro Colorado Island in August 1978, eight species of these flies were found on a single fallen *Tachigalia versicolor* within a few days; six were seen on a downed branch of *Enterolobium cyclocarpum* at this same time (other, much smaller, robber flies also occur on these dead trees, but they are not closely related to *Pilica*). How these different species of flies partition the resources of the tree-fall habitat is an interesting problem. *P. formidolosa* is considerably larger than any of these other flies and thus can utilize food items unavailable to the other species. Although prey records are scarce, the species definitely consumes insects, like large wasps, that its relatives are unable to capture. *Pilica erythrogaster* (Wied.), which is 12 to 19 mm long, feeds mainly on small beetles, especially Platypodidae (which are probably the most abundant insects on the fallen trees), but occasionally on small wasps. The twelve recorded prey items of this species ranged from 2 to 6.5 mm long and averaged about 35% of the length of their captors. Observations on feeding preferences for the various *Andrenosoma* species are even more limited, but only small Hymenoptera and Diptera (5 to 7 mm in length) were seen taken by them. The apparent trends in prey selection among these flies can also be correlated with mouthpart structure. The two *Pilica* species have an upward-curving proboscis that tapers to a sharp point (awl shaped), while that of *Andrenosoma* is straight, flattened, and blunt (wedge shaped). The species of *Andrenosoma*, which are mostly about the same size (15 to 20 mm long), further differentiate between themselves by each having a proboscis of unique width. Such diversity of mouthpart structure is unusual among closely related species of Asilidae. Although the functional relationship between proboscis shape and prey selection is unknown in this group, it does seem possible that this structural diversity (character divergence) is evidence for selective pressures—that is, for specialized feeding—to lessen competition between these species.

Temporal and microhabitat preferences possibly are involved with *Pilica* and *Andrenosoma*. The species of *Pilica* are characteristically seen on the larger, more exposed, dead stems of tree falls and tend to occupy these sites for longer periods of the day. *Andrenosoma* are seen less often on the principal stems, frequenting instead the smaller, more shaded, branches underneath and at the edges of the fallen trees. One species of *Andrenosoma* shows a preference for older, dead trees—those with the bark falling off; the other species of this group are almost always found on less decayed trees. Seasonality is apparently similar among these species, since the adults of all of them appear to be active during both the dry and the rainy seasons.

Knowledge of the larval biologies, unknown for 99.9% of the Neotropical species of Asilidae, is probably essential for proper evaluation of the ecological interactions of these flies. However, obtaining biological information even on the adults is difficult. *Pilica*, especially *P. formidolosa*, and *Andrenosoma* are extremely wary insects and fly at the slightest disturbance. As with many tropical species, their populations are small, and at most a few individuals are present in a given light gap at any one time. Field identification of *Andrenosoma* is also a problem, since most species of this genus are not easily differentiated. Prey species identification involves collecting the fly with its food, a difficult task at best as it flits around in a tree-fall tangle. Despite these drawbacks, *P. formidolosa* and its relatives are very important and interesting components of the tree-fall community and as such are worth considerable study.

*

Hespenheide, H. A., and Rubke, M. A. 1978. Prey, predatory behavior, and the daily cycle of *Holopogon wilcoxi* Martin (Diptera: Asilidae). *Pan-Pac. Ent.* 53:277–85.

Kahan, D. 1964. The toxic effect of the bite and the proteolytic activity of the saliva and stomach contents of the robber flies (Diptera, Asilidae). *Israel J. Zool.* 13:47–57.

Lavigne, R. J., and Holland, F. R. 1969. Comparative behavior of eleven species of Wyoming robber flies (Diptera: Asilidae). *Univ. Wyoming Agr. Exp. Sta. Sci. Monogr.* 18:1–61.

Musso, J.-J. 1971. Etude préliminaire sur les activités journalieres d'une population d'*Andrenosoma bayardi* Séguy. *Bull. Soc. Ent. France* 76:175–82.

Polistes (Quita Calzón, Lengua de Vaca [name of nest], Paper Wasp)

M. J. West-Eberhard

Several species of *Polistes* (fig. 11.55) are common in Costa Rica, including *P. canadensis* (L.), *P. versicolor* (Olivier), *P. carnifex* (F.), and *P. erythrocephalus* La-treille. The latter two species have been briefly studied in Costa Rica (Corn 1972; Nelson 1971) (the behavior of some Colombian *P. erythrocephalus* is described by West-Eberhard 1969 under the older name *P. canadensis erythrocephalus*). Skutch (1971, pp. 266–68) reports some long-term observations of a Costa Rican *Polistes*, which from his description (black, red-mandibled, highland species) is probably *P. aterrimus* de Saussure (this species, incidentally, is absent from the key given in Nelson 1971). Since *Polistes* species, and even regional variants within species, have proved surprisingly (and interestingly) diverse regarding the details of their social behavior and ecology, students can assume that observations of local populations are likely to yield new information.

It is easy to recognize *Polistes* by obvious features of nests and adults. All *Polistes* species build simple, naked

FIGURE 11.55. *Polistes. a,* Several-month-old nest with capped cells at bottom and workers on side. *b,* Young nest with foundress female; various-aged larvae in cells and one cell with newly spun silk cap. Santa Rosa National Park, Guanacaste Province, Costa Rica, July 1980 (photos, D. H. Janzen).

(unenveloped) paper combs of hexagonal cells suspended by one or more short stems or "pedicels." Most tropical species make nests having only one pedicel, situated at the topmost edge of the comb. Nests are commonly found on branches in dense shrubbery or beneath overhanging rocks or on man-made structures. The only genus that might be confused with *Polistes* on the basis of nest structure is *Mischocyttarus,* which also builds unenveloped paper nests. But *Mischocyttarus* wasps are generally either small (1–1.5 cm long) or have a pedunculate abdomen (elongate first gastral segment). They can be certainly separated from *Polistes* by having asymmetrical lengths of the lateral spines of the mid and hind tarsi (terminal segments of the legs). Nelson (1971) gives a key to Costa Rican *Polistes* in both Spanish and English. The most recent revision of the genus is by Richards (1978).

Polistes and *Mischocyttarus* differ from other Neotropical paper wasps (e.g., *Polybia, Metapolybia, Synoeca, Brachygastra*) in very seldom having more than one egg-laying member per nest and in lacking the capacity to found nests in large swarms. In general, *Polistes* colonies are founded by a single female ("foundress") that in most tropical species is soon joined by one or more additional females. *Polistes* is famous for the development of a dominance hierarchy among foundresses, most of which are mated females with somewhat developed ovaries. However, in the tropical species I have observed in Colombia, the competitive situation might better be described as territoriality on the nest by a hyperaggressive female, whose physical dominance (attacks and chasing) keeps other fertile females from laying eggs or (usually) even coming onto the nest, especially the portion containing newly started cells where they might lay eggs. As a result, many of the dominated females spend most of their time sitting idle beside newly founded nests, rather than *on* them as is typical in older colonies. There is often much movement among newly founded nests (e.g., in the vicinity of a declining old nest—see West-Eberhard 1969). As a result, most of the egg laying is done by a single territorial female, often (but not always) the one that initiated the nest. The primary egg layer is usually also the primary initiator of new cells, while most foraging and cell enlargement is done by other females ("workers").

Males are frequently seen in the vicinity of newly founded nests (some foundresses are unmated), where they come and go and, at least in some species, sometimes appear to chemically mark the region by rubbing surfaces near the nest with the underside of the abdomen (pers. obs.). Males can be distinguished from females by three characteristics: they have longer antennae (thirteen segments instead of the twelve found in females), which

at their extremities are slenderer and more curved than those of females; their "faces" (clypei) appear shorter and flatter than those of females, and in some species are strikingly lighter in color; and the male abdomen is rather blunt and rounded at its tip rather than pointed as in the female (as in all aculeate Hymenoptera, the males lack a sting, which in the female is derived from the ancestral ovipositor). Males are usually produced late in the nesting cycle, after some females (some or all of them "workers") have emerged.

The young develop, one per cell, via a "complete" metamorphosis (egg, larval, and pupal stages). The egg is attached to the side of a cell. After a variable period (usually 1 to 2 weeks) the egg transforms to a larva, which is progressively fed by the adult females for about a month, when it stops feeding and begins to spin a silken cocoon that closes the mouth of the cell with a white "cap." The larva pupates for 3 to 4 weeks, then chews its way out of the cell when mature. In many species cells are then reused to rear additional brood.

Polistes wasps feed on nectar (sometimes found stored as viscous drops of "honey"—really unconverted nectar—in egg-containing cells) and lepidopterous larvae (caterpillars) of various kinds. I have occasionally seen males visiting flowers, and collected males are sometimes covered with pollen, which they may consume (an unproved suspicion that could be investigated by simple dissection of the gut). Females often extensively masticate caterpillars at the capture site, so that by the time they take flight to return to the nest their abdomens are heavy with ingested body fluids, and the solid pellet they carry in the mouth is relatively dry and well chewed. The ingested fluids are regurgitated to adults and larvae at the nest, and solid food is also extensively divided among adults and larvae. Large larvae have well-developed, chitinous mandibles and, unlike the larvae of some other social wasps (Vespidae), are capable of ingesting solid food. Because *Polistes* is a common insect in many areas, and an efficient-looking predator of lepidopterous larvae, it has occasionally been considered of potential use in the control of certain crop pests (e.g., the tobacco hornworm).

In addition to caterpillar meat and honey, females forage for wood fiber, which they masticate with water and a clear oral secretion to form a crude pulp from which they build the nest.

Polistes wasps actively defend their nests against various predators and insect parasitoids, the most common being ants, ichneumon wasps (*Pachysomoides* spp.), and flies (e.g., Sarcophagidae) (see Nelson 1968). In Costa Rica, a large nocturnally foraging katydid, *Ancistrocercus inficitus,* often rests ("hides") during the day next to *Polistes* (and other) wasp nests, presumably to avoid predation by birds (Downhower and Wilson 1973).

Polistes wasps are particularly easy to study for anyone with a little patience, a pencil, and a notebook. Individuals can be marked with quick-drying lacquers (e.g., model airplane paints or typewriter correction fluids). Perhaps the most quickly and surely rewarding aspect of their complex social behavior to study is the nature of interactions among females at newly founded nests. Although much emphasis has been given to sibling associations in temperate-zone species, it is clear that cooperation among kin is only one factor underlying foundress associations, and there are many indications that in tropical species nonsibs may associate and compete to lay eggs. Many other easy-to-observe aspects of Neotropical *Polistes* biology are inadequately studied, including intracolony communication, foraging behavior, and the division of labor among nestmates. Dissection of collected females (especially whole colonies) can reveal much about the age and reproductive condition of individuals and the social organization of colonies. A great deal can be learned from dissections alone, and they often facilitate the interpretation of behavioral observations in terms of reproductive competition. Collection and dissection techniques are outlined in West-Eberhard (1975).

A list of persons currently doing research on *Polistes,* as well as references to recent publications on specialized topics, is available from Chris Starr, Department of Entomology, University of Georgia, Athens, Georgia 30602 (editor of the *Polistes Newsletter*).

*

Corn, M. L. 1972. Notes on the biology of *Polistes carnifex* (Hymenoptera, Vespidae) in Costa Rica and Colombia. *Psyche* 79:150–57.

Downhower, J. J., and Wilson, D. E. 1973. Wasps as a defense mechanism of katydids. *Am. Midl. Nat.* 89:451–55.

Evans, H. E., and West-Eberhard, M. J. 1970. *The wasps.* Ann Arbor: University of Michigan Press.

Nelson, J. M. 1968. Parasites and symbionts of *Polistes* wasps. *Ann. Ent. Soc. Am.* 61:1528–39.

———. 1971. Nesting habits and nest symbionts of *Polistes erythrocephalus* Latreille (Hymenoptera, Vespidae) in Costa Rica. *Rev. Biol. Trop.* 18:89–98.

Richards, O. W. 1978. *The social wasps of the Americas excluding the Vespinae.* London: British Museum (Natural History).

Skutch, A. F. 1971. *A naturalist in Costa Rica.* Gainesville: University of Florida Press.

West-Eberhard, M. J. 1969. The social biology of polistine wasps. *Misc. Publ. Univ. Michigan Mus. Zool.* 140:1–101.

———. 1975. Estudios de las avispas sociales (Himenmétodos y notas para facilitar la identificación de especies comunes. *Cespedesia* 4:245–68.

Wilson, E. O. 1971. *The insect societies.* Cambridge: Harvard University Press.

Polybia occidentalis (Cojones de Toro [name of nest], Paper Wasp)

D. M. Windsor

Polybia occidentalis bohemani Holmgren (Vespidae: Polistinae: Polybiini) is the most common social wasp constructing enclosed carton nests in the Pacific lowlands of northwestern Costa Rica (fig. 11.56). The species ranges from the southwestern United States to Argentina. The subspecies is recognized throughout Central America and the northern cap of South America (Richards 1978). Nests of this and other wasp species can usually be found in substantial numbers under the bridges along the Inter-American Highway. Nests in more natural circumstances are usually found in tangles of thorny evergreen vegetation. They are commonly found hanging from the leaf rachises of the palm *Acrocomia vinifera* or on the thorn-clad branches of *Acacia farnesiana, Parkinsonia aculeata* (Leguminosae), and *Pisonia macranthocarpa* (Nyctaginaceae).

There are three species of *Polybia* in northwestern Costa Rica that one is likely to encounter; each can be identified on the basis of colony architecture, or adult morphology, or both. The most common species is *P. occidentalis,* the least common is *P. rejecta.* The nests of all *Polybia* species vary considerably depending on age, size of the founding swarm, and seasonal conditions. Nests of *P. diguetana* (fig. 11.56a) are often cylindrical, light tan, and placed in shadier situations than nests of *P. occidentalis.* The nests of *P. occidentalis* and *P. rejecta* (fig. 11.56b,c) are often slightly coneshaped; the newest and largest cell layers are toward the bottom of the nest. Large *P. rejecta* nests, 60–70 cm deep, are at least twice the size of large *P. occidentalis* or *P. diguetana* nests. *P. rejecta* is also the only species of these three that habitually nests in association with ants. In savanna and forest-edge situations, *P. rejecta* nests in large, healthy antacacias inhabited by aggressive *Pseudomyrmex* ants. In forests, *P. rejecta* nests occur on large tree limbs amid the multiple carton nests of dolichoderine ants (*Azteca sp.*). By so nesting, *P. rejecta* may be avoiding column-raiding army ants.

Adults of these three *Polybia* species are roughly equal in size (8–10 mm), and all attack and sting in defense of a nest containing brood. The workers of *P. rejecta* are remarkably easy to provoke—merely walking by a nest at 5–10 m away is sometimes sufficient stimulus. Adults of *P. occidentalis* are black with yellow markings, including a rich gold spot on the propodeum (dorsal area immediately posterior to the metathorax); *P. diguetana* adults are black with light lemon yellow markings, and *P. rejecta* workers are all black with a reddish sheen in the wings visible in sunlight.

FIGURE 11.56. *Polybia. a,* Nest of *Polybia diguetana. b,* Nest of *Polybia occidentalis. c,* Nest of *Polybia rejecta.* Costa Rica (photos, D. M. Windsor).

P. occidentalis nests remain intact for a relatively short time, an average of 1 month during the dry season, 3 months during the wet season. Only one of 273 nests observed at Santa Rosa National Park lasted more than 12 months. Most nests are destroyed by vertebrate predators, especially tanagers and the gray-headed kite (*Leptodon cavanensis*) (Windsor 1976). While the brood is eaten by these avian predators, most of the adult population is able to form a swarm, move to a new site, and complete the rudiments of a new two-cell-layer nest within a week. *Polybia* nests are generally rare in forests and abundant in open savanna and scrub, reflecting the frequency of army-ant foraging in these two habitats. Colonies are most abundant during the favorable wet season, least abundant during the early dry season. Average nest size in the population declines during the dry season.

The prey of *P. occidentalis* includes a wide range of soft-bodied arthropods, chiefly larval Lepidoptera and Coleoptera, as for other polistine wasps. *Polybia* workers capitalize on at least one important prey item, alate termites during the early wet season. Following the early soaking rains of May and June and the release of termite reproductives, there are dramatic increases in foraging by adults of *Polybia*. Hundreds or thousands of termites are caught in the air or off the ground and carried back to the nest, where they are cached until they can be eaten by the developing brood (Forsyth 1978).

The nests of *P. occidentalis* are commonly sought out by the founding females of another polybiine wasp, *Mischocyttarus immarginatus* (Windsor 1972). This timid wasp constructs its small, open, pediceled nests usually within 5–15 cm of *Polybia* nests. As many as seven satellite nests of *M. immarginatus* have been observed surrounding a single *Polybia* colony. Usually more than 90% of all *M. immarginatus* nests in the habitat are associated with *Polybia* colonies. Associated *M. immarginatus* colonies are roughly twice as successful in rearing brood as unassociated colonies. How nest survival and productivity are so greatly enhanced by proximity to *Polybia* colonies is still uncertain. *M. immarginatus* also has the curious habit of establishing nests attached to the fibers protruding from the bottom of the black, pendulous nests of a flycatcher that commonly nests in ant-acacias. *M. immarginatus* nests are dark brown and consequently are very difficult to perceive within the outline of the bird's nest. Such colonies must benefit from their isolation from pedestrian predators, few if any of whom would be capable of passing over limbs patrolled by acacia-ants.

The colony cycle and demography of *P. occidentalis* colonies has been studied by Forsyth (1978). Most colonies are polygynous, containing from two to twenty laying, inseminated females or "gynes." Worker laying of male eggs is apparently absent or else extremely rare. Nests are founded by swarms of workers and young egg-laying females that rapidly construct two to three layers of cells and then fill them with eggs so that the brood develops in a large synchronous wave. Several such pulses of worker production occur together with episodes of nest enlargement. The number of original queens declines with time as some become dominant, others become submissive, adopting worker roles, and still others leave or are ejected from the nest. As the number of queens continues to drop, male production begins, and young, inseminated females exhibiting queenlike behavior begin to appear in the colony. Aggressive interactions and cannibalism then follow, leading eventually to the mass exodus of young queens and workers in founding swarms. Some workers and young queens remain behind to continue the cycle in the parental nest. Colony fissioning appears most common during the favorable months of the early and late wet season.

*

Forsyth, A. D. 1978. Studies on the behavioral ecology of polygynous wasps. Ph.D. diss. Harvard University.

Richards, O. W. 1978. *The social wasps of the Americas.* London: British Museum (Natural History).

Windsor, D. M. 1972. Nesting association between two Neotropcial polybiine wasps (Hymenoptera, Vespidae). *Biotropica* 4:1–3.

———. 1976. Birds as predators on the brood of *Polybia* wasps (Hymenoptera: Vespidae: Polistinae) in a Costa Rican deciduous forest. *Biotropica* 8:111–16.

Pseudomyrmex ferruginea (Hormiga del Cornizuelo, Acacia-Ant)

D. H. Janzen

This rust-colored, 6 mm long ant (fig. 11.57a) is a common occupant of ant-acacias in the Pacific coastal lowlands. In Guanacaste Province and northern Puntarenas Province (and a patch of subdeciduous forest in the hills above Palmar Norte) it occupies *Acacia collinsii;* in northern Guanacaste it also occupies the much rarer *Acacia cornigera.* In the Meseta Central, where *A. collinsii* used to be common (e.g., in the Villa Colón–Santa Ana area), it also occupied *A. collinsii.* In the Golfito–Osa Peninsula region, it is the exclusive obligate occupant of *Acacia allenii,* the rain-forest ant-acacia (Janzen 1974). This ant ranges from the dry lowlands of Colombia to the vicinity of Acapulco and Tampico, Mexico, and occupies all known species of ant-acacia. In its occupation of *A. collinsii* in Costa Rica, it shares the plant population (though not individual trees) with two other acacia-ants, *Pseudomyrmex belti* (solid black) and *Pseudomyrmex nigrocincta* (smaller workers than *P. ferruginea,* more yellow, queens with a black belt across the anterior dorsum of the gaster; workers hold the gaster straight out behind, where *P. ferruginea* often curls the gaster under toward the head).

It appears that, in general, *P. belti* occupies acacias more frequently in open sun (pastures), *P. nigrocincta* is more frequently found in deep shade (forest understory), and *P. ferruginea* is spread over all habitats.

Alate virgin queens of *P. ferruginea* leave the parent acacia (all days of the year) 1–2 h before dawn, fly to a nearby tall object (a tree on a hilltop, the tallest treetop on a flat plain), and perch there, releasing a pheromone downwind (see Janzen 1966, 1967 for more detail on this and the following). Males have left the acacias earlier and fly upwind to mate with these queens about half an hour before it is light enough to see them. Predation on males by social wasps (*Polybia* spp.) is common in these mating swarms as dawn's light illuminates them. A queen mates once and then drops from the tree, shedding the male in the air. It is not known whether he can mate again. After landing on the ground, she flies a short distance, then pulls/bites off her wings and searches for an unoccupied ant-acacia on foot. When she finds one (she can search at least a month without food), if there is a new green thorn she cuts an entrance hole and hollows out the thorn (fig. 11.57b). She lays her eggs inside and rears her first workers there. She leaves the thorn to harvest Beltian bodies (fig. 11.57d,e) and petiolar nectar (fig. 11.57c); if a thornless queen finds the first queen's thorn unoccupied, she takes it over, discards the original owner's brood, and tries to rear her own. In areas of high ant-acacia density, a seedling acacia normally has its several thorns each occupied by one founding queen and up to several dozen searching queens on its surface. When one queen gets a young colony started, her workers kill or evict by force the other queens and young colonies in the acacia, and only one colony with a single queen occupies the tree from this time on (see Janzen 1973 for a discussion of the multiple-queen acacia-ant species). A colony begins producing males about a year later, and the first virgin queens appear in the second year.

The colony may enlarge to occupy as many as ten to thirty acacia shoots. In general, all the shoots within the bare basal circle are occupied by only one colony. However, in late successional vegetation several meters in height, a very large basal circle (e.g., 3 m × 6 m) may contain two colonies, each in possession of a subset of the shoots. It appears that a normal life-span of a queen, and therefore a colony, is about twenty years (there is no evidence of supersedure in nature). In Guanacaste in delayed succession in pastures, and in some low swamp vegetation, clumps of ant-acacias may live well past this age and therefore lose their ant colonies before they sensesce. These enigmatic plants are often occupied by *Crematogaster,* small black ants with turned-up gasters that aggressively resist recolonization by even large colonies of acacia-ants. Unoccupied ant-acacias may be ten-

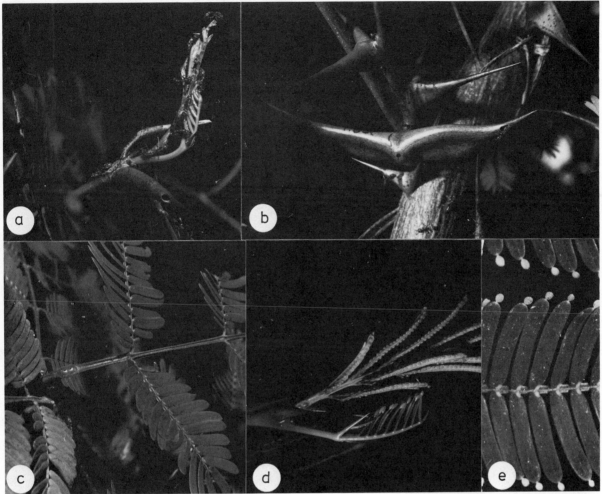

FIGURE 11.57. *Pseudomyrmex ferruginea* on *Acacia collinsii*. *a*, New leaf being patrolled by eight worker ants. *b*, Mature swollen thorn with entrance hole near tip; the colony queen is usually in a thorn of this size. *c*, Two petiolar nectaries at the base of a mature leaf. *d*, Newly expanding leaf with very large Beltian bodies on the tips of the pinnae. *e*, Expanded mature leaf with unharvested Beltian bodies on pinnule tips. Santa Rosa National Park, Guanacaste Province, Costa Rica (photos, D. H. Janzen).

anted by a variety of other ants, ranging from those obligatorily parasitic on the system (e.g., *Pseudomyrex nigropilosa*—large yellow red, large-eyed, unaggressive, Janzen 1975) to those that treat the hollow thorn as if it were just a hollow twig (e.g., *Camponotus, Paracryptocerus*).

A large adult *P. ferruginea* colony contains about ten thousand to fifteen thousand workers, two thousand males, one thousand virgin queens, and fifty thousand larvae in the early rainy season.

A. collinsii and its attendant ant colony in Guanacaste are parasitized by a large shoot-tip eating ruteline scarab (*Pelidnota punctulata*), a large leaf-eating ceratocampine moth larva (*Sphingicampa mexicana*), a fast-moving shoot-tip-eating moth larva (*Coxina hadenoides*), and one seed-eating bruchid larva (*Mimosestes* sp.). Unoccupied acacias are attacked by the coreid bug *Mozena tomentosa*

(distinct from the *Mozena* sp. that attacks *Acacia farnesiana* shoot tips). *P. ferruginea* colonies in the Cañas area were commonly found to contain the larvae of a coccinellid beetle that mimics the larvae and apparently feeds on them. The unopened thorns sometimes contained the larvae of a zygopine weevil, the adults of which run on the acacia surface.

In Guanacaste, orioles (*Icterus* sp.) and kiskadees (*Pitangus sulphuratus*) commonly nest in occupied ant-acacias. The ants first attack the developing nest but later grow accustomed to it and do not attack bird or nest. They do, however, attack climbing vertebrates, and so these nests, even though very close to the ground, have high fledging success.

Seeds of *Acacia collinsii* are embedded in a sweet and relatively dry yellow aril that is exposed when the pod dehisces; the aril is eaten by birds or bats, and the seeds are dispersed by transit through their guts. All ant-acacias are bird or bat dispersed, either because they are the animals most likely to be able to enter an ant-rich tree or because they are the most likely to carry the seeds to a new patch of bare ground, or for both reasons.

P. ferruginea, like other acacia-ants, produce very noticeable alarm pheromone that can easily be smelled by crushing a worker between the fingers. A disturbed colony can be smelled several meters downwind by humans, and much farther by another colony. The workers in a disturbed colony run much faster, more workers come out of the thorns, and they turn more often as they run. Livestock avoid the acacias day and night and probably use these chemicals to recognize their presence.

The acacia-ants quite thoroughly protect the acacia from most species of arthropod herbivores (Janzen 1966, 1967). *P. ferruginea*, with more vigor than *P. belti* and sometimes with less vigor than *P. nigrocincta*, kills foreign vegetation that touches the acacia and clears a circle about 1–4 m in diameter around the acacia(s). In Nicaragua it even prunes the shoot tips of the acacia to produce a dense, hedgelike crown; these tangled masses of thorns apparently protect them from predation by birds (Janzen 1974). Predation by birds (by thorn splitting) of acacia-ants is rare in Guanacaste but common to occasional in other parts of their range. White-faced monkeys may prey on acacia-ant larvae during the dry season (Freese 1976).

*

Freese, C. H. 1976. Predation on swollen-thorn acacia ants by white-faced monkeys, *Cebus capucinus*. *Biotropica* 8:278–81.

Janzen, D. H. 1966. Coevolution between ants and acacias in Central America. *Evolution* 20:249–75.

———. 1967. Interaction of the bull's horn acacia (*Acacia cornigera* L.) with an ant inhabitant (*Pseudomyrmex ferruginea* F. Smith) in eastern Mexico. *Univ. Kansas Sci. Bull.* 47:315–558.

———. 1973. Evolution of polygynous obligate acacia-ants in western Mexico. *J. Anim. Ecol.* 42:727–50.

———. 1974. Swollen-thorn acacias of Central America. *Smithsonian Contrib. Bot.* 13:1–131.

———. 1975. *Pseudomyrmex nigropilosa*: A parasite of a mutualism. *Science* 188:936–37.

Pseudosphinx tetrio (Oruga Falso-Coral, Frangipani Sphinx)

D. H. Janzen

The most conspicuous large moth larva (fig. 11.58) in the deciduous forests of Guanacaste Province, Costa Rica, is the larva of a large gray-mottled sphinx moth (Sphingidae). Weighing as much as 15 g when full-sized, the black larva is ringed with bright yellow and has a red

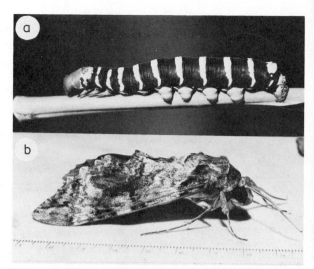

FIGURE 11.58. *a, Pseudosphinx tetrio,* last-instar caterpillar on petiole of its host plant, *Plumeria rubra. b,* Adult *P. tetrio.* Santa Rosa National Park, Guanacaste, Costa Rica (photos, D. H. Janzen).

orange head and first thoracic segment. Since it is as much as 10 cm long and 11–15 mm in diameter, it is not hard to imagine that it might be a coral-snake mimic (Janzen 1980). The larva perches during the day on the large bare stems of *Plumeria rubra* (Apocynaceae) or frangipani (flor blanca, sanjuanjoche), on whose leaves it feeds at night. In addition to its ostentatious coloring, the larva thrashes back and forth when touched, as do pinioned coral snakes, and bites viciously (most unusual behavior for a caterpillar). The larvae are colored in the same manner from the first instar onward. On the same plant, the larvae of the closely related sphinx *Isognathus rimosus* are extremely cryptic (when young they are white and feed on the flowers; W. A. Haber, pers. comm.), and when old they look like dead branches and walk off the plant to hide in the litter during the daytime. If the larva of *P. tetrio* is a coral-snake mimic, then it is likely to be depending on genetically programmed avoidance responses by birds to this color pattern rather than on some sort of learned response. However, since the host plant of *P. tetrio* is a member of a family whose members are generally viewed as containing toxic compounds, it may be that the bright coloring of *P. tetrio* larvae is merely aposematic. Whatever the case, *P. tetrio* is nearly unique among sphinx moth larvae in being visually very conspicuous.

In Santa Rosa National Park, most *Plumeria* trees are fed on sometime during the rainy season by *P. tetrio* larvae. The larvae take about 6 weeks to attain full size, then they wander off the host plant to pupate in the litter. The larva burrows into the leaf layer and produces a huge, shiny pupa above the soil. The adult emerges 1–2 months later, and adults may be taken at lights in deciduous forest from the beginning of the rainy season (May) to the end (January). Since *P. rubra* is thoroughly deciduous in the dry season, the last larvae are found feeding on the leaves in December. However, I found one larva that had grown to full size feeding on *P. rubra* flowers in March.

Of twenty-six larvae brought in from the field at medium to large size and reared, only one was parasitized by tachinid fly larvae (Santa Rosa), but they frequently die in captivity if not provided with very fresh foliage to eat, appearing to succumb to a microbial disease.

*

Janzen, D. H. 1980. Two potential coral snake mimics in a tropical deciduous forest. *Biotropica* 12:77–78.

Pseudoxychila tarsalis (Abejón Tigre, Tiger Beetle)

M. K. Palmer

Adults of this cicindelid species (fig. 11.59) are about 13 mm long and velvety blue green, with a single white spot ringed with black on each elytron. Essentially blind and flightless, these adults may be found on or near bare soil at almost any time of year but are more numerous at the beginning of the wet season. This species probably occurs throughout the country between 600 and 2,000 m elevation, exact limits being determined (apparently) by moisture.

I have seen either adults or confirmed larvae at San Vito, Monteverde, near the towns of Zapote, Quesada, and San Carlos, and along the road to Puerto Viejo down to about 600 m elevation. Highest recorded elevation is 1,970 m (near Poás), with none ever seen on Cerro de la

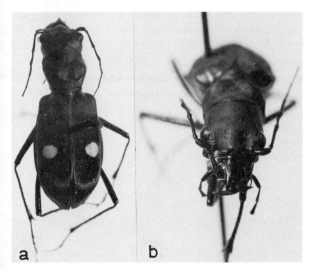

FIGURE 11.59. *a,* Dorsal view of adult *Pseudoxychila tarsalis. b,* Frontal view of *a;* note large and long mandibles crossed under head. Finca Las Cruces, San Vito de Java, Costa Rica (photos, D. H. Janzen).

Muerte. Below about 600 m, another similar-sized tiger beetle, *Megacephala* sp., occupies similar habitats; adults of this species are easily distinguished from *P. tarsalis* by their pale brown legs and purplish-and-yellow body markings. This species is also flightless and is crepuscular or nocturnal, whereas *P. tarsalis* is strictly diurnal.

Females in the field were observed to lay an average of 0.47 eggs per day (2.05 eggs per day was the laboratory average). Eggs are 1.5 mm in length, cream-colored, and sticky; they are laid at the bottoms of egg shafts 5–7 mm long dug by the female in vertical or steeply sloping clay banks. Eggs are dormant during the dry season at San Vito and hatch in abundance at the beginning of the wet season; eggs laid during the wet season hatch in a mean of 34 days.

All three larval stages of *P. tarsalis* occupy burrows at the site where the female laid the egg. Mean times required for first, second, and third instars are 70.25, 60.7, and 94.3 days; variance in instar length is large. Entrances to larval burrows are more or less circular with a tamped-down area surrounding them and are plugged during molting and pupation. Pupation occurs in a specially enlarged and (apparently) sealed portion of the rear of the larval burrow.

The generation time of *P. tarsalis* is about one year, with adults living a maximum of about 2 months (median adult life-span is 8 days). Survivorship is high through egg and larval stages and is type I (convex) overall. Second- and third-instar larvae are attacked by a parasitoid wasp, *Pterombrus piceus* Krombein (Tiphiidae), and the late third instar or prepupal stage is attacked by a fly, *Anthrax gideon* Fab. (Bombyliidae). Sources of mortality on adults are unknown but may include lizards (*Ameiva* sp.), which are common in similar habitats.

Larvae are sit-and-wait predators and are well camouflaged when the flattened head-and-thorax plate is fitted into the burrow entrance. Mandibles are curved upward and spread open when the larva is in feeding position; larvae maintain this position essentially any time they are not eating, molting, or avoiding human observers (this position being the safest; it may also prevent parasites and predators from entering the burrow). Any small animal that passes close to the burrow may serve as prey; I have seen larvae eating butterflies, caterpillars, spiders, orthopterans, small frogs, and (almost) an adult of its species (the adult ultimately won and ate the larva instead). Inedible remains of a meal are tossed out of the burrow.

Adults are both predators and scavengers; I have seen adults eating earthworms, caterpillars, ants, orthopterans, gelastochorids, frogs, and other adults (which they found dead?). Adults chew on vegetation or soil for moisture.

*

Palmer, M. K. 1976. Natural history and behavior of *Pseudoxychila tarsalis* Bates. *Cicindela* 8:61–92.

———. 1977. Natural history and population dynamics of *Pseudoxychila tarsalis* Bates (Coleoptera: Cicindelidae). Ph.D. diss., University of Michigan.

Pterombrus piceus (Avispa Escarabajo, Tiphiid Wasp, Beetle Wasp)

M. K. Palmer

Like other members of its genus, this tiphiid wasp is an ectoparasitoid of tiger-beetle larvae (*Pseudoxychila tarsalis* is the only known host). Females are black, winged, about 1 cm in length, and somewhat antlike in appearance. The range is virtually unknown, the species having been first described in 1976. I have collected specimens from San Vito (type locality), Monteverde, and between 1,665 and 1,350 m elevation along the road to Puerto Viejo; aside from the San Vito adults, all were collected as larvae or pupae from the burrows of *P. tarsalis* larvae.

Adult females actively search out second-instar (and some third-instar) beetle burrows during the wet season. Female wasps usually pass by empty burrow entrances (even when larvae are inside) and will also pass burrows with larvae immobile at the entrances. Wasps will sometimes circle the burrow entrance or tap with their antennae near the edges until the beetle retreats (apparently frightened by the wasp), at which point the wasp darts into the hole. Entering a burrow only when the larva is retreating is probably associated with possible attack by the beetle.

Larvae of this beetle apparently have no defense against the wasp once it is inside the burrow. Other species of cicindelid beetle larvae often flip out of their holes when a wasp enters and sometime avoid predation in this way. The wasp parasites of these temperate-zone species (*Methocha stycia,* also a tiphiid) will readily sting beetle larvae they find crawling on the ground and will drag them to nearby holes or depressions and oviposit on them. Females of *P. piceus,* however, display no interest in beetle larvae outside their burrows, even in the one observed case where larva and wasp fell from a burrow together while the wasp was stinging the larva.

Having paralyzed its prey by stinging it several times on the thorax, the wasp positions the larva ventral side up about 3 cm from the burrow entrance and lays a single cream-colored egg on its abdomen. The female then closes the hole with a plug of loose soil and searches for new hosts.

Eggs are about 1 mm long and hatch in 5 days in the laboratory. The salmon-colored larva feeds by inserting its head beneath the host's integument. Wasp larvae grow an average of 1 mm per day in the laboratory, until they are between 7 and 10 mm long. Larval development in the field requires between 8 and 13 days. When development is complete, the larva constructs a cocoon composed of many layers of reddish brown to white silk immediately behind and attached to the host's head capsule. A prepupal stage of about 20 days is followed by a pupal stage of 25–30 days, and adults emerge in the field approximately 65 days after the egg was laid.

Of the few third-instar hosts seen parasitized by this wasp, almost all were collected in late November or December, indicating a possible switch to larger prey near the end of the wet season, when few second-instar hosts remain in the population. The cocoons of these wasps are much larger (about 3 cm) than those of second-instar hosts (1.5 to 2 cm) but contain wasp pupae roughly equal in size to those found on second-instar hosts. Most of the size difference is thus due to additional layers of silk in the cocoon, which may help the pupa resist desiccation during the dry season.

*

Palmer, M. K. 1976. Notes on the biology of *Pterombrus piceus* Krombein (Hymenoptera: Tiphiidae). *Proc. Ent. Soc. Washington* 78:369–75.

Quichuana angustriventris (Mosca Abeja, Cola de Ratón, Rat-tailed Maggot, Syrphid Fly)

R. P. Seifert

Quichuana angustriventris (= *Q. picadoi* Knab and *Q. aurata* Walker) is one of several species of syrphids whose larvae live in the water-filled floral bracts of Neotropical *Heliconia* plants (see chap. 7 for details on *H. latispatha*). In Costa Rica the larvae of *Q. angustriventris* commonly live inside the flower bracts of *H. wagneriana* and *H. imbricata* and occasionally in *H. latispatha*. The larvae live below the waterline in the bracts and breathe air primarily through an elongate abdominal respiratory tube that can be extended to about twice the length of the insect's body. Newly hatched larvae move in the bract primarily by swimming through the water with an undulating, serpentine motion, but larger larvae can crawl underwater along the bract and flower edge and will crawl from bract to bract on the same inflorescence.

The developmental time for *Q. angustriventris* from oviposition to eclosion is about 55 days. The locations where mating occurs are unknown, but for many syrphids courtship occurs near the adult food sources, which are nectar and pollen of various plants. Adults of *Quichuana* species do not feed on *Heliconia* flowers, and the species of flowers used as adult food are not known. Females oviposit on the newly opening bracts of *Heliconia* plants, bracts that are only slightly reflected from the rachis of the inflorescence. The female lands on the bract and extends a three-pronged ovipositor into it. She apparently tests the inside of the bract tactilely and rejects bracts in which oviposition has already occurred. A female will lay eggs on several inflorescences in a *Heliconia* clump, with each clutch ranging in number from eight to thirty-two. The eggs hatch in 2 days, and the larvae feed on detritus and floral parts and sometimes enter open flowers to feed on nectar. Larval development takes about 45 days in lowland Costa Rica. The pupae are placed on the bract edge or at the union of the rachis and leaf. Pupal life lasts 8 days, and eclosion always occurs in the morning. Apparently morning eclosion is a response to the afternoon rains: adults that hatch but get wet before their wings dry are never able to fly. The adults of *Q. angustriventris* can be distinguished from other species in the same genus in Costa Rica by the bright golden pile on the thorax.

Larvae of *Q. angustriventris* are found in *H. wagneriana* inflorescences throughout the *H. wagneriana* blooming season (the dry season), but in *H. imbricata* most reproduction occurs early in the wet season. The larvae are found in *H. latispatha* throughout the year, but *H. latispatha* inflorescences are too small to support large larval populations. The adults appear to be long-lived. Large adult populations are found even after several months when no *Heliconia* plants have been blooming and reproduction thus could not occur.

Although ants will sometimes eat the eggs on the bracts and earwigs occasionally eat larvae, the larval life form seems to suffer little from predation. Adults are fed on by spiders and anoles when they hatch from the pupa and when they return to *Heliconia* to oviposit. Other predators, including robber flies, dragonflies, and small birds, probably eat *Q. angustriventris* adults.

Species in the genus *Quichuana* are obligate associates of *Heliconia* in Colombia, Ecuador, Venezuela, and Martinique. It is likely that most *Heliconia* species with large, erect bracts serve as larval feeding locations for *Quichuana* species. The associations of *Q. angustriventris* with other *Heliconia* -inhabiting insects have been studied in both Costa Rica and Venezuela.

*

Seifert, R. P., and Seifert, F. H. 1976a. A community matrix analysis of *Heliconia* insect communities. *Am. Nat.* 110:461–83.

———. 1976b. Natural history of insects living in inflorescences of two species of *Heliconia. J. N.Y. Ent. Soc.* 84:233–42.

———. 1979. A *Heliconia* insect community in a Venezuelan cloud forest. *Ecology* 60:462–67.

Rhinoseius colwelli (Acaro Floral del Colibrí, Totolate Floral de Colibrí, Hummingbird Flower Mite)

R. K. Colwell

Dependent on the mutualism between hummingbirds and bird-pollinated plants, this 0.6 mm long mite (order Mesostigmata: Ascidae) feeds and reproduces within the flowers of several species, chiefly of the genus *Centropogon* (Lobeliaceae) in the highlands of Costa Rica. The mites ride between flowers in the nasal passages of hummingbirds. Hunter (1972) described this species from specimens collected during an OTS field problem at Cerro de la Muerte, where the species is easily found in the rose lavender flowers of *C. talamancensis* Wilbur, the orange red flowers of *C. valerii* (Standl.) McVaugh, and the orange flowers of two species of *Bomarea* (Amaryllidaceae) (Colwell 1973). Eggs laid in small groups in the nectary region of flowers produce an active, six-legged larval instar, followed by the eight-legged protonymph, deutonymph, and adult. Generation time is about 7–10 days. Eggs are bathed in nectar, and all other life stages feed on nectar and perhaps on pollen exudates. At Cerro de la Muerte, deutonymphs and adults of both sexes can be found in the nasal cavities of *Eugenes fulgens* (magnificent or Rivoli's hummingbird), *Colibri thalassinus* (green violet-ear) (Colwell et al. 1974), and *Panterpe insignis* (fiery-throated hummingbird). (Mites may be removed from netted birds by aspiration without harming the birds.) In response to olfactory cues, mites disembark while their carrier feeds on a flower of an appropriate species. They do not obtain any nutriment from birds but must eventually rely on avian transport to disperse. (Local travel on foot is probably limited to nearby flowers on the same plant.)

These are very active mites, easy to see with the naked eye in a dissected flower or alive in a vial (they are whitish). For their size, they run about as fast as a cheetah—a useful ability when they have only 2 or 3 sec to disembark from a long-billed hummingbird. Under the microscope, the males appear more heavily sclerotized than the females, with opposable spines on the second set of legs and longer setae on the dorsum. They can often be seen actively courting and copulating with the calmer females. (Under the microscope it is best to include a piece of the corolla in the vial or dish and to use cool light if possible.) The adult sex ratio is this species is about two or three females per male, thought to be a group-selected phenomenon (Colwell 1981). *Rhinoseius* mites are almost certainly functionally haplodiploid (haploid males, diploid females), but it is not yet known how sex is determined genetically or regulated behaviorally.

At Cerro de la Muerte, *R. colwelli* coexists with a

single congener, *R. richardsoni* Hunter, whose host plants are the red-flowered epiphytes *Cavendishia smithii* Hoer. and *Macleania glabra* (Klotzsch) Hoer. (both Ericaceae) and whose avian carriers are *Panterpe* and *Eugenes*. Individual hummingbirds often carry mites of both species simultaneously, yet there is no mixing of species whatever on host plants, even though experiments show that each species is able to survive and reproduce in the other's host plant species if forcibly introduced into unoccupied flowers (Colwell 1973). This rigid segregation is made possible by olfactory discrimination of host plants and is enforced by lethal attacks by resident males on alien intruders of either sex. *R. colwelli* males crush their victims with their second set of raptorial legs, and male *R. richardsoni* are armed with four greatly enlarged spinelike setae in the center of the dorsum (easily seen under a dissecting microscope). This behavior can usually be observed among captive mites under a microscope.

Host-plant repertoires of hummingbird flower mites are a complicated function of hummingbird foraging patterns, flowering phenology, and host-plant dispersion (Colwell 1973). The taxonomic affinities of the plants are of little direct influence, in contrast with host-plant repertoires among Lepidoptera and Coleoptera. For example, near Monteverde, Costa Rica, *R. colwelli* occupies two species of *Centropogon* (Lobeliaceae), a *Bomarea* (Amaryllidaceae), a bromeliad, and a species of *Columnea* (Gesneriaceae)—a repertoire spanning two dicot orders and two monocot orders. In the same area, *R. chiriquensis* (Baker and Yunker) occupies another lobeliad, *Lobelia laxiflora*, as well as *Hamelia patens* (Rubiaceae) and *Cuphea* sp. (Lithraceae). The explanation is that all of *R. colwelli*'s host species at Monteverde are heavily visited by the long-billed *Campylopterus hemileucurus* (violet sabrewing), while the host species of *R. chiriquensis* are visited by several opportunistic, short-billed species (see Feinsinger 1976). (*R. richardsoni* also occurs at Monteverde, along with a fourth species of *Rhinoseius* and a species of the closely related genus *Proctolaelaps*.)

At this time, hummingbird flower mites (*Rhinoseius* and *Proctolaelaps*) have been found on more than fifty hummingbird species and in the flowers of more than one hundred plant species in some twenty families, from northern California (Colwell and Naeem 1979) to central Chile, and from sea level to over 4,500 m (Ecuador). Although there are doubtless several thousand host-plant species, I estimate that fewer than five hundred species of hummingbird flower mites exist—of which only about fifty have been described so far (Colwell 1979). In the lowland forests of Trinidad at least sixteen species of these mites coexist, each monopolizing one to three host-plant species while sharing hummingbird carriers with several other species in the group. At least some twenty host-plant species are involved, and eight or more hummingbird species. This community, and the one at Monteverde, are currently under study. Adaptive radiation in morphology, sex ratio, dispersal, and behavior among hummingbird flower mites, in relation to spatial and temporal patterns in potential host plants and their avian carriers (Feinsinger and Colwell 1978), provides a richly detailed portrait of coevolution.

*

Colwell, R. K. 1973. Competition and coexistence in a simple tropical community. *Am. Nat.* 107:737–60.

———. 1979. The geographical ecology of hummingbird flower mites in relation to their host plants and carriers. *Rec. Adv. Acarol.* 2:461–68.

———. 1981. Group selection is implicated in the evolution of female-biased sex ratios. *Nature*, in press.

Colwell, R. K.; Betts, B. J.; Bunnell, P.; Carpenter, F. L.; and Feinsinger, P. 1974. Competition for the nectar of *Centropogon valerii* by the hummingbird *Colibri thalassinus* and the flower-piercer *Diglossa plumbea*, and its evolutionary implications. *Condor* 76:447–52.

Colwell, R. K., and Naeem, S. 1979. The first known species of hummingbird flower mite north of Mexico: *Rhinoseius epoecus* sp. nov. (Mesostigmata: Ascidae). *Ann. Ent. Soc. Am.* 72:485–91.

Feinsinger, P. 1976. Organization of a tropical guild of nectivorous birds. *Ecol. Monogr.* 46:257–91.

Feinsinger, P., and Colwell, R. K. 1978. Community organization among Neotropical nectar-feeding birds. *Am. Zool.* 18:779–95.

Hunter, P. E. 1972. New *Rhinoseius* species (Mesostigmata: Ascidae) from Costa Rican hummingbirds. *J. Georgia Ent. Soc.* 7:27–36.

Scolytodes atratus panamensis
(Escarabajito de Guarumo, Cecropia Petiole Borer)

S. L. Wood

This is one of the most common and widely distributed bark beetles in Costa Rica (fig. 11.60). It is 2.5–3.5 mm long and dark brown to black. It breeds exclusively in petioles of recently fallen *Cecropia* leaves. *Cecropia* trees grow throughout Costa Rica at elevations below 2,000 m and shed a few leaves in all months of the year. About 80% of the leaves that catch on vegetation and are suspended above the forest floor become infested by this insect. Like scolytids everywhere, this species has secretive habits, but they differ significantly from those of scolytids in north-temperate areas.

The petioles are infested from 3 to 15 days after they

FIGURE 11.60. Adults of a cecropia petiole borer (Scolytidae) exposed in their galleries by splitting the petiole (*lower*) and exit holes of the beetles (*upper*). Corcovado National Park, Osa Peninsula, Costa Rica (photos, D. H. Janzen).

fall. Competition has partitioned this microhabitat in such a way that several other species of *Scolytodes* live harmoniously with *S. a. panamensis* in most of Costa Rica, but it evidently cannot compete successfully with *S. glabrescens* in most of Panama and extreme southeastern Costa Rica. The basal 3 to 5 cm of the *Crecopia* petiole is more dense and is filled by little if any soft pith; this area is occupied by *S. maurus,* a species 1.5–2.1 mm in length. The remaining portion of the basal third is occupied by *S. a. panamensis,* although in 10% of the petioles the infestation may reach the middle of the petiole and in 1% the distal third. Any one or more of a dozen smaller species of *Scolytodes,* all less than 1.2 mm in length, may occupy the distal half of the petiole.

A male bores an entrance hole through the hard cortex and into the soft pith near the base on the underside of the petiole. By the time his tunnel has reached a depth of 3 to 5 mm he is joined by one female. (Attraction is presumed to be by pheromones, as in other scolytids.) The basically cylindrical tunnel includes, near the entrance hole, a turning niche into which the male moves to allow the female to pass. She then extends the tunnel. Copulation takes place at the turning niche and may be repeated several times. Following copulation, the male expels frass from the gallery and blocks the entrance hole to obstruct invasion by predators and parasites. The female extends the tunnel through the pith, often branching the system of tunnels in an irregular pattern. She deposits clusters of one to twenty eggs in loose frass that is left in various areas of the tunnel. The eggs apparently hatch in 3 to 5 days. The white legless, grublike larvae consume the pith in congress, extending the parental chambers. Pupation occurs in the tunnels, and the young adults usually feed for some time before emerging. The entire life cycle may be completed in as little as 25 days.

Usually no more than one to four pairs of parent adults infest a petiole. Rarely do more than one hundred offspring emerge from one petiole.

*

Wood, S. L. 1982. The bark and ambrosia beetles of North and Central America (Coleoptera: Scolytidae), a taxonomic monograph. *Great Basin Nat. Mem.,* no. 6.

Simulium (Mosca de Café, Mosca Negra, Black Fly)

M. Vargas V. and F. Fallas B.

The Simuliidae are a very homogeneous group of flies that have adapted well and flourished, presenting us with unique evolutionary patterns in habitat exploitation and behavior. They are of recent geologic origin, and their potential for dispersion and speciation offers an array of interesting features to those interested in understanding biological phenomena in the Neotropics.

The black flies, or "moscas de café" as they are locally known, are rather small (2–5 mm in length) but compact and robust flies that are characteristically humpbacked in appearance and have short, broad wings and legs. They are frequently encountered near streams, where the females of some species readily attack humans for a blood meal, causing great annoyance and distress, especially to those who react severely to their painful bites. Other species prefer the blood of reptiles, birds, and other mammals. Males are not bloodsuckers but feed on nectar and other exposed plant secretions. These insects are active mainly during the daytime. They are powerful fliers and can cover long distances, aided in part by wind currents.

The immature forms normally require lotic habitats for development and are typically found in well-aerated, nonpolluted flowing water; in Costa Rica, however, the highest larval populations of certain species are associated with very polluted streams. The eggs are laid in masses of two hundred to five hundred on vegetation or rocks on or below the surface of the water, but plastic, fabric, or almost any object may serve as a suitable substrate for oviposition. Some species prefer leaves of plants trailing in the water for ovipositing, for example, *Simulium panamense,* a species that is widely distributed and tolerates a wide range of ecological conditions. *Simulium paynei,* also common in the Central Valley, lays its eggs on rocks and larger boulders where the current is stronger and faster.

Larvae hatching from the eggs pass through six or seven instars to reach maturity. Large salivary glands produce a secretion that allows them to spin silk threads that they use as a means of attaching themselves to the substrate or even for moving or drifting to more convenient habitats. They are filter feeders and possess two fanlike organs on the head that add to their peculiar bottle-shaped aspect, rendering them easily recognizable among the benthic macroinvertebrates, of which they are some of the most successful. Larval and pupal populations are often so abundant that they cover large sections of rocks and submerged leaves. When they mature, larvae spin a silken cocoon that they attach firmly to the substrate. The pupae have long, branching respiratory filaments that vary in shape, form, and number and are extremely helpful in identifying species, as are the shape and size of the cocoon.

Black flies are of considerable medical and economic importance, not only because of their painful bites and persistent attacks, which may cause heavy blood losses in domestic and wild vertebrates, but also because they can transmit disease organisms, mainly *Onchocerca volvulus,* a filarial worm responsible for onchocerciasis in man, and can serve as vectors of protozoan diseases of birds. More recently they have been also incriminated in the transmission of viruses. Biologists who intend to do fieldwork in Costa Rica, especially in the Central Valley where the hilly landscape favors breeding habitats for two important anthropophilic species, *Simulium metallicum* and *Simulium quadrivittatum,* should avoid severe allergic reactions by protecting themselves with an efficient repellent, since no better control methods are available.

At present, exposure to onchocerciasis is not to be feared, though the disease is present in some countries of Latin America north and south of Costa Rica, for it has not been found in this country. There is as yet no adequate explanation for this.

A project to study the bionomics of simuliids in this country has been under way since 1968. Immature and adult populations have been observed and collected in a hundred representative streams inside and outside the Central Valley.

The biometric data obtained have been helpful in understanding the biology and distribution of these insects and may help us interpret the epidemiological aspects of pathogen transmission by these flies. The taxonomic complexities of this group pose great difficulty for the nonspecialist but should not discourage ecological work at the level of populations.

The feasibility of using predators and pathogens in the biocontrol of simuliid populations is gaining interest. The role of *Neomesomermis travisi* n. sp., a mermithid nematode described from Costa Rican material, in regulating immature stages of black flies is being evaluated at present, and the information may prove useful in countries where transmission of onchocerciasis occurs and different control methods are needed.

*

Travis, B. V., and Vargas V., M. 1970. Bionomics of black flies in Costa Rica. 2. An ecological consideration. *Proc. Fifty-seventh Ann. Meet. New Jersey Mosq. Exterm. Assoc.,* pp. 111–12.

————. 1978. Bionomics of black flies (Diptera: Simuliidae) in Costa Rica. 6. Correlations with ecological factors. *Rev. Biol. Trop.* 26:335–45.

Travis, B. V.; Vargas V., M.; and Fallas N., F. 1979. Bionomics of black flies (Diptera: Simuliidae) in Costa Rica. 3. Larval population dynamics in five selected streams. *Rev. Biol. Trop.* 27:135–43.

Travis, B. V.; Vargas V., M.; and Swartzwelder, J. C. 1974. Bionomics of black flies (Diptera: Simuliidae) in Costa Rica. 1. Species biting man, with an epidemiological summary for the Western Hemisphere. *Rev. Biol. Trop.* 22:187–200.

Vargas V., M.; Rubtsov, I. A.; and Fallas B., F. 1980. Bionomics of black flies in Costa Rica (Diptera: Simuliidae). 5. Description of *Neomesomermis travisi* n. sp. (Nematoda: Mermithidae). *Rev. Biol. Trop.,* in press.

Vargas V., M., and Travis, B. V. 1973. Bionomía de los Simúlidos (Diptera: Simuliidae) en Costa Rica. 4. Localización y descripción de los lugares de recolección. *Rev. Biol. Trop.* 21:143–75.

Vargas V., M.; Travis, B. V.; Díaz Nájera, A.; and Fallas N., F. 1977. Bionomics of black flies (Diptera: Simuliidae) in Costa Rica. 7. Genus *Simulium* subgenus *Hearlea. Rev. Biol. Trop.* 25:137–49.

Trigona fulviventris (Abeja Atarrá, Abeja Jicote, Culo de Vaca, Trigona, Stingless Bee)

L. K. Johnson

Trigona fulviventris fulviventris Guérin (Hymenoptera: Apidae) ranges from Colima, Mexico, and the Yucatan Peninsula to São Paulo, Brazil. In Costa Rica it is common at low to mid elevations and occurs in habitats ranging from tropical dry forest to tropical wet forest. It can be distinguished from the more than sixty other *Trigona* species in Costa Rica by a combination of its size (5–6.5 mm) and its coloration (black with slender orange abdomen).

Like all stingless bees, or Meliponinae, *Trigona fulviventris* is eusocial and lives in colonies, in the case of *T. fulviventris* numbering from several thousand to ten thousand individuals. Nests are found at the bases of trees with a dbh of 85 cm or greater. The nest interior may open into a hollow at the base of the trunk, but more often it is subterranean, occurring among the roots of the tree. Nests among tree roots are virtually inaccessible to *Trigona* predators such as parrots, woodpeckers, tayras, armadillos, and anteaters, which may be why *T. fulviventris* does not defend its nest by mass biting as other members of its subgenus do. The workers possess an alarm pheromone (principally nerol) in the mandibular gland, which can be smelled if a bee is pressed between the fingers. Release of the pheromone, however, rarely elicits a response from other workers. Even if a bee is seized at the nest entrance by an ant or assassin bug, one worker at most will be drawn to the site of the pheromone release.

Some nest entrances, flush with the ground and roughly oval, are hard to find. More readily located are entrances that open within a sheltering hollow at the base of a tree. In such cases the bees construct an entrance tube perpendicular to the trunk, of an irregular funnel shape, sometimes with a lower lip that serves as a landing platform. The walls of the entrance funnel are about 0.2 cm thick, firm to slightly brittle, and grainy with sand, dirt, and bits of resin. The entrance is 3–4 cm wide, which permits many bees to enter and leave at the same time, either when the bees are foraging or in the event of a nest raid by other meliponine species. As the day gets hotter, bees may be seen fanning their wings in the throat of the funnel in what is presumably a method of temperature control.

The bees forage from dawn to dusk. Efflux appears to be stimulated by light level, since colonies at the edges of clearings begin foraging up to a quarter of an hour earlier than colonies deep in the woods. At dawn the bees pour out until about two thousand are in the field at any one time. This number remains constant until midmorning, then declines slowly until late afternoon, at which time there is a minor burst of activity. In late morning and midday, when flowers are depleted, foragers take more time per trip and spend less time at each flower. In Guanacaste this diel pattern of activity persists throughout both the wet and the dry seasons, although in the dry season in arid years activity may be drastically cut back between 0800 and 1630.

Among stingless bees, *T. fulviventris* is unusual for the diversity of loads it carries into the nest on any given day. As building material, it collects mud, fungi, feces, and a variety of plant exudates including resin from *Bursera, Bombacopsis, Hymenaea,* and *Machaerium.* As food, it collects pollen and nectar from nearly all flowering species in its environment, and it may bring in more than twenty kinds of pollen in a day. Despite the high diversity of resource types of colony collects, individual bees are relatively faithful to one resource type and resource location, and if switching occurs it is more likely to occur between days than within a day.

Most of the time *T. fulviventris* workers forage solitarily on small dispersed flowers, but if a forager is rewarded several times at one site, it may be stimulated to bring recruits. Before the onset of recruitment behavior, the bee will fly straight in, hover, land and collect, and return directly to the nest. But after a number of rewards a change suddenly comes over the insect. Now the bee flies in and hovers but does not collect. It alights instead

about once per second on the food source and on nearby leaves and twigs, depositing an oily bit of pheromone from its mandibular gland each time it touches down. At intervals it inspects or samples the food source, then restlessly resumes marking, favoring certain prominent leaves. Occasionally the marks attract another bee from the same colony that happens by, and such a bee may itself begin marking before finding or sampling the resource. The original scout finally returns to the nest, sometimes marking a leaf or two on the way back. On the next visit the scout arrives leading a group of one to a dozen recruits. These bees, if rewarded, recruit others in turn, and in this way, more than two hundred bees may learn of a resource location.

Experiments with sugar-water baits reveal that the number of recruits led by the scout is a function of molar sucrose concentration, or resource quality. This and the fact that recruitment is not initiated until a number of visits have been successfully completed ensures that recruitment occurs only when there is an ample supply of a fairly rich resource.

When two or more colonies of *T. fulviventris* are attracted to the same resource, the bees will readily threaten and sometimes fight, especially if the resource is concentrated in a small area. Display behaviors include rising up on the legs, holding the wings out, and opening the mandibles. Two bees may face off in the air and slowly rise together to a height of 7 m or more. Flights may include brief tussles, tugs at extremities, and prolonged fights to the death in which the bees chew each other's mandibles and necks (fig. 11.61). Severe colony encounters over resources are rare, however, since the colonies tend to be uniformly spaced (about 180 m apart in the dry forest of Guanacaste), so that most of a colony's foraging takes place in an intraspecifically exclusive area.

In contrast to its readiness to engage conspecifics in intercolony fights, *T. fulviventris* is reluctant to battle the aggressive members of its subgenus, namely *T. fuscipennis, T. silvestriana,* and *T. corvina.* Interspecific

FIGURE 11.61. *Trigona fulviventris* fighting to the death with mandibles armed with four pointed teeth. During a fight the antennae and legs are continuously in play. Costa Rica (redrawn by L. Johnson from an illustration by S. Abbott).

fights that do occur over rich, clumped resources usually end badly for *T. fulviventris*. The aggressive species mentioned are black and conspicuous, larger or at least stockier in build, and have toothier mandibles. They are good at recruiting and possess their own marking pheromones, the perception of which alarms foraging *T. fulviventris* and causes them to take to the air. This flight off the resource aids takeover by the aggressive rivals.

Despite the likelihood that one or more of these aggressive competitors will be present in any lowland habitat in Costa Rica, *Trigona fulviventris* is still able to exploit large, clumped resources because it finds new resources more quickly than any other species. Quick discovery occurs in part because *T. fulviventris* has a large, solitary, well-dispersed foraging force out in the field at any given time. Quick discovery is also promoted because a large proportion of the foragers can function as scouts—that is, they are prone to visit and sample novel sights and smells and, if rewarded, can mark the discovered site and recruit others. This habit of quick discovery gives *T. fulviventris* an initial period free of competition, during which time it can harvest much of the resource. Most of the time, though, single bees visit dispersed resources.

Attempts at colony multiplication take place principally in the Guanacaste dry season, when tree crowns flower, which suggests that multiplication efforts are stimulated in times of plenty, when the colony is growing. In meliponines, workers from the mother colony locate potential new sites and hover in and about them. If a site is favored by most of the scouting workers, the workers begin supplying it with pollen, nectar, and building materials carried from the mother nest. In a few weeks one or more gynes emerge from the mother colony and make a mating flight with males that have been sitting and swarming outside the entrances of the new and old nests. The new provisioned nest is then occupied by one of the new queens and a cohort of workers.

In *Trigona fulviventris,* a scout that has discovered a potential new nest will mark the site and recruit other bees. Sometimes bees from a second colony are attracted, and aggressive displays ensue. In one case a large-scale battle developed when several hundred bees from one colony were recruited to a hollow in a tree that already possessed a *T. fulviventris* nest. More than a thousand deaths were recorded, and the once-promising site was forsaken. This suggests that an important mechanism spacing the nests of *T. fulviventris* may be agonistic encounters over new nest sites that are too close to a rival colony.

The rate of establishment of new *T. fulviventris* colonies is at best slow, and existing colonies are likely to persist for years. Of eight Costa Rican nests that have been followed for as many years, five are still in existence, one was abandoned, one was killed by man, and one was destroyed by a colony of the robber bee *Lestrimelitta limao.*

*

Hubbell, S. P., and Johnson, L. K. 1977. Competition and nest spacing in a tropical stingless bee community. *Ecology* 58:949–63.

———. 1978. Comparative foraging behavior of six stingless bee species exploiting a standardized resource. *Ecology* 59:1123–36.

Johnson, L. K. 1980. Alarm response of foraging *Trigona fulviventris* (Hymenoptera: Apidae) to mandibular gland components of competing bee species. *J. Kansas Ent. Soc.* 53:357–62.

———. 1982a. The costly extermination of a *Trigona fulviventris* colony by nest-robbing bees. *Biotropica,* in press.

———. 1982b. Foraging strategies and the structure of stingless bee communities in Costa Rica. In *Social insects in the tropics,* ed. P. Jaisson. Paris: University of Paris Press. Forthcoming.

Johnson, L. K., and Hubbell, S. P. 1974. Aggression and competition among stingless bees: Field studies. *Ecology* 55:120–27.

———. 1975. Contrasting foraging strategies and coexistence of two bee species on a single resource. *Ecology* 56:1398–1406.

———. 1982. Solitary foraging by *Trigona fulviventris* bees: Evolved or enforced? In manuscript.

Johnson, L. K., and Wiemer, D. F. 1982. Nerol: An alarm substance of the stingless bee, *Trigona fulviventris* (Hymenoptera: Apidae). In manuscript.

Schwarz, H. F. 1948. Stingless bees (Meliponidae) of the Western Hemisphere. *Bull. Am. Mus. Nat. Hist.* 90:1–546.

Wille, A. 1965. Las abejas atarrá de la región mesoamericana del género y subgénero *Trigona* (Apidae-Meliponini). *Rev. Biol. Trop.* 13:271–91.

Wille, A., and Michener, C. D. 1973. The nest architecture of stingless bees with special reference to those of Costa Rica (Hymenoptera: Apidae). *Rev. Biol. Trop.* 21:1–278.

Tropidacris cristata (Saltamonte o Chapulín Gigante, Giant Red-winged Grasshopper)

H. F. Rowell

The genus *Tropidacris* comprises three species that are among the largest known acridids, and it is confined to the New World tropics. The adult female of *T. cristata* (fig. 11.62) reaches 14.5 cm in length from head to wingtips and nearly 25 cm across the spread wings; it weighs nearly 30 g. Gary Stiles once confessed to having shot one, thinking it was a hummingbird. It is mottled

FIGURE 11.62. *Tropidacris cristata,* female. Sirena, Corcovado National Park, Osa Peninsula, Costa Rica (photo, H. F. Rowell).

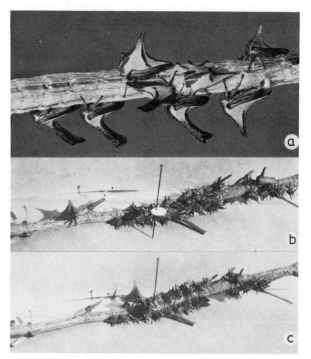

FIGURE 11.63. *Umbonia crassicornis. a,* Aggregation of adults; dark-colored individual in upper right is parent of all. *b,* Position of parent (to left of pin) away from nymphs before presenting a crushed nymph on pin. *c,* Position of parent (near pin) after presenting a crushed nymph on pin (photos, T. K. Wood).

dark green and yellow, except for the hind wings, which are crimson mottled with blue black spots. Because of this dramatic appearance, it is included here even though it is rarely very common; most OTS courses turn up two or three in two months' fieldwork. It is of the subfamily Romaleinae, family Romaleidae, superfamily Acridoidea.

The larvae are yellow, vertically tiger-striped with reddish brown. They and the adults eat a wide range of shrubs and trees. Like many of their subfamily, they seem to prefer plants rich in secondary chemicals that many herbivores find difficult to cope with. In Costa Rica the species is often found on *Quassia* of the Simarubaceae. Occasionally it is abundant, and forests in Trinidad have been sprayed with insecticide because of a perceived threat to timber trees from this species. The adults are powerful fliers, and the breeding range of the insect extends from Amazonia to Mexico; vagrants have been reported from as far north as urban Illinois. Adults are recorded from virtually everywhere in Costa Rica, and the species sometimes comes to lights at night. I have found larvae at La Selva and in Guanacaste.

There are a number of romaleine genera of this habit, large powerful fliers, all living in Neotropical rain forest. Nothing very much is known of any of them.

Umbonia crassicornis (Bicho Espino, Thorn Bug, Treehopper)

T. K. Wood

Umbonia crassicornis Amyot and Serville (*U. oziombe* of older literature) (fig. 11.63) is a membracid (Homoptera) frequently encountered in Costa Rica in a number of ecologically diverse habitats. Ballou (1936*a, b*) found this species in Guadalupe, Paso Ancho, San Lucas, and San Pedro, and I have collected it at La Selva, San José,

and La Pacifica. Its overall geographic range is extensive; it occurs from Brazil to South Florida. The north-south limits of the distribution are probably related to its inability to withstand prolonged freezing temperatures.

Although found in a variety of habitats, it is most common along the edges of forests and in successional or highly disturbed areas. I have never found this species in dense forests. High population densities may be encountered along the streets of San José on various ornamental trees and shrubs.

Umbonia crassicornis utilizes a wide variety of host plants from a number of families. My experience suggests that it is most common on hosts in the Leguminosae. Ballou (1936*a,b*) reports that Costa Rican host plants are *Citrus, Inga, Calliandra grandiflora, Parkinsonia, Enterolobium cyclocarpum, Pyrus communis,* and *Guazuma.* In Florida *U. crassicornis* has been reported from a number of hosts (Mead 1962), but I have found *Calliandra* sp., *Albizzia lebbek,* and *Lysiloma bahamensis* to be the most common host plants.

The biology of *U. crassicornis* is particularly interesting because of the high degree of parental investment females place in offspring. Fecund females of *U. crassicornis* insert eggs into branches or petioles of their host plants and remain there until their eggs hatch. During this

773

period females are inactive (Wood 1974), and if physically disturbed by probing with a pencil, they may fan their wings but do not desert the eggs. Females that are physically displaced can relocate egg masses, but when given a choice between their own eggs and others, they do not differentiate (Wood, unpub. data). Experimental removal of females in the field showed that egg masses without females suffer a higher predator-associated mortality than those with females (Wood 1976).

Before eggs hatch, females move off egg masses and with the ovipositor make a series of slits in the bark. These slits are arranged in a spiral around the branch and extend 3 to 6 cm below the egg mass. At egg hatch, the female positions herself about 4 cm below the egg mass. As first instars move off the egg mass, they line up along the spiral slits in front of the female. Nymphs walking down the branch are stopped by the parent female's tapping their dorsum with her front legs. Nymphs respond by either stopping or returning to the aggregation. As nymphs mature and grow larger, the female moves farther down the branch but remains with her offspring until they mature to adults. Removal of females from first-instar aggregations results in some nymphal dispersal and high predator-associated mortality; females are provoked to aggressive displays by the presence of adult coccinelid beetles and other invertebrate predators near their offspring. Aggressive female behavior is also evoked when an alarm pheromone(s) is released when the body wall of a nymph is experimentally injured (fig. 11.63). Females are attracted to the injured nymph, and presumably a potential predator, and they go through the same aggressive displays as if a predator were present. Nymphs do not respond to alarm pheronomnes from injured siblings (Wood 1974, 1976).

The vulnerability of parent females to vertebrate predators while on eggs and with offspring is reduced in several ways. During egg maturation, the female's lack of movement enhances her dark green cryptic coloration and presumably reduces danger from predators such as *Anolis* that capture moving prey. The highly sclerotized pronotum with its sharp dorsal horn is a physical deterrent to such a predator. Removing pronotum from mature females makes them acceptable prey to *Anolis* (Wood 1975, 1977a).

Sociality is not restricted to female-offspring interaction but continues between teneral adult siblings, which maintain aggregations that may last 20 to 30 days. Apparently the maintenance of these aggregations involves the dorsal horn of the pronotum (Wood 1977a). Teneral adult aggregates may enhance feeding but also have a defensive function. The coloration of the teneral adult pronotum is aposematic, with a light yellow ground color contrasted with black stripes and red tip of the dorsal horn. The pronotum at this stage is soft and pli-

able, presenting no physical obstacle to a potential vertebrate predator such as *Anolis*. When inexperienced anoles are released at the base of trees with adult aggregations, anole movement on branches triggers a cataleptic response by individual insects. Anoles may walk over or even sit on top of insects without disrupting the aggregation. Anoles may even "lick" the pronota of individual insects within the aggregation. Teneral females, when presented individually to caged anoles, were rejected. The chemical basis of this avoidance is under investigation. As adults mature and become more heavily sclerotized, individuals within the aggregation or the entire aggregation may disperse explosively when disturbed. Such rapid dispersal may produce a startle response in some types of predators. At the time females are sexually mature, they have lost their aposematic coloration, and the pronotum is hard enough to provide protection from anoles (Wood 1975, 1977a).

Umbonia crassicornis is only one of approximately thirty Costa Rican species that provide parental care (Wood, in prep.). The nature of parental care in these species is variable but is consistent along generic lines. Both *U. crassicornis* and *Guayaquila compressa* Walker (Wood 1978) represent a trend in membracid parental care that emphasizes female investment in offspring. In these species there are usually no associations with mutualistic organisms such as ants, *Trigona* bees, or wasps. A second trend in membracid parental care is represented by *Entylia bactriana* (Wood 1977b) and appears to be typical of many tropical species. Parental investment in this group is restricted to protection of eggs and first-instar nymphs. Parent females on egg masses are attended by ants, which establishes ant presence at egg hatch. Since females desert offspring shortly after egg hatch, nymphal survival in the field depends on being located and consistently attended by ants, which reduces predator-associated mortality.

The ecology of tropical membracids is generally unknown, which is surprising considering their diversity and abundance. The importance of ants of some tropical tree associations has been documented by Janzen (1966, 1969). In more general terms, Leston (1973a,b, 1978) proposes an ant mosaic theory for the humid tropics in which dominant ant species control a limited vegetational area. According to this theory, to coexist, insects must be positively or negatively associated with these dominant ants, and, according to Leston (1978), this has resulted in the coevolution of ant-Homoptera-plant mutualism.

A large portion of tropical membracids at least in Costa Rica appears to be positively associated with some ants, in particular *Ectatomma ruidum* and *E. tuberculatum*. These associations take a variety of forms. Some species appear to be like the North American *Enchenopa binotata*, where mated females are attracted to branches by an ovipositional stimulant in a waxy egg covering. Once an egg mass is placed on a branch, other females are attracted and deposit eggs. At the end of oviposition branches may have fifty to one hundred egg masses from a number of different females. When eggs hatch, the aggregation of nymphs provides a concentrated honeydew source that apparently attracts and maintains ant attendance (Wood, unpub. data). In other associations membracid nymphs and adults may be found in shelters made by ants. At La Selva aggregations of nymphs and adults of three species were found in shelters made by the ant *Monacis* sp. around the flowers of a *Markia* vine. This association is fairly permanent, since ants and treehoppers coexisted on the same vine over a 1-year period. Solitary membracid nymphs have also been found on *Vismia* in shelters made by *Pheidole* ants, and they were consistently attended. In other species such as *Sphonogophorus* sp., nymphs may be solitary or occur in groups of two or three. Ants may collect honeydew from these nymphs, but attendance may not be consistent day to day (Wood, unpub. data). This appears to support the idea that a critical number of nymphs must be present to produce a sufficient volume of honeydew to consistently attract protective ants.

The importance of membracids in tropical ecosystems cannot be determined with our present knowledge. What is very clear is that their host-plant specificity and interaction with ants may be clues. Bentley (1977) points out that plant extrafloral nectaries provide an energy resource to ants, which in turn reduce damage to plants by driving off some types of insect herbivores. A membracid nymph feeding on plant sap and producing honeydew is in many ways similar to an extrafloral nectary. Since membracids seldom reach population levels that appear to stress a plant, it is tempting to speculate that they may, in fact, be beneficial to their host plant in the same manner as extrafloral nectaries. This would be especially true for plants without extrafloral nectaries or other defense mechanisms in successional areas where plant competition may be intense.

*

Ballou, C. H. 1936a. Insectos observados durante el año 1934. *Cent. Nac. Agr. Bol.* 20:1–60.

———. 1936b. Insect notes from Costa Rica in 1935. *Insect Pest. Surv. Bull.* 16:437–97.

Bentley, B. L. 1977. Extrafloral nectaries and protection by pugnacious bodyguards. *Ann. Rev. Ecol. Syst.* 8:407–27.

Janzen, D. H. 1966. Coevolution of mutualism between ants and acacias in Central America. *Evolution* 20:249–75.

———. 1969. Allelopathy by myrmecophytes: The ant *Azteca* as an allelopathic agent of *Cecropia. Ecology* 50:147–53.

Leston, D. 1973a. The ant mosaic, tropical tree crops and the limiting of pests and diseases. *PANS* (London) 19:311–41.

———. 1973b. Ecological consequences of the tropical ant mosaic. *Proc. Seventh Congr. Int. Union Study Social Insects* (London) 1973:235–42.

———. 1978. A Neotropical ant mosaic. *Ann. Ent. Soc. Am.* 71:649–53.

Mead, F. W. 1962. The thorn bug, *Umbonia crassicornis* (Amyot and Serville) (Homoptera: Membracidae). *Florida Dept. Agr. Div. Plant Industry, Ent. Circ.* no. 8.

Wood, T. K. 1974. Aggregating behavior of *Umbonia crassicornis* (Homoptera: Membracidae). *Can. Ent.* 106:169–73.

———. 1975. Defense in presocial membracids (Homoptera: Membracidae). *Can. Ent.* 107:1227–31.

———. 1976. Alarm behavior of brooding female *Umbonia crassicornis* (Membracidae: Homoptera). *Ann. Ent. Soc. Am.* 69:340–44.

———. 1977a. Defense in *Umbonia crassicornis:* The role of the pronotum and adult aggregations. *Ann. Ent. Soc. Am.* 70:524–28.

———. 1977b. Role of parent females and attendant ants in the maturation of the treehopper, *Entylia bactriana* (Homoptera: Membracidae). *Sociobiology* 2:257–72.

———. 1978. Parental care in *Guayaquila compressa. Psyche* 85:135–45.

Urania fulgens (Colipato Verde, Green Urania)

N. G. Smith

This diurnal moth (Uraniidae) (fig. 11.64) resembles a swallowtail butterfly. It is black with iridescent green bars across each wing and white "tails" on the hind wings. Sexes may be distinguished in the field, for the females are larger (gravid females weigh 0.9–1.2 g; males weigh 0.2–0.3 g) and thus more ponderous fliers, have bright green wing bars rather than the bronzy green bars of the males, and have broader hind wings than the rather kitelike males.

Urania fulgens, like all uraniids, undergoes population explosions and massive migrations that may be unsurpassed by any other insect in the Neotropics. In some years these populations and subsequent migrations have occurred more or less simultaneously (in the same week) over 34° of transequatorial latitude, from Mexico to Bolivia. The factors producing such synchrony are not known.

Urania is restricted to the Neotropics, but the family skips Africa and occurs on Madagascar (*Chrysiridia madagascariensis,* perhaps the most handsome lepidopteran in the world), on Papua, and in the southern Philippines. This peculiar pattern reflects the distribution of the larval

FIGURE 11.64. *Urania fulgens*, upper side (*bottom*) and with folded wings (*top*, but upper wing is in abnormal position of having its base outside lower wing). Panama (photo, N. G. Smith).

food plants, species of the genus *Omphalea* (Euphorbiaceae) that are mainly lianas, but occasionally trees.

Current classification considers that there are four species of *Urania: U. fulgens* (Veracruz, Mexico, throughout Central America to northern Ecuador west of the Andes); *U. boisduvalii* (Cuba); *U. sloanus* (Jamaica, and rare); and finally *U. leilus* (South America east of the Andes). The morphological differences are slight, and they might be best treated as races of one biological species. This distribution in the lowland Neotropics tracks the occurrence of *Omphalea* spp. exactly.

In Costa Rica and Panama, *Omphalea diandra* is an often huge canopy liana of wet and swamp forest, usually occurring in coastal areas behind the white mangrove (*Laguncularia*) zone. It is patchily distributed throughout its range (reason?), being most abundant in pockets of relatively nonseasonal climate (Osa Peninsula, Atlantic lowlands of Panama). *Urania fulgens* is endemic to these areas, and individuals survive the dry season there as adults, usually in reproductive diapause. Breeding commences in May, and there may be up to five generations before the onset of the next dry season. In Costa Rica and Panama, the first population movements may begin in July and early August and, depending on the year, may be very massive indeed, continuing unabated for as long

as five months. The movement is "down through" Central America, being southward, southeastward, or eastward depending on the locale. In Cuba the movement is from the north coast to the south, and in South America it is to the east, from the base of the Andes toward the Atlantic.

Not all the recently eclosed adults leave any one area. For example, the northernmost population near Veracruz, Mexico, will at times produce five generations of migrant individuals, and there is no remigration during this period. The question why some move out and others remain has not yet been satisfactorily answered.

Analysis of the records since 1850 suggests that the commonest interval between really big flights was 8 years, but from the mid-1950s to the present this interval seems in the order of 4 years (reason?). There are no records of a large flight in a year following a large movement, but there is almost always an annual "return" movement in the dry season (usually March). Such return flights ("up through" Central America and westward in South America) are characterized as being usually less than 2 weeks in duration, fairly local, and composed of individuals showing no reproductive activity. They are the offspring of the individuals that in November flew in the opposite direction.

Urania females lay eggs in clutches (why?) of up to eighty on the undersides of relatively new leaves. These hatch in 3 or 4 days, and there are five larval instars. In the first and second instars the larvae are somewhat gregarious and are banded black and white. When touched, they flip off the leaf on a silken thread, which is apparently an anti-ant adaptation. By the third or fourth instar they acquire a red head and long plumes, become dispersed, feed on the tops of the leaves, and are less likely to jump when disturbed. They may have acquired some chemical protection by that time or may simply be too large for individual ants to attack. Fifth-instar larvae descend at night from the vine by long threads and pupate in various places, often under the clinging mature leaves of *Monstera* vines. The period from egg to eclosion may be as short as 31 days (in the laboratory), but 42 days appears to be the average in the wild.

Uranias feed as adults, showing a strong attraction to white "fluffy" flowers like those of the mimosoid legumes, such as *Inga* sp., *Leucania*, and the composite *Eupatorium* (Why?). Adults in the laboratory will not live longer than 4 days without a source of carbohydrates. Water alone is apparently insufficient. Females are not receptive to males until 9 days after eclosion. Hence, if they do not feed, they do not breed. The presence or absence of an adult food supply must be considered when asking the question Why do they migrate? The adults are strong fliers and can exceed 40 km/h, but 20 km/h for a 12-h day is the average speed while on migration. That they emerge with large amounts of fat and feed during the migration suggests that they can and do fly enormous distances. They are little influenced by the variable winds of the rainy season and can fly distances of 240 km over open water.

Why do they all fly basically in the same direction over 34° of latitude? Clearly, if one considers the Veracruz population, selection must have acted to produce individuals programmed to go east and south, for there is no *Omphalea* to the north and west. But it is less clear why the uranias in mid-Amazonia also go to the east when they presumedly have an equal probability of finding *Omphalea* in other directions. A "leapfrog" phenomenon may be occurring, but this is not certain.

The central question concerning *Urania* is Why do they migrate? Some individuals do migrate and others do not, and this varies within and between years. Part, perhaps the major portion, of the answer lies with *Omphalea* —in its abundance and, most important, in its edibility. Research still in progress suggests that an individual plant having experienced three generations of *Urania* larvae may increase the level of secondary defense compounds (presumably at some cost) to a point that the next generation of uranias cannot detoxify it. Circumstantial evidence suggests that adult females can discriminate between supertoxic plants and those of lesser toxicity. Hence, uranias migrate to find *Omphalea* vines that have not been recently attacked and have dropped their defenses. The May following a huge *Urania* outbreak is indeed a "silent spring," for, though the *Omphalea* vines are there, they cannot for the most part be eaten.

*

Gillott, A. G. M. 1954. Peregrinatory flights of lepidoptera in Costa Rica. *Entomology* 57:45–46.

Guppy, L. 1907. Life history of *Cydimon (Urania) leilus* (L.). *Trans. Ent. Soc. London* 1907:405–12.

Skutch, A. F. 1971. *A naturalist in Costa Rica*. Gainesville: University of Florida Press.

Smith, N. G. 1972. Migrations of the day-flying moth *Urania* in Central and South America. *Carib. J. Sci.* 12:45–58.

Valerio, C. E. 1966. La colipato verde (*Urania fulgens*). *Kratera* (Universidad de Costa Rica) 1:40–47.

Williams, C. B. 1958. *Insect migration*. London: Collins.

Xylocopa gualanensis (Xicote, Avispa Carpintera, Carpenter Bee)

G. W. Frankie and H. V. Daly

The subgenus *Neoxylocopa* Michener includes the largest number of species of carpenter bees in the Western Hemisphere, ranging from Argentina to Texas and California (Hurd 1978). One of these, *Xylocopa gualanensis* Coc-

kerell, occurs in Central America. It is common in Costa Rica, particularly in the lowland dry forest of Guanacaste Province (Hurd 1978; Frankie and P. A. Opler, field collections).

Females of *X. gualanensis* are large, glossy black bees, ranging in length from 24 to 28 mm. The dorsal surface of the abdomen is flattened and relatively hairless. Males are about the same size but differ markedly from the females in appearance, being hairier and light yellowish brown.

Females, which are common in Guanacaste, may be confused at a distance with a similar carpenter bee, *X. fimbriata* (fig. 11.65). However, *X. fimbriata* may be distinguished from *X. gualanensis* by its larger size, usually 30–32 mm long. Bumblebees, genus *Bombus*, may also be confused with *Xylocopa*. Females of *Xylocopa*, however, have the hind leg completely covered with stiff pollen-collecting hairs, whereas *Bombus* has a "pollen basket" or corbicula on the outer side of the leg, a bare area surrounded by hairs.

Nests of *X. gualanensis* are constructed in dead branches of live trees, in trunks of dead trees, and in dry wooden fence material that is oriented vertically or horizontally (Frankie, field notes; Sage 1968) (fig. 11.66).

FIGURE 11.65. *a*, Adult female (*left*) and male (*right*) of *Xylocopa fimbriata*, the largest carpenter bee in Guanacaste (colon coin is 28 mm diameter). *b*, Face of male (*left*) and female (*right*) of *a*. Santa Rosa National Park, Guanacaste, Costa Rica (photos, D. H. Janzen).

FIGURE 11.66. *Xylocopa gualanensis* nest in split log; larva on left is feeding on pollen ball; note wood chip plug between cells (photo, G. W. Frankie).

Individual nests are simply constructed, each having one or possibly as many as four excavated tunnels, each 1.5–1.8 cm in diameter and up to about 30 cm long. Tunnels largely follow the wood grain. They usually open to the outside by one hole, which may be at the end or the middle of an excavation. In horizontally oriented wood, the entrance hole is on the underside of the substrate (Sage 1968).

New nest construction and provisioning of cells may occur primarily during the dry season in Guanacaste (Sage 1968), when ample floral resources are available for large bees (Frankie 1975; Frankie and Coville 1979; Frankie et al 1980; Janzen 1977). The female typically deposits pollen and nectar at the extreme end of a tunnel. This is shaped into a loaf of characteristic form with dimensions of 1.5 × 1 × 1 cm. The large egg (1.25 cm long) is laid on top of the loaf, and the chamber or "cell" is sealed with a thin partition of packed wood particles. The process is repeated until several such cells are constructed in a single tunnel. The immature stages of carpenter bees are attacked by various natural enemies. *X. gualanensis* is the confirmed host (P. Hurd, pers. comm.) for *Leucospis klugii* Westwood, a chalcidoid parasitoid of bees (Daly 1976; Hurd 1978, p. 62).

Sage (1968) noted that during the wet months of June through August most nests of *X. gualanensis* and other *Xylocopa* species had variable numbers of adult male and female bees. He suggested that this may be a nonbreeding period for the bees. During this period the nest serves as a refuge for both sexes.

X. gualanensis visits flowers of many native and some ornamental plant species (Opler, field collections; Sage 1968). Only the natives are listed below. Females commonly forage from the following tree species during the

dry season (N = nectar host, P = pollen host): *Andira inermis* (N), *Caesalpinia eriostachys* (N), *Cochlospermum vitifolium* (P), *Dalbergia retusa* (P, N), *Gliricidia sepium* (N), *Inga vera* (P, N), *Parkinsonia aculeata* (P, ?N), and *Tabebuia ochracea* (N). At this time of year they also are frequent visitors to the second-growth shrub *Cassia biflora* (P) (Frankie and Coville 1979; Wille 1963). During the wet season females visit flowers from a number of tree, shrub, and vine/liana species (Opler, field collections; Sage 1968). These include: *Genipa americana* (N), *Bixa orellana* (P), *Calliandra portoricensis* (N), *Cordia pringlei* (N), *Stachytarpheta jamaicensis* (N), *Crotalaria retusa* (P), *Canavalia maritima* (P), *Passiflora pulchella* (N) and *Cucurbita* sp. (N). Males have only rarely been seen at flowers. Examples of these visits include *Andira inermis* (N), *Caesalpinia eriostachys* (N), *Myrospermum fructescens* (N), *Waltheria indica* (N), and *Ipomoea* sp. (N) during the dry season and *Cucurbita* sp. (N) and an asclepiad liana (N) during the wet season.

Males of *X. gualanensis* have been observed patrolling small territories within or at the tops of trees during the dry season in Guanacaste. In some locations this behavior can be viewed regularly in the morning year after year. For example, at a site near Liberia (see site description in Vinson and Frankie 1977) males frequently can be observed patrolling territories within the canopies of oak trees (*Quercus oleoides* Cham & Schlecht.) that are growing on top of a small hill (Frankie, Vinson, and Lewis 1979). The function of the territories is not clear, but it is thought that they may play some role in mating.

*

Daly, H. V. 1976. *Leucopsis* [sic] *klugii* (Hymenoptera, Chalcidoidea) reared from *Xylocopa brasilianorum* (Hymenoptera, Apoidea) in Costa Rica. *Pan-Pacific Ent.* 52:271.

Frankie, G. W. 1975. Tropical forest phenology and pollinator plant coevolution. In *Coevolution of animals and plants,* ed. L. E. Gilbert and P. H. Raven, pp. 192–209. Austin: University of Texas Press.

Frankie, G. W. and Coville, R. 1979. An experimental study of the foraging behavior of selected solitary bee species in the Costa Rican dry forest. *J. Kansas Ent. Soc.* 52:591–602.

Frankie, G. W.; Haber, W. A.; Opler, P. A.; and Bawa, K. S. 1980. Characteristics and organization of large bee pollination systems in the Costa Rican dry forest. *Biotropica,* in review.

Frankie, G. W.; Vinson, S. B.; and Lewis, A. 1979. Territorial behavior in male *Xylocopa micans* (Hymenoptera: Anthophoridae). *J. Kansas Ent. Soc.* 52: 313–23.

Hurd, P. D., Jr. 1978. *An annotated catalog of the carpenter bees (Genus* Xylocopa *Latreille) of the Western*

Hemisphere (Hymenoptera: Anthophoridae). Washington, D.C.: Smithsonian Institution Press.

Janzen, D. H. 1967. Synchronization of sexual reproduction of trees within the dry season in Central America. *Evolution*. 21:620–37.

Sage, R. D. 1968. Observations on feeding, nesting, and territorial behavior of carpenter bees genus *Xylocopa* in Costa Rica. *Ann. Ent. Soc. Am*. 61:884–89.

Vinson, S. B., and Frankie, G. W. 1977. Nests of *Centris aethyctera* (Hymenoptera: Apoidea: Anthophoridae) in the dry forest of Costa Rica. *J. Kansas Ent. Soc*. 50:301–11.

Wille, A. 1963. Behavioral adaptations of bees for pollen collecting from *Cassia* flowers. *Rev. Biol. Trop*. 11: 205–10.

ADDRESSES
OF CONTRIBUTORS

D. Amadon
American Museum of Natural History
Central Park West at 79th Street
New York, New York   10024

W. R. Anderson
Herbarium, North University Building
University of Michigan
Ann Arbor, Michigan   48109

C. C. Andrews
88 Standish Street
Cambridge, Massachusetts   02138

R. M. Andrews
Department of Biology
Virginia Polytechnic Institute and State University
Blacksburg, Virginia   24061

W. S. Armbruster
Department of Biology
University of Alaska
Fairbanks, Alaska   99701

K. A. Arnold
Department of Wildlife and Fisheries Sciences
Texas A. & M. University
College Station, Texas   77843

H. G. Baker
Department of Botany
University of California
Berkeley, California   94720

R. H. Baker (Retired)
302 North Strickland
Eagle Lake, Texas   77434

S. C. H. Barrett
Department of Botany
University of Toronto
Toronto, Ontario M5S 1A1
Canada

K. S. Bawa
Biology II Department
University of Massachusetts
Harbor Campus
Boston, Massachusetts   02125

J. H. Beach
Department of Botany
University of Massachusetts
Amherst, Massachusetts   01003

J. M. Beitel
Department of Botany
University of Michigan
Ann Arbor, Michigan   48109

B. L. Bentley
Department of Ecology and Evolution
State University of New York
Stony Brook, New York   11794

E. G. Bolen
Department of Range and Wildlife Management
Texas Tech University
Lubbock, Texas   79409

D. H. Boucher
Département de Sciences Biologiques
Université du Québec
Montréal, Québec H3C 3P8
Canada

J. W. Bradbury
Department of Biology, C-016
University of California
La Jolla, California   92093

C. Brandon
Science Department
Vermont Technical College
Randolph Center, Vermont   05061

S. H. Bullock
Estación de Biología Chamela
Universidad Nacional Autónoma de Mexico
Apdo. 21
San Patricio, Jalisco   48980
Mexico

W. C. Burger
Field Museum of Natural History
Roosevelt Road at Lake Shore Drive
Chicago, Illinois   60605

K. Burt-Utley
Department of Biological Sciences
University of New Orleans
New Orleans, Louisiana   70122

G. W. Byers
Department of Entomology
University of Kansas
Lawrence, Kansas   66045

A. Carr
Department of Zoology
University of Florida
Gainesville, Florida   32611

C. R. Carroll
Institute of Environmental Studies
Baylor University
Waco, Texas   76798

R. Castillo-Muñoz
Escuela Centroamericana de Geología
Universidad de Costa Rica
Ciudad Universitaria
Costa Rica

J. A. Chapman
Appalachian Environmental Laboratory
University of Maryland
Frostburg, Maryland   21532

J. A. Chemsak
Department of Entomology
University of California
Berkeley, California 94720

E. Coen
Apdo. 1028
San José, 1000
Costa Rica

C. T. Collins
Department of Botany
California State University
Long Beach, California 90840

R. K. Colwell
Department of Zoology
University of California
Berkeley, California 94720

S. E. Cornelius
R.R. 3, Box 216
Mountain View, Missouri 65548

T. B. Croat
Missouri Botanical Garden
P.O. Box 299
Saint Louis, Missouri 63166

M. L. Crump
Department of Zoology
University of Florida
Gainesville, Florida 32611

H. V. Daly
Department of Entomology
University of California
Berkeley, California 94720

P. J. DeVries
Department of Zoology
University of Texas
Austin, Texas 78712

J. R. Dixon
Department of Wildlife and Fisheries Science
Texas A. & M. University
College Station, Texas 77843

A. C. Echternacht
Department of Zoology
University of Tennessee
Knoxville, Tennessee 37996

E. P. Edwards
Department of Biology
Sweet Briar College
Sweet Briar, Virginia 24595

J. F. Eisenberg
Florida State Museum
University of Florida
Gainesville, Florida 32611

C. H. Ernst
Department of Biology
George Mason University
Fairfax, Virginia 22030

F. Fallas B.
Escuela de Microbiología
Universidad de Costa Rica
Ciudad Universitaria
Costa Rica

E. M. Fisher
California Department of Food and Agriculture
1220 N Street
Sacramento, California 95814

H. S. Fitch
Division of Biological Sciences
University of Kansas
Lawrence, Kansas 66045

J. W. Fitzpatrick
Field Museum of Natural History
Roosevelt Road at Lake Shore Drive
Chicago, Illinois 60605

T. H. Fleming
Department of Biology
University of Miami
Coral Gables, Florida 33124

M. S. Foster
Museum Section
U.S. Fish and Wildlife Service
National Museum of Natural History
Washington, D.C. 20560

G. W. Frankie
Department of Entomology
University of California
Berkeley, California 94720

C. H. Freese
International Affairs
Fish and Wildlife Service
U.S. Department of Interior
Washington, D.C. 20240

A. L. Gardner
Museum Section
U.S. Fish and Wildlife Service
National Museum of Natural History
Washington, D.C. 20560

A. H. Gentry
Missouri Botanical Garden
P.O. Box 299
Saint Louis, Missouri 63166

L. E. Gilbert
Department of Zoology
University of Texas
Austin, Texas 78712

D. E. Gladstone
1935 Mount Vernon
Philadelphia, Pennsylvania 19130

K. E. Glander
Department of Anthropology
Duke University
Durham, North Carolina 27706

L. D. Gómez
Museo Nacional de Costa Rica
Apdo. 749
San José
Costa Rica

H. W. Greene
Museum of Vertebrate Zoology
University of California
Berkeley, California 94720

W. A. Haber
  Department of Entomology
  University of California
  Berkeley, California 94720
J. Hackforth-Jones
  1210 North Gammon Road
  Middletown, Wisconsin 53562
W. Hallwachs
  Section of Ecology and Systematics
  Cornell University
  Ithaca, New York 14853
M. Hanson
  Division of Biological Sciences
  University of Michigan
  Ann Arbor, Michigan 48109
A. R. Hardy
  California Department of Agriculture
  915 Capitol Mall
  Sacramento, California 95814
G. S. Hartshorn
  Tropical Science Center
  Apdo. 8-3870
  San José
  Costa Rica
D. J. Harvey
  Department of Zoology
  University of Texas
  Austin, Texas 78712
L. R. Heaney
  Museum of Zoology
  University of Michigan
  Ann Arbor, Michigan 48104
I. L. Heisler
  Rutgers University
  Institute of Animal Behavior
  101 Warren Street
  Newark, New Jersey 07102
R. Heithaus
  Department of Biology
  Kenyon College
  Gambier, Ohio 43022
H. A. Hespenheide
  Department of Biology
  University of California
  Los Angeles, California 90024
C. L. Hogue
  Los Angeles County Museum of Natural History
  900 Exposition Boulevard
  Los Angeles, California 90007
M. Holle
  Centro Internacional de Recursos
  Fitogenéticos CIRF
  CIAT, Apdo. Aereo 6713
  Cali
  Colombia
H. F. Howden
  Department of Biology
  Carlton University
  Ottawa, Ontario K1S 5B6
  Canada

H. F. Howe
  Department of Zoology
  University of Iowa
  Iowa City, Iowa 52242
D. J. Howell
  Department of Biology
  Southern Methodist University
  Dallas, Texas 75275
J. H. Hunt
  Department of Biology
  University of Missouri
  Saint Louis, Missouri 63121
M. T. Jackson
  Department of Plant Biology
  University of Birmingham
  Birmingham B15 2TT
  England
D. P. Janos
  Department of Biology
  University of Miami
  Coral Gables, Florida 33124
D. H. Janzen
  Department of Biology
  University of Pennsylvania
  Philadelphia, Pennsylvania 19104
D. A. Jenni
  Department of Zoology
  University of Montana
  Missoula, Montana 59812
L. K. Johnson
  Department of Zoology
  University of Iowa
  Iowa City, Iowa 52242
J. H. Kaufmann
  Department of Zoology
  University of Florida
  Gainesville, Florida 32611
H. Kennedy
  Department of Botany
  University of Manitoba
  Winnipeg, Manitoba R3T 2N2
  Canada
C. B. Koford (Deceased)
  Museum of Vertebrate Zoology
  University of California
  Berkeley, California 94720
S. Koptur
  Department of Zoology
  University of Iowa
  Iowa City, Iowa 52242
A. LaBastille
  West of the Wind Publications
  Big Moose, New York 13331
D. A. Lancaster
  Box 447
  Etna, New York 13062
M. F. Lawton
  4316 Chickasaw Drive S.E.
  Huntsville, Alabama 35801

R. O. Lawton
  Department of Biological Sciences
  University of Alabama
  Huntsville, Alabama   35899

C. F. Leck
  Nelson Biological Laboratories
  Rutgers University
  New Brunswick, New Jersey   08903

S. H. Ligon
  Department of Biology
  University of New Mexico
  Albuquerque, New Mexico   87131

S. Limerick
  U.S. Fish and Wildlife Service
  Denver Wildlife Research Center
  Department of Biology
  University of New Mexico
  Albuquerque, New Mexico   87131

Y. D. Lubin
  Estación Científica Charles Darwin
  Casilla 58–39
  Guayaquil
  Ecuador

C. Lumer
  New York Botanical Garden
  Bronx, New York   10458

M. S. McClure
  Department of Entomology
  Connecticut Agricultural Experiment Station
  123 Huntington Street
  New Haven, Connecticut   06504

E. D. McCoy
  Department of Biology
  University of South Florida
  Tampa, Florida   33620

M. B. McCoy
  780 L Street
  Arcata, California   95521

R. W. McDiarmid
  Museum Section
  U.S. Fish and Wildlife Service
  National Museum of Natural History
  Washington, D.C.   20560

L. A. McHargue
  5820 Southwest 38th Street
  Miami, Florida   33155

A. Massey
  Department of Zoology
  North Carolina State University
  Raleigh, North Carolina   27650

R. W. Matthews
  Department of Entomology
  University of Georgia
  Athens, Georgia   30602

M. N. Melampy
  Department of Ecology, Ethology, and Evolution
  University of Illinois at Urbana-Champaign
  Champaign, Illinois   61820

C. D. Michener
  Department of Entomology
  University of Kansas
  Lawrence, Kansas   66045

D. W. Mock
  Department of Zoology
  University of Oklahoma
  Norman, Oklahoma   73019

G. G. Montgomery
  Smithsonian Tropical Research Institute
  APO Miami   34002

E. Morales M.
  Ministerio de Agricultura y Ganaderiá
  San José
  Costa Rica

D. W. Morrison
  Department of Zoology
  Rutgers University
  Newark, New Jersey   07102

E. S. Morton
  Department of Zoological Research
  National Zoological Park
  Washington, D.C.   20008

P. A. Opler
  Division of Biological Services
  U.S. Fish and Wildlife Service
  Department of the Interior
  Washington, D.C.   20240

G. H. Orians
  Department of Zoology
  University of Washington
  Seattle, Washington   98195

M. K. Palmer
  Department of Biology
  Vassar College
  Poughkeepsie, New York   12601

J. J. Parsons
  Department of Geography
  University of California
  Berkeley, California   94720

R. W. Pohl
  Department of Botany and Plant Pathology
  Iowa State University
  Ames, Iowa   50011

L. J. Poveda
  Tropical Science Center
  Apdo. 8-3870
  San José
  Costa Rica

G. V. N. Powell
  National Audubon Society Research Department
  115 Indian Mound Trail
  Tavernier, Florida   33070

A. S. Rand
  Smithsonian Tropical Research Institute
  P.O. Box 2072
  Balboa
  Panama

T. Ray
School of Life and Health Sciences
University of Delaware
Newark, Delaware   19711

J. V. Remsen, Jr.
Museum of Zoology
Louisiana State University
Baton Rouge, Louisiana   70803

D. C. F. Rentz
Division of Entomology
CSIRO
P.O. Box 1700
Canberra City ACT 2601
Australia

C. W. Rettenmeyer
Biological Sciences Group
University of Connecticut
Storrs, Connecticut   06268

R. A. Rice
Department of Geography
University of California
Berkeley, California   94720

P. V. Rich
Earth Sciences Department
Monash University
Clayton, Victoria 3168
Australia

T. H. Rich
National Museum of Victoria
Russell Street
Melbourne, Victoria 3000
Australia

R. E. Ricklefs
Department of Biology
University of Pennsylvania
Philadelphia, Pennsylvania   19104

S. Risch
Section of Ecology and Systematics
Cornell University
Ithaca, New York   14853

D. C. Robinson
Escuela de Biología
Universidad de Costa Rica
Ciudad Universitaria
Costa Rica

H. F. Rowell
Zoologisches Institut der Universität
Rheinsprung 9
4501 Basel
Switzerland

G. C. Sanderson
Section of Wildlife Research
Illinois Natural History Survey
607 East Peabody
Champaign, Illinois   61820

J. D. Sauer
Department of Geography
University of California
Los Angeles, California   90024

J. M. Savage
Department of Biology
University of Miami
Coral Gables, Florida   33124

C. Schal
Department of Entomology
University of Massachusetts
Amherst, Massachusetts   01003

D. W. Schemske
Department of Biology
University of Chicago
Chicago, Illinois   60637

R. W. Schreiber
Los Angeles County Museum of Natural History
900 Exposition Boulevard
Los Angeles, California   90007

N. J. Scott
U.S. Fish and Wildlife Service
Denver Wildlife Research Center
Department of Biology
University of New Mexico
Albuquerque, New Mexico   87131

R. L. Seib
Museum of Vertebrate Zoology
University of California
Berkeley, California   94720

R. P. Seifert (Deceased)
Department of Biological Sciences
George Washington University
Washington, D.C.   20052

T. W. Sherry
Department of Biological Sciences
Dartmouth College
Hanover, New Hampshire   03755

L. L. Short
American Museum of Natural History
Central Park West at 79th Street
New York, New York   10024

R. Silberglied (Deceased)
Smithsonian Tropical Research Institute
APO Miami   34002

D. S. Simberloff
Department of Biological Sciences
Florida State University
Tallahassee, Florida   32306

A. F. Skutch
Quizarra
San Isidro del General
Costa Rica

J. T. Smiley
Department of Ecology and Evolutionary Biology
University of California
Irvine, California   92717

N. G. Smith
Smithsonian Tropical Research Institute
APO Miami   34002

S. M. Smith
  Department of Biology
  Mount Holyoke College
  South Hadley, Massachusetts   01075

N. Smythe
  Smithsonian Tropical Research Institute
  APO Miami   34002

L. K. Sowls
  Arizona Cooperative Wildlife Research Unit
  University of Arizona
  Tucson, Arizona   85721

M. A. Staton
  Feather Crest Farms
  Route 1, Box 2250
  Douglass, Texas   75943

G. Stevens
  Department of Biology
  University of Pennsylvania
  Philadelphia, Pennsylvania   19104

F. G. Stiles
  Escuela de Biología
  Universidad de Costa Rica
  Ciudad Universitaria
  Costa Rica

D. E. Stone
  Department of Botany
  Duke University
  Durham, North Carolina   27706

J. Stout
  Department of Zoology
  Michigan State University
  East Lansing, Michigan   48824

J. G. Strauch, Jr.
  University Museum
  University of Colorado
  Boulder, Colorado   80309

D. R. Strong
  Department of Biological Sciences
  Florida State University
  Tallahassee, Florida   32306

C. A. Todzia
  Department of Botany
  University of Texas
  Austin, Texas   78712

D. C. Turner
  Ethologie und Wildforschung
  Universität Zurich
  Birchstrasse 95
  8050 Zurich
  Switzerland

J. F. Utley
  Department of Biological Sciences
  University of New Orleans
  New Orleans, Louisiana   70122

J. H. Vandermeer
  Division of Biological Sciences
  University of Michigan
  Ann Arbor, Michigan 48109

R. W. Van Devender
  Department of Biology
  Appalachian State University
  Boone, North Carolina   28608

M. Vargas V.
  Escuela de Microbiología
  Universidad de Costa Rica
  Ciudad Universitaria
  Costa Rica

A. Vásquez Morera
  Unidad de Suelos
  Ministerio de Agricultura y Ganadería
  San José
  Costa Rica

S. L. Vehrencamp
  Department of Biology, C-016
  University of California
  La Jolla, California   92093

S. B. Vinson
  Department of Entomology
  Texas A. & M. University
  College Station, Texas   77843

H. K. Voris
  Field Museum of Natural History
  Roosevelt Road at Lake Shore Drive
  Chicago, Illinois   60605

H. B. Wagner
  Smithsonian Tropical Research Institute
  APO Miami   34002

W. H. Wagner
  Department of Botany
  University of Michigan
  Ann Arbor, Michigan   48109

M. H. Wake
  Department of Zoology
  University of California
  Berkeley, California   94720

K. S. Walter
  New York Botanical Garden
  Bronx, New York   10458

M. J. West-Eberhard
  Escuela de Biología
  Universidad de Costa Rica
  Ciudad Universitaria
  Costa Rica

R. M. Wetzel
  Florida State Museum
  University of Florida
  Gainesville, Florida   32611

J. L. Whitmore
  U.S. Department of Agriculture
  International Forestry
  P.O. Box 2417
  Washington, D.C.   20013

R. H. Wiley
  Department of Biology
  University of North Carolina
  Chapel Hill, North Carolina   27514

G. B. Williamson
Department of Botany
Louisiana State University
Baton Rouge, Louisiana   70803

E. O. Willis
UNESP—Zoologia
13500 Rio Claro, S.P.
Brazil

M. F. Willson
Department of Ecology, Ethology, and Evolution
University of Illinois at Urbana-Champaign
Champaign, Illinois   61820

D. E. Wilson
Museum Section
U.S. Fish and Wildlife Service
National Museum of Natural History, NHB 382
Washington, D.C.   20560

D. M. Windsor
Smithsonian Tropical Research Institute
APO Miami   34002

M. Winston
Department of Biological Sciences
Simon Fraser University
Burnaby, British Columbia V5A 1S6
Canada

S. L. Wood
Life Sciences Museum
Brigham Young University
Provo, Utah   84602

T. K. Wood
Department of Entomology and Applied Ecology
University of Delaware
Newark, Delaware   19711

A. M. Young
Milwaukee Public Museum
800 West Wells Street
Milwaukee, Wisconsin   53233

G. R. Zug
National Museum of Natural History
Smithsonian Institution
Washington, D.C.   20560

INDEX

Since common names of large taxonomic groups (e.g., birds, vines, bugs, orchids) are frequently mentioned in a rather offhand manner (e.g., "flycatchers eat a variety of small insects such as flies, moths, beetles, orthopterans"), the indexing has been selective. I have attempted to include those uses of words most central to the story being told. All species-level Latin names have been indexed at the generic or species level, *except that the checklists have not been indexed to a level below family* (and the bird checklist is not indexed at all).

Not all occurrences of a taxon are indexed if they have already been indexed for lower taxonomic categories. For example, to get all references to rodents, one must check both Rodents and the entries for specific rodents commonly referred to (e.g., agouti, paca, mice, squirrel). Common names that are direct synonyms of family names are often pooled under one name (e.g., anthophorids = Anthophoridae) and the reverse (e.g., curculionids = weevils). If several species in the same genus are discussed at only one place in the book, they are often indexed only by genus.

All the species accounts have been indexed to the one or more standard field sites to which they are most relevant: a list of the species accounts most relevant to La Selva, for example, can be made by extracting its entries for plants, insects, mammals, and so forth.

Italic numbers indicate species accounts.